Introduction to Management Science

ECON 3300 - Kennesaw State University

David R. Anderson
University of Cincinnati

Dennis J. Sweeney
University of Cincinnati

Thomas A. Williams
Rochester Institute of Technology

Australia · Canada · Mexico · Singapore · Spain · United Kingdom · United States

Introduction to Management Science
Anderson/Sweeney/Williams

Executive Editors:
Michele Baird, Maureen Staudt &
Michael Stranz

Project Development Manager:
Linda deStefano

Sr. Marketing Coordinators:
Lindsay Annett and Sara Mercurio

Production/Manufacturing Manager:
Donna M. Brown

Production Editorial Manager:
Dan Plofchan

Pre-Media Services Supervisor:
Becki Walker

Rights and Permissions Specialist:
Kalina Ingham Hintz

Cover Image
Getty Images*

Printed in the
United States of America
1 2 3 4 5 6 7 10 09 08 07

For more information, please contact Thomson Custom Solutions, 5191 Natorp Boulevard, Mason, OH 45040. Or you can visit our Internet site at http://www.thomsoncustom.com

The Adaptable Courseware Program consists of products and additions to existing Thomson products that are produced from camera-ready copy. Peer review, class testing, and accuracy are primarily the responsibility of the author(s).

Introduction to Management Science / Anderson/Sweeney/Williams

ISBN: 978-0-324-67810-9
ISBN: 0-324-67810-X

International Divisions List

Asia (Including India):
Thomson Learning
(a division of Thomson Asia Pte Ltd)
5 Shenton Way #01-01
UIC Building
Singapore 068808
Tel: (65) 6410-1200
Fax: (65) 6410-1208

Australia/New Zealand:
Thomson Learning Australia
102 Dodds Street
Southbank, Victoria 3006
Australia

Latin America:
Thomson Learning
Seneca 53
Colonia Polano
11560 Mexico, D.F., Mexico
Tel (525) 281-2906
Fax (525) 281-2656

Canada:
Thomson Nelson
1120 Birchmount Road
Toronto, Ontario
Canada M1K 5G4
Tel (416) 752-9100
Fax (416) 752-8102

UK/Europe/Middle East/Africa:
Thomson Learning
High Holborn House
50-51 Bedford Row
London, WC1R 4LS
United Kingdom
Tel 44 (020) 7067-2500
Fax 44 (020) 7067-2600

Spain (Includes Portugal):
Thomson Paraninfo
Calle Magallanes 25
28015 Madrid
España
Tel 34 (0)91 446-3350
Fax 34 (0)91 445-6218

*Unless otherwise noted, all cover images used by Thomson Custom Solutions have been supplied courtesy of Getty Images with the exception of the *Earthview* cover image, which has been supplied by the National Aeronautics and Space Administration (NASA).

Table of Contents

An Introduction to Management Science: Quantitative Approaches to Decision Making

Essentials of Statistics for Business and Economics

TWELFTH EDITION

AN INTRODUCTION TO MANAGEMENT SCIENCE

QUANTITATIVE APPROACHES TO DECISION MAKING

An Introduction to Management Science:
Quantitative Approaches to Decision Making, Twelfth Edition

David R. Anderson, Dennis J. Sweeney, Thomas A. Williams, Kipp Martin

VP/Editorial Director:
Jack W. Calhoun

Editor-in-Chief:
Alex von Rosenberg

Senior Acquisitions Editor:
Charles McCormick, Jr.

Senior Developmental Editor:
Alice Denny

Senior Marketing Manager:
Larry Qualls

Marketing Communications Manager:
Libby Shipp

Content Project Manager:
Amy Hackett

Manager, Editorial Media:
John Barans

Technology Project Manager:
John Rich

Senior Manufacturing Coordinator:
Diane Gibbons

Production House:
ICC Macmillan Inc.

Printer:
Courier Corporation
Kendallville, IN

Art Director:
Stacy Jenkins Shirley

Internal Designer:
Michael Stratton/cmiller design

Cover Designer:
Paul Neff

Cover Image:
© Getty Images/Brand X

Printed in the United States of America
1 2 3 4 5 10 09 08 07

Student Edition:
ISBN 13: 978-0-324-39979-0
ISBN 10: 0-324-39979-0
Student Edition with CD:
ISBN 13: 978-0-324-39980-6
ISBN 10: 0-324-39980-4

Library of Congress Control Number:
2007900084

For more information about our products, contact us at:
Thomson Learning Academic Resource Center
1-800-423-0563

Thomson Higher Education
5191 Natorp Boulevard
Mason, OH 45040
USA

CHAPTER 1

Introduction

CONTENTS

Management science, an approach to decision making based on the scientific method, makes extensive use of quantitative analysis. A variety of names exists for the body of knowledge involving quantitative approaches to decision making; in addition to management science, two other widely known and accepted names are operations research and decision science. Today, many use the terms *management science, operations research,* and *decision science* interchangeably.

The scientific management revolution of the early 1900s, initiated by Frederic W. Taylor, provided the foundation for the use of quantitative methods in management. But modern management science research is generally considered to have originated during the World War II period, when teams were formed to deal with strategic and tactical problems faced by the military. These teams, which often consisted of people with diverse specialties (e.g., mathematicians, engineers, and behavioral scientists), were joined together to solve a common problem through the utilization of the scientific method. After the war, many of these team members continued their research in the field of management science.

According to Irv Lustig of ILOG, Inc., solution methods developed today are 10,000 times faster than the ones used 15 years ago.

Two developments that occurred during the post–World War II period led to the growth and use of management science in nonmilitary applications. First, continued research resulted in numerous methodological developments. Probably the most significant development was the discovery by George Dantzig, in 1947, of the simplex method for solving linear programming problems. At the same time these methodological developments were taking place, digital computers prompted a virtual explosion in computing power. Computers enabled practitioners to use the methodological advances to solve a large variety of problems. The computer technology explosion continues, and personal computers can now be used to solve problems larger than those solved on mainframe computers in the 1990s.

As stated in the Preface, the purpose of the text is to provide students with a sound conceptual understanding of the role that management science plays in the decision-making process. We also said that the text is applications oriented. To reinforce the applications nature of the text and to provide a better understanding of the variety of applications in which management science has been used successfully, Management Science in Action articles are presented throughout the text. Each Management Science in Action article summarizes an application of management science in practice. The first Management Science in Action in this chapter, Revenue Management at American Airlines, describes one of the most significant applications of management science in the airline industry.

MANAGEMENT SCIENCE IN ACTION

REVENUE MANAGEMENT AT AMERICAN AIRLINES*

One of the great success stories in management science involves the work done by the operations research (OR) group at American Airlines. In 1982, Thomas M. Cook joined a group of 12 operations research analysts at American Airlines. Under Cook's guidance, the OR group quickly grew to a staff of 75 professionals who developed models and conducted studies to support senior management decision making. Today the OR group is called Sabre and employs 10,000 professionals worldwide.

One of the most significant applications developed by the OR group came about because of the deregulation of the airline industry in the late 1970s. As a result of deregulation, a number of low-cost airlines were able to move into the market by selling seats at a fraction of the price charged by established carriers such as American Airlines. Facing the question of how to compete, the OR group suggested offering different fare classes (discount and full fare) and in the process created a new area of management science referred to as yield or revenue management.

The OR group used forecasting and optimization techniques to determine how many seats to sell at a discount and how many seats to hold for full fare. Although the initial implementation was relatively crude, the group continued to improve the forecasting and optimization models that drive the system and to obtain better data. Tom Cook counts at least four basic generations of revenue management during his tenure. Each produced in excess of $100 million in incremental profitability over its predecessor. This revenue management system at American Airlines generates nearly $1 billion annually in incremental revenue.

Today, virtually every airline uses some sort of revenue management system. The cruise, hotel, and car rental industries also now apply revenue management methods, a further tribute to the pioneering efforts of the OR group at American Airlines and its leader, Thomas M. Cook.

*Based on Peter Horner, "The Sabre Story," *OR/MS Today* (June 2000).

1.1 PROBLEM SOLVING AND DECISION MAKING

Problem solving can be defined as the process of identifying a difference between the actual and the desired state of affairs and then taking action to resolve the difference. For problems important enough to justify the time and effort of careful analysis, the problem-solving process involves the following seven steps:

1. Identify and define the problem.
2. Determine the set of alternative solutions.
3. Determine the criterion or criteria that will be used to evaluate the alternatives.
4. Evaluate the alternatives.
5. Choose an alternative.
6. Implement the selected alternative.
7. Evaluate the results to determine whether a satisfactory solution has been obtained.

Decision making is the term generally associated with the first five steps of the problem-solving process. Thus, the first step of decision making is to identify and define the problem. Decision making ends with the choosing of an alternative, which is the act of making the decision.

Let us consider the following example of the decision-making process. For the moment assume that you are currently unemployed and that you would like a position that will lead to a satisfying career. Suppose that your job search has resulted in offers from companies in Rochester, New York; Dallas, Texas; Greensboro, North Carolina; and Pittsburgh, Pennsylvania. Thus, the alternatives for your decision problem can be stated as follows:

1. Accept the position in Rochester.
2. Accept the position in Dallas.
3. Accept the position in Greensboro.
4. Accept the position in Pittsburgh.

The next step of the problem-solving process involves determining the criteria that will be used to evaluate the four alternatives. Obviously, the starting salary is a factor of some importance. If salary were the only criterion of importance to you, the alternative selected as "best" would be the one with the highest starting salary. Problems in which the objective is to find the best solution with respect to one criterion are referred to as **single-criterion decision problems.**

Suppose that you also conclude that the potential for advancement and the location of the job are two other criteria of major importance. Thus, the three criteria in your decision problem are starting salary, potential for advancement, and location. Problems that involve more than one criterion are referred to as **multicriteria decision problems.**

The next step of the decision-making process is to evaluate each of the alternatives with respect to each criterion. For example, evaluating each alternative relative to the starting

TABLE 1.1 DATA FOR THE JOB EVALUATION DECISION-MAKING PROBLEM

Alternative	Starting Salary	Potential for Advancement	Job Location
1. Rochester	$48,500	Average	Average
2. Dallas	$46,000	Excellent	Good
3. Greensboro	$46,000	Good	Excellent
4. Pittsburgh	$47,000	Average	Good

salary criterion is done simply by recording the starting salary for each job alternative. Evaluating each alternative with respect to the potential for advancement and the location of the job is more difficult to do, however, because these evaluations are based primarily on subjective factors that are often difficult to quantify. Suppose for now that you decide to measure potential for advancement and job location by rating each of these criteria as poor, fair, average, good, or excellent. The data that you compile are shown in Table 1.1.

You are now ready to make a choice from the available alternatives. What makes this choice phase so difficult is that the criteria are probably not all equally important, and no one alternative is "best" with regard to all criteria. Although we will present a method for dealing with situations like this one later in the text, for now let us suppose that after a careful evaluation of the data in Table 1.1, you decide to select alternative 3; alternative 3 is thus referred to as the **decision.**

At this point in time, the decision-making process is complete. In summary, we see that this process involves five steps:

1. Define the problem.
2. Identify the alternatives.
3. Determine the criteria.
4. Evaluate the alternatives.
5. Choose an alternative.

Note that missing from this list are the last two steps in the problem-solving process: implementing the selected alternative and evaluating the results to determine whether a satisfactory solution has been obtained. This omission is not meant to diminish the importance of each of these activities, but to emphasize the more limited scope of the term *decision making* as compared to the term *problem solving.* Figure 1.1 summarizes the relationship between these two concepts.

1.2 QUANTITATIVE ANALYSIS AND DECISION MAKING

Consider the flowchart presented in Figure 1.2. Note that it combines the first three steps of the decision-making process under the heading of "Structuring the Problem" and the latter two steps under the heading "Analyzing the Problem." Let us now consider in greater detail how to carry out the set of activities that make up the decision-making process.

Figure 1.3 shows that the analysis phase of the decision-making process may take two basic forms: qualitative and quantitative. Qualitative analysis is based primarily on the manager's judgment and experience; it includes the manager's intuitive "feel" for the problem and is more an art than a science. If the manager has had experience with similar

FIGURE 1.1 THE RELATIONSHIP BETWEEN PROBLEM SOLVING AND DECISION MAKING

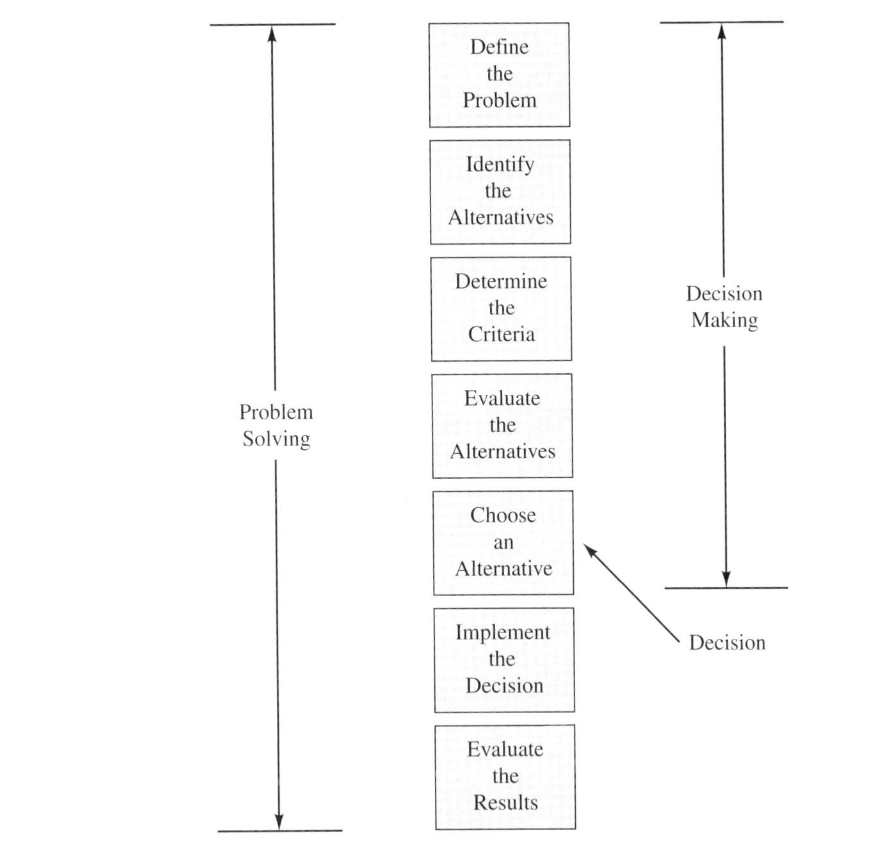

problems, or if the problem is relatively simple, heavy emphasis may be placed upon a qualitative analysis. However, if the manager has had little experience with similar problems, or if the problem is sufficiently complex, then a quantitative analysis of the problem can be an especially important consideration in the manager's final decision.

When using the quantitative approach, an analyst will concentrate on the quantitative facts or data associated with the problem and develop mathematical expressions that

FIGURE 1.2 AN ALTERNATE CLASSIFICATION OF THE DECISION-MAKING PROCESS

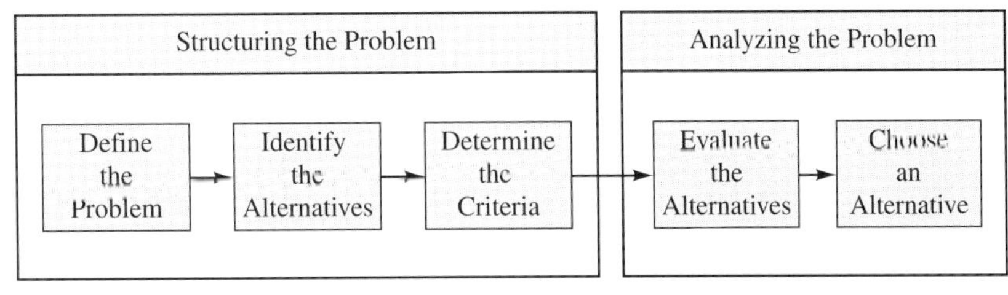

FIGURE 1.3 THE ROLE OF QUALITATIVE AND QUANTITATIVE ANALYSIS

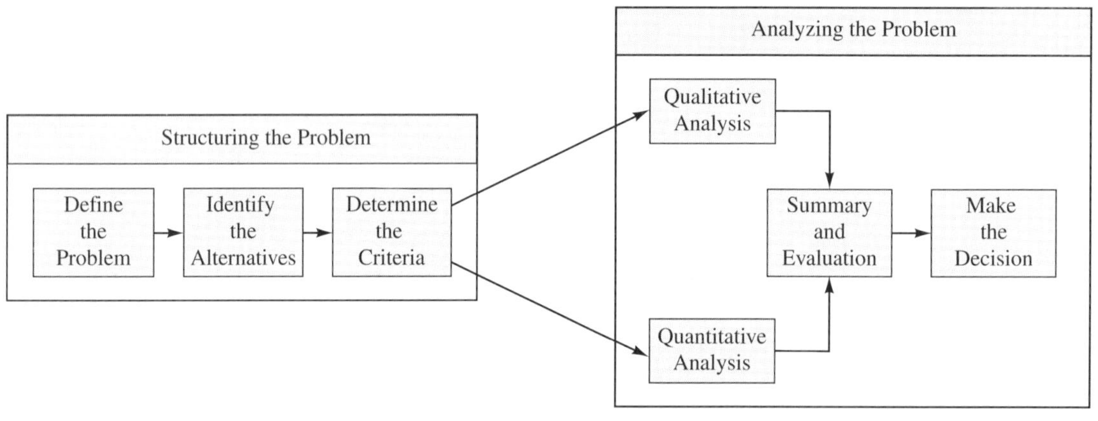

Quantitative methods are especially helpful with large, complex problems. For example, in the coordination of the thousands of tasks associated with landing Apollo 11 safely on the moon, quantitative techniques helped to ensure that more than 300,000 pieces of work performed by more than 400,000 people were integrated smoothly.

describe the objectives, constraints, and other relationships that exist in the problem. Then, by using one or more quantitative methods, the analyst will make a recommendation based on the quantitative aspects of the problem.

Although skills in the qualitative approach are inherent in the manager and usually increase with experience, the skills of the quantitative approach can be learned only by studying the assumptions and methods of management science. A manager can increase decision-making effectiveness by learning more about quantitative methodology and by better understanding its contribution to the decision-making process. A manager who is knowledgeable in quantitative decision-making procedures is in a much better position to compare and evaluate the qualitative and quantitative sources of recommendations and ultimately to combine the two sources in order to make the best possible decision.

The box in Figure 1.3 entitled "Quantitative Analysis" encompasses most of the subject matter of this text. We will consider a managerial problem, introduce the appropriate quantitative methodology, and then develop the recommended decision.

In closing this section, let us briefly state some of the reasons why a quantitative approach might be used in the decision-making process:

Try Problem 4 to test your understanding of why quantitative approaches might be needed in a particular problem.

1. The problem is complex, and the manager cannot develop a good solution without the aid of quantitative analysis.
2. The problem is especially important (e.g., a great deal of money is involved), and the manager desires a thorough analysis before attempting to make a decision.
3. The problem is new, and the manager has no previous experience from which to draw.
4. The problem is repetitive, and the manager saves time and effort by relying on quantitative procedures to make routine decision recommendations.

1.3 QUANTITATIVE ANALYSIS

From Figure 1.3 we see that quantitative analysis begins once the problem has been structured. It usually takes imagination, teamwork, and considerable effort to transform a rather general problem description into a well-defined problem that can be approached via quantitative analysis. The more the analyst is involved in the process of structuring the problem, the more likely the ensuing quantitative analysis will make an important contribution to the decision-making process.

To successfully apply quantitative analysis to decision making, the management scientist must work closely with the manager or user of the results. When both the management scientist and the manager agree that the problem has been adequately structured, work can begin on developing a model to represent the problem mathematically. Solution procedures can then be employed to find the best solution for the model. This best solution for the model then becomes a recommendation to the decision maker. The process of developing and solving models is the essence of the quantitative analysis process.

Model Development

Models are representations of real objects or situations and can be presented in various forms. For example, a scale model of an airplane is a representation of a real airplane. Similarly, a child's toy truck is a model of a real truck. The model airplane and toy truck are examples of models that are physical replicas of real objects. In modeling terminology, physical replicas are referred to as **iconic models.**

A second classification includes models that are physical in form but do not have the same physical appearance as the object being modeled. Such models are referred to as **analog models.** The speedometer of an automobile is an analog model; the position of the needle on the dial represents the speed of the automobile. A thermometer is another analog model representing temperature.

A third classification of models—the type we will primarily be studying—includes representations of a problem by a system of symbols and mathematical relationships or expressions. Such models are referred to as **mathematical models** and are a critical part of any quantitative approach to decision making. For example, the total profit from the sale of a product can be determined by multiplying the profit per unit by the quantity sold. If we let x represent the number of units sold and P the total profit, then, with a profit of \$10 per unit, the following mathematical model defines the total profit earned by selling x units:

$$P = 10x \tag{1.1}$$

The purpose, or value, of any model is that it enables us to make inferences about the real situation by studying and analyzing the model. For example, an airplane designer might test an iconic model of a new airplane in a wind tunnel to learn about the potential flying characteristics of the full-size airplane. Similarly, a mathematical model may be used to make inferences about how much profit will be earned if a specified quantity of a particular product is sold. According to the mathematical model of equation (1.1), we would expect selling three units of the product ($x = 3$) would provide a profit of $P = 10(3) = \$30$.

In general, experimenting with models requires less time and is less expensive than experimenting with the real object or situation. A model airplane is certainly quicker and less expensive to build and study than the full-size airplane. Similarly, the mathematical model in equation (1.1) allows a quick identification of profit expectations without actually requiring the manager to produce and sell x units. Models also have the advantage of reducing the risk associated with experimenting with the real situation. In particular, bad designs or bad decisions that cause the model airplane to crash or a mathematical model to project a \$10,000 loss can be avoided in the real situation.

The value of model-based conclusions and decisions is dependent on how well the model represents the real situation. The more closely the model airplane represents the real

Herbert A. Simon, a Nobel Prize winner in economics and an expert in decision making, said that a mathematical model does not have to be exact; it just has to be close enough to provide better results than can be obtained by common sense.

airplane, the more accurate the conclusions and predictions will be. Similarly, the more closely the mathematical model represents the company's true profit-volume relationship, the more accurate the profit projections will be.

Because this text deals with quantitative analysis based on mathematical models, let us look more closely at the mathematical modeling process. When initially considering a managerial problem, we usually find that the problem definition phase leads to a specific objective, such as maximization of profit or minimization of cost, and possibly a set of restrictions or **constraints,** such as production capacities. The success of the mathematical model and quantitative approach will depend heavily on how accurately the objective and constraints can be expressed in terms of mathematical equations or relationships.

A mathematical expression that describes the problem's objective is referred to as the **objective function.** For example, the profit equation $P = 10x$ would be an objective function for a firm attempting to maximize profit. A production capacity constraint would be necessary if, for instance, 5 hours are required to produce each unit and only 40 hours of production time are available per week. Let x indicate the number of units produced each week. The production time constraint is given by

$$5x \leq 40 \tag{1.2}$$

The value of $5x$ is the total time required to produce x units; the symbol $\leq$ indicates that the production time required must be less than or equal to the 40 hours available.

The decision problem or question is the following: How many units of the product should be scheduled each week to maximize profit? A complete mathematical model for this simple production problem is

$$\begin{aligned} &\text{Maximize} \quad && P = 10x \quad \text{objective function} \\ &\text{subject to (s.t.)} && \\ & && \left.\begin{aligned} 5x &\leq 40 \\ x &\geq 0 \end{aligned}\right\} \text{constraints} \end{aligned}$$

The $x \geq 0$ constraint requires the production quantity x to be greater than or equal to zero, which simply recognizes the fact that it is not possible to manufacture a negative number of units. The optimal solution to this model can be easily calculated and is given by $x = 8$, with an associated profit of \$80. This model is an example of a linear programming model. In subsequent chapters we will discuss more complicated mathematical models and learn how to solve them in situations where the answers are not nearly so obvious.

In the preceding mathematical model, the profit per unit (\$10), the production time per unit (5 hours), and the production capacity (40 hours) are environmental factors that are not under the control of the manager or decision maker. Such environmental factors, which can affect both the objective function and the constraints, are referred to as **uncontrollable inputs** to the model. Inputs that are controlled or determined by the decision maker are referred to as **controllable inputs** to the model. In the example given, the production quantity x is the controllable input to the model. Controllable inputs are the decision alternatives specified by the manager and thus are also referred to as the **decision variables** of the model.

Once all controllable and uncontrollable inputs are specified, the objective function and constraints can be evaluated and the output of the model determined. In this sense, the output of the model is simply the projection of what would happen if those particular

FIGURE 1.4 FLOWCHART OF THE PROCESS OF TRANSFORMING MODEL INPUTS INTO OUTPUT

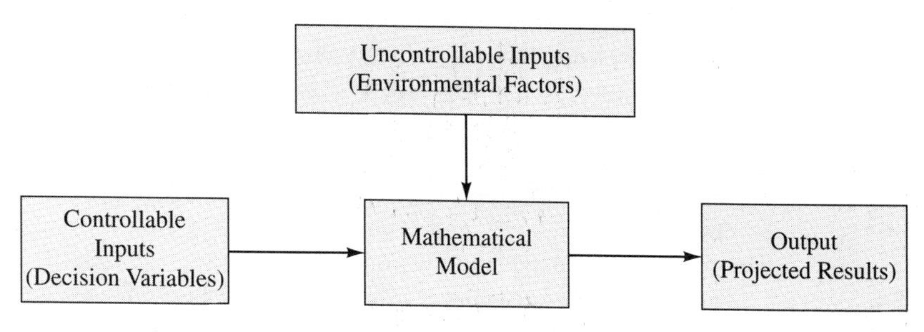

environmental factors and decisions occurred in the real situation. A flowchart of how controllable and uncontrollable inputs are transformed by the mathematical model into output is shown in Figure 1.4. A similar flowchart showing the specific details of the production model is shown in Figure 1.5.

As stated earlier, the uncontrollable inputs are those the decision maker cannot influence. The specific controllable and uncontrollable inputs of a model depend on the particular problem or decision-making situation. In the production problem, the production time available (40) is an uncontrollable input. However, if it were possible to hire more employees or use overtime, the number of hours of production time would become a controllable input and therefore a decision variable in the model.

Uncontrollable inputs can either be known exactly or be uncertain and subject to variation. If all uncontrollable inputs to a model are known and cannot vary, the model is referred to as a **deterministic model.** Corporate income tax rates are not under the influence of the manager and thus constitute an uncontrollable input in many decision models. Because these rates are known and fixed (at least in the short run), a mathematical model with corporate income tax rates as the only uncontrollable input would be a deterministic model.

FIGURE 1.5 FLOWCHART FOR THE PRODUCTION MODEL

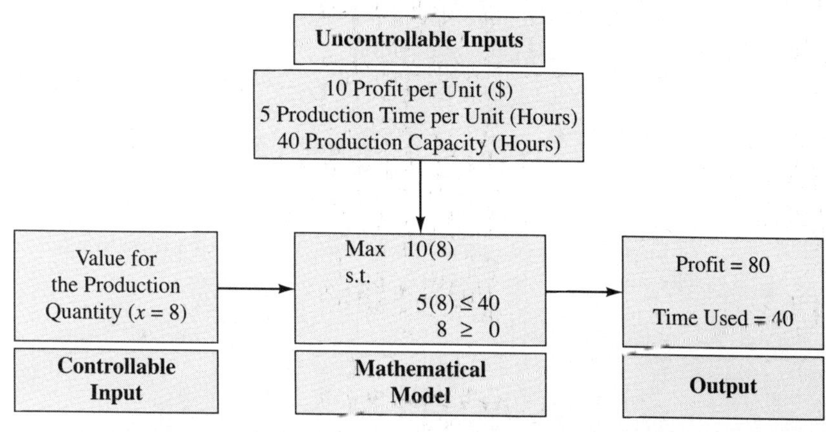

The distinguishing feature of a deterministic model is that the uncontrollable input values are known in advance.

If any of the uncontrollable inputs are uncertain and subject to variation, the model is referred to as a **stochastic** or **probabilistic model.** An uncontrollable input to many production planning models is demand for the product. A mathematical model that treats future demand—which may be any of a range of values—with uncertainty would be called a stochastic model. In the production model, the number of hours of production time required per unit, the total hours available, and the unit profit were all uncontrollable inputs. Because the uncontrollable inputs were all known to take on fixed values, the model was deterministic. If, however, the number of hours of production time per unit could vary from 3 to 6 hours depending on the quality of the raw material, the model would be stochastic. The distinguishing feature of a stochastic model is that the value of the output cannot be determined even if the value of the controllable input is known because the specific values of the uncontrollable inputs are unknown. In this respect, stochastic models are often more difficult to analyze.

Data Preparation

Another step in the quantitative analysis of a problem is the preparation of the data required by the model. Data in this sense refer to the values of the uncontrollable inputs to the model. All uncontrollable inputs or data must be specified before we can analyze the model and recommend a decision or solution for the problem.

In the production model, the values of the uncontrollable inputs or data were \$10 per unit for profit, 5 hours per unit for production time, and 40 hours for production capacity. In the development of the model, these data values were known and incorporated into the model as it was being developed. If the model is relatively small and the uncontrollable input values or data required are few, the quantitative analyst will probably combine model development and data preparation into one step. In these situations the data values are inserted as the equations of the mathematical model are developed.

However, in many mathematical modeling situations, the data or uncontrollable input values are not readily available. In these situations the management scientist may know that the model will need profit per unit, production time, and production capacity data, but the values will not be known until the accounting, production, and engineering departments can be consulted. Rather than attempting to collect the required data as the model is being developed, the analyst will usually adopt a general notation for the model development step and then a separate data preparation step will be performed to obtain the uncontrollable input values required by the model.

Using the general notation

$$
\begin{aligned}
c &= \text{profit per unit} \\
a &= \text{production time in hours per unit} \\
b &= \text{production capacity in hours}
\end{aligned}
$$

the model development step of the production problem would result in the following general model:

$$
\begin{aligned}
\text{Max} \quad & cx \\
\text{s.t.} \quad & \\
& ax \leq b \\
& x \geq 0
\end{aligned}
$$

A separate data preparation step to identify the values for c, a, and b would then be necessary to complete the model.

Many inexperienced quantitative analysts assume that once the problem has been defined and a general model developed, the problem is essentially solved. These individuals tend to believe that data preparation is a trivial step in the process and can be easily handled by clerical staff. Actually, this assumption could not be further from the truth, especially with large-scale models that have numerous data input values. For example, a moderately sized linear programming model with 50 decision variables and 25 constraints could have more than 1300 data elements that must be identified in the data preparation step. The time required to prepare these data and the possibility of data collection errors will make the data preparation step a critical part of the quantitative analysis process. Often, a fairly large database is needed to support a mathematical model, and information systems specialists may become involved in the data preparation step.

Model Solution

Once the model development and data preparation steps are completed, we can proceed to the model solution step. In this step, the analyst will attempt to identify the values of the decision variables that provide the "best" output for the model. The specific decision-variable value or values providing the "best" output will be referred to as the **optimal solution** for the model. For the production problem, the model solution step involves finding the value of the production quantity decision variable x that maximizes profit while not causing a violation of the production capacity constraint.

One procedure that might be used in the model solution step involves a trial-and-error approach in which the model is used to test and evaluate various decision alternatives. In the production model, this procedure would mean testing and evaluating the model under various production quantities or values of x. Note, in Figure 1.5, that we could input trial values for x and check the corresponding output for projected profit and satisfaction of the production capacity constraint. If a particular decision alternative does not satisfy one or more of the model constraints, the decision alternative is rejected as being **infeasible,** regardless of the objective function value. If all constraints are satisfied, the decision alternative is **feasible** and a candidate for the "best" solution or recommended decision. Through this trial-and-error process of evaluating selected decision alternatives, a decision maker can identify a good—and possibly the best—feasible solution to the problem. This solution would then be the recommended decision for the problem.

Table 1.2 shows the results of a trial-and-error approach to solving the production model of Figure 1.5. The recommended decision is a production quantity of 8 because the feasible solution with the highest projected profit occurs at $x = 8$.

Although the trial-and-error solution process is often acceptable and can provide valuable information for the manager, it has the drawbacks of not necessarily providing the best solution and of being inefficient in terms of requiring numerous calculations if many decision alternatives are tried. Thus, quantitative analysts have developed special solution procedures for many models that are much more efficient than the trial-and-error approach. Throughout this text, you will be introduced to solution procedures that are applicable to the specific mathematical models that will be formulated. Some relatively small models or problems can be solved by hand computations, but most practical applications require the use of a computer.

Model development and model solution steps are not completely separable. An analyst will want both to develop an accurate model or representation of the actual problem situation and to be able to find a solution to the model. If we approach the model development

TABLE 1.2 TRIAL-AND-ERROR SOLUTION FOR THE PRODUCTION MODEL OF FIGURE 1.5

Decision Alternative (Production Quantity) x	Projected Profit	Total Hours of Production	Feasible Solution? (Hours Used ≤ 40)
0	0	0	Yes
2	20	10	Yes
4	40	20	Yes
6	60	30	Yes
8	80	40	Yes
10	100	50	No
12	120	60	No

step by attempting to find the most accurate and realistic mathematical model, we may find the model so large and complex that it is impossible to obtain a solution. In this case, a simpler and perhaps more easily understood model with a readily available solution procedure is preferred even if the recommended solution is only a rough approximation of the best decision. As you learn more about quantitative solution procedures, you will have a better idea of the types of mathematical models that can be developed and solved.

Try Problem 8 to test your understanding of the concept of a mathematical model and what is referred to as the optimal solution to the model.

After a model solution is obtained, both the management scientist and the manager will be interested in determining how good the solution really is. Even though the analyst has undoubtedly taken many precautions to develop a realistic model, often the goodness or accuracy of the model cannot be assessed until model solutions are generated. Model testing and validation are frequently conducted with relatively small "test" problems that have known or at least expected solutions. If the model generates the expected solutions, and if other output information appears correct, the go-ahead may be given to use the model on the full-scale problem. However, if the model test and validation identify potential problems or inaccuracies inherent in the model, corrective action, such as model modification and/or collection of more accurate input data, may be taken. Whatever the corrective action, the model solution will not be used in practice until the model has satisfactorily passed testing and validation.

Report Generation

An important part of the quantitative analysis process is the preparation of managerial reports based on the model's solution. In Figure 1.3, we see that the solution based on the quantitative analysis of a problem is one of the inputs the manager considers before making a final decision. Thus, the results of the model must appear in a managerial report that can be easily understood by the decision maker. The report includes the recommended decision and other pertinent information about the results that may be helpful to the decision maker.

A Note Regarding Implementation

As discussed in Section 1.2, the manager is responsible for integrating the quantitative solution with qualitative considerations in order to make the best possible decision. After completing the decision-making process, the manager must oversee the implementation and follow-up evaluation of the decision. The manager should continue to monitor the contribution of the model during the implementation and follow-up. At times, this process may lead to requests for model expansion or refinement that will cause the management scientist to return to an earlier step of the quantitative analysis process.

Successful implementation of results is of critical importance to the management scientist as well as the manager. If the results of the quantitative analysis process are not correctly implemented, the entire effort may be of no value. It doesn't take too many unsuccessful implementations before the management scientist is out of work. Because implementation often requires people to do things differently, it often meets with resistance. People want to know, "What's wrong with the way we've been doing it?" and so on. One of the most effective ways to ensure successful implementation is to include users throughout the modeling process. A user who feels a part of identifying the problem and developing the solution is much more likely to enthusiastically implement the results. The success rate for implementing the results of a management science project is much greater for those projects characterized by extensive user involvement. The Management Science in Action, Quantitative Analysis at Merrill Lynch, discusses some of the reasons behind the success Merrill Lynch realized from using quantitative analysis.

MANAGEMENT SCIENCE IN ACTION

QUANTITATIVE ANALYSIS AT MERRILL LYNCH*

Merrill Lynch, a brokerage and financial services firm with more than 56,000 employees in 45 countries, serves its client base through two business units. The Merrill Lynch Corporate and Institutional Client Group serves more than 7000 corporations, institutions, and governments. The Merrill Lynch Private Client Group (MLPC) serves approximately 4 million households, as well as 225,000 small to mid-sized businesses and regional financial institutions, through more than 14,000 financial consultants in 600-plus branch offices. The management science group, established in 1986, has been part of MLPC since 1991. The mission of this group is to provide high-end quantitative analysis to support strategic management decisions and to enhance the financial consultant–client relationship.

The management science group has successfully implemented models and developed systems for asset allocation, financial planning, marketing information technology, database marketing, and portfolio performance measurement. Although technical expertise and objectivity are clearly important factors in any analytical group, the management science group attributes much of its success to communications skills, teamwork, and consulting skills.

Each project begins with face-to-face meetings with the client. A proposal is then prepared to outline the background of the problem, the objectives of the project, the approach, the required resources, the time schedule, and the implementation issues. At this stage, analysts focus on developing solutions that provide significant value and are easily implemented.

As the work progresses, frequent meetings keep the clients up-to-date. Because people with different skills, perspectives, and motivations must work together for a common goal, teamwork is essential. The group's members take classes in team approaches, facilitation, and conflict resolution. They possess a broad range of multifunctional and multidisciplinary capabilities and are motivated to provide solutions that focus on the goals of the firm. This approach to problem solving and the implementation of quantitative analysis has been a hallmark of the management science group. The impact and success of the group translates into hard dollars and repeat business. The group recently received the annual Edelman award given by the Institute for Operations Research and the Management Sciences for effective use of management science for organizational success.

*Based on Russ Labe, Raj Nigam, and Steve Spence, "Management Science at Merrill Lynch Private Client Group," *Interfaces* 29, no. 2 (March/April 1999): 1–14.

NOTES AND COMMENTS

1. Developments in computer technology have increased the availability of management science techniques to decision makers. Many software packages are now available for personal computers. Versions of The Management Scientist, Microsoft Excel, and LINGO are widely used in management science courses.
2. The Management Scientist (Version 6.0) is a software package developed by the authors of this text. This software can be used to solve problems in the text as well as small-scale problems encountered in practice. Appendix 1.1 provides an overview of the features and use of The Management Scientist.
3. Various chapter appendixes provide step-by-step instructions for using The Management Scientist, Excel, and LINGO to solve problems in the text.

1.4 MODELS OF COST, REVENUE, AND PROFIT

Some of the most basic quantitative models arising in business and economic applications are those involving the relationship between a volume variable—such as production volume or sales volume—and cost, revenue, and profit. Through the use of these models, a manager can determine the projected cost, revenue, and/or profit associated with an established production quantity or a forecasted sales volume. Financial planning, production planning, sales quotas, and other areas of decision making can benefit from such cost, revenue, and profit models.

Cost and Volume Models

The cost of manufacturing or producing a product is a function of the volume produced. This cost can usually be defined as a sum of two costs: fixed cost and variable cost. **Fixed cost** is the portion of the total cost that does not depend on the production volume; this cost remains the same no matter how much is produced. **Variable cost,** on the other hand, is the portion of the total cost that is dependent on and varies with the production volume. To illustrate how cost and volume models can be developed, we will consider a manufacturing problem faced by Nowlin Plastics.

Nowlin Plastics produces a variety of compact disc (CD) storage cases. Nowlin's best-selling product is the CD-50, a slim, plastic CD holder with a specially designed lining that protects the optical surface of the disc. Several products are produced on the same manufacturing line, and a setup cost is incurred each time a changeover is made for a new product. Suppose that the setup cost for the CD-50 is \$3000. This setup cost is a fixed cost that is incurred regardless of the number of units eventually produced. In addition, suppose that variable labor and material costs are \$2 for each unit produced. The cost-volume model for producing x units of the CD-50 can be written as

$$C(x) = 3000 + 2x \tag{1.3}$$

where

$$\begin{aligned} x &= \text{production volume in units} \\ C(x) &= \text{total cost of producing } x \text{ units} \end{aligned}$$

Once a production volume is established, the model in equation (1.3) can be used to compute the total production cost. For example, the decision to produce $x = 1200$ units would result in a total cost of $C(1200) = 3000 + 2(1200) = \$5400$.

Marginal cost is defined as the rate of change of the total cost with respect to production volume. That is, it is the cost increase associated with a one-unit increase in the production volume. In the cost model of equation (1.3), we see that the total cost $C(x)$ will increase by \$2 for each unit increase in the production volume. Thus, the marginal cost is \$2. With more complex total cost models, marginal cost may depend on the production volume. In such cases, we could have marginal cost increasing or decreasing with the production volume x.

Revenue and Volume Models

Management of Nowlin Plastics will also want information on the projected revenue associated with selling a specified number of units. Thus, a model of the relationship between revenue and volume is also needed. Suppose that each CD-50 storage unit sells for \$5. The model for total revenue can be written as

$$R(x) = 5x \tag{1.4}$$

where

$$\begin{aligned} x &= \text{sales volume in units} \\ R(x) &= \text{total revenue associated with selling } x \text{ units} \end{aligned}$$

Marginal revenue is defined as the rate of change of total revenue with respect to sales volume. That is, it is the increase in total revenue resulting from a one-unit increase in sales volume. In the model of equation (1.4), we see that the marginal revenue is \$5. In this case, marginal revenue is constant and does not vary with the sales volume. With more complex models, we may find that marginal revenue increases or decreases as the sales volume x increases.

Profit and Volume Models

One of the most important criteria for management decision making is profit. Managers need to be able to know the profit implications of their decisions. If we assume that we will only produce what can be sold, the production volume and sales volume will be equal. We can combine equations (1.3) and (1.4) to develop a profit-volume model that will determine the total profit associated with a specified production-sales volume. Total profit, denoted $P(x)$, is total revenue minus total cost; therefore, the following model provides the total profit associated with producing and selling x units:

$$\begin{aligned} P(x) &= R(x) - C(x) \\ &= 5x - (3000 + 2x) = -3000 + 3x \end{aligned} \tag{1.5}$$

Thus, the profit-volume model can be derived from the revenue-volume and cost-volume models.

Breakeven Analysis

Using equation (1.5), we can now determine the total profit associated with any production volume x. For example, suppose that a demand forecast indicates that 500 units of the product can be sold. The decision to produce and sell the 500 units results in a projected profit of

$$P(500) = -3000 + 3(500) = -1500$$

In other words, a loss of \$1500 is predicted. If sales are expected to be 500 units, the manager may decide against producing the product. However, a demand forecast of 1800 units would show a projected profit of

$$P(1800) = -3000 + 3(1800) = 2400$$

This profit may be enough to justify proceeding with the production and sale of the product.

We see that a volume of 500 units will yield a loss, whereas a volume of 1800 provides a profit. The volume that results in total revenue equaling total cost (providing \$0 profit) is called the **breakeven point.** If the breakeven point is known, a manager can quickly infer that a volume above the breakeven point will result in a profit, while a volume below the breakeven point will result in a loss. Thus, the breakeven point for a product provides valuable information for a manager who must make a yes/no decision concerning production of the product.

Let us now return to the Nowlin Plastics example and show how the total profit model in equation (1.5) can be used to compute the breakeven point. The breakeven point can be found by setting the total profit expression equal to zero and solving for the production volume. Using equation (1.5), we have

$$\begin{aligned} P(x) = -3000 + 3x &= 0 \\ 3x &= 3000 \\ x &= 1000 \end{aligned}$$

Try Problem 12 to test your ability to determine the breakeven point for a quantitative model.

With this information, we know that production and sales of the product must be greater than 1000 units before a profit can be expected. The graphs of the total cost model, the total revenue model, and the location of the breakeven point are shown in Figure 1.6. In Appendix 1.2 we also show how Excel can be used to perform a breakeven analysis for the Nowlin Plastics production example.

1.5 MANAGEMENT SCIENCE TECHNIQUES

In this section we present a brief overview of the management science techniques covered in this text. Over the years, practitioners have found numerous applications for the following techniques:

Linear Programming Linear programming is a problem-solving approach developed for situations involving maximizing or minimizing a linear function subject to linear constraints that limit the degree to which the objective can be pursued. The production model developed in Section 1.3 (see Figure 1.5) is an example of a simple linear programming model.

Integer Linear Programming Integer linear programming is an approach used for problems that can be set up as linear programs with the additional requirement that some or all of the decision variables be integer values.

FIGURE 1.6 GRAPH OF THE BREAKEVEN ANALYSIS FOR NOWLIN PLASTICS

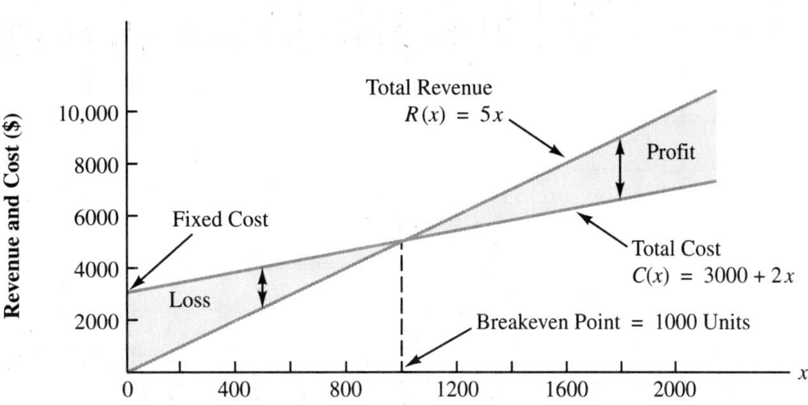

Network Models A network is a graphical description of a problem consisting of circles called nodes that are interconnected by lines called arcs. Specialized solution procedures exist for these types of problems, enabling us to quickly solve problems in such areas as transportation system design, information system design, and project scheduling.

Project Scheduling: PERT/CPM In many situations, managers are responsible for planning, scheduling, and controlling projects that consist of numerous separate jobs or tasks performed by a variety of departments, individuals, and so forth. The PERT (Program Evaluation and Review Technique) and CPM (Critical Path Method) techniques help managers carry out their project scheduling responsibilities.

Inventory Models Inventory models are used by managers faced with the dual problems of maintaining sufficient inventories to meet demand for goods and, at the same time, incurring the lowest possible inventory holding costs.

Waiting Line or Queueing Models Waiting-line or queueing models have been developed to help managers understand and make better decisions concerning the operation of systems involving waiting lines.

Simulation Simulation is a technique used to model the operation of a system. This technique employs a computer program to model the operation and perform simulation computations.

Decision Analysis Decision analysis can be used to determine optimal strategies in situations involving several decision alternatives and an uncertain or risk-filled pattern of events.

Goal Programming Goal programming is a technique for solving multicriteria decision problems, usually within the framework of linear programming.

Analytic Hierarchy Process This multicriteria decision-making technique permits the inclusion of subjective factors in arriving at a recommended decision.

Forecasting Forecasting methods are techniques that can be used to predict future aspects of a business operation.

Markov Process Models Markov process models are useful in studying the evolution of certain systems over repeated trials. For example, Markov processes have been used to describe the probability that a machine, functioning in one period, will function or break down in another period.

Dynamic Programming Dynamic programming is an approach that allows us to break up a large problem in such a fashion that once all the smaller problems have been solved, we are left with an optimal solution to the large problem.

Methods Used Most Frequently

Our experience as both practitioners and educators has been that the most frequently used management science techniques are linear programming, integer programming, network models (including transportation and transshipment models), and simulation. Depending upon the industry, the other methods in the preceding list are used more or less frequently.

Helping to bridge the gap between the manager and the management scientist is a major focus of the text. We believe that the barriers to the use of management science can best be removed by increasing the manager's understanding of how management science can be applied. The text will help you develop an understanding of which management science techniques are most useful, how they are used, and, most importantly, how they can assist managers in making better decisions.

The Management Science in Action, Impact of Operations Research on Everyday Living, describes some of the many ways quantitative analysis affects our everyday lives.

MANAGEMENT SCIENCE IN ACTION

IMPACT OF OPERATIONS RESEARCH ON EVERYDAY LIVING*

Mark Eisner, associate director of the School of Operations Research and Industrial Engineering at Cornell University, once said that operations research "is probably the most important field nobody's ever heard of." The impact of operations research on everyday living over the past 20 years is substantial.

Suppose you schedule a vacation to Florida and use Orbitz to book your flights. An algorithm developed by operations researchers will search among millions of options to find the cheapest fare. Another algorithm will schedule the flight crews and aircraft used by the airline. If you rent a car in Florida, the price you pay for the car is determined by a mathematical model that seeks to maximize revenue for the car rental firm. If you do some shopping on your trip and decide to ship your purchases home using UPS, another algorithm tells UPS which truck to put the packages on, the route the truck should follow, and where the packages should be placed on the truck to minimize loading and unloading time.

If you enjoy watching college basketball, operations research plays a role in what games you see. Michael Trick, a professor at the Tepper School of Business at Carnegie-Mellon, designed a system for scheduling each year's Atlantic Coast Conference men's and women's basketball games. Even though it might initially appear that scheduling 16 games among the nine men's teams would be easy, it requires sorting through hundreds of millions of possible combinations of possible schedules. Each of those possibilities entails some desirable and some undesirable characteristics. For example, you do not want to schedule too many consecutive home games, and you want to ensure that each team plays the same number of weekend games.

*Based on Virginia Postrel, "Operations Everything," *The Boston Globe,* June 27, 2004.

NOTES AND COMMENTS

The Institute for Operations Research and the Management Sciences (INFORMS) and the Decision Sciences Institute (DSI) are two professional societies that publish journals and newsletters dealing with current research and applications of operations research and management science techniques.

SUMMARY

This text is about how management science may be used to help managers make better decisions. The focus of this text is on the decision-making process and on the role of management science in that process. We discussed the problem orientation of this process and in an overview showed how mathematical models can be used in this type of analysis.

The difference between the model and the situation or managerial problem it represents is an important point. Mathematical models are abstractions of real-world situations and, as such, cannot capture all the aspects of the real situation. However, if a model can capture the major relevant aspects of the problem and can then provide a solution recommendation, it can be a valuable aid to decision making.

One of the characteristics of management science that will become increasingly apparent as we proceed through the text is the search for a best solution to the problem. In carrying out the quantitative analysis, we shall be attempting to develop procedures for finding the "best" or optimal solution.

GLOSSARY

Problem solving The process of identifying a difference between the actual and the desired state of affairs and then taking action to resolve the difference.

Decision making The process of defining the problem, identifying the alternatives, determining the criteria, evaluating the alternatives, and choosing an alternative.

Single-criterion decision problem A problem in which the objective is to find the "best" solution with respect to just one criterion.

Multicriteria decision problem A problem that involves more than one criterion; the objective is to find the "best" solution, taking into account all the criteria.

Decision The alternative selected.

Model A representation of a real object or situation.

Iconic model A physical replica, or representation, of a real object.

Analog model Although physical in form, an analog model does not have a physical appearance similar to the real object or situation it represents.

Mathematical model Mathematical symbols and expressions used to represent a real situation.

Constraints Restrictions or limitations imposed on a problem.

Objective function A mathematical expression that describes the problem's objective.

Uncontrollable inputs The environmental factors or inputs that cannot be controlled by the decision maker.

Controllable inputs The inputs that are controlled or determined by the decision maker.

Decision variable Another term for controllable input.

Deterministic model A model in which all uncontrollable inputs are known and cannot vary.

Stochastic (probabilistic) model A model in which at least one uncontrollable input is uncertain and subject to variation; stochastic models are also referred to as probabilistic models.

Optimal solution The specific decision-variable value or values that provide the "best" output for the model.

Infeasible solution A decision alternative or solution that does not satisfy one or more constraints.

Feasible solution A decision alternative or solution that satisfies all constraints.

Fixed cost The portion of the total cost that does not depend on the volume; this cost remains the same no matter how much is produced.

Variable cost The portion of the total cost that is dependent on and varies with the volume.

Marginal cost The rate of change of the total cost with respect to volume.

Marginal revenue The rate of change of total revenue with respect to volume.

Breakeven point The volume at which total revenue equals total cost.

PROBLEMS

1. Define the terms *management science* and *operations research.*
2. List and discuss the steps of the decision-making process.
3. Discuss the different roles played by the qualitative and quantitative approaches to managerial decision making. Why is it important for a manager or decision maker to have a good understanding of both of these approaches to decision making?

4. A firm just completed a new plant that will produce more than 500 different products, using more than 50 different production lines and machines. The production scheduling decisions are critical in that sales will be lost if customer demands are not met on time. If no individual in the firm has experience with this production operation, and if new production schedules must be generated each week, why should the firm consider a quantitative approach to the production scheduling problem?
5. What are the advantages of analyzing and experimenting with a model as opposed to a real object or situation?
6. Suppose that a manager has a choice between the following two mathematical models of a given situation: (a) a relatively simple model that is a reasonable approximation of the real situation, and (b) a thorough and complex model that is the most accurate mathematical representation of the real situation possible. Why might the model described in part (a) be preferred by the manager?
7. Suppose you are going on a weekend trip to a city that is d miles away. Develop a model that determines your round-trip gasoline costs. What assumptions or approximations are necessary to treat this model as a deterministic model? Are these assumptions or approximations acceptable to you?

8. Recall the production model from Section 1.3:

$$\begin{aligned} &\text{Max} \quad 10x \\ &\text{s.t.} \\ &\qquad 5x \leq 40 \\ &\qquad\ \ x \geq 0 \end{aligned}$$

Suppose the firm in this example considers a second product that has a unit profit of \$5 and requires 2 hours of production time for each unit produced. Use y as the number of units of product 2 produced.

a. Show the mathematical model when both products are considered simultaneously.
b. Identify the controllable and uncontrollable inputs for this model.
c. Draw the flowchart of the input-output process for this model (see Figure 1.5).
d. What are the optimal solution values of x and y?
e. Is the model developed in part (a) a deterministic or a stochastic model? Explain.

9. Suppose we modify the production model in Section 1.3 to obtain the following mathematical model:

$$\begin{aligned} \text{Max} \quad & 10x \\ \text{s.t.} \quad & \\ & ax \leq 40 \\ & x \geq 0 \end{aligned}$$

where a is the number of hours of production time required for each unit produced. With $a = 5$, the optimal solution is $x = 8$. If we have a stochastic model with $a = 3$, $a = 4$, $a = 5$, or $a = 6$ as the possible values for the number of hours required per unit, what is the optimal value for x? What problems does this stochastic model cause?

10. A retail store in Des Moines, Iowa, receives shipments of a particular product from Kansas City and Minneapolis. Let

$$\begin{aligned} x &= \text{number of units of the product received from Kansas City} \\ y &= \text{number of units of the product received from Minneapolis} \end{aligned}$$

a. Write an expression for the total number of units of the product received by the retail store in Des Moines.
b. Shipments from Kansas City cost \$0.20 per unit, and shipments from Minneapolis cost \$0.25 per unit. Develop an objective function representing the total cost of shipments to Des Moines.
c. Assuming the monthly demand at the retail store is 5000 units, develop a constraint that requires 5000 units to be shipped to Des Moines.
d. No more than 4000 units can be shipped from Kansas City, and no more than 3000 units can be shipped from Minneapolis in a month. Develop constraints to model this situation.
e. Of course, negative amounts cannot be shipped. Combine the objective function and constraints developed to state a mathematical model for satisfying the demand at the Des Moines retail store at minimum cost.

11. For most products, higher prices result in a decreased demand, whereas lower prices result in an increased demand. Let

$$\begin{aligned} d &= \text{annual demand for a product in units} \\ p &= \text{price per unit} \end{aligned}$$

Assume that a firm accepts the following price-demand relationship as being realistic:

$$d = 800 - 10p$$

where p must be between \$20 and \$70.

a. How many units can the firm sell at the \$20 per-unit price? At the \$70 per-unit price?
b. Show the mathematical model for the total revenue (TR), which is the annual demand multiplied by the unit price.

c. Based on other considerations, the firm's management will only consider price alternatives of \$30, \$40, and \$50. Use your model from part (b) to determine the price alternative that will maximize the total revenue.
d. What are the expected annual demand and the total revenue corresponding to your recommended price?

12. The O'Neill Shoe Manufacturing Company will produce a special-style shoe if the order size is large enough to provide a reasonable profit. For each special-style order, the company incurs a fixed cost of \$1000 for the production setup. The variable cost is \$30 per pair, and each pair sells for \$40.
    a. Let x indicate the number of pairs of shoes produced. Develop a mathematical model for the total cost of producing x pairs of shoes.
    b. Let P indicate the total profit. Develop a mathematical model for the total profit realized from an order for x pairs of shoes.
    c. How large must the shoe order be before O'Neill will break even?
13. Micromedia offers computer training seminars on a variety of topics. In the seminars each student works at a personal computer, practicing the particular activity that the instructor is presenting. Micromedia is currently planning a two-day seminar on the use of Microsoft Excel in statistical analysis. The projected fee for the seminar is \$300 per student. The cost for the conference room, instructor compensation, lab assistants, and promotion is \$4800. Micromedia rents computers for its seminars at a cost of \$30 per computer per day.
    a. Develop a model for the total cost to put on the seminar. Let x represent the number of students who enroll in the seminar.
    b. Develop a model for the total profit if x students enroll in the seminar.
    c. Micromedia has forecasted an enrollment of 30 students for the seminar. How much profit will be earned if their forecast is accurate?
    d. Compute the breakeven point.
14. Eastman Publishing Company is considering publishing a paperback textbook on spreadsheet applications for business. The fixed cost of manuscript preparation, textbook design, and production setup is estimated to be \$80,000. Variable production and material costs are estimated to be \$3 per book. Demand over the life of the book is estimated to be 4000 copies. The publisher plans to sell the text to college and university bookstores for \$20 each.
    a. What is the breakeven point?
    b. What profit or loss can be anticipated with a demand of 4000 copies?
    c. With a demand of 4000 copies, what is the minimum price per copy that the publisher must charge to break even?
    d. If the publisher believes that the price per copy could be increased to \$25.95 and not affect the anticipated demand of 4000 copies, what action would you recommend? What profit or loss can be anticipated?
15. Preliminary plans are under way for the construction of a new stadium for a major league baseball team. City officials have questioned the number and profitability of the luxury corporate boxes planned for the upper deck of the stadium. Corporations and selected individuals may buy the boxes for \$100,000 each. The fixed construction cost for the upper-deck area is estimated to be \$1,500,000, with a variable cost of \$50,000 for each box constructed.
    a. What is the breakeven point for the number of luxury boxes in the new stadium?
    b. Preliminary drawings for the stadium show that space is available for the construction of up to 50 luxury boxes. Promoters indicate that buyers are available and that all 50 could be sold if constructed. What is your recommendation concerning the construction of luxury boxes? What profit is anticipated?

16. Financial Analysts, Inc., is an investment firm that manages stock portfolios for a number of clients. A new client is requesting that the firm handle an $80,000 portfolio. As an initial investment strategy, the client would like to restrict the portfolio to a mix of the following two stocks:

Stock	Price/ Share	Estimated Annual Return/Share	Maximum Possible Investment
Oil Alaska	$50	$6	$50,000
Southwest Petroleum	$30	$4	$45,000

Let

$$x = \text{number of shares of Oil Alaska}$$
$$y = \text{number of shares of Southwest Petroleum}$$

a. Develop the objective function, assuming that the client desires to maximize the total annual return.
b. Show the mathematical expression for each of the following three constraints:
(1) Total investment funds available are $80,000.
(2) Maximum Oil Alaska investment is $50,000.
(3) Maximum Southwest Petroleum investment is $45,000.

Note: Adding the $x \geq 0$ and $y \geq 0$ constraints provides a linear programming model for the investment problem. A solution procedure for this model will be discussed in Chapter 2.

17. Models of inventory systems frequently consider the relationships among a beginning inventory, a production quantity, a demand or sales, and an ending inventory. For a given production period j, let

s_{j-1} = ending inventory from the previous period (beginning inventory for period j)
x_j = production quantity in period j
d_j = demand in period j
s_j = ending inventory for period j

a. Write the mathematical relationship or model that describes how these four variables are related.
b. What constraint should be added if production capacity for period j is given by C_j?
c. What constraint should be added if inventory requirements for period j mandate an ending inventory of at least I_j?

Case Problem SCHEDULING A GOLF LEAGUE

Chris Lane, the head professional at Royal Oak Country Club, must develop a schedule of matches for the couples' golf league that begins its season at 4:00 P.M. tomorrow. Eighteen couples signed up for the league, and each couple must play every other couple over the course of the 17-week season. Chris thought it would be fairly easy to develop a schedule, but after working on it for a couple of hours, he has been unable to come up with a schedule. Because Chris must have a schedule ready by tomorrow afternoon, he asked you to help him. A possible complication is that one of the couples told Chris that they may have to cancel for the season. They told Chris they will let him know by 1:00 P.M. tomorrow whether they will be able to play this season.

Managerial Report

Prepare a report for Chris Lane. Your report should include, at a minimum, the following items:

1. A schedule that will enable each of the 18 couples to play every other couple over the 17-week season.
2. A contingency schedule that can be used if the couple that contacted Chris decides to cancel for the season.

Appendix 1.1 THE MANAGEMENT SCIENTIST SOFTWARE

Developments in computer technology play a major role in making management science techniques available to decision makers. A software package called *The Management Scientist* (Version 6.0) accompanies this text. This software can be used to solve problems in the text as well as small-scale problems encountered in practice. Using The Management Scientist will give you an understanding and appreciation of the role of the computer in applying management science to decision problems.

The Management Scientist contains 12 modules, or programs, that will enable you to solve problems in the following areas:

Chapters 2–6	Linear programming
Chapter 7	Transportation and assignment
Chapter 8	Integer linear programming
Chapter 9	Shortest route and minimal spanning tree
Chapter 10	PERT/CPM
Chapter 11	Inventory models
Chapter 12	Waiting line models
Chapter 14	Decision analysis
Chapter 16	Forecasting
Chapter 17	Markov processes

Use of The Management Scientist with the text is optional. Occasionally, we insert a figure in the text that shows the output The Management Scientist provides for a problem. However, familiarity with the use of the software is not necessary to understand the figure and the text material. The remainder of this appendix provides an overview of the features and the use of the software.

Selecting a Module

After starting The Management Scientist, you will encounter the module selection screen as shown in Figure 1.7. The choices provide access to the 12 modules. Simply click the desired module and select OK to load the requested module into the computer's memory.

FIGURE 1.7 MODULE SELECTION SCREEN FOR THE MANAGEMENT SCIENTIST VERSION 6.0

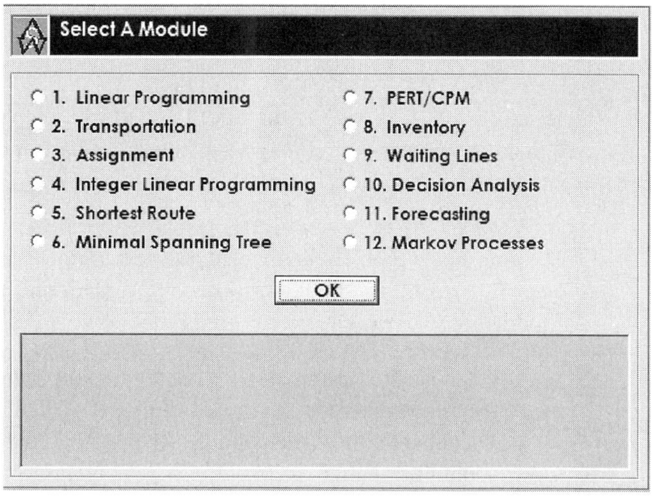

Select A Module

1. Linear Programming
2. Transportation
3. Assignment
4. Integer Linear Programming
5. Shortest Route
6. Minimal Spanning Tree
7. PERT/CPM
8. Inventory
9. Waiting Lines
10. Decision Analysis
11. Forecasting
12. Markov Processes

OK

The File Menu

After a module is loaded, you will need to click the File menu to begin working with a problem. The File menu provides the following options.

New Select this option to begin a new problem. Dialog boxes and input templates will guide you through the data input process.

Open Select this option to retrieve a problem that has been previously saved. When the problem is selected it will be displayed on the screen for you to verify as the problem you want to solve.

Save Once a new problem has been entered, you may want to save it for future use or modification. The Save option will guide you through the naming and saving process. If you create a folder named Problems, the Open and Save options will take you automatically to the Problems folder.

Change Modules This option returns control to the screen in Figure 1.7 and another module may be selected.

Exit This option will exit The Management Scientist.

The Edit Menu

After a new problem has been solved, you may want to make one or more modifications to the problem before re-solving. The Edit menu provides the option to display the problem and then make revisions in the problem before solving or saving. In the linear and integer programming modules, the Edit menu also includes options to change the problem size by adding or deleting variables and adding or deleting constraints. Similar options to change the problem size are provided in the Edit menu of the transportation and assignment modules.

The Solution Menu

The Solution menu provides three options.

Solve This option solves the current problem and displays the solution on the screen.

Print Once the solution is on the screen, the Print option sends the solution to a printer.

Save As Text File Once the solution is on the screen, the Save As Text File option enables the solution to be saved as a text file. The text file can be accessed later by a word processor so that the solution output may be displayed as part of a solution report.

Advice About Data Input

Any time a new problem is selected, the appropriate module will provide dialog boxes and forms for describing the features of the problem and for entering data. When using The Management Scientist, you may find the following data input suggestions helpful.

1. Do not enter commas (,) with your input data. For example, the value 104,000 should be entered with the six digits: 104000.
2. Do not enter the dollar sign ($) for profit or cost data. For example, a cost of $20.00 should be entered as 20.
3. Do not enter the percent sign (%) if percentage is requested. For example, 25% should be entered as 25, not 25% or .25.
4. Occasionally, a model may be formulated with fractional values such as ¼, ⅔, ⅚, and so on. The data input for The Management Scientist must be in decimal form. The fraction ¼ can be entered as .25. However, fractions such as ⅔ and ⅚ have repeating decimal forms. In these cases, we recommend the convention of rounding to five places such as .66667 and .83333.
5. Finally, we recommend that in general you attempt to scale extremely large input data so that smaller numbers may be input and operated on by the computer. For example, costs such as $2,500,000 may be scaled to 2.5 with the understanding that the data used in the problem reflect millions of dollars.

Appendix 1.2 USING EXCEL FOR BREAKEVEN ANALYSIS

In Section 1.4 we introduced the Nowlin Plastics production example to illustrate how quantitative models can be used to help a manager determine the projected cost, revenue, and/or profit associated with an established production quantity or a forecasted sales volume. In this appendix we introduce spreadsheet applications by showing how to use Microsoft Excel to perform a quantitative analysis of the Nowlin Plastics example.

Refer to the worksheet shown in Figure 1.8. We begin by entering the problem data into the top portion of the worksheet. The value of 3000 in cell B3 is the setup cost, the value of 2 in cell B5 is the variable labor and material costs per unit, and the value of 5 in cell B7 is the selling price per unit. In general, whenever we perform a quantitative analysis using Excel, we will enter the problem data in the top portion of the worksheet and reserve the bottom portion for model development. The label "Models" in cell A10 helps to provide a visual reminder of this convention.

Cell B12 in the models portion of the worksheet contains the proposed production volume in units. Because the values for total cost, total revenue, and total profit depend upon the value of this decision variable, we have placed a border around cell B12 and screened the cell for emphasis. Based upon the value in cell B12, the cell formulas in cells B14, B16, and B18 are used to compute values for total cost, total revenue, and total profit (loss),

FIGURE 1.8 FORMULA WORKSHEET FOR THE NOWLIN PLASTICS PRODUCTION EXAMPLE

	A	B
1	**Nowlin Plastics**	
2		
3	**Fixed Cost**	3000
4		
5	**Variable Cost Per Unit**	2
6		
7	**Selling Price Per Unit**	5
8		
9		
10	**Models**	
11		
12	**Production Volume**	800
13		
14	**Total Cost**	=B3+B5*B12
15		
16	**Total Revenue**	=B7*B12
17		
18	**Total Profit (Loss)**	=B16-B14

respectively. First, recall that the value of total cost is the sum of the fixed cost (cell B3) and the total variable cost. The total variable cost—the product of the variable cost per unit (cell B5) and the production volume (cell B12)—is given by B5*B12. Thus, to compute the value of total cost we entered the formula =B3+B5*B12 in cell B14. Next, total revenue is the product of the selling price per unit (cell B7) and the number of units produced (cell B12), which is entered in cell B16 as the formula =B7*B12. Finally, the total profit (or loss) is the difference between the total revenue (cell B16) and the total cost (cell B14). Thus, in cell B18 we have entered the formula =B16−B14. The worksheet shown in Figure 1.8 shows the formulas used to make these computations; we refer to it as a formula worksheet.

To examine the effect of selecting a particular value for the production volume, we entered a value of 800 in cell B12. The worksheet shown in Figure 1.9 shows the values obtained by the formulas; a production volume of 800 units results in a total cost of $4600, a total revenue of $4000, and a loss of $600. To examine the effect of other production volumes, we only need to enter a different value into cell B12. To examine the effect of different costs and selling prices, we simply enter the appropriate values in the data portion of the worksheet; the results will be displayed in the model section of the worksheet.

In Section 1.4 we illustrated breakeven analysis. Let us now see how Excel's Goal Seek tool can be used to compute the breakeven point for the Nowlin Plastics production example.

Determining the Breakeven Point Using Excel's Goal Seek Tool

The breakeven point is the production volume that results in total revenue equal to total cost and hence a profit of $0. One way to determine the breakeven point is to use a trial-and-error approach. For example, in Figure 1.9 we saw that a trial production volume of 800 units

FIGURE 1.9 SOLUTION USING A PRODUCTION VOLUME OF 800 UNITS FOR THE NOWLIN PLASTICS PRODUCTION EXAMPLE

	A	B
1	**Nowlin Plastics**	
2		
3	**Fixed Cost**	$3,000
4		
5	**Variable Cost Per Unit**	$2
6		
7	**Selling Price Per Unit**	$5
8		
9		
10	**Models**	
11		
12	**Production Volume**	800
13		
14	**Total Cost**	$4,600
15		
16	**Total Revenue**	$4,000
17		
18	**Total Profit (Loss)**	−$600

Tutorial 1: Breakeven Analysis

resulted in a loss of $600. Because this trial solution resulted in a loss, a production volume of 800 units cannot be the breakeven point. We could continue to experiment with other production volumes by simply entering different values into cell B12 and observing the resulting profit or loss in cell B18. A better approach is to use Excel's Goal Seek tool to determine the breakeven point.

Excel's Goal Seek tool allows the user to determine the value for an input cell that will cause the value of a related output cell to equal some specified value (called the *goal*). In the case of breakeven analysis, the "goal" is to set Total Profit to zero by "seeking" an appropriate value for Production Volume. Goal Seek will allow us to find the value of production volume that will set Nowlin Plastics' total profit to zero. The following steps describe how to use Goal Seek to find the breakeven point for Nowlin Plastics:

Step 1. Select the **Tools** menu
Step 2. Choose the **Goal Seek** option
Step 3. When the **Goal Seek** dialog box appears:
Enter B18 in the **Set cell** box
Enter 0 in the **To value** box
Enter B12 in the **By changing cell** box
Click **OK**

The completed Goal Seek dialog box is shown in Figure 1.10, and the worksheet obtained after selecting **OK** is shown in Figure 1.11. The Total Profit in cell B18 is zero, and the Production Volume in cell B12 has been set to the breakeven point of 1000.

FIGURE 1.10 GOAL SEEK DIALOG BOX FOR THE NOWLIN PLASTICS PRODUCTION EXAMPLE

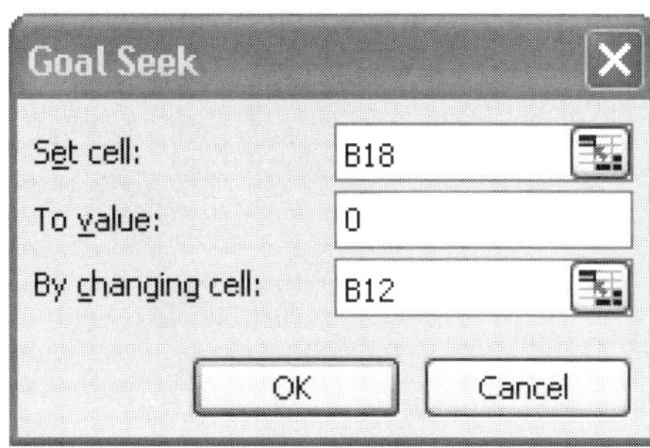

FIGURE 1.11 BREAKEVEN POINT FOUND USING EXCEL'S GOAL SEEK TOOL FOR THE NOWLIN PLASTICS PRODUCTION EXAMPLE

	A	B
1	**Nowlin Plastics**	
2		
3	**Fixed Cost**	$3,000
4		
5	**Variable Cost Per Unit**	$2
6		
7	**Selling Price Per Unit**	$5
8		
9		
10	**Models**	
11		
12	**Production Volume**	1000
13		
14	**Total Cost**	$5,000
15		
16	**Total Revenue**	$5,000
17		
18	**Total Profit (Loss)**	$0

CHAPTER 2

An Introduction to Linear Programming

CONTENTS

Linear programming is a problem-solving approach developed to help managers make decisions. Numerous applications of linear programming can be found in today's competitive business environment. For instance, Eastman Kodak uses linear programming to determine where to manufacture products throughout their worldwide facilities, and GE Capital uses linear programming to help determine optimal lease structuring. Marathon Oil Company uses linear programming for gasoline blending and to evaluate the economics of a new terminal or pipeline. The Management Science in Action, Timber Harvesting Model at MeadWestvaco Corporation, provides another example of the use of linear programming. Later in the chapter another Management Science in Action illustrates how the Hanshin Expressway Public Corporation uses linear programming for traffic control on an urban toll expressway in Osaka, Japan.

To illustrate some of the properties that all linear programming problems have in common, consider the following typical applications:

1. A manufacturer wants to develop a production schedule and an inventory policy that will satisfy sales demand in future periods. Ideally, the schedule and policy will enable the company to satisfy demand and at the same time *minimize* the total production and inventory costs.
2. A financial analyst must select an investment portfolio from a variety of stock and bond investment alternatives. The analyst would like to establish the portfolio that *maximizes* the return on investment.
3. A marketing manager wants to determine how best to allocate a fixed advertising budget among alternative advertising media such as radio, television, newspaper, and magazine. The manager would like to determine the media mix that *maximizes* advertising effectiveness.
4. A company has warehouses in a number of locations throughout the United States. For a set of customer demands, the company would like to determine how much each warehouse should ship to each customer so that total transportation costs are *minimized.*

MANAGEMENT SCIENCE IN ACTION

TIMBER HARVESTING MODEL AT MEADWESTVACO CORPORATION*

MeadWestvaco Corporation is a major producer of premium papers for periodicals, books, commercial printing, and business forms. The company also produces pulp and lumber, designs and manufactures packaging systems for beverage and other consumables markets, and is a world leader in the production of coated board and shipping containers. Quantitative analyses at MeadWestvaco are developed and implemented by the company's Decision Analysis Department. The department assists decision makers by providing them with analytical tools of quantitative methods as well as personal analysis and recommendations.

MeadWestvaco uses quantitative models to assist with the long-range management of the company's timberland. Through the use of large-scale linear programs, timber harvesting plans are developed to cover a substantial time horizon. These models consider wood market conditions, mill pulpwood requirements, harvesting capacities, and general forest management principles. Within these constraints, the model arrives at an optimal harvesting and purchasing schedule based on discounted cash flow. Alternative schedules reflect changes in the various assumptions concerning forest growth, wood availability, and general economic conditions.

Quantitative methods are also used in the development of the inputs for the linear programming models. Timber prices and supplies as well as mill requirements must be forecast over the time horizon, and advanced sampling techniques are used to evaluate land holdings and to project forest growth. The harvest schedule is then developed using quantitative methods.

*Based on information provided by Dr. Edward P. Winkofsky of MeadWestvaco Corporation.

Linear programming was initially referred to as "programming in a linear structure." In 1948 Tjalling Koopmans suggested to George Dantzig that the name was much too long; Koopmans suggested shortening it to linear programming. George Dantzig agreed and the field we now know as linear programming was named.

These examples are only a few of the situations in which linear programming has been used successfully, but they illustrate the diversity of linear programming applications. A close scrutiny reveals one basic property they all have in common. In each example, we were concerned with *maximizing* or *minimizing* some quantity. In example 1, the manufacturer wanted to minimize costs; in example 2, the financial analyst wanted to maximize return on investment; in example 3, the marketing manager wanted to maximize advertising effectiveness; and in example 4, the company wanted to minimize total transportation costs. *In all linear programming problems, the maximization or minimization of some quantity is the objective.*

All linear programming problems also have a second property: restrictions or **constraints** that limit the degree to which the objective can be pursued. In example 1, the manufacturer is restricted by constraints requiring product demand to be satisfied and by the constraints limiting production capacity. The financial analyst's portfolio problem is constrained by the total amount of investment funds available and the maximum amounts that can be invested in each stock or bond. The marketing manager's media selection decision is constrained by a fixed advertising budget and the availability of the various media. In the transportation problem, the minimum-cost shipping schedule is constrained by the supply of product available at each warehouse. *Thus, constraints are another general feature of every linear programming problem.*

2.1 A SIMPLE MAXIMIZATION PROBLEM

Par, Inc., is a small manufacturer of golf equipment and supplies whose management has decided to move into the market for medium- and high-priced golf bags. Par's distributor is enthusiastic about the new product line and has agreed to buy all the golf bags Par produces over the next three months.

After a thorough investigation of the steps involved in manufacturing a golf bag, management determined that each golf bag produced will require the following operations:

1. Cutting and dyeing the material
2. Sewing
3. Finishing (inserting umbrella holder, club separators, etc.)
4. Inspection and packaging

The director of manufacturing analyzed each of the operations and concluded that if the company produces a medium-priced standard model, each bag will require $\frac{7}{10}$ hour in the cutting and dyeing department, $\frac{1}{2}$ hour in the sewing department, 1 hour in the finishing department, and $\frac{1}{10}$ hour in the inspection and packaging department. The more expensive deluxe model will require 1 hour for cutting and dyeing, $\frac{5}{6}$ hour for sewing, $\frac{2}{3}$ hour for finishing, and $\frac{1}{4}$ hour for inspection and packaging. This production information is summarized in Table 2.1.

Par's production is constrained by a limited number of hours available in each department. After studying departmental workload projections, the director of manufacturing estimates that 630 hours for cutting and dyeing, 600 hours for sewing, 708 hours for finishing, and 135 hours for inspection and packaging will be available for the production of golf bags during the next three months.

The accounting department analyzed the production data, assigned all relevant variable costs, and arrived at prices for both bags that will result in a profit contribution[1] of $10 for every standard bag and $9 for every deluxe bag produced. Let us now develop a mathematical model

[1]From an accounting perspective, profit contribution is more correctly described as the contribution margin per bag; for example, overhead and other shared costs have not been allocated.

TABLE 2.1 PRODUCTION REQUIREMENTS PER GOLF BAG

	Production Time (hours)	
Department	**Standard Bag**	**Deluxe Bag**
Cutting and Dyeing	$7/10$	1
Sewing	$1/2$	$5/6$
Finishing	1	$2/3$
Inspection and Packaging	$1/10$	$1/4$

It is important to understand that we are maximizing profit contribution, not profit. Overhead and other shared costs must be deducted before arriving at a profit figure.

of the Par, Inc., problem that can be used to determine the number of standard bags and the number of deluxe bags to produce in order to maximize total profit contribution.

Problem Formulation

Problem formulation or **modeling** is the process of translating the verbal statement of a problem into a mathematical statement. Formulating models is an art that can only be mastered with practice and experience. Even though every problem has some unique features, most problems also have common features. As a result, *some* general guidelines for model formulation can be helpful, especially for beginners. We will illustrate these general guidelines by developing a mathematical model for the Par, Inc., problem.

Understand the Problem Thoroughly. We selected the Par, Inc., problem to introduce linear programming because it is easy to understand. However, more complex problems will require much more thinking in order to identify the items that need to be included in the model. In such cases, read the problem description quickly to get a feel for what is involved. Taking notes will help you focus on the key issues and facts.

Describe the Objective. The objective is to maximize the total contribution to profit.

Describe Each Constraint. Four constraints relate to the number of hours of manufacturing time available; they restrict the number of standard bags and the number of deluxe bags that can be produced.

Constraint 1 Number of hours of cutting and dyeing time used must be less than or equal to the number of hours of cutting and dyeing time available.

Constraint 2 Number of hours of sewing time used must be less than or equal to the number of hours of sewing time available.

Constraint 3 Number of hours of finishing time used must be less than or equal to the number of hours of finishing time available.

Constraint 4 Number of hours of inspection and packaging time used must be less than or equal to the number of hours of inspection and packaging time available.

Define the Decision Variables. The controllable inputs for Par, Inc., are (1) the number of standard bags produced, and (2) the number of deluxe bags produced. Let

$$S = \text{number of standard bags}$$
$$D = \text{number of deluxe bags}$$

In linear programming terminology, S and D are referred to as the **decision variables.**

Write the Objective in Terms of the Decision Variables. Par's profit contribution comes from two sources: (1) the profit contribution made by producing S standard bags, and (2) the profit contribution made by producing D deluxe bags. If Par makes \$10 for every standard bag, the company will make \$10S if S standard bags are produced. Also, if Par makes \$9 for every deluxe bag, the company will make \$9D if D deluxe bags are produced. Thus, we have

$$\text{Total Profit Contribution} = 10S + 9D$$

Because the objective—maximize total profit contribution—is a function of the decision variables S and D, we refer to $10S + 9D$ as the *objective function.* Using "Max" as an abbreviation for maximize, we write Par's objective as follows:

$$\text{Max } 10S + 9D$$

Write the Constraints in Terms of the Decision Variables

Constraint 1:

$$\begin{pmatrix}\text{Hours of cutting and}\\ \text{dyeing time used}\end{pmatrix} \leq \begin{pmatrix}\text{Hours of cutting and}\\ \text{dyeing time available}\end{pmatrix}$$

Every standard bag Par produces will use $\frac{7}{10}$ hour cutting and dyeing time; therefore, the total number of hours of cutting and dyeing time used in the manufacture of S standard bags is $\frac{7}{10}S$. In addition, because every deluxe bag produced uses 1 hour of cutting and dyeing time, the production of D deluxe bags will use $1D$ hours of cutting and dyeing time. Thus, the total cutting and dyeing time required for the production of S standard bags and D deluxe bags is given by

$$\text{Total hours of cutting and dyeing time used} = \tfrac{7}{10}S + 1D$$

The units of measurement on the left-hand side of the constraint must match the units of measurement on the right-hand side.

The director of manufacturing stated that Par has at most 630 hours of cutting and dyeing time available. Therefore, the production combination we select must satisfy the requirement

$$\tfrac{7}{10}S + 1D \leq 630 \qquad (2.1)$$

Constraint 2:

$$\begin{pmatrix}\text{Hours of sewing}\\ \text{time used}\end{pmatrix} \leq \begin{pmatrix}\text{Hours of sewing}\\ \text{time available}\end{pmatrix}$$

From Table 2.1 we see that every standard bag manufactured will require $\frac{1}{2}$ hour for sewing, and every deluxe bag will require $\frac{5}{6}$ hour for sewing. Because 600 hours of sewing time are available, it follows that

$$\tfrac{1}{2}S + \tfrac{5}{6}D \leq 600 \qquad (2.2)$$

Constraint 3:

$$\begin{pmatrix}\text{Hours of finishing} \\ \text{time used}\end{pmatrix} \leq \begin{pmatrix}\text{Hours of finishing} \\ \text{time available}\end{pmatrix}$$

Every standard bag manufactured will require 1 hour for finishing, and every deluxe bag will require ⅔ hour for finishing. With 708 hours of finishing time available, it follows that

$$1S + \tfrac{2}{3}D \leq 708 \tag{2.3}$$

Constraint 4:

$$\begin{pmatrix}\text{Hours of inspection and} \\ \text{packaging time used}\end{pmatrix} \leq \begin{pmatrix}\text{Hours of inspection and} \\ \text{packaging time available}\end{pmatrix}$$

Every standard bag manufactured will require $\frac{1}{10}$ hour for inspection and packaging, and every deluxe bag will require ¼ hour for inspection and packaging. Because 135 hours of inspection and packaging time are available, it follows that

$$\tfrac{1}{10}S + \tfrac{1}{4}D \leq 135 \tag{2.4}$$

We have now specified the mathematical relationships for the constraints associated with the four departments. Have we forgotten any other constraints? Can Par produce a negative number of standard or deluxe bags? Clearly, the answer is no. Thus, to prevent the decision variables S and D from having negative values, two constraints,

$$S \geq 0 \quad \text{and} \quad D \geq 0 \tag{2.5}$$

must be added. These constraints ensure that the solution to the problem will contain nonnegative values for the decision variables and are thus referred to as the **nonnegativity constraints.** Nonnegativity constraints are a general feature of all linear programming problems and may be written in the abbreviated form:

$$S, D \geq 0$$

Try Problem 24(a) to test your ability to formulate a mathematical model for a maximization linear programming problem with less-than-or-equal-to constraints.

Mathematical Statement of the Par, Inc., Problem

The mathematical statement or mathematical formulation of the Par, Inc., problem is now complete. We succeeded in translating the objective and constraints of the problem into a set of mathematical relationships referred to as a **mathematical model.** The complete mathematical model for the Par problem is as follows:

$$
\begin{aligned}
\text{Max} \quad & 10S + 9D \\
\text{subject to (s.t.)} & \\
& \tfrac{7}{10}S + 1D \le 630 \quad \text{Cutting and dyeing} \\
& \tfrac{1}{2}S + \tfrac{5}{6}D \le 600 \quad \text{Sewing} \\
& 1S + \tfrac{2}{3}D \le 708 \quad \text{Finishing} \\
& \tfrac{1}{10}S + \tfrac{1}{4}D \le 135 \quad \text{Inspection and packaging} \\
& S, D \ge 0
\end{aligned}
\tag{2.6}
$$

Our job now is to find the product mix (i.e., the combination of S and D) that satisfies all the constraints and, at the same time, yields a value for the objective function that is greater than or equal to the value given by any other feasible solution. Once these values are calculated, we will have found the optimal solution to the problem.

This mathematical model of the Par problem is a **linear programming model,** or **linear program.** The problem has the objective and constraints that, as we said earlier, are common properties of all *linear* programs. But what is the special feature of this mathematical model that makes it a linear program? The special feature that makes it a linear program is that the objective function and all constraint functions (the left-hand sides of the constraint inequalities) are linear functions of the decision variables.

Mathematical functions in which each variable appears in a separate term and is raised to the first power are called **linear functions.** The objective function ($10S + 9D$) is linear because each decision variable appears in a separate term and has an exponent of 1. The amount of production time required in the cutting and dyeing department ($\tfrac{7}{10}S + 1D$) is also a linear function of the decision variables for the same reason. Similarly, the functions on the left-hand side of all the constraint inequalities (the constraint functions) are linear functions. Thus, the mathematical formulation of this problem is referred to as a linear program.

Try Problem 1 to test your ability to recognize the types of mathematical relationships that can be found in a linear program.

Linear *programming* has nothing to do with computer programming. The use of the word *programming* here means "choosing a course of action." Linear programming involves choosing a course of action when the mathematical model of the problem contains only linear functions.

NOTES AND COMMENTS

1. The three assumptions necessary for a linear programming model to be appropriate are proportionality, additivity, and divisibility. *Proportionality* means that the contribution to the objective function and the amount of resources used in each constraint are proportional to the value of each decision variable. *Additivity* means that the value of the objective function and the total resources used can be found by summing the objective function contribution and the resources used for all decision variables. *Divisibility* means that the decision variables are continuous. The divisibility assumption plus the nonnegativity constraints mean that decision variables can take on any value greater than or equal to zero.
2. Management scientists formulate and solve a variety of mathematical models that contain an objective function and a set of constraints. Models of this type are referred to as *mathematical programming models.* Linear programming models are a special type of mathematical programming model in that the objective function and all constraint functions are linear.

2.2 GRAPHICAL SOLUTION PROCEDURE

A linear programming problem involving only two decision variables can be solved using a graphical solution procedure. Let us begin the graphical solution procedure by developing a graph that displays the possible solutions (S and D values) for the Par problem. The graph (Figure 2.1) will have values of S on the horizontal axis and values of D on the vertical axis. Any point on the graph can be identified by the S and D values, which indicate the position of the point along the horizontal and vertical axes, respectively. Because every point (S, D) corresponds to a possible solution, every point on the graph is called a *solution point.* The solution point where $S = 0$ and $D = 0$ is referred to as the origin. Because S and D must be nonnegative, the graph in Figure 2.1 only displays solutions where $S \geq 0$ and $D \geq 0$.

Earlier, we saw that the inequality representing the cutting and dyeing constraint is

$$\tfrac{7}{10}S + 1D \leq 630$$

To show all solution points that satisfy this relationship, we start by graphing the solution points satisfying the constraint as an equality. That is, the points where $\tfrac{7}{10}S + 1D = 630$. Because the graph of this equation is a line, it can be obtained by identifying two points that satisfy the equation and then drawing a line through the points. Setting $S = 0$ and solving for D, we see that the point ($S = 0$, $D = 630$) satisfies the equation. To find a second point satisfying this equation, we set $D = 0$ and solve for S. By doing so, we obtain

FIGURE 2.1 SOLUTION POINTS FOR THE TWO-VARIABLE PAR, INC., PROBLEM

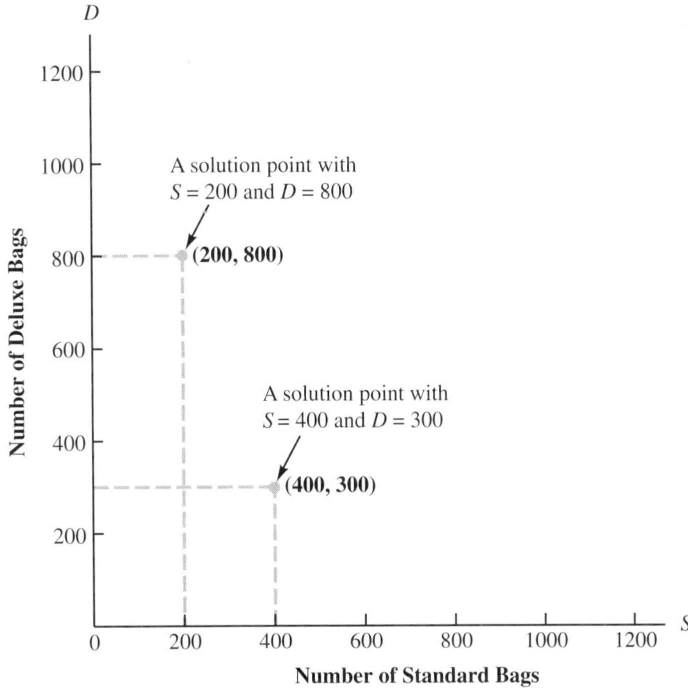

$^7\!/_{10}S + 1(0) = 630$, or $S = 900$. Thus, a second point satisfying the equation is ($S = 900$, $D = 0$). Given these two points, we can now graph the line corresponding to the equation

$$^7\!/_{10}S + 1D = 630$$

This line, which will be called the cutting and dyeing *constraint line,* is shown in Figure 2.2. We label this line "C & D" to indicate that it represents the cutting and dyeing constraint line.

Recall that the inequality representing the cutting and dyeing constraint is

$$^7\!/_{10}S + 1D \leq 630$$

Can you identify all of the solution points that satisfy this constraint? Because all points on the line satisfy $^7\!/_{10}S + 1D = 630$, we know any point on this line must satisfy the constraint. But where are the solution points satisfying $^7\!/_{10}S + 1D < 630$? Consider two solution points: ($S = 200$, $D = 200$) and ($S = 600$, $D = 500$). You can see from Figure 2.2 that the first solution point is below the constraint line and the second is above the constraint line. Which of these solutions will satisfy the cutting and dyeing constraint? For the point ($S = 200$, $D = 200$), we see that

$$^7\!/_{10}S + 1D = {}^7\!/_{10}(200) + 1(200) = 340$$

FIGURE 2.2 THE CUTTING AND DYEING CONSTRAINT LINE

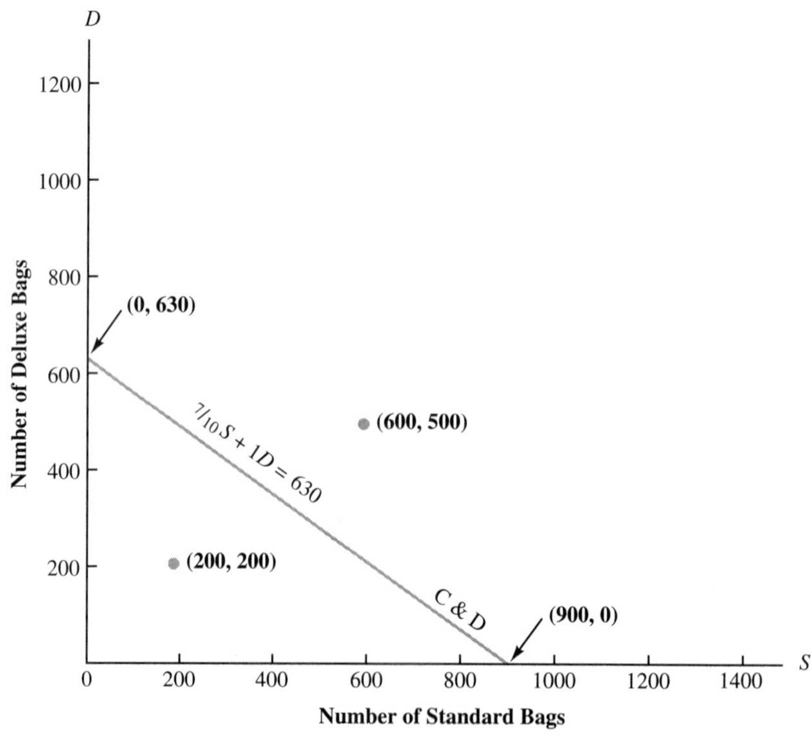

Because the 340 hours is less than the 630 hours available, the ($S = 200$, $D = 200$) production combination, or solution point, satisfies the constraint. For the point ($S = 600$, $D = 500$), we have

$$\tfrac{7}{10}S + 1D = \tfrac{7}{10}(600) + 1(500) = 920$$

The 920 hours is greater than the 630 hours available, so the ($S = 600$, $D = 500$) solution point does not satisfy the constraint and is thus not feasible.

Can you graph a constraint line and find the solution points that are feasible? Try Problem 2.

If a solution point is not feasible for a particular constraint, then all other solution points on the same side of that constraint line are not feasible. If a solution point is feasible for a particular constraint, then all other solution points on the same side of the constraint line are feasible for that constraint. Thus, one needs to evaluate the constraint function for only one solution point to determine which side of a constraint line is feasible. In Figure 2.3 we indicate all points satisfying the cutting and dyeing constraint by the shaded region.

We continue by identifying the solution points satisfying each of the other three constraints. The solutions that are feasible for each of these constraints are shown in Figure 2.4.

Four separate graphs now show the feasible solution points for each of the four constraints. In a linear programming problem, we need to identify the solution points that satisfy *all* the constraints *simultaneously.* To find these solution points, we can draw all four constraints on one graph and observe the region containing the points that do in fact satisfy all the constraints simultaneously.

FIGURE 2.3 FEASIBLE SOLUTIONS FOR THE CUTTING AND DYEING CONSTRAINT, REPRESENTED BY THE SHADED REGION

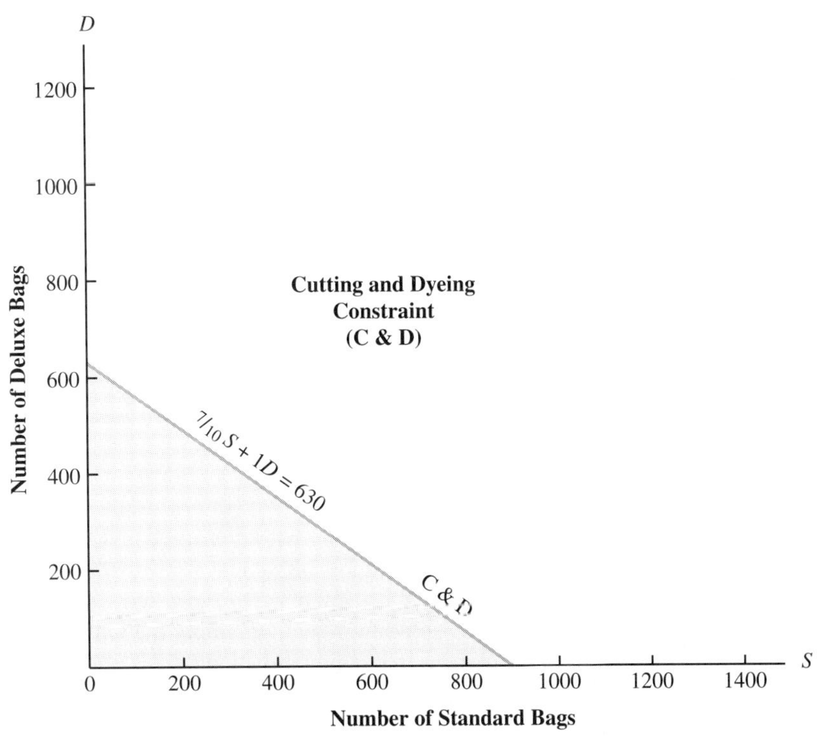

FIGURE 2.4 FEASIBLE SOLUTIONS FOR THE SEWING, FINISHING, AND INSPECTION AND PACKAGING CONSTRAINTS, REPRESENTED BY THE SHADED REGIONS

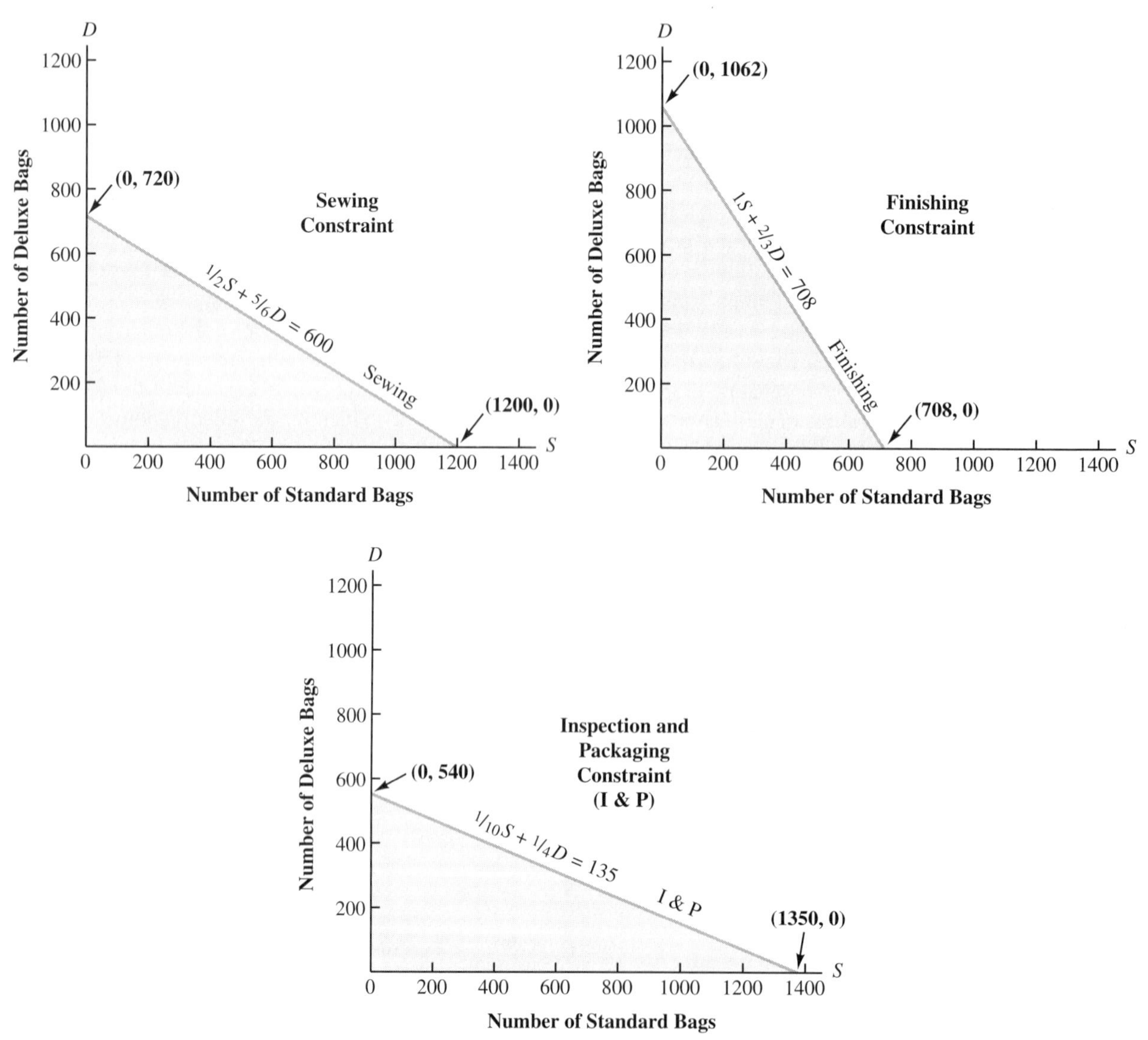

Try Problem 7 to test your ability to find the feasible region given several constraints.

The graphs in Figures 2.3 and 2.4 can be superimposed to obtain one graph with all four constraints. This combined-constraint graph is shown in Figure 2.5. The shaded region in this figure includes every solution point that satisfies all the constraints simultaneously. Solutions that satisfy all the constraints are termed **feasible solutions,** and the shaded region is called the feasible solution region, or simply the **feasible region.** Any solution point on the boundary of the feasible region or within the feasible region is a *feasible solution point.*

Now that we have identified the feasible region, we are ready to proceed with the graphical solution procedure and find the optimal solution to the Par, Inc., problem. Recall that the optimal solution for a linear programming problem is the feasible solution that provides

FIGURE 2.5 COMBINED-CONSTRAINT GRAPH SHOWING THE FEASIBLE REGION FOR THE PAR, INC., PROBLEM

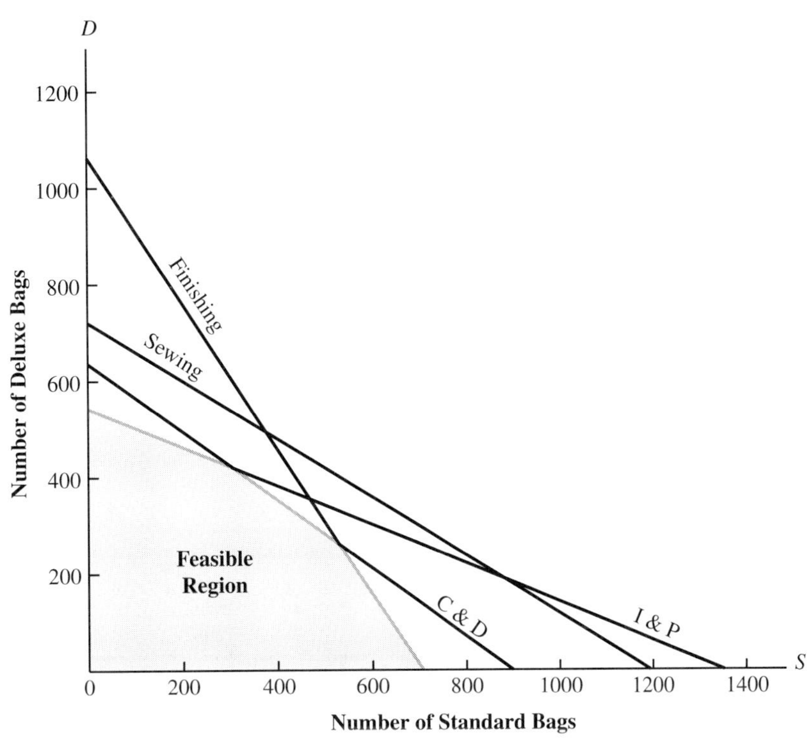

the best possible value of the objective function. Let us start the optimizing step of the graphical solution procedure by redrawing the feasible region on a separate graph. The graph is shown in Figure 2.6.

One approach to finding the optimal solution would be to evaluate the objective function for each feasible solution; the optimal solution would then be the one yielding the largest value. The difficulty with this approach is the infinite number of feasible solutions; thus, because one cannot possibly evaluate an infinite number of feasible solutions, this trial-and-error procedure cannot be used to identify the optimal solution.

Rather than trying to compute the profit contribution for each feasible solution, we select an arbitrary value for profit contribution and identify all the feasible solutions (S, D) that yield the selected value. For example, what feasible solutions provide a profit contribution of \$1800? These solutions are given by the values of S and D in the feasible region that will make the objective function

$$10S + 9D = 1800$$

This expression is simply the equation of a line. Thus, all feasible solution points (S, D) yielding a profit contribution of \$1800 must be on the line. We learned earlier in this section how to graph a constraint line. The procedure for graphing the profit or objective function line is the same. Letting $S = 0$, we see that D must be 200; thus, the solution point

FIGURE 2.6 FEASIBLE REGION FOR THE PAR, INC., PROBLEM

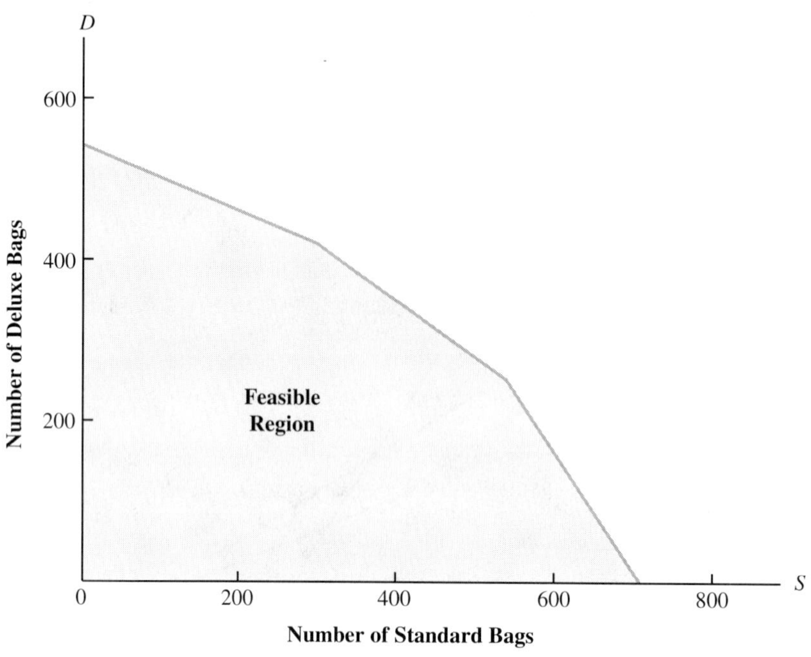

($S = 0, D = 200$) is on the line. Similarly, by letting $D = 0$, we see that the solution point ($S = 180, D = 0$) is also on the line. Drawing the line through these two points identifies all the solutions that have a profit contribution of \$1800. A graph of this profit line is presented in Figure 2.7.

Because the objective is to find the feasible solution yielding the largest profit contribution, let us proceed by selecting higher profit contributions and finding the solutions yielding the selected values. For instance, let us find all solutions yielding profit contributions of \$3600 and \$5400. To do so, we must find the S and D values that are on the following lines:

$$10S + 9D = 3600$$

and

$$10S + 9D = 5400$$

Using the previous procedure for graphing profit and constraint lines, we draw the \$3600 and \$5400 profit lines as shown on the graph in Figure 2.8. Although not all solution points on the \$5400 profit line are in the feasible region, at least some points on the line are, and it is therefore possible to obtain a feasible solution that provides a \$5400 profit contribution.

Can we find a feasible solution yielding an even higher profit contribution? Look at Figure 2.8, and see what general observations you can make about the profit lines already drawn. Note the following: (1) the profit lines are *parallel* to each other, and (2) higher

FIGURE 2.7 $1800 PROFIT LINE FOR THE PAR, INC., PROBLEM

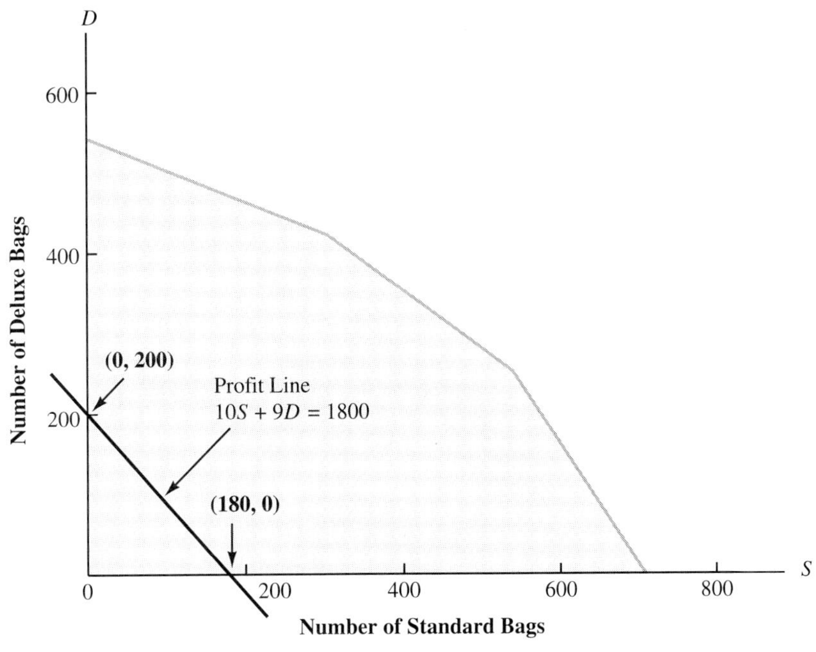

FIGURE 2.8 SELECTED PROFIT LINES FOR THE PAR, INC., PROBLEM

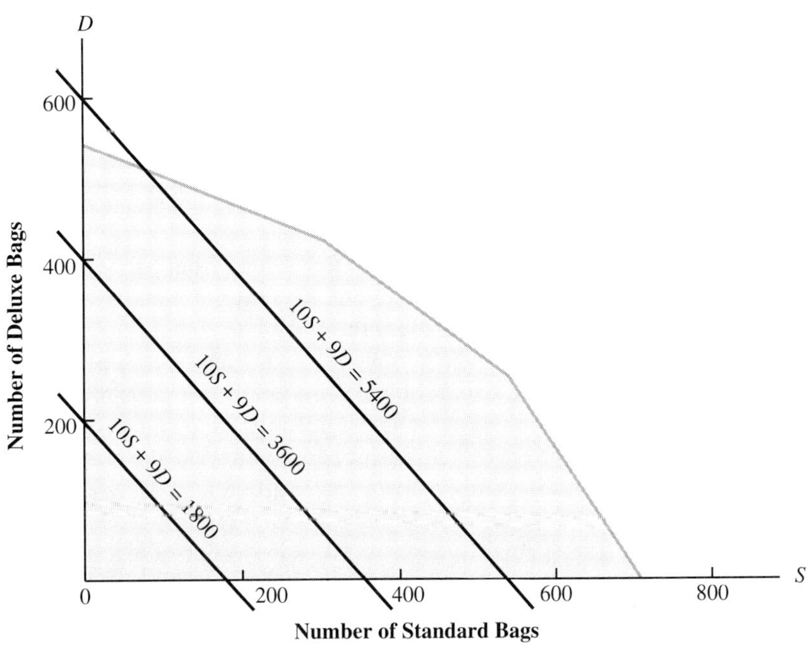

profit lines are obtained as we move farther from the origin. These observations can also be expressed algebraically. Let P represent total profit contribution. The objective function is

$$P = 10S + 9D$$

Solving for D in terms of S and P, we obtain

$$9D = -10S + P$$
$$D = -\tfrac{10}{9}S + \tfrac{1}{9}P \tag{2.7}$$

Equation (2.7) is the *slope-intercept form* of the linear equation relating S and D. The coefficient of S, $-\tfrac{10}{9}$, is the slope of the line, and the term $\tfrac{1}{9}P$ is the D intercept (i.e., the value of D where the graph of equation [2.7] crosses the D axis). Substituting the profit contributions of $P = 1800$, $P = 3600$, and $P = 5400$ into equation (2.7) yields the following slope-intercept equations for the profit lines shown in Figure 2.8:

For $P = 1800$,

$$D = -\tfrac{10}{9}S + 200$$

For $P = 3600$,

$$D = -\tfrac{10}{9}S + 400$$

For $P = 5400$,

$$D = -\tfrac{10}{9}S + 600$$

Can you graph the profit line for a linear program? Try Problem 6.

The slope $(-\tfrac{10}{9})$ is the same for each profit line because the profit lines are parallel. Further, we see that the D intercept increases with larger profit contributions. Thus, higher profit lines are farther from the origin.

Because the profit lines are parallel and higher profit lines are farther from the origin, we can obtain solutions that yield increasingly larger values for the objective function by continuing to move the profit line farther from the origin in such a fashion that it remains parallel to the other profit lines. However, at some point we will find that any further outward movement will place the profit line completely outside the feasible region. Because solutions outside the feasible region are unacceptable, the point in the feasible region that lies on the highest profit line is the optimal solution to the linear program.

You should now be able to identify the optimal solution point for this problem. Use a ruler or the edge of a piece of paper, and move the profit line as far from the origin as you can. What is the last point in the feasible region that you reach? This point, which is the optimal solution, is shown graphically in Figure 2.9.

The optimal values of the decision variables are the S and D values at the optimal solution. Depending on the accuracy of the graph, you may or may not be able to determine the *exact* S and D values. Based on the graph in Figure 2.9, the best we can do is conclude that the optimal production combination consists of approximately 550 standard bags (S) and approximately 250 deluxe bags (D).

FIGURE 2.9 OPTIMAL SOLUTION FOR THE PAR, INC., PROBLEM

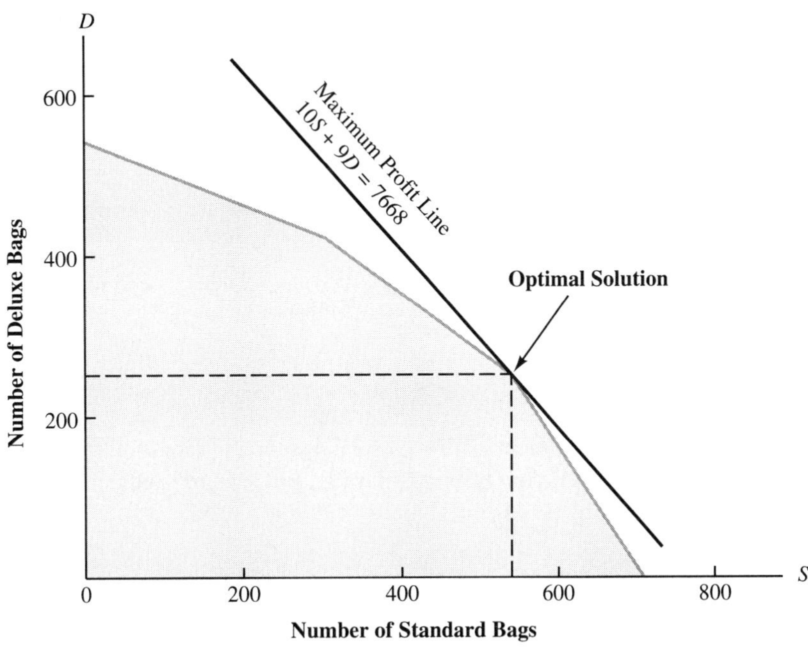

A closer inspection of Figures 2.5 and 2.9 shows that the optimal solution point is at the intersection of the cutting and dyeing and the finishing constraint lines. That is, the optimal solution point is on both the cutting and dyeing constraint line

$$\tfrac{7}{10}S + 1D = 630 \tag{2.8}$$

and the finishing constraint line

$$1S + \tfrac{2}{3}D = 708 \tag{2.9}$$

Thus, the optimal values of the decision variables S and D must satisfy both equations (2.8) and (2.9) simultaneously. Using equation (2.8) and solving for S gives

$$\tfrac{7}{10}S = 630 - 1D$$

or

$$S = 900 - \tfrac{10}{7}D \tag{2.10}$$

Substituting this expression for S into equation (2.9) and solving for D provides the following:

$$\begin{aligned} 1(900 - \tfrac{10}{7}D) + \tfrac{2}{3}D &= 708 \\ 900 - \tfrac{10}{7}D + \tfrac{2}{3}D &= 708 \\ 900 - \tfrac{30}{21}D + \tfrac{14}{21}D &= 708 \\ -\tfrac{16}{21}D &= -192 \\ D &= \frac{192}{16/21} = 252 \end{aligned}$$

Using $D = 252$ in equation (2.10) and solving for S, we obtain

$$\begin{aligned} S &= 900 - \tfrac{10}{7}(252) \\ &= 900 - 360 = 540 \end{aligned}$$

Although the optimal solution to the Par, Inc., problem consists of integer values for the decision variables, this result will not always be the case.

The exact location of the optimal solution point is $S = 540$ and $D = 252$. Hence, the optimal production quantities for Par, Inc., are 540 standard bags and 252 deluxe bags, with a resulting profit contribution of $10(540) + 9(252) = \$7668$.

For a linear programming problem with two decision variables, the exact values of the decision variables can be determined by first using the graphical solution procedure to identify the optimal solution point and then solving the two simultaneous constraint equations associated with it.

A Note on Graphing Lines

Try Problem 10 to test your ability to use the graphical solution procedure to identify the optimal solution and find the exact values of the decision variables at the optimal solution.

An important aspect of the graphical method is the ability to graph lines showing the constraints and the objective function of the linear program. The procedure we used for graphing the equation of a line is to find any two points satisfying the equation and then draw the line through the two points. For the Par, Inc., constraints, the two points were easily found by first setting $S = 0$ and solving the constraint equation for D. Then we set $D = 0$ and solved for S. For the cutting and dyeing constraint line

$$\tfrac{7}{10}S + 1D = 630$$

this procedure identified the two points ($S = 0, D = 630$) and ($S = 900, D = 0$). The cutting and dyeing constraint line was then graphed by drawing a line through these two points.

All constraints and objective function lines in two-variable linear programs can be graphed if two points on the line can be identified. However, finding the two points on the line is not always as easy as shown in the Par, Inc., problem. For example, suppose a company manufactures two models of a small handheld computer: the Assistant (A) and the Professional (P). Management needs 50 units of the Professional model for its own salesforce, and expects sales of the Professional to be at most one-half of the sales of the Assistant. A constraint enforcing this requirement is

$$P - 50 \leq \tfrac{1}{2}A$$

or

$$2P - 100 \leq A$$

or

$$2P - A \leq 100$$

Using the equality form and setting $P = 0$, we find the point ($P = 0, A = -100$) is on the constraint line. Setting $A = 0$, we find a second point ($P = 50, A = 0$) on the constraint line. If we have drawn only the nonnegative ($P \geq 0, A \geq 0$) portion of the graph, the first point ($P = 0$, $A = -100$) cannot be plotted because $A = -100$ is not on the graph. Whenever we have two points on the line, but one or both of the points cannot be plotted in the nonnegative portion of the graph, the simplest approach is to enlarge the graph. In this example, the point ($P = 0$, $A = -100$) can be plotted by extending the graph to include the negative A axis. Once both points satisfying the constraint equation have been located, the line can be drawn. The constraint line and the feasible solutions for the constraint $2P - A \leq 100$ are shown in Figure 2.10.

As another example, consider a problem involving two decision variables, R and T. Suppose that the number of units of R produced had to be at least equal to the number of units of T produced. A constraint enforcing this requirement is

$$R \geq T$$

or

$$R - T \geq 0$$

FIGURE 2.10 FEASIBLE SOLUTIONS FOR THE CONSTRAINT $2P - A \leq 100$

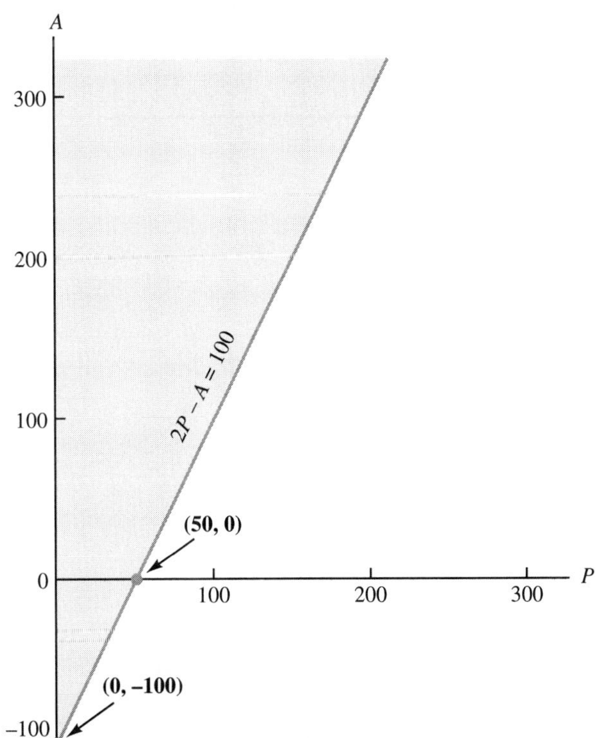

Can you graph a constraint line when the origin is on the constraint line? Try Problem 5.

To find all solutions satisfying the constraint as an equality, we first set $R = 0$ and solve for T. This result shows that the origin ($T = 0$, $R = 0$) is on the constraint line. Setting $T = 0$ and solving for R provides the same point. However, we can obtain a second point on the line by setting T equal to any value other than zero and then solving for R. For instance, setting $T = 100$ and solving for R, we find that the point ($T = 100$, $R = 100$) is on the line. With the two points ($R = 0$, $T = 0$) and ($R = 100$, $T = 100$), the constraint line $R - T = 0$ and the feasible solutions for $R - T \geq 0$ can be plotted as shown in Figure 2.11.

Summary of the Graphical Solution Procedure for Maximization Problems

For additional practice in using the graphical solution procedure, try Problem 24(b), 24(c), and 24(d).

As we have seen, the graphical solution procedure is a method for solving two-variable linear programming problems such as the Par, Inc., problem. The steps of the graphical solution procedure for a maximization problem are summarized here:

1. Prepare a graph of the feasible solutions for each of the constraints.
2. Determine the feasible region by identifying the solutions that satisfy all the constraints simultaneously.
3. Draw an objective function line showing the values of the decision variables that yield a specified value of the objective function.
4. Move parallel objective function lines toward larger objective function values until further movement would take the line completely outside the feasible region.
5. Any feasible solution on the objective function line with the largest value is an optimal solution.

FIGURE 2.11 FEASIBLE SOLUTIONS FOR THE CONSTRAINT $R - T \geq 0$

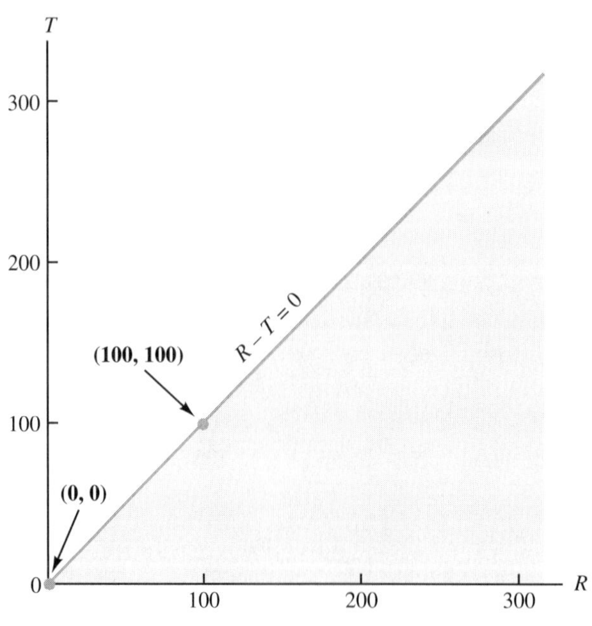

Slack Variables

In addition to the optimal solution and its associated profit contribution, Par's management will probably want information about the production time requirements for each production operation. We can determine this information by substituting the optimal solution values (S = 540, D = 252) into the constraints of the linear program.

Constraint	Hours Required for S = 540 and D = 252	Hours Available	Unused Hours
Cutting and dyeing	$\frac{7}{10}(540) + 1(252) = 630$	630	0
Sewing	$\frac{1}{2}(540) + \frac{5}{6}(252) = 480$	600	120
Finishing	$1(540) + \frac{2}{3}(252) = 708$	708	0
Inspection and packaging	$\frac{1}{10}(540) + \frac{1}{4}(252) = 117$	135	18

Thus, the complete solution tells management that the production of 540 standard bags and 252 deluxe bags will require all available cutting and dyeing time (630 hours) and all available finishing time (708 hours), while 600 − 480 = 120 hours of sewing time and 135 − 117 = 18 hours of inspection and packaging time will remain unused. The 120 hours of unused sewing time and 18 hours of unused inspection and packaging time are referred to as *slack* for the two departments. In linear programming terminology, any unused capacity for a ≤ constraint is referred to as the *slack* associated with the constraint.

Can you identify the slack associated with a constraint? Try Problem 24(e).

Often variables, called **slack variables,** are added to the formulation of a linear programming problem to represent the slack, or idle capacity. Unused capacity makes no contribution to profit; thus, slack variables have coefficients of zero in the objective function. After the addition of four slack variables, denoted S_1, S_2, S_3, and S_4, the mathematical model of the Par, Inc., problem becomes

$$\begin{aligned}
\text{Max} \quad & 10S + 9D + 0S_1 + 0S_2 + 0S_3 + 0S_4 \\
\text{s.t.} \quad & \\
& \tfrac{7}{10}S + 1D + 1S_1 = 630 \\
& \tfrac{1}{2}S + \tfrac{5}{6}D + 1S_2 = 600 \\
& 1S + \tfrac{2}{3}D + 1S_3 = 708 \\
& \tfrac{1}{10}S + \tfrac{1}{4}D + 1S_4 = 135 \\
& S, D, S_1, S_2, S_3, S_4 \geq 0
\end{aligned}$$

Can you write a linear program in standard form? Try Problem 18.

Whenever a linear program is written in a form with all constraints expressed as equalities, it is said to be written in **standard form.**

Referring to the standard form of the Par, Inc., problem, we see that at the optimal solution (S = 540 and D = 252), the values for the slack variables are

Constraint	Value of Slack Variable
Cutting and dyeing	$S_1 = 0$
Sewing	$S_2 = 120$
Finishing	$S_3 = 0$
Inspection and packaging	$S_4 = 18$

Could we have used the graphical solution to provide some of this information? The answer is yes. By finding the optimal solution point on Figure 2.5, we can see that the cutting and dyeing and the finishing constraints restrict, or *bind,* the feasible region at this point. Thus, this solution requires the use of all available time for these two operations. In other words, the graph shows us that the cutting and dyeing and the finishing departments will have zero slack. On the other hand, the sewing and the inspection and packaging constraints are not binding the feasible region at the optimal solution, which means we can expect some unused time or slack for these two operations.

As a final comment on the graphical analysis of this problem, we call your attention to the sewing capacity constraint as shown in Figure 2.5. Note, in particular, that this constraint did not affect the feasible region. That is, the feasible region would be the same whether the sewing capacity constraint were included or not, which tells us that enough sewing time is available to accommodate any production level that can be achieved by the other three departments. The sewing constraint does not affect the feasible region and thus cannot affect the optimal solution; it is called a **redundant constraint.**

NOTES AND COMMENTS

1. In the standard-form representation of a linear programming model, the objective function coefficients for slack variables are zero. This zero coefficient implies that slack variables, which represent unused resources, do not affect the value of the objective function. However, in some applications, unused resources can be sold and contribute to profit. In such cases, the corresponding slack variables become decision variables representing the amount of unused resources to be sold. For each of these variables, a nonzero coefficient in the objective function would reflect the profit associated with selling a unit of the corresponding resource.
2. Redundant constraints do not affect the feasible region; as a result, they can be removed from a linear programming model without affecting the optimal solution. However, if the linear programming model is to be re-solved later, changes in some of the data might make a previously redundant constraint a binding constraint. Thus, we recommend keeping all constraints in the linear programming model even though at some point in time one or more of the constraints may be redundant.

2.3 EXTREME POINTS AND THE OPTIMAL SOLUTION

Suppose that the profit contribution for Par's standard golf bag is reduced from \$10 to \$5 per bag, while the profit contribution for the deluxe golf bag and all the constraints remain unchanged. The complete linear programming model of this new problem is identical to the mathematical model in Section 2.1, except for the revised objective function:

$$\text{Max } 5S + 9D$$

How does this change in the objective function affect the optimal solution to the Par, Inc., problem? Figure 2.12 shows the graphical solution of this new problem with the revised objective function. Note that without any change in the constraints, the feasible region does not change. However, the profit lines have been altered to reflect the new objective function.

By moving the profit line in a parallel manner toward higher profit values, we find the optimal solution as shown in Figure 2.12. The values of the decision variables at this point

FIGURE 2.12 OPTIMAL SOLUTION FOR THE PAR, INC., PROBLEM WITH AN OBJECTIVE FUNCTION OF $5S + 9D$

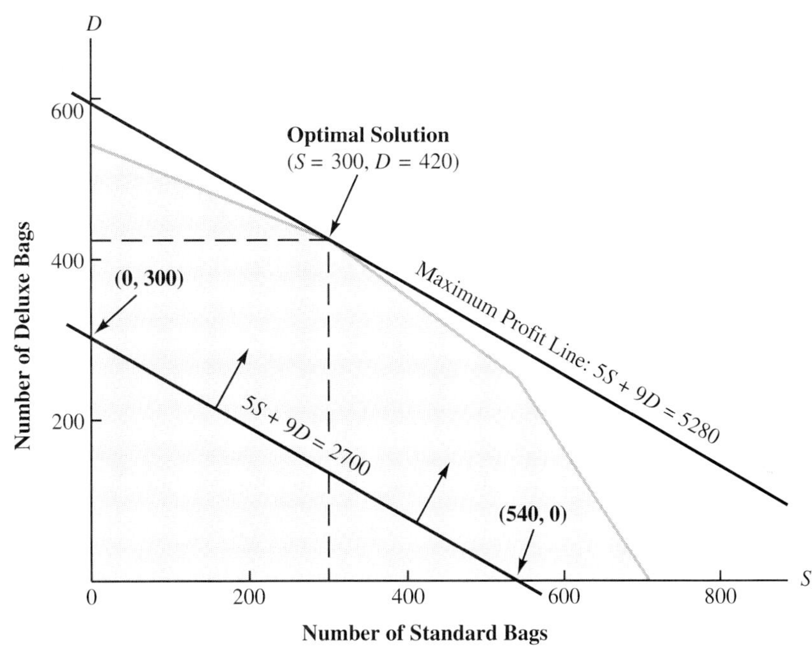

are $S = 300$ and $D = 420$. The reduced profit contribution for the standard bag caused a change in the optimal solution. In fact, as you may have suspected, we are cutting back the production of the lower-profit standard bags and increasing the production of the higher-profit deluxe bags.

What observations can you make about the location of the optimal solutions in the two linear programming problems solved thus far? Look closely at the graphical solutions in Figures 2.9 and 2.12. Notice that the optimal solutions occur at one of the vertices or "corners" of the feasible region. In linear programming terminology, these vertices are referred to as the **extreme points** of the feasible region. The Par, Inc., feasible region has five vertices, or five extreme points (see Figure 2.13). We can now formally state our observation about the location of optimal solutions as follows:

For additional practice in identifying the extreme points of the feasible region and determining the optimal solution by computing and comparing the objective function value at each extreme point, try Problem 13.

The optimal solution to a linear program can be found at an extreme point of the feasible region.[2]

This property means that if you are looking for the optimal solution to a linear program, you do not have to evaluate all feasible solution points. In fact, you have to consider *only*

[2]We will discuss in Section 2.6 the two special cases (infeasibility and unboundedness) in linear programming that have no optimal solution, and for which this statement does not apply.

FIGURE 2.13 THE FIVE EXTREME POINTS OF THE FEASIBLE REGION FOR THE PAR, INC., PROBLEM

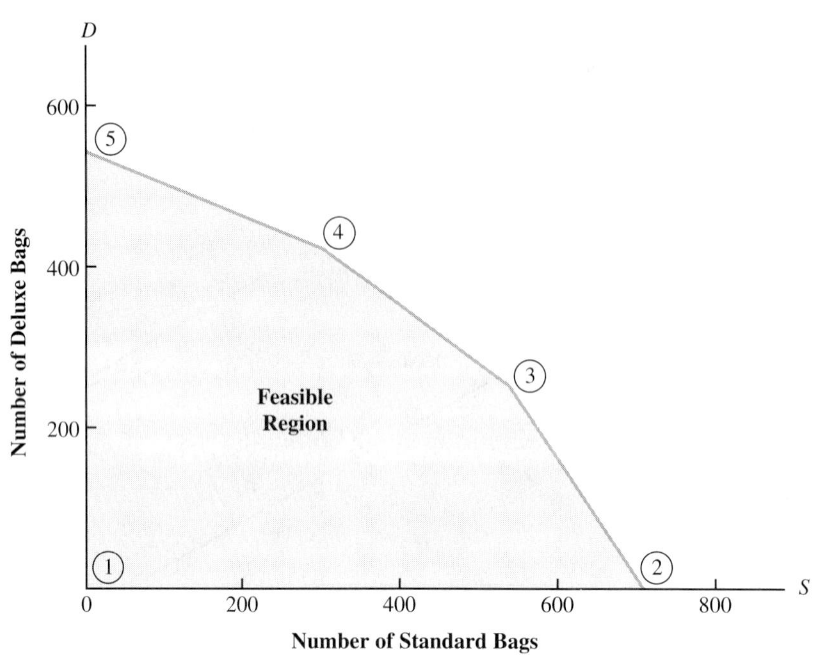

the feasible solutions that occur at the extreme points of the feasible region. Thus, for the Par, Inc., problem, instead of computing and comparing the profit contributions for all feasible solutions, we can find the optimal solution by evaluating the five extreme-point solutions and selecting the one that provides the largest profit contribution. Actually, the graphical solution procedure is nothing more than a convenient way of identifying an optimal extreme point for two-variable problems.

2.4 COMPUTER SOLUTION OF THE PAR, INC., PROBLEM

In January 1952 the first successful computer solution of a linear programming problem was performed on the SEAC (Standards Eastern Automatic Computer). The SEAC, the first digital computer built by the National Bureau of Standards under U.S. Air Force sponsorship, had a 512-word memory and magnetic tape for external storage.

Computer programs designed to solve linear programming problems are now widely available. Most companies and universities have access to these computer programs. After a short period of familiarization with the specific features of the package, users are able to solve linear programming problems with few difficulties. Problems involving thousands of variables and thousands of constraints are now routinely solved with computer packages. Some of the leading commercial packages include CPLEX, LINGO, MOSEK, Premium Solver for Excel, and Xpress-MP. Packages are also available for free download. A good example is Clp (COIN-OR linear programming) available from the COIN-OR organization at www.coin-or.org.

The Management Scientist, a software package developed by the authors of this text, contains a linear programming module. Let us demonstrate its use by solving the Par, Inc., problem introduced in Section 2.1. Because computer input must utilize decimal rather than fractional data values, we restate the linear program with decimal coefficients:

Instructions on how to solve linear programs using The Management Scientist, LINGO, and Excel are provided in appendixes at the end of the chapter.

$$
\begin{array}{llll}
\text{Max} & 10S + 9D & & \\
\text{s.t.} & & & \\
& 0.7S + 1D \leq 630 & & \text{Cutting and dyeing} \\
& 0.5S + 0.83333D \leq 600 & & \text{Sewing} \\
& 1.0S + 0.66667D \leq 708 & & \text{Finishing} \\
& 0.1S + 0.25D \leq 135 & & \text{Inspection and packaging} \\
& S, D \geq 0 & &
\end{array}
$$

Note that in the preceding form, the coefficient of D in the sewing constraint is written as 0.83333, which is the closest five-place decimal value to the fraction $\frac{5}{6}$. A similar rounding occurs for the D coefficient in the finishing constraint, where the decimal 0.66667 is used as the closest five-place decimal value to the fraction $\frac{2}{3}$. When this rounding of the input data is required, we may expect the computer solution to be slightly different from the hand-calculated solution based on the exact fractional values. However, as you will see, the two solutions are extremely close, and the slight rounding of the input data causes no serious problem. The solution generated by The Management Scientist is shown in Figure 2.14. The steps required to generate this solution are described in Appendix 2.1. In Appendix 2.2 we also show how to solve the Par, Inc., problem using LINGO. In Appendix 2.3 we show how to formulate a worksheet model for the Par, Inc., problem and use Frontline Systems' Premium Solver for Education to solve the problem.

Interpretation of Computer Output

Let us look more closely at The Management Scientist output in Figure 2.14 and interpret the computer solution provided for the Par, Inc., problem. First, note the number 7667.99417, which appears to the right of Objective Function Value. Rounding this value, we can conclude that the optimal solution to this problem will provide a profit of $7668. Directly below the objective function value, we find the values of the decision variables at the optimal solution. After rounding we have $S = 540$ standard bags and $D = 252$ deluxe bags as the optimal production quantities.

The information in the Reduced Costs column indicates how much the objective function coefficient of each decision variable would have to improve[3] before it would be possible for that variable to assume a positive value in the optimal solution. If a decision variable is already positive in the optimal solution, its reduced cost is zero. For the Par, Inc., problem, the optimal solution is $S = 540$ and $D = 252$. Both variables already have positive values; therefore, their corresponding reduced costs are zero. In Chapter 3 we will interpret the reduced cost for a decision variable that does not have a positive value in the optimal solution.

Immediately following the optimal S and D values and the reduced cost information, the computer output provides information about the status of the constraints. Recall that the Par, Inc., problem had four less-than-or-equal-to constraints corresponding to the hours available in each of four production departments. The information shown in the Slack/Surplus column

[3]For a maximization problem, improve means get bigger; for a minimization problem, improve means get smaller.

FIGURE 2.14 THE MANAGEMENT SCIENTIST SOLUTION FOR THE PAR, INC., PROBLEM

```
Objective Function Value =              7667.99417

      Variable                Value              Reduced Costs
   --------------      ---------------      ------------------
          S               539.99842                0.00000
          D               252.00110                0.00000

     Constraint          Slack/Surplus           Dual Prices
   --------------      ---------------      ------------------
          1                 0.00000                4.37496
          2               120.00071                0.00000
          3                 0.00000                6.93753
          4                17.99988                0.00000

OBJECTIVE COEFFICIENT RANGES

  Variable        Lower Limit       Current Value       Upper Limit
------------   ---------------   ---------------   ---------------
      S              6.30000          10.00000          13.49993
      D              6.66670           9.00000          14.28571

RIGHT HAND SIDE RANGES

 Constraint       Lower Limit       Current Value       Upper Limit
------------   ---------------   ---------------   ---------------
      1            495.60000         630.00000         682.36316
      2            479.99929         600.00000    No Upper Limit
      3            580.00140         708.00000         900.00000
      4            117.00012         135.00000    No Upper Limit
```

EXCELfile
Par

provides the value of the slack variable for each of the departments. This information (after rounding) is summarized here:

Constraint Number	Constraint Name	Slack
1	Cutting and dyeing	0
2	Sewing	120
3	Finishing	0
4	Inspection and packaging	18

From this information, we see that the binding constraints (the cutting and dyeing and the finishing constraints) have zero slack at the optimal solution. The sewing department has 120 hours of slack or unused capacity, and the inspection and packaging department has 18 hours of slack or unused capacity.

The rest of the output in Figure 2.14 can be used to determine how a change in a coefficient of the objective function or a change in the right-hand-side value of a constraint will affect the optimal solution. We will discuss the use of this information in Chapter 3 when we study the topic of sensitivity analysis.

NOTES AND COMMENTS

Linear programming solvers are now a standard feature of most spreadsheet packages. In Appendix 2.3 we show how spreadsheets can be used to solve linear programs by using Excel to solve the Par, Inc., problem.

2.5 A SIMPLE MINIMIZATION PROBLEM

M&D Chemicals produces two products that are sold as raw materials to companies manufacturing bath soaps and laundry detergents. Based on an analysis of current inventory levels and potential demand for the coming month, M&D's management specified that the combined production for products A and B must total at least 350 gallons. Separately, a major customer's order for 125 gallons of product A must also be satisfied. Product A requires 2 hours of processing time per gallon and product B requires 1 hour of processing time per gallon. For the coming month, 600 hours of processing time are available. M&D's objective is to satisfy these requirements at a minimum total production cost. Production costs are \$2 per gallon for product A and \$3 per gallon for product B.

To find the minimum-cost production schedule, we will formulate the M&D Chemicals problem as a linear program. Following a procedure similar to the one used for the Par, Inc., problem, we first define the decision variables and the objective function for the problem. Let

$$A = \text{number of gallons of product A}$$
$$B = \text{number of gallons of product B}$$

With production costs at \$2 per gallon for product A and \$3 per gallon for product B, the objective function that corresponds to the minimization of the total production cost can be written as

$$\text{Min } 2A + 3B$$

Next consider the constraints placed on the M&D Chemicals problem. To satisfy the major customer's demand for 125 gallons of product A, we know A must be at least 125. Thus, we write the constraint

$$1A \geq 125$$

For the combined production for both products, which must total at least 350 gallons, we can write the constraint

$$1A + 1B \geq 350$$

Finally, for the limitation of 600 hours on available processing time, we add the constraint

$$2A + 1B \leq 600$$

After adding the nonnegativity constraints ($A, B \geq 0$), we arrive at the following linear program for the M&D Chemicals problem:

$$\begin{aligned}
\text{Min} \quad & 2A + 3B \\
\text{s.t.} \quad & \\
& 1A \geq 125 && \text{Demand for product A} \\
& 1A + 1B \geq 350 && \text{Total production} \\
& 2A + 1B \leq 600 && \text{Processing time} \\
& A, B \geq 0
\end{aligned}$$

Because the linear programming model has only two decision variables, the graphical solution procedure can be used to find the optimal production quantities. The graphical solution procedure for this problem, just as in the Par problem, requires us to first graph the constraint lines to find the feasible region. By graphing each constraint line separately and then checking points on either side of the constraint line, the feasible solutions for each constraint can be identified. By combining the feasible solutions for each constraint on the same graph, we obtain the feasible region shown in Figure 2.15.

FIGURE 2.15 THE FEASIBLE REGION FOR THE M&D CHEMICALS PROBLEM

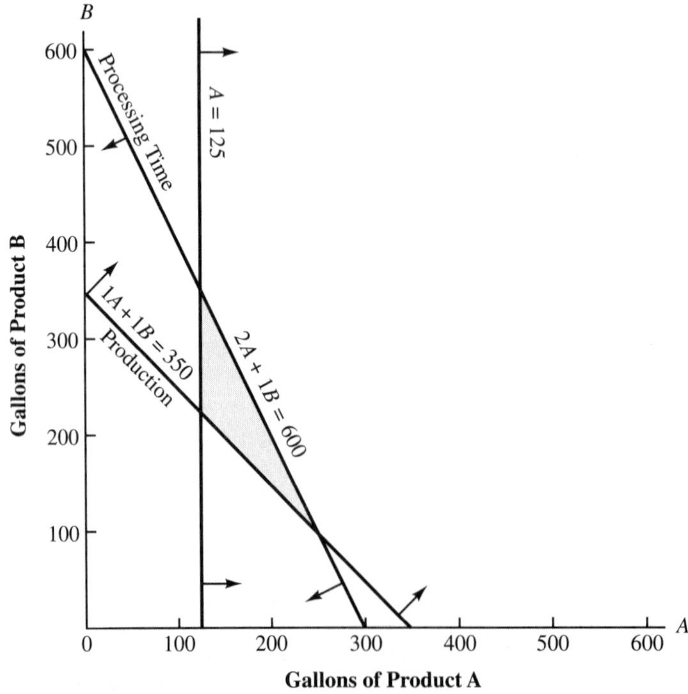

FIGURE 2.16 GRAPHICAL SOLUTION FOR THE M&D CHEMICALS PROBLEM

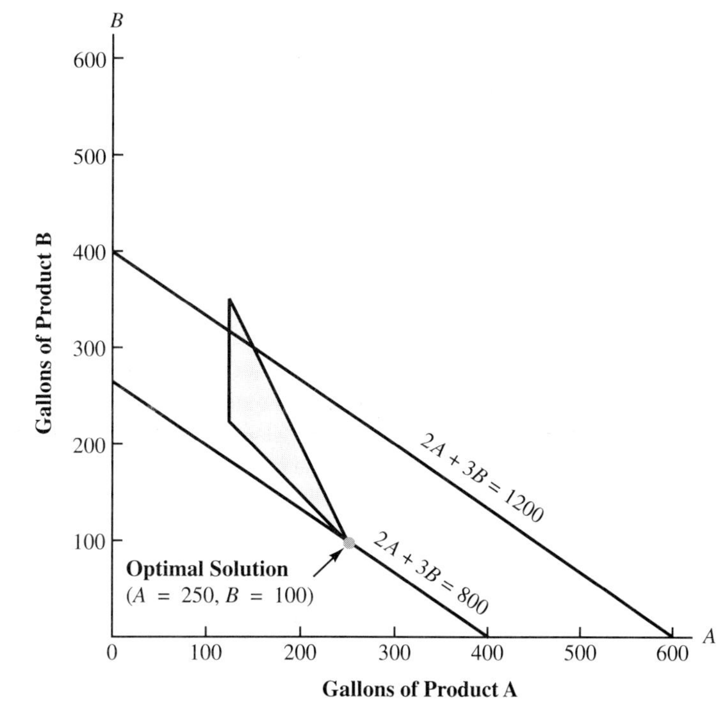

To find the minimum-cost solution, we now draw the objective function line corresponding to a particular total cost value. For example, we might start by drawing the line $2A + 3B = 1200$. This line is shown in Figure 2.16. Clearly some points in the feasible region would provide a total cost of \$1200. To find the values of A and B that provide smaller total cost values, we move the objective function line in a lower left direction until, if we moved it any farther, it would be entirely outside the feasible region. Note that the objective function line $2A + 3B = 800$ intersects the feasible region at the extreme point $A = 250$ and $B = 100$. This extreme point provides the minimum-cost solution with an objective function value of 800. From Figures 2.15 and 2.16, we can see that the total production constraint and the processing time constraint are binding. Just as in every linear programming problem, the optimal solution occurs at an extreme point of the feasible region.

Summary of the Graphical Solution Procedure for Minimization Problems

Can you use the graphical solution procedure to determine the optimal solution for a minimization problem? Try Problem 31.

The steps of the graphical solution procedure for a minimization problem are summarized here:

1. Prepare a graph of the feasible solutions for each of the constraints.
2. Determine the feasible region by identifying the solutions that satisfy all the constraints simultaneously.
3. Draw an objective function line showing the values of the decision variables that yield a specified value of the objective function.

4. Move parallel objective function lines toward smaller objective function values until further movement would take the line completely outside the feasible region.
5. Any feasible solution on the objective function line with the smallest value is an optimal solution.

Surplus Variables

The optimal solution to the M&D Chemicals problem shows that the desired total production of $A + B = 350$ gallons has been achieved by using all available processing time of $2A + 1B = 2(250) + 1(100) = 600$ hours. In addition, note that the constraint requiring that product A demand be met has been satisfied with $A = 250$ gallons. In fact, the production of product A exceeds its minimum level by $250 - 125 = 125$ gallons. This excess production for product A is referred to as *surplus.* In linear programming terminology, any excess quantity corresponding to a $\geq$ constraint is referred to as surplus.

Recall that with a $\leq$ constraint, a slack variable can be added to the left-hand side of the inequality to convert the constraint to equality form. With a $\geq$ constraint, a **surplus variable** can be subtracted from the left-hand side of the inequality to convert the constraint to equality form. Just as with slack variables, surplus variables are given a coefficient of zero in the objective function because they have no effect on its value. After including two surplus variables, S_1 and S_2, for the $\geq$ constraints and one slack variable, S_3, for the $\leq$ constraint, the linear programming model of the M&D Chemicals problem becomes

$$\begin{aligned}
\text{Min} \quad & 2A + 3B + 0S_1 + 0S_2 + 0S_3 \\
\text{s.t.} \quad & \\
& 1A \qquad\quad - 1S_1 \qquad\qquad\qquad = 125 \\
& 1A + 1B \qquad\quad - 1S_2 \qquad\quad = 350 \\
& 2A + 1B \qquad\qquad\qquad + 1S_3 = 600 \\
& A, B, S_1, S_2, S_3 \geq 0
\end{aligned}$$

Try Problem 35 to test your ability to use slack and surplus variables to write a linear program in standard form.

All the constraints are now equalities. Hence, the preceding formulation is the standard-form representation of the M&D Chemicals problem. At the optimal solution of $A = 250$ and $B = 100$, the values of the surplus and slack variables are as follows:

Constraint	Value of Surplus or Slack Variables
Demand for product A	$S_1 = 125$
Total production	$S_2 = 0$
Processing time	$S_3 = 0$

Refer to Figures 2.15 and 2.16. Note that the zero surplus and slack variables are associated with the constraints that are binding at the optimal solution—that is, the total production and processing time constraints. The surplus of 125 units is associated with the nonbinding constraint on the demand for product A.

In the Par, Inc., problem all the constraints were of the $\leq$ type, and in the M&D Chemicals problem the constraints were a mixture of $\geq$ and $\leq$ types. The number and types of constraints encountered in a particular linear programming problem depend on the specific conditions existing in the problem. Linear programming problems may have some $\leq$ constraints, some $\geq$ constraints, and some $=$ constraints. For an equality constraint, feasible solutions must lie directly on the constraint line.

Try Problem 34 to practice solving a linear program with all three constraint forms.

An example of a linear program with two decision variables, G and H, and all three constraint forms is given here:

$$\begin{aligned} \text{Min} \quad & 2G + 2H \\ \text{s.t.} \quad & \\ & 1G + 3H \leq 12 \\ & 3G + 1H \geq 13 \\ & 1G - 1H = 3 \\ & G, H \geq 0 \end{aligned}$$

The standard-form representation of this problem is

$$\begin{aligned} \text{Min} \quad & 2G + 2H + 0S_1 + 0S_2 \\ \text{s.t.} \quad & \\ & 1G + 3H + 1S_1 \qquad\quad = 12 \\ & 3G + 1H \qquad\quad - 1S_2 = 13 \\ & 1G - 1H \qquad\qquad\qquad = 3 \\ & G, H, S_1, S_2 \geq 0 \end{aligned}$$

The standard form requires a slack variable for the $\leq$ constraint and a surplus variable for the $\geq$ constraint. However, neither a slack nor a surplus variable is required for the third constraint because it is already in equality form.

The Student CD contains the file for Chapter 17, Linear Programming: Simplex Method.

When solving linear programs graphically, it is not necessary to write the problem in its standard form. Nevertheless, you should be able to compute the values of the slack and surplus variables and understand what they mean, because the values of slack and surplus variables are included in the computer solution of linear programs. In Chapter 17 we will introduce an algebraic solution procedure, the simplex method, which can be used to find optimal extreme-point solutions for linear programming problems with as many as several thousand decision variables. The mathematical steps of the simplex method involve solving simultaneous equations that represent the constraints of the linear program. Thus, in setting up a linear program for solution by the simplex method, we must have one linear equation for each constraint in the problem; therefore, the problem must be in its standard form.

A final point: The standard form of the linear programming problem is equivalent to the original formulation of the problem. That is, the optimal solution to any linear programming problem is the same as the optimal solution to the standard form of the problem. The standard form has not changed the basic problem; it has only changed how we write the constraints for the problem.

Computer Solution of the M&D Chemicals Problem

The solution obtained using The Management Scientist is presented in Figure 2.17. The computer output shows that the minimum-cost solution yields an objective function value of \$800. The values of the decision variables show that 250 gallons of product A and 100 gallons of product B provide the minimum-cost solution.

The Slack/Surplus column shows that the $\geq$ constraint corresponding to the demand for product A (see constraint 1) has a surplus of 125 units. This column tells us that production of product A in the optimal solution exceeds demand by 125 gallons. The Slack/Surplus values are zero for the total production requirement (constraint 2) and the processing time limitation (constraint 3), which indicates that these constraints are binding at the

FIGURE 2.17 THE MANAGEMENT SCIENTIST SOLUTION FOR THE M&D CHEMICALS PROBLEM

```
Objective Function Value =                    800.000

      Variable              Value              Reduced Costs
   --------------     ---------------     -----------------
            A                250.000                  0.000
            B                100.000                  0.000

     Constraint          Slack/Surplus          Dual Prices
   --------------     ---------------     -----------------
             1               125.000                  0.000
             2                 0.000                 -4.000
             3                 0.000                  1.000

OBJECTIVE COEFFICIENT RANGES

   Variable        Lower Limit      Current Value      Upper Limit
 ------------   ---------------   ---------------   ---------------
        A       No Lower Limit             2.000             3.000
        B                2.000             3.000    No Upper Limit

RIGHT HAND SIDE RANGES

  Constraint       Lower Limit      Current Value      Upper Limit
 ------------   ---------------   ---------------   ---------------
        1       No Lower Limit           125.000           250.000
        2              300.000           350.000           475.000
        3              475.000           600.000           700.000
```

EXCELfile
M&D

optimal solution. We will discuss the rest of the computer output that appears in Figure 2.17 in Chapter 3 when we study the topic of sensitivity analysis.

2.6 SPECIAL CASES

In this section we discuss three special situations that can arise when we attempt to solve linear programming problems.

Alternative Optimal Solutions

From the discussion of the graphical solution procedure, we know that optimal solutions can be found at the extreme points of the feasible region. Now let us consider the special case in which the optimal objective function line coincides with one of the binding constraint lines on the boundary of the feasible region. We will see that this situation can lead to the case of **alternative optimal solutions;** in such cases, more than one solution provides the optimal value for the objective function.

FIGURE 2.18 PAR, INC., PROBLEM WITH AN OBJECTIVE FUNCTION OF $6.3S + 9D$ (ALTERNATIVE OPTIMAL SOLUTIONS)

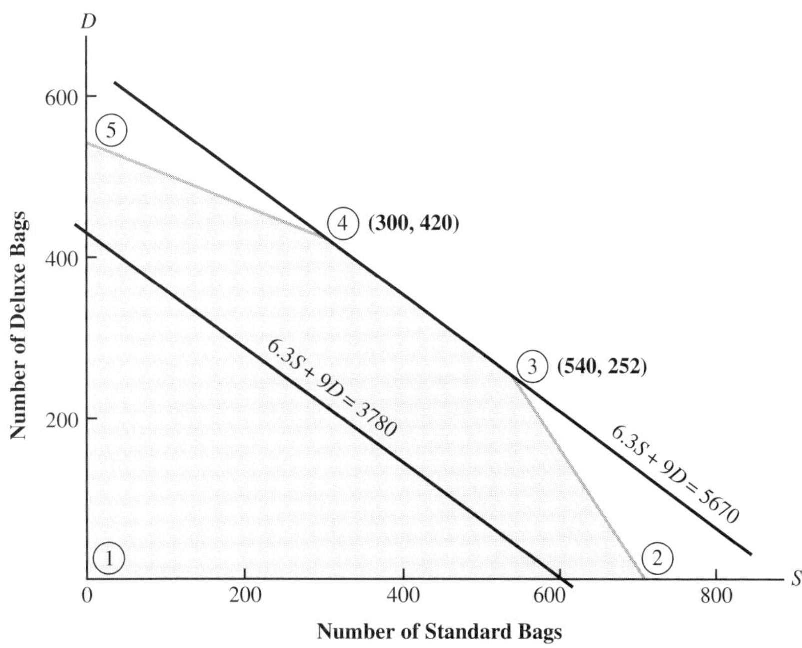

To illustrate the case of alternative optimal solutions, we return to the Par, Inc., problem. However, let us assume that the profit for the standard golf bag (S) has been decreased to \$6.30. The revised objective function becomes $6.3S + 9D$. The graphical solution of this problem is shown in Figure 2.18. Note that the optimal solution still occurs at an extreme point. In fact, it occurs at two extreme points: extreme point ④ ($S = 300$, $D = 420$) and extreme point ③ ($S = 540$, $D = 252$).

The objective function values at these two extreme points are identical; that is,

$$6.3S + 9D = 6.3(300) + 9(420) = 5670$$

and

$$6.3S + 9D = 6.3(540) + 9(252) = 5670$$

Furthermore, any point on the line connecting the two optimal extreme points also provides an optimal solution. For example, the solution point ($S = 420$, $D = 336$), which is halfway between the two extreme points, also provides the optimal objective function value of

$$6.3S + 9D = 6.3(420) + 9(336) = 5670$$

A linear programming problem with alternative optimal solutions is generally a good situation for the manager or decision maker. It means that several combinations of the decision variables are optimal and that the manager can select the most desirable optimal solution. Unfortunately, determining whether a problem has alternative optimal solutions is not a simple matter.

Infeasibility

Problems with no feasible solution do arise in practice, most often because management's expectations are too high or because too many restrictions have been placed on the problem.

Infeasibility means that no solution to the linear programming problem satisfies all the constraints, including the nonnegativity conditions. Graphically, infeasibility means that a feasible region does not exist; that is, no points satisfy all the constraints and the nonnegativity conditions simultaneously. To illustrate this situation, let us look again at the problem faced by Par, Inc.

Suppose that management specified that at least 500 of the standard bags and at least 360 of the deluxe bags must be manufactured. The graph of the solution region may now be constructed to reflect these new requirements (see Figure 2.19). The shaded area in the lower left-hand portion of the graph depicts those points satisfying the departmental constraints on the availability of time. The shaded area in the upper right-hand portion depicts those points satisfying the minimum production requirements of 500 standard and 360 deluxe bags. But no points satisfy both sets of constraints. Thus, we see that if management imposes these minimum production requirements, no feasible region exists for the problem.

How should we interpret infeasibility in terms of this current problem? First, we should tell management that given the resources available (i.e., production time for cutting and dyeing, sewing, finishing, and inspection and packaging), it is not possible to make 500 standard bags and 360 deluxe bags. Moreover, we can tell management exactly how much of each resource must be expended to make it possible to manufacture 500 standard and 360 deluxe

FIGURE 2.19 NO FEASIBLE REGION FOR THE PAR, INC., PROBLEM WITH MINIMUM PRODUCTION REQUIREMENTS OF 500 STANDARD AND 360 DELUXE BAGS

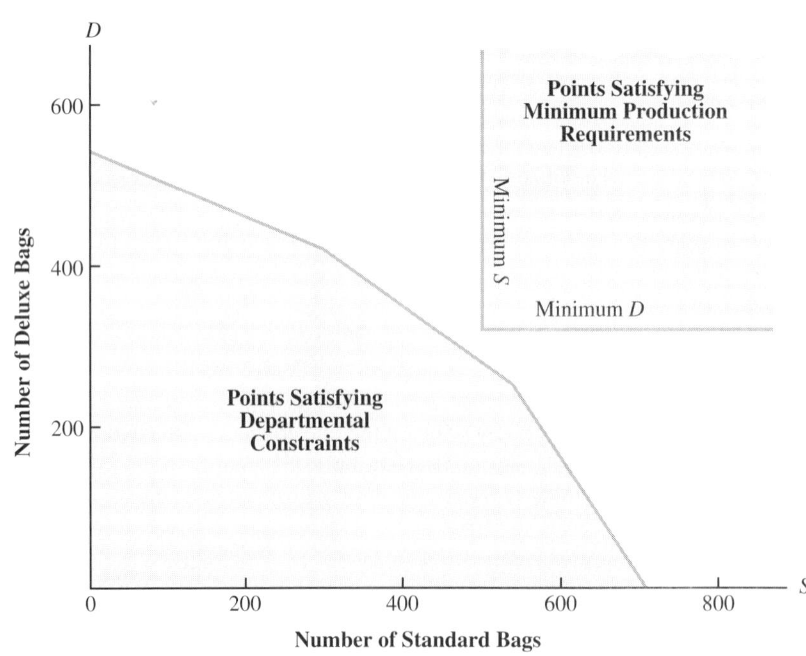

TABLE 2.2 RESOURCES NEEDED TO MANUFACTURE 500 STANDARD BAGS AND 360 DELUXE BAGS

Operation	Minimum Required Resources (hours)	Available Resources (hours)	Additional Resources Needed (hours)
Cutting and dyeing	$\frac{7}{10}(500) + 1(360) = 710$	630	80
Sewing	$\frac{1}{2}(500) + \frac{5}{6}(360) = 550$	600	None
Finishing	$1(500) + \frac{2}{3}(360) = 740$	708	32
Inspection and packaging	$\frac{1}{10}(500) + \frac{1}{4}(360) = 140$	135	5

bags. Table 2.2 shows the minimum amounts of resources that must be available, the amounts currently available, and additional amounts that would be required to accomplish this level of production. Thus, we need 80 more hours for cutting and dyeing, 32 more hours for finishing, and 5 more hours for inspection and packaging to meet management's minimum production requirements.

If, after reviewing this information, management still wants to manufacture 500 standard and 360 deluxe bags, additional resources must be provided. Perhaps by hiring another person to work in the cutting and dyeing department, transferring a person from elsewhere in the plant to work part-time in the finishing department, or having the sewing people help out periodically with the inspection and packaging, the resource requirements can be met. As you can see, many possibilities are available for corrective management action, once we discover the lack of a feasible solution. The important thing to realize is that linear programming analysis can help determine whether management's plans are feasible. By analyzing the problem using linear programming, we are often able to point out infeasible conditions and initiate corrective action.

Whenever you attempt to solve a problem that is infeasible using The Management Scientist, you will obtain a message that says "No Feasible Solution." In this case you know that no solution to the linear programming problem will satisfy all constraints, including the nonnegativity conditions. Careful inspection of your formulation is necessary to try to identify why the problem is infeasible. In some situations, the only reasonable approach is to drop one or more constraints and re-solve the problem. If you are able to find an optimal solution for this revised problem, you will know that the constraint(s) that were omitted, in conjunction with the others, are causing the problem to be infeasible.

Unbounded

The solution to a maximization linear programming problem is **unbounded** if the value of the solution may be made infinitely large without violating any of the constraints; for a minimization problem, the solution is unbounded if the value may be made infinitely small. This condition might be termed *managerial utopia;* for example, if this condition were to occur in a profit maximization problem, the manager could achieve an unlimited profit.

However, in linear programming models of real problems, the occurrence of an unbounded solution means that the problem has been improperly formulated. We know it is not possible to increase profits indefinitely. Therefore, we must conclude that if a profit maximization problem results in an unbounded solution, the mathematical model doesn't represent the real-world problem sufficiently. Usually, what has happened is that a constraint has been inadvertently omitted during problem formulation.

As an illustration, consider the following linear program with two decision variables, X and Y.

$$
\begin{aligned}
\text{Max} \quad & 20X + 10Y \\
\text{s.t.} \quad & \\
& 1X \geq 2 \\
& 1Y \leq 5 \\
& X, Y \geq 0
\end{aligned}
$$

In Figure 2.20 we graphed the feasible region associated with this problem. Note that we can only indicate part of the feasible region because the feasible region extends indefinitely in the direction of the X axis. Looking at the objective function lines in Figure 2.20, we see that the solution to this problem may be made as large as we desire. That is, no matter what solution we pick, we will always be able to reach some feasible solution with a larger value. Thus, we say that the solution to this linear program is *unbounded.*

FIGURE 2.20 EXAMPLE OF AN UNBOUNDED PROBLEM

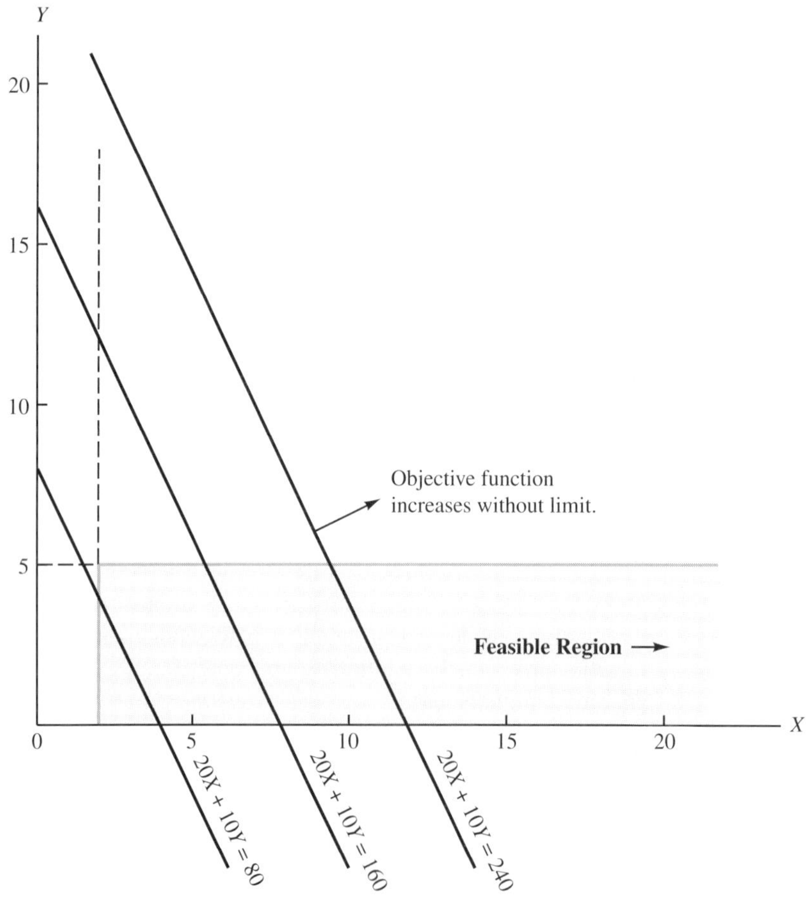

Can you recognize whether a linear program involves alternative optimal solutions, infeasibility, or is unbounded? Try Problems 42 and 43.

Whenever you attempt to solve a problem that is unbounded using The Management Scientist, you will obtain a message that says, "Problem is Unbounded." Because unbounded solutions cannot occur in real problems, the first thing you should do is to review your model to determine whether you incorrectly formulated the problem. In many cases, this error is the result of inadvertently omitting a constraint during problem formulation.

NOTES AND COMMENTS

1. Infeasibility is independent of the objective function. It exists because the constraints are so restrictive that no feasible region for the linear programming model is possible. Thus, when you encounter infeasibility, making changes in the coefficients of the objective function will not help; the problem will remain infeasible.
2. The occurrence of an unbounded solution is often the result of a missing constraint. However, a change in the objective function may cause a previously unbounded problem to become bounded with an optimal solution. For example, the graph in Figure 2.20 shows an unbounded solution for the objective function Max $20X + 10Y$. However, changing the objective function to Max $-20X - 10Y$ will provide the optimal solution $X = 2$ and $Y = 0$ even though no changes have been made in the constraints.

2.7 GENERAL LINEAR PROGRAMMING NOTATION

In this chapter we showed how to formulate linear programming models for the Par, Inc., and M&D Chemicals problems. To formulate a linear programming model of the Par, Inc., problem we began by defining two decision variables: S = number of standard bags, and D = number of deluxe bags. In the M&D Chemicals problem, the two decision variables were defined as A = number of gallons of product A and B = number of gallons of product B. We selected decision-variable names of S and D in the Par, Inc., problem and A and B in the M&D Chemicals problem to make it easier to recall what these decision variables represented in the problem. Although this approach works well for linear programs involving a small number of decision variables, it can become difficult when dealing with problems involving a large number of decision variables.

A more general notation that is often used for linear programs uses the letter x with a subscript. For instance, in the Par, Inc., problem, we could have defined the decision variables as follows:

$$x_1 = \text{number of standard bags}$$
$$x_2 = \text{number of deluxe bags}$$

In the M&D Chemicals problem, the same variable names would be used, but their definitions would change:

$$x_1 = \text{number of gallons of product A}$$
$$x_2 = \text{number of gallons of product B}$$

A disadvantage of using general notation for decision variables is that we are no longer able to easily identify what the decision variables actually represent in the mathematical model. However, the advantage of general notation is that formulating a mathematical model for a problem that involves a large number of decision variables is much easier. For instance, for a linear programming model with three decision variables, we would use variable names of x_1, x_2, and x_3; for a problem with four decision variables, we would use variable names of x_1, x_2, x_3, and x_4, and so on. Clearly, if a problem involved 1000 decision variables, trying to identify 1000 unique names would be difficult. However, using the general linear programming notation, the decision variables would be defined as $x_1, x_2, x_3, \ldots, x_{1000}$.

To illustrate the graphical solution procedure for a linear program written using general linear programming notation, consider the following mathematical model for a maximization problem involving two decision variables:

$$
\begin{aligned}
\text{Max} \quad & 3x_1 + 2x_2 \\
\text{s.t.} \quad & \\
& 2x_1 + 2x_2 \leq 8 \\
& 1x_1 + 0.5x_2 \leq 3 \\
& x_1, x_2 \geq 0
\end{aligned}
$$

We must first develop a graph that displays the possible solutions (x_1 and x_2 values) for the problem. The usual convention is to plot values of x_1 along the horizontal axis and values of x_2 along the vertical axis. Figure 2.21 shows the graphical solution for this two-variable problem. Note that for this problem the optimal solution is $x_1 = 2$ and $x_2 = 2$, with an objective function value of 10.

Using general linear programming notation, we can write the standard form of the preceding linear program as follows:

$$
\begin{aligned}
\text{Max} \quad & 3x_1 + 2x_2 + 0s_1 + 0s_2 \\
\text{s.t.} \quad & \\
& 2x_1 + 2x_2 + 1s_1 \qquad\quad = 8 \\
& 1x_1 + 0.5x_2 + \qquad\quad 1s_2 = 3 \\
& x_1, x_2, s_1, s_2 \geq 0
\end{aligned}
$$

Thus, at the optimal solution $x_1 = 2$ and $x_2 = 2$; the values of the slack variables are $s_1 = s_2 = 0$.

SUMMARY

We formulated linear programming models for two problems: the Par, Inc., maximization problem and the M&D Chemicals minimization problem. For both problems we showed how a graphical solution procedure and The Management Scientist software package can be used to identify an optimal solution. In formulating a mathematical model of these problems, we developed a general definition of a linear programming model.

A linear programming model is a mathematical model with the following characteristics:

1. A linear objective function that is to be maximized or minimized
2. A set of linear constraints
3. Variables that are all restricted to nonnegative values

Slack variables may be used to write less-than-or-equal-to constraints in equality form and surplus variables may be used to write greater-than-or-equal-to constraints in equality form. The value of a slack variable can usually be interpreted as the amount of unused resource, while the value of a surplus variable indicates the amount over and above some

FIGURE 2.21 GRAPHICAL SOLUTION OF A TWO-VARIABLE LINEAR PROGRAM WITH GENERAL NOTATION

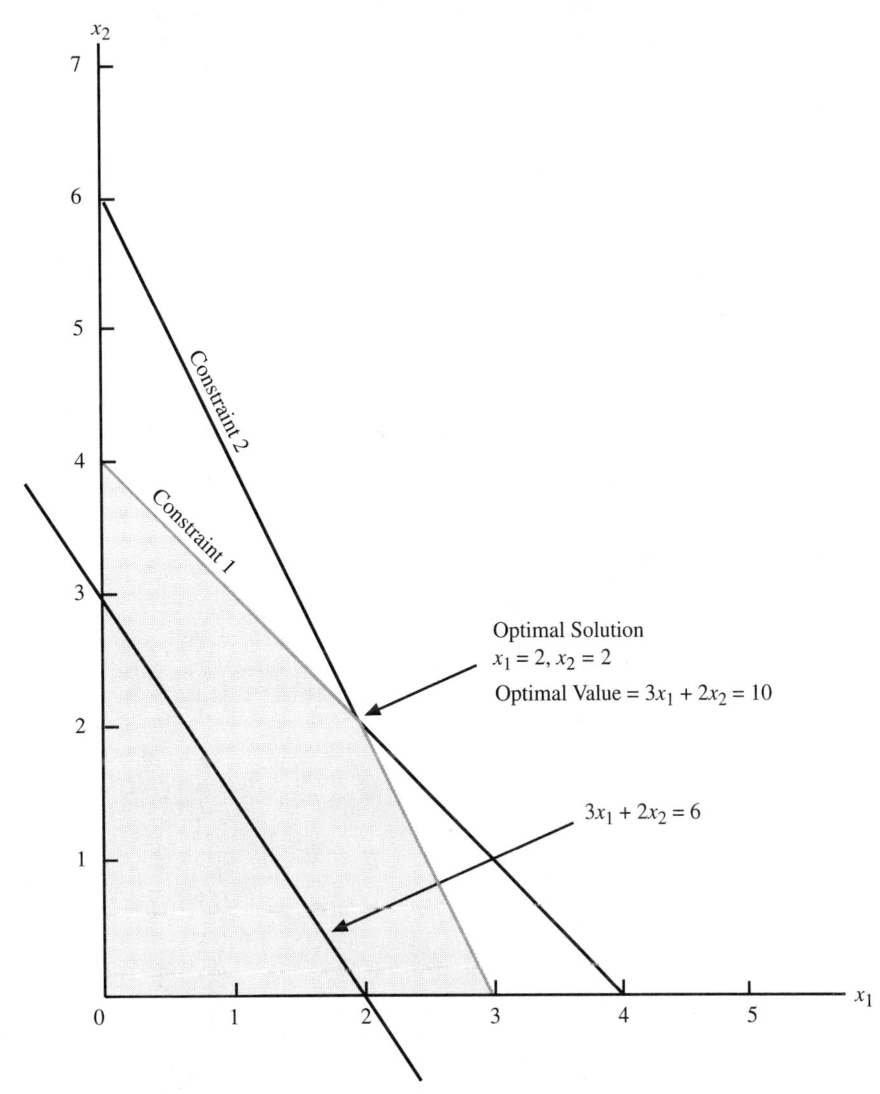

stated minimum requirement. When all constraints have been written as equalities, the linear program has been written in its standard form.

If the solution to a linear program is infeasible or unbounded, no optimal solution to the problem can be found. In the case of infeasibility, no feasible solutions are possible, whereas, in the case of an unbounded solution, the objective function can be made infinitely large for a maximization problem and infinitely small for a minimization problem. In the case of alternative optimal solutions, two or more optimal extreme points exist, and all the points on the line segment connecting them are also optimal.

This chapter concludes with a section showing how to write a linear program using general linear programming notation. The Management Science in Action, Using Linear Programming for Traffic Control, provides another example of the widespread use of linear programming. In the next two chapters we will see many more applications of linear programming.

MANAGEMENT SCIENCE IN ACTION

USING LINEAR PROGRAMMING FOR TRAFFIC CONTROL*

The Hanshin Expressway was the first urban toll expressway in Osaka, Japan. Although in 1964 its length was only 2.3 kilometers, today it is a large-scale urban expressway network of 200 kilometers. The Hanshin Expressway provides service for the Hanshin (Osaka-Kobe) area, the second-most populated area in Japan. An average of 828,000 vehicles use the expressway each day, with daily traffic sometimes exceeding 1 million vehicles. In 1990, the Hanshin Expressway Public Corporation started using an automated traffic control system in order to maximize the number of vehicles flowing into the expressway network.

The automated traffic control system relies on two control methods: (1) limiting the number of cars that enter the expressway at each entrance ramp; and (2) providing drivers with up-to-date and accurate traffic information, including expected travel times and information about accidents. The approach used to limit the number of vehicles depends upon whether the expressway is in a normal or steady state of operation, or whether some type of unusual event, such as an accident or a breakdown, has occurred.

In the first phase of the steady-state case, the Hanshin system uses a linear programming model to maximize the total number of vehicles entering the system, while preventing traffic congestion and adverse effects on surrounding road networks. The data that drive the linear programming model are collected from detectors installed every 500 meters along the expressway and at all entrance and exit ramps. Every five minutes the real-time data collected from the detectors are used to update the model coefficients, and a new linear program computes the maximum number of vehicles the expressway can accommodate.

The automated traffic control system has been successful. According to surveys, traffic control decreased the length of congested portions of the expressway by 30 percent and the duration by 20 percent. It proved to be extremely cost effective, and drivers consider it an indispensable service.

*Based on T. Yoshino, T. Sasaki, and T. Hasegawa, "The Traffic-Control System on the Hanshin Expressway," *Interfaces* (January/February 1995): 94–108.

GLOSSARY

Constraint An equation or inequality that rules out certain combinations of decision variables as feasible solutions.

Problem formulation The process of translating the verbal statement of a problem into a mathematical statement called the *mathematical model.*

Decision variable A controllable input for a linear programming model.

Nonnegativity constraints A set of constraints that requires all variables to be nonnegative.

Mathematical model A representation of a problem where the objective and all constraint conditions are described by mathematical expressions.

Linear programming model A mathematical model with a linear objective function, a set of linear constraints, and nonnegative variables.

Linear program Another term for linear programming model.

Linear functions Mathematical expressions in which the variables appear in separate terms and are raised to the first power.

Feasible solution A solution that satisfies all the constraints.

Feasible region The set of all feasible solutions.

Slack variable A variable added to the left-hand side of a less-than-or-equal-to constraint to convert the constraint into an equality. The value of this variable can usually be interpreted as the amount of unused resource.

Standard form A linear program in which all the constraints are written as equalities. The optimal solution of the standard form of a linear program is the same as the optimal solution of the original formulation of the linear program.

Redundant constraint A constraint that does not affect the feasible region. If a constraint is redundant, it can be removed from the problem without affecting the feasible region.

Extreme point Graphically speaking, extreme points are the feasible solution points occurring at the vertices or "corners" of the feasible region. With two-variable problems, extreme points are determined by the intersection of the constraint lines.

Surplus variable A variable subtracted from the left-hand side of a greater-than-or-equal-to constraint to convert the constraint into an equality. The value of this variable can usually be interpreted as the amount over and above some required minimum level.

Alternative optimal solutions The case in which more than one solution provides the optimal value for the objective function.

Infeasibility The situation in which no solution to the linear programming problem satisfies all the constraints.

Unbounded If the value of the solution may be made infinitely large in a maximization linear programming problem or infinitely small in a minimization problem without violating any of the constraints, the problem is said to be unbounded.

PROBLEMS

1. Which of the following mathematical relationships could be found in a linear programming model, and which could not? For the relationships that are unacceptable for linear programs, state why.
   a. $-1A + 2B \leq 70$
   b. $2A - 2B = 50$
   c. $1A - 2B^2 \leq 10$
   d. $3\sqrt{A} + 2B \geq 15$
   e. $1A + 1B = 6$
   f. $2A + 5B + 1AB \leq 25$

2. Find the solutions that satisfy the following constraints:
   a. $4A + 2B \leq 16$
   b. $4A + 2B \geq 16$
   c. $4A + 2B = 16$
3. Show a separate graph of the constraint lines and the solutions that satisfy each of the following constraints:
   a. $3A + 2B \leq 18$
   b. $12A + 8B \geq 480$
   c. $5A + 10B = 200$

4. Show a separate graph of the constraint lines and the solutions that satisfy each of the following constraints:
   a. $3A - 4B \geq 60$
   b. $-6A + 5B \leq 60$
   c. $5A - 2B \leq 0$

5. Show a separate graph of the constraint lines and the solutions that satisfy each of the following constraints:
   a. $A \geq 0.25\,(A + B)$
   b. $B \leq 0.10\,(A + B)$
   c. $A \leq 0.50\,(A + B)$

SELF test

6. Three objective functions for linear programming problems are $7A + 10B$, $6A + 4B$, and $-4A + 7B$. Show the graph of each for objective function values equal to 420.

SELF test

7. Identify the feasible region for the following set of constraints:

$$\begin{aligned} 0.5A + 0.25B &\geq 30 \\ 1A + 5B &\geq 250 \\ 0.25A + 0.5B &\leq 50 \\ A, B &\geq 0 \end{aligned}$$

8. Identify the feasible region for the following set of constraints:

$$\begin{aligned} 2A - 1B &\leq 0 \\ -1A + 1.5B &\leq 200 \\ A, B &\geq 0 \end{aligned}$$

9. Identify the feasible region for the following set of constraints:

$$\begin{aligned} 3A - 2B &\geq 0 \\ 2A - 1B &\leq 200 \\ 1A &\leq 150 \\ A, B &\geq 0 \end{aligned}$$

10. For the linear program

$$\begin{aligned} \text{Max} \quad & 2A + 3B \\ \text{s.t.} \quad & \\ & 1A + 2B \leq 6 \\ & 5A + 3B \leq 15 \\ & A, B \geq 0 \end{aligned}$$

find the optimal solution using the graphical solution procedure. What is the value of the objective function at the optimal solution?

11. Solve the following linear program using the graphical solution procedure.

$$\begin{aligned} \text{Max} \quad & 5A + 5B \\ \text{s.t.} \quad & \\ & 1A \leq 100 \\ & 1B \leq 80 \\ & 2A + 4B \leq 400 \\ & A, B \geq 0 \end{aligned}$$

12. Consider the following linear programming problem:

$$\begin{aligned} \text{Max} \quad & 3A + 3B \\ \text{s.t.} \quad & \\ & 2A + 4B \leq 12 \\ & 6A + 4B \leq 24 \\ & A, B \geq 0 \end{aligned}$$

a. Find the optimal solution using the graphical solution procedure.
b. If the objective function is changed to $2A + 6B$, what will the optimal solution be?
c. How many extreme points are there? What are the values of A and B at each extreme point?

13. Consider the following linear program:

$$\begin{aligned} \text{Max} \quad & 1A + 2B \\ \text{s.t.} \quad & \\ & 1A \leq 5 \\ & 1B \leq 4 \\ & 2A + 2B = 12 \\ & A, B \geq 0 \end{aligned}$$

a. Show the feasible region.
b. What are the extreme points of the feasible region?
c. Find the optimal solution using the graphical procedure.

14. RMC, Inc., is a small firm that produces a variety of chemical products. In a particular production process, three raw materials are blended (mixed together) to produce two products: a fuel additive and a solvent base. Each ton of fuel additive is a mixture of $\frac{2}{5}$ ton of material 1 and $\frac{3}{5}$ of material 3. A ton of solvent base is a mixture of $\frac{1}{2}$ ton of material 1, $\frac{1}{5}$ ton of material 2, and $\frac{3}{10}$ ton of material 3. After deducting relevant costs, the profit contribution is \$40 for every ton of fuel additive produced and \$30 for every ton of solvent base produced.

RMC's production is constrained by a limited availability of the three raw materials. For the current production period, RMC has available the following quantities of each raw material:

Raw Material	Amount Available for Production
Material 1	20 tons
Material 2	5 tons
Material 3	21 tons

Assuming that RMC is interested in maximizing the total profit contribution, answer the following:

a. What is the linear programming model for this problem?
b. Find the optimal solution using the graphical solution procedure. How many tons of each product should be produced, and what is the projected total profit contribution?
c. Is there any unused material? If so, how much?
d. Are any of the constraints redundant? If so, which ones?

15. Refer to the Par, Inc., problem described in Section 2.1. Suppose that Par's management encounters the following situations.
    a. The accounting department revises its estimate of the profit contribution for the deluxe bag to \$18 per bag.
    b. A new low-cost material is available for the standard bag, and the profit contribution per standard bag can be increased to \$20 per bag. (Assume that the profit contribution of the deluxe bag is the original \$9 value.)
    c. New sewing equipment is available that would increase the sewing operation capacity to 750 hours. (Assume that $10A + 9B$ is the appropriate objective function.)

    If each of these situations is encountered separately, what is the optimal solution and the total profit contribution?
16. Refer to the feasible region for Par, Inc., problem in Figure 2.13.
    a. Develop an objective function that will make extreme point (5) the optimal extreme point.
    b. What is the optimal solution for the objective function you selected in part (a)?
    c. What are the values of the slack variables associated with this solution?

17. Write the following linear program in standard form:

$$
\begin{aligned}
\text{Max} \quad & 5A + 2B \\
\text{s.t.} \quad & \\
& 1A - 2B \le 420 \\
& 2A + 3B \le 610 \\
& 6A - 1B \le 125 \\
& A, B \ge 0
\end{aligned}
$$

18. For the linear program

$$
\begin{aligned}
\text{Max} \quad & 4A + 1B \\
\text{s.t.} \quad & \\
& 10A + 2B \le 30 \\
& 3A + 2B \le 12 \\
& 2A + 2B \le 10 \\
& A, B \ge 0
\end{aligned}
$$

    a. Write this problem in standard form.
    b. Solve the problem using the graphical solution procedure.
    c. What are the values of the three slack variables at the optimal solution?
19. Given the linear program

$$
\begin{aligned}
\text{Max} \quad & 3A + 4B \\
\text{s.t.} \quad & \\
& -1A + 2B \le 8 \\
& 1A + 2B \le 12 \\
& 2A + 1B \le 16 \\
& A, B \ge 0
\end{aligned}
$$

    a. Write the problem in standard form.
    b. Solve the problem using the graphical solution procedure.
    c. What are the values of the three slack variables at the optimal solution?

20. For the linear program

$$
\begin{aligned}
\text{Max} \quad & 3A + 2B \\
\text{s.t.} \quad & \\
& A + B \geq 4 \\
& 3A + 4B \leq 24 \\
& A \geq 2 \\
& A - B \leq 0 \\
& A, B \geq 0
\end{aligned}
$$

a. Write the problem in standard form.
b. Solve the problem.
c. What are the values of the slack and surplus variables at the optimal solution?

21. Consider the following linear program:

$$
\begin{aligned}
\text{Max} \quad & 2A + 3B \\
\text{s.t.} \quad & \\
& 5A + 5B \leq 400 \quad \text{Constraint 1} \\
& -1A + 1B \leq 10 \quad \text{Constraint 2} \\
& 1A + 3B \geq 90 \quad \text{Constraint 3} \\
& A, B \geq 0
\end{aligned}
$$

Figure 2.22 shows a graph of the constraint lines.

a. Place a number (1, 2, or 3) next to each constraint line to identify which constraint it represents.
b. Shade in the feasible region on the graph.
c. Identify the optimal extreme point. What is the optimal solution?

FIGURE 2.22 GRAPH OF THE CONSTRAINT LINES FOR EXERCISE 21

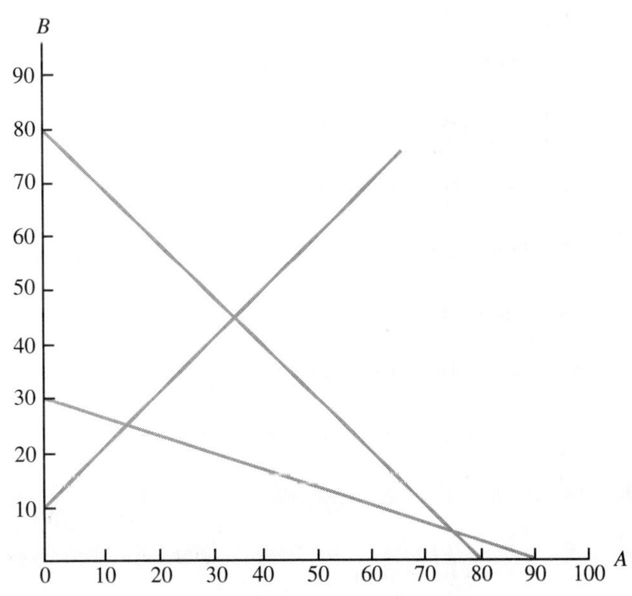

d. Which constraints are binding? Explain.
e. How much slack or surplus is associated with the nonbinding constraint?

22. Reiser Sports Products wants to determine the number of All-Pro (A) and College (C) footballs to produce in order to maximize profit over the next four-week planning horizon. Constraints affecting the production quantities are the production capacities in three departments: cutting and dyeing; sewing; and inspection and packaging. For the four-week planning period, 340 hours of cutting and dyeing time, 420 hours of sewing time, and 200 hours of inspection and packaging time are available. All-Pro footballs provide a profit of $5 per unit and College footballs provide a profit of $4 per unit. The linear programming model with production times expressed in minutes is as follows:

$$\text{Max} \quad 5A + 4C$$

s.t.

$$12A + 6C \leq 20{,}400 \quad \text{Cutting and dyeing}$$
$$9A + 15C \leq 25{,}200 \quad \text{Sewing}$$
$$6A + 6C \leq 12{,}000 \quad \text{Inspection and packaging}$$
$$A, C \geq 0$$

A portion of the graphical solution to the Reiser problem is shown in Figure 2.23.

a. Shade the feasible region for this problem.
b. Determine the coordinates of each extreme point and the corresponding profit. Which extreme point generates the highest profit?

FIGURE 2.23 PORTION OF THE GRAPHICAL SOLUTION FOR EXERCISE 22

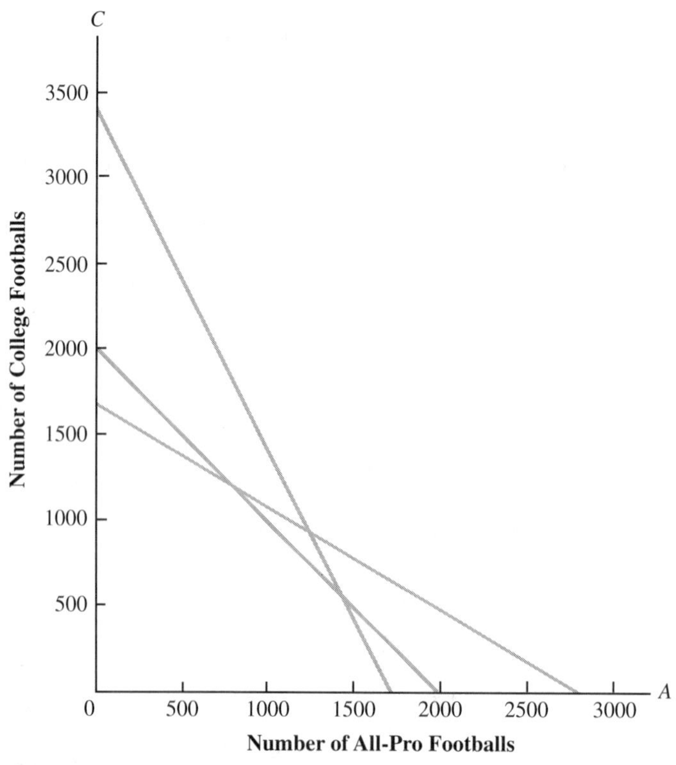

c. Draw the profit line corresponding to a profit of \$4000. Move the profit line as far from the origin as you can in order to determine which extreme point will provide the optimal solution. Compare your answer with the approach you used in part (b).
d. Which constraints are binding? Explain.
e. Suppose that the values of the objective function coefficients are \$4 for each All-Pro model produced and \$5 for each College model. Use the graphical solution procedure to determine the new optimal solution and the corresponding value of profit.

23. Embassy Motorcycles (EM) manufacturers two lightweight motorcycles designed for easy handling and safety. The EZ-Rider model has a new engine and a low profile that make it easy to balance. The Lady-Sport model is slightly larger, uses a more traditional engine, and is specifically designed to appeal to women riders. Embassy produces the engines for both models at its Des Moines, Iowa, plant. Each EZ-Rider engine requires 6 hours of manufacturing time and each Lady-Sport engine requires 3 hours of manufacturing time. The Des Moines plant has 2100 hours of engine manufacturing time available for the next production period. Embassy's motorcycle frame supplier can supply as many EZ-Rider frames as needed. However, the Lady-Sport frame is more complex and the supplier can only provide up to 280 Lady-Sport frames for the next production period. Final assembly and testing requires 2 hours for each EZ-Rider model and 2.5 hours for each Lady-Sport model. A maximum of 1000 hours of assembly and testing time are available for the next production period. The company's accounting department projects a profit contribution of \$2400 for each EZ-Rider produced and \$1800 for each Lady-Sport produced.
a. Formulate a linear programming model that can be used to determine the number of units of each model that should be produced in order to maximize the total contribution to profit.
b. Solve the problem graphically. What is the optimal solution?
c. Which constraints are binding?

24. Kelson Sporting Equipment, Inc., makes two different types of baseball gloves: a regular model and a catcher's model. The firm has 900 hours of production time available in its cutting and sewing department, 300 hours available in its finishing department, and 100 hours available in its packaging and shipping department. The production time requirements and the profit contribution per glove are given in the following table.

	Production Time (hours)			
Model	**Cutting and Sewing**	**Finishing**	**Packaging and Shipping**	**Profit/Glove**
Regular model	1	$\frac{1}{2}$	$\frac{1}{8}$	\$5
Catcher's model	$\frac{3}{2}$	$\frac{1}{3}$	$\frac{1}{4}$	\$8

Assuming that the company is interested in maximizing the total profit contribution, answer the following:
a. What is the linear programming model for this problem?
b. Find the optimal solution using the graphical solution procedure. How many gloves of each model should Kelson manufacture?
c. What is the total profit contribution Kelson can earn with the given production quantities?
d. How many hours of production time will be scheduled in each department?
e. What is the slack time in each department?

25. George Johnson recently inherited a large sum of money; he wants to use a portion of this money to set up a trust fund for his two children. The trust fund has two investment options: (1) a bond fund and (2) a stock fund. The projected returns over the life of the investments are 6% for the bond fund and 10% for the stock fund. Whatever portion of the inheritance he finally decides to commit to the trust fund, he wants to invest at least 30% of that amount in the bond fund. In addition, he wants to select a mix that will enable him to obtain a total return of at least 7.5%.

    a. Formulate a linear programming model that can be used to determine the percentage that should be allocated to each of the possible investment alternatives.
    b. Solve the problem using the graphical solution procedure.

26. The Sea Wharf Restaurant would like to determine the best way to allocate a monthly advertising budget of $1000 between newspaper advertising and radio advertising. Management decided that at least 25% of the budget must be spent on each type of media, and that the amount of money spent on local newspaper advertising must be at least twice the amount spent on radio advertising. A marketing consultant developed an index that measures audience exposure per dollar of advertising on a scale from 0 to 100, with higher values implying greater audience exposure. If the value of the index for local newspaper advertising is 50 and the value of the index for spot radio advertising is 80, how should the restaurant allocate its advertising budget in order to maximize the value of total audience exposure?

    a. Formulate a linear programming model that can be used to determine how the restaurant should allocate its advertising budget in order to maximize the value of total audience exposure.
    b. Solve the problem using the graphical solution procedure.

27. Blair & Rosen, Inc. (B&R), is a brokerage firm that specializes in investment portfolios designed to meet the specific risk tolerances of its clients. A client who contacted B&R this past week has a maximum of $50,000 to invest. B&R's investment advisor decides to recommend a portfolio consisting of two investment funds: an Internet fund and a Blue Chip fund. The Internet fund has a projected annual return of 12%, while the Blue Chip fund has a projected annual return of 9%. The investment advisor requires that at most $35,000 of the client's funds should be invested in the Internet fund. B&R services include a risk rating for each investment alternative. The Internet fund, which is the more risky of the two investment alternatives, has a risk rating of 6 per thousand dollars invested. The Blue Chip fund has a risk rating of 4 per thousand dollars invested. For example, if $10,000 is invested in each of the two investment funds, B&R's risk rating for the portfolio would be $6(10) + 4(10) = 100$. Finally, B&R developed a questionnaire to measure each client's risk tolerance. Based on the responses, each client is classified as a conservative, moderate, or aggressive investor. Suppose that the questionnaire results classified the current client as a moderate investor. B&R recommends that a client who is a moderate investor limit his or her portfolio to a maximum risk rating of 240.

    a. What is the recommended investment portfolio for this client? What is the annual return for the portfolio?
    b. Suppose that a second client with $50,000 to invest has been classified as an aggressive investor. B&R recommends that the maximum portfolio risk rating for an aggressive investor is 320. What is the recommended investment portfolio for this aggressive investor? Discuss what happens to the portfolio under the aggressive investor strategy.
    c. Suppose that a third client with $50,000 to invest has been classified as a conservative investor. B&R recommends that the maximum portfolio risk rating for a conservative investor is 160. Develop the recommended investment portfolio for the

conservative investor. Discuss the interpretation of the slack variable for the total investment fund constraint.

28. Tom's, Inc., produces various Mexican food products and sells them to Western Foods, a chain of grocery stores located in Texas and New Mexico. Tom's, Inc., makes two salsa products: Western Foods Salsa and Mexico City Salsa. Essentially, the two products have different blends of whole tomatoes, tomato sauce, and tomato paste. The Western Foods Salsa is a blend of 50% whole tomatoes, 30% tomato sauce, and 20% tomato paste. The Mexico City Salsa, which has a thicker and chunkier consistency, consists of 70% whole tomatoes, 10% tomato sauce, and 20% tomato paste. Each jar of salsa produced weighs 10 ounces. For the current production period Tom's, Inc., can purchase up to 280 pounds of whole tomatoes, 130 pounds of tomato sauce, and 100 pounds of tomato paste; the price per pound for these ingredients is \$0.96, \$0.64, and \$0.56, respectively. The cost of the spices and the other ingredients is approximately \$0.10 per jar. Tom's, Inc., buys empty glass jars for \$0.02 each, and labeling and filling costs are estimated to be \$0.03 for each jar of salsa produced. Tom's contract with Western Foods results in sales revenue of \$1.64 for each jar of Western Foods Salsa and \$1.93 for each jar of Mexico City Salsa.
   a. Develop a linear programming model that will enable Tom's to determine the mix of salsa products that will maximize the total profit contribution.
   b. Find the optimal solution.

29. AutoIgnite produces electronic ignition systems for automobiles at a plant in Cleveland, Ohio. Each ignition system is assembled from two components produced at AutoIgnite's plants in Buffalo, New York, and Dayton, Ohio. The Buffalo plant can produce 2000 units of component 1, 1000 units of component 2, or any combination of the two components each day. For instance, 60% of Buffalo's production time could be used to produce component 1 and 40% of Buffalo's production time could be used to produce component 2; in this case, the Buffalo plant would be able to produce 0.6(2000) = 1200 units of component 1 each day and 0.4(1000) = 400 units of component 2 each day. The Dayton plant can produce 600 units of component 1, 1400 units of component 2, or any combination of the two components each day. At the end of each day, the component production at Buffalo and Dayton is sent to Cleveland for assembly of the ignition systems on the following work day.
   a. Formulate a linear programming model that can be used to develop a daily production schedule for the Buffalo and Dayton plants that will maximize daily production of ignition systems at Cleveland.
   b. Find the optimal solution.

30. A financial advisor at Diehl Investments identified two companies that are likely candidates for a takeover in the near future. Eastern Cable is a leading manufacturer of flexible cable systems used in the construction industry, and ComSwitch is a new firm specializing in digital switching systems. Eastern Cable is currently trading for \$40 per share, and ComSwitch is currently trading for \$25 per share. If the takeovers occur, the financial advisor estimates that the price of Eastern Cable will go to \$55 per share and ComSwitch will go to \$43 per share. At this point in time, the financial advisor has identified ComSwitch as the higher risk alternative. Assume that a client indicated a willingness to invest a maximum of \$50,000 in the two companies. The client wants to invest at least \$15,000 in Eastern Cable and at least \$10,000 in ComSwitch. Because of the higher risk associated with ComSwitch, the financial advisor has recommended that at most \$25,000 should be invested in ComSwitch.
   a. Formulate a linear programming model that can be used to determine the number of shares of Eastern Cable and the number of shares of ComSwitch that will meet the investment constraints and maximize the total return for the investment.
   b. Graph the feasible region.

c. Determine the coordinates of each extreme point.
d. Find the optimal solution.

31. Consider the following linear program:

$$\begin{aligned} \text{Min} \quad & 3A + 4B \\ \text{s.t.} \quad & \\ & 1A + 3B \geq 6 \\ & 1A + 1B \geq 4 \\ & A, B \geq 0 \end{aligned}$$

Identify the feasible region and find the optimal solution using the graphical solution procedure. What is the value of the objective function?

32. Identify the three extreme-point solutions for the M&D Chemicals problem (see Section 2.5). Identify the value of the objective function and the values of the slack and surplus variables at each extreme point.

33. Consider the following linear programming problem:

$$\begin{aligned} \text{Min} \quad & A + 2B \\ \text{s.t.} \quad & \\ & A + 4B \leq 21 \\ & 2A + B \geq 7 \\ & 3A + 1.5B \leq 21 \\ & -2A + 6B \geq 0 \\ & A, B \geq 0 \end{aligned}$$

a. Find the optimal solution using the graphical solution procedure and the value of the objective function.
b. Determine the amount of slack or surplus for each constraint.
c. Suppose the objective function is changed to max $5A + 2B$. Find the optimal solution and the value of the objective function.

34. Consider the following linear program:

$$\begin{aligned} \text{Min} \quad & 2A + 2B \\ \text{s.t.} \quad & \\ & 1A + 3B \leq 12 \\ & 3A + 1B \geq 13 \\ & 1A - 1B = 3 \\ & A, B \geq 0 \end{aligned}$$

a. Show the feasible region.
b. What are the extreme points of the feasible region?
c. Find the optimal solution using the graphical solution procedure.

SELF test

35. For the linear program

$$\begin{aligned} \text{Min} \quad & 6A + 4B \\ \text{s.t.} \quad & \\ & 2A + 1B \geq 12 \\ & 1A + 1B \geq 10 \\ & 1B \leq 4 \\ & A, B \geq 0 \end{aligned}$$

a. Write the problem in standard form.
b. Solve the problem using the graphical solution procedure.
c. What are the values of the slack and surplus variables?

36. As part of a quality improvement initiative, Consolidated Electronics employees complete a three-day training program on teaming and a two-day training program on problem solving. The manager of quality improvement has requested that at least 8 training programs on teaming and at least 10 training programs on problem solving be offered during the next six months. In addition, senior-level management has specified that at least 25 training programs must be offered during this period. Consolidated Electronics uses a consultant to teach the training programs. During the next quarter, the consultant has 84 days of training time available. Each training program on teaming costs $10,000 and each training program on problem solving costs $8000.
   a. Formulate a linear programming model that can be used to determine the number of training programs on teaming and the number of training programs on problem solving that should be offered in order to minimize total cost.
   b. Graph the feasible region.
   c. Determine the coordinates of each extreme point.
   d. Solve for the minimum cost solution.

37. The New England Cheese Company produces two cheese spreads by blending mild cheddar cheese with extra sharp cheddar cheese. The cheese spreads are packaged in 12-ounce containers, which are then sold to distributors throughout the Northeast. The Regular blend contains 80% mild cheddar and 20% extra sharp, and the Zesty blend contains 60% mild cheddar and 40% extra sharp. This year, a local dairy cooperative offered to provide up to 8100 pounds of mild cheddar cheese for $1.20 per pound and up to 3000 pounds of extra sharp cheddar cheese for $1.40 per pound. The cost to blend and package the cheese spreads, excluding the cost of the cheese, is $0.20 per container. If each container of Regular is sold for $1.95 and each container of Zesty is sold for $2.20, how many containers of Regular and Zesty should New England Cheese produce?

38. Applied Technology, Inc. (ATI), produces bicycle frames using two fiberglass materials that improve the strength-to-weight ratio of the frames. The cost of the standard grade material is $7.50 per yard and the cost of the professional grade material is $9.00 per yard. The standard and professional grade materials contain different amounts of fiberglass, carbon fiber, and Kevlar as shown in the following table.

	Standard Grade	**Professional Grade**
Fiberglass	84%	58%
Carbon fiber	10%	30%
Kevlar	6%	12%

ATI signed a contract with a bicycle manufacturer to produce a new frame with a carbon fiber content of at least 20% and a Kevlar content of not greater than 10%. To meet the required weight specification, a total of 30 yards of material must be used for each frame.
   a. Formulate a linear program to determine the number of yards of each grade of fiberglass material that ATI should use in each frame in order to minimize total cost. Define the decision variables and indicate the purpose of each constraint.
   b. Use the graphical solution procedure to determine the feasible region. What are the coordinates of the extreme points?
   c. Compute the total cost at each extreme point. What is the optimal solution?

d. The distributor of the fiberglass material is currently overstocked with the professional grade material. To reduce inventory, the distributor offered ATI the opportunity to purchase the professional grade for $8 per yard. Will the optimal solution change?
e. Suppose that the distributor further lowers the price of the professional grade material to $7.40 per yard. Will the optimal solution change? What effect would an even lower price for the professional grade material have on the optimal solution? Explain.

39. Innis Investments manages funds for a number of companies and wealthy clients. The investment strategy is tailored to each client's needs. For a new client, Innis has been authorized to invest up to $1.2 million in two investment funds: a stock fund and a money market fund. Each unit of the stock fund costs $50 and provides an annual rate of return of 10%; each unit of the money market fund costs $100 and provides an annual rate of return of 4%.

The client wants to minimize risk subject to the requirement that the annual income from the investment be at least $60,000. According to Innis's risk measurement system, each unit invested in the stock fund has a risk index of 8, and each unit invested in the money market fund has a risk index of 3; the higher risk index associated with the stock fund simply indicates that it is the riskier investment. Innis's client also specified that at least $300,000 be invested in the money market fund.

a. Determine how many units of each fund Innis should purchase for the client to minimize the total risk index for the portfolio.
b. How much annual income will this investment strategy generate?
c. Suppose the client desires to maximize annual return. How should the funds be invested?

40. Photo Chemicals produces two types of photographic developing fluids. Both products cost Photo Chemicals $1 per gallon to produce. Based on an analysis of current inventory levels and outstanding orders for the next month, Photo Chemicals' management specified that at least 30 gallons of product 1 and at least 20 gallons of product 2 must be produced during the next two weeks. Management also stated that an existing inventory of highly perishable raw material required in the production of both fluids must be used within the next two weeks. The current inventory of the perishable raw material is 80 pounds. Although more of this raw material can be ordered if necessary, any of the current inventory that is not used within the next two weeks will spoil—hence, the management requirement that at least 80 pounds be used in the next two weeks. Furthermore, it is known that product 1 requires 1 pound of this perishable raw material per gallon and product 2 requires 2 pounds of the raw material per gallon. Because Photo Chemicals' objective is to keep its production costs at the minimum possible level, the firm's management is looking for a minimum cost production plan that uses all the 80 pounds of perishable raw material and provides at least 30 gallons of product 1 and at least 20 gallons of product 2. What is the minimum cost solution?

41. Southern Oil Company produces two grades of gasoline: regular and premium. The profit contributions are $0.30 per gallon for regular gasoline and $0.50 per gallon for premium gasoline. Each gallon of regular gasoline contains 0.3 gallons of grade A crude oil and each gallon of premium gasoline contains 0.6 gallons of grade A crude oil. For the next production period, Southern has 18,000 gallons of grade A crude oil available. The refinery used to produce the gasolines has a production capacity of 50,000 gallons for the next production period. Southern Oil's distributors have indicated that demand for the premium gasoline for the next production period will be at most 20,000 gallons.

a. Formulate a linear programming model that can be used to determine the number of gallons of regular gasoline and the number of gallons of premium gasoline that should be produced in order to maximize total profit contribution.
b. What is the optimal solution?

c. What are the values and interpretations of the slack variables?
d. What are the binding constraints?

42. Does the following linear program involve infeasibility, unbounded, and/or alternative optimal solutions? Explain.

$$\begin{aligned} \text{Max} \quad & 4A + 8B \\ \text{s.t.} \quad & \\ & 2A + 2B \leq 10 \\ & -1A + 1B \geq 8 \\ & A, B \geq 0 \end{aligned}$$

43. Does the following linear program involve infeasibility, unbounded, and/or alternative optimal solutions? Explain.

$$\begin{aligned} \text{Max} \quad & 1A + 1B \\ \text{s.t.} \quad & \\ & 8A + 6B \geq 24 \\ & 2B \geq 4 \\ & A, B \geq 0 \end{aligned}$$

44. Consider the following linear program:

$$\begin{aligned} \text{Max} \quad & 1A + 1B \\ \text{s.t.} \quad & \\ & 5A + 3B \leq 15 \\ & 3A + 5B \leq 15 \\ & A, B \geq 0 \end{aligned}$$

a. What is the optimal solution for this problem?
b. Suppose that the objective function is changed to $1A + 2B$. Find the new optimal solution.

45. Consider the following linear program:

$$\begin{aligned} \text{Max} \quad & 1A - 2B \\ \text{s.t.} \quad & \\ & -4A + 3B \leq 3 \\ & 1A - 1B \leq 3 \\ & A, B \geq 0 \end{aligned}$$

a. Graph the feasible region for the problem.
b. Is the feasible region unbounded? Explain.
c. Find the optimal solution.
d. Does an unbounded feasible region imply that the optimal solution to the linear program will be unbounded?

46. The manager of a small independent grocery store is trying to determine the best use of her shelf space for soft drinks. The store carries national and generic brands and currently has 200 square feet of shelf space available. The manager wants to allocate at least 60% of the space to the national brands and, regardless of the profitability, allocate at least 10% of the

space to the generic brands. How many square feet of space should the manager allocate to the national brands and the generic brands under the following circumstances?

a. The national brands are more profitable than the generic brands.
b. Both brands are equally profitable.
c. The generic brand is more profitable than the national brand.

47. Discuss what happens to the M&D Chemicals problem (see Section 2.5) if the cost per gallon for product A is increased to $3.00 per gallon. What would you recommend? Explain.

48. For the M&D Chemicals problem in Section 2.5, discuss the effect of management's requiring total production of 500 gallons for the two products. List two or three actions M&D should consider to correct the situation you encounter.

49. PharmaPlus operates a chain of 30 pharmacies. The pharmacies are staffed by licensed pharmacists and pharmacy technicians. The company currently employs 85 full-time equivalent pharmacists (combination of full time and part time) and 175 full-time equivalent technicians. Each spring management reviews current staffing levels and makes hiring plans for the year. A recent forecast of the prescription load for the next year shows that at least 250 full-time equivalent employees (pharmacists and technicians) will be required to staff the pharmacies. The personnel department expects 10 pharmacists and 30 technicians to leave over the next year. To accommodate the expected attrition and prepare for future growth, management stated that at least 15 new pharmacists must be hired. In addition, PharmaPlus's new service quality guidelines specify no more than two technicians per licensed pharmacist. The average salary for licensed pharmacists is $40 per hour and the average salary for technicians is $10 per hour.

a. Determine a minimum-cost staffing plan for PharmaPlus. How many pharmacists and technicians are needed?
b. Given current staffing levels and expected attrition, how many new hires (if any) must be made to reach the level recommended in part (a)? What will be the impact on the payroll?

50. Expedition Outfitters manufactures a variety of specialty clothing for hiking, skiing, and mountain climbing. Its management decided to begin production on two new parkas designed for use in extremely cold weather: the Mount Everest Parka and the Rocky Mountain Parka. The manufacturing plant has 120 hours of cutting time and 120 hours of sewing time available for producing these two parkas. Each Mount Everest Parka requires 30 minutes of cutting time and 45 minutes of sewing time, and each Rocky Mountain Parka requires 20 minutes of cutting time and 15 minutes of sewing time. The labor and material cost is $150 for each Mount Everest Parka and $50 for each Rocky Mountain Parka, and the retail prices through the firm's mail order catalog are $250 for the Mount Everest Parka and $200 for the Rocky Mountain Parka. Because management believes that the Mount Everest Parka is a unique coat that will enhance the image of the firm, they specified that at least 20% of the total production must consist of this model. Assuming that Expedition Outfitters can sell as many coats of each type as it can produce, how many units of each model should it manufacture to maximize the total profit contribution?

51. English Motors, Ltd. (EML), developed a new all-wheel-drive sports utility vehicle. As part of the marketing campaign, EML produced a video tape sales presentation to send to both owners of current EML four-wheel-drive vehicles as well as to owners of four-wheel-drive sports utility vehicles offered by competitors; EML refers to these two target markets as the current customer market and the new customer market. Individuals who receive the new promotion video will also receive a coupon for a test drive of the new EML model for one weekend. A key factor in the success of the new promotion is the response rate, the percentage of individuals who receive the new promotion and test drive the new model. EML estimates that the response rate for the current customer market is 25% and the response rate for the new customer market is 20%. For the customers who test drive the new model

the sales rate is the percentage of individuals that make a purchase. Marketing research studies indicate that the sales rate is 12% for the current customer market and 20% for the new customer market. The cost for each promotion, excluding the test drive costs, is $4 for each promotion sent to the current customer market and $6 for each promotion sent to the new customer market. Management also specified that a minimum of 30,000 current customers should test drive the new model and a minimum of 10,000 new customers should test drive the new model. In addition, the number of current customers who test drive the new vehicle must be at least twice the number of new customers who test drive the new vehicle. If the marketing budget, excluding test drive costs, is $1.2 million how many promotions should be sent to each group of customers in order to maximize total sales?

52. Creative Sports Design (CSD) manufactures a standard-size racket and an oversize racket. The firm's rackets are extremely light due to the use of a magnesium-graphite alloy that was invented by the firm's founder. Each standard-size racket uses 0.125 kilograms of the alloy and each oversize racket uses 0.4 kilograms; over the next two-week production period only 80 kilograms of the alloy are available. Each standard-size racket uses 10 minutes of manufacturing time and each oversize racket uses 12 minutes. The profit contributions are $10 for each standard-size racket and $15 for each oversize racket, and 40 hours of manufacturing time are available each week. Management specified that at least 20% of the total production must be the standard-size racket. How many rackets of each type should CSD manufacture over the next two weeks to maximize the total profit contribution? Assume that because of the unique nature of their products, CSD can sell as many rackets as they can produce.

53. Management of High Tech Services (HTS) would like to develop a model that will help allocate their technicians' time between service calls to regular contract customers and new customers. A maximum of 80 hours of technician time is available over the two-week planning period. To satisfy cash flow requirements, at least $800 in revenue (per technician) must be generated during the two-week period. Technician time for regular customers generates $25 per hour. However, technician time for new customers only generates an average of $8 per hour because in many cases a new customer contact does not provide billable services. To ensure that new customer contacts are being maintained, the technician time spent on new customer contacts must be at least 60% of the time spent on regular customer contacts. Given these revenue and policy requirements, HTS would like to determine how to allocate technician time between regular customers and new customers so that the total number of customers contacted during the two-week period will be maximized. Technicians require an average of 50 minutes for each regular customer contact and 1 hour for each new customer contact.

a. Develop a linear programming model that will enable HTS to allocate technician time between regular customers and new customers.
b. Find the optimal solution.

54. Jackson Hole Manufacturing is a small manufacturer of plastic products used in the automotive and computer industries. One of its major contracts is with a large computer company and involves the production of plastic printer cases for the computer company's portable printers. The printer cases are produced on two injection molding machines. The M-100 machine has a production capacity of 25 printer cases per hour, and the M-200 machine has a production capacity of 40 cases per hour. Both machines use the same chemical material to produce the printer cases; the M-100 uses 40 pounds of the raw material per hour and the M-200 uses 50 pounds per hour. The computer company asked Jackson Hole to produce as many of the cases during the upcoming week as possible; it will pay $18 for each case Jackson Hole can deliver. However, next week is a regularly scheduled vacation period for most of Jackson Hole's production employees; during this time, annual maintenance is performed for all equipment in the plant. Because of the downtime for maintenance, the M-100 will be available for no more than 15 hours, and the M-200 will be

available for no more than 10 hours. However, because of the high setup cost involved with both machines, management requires that, if production is scheduled on either machine, the machine must be operated for at least 5 hours. The supplier of the chemical material used in the production process informed Jackson Hole that a maximum of 1000 pounds of the chemical material will be available for next week's production; the cost for this raw material is $6 per pound. In addition to the raw material cost, Jackson Hole estimates that the hourly cost of operating the M-100 and the M-200 are $50 and $75, respectively.

a. Formulate a linear programming model that can be used to maximize the contribution to profit.
b. Find the optimal solution.

Case Problem 1 WORKLOAD BALANCING

Digital Imaging (DI) produces photo printers for both the professional and consumer markets. The DI consumer division recently introduced two photo printers that provide color prints rivaling those produced by a professional processing lab. The DI-910 model can produce a 4″ × 6″ borderless print in approximately 37 seconds. The more sophisticated and faster DI-950 can even produce a 13″ × 19″ borderless print. Financial projections show profit contributions of $42 for each DI-910 and $87 for each DI-950.

The printers are assembled, tested, and packaged at DI's plant located in New Bern, North Carolina. This plant is highly automated and uses two manufacturing lines to produce the printers. Line 1 performs the assembly operation with times of 3 minutes per DI-910 printer and 6 minutes per DI-950 printer. Line 2 performs both the testing and packaging operations. Times are 4 minutes per DI-910 printer and 2 minutes per DI-950 printer. The shorter time for the DI-950 printer is a result of its faster print speed. Both manufacturing lines are in operation one 8-hour shift per day.

Managerial Report

Perform an analysis for Digital Imaging in order to determine how many units of each printer to produce. Prepare a report to DI's president presenting your findings and recommendations. Include (but do not limit your discussion to) a consideration of the following:

1. The recommended number of units of each printer to produce to maximize the total contribution to profit for an 8-hour shift. What reasons might management have for not implementing your recommendation?
2. Suppose that management also states that the number of DI-910 printers produced must be at least as great as the number of DI-950 units produced. Assuming that the objective is to maximize the total contribution to profit for an 8-hour shift, how many units of each printer should be produced?
3. Does the solution you developed in part (2) balance the total time spent on line 1 and the total time spent on line 2? Why might this balance or lack of it be a concern to management?
4. Management requested an expansion of the model in part (2) that would provide a better balance between the total time on line 1 and the total time on line 2. Management wants to limit the difference between the total time on line 1 and the total time on line 2 to 30 minutes or less. If the objective is still to maximize the total contribution to profit, how many units of each printer should be produced? What effect does this workload balancing have on total profit in part (2)?
5. Suppose that in part (1) management specified the objective of maximizing the total number of printers produced each shift rather than total profit contribution. With this

objective, how many units of each printer should be produced per shift? What effect does this objective have on total profit and workload balancing?

For each solution that you develop include a copy of your linear programming model and graphical solution in the appendix to your report.

Case Problem 2 PRODUCTION STRATEGY

Better Fitness, Inc. (BFI), manufactures exercise equipment at its plant in Freeport, Long Island. It recently designed two universal weight machines for the home exercise market. Both machines use BFI-patented technology that provides the user with an extremely wide range of motion capability for each type of exercise performed. Until now, such capabilities have been available only on expensive weight machines used primarily by physical therapists.

At a recent trade show, demonstrations of the machines resulted in significant dealer interest. In fact, the number of orders that BFI received at the trade show far exceeded its manufacturing capabilities for the current production period. As a result, management decided to begin production of the two machines. The two machines, which BFI named the BodyPlus 100 and the BodyPlus 200, require different amounts of resources to produce.

The BodyPlus 100 consists of a frame unit, a press station, and a pec-dec station. Each frame produced uses 4 hours of machining and welding time and 2 hours of painting and finishing time. Each press station requires 2 hours of machining and welding time and 1 hour of painting and finishing time, and each pec-dec station uses 2 hours of machining and welding time and 2 hours of painting and finishing time. In addition, 2 hours are spent assembling, testing, and packaging each BodyPlus 100. The raw material costs are \$450 for each frame, \$300 for each press station, and \$250 for each pec-dec station; packaging costs are estimated to be \$50 per unit.

The BodyPlus 200 consists of a frame unit, a press station, a pec-dec station, and a leg-press station. Each frame produced uses 5 hours of machining and welding time and 4 hours of painting and finishing time. Each press station requires 3 hours machining and welding time and 2 hours of painting and finishing time, each pec-dec station uses 2 hours of machining and welding time and 2 hours of painting and finishing time, and each leg-press station requires 2 hours of machining and welding time and 2 hours of painting and finishing time. In addition, 2 hours are spent assembling, testing, and packaging each BodyPlus 200. The raw material costs are \$650 for each frame, \$400 for each press station, \$250 for each pec-dec station, and \$200 for each leg-press station; packaging costs are estimated to be \$75 per unit.

For the next production period, management estimates that 600 hours of machining and welding time, 450 hours of painting and finishing time, and 140 hours of assembly, testing, and packaging time will be available. Current labor costs are \$20 per hour for machining and welding time, \$15 per hour for painting and finishing time, and \$12 per hour for assembly, testing, and packaging time. The market in which the two machines must compete suggests a retail price of \$2400 for the BodyPlus 100 and \$3500 for the BodyPlus 200, although some flexibility may be available to BFI because of the unique capabilities of the new machines. Authorized BFI dealers can purchase machines for 70 percent of the suggested retail price.

BFI's president believes that the unique capabilities of the BodyPlus 200 can help position BFI as one of the leaders in high-end exercise equipment. Consequently, he has stated that the number of units of the BodyPlus 200 produced must be at least 25 percent of the total production.

Managerial Report

Analyze the production problem at Better Fitness, Inc., and prepare a report for BFI's president presenting your findings and recommendations. Include (but do not limit your discussion to) a consideration of the following items:

1. What is the recommended number of BodyPlus 100 and BodyPlus 200 machines to produce?
2. How does the requirement that the number of units of the BodyPlus 200 produced be at least 25 percent of the total production affect profits?
3. Where should efforts be expended in order to increase profits?

Include a copy of your linear programming model and graphical solution in an appendix to your report.

Case Problem 3 HART VENTURE CAPITAL

Hart Venture Capital (HVC) specializes in providing venture capital for software development and Internet applications. Currently HVC has two investment opportunities: (1) Security Systems, a firm that needs additional capital to develop an Internet security software package; (2) Market Analysis, a market research company that needs additional capital to develop a software package for conducting customer satisfaction surveys. In exchange for Security Systems stock, the firm has asked HVC to provide \$600,000 in year 1, \$600,000 in year 2, and \$250,000 in year 3 over the coming three-year period. In exchange for their stock, Market Analysis has asked HVC to provide \$500,000 in year 1, \$350,000 in year 2, and \$400,000 in year 3 over the same three-year period. HVC believes that both investment opportunities are worth pursuing. However, because of other investments, they are willing to commit at most \$800,000 for both projects in the first year, at most \$700,000 in the second year, and \$500,000 in the third year.

HVC's financial analysis team reviewed both projects and recommended that the company's objective should be to maximize the net present value of the total investment in Security Systems and Market Analysis. The net present value takes into account the estimated value of the stock at the end of the three-year period as well as the capital outflows that are necessary during each of the three years. Using an 8% rate of return, HVC's financial analysis team estimates that 100 percent funding of the Security Systems project has a net present value of \$1,800,000 and 100 percent funding of the Market Analysis project has a net present value of \$1,600,000.

HVC has the option to fund any percentage of the Security Systems and Market Analysis projects. For example, if HVC decides to fund 40% of the Security Systems project, investments of 0.40(\$600,000) = \$240,000 would be required in year 1, 0.40(\$600,000) = \$240,000 would be required in year 2, and 0.40(\$250,000) = \$100,000 would be required in year 3. In this case, the net present value of the Security Systems project would be 0.40(\$1,800,000) = \$720,000. The investment amounts and the net present value for partial funding of the Market Analysis project would be computed in the same manner.

Managerial Report

Perform an analysis of HVC's investment problem and prepare a report that presents your findings and recommendations. Include (but do not limit your discussion to) a consideration of the following items:

1. What is the recommended percentage of each project that HVC should fund and the net present value of the total investment?

2. What capital allocation plan for Security Systems and Market Analysis for the coming three-year period and the total HVC investment each year would you recommend?
3. What effect, if any, would HVC's willingness to commit an additional \$100,000 during the first year have on the recommended percentage of each project that HVC should fund?
4. What would the capital allocation plan look like if an additional \$100,000 is made available?
5. What is your recommendation as to whether HVC should commit the additional \$100,000 in the first year?

Provide model details and relevant computer output in a report appendix.

Appendix 2.1 SOLVING LINEAR PROGRAMS WITH THE MANAGEMENT SCIENTIST

In this appendix we describe how The Management Scientist software package can be used to solve the Par, Inc., linear programming problem. After starting The Management Scientist, execute the following steps.

Step 1. Select the **Linear Programming** module
Step 2. Select the **File** menu
Choose **New**
Step 3. When the **Problem Features** dialog box appears:
Enter 2 in the **Number of Decision Variables** box
Enter 4 in the **Number of Constraints** box
Select Maximize in the **Optimization Type** box
Click **OK**
Step 4. When the data input worksheet appears (see Figure 2.24):
Change **Variable Names** from X1 and X2 to S and D, respectively.
Enter the **Objective Function Coefficients**
For each constraint:
Enter the **Coefficients**
Enter the **Relation** (<, =, >)
Enter the **Right-Hand-Side** value
Step 5. Select the **Solution** menu
Choose **Solve**

The Management Scientist interprets the < symbol as ≤ and the > symbol as ≥.

FIGURE 2.24 DATA INPUT WORKSHEET FOR THE PAR, INC., PROBLEM

Optimization Type: Max

	Objective Function	
Variable Names:	S	D
Coefficients:	10	9

	Constraints			
Subject To	S	D	Relation(<,=,>)	Right-Hand-Side
Constraint 1	0.7	1	<	630
Constraint 2	0.5	0.83333	<	600
Constraint 3	1	0.66667	<	708
Constraint 4	0.1	0.25	<	135

The user entries in the data input worksheet are shown in Figure 2.24. The output from The Management Scientist is shown in Figure 2.14. When entering the problem data, zero coefficients do not have to be entered. The original problem can be edited or changed by selecting the **Edit** menu. Finally, printed output can be obtained by selecting the **Solution** menu and then selecting the **Print** option.

Appendix 2.2 SOLVING LINEAR PROGRAMS WITH LINGO

LINGO was developed by Linus E. Schrage at the University of Chicago.

In this appendix we describe how to use LINGO to solve the Par, Inc., problem. When you start LINGO, two windows are immediately displayed. The outer or main frame window contains all the command menus and the command toolbar. The smaller window is the model window; this window is used to enter and edit the linear programming model you want to solve. The first item we enter into the model window is the objective function. Recall that the objective function for the Par, Inc., problem is Max $10S + 9D$. Thus, in the first line of the LINGO model window, we enter the following expression:

$$\text{MAX} = 10{*}S + 9{*}D;$$

Note that in LINGO the symbol * is used to denote multiplication and that the objective function line ends with a semicolon. In general, each mathematical expression (objective function and constraints) in LINGO is terminated with a semicolon.

Next, we press the enter key to move to a new line. The first constraint in the Par, Inc., problem is $0.7S + 1D \leq 630$. Thus, in the second line of the LINGO model window we enter the following expression:

$$0.7{*}S + 1{*}D <= 630;$$

Note that LINGO interprets the <= symbol as ≤. Alternatively, we could enter < instead of <=. As was the case when entering the objective function, a semicolon is required at the end of the first constraint. Pressing the enter key moves us to a new line as we continue the process by entering the remaining constraints as shown here:

$$\begin{aligned} 0.5{*}S + 0.83333{*}D &<= 600; \\ 1{*}S + 0.66667{*}D &<= 708; \\ 0.1{*}S + 0.25{*}D &<= 135; \end{aligned}$$

The model window will now appear as follows:

$$\begin{aligned} \text{MAX} &= 10{*}S + 9{*}D; \\ 0.7{*}S + 1{*}D &<= 630; \\ 0.5{*}S + 0.83333{*}D &<= 600; \\ 1{*}S + 0.66667{*}D &<= 708; \\ 0.1{*}S + 0.25{*}D &<= 135; \end{aligned}$$

If you make an error in entering the model, you can correct it at any time by simply positioning the cursor where you made the error and entering the necessary correction.

To solve the model, select the Solve command from the LINGO menu or press the Solve button on the toolbar at the top of the main frame window. LINGO will begin the solution process by determining whether the model conforms to all syntax requirements. If the LINGO model doesn't pass these tests, you will be informed by an error message. If LINGO

FIGURE 2.25 PAR, INC., SOLUTION REPORT USING LINGO

```
Global optimal solution found.
Objective value:                                7667.994
Total solver iterations:                               2

      Variable              Value          Reduced Cost
--------------     --------------     -----------------
             S           539.9984              0.000000
             D           252.0011              0.000000

           Row   Slack or Surplus            Dual Price
--------------   ----------------     -----------------
             1           7667.994              1.000000
             2           0.000000              4.374957
             3           120.0007              0.000000
             4           0.000000              6.937530
             5           17.99988              0.000000
```

does not find any errors in the model input, it will begin to solve the model. As part of the solution process, LINGO displays a Solver Status window that allows you to monitor the progress of the solver. LINGO displays the solution in a new window titled "Solution Report." The output that appears in the Solution Report window for the Par, Inc., problem is shown in Figure 2.25.

The first part of the output shown in Figure 2.25 indicates that an optimal solution has been found and that the value of the objective function is, after rounding, 7668. We see that the optimal solution is $S = 540$ and $D = 252$, and that the slack variables for the four constraints (rows 2–5) are 0, 120, 0, and 18. We will discuss the use of the information in the Reduced Cost column and the Dual Price column in Chapter 3 when we study the topic of sensitivity analysis.

Appendix 2.3 SOLVING LINEAR PROGRAMS WITH EXCEL

In this appendix, we will use an Excel worksheet to solve the Par, Inc., linear programming problem. We will enter the problem data for the Par problem in the top part of the worksheet and develop the linear programming model in the bottom part of the worksheet.

Formulation

Whenever we formulate a worksheet model of a linear program, we perform the following steps:

Step 1. Enter the problem data in the top part of the worksheet.
Step 2. Specify cell locations for the decision variables.
Step 3. Select a cell and enter a formula for computing the value of the objective function.
Step 4. Select a cell and enter a formula for computing the left-hand side of each constraint.

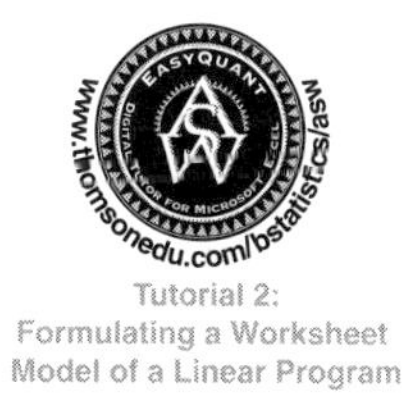

Tutorial 2: Formulating a Worksheet Model of a Linear Program

FIGURE 2.26 FORMULA WORKSHEET FOR THE PAR, INC., PROBLEM

	A	B	C	D
1	**Par, Inc.**			
2				
3		**Production Time**		
4	**Operation**	**Standard**	**Deluxe**	**Time Available**
5	Cutting and Dyeing	0.7	1	630
6	Sewing	0.5	0.83333	600
7	Finishing	1	0.66667	708
8	Inspection and Packaging	0.1	0.25	135
9	**Profit Per Bag**	10	9	
10				
11				
12	**Model**			
13				
14		**Decision Variables**		
15		**Standard**	**Deluxe**	
16	**Bags Produced**			
17				
18	**Maximize Total Profit**	=B9*B16+C9*C16		
19				
20	**Constraints**	**Hours Used (LHS)**		**Hours Available (RHS)**
21	Cutting and Dyeing	=B5*B16+C5*C16	<=	=D5
22	Sewing	=B6*B16+C6*C16	<=	=D6
23	Finishing	=B7*B16+C7*C16	<=	=D7
24	Inspection and Packaging	=B8*B16+C8*C16	<=	=D8

Step 5. Select a cell and enter a formula for computing the right-hand side of each constraint.

The formula worksheet that we developed for the Par, Inc., problem using these five steps is shown in Figure 2.26. Note that the worksheet consists of two sections: a data section and a model section. The four components of the model are screened, and the cells reserved for the decision variables are enclosed in a boldface box. Figure 2.26 is called a formula worksheet because it displays the formulas that we have entered and not the values computed from those formulas. In a moment we will see how Excel's Solver is used to find the optimal solution to the Par, Inc., problem. But first, let's review each of the preceding steps as they apply to the Par, Inc., problem.

Step 1. Enter the problem data in the top part of the worksheet.
Cells B5:C8 show the production requirements per unit for each product.
Cells B9:C9 show the profit contribution per unit for the two products.
Cells D5:D8 show the number of hours available in each department.

Step 2. Specify cell locations for the decision variables.
Cell B16 will contain the number of standard bags produced, and cell C16 will contain the number of deluxe bags produced.

Step 3. Select a cell and enter a formula for computing the value of the objective function.
Cell B18: =B9*B16+C9*C16

Step 4. Select a cell and enter a formula for computing the left-hand side of each constraint.
With four constraints, we have
Cell B21: =B5*B16+C5*C16
Cell B22: =B6*B16+C6*C16
Cell B23: =B7*B16+C7*C16
Cell B24: =B8*B16+C8*C16

Step 5. Select a cell and enter a formula for computing the right-hand side of each constraint.
With four constraints, we have
Cell D21: =D5
Cell D22: =D6
Cell D23: =D7
Cell D24: =D8

Note that descriptive labels make the model section of the worksheet easier to read and understand. For example, we added "Standard," "Deluxe," and "Bags Produced" in rows 15 and 16 so that the values of the decision variables appearing in cells B16 and C16 can be easily interpreted. In addition, we entered "Maximize Total Profit" in cell A18 to indicate that the value of the objective function appearing in cell B18 is the maximum profit contribution. In the constraint section of the worksheet we added the constraint names as well as the "<=" symbols to show the relationship that exists between the left-hand side and the right-hand side of each constraint. Although these descriptive labels are not necessary to use Excel Solver to find a solution to the Par, Inc., problem, the labels make it easier for the user to understand and interpret the optimal solution.

Excel Solution

Tutorial 3: Solving a Linear Program Using Excel Solver

The standard Excel Solver developed by Frontline Systems can be used to solve all of the linear programming problems presented in this text. However, the CD that accompanies this text includes a more powerful version referred to as Premium Solver for Education. When first started, Premium Solver for Education looks similar to the standard Excel Solver. But, the Premium Solver Parameters dialog box provides a variety of new features, including an online user's guide. We recommend that you use Premium Solver when developing and solving spreadsheet models of linear programs.

The following steps describe how Frontline Systems' Premium Solver for Education can be used to obtain the optimal solution to the Par, Inc., problem.

Excel 2007 Users: Replace Step 1 with Select the ***Ad-Ins*** *tab.*

Step 1. Select the **Tools** menu

Step 2. Select the **Premium Solver** option

Step 3. When the **Solver Parameters** dialog box appears (see Figure 2.27):
Make sure **Standard LP Simplex** is displayed
Enter B18 into the **Set Cell** box
Select the **Equal To: Max** option
Enter B16:C16 into the **By Changing Variable Cells** box
Select **Add**

FIGURE 2.27 SOLVER PARAMETERS DIALOG BOX FOR THE PAR, INC., PROBLEM

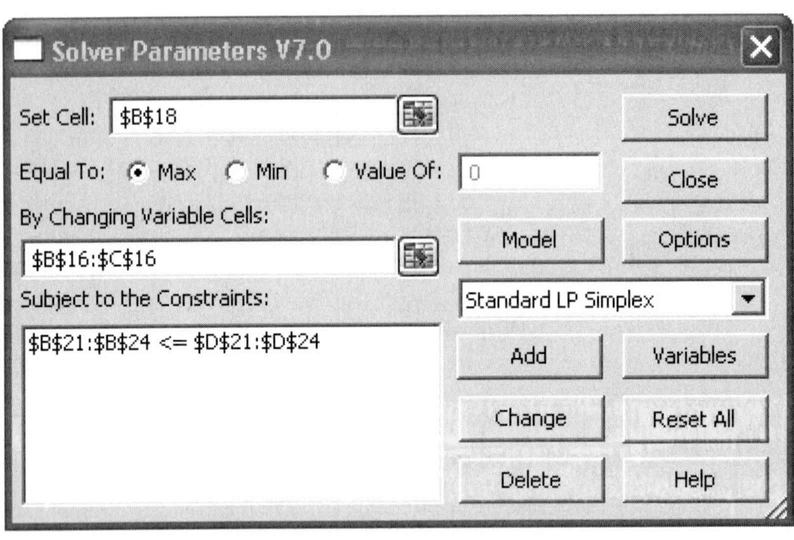

Step 4. When the **Add Constraint** dialog box appears:
Enter B21:B24 in the left-hand box of the **Cell Reference** area
Select <=
Enter D21:D24 in the right-hand box
Click **OK**

Step 5. When the **Solver Parameters** dialog box reappears:
Choose **Options**

Step 6. When the LP Simplex **Solver Options** dialog box appears:
Select **Assume Non-Negative**
Click **OK**

Step 7. When the **Solver Parameters** dialog box appears:
Choose **Solve**

Step 8. When the **Solver Results** dialog box appears:
Select **Keep Solver Solution**
Click **OK**

Figure 2.27 shows the completed **Solver Parameters** dialog box, and Figure 2.28 shows the optimal solution in the worksheet. Note that after rounding, the optimal solution of 540 standard bags and 252 deluxe bags is the same as we obtained using the graphical solution procedure. In addition to the output information shown in Figure 2.28, Solver has an option to provide sensitivity analysis information. We discuss sensitivity analysis in Chapter 3.

In Step 6 we selected the **Assume Non-Negative** option in the **Solver Options** dialog box to avoid having to enter nonnegativity constraints for the decision variables. In general, whenever we want to solve a linear programming model in which the decision variables are all restricted to be nonnegative, we will select this option. In addition, in Step 4 we entered all four less-than-or-equal-to constraints simultaneously by entering B21:B24 in the left-hand box of the **Cell Reference** area, selecting <=, and entering D21:D24 in the right-hand box. Alternatively, we could have entered the four constraints one at a time.

FIGURE 2.28 EXCEL SOLUTION FOR THE PAR, INC., PROBLEM

	A	B	C	D
1	**Par, Inc.**			
2				
3		**Production Time**		
4	**Operation**	**Standard**	**Deluxe**	**Time Available**
5	Cutting and Dyeing	0.7	1	630
6	Sewing	0.5	0.83333	600
7	Finishing	1	0.66667	708
8	Inspection and Packaging	0.1	0.25	135
9	**Profit Per Bag**	10	9	
10				
11				
12	**Model**			
13				
14		**Decision Variables**		
15		**Standard**	**Deluxe**	
16	**Bags Produced**	539.99842	252.00110	
17				
18	**Maximize Total Profit**	7668		
19				
20	**Constraints**	**Hours Used (LHS)**		**Hours Available (RHS)**
21	Cutting and Dyeing	630	<=	630
22	Sewing	479.99929	<=	600
23	Finishing	708	<=	708
24	Inspection and Packaging	117.00012	<=	135

CHAPTER 3

Linear Programming: Sensitivity Analysis and Interpretation of Solution

CONTENTS

Sensitivity analysis is the study of how the changes in the coefficients of a linear program affect the optimal solution. Using sensitivity analysis, we can answer questions such as the following:

1. How will a change *in a coefficient of the objective function* affect the optimal solution?
2. How will a change in the *right-hand-side value for a constraint* affect the optimal solution?

Because sensitivity analysis is concerned with how these changes affect the optimal solution, the analysis does not begin until the optimal solution to the original linear programming problem has been obtained. For that reason, sensitivity analysis is often referred to as *postoptimality analysis.*

Our approach to sensitivity analysis parallels the approach used to introduce linear programming in Chapter 2. We begin by showing how a graphical method can be used to perform sensitivity analysis for linear programming problems with two decision variables. Then, we show how The Management Scientist provides sensitivity analysis information.

Finally, we extend the discussion of problem formulation started in Chapter 2 by formulating and solving three larger linear programming problems. In discussing the solution for each of these problems, we focus on managerial interpretation of the optimal solution and sensitivity analysis information.

Sensitivity analysis and the interpretation of the optimal solution are important aspects of applying linear programming. The Management Science in Action, Assigning Products to Worldwide Facilities at Eastman Kodak, shows some of the sensitivity analysis and interpretation issues encountered at Kodak in determining the optimal product assignments. Later in the chapter other Management Science in Action articles illustrate how Performance Analysis Corporation uses sensitivity analysis as part of an evaluation model for a chain of fast-food outlets, how GE Plastics uses a linear programming model involving thousands of variables and constraints to determine optimal production quantities, how the Nutrition Coordinating Center of the University of Minnesota uses a linear programming model to estimate the nutrient amounts in new food products, and how Duncan Industries Limited's linear programming model for tea distribution convinced management of the benefits of using quantitative analysis techniques to support the decision-making process.

MANAGEMENT SCIENCE IN ACTION

ASSIGNING PRODUCTS TO WORLDWIDE FACILITIES AT EASTMAN KODAK*

One of the major planning issues at Eastman Kodak involves the determination of what products should be manufactured at Kodak's facilities located throughout the world. The assignment of products to facilities is called the "world load." In determining the world load, Kodak faces a number of interesting trade-offs. For instance, not all manufacturing facilities are equally efficient for all products, and the margins by which some facilities are better varies from product to product. In addition to manufacturing costs, the transportation costs and the effects of duty and duty drawbacks can significantly affect the allocation decision.

To assist in determining the world load, Kodak developed a linear programming model that accounts for the physical nature of the distribution problem and the various costs (manufacturing, transportation, and duties) involved. The model's objective is to minimize the total cost subject to constraints such as satisfying demand and capacity constraints for each facility.

The linear programming model is a static representation of the problem situation, and the real world is always changing. Thus, the linear programming model must be used in a dynamic way. For instance, when demand expectations change, the model can be used to determine the effect the change will have on the world load. Suppose that the currency of country A rises compared to the currency of country B. How should the world load

(*continued*)

be modified? In addition to using the linear programming model in a "how-to-react" mode, the model is useful in a more active mode by considering questions such as the following: Is it worthwhile for facility F to spend d dollars to lower the unit manufacturing cost of product P from x to y? The linear programming model helps Kodak evaluate the overall effect of possible changes at any facility.

In the final analysis, managers recognize that they cannot use the model by simply turning it on, reading the results, and executing the solution. The model's recommendation combined with managerial judgment provide the final decision.

*Based on information provided by Greg Sampson of Eastman Kodak.

3.1 INTRODUCTION TO SENSITIVITY ANALYSIS

Sensitivity analysis is important to decision makers because real-world problems exist in a changing environment. Prices of raw materials change, product demand changes, companies purchase new machinery, stock prices fluctuate, employee turnover occurs, and so on. If a linear programming model has been used in such an environment, we can expect some of the coefficients to change over time. We will then want to determine how these changes affect the optimal solution to the original linear programming problem. Sensitivity analysis provides us with the information needed to respond to such changes without requiring the complete solution of a revised linear program.

Recall the Par, Inc., problem:

$$\begin{aligned}
\text{Max} \quad & 10S + 9D \\
\text{s.t.} \quad & \\
& \tfrac{7}{10}S + 1D \leq 630 \quad \text{Cutting and dyeing} \\
& \tfrac{1}{2}S + \tfrac{5}{6}D \leq 600 \quad \text{Sewing} \\
& 1S + \tfrac{2}{3}D \leq 708 \quad \text{Finishing} \\
& \tfrac{1}{10}S + \tfrac{1}{4}D \leq 135 \quad \text{Inspection and packaging} \\
& S, D \geq 0
\end{aligned}$$

The optimal solution, $S = 540$ standard bags and $D = 252$ deluxe bags, was based on profit contribution figures of \$10 per standard bag and \$9 per deluxe bag. Suppose we later learn that a price reduction causes the profit contribution for the standard bag to fall from \$10 to \$8.50. Sensitivity analysis can be used to determine whether the production schedule calling for 540 standard bags and 252 deluxe bags is still best. If it is, solving a modified linear programming problem with $8.50S + 9D$ as the new objective function will not be necessary.

Sensitivity analysis can also be used to determine which coefficients in a linear programming model are crucial. For example, suppose that management believes the \$9 profit contribution for the deluxe bag is only a rough estimate of the profit contribution that will actually be obtained. If sensitivity analysis shows that 540 standard bags and 252 deluxe bags will be the optimal solution as long as the profit contribution for the deluxe bag is between \$6.67 and \$14.29, management should feel comfortable with the \$9 per bag estimate and the recommended production quantities. However, if sensitivity analysis shows that 540 standard bags and 252 deluxe bags will be the optimal solution only if the profit contribution for the deluxe bags is between \$8.90 and \$9.25, management may want to review the accuracy of the \$9 per bag estimate. Management would especially want to consider how the optimal production quantities should be revised if the profit contribution per deluxe bag were to drop.

Another aspect of sensitivity analysis concerns changes in the right-hand-side values of the constraints. Recall that in the Par, Inc., problem the optimal solution used all available time in the cutting and dyeing department and the finishing department. What would happen to the optimal solution and total profit contribution if Par could obtain additional quantities of either of these resources? Sensitivity analysis can help determine how much each additional hour of production time is worth and how many hours can be added before diminishing returns set in.

3.2 GRAPHICAL SENSITIVITY ANALYSIS

For linear programming problems with two decision variables, graphical solution methods can be used to perform sensitivity analysis on the objective function coefficients and the right-hand-side values for the constraints.

Objective Function Coefficients

Let us consider how changes in the objective function coefficients might affect the optimal solution to the Par, Inc., problem. The current contribution to profit is $10 per unit for the standard bag and $9 per unit for the deluxe bag. It seems obvious that an increase in the profit contribution for one of the bags might lead management to increase production of that bag, and a decrease in the profit contribution for one of the bags might lead management to decrease production of that bag. It is not as obvious, however, how much the profit contribution would have to change before management would want to change the production quantities.

The current optimal solution to this problem calls for producing 540 standard golf bags and 252 deluxe golf bags. The **range of optimality** for each objective function coefficient provides the range of values over which the current solution will remain optimal. Managerial attention needs to be focused on those objective function coefficients that have a narrow range of optimality and coefficients near the end points of the range. With these coefficients, a small change can necessitate modifying the optimal solution. Let us now compute the ranges of optimality for this problem.

Figure 3.1 shows the graphical solution. A careful inspection of this graph shows that as long as the slope of the objective function line is between the slope of line A (which coincides with the cutting and dyeing constraint line) and the slope of line B (which coincides with the finishing constraint line), extreme point ③ with $S = 540$ and $D = 252$ will be optimal. Changing an objective function coefficient for S or D will cause the slope of the objective function line to change. In Figure 3.1 we see that such changes cause the objective function line to rotate around extreme point ③. However, as long as the objective function line stays within the shaded region, extreme point ③ will remain optimal.

Rotating the objective function line *counterclockwise* causes the slope to become less negative, and the slope increases. When the objective function line rotates counterclockwise (slope increased) enough to coincide with line A, we obtain alternative optimal solutions between extreme points ③ and ④. Any further counterclockwise rotation of the objective function line will cause extreme point ③ to be nonoptimal. Hence, the slope of line A provides an upper limit for the slope of the objective function line.

The slope of the objective function line usually is negative; hence, rotating the objective function line clockwise makes the line steeper even though the slope is getting smaller (more negative).

Rotating the objective function line *clockwise* causes the slope to become more negative, and the slope decreases. When the objective function line rotates clockwise (slope decreases) enough to coincide with line B, we obtain alternative optimal solutions between extreme points ③ and ②. Any further clockwise rotation of the objective function line will cause extreme point ③ to be nonoptimal. Hence, the slope of line B provides a lower limit for the slope of the objective function line.

FIGURE 3.1 GRAPHICAL SOLUTION OF PAR, INC., PROBLEM WITH SLOPE OF OBJECTIVE FUNCTION LINE BETWEEN SLOPES OF LINES A AND B; EXTREME POINT ③ IS OPTIMAL

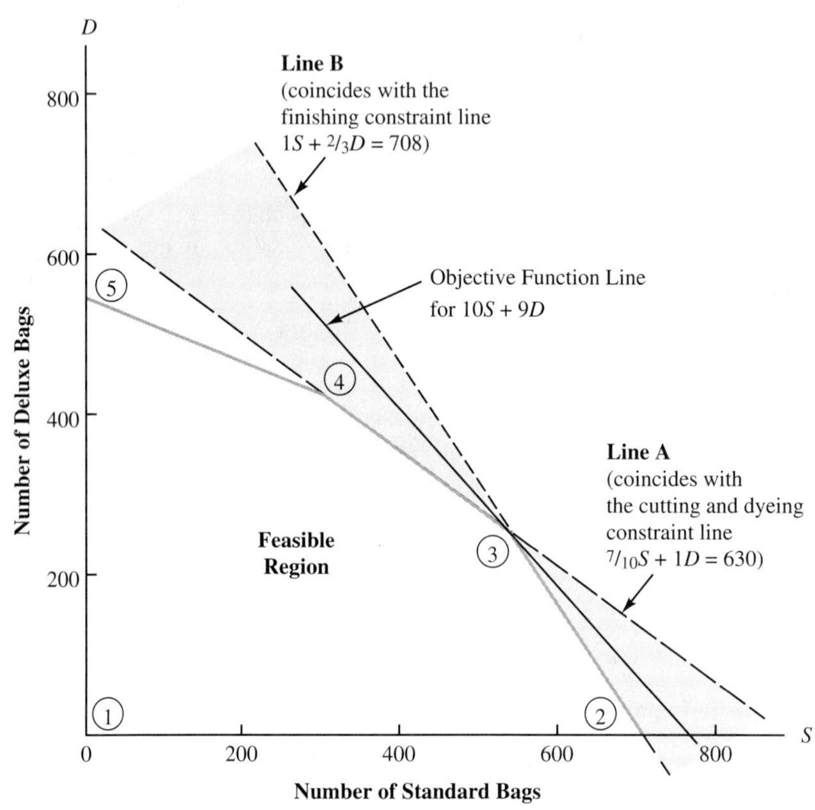

Thus, extreme point ③ will be the optimal solution as long as

$$\text{Slope of line B} \leq \text{slope of the objective function line} \leq \text{slope of line A}$$

In Figure 3.1 we see that the equation for line A, the cutting and dyeing constraint line, is as follows:

$$\tfrac{7}{10}S + 1D = 630$$

By solving this equation for D, we can write the equation for line A in its slope-intercept form, which yields

$$D = -\tfrac{7}{10}S + 630$$

↑ Slope of line A ↑ Intercept of line A on D axis

Thus, the slope for line A is $-\tfrac{7}{10}$, and its intercept on the D axis is 630.

The equation for line B in Figure 3.1 is

$$1S + \tfrac{2}{3}D = 708$$

Solving for D provides the slope-intercept form for line B. Doing so yields

$$\tfrac{2}{3}D = -1S + 708$$
$$D = -\tfrac{3}{2}S + 1062$$

Thus, the slope of line B is $-\tfrac{3}{2}$, and its intercept on the D axis is 1062.

Now that the slopes of lines A and B have been computed, we see that for extreme point ③ to remain optimal we must have

$$-\tfrac{3}{2} \leq \text{slope of objective function} \leq -\tfrac{7}{10} \tag{3.1}$$

Let us now consider the general form of the slope of the objective function line. Let C_S denote the profit of a standard bag, C_D denote the profit of a deluxe bag, and P denote the value of the objective function. Using this notation, the objective function line can be written as

$$P = C_S S + C_D D$$

Writing this equation in slope-intercept form, we obtain

$$C_D D = -C_S S + P$$

and

$$D = \frac{C_S}{C_D} S + \frac{P}{C_D}$$

Thus, we see that the slope of the objective function line is given by $-C_S/C_D$. Substituting $-C_S/C_D$ into expression (3.1), we see that extreme point ③ will be optimal as long as the following expression is satisfied:

$$-\tfrac{3}{2} \leq -\frac{C_S}{C_D} \leq -\tfrac{7}{10} \tag{3.2}$$

To compute the range of optimality for the standard-bag profit contribution, we hold the profit contribution for the deluxe bag fixed at its initial value $C_D = 9$. Doing so in expression (3.2), we obtain

$$-\tfrac{3}{2} \leq -\frac{C_S}{9} \leq -\tfrac{7}{10}$$

From the left-hand inequality, we have

$$-3/2 \le -\frac{C_S}{9} \quad \text{or} \quad 3/2 \ge \frac{C_S}{9}$$

Thus,

$$27/2 \ge C_S \quad \text{or} \quad C_S \le 27/2 = 13.5$$

From the right-hand inequality, we have

$$-\frac{C_S}{9} \le -7/10 \quad \text{or} \quad \frac{C_S}{9} \ge 7/10$$

Thus,

$$C_S \ge 63/10 \quad \text{or} \quad C_S \ge 6.3$$

Combining the calculated limits for C_S provides the following range of optimality for the standard-bag profit contribution:

$$6.3 \le C_S \le 13.5$$

In the original problem for Par, Inc., the standard bag had a profit contribution of \$10. The resulting optimal solution was 540 standard bags and 252 deluxe bags. The range of optimality for C_S tells Par's management that, with other coefficients unchanged, the profit contribution for the standard bag can be anywhere between \$6.30 and \$13.50 and the production quantities of 540 standard bags and 252 deluxe bags will remain optimal. Note, however, that even though the production quantities will not change, the total profit contribution (value of objective function) will change due to the change in profit contribution per standard bag.

These computations can be repeated, holding the profit contribution for standard bags constant at $C_S = 10$. In this case, the range of optimality for the deluxe-bag profit contribution can be determined. Check to see that this range is $6.67 \le C_D \le 14.29$.

In cases where the rotation of the objective function line about an optimal extreme point causes the objective function line to become *vertical,* there will be either no upper limit or no lower limit for the slope as it appears in the form of expression (3.2). To show how this special situation can occur, suppose that the objective function for the Par, Inc., problem is $18C_S + 9C_D$; in this case, extreme point (2) in Figure 3.2 provides the optimal solution. Rotating the objective function line counterclockwise around extreme point (2) provides an upper limit for the slope when the objective function line coincides with line B. We showed previously that the slope of line B is $-3/2$, so the upper limit for the slope of the objective function line must be $-3/2$. However, rotating the objective function line clockwise results in the slope becoming more and more negative, approaching a value of minus infinity as the objective function line becomes vertical; in this case, the slope of the objective function has no lower limit. Using the upper limit of $-3/2$, we can write

$$-\frac{C_S}{C_D} \le -3/2$$

Slope of the objective function line ↗

FIGURE 3.2 GRAPHICAL SOLUTION OF PAR, INC., PROBLEM WITH AN OBJECTIVE FUNCTION OF $18S + 9D$; OPTIMAL SOLUTION AT EXTREME POINT (2)

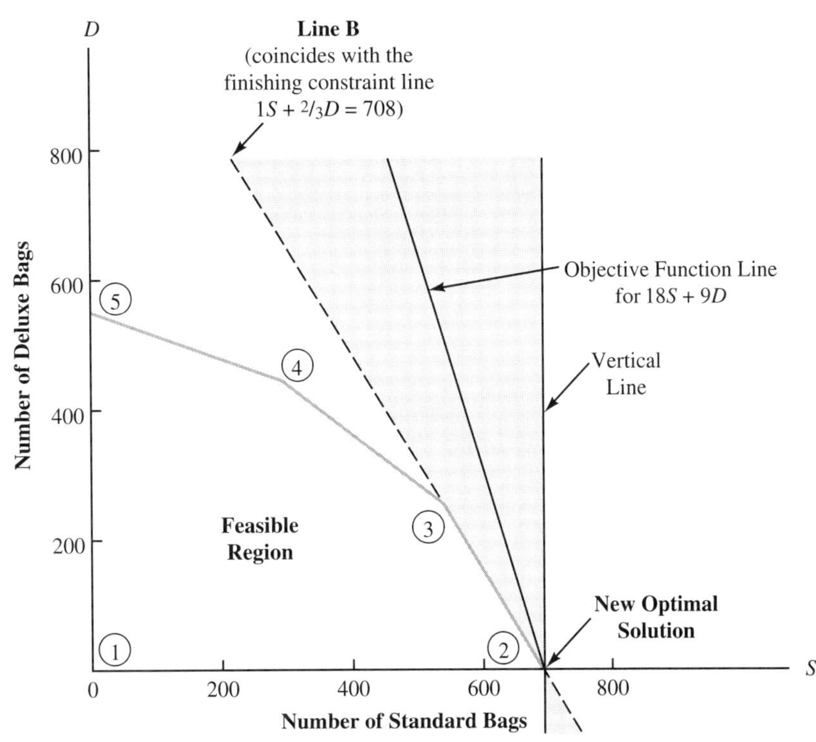

Following the previous procedure of holding C_D constant at its original value, $C_D = 9$, we have

$$-\frac{C_S}{9} \leq -\tfrac{3}{2} \qquad \text{or} \qquad \frac{C_S}{9} \geq \tfrac{3}{2}$$

Solving for C_S provides the following result:

$$C_S \geq \tfrac{27}{2} = 13.5$$

In reviewing Figure 3.2 we note that extreme point (2) remains optimal for all values of C_S above 13.5. Thus, we obtain the following range of optimality for C_S at extreme point (2):

$$13.5 \leq C_S < \infty$$

Simultaneous Changes The range of optimality for objective function coefficients is only applicable for changes made to one coefficient at a time. All other coefficients are assumed to be fixed at their initial values. If two or more objective function coefficients are changed simultaneously, further analysis is necessary to determine whether the optimal solution will change. However, when solving two-variable problems graphically, expression (3.2) suggests an easy way to determine whether simultaneous changes in both objective function coefficients will cause a change in the optimal solution. Simply compute the slope of the objective function ($-C_S/C_D$) for the new coefficient values. If this ratio is greater than or equal to the lower limit on the slope of the objective function and less than or equal to the upper limit, then the changes made will not cause a change in the optimal solution.

Consider changes in both of the objective function coefficients for the Par, Inc., problem. Suppose the profit contribution per standard bag is increased to \$13 and the profit contribution per deluxe bag is simultaneously reduced to \$8. Recall that the ranges of optimality for C_S and C_D (both computed in a one-at-a-time manner) are

$$6.3 \leq C_S \leq 13.5 \tag{3.3}$$

$$6.67 \leq C_D \leq 14.29 \tag{3.4}$$

For these ranges of optimality, we can conclude that changing either C_S to \$13 or C_D to \$8 (but not both) would not cause a change in the optimal solution of $S = 540$ and $D = 252$. But we cannot conclude from the ranges of optimality that changing both coefficients simultaneously would not result in a change in the optimal solution.

In expression (3.2) we showed that extreme point (3) remains optimal as long as

$$-3/2 \leq -\frac{C_S}{C_D} \leq -7/10$$

If C_S is changed to 13 and simultaneously C_D is changed to 8, the new objective function slope will be given by

$$-\frac{C_S}{C_D} = -\frac{13}{8} = -1.625$$

Because this value is less than the lower limit of $-3/2$, the current solution of $S = 540$ and $D = 252$ will no longer be optimal. By resolving the problem with $C_S = 13$ and $C_D = 8$ we will find that extreme point (2) is the new optimal solution.

Looking at the ranges of optimality, we concluded that changing either C_S to \$13 or C_D to \$8 (but not both) would not cause a change in the optimal solution. But in recomputing the slope of the objective function with simultaneous changes for both C_S and C_D, we saw that the optimal solution did change. This result emphasizes the fact that a range of optimality, by itself, can only be used to draw a conclusion about changes made to *one objective function coefficient at a time.*

Right-Hand Sides

Let us now consider how a change in the right-hand side for a constraint may affect the feasible region and perhaps cause a change in the optimal solution to the problem. To illustrate this aspect of sensitivity analysis, let us consider what happens if an additional 10 hours of production time become available in the cutting and dyeing department of Par, Inc. The right-hand side of the cutting and dyeing constraint is changed from 630 to 640, and the constraint is rewritten as

$$7/10S + 1D \leq 640$$

FIGURE 3.3 EFFECT OF A 10-UNIT CHANGE IN THE RIGHT-HAND SIDE OF THE CUTTING AND DYEING CONSTRAINT

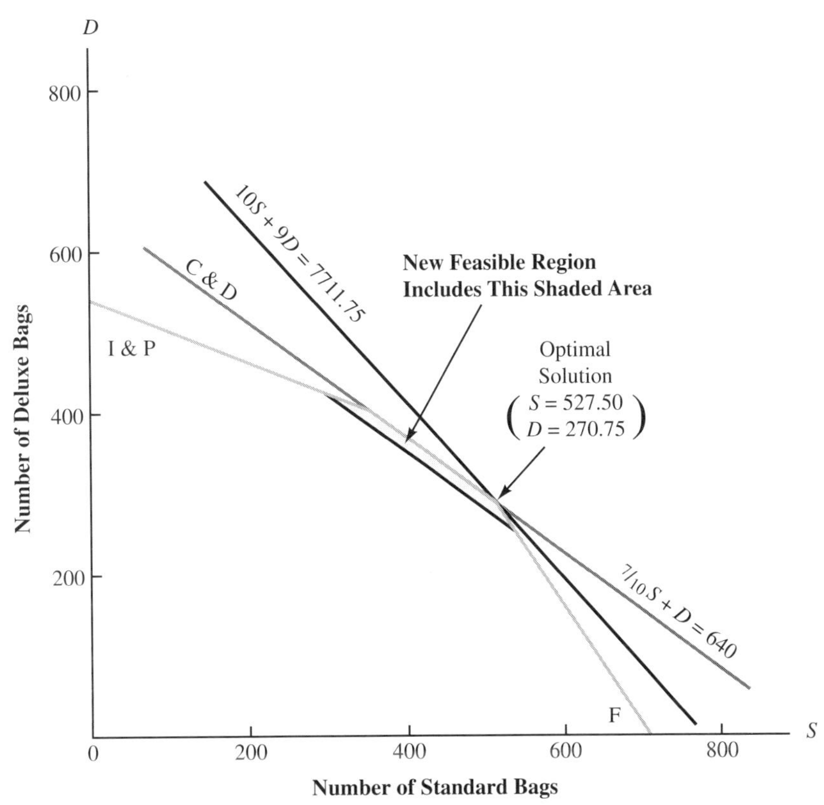

By obtaining an additional 10 hours of cutting and dyeing time, we expand the feasible region for the problem, as shown in Figure 3.3. With an enlarged feasible region, we now want to determine whether one of the new feasible solutions provides an improvement in the value of the objective function. Application of the graphical solution procedure to the problem with the enlarged feasible region shows that the extreme point with $S = 527.5$ and $D = 270.75$ now provides the optimal solution. The new value for the objective function is $10(527.5) + 9(270.75) = \$7711.75$, with an increase in profit of $\$7711.75 - \$7668.00 = \$43.75$. Thus, the increased profit occurs at a rate of $\$43.75/10$ hours $= \$4.375$ per hour added.

The *improvement* in the value of the optimal solution per unit increase in the right-hand side of the constraint is called the **dual price.** Here, the dual price for the cutting and dyeing constraint is \$4.375; in other words, if we increase the right-hand side of the cutting and dyeing constraint by 1 hour, the value of the objective function will improve by \$4.375. Conversely, if the right-hand side of the cutting and dyeing constraint were to decrease by 1 hour, the objective function would get worse by \$4.375. The dual price can generally be used to determine what will happen to the value of the objective function when we make a one-unit change in the right-hand side of a constraint.

We caution here that the value of the dual price may be applicable only for small changes in the right-hand side. As more and more resources are obtained and the right-hand-side value continues to increase, other constraints will become binding and limit the change in the value of the objective function. For example, in the problem for Par, Inc., we would eventually reach a point where more cutting and dyeing time would be of no value; it would occur at the point where the cutting and dyeing constraint becomes nonbinding. At this point, the dual price would equal zero. In the next section we will show how to determine the range of values for a right-hand side over which the dual price will accurately predict the improvement in the objective function. Finally, we note that the dual price for any nonbinding constraint will be zero because an increase in the right-hand side of such a constraint will affect only the value of the slack or surplus variable for that constraint.

To illustrate the correct interpretation of dual prices for a minimization problem, suppose we had solved a problem involving the minimization of total cost and that the value of the optimal solution was \$100. Furthermore, suppose that the dual price for a particular constraint was −\$10. The *negative dual price* tells us that the objective function *will not improve* if the value of the right-hand side is increased by one unit. Thus, if the right-hand side of this constraint is increased by one unit, the value of the objective function will get worse by the amount of \$10. Becoming worse in a minimization problem means an increase in the total cost. In this case, the value of the objective function will become \$110 if the right-hand side is increased by one unit. Conversely, a decrease in the right-hand side of one unit will decrease the total cost by \$10.

The Management Science in Action, Evaluating Efficiency at Performance Analysis Corporation, illustrates the use of dual prices as part of an evaluation model for a chain of fast-food outlets. This type of model will be studied in more detail in Chapter 5 when we discuss an application referred to as data envelopment analysis.

MANAGEMENT SCIENCE IN ACTION

EVALUATING EFFICIENCY AT PERFORMANCE ANALYSIS CORPORATION*

Performance Analysis Corporation specializes in the use of management science to design more efficient and effective operations for a wide variety of chain stores. One such application uses linear programming methodology to provide an evaluation model for a chain of fast-food outlets.

According to the concept of Pareto optimality, a restaurant in a given chain is relatively inefficient if other restaurants in the same chain exhibit the following characteristics:

1. Operates in the same or worse environment.
2. Produces at least the same level of *all* outputs.
3. Utilizes no more of *any* resource and *less* of at least one of the resources.

To determine which of the restaurants are Pareto inefficient, Performance Analysis Corporation developed and solved a linear programming model. Model constraints involve requirements concerning the minimum acceptable levels of output and conditions imposed by uncontrollable elements in the environment, and the objective function calls for the minimization of the resources necessary to produce the output. Solving the model produces the following output for each restaurant:

1. A score that assesses the level of so-called relative technical efficiency achieved by the particular restaurant over the time period in question.
2. The reduction in controllable resources or the increase of outputs over the time period in question needed for an inefficient restaurant to be rated as efficient.
3. A peer group of other restaurants with which each restaurant can be compared in the future.

Sensitivity analysis provides important managerial information. For example, for each constraint concerning a minimum acceptable output level, the dual price tells the manager how much one more unit of output would increase the efficiency measure.

The analysis typically identifies 40% to 50% of the restaurants as underperforming, given the previously stated conditions concerning the inputs available and outputs produced. Performance Analysis Corporation finds that if all the relative inefficiencies identified are eliminated simultaneously, corporate profits typically increase approximately 5% to 10%. This increase is truly substantial given the large scale of operations involved.

*Based on information provided by Richard C. Morey of Performance Analysis Corporation.

NOTES AND COMMENTS

1. If two objective function coefficients change simultaneously, both may move outside their respective ranges of optimality and not affect the optimal solution. For instance, in a two-variable linear program, the slope of the objective function will not change at all if both coefficients are changed by the same percentage.
2. Some texts associate the term *shadow price* with each constraint. The concept of a shadow price is closely related to the concept of a dual price. The shadow price associated with a constraint is the *change* in the value of the optimal solution per unit increase in the right-hand side of the constraint. In general, the dual price and the shadow price are the *same* for all *maximization* linear programs. In *minimization* linear programs, the shadow price is the *negative* of the corresponding dual price.

3.3 SENSITIVITY ANALYSIS: COMPUTER SOLUTION

In Section 2.4 we showed how The Management Scientist can be used to solve the Par, Inc., linear program. Recall that in order to use The Management Scientist, we must use decimal rather than fractional values. The Par, Inc., problem with decimal coefficients is restated here:

$$
\begin{array}{lrll}
\text{Max} & 10S + 9D & & \\
\text{s.t.} & & & \\
& 0.7S + 1D & \leq 630 & \text{Cutting and dyeing} \\
& 0.5S + 0.83333D & \leq 600 & \text{Sewing} \\
& 1.0S + 0.66667D & \leq 708 & \text{Finishing} \\
& 0.1S + 0.25D & \leq 135 & \text{Inspection and packaging} \\
& S, D \geq 0 & &
\end{array}
$$

Let us demonstrate the use of The Management Scientist in performing sensitivity analysis by considering the solution to the Par, Inc., linear program shown in Figure 3.4.

Interpretation of Computer Output

In Section 2.4 we discussed the output in the top portion of Figure 3.4. Thus, after rounding, we see that the optimal solution is $S = 540$ standard bags and $D = 252$ deluxe bags; the value of the optimal solution is \$7668. As we discussed in Section 2.4, the **reduced costs** indicate how much the objective function coefficient of each decision variable would have to improve before that variable could assume a positive value in the optimal solution. For the Par, Inc., problem, both variables already have positive values, and thus their corresponding reduced costs are zero. In Section 3.4 we will interpret the reduced cost for a decision variable that does not have a positive value in the optimal solution.

FIGURE 3.4 THE MANAGEMENT SCIENTIST SOLUTION FOR THE PAR, INC., PROBLEM

```
Objective Function Value =          7667.99463

     Variable            Value             Reduced Costs
  --------------    ---------------    -----------------
        S              539.99841            0.00000
        D              252.00113            0.00000

    Constraint        Slack/Surplus        Dual Prices
  --------------    ---------------    -----------------
        1                0.00000            4.37496
        2              120.00070            0.00000
        3                0.00000            6.93753
        4               17.99988            0.00000

OBJECTIVE COEFFICIENT RANGES

  Variable       Lower Limit      Current Value      Upper Limit
 ------------  ---------------  ---------------  ---------------
      S             6.30000         10.00000          13.49993
      D             6.66670          9.00000          14.28572

RIGHT HAND SIDE RANGES

 Constraint      Lower Limit      Current Value      Upper Limit
 ------------  ---------------  ---------------  ---------------
      1           495.59998        630.00000         682.36316
      2           479.99930        600.00000      No Upper Limit
      3           580.00146        708.00000         900.00000
      4           117.00012        135.00000      No Upper Limit
```

EXCEL file
Par

Immediately following the optimal S and D values and the reduced cost information, the computer output provides information about the constraints. Recall that the Par, Inc., problem had four less-than-or-equal-to constraints corresponding to the hours available in each of four production departments. The information shown in the Slack/Surplus column provides the value of the slack variable for each of the departments. This information (after rounding) is summarized here:

Constraint Number	Constraint Name	Slack
1	Cutting and dyeing	0
2	Sewing	120
3	Finishing	0
4	Inspection and packaging	18

From this information, we see that the binding constraints (the cutting and dyeing and the finishing constraints) have zero slack at the optimal solution. The sewing department has

120 hours of slack, or unused capacity, and the inspection and packaging department has 18 hours of slack or unused capacity.

The Dual Prices column contains information about the marginal value of each of the four resources at the optimal solution. In Section 3.2 we defined the *dual price* as follows.

The dual price associated with a constraint is the *improvement* in the value of the solution per unit increase in the right-hand side of the constraint.

Try Problem 5 to test your ability to use computer output to determine the optimal solution and to interpret the values of the dual prices.

Thus, the nonzero dual prices of 4.37496 for constraint 1 (cutting and dyeing constraint) and 6.93753 for constraint 3 (finishing constraint) tell us that an additional hour of cutting and dyeing time improves (increases) the value of the optimal solution by $4.37 and an additional hour of finishing time improves (increases) the value of the optimal solution by $6.94. Thus, if the cutting and dyeing time were increased from 630 to 631 hours, with all other coefficients in the problem remaining the same, Par's profit would be increased by $4.37 from $7668 to $7668 + $4.37 = $7672.37. A similar interpretation for the finishing constraint implies that an increase from 708 to 709 hours of available finishing time, with all other coefficients in the problem remaining the same, would increase Par's profit to $7668 + $6.94 = $7674.94. Because the sewing and the inspection and packaging constraints both have slack or unused capacity available, the dual prices of zero show that additional hours of these two resources will not improve the value of the objective function.

Referring again to the computer output in Figure 3.4, we see that after providing the constraint information on slack/surplus variables and dual prices, The Management Scientist provides ranges for the objective function coefficients and the right-hand sides of the constraints.

Considering the information provided under the computer output heading labeled OBJECTIVE COEFFICIENT RANGES, we see that variable S, which has a current profit coefficient of 10, has the following *range of optimality* for C_S:

$$6.30 \leq C_S \leq 13.50$$

Therefore, as long as the profit contribution associated with the standard bag is between $6.30 and $13.50, the production of $S = 540$ standard bags and $D = 252$ deluxe bags will remain the optimal solution. Note that the range of optimality is the same as obtained by performing graphical sensitivity analysis for C_S in Section 3.2.

Using the objective function coefficient range information for deluxe bags, we see that The Management Scientist computed the following range of optimality:

$$6.67 \leq C_D \leq 14.29$$

This result tells us that as long as the profit contribution associated with the deluxe bag is between $6.67 and $14.29, the production of $S = 540$ standard bags and $D = 252$ deluxe bags will remain the optimal solution.

Try Problem 6 to test your ability to use computer output to determine the ranges of optimality and the ranges of feasibility.

The final section of the computer output (RIGHT HAND SIDE RANGES) provides the limits within which the dual prices are applicable. As long as the constraint right-hand side is between the lower and upper limit values, the associated dual price gives the improvement in the value of the optimal solution per unit increase in the right-hand side. For example, let us consider the cutting and dyeing constraint with a current right-hand-side value of 630. Because the dual price for this constraint is $4.37, we can conclude that additional hours will increase the objective function by \$4.37 per hour. It is also true that a reduction in the hours available will reduce the value of the objective function by \$4.37 per hour. From the range information given, we see that the dual price of \$4.37 is valid for increases up to 682.36316 and decreases down to 495.59998. A similar interpretation for the finishing constraint's right-hand side (constraint 3) shows that the dual price of \$6.94 is applicable for increases up to 900 hours and decreases down to 580.00146 hours.

As mentioned, the right-hand-side ranges provide limits within which the dual prices are applicable. For changes outside the range, the problem must be re-solved to find the new optimal solution and the new dual price. We shall call the range over which the dual price is applicable the **range of feasibility.** The ranges of feasibility for the Par, Inc., problem are summarized here:

Constraint	Min RHS	Max RHS
Cutting and dyeing	495.6	682.4
Sewing	480.0	No upper limit
Finishing	580.0	900.0
Inspection and packaging	117.0	No upper limit

As long as the values of the right-hand sides are within these ranges, the dual prices shown on the computer output will not change. Right-hand-side values outside these limits will result in changes in the dual price information.

Simultaneous Changes

The sensitivity analysis information in computer output is based on the assumption that only one coefficient changes; it is assumed that all other coefficients will remain as stated in the original problem. Thus, the ranges for the objective function coefficients and the constraint right-hand sides are only applicable for changes in a single coefficient. In many cases, however, we may be interested in what would happen if two or more coefficients are changed simultaneously. As we will demonstrate, some analysis of simultaneous changes is possible with the help of the **100 percent rule.** We begin by showing how the 100 percent rule applies to simultaneous changes in the objective function coefficients.

Suppose that in the Par, Inc., problem the accounting department concluded that the original profit contributions of \$10 and \$9 for the standard and deluxe bags, respectively, were incorrectly computed; the correct values should have been \$11.50 and \$8.25. To determine what effect, if any, these simultaneous changes have on the optimal solution, we need to first define the terms *allowable increase* and *allowable decrease.* For an objective function coefficient, the allowable increase is the maximum amount the coefficient may increase without exceeding the upper limit of the range of optimality; the allowable decrease is the maximum amount the coefficient may decrease without dropping below the lower limit of the range of optimality.

From Figure 3.4 we see that the upper limit for the objective function coefficient of S is 13.49993; thus, the allowable increase is $3.49993 = 13.49993 - 10$. In terms of percentage change, the increase of \$1.50 in the objective function coefficient (from 10 to 11.50) for the standard bags is $(1.50/3.49993)(100) = 42.86\%$ of the allowable increase. Given the lower limit of 6.66670 for D, the allowable decrease for D is $2.33330 = 9 - 6.66670$. In terms of percentage change, the decrease of \$0.75 in the objective function coefficient (from 9 to 8.25) for the deluxe bags is (0.75/2.33330)(100) = 32.14% of the allowable decrease. The sum of the percentage change of the allowable increase (42.86%) and the percentage change of the allowable decrease (32.14%) is 75.00%.

Let us now state the 100 percent rule as it applies to simultaneous changes in the objective function coefficients.

100 Percent Rule for Objective Function Coefficients

For all objective function coefficients that are changed, sum the percentages of the allowable increases and the allowable decreases represented by the changes. If the sum of the percentage changes does not exceed 100%, the optimal solution will not change.

Thus, because the sum of the two percentage changes in the objective function coefficients for the Par, Inc., problem is 75%, these simultaneous changes will not affect the optimal solution. Note, however, that although the optimal solution is still $S = 539.99841$ and $D = 252.00113$, the value of the optimal solution will change because the profit contribution for the standard bags has increased to \$11.50 and the profit contribution of the deluxe bags has decreased to \$8.25.

The 100 percent rule does not, however, say that the optimal solution will change if the sum of the percentage changes exceeds 100%. It is possible that the optimal solution will not change even though the sum of the percentage changes exceeds 100%. When the 100 percent rule is not satisfied, we must re-solve the problem to determine what effect such changes will have on the optimal solution.

A similar version of the 100 percent rule also applies to simultaneous changes in the constraint right-hand sides.

100 Percent Rule for Constraint Right-Hand Sides

For all right-hand sides that are changed, sum the percentages of allowable increases and allowable decreases. If the sum of percentages does not exceed 100%, then the dual prices will not change.

Let us illustrate the 100 percent rule for constraint right-hand sides by considering simultaneous changes in the right-hand sides for the Par, Inc., problem. Suppose, for instance, that in this problem we could obtain 20 additional hours of cutting and dyeing time and 100 additional hours of finishing time. The allowable increase for cutting and dyeing time is 682.36316 − 630.0 = 52.36316, and the allowable increase for finishing time is 900.0 − 708.0 = 192.0 (see Figure 3.4). The 20 additional hours of cutting and dyeing time are (20/52.36316)(100) = 38.19% of the allowable increase in the constraint's right-hand side. The 100 additional hours of finishing time are (100/192)(100) = 52.08% of the allowable increase in the finishing time constraint's right-hand side. The sum of the percentage changes is 38.19% + 52.08% = 90.27%. The sum of the percentage changes does not exceed 100%; therefore, we can conclude that the dual prices are applicable and that the objective function will improve by (20)(4.37) + (100)(6.94) = 781.40.

Interpretation of Computer Output—A Second Example

As another example of interpreting computer output, let us reconsider the M&D Chemicals problem introduced in Section 2.5. M&D's objective was to find the minimum-cost production schedule for products A and B. The linear programming model for this problem is restated as follows, where A = number of gallons of product A and B = number of gallons of product B.

$$
\begin{array}{ll}
\text{Min} & 2A + 3B \\
\text{s.t.} & \\
& 1A \qquad\quad \geq 125 \quad \text{Demand for product A} \\
& 1A + 1B \geq 350 \quad \text{Total production} \\
& 2A + 1B \leq 600 \quad \text{Processing time} \\
& A, B \geq 0
\end{array}
$$

The solution obtained using The Management Scientist is presented in Figure 3.5. The computer output shows that the minimum-cost solution yields an objective function

FIGURE 3.5 THE MANAGEMENT SCIENTIST SOLUTION FOR THE M&D CHEMICALS PROBLEM

```
Objective Function Value =                 800.000

     Variable              Value              Reduced Costs
  --------------      ---------------      ------------------
        A                 250.000                 0.000
        B                 100.000                 0.000

    Constraint          Slack/Surplus          Dual Prices
  --------------      ---------------      ------------------
        1                 125.000                 0.000
        2                   0.000                -4.000
        3                   0.000                 1.000

OBJECTIVE COEFFICIENT RANGES

  Variable       Lower Limit       Current Value      Upper Limit
 ------------  ---------------   ---------------   ---------------
      A        No Lower Limit             2.000             3.000
      B                 2.000             3.000    No Upper Limit

RIGHT HAND SIDE RANGES

  Constraint     Lower Limit       Current Value      Upper Limit
 ------------  ---------------   ---------------   ---------------
      1        No Lower Limit           125.000           250.000
      2               300.000           350.000           475.000
      3               475.000           600.000           700.000
```

value of $800. The values of the decision variables show that 250 gallons of product A and 100 gallons of product B provide the minimum-cost production schedule.

The Slack/Surplus column shows that the ≥ constraint corresponding to the demand for product A (see constraint 1) has a surplus of 125 units. It tells us that production of product A in the optimal solution exceeds demand by 125 gallons. The Slack/Surplus values are zero for the total production requirement (constraint 2) and the processing time limitation (constraint 3), which indicates that these constraints are binding at the optimal solution.

The Dual Prices column again shows us the *improvement* in the value of the optimal solution per unit increase in the right-hand side of the constraint. Focusing first on the dual price of 1.00 for the processing time constraint (constraint 3), we see that if we can increase the processing time from 600 to 601 hours, the objective function value will *improve* by $1. Because the objective is to minimize costs, improvement in this case means a lowering of costs. Thus, if 601 hours of processing time are available, the value of the optimal solution will improve to $800 − $1 = $799. The RIGHT HAND SIDE RANGES section of the output shows that the upper limit for the processing time constraint (constraint 3) is 700 hours. Thus, the dual price of $1 per unit would be applicable for every additional hour of processing time up to a total of 700 hours.

Let us again return to the Dual Prices section of the output and consider the dual price for the total production constraint (constraint 2). The *negative dual price* tells us that the value of the optimal solution *will not improve* if the value of the right-hand side is increased by one unit. In fact, the dual price of −4.00 tells us that if the right-hand side of the total production constraint is increased from 350 to 351 units, the value of the optimal solution will worsen by the amount of $4. A worsening means an increase in cost, which also means the value of the optimal solution will become $800 + $4 = $804 if the one-unit increase in the total production requirement is made.

Because the dual price refers to improvement in the value of the optimal solution per unit increase in the right-hand side, a constraint with a negative dual price should not have its right-hand side increased. In fact, if the dual price is negative, efforts should be made to reduce the right-hand side of the constraint. If the right-hand side of the total production constraint were decreased from 350 to 349 units, the dual price tells us the total cost could be lowered by $4 to $800 − $4 = $796.

Even though the dual price is the improvement in the value of the optimal solution per unit increase in the right-hand side of a constraint, the interpretation of an *improvement* in the value of an objective function depends on whether we are solving a maximization or a minimization problem. The dual price for a ≤ constraint will always be greater than or equal to zero because increasing the right-hand side cannot make the value of the objective function worse. Similarly, the dual price for a ≥ constraint will always be less than or equal to zero because increasing the right-hand side cannot improve the value of the optimal solution.

Finally, consider the right-hand-side ranges provided in Figure 3.5. The ranges of feasibility for the M&D Chemicals problem are summarized here:

Constraint	**Min RHS**	**Max RHS**
Demand for product A	No lower limit	250
Total production	300	475
Processing time	475	700

Try Problem 10 to test your ability to interpret the computer output for a minimization problem.

As long as the right-hand sides are within these ranges, the dual prices shown on the computer printout are applicable.

Cautionary Note on the Interpretation of Dual Prices

As stated previously, the dual price is the improvement in the value of the optimal solution per unit increase in the right-hand side of a constraint. When the right-hand side of the constraint represents the amount of a resource available, the associated dual price is often interpreted as the maximum amount one should be willing to pay for one additional unit of the resource. However, such an interpretation is not always correct. To see why, we need to understand the difference between sunk and relevant costs. A **sunk cost** is one that is not affected by the decision made. It will be incurred no matter what values the decision variables assume. A **relevant cost** is one that depends on the decision made. The amount of a relevant cost will vary depending on the values of the decision variables.

Let us reconsider the Par, Inc., problem. The amount of cutting and dyeing time available is 630 hours. The cost of the time available is a sunk cost if it must be paid regardless of the number of standard and deluxe golf bags produced. It would be a relevant cost if Par only had to pay for the number of hours of cutting and dyeing time actually used to produce golf bags. All relevant costs should be reflected in the objective function of a linear program. Sunk costs should not be reflected in the objective function. For Par, Inc., we have been assuming that the company must pay its employees' wages regardless of whether their time on the job is completely utilized. Therefore, the cost of the labor-hours resource for Par, Inc., is a sunk cost and has not been reflected in the objective function.

Only relevant costs should be included in the objective function.

When the cost of a resource is *sunk,* the dual price can be interpreted as the maximum amount the company should be willing to pay for one additional unit of the resource. When the cost of a resource used is relevant, the dual price can be interpreted as the amount by which the value of the resource exceeds its cost. Thus, when the resource cost is relevant, the dual price can be interpreted as the maximum premium over the normal cost that the company should be willing to pay for one unit of the resource.

NOTES AND COMMENTS

1. Computer software packages for solving linear programs are readily available. Most of these provide the optimal solution, dual or shadow price information, the range of optimality for the objective function coefficients, and the range of feasibility for the right-hand sides. The labels used for the ranges of optimality and feasibility may vary, but the meaning is the same as what we have described here.
2. Whenever one of the right-hand sides is at an end point of its range of feasibility, the dual and shadow prices only provide one-sided information. In this case, they only predict the change in the optimal value of the objective function for changes toward the interior of the range.
3. A condition called *degeneracy* can cause a subtle difference in how we interpret changes in the objective function coefficients beyond the end points of the range of optimality. Degeneracy occurs when the dual price equals zero for one of the binding constraints. Degeneracy does not affect the interpretation of changes toward the interior of the range of optimality. However, when degeneracy is present, changes beyond the end points of the range do not necessarily mean a different solution will be optimal. From a practical point of view, changes beyond the end points of the range of optimality necessitate re-solving the problem.
4. The 100 percent rule permits an analysis of multiple changes in the right-hand sides or multiple changes in the objective function coefficients. But the 100 percent rule cannot be applied to changes in both objective function coefficients *and* right-hand sides at the same time. In order to consider simultaneous changes for *both* right-hand-side values and objective function coefficients, the problem must be re-solved.

5. Managers are frequently called on to provide an economic justification for new technology. Often the new technology is developed, or purchased, in order to conserve resources. The dual price can be helpful in such cases because it can be used to determine the savings attributable to the new technology by showing the savings per unit of resource conserved.

3.4 MORE THAN TWO DECISION VARIABLES

The graphical solution procedure is useful only for linear programs involving two decision variables. In practice, the problems solved using linear programming usually involve large numbers of variables and constraints. For instance, the Management Science in Action, Determining Optimal Production Quantities at GE Plastics, describes how a linear programming model with 3100 variables and 1100 constraints was solved in less than 10 seconds to determine the optimal production quantities at GE Plastics. In this section we discuss the formulation and computer solution for two linear programs with three decision variables. In doing so, we will show how to interpret the reduced-cost portion of the computer output and will also illustrate the interpretation of dual prices for constraints that involve percentages.

The Modified Par, Inc., Problem

The original Par, Inc., problem is restated as follows:

$$
\begin{aligned}
\text{Max} \quad & 10S + 9D \\
\text{s.t.} \quad & \\
& 0.7S + 1D \leq 630 \quad \text{Cutting and dyeing} \\
& 0.5S + 0.83333D \leq 600 \quad \text{Sewing} \\
& 1S + 0.66667D \leq 708 \quad \text{Finishing} \\
& 0.1S + 0.25D \leq 135 \quad \text{Inspection and packaging} \\
& S, D \geq 0
\end{aligned}
$$

Recall that S is the number of standard golf bags produced and D is the number of deluxe golf bags produced. Suppose that management is also considering producing a lightweight model designed specifically for golfers who prefer to carry their bags. The design department estimates that each new lightweight model will require 0.8 hours for cutting and dyeing, 1 hour for sewing, 1 hour for finishing, and 0.25 hours for inspection and packaging. Because of the unique capabilities designed into the new model, Par's management feels they will realize a profit contribution of $12.85 for each lightweight model produced during the current production period.

Let us consider the modifications in the original linear programming model that are needed to incorporate the effect of this additional decision variable. We will let L denote the number of lightweight bags produced. After adding L to the objective function and to each of the four constraints, we obtain the following linear program for the modified problem:

$$
\begin{aligned}
\text{Max} \quad & 10S + 9D + 12.85L \\
\text{s.t.} \quad & \\
& 0.7S + 1D + 0.8L \leq 630 \quad \text{Cutting and dyeing} \\
& 0.5S + 0.83333D + 1L \leq 630 \quad \text{Sewing} \\
& 1S + 0.66667D + 1L \leq 708 \quad \text{Finishing} \\
& 0.1S + 0.25D + 0.25L \leq 135 \quad \text{Inspection and packaging} \\
& S, D, L \geq 0
\end{aligned}
$$

MANAGEMENT SCIENCE IN ACTION

DETERMINING OPTIMAL PRODUCTION QUANTITIES AT GE PLASTICS*

General Electric Plastics (GEP) is a $5 billion global materials supplier of plastics and raw materials to many industries (e.g., automotive, computer, and medical equipment). GEP has plants all over the globe. In the past, GEP followed a pole-centric manufacturing approach wherein each product was manufactured in the geographic area (Americas, Europe, or Pacific) where it was to be delivered. When many of GEP's customers started shifting their manufacturing operations to the Pacific, a geographic imbalance was created between GEP's capacity and demand in the form of overcapacity in the Americas and undercapacity in the Pacific.

Recognizing that a pole-centric approach was no longer effective, GEP adopted a global approach to its manufacturing operations. Initial work focused on the high-performance polymers (HPP) division. Using a linear programming model, GEP was able to determine the optimal production quantities at each HPP plant to maximize the total contribution margin for the division. The model included demand constraints, manufacturing capacity constraints, and constraints that modeled the flow of materials produced at resin plants to the finishing plants and on to warehouses in three geographical regions (Americas, Europe, and Pacific). The mathematical model for a one-year problem has 3100 variables and 1100 constraints, and can be solved in less than 10 seconds. The new system proved successful at the HPP division, and other GE Plastics divisions are adapting it for their supply chain planning.

*Based on R. Tyagi, P. Kalish, and K. Akbay, "GE Plastics Optimizes the Two-Echelon Global Fulfillment Network at Its High-Performance Polymers Division," *Interfaces* (September/October 2004): 359–366.

Figure 3.6 shows the solution to the modified problem using The Management Scientist. We see that the optimal solution calls for the production of 280 standard bags, 0 deluxe bags, and 428 of the new lightweight bags; the value of the optimal solution after rounding is $8299.80.

Let us now look at the information contained in the Reduced Costs column. Recall that the reduced costs indicate how much each objective function coefficient would have to improve before the corresponding decision variable could assume a positive value in the optimal solution. As the computer output shows, the reduced costs for S and L are zero because the corresponding decision variables already have positive values in the optimal solution. The reduced cost of 1.15003 for decision variable D tells us that the profit contribution for the deluxe bag would have to increase to at least $9 + $1.15003 = $10.15003 before D *could* assume a positive value in the optimal solution.[1] In other words, unless the profit contribution for D increases by at least $1.15 the value of D will remain at zero in the optimal solution.

Suppose we increase the coefficient of D by exactly $1.15003 and then re-solve the problem using The Management Scientist. Figure 3.7 shows the new solution. Note that although D assumes a positive value in the new solution, the value of the optimal solution has not changed. In other words, increasing the profit contribution of D by *exactly* the amount of the reduced cost has resulted in alternative optimal solutions. Using a different computer software package, you may not see D assume a positive value if you re-solve the problem with an objective function coefficient of exactly 10.15003 for D—that is, the software package may show a different alternative optimal solution. However, if the profit contribution of D is increased by *more than* $1.15003, then D will not remain at zero in the optimal solution.

---

[1]In the case of degeneracy, a variable may not assume a positive value in the optimal solution even when the improvement in the profit contribution exceeds the value of the reduced cost. Our definition of reduced costs, stated as ". . . could assume a positive value . . . ," provides for such special cases. More advanced texts on mathematical programming discuss these special types of situations.

FIGURE 3.6 THE MANAGEMENT SCIENTIST SOLUTION FOR THE MODIFIED PAR, INC., PROBLEM

```
Objective Function Value =            8299.80078

      Variable              Value               Reduced Costs
    --------------     ---------------     ------------------
           S              280.00000                 0.00000
           D                0.00000                 1.15003
           L              428.00000                 0.00000

     Constraint         Slack/Surplus             Dual Prices
    --------------     ---------------     ------------------
           1               91.60001                 0.00000
           2               32.00000                 0.00000
           3                0.00000                 8.10000
           4                0.00000                19.00000

OBJECTIVE COEFFICIENT RANGES

  Variable        Lower Limit       Current Value      Upper Limit
------------    ---------------   ---------------   ---------------
     S                5.14000          10.00000          12.07007
     D         No Lower Limit           9.00000          10.15003
     L               11.90907          12.85000          25.00000

RIGHT HAND SIDE RANGES

 Constraint       Lower Limit       Current Value      Upper Limit
------------    ---------------   ---------------   ---------------
      1             538.40002         630.00000    No Upper Limit
      2             568.00000         600.00000    No Upper Limit
      3             540.00000         708.00000         852.63159
      4              70.80000         135.00000         144.60001
```

We also note from Figure 3.6 that the dual prices for constraints 3 and 4 are 8.1 and 19, respectively, indicating that these two constraints are binding in the optimal solution. Thus, each additional hour in the finishing department would increase the value of the optimal solution by $8.10 and each additional hour in the inspection and packaging department would increase the value of the optimal solution by $19.00. Because of a slack of 91.6 hours in the cutting and dyeing department and 32 hours in the sewing department (see Figure 3.6), management might want to consider the possibility of utilizing these unused labor-hours in the finishing or inspection and packaging departments. For example, some of the employees in the cutting and dyeing department could be used to perform certain operations in either the finishing department or the inspection and packaging department. In the future, Par's management may want to explore the possibility of cross-training employees so that unused capacity in one department could be shifted to other departments. In the next chapter we will consider similar modeling situations.

FIGURE 3.7 THE MANAGEMENT SCIENTIST SOLUTION FOR THE MODIFIED PAR, INC., PROBLEM WITH THE COEFFICIENT OF *D* INCREASED BY $1.15003

```
Objective Function Value =           8299.80078

     Variable             Value             Reduced Costs
  --------------    ---------------    ------------------
        S              403.78317              0.00000
        D              222.81198              0.00000
        L              155.67476              0.00000

    Constraint        Slack/Surplus          Dual Prices
  --------------    ---------------    ------------------
        1                0.00000              0.00000
        2               56.75776              0.00000
        3                0.00000              8.10000
        4                0.00000             19.00000

OBJECTIVE COEFFICIENT RANGES

  Variable       Lower Limit      Current Value      Upper Limit
------------   ---------------   ---------------   ---------------
      S             10.00000          10.00000          12.51072
      D             10.15003          10.15003          15.40790
      L             10.65313          12.85000          12.85000

RIGHT HAND SIDE RANGES

 Constraint      Lower Limit      Current Value      Upper Limit
------------   ---------------   ---------------   ---------------
      1            538.40002         630.00000         682.36316
      2            543.24225         600.00000    No Upper Limit
      3            580.00140         708.00000         852.63159
      4            117.00012         135.00000         151.15410
```

Suppose that after reviewing the solution shown in Figure 3.6, management states that they will not consider any solution that does not include the production of some deluxe bags. Management then decides to add the requirement that the number of deluxe bags produced must be at least 30% of the number of standard bags produced. Writing this requirement using the decision variables *S* and *D*, we obtain

$$D \geq 0.3S$$

or

$$-0.3S + D \geq 0$$

Adding this new constraint to the modified Par, Inc., linear program and resolving the problem using The Management Scientist, we obtain the optimal solution shown in Figure 3.8.

Let us consider the interpretation of the dual price for constraint 5, the requirement that the number of deluxe bags produced must be at least 30% of the number of standard bags

FIGURE 3.8 THE MANAGEMENT SCIENTIST SOLUTION FOR THE MODIFIED PAR, INC., PROBLEM WITH THE 30% DELUXE BAG REQUIREMENT

```
Objective Function Value =          8183.87793

     Variable              Value              Reduced Costs
   --------------    ---------------    ------------------
           S             335.99933               0.00000
           D             100.79980               0.00000
           L             304.80048               0.00000

    Constraint         Slack/Surplus          Dual Prices
   --------------    ---------------    ------------------
            1             50.16031               0.00000
            2             43.20037               0.00000
            3              0.00000               7.40998
            4              0.00000              21.76006
            5              0.00000              -1.38003

OBJECTIVE COEFFICIENT RANGES

  Variable         Lower Limit       Current Value       Upper Limit
------------   ---------------   ---------------   ---------------
      S               6.29500          10.00000          12.07007
      D              -3.35000           9.00000          10.15003
      L              11.90907          12.85000          18.14286

RIGHT HAND SIDE RANGES

 Constraint        Lower Limit       Current Value       Upper Limit
------------   ---------------   ---------------   ---------------
      1             579.83972         630.00000    No Upper Limit
      2             556.79962         600.00000    No Upper Limit
      3             540.00000         708.00000         765.00049
      4             103.24991         135.00000         147.00008
      5             -84.00000           0.00000         101.67704
```

produced. The dual price of -1.38 indicates that a one-unit increase in the right-hand side of the constraint will lower profits by \$1.38. Thus, what the dual price of -1.38 is really telling us is what will happen to the value of the optimal solution if the constraint is changed to

$$D \geq 0.3S + 1$$

The correct interpretation of the dual price of -1.38 can now be stated as follows: If we are forced to produce one deluxe bag over and above the minimum 30% requirement, total profits will decrease by \$1.38. Conversely, if we relax the minimum 30% requirement by one bag ($D \geq 0.3S - 1$), total profits will increase by \$1.38.

The dual price for similar percentage (or ratio) constraints will not directly provide answers to questions concerning a percentage increase or decrease in the right-hand side of the constraint. For example, we might wonder what would happen to the value of the optimal solution if the number of deluxe bags has to be at least 31% of the number of standard bags. To answer such a question, we would re-solve the problem using the constraint $-0.31S + D \geq 0$.

Because percentage (or ratio) constraints frequently occur in linear programming models, let us consider another example. For instance, suppose that Par's management states that the number of lightweight bags produced may not exceed 20% of the total golf bag production. If the total production of golf bags is $S + D + L$, we can write this constraint as

$$L \leq 0.2(S + D + L)$$
$$L \leq 0.2S + 0.2D + 0.2L$$
$$-0.2S - 0.2D + 0.8L \leq 0$$

The solution obtained using The Management Scientist for the model that incorporates both the effects of this new percentage requirement and the previous requirement ($-0.3S + D \geq 0$) is shown in Figure 3.9. After rounding, the dual price corresponding to the new constraint (constraint 6) is 0.89. Thus, every additional lightweight bag we are allowed to produce over the current 20% limit will increase the value of the objective function by \$0.89; moreover, the right-hand-side range for this constraint shows that this interpretation is valid for increases of up to 156 units.

The Bluegrass Farms Problem

To provide additional practice in formulating and interpreting the computer solution for linear programs involving more than two decision variables, we consider a minimization problem involving three decision variables. Bluegrass Farms, located in Lexington, Kentucky, has been experimenting with a special diet for its racehorses. The feed components available for the diet are a standard horse feed product, a vitamin-enriched oat product, and a new vitamin and mineral feed additive. The nutritional values in units per pound and the costs for the three feed components are summarized in Table 3.1; for example, each pound of the standard feed component contains 0.8 unit of ingredient A, 1 unit of ingredient B, and 0.1 unit of ingredient C. The minimum daily diet requirements for each horse are three units of ingredient A, six units of ingredient B, and four units of ingredient C. In addition, to control the weight of the horses, the total daily feed for a horse should not exceed 6 pounds. Bluegrass Farms would like to determine the minimum-cost mix that will satisfy the daily diet requirements.

Formulation of the Bluegrass Farms Problem

To formulate a linear programming model for the Bluegrass Farms problem, we introduce the following three decision variables:

S = number of pounds of the standard horse feed product
E = number of pounds of the enriched oat product
A = number of pounds of the vitamin and mineral feed additive

Using the data in Table 3.1, the objective function for minimizing the total cost associated with the daily feed can be written as follows:

$$\min 0.25S + 0.50E + 3A$$

For a minimum daily requirement for ingredient A of three units, we obtain the constraint

$$0.8S + 0.2E \geq 3$$

FIGURE 3.9 THE MANAGEMENT SCIENTIST SOLUTION FOR THE MODIFIED PAR, INC., PROBLEM INCORPORATING THE 20% LIGHTWEIGHT BAG REQUIREMENT AND THE 30% DELUXE BAG REQUIREMENT

Objective Function Value = 8044.25488

Variable	Value	Reduced Costs
S	403.44730	0.00000
D	222.20738	0.00000
L	156.41367	0.00000

Constraint	Slack/Surplus	Dual Prices
1	0.24859	0.00000
2	56.69057	0.00000
3	0.00000	8.87330
4	0.00000	13.05157
5	101.17319	0.00000
6	0.00000	0.89226

OBJECTIVE COEFFICIENT RANGES

Variable	Lower Limit	Current Value	Upper Limit
S	3.13800	10.00000	12.07007
D	6.47670	9.00000	10.15003
L	11.90907	12.85000	No Upper Limit

RIGHT HAND SIDE RANGES

Constraint	Lower Limit	Current Value	Upper Limit
1	629.75140	630.00000	No Upper Limit
2	543.30945	600.00000	No Upper Limit
3	396.00146	708.00000	708.69653
4	118.96714	135.00000	135.08900
5	No Lower Limit	0.00000	101.17319
6	-0.77936	0.00000	156.48053

TABLE 3.1 NUTRITIONAL VALUE AND COST DATA FOR THE BLUEGRASS FARMS PROBLEM

Feed Component	Standard	Enriched Oat	Additive
Ingredient A	0.8	0.2	0.0
Ingredient B	1.0	1.5	3.0
Ingredient C	0.1	0.6	2.0
Cost per pound	$0.25	$0.50	$3.00

The constraint for ingredient B is

$$1.0S + 1.5E + 3.0A \geq 6$$

and the constraint for ingredient C is

$$0.1S + 0.6E + 2.0A \geq 4$$

Finally, the constraint that restricts the mix to at most 6 pounds is

$$S + E + A \leq 6$$

Combining all the constraints with the nonnegativity requirements enables us to write the complete linear programming model for the Bluegrass Farms problem as follows:

$$\begin{aligned}
\text{Min}\quad & 0.25S + 0.50E + 3A \\
\text{s.t.}\quad & \\
& 0.8S + 0.2E \geq 3 \quad \text{Ingredient A} \\
& 1.0S + 1.5E + 3.0A \geq 6 \quad \text{Ingredient B} \\
& 0.1S + 0.6E + 2.0A \geq 4 \quad \text{Ingredient C} \\
& S + E + A \leq 6 \quad \text{Weight} \\
& S, E, A \geq 0
\end{aligned}$$

Computer Solution and Interpretation for the Bluegrass Farms Problem

The output obtained using The Management Scientist to solve the Bluegrass Farms problem is shown in Figure 3.10. After rounding, we see that the optimal solution calls for a daily diet consisting of 3.51 pounds of the standard horse feed product, 0.95 pound of the enriched oat product, and 1.54 pounds of the vitamin and mineral feed additive. Thus, with feed component costs of \$0.25, \$0.50, and \$3.00, the total cost of the optimal diet is

3.51 pounds @ \$0.25 per pound	=	\$0.88
0.95 pounds @ \$0.50 per pound	=	0.47
1.54 pounds @ \$3.00 per pound	=	4.62
Total cost	=	\$5.97

Note that after rounding, this result is the same as the objective function value in the computer output (Figure 3.10).

Looking at the Slack/Surplus section of the computer output, we find a value of 3.554 for constraint 2. Because constraint 2 is a greater-than-or-equal-to constraint, 3.554 is the surplus; the optimal solution exceeds the minimum daily diet requirement for ingredient B (six units) by 3.554 units. Because the surplus values for constraints 1 and 3 are both zero, we see that the optimal diet just meets the minimum requirements for ingredients A and C; moreover, a slack value of zero for constraint 4 shows that the optimal solution provides a total daily feed weight of 6 pounds.

The dual price (after rounding) for the ingredient A constraint (constraint 1) is -1.22. To interpret this value properly, we first look at the sign; it is negative, and therefore we know that increasing the right-hand side of constraint 1 will cause the solution value to worsen. In a minimization problem, "worsen" means that the total daily cost will increase,

FIGURE 3.10 THE MANAGEMENT SCIENTIST SOLUTION FOR THE BLUEGRASS FARMS PROBLEM

EXCEL file
Bluegrass

```
Objective Function Value =                    5.973

      Variable             Value            Reduced Costs
    --------------    ---------------    -----------------
            S                3.514                0.000
            E                0.946                0.000
            A                1.541                0.000

     Constraint          Slack/Surplus        Dual Prices
    --------------    ---------------    -----------------
            1                0.000               -1.216
            2                3.554                0.000
            3                0.000               -1.959
            4                0.000                0.919

OBJECTIVE COEFFICIENT RANGES

  Variable       Lower Limit       Current Value      Upper Limit
 ------------  ---------------  ---------------  ---------------
       S              -0.393            0.250     No Upper Limit
       E        No Lower Limit          0.500              0.925
       A               1.522            3.000     No Upper Limit

RIGHT HAND SIDE RANGES

 Constraint      Lower Limit       Current Value      Upper Limit
 ------------  ---------------  ---------------  ---------------
       1               1.143            3.000              3.368
       2        No Lower Limit          6.000              9.554
       3               2.100            4.000              4.875
       4               5.562            6.000              8.478
```

and therefore, a one-unit increase in the right-hand side of constraint 1 will increase the total cost of the daily diet by \$1.22. Conversely, it is also correct to conclude that a decrease of one unit in the right-hand side will decrease the total cost by \$1.22. Looking at the RIGHT HAND SIDE RANGES section of the computer output, we see that these interpretations are correct as long as the right-hand side is between 1.143 and 3.368.

Suppose that the Bluegrass management is willing to reconsider their position regarding the maximum weight of the daily diet. The dual price of 0.92 (after rounding) for constraint 4 shows that a one-unit increase in the right-hand side of constraint 4 will reduce total cost by \$0.92. The RIGHT HAND SIDE RANGES section of the output shows that this interpretation is correct for increases in the right-hand side up to a maximum of 8.478 pounds. Thus, the effect of increasing the right-hand side of constraint 4 from 6 to 8 pounds is a decrease in the total daily cost of $2 \times \$0.92$ or \$1.84. Keep in mind that if this change were made, the feasible region would change, and we would obtain a new optimal solution.

The OBJECTIVE COEFFICIENT RANGES section of the computer output shows a lower limit of -0.393 for S. Clearly, in a real problem, the objective function coefficient of

S (the cost of the standard horse feed product) cannot take on a negative value. So, from a practical point of view, we can think of the lower limit for the objective function coefficient of S as being zero. We can thus conclude that no matter how much the cost of the standard mix were to decrease, the optimal solution would not change. Even if Bluegrass Farms could obtain the standard horse feed product for free, the optimal solution would still specify a daily diet of 3.51 pounds of the standard horse feed product, 0.95 pound of the enriched oat product, and 1.54 pounds of the vitamin and mineral feed additive. However, any decrease in the per-unit cost of the standard feed would result in a decrease in the total cost for the optimal daily diet.

Note that the objective function coefficient values for S and A have no upper limit. Even if the cost of A were to increase, for example, from \$3.00 to \$13.00 per pound, the optimal solution would not change; the total cost of the solution, however, would increase by \$10 (the amount of the increase) times 1.541 or \$15.41. You must always keep in mind that the interpretations we have made using the sensitivity analysis information in the computer output are only appropriate if all other coefficients in the problem do not change. To consider simultaneous changes we must use the 100 percent rule or re-solve the problem after making the changes.

Linear programming has been successfully applied to a variety of applications involving food products and information. The Management Science in Action, Estimation of Food Nutrient Values, discusses how the Nutrition Coordinating Center of the University of Minnesota uses linear programming to help estimate the nutrient amounts in new food products.

MANAGEMENT SCIENCE IN ACTION

ESTIMATION OF FOOD NUTRIENT VALUES*

The Nutrition Coordinating Center (NCC) of the University of Minnesota maintains a food-composition database that is used by nutritionists and researchers throughout the world. Nutrient information provided by NCC is used to estimate the nutrient intake of individuals, to plan menus, to research links between diet and disease, and to meet regulatory requirements.

Nutrient intake calculations require data on an enormous number of food nutrient values. NCC's food composition database contains information on 93 different nutrients for each food product. With many new brand-name products introduced each year, NCC has the significant task of maintaining an accurate and timely database. The task is made more difficult by the fact that new brand-name products only provide data on a relatively small number of nutrients. Because of the high cost of chemically analyzing the new products, NCC uses a linear programming model to help estimate thousands of nutrient values per year.

The decision variables in the linear programming model are the amounts of each ingredient in a food product. The objective is to minimize the differences between the estimated nutrient values and the known nutrient values for the food product. Constraints are that ingredients must be in descending order by weight, ingredients must be within nutritionist-specified bounds, and the differences between the calculated nutrient values and the known nutrient values must be within specified tolerances.

In practice, an NCC nutritionist employs the linear programming model to derive estimates of the amounts of each ingredient in a new food product. Given these estimates, the nutritionist refines the estimates based on his or her knowledge of the product formulation and the food composition. Once the amounts of each ingredient are obtained, the amounts of each nutrient in the food product can be calculated. With approximately 1000 products evaluated each year, the time and cost savings provided by using linear programming to help estimate the nutrient values are significant.

*Based on Brian J. Westrich, Michael A. Altmann, and Sandra J. Potthoff, "Minnesota's Nutrition Coordinating Center Uses Mathematical Optimization to Estimate Food Nutrient Values," *Interfaces* (September/October 1998): 86–99.

3.5 THE ELECTRONIC COMMUNICATIONS PROBLEM

The Electronic Communications problem introduced in this section is a maximization problem involving four decision variables, two less-than-or-equal-to constraints, one equality constraint, and one greater-than-or-equal-to constraint. Our objective is to provide a summary of the process of formulating a mathematical model, using The Management Scientist to obtain an optimal solution, and interpreting the solution and sensitivity report information. In the next chapter we will continue to illustrate how linear programming can be applied by showing additional examples from the areas of marketing, finance, and production management. Your ability to formulate, solve, and interpret the solution to problems like the Electronic Communications problem is critical to understanding how more complex problems can be modeled using linear programming.

Electronic Communications manufactures portable radio systems that can be used for two-way communications. The company's new product, which has a range of up to 25 miles, is particularly suitable for use in a variety of business and personal applications. The distribution channels for the new radio are as follows:

1. Marine equipment distributors
2. Business equipment distributors
3. National chain of retail stores
4. Direct mail

Because of differing distribution and promotional costs, the profitability of the product will vary with the distribution channel. In addition, the advertising cost and the personal sales effort required will vary with the distribution channels. Table 3.2 summarizes the contribution to profit, advertising cost, and personal sales effort data pertaining to the Electronic Communications problem. The firm set the advertising budget at $5000, and a maximum of 1800 hours of salesforce time is available for allocation to the sales effort. Management also decided to produce exactly 600 units for the current production period. Finally, an ongoing contract with the national chain of retail stores requires that at least 150 units be distributed through this distribution channel.

Electronic Communications is now faced with the problem of establishing a strategy that will provide for the distribution of the radios in such a way that overall profitability of the new radio production will be maximized. Decisions must be made as to how many units should be allocated to each of the four distribution channels, as well as how to allocate the advertising budget and salesforce effort to each of the four distribution channels.

TABLE 3.2 PROFIT, ADVERTISING COST, AND PERSONAL SALES TIME DATA FOR THE ELECTRONIC COMMUNICATIONS PROBLEM

Distribution Channel	Profit per Unit Sold ($)	Advertising Cost per Unit Sold ($)	Personal Sales Effort per Unit Sold (hours)
Marine distributors	90	10	2
Business distributors	84	8	3
National retail stores	70	9	3
Direct mail	60	15	None

Problem Formulation

We will now write the objective function and the constraints for the Electronic Communications problem. For the objective function, we can write

Objective function: Maximize profit

Four constraints appear necessary for this problem. They are necessary because of (1) a limited advertising budget, (2) limited salesforce availability, (3) a production requirement, and (4) a retail stores distribution requirement.

Constraint 1 Advertising expenditures $\leq$ Budget

Constraint 2 Sales time used $\leq$ Time available

Constraint 3 Radios produced $=$ Management requirement

Constraint 4 Retail distribution $\geq$ Contract requirement

These expressions provide descriptions of the objective function and the constraints. We are now ready to define the decision variables that will represent the decisions the manager must make.

For the Electronic Communications problem, we introduce the following four decision variables:

M = the number of units produced for the marine equipment distribution channel

B = the number of units produced for the business equipment distribution channel

R = the number of units produced for the national retail chain distribution channel

D = the number of units produced for the direct mail distribution channel

Using the data in Table 3.2, the objective function for maximizing the total contribution to profit associated with the radios can be written as follows:

$$\text{Max } 90M + 84B + 70R + 60D$$

Let us now develop a mathematical statement of the constraints for the problem. Because the advertising budget is set at \$5000, the constraint that limits the amount of advertising expenditure can be written as follows:

$$10M + 8B + 9R + 15D \leq 5000$$

Similarly, because the sales time is limited to 1800 hours, we obtain the constraint

$$2M + 3B + 3R \leq 1800$$

Management's decision to produce exactly 600 units during the current production period is expressed as

$$M + B + R + D = 600$$

Finally, to account for the fact that the number of units distributed by the national chain of retail stores must be at least 150, we add the constraint

$$R \geq 150$$

Combining all of the constraints with the nonnegativity requirements enables us to write the complete linear programming model for the Electronic Communications problem as follows:

$$
\begin{aligned}
\text{Max} \quad & 90M + 84B + 70R + 60D \\
\text{s.t.} \quad & \\
& 10M + 8B + 9R + 15D \leq 5000 \quad \text{Advertising budget} \\
& 2M + 3B + 3R \leq 1800 \quad \text{Salesforce availability} \\
& M + B + R + D = 600 \quad \text{Production level} \\
& R \geq 150 \quad \text{Retail stores requirement} \\
& M, B, R, D \geq 0
\end{aligned}
$$

Computer Solution and Interpretation

A portion of the output obtained using The Management Scientist to solve the Electronic Communications problem is shown in Figure 3.11. The Objective Function Value section shows that the optimal solution to the problem will provide a maximum profit of $48,450. The optimal values of the decision variables are given by $M = 25$, $B = 425$, $R = 150$, and $D = 0$. Thus, the optimal strategy for Electronic Communications is to concentrate on the business equipment distribution channel with $B = 425$ units. In addition, the firm should allocate 25 units to the marine distribution channel ($M = 25$) and meet its 150-unit commitment to the national retail chain store distribution channel ($R = 150$). With $D = 0$, the optimal solution indicates that the firm should not use the direct mail distribution channel.

Now consider the information contained in the Reduced Costs column. Recall that the reduced costs indicate how much each objective function coefficient would have to improve before the corresponding decision variable could assume a positive value in the optimal solution. As the computer output shows, the first three reduced costs are zero because the corresponding decision variables already have positive values in the optimal solution. However, the reduced cost of 45 for decision variable D tells us that the profit for the new radios distributed via the direct mail channel would have to increase from its current value of $60 per unit to at least $60 + $45 = $105 per unit before it would be profitable to use the direct mail distribution channel.

FIGURE 3.11 A PORTION OF THE MANAGEMENT SCIENTIST COMPUTER OUTPUT FOR THE ELECTRONIC COMMUNICATIONS PROBLEM

EXCELfile
Electronic

```
Objective Function Value =          48450.000

      Variable              Value              Reduced Costs
   --------------      ---------------      -----------------
         M                    25.000                  0.000
         B                   425.000                  0.000
         R                   150.000                  0.000
         D                     0.000                 45.000

     Constraint          Slack/Surplus          Dual Prices
   --------------      ---------------      -----------------
          1                    0.000                  3.000
          2                   25.000                  0.000
          3                    0.000                 60.000
          4                    0.000                -17.000
```

The computer output information for the slack/surplus variables and the dual prices is restated here:

Constraint Number	Constraint Name	Type of Constraint	Slack or Surplus	Dual Price
1	Advertising budget	$\leq$	0	3
2	Salesforce availability	$\leq$	25	0
3	Production level	$=$	0	60
4	Retail stores requirement	$\geq$	0	−17

The advertising budget constraint has a slack of zero, indicating that the entire budget of $5000 has been used. The corresponding dual price of 3 tells us that an additional dollar added to the advertising budget will improve the objective function (increase the profit) by $3. Thus, the possibility of increasing the advertising budget should be seriously considered by the firm. The slack of 25 hours for the salesforce availability constraint shows that the allocated 1800 hours of sales time are adequate to distribute the radios produced and that 25 hours of sales time will remain unused. Because the production level constraint is an equality constraint, the zero slack/surplus shown on the output is expected. However, the dual price of 60 associated with this constraint shows that if the firm were to consider increasing the production level for the radios, the value of the objective function, or profit, would improve at the rate of $60 per radio produced. Finally, the surplus of zero associated with the retail store distribution channel commitment is a result of this constraint being binding. The negative dual price indicates that increasing the commitment from 150 to 151 units will actually decrease the profit by $17. Thus, Electronic Communications may want to consider reducing its commitment to the retail store distribution channel. A *decrease* in the commitment will actually improve profit at the rate of $17 per unit.

We now consider the additional sensitivity analysis information provided by the computer output shown in Figure 3.12. The ranges of optimality for the objective function coefficients are

$$84 \leq C_M < \text{No upper limit}$$
$$50 \leq C_B \leq 90$$
$$\text{No lower limit} < C_R \leq 87$$
$$\text{No lower limit} < C_D \leq 105$$

The current solution or strategy remains optimal, provided that the objective function coefficients remain in the given ranges of optimality. Note in particular the range of optimality associated with the direct mail distribution channel coefficient, C_D. This information is consistent with the earlier observation for the Reduced Costs portion of the output. In both instances, we see that the per-unit profit would have to increase to $105 before the direct mail distribution channel could be in the optimal solution with a positive value.

Finally, the sensitivity analysis information on RIGHT HAND SIDE RANGES, as shown in Figure 3.12, provides the ranges of feasibility for the right-hand-side values.

Constraint	Min RHS	Current Value	Max RHS
Advertising budget	4950	5000	5850
Salesforce availability	1775	1800	No upper limit
Production level	515	600	603.57
Retail stores requirement	0	150	200

FIGURE 3.12 OBJECTIVE COEFFICIENT AND RIGHT-HAND-SIDE RANGES PROVIDED BY THE MANAGEMENT SCIENTIST FOR THE ELECTRONIC COMMUNICATIONS PROBLEM

OBJECTIVE COEFFICIENT RANGES

Variable	Lower Limit	Current Value	Upper Limit
M	84.000	90.000	No Upper Limit
B	50.000	84.000	90.000
R	No Lower Limit	70.000	87.000
D	No Lower Limit	60.000	105.000

RIGHT HAND SIDE RANGES

Constraint	Lower Limit	Current Value	Upper Limit
1	4950.000	5000.000	5850.000
2	1775.000	1800.000	No Upper Limit
3	515.000	600.000	603.571
4	0.000	150.000	200.000

Try Problems 12 and 13 to test your ability at interpreting the computer output for problems involving more than two decision variables.

Several interpretations of these ranges are possible. In particular, recall that the dual price for the advertising budget enabled us to conclude that each \$1 increase in the budget would improve the profit by \$3. The range for the advertising budget shows that this statement about the value of increasing the budget is appropriate up to an advertising budget of \$5850. Increases above this level would not necessarily be beneficial. Also note that the dual price of -17 for the retail stores requirement suggested the desirability of reducing this commitment. The range of feasibility for this constraint shows that the commitment could be reduced to zero and the value of the reduction would be at the rate of \$17 per unit.

Again, the *sensitivity analysis* or *postoptimality analysis* provided by computer software packages for linear programming problems considers only *one change at a time,* with all other coefficients of the problem remaining as originally specified. As mentioned earlier, simultaneous changes can sometimes be analyzed without resolving the problem, provided that the cumulative changes are not large enough to violate the 100 percent rule.

Finally, recall that the complete solution to the Electronic Communications problem requested information not only on the number of units to be distributed over each channel, but also on the allocation of the advertising budget and the salesforce effort to each distribution channel. For the optimal solution of $M = 25$, $B = 425$, $R = 150$, and $D = 0$, we can simply evaluate each term in a given constraint to determine how much of the constraint resource is allocated to each distribution channel. For example, the advertising budget constraint of

$$10M + 8B + 9R + 15D \leq 5000$$

shows that $10M = 10(25) = \$250$, $8B = 8(425) = \$3400$, $9R = 9(150) = \$1350$, and $15D = 15(0) = \$0$. Thus, the advertising budget allocations are, respectively, \$250, \$3400, \$1350, and \$0 for each of the four distribution channels. Making similar calculations for the salesforce constraint results in the managerial summary of the Electronic Communications optimal solution as shown in Table 3.3.

TABLE 3.3 PROFIT-MAXIMIZING STRATEGY FOR THE ELECTRONIC COMMUNICATIONS PROBLEM

Distribution Channel	Volume	Advertising Allocation	Salesforce Allocation (hours)
Marine distributors	25	$ 250	50
Business distributors	425	3400	1275
National retail stores	150	1350	450
Direct mail	0	0	0
Totals	600	$5000	1775
Projected total profit = $48,450			

SUMMARY

We began the chapter with a discussion of sensitivity analysis: the study of how changes in the coefficients of a linear program affect the optimal solution. First, we showed how a graphical method can be used to determine how a change in one of the objective function coefficients or a change in the right-hand-side value for a constraint will affect the optimal solution to the problem. Because graphical sensitivity analysis is limited to linear programs with two decision variables, we showed how The Management Scientist can be used to produce a sensitivity report containing the same information.

We continued our discussion of problem formulation, sensitivity analysis, and the interpretation of the solution by introducing several modifications of the Par, Inc., problem. They involved an additional decision variable and several types of percentage, or ratio, constraints. Then, in order to provide additional practice in formulating and interpreting the solution for linear programs involving more than two decision variables, we introduced the Bluegrass Farms problem, a minimization problem involving three decision variables. In the last section we summarized all the work to date using the Electronic Communications problem, a maximization problem with four decision variables, two less-than-or-equal-to constraints, one equality constraint, and one greater-than-or-equal-to constraint.

The Management Science in Action, Tea Production and Distribution in India, illustrates the diversity of problems in which linear programming can be applied and the importance of sensitivity analysis. In the next chapter we will see many more applications of linear programming.

MANAGEMENT SCIENCE IN ACTION

TEA PRODUCTION AND DISTRIBUTION IN INDIA*

In India, one of the largest tea producers in the world, approximately $1 billion of tea packets and loose tea are sold. Duncan Industries Limited (DIL), the third largest producer of tea in the Indian tea market, sells about $37.5 million of tea, almost all of which is sold in packets.

DIL has 16 tea gardens, three blending units, six packing units, and 22 depots. Tea from the gardens is sent to blending units, which then mix various grades of tea to produce blends such as Sargam, Double Diamond, and Runglee Rungliot. The blended tea is transported to packing units, where it is placed in packets of different sizes and shapes to produce about 120 different product lines. For example, one line is Sargam tea packed in 500-gram cartons, another line is Double Diamond packed in 100-gram pouches, and so on. The tea is then shipped to the depots that supply 11,500 distributors through whom the needs of approximately 325,000 retailers are satisfied.

For the coming month, sales managers provide estimates of the demand for each line of tea at each depot. Using these estimates, a team of senior managers would determine the amounts of loose tea of each blend to ship to each packing unit, the quantity of each line of tea to be packed at each packing unit, and the amounts of packed tea of each line to be transported from each packing unit to the various depots. This process requires two to three days each month and often results in stockouts of lines in demand at specific depots.

Consequently, a linear programming model involving approximately 7000 decision variables and 1500 constraints was developed to minimize the company's freight cost while satisfying demand, supply, and all operational constraints. The model was tested on past data and showed that stockouts could be prevented at little or no additional cost. Moreover, the model was able to provide management with the ability to perform various what-if types of exercises, convincing them of the potential benefits of using management science techniques to support the decision-making process.

*Based on Nilotpal Chakravarti, "Tea Company Steeped in OR," *OR/MS Today* (April 2000).

GLOSSARY

Sensitivity analysis The study of how changes in the coefficients of a linear programming problem affect the optimal solution.

Range of optimality The range of values over which an objective function coefficient may vary without causing any change in the values of the decision variables in the optimal solution.

Dual price The improvement in the value of the objective function per unit increase in the right-hand side of a constraint.

Reduced cost The amount by which an objective function coefficient would have to improve (increase for a maximization problem, decrease for a minimization problem) before it would be possible for the corresponding variable to assume a positive value in the optimal solution.

Range of feasibility The range of values over which the dual price is applicable.

100 percent rule A rule indicating when simultaneous changes in two or more objective function coefficients will not cause a change in the optimal solution. It can also be applied to indicate when two or more right-hand-side changes will not cause a change in any of the dual prices.

Sunk cost A cost that is not affected by the decision made. It will be incurred no matter what values the decision variables assume.

Relevant cost A cost that depends upon the decision made. The amount of a relevant cost will vary depending on the values of the decision variables.

PROBLEMS

1. Consider the following linear program:

$$\begin{aligned} \text{Max} \quad & 3A + 2B \\ \text{s.t.} \quad & \\ & 1A + 1B \leq 10 \\ & 3A + 1B \leq 24 \\ & 1A + 2B \leq 16 \\ & A, B \geq 0 \end{aligned}$$

a. Use the graphical solution procedure to find the optimal solution.
b. Assume that the objective function coefficient for A changes from 3 to 5. Does the optimal solution change? Use the graphical solution procedure to find the new optimal solution.
c. Assume that the objective function coefficient for A remains 3, but the objective function coefficient for B changes from 2 to 4. Does the optimal solution change? Use the graphical solution procedure to find the new optimal solution.
d. The Management Scientist computer solution for the linear program in part (a) provides the following objective coefficient range information:

Variable	Lower Limit	Current Value	Upper Limit
A	2	3	6
B	1	2	3

Use this objective coefficient range information to answer parts (b) and (c).

2. Consider the linear program in Problem 1. The value of the optimal solution is 27. Suppose that the right-hand side for constraint 1 is increased from 10 to 11.
a. Use the graphical solution procedure to find the new optimal solution.
b. Use the solution to part (a) to determine the dual price for constraint 1.
c. The Management Scientist computer solution for the linear program in Problem 1 provides the following right-hand-side range information:

Constraint	Lower Limit	Current Value	Upper Limit
1	8	10	11.2
2	18	24	30
3	13	16	No Upper Limit

What does the right-hand-side range information for constraint 1 tell you about the dual price for constraint 1?
d. The dual price for constraint 2 is 0.5. Using this dual price and the right-hand-side range information in part (c), what conclusion can be drawn about the effect of changes to the right-hand side of constraint 2?

3. Consider the following linear program:

$$
\begin{aligned}
\text{Min}\quad & 8X + 12Y \\
\text{s.t.}\quad & \\
& 1X + 3Y \geq 9 \\
& 2X + 2Y \geq 10 \\
& 6X + 2Y \geq 18 \\
& X, Y \geq 0
\end{aligned}
$$

a. Use the graphical solution procedure to find the optimal solution.
b. Assume that the objective function coefficient for X changes from 8 to 6. Does the optimal solution change? Use the graphical solution procedure to find the new optimal solution.

c. Assume that the objective function coefficient for X remains 8, but the objective function coefficient for Y changes from 12 to 6. Does the optimal solution change? Use the graphical solution procedure to find the new optimal solution.
d. The Management Scientist computer solution for the linear program in part (a) provides the following objective coefficient range information:

Variable	Lower Limit	Current Value	Upper Limit
X	4	8	12
Y	8	12	24

How would this objective coefficient range information help you answer parts (b) and (c) prior to resolving the problem?

4. Consider the linear program in Problem 3. The value of the optimal solution is 48. Suppose that the right-hand side for constraint 1 is increased from 9 to 10.
   a. Use the graphical solution procedure to find the new optimal solution.
   b. Use the solution to part (a) to determine the dual price for constraint 1.
   c. The Management Scientist computer solution for the linear program in Problem 3 provides the following right-hand-side range information:

Constraint	Lower Limit	Current Value	Upper Limit
1	5	9	11
2	9	10	18
3	No Lower Limit	18	22

What does the right-hand-side range information for constraint 1 tell you about the dual price for constraint 1?
   d. The dual price for constraint 2 is -3. Using this dual price and the right-hand-side range information in part (c), what conclusion can be drawn about the effect of changes to the right-hand side of constraint 2?

5. Refer to the Kelson Sporting Equipment problem (Chapter 2, Problem 24). Letting

$$R = \text{number of regular gloves}$$
$$C = \text{number of catcher's mitts}$$

leads to the following formulation:

$$\begin{aligned} \text{Max} \quad & 5R + 8C \\ \text{s.t.} \quad & \\ & R + \tfrac{3}{2}C \le 900 \quad \text{Cutting and sewing} \\ & \tfrac{1}{2}R + \tfrac{1}{3}C \le 300 \quad \text{Finishing} \\ & \tfrac{1}{8}R + \tfrac{1}{4}C \le 100 \quad \text{Packaging and shipping} \\ & R, C \ge 0 \end{aligned}$$

The computer solution obtained using The Management Scientist is shown in Figure 3.13.
   a. What is the optimal solution, and what is the value of the total profit contribution?
   b. Which constraints are binding?

FIGURE 3.13 THE MANAGEMENT SCIENTIST SOLUTION FOR THE KELSON SPORTING EQUIPMENT PROBLEM

```
Objective Function Value =        3700.00146

      Variable              Value              Reduced Costs
    --------------     ---------------     -----------------
           R               500.00153                0.00000
           C               149.99924                0.00000

     Constraint         Slack/Surplus          Dual Prices
    --------------     ---------------     -----------------
           1               174.99962                0.00000
           2                 0.00000                2.99999
           3                 0.00000               28.00006

OBJECTIVE COEFFICIENT RANGES

  Variable      Lower Limit        Current Value     Upper Limit
 ------------  ---------------   ---------------   ---------------
      R                4.00000           5.00000          12.00012
      C                3.33330           8.00000          10.00000

RIGHT HAND SIDE RANGES

 Constraint     Lower Limit        Current Value     Upper Limit
 ------------  ---------------   ---------------   ---------------
      1              725.00037         900.00000   No Upper Limit
      2              133.33199         300.00000         400.00000
      3               75.00000         100.00000         134.99982
```

c. What are the dual prices for the resources? Interpret each.
d. If overtime can be scheduled in one of the departments, where would you recommend doing so?

6. Refer to the computer solution of the Kelson Sporting Equipment problem in Figure 3.13 (see Problem 5).
   a. Determine the objective coefficient ranges.
   b. Interpret the ranges in part (a).
   c. Interpret the right-hand-side ranges.
   d. How much will the value of the optimal solution improve if 20 extra hours of packaging and shipping time are made available?

7. Investment Advisors, Inc., is a brokerage firm that manages stock portfolios for a number of clients. A particular portfolio consists of U shares of U.S. Oil and H shares of Huber Steel. The annual return for U.S. Oil is \$3 per share and the annual return for Huber Steel is \$5 per share. U.S. Oil sells for \$25 per share and Huber Steel sells for \$50 per share. The portfolio has \$80,000 to be invested. The portfolio risk index (0.50 per share of U.S. Oil and 0.25 per share for Huber Steel) has a maximum of 700. In addition, the portfolio is

limited to a maximum of 1000 shares of U.S. Oil. The linear programming formation that will maximize the total annual return of the portfolio is as follows:

$$
\begin{array}{llll}
\text{Max} & 3U + 5H & & \text{Maximize total annual return} \\
\text{s.t.} & & & \\
& 25U + 50H \leq & 80{,}000 & \text{Funds available} \\
& 0.50U + 0.25H \leq & 700 & \text{Risk maximum} \\
& 1U \leq & 1000 & \text{U.S. Oil maximum} \\
& U, H \geq 0 & &
\end{array}
$$

The computer solution of this problem is shown in Figure 3.14.

a. What is the optimal solution, and what is the value of the total annual return?
b. Which constraints are binding? What is your interpretation of these constraints in terms of the problem?
c. What are the dual prices for the constraints? Interpret each.
d. Would it be beneficial to increase the maximum amount invested in U.S. Oil? Why or why not?

FIGURE 3.14 THE MANAGEMENT SCIENTIST SOLUTION FOR THE INVESTMENT ADVISORS PROBLEM

```
Objective Function Value =                8400.000

      Variable                Value              Reduced Costs
   --------------        ---------------       ------------------
          U                     800.000                   0.000
          H                    1200.000                   0.000

     Constraint            Slack/Surplus            Dual Prices
   --------------        ---------------       ------------------
          1                       0.000                   0.093
          2                       0.000                   1.333
          3                     200.000                   0.000

OBJECTIVE COEFFICIENT RANGES

  Variable        Lower Limit        Current Value        Upper Limit
 ------------   ---------------    ---------------    ---------------
      U                 2.500              3.000             10.000
      H                 1.500              5.000              6.000

RIGHT HAND SIDE RANGES

  Constraint       Lower Limit        Current Value        Upper Limit
 ------------   ---------------    ---------------    ---------------
      1             65000.000          80000.000         140000.000
      2               400.000            700.000            775.000
      3               800.000           1000.000     No Upper Limit
```

8. Refer to Figure 3.14, which shows the computer solution of Problem 7.
   a. How much would the return for U.S. Oil have to increase before it would be beneficial to increase the investment in this stock?
   b. How much would the return for Huber Steel have to decrease before it would be beneficial to reduce the investment in this stock?
   c. How much would the total annual return be reduced if the U.S. Oil maximum were reduced to 900 shares?
9. Recall the Tom's, Inc., problem (Chapter 2, Problem 28). Letting

$$W = \text{jars of Western Foods Salsa}$$
$$M = \text{jars of Mexico City Salsa}$$

leads to the formulation:

$$\begin{array}{lrcll} \text{Max} & 1W + 1.25M & & & \\ \text{s.t.} & & & & \\ & 5W + 7M & \leq & 4480 & \text{Whole tomatoes} \\ & 3W + 1M & \leq & 2080 & \text{Tomato sauce} \\ & 2W + 2M & \leq & 1600 & \text{Tomato paste} \\ & W, M & \geq & 0 & \end{array}$$

The Management Scientist solution is shown in Figure 3.15.
   a. What is the optimal solution, and what are the optimal production quantities?
   b. Specify the objective function ranges.
   c. What are the dual prices for each constraint? Interpret each.
   d. Identify each of the right-hand-side ranges.

10. Recall the Innis Investments problem (Chapter 2, Problem 39). Letting

$$S = \text{units purchased in the stock fund}$$
$$M = \text{units purchased in the money market fund}$$

leads to the following formulation:

$$\begin{array}{lrcll} \text{Min} & 8S + 3M & & & \\ \text{s.t.} & & & & \\ & 50S + 100M & \leq & 1{,}200{,}000 & \text{Funds available} \\ & 5S + 4M & \geq & 60{,}000 & \text{Annual income} \\ & M & \geq & 3{,}000 & \text{Units in money market} \\ & S, M & \geq & 0 & \end{array}$$

The computer solution is shown in Figure 3.16.
   a. What is the optimal solution, and what is the minimum total risk?
   b. Specify the objective coefficient ranges.
   c. How much annual income will be earned by the portfolio?
   d. What is the rate of return for the portfolio?
   e. What is the dual price for the funds available constraint?
   f. What is the marginal rate of return on extra funds added to the portfolio?
11. Refer to Problem 10 and the computer solution shown in Figure 3.16.
   a. Suppose the risk index for the stock fund (the value of C_S) increases from its current value of 8 to 12. How does the optimal solution change, if at all?

FIGURE 3.15 THE MANAGEMENT SCIENTIST SOLUTION FOR THE TOM'S, INC., PROBLEM

```
OPTIMAL SOLUTION

Objective Function Value =                 860.000

     Variable              Value              Reduced Costs
   --------------     ---------------      -----------------
          W                 560.000                   0.000
          M                 240.000                   0.000

    Constraint           Slack/Surplus          Dual Prices
   --------------     ---------------      -----------------
          1                   0.000                   0.125
          2                 160.000                   0.000
          3                   0.000                   0.187

OBJECTIVE COEFFICIENT RANGES

  Variable      Lower Limit       Current Value     Upper Limit
 ------------  ---------------   ---------------   ---------------
     M                0.893             1.000            1.250
     W                1.000             1.250            1.400

RIGHT HAND SIDE RANGES

  Constraint    Lower Limit       Current Value     Upper Limit
 ------------  ---------------   ---------------   ---------------
     1             4320.000          4480.000         5600.000
     2             1920.000          2080.000   No Upper Limit
     3             1280.000          1600.000         1640.000
```

b. Suppose the risk index for the money market fund (the value of C_M) increases from its current value of 3 to 3.5. How does the optimal solution change, if at all?

c. Suppose C_S increases to 12 and C_M increases to 3.5. How does the optimal solution change, if at all?

12. Quality Air Conditioning manufactures three home air conditioners: an economy model, a standard model, and a deluxe model. The profits per unit are $63, $95, and $135, respectively. The production requirements per unit are as follows:

	Number of Fans	Number of Cooling Coils	Manufacturing Time (hours)
Economy	1	1	8
Standard	1	2	12
Deluxe	1	4	14

FIGURE 3.16 THE MANAGEMENT SCIENTIST SOLUTION FOR THE INNIS INVESTMENTS PROBLEM

```
Objective Function Value =              62000.000

      Variable               Value              Reduced Costs
    --------------      ---------------      -----------------
          S                  4000.000                   0.000
          M                 10000.000                   0.000

     Constraint          Slack/Surplus          Dual Prices
    --------------      ---------------      -----------------
          1                     0.000                   0.057
          2                     0.000                  -2.167
          3                  7000.000                   0.000

OBJECTIVE COEFFICIENT RANGES

  Variable       Lower Limit        Current Value      Upper Limit
 ------------  ---------------    ---------------    ---------------
      S                  3.750              8.000     No Upper Limit
      M         No Lower Limit              3.000              6.400

RIGHT HAND SIDE RANGES

 Constraint       Lower Limit        Current Value      Upper Limit
 ------------  ---------------    ---------------    ---------------
      1             780000.000        1200000.000        1500000.000
      2              48000.000          60000.000         102000.000
      3         No Lower Limit           3000.000          10000.000
```

For the coming production period, the company has 200 fan motors, 320 cooling coils, and 2400 hours of manufacturing time available. How many economy models (E), standard models (S), and deluxe models (D) should the company produce in order to maximize profit? The linear programming model for the problem is as follows.

$$
\begin{aligned}
\text{Max} \quad & 63E + 95S + 135D \\
\text{s.t.} \quad & \\
& 1E + 1S + 1D \leq 200 \quad \text{Fan motors} \\
& 1E + 2S + 4D \leq 320 \quad \text{Cooling coils} \\
& 8E + 12S + 14D \leq 2400 \quad \text{Manufacturing time} \\
& E, S, D \geq 0
\end{aligned}
$$

The computer solution using The Management Scientist is shown in Figure 3.17.

a. What is the optimal solution, and what is the value of the objective function?
b. Which constraints are binding?
c. Which constraint shows extra capacity? How much?
d. If the profit for the deluxe model were increased to $150 per unit, would the optimal solution change? Use the information in Figure 3.17 to answer this question.

FIGURE 3.17 THE MANAGEMENT SCIENTIST SOLUTION FOR THE QUALITY AIR CONDITIONING PROBLEM

```
Objective Function Value =                 16440.000

     Variable              Value              Reduced Costs
   --------------     ---------------      -----------------
          E                  80.000                  0.000
          S                 120.000                  0.000
          D                   0.000                 24.000

     Constraint          Slack/Surplus          Dual Prices
   --------------     ---------------      -----------------
          1                   0.000                 31.000
          2                   0.000                 32.000
          3                 320.000                  0.000

OBJECTIVE COEFFICIENT RANGES

  Variable      Lower Limit      Current Value     Upper Limit
 ------------  ---------------  ---------------  ---------------
      E                47.500           63.000           75.000
      S                87.000           95.000          126.000
      D        No Lower Limit          135.000          159.000

RIGHT HAND SIDE RANGES

  Constraint     Lower Limit      Current Value     Upper Limit
 ------------  ---------------  ---------------  ---------------
      1               160.000          200.000          280.000
      2               200.000          320.000          400.000
      3              2080.000         2400.000   No Upper Limit
```

13. Refer to the computer solution of Problem 12 in Figure 3.17.
    a. Identify the range of optimality for each objective function coefficient.
    b. Suppose the profit for the economy model is increased by $6 per unit, the profit for the standard model is decreased by $2 per unit, and the profit for the deluxe model is increased by $4 per unit. What will the new optimal solution be?
    c. Identify the range of feasibility for the right-hand-side values.
    d. If the number of fan motors available for production is increased by 100, will the dual price for that constraint change? Explain.

14. Digital Controls, Inc. (DCI), manufactures two models of a radar gun used by police to monitor the speed of automobiles. Model A has an accuracy of plus or minus 1 mile per hour, whereas the smaller model B has an accuracy of plus or minus 3 miles per hour. For the next week, the company has orders for 100 units of model A and 150 units of model B. Although DCI purchases all the electronic components used in both models, the plastic cases for both models are manufactured at a DCI plant in Newark, New Jersey. Each model A case requires 4 minutes of injection-molding time and 6 minutes of assembly time.

Each model B case requires 3 minutes of injection-molding time and 8 minutes of assembly time. For next week, the Newark plant has 600 minutes of injection-molding time available and 1080 minutes of assembly time available. The manufacturing cost is \$10 per case for model A and \$6 per case for model B. Depending upon demand and the time available at the Newark plant, DCI occasionally purchases cases for one or both models from an outside supplier in order to fill customer orders that could not be filled otherwise. The purchase cost is \$14 for each model A case and \$9 for each model B case. Management wants to develop a minimum cost plan that will determine how many cases of each model should be produced at the Newark plant and how many cases of each model should be purchased. The following decision variables were used to formulate a linear programming model for this problem:

$$\begin{aligned} AM &= \text{number of cases of model A manufactured} \\ BM &= \text{number of cases of model B manufactured} \\ AP &= \text{number of cases of model A purchased} \\ BP &= \text{number of cases of model B purchased} \end{aligned}$$

The linear programming model that can be used to solve this problem is as follows:

$$\begin{array}{lllll} \text{Min} & 10AM + 6BM + 14AP + 9BP & & & \\ \text{s.t.} & & & & \\ & 1AM + \quad\quad + 1AP + & = & 100 & \text{Demand for model A} \\ & \quad\quad 1BM + \quad\quad\quad 1BP & = & 150 & \text{Demand for model B} \\ & 4AM + 3BM & \leq & 600 & \text{Injection molding time} \\ & 6AM + 8BM & \leq & 1080 & \text{Assembly time} \\ & AM, BM, AP, BP \geq 0 & & & \end{array}$$

The computer solution developed using The Management Scientist is shown in Figure 3.18.

a. What is the optimal solution and what is the optimal value of the objective function?
b. Which constraints are binding?
c. What are the dual prices? Interpret each.
d. If you could change the right-hand side of one constraint by one unit, which one would you choose? Why?

15. Refer to the computer solution to Problem 14 in Figure 3.18.
    a. Interpret the ranges of optimality for the objective function coefficients.
    b. Suppose that the manufacturing cost increases to \$11.20 per case for model A. What is the new optimal solution?
    c. Suppose that the manufacturing cost increases to \$11.20 per case for model A and the manufacturing cost for model B decreases to \$5 per unit. Would the optimal solution change? Use the 100 percent rule and discuss.

16. Tucker Inc. produces high-quality suits and sport coats for men. Each suit requires 1.2 hours of cutting time and 0.7 hours of sewing time, uses 6 yards of material, and provides a profit contribution of \$190. Each sport coat requires 0.8 hours of cutting time and 0.6 hours of sewing time, uses 4 yards of material, and provides a profit contribution of \$150. For the coming week, 200 hours of cutting time, 180 hours of sewing time, and 1200 yards of fabric are available. Additional cutting and sewing time can be obtained by scheduling overtime for these operations. Each hour of overtime for the cutting operation increases the hourly cost by \$15, and each hour of overtime for the sewing operation increases the hourly cost

FIGURE 3.18 THE MANAGEMENT SCIENTIST SOLUTION FOR THE DIGITAL CONTROLS, INC., PROBLEM

```
Objective Function Value =                 2170.000

     Variable              Value             Reduced Costs
   --------------     ---------------     ------------------
        AM                100.000                  0.000
        BM                 60.000                  0.000
        AP                  0.000                  1.750
        BP                 90.000                  0.000

    Constraint         Slack/Surplus           Dual Prices
   --------------     ---------------     ------------------
         1                  0.000                -12.250
         2                  0.000                 -9.000
         3                 20.000                  0.000
         4                  0.000                  0.375

OBJECTIVE COEFFICIENT RANGES

  Variable        Lower Limit        Current Value      Upper Limit
 ------------   ---------------     ---------------   ---------------
     AM         No Lower Limit              10.000             11.750
     BM                  3.667               6.000              9.000
     AP                 12.250              14.000     No Upper Limit
     BP                  6.000               9.000             11.333

RIGHT HAND SIDE RANGES

 Constraint        Lower Limit        Current Value       Upper Limit
 ------------   ---------------     ---------------   ---------------
      1                  0.000             100.000            111.429
      2                 60.000             150.000     No Upper Limit
      3                580.000             600.000     No Upper Limit
      4                600.000            1080.000           1133.333
```

by \$10. A maximum of 100 hours of overtime can be scheduled. Marketing requirements specify a minimum production of 100 suits and 75 sport coats. Let

S = number of suits produced
SC = number of sport coats produced
$D1$ = hours of overtime for the cutting operation
$D2$ = hours of overtime for the sewing operation

The computer solution developed using The Management Scientist is shown in Figure 3.19.

a. What is the optimal solution, and what is the total profit? What is the plan for the use of overtime?

FIGURE 3.19 THE MANAGEMENT SCIENTIST SOLUTION FOR THE TUCKER INC. PROBLEM

```
Objective Function Value =          40900.000

      Variable              Value              Reduced Costs
   --------------     ---------------      ------------------
         S                  100.000                  0.000
         SC                 150.000                  0.000
         D1                  40.000                  0.000
         D2                   0.000                 10.000

     Constraint         Slack/Surplus           Dual Prices
   --------------     ---------------      ------------------
         1                    0.000                 15.000
         2                   20.000                  0.000
         3                    0.000                 34.500
         4                   60.000                  0.000
         5                    0.000                -35.000
         6                   75.000                  0.000

OBJECTIVE COEFFICIENT RANGES

  Variable        Lower Limit       Current Value       Upper Limit
------------   ---------------   ---------------   ---------------
      S         No Lower Limit           190.000           225.000
      SC               126.667           150.000    No Upper Limit
      D1              -187.500           -15.000             0.000
      D2        No Lower Limit           -10.000             0.000

RIGHT HAND SIDE RANGES

  Constraint      Lower Limit       Current Value       Upper Limit
------------   ---------------   ---------------   ---------------
      1                140.000           200.000           240.000
      2                160.000           180.000    No Upper Limit
      3               1000.000          1200.000          1333.333
      4                 40.000           100.000    No Upper Limit
      5                  0.000           100.000           150.000
      6         No Lower Limit            75.000           150.000
```

b. A price increase for suits is being considered that would result in a profit contribution of \$210 per suit. If this price increase is undertaken, how will the optimal solution change?

c. Discuss the need for additional material during the coming week. If a rush order for material can be placed at the usual price plus an extra \$8 per yard for handling, would you recommend the company consider placing a rush order for material? What is the maximum price Tucker would be willing to pay for an additional yard of material? How many additional yards of material should Tucker consider ordering?

d. Suppose the minimum production requirement for suits is lowered to 75. Would this change help or hurt profit? Explain.

17. The Porsche Club of America sponsors driver education events that provide high-performance driving instruction on actual race tracks. Because safety is a primary consid-

eration at such events, many owners elect to install roll bars in their cars. Deegan Industries manufactures two types of roll bars for Porsches. Model DRB is bolted to the car using existing holes in the car's frame. Model DRW is a heavier roll bar that must be welded to the car's frame. Model DRB requires 20 pounds of a special high alloy steel, 40 minutes of manufacturing time, and 60 minutes of assembly time. Model DRW requires 25 pounds of the special high alloy steel, 100 minutes of manufacturing time, and 40 minutes of assembly time. Deegan's steel supplier indicated that at most 40,000 pounds of the high alloy steel will be available next quarter. In addition, Deegan estimates that 2000 hours of manufacturing time and 1600 hours of assembly time will be available next quarter. The profit contributions are \$200 per unit for model DRB and \$280 per unit for model DRW. The linear programming model for this problem is as follows:

$$
\begin{aligned}
\text{Max} \quad & 200DRB + 280DRW \\
\text{s.t.} \quad & \\
& 20DRB + 25DRW \leq 40{,}000 \quad \text{Steel available} \\
& 40DRB + 100DRW \leq 120{,}000 \quad \text{Manufacturing minutes} \\
& 60DRB + 40DRW \leq 96{,}000 \quad \text{Assembly minutes} \\
& DRB, DRW \geq 0
\end{aligned}
$$

The Management Scientist solution is shown in Figure 3.20.

a. What are the optimal solution and the total profit contribution?
b. Another supplier offered to provide Deegan Industries with an additional 500 pounds of the steel alloy at \$2 per pound. Should Deegan purchase the additional pounds of the steel alloy? Explain.
c. Deegan is considering using overtime to increase the available assembly time. What would you advise Deegan to do regarding this option? Explain.
d. Because of increased competition, Deegan is considering reducing the price of model DRB such that the new contribution to profit is \$175 per unit. How would this change in price affect the optimal solution? Explain.
e. If the available manufacturing time is increased by 500 hours, will the dual price for the manufacturing time constraint change? Explain.

18. Davison Electronics manufactures two LCD television monitors, identified as model A and model B. Each model has its lowest possible production cost when produced on Davison's new production line. However, the new production line does not have the capacity to handle the total production of both models. As a result, at least some of the production must be routed to a higher-cost, old production line. The following table shows the minimum production requirements for next month, the production line capacities in units per month, and the production cost per unit for each production line.

Model	Production Cost per Unit		Minimum Production Requirements
	New Line	Old Line	
A	\$30	\$50	50,000
B	\$25	\$40	70,000
Production Line Capacity	80,000	60,000	

Let

AN = Units of model A produced on the new production line
AO = Units of model A produced on the old production line
BN = Units of model B produced on the new production line
BO = Units of model B produced on the old production line

FIGURE 3.20 THE MANAGEMENT SCIENTIST SOLUTION FOR THE DEEGAN INDUSTRIES PROBLEM

```
OPTIMAL SOLUTION

Objective Function Value =          424000.000

    Variable             Value            Reduced Costs
  --------------    ---------------    -----------------
      DRB               1000.000              0.000
      DRW                800.000              0.000

   Constraint        Slack/Surplus       Dual Prices
  --------------    ---------------    -----------------
       1                   0.000              8.800
       2                   0.000              0.600
       3                4000.000              0.000

OBJECTIVE COEFFICIENT RANGES

 Variable     Lower Limit       Current Value     Upper Limit
------------ ---------------   ---------------  ---------------
   DRB           112.000           200.000          224.000
   DRW           250.000           280.000          500.000

RIGHT HAND SIDE RANGES

 Constraint   Lower Limit       Current Value     Upper Limit
------------ ---------------   ---------------  ---------------
     1         30000.000         40000.000        40909.091
     2        114285.714        120000.000       160000.000
     3         92000.000         96000.000   No Upper Limit
```

Davison's objective is to determine the minimum cost production plan. The computer solution obtained using The Management Scientist is shown in Figure 3.21.

a. Formulate the linear programming model for this problem using the following four constraints:

Constraint 1: Minimum production for model A
Constraint 2: Minimum production for model B
Constraint 3: Capacity of the new production line
Constraint 4: Capacity of the old production line

b. Using The Management Scientist solution in Figure 3.21, what is the optimal solution, and what is the total production cost associated with this solution?
c. Which constraints are binding? Explain.
d. The production manager noted that the only constraint with a positive dual price is the constraint on the capacity of the new production line. The manager's interpretation of the dual price was that a one-unit increase in the right-hand side of this constraint would actually increase the total production cost by $15 per unit. Do you agree with this

FIGURE 3.21 THE MANAGEMENT SCIENTIST SOLUTION TO THE DAVISON ELECTRONICS PROBLEM

OPTIMAL SOLUTION

Objective Function Value = 3850000.000

Variable	Value	Reduced Costs
AN	50000.000	0.000
AO	0.000	5.000
BN	30000.000	0.000
BO	40000.000	0.000

Constraint	Slack/Surplus	Dual Prices
1	0.000	-45.000
2	0.000	-40.000
3	0.000	15.000
4	20000.000	0.000

OBJECTIVE COEFFICIENT RANGES

Variable	Lower Limit	Current Value	Upper Limit
AN	-15.000	30.000	35.000
AO	45.000	50.000	No Upper Limit
BN	20.000	25.000	40.000
BO	25.000	40.000	45.000

RIGHT HAND SIDE RANGES

Constraint	Lower Limit	Current Value	Upper Limit
1	10000.000	50000.000	70000.000
2	30000.000	70000.000	90000.000
3	60000.000	80000.000	120000.000
4	40000.000	60000.000	No Upper Limit

interpretation? Would an increase in capacity for the new production line be desirable? Explain.

e. Would you recommend increasing the capacity of the old production line? Explain.

f. The production cost for model A on the old production line is $50 per unit. How much would this cost have to change to make it worthwhile to produce model A on the old production line? Explain.

g. Suppose that the minimum production requirement for model B is reduced from 70,000 units to 60,000 units. What effect would this change have on the total production cost? Explain.

19. Better Products, Inc., manufactures three products on two machines. In a typical week, 40 hours are available on each machine. The profit contribution and production time in hours per unit are as follows:

Category	Product 1	Product 2	Product 3
Profit/unit	$30	$50	$20
Machine 1 time/unit	0.5	2.0	0.75
Machine 2 time/unit	1.0	1.0	0.5

Two operators are required for machine 1; thus, 2 hours of labor must be scheduled for each hour of machine 1 time. Only one operator is required for machine 2. A maximum of 100 labor-hours is available for assignment to the machines during the coming week. Other production requirements are that product 1 cannot account for more than 50% of the units produced and that product 3 must account for at least 20% of the units produced.

a. How many units of each product should be produced to maximize the total profit contribution? What is the projected weekly profit associated with your solution?
b. How many hours of production time will be scheduled on each machine?
c. What is the value of an additional hour of labor?
d. Assume that labor capacity can be increased to 120 hours. Would you be interested in using the additional 20 hours available for this resource? Develop the optimal product mix assuming the extra hours are made available.

20. Adirondack Savings Bank (ASB) has $1 million in new funds that must be allocated to home loans, personal loans, and automobile loans. The annual rates of return for the three types of loans are 7% for home loans, 12% for personal loans, and 9% for automobile loans. The bank's planning committee has decided that at least 40% of the new funds must be allocated to home loans. In addition, the planning committee has specified that the amount allocated to personal loans cannot exceed 60% of the amount allocated to automobile loans.

a. Formulate a linear programming model that can be used to determine the amount of funds ASB should allocate to each type of loan in order to maximize the total annual return for the new funds.
b. How much should be allocated to each type of loan? What is the total annual return? What is the annual percentage return?
c. If the interest rate on home loans increased to 9%, would the amount allocated to each type of loan change? Explain.
d. Suppose the total amount of new funds available was increased by $10,000. What effect would this have on the total annual return? Explain.
e. Assume that ASB has the original $1 million in new funds available and that the planning committee has agreed to relax the requirement that at least 40% of the new funds must be allocated to home loans by 1%. How much would the annual return change? How much would the annual percentage return change?

21. Round Tree Manor is a hotel that provides two types of rooms with three rental classes: Super Saver, Deluxe, and Business. The profit per night for each type of room and rental class is as follows:

		Rental Class		
		Super Saver	Deluxe	Business
Room	Type I	$30	$35	—
	Type II	$20	$30	$40

Type I rooms do not have Internet access and are not available for the Business rental class.

Round Tree's management makes a forecast of the demand by rental class for each night in the future. A linear programming model developed to maximize profit is used to determine how many reservations to accept for each rental class. The demand forecast for a particular night is 130 rentals in the Super Saver class, 60 rentals in the Deluxe class, and 50 rentals in the Business class. Round Tree has 100 Type I rooms and 120 Type II rooms.

a. Use linear programming to determine how many reservations to accept in each rental class and how the reservations should be allocated to room types. Is the demand by any rental class not satisfied? Explain.
b. How many reservations can be accommodated in each rental class?
c. Management is considering offering a free breakfast to anyone upgrading from a Super Saver reservation to Deluxe class. If the cost of the breakfast to Round Tree is $5, should this incentive be offered?
d. With a little work, an unused office area could be converted to a rental room. If the conversion cost is the same for both types of rooms, would you recommend converting the office to a Type I or a Type II room? Why?
e. Could the linear programming model be modified to plan for the allocation of rental demand for the next night? What information would be needed and how would the model change?

22. Industrial Designs has been awarded a contract to design a label for a new wine produced by Lake View Winery. The company estimates that 150 hours will be required to complete the project. The firm's three graphics designers available for assignment to this project are Lisa, a senior designer and team leader; David, a senior designer; and Sarah, a junior designer. Because Lisa has worked on several projects for Lake View Winery, management specified that Lisa must be assigned at least 40% of the total number of hours assigned to the two senior designers. To provide label-designing experience for Sarah, Sarah must be assigned at least 15% of the total project time. However, the number of hours assigned to Sarah must not exceed 25% of the total number of hours assigned to the two senior designers. Due to other project commitments, Lisa has a maximum of 50 hours available to work on this project. Hourly wage rates are $30 for Lisa, $25 for David, and $18 for Sarah.
    a. Formulate a linear program that can be used to determine the number of hours each graphic designer should be assigned to the project in order to minimize total cost.
    b. How many hours should each graphic designer be assigned to the project? What is the total cost?
    c. Suppose Lisa could be assigned more than 50 hours. What effect would this have on the optimal solution? Explain.
    d. If Sarah were not required to work a minimum number of hours on this project, would the optimal solution change? Explain.

23. Vollmer Manufacturing makes three components for sale to refrigeration companies. The components are processed on two machines: a shaper and a grinder. The times (in minutes) required on each machine are as follows:

	Machine	
Component	**Shaper**	**Grinder**
1	6	4
2	4	5
3	4	2

The shaper is available for 120 hours, and the grinder is available for 110 hours. No more than 200 units of component 3 can be sold, but up to 1000 units of each of the other components can be sold. In fact, the company already has orders for 600 units of component 1 that must be satisfied. The profit contributions for components 1, 2, and 3 are \$8, \$6, and \$9, respectively.

a. Formulate and solve for the recommended production quantities.
b. What are the objective coefficient ranges for the three components? Interpret these ranges for company management.
c. What are the right-hand-side ranges? Interpret these ranges for company management.
d. If more time could be made available on the grinder, how much would it be worth?
e. If more units of component 3 can be sold by reducing the sales price by \$4, should the company reduce the price?

24. National Insurance Associates carries an investment portfolio of stocks, bonds, and other investment alternatives. Currently \$200,000 of funds are available and must be considered for new investment opportunities. The four stock options National is considering and the relevant financial data are as follows:

	Stock			
	A	B	C	D
Price per share	\$100	\$50	\$80	\$40
Annual rate of return	0.12	0.08	0.06	0.10
Risk measure per dollar invested	0.10	0.07	0.05	0.08

The risk measure indicates the relative uncertainty associated with the stock in terms of its realizing the projected annual return; higher values indicate greater risk. The risk measures are provided by the firm's top financial advisor.

National's top management has stipulated the following investment guidelines: the annual rate of return for the portfolio must be at least 9% and no one stock can account for more than 50% of the total dollar investment.

a. Use linear programming to develop an investment portfolio that minimizes risk.
b. If the firm ignores risk and uses a maximum return-on-investment strategy, what is the investment portfolio?
c. What is the dollar difference between the portfolios in parts (a) and (b)? Why might the company prefer the solution developed in part (a)?

25. Georgia Cabinets manufactures kitchen cabinets that are sold to local dealers throughout the Southeast. Because of a large backlog of orders for oak and cherry cabinets, the company decided to contract with three smaller cabinetmakers to do the final finishing operation. For the three cabinetmakers, the number of hours required to complete all the oak cabinets, the number of hours required to complete all the cherry cabinets, the number of hours available for the final finishing operation, and the cost per hour to perform the work are shown here.

	Cabinetmaker 1	Cabinetmaker 2	Cabinetmaker 3
Hours required to complete all the oak cabinets	50	42	30
Hours required to complete all the cherry cabinets	60	48	35
Hours available	40	30	35
Cost per hour	\$36	\$42	\$55

For example, Cabinetmaker 1 estimates it will take 50 hours to complete all the oak cabinets and 60 hours to complete all the cherry cabinets. However, Cabinetmaker 1 only has 40 hours available for the final finishing operation. Thus, Cabinetmaker 1 can only complete 40/50 = 0.80 or 80% of the oak cabinets if it worked only on oak cabinets. Similarly, Cabinetmaker 1 can only complete 40/60 = 0.67 or 67% of the cherry cabinets if it worked only on cherry cabinets.

a. Formulate a linear programming model that can be used to determine the percentage of the oak cabinets and the percentage of the cherry cabinets that should be given to each of the three cabinetmakers in order to minimize the total cost of completing both projects.
b. Solve the model formulated in part (a). What percentage of the oak cabinets and what percentage of the cherry cabinets should be assigned to each cabinetmaker? What is the total cost of completing both projects?
c. If Cabinetmaker 1 has additional hours available, would the optimal solution change? Explain.
d. If Cabinetmaker 2 has additional hours available, would the optimal solution change? Explain.
e. Suppose Cabinetmaker 2 reduced its cost to $38 per hour. What effect would this change have on the optimal solution? Explain.

26. Benson Electronics manufactures three components used to produce cell telephones and other communication devices. In a given production period, demand for the three components may exceed Benson's manufacturing capacity. In this case, the company meets demand by purchasing the components from another manufacturer at an increased cost per unit. Benson's manufacturing cost per unit and purchasing cost per unit for the three components are as follows:

Source	Component 1	Component 2	Component 3
Manufacture	$4.50	$5.00	$2.75
Purchase	$6.50	$8.80	$7.00

Manufacturing times in minutes per unit for Benson's three departments are as follows:

Department	Component 1	Component 2	Component 3
Production	2	3	4
Assembly	1	1.5	3
Testing & Packaging	1.5	2	5

For instance, each unit of component 1 that Benson manufactures requires 2 minutes of production time, 1 minute of assembly time, and 1.5 minutes of testing and packaging time. For the next production period, Benson has capacities of 360 hours in the production department, 250 hours in the assembly department, and 300 hours in the testing and packaging department.

a. Formulate a linear programming model that can be used to determine how many units of each component to manufacture and how many units of each component to purchase. Assume that component demands that must be satisfied are 6000 units for component 1, 4000 units for component 2, and 3500 units for component 3. The objective is to minimize the total manufacturing and purchasing costs.

b. What is the optimal solution? How many units of each component should be manufactured and how many units of each component should be purchased?
c. Which departments are limiting Benson's manufacturing quantities? Use the dual price to determine the value of an *extra hour* in each of these departments.
d. Suppose that Benson had to obtain one additional unit of component 2. Discuss what the dual price for the component 2 constraint tells us about the cost to obtain the additional unit.

27. Golf Shafts, Inc. (GSI), produces graphite shafts for several manufacturers of golf clubs. Two GSI manufacturing facilities, one located in San Diego and the other in Tampa, have the capability to produce shafts in varying degrees of stiffness, ranging from regular models used primarily by average golfers to extra stiff models used primarily by low-handicap and professional golfers. GSI just received a contract for the production of 200,000 regular shafts and 75,000 stiff shafts. Because both plants are currently producing shafts for previous orders, neither plant has sufficient capacity by itself to fill the new order. The San Diego plant can produce up to a total of 120,000 shafts and the Tampa plant can produce up to a total of 180,000 shafts. Because of equipment differences at each of the plants and differing labor costs, the per-unit production costs vary as shown here:

	San Diego Cost	**Tampa Cost**
Regular shaft	\$5.25	\$4.95
Stiff shaft	\$5.45	\$5.70

a. Formulate a linear programming model to determine how GSI should schedule production for the new order in order to minimize the total production cost.
b. Solve the model that you developed in part (a).
c. Suppose that some of the previous orders at the Tampa plant could be rescheduled in order to free up additional capacity for the new order. Would this option be worthwhile? Explain.
d. Suppose that the cost to produce a stiff shaft in Tampa had been incorrectly computed, and that the correct cost is \$5.30 per shaft. What effect, if any, would the correct cost have on the optimal solution developed in part (b)? What effect would it have on total production cost?

28. The Pfeiffer Company manages approximately \$15 million for clients. For each client, Pfeiffer chooses a mix of three investment vehicles: a growth stock fund, an income fund, and a money market fund. Each client has different investment objectives and different tolerances for risk. To accommodate these differences, Pfeiffer places limits on the percentage of each portfolio that may be invested in the three funds and assigns a portfolio risk index to each client.

Here's how the system works for Dennis Hartmann, one of Pfeiffer's clients. Based on an evaluation of Hartmann's risk tolerance, Pfeiffer has assigned Hartmann's portfolio a risk index of 0.05. Furthermore, to maintain diversity, the fraction of Hartmann's portfolio invested in the growth and income funds must be at least 10% for each, and at least 20% must be in the money market fund.

The risk ratings for the growth, income, and money market funds are 0.10, 0.05, and 0.01, respectively. A portfolio risk index is computed as a weighted average of the risk ratings for the three funds where the weights are the fraction of the portfolio invested in each of the funds. Hartmann has given Pfeiffer \$300,000 to manage. Pfeiffer is currently forecasting a yield of 20% on the growth fund, 10% on the income fund, and 6% on the money market fund.

a. Develop a linear programming model to select the best mix of investments for Hartmann's portfolio.
b. Solve the model you developed in part (a).
c. How much may the yields on the three funds vary before it will be necessary for Pfeiffer to modify Hartmann's portfolio?
d. If Hartmann were more risk tolerant, how much of a yield increase could he expect? For instance, what if his portfolio risk index is increased to 0.06?
e. If Pfeiffer revised the yield estimate for the growth fund downward to 0.10, how would you recommend modifying Hartmann's portfolio?
f. What information must Pfeiffer maintain on each client in order to use this system to manage client portfolios?
g. On a weekly basis Pfeiffer revises the yield estimates for the three funds. Suppose Pfeiffer has 50 clients. Describe how you would envision Pfeiffer making weekly modifications in each client's portfolio and allocating the total funds managed among the three investment funds.

29. La Jolla Beverage Products is considering producing a wine cooler that would be a blend of a white wine, a rosé wine, and fruit juice. To meet taste specifications, the wine cooler must consist of at least 50% white wine, at least 20% and no more than 30% rosé, and exactly 20% fruit juice. La Jolla purchases the wine from local wineries and the fruit juice from a processing plant in San Francisco. For the current production period, 10,000 gallons of white wine and 8000 gallons of rosé wine can be purchased; an unlimited amount of fruit juice can be ordered. The costs for the wine are $1.00 per gallon for the white and $1.50 per gallon for the rosé; the fruit juice can be purchased for $0.50 per gallon. La Jolla Beverage Products can sell all of the wine cooler they can produce for $2.50 per gallon.
a. Is the cost of the wine and fruit juice a sunk cost or a relevant cost in this situation? Explain.
b. Formulate a linear program to determine the blend of the three ingredients that will maximize the total profit contribution. Solve the linear program to determine the number of gallons of each ingredient La Jolla should purchase and the total profit contribution they will realize from this blend.
c. If La Jolla could obtain additional amounts of the white wine, should they do so? If so, how much should they be willing to pay for each additional gallon, and how many additional gallons would they want to purchase?
d. If La Jolla Beverage Products could obtain additional amounts of the rosé wine, should they do so? If so, how much should they be willing to pay for each additional gallon, and how many additional gallons would they want to purchase?
e. Interpret the dual price for the constraint corresponding to the requirement that the wine cooler must contain at least 50% white wine. What is your advice to management given this dual price?
f. Interpret the dual price for the constraint corresponding to the requirement that the wine cooler must contain exactly 20% fruit juice. What is your advice to management given this dual price?

30. The program manager for Channel 10 would like to determine the best way to allocate the time for the 11:00–11:30 evening news broadcast. Specifically, she would like to determine the number of minutes of broadcast time to devote to local news, national news, weather, and sports. Over the 30-minute broadcast, 10 minutes are set aside for advertising. The station's broadcast policy states that at least 15% of the time available should be devoted to local news coverage; the time devoted to local news or national news must be at least 50% of the total broadcast time; the time devoted to the weather segment must be less than or equal to the time devoted to the sports segment; the time devoted to the

sports segment should be no longer than the total time spent on the local and national news; and at least 20% of the time should be devoted to the weather segment. The production costs per minute are $300 for local news, $200 for national news, $100 for weather, and $100 for sports.

a. Formulate and solve a linear program that can determine how the 20 available minutes should be used to minimize the total cost of producing the program.
b. Interpret the dual price for the constraint corresponding to the available time. What advice would you give the station manager given this dual price?
c. Interpret the dual price for the constraint corresponding to the requirement that at least 15% of the available time should be devoted to local coverage. What advice would you give the station manager given this dual price?
d. Interpret the dual price for the constraint corresponding to the requirement that the time devoted to the local and the national news must be at least 50% of the total broadcast time. What advice would you give the station manager given this dual price?
e. Interpret the dual price for the constraint corresponding to the requirement that the time devoted to the weather segment must be less than or equal to the time devoted to the sports segment. What advice would you give the station manager given this dual price?

31. Gulf Coast Electronics is ready to award contracts for printing their annual report. For the past several years, the four-color annual report has been printed by Johnson Printing and Lakeside Litho. A new firm, Benson Printing, inquired into the possibility of doing a portion of the printing. The quality and service level provided by Lakeside Litho has been extremely high; in fact, only 0.5% of their reports have had to be discarded because of quality problems. Johnson Printing has also had a high quality level historically, producing an average of only 1% unacceptable reports. Because Gulf Coast Electronics has had no experience with Benson Printing, they estimated their defective rate to be 10%. Gulf Coast would like to determine how many reports should be printed by each firm to obtain 75,000 acceptable-quality reports. To ensure that Benson Printing will receive some of the contract, management specified that the number of reports awarded to Benson Printing must be at least 10% of the volume given to Johnson Printing. In addition, the total volume assigned to Benson Printing, Johnson Printing, and Lakeside Litho should not exceed 30,000, 50,000, and 50,000 copies, respectively. Because of the long-term relationship with Lakeside Litho, management also specified that at least 30,000 reports should be awarded to Lakeside Litho. The cost per copy is $2.45 for Benson Printing, $2.50 for Johnson Printing, and $2.75 for Lakeside Litho.

a. Formulate and solve a linear program for determining how many copies should be assigned to each printing firm to minimize the total cost of obtaining 75,000 acceptable-quality reports.
b. Suppose that the quality level for Benson Printing is much better than estimated. What effect, if any, would this quality level have?
c. Suppose that management is willing to reconsider their requirement that Lakeside Litho be awarded at least 30,000 reports. What effect, if any, would this consideration have?

32. PhotoTech, Inc., a manufacturer of rechargeable batteries for digital cameras, signed a contract with a digital photography company to produce three different lithium-ion battery packs for a new line of digital cameras. The contract calls for the following:

Battery Pack	Production Quantity
PT-100	200,000
PT-200	100,000
PT-300	150,000

PhotoTech can manufacture the battery packs at manufacturing plants located in the Philippines and Mexico. The unit cost of the battery packs differ at the two plants because of differences in production equipment and wage rates. The unit costs for each battery pack at each manufacturing plant are as follows:

	Plant	
Product	**Philippines**	**Mexico**
PT-100	$0.95	$0.98
PT-200	$0.98	$1.06
PT-300	$1.34	$1.15

The PT-100 and PT-200 battery packs are produced using similar production equipment available at both plants. However, each plant has a limited capacity for the total number of PT-100 and PT-200 battery packs produced. The combined PT-100 and PT-200 production capacities are 175,000 units at the Philippines plant and 160,000 units at the Mexico plant. The PT-300 production capacities are 75,000 units at the Philippines plant and 100,000 units at the Mexico plant. The cost of shipping from the Philippines plant is $0.18 per unit, and the cost of shipping from the Mexico plant is $0.10 per unit.

a. Develop a linear program that PhotoTech can use to determine how many units of each battery pack to produce at each plant in order to minimize the total production and shipping cost associated with the new contract.
b. Solve the linear program developed in part (a) to determine the optimal production plan.
c. Use sensitivity analysis to determine how much the production and/or shipping cost per unit would have to change in order to produce additional units of the PT-100 in the Philippines plant.
d. Use sensitivity analysis to determine how much the production and/or shipping cost per unit would have to change in order to produce additional units of the PT-200 in the Mexico plant.

Case Problem 1 PRODUCT MIX

TJ's, Inc., makes three nut mixes for sale to grocery chains located in the Southeast. The three mixes, referred to as the Regular Mix, the Deluxe Mix, and the Holiday Mix, are made by mixing different percentages of five types of nuts.

In preparation for the fall season, TJ's has just purchased the following shipments of nuts at the prices shown:

Type of Nut	Shipment Amount (pounds)	Cost per Shipment ($)
Almond	6000	7500
Brazil	7500	7125
Filbert	7500	6750
Pecan	6000	7200
Walnut	7500	7875

The Regular Mix consists of 15% almonds, 25% Brazil nuts, 25% filberts, 10% pecans, and 25% walnuts. The Deluxe Mix consists of 20% of each type of nut, and the Holiday Mix consists of 25% almonds, 15% Brazil nuts, 15% filberts, 25% pecans, and 20% walnuts.

TJ's accountant analyzed the cost of packaging materials, sales price per pound, and so forth, and determined that the profit contribution per pound is $1.65 for the Regular Mix, $2.00 for the Deluxe Mix, and $2.25 for the Holiday Mix. These figures do not include the cost of specific types of nuts in the different mixes because that cost can vary greatly in the commodity markets.

Customer orders already received are summarized here:

Type of Mix	Orders (pounds)
Regular	10,000
Deluxe	3,000
Holiday	5,000

Because demand is running high, it is expected that TJ's will receive many more orders than can be satisfied.

TJ's is committed to using the available nuts to maximize profit over the fall season; nuts not used will be given to a local charity. Even if it is not profitable to do so, TJ's president indicated that the orders already received must be satisfied.

Managerial Report

Perform an analysis of TJ's product-mix problem, and prepare a report for TJ's president that summarizes your findings. Be sure to include information and analysis on the following:

1. The cost per pound of the nuts included in the Regular, Deluxe, and Holiday mixes
2. The optimal product mix and the total profit contribution
3. Recommendations regarding how the total profit contribution can be increased if additional quantities of nuts can be purchased
4. A recommendation as to whether TJ's should purchase an additional 1000 pounds of almonds for $1000 from a supplier who overbought
5. Recommendations on how profit contribution could be increased (if at all) if TJ's does not satisfy all existing orders

Case Problem 2 INVESTMENT STRATEGY

J. D. Williams, Inc., is an investment advisory firm that manages more than $120 million in funds for its numerous clients. The company uses an asset allocation model that recommends the portion of each client's portfolio to be invested in a growth stock fund, an income fund, and a money market fund. To maintain diversity in each client's portfolio, the firm places limits on the percentage of each portfolio that may be invested in each of the three funds. General guidelines indicate that the amount invested in the growth fund must be between 20% and 40% of the total portfolio value. Similar percentages for the other two funds stipulate that between 20% and 50% of the total portfolio value must be in the income fund and at least 30% of the total portfolio value must be in the money market fund.

In addition, the company attempts to assess the risk tolerance of each client and adjust the portfolio to meet the needs of the individual investor. For example, Williams just contracted with a new client who has $800,000 to invest. Based on an evaluation of the client's risk tolerance, Williams assigned a maximum risk index of 0.05 for the client. The firm's risk indicators show the risk of the growth fund at 0.10, the income fund at 0.07, and the money market fund at 0.01. An overall portfolio risk index is computed as a weighted average of the risk rating for the three funds where the weights are the fraction of the client's portfolio invested in each of the funds.

Additionally, Williams is currently forecasting annual yields of 18% for the growth fund, 12.5% for the income fund, and 7.5% for the money market fund. Based on the information provided, how should the new client be advised to allocate the $800,000 among the growth, income, and money market funds? Develop a linear programming model that will provide the maximum yield for the portfolio. Use your model to develop a managerial report.

Managerial Report

1. Recommend how much of the $800,000 should be invested in each of the three funds. What is the annual yield you anticipate for the investment recommendation?
2. Assume that the client's risk index could be increased to 0.055. How much would the yield increase and how would the investment recommendation change?
3. Refer again to the original situation where the client's risk index was assessed to be 0.05. How would your investment recommendation change if the annual yield for the growth fund were revised downward to 16% or even to 14%?
4. Assume that the client expressed some concern about having too much money in the growth fund. How would the original recommendation change if the amount invested in the growth fund is not allowed to exceed the amount invested in the income fund?
5. The asset allocation model you developed may be useful in modifying the portfolios for all of the firm's clients whenever the anticipated yields for the three funds are periodically revised. What is your recommendation as to whether use of this model is possible?

Case Problem 3 TRUCK LEASING STRATEGY

Reep Construction recently won a contract for the excavation and site preparation of a new rest area on the Pennsylvania Turnpike. In preparing his bid for the job, Bob Reep, founder and president of Reep Construction, estimated that it would take four months to perform the work and that 10, 12, 14, and 8 trucks would be needed in months 1 through 4, respectively.

The firm currently has 20 trucks of the type needed to perform the work on the new project. These trucks were obtained last year when Bob signed a long-term lease with PennState Leasing. Although most of these trucks are currently being used on existing jobs, Bob estimates that one truck will be available for use on the new project in month 1, two trucks will be available in month 2, three trucks will be available in month 3, and one truck will be available in month 4. Thus, to complete the project, Bob will have to lease additional trucks.

The long-term leasing contract with PennState has a monthly cost of $600 per truck. Reep Construction pays its truck drivers $20 an hour, and daily fuel costs are approximately $100 per truck. All maintenance costs are paid by PennState Leasing. For planning purposes, Bob estimates that each truck used on the new project will be operating eight hours a day, five days a week for approximately four weeks each month.

Bob does not believe that current business conditions justify committing the firm to additional long-term leases. In discussing the short-term leasing possibilities with PennState Leasing, Bob learned that he can obtain short-term leases of 1–4 months. Short-term leases differ from long-term leases in that the short-term leasing plans include the cost of both a truck and a driver. Maintenance costs for short-term leases also are paid by PennState Leasing. The following costs for each of the four months cover the lease of a truck and driver.

Length of Lease	Cost per Month ($)
1	4000
2	3700
3	3225
4	3040

Bob Reep would like to acquire a lease that would minimize the cost of meeting the monthly trucking requirements for his new project, but he also takes great pride in the fact that his company has never laid off employees. Bob is committed to maintaining his no-layoff policy; that is, he will use his own drivers even if costs are higher.

Managerial Report

Perform an analysis of Reep Construction's leasing problem and prepare a report for Bob Reep that summarizes your findings. Be sure to include information on and analysis of the following items.

1. The optimal leasing plan
2. The costs associated with the optimal leasing plan
3. The cost for Reep Construction to maintain its current policy of no layoffs

Appendix 3.1 SENSITIVITY ANALYSIS WITH EXCEL

Tutorial 4: Sensitivity Analysis Using Excel Solver

In Appendix 2.3 we showed how Frontline Systems' Premium Solver for Education can be used to solve a linear program by using it to solve the Par, Inc., problem. Let us now see how it can be used to provide sensitivity analysis.

When Premium Solver finds the optimal solution to a linear program, the **Solver Results** dialog box (see Figure 3.22) will appear on the screen. If only the solution is desired you simply click **OK.** To obtain the optimal solution and the sensitivity analysis output, you must select **Sensitivity** in the **Reports** box before clicking **OK;** the sensitivity report is created on another worksheet in the same Excel workbook. Using this procedure for the Par problem, we obtained the optimal solution shown in Figure 3.23 and the sensitivity report shown in Figure 3.24.

Interpretation of Excel Sensitivity Report

In the Adjustable Cells section of the Sensitivity Report, the column labeled Final Value contains the optimal values of the decision variables. For the Par, Inc., problem the optimal solution is 540 standard bags and 252 deluxe bags. Next, let us consider the values in the Reduced Cost column. In Excel, the value of a nonzero reduced cost indicates how much the value of the objective function would change[2] if the corresponding variable was increased by one unit. For the Par, Inc., problem, the reduced costs for both decision variables are zero; they are at their optimal values.

To the right of the Reduced Cost column in Figure 3.24, we find three columns labeled Objective Coefficient, Allowable Increase, and Allowable Decrease. Note that for the standard bag decision variable, the objective function coefficient value is 10, the allowable

[2]This definition of reduced cost is slightly different from (but equivalent to) the one in the glossary. Excel's solution algorithm permits variables in solution at their upper bound to have a nonzero reduced cost.

FIGURE 3.22 PREMIUM SOLVER RESULTS DIALOG BOX

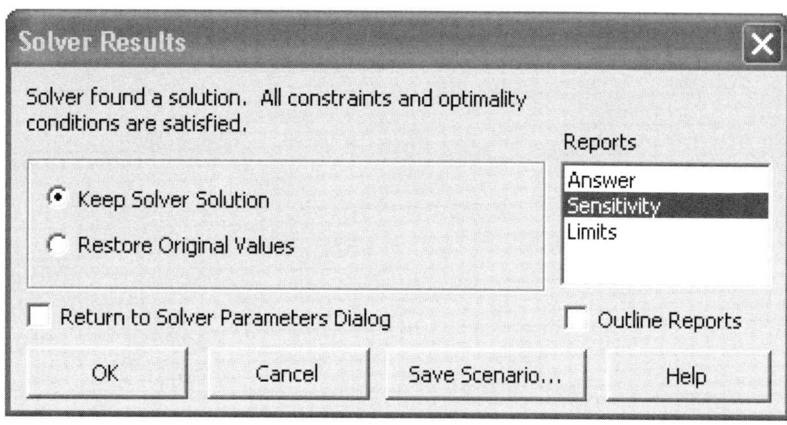

FIGURE 3.23 EXCEL SOLUTION FOR THE PAR, INC., PROBLEM

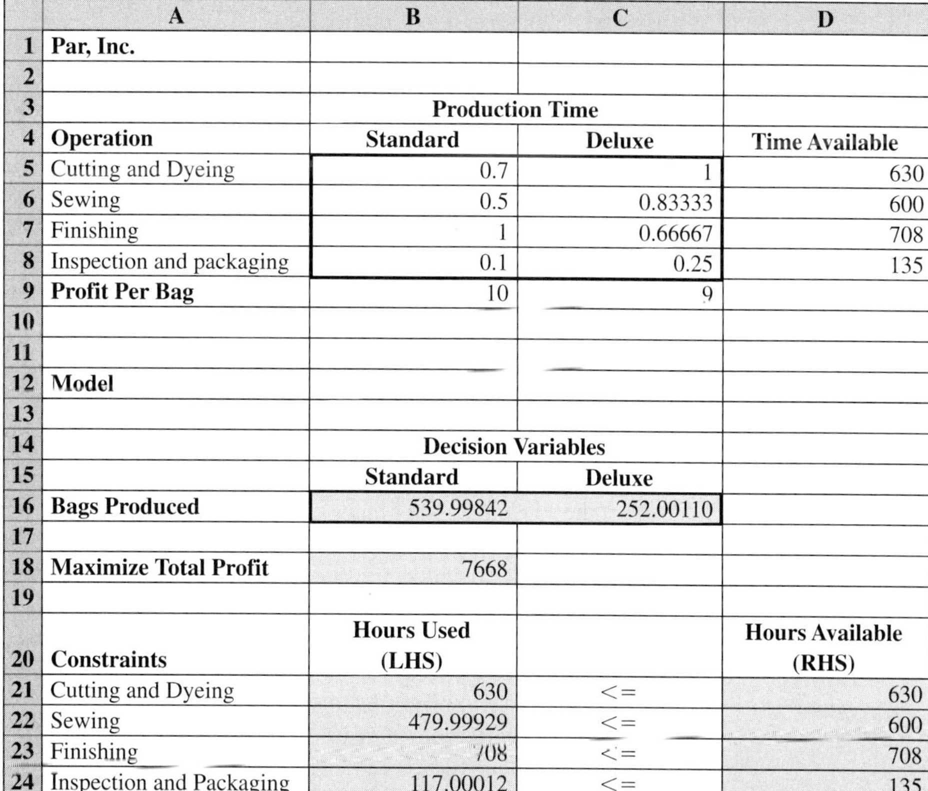

	A	B	C	D
1	**Par, Inc.**			
2				
3		**Production Time**		
4	**Operation**	**Standard**	**Deluxe**	**Time Available**
5	Cutting and Dyeing	0.7	1	630
6	Sewing	0.5	0.83333	600
7	Finishing	1	0.66667	708
8	Inspection and packaging	0.1	0.25	135
9	**Profit Per Bag**	10	9	
10				
11				
12	**Model**			
13				
14		**Decision Variables**		
15		**Standard**	**Deluxe**	
16	**Bags Produced**	539.99842	252.00110	
17				
18	**Maximize Total Profit**	7668		
19				
20	**Constraints**	**Hours Used (LHS)**		**Hours Available (RHS)**
21	Cutting and Dyeing	630	<=	630
22	Sewing	479.99929	<=	600
23	Finishing	708	<=	708
24	Inspection and Packaging	117.00012	<=	135

FIGURE 3.24 EXCEL SENSITIVITY REPORT FOR THE PAR, INC., PROBLEM

Adjustable Cells

Cell	Name	Final Value	Reduced Cost	Objective Coefficient	Allowable Increase	Allowable Decrease
$B$16	Bags Produced Standard	539.99842	0.00000	10	3.4999325	3.7
$C$16	Bags Produced Deluxe	252.00110	0.00000	9	5.285714286	2.3333

Constraints

Cell	Name	Final Value	Shadow Price	Constraint R.H. Side	Allowable Increase	Allowable Decrease
$B$21	Cutting and Dyeing Hours Used (LHS)	630	4.37495664	630	52.36315884	134.4
$B$22	Sewing Hours Used (LHS)	479.99929	0.00000	600	1E+30	120.0007088
$B$23	Finishing Hours Used (LHS)	708	6.937530352	708	192	127.9986
$B$24	Inspection and Packaging Hours Used (LHS)	117.00012	0.00000	135	1E+30	17.99988187

increase is 3.5, and the allowable decrease is 3.7. Adding 3.5 to and subtracting 3.7 from the current coefficient of 10 provides the range of optimality for C_S.

$$6.3 \leq C_S \leq 13.5$$

Similarly, the range of optimality for C_D is

$$6.67 \leq C_D \leq 14.29$$

Next, consider the information in the Constraints section of the report. The entries in the Final Value column are the number of hours needed in each department to produce the optimal production quantities of 540 standard bags and 252 deluxe bags. Thus, at the optimal solution, 630 hours of cutting and dyeing time, 480 hours of sewing time, 708 hours of finishing time, and 117 hours of inspection and packaging time are required. The values in the Constraint R.H. Side column are just the original right-hand-side values: 630 hours of cutting and dyeing time, 600 hours of sewing time, 708 hours of finishing time, and 135 hours of inspection and packaging time. Note that for the Par, Inc., problem, the values of the slack variables for each constraint are simply the differences between the entries in the Constraint R.H. Side column and the corresponding entries in the Final Value column.

The entries in the Shadow Price column provide the *shadow price* for each constraint. The shadow price is the *change* in the value of the solution per unit increase in the right-hand side of the constraint. The Management Scientist uses the term *dual price* to describe the *improvement* in the value of the solution per unit increase in the right-hand side of a constraint. The shadow price and dual price are the same for maximization problems because improvement is an increase in value. For minimization problems, improvement is a decrease in value; thus, for minimization problems, the shadow price and dual price have opposite signs.

The sensitivity analysis interpretations provided in this appendix are based on the assumption that only one objective function coefficient or only one right-hand-side change occurs at a time.

The last two columns of the Sensitivity Report contain the range of feasibility information for the constraint right-hand sides. For example, consider the cutting and dyeing constraint with an allowable increase value of 52.4 and an allowable decrease value of 134.4. The values in the Allowable Increase and Allowable Decrease columns indicate that the shadow price of $4.375 is valid for increases up to 52.4 hours and decreases to 134.4 hours. Thus, the shadow price of $4.375 is applicable for increases up to 630 + 52.4 = 682.4 and decreases down to 630 − 134.4 = 495.6 hours.

In summary, the range of feasibility information provides the limits where the shadow prices are applicable. For changes outside the range, the problem must be re-solved to find the new optimal solution and the new shadow price.

Appendix 3.2 SENSITIVITY ANALYSIS WITH LINGO

In Appendix 2.2 we showed how LINGO can be used to solve a linear program by using it to solve the Par, Inc., problem. A copy of the Solution Report is shown in Figure 3.25. As we discussed previously, the value of the objective function is 7668, the optimal solution is $S = 540$ and $D = 252$, and the values of the slack variables corresponding to the four constraints (rows 2–5) are 0, 120, 0, and 18. Now, let us consider the information in the Reduced Cost column and the Dual Price column.

In LINGO, the value of a nonzero reduced cost indicates how much the value of the corresponding objective function coefficient would have to improve before that variable could assume a positive value in the optimal solution. For the Par, Inc., problem, the reduced costs for both decision variables are zero because both variables are at their optimal values. The nonzero dual prices of 4.374957 for constraint 1 (cutting and dyeing constraint in row 2) and 6.937530 for constraint 3 (finishing constraint in row 4) tell us that an additional hour of cutting and dyeing time improves (increases) the value of the optimal solution by $4.37 and an additional hour of finishing time improves (increases) the value of the optimal solution by $6.94.

Next, let us consider how LINGO can be used to compute the range of optimality for each objective function coefficient and the range of feasibility for each of the dual prices. By default, range computations are not enabled in LINGO. To enable range computations, perform the following steps:

Step 1. Choose the **LINGO** menu
Step 2. Select **Options**

FIGURE 3.25 PAR, INC., SOLUTION REPORT USING LINGO

```
Global optimal solution found.
  Objective value:                 7667.994
  Total solver iterations:                2

     Variable              Value              Reduced Cost
   --------------    ----------------    ------------------
         S                539.9984             0.000000
         D                252.0011             0.000000

        Row          Slack or Surplus         Dual Price
   --------------    ----------------    ------------------
         1                7667.994              1.000000
         2                0.000000              4.374957
         3                120.0007              0.000000
         4                0.000000              6.937530
         5                17.99988              0.000000
```

Step 3. When the LINGO Options dialog box appears:
Select the **General Solver** tab
Choose **Prices and Ranges** in the **Dual Computations** box
Click **Apply**
Click **OK**

You will now have to re-solve the Par, Inc., problem in order for LINGO to perform the range computations. After re-solving the problem, close or minimize the Solution Report window. To display the range information, select the Range command from the LINGO menu. LINGO displays the range information in a new window titled Range Report. The output that appears in the Range Report window for the Par, Inc., problem is shown in Figure 3.26.

We will use the information in the Objective Coefficient Ranges section of the range report to compute the range of optimality for the objective function coefficients. For example, the current objective function coefficient for S is 10. Note that the corresponding allowable increase is 3.499933 and the corresponding allowable decrease is 3.700000. Thus the range of optimality for C_S, the objective function coefficient for S, is $10 - 3.700000 = 6.300000$ to $10 + 3.499933 = 13.499933$. After rounding, the range of optimality for C_S is $6.30 \leq C_S \leq 13.50$. Similarly, with an allowable increase of 5.285714 and an allowable decrease of 2.333300, the range of optimality for C_D is $6.67 \leq C_S \leq 14.29$.

To compute the range of feasibility for each dual price we will use the information in the "Righthand Side Ranges" section of the range report. For example, the current right-hand-side value for the cutting and dyeing constraint (row 2) is 630, the allowable increase is 52.36316, and the allowable decrease is 134.40000. Because the dual price for this constraint is 4.374957 (shown in the LINGO solution report), we can conclude that additional hours will increase the objective function by \$4.37 per hour. From the range information given, we see that after rounding the dual price of \$4.37 is valid for increases up to $630 + 52.36 = 682.4$ and decreases to $630 - 134.4 = 495.6$. Thus, the range of feasibility for the cutting and dyeing constraint is 495.6 to 682.4. The ranges of feasibility for the other constraints can be determined in a similar manner.

FIGURE 3.26 PAR, INC., SENSITIVITY REPORT USING LINGO

Ranges in which the basis is unchanged:

OBJECTIVE COEFFICIENT RANGES

Variable	Current Coefficient	Allowable Increase	Allowable Decrease
S	10.00000	3.499933	3.700000
D	9.000000	5.285714	2.333300

RIGHTHAND SIDE RANGES

Row	Current RHS	Allowable Increase	Allowable Decrease
2	630.0000	52.36316	134.4000
3	600.0000	INFINITY	120.0007
4	708.0000	192.0000	127.9986
5	135.0000	INFINITY	17.99988

CHAPTER 4

Linear Programming Applications in Marketing, Finance, and Operations Management

CONTENTS

Linear programming has proven to be one of the most successful quantitative approaches to decision making. Applications have been reported in almost every industry. These applications include production scheduling, media selection, financial planning, capital budgeting, transportation, distribution system design, product mix, staffing, and blending.

The wide variety of Management Science in Actions presented in Chapters 2 and 3 illustrated the use of linear programming as a flexible problem-solving tool. The Management Science in Action, A Marketing Planning Model at Marathon Oil Company, provides another example of the use of linear programming by showing how Marathon uses a large-scale linear programming model to solve a wide variety of planning problems. Later in the chapter other Management Science in Action features illustrate how GE Capital uses linear programming for optimal lease structuring; how Jeppesen Sanderson use linear programming to optimize production of flight manuals; and how the Kellogg Company uses a large-scale linear programming model to integrate production, distribution, and inventory planning.

In this chapter we present a variety of applications from the traditional business areas of marketing, finance, and operations management. Modeling, computer solution, and interpretation of output are emphasized. A mathematical model is developed for each problem studied, and solutions obtained using The Management Scientist are presented for most of the applications. In the chapter appendix we illustrate the use of Excel Solver by solving a financial planning problem.

MANAGEMENT SCIENCE IN ACTION

A MARKETING PLANNING MODEL AT MARATHON OIL COMPANY*

Marathon Oil Company has four refineries within the United States, operates 50 light products terminals, and has product demand at more than 95 locations. The Supply and Transportation Division faces the problem of determining which refinery should supply which terminal and, at the same time, determining which products should be transported via pipeline, barge, or tanker to minimize cost. Product demand must be satisfied, and the supply capability of each refinery must not be exceeded. To help solve this difficult problem, Marathon Oil developed a marketing planning model.

The marketing planning model is a large-scale linear programming model that takes into account sales not only at Marathon product terminals but also at all exchange locations. An exchange contract is an agreement with other oil product marketers that involves exchanging or trading Marathon's products for theirs at different locations. All pipelines, barges, and tankers within Marathon's marketing area are also represented in the linear programming model. The objective of the model is to minimize the cost of meeting a given demand structure, taking into account sales price, pipeline tariffs, exchange contract costs, product demand, terminal operating costs, refining costs, and product purchases.

The marketing planning model is used to solve a wide variety of planning problems that vary from evaluating gasoline blending economics to analyzing the economics of a new terminal or pipeline. With daily sales of about 10 million gallons of refined light product, a savings of even one-thousandth of a cent per gallon can result in significant long-term savings. At the same time, what may appear to be a savings in one area, such as refining or transportation, may actually add to overall costs when the effects are fully realized throughout the system. The marketing planning model allows a simultaneous examination of this total effect.

*Based on information provided by Robert W. Wernert at Marathon Oil Company, Findlay, Ohio.

4.1 MARKETING APPLICATIONS

Applications of linear programming in marketing are numerous. In this section we discuss applications in media selection and marketing research.

Media Selection

In Section 2.1 we provided some general guidelines for modeling linear programming problems. You may want to review Section 2.1 before proceeding with the linear programming applications in this chapter.

Media selection applications of linear programming are designed to help marketing managers allocate a fixed advertising budget to various advertising media. Potential media include newspapers, magazines, radio, television, and direct mail. In these applications, the objective is to maximize reach, frequency, and quality of exposure. Restrictions on the allowable allocation usually arise during consideration of company policy, contract requirements, and media availability. In the application that follows, we illustrate how a media selection problem might be formulated and solved using a linear programming model.

Relax-and-Enjoy Lake Development Corporation is developing a lakeside community at a privately owned lake. The primary market for the lakeside lots and homes includes all middle- and upper-income families within approximately 100 miles of the development. Relax-and-Enjoy employed the advertising firm of Boone, Phillips, and Jackson (BP&J) to design the promotional campaign.

After considering possible advertising media and the market to be covered, BP&J recommended that the first month's advertising be restricted to five media. At the end of the month, BP&J will then reevaluate its strategy based on the month's results. BP&J collected data on the number of potential customers reached, the cost per advertisement, the maximum number of times each medium is available, and the exposure quality rating for each of the five media. The quality rating is measured in terms of an exposure quality unit, a measure of the relative value of one advertisement in each of the media. This measure, based on BP&J's experience in the advertising business, takes into account factors such as audience demographics (age, income, and education of the audience reached), image presented, and quality of the advertisement. The information collected is presented in Table 4.1.

Relax-and-Enjoy provided BP&J with an advertising budget of $30,000 for the first month's campaign. In addition, Relax-and-Enjoy imposed the following restrictions on how BP&J may allocate these funds: At least 10 television commercials must be used, at least 50,000 potential customers must be reached, and no more than $18,000 may be spent on television advertisements. What advertising media selection plan should be recommended?

TABLE 4.1 ADVERTISING MEDIA ALTERNATIVES FOR THE RELAX-AND-ENJOY LAKE DEVELOPMENT CORPORATION

Advertising Media	Number of Potential Customers Reached	Cost ($) per Advertisement	Maximum Times Available per Month*	Exposure Quality Units
1. Daytime TV (1 min), station WKLA	1000	1500	15	65
2. Evening TV (30 sec), station WKLA	2000	3000	10	90
3. Daily newspaper (full page), *The Morning Journal*	1500	400	25	40
4. Sunday newspaper magazine (½ page color), *The Sunday Press*	2500	1000	4	60
5. Radio, 8:00 A.M. or 5:00 P.M. news (30 sec), station KNOP	300	100	30	20

*The maximum number of times the medium is available is either the maximum number of times the advertising medium occurs (e.g., four Sundays per month) or the maximum number of times BP&J recommends that the medium be used.

The decision to be made is how many times to use each medium. We begin by defining the decision variables:

$$\begin{aligned} DTV &= \text{number of times daytime TV is used} \\ ETV &= \text{number of times evening TV is used} \\ DN &= \text{number of times daily newspaper is used} \\ SN &= \text{number of times Sunday newspaper is used} \\ R &= \text{number of times radio is used} \end{aligned}$$

The data on quality of exposure in Table 4.1 show that each daytime TV (DTV) advertisement is rated at 65 exposure quality units. Thus, an advertising plan with DTV advertisements will provide a total of $65DTV$ exposure quality units. Continuing with the data in Table 4.1, we find evening TV (ETV) rated at 90 exposure quality units, daily newspaper (DN) rated at 40 exposure quality units, Sunday newspaper (SN) rated at 60 exposure quality units, and radio (R) rated at 20 exposure quality units. With the objective of maximizing the total exposure quality units for the overall media selection plan, the objective function becomes

$$\text{Max} \quad 65DTV + 90ETV + 40DN + 60SN + 20R \qquad \text{Exposure quality}$$

Care must be taken to ensure the linear programming model accurately reflects the real problem. Always review your formulation thoroughly before attempting to solve the model.

We now formulate the constraints for the model from the information given:

$$\begin{array}{lllllll}
DTV & & & & & \leq & 15 \\
& ETV & & & & \leq & 10 \\
& & DN & & & \leq & 25 \\
& & & SN & & \leq & 4 \\
& & & & R & \leq & 30 \\
\end{array} \left.\right\} \text{Availability of media}$$

$$\begin{array}{ll}
1500DTV + 3000ETV + 400DN + 1000SN + 100R \leq 30{,}000 & \text{Budget} \\
DTV + ETV \geq 10 & \text{Television} \\
1500DTV + 3000ETV \leq 18{,}000 & \text{restrictions} \\
1000DTV + 2000ETV + 1500DN + 2500SN + 300R \geq 50{,}000 & \text{Customers reached} \\
DTV, ETV, DN, SN, R \geq 0 &
\end{array}$$

Problem 1 provides practice at formulating a similar media selection model.

The optimal solution to this five-variable, nine-constraint linear programming model is shown in Figure 4.1; a summary is presented in Table 4.2.

The optimal solution calls for advertisements to be distributed among daytime TV, daily newspaper, Sunday newspaper, and radio. The maximum number of exposure quality units is 2370, and the total number of customers reached is 61,500. The Reduced Costs column in Figure 4.1 indicates that the number of exposure quality units for evening TV would have to increase by at least 65 before this media alternative could appear in the optimal solution. Note that the budget constraint (constraint 6) has a dual price of 0.060. Therefore, a \$1.00 increase in the advertising budget will lead to an increase of 0.06 exposure quality units. The dual price of -25.000 for constraint 7 indicates that reducing the number of television commercials by 1 will increase the exposure quality of the advertising plan by 25 units. Thus, Relax-and-Enjoy should consider reducing the requirement of having at least 10 television commercials.

More complex media selection models may include considerations such as the reduced exposure quality value for repeat media usage, cost discounts for repeat media usage, audience overlap by different media, and/or timing recommendations for the advertisements.

A possible shortcoming of this model is that, even if the exposure quality measure were not subject to error, it offers no guarantee that maximization of total exposure quality will lead to a maximization of profit or of sales (a common surrogate for profit). However, this issue is not a shortcoming of linear programming; rather, it is a shortcoming of the use of exposure quality as a criterion. If we could directly measure the effect of an advertisement on profit, we could use total profit as the objective to be maximized.

FIGURE 4.1 THE MANAGEMENT SCIENTIST SOLUTION FOR THE RELAX-AND-ENJOY LAKE DEVELOPMENT CORPORATION PROBLEM

EXCELfile
Relax

```
Objective Function Value =        2370.000

    Variable              Value              Reduced Costs
 --------------     ---------------     -----------------
      DTV                10.000                  0.000
      ETV                 0.000                 65.000
      DN                 25.000                  0.000
      SN                  2.000                  0.000
      R                  30.000                  0.000

   Constraint          Slack/Surplus         Dual Prices
 --------------     ---------------     -----------------
       1                  5.000                  0.000
       2                 10.000                  0.000
       3                  0.000                 16.000
       4                  2.000                  0.000
       5                  0.000                 14.000
       6                  0.000                  0.060
       7                  0.000                -25.000
       8               3000.000                  0.000
       9              11500.003                  0.000
```


TABLE 4.2 ADVERTISING PLAN FOR THE RELAX-AND-ENJOY LAKE DEVELOPMENT CORPORATION

Media	Frequency	Budget
Daytime TV	10	$15,000
Daily newspaper	25	10,000
Sunday newspaper	2	2,000
Radio	30	3,000
		$30,000

Exposure quality units = 2370
Total customers reached = 61,500

NOTES AND COMMENTS

1. The media selection model required subjective evaluations of the exposure quality for the media alternatives. Marketing managers may have substantial data concerning exposure quality, but the final coefficients used in the objective function may also include considerations based primarily on managerial judgment. Judgment is an acceptable way of obtaining input for a linear programming model.

2. The media selection model presented in this section uses exposure quality as the objective function and places a constraint on the number of customers reached. An alternative formulation of this problem would be to use the number of customers reached as the objective function and add a constraint indicating the minimum total exposure quality required for the media plan.

Marketing Research

An organization conducts marketing research to learn about consumer characteristics, attitudes, and preferences. Marketing research firms that specialize in providing such information often do the actual research for client organizations. Typical services offered by a marketing research firm include designing the study, conducting market surveys, analyzing the data collected, and providing summary reports and recommendations for the client. In the research design phase, targets or quotas may be established for the number and types of respondents to be surveyed. The marketing research firm's objective is to conduct the survey so as to meet the client's needs at a minimum cost.

Market Survey, Inc. (MSI), specializes in evaluating consumer reaction to new products, services, and advertising campaigns. A client firm requested MSI's assistance in ascertaining consumer reaction to a recently marketed household product. During meetings with the client, MSI agreed to conduct door-to-door personal interviews to obtain responses from households with children and households without children. In addition, MSI agreed to conduct both day and evening interviews. Specifically, the client's contract called for MSI to conduct 1000 interviews under the following quota guidelines.

1. Interview at least 400 households with children.
2. Interview at least 400 households without children.
3. The total number of households interviewed during the evening must be at least as great as the number of households interviewed during the day.
4. At least 40 percent of the interviews for households with children must be conducted during the evening.
5. At least 60 percent of the interviews for households without children must be conducted during the evening.

Because the interviews for households with children take additional interviewer time and because evening interviewers are paid more than daytime interviewers, the cost varies with the type of interview. Based on previous research studies, estimates of the interview costs are as follows:

	Interview Cost	
Household	**Day**	**Evening**
Children	\$20	\$25
No children	\$18	\$20

What is the household, time-of-day interview plan that will satisfy the contract requirements at a minimum total interviewing cost?

In formulating the linear programming model for the MSI problem, we utilize the following decision-variable notation:

DC = the number of daytime interviews of households with children
EC = the number of evening interviews of households with children
DNC = the number of daytime interviews of households without children
ENC = the number of evening interviews of households without children

We begin the linear programming model formulation by using the cost-per-interview data to develop the objective function:

$$\text{Min} \quad 20DC + 25EC + 18DNC + 20ENC$$

The constraint requiring a total of 1000 interviews is

$$DC + EC + DNC + ENC = 1000$$

The five specifications concerning the types of interviews are as follows.

- Households with children:

$$DC + EC \geq 400$$

- Households without children:

$$DNC + ENC \geq 400$$

- At least as many evening interviews as day interviews:

$$EC + ENC \geq DC + DNC$$

  The usual format for linear programming model formulation and computer input places all decision variables on the left side of the inequality and a constant (possibly zero) on the right side. Thus, we rewrite this constraint as

$$-DC + EC - DNC + ENC \geq 0$$

- At least 40 percent of interviews of households with children during the evening:

$$EC \geq 0.4(DC + EC) \quad \text{or} \quad -0.4DC + 0.6EC \geq 0$$

- At least 60 percent of interviews of households without children during the evening:

$$ENC \geq 0.6(DNC + ENC) \quad \text{or} \quad -0.6DNC + 0.4ENC \geq 0$$

When we add the nonnegativity requirements, the four-variable and six-constraint linear programming model becomes

$$\begin{array}{llll}
\text{Min} & 20DC + 25EC + 18DNC + 20ENC & & \\
\text{s.t.} & & & \\
& DC + EC + DNC + ENC = 1000 & & \text{Total interviews} \\
& DC + EC \geq 400 & & \text{Households with children} \\
& DNC + ENC \geq 400 & & \text{Households without children} \\
& -DC + EC - DNC + ENC \geq 0 & & \text{Evening interviews} \\
& -0.4DC + 0.6EC \geq 0 & & \text{Evening interviews in households with children} \\
& -0.6DNC + 0.4ENC \geq 0 & & \text{Evening interviews in households without children} \\
& DC, EC, DNC, ENC \geq 0 & &
\end{array}$$

The optimal solution to this linear program is shown in Figure 4.2. The solution reveals that the minimum cost of \$20,320 occurs with the following interview schedule.

	Number of Interviews		
Household	**Day**	**Evening**	**Totals**
Children	240	160	400
No children	240	360	600
Totals	480	520	1000

FIGURE 4.2 THE MANAGEMENT SCIENTIST SOLUTION FOR THE MARKET SURVEY PROBLEM

```
Objective Function Value =          20320.000

     Variable            Value           Reduced Costs
  --------------    ---------------    -----------------
        DC               240.000               0.000
        EC               160.000               0.000
        DNC              240.000               0.000
        ENC              360.000               0.000

    Constraint       Slack/Surplus        Dual Prices
  --------------    ---------------    -----------------
         1                 0.000             -19.200
         2                 0.000              -2.800
         3               200.000               0.000
         4                40.000               0.000
         5                 0.000              -5.000
         6                 0.000              -2.000
```

EXCELfile
Market

Hence, 480 interviews will be scheduled during the day and 520 during the evening. Households with children will be covered by 400 interviews, and households without children will be covered by 600 interviews.

Selected sensitivity analysis information from Figure 4.2 shows a dual price of -19.200 for constraint 1. In other words, the value of the optimal solution will get worse (the total interviewing cost will increase) by \$19.20 if the number of interviews is increased from 1000 to 1001. Thus, \$19.20 is the incremental cost of obtaining additional interviews. It also is the savings that could be realized by reducing the number of interviews from 1000 to 999.

The surplus variable, with a value of 200.000, for constraint 3 shows that 200 more households without children will be interviewed than required. Similarly, the surplus variable, with a value of 40.000, for constraint 4 shows that the number of evening interviews exceeds the number of daytime interviews by 40. The zero values for the surplus variables in constraints 5 and 6 indicate that the more expensive evening interviews are being held at a minimum. Indeed, the dual price of -5.000 for constraint 5 indicates that if one more household (with children) than the minimum requirement must be interviewed during the evening, the total interviewing cost will go up by \$5.00. Similarly, constraint 6 shows that requiring one more household (without children) to be interviewed during the evening will increase costs by \$2.00.

4.2 FINANCIAL APPLICATIONS

In finance, linear programming can be applied in problem situations involving capital budgeting, make-or-buy decisions, asset allocation, portfolio selection, financial planning, and many more. In this section, we describe a portfolio selection problem and a problem involving funding of an early retirement program.

Portfolio Selection

Portfolio selection problems involve situations in which a financial manager must select specific investments—for example, stocks and bonds—from a variety of investment alternatives. Managers of mutual funds, credit unions, insurance companies, and banks frequently encounter this type of problem. The objective function for portfolio selection problems usually is maximization of expected return or minimization of risk. The constraints usually take the form of restrictions on the type of permissible investments, state laws, company policy, maximum permissible risk, and so on. Problems of this type have been formulated and solved using a variety of mathematical programming techniques. In this section we formulate and solve a portfolio selection problem as a linear program.

Consider the case of Welte Mutual Funds, Inc., located in New York City. Welte just obtained \$100,000 by converting industrial bonds to cash and is now looking for other investment opportunities for these funds. Based on Welte's current investments, the firm's top financial analyst recommends that all new investments be made in the oil industry, steel industry, or in government bonds. Specifically, the analyst identified five investment opportunities and projected their annual rates of return. The investments and rates of return are shown in Table 4.3.

Management of Welte imposed the following investment guidelines.

1. Neither industry (oil or steel) should receive more than \$50,000.
2. Government bonds should be at least 25% of the steel industry investments.
3. The investment in Pacific Oil, the high-return but high-risk investment, cannot be more than 60% of the total oil industry investment.

What portfolio recommendations—investments and amounts—should be made for the available \$100,000? Given the objective of maximizing projected return subject to the budgetary and managerially imposed constraints, we can answer this question by formulating and solving a linear programming model of the problem. The solution will provide investment recommendations for the management of Welte Mutual Funds.

Let

$$
\begin{aligned}
A &= \text{dollars invested in Atlantic Oil} \\
P &= \text{dollars invested in Pacific Oil} \\
M &= \text{dollars invested in Midwest Steel} \\
H &= \text{dollars invested in Huber Steel} \\
G &= \text{dollars invested in government bonds}
\end{aligned}
$$

Using the projected rates of return shown in Table 4.3, we write the objective function for maximizing the total return for the portfolio as

$$\text{Max} \quad 0.073A + 0.103P + 0.064M + 0.075H + 0.045G$$

The constraint specifying investment of the available \$100,000 is

$$A + P + M + H + G = 100{,}000$$

TABLE 4.3 INVESTMENT OPPORTUNITIES FOR WELTE MUTUAL FUNDS

Investment	**Projected Rate of Return (%)**
Atlantic Oil	7.3
Pacific Oil	10.3
Midwest Steel	6.4
Huber Steel	7.5
Government bonds	4.5

The requirements that neither the oil nor the steel industry should receive more than \$50,000 are

$$A + P \leq 50{,}000$$
$$M + H \leq 50{,}000$$

The requirement that government bonds be at least 25% of the steel industry investment is expressed as

$$G \geq 0.25(M + H) \qquad \text{or} \qquad -0.25M - 0.25H + G \geq 0$$

Finally, the constraint that Pacific Oil cannot be more than 60% of the total oil industry investment is

$$P \leq 0.60(A + P) \qquad \text{or} \qquad -0.60A + 0.40P \leq 0$$

By adding the nonnegativity restrictions, we obtain the complete linear programming model for the Welte Mutual Funds investment problem:

$$\text{Max} \quad 0.073A + 0.103P + 0.064M + 0.075H + 0.045G$$

s.t.

$$\begin{aligned}
A + P + M + H + G &= 100{,}000 && \text{Available funds} \\
A + P &\leq 50{,}000 && \text{Oil industry maximum} \\
M + H &\leq 50{,}000 && \text{Steel industry maximum} \\
-0.25M - 0.25H + G &\geq 0 && \text{Government bonds minimum} \\
-0.6A + 0.4P &\leq 0 && \text{Pacific Oil restriction}
\end{aligned}$$

$$A, P, M, H, G \geq 0$$

The optimal solution to this linear program is shown in Figure 4.3. Table 4.4 shows how the funds are divided among the securities. Note that the optimal solution indicates that the portfolio should be diversified among all the investment opportunities except Midwest Steel. The projected annual return for this portfolio is \$8000, which is an overall return of 8%.

The optimal solution shows the dual price for constraint 3 is zero. The reason is that the steel industry maximum isn't a binding constraint; increases in the steel industry limit of \$50,000 will not improve the value of the optimal solution. Indeed, the slack variable for this constraint shows that the current steel industry investment is \$10,000 below its limit of \$50,000. The dual prices for the other constraints are nonzero, indicating that these constraints are binding.

The dual price for the available funds constraint provides information on the rate of return from additional investment funds.

The dual price of 0.069 for constraint 1 shows that the value of the optimal solution can be increased by 0.069 if one more dollar can be made available for the portfolio investment. If more funds can be obtained at a cost of less than 6.9%, management should consider obtaining them. However, if a return in excess of 6.9% can be obtained by investing funds elsewhere (other than in these five securities), management should question the wisdom of investing the entire \$100,000 in this portfolio.

Similar interpretations can be given to the other dual prices. Note that the dual price for constraint 4 is negative at −0.024. This result indicates that increasing the value on the right-hand side of the constraint by one unit can be expected to worsen the value of the optimal solution by 0.024. In terms of the optimal portfolio, then, if Welte invests one more dollar in government bonds (beyond the minimum requirement), the total return will decrease by

FIGURE 4.3 THE MANAGEMENT SCIENTIST SOLUTION FOR THE WELTE MUTUAL FUNDS PROBLEM

EXCELfile
Welte

```
Objective Function Value =                8000.000

   Variable              Value              Reduced Costs
--------------     ---------------     -----------------
      A               20000.000                 0.000
      P               30000.000                 0.000
      M                   0.000                 0.011
      H               40000.000                 0.000
      G               10000.000                 0.000

  Constraint         Slack/Surplus          Dual Prices
--------------     ---------------     -----------------
      1                   0.000                 0.069
      2                   0.000                 0.022
      3               10000.000                 0.000
      4                   0.000                -0.024
      5                   0.000                 0.030
```

$0.024. To see why this decrease occurs, note again from the dual price for constraint 1 that the marginal return on the funds invested in the portfolio is 6.9% (the average return is 8%). The rate of return on government bonds is 4.5%. Thus, the cost of investing one more dollar in government bonds is the difference between the marginal return on the portfolio and the marginal return on government bonds: 6.9% − 4.5% = 2.4%.

Practice formulating a variation of the Welte problem by working Problem 9.

Note that the optimal solution shows that Midwest Steel should not be included in the portfolio ($M = 0$). The associated reduced cost for M of 0.011 tells us that the objective function coefficient for Midwest Steel would have to increase by 0.011 before considering the Midwest Steel investment alternative would be advisable. With such an increase the Midwest Steel return would be $0.064 + 0.011 = 0.075$, making this investment just as desirable as the currently used Huber Steel investment alternative.

Finally, a simple modification of the Welte linear programming model permits determining the fraction of available funds invested in each security. That is, we divide each of the right-hand-side values by 100,000. Then the optimal values for the variables will give the fraction of funds that should be invested in each security for a portfolio of any size.

TABLE 4.4 OPTIMAL PORTFOLIO SELECTION FOR WELTE MUTUAL FUNDS

Investment	Amount	Expected Annual Return
Atlantic Oil	$ 20,000	$1460
Pacific Oil	30,000	3090
Huber Steel	40,000	3000
Government bonds	10,000	450
Totals	$100,000	$8000

Expected annual return of $8000
Overall rate of return = 8%

NOTES AND COMMENTS

1. The optimal solution to the Welte Mutual Funds problem indicates that $20,000 is to be spent on the Atlantic Oil stock. If Atlantic Oil sells for $75 per share, we would have to purchase exactly 266⅔ shares in order to spend exactly $20,000. The difficulty of purchasing fractional shares can be handled by purchasing the largest possible integer number of shares with the allotted funds (e.g., 266 shares of Atlantic Oil). This approach guarantees that the budget constraint will not be violated. This approach, of course, introduces the possibility that the solution will no longer be optimal, but the danger is slight if a large number of securities are involved. In cases where the analyst believes that the decision variables *must* have integer values, the problem must be formulated as an integer linear programming model. Integer linear programming is the topic of Chapter 7.
2. Financial portfolio theory stresses obtaining a proper balance between risk and return. In the Welte problem, we explicitly considered return in the objective function. Risk is controlled by choosing constraints that ensure diversity among oil and steel stocks and a balance between government bonds and the steel industry investment.

Financial Planning

Linear programming has been used for a variety of financial planning applications. The Management Science in Action, Optimal Lease Structuring at GE Capital, describes how linear programming is used to optimize the structure of a leveraged lease.

MANAGEMENT SCIENCE IN ACTION

OPTIMAL LEASE STRUCTURING AT GE CAPITAL*

GE Capital is a $70 billion subsidiary of General Electric. As one of the nation's largest and most diverse financial services companies, GE Capital arranges leases in both domestic and international markets, including leases for telecommunications; data processing; construction; and fleets of cars, trucks, and commercial aircraft. To help allocate and schedule the rental and debt payments of a leveraged lease, GE Capital analysts developed an optimization model, which is available as an optional component of the company's lease analysis proprietary software.

Leveraged leases are designed to provide financing for assets with economic lives of at least five years, which require large capital outlays. A leveraged lease represents an agreement among the lessor (the owner of the asset), the lessee (the user of the asset), and the lender who provides a nonrecourse loan of 50% to 80% of the lessor's purchase price. In a nonrecourse loan, the lenders cannot turn to the lessor for repayment in the event of default. As the lessor in such arrangements, GE Capital is able to claim ownership and realize income tax benefits such as depreciation and interest deductions. These deductions usually produce tax losses during the early years of the lease, which reduces the total tax liability. Approximately 85% of all financial leases in the United States are leveraged leases.

In its simplest form, the leveraged lease structuring problem can be formulated as a linear program. The linear program models the after-tax cash flow for the lessor, taking into consideration rental receipts, borrowing and repaying of the loan, and income taxes. Constraints are formulated to ensure compliance with IRS guidelines and to enable customizing of leases to meet lessee and lessor requirements. The objective function can be entered in a custom fashion or selected from a predefined list. Typically, the objective is to minimize the lessee's cost, expressed as the net present value of rental payments, or to maximize the lessor's after-tax yield.

GE Capital developed an optimization approach that could be applied to single-investor lease structuring. In a study with the department most involved with these transactions, the optimization approach yielded substantial benefits. The approach helped GE Capital win some single-investor transactions ranging in size from $1 million to $20 million.

*Based on C. J. Litty, "Optimal Lease Structuring at GE Capital," *Interfaces* (May/June 1994): 34–45.

Hewlitt Corporation established an early retirement program as part of its corporate restructuring. At the close of the voluntary sign-up period, 68 employees had elected early retirement. As a result of these early retirements, the company incurs the following obligations over the next eight years.

Year	1	2	3	4	5	6	7	8
Cash Requirement	430	210	222	231	240	195	225	255

The cash requirements (in thousands of dollars) are due at the beginning of each year.

The corporate treasurer must determine how much money must be set aside today to meet the eight yearly financial obligations as they come due. The financing plan for the retirement program includes investments in government bonds as well as savings. The investments in government bonds are limited to three choices:

Bond	Price	Rate (%)	Years to Maturity
1	\$1150	8.875	5
2	1000	5.500	6
3	1350	11.750	7

The government bonds have a par value of \$1000, which means that even with different prices each bond pays \$1000 at maturity. The rates shown are based on the par value. For purposes of planning, the treasurer assumed that any funds not invested in bonds will be placed in savings and earn interest at an annual rate of 4%.

We define the decision variables as follows:

F = total dollars required to meet the retirement plan's eight-year obligation
B_1 = units of bond 1 purchased at the beginning of year 1
B_2 = units of bond 2 purchased at the beginning of year 1
B_3 = units of bond 3 purchased at the beginning of year 1
S_i = amount placed in savings at the beginning of year i for $i = 1, \ldots, 8$

The objective function is to minimize the total dollars needed to meet the retirement plan's eight-year obligation, or

$$\text{Min} \quad F$$

A key feature of this type of financial planning problem is that a constraint must be formulated for each year of the planning horizon. In general, each constraint takes the form:

$$\begin{pmatrix}\text{Funds available at}\\ \text{the beginning of the year}\end{pmatrix} - \begin{pmatrix}\text{Funds invested in bonds}\\ \text{and placed in savings}\end{pmatrix} = \begin{pmatrix}\text{Cash obligation for}\\ \text{the current year}\end{pmatrix}$$

The funds available at the beginning of year 1 are given by F. With a current price of \$1150 for bond 1 and investments expressed in thousands of dollars, the total investment for B_1 units of bond 1 would be $1.15B_1$. Similarly, the total investment in bonds 2 and 3 would be $1B_2$ and $1.35B_3$, respectively. The investment in savings for year 1 is S_1. Using these results and the first-year obligation of 430, we obtain the constraint for year 1:

$$F - 1.15B_1 - 1B_2 - 1.35B_3 - S_1 = 430 \quad \text{Year 1}$$

We do not consider future investments in bonds because the future price of bonds depends on interest rates and cannot be known in advance.

Investments in bonds can take place only in this first year, and the bonds will be held until maturity.

The funds available at the beginning of year 2 include the investment returns of 8.875% on the par value of bond 1, 5.5% on the par value of bond 2, 11.75% on the par value of bond 3, and 4% on savings. The new amount to be invested in savings for year 2 is S_2. With an obligation of 210, the constraint for year 2 is

$$0.08875B_1 + 0.055B_2 + 0.1175B_3 + 1.04S_1 - S_2 = 210 \quad \text{Year 2}$$

Similarly, the constraints for years 3 to 8 are

$$\begin{aligned}
0.08875B_1 + 0.055B_2 + 0.1175B_3 + 1.04S_2 - S_3 &= 222 \quad \text{Year 3}\\
0.08875B_1 + 0.055B_2 + 0.1175B_3 + 1.04S_3 - S_4 &= 231 \quad \text{Year 4}\\
0.08875B_1 + 0.055B_2 + 0.1175B_3 + 1.04S_4 - S_5 &= 240 \quad \text{Year 5}\\
1.08875B_1 + 0.055B_2 + 0.1175B_3 + 1.04S_5 - S_6 &= 195 \quad \text{Year 6}\\
1.055B_2 + 0.1175B_3 + 1.04S_6 - S_7 &= 225 \quad \text{Year 7}\\
1.1175B_3 + 1.04S_7 - S_8 &= 255 \quad \text{Year 8}
\end{aligned}$$

Note that the constraint for year 6 shows that funds available from bond 1 are $1.08875B_1$. The coefficient of 1.08875 reflects the fact that bond 1 matures at the end of year 5. As a result, the par value plus the interest from bond 1 during year 5 is available at the beginning of year 6. Also, because bond 1 matures in year 5 and becomes available for use at the beginning of year 6, the variable B_1 does not appear in the constraints for years 7 and 8. Note the similar interpretation for bond 2, which matures at the end of year 6 and has the par value plus interest available at the beginning of year 7. In addition, bond 3 matures at the end of year 7 and has the par value plus interest available at the beginning of year 8.

Finally, note that a variable S_8 appears in the constraint for year 8. The retirement fund obligation will be completed at the beginning of year 8, so we anticipate that S_8 will be zero and no funds will be put into savings. However, the formulation includes S_8 in the event that the bond income plus interest from the savings in year 7 exceed the 255 cash requirement for year 8. Thus, S_8 is a surplus variable that shows any funds remaining after the eight-year cash requirements have been satisfied.

The optimal solution to this 12-variable, 8-constraint linear program is shown in Figure 4.4. With an objective function value of 1728.79385, the total investment required to meet the retirement plan's eight-year obligation is $1,728,794. Using the current prices of $1150, $1000, and $1350 for each of the bonds respectively, we can summarize the initial investments in the three bonds as follows:

Bond	Units Purchased	Investment Amount
1	$B_1 = 144.988$	$1150(144.988) = $166,736
2	$B_2 = 187.856$	$1000(187.856) = $187,856
3	$B_3 = 228.188$	$1350(228.188) = $308,054

The solution also shows that $636,148 (see S_1) will be placed in savings at the beginning of the first year. By starting with $1,728,794, the company can make the specified bond and savings investments and have enough left over to meet the retirement program's first-year cash requirement of $430,000.

The optimal solution in Figure 4.4 shows that the decision variables S_1, S_2, S_3, and S_4 all are greater than zero, indicating investments in savings are required in each of the first

FIGURE 4.4 THE MANAGEMENT SCIENTIST SOLUTION FOR THE HEWLITT CORPORATION CASH REQUIREMENTS PROBLEM

```
Objective Function Value =          1728.79385

      Variable              Value           Reduced Costs
   --------------      ---------------    -----------------
          F              1728.79385             0.00000
          B1              144.98815             0.00000
          B2              187.85585             0.00000
          B3              228.18792             0.00000
          S1              636.14794             0.00000
          S2              501.60571             0.00000
          S3              349.68179             0.00000
          S4              182.68091             0.00000
          S5                0.00000             0.06403
          S6                0.00000             0.01261
          S7                0.00000             0.02132
          S8                0.00000             0.67084

     Constraint          Slack/Surplus          Dual Prices
   --------------      ---------------    -----------------
          1                 0.00000            -1.00000
          2                 0.00000            -0.96154
          3                 0.00000            -0.92456
          4                 0.00000            -0.88900
          5                 0.00000            -0.85480
          6                 0.00000            -0.76036
          7                 0.00000            -0.71899
          8                 0.00000            -0.67084
```

EXCELfile
Hewlitt

four years. However, interest from the bonds plus the bond maturity incomes will be sufficient to cover the retirement program's cash requirements in years 5 through 8.

In this application, the dual price can be thought of as the negative of the present value of each dollar in the cash requirement. For example, each dollar that must be paid in year 8 has a present value of \$0.67084.

The dual prices have an interesting interpretation in this application. Each right-hand-side value corresponds to the payment that must be made in that year. Note that the dual prices are negative, indicating that reducing the payment in any year would be beneficial because the total funds required for the retirement program's obligation would be less. Also note that the dual prices show that reductions are more beneficial in the early years, with decreasing benefits in subsequent years. As a result, Hewlitt would benefit by reducing cash requirements in the early years even if it had to make equivalently larger cash payments in later years.

NOTES AND COMMENTS

1. The optimal solution for the Hewlitt Corporation problem shows fractional numbers of government bonds at 144.988, 187.856, and 228.188 units, respectively. However, fractional bond units usually are not available. If we were conservative and rounded up to 145, 188, and 229 units, respectively, the total funds required for the eight-year retirement program obligation would be approximately \$1254 more than the total funds indicated by the objective function. Because of the magnitude of the funds involved, rounding up probably would provide a workable solution.

(continued)

If an optimal integer solution were required, the methods of integer linear programming covered in Chapter 7 would have to be used.

2. We implicitly assumed that interest from the government bonds is paid annually. Investments such as treasury notes actually provide interest payments every six months. In such cases, the model can be reformulated with six-month periods, with interest and/or cash payments occurring every six months.

4.3 OPERATIONS MANAGEMENT APPLICATIONS

Linear programming applications developed for production and operations management include scheduling, staffing, inventory control, and capacity planning. In this section we describe examples with make-or-buy decisions, production scheduling, and workforce assignments.

A Make-or-Buy Decision

We illustrate the use of a linear programming model to determine how much of each of several component parts a company should manufacture and how much it should purchase from an outside supplier. Such a decision is referred to as a make-or-buy decision.

The Janders Company markets various business and engineering products. Currently, Janders is preparing to introduce two new calculators: one for the business market called the Financial Manager and one for the engineering market called the Technician. Each calculator has three components: a base, an electronic cartridge, and a faceplate or top. The same base is used for both calculators, but the cartridges and tops are different. All components can be manufactured by the company or purchased from outside suppliers. The manufacturing costs and purchase prices for the components are summarized in Table 4.5.

Company forecasters indicate that 3000 Financial Manager calculators and 2000 Technician calculators will be needed. However, manufacturing capacity is limited. The company has 200 hours of regular manufacturing time and 50 hours of overtime that can be scheduled for the calculators. Overtime involves a premium at the additional cost of \$9 per hour. Table 4.6 shows manufacturing times (in minutes) for the components.

The problem for Janders is to determine how many units of each component to manufacture and how many units of each component to purchase. We define the decision variables as follows:

$$
\begin{aligned}
BM &= \text{number of bases manufactured} \\
BP &= \text{number of bases purchased} \\
FCM &= \text{number of Financial cartridges manufactured} \\
FCP &= \text{number of Financial cartridges purchased} \\
TCM &= \text{number of Technician cartridges manufactured} \\
TCP &= \text{number of Technician cartridges purchased} \\
FTM &= \text{number of Financial tops manufactured} \\
FTP &= \text{number of Financial tops purchased} \\
TTM &= \text{number of Technician tops manufactured} \\
TTP &= \text{number of Technician tops purchased}
\end{aligned}
$$

One additional decision variable is needed to determine the hours of overtime that must be scheduled:

$$OT = \text{number of hours of overtime to be scheduled}$$

TABLE 4.5 MANUFACTURING COSTS AND PURCHASE PRICES FOR JANDERS CALCULATOR COMPONENTS

	Cost per Unit	
Component	Manufacture (regular time)	Purchase
Base	\$0.50	\$0.60
Financial cartridge	\$3.75	\$4.00
Technician cartridge	\$3.30	\$3.90
Financial top	\$0.60	\$0.65
Technician top	\$0.75	\$0.78

The objective function is to minimize the total cost, including manufacturing costs, purchase costs, and overtime costs. Using the cost-per-unit data in Table 4.5 and the overtime premium cost rate of \$9 per hour, we write the objective function as

$$\begin{aligned}\text{Min} \quad & 0.5BM + 0.6BP + 3.75FCM + 4FCP + 3.3TCM + 3.9TCP + 0.6FTM \\ & + 0.65FTP + 0.75TTM + 0.78TTP + 9OT\end{aligned}$$

The first five constraints specify the number of each component needed to satisfy the demand for 3000 Financial Manager calculators and 2000 Technician calculators. A total of 5000 base components are needed, with the number of other components depending on the demand for the particular calculator. The five demand constraints are

$$\begin{aligned} BM + BP &= 5000 \quad \text{Bases} \\ FCM + FCP &= 3000 \quad \text{Financial cartridges} \\ TCM + TCP &= 2000 \quad \text{Technician cartridges} \\ FTM + FTP &= 3000 \quad \text{Financial tops} \\ TTM + TTP &= 2000 \quad \text{Technician tops} \end{aligned}$$

Two constraints are needed to guarantee that manufacturing capacities for regular time and overtime cannot be exceeded. The first constraint limits overtime capacity to 50 hours, or

$$OT \leq 50$$

The second constraint states that the total manufacturing time required for all components must be less than or equal to the total manufacturing capacity, including regular time plus

TABLE 4.6 MANUFACTURING TIMES IN MINUTES PER UNIT FOR JANDERS CALCULATOR COMPONENTS

Component	Manufacturing Time
Base	1.0
Financial cartridge	3.0
Technician cartridge	2.5
Financial top	1.0
Technician top	1.5

The same units of measure must be used for both the left-hand side and right-hand side of the constraint. In this case, minutes are used.

overtime. The manufacturing times for the components are expressed in minutes, so we state the total manufacturing capacity constraint in minutes, with the 200 hours of regular time capacity becoming 60(200) = 12,000 minutes. The actual overtime required is unknown at this point, so we write the overtime as $60OT$ minutes. Using the manufacturing times from Table 4.6, we have

$$BM + 3FCM + 2.5TCM + FTM + 1.5TTM \leq 12{,}000 + 60OT$$

Moving the decision variable for overtime to the left-hand side of the constraint provides the manufacturing capacity constraint:

$$BM + 3FCM + 2.5TCM + FTM + 1.5TTM - 60OT \leq 12{,}000$$

The complete formulation of the Janders make-or-buy problem with all decision variables greater than or equal to zero is

$$\begin{aligned} \text{Min} \quad & 0.5BM + 0.6BP + 3.75FCM + 4FCP + 3.3TCM + 3.9TCP \\ & + 0.6FTM + 0.65FTP + 0.75TTM + 0.78TTP + 9OT \end{aligned}$$

s.t.

$$\begin{array}{lllllllll} BM & & & & & + & BP = & 5000 & \text{Bases} \\ & FCM & & & & + & FCP = & 3000 & \text{Financial cartridges} \\ & & TCM & & & + & TCP = & 2000 & \text{Technician cartridges} \\ & & & FTM & & + & FTP = & 3000 & \text{Financial tops} \\ & & & & TTM & + & TTP = & 2000 & \text{Technician tops} \\ & & & & & & OT \leq & 50 & \text{Overtime hours} \\ BM & + 3FCM & + 2.5TCM & + FTM & + 1.5TTM & - & 60OT \leq & 12{,}000 & \text{Manufacturing capacity} \end{array}$$

The optimal solution to this 11-variable, 7-constraint linear program is shown in Figure 4.5. The optimal solution indicates that all 5000 bases (BM), 667 Financial Manager cartridges (FCM), and 2000 Technician cartridges (TCM) should be manufactured. The remaining 2333 Financial Manager cartridges (FCP), all the Financial Manager tops (FTP), and all Technician tops (TTP) should be purchased. No overtime manufacturing is necessary, and the total cost associated with the optimal make-or-buy plan is $24,443.33.

Sensitivity analysis provides some additional information about the unused overtime capacity. The Reduced Costs column shows that the overtime (OT) premium would have to decrease by $4 per hour before overtime production should be considered. That is, if the overtime premium is $9 − $4 = $5 or less, Janders may want to replace some of the purchased components with components manufactured on overtime.

The dual price for the manufacturing capacity constraint 7 is 0.083. This price indicates that an additional hour of manufacturing capacity is worth $0.083 per minute or ($0.083)(60) = $5 per hour. The right-hand-side range for constraint 7 shows that this conclusion is valid until the amount of regular time increases to 19,000 minutes, or 316.7 hours.

Sensitivity analysis also indicates that a change in prices charged by the outside suppliers can affect the optimal solution. For instance, the objective coefficient range for BP is 0.583 to no upper limit. If the purchase price for bases remains at $0.583 or more, the number of bases purchased (BP) will remain at zero. However, if the purchase price drops below $0.583, Janders should begin to purchase rather than manufacture the base component. Similar sensitivity analysis conclusions about the purchase price ranges can be drawn for the other components.

FIGURE 4.5 THE MANAGEMENT SCIENTIST SOLUTION FOR THE JANDERS MAKE-OR-BUY PROBLEM

EXCEL file
Janders

```
Objective Function Value =            24443.333

   Variable             Value             Reduced Costs
 --------------     ---------------     -----------------
     BM                  5000.000                 0.000
     BP                     0.000                 0.017
     FCM                  666.667                 0.000
     FCP                 2333.333                 0.000
     TCM                 2000.000                 0.000
     TCP                    0.000                 0.392
     FTM                    0.000                 0.033
     FTP                 3000.000                 0.000
     TTM                    0.000                 0.095
     TTP                 2000.000                 0.000
     OT                     0.000                 4.000

  Constraint          Slack/Surplus          Dual Prices
 --------------     ---------------     -----------------
      1                     0.000                -0.583
      2                     0.000                -4.000
      3                     0.000                -3.508
      4                     0.000                -0.650
      5                     0.000                -0.780
      6                    50.000                 0.000
      7                     0.000                 0.083

OBJECTIVE COEFFICIENT RANGES

 Variable       Lower Limit     Current Value      Upper Limit
------------  ---------------  ---------------  ---------------
    BM        No Lower Limit             0.500            0.517
    BP                 0.583             0.600   No Upper Limit
    FCM                3.700             3.750            3.850
    FCP                3.900             4.000            4.050
    TCM       No Lower Limit             3.300            3.692
    TCP                3.508             3.900   No Upper Limit
    FTM                0.567             0.600   No Upper Limit
    FTP       No Lower Limit             0.650            0.683
    TTM                0.655             0.750   No Upper Limit
    TTP       No Lower Limit             0.780            0.875
    OT                 5.000             9.000   No Upper Limit

RIGHT HAND SIDE RANGES

 Constraint     Lower Limit     Current Value      Upper Limit
------------  ---------------  ---------------  ---------------
    1                  0.000          5000.000         7000.000
    2                666.667          3000.000   No Upper Limit
    3                  0.000          2000.000         2800.000
    4                  0.000          3000.000   No Upper Limit
    5                  0.000          2000.000   No Upper Limit
    6                  0.000            50.000   No Upper Limit
    7              10000.000         12000.000        19000.000
```

NOTES AND COMMENTS

The proper interpretation of the dual price for manufacturing capacity (constraint 7) in the Janders problem is that an additional hour of manufacturing capacity is worth (\$0.083)(60) = \$5 per hour. Thus, the company should be willing to pay a premium of \$5 per hour over and above the current regular time cost per hour, which is already included in the manufacturing cost of the product. Thus, if the regular time cost is \$18 per hour, Janders should be willing to pay up to \$18 + \$5 = \$23 per hour to obtain additional labor capacity.

Production Scheduling

One of the most important applications of linear programming deals with multiperiod planning such as production scheduling. The solution to a production scheduling problem enables the manager to establish an efficient low-cost production schedule for one or more products over several time periods (weeks or months). Essentially, a production scheduling problem can be viewed as a product-mix problem for each of several periods in the future. The manager must determine the production levels that will allow the company to meet product demand requirements, given limitations on production capacity, labor capacity, and storage space, while minimizing total production costs.

One advantage of using linear programming for production scheduling problems is that they recur. A production schedule must be established for the current month, then again for the next month, for the month after that, and so on. When looking at the problem each month, the production manager will find that, although demand for the products has changed, production times, production capacities, storage space limitations, and so on are roughly the same. Thus, the production manager is basically resolving the same problem handled in previous months, and a general linear programming model of the production scheduling procedure may be frequently applied. Once the model has been formulated, the manager can simply supply the data—demand, capacities, and so on—for the given production period and use the linear programming model repeatedly to develop the production schedule. The Management Science in Action, Optimizing Production of Flight Manuals at Jeppesen Sanderson, Inc., describes how linear programming is used to minimize the cost of producing weekly revisions to flight manuals.

Let us consider the case of the Bollinger Electronics Company, which produces two different electronic components for a major airplane engine manufacturer. The airplane engine manufacturer notifies the Bollinger sales office each quarter of its monthly requirements for components for each of the next three months. The monthly requirements for the components may vary considerably, depending on the type of engine the airplane engine manufacturer is producing. The order shown in Table 4.7 has just been received for the next three-month period.

After the order is processed, a demand statement is sent to the production control department. The production control department must then develop a three-month production plan for the components. In arriving at the desired schedule, the production manager will want to identify the following:

1. Total production cost
2. Inventory holding cost
3. Change-in-production-level costs

In the remainder of this section, we show how to formulate a linear programming model of the production and inventory process for Bollinger Electronics to minimize the total cost.

To develop the model, we let x_{im} denote the production volume in units for product i in month m. Here $i = 1, 2$, and $m = 1, 2, 3$; $i = 1$ refers to component 322A, $i = 2$ refers to

MANAGEMENT SCIENCE IN ACTION

OPTIMIZING PRODUCTION OF FLIGHT MANUALS AT JEPPESEN SANDERSON, INC.*

Jeppesen Sanderson, Inc., manufactures and distributes flight manuals that contain safety information to more than 300,000 pilots and 4000 airlines. Every week Jeppesen mails between 5 and 30 million pages of chart revisions to 200,000 customers worldwide, and receives about 1,500 new orders each week. In the late 1990s, its customer service deteriorated as its existing production and supporting systems failed to keep up with this level of activity. To meet customer service goals, Jeppesen turned to optimization-based decision support tools for production planning.

Jeppesen developed a large-scale linear program called Scheduler to minimize the cost of producing the weekly revisions. Model constraints included capacity constraints and numerous internal business rules. The model includes 250,000 variables, and 40,000–50,000 constraints. Immediately after introducing the model, Jeppesen established a new record for the number of consecutive weeks with 100% on-time revisions. Scheduler decreased tardiness of revisions from approximately 9% to 3% and dramatically improved customer satisfaction. Even more importantly, Scheduler provided a model of the production system for Jeppesen to use in strategic economic analysis. Overall, the use of optimization techniques at Jeppesen resulted in cost reductions of nearly 10% and a 24% increase in profit.

*Based on E. Katok, W. Tarantino, and R. Tiedman, "Improving Performance and Flexibility at Jeppesen: The World's Leading Aviation-Information Company," *Interfaces* (January/February 2001): 7–29.

component 802B, $m = 1$ refers to April, $m = 2$ refers to May, and $m = 3$ refers to June. The purpose of the double subscript is to provide a more descriptive notation. We could simply use x_6 to represent the number of units of product 2 produced in month 3, but x_{23} is more descriptive, identifying directly the product and month represented by the variable.

If component 322A costs \$20 per unit produced and component 802B costs \$10 per unit produced, the total production cost part of the objective function is

$$\text{Total production cost} = 20x_{11} + 20x_{12} + 20x_{13} + 10x_{21} + 10x_{22} + 10x_{23}$$

Because the production cost per unit is the same each month, we don't need to include the production costs in the objective function; that is, regardless of the production schedule selected, the total production cost will remain the same. In other words, production costs are not relevant costs for the production scheduling decision under consideration. In cases in which the production cost per unit is expected to change each month, the variable production costs per unit per month must be included in the objective function. The solution for the Bollinger Electronics problem will be the same regardless of whether these costs are included, therefore, we included them so that the value of the linear programming objective function will include all the costs associated with the problem.

To incorporate the relevant inventory holding costs into the model, we let s_{im} denote the inventory level for product i at the end of month m. Bollinger determined that on a

TABLE 4.7 THREE-MONTH DEMAND SCHEDULE FOR BOLLINGER ELECTRONICS COMPANY

Component	April	May	June
322A	1000	3000	5000
802B	1000	500	3000

monthly basis inventory holding costs are 1.5% of the cost of the product; that is, (0.015)($20) = $0.30 per unit for component 322A and (0.015)($10) = $0.15 per unit for component 802B. A common assumption made in using the linear programming approach to production scheduling is that monthly ending inventories are an acceptable approximation to the average inventory levels throughout the month. Making this assumption, we write the inventory holding cost portion of the objective function as

$$\text{Inventory holding cost} = 0.30s_{11} + 0.30s_{12} + 0.30s_{13} + 0.15s_{21} + 0.15s_{22} + 0.15s_{23}$$

To incorporate the costs of fluctuations in production levels from month to month, we need to define two additional variables:

$$I_m = \text{increase in the total production level necessary during month } m$$
$$D_m = \text{decrease in the total production level necessary during month } m$$

After estimating the effects of employee layoffs, turnovers, reassignment training costs, and other costs associated with fluctuating production levels, Bollinger estimates that the cost associated with increasing the production level for any month is $0.50 per unit increase. A similar cost associated with decreasing the production level for any month is $0.20 per unit. Thus, we write the third portion of the objective function as

$$\begin{aligned}\text{Change-in-production-level costs} = {} & 0.50I_1 + 0.50I_2 + 0.50I_3 \\ & + 0.20D_1 + 0.20D_2 + 0.20D_3\end{aligned}$$

Note that the cost associated with changes in production level is a function of the change in the total number of units produced in month m compared to the total number of units produced in month $m - 1$. In other production scheduling applications, fluctuations in production level might be measured in terms of machine hours or labor-hours required rather than in terms of the total number of units produced.

Combining all three costs, the complete objective function becomes

$$\begin{aligned}\text{Min} \quad & 20x_{11} + 20x_{12} + 20x_{13} + 10x_{21} + 10x_{22} + 10x_{23} + 0.30s_{11} \\ & + 0.30s_{12} + 0.30s_{13} + 0.15s_{21} + 0.15s_{22} + 0.15s_{23} + 0.50I_1 \\ & + 0.50I_2 + 0.50I_3 + 0.20D_1 + 0.20D_2 + 0.20D_3\end{aligned}$$

We now consider the constraints. First, we must guarantee that the schedule meets customer demand. Because the units shipped can come from the current month's production or from inventory carried over from previous months, the demand requirement takes the form

$$\begin{pmatrix}\text{Ending}\\ \text{inventory}\\ \text{from previous}\\ \text{month}\end{pmatrix} + \begin{pmatrix}\text{Current}\\ \text{production}\end{pmatrix} - \begin{pmatrix}\text{Ending}\\ \text{inventory}\\ \text{for this}\\ \text{month}\end{pmatrix} = \begin{pmatrix}\text{This month's}\\ \text{demand}\end{pmatrix}$$

Suppose that the inventories at the beginning of the three-month scheduling period were 500 units for component 322A and 200 units for component 802B. The demand for both products in the first month (April) was 1000 units, so the constraints for meeting demand in the first month become

$$500 + x_{11} - s_{11} = 1000$$
$$200 + x_{21} - s_{21} = 1000$$

Moving the constants to the right-hand side, we have

$$\begin{aligned} x_{11} - s_{11} &= 500 \\ x_{21} - s_{21} &= 800 \end{aligned}$$

Similarly, we need demand constraints for both products in the second and third months. We write them as follows.

Month 2

$$\begin{aligned} s_{11} + x_{12} - s_{12} &= 3000 \\ s_{21} + x_{22} - s_{22} &= 500 \end{aligned}$$

Month 3

$$\begin{aligned} s_{12} + x_{13} - s_{13} &= 5000 \\ s_{22} + x_{23} - s_{23} &= 3000 \end{aligned}$$

If the company specifies a minimum inventory level at the end of the three-month period of at least 400 units of component 322A and at least 200 units of component 802B, we can add the constraints

$$\begin{aligned} s_{13} &\geq 400 \\ s_{23} &\geq 200 \end{aligned}$$

Suppose that we have the additional information on machine, labor, and storage capacity shown in Table 4.8. Machine, labor, and storage space requirements are given in Table 4.9. To reflect these limitations, the following constraints are necessary.

Machine Capacity

$$\begin{aligned} 0.10x_{11} + 0.08x_{21} &\leq 400 \quad \text{Month 1} \\ 0.10x_{12} + 0.08x_{22} &\leq 500 \quad \text{Month 2} \\ 0.10x_{13} + 0.08x_{23} &\leq 600 \quad \text{Month 3} \end{aligned}$$

Labor Capacity

$$\begin{aligned} 0.05x_{11} + 0.07x_{21} &\leq 300 \quad \text{Month 1} \\ 0.05x_{12} + 0.07x_{22} &\leq 300 \quad \text{Month 2} \\ 0.05x_{13} + 0.07x_{23} &\leq 300 \quad \text{Month 3} \end{aligned}$$

TABLE 4.8 MACHINE, LABOR, AND STORAGE CAPACITIES FOR BOLLINGER ELECTRONICS

Month	Machine Capacity (hours)	Labor Capacity (hours)	Storage Capacity (square feet)
April	400	300	10,000
May	500	300	10,000
June	600	300	10,000

TABLE 4.9 MACHINE, LABOR, AND STORAGE REQUIREMENTS FOR COMPONENTS 322A AND 802B

Component	Machine (hours/unit)	Labor (hours/unit)	Storage (square feet/unit)
322A	0.10	0.05	2
802B	0.08	0.07	3

Storage Capacity

$$2s_{11} + 3s_{21} \leq 10{,}000 \quad \text{Month 1}$$
$$2s_{12} + 3s_{22} \leq 10{,}000 \quad \text{Month 2}$$
$$2s_{13} + 3s_{23} \leq 10{,}000 \quad \text{Month 3}$$

One final set of constraints must be added to guarantee that I_m and D_m will reflect the increase or decrease in the total production level for month m. Suppose that the production levels for March, the month before the start of the current production scheduling period, had been 1500 units of component 322A and 1000 units of component 802B for a total production level of 1500 + 1000 = 2500 units. We can find the amount of the change in production for April from the relationship

$$\text{April production} - \text{March production} = \text{Change}$$

Using the April production variables, x_{11} and x_{21}, and the March production of 2500 units, we have

$$(x_{11} + x_{21}) - 2500 = \text{Change}$$

Note that the change can be positive or negative. A positive change reflects an increase in the total production level, and a negative change reflects a decrease in the total production level. We can use the increase in production for April, I_1, and the decrease in production for April, D_1, to specify the constraint for the change in total production for the month of April:

$$(x_{11} + x_{21}) - 2500 = I_1 - D_1$$

Of course, we cannot have an increase in production and a decrease in production during the same one-month period; thus, either, I_1 or D_1 will be zero. If April requires 3000 units of production, $I_1 = 500$ and $D_1 = 0$. If April requires 2200 units of production, $I_1 = 0$ and $D_1 = 300$. This approach of denoting the change in production level as the difference between two nonnegative variables, I_1 and D_1, permits both positive and negative changes in the total production level. If a single variable (say, c_m) had been used to represent the change in production level, only positive changes would be possible because of the nonnegativity requirement.

Using the same approach in May and June (always subtracting the previous month's total production from the current month's total production), we obtain the constraints for the second and third months of the production scheduling period:

$$(x_{12} + x_{22}) - (x_{11} + x_{21}) = I_2 - D_2$$
$$(x_{13} + x_{23}) - (x_{12} + x_{22}) = I_3 - D_3$$

Placing the variables on the left-hand side and the constants on the right-hand side yields the complete set of what are commonly referred to as production-smoothing constraints:

Problem 19 involves a production scheduling application with labor-smoothing constraints.

$$
\begin{aligned}
x_{11} + x_{21} \qquad\qquad\qquad\qquad\qquad\quad - I_1 + D_1 &= 2500 \\
-x_{11} - x_{21} + x_{12} + x_{22} \qquad\qquad\qquad - I_2 + D_2 &= 0 \\
-x_{12} - x_{22} + x_{13} + x_{23} - I_3 + D_3 &= 0
\end{aligned}
$$

Linear programming models for production scheduling are often very large. Thousands of decision variables and constraints are necessary when the problem involves numerous products, machines, and time periods. Data collection for large-scale models can be more time-consuming than either the formulation of the model or the development of the computer solution.

The initially rather small, two-product, three-month scheduling problem has now developed into an 18-variable, 20-constraint linear programming problem. Note that in this problem we were concerned only with one type of machine process, one type of labor, and one type of storage area. Actual production scheduling problems usually involve several machine types, several labor grades, and/or several storage areas, requiring large-scale linear programs. For instance, a problem involving 100 products over a 12-month period could have more than 1000 variables and constraints.

Figure 4.6 shows the optimal solution to the Bollinger Electronics production scheduling problem. Table 4.10 contains a portion of the managerial report based on the optimal solution.

Consider the monthly variation in the production and inventory schedule shown in Table 4.10. Recall that the inventory cost for component 802B is one-half the inventory cost for component 322A. Therefore, as might be expected, component 802B is produced heavily in the first month (April) and then held in inventory for the demand that will occur in future months. Component 322A tends to be produced when needed, and only small amounts are carried in inventory.

The costs of increasing and decreasing the total production volume tend to smooth the monthly variations. In fact, the minimum-cost schedule calls for a 500-unit increase in total production in April and a 2200-unit increase in total production in May. The May production level of 5200 units is then maintained during June.

The machine usage section of the report shows ample machine capacity in all three months. However, labor capacity is at full utilization (slack = 0 for constraint 13 in Figure 4.6) in the month of May. The dual price shows that an additional hour of labor capacity in May will improve the value of the optimal solution (lower cost) by approximately \$1.11.

A linear programming model of a two-product, three-month production system can provide valuable information in terms of identifying a minimum-cost production schedule. In larger production systems, where the number of variables and constraints is too large to track manually, linear programming models can provide a significant advantage in developing cost-saving production schedules. The Management Science in Action, Optimizing Production, Inventory, and Distribution at the Kellogg Company, illustrates the use of a large-scale multiperiod linear program for production planning and distribution.

Workforce Assignment

Workforce assignment problems frequently occur when production managers must make decisions involving staffing requirements for a given planning period. Workforce assignments often have some flexibility, and at least some personnel can be assigned to more than one department or work center. Such is the case when employees have been cross-trained on two or more jobs or, for instance, when sales personnel can be transferred between stores. In the following application, we show how linear programming can be used to determine not only an optimal product mix, but also an optimal workforce assignment.

McCormick Manufacturing Company produces two products with contributions to profit per unit of \$10 and \$9, respectively. The labor requirements per unit produced and the total hours of labor available from personnel assigned to each of four departments are

FIGURE 4.6 THE MANAGEMENT SCIENTIST SOLUTION FOR THE BOLLINGER ELECTRONICS PROBLEM

EXCELfile
Bollinger

```
Objective Function Value =          225295.000

     Variable            Value          Reduced Costs
  --------------    ---------------    ------------------
       X11                 500.000                 0.000
       X12                3200.000                 0.000
       X13                5200.000                 0.000
       X21                2500.000                 0.000
       X22                2000.000                 0.000
       X23                   0.000                 0.128
       S11                   0.000                 0.172
       S12                 200.000                 0.000
       S13                 400.000                 0.000
       S21                1700.000                 0.000
       S22                3200.000                 0.000
       S23                 200.000                 0.000
       I1                  500.000                 0.000
       I2                 2200.000                 0.000
       I3                    0.000                 0.072
       D1                    0.000                 0.700
       D2                    0.000                 0.700
       D3                    0.000                 0.628

    Constraint       Slack/Surplus         Dual Prices
  --------------    ---------------    ------------------
        1                    0.000               -20.000
        2                    0.000               -10.000
        3                    0.000               -20.128
        4                    0.000               -10.150
        5                    0.000               -20.428
        6                    0.000               -10.300
        7                    0.000               -20.728
        8                    0.000               -10.450
        9                  150.000                 0.000
       10                   20.000                 0.000
       11                   80.000                 0.000
       12                  100.000                 0.000
       13                    0.000                 1.111
       14                   40.000                 0.000
       15                 4900.000                 0.000
       16                    0.000                 0.000
       17                 8600.000                 0.000
       18                    0.000                 0.500
       19                    0.000                 0.500
       20                    0.000                 0.428
```

TABLE 4.10 MINIMUM COST PRODUCTION SCHEDULE INFORMATION FOR THE BOLLINGER ELECTRONICS PROBLEM

Activity	April	May	June
Production			
Component 322A	500	3200	5200
Component 802B	2500	2000	0
Totals	3000	5200	5200
Ending inventory			
Component 322A	0	200	400
Component 802B	1700	3200	200
Machine usage			
Scheduled hours	250	480	520
Slack capacity hours	150	20	80
Labor usage			
Scheduled hours	200	300	260
Slack capacity hours	100	0	40
Storage usage			
Scheduled storage	5100	10,000	1400
Slack capacity	4900	0	8600
Total production, inventory, and production-smoothing cost = $225,295			

MANAGEMENT SCIENCE IN ACTION

OPTIMIZING PRODUCTION, INVENTORY, AND DISTRIBUTION AT THE KELLOGG COMPANY*

The Kellogg Company is the largest cereal producer in the world and a leading producer of convenience foods, such as Kellogg's Pop-Tarts and Nutri-Grain cereal bars. Kellogg produces more than 40 different cereals at plants in 19 countries, on six continents. The company markets its products in more than 160 countries and employs more than 15,600 people in its worldwide organization. In the cereal business alone, Kellogg coordinates the production of about 80 products using a total of approximately 90 production lines and 180 packaging lines.

Kellogg has a long history of using linear programming for production planning and distribution. The Kellogg Planning System (KPS) is a large-scale, multiperiod linear program. The operational version of KPS makes production, packaging, inventory, and distribution decisions on a weekly basis. The primary objective of the system is to minimize the total cost of meeting estimated demand; constraints involve processing line capacities, packaging line capacities, and satisfying safety stock requirements.

A tactical version of KPS helps to establish plant budgets and make capacity-expansion and consolidation decisions on a monthly basis. The tactical version was recently used to guide a consolidation of production capacity that resulted in projected savings of $35 to $40 million per year. Because of the success Kellogg has had using KPS in their North American operations, the company is now introducing KPS into Latin America, and is studying the development of a global KPS model.

*Based on G. Brown, J. Keegan, B. Vigus, and K. Wood, "The Kellogg Company Optimizes Production, Inventory, and Distribution," *Interfaces* (November/December 2001): 1–15.

TABLE 4.11 DEPARTMENTAL LABOR-HOURS PER UNIT AND TOTAL HOURS AVAILABLE FOR THE McCORMICK MANUFACTURING COMPANY

	Labor-Hours per Unit		
Department	Product 1	Product 2	Total Hours Available
1	0.65	0.95	6500
2	0.45	0.85	6000
3	1.00	0.70	7000
4	0.15	0.30	1400

shown in Table 4.11. Assuming that the number of hours available in each department is fixed, we can formulate McCormick's problem as a standard product-mix linear program with the following decision variables:

$$P_1 = \text{units of product 1}$$
$$P_2 = \text{units of product 2}$$

The linear program is

$$\begin{aligned} \text{Max} \quad & 10P_1 + 9P_2 \\ \text{s.t.} \quad & \\ & 0.65P_1 + 0.95P_2 \leq 6500 \\ & 0.45P_1 + 0.85P_2 \leq 6000 \\ & 1.00P_1 + 0.70P_2 \leq 7000 \\ & 0.15P_1 + 0.30P_2 \leq 1400 \\ & P_1, P_2 \geq 0 \end{aligned}$$

The optimal solution to the linear programming model is shown in Figure 4.7. After rounding, it calls for 5744 units of product 1, 1795 units of product 2, and a total profit of

FIGURE 4.7 THE MANAGEMENT SCIENTIST SOLUTION FOR THE McCORMICK MANUFACTURING COMPANY PROBLEM WITH NO WORKFORCE TRANSFERS PERMITTED

EXCELfile
McCormick

```
Objective Function Value =          73589.744

    Variable            Value           Reduced Costs
  --------------   ---------------   -----------------
       P1              5743.590               0.000
       P2              1794.872               0.000

   Constraint       Slack/Surplus        Dual Prices
  --------------   ---------------   -----------------
       1               1061.538               0.000
       2               1889.744               0.000
       3                  0.000               8.462
       4                  0.000              10.256
```

$73,590. With this optimal solution, departments 3 and 4 are operating at capacity, and departments 1 and 2 have a slack of approximately 1062 and 1890 hours, respectively. We would anticipate that the product mix would change and that the total profit would increase if the workforce assignment could be revised so that the slack, or unused hours, in departments 1 and 2 could be transferred to the departments currently working at capacity. However, the production manager may be uncertain as to how the workforce should be reallocated among the four departments. Let us expand the linear programming model to include decision variables that will help determine the optimal workforce assignment in addition to the profit-maximizing product mix.

Suppose that McCormick has a cross-training program that enables some employees to be transferred between departments. By taking advantage of the cross-training skills, a limited number of employees and labor-hours may be transferred from one department to another. For example, suppose that the cross-training permits transfers as shown in Table 4.12. Row 1 of this table shows that some employees assigned to department 1 have cross-training skills that permit them to be transferred to department 2 or 3. The right-hand column shows that, for the current production planning period, a maximum of 400 hours can be transferred from department 1. Similar cross-training transfer capabilities and capacities are shown for departments 2, 3, and 4.

When workforce assignments are flexible, we do not automatically know how many hours of labor should be assigned to or be transferred from each department. We need to add decision variables to the linear programming model to account for such changes.

$$b_i = \text{the labor-hours allocated to department } i \text{ for } i = 1, 2, 3, \text{ and } 4$$
$$t_{ij} = \text{the labor-hours transferred from department } i \text{ to department } j$$

The right-hand sides are now treated as decision variables.

With the addition of decision variables b_1, b_2, b_3, and b_4, we write the capacity restrictions for the four departments as follows:

$$\begin{aligned}
0.65P_1 + 0.95P_2 &\le b_1 \\
0.45P_1 + 0.85P_2 &\le b_2 \\
1.00P_1 + 0.70P_2 &\le b_3 \\
0.15P_1 + 0.30P_2 &\le b_4
\end{aligned}$$

Because b_1, b_2, b_3, and b_4 are now decision variables, we follow the standard practice of placing these variables on the left side of the inequalities, and the first four constraints of the linear programming model become

$$\begin{array}{llllll}
0.65P_1 + 0.95P_2 & - b_1 & & & & \le 0 \\
0.45P_1 + 0.85P_2 & & - b_2 & & & \le 0 \\
1.00P_1 + 0.70P_2 & & & - b_3 & & \le 0 \\
0.15P_1 + 0.30P_2 & & & & - b_4 & \le 0
\end{array}$$

The labor-hours ultimately allocated to each department must be determined by a series of labor balance equations, or constraints, that include the number of hours initially assigned to each department plus the number of hours transferred into the department minus the number of hours transferred out of the department. Using department 1 as an example, we determine the workforce allocation as follows:

$$b_1 = \begin{pmatrix}\text{Hours} \\ \text{initially in} \\ \text{department 1}\end{pmatrix} + \begin{pmatrix}\text{Hours} \\ \text{transferred into} \\ \text{department 1}\end{pmatrix} - \begin{pmatrix}\text{Hours} \\ \text{transferred out of} \\ \text{department 1}\end{pmatrix}$$

TABLE 4.12 CROSS-TRAINING ABILITY AND CAPACITY INFORMATION

From Department	Cross-Training Transfers Permitted to Department 1	2	3	4	Maximum Hours Transferable
1	—	yes	yes	—	400
2	—	—	yes	yes	800
3	—	—	—	yes	100
4	yes	yes	—	—	200

Table 4.11 shows 6500 hours initially assigned to department 1. We use the transfer decision variables t_{i1} to denote transfers into department 1 and t_{1j} to denote transfers from department 1. Table 4.12 shows that the cross-training capabilities involving department 1 are restricted to transfers from department 4 (variable t_{41}) and transfers to either department 2 or department 3 (variables t_{12} and t_{13}). Thus, we can express the total workforce allocation for department 1 as

$$b_1 = 6500 + t_{41} - t_{12} - t_{13}$$

Moving the decision variables for the workforce transfers to the left-hand side, we have the labor balance equation or constraint

$$b_1 - t_{41} + t_{12} + t_{13} = 6500$$

This form of constraint will be needed for each of the four departments. Thus, the following labor balance constraints for departments 2, 3, and 4 would be added to the model.

$$\begin{aligned} b_2 - t_{12} - t_{42} + t_{23} + t_{24} &= 6000 \\ b_3 - t_{13} - t_{23} + t_{34} &= 7000 \\ b_4 - t_{24} - t_{34} + t_{41} + t_{42} &= 1400 \end{aligned}$$

Finally, Table 4.12 shows the number of hours that may be transferred from each department is limited, indicating that a transfer capacity constraint must be added for each of the four departments. The additional constraints are

$$\begin{aligned} t_{12} + t_{13} &\leq 400 \\ t_{23} + t_{24} &\leq 800 \\ t_{34} &\leq 100 \\ t_{41} + t_{42} &\leq 200 \end{aligned}$$

Variations in the workforce assignment model could be used in situations such as allocating raw material resources to products, allocating machine time to products, and allocating salesforce time to stores or sales territories.

The complete linear programming model has two product decision variables (P_1 and P_2), four department workforce assignment variables (b_1, b_2, b_3, and b_4), seven transfer variables ($t_{12}, t_{13}, t_{23}, t_{24}, t_{34}, t_{41}$, and t_{42}), and 12 constraints. Figure 4.8 shows the optimal solution to this linear program.

McCormick's profit can be increased by \$84,011 − \$73,590 = \$10,421 by taking advantage of cross-training and workforce transfers. The optimal product mix of 6825 units of product 1 and 1751 units of product 2 can be achieved if $t_{13} = 400$ hours are transferred from department 1 to department 3; $t_{23} = 651$ hours are transferred from department 2 to department 3; and $t_{24} = 149$ hours are transferred from department 2 to department 4. The

FIGURE 4.8 THE MANAGEMENT SCIENTIST SOLUTION FOR THE McCORMICK MANUFACTURING COMPANY PROBLEM

EXCELfile McCormick

```
Objective Function Value =          84011.299

     Variable              Value            Reduced Costs
  --------------     ---------------     -----------------
        P1                6824.859                0.000
        P2                1751.412                0.000
        B1                6100.000                0.000
        B2                5200.000                0.000
        B3                8050.847                0.000
        B4                1549.153                0.000
        T12                  0.000                8.249
        T13                400.000                0.000
        T23                650.847                0.000
        T24                149.153                0.000
        T34                  0.000                0.000
        T41                  0.000                7.458
        T42                  0.000                8.249

    Constraint          Slack/Surplus          Dual Prices
  --------------     ---------------     -----------------
         1                   0.000                0.791
         2                 640.113                0.000
         3                   0.000                8.249
         4                   0.000                8.249
         5                   0.000                0.791
         6                   0.000                0.000
         7                   0.000                8.249
         8                   0.000                8.249
         9                   0.000                7.458
        10                   0.000                8.249
        11                 100.000                0.000
        12                 200.000                0.000
```

resulting workforce assignments for departments 1–4 would provide 6100, 5200, 8051, and 1549 hours, respectively.

If a manager has the flexibility to assign personnel to different departments, reduced workforce idle time, improved workforce utilization, and improved profit should result. The linear programming model in this section automatically assigns employees and labor-hours to the departments in the most profitable manner.

Blending Problems

Blending problems arise whenever a manager must decide how to blend two or more resources to produce one or more products. In these situations, the resources contain one or more essential ingredients that must be blended into final products that will contain specific percentages of each. In most of these applications, then, management must decide how much of each resource to purchase to satisfy product specifications and product demands at minimum cost.

Blending problems occur frequently in the petroleum industry (e.g., blending crude oil to produce different octane gasolines), chemical industry (e.g., blending chemicals to produce fertilizers and weed killers), and food industry (e.g., blending ingredients to produce soft drinks and soups). In this section we illustrate how to apply linear programming to a blending problem in the petroleum industry.

The Grand Strand Oil Company produces regular and premium gasoline for independent service stations in the southeastern United States. The Grand Strand refinery manufactures the gasoline products by blending three petroleum components. The gasolines are sold at different prices, and the petroleum components have different costs. The firm wants to determine how to mix or blend the three components into the two gasoline products and maximize profits.

Data available show that regular gasoline can be sold for $2.90 per gallon and premium gasoline for $3.00 per gallon. For the current production planning period, Grand Strand can obtain the three petroleum components at the cost per gallon and in the quantities shown in Table 4.13.

Product specifications for the regular and premium gasolines restrict the amounts of each component that can be used in each gasoline product. Table 4.14 lists the product specifications. Current commitments to distributors require Grand Strand to produce at least 10,000 gallons of regular gasoline.

The Grand Strand blending problem is to determine how many gallons of each component should be used in the regular gasoline blend and how many should be used in the premium gasoline blend. The optimal blending solution should maximize the firm's profit, subject to the constraints on the available petroleum supplies shown in Table 4.13, the product specifications shown in Table 4.14, and the required 10,000 gallons of regular gasoline.

We define the decision variables as

$$
\begin{aligned}
x_{ij} = {} & \text{gallons of component } i \text{ used in gasoline } j, \\
& \text{where } i = 1, 2, \text{ or } 3 \text{ for components } 1, 2, \text{ or } 3, \\
& \text{and } j = r \text{ if regular or } j = p \text{ if premium}
\end{aligned}
$$

The six decision variables are

$$
\begin{aligned}
x_{1r} &= \text{gallons of component 1 in regular gasoline} \\
x_{2r} &= \text{gallons of component 2 in regular gasoline} \\
x_{3r} &= \text{gallons of component 3 in regular gasoline} \\
x_{1p} &= \text{gallons of component 1 in premium gasoline} \\
x_{2p} &= \text{gallons of component 2 in premium gasoline} \\
x_{3p} &= \text{gallons of component 3 in premium gasoline}
\end{aligned}
$$

TABLE 4.13 PETROLEUM COST AND SUPPLY FOR THE GRAND STRAND BLENDING PROBLEM

Petroleum Component	Cost/Gallon	Maximum Available
1	$2.50	5,000 gallons
2	$2.60	10,000 gallons
3	$2.84	10,000 gallons

TABLE 4.14 PRODUCT SPECIFICATIONS FOR THE GRAND STRAND BLENDING PROBLEM

Product	Specifications
Regular gasoline	At most 30% component 1
	At least 40% component 2
	At most 20% component 3
Premium gasoline	At least 25% component 1
	At most 45% component 2
	At least 30% component 3

The total number of gallons of each type of gasoline produced is the sum of the number of gallons produced using each of the three petroleum components.

Total Gallons Produced

$$\text{Regular gasoline} = x_{1r} + x_{2r} + x_{3r}$$
$$\text{Premium gasoline} = x_{1p} + x_{2p} + x_{3p}$$

The total gallons of each petroleum component are computed in a similar fashion.

Total Petroleum Component Use

$$\text{Component 1} = x_{1r} + x_{1p}$$
$$\text{Component 2} = x_{2r} + x_{2p}$$
$$\text{Component 3} = x_{3r} + x_{3p}$$

We develop the objective function of maximizing the profit contribution by identifying the difference between the total revenue from both gasolines and the total cost of the three petroleum components. By multiplying the \$2.90 per gallon price by the total gallons of regular gasoline, the \$3.00 per gallon price by the total gallons of premium gasoline, and the component cost per gallon figures in Table 4.13 by the total gallons of each component used, we obtain the objective function:

$$\begin{aligned} \text{Max} \quad & 2.90(x_{1r} + x_{2r} + x_{3r}) + 3.00(x_{1p} + x_{2p} + x_{3p}) \\ & - 2.50(x_{1r} + x_{1p}) - 2.60(x_{2r} + x_{2p}) - 2.84(x_{3r} + x_{3p}) \end{aligned}$$

When we combine terms, the objective function becomes

$$\text{Max} \quad 0.40x_{1r} + 0.30x_{2r} + 0.06x_{3r} + 0.50x_{1p} + 0.40x_{2p} + 0.16x_{3p}$$

The limitations on the availability of the three petroleum components are

$$\begin{aligned} x_{1r} + x_{1p} &\le 5{,}000 \quad \text{Component 1} \\ x_{2r} + x_{2p} &\le 10{,}000 \quad \text{Component 2} \\ x_{3r} + x_{3p} &\le 10{,}000 \quad \text{Component 3} \end{aligned}$$

Six constraints are now required to meet the product specifications stated in Table 4.14. The first specification states that component 1 can account for no more than 30 percent of the total gallons of regular gasoline produced. That is,

$$x_{1r} \le 0.30(x_{1r} + x_{2r} + x_{3r})$$

Rewriting this constraint with the variables on the left-hand side and a constant on the right-hand side yields

$$0.70x_{1_r} - 0.30x_{2_r} - 0.30x_{3_r} \leq 0$$

The second product specification listed in Table 4.14 becomes

$$x_{2_r} \geq 0.40(x_{1_r} + x_{2_r} + x_{3_r})$$

and thus

$$-0.40x_{1_r} + 0.60x_{2_r} - 0.40x_{3_r} \geq 0$$

Similarly, we write the four remaining blending specifications listed in Table 4.14 as

$$\begin{aligned}
-0.20x_{1_r} - 0.20x_{2_r} + 0.80x_{3_r} &\leq 0 \\
+0.75x_{1_p} - 0.25x_{2_p} - 0.25x_{3_p} &\geq 0 \\
-0.45x_{1_p} + 0.55x_{2_p} - 0.45x_{3_p} &\leq 0 \\
-0.30x_{1_p} - 0.30x_{2_p} + 0.70x_{3_p} &\geq 0
\end{aligned}$$

The constraint for at least 10,000 gallons of regular gasoline is

$$x_{1_r} + x_{2_r} + x_{3_r} \geq 10{,}000$$

The complete linear programming model with six decision variables and 10 constraints is

$$\begin{array}{llr}
\text{Max} & 0.40x_{1_r} + 0.30x_{2_r} + 0.06x_{3_r} + 0.50x_{1_p} + 0.40x_{2_p} + 0.16x_{3_p} & \\
\text{s.t.} & & \\
& x_{1_r} + x_{1_p} & \leq 5{,}000 \\
& x_{2_r} + x_{2_p} & \leq 10{,}000 \\
& x_{3_r} + x_{3_p} & \leq 10{,}000 \\
& 0.70x_{1_r} - 0.30x_{2_r} - 0.30x_{3_r} & \leq 0 \\
& -0.40x_{1_r} + 0.60x_{2_r} - 0.40x_{3_r} & \geq 0 \\
& -0.20x_{1_r} - 0.20x_{2_r} + 0.80x_{3_r} & \leq 0 \\
& 0.75x_{1_p} - 0.25x_{2_p} - 0.25x_{3_p} & \geq 0 \\
& -0.45x_{1_p} + 0.55x_{2_p} - 0.45x_{3_p} & \leq 0 \\
& -0.30x_{1_p} - 0.30x_{2_p} + 0.70x_{3_p} & \geq 0 \\
& x_{1_r} + x_{2_r} + x_{3_r} & \geq 10{,}000 \\
& x_{1_r}, x_{2_r}, x_{3_r}, x_{1_p}, x_{2_p}, x_{3_p} \geq 0 &
\end{array}$$

Try Problem 15 as another example of a blending model.

The optimal solution to the Grand Strand blending problem is shown in Figure 4.9. The optimal solution, which provides a profit of $7100, is summarized in Table 4.15. The optimal blending strategy shows that 10,000 gallons of regular gasoline should be produced. The regular gasoline will be manufactured as a blend of 1250 gallons of component 1, 6750 gallons of component 2, and 2000 gallons of component 3. The 15,000 gallons of premium gasoline will be manufactured as a blend of 3750 gallons of component 1, 3250 gallons of component 2, and 8000 gallons of component 3.

FIGURE 4.9 THE MANAGEMENT SCIENTIST SOLUTION FOR THE GRAND STRAND BLENDING PROBLEM

EXCELfile
Grand

```
Objective Function Value =              7100.000

     Variable              Value              Reduced Costs
  --------------      ---------------      ------------------
        X1R              1250.000                  0.000
        X2R              6750.000                  0.000
        X3R              2000.000                  0.000
        X1P              3750.000                  0.000
        X2P              3250.000                  0.000
        X3P              8000.000                  0.000

    Constraint          Slack/Surplus          Dual Prices
  --------------      ---------------      ------------------
         1                  0.000                  0.500
         2                  0.000                  0.400
         3                  0.000                  0.160
         4               1750.000                  0.000
         5               2750.000                  0.000
         6                  0.000                  0.000
         7                  0.000                  0.000
         8               3500.000                  0.000
         9               3500.000                  0.000
        10                  0.000                 -0.100
```

The interpretation of the slack and surplus variables associated with the product specification constraints (constraints 4–9) in Figure 4.9 needs some clarification. If the constraint is a $\leq$ constraint, the value of the slack variable can be interpreted as the gallons of component use below the maximum amount of the component use specified by the constraint. For example, the slack of 1750.000 for constraint 4 shows that component 1 use is 1750 gallons below the maximum amount of component 1 that could have been used in the production of 10,000 gallons of regular gasoline. If the product specification constraint is a $\geq$ constraint, a surplus variable shows the gallons of component use above the minimum amount of component use specified by the blending constraint. For example, the surplus of 2750.000 for constraint 5 shows that component 2 use is 2750 gallons above the minimum amount of component 2 that must be used in the production of 10,000 gallons of regular gasoline.

TABLE 4.15 GRAND STRAND GASOLINE BLENDING SOLUTION

	Gallons of Component (percentage)			
Gasoline	**Component 1**	**Component 2**	**Component 3**	Total
Regular	1250 (12.5%)	6750 (67.5%)	2000 (20%)	10,000
Premium	3750 (25%)	3250 (21⅔%)	8000 (53⅓%)	15,000

NOTES AND COMMENTS

A convenient way to define the decision variables in a blending problem is to use a matrix in which the rows correspond to the raw materials and the columns correspond to the final products. For example, in the Grand Strand blending problem, we define the decision variables as follows:

This approach has two advantages: (1) it provides a systematic way to define the decision variables for any blending problem; and (2) it provides a visual image of the decision variables in terms of how they are related to the raw materials, products, and each other.

		Final Products	
		Regular Gasoline	**Premium Gasoline**
Raw Materials	**Component 1**	x_{1r}	x_{1p}
	Component 2	x_{2r}	x_{2p}
	Component 3	x_{3r}	x_{3p}

SUMMARY

In this chapter we presented a broad range of applications that demonstrate how to use linear programming to assist in the decision-making process. We formulated and solved problems from marketing, finance, and operations management, and interpreted the computer output.

Many of the illustrations presented in this chapter are scaled-down versions of actual situations in which linear programming has been applied. In real-world applications, the problem may not be so concisely stated, the data for the problem may not be as readily available, and the problem most likely will involve numerous decision variables and/or constraints. However, a thorough study of the applications in this chapter is a good place to begin in applying linear programming to real problems.

PROBLEMS

Note: The following problems have been designed to give you an understanding and appreciation of the broad range of problems that can be formulated as linear programs. You should be able to formulate a linear programming model for each of the problems. However, you will need access to a linear programming computer package to develop the solutions and make the requested interpretations.

1. The Westchester Chamber of Commerce periodically sponsors public service seminars and programs. Currently, promotional plans are under way for this year's program. Advertising alternatives include television, radio, and newspaper. Audience estimates, costs, and maximum media usage limitations are as shown.

Constraint	Television	Radio	Newspaper
Audience per advertisement	100,000	18,000	40,000
Cost per advertisement	\$2000	\$300	\$600
Maximum media usage	10	20	10

To ensure a balanced use of advertising media, radio advertisements must not exceed 50% of the total number of advertisements authorized. In addition, television should account for at least 10% of the total number of advertisements authorized.

a. If the promotional budget is limited to $18,200, how many commercial messages should be run on each medium to maximize total audience contact? What is the allocation of the budget among the three media, and what is the total audience reached?
b. By how much would audience contact increase if an extra $100 were allocated to the promotional budget?

2. The management of Hartman Company is trying to determine the amount of each of two products to produce over the coming planning period. The following information concerns labor availability, labor utilization, and product profitability.

Department	Product (hours/unit) 1	2	Labor-Hours Available
A	1.00	0.35	100
B	0.30	0.20	36
C	0.20	0.50	50
Profit contribution/unit	$30.00	$15.00	

a. Develop a linear programming model of the Hartman Company problem. Solve the model to determine the optimal production quantities of products 1 and 2.
b. In computing the profit contribution per unit, management doesn't deduct labor costs because they are considered fixed for the upcoming planning period. However, suppose that overtime can be scheduled in some of the departments. Which departments would you recommend scheduling for overtime? How much would you be willing to pay per hour of overtime in each department?
c. Suppose that 10, 6, and 8 hours of overtime may be scheduled in departments A, B, and C, respectively. The cost per hour of overtime is $18 in department A, $22.50 in department B, and $12 in department C. Formulate a linear programming model that can be used to determine the optimal production quantities if overtime is made available. What are the optimal production quantities, and what is the revised total contribution to profit? How much overtime do you recommend using in each department? What is the increase in the total contribution to profit if overtime is used?

3. The employee credit union at State University is planning the allocation of funds for the coming year. The credit union makes four types of loans to its members. In addition, the credit union invests in risk-free securities to stabilize income. The various revenue-producing investments together with annual rates of return are as follows:

Type of Loan/Investment	**Annual Rate of Return (%)**
Automobile loans	8
Furniture loans	10
Other secured loans	11
Signature loans	12
Risk-free securities	9

The credit union will have $2 million available for investment during the coming year. State laws and credit union policies impose the following restrictions on the composition of the loans and investments.

- Risk-free securities may not exceed 30% of the total funds available for investment.
- Signature loans may not exceed 10% of the funds invested in all loans (automobile, furniture, other secured, and signature loans).
- Furniture loans plus other secured loans may not exceed the automobile loans.

- Other secured loans plus signature loans may not exceed the funds invested in risk-free securities.

How should the $2 million be allocated to each of the loan/investment alternatives to maximize total annual return? What is the projected total annual return?

4. Hilltop Coffee manufactures a coffee product by blending three types of coffee beans. The cost per pound and the available pounds of each bean are as follows:

Bean	Cost per Pound	Available Pounds
1	$0.50	500
2	$0.70	600
3	$0.45	400

Consumer tests with coffee products were used to provide ratings on a scale of 0–100, with higher ratings indicating higher quality. Product quality standards for the blended coffee require a consumer rating for aroma to be at least 75 and a consumer rating for taste to be at least 80. The individual ratings of the aroma and taste for coffee made from 100% of each bean are as follows.

Bean	Aroma Rating	Taste Rating
1	75	86
2	85	88
3	60	75

Assume that the aroma and taste attributes of the coffee blend will be a weighted average of the attributes of the beans used in the blend.

a. What is the minimum-cost blend that will meet the quality standards and provide 1000 pounds of the blended coffee product?
b. What is the cost per pound for the coffee blend?
c. Determine the aroma and taste ratings for the coffee blend.
d. If additional coffee were to be produced, what would be the expected cost per pound?

5. Ajax Fuels, Inc., is developing a new additive for airplane fuels. The additive is a mixture of three ingredients: A, B, and C. For proper performance, the total amount of additive (amount of A + amount of B + amount of C) must be at least 10 ounces per gallon of fuel. However, because of safety reasons, the amount of additive must not exceed 15 ounces per gallon of fuel. The mix or blend of the three ingredients is critical. At least 1 ounce of ingredient A must be used for every ounce of ingredient B. The amount of ingredient C must be at least one-half the amount of ingredient A. If the costs per ounce for ingredients A, B, and C are $0.10, $0.03, and $0.09, respectively, find the minimum-cost mixture of A, B, and C for each gallon of airplane fuel.

6. G. Kunz and Sons, Inc., manufactures two products used in the heavy equipment industry. Both products require manufacturing operations in two departments. The following are the production time (in hours) and profit contribution figures for the two products.

		Labor-Hours	
Product	Profit per Unit	Dept. A	Dept. B
1	$25	6	12
2	$20	8	10

For the coming production period, Kunz has available a total of 900 hours of labor that can be allocated to either of the two departments. Find the production plan and labor allocation (hours assigned in each department) that will maximize the total contribution to profit.

7. As part of the settlement for a class action lawsuit, Hoxworth Corporation must provide sufficient cash to make the following annual payments (in thousands of dollars).

Year	1	2	3	4	5	6
Payment	190	215	240	285	315	460

The annual payments must be made at the beginning of each year. The judge will approve an amount that, along with earnings on its investment, will cover the annual payments. Investment of the funds will be limited to savings (at 4% annually) and government securities, at prices and rates currently quoted in *The Wall Street Journal.*

Hoxworth wants to develop a plan for making the annual payments by investing in the following securities (par value = \$1000). Funds not invested in these securities will be placed in savings.

Security	Current Price	Rate (%)	Years to Maturity
1	\$1055	6.750	3
2	\$1000	5.125	4

Assume that interest is paid annually. The plan will be submitted to the judge and, if approved, Hoxworth will be required to pay a trustee the amount that will be required to fund the plan.

a. Use linear programming to find the minimum cash settlement necessary to fund the annual payments.
b. Use the dual price to determine how much more Hoxworth should be willing to pay now to reduce the payment at the beginning of year 6 to \$400,000.
c. Use the dual price to determine how much more Hoxworth should be willing to pay to reduce the year 1 payment to \$150,000.
d. Suppose that the annual payments are to be made at the end of each year. Reformulate the model to accommodate this change. How much would Hoxworth save if this change could be negotiated?

8. The Clark County Sheriff's Department schedules police officers for 8-hour shifts. The beginning times for the shifts are 8:00 A.M., noon, 4:00 P.M., 8:00 P.M., midnight, and 4:00 A.M. An officer beginning a shift at one of these times works for the next 8 hours. During normal weekday operations, the number of officers needed varies depending on the time of day. The department staffing guidelines require the following minimum number of officers on duty:

Time of Day	Minimum Officers on Duty
8:00 A.M.–Noon	5
Noon–4:00 P.M.	6
4:00 P.M.–8:00 P.M.	10
8:00 P.M.–Midnight	7
Midnight–4:00 A.M.	4
4:00 A.M.–8:00 A.M.	6

Determine the number of police officers that should be scheduled to begin the 8-hour shifts at each of the six times (8:00 A.M., noon, 4:00 P.M., 8:00 P.M., midnight, and 4:00 A.M.) to minimize the total number of officers required. (*Hint:* Let x_1 = the number of officers beginning work at 8:00 A.M., x_2 = the number of officers beginning work at noon, and so on.)

9. Reconsider the Welte Mutual Funds problem from Section 4.2. Define your decision variables as the fraction of funds invested in each security. Also, modify the constraints limiting investments in the oil and steel industries as follows: No more than 50% of the total funds invested in stock (oil and steel) may be invested in the oil industry, and no more than 50% of the funds invested in stock (oil and steel) may be invested in the steel industry.
   a. Solve the revised linear programming model. What fraction of the portfolio should be invested in each type of security?
   b. How much should be invested in each type of security?
   c. What are the total earnings for the portfolio?
   d. What is the marginal rate of return on the portfolio? That is, how much more could be earned by investing one more dollar in the portfolio?

10. An investment advisor at Shore Financial Services wants to develop a model that can be used to allocate investment funds among four alternatives: stocks, bonds, mutual funds, and cash. For the coming investment period, the company developed estimates of the annual rate of return and the associated risk for each alternative. Risk is measured using an index between 0 and 1, with higher risk values denoting more volatility and thus more uncertainty.

Investment	Annual Rate of Return (%)	Risk
Stocks	10	0.8
Bonds	3	0.2
Mutual funds	4	0.3
Cash	1	0.0

Because cash is held in a money market fund, the annual return is lower, but it carries essentially no risk. The objective is to determine the portion of funds allocated to each investment alternative in order to maximize the total annual return for the portfolio subject to the risk level the client is willing to tolerate.

Total risk is the sum of the risk for all investment alternatives. For instance, if 40% of a client's funds are invested in stocks, 30% in bonds, 20% in mutual funds, and 10% in cash, the total risk for the portfolio would be $0.40(0.8) + 0.30(0.2) + 0.20(0.3) + 0.10(0.0) = 0.44$. An investment advisor will meet with each client to discuss the client's investment objectives and to determine a maximum total risk value for the client. A maximum total risk value of less than 0.3 would be assigned to a conservative investor; a maximum total risk value of between 0.3 and 0.5 would be assigned to a moderate tolerance to risk; and a maximum total risk value greater than 0.5 would be assigned to a more aggressive investor.

Shore Financial Services specified additional guidelines that must be applied to all clients. The guidelines are as follows:

- No more than 75% of the total investment may be in stocks.
- The amount invested in mutual funds must be at least as much as invested in bonds.
- The amount of cash must be at least 10%, but no more than 30% of the total investment funds.

a. Suppose the maximum risk value for a particular client is 0.4. What is the optimal allocation of investment funds among stocks, bonds, mutual funds, and cash? What is the annual rate of return and the total risk for the optimal portfolio?
b. Suppose the maximum risk value for a more conservative client is 0.18. What is the optimal allocation of investment funds for this client? What is the annual rate of return and the total risk for the optimal portfolio?
c. Another more aggressive client has a maximum risk value of 0.7. What is the optimal allocation of investment funds for this client? What is the annual rate of return and the total risk for the optimal portfolio?

d. Refer to the solution for the more aggressive client in part (c). Would this client be interested in having the investment advisor increase the maximum percentage allowed in stocks or decrease the requirement that the amount of cash must be at least 10% of the funds invested? Explain.

e. What is the advantage of defining the decision variables as is done in this model rather than stating the amount to be invested and expressing the decision variables directly in dollar amounts?

11. Edwards Manufacturing Company purchases two component parts from three different suppliers. The suppliers have limited capacity, and no one supplier can meet all the company's needs. In addition, the suppliers charge different prices for the components. Component price data (in price per unit) are as follows:

	Supplier		
Component	1	2	3
1	$12	$13	$14
2	$10	$11	$10

Each supplier has a limited capacity in terms of the total number of components it can supply. However, as long as Edwards provides sufficient advance orders, each supplier can devote its capacity to component 1, component 2, or any combination of the two components, if the total number of units ordered is within its capacity. Supplier capacities are as follows.

Supplier	1	2	3
Capacity	600	1000	800

If the Edwards production plan for the next period includes 1000 units of component 1 and 800 units of component 2, what purchases do you recommend? That is, how many units of each component should be ordered from each supplier? What is the total purchase cost for the components?

12. The Atlantic Seafood Company (ASC) is a buyer and distributor of seafood products that are sold to restaurants and specialty seafood outlets throughout the Northeast. ASC has a frozen storage facility in New York City that serves as the primary distribution point for all products. One of the ASC products is frozen large black tiger shrimp, which are sized at 16–20 pieces per pound. Each Saturday ASC can purchase more tiger shrimp or sell the tiger shrimp at the existing New York City warehouse market price. The ASC goal is to buy tiger shrimp at a low weekly price and sell it later at a higher price. ASC currently has 20,000 pounds of tiger shrimp in storage. Space is available to store a maximum of 100,000 pounds of tiger shrimp each week. In addition, ASC developed the following estimates of tiger shrimp prices for the next four weeks:

Week	Price/lb.
1	$6.00
2	$6.20
3	$6.65
4	$5.55

ASC would like to determine the optimal buying-storing-selling strategy for the next four weeks. The cost to store a pound of shrimp for one week is $0.15, and to account for unforeseen changes in supply or demand, management also indicated that 25,000 pounds of tiger shrimp must be in storage at the end of week 4. Determine the optimal buying-storing-selling strategy for ASC. What is the projected four-week profit?

13. Romans Food Market, located in Saratoga, New York, carries a variety of specialty foods from around the world. Two of the store's leading products use the Romans Food Market name: Romans Regular Coffee and Romans DeCaf Coffee. These coffees are blends of Brazilian Natural and Colombian Mild coffee beans, which are purchased from a distributor located in New York City. Because Romans purchases large quantities, the coffee beans may be purchased on an as-needed basis for a price 10% higher than the market price the distributor pays for the beans. The current market price is \$0.47 per pound for Brazilian Natural and \$0.62 per pound for Colombian Mild. The compositions of each coffee blend are as follows:

	Blend	
Bean	**Regular**	**DeCaf**
Brazilian Natural	75%	40%
Colombian Mild	25%	60%

Romans sells the Regular blend for \$3.60 per pound and the DeCaf blend for \$4.40 per pound. Romans would like to place an order for the Brazilian and Colombian coffee beans that will enable the production of 1000 pounds of Romans Regular coffee and 500 pounds of Romans DeCaf coffee. The production cost is \$0.80 per pound for the Regular blend. Because of the extra steps required to produce DeCaf, the production cost for the DeCaf blend is \$1.05 per pound. Packaging costs for both products are \$0.25 per pound. Formulate a linear programming model that can be used to determine the pounds of Brazilian Natural and Colombian Mild that will maximize the total contribution to profit. What is the optimal solution and what is the contribution to profit?

14. The production manager for the Classic Boat Corporation must determine how many units of the Classic 21 model to produce over the next four quarters. The company has a beginning inventory of 100 Classic 21 boats, and demand for the four quarters is 2000 units in quarter 1, 4000 units in quarter 2, 3000 units in quarter 3, and 1500 units in quarter 4. The firm has limited production capacity in each quarter. That is, up to 4000 units can be produced in quarter 1, 3000 units in quarter 2, 2000 units in quarter 3, and 4000 units in quarter 4. Each boat held in inventory in quarters 1 and 2 incurs an inventory holding cost of \$250 per unit; the holding cost for quarters 3 and 4 is \$300 per unit. The production costs for the first quarter are \$10,000 per unit; these costs are expected to increase by 10% each quarter because of increases in labor and material costs. Management specified that the ending inventory for quarter 4 must be at least 500 boats.
   a. Formulate a linear programming model that can be used to determine the production schedule that will minimize the total cost of meeting demand in each quarter subject to the production capacities in each quarter and also to the required ending inventory in quarter 4.
   b. Solve the linear program formulated in part (a). Then develop a table that will show for each quarter the number of units to manufacture, the ending inventory, and the costs incurred.
   c. Interpret each of the dual prices corresponding to the constraints developed to meet demand in each quarter. Based on these dual prices, what advice would you give the production manager?
   d. Interpret each of the dual prices corresponding to the production capacity in each quarter. Based on each of these dual prices, what advice would you give the production manager?

15. Seastrand Oil Company produces two grades of gasoline: regular and high octane. Both gasolines are produced by blending two types of crude oil. Although both types of crude oil contain the two important ingredients required to produce both gasolines, the

percentage of important ingredients in each type of crude oil differs, as does the cost per gallon. The percentage of ingredients A and B in each type of crude oil and the cost per gallon are shown.

Crude Oil	Cost	Ingredient A	Ingredient B	
1	$0.10	20%	60%	← Crude oil 1 is 60% ingredient B
2	$0.15	50%	30%	

Each gallon of regular gasoline must contain at least 40% of ingredient A, whereas each gallon of high octane can contain at most 50% of ingredient B. Daily demand for regular and high-octane gasoline is 800,000 and 500,000 gallons, respectively. How many gallons of each type of crude oil should be used in the two gasolines to satisfy daily demand at a minimum cost?

16. The Ferguson Paper Company produces rolls of paper for use in adding machines, desk calculators, and cash registers. The rolls, which are 200 feet long, are produced in widths of 1½, 2½, and 3½ inches. The production process provides 200-foot rolls in 10-inch widths only. The firm must therefore cut the rolls to the desired final product sizes. The seven cutting alternatives and the amount of waste generated by each are as follows.

Cutting Alternative	Number of Rolls 1½ in.	2½ in.	3½ in.	Waste (inches)
1	6	0	0	1
2	0	4	0	0
3	2	0	2	0
4	0	1	2	½
5	1	3	0	1
6	1	2	1	0
7	4	0	1	½

The minimum requirements for the three products are

Roll Width (inches)	1½	2½	3½
Units	1000	2000	4000

a. If the company wants to minimize the number of 10-inch rolls that must be manufactured, how many 10-inch rolls will be processed on each cutting alternative? How many rolls are required, and what is the total waste (inches)?

b. If the company wants to minimize the waste generated, how many 10-inch rolls will be processed on each cutting alternative? How many rolls are required, and what is the total waste (inches)?

c. What are the differences in parts (a) and (b) to this problem? In this case, which objective do you prefer? Explain. What types of situations would make the other objective more desirable?

17. Frandec Company manufactures, assembles, and rebuilds material handling equipment used in warehouses and distribution centers. One product, called a Liftmaster, is assembled from four components: a frame, a motor, two supports, and a metal strap. Frandec's production schedule calls for 5000 Liftmasters to be made next month. Frandec purchases

the motors from an outside supplier, but the frames, supports, and straps may be either manufactured by the company or purchased from an outside supplier. Manufacturing and purchase costs per unit are shown.

Component	Manufacturing Cost	Purchase Cost
Frame	$38.00	$51.00
Support	$11.50	$15.00
Strap	$ 6.50	$ 7.50

Three departments are involved in the production of these components. The time (in minutes per unit) required to process each component in each department and the available capacity (in hours) for the three departments are as follows.

	Department		
Component	Cutting	Milling	Shaping
Frame	3.5	2.2	3.1
Support	1.3	1.7	2.6
Strap	0.8	—	1.7
Capacity (hours)	350	420	680

a. Formulate and solve a linear programming model for this make-or-buy application. How many of each component should be manufactured and how many should be purchased?
b. What is the total cost of the manufacturing and purchasing plan?
c. How many hours of production time are used in each department?
d. How much should Frandec be willing to pay for an additional hour of time in the shaping department?
e. Another manufacturer has offered to sell frames to Frandec for $45 each. Could Frandec improve its position by pursuing this opportunity? Why or why not?

18. The Two-Rivers Oil Company near Pittsburgh transports gasoline to its distributors by truck. The company recently contracted to supply gasoline distributors in southern Ohio, and it has $600,000 available to spend on the necessary expansion of its fleet of gasoline tank trucks. Three models of gasoline tank trucks are available.

Truck Model	Capacity (gallons)	Purchase Cost	Monthly Operating Cost, Including Depreciation
Super Tanker	5000	$67,000	$550
Regular Line	2500	$55,000	$425
Econo-Tanker	1000	$46,000	$350

The company estimates that the monthly demand for the region will be 550,000 gallons of gasoline. Because of the size and speed differences of the trucks, the number of deliveries or round trips possible per month for each truck model will vary. Trip capacities are estimated at 15 trips per month for the Super Tanker, 20 trips per month for the Regular Line, and 25 trips per month for the Econo-Tanker. Based on maintenance and driver availability, the firm does not want to add more than 15 new vehicles to its fleet. In addition, the company has decided to purchase at least three of the new Econo-Tankers for use on short-run, low-demand routes. As a final constraint, the company does not want more than half the new models to be Super Tankers.

a. If the company wishes to satisfy the gasoline demand with a minimum monthly operating expense, how many models of each truck should be purchased?
b. If the company did not require at least three Econo-Tankers and did not limit the number of Super Tankers to at most half the new models, how many models of each truck should be purchased?

19. The Silver Star Bicycle Company will be manufacturing both men's and women's models for its Easy-Pedal 10-speed bicycles during the next two months. Management wants to develop a production schedule indicating how many bicycles of each model should be produced in each month. Current demand forecasts call for 150 men's and 125 women's models to be shipped during the first month and 200 men's and 150 women's models to be shipped during the second month. Additional data are shown.

Model	Production Costs	Labor Requirements (hours)		Current Inventory
		Manufacturing	**Assembly**	
Men's	$120	2.0	1.5	20
Women's	$ 90	1.6	1.0	30

Last month the company used a total of 1000 hours of labor. The company's labor relations policy will not allow the combined total hours of labor (manufacturing plus assembly) to increase or decrease by more than 100 hours from month to month. In addition, the company charges monthly inventory at the rate of 2% of the production cost based on the inventory levels at the end of the month. The company would like to have at least 25 units of each model in inventory at the end of the two months.

a. Establish a production schedule that minimizes production and inventory costs and satisfies the labor-smoothing, demand, and inventory requirements. What inventories will be maintained and what are the monthly labor requirements?
b. If the company changed the constraints so that monthly labor increases and decreases could not exceed 50 hours, what would happen to the production schedule? How much will the cost increase? What would you recommend?

20. Filtron Corporation produces filtration containers used in water treatment systems. Although business has been growing, the demand each month varies considerably. As a result, the company utilizes a mix of part-time and full-time employees to meet production demands. Although this approach provides Filtron with great flexibility, it resulted in increased costs and morale problems among employees. For instance, if Filtron needs to increase production from one month to the next, additional part-time employees have to be hired and trained, and costs go up. If Filtron has to decrease production, the workforce has to be reduced and Filtron incurs additional costs in terms of unemployment benefits and decreased morale. Best estimates are that increasing the number of units produced from one month to the next will increase production costs by $1.25 per unit, and that decreasing the number of units produced will increase production costs by $1.00 per unit. In February Filtron produced 10,000 filtration containers but only sold 7500 units; 2500 units are currently in inventory. The sales forecasts for March, April, and May are for 12,000 units, 8000 units, and 15,000 units, respectively. In addition, Filtron has the capacity to store up to 3000 filtration containers at the end of any month. Management would like to determine the number of units to be produced in March, April, and May that will minimize the total cost of the monthly production increases and decreases.

21. Greenville Cabinets received a contract to produce speaker cabinets for a major speaker manufacturer. The contract calls for the production of 3300 bookshelf speakers and 4100 floor speakers over the next two months, with the following delivery schedule.

Model	Month 1	Month 2
Bookshelf	2100	1200
Floor	1500	2600

Greenville estimates that the production time for each bookshelf model is 0.7 hour and the production time for each floor model is 1 hour. The raw material costs are $10 for each bookshelf model and $12 for each floor model. Labor costs are $22 per hour using regular production time and $33 using overtime. Greenville has up to 2400 hours of regular production time available each month and up to 1000 additional hours of overtime available each month. If production for either cabinet exceeds demand in month 1, the cabinets can be stored at a cost of $5 per cabinet. For each product, determine the number of units that should be manufactured each month on regular time and on overtime to minimize total production and storage costs.

22. TriCity Manufacturing (TCM) makes Styrofoam cups, plates, and sandwich and meal containers. Next week's schedule calls for the production of 80,000 small sandwich containers, 80,000 large sandwich containers, and 65,000 meal containers. To make these containers, Styrofoam sheets are melted and formed into final products using three machines: M1, M2, and M3. Machine M1 can process Styrofoam sheets with a maximum width of 12 inches. The width capacity of machine M2 is 16 inches, and the width capacity of machine M3 is 20 inches. The small sandwich containers require 10-inch-wide Styrofoam sheets; thus, these containers can be produced on each of the three machines. The large sandwich containers require 12-inch-wide sheets; thus, these containers can also be produced on each of the three machines. However, the meal containers require 16-inch-wide Styrofoam sheets, so the meal containers cannot be produced on machine M1. Waste is incurred in the production of all three containers because Styrofoam is lost in the heating and forming process as well as in the final trimming of the product. The amount of waste generated varies depending upon the container produced and the machine used. The following table shows the waste in square inches for each machine and product combination. The waste material is recycled for future use.

Machine	Small Sandwich	Large Sandwich	Meal
M1	20	15	—
M2	24	28	18
M3	32	35	36

Production rates also depend upon the container produced and the machine used. The following table shows the production rates in units per minute for each machine and product combination. Machine capacities are limited for the next week. Time available is 35 hours for machine M1, 35 hours for machine M2, and 40 hours for machine M3.

Machine	Small Sandwich	Large Sandwich	Meal
M1	30	25	—
M2	45	40	30
M3	60	52	44

a. Costs associated with reprocessing the waste material have been increasing. Thus, TCM would like to minimize the amount of waste generated in meeting next week's production schedule. Formulate a linear programming model that can be used to determine the best production schedule.
b. Solve the linear program formulated in part (a) to determine the production schedule. How much waste is generated? Which machines, if any, have idle capacity?

23. EZ-Windows, Inc., manufactures replacement windows for the home remodeling business. In January, the company produced 15,000 windows and ended the month with 9000 windows in inventory. EZ-Windows' management team would like to develop a production schedule for the next three months. A smooth production schedule is obviously desirable because it maintains the current workforce and provides a similar month-to-month operation. However, given the sales forecasts, the production capacities, and the storage capabilities as shown, the management team does not think a smooth production schedule with the same production quantity each month possible.

	February	**March**	**April**
Sales forecast	15,000	16,500	20,000
Production capacity	14,000	14,000	18,000
Storage capacity	6,000	6,000	6,000

The company's cost accounting department estimates that increasing production by one window from one month to the next will increase total costs by \$1.00 for each unit increase in the production level. In addition, decreasing production by one unit from one month to the next will increase total costs by \$0.65 for each unit decrease in the production level. Ignoring production and inventory carrying costs, formulate and solve a linear programming model that will minimize the cost of changing production levels while still satisfying the monthly sales forecasts.

24. Morton Financial must decide on the percentage of available funds to commit to each of two investments, referred to as A and B, over the next four periods. The following table shows the amount of new funds available for each of the four periods, as well as the cash expenditure required for each investment (negative values) or the cash income from the investment (positive values). The data shown (in thousands of dollars) reflect the amount of expenditure or income if 100% of the funds available in any period are invested in either A or B. For example, if Morton decides to invest 100% of the funds available in any period in investment A, it will incur cash expenditures of \$1000 in period 1, \$800 in period 2, \$200 in period 3, and income of \$200 in period 4. Note, however, if Morton made the decision to invest 80% in investment A, the cash expenditures or income would be 80% of the values shown.

		Investment	
Period	New Investment Funds Available	A	B
1	1500	−1000	−800
2	400	−800	−500
3	500	−200	−300
4	100	200	300

The amount of funds available in any period is the sum of the new investment funds for the period, the new loan funds, the savings from the previous period, the cash income from investment A, and the cash income from investment B. The funds available in any period can be used to pay the loan and interest from the previous period, placed in savings, used to pay the cash expenditures for investment A, or used to pay the cash expenditures for investment B.

Assume an interest rate of 10% per period for savings and an interest rate of 18% per period on borrowed funds. Let

$$S(t) = \text{the savings for period } t$$
$$L(t) = \text{the new loan funds for period } t$$

Then, in any period t, the savings income from the previous period is $1.1S(t - 1)$ and the loan and interest expenditure from the previous period is $1.18L(t - 1)$.

At the end of period 4, investment A is expected to have a cash value of $3200 (assuming a 100% investment in A), and investment B is expected to have a cash value of $2500 (assuming a 100% investment in B). Additional income and expenses at the end of period 4 will be income from savings in period 4 less the repayment of the period 4 loan plus interest.

Suppose that the decision variables are defined as

$$x_1 = \text{the proportion of investment A undertaken}$$
$$x_2 = \text{the proportion of investment B undertaken}$$

For example, if $x_1 = 0.5$, $500 would be invested in investment A during the first period, and all remaining cash flows and ending investment A values would be multiplied by 0.5. The same holds for investment B. The model must include constraints $x_1 \leq 1$ and $x_2 \leq 1$ to make sure that no more than 100% of the investments can be undertaken.

If no more than $200 can be borrowed in any period, determine the proportions of investments A and B and the amount of savings and borrowing in each period that will maximize the cash value for the firm at the end of the four periods.

25. Western Family Steakhouse offers a variety of low-cost meals and quick service. Other than management, the steakhouse operates with two full-time employees who work 8 hours per day. The rest of the employees are part-time employees who are scheduled for 4-hour shifts during peak meal times. On Saturdays the steakhouse is open from 11:00 A.M. to 10:00 P.M. Management wants to develop a schedule for part-time employees that will minimize labor costs and still provide excellent customer service. The average wage rate for the part-time employees is $7.60 per hour. The total number of full-time and part-time employees needed varies with the time of day as shown.

Time	Total Number of Employees Needed
11:00 A.M.–Noon	9
Noon–1:00 P.M.	9
1:00 P.M.–2:00 P.M.	9
2:00 P.M.–3:00 P.M.	3
3:00 P.M.–4:00 P.M.	3
4:00 P.M.–5:00 P.M.	3
5:00 P.M.–6:00 P.M.	6
6:00 P.M.–7:00 P.M.	12
7:00 P.M.–8:00 P.M.	12
8:00 P.M.–9:00 P.M.	7
9:00 P.M.–10:00 P.M.	7

One full-time employee comes on duty at 11:00 A.M., works 4 hours, takes an hour off, and returns for another 4 hours. The other full-time employee comes to work at 1:00 P.M. and works the same 4-hours-on, 1-hour-off, 4-hours-on pattern.

a. Develop a minimum-cost schedule for part-time employees.

b. What is the total payroll for the part-time employees? How many part-time shifts are needed? Use the surplus variables to comment on the desirability of scheduling at least some of the part-time employees for 3-hour shifts.

c. Assume that part-time employees can be assigned either a 3-hour or a 4-hour shift. Develop a minimum-cost schedule for the part-time employees. How many part-time shifts are needed, and what is the cost savings compared to the previous schedule?

Case Problem 1 PLANNING AN ADVERTISING CAMPAIGN

The Flamingo Grill is an upscale restaurant located in St. Petersburg, Florida. To help plan an advertising campaign for the coming season, Flamingo's management team hired the advertising firm of Haskell & Johnson (HJ). The management team requested HJ's recommendation concerning how the advertising budget should be distributed across television, radio, and newspaper advertisements. The budget has been set at $279,000.

In a meeting with Flamingo's management team, HJ consultants provided the following information about the industry exposure effectiveness rating per ad, their estimate of the number of potential new customers reached per ad, and the cost for each ad.

Advertising Media	Exposure Rating per Ad	New Customers per Ad	Cost per Ad
Television	90	4000	$10,000
Radio	25	2000	$ 3,000
Newspaper	10	1000	$ 1,000

The exposure rating is viewed as a measure of the value of the ad to both existing customers and potential new customers. It is a function of such things as image, message recall, visual and audio appeal, and so on. As expected, the more expensive television advertisement has the highest exposure effectiveness rating along with the greatest potential for reaching new customers.

At this point, the HJ consultants pointed out that the data concerning exposure and reach were only applicable to the first few ads in each medium. For television, HJ stated that the exposure rating of 90 and the 4000 new customers reached per ad were reliable for the first 10 television ads. After 10 ads, the benefit is expected to decline. For planning purposes, HJ recommended reducing the exposure rating to 55 and the estimate of the potential new customers reached to 1500 for any television ads beyond 10. For radio ads, the preceding data are reliable up to a maximum of 15 ads. Beyond 15 ads, the exposure rating declines to 20 and the number of new customers reached declines to 1200 per ad. Similarly, for newspaper ads, the preceding data are reliable up to a maximum of 20; the exposure rating declines to 5 and the potential number of new customers reached declines to 800 for additional ads.

Flamingo's management team accepted maximizing the total exposure rating, across all media, as the objective of the advertising campaign. Because of management's concern with attracting new customers, management stated that the advertising campaign must reach at least 100,000 new customers. To balance the advertising campaign and make use of all advertising media, Flamingo's management team also adopted the following guidelines.

- Use at least twice as many radio advertisements as television advertisements.
- Use no more than 20 television advertisements.
- The television budget should be at least $140,000.
- The radio advertising budget is restricted to a maximum of $99,000.
- The newspaper budget is to be at least $30,000.

HJ agreed to work with these guidelines and provide a recommendation as to how the $279,000 advertising budget should be allocated among television, radio, and newspaper advertising.

Managerial Report

Develop a model that can be used to determine the advertising budget allocation for the Flamingo Grill. Include a discussion of the following in your report.

1. A schedule showing the recommended number of television, radio, and newspaper advertisements and the budget allocation for each medium. Show the total exposure and indicate the total number of potential new customers reached.
2. How would the total exposure change if an additional \$10,000 were added to the advertising budget?
3. A discussion of the ranges for the objective function coefficients. What do the ranges indicate about how sensitive the recommended solution is to HJ's exposure rating coefficients?
4. After reviewing HJ's recommendation, the Flamingo's management team asked how the recommendation would change if the objective of the advertising campaign was to maximize the number of potential new customers reached. Develop the media schedule under this objective.
5. Compare the recommendations from parts 1 and 4. What is your recommendation for the Flamingo Grill's advertising campaign?

Case Problem 2 PHOENIX COMPUTER

Phoenix Computer manufactures and sells personal computers directly to customers. Orders are accepted by phone and through the company's Web site. Phoenix will be introducing several new laptop models over the next few months and management recognizes a need to develop technical support personnel to specialize in the new laptop systems. One option being considered is to hire new employees and put them through a three-month training program. Another option is to put current customer service specialists through a two-month training program on the new laptop models. Phoenix estimates that the need for laptop specialists will grow from 0 to 100 during the months of May through September as follows: May—20; June—30; July—85; August—85; and September—100. After September, Phoenix expects that maintaining a staff of 100 laptop specialists will be sufficient.

The annual salary for a new employee is estimated to be \$27,000 whether the person is hired to enter the training program or to replace a current employee who is entering the training program. The annual salary for the current Phoenix employees who are being considered for the training program is approximately \$36,000. The cost of the three-month training program is \$1500 per person, and the cost of the two-month training program is \$1000 per person. Note that the length of the training program means that a lag will occur between the time when a new person is hired and the time a new laptop specialist is available. The number of current employees who will be available for training is limited. Phoenix estimates that the following numbers can be made available in the coming months: March—15; April—20; May—0; June—5; and July—10. The training center has the capacity to start new three-month and two-month training classes each month; however, the total number of students (new and current employees) that begin training each month cannot exceed 25.

Phoenix needs to determine the number of new hires that should begin the three-month training program each month and the number of current employees that should begin the two-month training program each month. The objective is to satisfy staffing needs during May through September at the lowest possible total cost; that is, minimize the incremental salary cost and the total training cost.

It is currently January, and Phoenix Computer would like to develop a plan for hiring new employees and determining the mix of new hires and current employees to place in the training program.

Managerial Report

Perform an analysis of the Phoenix Computer problem and prepare a report that summarizes your findings. Be sure to include information on and analysis of the following items.

1. The incremental salary and training cost associated with hiring a new employee and training him/her to be a laptop specialist.
2. The incremental salary and training cost associated with putting a current employee through the training program. (Don't forget that a replacement must be hired when the current employee enters the program.)
3. Recommendations regarding the hiring and training plan that will minimize the salary and training costs over the February through August period as well as answers to these questions: What is the total cost of providing technical support for the new laptop models? How much higher will monthly payroll costs be in September than in January?

Case Problem 3 TEXTILE MILL SCHEDULING

The Scottsville Textile Mill* produces five different fabrics. Each fabric can be woven on one or more of the mill's 38 looms. The sales department's forecast of demand for the next month is shown in Table 4.16, along with data on the selling price per yard, variable cost per yard, and purchase price per yard. The mill operates 24 hours a day and is scheduled for 30 days during the coming month.

The mill has two types of looms: dobbie and regular. The dobbie looms are more versatile and can be used for all five fabrics. The regular looms can produce only three of the fabrics. The mill has a total of 38 looms: 8 are dobbie and 30 are regular. The rate of production for each fabric on each type of loom is given in Table 4.17. The time required to change over from producing one fabric to another is negligible and does not have to be considered.

The Scottsville Textile Mill satisfies all demand with either its own fabric or fabric purchased from another mill. Fabrics that cannot be woven at the Scottsville Mill because of limited loom capacity will be purchased from another mill. The purchase price of each fabric is also shown in Table 4.16.

TABLE 4.16 MONTHLY DEMAND, SELLING PRICE, VARIABLE COST, AND PURCHASE PRICE DATA FOR SCOTTSVILLE TEXTILE MILL FABRICS

Fabric	Demand (yards)	Selling Price ($/yard)	Variable Cost ($/yard)	Purchase Price ($/yard)
1	16,500	0.99	0.66	0.80
2	22,000	0.86	0.55	0.70
3	62,000	1.10	0.49	0.60
4	7,500	1.24	0.51	0.70
5	62,000	0.70	0.50	0.70

*This case is based on the Calhoun Textile Mill Case by Jeffrey D. Camm, P. M. Dearing, and Suresh K. Tadisnia, 1987.

TABLE 4.17 LOOM PRODUCTION RATES FOR THE SCOTTSVILLE TEXTILE MILL

	Loom Rate (yards/hour)	
Fabric	**Dobbie**	**Regular**
1	4.63	—
2	4.63	—
3	5.23	5.23
4	5.23	5.23
5	4.17	4.17

Note: Fabrics 1 and 2 can be manufactured only on the dobbie loom.

Managerial Report

Develop a model that can be used to schedule production for the Scottsville Textile Mill, and at the same time, determine how many yards of each fabric must be purchased from another mill. Include a discussion and analysis of the following items in your report.

1. The final production schedule and loom assignments for each fabric.
2. The projected total contribution to profit.
3. A discussion of the value of additional loom time. (The mill is considering purchasing a ninth dobbie loom. What is your estimate of the monthly profit contribution of this additional loom?)
4. A discussion of the objective coefficients' ranges.
5. A discussion of how the objective of minimizing total costs would provide a different model than the objective of maximizing total profit contribution. (How would the interpretation of the objective coefficients' ranges differ for these two models?)

Case Problem 4 WORKFORCE SCHEDULING

Davis Instruments has two manufacturing plants located in Atlanta, Georgia. Product demand varies considerably from month to month, causing Davis extreme difficulty in workforce scheduling. Recently Davis started hiring temporary workers supplied by WorkForce Unlimited, a company that specializes in providing temporary employees for firms in the greater Atlanta area. WorkForce Unlimited offered to provide temporary employees under three contract options that differ in terms of the length of employment and the cost. The three options are summarized:

Option	Length of Employment	Cost
1	One month	$2000
2	Two months	$4800
3	Three months	$7500

The longer contract periods are more expensive because WorkForce Unlimited experiences greater difficulty finding temporary workers who are willing to commit to longer work assignments.

Over the next six months, Davis projects the following needs for additional employees.

Month	January	February	March	April	May	June
Employees Needed	10	23	19	26	20	14

Each month, Davis can hire as many temporary employees as needed under each of the three options. For instance, if Davis hires five employees in January under Option 2, WorkForce Unlimited will supply Davis with five temporary workers who will work two months: January and February. For these workers, Davis will have to pay 5($4800) = $24,000. Because of some merger negotiations under way, Davis does not want to commit to any contractual obligations for temporary employees that extend beyond June.

Davis's quality control program requires each temporary employee to receive training at the time of hire. The training program is required even if the person worked for Davis Instruments in the past. Davis estimates that the cost of training is $875 each time a temporary employee is hired. Thus, if a temporary employee is hired for one month, Davis will incur a training cost of $875, but will incur no additional training cost if the employee is on a two- or three-month contract.

Managerial Report

Develop a model that can be used to determine the number of temporary employees Davis should hire each month under each contract plan in order to meet the projected needs at a minimum total cost. Include the following items in your report:

1. A schedule that shows the number of temporary employees that Davis should hire each month for each contract option.
2. A summary table that shows the number of temporary employees that Davis should hire under each contract option, the associated contract cost for each option, and the associated training cost for each option. Provide summary totals showing the total number of temporary employees hired, total contract costs, and total training costs.
3. If the cost to train each temporary employee could be reduced to $700 per month, what effect would this change have on the hiring plan? Explain. Discuss the implications that this effect on the hiring plan has for identifying methods for reducing training costs. How much of a reduction in training costs would be required to change the hiring plan based on a training cost of $875 per temporary employee?
4. Suppose that Davis hired 10 full-time employees at the beginning of January in order to satisfy part of the labor requirements over the next six months. If Davis can hire full-time employees for $16.50 per hour, including fringe benefits, what effect would it have on total labor and training costs over the six-month period as compared to hiring only temporary employees? Assume that full-time and temporary employees both work approximately 160 hours per month. Provide a recommendation regarding the decision to hire additional full-time employees.

Case Problem 5 DUKE ENERGY COAL ALLOCATION*

Duke Energy manufactures and distributes electricity to customers in the United States and Latin America. Duke recently purchased Cinergy Corporation, which has generating facilities and energy customers in Indiana, Kentucky, and Ohio. For these customers Cinergy has been spending $725 to $750 million each year for the fuel needed to operate its coal-fired and gas-fired power plants; 92% to 95% of the fuel used is coal. In this region, Duke Energy uses 10 coal-burning generating plants: five located inland and five located on

*The authors are indebted to Thomas Mason and David Bossee of Duke Energy Corporation, formerly Cinergy Corp., for their contribution to this case problem.

the Ohio River. Some plants have more than one generating unit. Duke Energy uses 28–29 million tons of coal per year at a cost of approximately $2 million every day in this region.

The company purchases coal using fixed-tonnage or variable-tonnage contracts from mines in Indiana (49%), West Virginia (20%), Ohio (12%), Kentucky (11%), Illinois (5%), and Pennsylvania (3%). The company must purchase all of the coal contracted for on fixed-tonnage contracts, but on variable-tonnage contracts it can purchase varying amounts up to the limit specified in the contract. The coal is shipped from the mines to Duke Energy's generating facilities in Ohio, Kentucky, and Indiana. The cost of coal varies from $19 to $35 per ton and transportation/delivery charges range from $1.50 to $5.00 per ton.

A model is used to determine the megawatt-hours (mWh) of electricity that each generating unit is expected to produce and to provide a measure of each generating unit's efficiency, referred to as the heat rate. The heat rate is the total BTUs required to produce 1 kilowatt-hour (kWh) of electrical power.

Coal Allocation Model

Duke Energy uses a linear programming model, called the coal allocation model, to allocate coal to its generating facilities. The objective of the coal allocation model is to determine the lowest-cost method for purchasing and distributing coal to the generating units. The supply/availability of the coal is determined by the contracts with the various mines, and the demand for coal at the generating units is determined indirectly by the megawatt-hours of electricity each unit must produce.

The cost to process coal, called the add-on cost, depends upon the characteristics of the coal (moisture content, ash content, BTU content, sulfur content, and grindability) and the efficiency of the generating unit. The add-on cost plus the transportation cost are added to the purchase cost of the coal to determine the total cost to purchase and use the coal.

Current Problem

Duke Energy signed three fixed-tonnage contracts and four variable-tonnage contracts. The company would like to determine the least-cost way to allocate the coal available through these contracts to five generating units. The relevant data for the three fixed-tonnage contracts are as follows:

Supplier	Number of Tons Contracted For	Cost ($/ton)	BTUs/lb
RAG	350,000	22	13,000
Peabody Coal Sales	300,000	26	13,300
American Coal Sales	275,000	22	12,600

For example, the contract signed with RAG requires Duke Energy to purchase 350,000 tons of coal at a price of $22 per ton; each pound of this particular coal provides 13,000 BTUs.

The data for the four variable-tonnage contracts follow:

Supplier	Number of Tons Available	Cost ($/ton)	BTUs/lb
Consol, Inc.	200,000	32	12,250
Cyprus Amax	175,000	35	12,000
Addington Mining	200,000	31	12,000
Waterloo	180,000	33	11,300

For example, the contract with Consol, Inc., enables Duke Energy to purchase up to 200,000 tons of coal at a cost of $32 per ton; each pound of this coal provides 12,250 BTUs.

The number of megawatt-hours of electricity that each generating unit must produce and the heat rate provided are as follows:

Generating Unit	Electricity Produced (mWh)	Heat Rate (BTUs per kWh)
Miami Fort Unit 5	550,000	10,500
Miami Fort Unit 7	500,000	10,200
Beckjord Unit 1	650,000	10,100
East Bend Unit 2	750,000	10,000
Zimmer Unit 1	1,100,000	10,000

For example, Miami Fort Unit 5 must produce 550,000 megawatt-hours of electricity, and 10,500 BTUs are needed to produce each kilowatt-hour.

The transportation cost and the add-on cost in dollars per ton are shown here:

	Transportation Cost ($/ton)				
Supplier	Miami Fort Unit 5	Miami Fort Unit 7	Beckjord Unit 1	East Bend Unit 2	Zimmer Unit 1
RAG	5.00	5.00	4.75	5.00	4.75
Peabody	3.75	3.75	3.50	3.75	3.50
American	3.00	3.00	2.75	3.00	2.75
Consol	3.25	3.25	2.85	3.25	2.85
Cyprus	5.00	5.00	4.75	5.00	4.75
Addington	2.25	2.25	2.00	2.25	2.00
Waterloo	2.00	2.00	1.60	2.00	1.60

	Add-On Cost ($/ton)				
Supplier	Miami Fort Unit 5	Miami Fort Unit 7	Beckjord Unit 1	East Bend Unit 2	Zimmer Unit 1
RAG	10.00	10.00	10.00	5.00	6.00
Peabody	10.00	10.00	11.00	6.00	7.00
American	13.00	13.00	15.00	9.00	9.00
Consol	10.00	10.00	11.00	7.00	7.00
Cyprus	10.00	10.00	10.00	5.00	6.00
Addington	5.00	5.00	6.00	4.00	4.00
Waterloo	11.00	11.00	11.00	7.00	9.00

Managerial Report

Prepare a report that summarizes your recommendations regarding Duke Energy's coal allocation problem. Be sure to include information and analysis for the following issues.

1. Determine how much coal to purchase from each of the mining companies and how it should be allocated to the generating units. What is the cost to purchase, deliver, and process the coal?
2. Compute the average cost of coal in cents per million BTUs for each generating unit (a measure of the cost of fuel for the generating units).

3. Compute the average number of BTUs per pound of coal received at each generating unit (a measure of the energy efficiency of the coal received at each unit).
4. Suppose that Duke Energy can purchase an additional 80,000 tons of coal from American Coal Sales as an "all or nothing deal" for $30 per ton. Should Duke Energy purchase the additional 80,000 tons of coal?
5. Suppose that Duke Energy learns that the energy content of the coal from Cyprus Amax is actually 13,000 BTUs per pound. Should Duke Energy revise its procurement plan?
6. Duke Energy has learned from its trading group that Duke Energy can sell 50,000 megawatt-hours of electricity over the grid (to other electricity suppliers) at a price of $30 per megawatt-hour. Should Duke Energy sell the electricity? If so, which generating units should produce the additional electricity?

Appendix 4.1 EXCEL SOLUTION OF HEWLITT CORPORATION FINANCIAL PLANNING PROBLEM

In Appendix 2.3 we showed how Excel could be used to solve the Par, Inc. linear programming problem. To illustrate the use of Excel in solving a more complex linear programming problem, we show the solution to the Hewlitt Corporation financial planning problem presented in Section 4.2.

The spreadsheet formulation and solution of the Hewlitt Corporation problem are shown in Figure 4.10. As described in Appendix 2.3, our practice is to put the data required for the problem in the top part of the worksheet and build the model in the bottom part of

FIGURE 4.10 EXCEL SOLUTION FOR THE HEWLITT CORPORATION PROBLEM

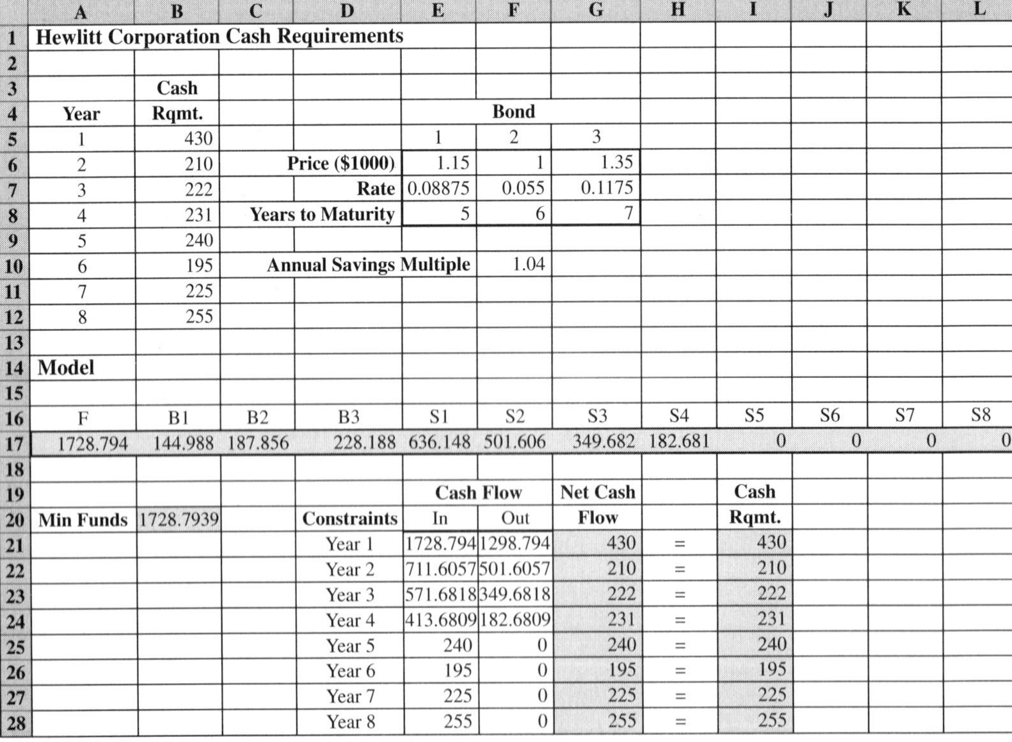

	A	B	C	D	E	F	G	H	I	J	K	L
1	Hewlitt Corporation Cash Requirements											
2												
3		Cash										
4	Year	Rqmt.				Bond						
5	1	430			1	2	3					
6	2	210		Price ($1000)	1.15	1	1.35					
7	3	222		Rate	0.08875	0.055	0.1175					
8	4	231		Years to Maturity	5	6	7					
9	5	240										
10	6	195		Annual Savings Multiple		1.04						
11	7	225										
12	8	255										
13												
14	Model											
15												
16	F	B1	B2	B3	S1	S2	S3	S4	S5	S6	S7	S8
17	1728.794	144.988	187.856	228.188	636.148	501.606	349.682	182.681	0	0	0	0
18												
19					Cash Flow		Net Cash		Cash			
20	Min Funds	1728.7939		Constraints	In	Out	Flow		Rqmt.			
21				Year 1	1728.794	1298.794	430	=	430			
22				Year 2	711.6057	501.6057	210	=	210			
23				Year 3	571.6818	349.6818	222	=	222			
24				Year 4	413.6809	182.6809	231	=	231			
25				Year 5	240	0	240	=	240			
26				Year 6	195	0	195	=	195			
27				Year 7	225	0	225	=	225			
28				Year 8	255	0	255	=	255			

the worksheet. The model consists of a set of cells for the decision variables, a cell for the objective function, a set of cells for the left-hand-side functions, and a set of cells for the right-hand sides of the constraints. The cells for each of these model components are screened; the cells for the decision variables are also enclosed by a boldface line. Descriptive labels are used to make the spreadsheet easy to read.

Formulation

The data and descriptive labels are contained in cells A1:G12. The screened cells in the bottom portion of the spreadsheet contain the key elements of the model required by the Excel Solver.

Decision Variables Cells A17:L17 are reserved for the decision variables. The optimal values (rounded to three places), are shown to be $F = 1728.794$, $B_1 = 144.988$, $B_2 = 187.856$, $B_3 = 228.188$, $S_1 = 636.148$, $S_2 = 501.606$, $S_3 = 349.682$, $S_4 = 182.681$, and $S_5 = S_6 = S_7 = S_8 = 0$.

Objective Function The formula =A17 has been placed into cell B20 to reflect the total funds required. It is simply the value of the decision variable, *F*. The total funds required by the optimal solution is shown to be $1,728,794.

Left-Hand Sides The left-hand sides for the eight constraints represent the annual net cash flow. They are placed into cells G21:G28.

Cell G21 = E21 − F21 (Copy to G22:G28)

For this problem, some of the left-hand-side cells reference other cells that contain formulas. These referenced cells provide Hewlitt's cash flow in and cash flow out for each of the eight years.* The cells and their formulas are as follows:

Cell E21 = A17
Cell E22 = SUMPRODUCT($E$7:$G$7,$B$17:$D$17)+$F$10*E17
Cell E23 = SUMPRODUCT($E$7:$G$7,$B$17:$D$17)+$F$10*F17
Cell E24 = SUMPRODUCT($E$7:$G$7,$B$17:$D$17)+$F$10*G17
Cell E25 = SUMPRODUCT($E$7:$G$7,$B$17:$D$17)+$F$10*H17
Cell E26 = (1+E7)*B17+F7*C17+G7*D17+F10*I17
Cell E27 = (1+F7)*C17+G7*D17+F10*J17
Cell E28 = (1+G7)*D17+F10*K17
Cell F21 = SUMPRODUCT(E6:G6,B17:D17)+E17
Cell F22 = F17
Cell F23 = G17
Cell F24 = H17
Cell F25 = I17
Cell F26 = J17
Cell F27 = K17
Cell F28 = L17

Right-Hand Sides The right-hand sides for the eight constraints represent the annual cash requirements. They are placed into cells I21:I28.

Cell I21 = B5 (Copy to I22:I28)

*The cash flow in is the sum of the positive terms in each constraint equation in the mathematical model, and the cash flow out is the sum of the negative terms in each constraint equation.

Excel Solution

We are now ready to use the information in the worksheet to determine the optimal solution to the Hewlitt Corporation problem. The following steps describe how to use Excel to obtain the optimal solution.

*Excel 2007 Users: Replace Step 1 with, select the **Add-Ins** tab.*

Step 1. Select the **Tools** menu
Step 2. Select the **Premium Solver** option
Step 3. When the **Solver Parameters** dialog box appears (see Figure 4.11):
Make sure **Standard LP Simplex** is displayed
Enter B20 in the **Set Cell** box
Select the **Equal to: Min** option
Enter A17:L17 in the **By Changing Variable Cells** box
Choose **Add**
Step 4. When the **Add Constraint** dialog box appears:
Enter G21:G28 in the left-hand box of the **Cell Reference** area
Select =
Enter I21:I28 in the right-hand box
Click **OK**
Step 5. When the **Solver Parameters** dialog box reappears (see Figure 4.11):
Choose **Options**
Step 6. When the **LP Simplex Solver Options** dialog box appears:
Select **Assume Non-Negative**
Click **OK**
Step 7. When the **Solver Parameters** dialog box reappears:
Choose **Solve**
Step 8. When the **Solver Results** dialog box appears:
Select **Keep Solver Solution**
Select **Sensitivity** in the **Reports** box
Click **OK**

The Solver Parameters dialog box is shown in Figure 4.11. The optimal solution is shown in Figure 4.10; the accompanying sensitivity report is shown in Figure 4.12.

FIGURE 4.11 SOLVER PARAMETERS DIALOG BOX FOR THE HEWLITT CORPORATION PROBLEM

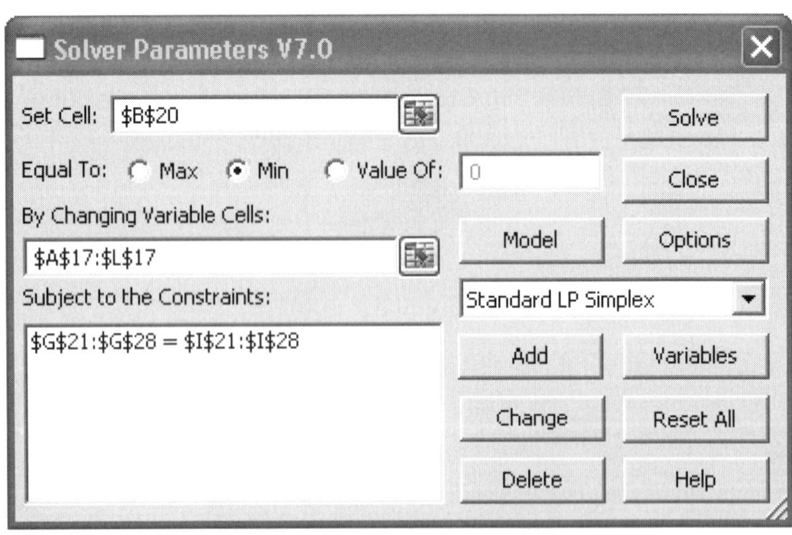

FIGURE 4.12 EXCEL'S SENSITIVITY REPORT FOR THE HEWLITT CORPORATION PROBLEM

Adjustable Cells

Cell	Name	Final Value	Reduced Cost	Objective Coefficient	Allowable Increase	Allowable Decrease
$A$17	F	1728.793855	0	1	1E + 30	1
$B$17	B1	144.9881496	0	0	0.067026339	0.013026775
$C$17	B2	187.8558478	0	0	0.012795531	0.020273774
$D$17	B3	228.1879195	0	0	0.022906851	0.749663022
$E$17	S1	636.1479438	0	0	0.109559907	0.05507386
$F$17	S2	501.605712	0	0	0.143307365	0.056948823
$G$17	S3	349.681791	0	0	0.210854199	0.059039182
$H$17	S4	182.680913	0	0	0.413598622	0.061382404
$I$17	S5	0	0.064025159	0	1E + 30	0.064025159
$J$17	S6	0	0.012613604	0	1E + 30	0.012613604
$K$17	S7	0	0.021318233	0	1E + 30	0.021318233
$L$17	S8	0	0.670839393	0	1E + 30	0.670839393

Constraints

Cell	Name	Final Value	Shadow Price	Constraint R.H. Side	Allowable Increase	Allowable Decrease
$G$21	Year 1 Flow	430	1	430	1E + 30	1728.793855
$G$22	Year 2 Flow	210	0.961538462	210	1E + 30	661.5938616
$G$23	Year 3 Flow	222	0.924556213	222	1E + 30	521.6699405
$G$24	Year 4 Flow	231	0.888996359	231	1E + 30	363.6690626
$G$25	Year 5 Flow	240	0.854804191	240	1E + 30	189.9881496
$G$26	Year 6 Flow	195	0.760364454	195	2149.927647	157.8558478
$G$27	Year 7 Flow	225	0.718991202	225	3027.962172	198.1879195
$G$28	Year 8 Flow	255	0.670839393	255	1583.881915	255

Discussion

Figures 4.10 and 4.12 contain essentially the same information as that provided by The Management Scientist solution in Figure 4.4. Recall that the Excel sensitivity report uses the term *shadow price* to describe the *change* in value of the solution per unit increase in the right-hand side of a constraint. The Management Scientist and LINGO use the term *dual price* to describe the *improvement* in value of the solution per unit increase in the right-hand side of a constraint. For maximization problems, the shadow price and dual price are the same; for minimization problems, the shadow price and dual price have opposite signs. Because the Hewlitt financial planning problem involves minimization, the shadow prices in the Excel sensitivity report (Figure 4.12) are the negative of the dual prices in The Management Scientist solution (Figure 4.4).

CHAPTER 5

Advanced Linear Programming Applications

CONTENTS

This chapter continues the study of linear programming applications. Four new applications of linear programming are introduced. We begin with data envelopment analysis (DEA), which is an application of linear programming used to measure the relative efficiency of operating units with the same goals and objectives. We illustrate how this technique is used to evaluate the performance of hospitals. In Section 5.2, we introduce the topic of revenue management. Revenue management involves managing the short-term demand for a fixed perishable inventory in order to maximize the revenue potential for an organization. Revenue management is critically important in the airline industry, and we illustrate the concept by determining the optimal full-fare and discount-fare seat allocations for flights among five cities.

Management science has a major impact in finance. Section 5.3 shows how linear programming is used to design portfolios that are consistent with a client's risk preferences. In Section 5.4, we introduce game theory, which is the study of how two or more decision makers (players) can compete against each other in an optimal fashion. We illustrate with a linear programming model for two firms competing against each other by trying to gain market share.

5.1 DATA ENVELOPMENT ANALYSIS

Data envelopment analysis (DEA) is an application of linear programming used to measure the relative efficiency of operating units with the same goals and objectives. For example, DEA has been used within individual fast-food outlets in the same chain. In this case, the goal of DEA was to identify the inefficient outlets that should be targeted for further study and, if necessary, corrective action. Other applications of DEA have measured the relative efficiencies of hospitals, banks, courts, schools, and so on. In these applications, the performance of each institution or organization was measured relative to the performance of all operating units in the same system. The Management Science in Action, Efficiency of Bank Branches, describes how a large nationally known bank used DEA to determine which branches were operating inefficiently.

MANAGEMENT SCIENCE IN ACTION

EFFICIENCY OF BANK BRANCHES*

Management of a large, nationally known bank wanted to improve operations at the branch level. A total of 182 branch banks located in four major cities were selected for the study. Data envelopment analysis (DEA) was used to determine which branches were operating inefficiently.

The DEA model compared the actual operating results of each branch with those of all other branches. A less-productive branch was one that required more resources to produce the same output as the best-performing branches. The best-performing branches are identified by a DEA efficiency rating of 100% ($E = 100$). The inefficient or less-productive branches are identified by an efficiency rating less than 100% ($E < 1.00$).

The inputs used for each branch were the number of teller full-time equivalents, the number of nonteller personnel full-time equivalents, the number of parking spaces, the number of ATMs, and the advertising expense per customer. The outputs were the amount of loans (direct, indirect, commercial, and equity), the amount of deposits (checking, savings, and CDs), the average number of accounts per customer, and the customer satisfaction score based on a quarterly customer survey. Data were collected over six consecutive quarters to determine how the branches were operating over time.

(continued)

The solution to the DEA linear programming model showed that 92 of the 182 branches were fully efficient. Only five branches fell below the 70% efficiency level, and approximately 25% of the branches had efficiency ratings between 80% to 89%. DEA identified the specific branches that were relatively inefficient and provided insights as to how these branches could improve productivity. Focusing on the less-productive branches, the bank was able to identify ways to reduce the input resources required without significantly reducing the volume and quality of service. In addition, the DEA analysis provided management with a better understanding of the factors that contribute most to the efficiency of the branch banks.

*Based on B. Golany and J. E. Storbeck, "A Data Envelopment Analysis of the Operational Efficiency of Bank Branches," *Interfaces* (May/June 1999): 14–26.

The operating units of most organizations have multiple inputs such as staff size, salaries, hours of operation, and advertising budget, as well as multiple outputs such as profit, market share, and growth rate. In these situations, it is often difficult for a manager to determine which operating units are inefficient in converting their multiple inputs into multiple outputs. This particular area is where data envelopment analysis has proven to be a helpful managerial tool. We illustrate the application of data envelopment analysis by evaluating the performance of a group of four hospitals.

Evaluating the Performance of Hospitals

The hospital administrators at General Hospital, University Hospital, County Hospital, and State Hospital have been meeting to discuss ways in which they can help one another improve the performance at each of their hospitals. A consultant suggested that they consider using DEA to measure the performance of each hospital relative to the performance of all four hospitals. In discussing how this evaluation could be done, the following three input measures and four output measures were identified:

Input Measures

1. The number of full-time equivalent (FTE) nonphysician personnel
2. The amount spent on supplies
3. The number of bed-days available

Output Measures

Problem 1 asks you to formulate and solve a linear program to assess the relative efficiency of General Hospital.

1. Patient-days of service under Medicare
2. Patient-days of service not under Medicare
3. Number of nurses trained
4. Number of interns trained

Summaries of the input and output measures for a one-year period at each of the four hospitals are shown in Tables 5.1 and 5.2. Let us show how DEA can use these data to identify relatively inefficient hospitals.

Overview of the DEA Approach

In this application of DEA, a linear programming model is developed for each hospital whose efficiency is to be evaluated. To illustrate the modeling process, we formulate a linear program that can be used to determine the relative efficiency of County Hospital.

First, using a linear programming model, we construct a **hypothetical composite,** in this case a composite hospital, based on the outputs and inputs for all operating units with

TABLE 5.1 ANNUAL RESOURCES CONSUMED (INPUTS) BY THE FOUR HOSPITALS

	Hospital			
Input Measure	**General**	**University**	**County**	**State**
Full-time equivalent nonphysicians	285.20	162.30	275.70	210.40
Supply expense ($1000s)	123.80	128.70	348.50	154.10
Bed-days available (1000s)	106.72	64.21	104.10	104.04

the same goals. For each of the four hospitals' output measures, the output for the composite hospital is determined by computing a weighted average of the corresponding outputs for all four hospitals. For each of the three input measures, the input for the composite hospital is determined by using the same weights to compute a weighted average of the corresponding inputs for all four hospitals. Constraints in the linear programming model require all outputs for the composite hospital to be *greater than or equal to* the outputs of County Hospital, the hospital being evaluated. If the inputs for the composite unit can be shown to be *less than* the inputs for County Hospital, the composite hospital is shown to have the same, or more, output for *less input.* In this case, the model shows that the composite hospital is more efficient than County Hospital. In other words, the hospital being evaluated is *less efficient* than the composite hospital. Because the composite hospital is based on all four hospitals, the hospital being evaluated can be judged *relatively inefficient* when compared to the other hospitals in the group.

DEA Linear Programming Model

To determine the weight that each hospital will have in computing the outputs and inputs for the composite hospital, we use the following decision variables:

wg = weight applied to inputs and outputs for General Hospital
wu = weight applied to inputs and outputs for University Hospital
wc = weight applied to inputs and outputs for County Hospital
ws = weight applied to inputs and outputs for State Hospital

The DEA approach requires that the sum of these weights equal 1. Thus, the first constraint is

$$wg + wu + wc + ws = 1$$

TABLE 5.2 ANNUAL SERVICES PROVIDED (OUTPUTS) BY THE FOUR HOSPITALS

	Hospital			
Output Measure	**General**	**University**	**County**	**State**
Medicare patient-days (1000s)	48.14	34.62	36.72	33.16
Non-Medicare patient-days (1000s)	43.10	27.11	45.98	56.46
Nurses trained	253	148	175	160
Interns trained	41	27	23	84

In general, every DEA linear programming model will include a constraint that requires the weights for the operating units to sum to 1.

As we stated previously, for each output measure, the output for the composite hospital is determined by computing a weighted average of the corresponding outputs for all four hospitals. For instance, for output measure 1, the number of patient days of service under Medicare, the output for the composite hospital is

$$\begin{matrix}\text{Medicare patient-days}\\ \text{for Composite Hospital}\end{matrix} = \begin{pmatrix}\text{Medicare patient-days}\\ \text{for General Hospital}\end{pmatrix} wg + \begin{pmatrix}\text{Medicare patient-days}\\ \text{for University Hospital}\end{pmatrix} wu$$
$$+ \begin{pmatrix}\text{Medicare patient-days}\\ \text{for County Hospital}\end{pmatrix} wc + \begin{pmatrix}\text{Medicare patient-days}\\ \text{for State Hospital}\end{pmatrix} ws$$

Substituting the number of medicare patient-days for each hospital as shown in Table 5.2, we obtain the following expression:

$$\begin{matrix}\text{Medicare patient-days}\\ \text{for Composite Hospital}\end{matrix} = 48.14wg + 34.62wu + 36.72wc + 33.16ws$$

The other output measures for the composite hospital are computed in a similar fashion. Figure 5.1 provides a summary of the results.

For each of the four output measures, we need to write a constraint that requires the output for the composite hospital to be greater than or equal to the output for County Hospital. Thus, the general form of the output constraints is

$$\begin{matrix}\text{Output for the}\\ \text{Composite Hospital}\end{matrix} \geq \begin{matrix}\text{Output for}\\ \text{County Hospital}\end{matrix}$$

FIGURE 5.1 RELATIONSHIP BETWEEN THE OUTPUT MEASURES FOR THE FOUR HOSPITALS AND THE OUTPUT MEASURES FOR THE COMPOSITE HOSPITAL

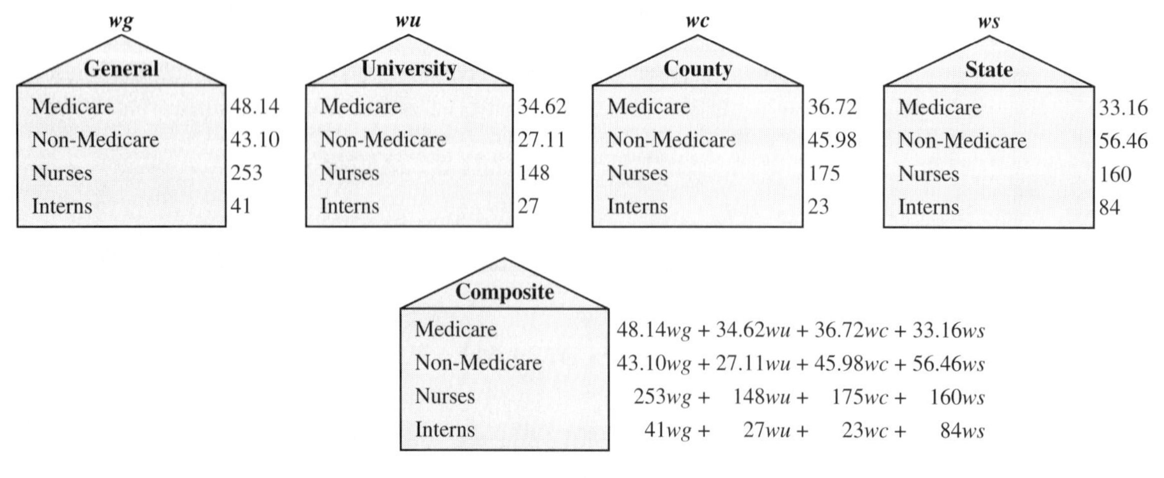

Because the number of Medicare patient-days for County Hospital is 36.72, the output constraint corresponding to the number of Medicare patient-days is

$$48.14wg + 34.62wu + 36.72wc + 33.16ws \geq 36.72$$

In a similar fashion, we formulated a constraint for each of the other three output measures, with the results as shown:

$$\begin{aligned} 43.10wg + 27.11wu + 45.98wc + 56.46ws &\geq 45.98 \quad \text{Non-Medicare} \\ 253wg + 148wu + 175wc + 160ws &\geq 175 \quad \text{Nurses} \\ 41wg + 27wu + 23wc + 84ws &\geq 23 \quad \text{Interns} \end{aligned}$$

The four output constraints require the linear programming solution to provide weights that will make each output measure for the composite hospital greater than or equal to the corresponding output measure for County Hospital. Thus, if a solution satisfying the output constraints can be found, the composite hospital will have produced at least as much of each output as County Hospital.

Next, we need to consider the constraints needed to model the relationship between the inputs for the composite hospital and the resources available to the composite hospital. A constraint is required for each of the three input measures. The general form for the input constraints is as follows:

$$\begin{pmatrix}\text{Input for the} \\ \text{Composite Hospital}\end{pmatrix} \leq \begin{pmatrix}\text{Resources available to} \\ \text{the Composite Hospital}\end{pmatrix}$$

For each input measure, the input for the composite hospital is a weighted average of the corresponding input for each of the four hospitals. Thus, for input measure 1, the number of full-time equivalent nonphysicians, the input for the composite hospital is

$$\begin{aligned} \begin{matrix}\text{FTE nonphysicians} \\ \text{for Composite Hospital}\end{matrix} = & \begin{pmatrix}\text{FTE nonphysicians} \\ \text{for General Hospital}\end{pmatrix} wg + \begin{pmatrix}\text{FTE nonphysicians} \\ \text{for University Hospital}\end{pmatrix} wu \\ & + \begin{pmatrix}\text{FTE nonphysicians} \\ \text{for County Hospital}\end{pmatrix} wc + \begin{pmatrix}\text{FTE nonphysicians} \\ \text{for State Hospital}\end{pmatrix} ws \end{aligned}$$

Substituting the values for the number of full-time equivalent nonphysicians for each hospital as shown in Table 5.1, we obtain the following expression for the number of full-time equivalent nonphysicians for the composite hospital:

$$285.20wg + 162.30wu + 275.70wc + 210.40ws$$

The logic of a DEA model is to determine whether a hypothetical composite facility can achieve the same or more output while requiring less input. If more output with less input can be achieved, the facility being evaluated is judged to be relatively inefficient.

In a similar manner, we can write expressions for each of the other two input measures as shown in Figure 5.2.

To complete the formulation of the input constraints, we must write expressions for the right-hand-side values for each constraint. First, note that the right-hand-side values are the resources available to the composite hospital. In the DEA approach, these right-hand-side values are a percentage of the input values for County Hospital. Thus, we must introduce the following decision variable:

E = the fraction of County Hospital's input available to the composite hospital

FIGURE 5.2 RELATIONSHIP BETWEEN THE INPUT MEASURES FOR THE FOUR HOSPITALS AND THE INPUT MEASURES FOR THE COMPOSITE HOSPITAL

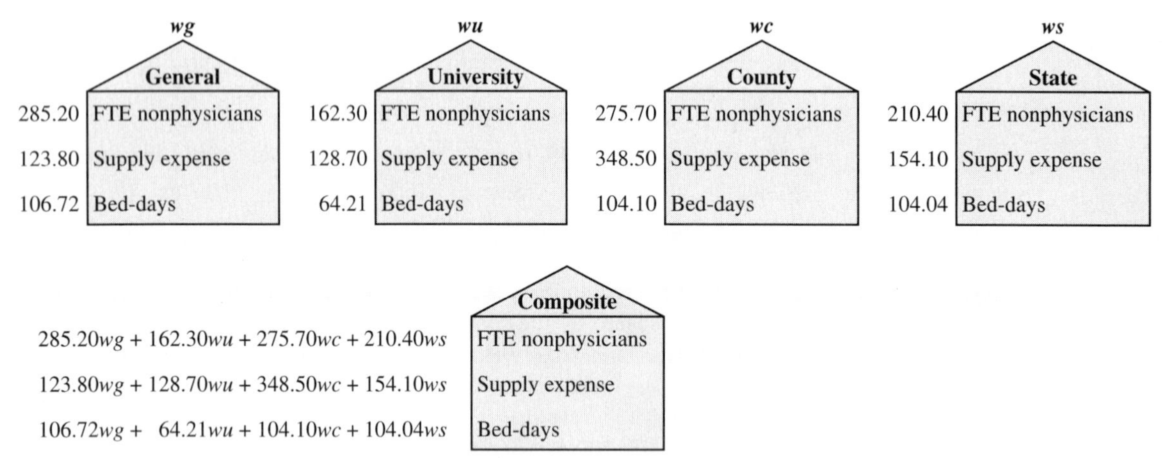

To illustrate the important role that E plays in the DEA approach, we show how to write the expression for the number of FTE nonphysicians available to the composite hospital. Table 5.1 shows that the number of FTE nonphysicians used by County Hospital was 275.70; thus, $275.70E$ is the number of FTE nonphysicians available to the composite hospital. If $E = 1$, the number of FTE nonphysicians available to the composite hospital is 275.70, the same as the number of FTE nonphysicians used by County Hospital. However, if E is greater than 1, the composite hospital would have available proportionally more nonphysicians, while if E is less than 1, the composite hospital would have available proportionally fewer FTE nonphysicians. Because of the effect that E has in determining the resources available to the composite hospital, E is referred to as the **efficiency index.**

We can now write the input constraint corresponding to the number of FTE nonphysicians available to the composite hospital:

$$285.20wg + 162.30wu + 275.70wc + 210.40ws \leq 275.70E$$

In a similar manner, we can write the input constraints for the supplies and bed-days available to the composite hospital. First, using the data in Table 5.1, we note that for each of these resources, the amount that is available to the composite hospital is $348.50E$ and $104.10E$, respectively. Thus, the input constraints for the supplies and bed-days are written as follows:

$$\begin{aligned} 123.80wg + 128.70wu + 348.50wc + 154.10ws &\leq 348.50E \quad \text{Supplies} \\ 106.72wg + 64.21wu + 104.10wc + 104.04ws &\leq 104.10E \quad \text{Bed-days} \end{aligned}$$

If a solution with $E < 1$ can be found, the composite hospital does not need as many resources as County Hospital needs to produce the same level of output.

The objective function for the DEA model is to minimize the value of E, which is equivalent to minimizing the input resources available to the composite hospital. Thus, the objective function is written as

$$\text{Min } E$$

The objective function in a DEA model is always Min E. The facility being evaluated (County Hospital in this example) can be judged relatively inefficient if the optimal solution provides E less than 1, indicating that the composite facility requires less in input resources.

The DEA efficiency conclusion is based on the optimal objective function value for E. The decision rule is as follows:

If $E = 1$, the composite hospital requires *as much input* as County Hospital does. There is no evidence that County Hospital is inefficient.

If $E < 1$, the composite hospital requires *less input* to obtain the output achieved by County Hospital. The composite hospital is more efficient; thus, County Hospital can be judged relatively inefficient.

The DEA linear programming model for the efficiency evaluation of County Hospital has five decision variables and eight constraints. The complete model is rewritten as follows:

$$
\begin{array}{lrrrrrl}
\text{Min} & E & & & & & \\
\text{s.t.} & & & & & & \\
& & wg + & wu + & wc + & ws = & 1 \\
& & 48.14wg + & 34.62wu + & 36.72wc + & 33.16ws \geq & 36.72 \\
& & 43.10wg + & 27.11wu + & 45.98wc + & 56.46ws \geq & 45.98 \\
& & 253wg + & 148wu + & 175wc + & 160ws \geq & 175 \\
& & 41wg + & 27wu + & 23wc + & 84ws \geq & 23 \\
& -275.70E + & 285.20wg + & 162.30wu + & 275.70wc + & 210.40ws \leq & 0 \\
& -348.50E + & 123.80wg + & 128.70wu + & 348.50wc + & 154.10ws \leq & 0 \\
& -104.10E + & 106.72wg + & 64.21wu + & 104.10wc + & 104.04ws \leq & 0 \\
& & E, wg, wu, wc, ws \geq 0 & & & &
\end{array}
$$

Note that in this formulation of the model, we moved the terms involving E to the left side of the three input constraints because E is a decision variable.

The optimal solution is shown in Figure 5.3. We first note that the value of the objective function shows that the efficiency score for County Hospital is 0.905. This score tells us that the composite hospital can obtain at least the level of each output that County Hospital obtains by having available no more than 90.5 percent of the input resources required by County Hospital. Thus, the composite hospital is more efficient, and the DEA analysis identified County Hospital as being relatively inefficient.

From the solution in Figure 5.3, we see that the composite hospital is formed from the weighted average of General Hospital ($wg = 0.212$), University Hospital ($wu = 0.260$), and State Hospital ($ws = 0.527$). Each input and output of the composite hospital is determined by the same weighted average of the inputs and outputs of these three hospitals.

The Slack/Surplus column provides some additional information about the efficiency of County Hospital compared to the composite hospital. Specifically, the composite hospital has at least as much of each output as County Hospital has (constraints 2–5) and provides 1.6 more nurses trained (surplus for constraint 4) and 37 more interns trained (surplus for constraint 5). The slack of zero from constraint 8 shows that the composite hospital uses approximately 90.5 percent of the bed-days used by County Hospital. The slack values for constraints 6 and 7 show that less than 90.5 percent of the FTE nonphysician and the supplies expense resources used at County Hospital are used by the composite hospital.

Clearly, the composite hospital is more efficient than County Hospital, and we are justified in concluding that County Hospital is relatively inefficient compared to the other hospitals in the group. Given the results of the DEA analysis, hospital administrators should examine operations to determine how County Hospital resources can be more effectively utilized.

FIGURE 5.3 THE MANAGEMENT SCIENTIST SOLUTION FOR THE COUNTY HOSPITAL DATA ENVELOPMENT ANALYSIS PROBLEM

EXCELfile
County

```
Objective Function Value =          0.905

    Variable              Value              Reduced Costs
 --------------      ---------------      -----------------
         E                 0.905                  0.000
        WG                 0.212                  0.000
        WU                 0.260                  0.000
        WC                 0.000                  0.095
        WS                 0.527                  0.000

   Constraint          Slack/Surplus           Dual Prices
 --------------      ---------------      -----------------
         1                 0.000                  0.239
         2                 0.000                 -0.014
         3                 0.000                 -0.014
         4                 1.615                  0.000
         5                37.027                  0.000
         6                35.824                  0.000
         7               174.422                  0.000
         8                 0.000                  0.010
```

Summary of the DEA Approach

To use data envelopment analysis to measure the relative efficiency of County Hospital, we used a linear programming model to construct a hypothetical composite hospital based on the outputs and inputs for the four hospitals in the problem. The approach to solving other types of problems using DEA is similar. For each operating unit that we want to measure the efficiency of, we must formulate and solve a linear programming model similar to the linear program we solved to measure the relative efficiency of County Hospital. The following step-by-step procedure should help you in formulating a linear programming model for other types of DEA applications. Note that the operating unit that we want to measure the relative efficiency of is referred to as the *j*th operating unit.

Step 1. Define decision variables or weights (one for each operating unit) that can be used to determine the inputs and outputs for the composite operating unit.
Step 2. Write a constraint that requires the weights to sum to 1.
Step 3. For each output measure, write a constraint that requires the output for the composite operating unit to be greater than or equal to the corresponding output for the *j*th operating unit.
Step 4. Define a decision variable, E, which determines the fraction of the *j*th operating unit's input available to the composite operating unit.
Step 5. For each input measure, write a constraint that requires the input for the composite operating unit to be less than or equal to the resources available to the composite operating unit.
Step 6. Write the objective function as Min E.

NOTES AND COMMENTS

1. Remember that the goal of data envelopment analysis is to identify operating units that are relatively inefficient. The method *does not* necessarily identify the operating units that are *relatively efficient.* Just because the efficiency index is $E = 1$, we cannot conclude that the unit being analyzed is relatively efficient. Indeed, any unit that has the largest output on any one of the output measures cannot be judged relatively inefficient.
2. It is possible for DEA to show all but one unit to be relatively inefficient. Such would be the case if a unit producing the most of every output also consumes the least of every input. Such cases are extremely rare in practice.
3. In applying data envelopment analysis to problems involving a large group of operating units, practitioners have found that roughly 50% of the operating units can be identified as inefficient. Comparing each relatively inefficient unit to the units contributing to the composite unit may be helpful in understanding how the operation of each relatively inefficient unit can be improved.

5.2 REVENUE MANAGEMENT

Revenue management involves managing the short-term demand for a fixed perishable inventory in order to maximize the revenue potential for an organization. The methodology, originally developed for American Airlines, was first used to determine how many airline flight seats to sell at an early reservation discount fare and how many airline flight seats to sell at a full fare. By making the optimal decision for the number of discount-fare seats and the number of full-fare seats on each flight, the airline is able to increase its average number of passengers per flight and maximize the total revenue generated by the combined sale of discount-fare and full-fare seats. Today, all major airlines use some form of revenue management.

Given the success of revenue management in the airline industry, it was not long before other industries began using this approach. Revenue management systems often include pricing strategies, overbooking policies, short-term supply decisions, and the management of nonperishable assets. Application areas now include hotels, apartment rentals, car rentals, cruise lines, and golf courses. The Management Science in Action, Revenue Management at National Car Rental, discusses how National implemented revenue management.

The development of a revenue management system can be expensive and time-consuming, but the potential payoffs may be substantial. For instance, the revenue management system used at American Airlines generates nearly $1 billion in annual incremental revenue. To illustrate the fundamentals of revenue management, we will use a linear programming model to develop a revenue management plan for Leisure Air, a regional airline that provides service for Pittsburgh, Newark, Charlotte, Myrtle Beach, and Orlando.

Leisure Air has two Boeing 737-400 airplanes, one based in Pittsburgh and the other in Newark. Both airplanes have a coach section with a 132-seat capacity. Each morning the Pittsburgh-based plane flies to Orlando with a stopover in Charlotte, and the Newark-based plane flies to Myrtle Beach, also with a stopover in Charlotte. At the end of the day, both planes return to their home bases. To keep the size of the problem reasonable we restrict our attention to the Pittsburgh–Charlotte, Charlotte–Orlando, Newark–Charlotte, and Charlotte–Myrtle Beach flight legs for the morning flights. Figure 5.4 illustrates the logistics of the Leisure Air problem situation.

MANAGEMENT SCIENCE IN ACTION

REVENUE MANAGEMENT AT NATIONAL CAR RENTAL*

During its recovery from a near liquidation in the mid-1990s, National Car Rental developed a revenue management system that uses linear programming and other analytical models to help manage rental car capacity, pricing, and reservations. The goal of the revenue management system is to develop procedures that identify unrealized revenue opportunities, improve utilization, and ultimately increase revenue for the company.

Management science models play a key role in revenue management at National. For instance, a linear programming model is used for length-of-rent control. An overbooking model identifies optimal overbooking levels subject to service level constraints, and a planned upgrade algorithm allows cars in a higher-priced class to be used to satisfy excess demand for cars in a lower-priced class.

Another model generates length-of-rent categories for each arrival day, which maximizes revenue. Pricing models are used to manage revenue by segmenting the market between business and leisure travel. For example, fares are adjusted to account for the fact that leisure travelers are willing to commit further in advance than business travelers and are willing to stay over a weekend.

The implementation of the revenue management system is credited with returning National Car Rental to profitability. In the first year of use, revenue management resulted in increased revenues of $56 million.

*Based on M. K. Geraghty and Ernest Johnson, "Revenue Management Saves National Car Rental," *Interfaces* 27, no. 1 (January/February 1997): 107–127.

Leisure Air uses two fare classes: a discount-fare Q class and a full-fare Y class. Reservations using the discount-fare Q class must be made 14 days in advance and must include a Saturday night stay in the destination city. Reservations using the full-fare Y class may be made anytime, with no penalty for changing the reservation at a later date. To determine

FIGURE 5.4 LOGISTICS OF THE LEISURE AIR PROBLEM

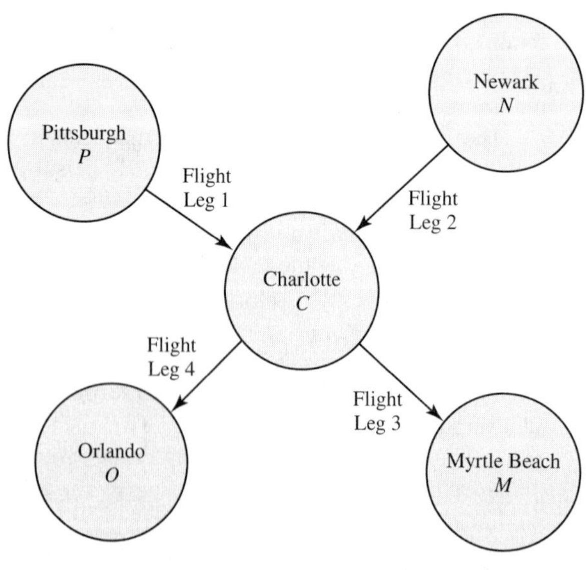

TABLE 5.3 FARE AND DEMAND DATA FOR 16 LEISURE AIR ORIGIN-DESTINATION-ITINERARY FARES (ODIFs)

ODIF	Origin	Destination	Fare Class	ODIF Code	Fare	Forecasted Demand
1	Pittsburgh	Charlotte	Q	PCQ	$178	33
2	Pittsburgh	Myrtle Beach	Q	PMQ	268	44
3	Pittsburgh	Orlando	Q	POQ	228	45
4	Pittsburgh	Charlotte	Y	PCY	380	16
5	Pittsburgh	Myrtle Beach	Y	PMY	456	6
6	Pittsburgh	Orlando	Y	POY	560	11
7	Newark	Charlotte	Q	NCQ	199	26
8	Newark	Myrtle Beach	Q	NMQ	249	56
9	Newark	Orlando	Q	NOQ	349	39
10	Newark	Charlotte	Y	NCY	385	15
11	Newark	Myrtle Beach	Y	NMY	444	7
12	Newark	Orlando	Y	NOY	580	9
13	Charlotte	Myrtle Beach	Q	CMQ	179	64
14	Charlotte	Myrtle Beach	Y	CMY	380	8
15	Charlotte	Orlando	Q	COQ	224	46
16	Charlotte	Orlando	Y	COY	582	10

the itinerary and fare alternatives that Leisure Air can offer its customers, we must consider not only the origin and the destination of each flight, but also the fare class. For instance, possible products include Pittsburgh to Charlotte using Q class, Newark to Orlando using Q class, Charlotte to Myrtle Beach using Y class, and so on. Each product is referred to as an origin-destination-itinerary fare (ODIF). For May 5, Leisure Air established fares and developed forecasts of customer demand for each of 16 ODIFs. These data are shown in Table 5.3.

Suppose that on April 4 a customer calls the Leisure Air reservation office and requests a Q class seat on the May 5 flight from Pittsburgh to Myrtle Beach. Should Leisure Air accept the reservation? The difficulty in making this decision is that even though Leisure Air may have seats available, the company may not want to accept this reservation at the Q class fare of $268, especially if it is possible to sell the same reservation later at the Y class fare of $456. Thus, determining how many Q and Y class seats to make available are important decisions that Leisure Air must make in order to operate its reservation system.

To develop a linear programming model that can be used to determine how many seats Leisure Air should allocate to each fare class we need to define 16 decision variables, one for each origin-destination-itinerary fare alternative. Using *P* for Pittsburgh, *N* for Newark, *C* for Charlotte, *M* for Myrtle Beach, and *O* for Orlando, the decision variables take the following form:

PCQ = number of seats allocated to Pittsburgh–Charlotte Q class
PMQ = number of seats allocated to Pittsburgh–Myrtle Beach Q class
POQ = number of seats allocated to Pittsburgh–Orlando Q class

$$PCY = \text{number of seats allocated to Pittsburgh–Charlotte Y class}$$
$$\vdots$$
$$NCQ = \text{number of seats allocated to Newark–Charlotte Q class}$$
$$\vdots$$
$$COY = \text{number of seats allocated to Charlotte–Orlando Y class}$$

The objective is to maximize total revenue. Using the fares shown in Table 5.3, we can write the objective function for the linear programming model as follows:

$$\begin{aligned} \text{Max} \quad & 178PCQ + 268PMQ + 228POQ + 380PCY + 456PMY + 560POY \\ & + 199NCQ + 249NMQ + 349NOQ + 385NCY + 444NMY \\ & + 580NOY + 179CMQ + 380CMY + 224COQ + 582COY \end{aligned}$$

Next we must write the constraints. We need two types of constraints: capacity and demand. We begin with the capacity constraints.

Consider the Pittsburgh–Charlotte flight leg in Figure 5.4. The Boeing 737-400 airplane has a 132-seat capacity. Three possible final destinations for passengers on this flight (Charlotte, Myrtle Beach, or Orlando) and two fare classes (Q and Y) provide six ODIF alternatives: (1) Pittsburgh–Charlotte Q class; (2) Pittsburgh–Myrtle Beach Q class; (3) Pittsburgh–Orlando Q class; (4) Pittsburgh–Charlotte Y class; (5) Pittsburgh–Myrtle Beach Y class; and (6) Pittsburgh–Orlando Y class. Thus, the number of seats allocated to the Pittsburgh–Charlotte flight leg is $PCQ + PMQ + POQ + PCY + PMY + POY$. With the capacity of 132 seats, the capacity constraint is as follows:

$$PCQ + PMQ + POQ + PCY + PMY + POY \leq 132 \quad \text{Pittsburgh–Charlotte}$$

The capacity constraints for the Newark–Charlotte, Charlotte–Myrtle Beach, and Charlotte–Orlando flight legs are developed in a similar manner. These three constraints are as follows:

$$\begin{aligned} NCQ + NMQ + NOQ + NCY + NMY + NOY &\leq 132 \quad \text{Newark–Charlotte} \\ PMQ + PMY + NMQ + NMY + CMQ + CMY &\leq 132 \quad \text{Charlotte–Myrtle Beach} \\ POQ + POY + NOQ + NOY + COQ + COY &\leq 132 \quad \text{Charlotte–Orlando} \end{aligned}$$

The demand constraints limit the number of seats for each ODIF based on the forecasted demand. Using the demand forecasts in Table 5.3, 16 demand constraints must be added to the model. The first four demand constraints are as follows:

$$\begin{aligned} PCQ &\leq 33 \quad \text{Pittsburgh–Charlotte Q class} \\ PMQ &\leq 44 \quad \text{Pittsburgh–Myrtle Beach Q class} \\ POQ &\leq 45 \quad \text{Pittsburgh–Orlando Q class} \\ PCY &\leq 16 \quad \text{Pittsburgh–Charlotte Y class} \end{aligned}$$

The complete linear programming model with 16 decision variables, 4 capacity constraints, and 16 demand constraints is as follows.

$$\begin{aligned} \text{Max} \quad & 178PCQ + 268PMQ + 228POQ + 380PCY + 456PMY + 560POY \\ & + 199NCQ + 249NMQ + 349NOQ + 385NCY + 444NMY \\ & + 580NOY + 179CMQ + 380CMY + 224COQ + 582COY \end{aligned}$$

s.t.

$$
\begin{aligned}
PCQ + PMQ + POQ + PCY + PMY + POY &\leq 132 \quad \text{Pittsburgh–Charlotte} \\
NCQ + NMQ + NOQ + NCY + NMY + NOY &\leq 132 \quad \text{Newark–Charlotte} \\
PMQ + PMY + NMQ + NMY + CMQ + CMY &\leq 132 \quad \text{Charlotte–Myrtle Beach} \\
POQ + POY + NOQ + NOY + COQ + COY &\leq 132 \quad \text{Charlotte–Orlando}
\end{aligned}
$$

$$
\left.
\begin{aligned}
PCQ &\leq 33 \\
PMQ &\leq 44 \\
POQ &\leq 45 \\
PCY &\leq 16 \\
PMY &\leq 6 \\
POY &\leq 11 \\
NCQ &\leq 26 \\
NMQ &\leq 56 \\
NOQ &\leq 39 \\
NCY &\leq 15 \\
NMY &\leq 7 \\
NOY &\leq 9 \\
CMQ &\leq 64 \\
CMY &\leq 8 \\
COQ &\leq 46 \\
COY &\leq 10
\end{aligned}
\right\} \text{Demand Constraints}
$$

$$PCQ, PMQ, POQ, PCY, \ldots, COY \geq 0$$

The optimal solution to the Leisure Air revenue management problem is shown in Figure 5.5. The value of the optimal solution is \$103,103. The optimal solution shows that $PCQ = 33$, $PMQ = 44$, $POQ = 22$, $PCY = 16$, and so on. Thus, to maximize revenue Leisure Air should allocate 33 Q class seats to Pittsburgh–Charlotte, 44 Q class seats to Pittsburgh–Myrtle Beach, 22 Q class seats to Pittsburgh–Orlando, 16 Y class seats to Pittsburgh–Charlotte, and so on.

Over time, reservations will come into the system and the number of remaining seats available for each ODIF will decrease. For example, the optimal solution allocated 44 Q class seats to Pittsburgh–Myrtle Beach. Suppose that two weeks prior to the departure date of May 5, all 44 seats have been sold. Now, suppose that a new customer calls the Leisure Air reservation office and requests a Q class seat for the Pittsburgh–Myrtle Beach flight. Should Leisure Air accept the new reservation even though it exceeds the original 44-seat allocation? The dual price for the Pittsburgh–Myrtle Beach Q class demand constraint will provide information that will help a Leisure Air reservation agent make this decision.

Dual prices tell reservation agents the additional revenue associated with overbooking each ODIF.

Constraint 6, $PMQ \leq 44$, restricts the number of Q class seats that can be allocated to Pittsburgh–Myrtle Beach to 44 seats. In Figure 5.5 we see that the dual price for constraint 6 is \$85. The dual price tells us that if one more Q class seat was available from Pittsburgh to Myrtle Beach, revenue would improve by \$85. This increase in revenue is referred to as the bid price for this origin-destination-itinerary fare. In general, the bid price for an ODIF tells a Leisure Air reservation agent the value of one additional reservation once a particular ODIF has been sold out.

By looking at the dual prices for the demand constraints in Figure 5.5, we see that the highest dual price (bid price) is \$376 for constraint 8, $PCY \leq 16$. This constraint corresponds

EXCELfile
Leisure

FIGURE 5.5 THE MANAGEMENT SCIENTIST SOLUTION FOR THE LEISURE AIR REVENUE MANAGEMENT PROBLEM

Objective Function Value = 103103.000

Variable	Value	Reduced Costs
PCQ	33.000	0.000
PMQ	44.000	0.000
POQ	22.000	0.000
PCY	16.000	0.000
PMY	6.000	0.000
POY	11.000	0.000
NCQ	26.000	0.000
NMQ	36.000	0.000
NOQ	39.000	0.000
NCY	15.000	0.000
NMY	7.000	0.000
NOY	9.000	0.000
CMQ	31.000	0.000
CMY	8.000	0.000
COQ	41.000	0.000
COY	10.000	0.000

Constraint	Slack/Surplus	Dual Prices
1	0.000	4.000
2	0.000	70.000
3	0.000	179.000
4	0.000	224.000
5	0.000	174.000
6	0.000	85.000
7	23.000	0.000
8	0.000	376.000
9	0.000	273.000
10	0.000	332.000
11	0.000	129.000
12	20.000	0.000
13	0.000	55.000
14	0.000	315.000
15	0.000	195.000
16	0.000	286.000
17	33.000	0.000
18	0.000	201.000
19	5.000	0.000
20	0.000	358.000

to the Pittsburgh–Charlotte Y class itinerary. Thus, if all 16 seats allocated to this itinerary have been sold, accepting another reservation will provide additional revenue of $376. Given this revenue contribution, a reservation agent would most likely accept the additional reservation even if it resulted in an overbooking of the flight. Other dual prices for the demand constraints show a bid price of $358 for constraint 20 ($COY$) and a bid price of $332 for constraint 10 ($POY$). Thus, accepting additional reservations for the Charlotte–Orlando Y class and the Pittsburgh–Orlando Y class itineraries is a good choice for increasing revenue.

A revenue management system like the one at Leisure Air must be flexible and adjust to the ever-changing reservation status. Conceptually, each time a reservation is accepted for an origin-destination-itinerary fare that is at its capacity, the linear programming model should be updated and re-solved to obtain new seat allocations along with the revised bid price information. In practice, updating the allocations on a real-time basis is not practical because of the large number of itineraries involved. However, the bid prices from a current solution and some simple decision rules enable reservation agents to make decisions that improve the revenue for the firm. Then, on a periodic basis such as once a day or once a week, the entire linear programming model can be updated and re-solved to generate new seat allocations and revised bid price information.

5.3 PORTFOLIO MODELS AND ASSET ALLOCATION

In 1952 Harry Markowitz showed how to develop a portfolio that optimized the trade-off between risk and return. His work earned him a share of the 1990 Nobel Prize in Economics.

Asset allocation refers to the process of determining how to allocate investment funds across a variety of asset classes such as stocks, bonds, mutual funds, real estate, and cash. Portfolio models are used to determine the percentage of the investment funds that should be made in each asset class. The goal is to create a portfolio that provides the best balance between risk and return. In this section we show how linear programming models can be developed to determine an optimal portfolio involving a mix of mutual funds. The first model is designed for conservative investors who are strongly averse to risk. The second model is designed for investors with a variety of risk tolerances.

A Portfolio of Mutual Funds

Hauck Investment Services designs annuities, IRAs, 401(k) plans, and other investment vehicles for investors with a variety of risk tolerances. Hauck would like to develop a portfolio model that can be used to determine an optimal portfolio involving a mix of six mutual funds. A variety of measures can be used to indicate risk, but for portfolios of financial assets all are related to variability in return. Table 5.4 shows the annual return (%) for five

TABLE 5.4 MUTUAL FUND PERFORMANCE IN FIVE SELECTED YEARS (USED AS PLANNING SCENARIOS FOR THE NEXT 12 MONTHS)

	Annual Return (%)				
Mutual Fund	**Year 1**	**Year 2**	**Year 3**	**Year 4**	**Year 5**
Foreign Stock	10.06	13.12	13.47	45.42	−21.93
Intermediate Term Bond	17.64	3.25	7.51	−1.33	7.36
Large-Cap Growth	32.41	18.71	33.28	41.46	−23.26
Large-Cap Value	32.36	20.61	12.93	7.06	−5.37
Small-Cap Growth	33.44	19.40	3.85	58.68	−9.02
Small-Cap Value	24.56	25.32	−6.70	5.43	17.31

1-year periods for the six mutual funds. Year 1 represents a year in which the annual returns are good for all the mutual funds. Year 2 is also a good year for most of the mutual funds. But year 3 is a bad year for the small-cap value fund; year 4 is a bad year for the intermediate-term bond fund; and year 5 is a bad year for four of the six mutual funds.

It is not possible to predict exactly the returns for any of the funds over the next 12 months, but the portfolio managers at Hauck Financial Services think that the returns for the five years shown in Table 5.4 are scenarios that can be used to represent the possibilities for the next year. For the purpose of building portfolios for their clients, Hauck's portfolio managers will choose a mix of these six mutual funds and assume that one of the five possible scenarios will describe the return over the next 12 months.

Conservative Portfolio

One of Hauck's portfolio managers has been asked to develop a portfolio for the firm's conservative clients who express a strong aversion to risk. The manager's task is to determine the proportion of the portfolio to invest in each of the six mutual funds so that the portfolio provides the best return possible with a minimum risk. Let us see how linear programming can be used to develop a portfolio for these clients.

In portfolio models, risk is minimized by diversification. To see the value of diversification, suppose we first consider investing the entire portfolio in just one of the six mutual funds. Assuming the data in Table 5.4 represent the possible outcomes over the next 12 months, the clients run the risk of losing 21.93% over the next 12 months if the entire portfolio is invested in the foreign stock mutual fund. Similarly, if the entire portfolio is invested in any one of the other five mutual funds, the clients will also run the risk of losing money; that is, the possible losses are 1.33% for the intermediate-term bond fund, 23.26% for the large-cap growth fund, 5.37% for the large-cap value fund, 9.02% for the small-cap growth fund, and 6.70% for the small-cap value fund. Let us now see how we can construct a diversified portfolio of these mutual funds that minimizes the risk of a loss.

To determine the proportion of the portfolio that will be invested in each of the mutual funds we use the following decision variables:

FS = proportion of portfolio invested in the foreign stock mutual fund
IB = proportion of portfolio invested in the intermediate-term bond fund
LG = proportion of portfolio invested in the large-cap growth fund
LV = proportion of portfolio invested in the large-cap value fund
SG = proportion of portfolio invested in the small-cap growth fund
SV = proportion of portfolio invested in the small-cap value fund

Because the sum of these proportions must equal 1, we need the following constraint:

$$FS + IB + LG + LV + SG + SV = 1$$

The other constraints are concerned with the return that the portfolio will earn under each of the planning scenarios in Table 5.4.

The portfolio return over the next 12 months depends on which of the possible scenarios (years 1 through 5) in Table 5.4 occurs. Let $R1$ denote the portfolio return if the scenario represented by year 1 occurs, $R2$ denote the portfolio return if the scenario represented by year 2 occurs, and so on. The portfolio returns for the five planning scenarios are as follows:

Scenario 1 return:

$$R1 = 10.06FS + 17.64IB + 32.41LG + 32.36LV + 33.44SG + 24.56SV$$

Scenario 2 return:

$$R2 = 13.12FS + 3.25IB + 18.71LG + 20.61LV + 19.40SG + 25.32SV$$

Scenario 3 return:

$$R3 = 13.47FS + 7.51IB + 33.28LG + 12.93LV + 3.85SG - 6.70SV$$

Scenario 4 return:

$$R4 = 45.42FS - 1.33IB + 41.46LG + 7.06LV + 58.68SG + 5.43SV$$

Scenario 5 return:

$$R5 = -21.93FS + 7.36IB - 23.26LG - 5.37LV - 9.02SG + 17.31SV$$

Let us now introduce a variable M to represent the minimum return for the portfolio. As we have already shown, one of the five possible scenarios in Table 5.4 will determine the portfolio return. Thus, the minimum possible return for the portfolio will be determined by the scenario which provides the worst case return. But we don't know which of the scenarios will turn out to represent what happens over the next 12 months. To ensure that the return under each scenario is at least as large as the minimum return M, we must add the following minimum-return constraints.

$$\begin{aligned} R1 &\geq M & &\text{Scenario 1 minimum return} \\ R2 &\geq M & &\text{Scenario 2 minimum return} \\ R3 &\geq M & &\text{Scenario 3 minimum return} \\ R4 &\geq M & &\text{Scenario 4 minimum return} \\ R5 &\geq M & &\text{Scenario 5 minimum return} \end{aligned}$$

Substituting the values shown previously for $R1$, $R2$, and so on, provides the following five minimum-return constraints:

$$\begin{aligned} 10.06FS + 17.64IB + 32.41LG + 32.36LV + 33.44SG + 24.56SV &\geq M & &\text{Scenario 1} \\ 13.12FS + 3.25IB + 18.71LG + 20.61LV + 19.40SG + 25.32SV &\geq M & &\text{Scenario 2} \\ 13.47FS + 7.51IB + 33.28LG + 12.93LV + 3.85SG - 6.70SV &\geq M & &\text{Scenario 3} \\ 45.42FS - 1.33IB + 41.46LG + 7.06LV + 58.68SG + 5.43SV &\geq M & &\text{Scenario 4} \\ -21.93FS + 7.36IB - 23.26LG - 5.37LV - 9.02SG + 17.31SV &\geq M & &\text{Scenario 5} \end{aligned}$$

To develop a portfolio that provides the best return possible with a minimum risk, we need to maximize the minimum return for the portfolio. Thus, the objective function is simple:

$$\text{Max } M$$

With the five minimum-return constraints present, the optimal value of M will equal the value of the minimum return scenario. The objective is to maximize the value of the minimum return scenario.

Because the linear programming model was designed to maximize the minimum return over all the scenarios considered, we refer to it as the *maximin* model. The complete maximin model for the problem of choosing a portfolio of mutual funds for a conservative, risk-averse investor involves seven variables and six constraints. After moving all the variables in the five minimum-return constraints to the left-hand side, the complete maximin model is rewritten as follows:

$$\begin{aligned}
\text{Max} \quad & M \\
\text{s.t.} \quad & \\
& -M + 10.06FS + 17.64IB + 32.41LG + 32.36LV + 33.44SG + 24.56SV \geq 0 \\
& -M + 13.12FS + 3.25IB + 18.71LG + 20.61LV + 19.40SG + 25.32SV \geq 0 \\
& -M + 13.47FS + 7.51IB + 33.28LG + 12.93LV + 3.85SG - 6.70SV \geq 0 \\
& -M + 45.42FS - 1.33IB + 41.46LG + 7.06LV + 58.68SG + 5.43SV \geq 0 \\
& -M - 21.93FS + 7.36IB - 23.26LG - 5.37LV - 9.02SG + 17.31SV \geq 0 \\
& FS + IB + LG + LV + SG + SV = 1 \\
& M, FS, IB, LG, LV, SG, SV \geq 0
\end{aligned}$$

Note that we have written the constraint that requires the sum of the proportion of the portfolio invested in each mutual fund as the last constraint in the model. In this way, when we interpret the computer solution of the model, constraint 1 will correspond to planning scenario 1, constraint 2 will correspond to planning scenario 2, and so on.

The optimal solution to the Hauck maximin model is shown in Figure 5.6. The optimal value of the objective function is 6.445; thus, the optimal portfolio will earn 6.445% in the worst-case scenario. The optimal solution calls for 55.4% of the portfolio to be invested

FIGURE 5.6 THE MANAGEMENT SCIENTIST SOLUTION FOR THE HAUCK MAXIMIN PORTFOLIO MODEL

```
OPTIMAL SOLUTION
Objective Function Value =               6.445

     Variable              Value            Reduced Costs
  --------------     ---------------    -----------------
       FS                  0.000                6.768
       IB                  0.554                0.000
       LG                  0.132                0.000
       LV                  0.000                3.156
       SG                  0.000                2.764
       SV                  0.314                0.000
       M                   6.445                0.000

    Constraint         Slack/Surplus        Dual Prices
  --------------     ---------------    -----------------
       1                  15.321                0.000
       2                   5.785                0.000
       3                   0.000               -0.397
       4                   0.000               -0.112
       5                   0.000               -0.491
       6                   0.000                6.445
```

in the intermediate-term bond fund, 13.2% of the portfolio to be invested in the large-cap growth fund, and 31.4% of the portfolio to be invested in the small-cap value fund.

Because we do not know at the time of solving the model which of the five possible scenarios will occur, we cannot say for sure that the portfolio return will be 6.445%. However, using the surplus variables, we can learn what the portfolio return will be under each of the scenarios. Constraints 3, 4, and 5 correspond to scenarios 3, 4, and 5 (years 3, 4, and 5 in Table 5.4). The surplus variables for these constraints are zero to indicate that the portfolio return will be $M = 6.445\%$ if any of these three scenarios occur. The surplus variable for constraint 1 is 15.321, indicating that the portfolio return will exceed $M = 6.445$ by 15.321 if scenario 1 occurs. So, if scenario 1 occurs, the portfolio return will be 6.445% + 15.321% = 21.766%. Referring to the surplus variable for constraint 2, we see that the portfolio return will be 6.445% + 5.785% = 12.230% if scenario 2 occurs.

We must also keep in mind that in order to develop the portfolio model, Hauck made the assumption that over the next 12 months one of the five possible scenarios in Table 5.4 will occur. But we also recognize that the actual scenario that occurs over the next 12 months may be different from the scenarios Hauck considered. Thus, Hauck's experience and judgment in selecting representative scenarios plays a key part in determining how valuable the model recommendations will be for the client.

Moderate Risk Portfolio

Hauck's portfolio manager would like to also construct a portfolio for clients who are willing to accept a moderate amount of risk in order to attempt to achieve better returns. Suppose that clients in this risk category are willing to accept some risk, but do not want the annual return for the portfolio to drop below 2%. By setting $M = 2$ in the minimum-return constraints in the maximin model we can constrain the model to provide a solution with an annual return of at least 2%. The minimum-return constraints needed to provide an annual return of at least 2% are as follows:

$$
\begin{aligned}
R1 &\geq 2 && \text{Scenario 1 minimum return} \\
R2 &\geq 2 && \text{Scenario 2 minimum return} \\
R3 &\geq 2 && \text{Scenario 3 minimum return} \\
R4 &\geq 2 && \text{Scenario 4 minimum return} \\
R5 &\geq 2 && \text{Scenario 5 minimum return}
\end{aligned}
$$

Substituting the expressions previously developed for $R1$, $R2$, and so on, provides the following five minimum-return constraints:

$$
\begin{aligned}
10.06FS + 17.64IB + 32.41LG + 32.36LV + 33.44SG + 24.56SV &\geq 2 && \text{Scenario 1} \\
13.12FS + 3.25IB + 18.71LG + 20.61LV + 19.40SG + 25.32SV &\geq 2 && \text{Scenario 2} \\
13.47FS + 7.51IB + 33.28LG + 12.93LV + 3.85SG - 6.70SV &\geq 2 && \text{Scenario 3} \\
45.42FS - 1.33IB + 41.46LG + 7.06LV + 58.68SG + 5.43SV &\geq 2 && \text{Scenario 4} \\
-21.93FS + 7.36IB - 23.26LG - 5.37LV - 9.02SG + 17.31SV &\geq 2 && \text{Scenario 5}
\end{aligned}
$$

In addition to these five minimum-return constraints, we still need the constraint that requires that the sum of the proportions invested in the separate mutual funds add to 1.

$$FS + IB + LG + LV + SG + SV = 1$$

A different objective is needed for this portfolio optimization problem. A common approach is to maximize the expected value of the return for the portfolio. For instance, if we assume that the planning scenarios are equally likely we would assign a probability of .20 to each scenario. In this case the objective function is

$$\text{Expected value of the return} = .2R1 + .2R2 + .2R3 + .2R4 + .2R5$$

The coefficient of FS in the objective function is given by $.2(10.06) + .2(13.12) + .2(13.47) + .2(45.42) + .2(-21.93) = 12.03$; the coefficient of IB is $.2(17.64) + .2(3.25) + .2(7.51) + .2(-1.33) + .2(7.36) = 6.89$; and so on. Thus, the objective function is

$$12.03FS + 6.89IB + 20.52LG + 13.52LV + 21.27SG + 13.18SV$$

Because the objective is to maximize the expected value of the return we write Hauck's objective as follows:

$$\text{Max } 12.03FS + 6.89IB + 20.52LG + 13.52LV + 21.27SG + 13.18SV$$

The complete linear programming formulation for this version of the portfolio optimization problem involves six variables and six constraints.

$$\begin{aligned}
\text{Max } & 12.03FS + 6.89IB + 20.52LG + 13.52LV + 21.27SG + 13.18SV \\
\text{s.t.} & \\
& 10.06FS + 17.64IB + 32.41LG + 32.36LV + 33.44SG + 24.56SV \geq 2 \\
& 13.12FS + 3.25IB + 18.71LG + 20.61LV + 19.40SG + 25.32SV \geq 2 \\
& 13.47FS + 7.51IB + 33.28LG + 12.93LV + 3.85SG - 6.70SV \geq 2 \\
& 45.42FS - 1.33IB + 41.46LG + 7.06LV + 58.68SG + 5.43SV \geq 2 \\
& -21.93FS + 7.36IB - 23.26LG - 5.37LV - 9.02SG + 17.31SV \geq 2 \\
& FS + IB + LG + LV + SG + SV = 1 \\
& FS, IB, LG, LV, SG, SV \geq 0
\end{aligned}$$

The optimal solution is shown in Figure 5.7. The optimal allocation is to invest 10.8% of the portfolio in a large-cap growth mutual fund, 41.5% in a small-cap growth mutual fund, and 47.7% in a small-cap value mutual fund. The objective function value shows that this allocation provides a maximum expected return of 17.33%. From the surplus variables, we see that the portfolio return will only be 2% if scenarios 3 or 5 occur (constraints 3 and 5 are binding). The returns will be excellent if scenarios 1, 2, or 4 occur: The portfolio return will be 29.093% if scenario 1 occurs, 22.149% if scenario 2 occurs, and 31.417% if scenario 4 occurs.

The moderate risk portfolio exposes Hauck's clients to more risk than the maximin portfolio developed for a conservative investor. With the maximin portfolio, the worst-case scenario provided a return of 6.44%. With this moderate risk portfolio, the worst-case scenarios (scenarios 3 and 5) only provide a return of 2%, but it also provides the possibility of higher returns.

The formulation we have developed for a moderate risk portfolio can be modified to account for other risk tolerances. If an investor can tolerate the risk of no return, the right-hand sides of the minimum-return constraints would be set to 0. If an investor can tolerate a *loss* of 3%, the right-hand side of the minimum-return constraints would be set equal to −3.

FIGURE 5.7 THE MANAGEMENT SCIENTIST SOLUTION FOR THE MODERATE RISK PORTFOLIO MODEL

EXCELfile
Moderate Risk

```
Objective Function Value =              17.330

    Variable              Value               Reduced Costs
 --------------      ---------------      -----------------
       FS                   0.000                  12.246
       IB                   0.000                   7.139
       LG                   0.108                   0.000
       LV                   0.000                   4.351
       SG                   0.415                   0.000
       SV                   0.477                   0.000

   Constraint          Slack/Surplus          Dual Prices
 --------------      ---------------      -----------------
        1                  27.093                   0.000
        2                  20.149                   0.000
        3                   0.000                  -0.216
        4                  29.417                   0.000
        5                   0.000                  -0.394
        6                   0.000                  18.550

OBJECTIVE COEFFICIENT RANGES

  Variable        Lower Limit        Current Value        Upper Limit
------------    ---------------     ---------------    ---------------
     FS         No Lower Limit              12.030              24.276
     IB         No Lower Limit               6.890              14.029
     LG                 10.729              20.520              25.645
     LV         No Lower Limit              13.520              17.871
     SG                 17.944              21.270              46.224
     SV                  4.832              13.180              21.539

RIGHT HAND SIDE RANGES

 Constraint       Lower Limit        Current Value        Upper Limit
------------    ---------------     ---------------    ---------------
     1          No Lower Limit               2.000              29.093
     2          No Lower Limit               2.000              22.149
     3                  -0.566               2.000               8.387
     4          No Lower Limit               2.000              31.417
     5                  -4.403               2.000               8.482
     6                   0.383               1.000              11.879
```

The dual prices for the minimum-return constraints have an interesting interpretation in this formulation. Changing the risk tolerance, and hence the minimum acceptable return, requires a simultaneous change in the right hand side of the five minimum-return constraints. Suppose we want to use the dual prices to determine how much the objective function will increase for an investor who is willing to tolerate a return as low as 1%. Notice that constraints 3 and 5 are binding (surplus variables = 0). The dual price for constraint 3 is −.216 and the dual price for constraint 5 is −.394. The question is: Can we conclude that

NOTES AND COMMENTS

1. The Management Science in Action, Asset Allocation and Variable Annuities, describes how insurance companies use asset allocation models to choose a portfolio of mutual funds for their clients' variable annuity investments.
2. Other constraints may be added to portfolio models to make them more flexible. For instance, if a client wanted to have at least 10% of the portfolio invested in foreign stocks, we would add the constraint $FS \geq .10$ to either the maximin or moderate risk portfolio models.
3. The portfolio models developed in this section are based on a working paper entitled "Decision Analysis, Diversification, and Financial Services" (December 2005) by George G. Polak and Dennis J. Sweeney. Related models can be found in "A Minimax Portfolio Selection Rule with Linear Programming," by Martin R. Young, *Management Science* (1998).
4. Harry Markowitz pioneered the use of mathematical models for portfolio selection. The primary model he developed is nonlinear and uses the statistical variance of returns for the portfolio as a measure of risk. We describe and illustrate the Markowitz model in Chapter 8 (Nonlinear Optimization Models).

the objective function will go up by .216 + .394 = .610 if an investor is willing to specify 1% as the minimum acceptable return? The answer is yes, because of the 100% rule.

The ranges for the right-hand sides are also shown in Figure 5.7. Note that the lower limit of the range for the right-hand side of constraint 3 is −.566 and the lower limit of the range for the right-hand side of constraint 5 is −4.403. The ranges for constraints 1, 2, and 4 do not have a lower limit. From the 100% rule, we need to compute the cumulative percentage of the allowable decreases corresponding to the changes in the right-hand sides. The allowable decreases for constraints 1, 2, and 4 are infinite. So the change in the right-hand side

MANAGEMENT SCIENCE IN ACTION

ASSET ALLOCATION AND VARIABLE ANNUITIES*

Insurance companies use portfolio models for asset allocation to structure a portfolio for their clients who purchase variable annuities. A variable annuity is an insurance contract that involves an accumulation phase and a distribution phase. In the accumulation phase the individual either makes a lump sum contribution or contributes to the annuity over a period of time. In the distribution phase the investor receives payments either in a lump sum or over a period of time. The distribution phase usually occurs at retirement, but because a variable annuity is an insurance product, a benefit is paid to a beneficiary should the annuitant die before or during the distribution period.

Most insurance companies selling variable annuities offer their clients the benefit of an asset allocation model to help them decide how to allocate their investment among a family of mutual funds. Usually the client fills out a questionnaire to assess his or her level of risk tolerance. Then, given that risk tolerance, the insurance company's asset allocation model recommends how the client's investment should be allocated over a family of mutual funds. American Skandia, a Prudential Financial Company, markets variable annuities that provide the types of services mentioned. A questionnaire is used to assess the client's risk tolerance, and the Morningstar Asset Allocator is used to develop portfolios for five levels of risk tolerance. Clients with low levels of risk tolerance are guided to portfolios consisting of bond funds and T-bills, and the most risk-tolerant investors are guided to portfolios consisting of a large proportion of growth stock mutual funds. Investors with intermediate, or moderate, risk tolerances are guided to portfolios that may consist of suitable mixtures of value and growth stock funds as well as some bond funds.

*Based on information provided by James R. Martin of the Martin Company, a financial services company.

Instead of using the 100% rule to determine the change in the value of the objective function, we can also resolve the model after changing the right-hand sides of constraints 1 to 5 from 2 to 1; the value of the optimal solution after making these changes is 17.940.

from 2 to 1 for those constraints is 0% of the allowable decrease. The allowable decrease for constraint 3 is 2.566 = 2 − (−.566), and the allowable decrease for constraint 5 is 6.403 = 2 − (−4.403). The percentage of the allowable decrease for constraint 3 represented by a decrease in the right-hand side from 2 to 1 is (1/2.566)(100%) = 39.0%. The percentage of the allowable decrease for constraint 5 represented by a decrease in the right-hand side from 2 to 1 is (1/6.403)(100%) = 15.6%. Thus, because changing the right-hand sides of constraints 1 to 5 from 2 to 1 results in a cumulative percentage decrease of 39.0% + 15.6% = 54.6%, the 100% rule is satisfied. This result tells us that the value of the objective function (the expected return for the portfolio) will go up by .610% to 17.940% if the minimal acceptable return is lowered by 1%.

5.4 GAME THEORY

In **game theory**, two or more decision makers, called players, compete against each other. Each player selects one of several strategies without knowing in advance the strategy selected by the other player or players. The combination of the competing strategies provides the value of the game to the players. Game theory applications have been developed for situations in which the competing players are teams, companies, political candidates, and contract bidders.

In this section, we describe **two-person, zero-sum games.** *Two-person* means that two players participate in the game. *Zero-sum* means that the gain (or loss) for one player is equal to the loss (or gain) for the other player. As a result, the gain and loss balance out (resulting in a zero-sum) for the game. What one player wins, the other player loses. Let us demonstrate a two-person, zero-sum game and its solution by considering two companies competing for market share.

Competing for Market Share

Suppose that two companies are the only manufacturers of a particular product; they compete against each other for market share. In planning a marketing strategy for the coming year, each company will select one of three strategies designed to take market share from the other company. The three strategies, which are assumed to be the same for both companies, are as follows:

Strategy 1: Increase advertising.
Strategy 2: Provide quantity discounts.
Strategy 3: Extend warranty.

A payoff table showing the percentage gain in the market share for Company A for each combination of strategies is shown in Table 5.5. Because it is a zero-sum game, any gain in market share for Company A is a loss in market share for Company B.

In interpreting the entries in the table, we see that if Company A increases advertising (a_1) and Company B increases advertising (b_1), Company A will come out ahead with an increase in market share of 4% while Company B will have a decrease in market share of 4%. On the other hand, if Company A provides quantity discounts (a_2) and Company B increases advertising (b_1), Company A will lose 1% of market share while Company B will gain 1% of market share. Therefore, Company A wants to maximize the payoff which is its increase in market share. Company B wants to minimize the payoff because the increase in market share for Company A is the decrease in market share for Company B.

TABLE 5.5 PAYOFF TABLE SHOWING THE PERCENTAGE GAIN IN MARKET SHARE FOR COMPANY A

		Company B		
		Increase Advertising b_1	**Quantity Discounts** b_2	**Extend Warranty** b_3
	Increase Advertising a_1	4	3	2
Company A	**Quantity Discounts** a_2	−1	4	1
	Extend Warranty a_3	5	−2	0

This market-share game meets the requirements of a two-person, zero-sum game. The two companies are the two players and the zero-sum occurs because the gain (or loss) in market share for Company A is the same as the loss (or gain) in market share for Company B. Each company will select one of its three alternative strategies. Because of the planning horizon, each company will have to select its strategy before knowing the other company's strategy. What is the optimal strategy for the each company?

The logic of game theory assumes that each player has the same information and will select a strategy that provides the best possible payoff from its point of view. Suppose Company A selects strategy a_1. Market share increases of 4%, 3%, or 2% are possible depending upon Company B's strategy. At this point, Company A assumes that Company B will select the strategy that is best for it. Thus, if Company A selects strategy a_1, Company A assumes Company B will select its best strategy b_3, which will limit Company A's increase in market share to 2%. Continuing with this logic, Company A analyzes the game by protecting itself against the strategy that may be taken by Company B. Doing so, Company A identifies the minimum payoff for each of its strategies, which is the minimum value in each row of the payoff table. These row minimums are shown in Table 5.6.

The player seeking to maximize the value of the game selects a maximin strategy.

Considering the entries in the Row Minimum column, we see that Company A can be guaranteed an increase in market share of at least 2% by selecting strategy a_1. Strategy a_2 could result in a decrease in market share of 1% and strategy a_3 could result in a decrease in market share of 2%. After comparing the row minimum values, Company A selects the strategy that provides the *maximum* of the row *minimum* values. This is called a **maximin** strategy. Thus, Company A selects strategy a_1 as its optimal strategy; an increase in market share of at least 2% is guaranteed.

TABLE 5.6 PAYOFF TABLE WITH ROW MINIMUMS

		Company B			
		Increase Advertising b_1	**Quantity Discounts** b_2	**Extend Warranty** b_3	**Row Minimum**
	Increase Advertising a_1	4	3	2	(2) ←Maximum
Company A	**Quantity Discounts** a_2	−1	4	1	−1
	Extend Warranty a_3	5	−2	0	−2

TABLE 5.7 PAYOFF TABLE WITH COLUMN MAXIMUMS

		Company B			
		Increase Advertising b_1	**Quantity Discounts** b_2	**Extend Warranty** b_3	**Row Minimum**
Company A	**Increase Advertising** a_1	4	3	2	(2) ←Maximum
	Quantity Discounts a_2	−1	4	1	−1
	Extend Warranty a_3	5	−2	0	−2
	Column Maximum	5	4	(2) ←Minimum	

Let us now look at the payoff table from the point of view of the other player, Company B. The entries in the payoff table represent gains in market share for Company A, which correspond to losses in market share for Company B. Consider what happens if Company B selects strategy b_1. Company B market share decreases of 4%, −1%, and 5% are possible. Under the assumption that Company A will select the strategy that is best for it, Company B assumes Company A will select strategy a_3, resulting in a gain in market share of 5% for Company A and a loss in market share of 5% for Company B. At this point, Company B analyzes the game by protecting itself against the strategy taken by Company A. Doing so, Company B identifies the maximum payoff to Company A for each of its strategies b_1, b_2, and b_3. This payoff value is the maximum value in each column of the payoff table. These column maximums are shown in Table 5.7.

The player seeking to minimize the value of the game selects a minimax strategy.

Considering the entries in the Column Maximum row, Company B can be guaranteed a decrease in market share of no more than 2% by selecting the strategy b_3. Strategy b_1 could result in a decrease in market share of 5% and strategy b_2 could result in a decrease in market share of 4%. After comparing the column maximum values, Company B selects the strategy that provides the *minimum* of the column *maximum* values. This is called a **minimax** strategy. Thus, Company B selects b_3 as its optimal strategy. Company B has guaranteed that Company A cannot gain more than 2% in market share.

Identifying a Pure Strategy Solution

If it is optimal for both players to select one strategy and stay with that strategy regardless of what the other player does, the game has a **pure strategy** solution. Whenever the maximum of the row minimums *equals* the minimum of the column maximums, the players cannot improve their payoff by changing to a different strategy. The game is said to have a **saddle point** or an equilibrium point. Thus, a pure strategy is the optimal strategy for the players. The requirement for a pure strategy solution is as follows:

A Game has a Pure Strategy Solution if:

Maximum(Row minimums) = Minimum(Column maximums)

Because this equality is the case in our example, the solution to the game is for Company A to increase advertising (strategy a_1) and for Company B to extend the warranty (strategy b_3). Company A's market share will increase by 2% and Company B's market share will decrease by 2%.

With Company A selecting its pure strategy a_1, let us see what happens if Company B tries to change from its pure strategy b_3. Company A's market share will increase 4% if b_1 is selected or will increase 3% if b_2 is selected. Company B must stay with its pure strategy b_3 to limit Company A to a 2% increase in market share. Similarly, with Company B selecting its pure strategy b_3, let us see what happens if Company A tries to change from its pure strategy a_1. Company A's market share will increase only 1% if a_2 is selected or will not increase at all if a_3 is selected. Company A must stay with its pure strategy a_1 in order to keep its 2% increase in market share. Thus, even if one of the companies discovers its opponent's pure strategy in advance, neither company can gain any advantage by switching from its pure strategy.

If a pure strategy solution exists, it is the optimal solution to the game. The following steps can be used to determine when a game has a pure strategy solution and to identify the optimal pure strategy for each player.

Analyze a two-person, zero-sum game by first checking to see whether a pure strategy solution exists.

Step 1. Compute the minimum payoff for each row (Player A).

Step 2. For Player A, select the strategy that provides the maximum of the row minimums.

Step 3. Compute the maximum payoff for each column (Player B).

Step 4. For Player B select the strategy that provides the minimum of the column maximums.

Step 5. If the maximum of the row minimums is equal to the minimum of the column maximums, this value is the value of the game and a pure strategy solution exists. The optimal pure strategy for Player A is identified in Step 2, and the optimal pure strategy for Player B is identified in Step 4.

If the maximum of the row minimums *does not equal* the minimum of the column maximums, a pure strategy solution does not exist. In this case, a mixed strategy solution becomes optimal. In the following discussion, we define a mixed strategy solution and show how linear programming can be used to identify the optimal mixed strategy for each player.

Identifying a Mixed Strategy Solution

Let us continue with the two-company market-share game and consider a slight modification in the payoff table as shown in Table 5.8. Only one payoff has changed. If both Company A and Company B choose the extended warranty strategy, the payoff to Company A

TABLE 5.8 MODIFIED PAYOFF TABLE SHOWING THE PERCENTAGE GAIN IN MARKET SHARE FOR COMPANY A

		Company B			
		Increase Advertising b_1	**Quantity Discounts b_2**	**Extend Warranty b_3**	**Row Minimum**
Company A	**Increase Advertising a_1**	4	3	2	(2) ←Maximum
	Quantity Discounts a_2	−1	4	1	−1
	Extend Warranty a_3	5	−2	5	−2
	Column Maximum	5	(4) ↑ Minimum	5	

is now a 5% increase in market share rather than the previous 0%. The row minimums do not change, but the column maximums do. Note that the column maximum for strategy b_3 is 5% instead of the previous 2%.

In analyzing the game to determine whether a pure strategy solution exists, we find that the maximum of the row minimums is 2% while the minimum of the row maximums is 4%. Because these values are not equal, a pure strategy solution does not exist. In this case, it is not optimal for each company to be predictable and select a pure strategy regardless of what the other company does. The optimal solution is for both players to adopt a mixed strategy.

With a **mixed strategy,** each player selects its strategy according to a probability distribution. In the market share example, each company will first determine an optimal probability distribution for selecting whether to increase advertising, provide quantity discounts, or extend warranty. Then, when the game is played, each company will use its probability distribution to randomly select one of its three strategies.

First consider the game from the point of view of Company A. Company A will select one of its three strategies based on the following probabilities.

$$PA1 = \text{the probability that Company A selects strategy } a_1$$
$$PA2 = \text{the probability that Company A selects strategy } a_2$$
$$PA3 = \text{the probability that Company A selects strategy } a_3$$

The expected value, computed by multiplying each payoff by its probability and summing, can be interpreted as a long-run average payoff for a mixed strategy.

Using these probabilities for Company A's mixed strategy, what happens if Company B selects strategy b_1? Using the payoffs in the b_1 column of Table 5.8, we see Company A will experience an increase in market share of 4% with probability $PA1$, a decrease in market share of 1% with probability $PA2$, and an increase in market share of 5% with probability $PA3$. Weighting each payoff by its probability and summing provides the **expected value** of the increase in market share for Company A. If Company B selects strategy b_1, this expected value, referred to as the *expected gain* if strategy b_1 is selected, can be written as follows.

$$EG(b_1) = 4PA1 - 1PA2 + 5PA3$$

The expression for the expected gain in market share for Company A for each Company B strategy is provided in Table 5.9.

For example, if Company A uses a mixed strategy with equal probabilities ($PA1 = 1/3$, $PA2 = 1/3$, and $PA3 = 1/3$), Company A's expected gain in market share for each Company B strategy is as follows.

$$EG(b_1) = 4PA1 - 1PA2 + 5PA3 = 4(1/3) - 1(1/3) + 5(1/3) = 8/3 = 2.67$$
$$EG(b_2) = 3PA1 + 4PA2 - 2PA3 = 3(1/3) + 4(1/3) - 2(1/3) = 5/3 = 1.67$$
$$EG(b_3) = 2PA1 + 1PA2 + 5PA3 = 2(1/3) + 1(1/3) + 5(1/3) = 8/3 = 2.67$$

TABLE 5.9 EXPECTED GAIN IN MARKET SHARE FOR COMPANY A FOR EACH COMPANY B STRATEGY

Company B Strategy	**Expected Gain for Company A**
b_1	$EG(b_1) = 4PA1 - 1PA2 + 5PA3$
b_2	$EG(b_2) = 3PA1 + 4PA2 - 2PA3$
b_3	$EG(b_3) = 2PA1 + 1PA2 + 5PA3$

The logic of game theory assumes that if Company A uses a mixed strategy, Company B will select the strategy that will minimize Company A's expected gain. Using these results, Company A assumes Company B will select strategy b_2 and limit Company A's expected gain in market share to 1.67%. Because Company A's pure strategy a_1 provides a 2% increase in market share, the mixed strategy with equal probabilities, $PA1 = 1/3$, $PA2 = 1/3$, and $PA3 = 1/3$, is not the optimal strategy for Company A.

Let us show how Company A can use linear programming to find its optimal mixed strategy. Our goal is to find probabilities, $PA1$, $PA2$, and $PA3$, that maximize the expected gain in market share for Company A regardless of the strategy selected by Company B. In effect, Company A will protect itself against any strategy selected by Company B by being sure its expected gain in market share is as large as possible even if Company B selects its own optimal strategy.

Given the probabilities $PA1$, $PA2$, and $PA3$ and the expected gain expressions in Table 5.9, game theory assumes that Company B will select a strategy that provides the minimum expected gain for Company A. Thus, Company B will select b_1, b_2, or b_3 based on

$$\text{Min}\ \{EG(b_1), EG(b_2), EG(b_3)\}$$

When Company B selects its strategy, the value of the game will be the minimum expected gain. This strategy will minimize Company A's expected gain in market share.

Company A will select its optimal mixed strategy using a *maximin* strategy, which will maximize the minimum expected gain. This objective is written as follows.

The player seeking to maximize the value of the game selects a maximin strategy by maximizing the minimum expected gain.

$$\text{Max}\ [\text{Min}\ \{EG(b_1), EG(b_2), EG(b_3)\}]$$

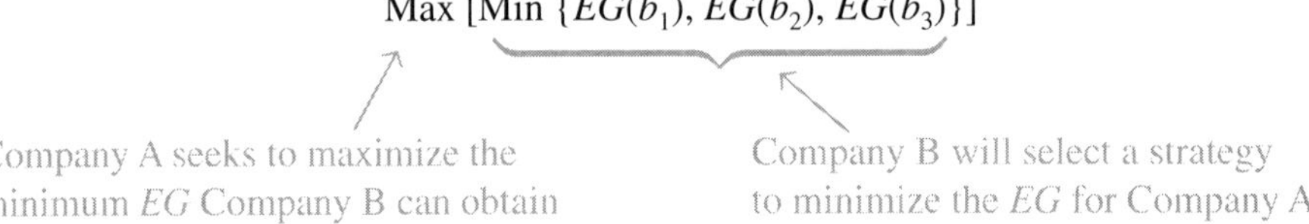

Define *GAINA* to be the optimal expected gain in market share for Company A. Because Company B will select a strategy that minimizes this expected gain, we know *GAINA* is equal to Min $\{EG(b_1), EG(b_2), EG(b_3)\}$. Thus, the individual expected gains, $EG(b_1)$, $EG(b_2)$, and $EG(b_3)$, must all be *greater than or equal* to *GAINA*. If Company B selects strategy b_1, we know

$$EG(b_1) \geq GAINA$$

Using the probabilities $PA1$, $PA2$, and $PA3$ and the expected gain expression in Table 5.9, this condition can be written as follows:

$$4PA1 - 1PA2 + 5PA3 \geq GAINA$$

or

$$4PA1 - 1PA2 + 5PA3 - GAINA \geq 0$$

Similarly, for Company B strategies b_2 and b_3, the fact that both $EG(b_2) \geq GAINA$ and $EG(b_3) \geq GAINA$ provides the following two expressions.

$$3PA1 + 4PA2 - 2PA3 - GAINA \geq 0$$
$$2PA1 + 1PA2 + 5PA3 - GAINA \geq 0$$

In addition, we know that the sum of the Company A's mixed strategy probabilities must equal 1.

$$PA1 + PA2 + PA3 = 1$$

Finally, realizing that the objective of Company A is to maximize its expected gain, *GAINA*, we have the following linear programming model. Solving this linear program will provide Company A's optimal mixed strategy.

$$\begin{array}{lll} \text{Max} & GAINA & \\ \text{s.t.} & & \text{Company B strategy} \\ & 4PA1 - 1PA2 + 5PA3 - GAINA \geq 0 & (\text{Strategy } b_1) \\ & 3PA1 + 4PA2 - 2PA3 - GAINA \geq 0 & (\text{Strategy } b_2) \\ & 2PA1 + 1PA2 + 5PA3 - GAINA \geq 0 & (\text{Strategy } b_3) \\ & PA1 + PA2 + PA3 = 1 & \\ & PA1, PA2, PA3, GAINA \geq 0 & \end{array}$$

The Management Scientist solution of Company A's linear program is shown in Figure 5.8.

From Figure 5.8, we see Company A's optimal mixed strategy is to increase advertising (a_1) with a probability of 0.875 and extend warranty (a_3) with a probability of 0.125. Company A should never provide quantity discounts (a_2) because $PA2 = 0$. The expected value of this mixed strategy is a 2.375% increase in market share for Company A.

Let us show what happens to the expected gain if Company A uses this optimal mixed strategy. Company A's expected gain for each Company B strategy follows.

$$EG(b_1) = 4PA1 - 1PA2 + 5PA3 = 4(0.875) - 1(0) + 5(0.125) = 4.125$$
$$EG(b_2) = 3PA1 + 4PA2 - 2PA3 = 3(0.875) + 4(0) - 2(0.125) = 2.375$$
$$EG(b_3) = 2PA1 + 1PA2 + 5PA3 = 2(0.875) + 1(0) + 5(0.125) = 2.375$$

FIGURE 5.8 THE MANAGEMENT SCIENTIST SOLUTION FOR COMPANY A'S OPTIMAL MIXED STRATEGY

```
OPTIMAL SOLUTION

Objective Function Value =              2.375

    Variable              Value            Reduced Costs
 --------------      ---------------    -----------------
       PA1                  0.875                0.000
       PA2                  0.000                0.250
       PA3                  0.125                0.000
      GAINA                 2.375                0.000

   Constraint         Slack/Surplus          Dual Prices
 --------------      ---------------    -----------------
        1                   1.750                0.000
        2                   0.000               -0.375
        3                   0.000               -0.625
        4                   0.000                2.375
```

Company B will minimize Company A's expected gain by selecting either strategy b_2 or b_3. However, Company A has selected its optimal mixed strategy by maximizing this minimum expected gain. Thus, Company A obtains an expected gain in market share of 2.375% regardless of the strategy selected by Company B. The mixed strategy with $PA1 = 0.875$, $PA2 = 0.0$, and $PA3 = 0.125$ is the optimal strategy for Company A. The expected gain of 2.375% is better than Company A's best pure strategy (a_1), which provides a 2% increase in market share.

Now consider the game from the point of view of Company B. Company B will select one of its strategies based on the following probabilities.

$$PB1 = \text{the probability that Company B selects strategy } b_1$$
$$PB2 = \text{the probability that Company B selects strategy } b_2$$
$$PB3 = \text{the probability that Company B selects strategy } b_3$$

Based on these probabilities for Company B's mixed strategy, what happens if Company A selects strategy a_1? Using the payoffs in the a_1 row of Table 5.8, Company B will experience a decrease in market share of 4% with probability $PB1$, a decrease in market share of 3% with probability $PB2$, and decrease in market share of 2% with probability $PB3$. If Company A selects strategy a_1, the expected value, referred to Company B's *expected loss* if strategy a_1 is selected, can be written as follows.

$$EL(a_1) = 4PB1 + 3PB2 + 2PB3$$

The expression for the expected loss in market share for Company B for each Company A strategy is provided in Table 5.10.

Let us show how Company B can use linear programming to find its optimal mixed strategy. Our goal is to find the probabilities, $PB1$, $PB2$, and $PB3$, that minimize the expected loss in market share to Company B regardless of the strategy selected by Company A. In effect, Company B will protect itself from any strategy selected by Company A by being sure its expected loss in market share is as small as possible even if Company A selects its own optimal strategy.

Given the probabilities $PB1$, $PB2$, and $PB3$ and the expected loss expressions in Table 5.10, game theory assumes that Company A will select a strategy that provides the maximum expected loss for Company B. Thus, Company A will select a_1, a_2, or a_3 based on

$$\text{Max } \{EL(a_1), EL(a_2), EL(a_3)\}$$

When Company A selects its strategy, the value of the game will be the expected loss, which will maximize Company B's expected loss in market share.

TABLE 5.10 EXPECTED LOSS IN MARKET SHARE FOR COMPANY B FOR EACH COMPANY A STRATEGY

Company A Strategy	Expected Loss for Company B
a_1	$4PB1 + 3PB2 + 2PB3$
a_2	$-1PB1 + 4PB2 + 1PB3$
a_3	$5PB1 - 2PB2 + 5PB3$

Company B will select its optimal mixed strategy using a *minimax* strategy to minimize the maximum expected loss. This objective is written as follows.

The player seeking to minimize the value of the game selects a minimax strategy by minimizing the maximum expected loss.

$$\text{Min}\ [\text{Max}\ \{EL(a_1), EL(a_2), EL(a_3)\}]$$

Company B seeks to minimize the maximum EL Company A can obtain

Company A will select a strategy to maximize the EL for Company B

Define *LOSSB* to be the optimal expected loss in market share for Company B. Because Company A will select a strategy that maximizes this expected loss, we know *LOSSB* is equal to Max $\{EL(a_1), EL(a_2), EL(a_3)\}$. Thus, the individual expected losses, $EL(a_1)$, $EL(a_2)$, and $EL(a_3)$, must all be *less than or equal to LOSSB*. If Company A selects strategy, a_1, we know

$$EL(a_1) \leq LOSSB$$

Using the probabilities $PB1$, $PB2$, and $PB3$ and the expected loss expression for $EL(a_1)$ in Table 5.10, this condition can be written as follows:

$$4PB1 + 3PB2 + 2PB3 \leq LOSSB$$

or

$$4PB1 + 3PB2 + 2PB3 - LOSSB \leq 0$$

Similarly, for Company A strategies a_2 and a_3, the fact that both $EL(a_2) \leq LOSSB$ and $EL(a_3) \leq LOSSB$ provides the following two expressions.

$$-1PB1 + 4PB2 + 1PB3 - LOSSB \leq 0$$
$$5PB1 - 2PB2 + 5PB3 - LOSSB \leq 0$$

In addition we know that the sum of the Company B's mixed strategy probabilities must equal 1.

$$PB1 + PB2 + PB3 = 1$$

Finally, realizing that the objective of Company B is to minimize its expected loss, *LOSSB*, we have the following linear programming model. Solving this linear program will provide Company B's optimal mixed strategy.

Min *LOSSB*

s.t.

	Company A strategy
$4PB1 + 3PB2 + 2PB3 - LOSSB \leq 0$	(Strategy a_1)
$-1PB1 + 4PB2 + 1PB3 - LOSSB \leq 0$	(Strategy a_2)
$5PB1 - 2PB2 + 5PB3 - LOSSB \leq 0$	(Strategy a_3)
$PB1 + PB2 + PB3 = 1$	
$PB1, PB2, PB3, LOSSB \geq 0$	

The Management Scientist solution of Company B's linear program is shown in Figure 5.9.

FIGURE 5.9 THE MANAGEMENT SCIENTIST SOLUTION FOR COMPANY B'S OPTIMAL MIXED STRATEGY

EXCELfile
Strategy B

```
OPTIMAL SOLUTION

Objective Function Value =                    2.375

       Variable              Value            Reduced Costs
    --------------     ---------------     -----------------
          PB1                 0.000                 1.750
          PB2                 0.375                 0.000
          PB3                 0.625                 0.000
         LOSSB                2.375                 0.000

      Constraint         Slack/Surplus         Dual Prices
    --------------     ---------------     -----------------
           1                  0.000                 0.875
           2                  0.250                 0.000
           3                  0.000                 0.125
           4                  0.000                -2.375
```

From Figure 5.9, we see Company B's optimal mixed strategy is to provide quantity discounts (b_2) with a probability of 0.375 and extend warranty (b_3) with a probability of 0.625. Company B should not increase advertising (b_1) because $PB1 = 0$. The expected value or expected loss of this mixed strategy is 2.375%. Note that the expected loss of 2.375% of the market share for Company B is the same as the expected gain in market share for Company A. The mixed strategy solution shows the zero-sum for the expected payoffs.

Let us show what happens to the expected loss if Company B uses this optimal mixed strategy. Company B's expected loss for each Company A strategy follows.

$$\begin{aligned}
EL(a_1) &= 4PB1 + 3PB2 + 2PB3 = 4(0) + 3(0.375) + 2(0.625) = 2.375 \\
EL(a_2) &= -1PB1 + 4PB2 + 1PB3 = -1(0) + 4(0.375) + 1(0.625) = 2.125 \\
EL(a_3) &= 5PB1 - 2PB2 + 5PB3 = 5(0) - 2(0.375) + 5(0.625) = 2.375
\end{aligned}$$

Company A will maximize Company B's expected loss by selecting either strategy a_1 or a_3. However, Company B has selected its optimal mixed strategy by minimizing this maximum expected loss. Thus, Company B obtains an expected loss in market share of 2.375% regardless of the strategy selected by Company A. The mixed strategy with $PB1 = 0.0$, $PB2 = 0.375$, and $PB3 = 0.625$ is the optimal strategy for Company B. The expected loss of 2.375% is better than Company B's best pure strategy (b_2), which provides a 4% loss in market share.

The optimal mixed strategy solution with a value of 2.375% is an equilibrium solution. Given Company A's mixed strategy probabilities, Company B cannot improve the value of the game by changing $PB1$, $PB2$, or $PB3$. Likewise, given Company B's mixed strategy probabilities, Company A cannot improve the value of the game by changing $PA1$, $PA2$, or $PA3$. In general, the solution to the linear program will provide an equilibrium optimal mixed strategy solution for the game.

With a mixed strategy game, only solve the linear program for one of the players. Provided the value of the game is greater than zero, the dual prices provide the optimal mixed strategy solution for the other player.

Let us conclude this linear programming application by making some observations and suggestions about using linear programming to solve mixed strategy two-person, zero-sum games. First of all, consider the dual price for constraint 2 in the solution of the Company A linear program in Figure 5.8. This dual price is −0.375. Recall that constraint 2 provides Company A's expected gain if Company B selects strategy b_2. The *absolute value* of the dual price is Company B's optimal probability for this strategy. Thus, we know $PB2 = 0.375$ without having to solve the Company B linear program. Using the absolute value of the dual prices for the Company A linear program in Figure 5.8, we know that the optimal mixed strategy solution for Company B is $PB1 = 0.0$, $PB2 = 0.375$, and $PB3 = 0.625$. Therefore, when a two-person, zero-sum game has a mixed strategy, we only need to solve the linear program for one of the players. The optimal mixed strategy for the other player can be found by using the absolute value of the dual prices.

Finally, note that a nonnegativity constraint in the linear program for Company A requires the value of the game, *GAINA*, to be greater than or equal to 0. A similar nonnegativity constraint in the linear program for Company B requires the value of the game, *LOSSB*, to be greater than or equal to 0. Because the value of the game in our example was 2.375%, we met these nonnegativity requirements. However, consider a two-person, zero-sum game where the payoff table contains several negative payoffs for player A. It may turn out that when player A selects an optimal mixed strategy, a negative value of the game is the best the player can do. In this case *GAINA* and *LOSSB* would be negative, which causes the linear program to have an infeasible solution.

If this condition exists or may exist, the following strategy can be used modify the game and ensure that the linear program has a feasible solution. Define a constant c as follows:

c = the absolute value of the largest negative payoff for player A

If the value of a mixed strategy game may be negative, this procedure will guarantee that the linear program used to determine the optimal mixed strategy will have a feasible solution.

A revised payoff table can be created by adding c to each payoff, turning it into an equivalent two-person, zero-sum game. Because the revised payoff table contains no negative payoffs, the nonnegativity constraint for the value of the game will be satisfied and a feasible solution will exist for the linear program. More importantly, the optimal mixed strategy using the revised payoffs *will be the same* as the optimal mixed strategy for the original game. By subtracting c from the optimal objective function value for game with the revised payoffs, you will obtain the objective function value for the original game.

NOTES AND COMMENTS

1. The analysis of a two-person, zero-sum game begins with checking to see whether a pure strategy solution exists. If the maximum of the row minimums for player A, V_A, is not equal to the minimum the column maximums for player B, V_B, a pure strategy solution does not exist. At this point, we can also conclude that a mixed strategy solution is optimal and that the value of the game will be *between* V_A and V_B. For example, in our mixed strategy market-share game, the maximum of the row minimums was 2% and the minimum of the column maximums was 4%. Thus, we can conclude that a mixed strategy solution exists and that the value of the game is between 2% and 4%. We would know this result before solving the mixed strategy linear program.

   If the maximum of the row minimums, V_A, is positive and the minimum of the column maximums, V_B, is positive, we know that the value of the mixed strategy game will be positive. In this case, it is not necessary to revise the payoff table by the constant c to obtain a feasible linear

(*continued*)

programming solution. However, if one or both V_A and V_B are negative, the value of the mixed strategy game can be negative. In this case, it is desirable to revise the payoff table by adding the constant c to all payoffs prior to solving the linear program.

2. The linear programming formulation presented in this section used nonnegativity constraints $GAINA \geq 0$ and $LOSSB \geq 0$ so that the two-person, mixed strategy game could be solved with traditional linear programming software such as The Management Scientist. If you are using software such as LINGO or Excel, these variables do not have to be nonnegative. In this case, eliminate the nonnegative requirements and make *GAINA* and *LOSSB* unrestricted in sign. This treatment guarantees that the linear program will have a feasible solution and eliminates the need to add a constant to the payoffs in situations where *GAINA* and *LOSSB* may be negative.

SUMMARY

In this chapter we presented selected advanced linear programming applications. In particular, we applied linear programming to evaluating the performance of hospitals, maximizing revenue for airlines, constructing mutual fund portfolios, and competing for market share. In practice, most of the modeling effort in these types of linear programming applications involves clearly understanding the problem, stating the problem mathematically, and then finding reliable data in the format required by the model.

GLOSSARY

Data envelopment analysis (DEA) A linear programming application used to measure the relative efficiency of operating units with the same goals and objectives.

Hypothetical composite A weighted average of outputs and inputs of all operating units with similar goals.

Efficiency index Percentage of an individual operating unit's resources that are available to the composite operating unit.

Game theory A decision-making situation in which two or more decision makers compete by each selecting one of several strategies. The combination of the competing strategies provides the value of the game to the players.

Two-person, zero-sum game A game with two players in which the gain to one player is equal to the loss to the other player.

Maximin strategy A strategy where the player seeking to maximize the value of the game selects the strategy that maximizes the minimum payoff obtainable by the other player.

Minimax strategy A strategy where the player seeking to minimize the value of the game selects the strategy that minimizes the maximum payoff obtainable by the other player.

Pure strategy When one of the available strategies is optimal and the player always selects this strategy regardless of the strategy selected by the other player.

Saddle point A condition that exists when pure strategies are optimal for both players. Neither player can improve the value of the game by changing from the optimal pure strategy.

Mixed strategy When a player randomly selects its strategy based on a probability distribution. The strategy selected can vary each time the game is played.

Expected value In a mixed strategy game, a value computed by multiplying each payoff by its probability and summing. It can be interpreted as the long-run average payoff for the mixed strategy.

PROBLEMS

Note: The following problems have been designed to give you an understanding and appreciation of the broad range of problems that can be formulated as linear programs. You should be able to formulate a linear programming model for each of the problems. However, you will need access to a linear programming computer package to develop the solutions and make the requested interpretations.

1. In Section 5.1 data envelopment analysis was used to evaluate the relative efficiencies of four hospitals. Data for three input measures and four output measures were provided in Tables 5.1 and 5.2.
   a. Use these data to develop a linear programming model that could be used to evaluate the performance of General Hospital.
   b. The following optimal solution was obtained using The Management Scientist. Does the solution indicate that General Hospital is relatively inefficient?

Objective Function Value = 1.000

Variable	Value	Reduced Costs
E	1.000	0.000
WG	1.000	0.000
WU	0.000	0.000
WC	0.000	0.331
WS	0.000	0.215

   c. Explain which hospital or hospitals make up the composite unit used to evaluate General Hospital and why.

2. Data envelopment analysis can measure the relative efficiency of a group of hospitals. The following data from a particular study involving seven teaching hospitals include three input measures and four output measures.
   a. Formulate a linear programming model so that data envelopment analysis can be used to evaluate the performance of hospital D.
   b. Solve the model.
   c. Is hospital D relatively inefficient? What is the interpretation of the value of the objective function?

	Input Measures		
Hospital	Full-Time Equivalent Nonphysicians	Supply Expense (1000s)	Bed-Days Available (1000s)
A	310.0	134.60	116.00
B	278.5	114.30	106.80
C	165.6	131.30	65.52
D	250.0	316.00	94.40
E	206.4	151.20	102.10
F	384.0	217.00	153.70
G	530.1	770.80	215.00

	Output Measures			
Hospital	Patient-Days (65 or older) (1000s)	Patient-Days (under 65) (1000s)	Nurses Trained	Interns Trained
A	55.31	49.52	291	47
B	37.64	55.63	156	3
C	32.91	25.77	141	26
D	33.53	41.99	160	21
E	32.48	55.30	157	82
F	48.78	81.92	285	92
G	58.41	119.70	111	89

d. How many patient-days of each type are produced by the composite hospital?
e. Which hospitals would you recommend hospital D consider emulating to improve the efficiency of its operation?

3. Refer again to the data presented in Problem 2.
   a. Formulate a linear programming model that can be used to perform data envelopment analysis for hospital E.
   b. Solve the model.
   c. Is hospital E relatively inefficient? What is the interpretation of the value of the objective function?
   d. Which hospitals are involved in making up the composite hospital? Can you make a general statement about which hospitals will make up the composite unit associated with a unit that is not inefficient?

4. The Ranch House, Inc., operates five fast-food restaurants. Input measures for the restaurants include weekly hours of operation, full-time equivalent staff, and weekly supply expenses. Output measures of performance include average weekly contribution to profit, market share, and annual growth rate. Data for the input and output measures are shown in the following tables.

	Input Measures		
Restaurant	Hours of Operation	FTE Staff	Supplies ($)
Bardstown	96	16	850
Clarksville	110	22	1400
Jeffersonville	100	18	1200
New Albany	125	25	1500
St. Matthews	120	24	1600

	Output Measures		
Restaurant	Weekly Profit	Market Share (%)	Growth Rate (%)
Bardstown	$3800	25	8.0
Clarksville	$4600	32	8.5
Jeffersonville	$4400	35	8.0
New Albany	$6500	30	10.0
St. Matthews	$6000	28	9.0

a. Develop a linear programming model that can be used to evaluate the performance of the Clarksville Ranch House restaurant.
b. Solve the model.
c. Is the Clarksville Ranch House restaurant relatively inefficient? Discuss.
d. Where does the composite restaurant have more output than the Clarksville restaurant? How much less of each input resource does the composite restaurant require when compared to the Clarksville restaurant?
e. What other restaurants should be studied to find suggested ways for the Clarksville restaurant to improve its efficiency?

5. Reconsider the Leisure Airlines problem from Section 5.2. The demand forecasts shown in Table 5.3 represent Leisure Air's best estimates of demand. But because demand cannot be forecasted perfectly, the number of seats actually sold for each origin-destination-itinerary fare (ODIF) may turn out to be smaller or larger than forecasted. Suppose that Leisure Air believes that economic conditions have improved and that their original forecast may be too low. To account for this possibility, Leisure Air is considering switching the Boeing 737-400 airplanes that are based in Pittsburgh and Newark with Boeing 757-200 airplanes that Leisure Air has available in other markets. The Boeing 757-200 airplane has a seating capacity of 158 in the coach section.
   a. Because of scheduling conflicts in other markets, suppose that Leisure Air is only able to obtain one Boeing 757-200. Should the larger plane be based in Pittsburgh or in Newark? Explain.
   b. Based upon your answer in part (a), determine a new allocation for the ODIFs. Briefly summarize the major differences between the new allocation using one Boeing 757-200 and the original allocation summarized in Figure 5.5.
   c. Suppose that two Boeing 757-200 airplanes are available. Determine a new allocation for the ODIF's using the two larger airplanes. Briefly summarize the major differences between the new allocation using two Boeing 757-200 airplanes and the original allocation shown in Figure 5.5.
   d. Consider the new solution obtained in part (b). Which ODIF has the highest bid price? What is the interpretation for this bid price?

6. Reconsider the Leisure Airlines problem from Section 5.2. Suppose that as of May 1 the following number of seats have been sold.

ODIF	1	2	3	4	5	6	7	8	9	10	11	12	13	14	15	16
Seats Sold	25	44	18	12	5	9	20	33	37	11	5	8	27	6	35	7

   a. Determine how many seats are still available for sale on each flight leg.
   b. Using the original demand forecasted for each ODIF, determine the remaining demand for each ODIF.
   c. Revise the linear programming model presented in Section 5.2 to account for the number of seats currently sold and a demand of one additional seat for the Pittsburgh–Myrtle Beach Q class ODIF. Resolve the linear programming model to determine a new allocation schedule for the ODIFs.

7. Hanson Inn is a 96-room hotel located near the airport and convention center in Louisville, Kentucky. When a convention or a special event is in town, Hanson increases its normal room rates and takes reservations based on a revenue management system. The Classic Corvette Owners Association scheduled its annual convention in Louisville for the first weekend in June. Hanson Inn agreed to make at least 50% of its rooms available for convention attendees at a special convention rate in order to be listed as a recommended hotel for the convention. Although the majority of attendees at the annual meeting typically requests a Friday and Saturday two-night package, some attendees may select a Friday night only or a Saturday night only reservation. Customers not attending the convention may also

request a Friday and Saturday two-night package, or make a Friday night only or Saturday night only reservation. Thus, six types of reservations are possible: Convention customers/two-night package; convention customers/Friday night only; convention customers/Saturday night only; regular customers/two-night package; regular customers/Friday night only; and regular customers/Saturday night only. The cost for each type of reservation is shown here.

	Two-Night Package	Friday Night Only	Saturday Night Only
Convention	$225	$123	$130
Regular	$295	$146	$152

The anticipated demand for each type of reservation is as follows:

	Two-Night Package	Friday Night Only	Saturday Night Only
Convention	40	20	15
Regular	20	30	25

Hanson Inn would like to determine how many rooms to make available for each type of reservation in order to maximize total revenue.

a. Define the decision variables and state the objective function.
b. Formulate a linear programming model for this revenue management application.
c. What is the optimal allocation and the anticipated total revenue?
d. Suppose that one week before the convention, the number of regular customers/Saturday night only rooms that were made available sell out. If another nonconvention customer calls and requests a Saturday only room, what is the value of accepting this additional reservation?

8. In the latter part of Section 5.3 we developed a moderate risk portfolio model for Hauck Investment Services. Modify the model given so that it can be used to construct a portfolio for more aggressive investors. In particular, do the following:
   a. Develop a portfolio model for investors who are willing to risk a portfolio with a return as low as 0%.
   b. What is the recommended allocation for this type of investor?
   c. How would you modify your recommendation in part (b) for an investor who also wants to have at least 10% of his or her portfolio invested in the foreign stock mutual fund? How does requiring at least 10% of the portfolio be invested in the foreign stock fund affect the expected return?

9. Table 5.11 shows data on the returns over five 1-year periods for six mutual funds. A firm's portfolio managers will assume that one of these scenarios will accurately reflect the investing climate over the next 12 months. The probabilities of each of the scenarios occurring are 0.1, 0.3, 0.1, 0.1, and 0.4 for years 1 to 5, respectively.
   a. Develop a portfolio model for investors who are willing to risk a portfolio with a return no lower than 2%.
   b. Solve the model in part (a) and recommend a portfolio allocation for the investor with this risk tolerance.

TABLE 5.11 RETURNS OVER FIVE 1-YEAR PERIODS FOR SIX MUTUAL FUNDS

	Planning Scenarios for Next 12 Months				
Mutual Funds	Year 1	Year 2	Year 3	Year 4	Year 5
Large-Cap Stock	35.3	20.0	28.3	10.4	−9.3
Mid-Cap Stock	32.3	23.2	−0.9	49.3	−22.8
Small-Cap Stock	20.8	22.5	6.0	33.3	6.1
Energy/Resources Sector	25.3	33.9	−20.5	20.9	−2.5
Health Sector	49.1	5.5	29.7	77.7	−24.9
Technology Sector	46.2	21.7	45.7	93.1	−20.1
Real Estate Sector	20.5	44.0	−21.1	2.6	5.1

c. Modify the portfolio model in part (a) and solve it to develop a portfolio for an investor with a risk tolerance of 0%.

d. Is the expected return higher for investors following the portfolio recommendations in part (c) as compared to the returns for the portfolio in part (b)? If so, do you believe the returns are enough higher to justify investing in that portfolio?

10. Consider the following two-person, zero-sum game. Payoffs are the winnings for Player A. Identify the pure strategy solution. What is the value of the game?

		Player B		
		b_1	b_2	b_3
Player A	a_1	8	5	7
	a_2	2	4	10

11. Assume that a two-person, zero-sum game has a pure strategy solution. If this game were solved using a linear programming formulation, how would you know from the linear programming solution that the game had a pure strategy solution?

12. Consider the payoff table below that shows the percentage increase in market share for Company A for each combination of Company A and Company B strategies. Assume that Company B implements a mixed strategy by using strategy b_2 with probability 0.5 and strategy b_3 with probability 0.5. Company B decides never to use strategy b_1. What is the expected payoff to Company A under each of its three strategies? If Company B were to always use the stated mixed strategy probabilities, what is the optimal strategy for Company A?

		Company B		
		Increase Advertising b_1	Quantity Discounts b_2	Extend Warranty b_3
Company A	**Increase Advertising a_1**	4	3	2
	Quantity Discounts a_2	−1	4	1
	Extend Warranty a_3	5	−2	5

13. Two television stations compete with each other for viewing audience. Local programming options for the 5:00 P.M. weekday time slot include a sitcom rerun, an early news program, or a home improvement show. Each station has the same programming options and must make its preseason program selection before knowing what the other television station will do. The viewing audience gains in thousands of viewers for Station A are shown in the payoff table.

		Station B		
		Sitcom Rerun b_1	**News Program** b_2	**Home Improvement** b_3
Station A	**Sitcom Rerun** a_1	10	−5	3
	News Program a_2	8	7	6
	Home Improvement a_3	4	8	7

Determine the optimal strategy for each station. What is the value of the game?

14. Two Indiana state senate candidates must decide which city to visit the day before the November election. The same four cities—Indianapolis, Evansville, Fort Wayne, and South Bend—are available for both candidates. Travel plans must be made in advance, so the candidates must decide which city to visit prior to knowing the city the other candidate will visit. Values in the payoff table show thousands of voters gained by the Republican candidate based on the strategies selected by the two candidates. Which city should each candidate visit and what is the value of the game?

		Democratic Candidate			
		Indianapolis b_1	**Evansville** b_2	**Fort Wayne** b_3	**South Bend** b_4
Republican Candidate	**Indianapolis** a_1	0	−15	−8	20
	Evansville a_2	30	−5	5	−10
	Fort Wayne a_3	10	−25	0	20
	South Bend a_4	20	20	10	15

15. Consider a game in which each player selects one of three colored poker chips: red, white or blue. The players must select a chip without knowing the color of the chip selected by the other player. The players then reveal their chips. Payoffs to Player A in dollars are as follows:

		Player B		
		Red b_1	**White** b_2	**Blue** b_3
Player A	**Red** a_1	0	−1	2
	White a_2	5	4	−3
	Blue a_3	2	3	−4

a. What is the optimal strategy for each player?
b. What is the value of the game?
c. Would you prefer to be Player A or Player B? Why?

16. Two companies compete for a share of the soft drink market. Each has worked with an advertising agency in order to develop alternative advertising strategies for the coming year. A variety of television advertisements, newspaper advertisements, product promotions, and in-store displays have provided four different strategies for each company. The payoff table summarizes the gain in market share for Company A projected for the various combinations of Company A and Company B strategies. What is the optimal strategy for each company? What is the value of the game?

		Company B			
		b_1	b_2	b_3	b_4
Company A	a_1	3	0	2	4
	a_2	2	−2	1	0
	a_3	4	2	5	6
	a_4	−2	6	−1	0

17. The offensive coordinator for the Chicago Bears professional football team is preparing a game plan for the upcoming game against the Green Bay Packers. A review of game tapes from previous Bears-Packers games provides data on the yardage gained for run plays and pass plays. Data show that when the Bears run against the Packers' run defense, the Bears gain an average of 2 yards. However, when the Bears run against the Packers' pass defense, the Bears gain an average of 6 yards. A similar analysis of pass plays reveals that if the Bears pass against the Packers' run defense, the Bears gain an average of 11 yards. However, if the Bears pass against the Packers' pass defense, the Bears average a loss of 1 yard. This loss, or negative gain of −1, includes the lost yardage due to quarterback sacks and interceptions. Develop a payoff table that shows the Bears' average yardage gain for each combination of the Bears' offensive strategy to run or pass and the Packers' strategy of using a run defense or a pass defense. What is the optimal strategy for the Chicago Bears during the upcoming game against the Green Bay Packers? What is the expected value of this strategy?

CHAPTER 7

Integer Linear Programming

CONTENTS

In this chapter we discuss a class of problems that are modeled as linear programs with the additional requirement that one or more variables must be integer. Such problems are called **integer linear programs.** If all variables must be integer, we have an all-integer linear program. If some, but not all, variables must be integer, we have a mixed-integer linear program. In many applications of integer linear programming, one or more integer variables are required to equal either 0 or 1. Such variables are called 0-1 or *binary variables.* If all variables are 0-1 variables, we have a 0-1 integer linear program.

Integer variables—especially 0-1 variables—provide substantial modeling flexibility. As a result, the number of applications that can be addressed with linear programming methodology is expanded. For instance, the Management Science in Action, Crew Scheduling at Air New Zealand, describes how that airline company employs 0-1 integer programming models to schedule its pilots and flight attendants. Later Management Science in Actions describe how Valley Metal Containers uses a mixed-integer program for scheduling aluminum can production for Coors beer, and how the modeling flexibility provided by 0-1 variables helped Ketron build a customer order allocation model for a sporting goods company. Many other applications of integer programming are described throughout the chapter.

The objective of this chapter is to provide an applications-oriented introduction to integer linear programming. First, we discuss the different types of integer linear programming models. Then we show the formulation, graphical solution, and computer solution of an all-integer linear program. In Section 7.3, we discuss five applications of integer linear programming that make use of 0-1 variables: capital budgeting, fixed cost, distribution system design, bank location, and market share optimization problems. In Section 7.4, we provide additional illustrations of the modeling flexibility provided by 0-1 variables. A chapter appendix illustrates the use of Excel for solving integer programs.

The cost of the added modeling flexibility provided by integer programming is that problems involving integer variables are often much more difficult to solve. A linear programming problem with several thousand continuous variables can be solved with any of several commercial linear programming solvers. However, an all-integer linear programming problem with less than 100 variables can be extremely difficult to solve. Experienced management scientists can help identify the types of integer linear programs that are easy, or at least reasonable, to solve. Commercial computer software packages, such as LINGO, CPLEX, Xpress-MP, and the commercial version of Premium Solver have extensive integer programming capability, and very robust open-source software packages for integer programming are also available. The Management Scientist and spreadsheet packages, such as Excel, have the capability for solving smaller integer linear programs.

Information about open-source software can be found at www.coin-or.org.

MANAGEMENT SCIENCE IN ACTION

CREW SCHEDULING AT AIR NEW ZEALAND*

As noted in Chapter 1, airlines make extensive use of management science (see Management Science in Action, Revenue Management at American Airlines). Air New Zealand is the largest national and international airline based in New Zealand. Over the past 15 years, Air New Zealand developed integer programming models for crew scheduling.

Air New Zealand finalizes flight schedules at least 12 weeks in advance of when the flights are to take place. At that point the process of assigning crews to implement the flight schedule begins. The crew-scheduling problem involves staffing the flight schedule with pilots and flight attendants. It is solved in two phases. In the first phase, tours of duty (ToD) are generated that will permit constructing sequences of flights for pilots and flight attendants that will allow the airline's flight schedule to be implemented. A tour of duty is a one-day or multiday alternating sequence of duty periods (flight legs, training, etc.) and rest periods (layovers).

(continued)

In the ToD problem, no consideration is given to which individual crew members will perform the tours of duty. In the second phase, individual crew members are assigned to the tours of duty, which is called the rostering problem.

Air New Zealand employs integer programming models to solve both the ToD problem and the rostering problem. In the integer programming model of the ToD problem, each variable is a 0-1 variable that corresponds to a possible tour of duty that could be flown by a crew member (e.g., pilot or flight attendant). Each constraint corresponds to a particular flight and ensures that the flight is included in exactly one tour of duty. The cost of variable *j* reflects the cost of operating the *j*th tour of duty, and the objective is to minimize total cost. Air New Zealand solves a separate ToD problem for each crew type (pilot type or flight attendant type).

In the rostering problem, the tours of duty from the solution to the ToD problem are used to construct lines of work (LoW) for each crew member. In the integer programming model of the rostering problem, a 0-1 variable represents the possible LoWs for each crew member. A separate constraint for each crew member guarantees that each will be assigned a single LoW. Other constraints correspond to the ToDs that must be covered by any feasible solution to the rostering problem.

The crew-scheduling optimizers developed by Air New Zealand showed a significant impact on profitability. Over the 15 years it took to develop these systems, the estimated development costs were approximately NZ$2 million. The estimated savings are NZ$15.6 million per year. In 1999 the savings from employing these integer programming models represented 11% of Air New Zealand's net operating profit. In addition to the direct dollar savings, the optimization systems provided many intangible benefits such as higher-quality solutions in less time, less dependence on a small number of highly skilled schedulers, flexibility to accommodate small changes in the schedule, and a guarantee that the airline satisfies legislative and contractual rules.

*Based on E. Rod Butchers et al., "Optimized Crew Scheduling at Air New Zealand," *Interfaces* (January/February 2001): 30–56.

NOTES AND COMMENTS

1. Because integer linear programs are harder to solve than linear programs, one should not try to solve a problem as an integer program if simply rounding the linear programming solution is adequate. In many linear programming problems, such as those in previous chapters, rounding has little economic consequence on the objective function, and feasibility is not an issue. But, in problems such as determining how many jet engines to manufacture, the consequences of rounding can be substantial and integer programming methodology should be employed.
2. Some linear programming problems have a special structure, which guarantees that the variables will have integer values. The assignment, transportation, and transshipment problems of Chapter 6 have such structures. If the supply and the demand for transportation and transshipment problems are integer, the optimal linear programming solution will provide integer amounts shipped. For the assignment problem, the optimal linear programming solution will consist of 0s and 1s. So, for these specially structured problems, linear programming methodology can be used to find optimal integer solutions. Integer linear programming algorithms are not necessary.

7.1 TYPES OF INTEGER LINEAR PROGRAMMING MODELS

The only difference between the problems studied in this chapter and the ones studied in earlier chapters on linear programming is that one or more variables are required to be integer. If all variables are required to be integer, we have an **all-integer linear program.** The following is a two-variable, all-integer linear programming model.

$$\begin{aligned} \text{Max} \quad & 2x_1 + 3x_2 \\ \text{s.t.} \quad & \\ & 3x_1 + 3x_2 \leq 12 \\ & \tfrac{2}{3}x_1 + 1x_2 \leq 4 \\ & 1x_1 + 2x_2 \leq 6 \\ & x_1, x_2 \geq 0 \text{ and integer} \end{aligned}$$

If we drop the phrase "and integer" from the last line of this model, we have the familiar two-variable linear program. The linear program that results from dropping the integer requirements is called the **LP Relaxation** of the integer linear program.

If some, but not necessarily all, variables are required to be integer, we have a **mixed-integer linear program.** The following is a two-variable, mixed-integer linear program.

$$\begin{aligned} \text{Max} \quad & 3x_1 + 4x_2 \\ \text{s.t.} \quad & \\ & -1x_1 + 2x_2 \leq 8 \\ & 1x_1 + 2x_2 \leq 12 \\ & 2x_1 + 1x_2 \leq 16 \\ & x_1, x_2 \geq 0 \textit{ and } x_2 \text{ integer} \end{aligned}$$

We obtain the LP Relaxation of this mixed-integer linear program by dropping the requirement that x_2 be integer.

In some applications, the integer variables may only take on the values 0 or 1. Then we have a **0-1 linear integer program.** As we see later in the chapter, 0-1 variables provide additional modeling capability. The Management Science in Action, Aluminum Can Production at Valley Metal Container, describes how a mixed-integer linear program involving 0-1 integer variables is used to schedule production of aluminum beer cans for Coors breweries. The 0-1 variables are used to model production line changeovers; the continuous variables model production quantities.

MANAGEMENT SCIENCE IN ACTION

ALUMINUM CAN PRODUCTION AT VALLEY METAL CONTAINER*

Valley Metal Container (VMC) produces cans for the seven brands of beer produced by the Coors breweries: Coors Extra Gold, Coors Light, Coors Original, Keystone Ale, Keystone Ice, Keystone Light, and Keystone Premium. VMC produces these cans on six production lines and stores them in three separate inventory storage areas from which they are shipped on to the Coors breweries in Golden, Colorado; Memphis, Tennessee; and Shenandoah, Virginia.

Two important issues face production scheduling at the VMC facility. First, each time a production line must be changed over from producing one type of can to another (label change), it takes time to get the color just right for the new label. As a result, downtime is incurred and scrap is generated. Second, proper scheduling can reduce the amount of inventory that must be transferred from long-term to short-term storage. Thus, two costs are critical in determining the best production schedule at the VMC facility: the label-change cost and the cost of transferring inventory from one type of storage to another. To determine a production schedule that will minimize these two costs, VMC developed a mixed-integer linear programming model of its production process.

The model's objective function calls for minimizing the sum of the weekly cost of changing labels

(continued)

and the cost of transferring inventory from long-term to short-term storage. Binary (0-1) variables are used to represent a label change in the production process. Continuous variables are used to represent the size of the production run for each type of label on each line during each shift; analogous variables are used to represent inventories for each type of can produced. Additional continuous variables are used to represent the amount of inventory transferred to short-term storage during the week.

The VMC production scheduling problem is solved weekly using a personal computer. Excel worksheets are used for input data preparation and for storing the output report. The GAMS mathematical programming system is used to solve the mixed-integer linear program. Susan Schultz, manager of Logistics for Coors Container Operations, reports that using the system resulted in documented annual savings of $169,230.

*Based on Elena Katok and Dennis Ott, "Using Mixed-Integer Programming to Reduce Label Changes in the Coors Aluminum Can Plant," *Interfaces* (March/April 2000): 1–12.

7.2 GRAPHICAL AND COMPUTER SOLUTIONS FOR AN ALL-INTEGER LINEAR PROGRAM

Eastborne Realty has $2 million available for the purchase of new rental property. After an initial screening, Eastborne reduced the investment alternatives to townhouses and apartment buildings. Each townhouse can be purchased for $282,000, and five are available. Each apartment building can be purchased for $400,000, and the developer will construct as many buildings as Eastborne wants to purchase.

Eastborne's property manager can devote up to 140 hours per month to these new properties; each townhouse is expected to require 4 hours per month, and each apartment building is expected to require 40 hours per month. The annual cash flow, after deducting mortgage payments and operating expenses, is estimated to be $10,000 per townhouse and $15,000 per apartment building. Eastborne's owner would like to determine the number of townhouses and the number of apartment buildings to purchase to maximize annual cash flow.

We begin by defining the decision variables as follows:

$$\begin{aligned} T &= \text{number of townhouses} \\ A &= \text{number of apartment buildings} \end{aligned}$$

The objective function for cash flow ($1000s) is

$$\text{Max} \quad 10T + 15A$$

Three constraints must be satisfied:

$$\begin{aligned} 282T + 400A &\leq 2000 \quad \text{Funds available (\$1000s)} \\ 4T + 40A &\leq 140 \quad \text{Manager's time (hours)} \\ T &\leq 5 \quad \text{Townhouses available} \end{aligned}$$

The variables T and A must be nonnegative. In addition, the purchase of a fractional number of townhouses and/or a fractional number of apartment buildings is unacceptable. Thus, T and A must be integer. The model for the Eastborne Realty problem is the following all-integer linear program.

$$
\begin{aligned}
\text{Max} \quad & 10T + 15A \\
\text{s.t.} \quad & \\
& 282T + 400A \le 2000 \\
& 4T + 40A \le 140 \\
& T \le 5 \\
& T, A \ge 0 \text{ and integer}
\end{aligned}
$$

Graphical Solution of the LP Relaxation

Suppose that we drop the integer requirements for T and A and solve the LP Relaxation of the Eastborne Realty problem. Using the graphical solution procedure, as presented in Chapter 2, the optimal linear programming solution is shown in Figure 7.1. It is $T = 2.479$ townhouses and $A = 3.252$ apartment buildings. The optimal value of the objective function is 73.574, which indicates an annual cash flow of $73,574. Unfortunately, Eastborne cannot purchase fractional numbers of townhouses and apartment buildings; further analysis is necessary.

FIGURE 7.1 GRAPHICAL SOLUTION TO THE LP RELAXATION OF THE EASTBORNE REALTY PROBLEM

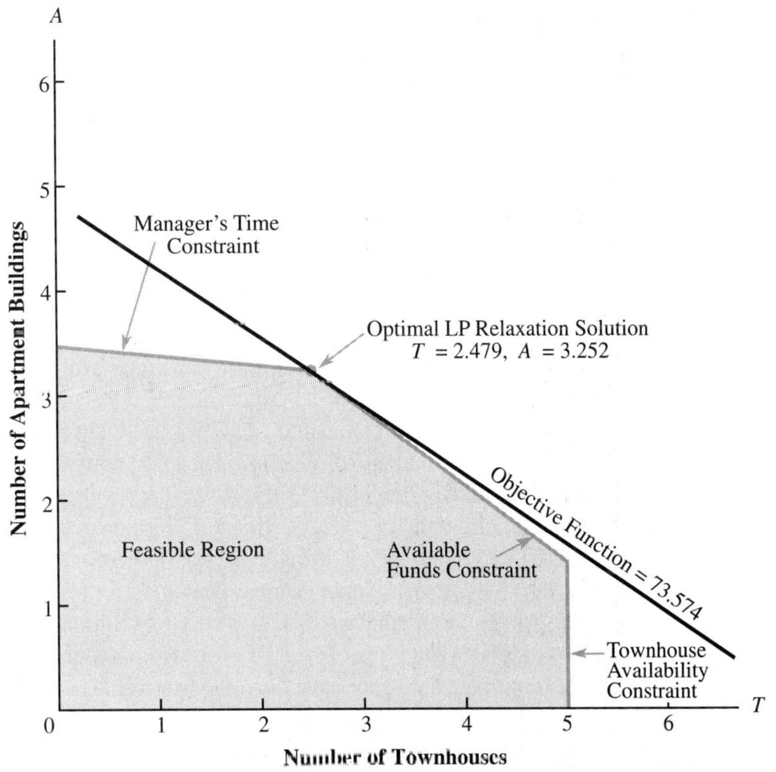

Rounding to Obtain an Integer Solution

In many cases, a noninteger solution can be rounded to obtain an acceptable integer solution. For instance, a linear programming solution to a production scheduling problem might call for the production of 15,132.4 cases of breakfast cereal. The rounded integer solution of 15,132 cases would probably have minimal impact on the value of the objective function and the feasibility of the solution. Rounding would be a sensible approach. Indeed, whenever rounding has a minimal impact on the objective function and constraints, most managers find it acceptable. A near-optimal solution is fine.

However, rounding may not always be a good strategy. When the decision variables take on small values that have a major impact on the value of the objective function or feasibility, an optimal integer solution is needed. Let us return to the Eastborne Realty problem and examine the impact of rounding. The optimal solution to the LP Relaxation for Eastborne Realty resulted in $T = 2.479$ townhouses and $A = 3.252$ apartment buildings. Because each townhouse costs $282,000 and each apartment building costs $400,000, rounding to an integer solution can be expected to have a significant economic impact on the problem.

If a problem has only less-than-or-equal-to constraints with nonnegative coefficients for the variables, rounding down will always provide a feasible integer solution.

Suppose that we round the solution to the LP Relaxation to obtain the integer solution $T = 2$ and $A = 3$, with an objective function value of $10(2) + 15(3) = 65$. The annual cash flow of $65,000 is substantially less than the annual cash flow of $73,574 provided by the solution to the LP Relaxation. Do other rounding possibilities exist? Exploring other rounding alternatives shows that the integer solution $T = 3$ and $A = 3$ is infeasible because it requires more funds than the $2,000,000 Eastborne has available. The rounded solution of $T = 2$ and $A = 4$ is also infeasible for the same reason. At this point, rounding has led to two townhouses and three apartment buildings with an annual cash flow of $65,000 as the best feasible integer solution to the problem. Unfortunately, we don't know whether this solution is the best integer solution to the problem.

Rounding to an integer solution is a trial-and-error approach. Each rounded solution must be evaluated for feasibility as well as for its impact on the value of the objective function. Even in cases where a rounded solution is feasible, we do not have a guarantee that we have found the optimal integer solution. We will see shortly that the rounded solution ($T = 2$ and $A = 3$) is not optimal for Eastborne Realty.

Graphical Solution of the All-Integer Problem

Figure 7.2 shows the changes in the linear programming graphical solution procedure required to solve the Eastborne Realty integer linear programming problem. First, the graph of the feasible region is drawn exactly as in the LP Relaxation of the problem. Then, because the optimal solution must have integer values, we identify the feasible integer solutions with the dots shown in Figure 7.2. Finally, instead of moving the objective function line to the best extreme point in the feasible region, we move it in an improving direction as far as possible until reaching the dot (feasible integer point) providing the best value for the objective function. Viewing Figure 7.2, we see that the optimal integer solution occurs at $T = 4$ townhouses and $A = 2$ apartment buildings. The objective function value is $10(4) + 15(2) = 70$, providing an annual cash flow of $70,000. This solution is significantly better than the best solution found by rounding: $T = 2$, $A = 3$, with an annual cash flow of $65,000. Thus, we see that rounding would not have been the best strategy for Eastborne Realty.

Try Problem 2 for practice with the graphical solution of an integer program.

Using the LP Relaxation to Establish Bounds

An important observation can be made from the analysis of the Eastborne Realty problem. It has to do with the relationship between the value of the optimal integer solution and the value of the optimal solution to the LP Relaxation.

FIGURE 7.2 GRAPHICAL SOLUTION OF THE EASTBORNE REALTY INTEGER PROBLEM

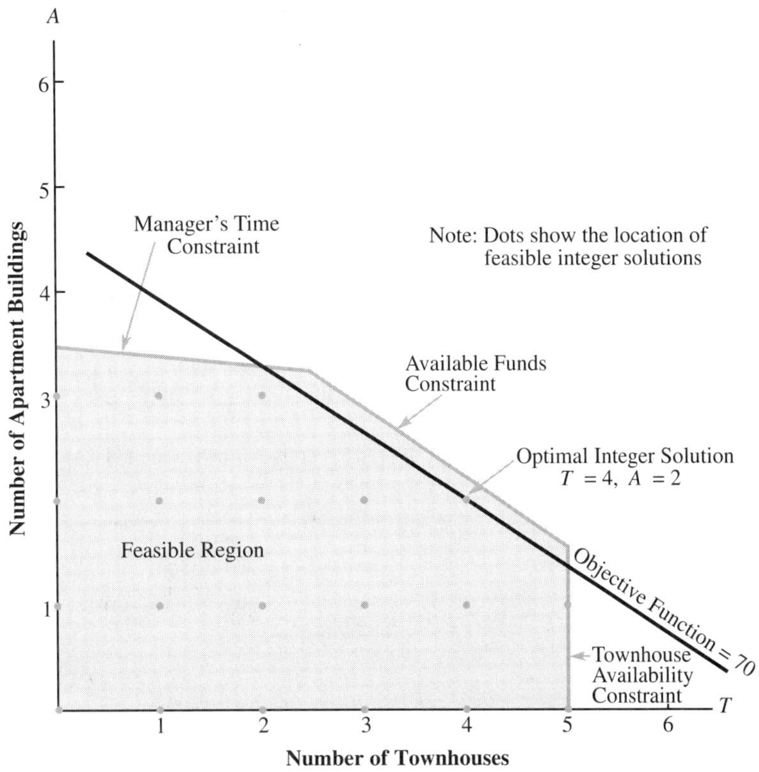

For integer linear programs involving maximization, the value of the optimal solution to the LP Relaxation provides an upper bound on the value of the optimal integer solution. For integer linear programs involving minimization, the value of the optimal solution to the LP Relaxation provides a lower bound on the value of the optimal integer solution.

This observation is valid for the Eastborne Realty problem. The value of the optimal integer solution is \$70,000, and the value of the optimal solution to the LP Relaxation is \$73,574. Thus, we know from the LP Relaxation solution that the upper bound for the value of the objective function is \$73,574.

The bounding property of the LP Relaxation allows us to conclude that if, by chance, the solution to an LP Relaxation turns out to be an integer solution, it is also optimal for the integer linear program. This bounding property can also be helpful in determining whether a rounded solution is "good enough." If a rounded LP Relaxation solution is feasible and provides a value of the objective function that is "almost as good as" the value of the objective function for the LP Relaxation, we know the rounded solution is a near-optimal integer solution. In this case, we can avoid having to solve the problem as an integer linear program.

Try Problem 5 for the graphical solution of a mixed-integer program.

Computer Solution

As mentioned earlier, commercial software packages that can solve integer linear programs are widely available. Generally, these packages are reliable for problems having up to approximately 100 integer variables and may be used to solve specially structured problems with several thousand integer variables.

The Management Scientist, LINGO, or Frontline Systems' Premium Solver for Education can be used to solve most of the integer linear programs in this chapter. To use The Management Scientist to solve the Eastborne Realty problem, the data input worksheet is completed in the same way as for any linear program (see Appendix 2.1). Then after instructing the computer to solve the problem, the user will be asked to indicate which of the variables are integer. Specifying both T and A as integers provides the optimal integer solution shown in Figure 7.3. The solution of $T = 4$ townhouses and $A = 2$ apartment buildings has a maximum annual cash flow of \$70,000. The values of the slack variables tell us that the optimal solution has \$72,000 of available funds unused, 44 hours of the manager's time still available, and 1 of the available townhouses not purchased.

FIGURE 7.3 THE MANAGEMENT SCIENTIST SOLUTION FOR THE EASTBORNE REALTY PROBLEM

EXCELfile
Eastborne

```
Objective Function Value = 70.000

   Variable            Value
--------------    ---------------
      T                 4.000
      A                 2.000

  Constraint       Slack/Surplus
--------------    ---------------
      1                72.000
      2                44.000
      3                 1.000
```

NOTES AND COMMENTS

In Appendix 7.1 we show how Premium Solver for Education can be used to solve integer linear programs such as the Eastborne Realty problem.

7.3 APPLICATIONS INVOLVING 0-1 VARIABLES

Much of the modeling flexibility provided by integer linear programming is due to the use of 0-1 variables. In many applications, 0-1 variables provide selections or choices with the value of the variable equal to 1 if a corresponding activity is undertaken and equal to 0 if the corresponding activity is not undertaken. The capital budgeting, fixed cost, distribution system design, bank location, and product design/market share applications presented in this section make use of 0-1 variables.

Capital Budgeting

The Ice-Cold Refrigerator Company is considering investing in several projects that have varying capital requirements over the next four years. Faced with limited capital each year, management would like to select the most profitable projects. The estimated net present value for each project,[1] the capital requirements, and the available capital over the four-year period are shown in Table 7.1.

The four 0-1 decision variables are as follows:

$$\begin{aligned} P &= 1 \text{ if the plant expansion project is accepted; 0 if rejected} \\ W &= 1 \text{ if the warehouse expansion project is accepted; 0 if rejected} \\ M &= 1 \text{ if the new machinery project is accepted; 0 if rejected} \\ R &= 1 \text{ if the new product research project is accepted; 0 if rejected} \end{aligned}$$

In a **capital budgeting problem,** the company's objective function is to maximize the net present value of the capital budgeting projects. This problem has four constraints: one for the funds available in each of the next four years.

A 0-1 integer linear programming model with dollars in thousands is as follows:

$$\begin{aligned} \text{Max} \quad & 90P + 40W + 10M + 37R \\ \text{s.t.} \quad & \\ & 15P + 10W + 10M + 15R \leq 40 \quad \text{(Year 1 capital available)} \\ & 20P + 15W + 10R \leq 50 \quad \text{(Year 2 capital available)} \\ & 20P + 20W + 10R \leq 40 \quad \text{(Year 3 capital available)} \\ & 15P + 5W + 4M + 10R \leq 35 \quad \text{(Year 4 capital available)} \\ & P, W, M, R = 0, 1 \end{aligned}$$

The integer programming solution from The Management Scientist is shown in Figure 7.4. The optimal solution is $P = 1, W = 1, M = 1, R = 0$, with a total estimated net present value of \$140,000. Thus, the company should fund the plant expansion, the warehouse expansion, and the new machinery projects. The new product research project should be put on hold unless additional capital funds become available. The values of the slack variables (see

TABLE 7.1 PROJECT NET PRESENT VALUE, CAPITAL REQUIREMENTS, AND AVAILABLE CAPITAL FOR THE ICE-COLD REFRIGERATOR COMPANY

	Project				
	Plant Expansion	**Warehouse Expansion**	**New Machinery**	**New Product Research**	Total Capital Available
Present Value	\$90,000	\$40,000	\$10,000	\$37,000	
Year 1 Cap Rqmt	\$15,000	\$10,000	\$10,000	\$15,000	\$40,000
Year 2 Cap Rqmt	\$20,000	\$15,000		\$10,000	\$50,000
Year 3 Cap Rqmt	\$20,000	\$20,000		\$10,000	\$40,000
Year 4 Cap Rqmt	\$15,000	\$ 5,000	\$ 4,000	\$10,000	\$35,000

[1]The estimated net present value is the net cash flow discounted back to the beginning of year 1.

FIGURE 7.4 THE MANAGEMENT SCIENTIST SOLUTION FOR THE ICE-COLD REFRIGERATOR COMPANY PROBLEM

EXCELfile
Ice-Cold

```
Objective Function Value = 140.000

     Variable               Value
  --------------     ---------------
         P                    1.000
         W                    1.000
         M                    1.000
         R                    0.000

    Constraint          Slack/Surplus
  --------------     ---------------
         1                    5.000
         2                   15.000
         3                    0.000
         4                   11.000
```

Figure 7.4) show that the company will have \$5,000 remaining in year 1, \$15,000 remaining in year 2, and \$11,000 remaining in year 4. Checking the capital requirements for the new product research project, we see that enough funds are available for this project in year 2 and year 4. However, the company would have to find additional capital funds of \$10,000 in year 1 and \$10,000 in year 3 to fund the new product research project.

Fixed Cost

In many applications, the cost of production has two components: a setup cost, which is a fixed cost, and a variable cost, which is directly related to the production quantity. The use of 0-1 variables makes including the setup cost possible in a model for a production application.

As an example of a **fixed cost problem,** consider the RMC problem. Three raw materials are used to produce three products: a fuel additive, a solvent base, and a carpet cleaning fluid. The following decision variables are used.

F = tons of fuel additive produced
S = tons of solvent base produced
C = tons of carpet cleaning fluid produced

The profit contributions are \$40 per ton for the fuel additive, \$30 per ton for the solvent base, and \$50 per ton for the carpet cleaning fluid. Each ton of fuel additive is a blend of 0.4 tons of material 1 and 0.6 tons of material 3. Each ton of solvent base requires 0.5 tons of material 1, 0.2 tons of material 2, and 0.3 tons of material 3. Each ton of carpet cleaning fluid is a blend of 0.6 tons of material 1, 0.1 tons of material 2, and 0.3 tons of material 3. RMC has 20 tons of material 1, 5 tons of material 2, and 21 tons of material 3 and is interested in determining the optimal production quantities for the upcoming planning period.

A linear programming model of the RMC problem is shown.

$$\begin{aligned} \text{Max} \quad & 40F + 30S + 50C \\ \text{s.t.} \quad & \\ & 0.4F + 0.5S + 0.6C \leq 20 \quad \text{Material 1} \\ & 0.2S + 0.1C \leq 5 \quad \text{Material 2} \\ & 0.6F + 0.3S + 0.3C \leq 21 \quad \text{Material 3} \\ & F, S, C \geq 0 \end{aligned}$$

Using the linear programming module of The Management Scientist, we obtained an optimal solution consisting of 27.5 tons of fuel additive, 0 tons of solvent base, and 15 tons of carpet cleaning fluid, with a value of \$1850, as shown in Figure 7.5.

This linear programming formulation of the RMC problem does not include a fixed cost for production setup of the products. Suppose that the following data are available concerning the setup cost and the maximum production quantity for each of the three products.

Product	Setup Cost	Maximum Production
Fuel additive	\$200	50 tons
Solvent base	\$ 50	25 tons
Carpet cleaning fluid	\$400	40 tons

The modeling flexibility provided by 0-1 variables can now be used to incorporate the fixed setup costs into the production model. The 0-1 variables are defined as follows:

SF = 1 if the fuel additive is produced; 0 if not
SS = 1 if the solvent base is produced; 0 if not
SC = 1 if the carpet cleaning fluid is produced; 0 if not

Using these setup variables, the total setup cost is

$$200SF + 50SS + 400SC$$

We can now rewrite the objective function to include the setup cost. Thus, the net profit objective function becomes

$$\text{Max} \quad 40F + 30S + 50C - 200SF - 50SS - 400SC$$

FIGURE 7.5 THE MANAGEMENT SCIENTIST SOLUTION TO THE RMC PROBLEM

```
Objective Function Value =     1850.00

     Variable              Value           Reduced Costs
  --------------     ---------------     -----------------
        F                  27.500                 0.000
        S                   0.000                12.500
        C                  15.000                 0.000
```

Next, we must write production capacity constraints so that if a setup variable equals 0, production of the corresponding product is not permitted and, if a setup variable equals 1, production is permitted up to the maximum quantity. For the fuel additive, we do so by adding the following constraint:

$$F \leq 50SF$$

Note that, with this constraint present, production of the fuel additive is not permitted when $SF = 0$. When $SF = 1$, production of up to 50 tons of fuel additive is permitted. We can think of the setup variable as a switch. When it is off ($SF = 0$), production is not permitted; when it is on ($SF = 1$), production is permitted.

Similar production capacity constraints, using 0-1 variables, are added for the solvent base and carpet cleaning products

$$S \leq 25SS$$
$$C \leq 40SC$$

Moving all the variables to the left-hand side of the constraints provides the following fixed cost model for the RMC problem.

$$\begin{array}{llr}
\text{Max} & 40F + 30S + 50C - 200SF - 50SS - 400SC & \\
\text{s.t.} & & \\
& 0.4F + 0.5S + 0.6C \leq 20 & \text{Material 1} \\
& 0.2S + 0.1C \leq 5 & \text{Material 2} \\
& 0.6F + 0.3S + 0.3C \leq 21 & \text{Material 3} \\
& F - 50SF \leq 0 & \text{Maximum } F \\
& S - 25SS \leq 0 & \text{Maximum } S \\
& C - 40SC \leq 0 & \text{Maximum } C \\
& F, S, C \geq 0;\ SF, SS, SC = 0, 1 &
\end{array}$$

We solved the RMC problem with setup costs using The Management Scientist. As shown in Figure 7.6, the optimal solution shows 25 tons of fuel additive and 20 tons of solvent base. The value of the objective function after deducting the setup cost is \$1350. The setup cost for the fuel additive and the solvent base is \$200 + \$50 = \$250. The optimal solution shows $SC = 0$, which indicates that the more expensive \$400 setup cost for the carpet cleaning fluid should be avoided. Thus the carpet cleaning fluid is not produced.

The Management Science in Action, Aluminum Can Production at Valley Metal Containers (see Section 7.1), employs 0-1 fixed cost variables for production line changeovers.

The key to developing a fixed cost model is the introduction of a 0-1 variable for each fixed cost and the specification of an upper bound for the corresponding production variable. For a production quantity x, a constraint of the form $x \leq My$ can then be used to allow production when the setup variable $y = 1$ and not to allow production when the setup variable $y = 0$. The value of the maximum production quantity M should be large enough to allow for all reasonable levels of production. But research has shown that choosing values of M excessively large will slow the solution procedure.

Distribution System Design

The Martin-Beck Company operates a plant in St. Louis with an annual capacity of 30,000 units. Product is shipped to regional distribution centers located in Boston, Atlanta, and Houston. Because of an anticipated increase in demand, Martin-Beck plans to increase capacity by constructing a new plant in one or more of the following cities: Detroit, Toledo,

FIGURE 7.6 THE MANAGEMENT SCIENTIST SOLUTION TO THE RMC PROBLEM WITH SETUP COSTS

```
Objective Function Value = 1350.000

     Variable              Value
  --------------      ---------------
         F                  25.000
         S                  20.000
         C                   0.000
         SF                  1.000
         SS                  1.000
         SC                  0.000
```

EXCELfile
RMC Setup

Denver, or Kansas City. The estimated annual fixed cost and the annual capacity for the four proposed plants are as follows:

Proposed Plant	Annual Fixed Cost	Annual Capacity
Detroit	$175,000	10,000
Toledo	$300,000	20,000
Denver	$375,000	30,000
Kansas City	$500,000	40,000

The company's long-range planning group developed forecasts of the anticipated annual demand at the distribution centers as follows:

Distribution Center	Annual Demand
Boston	30,000
Atlanta	20,000
Houston	20,000

The shipping cost per unit from each plant to each distribution center is shown in Table 7.2. A network representation of the potential Martin-Beck distribution system is shown in

TABLE 7.2 SHIPPING COST PER UNIT FOR THE MARTIN-BECK DISTRIBUTION SYSTEM

	Distribution Centers		
Plant Site	**Boston**	**Atlanta**	**Houston**
Detroit	5	2	3
Toledo	4	3	4
Denver	9	7	5
Kansas City	10	4	2
St. Louis	8	4	3

Figure 7.7. Each potential plant location is shown; capacities and demands are shown in thousands of units. This network representation is for a transportation problem with a plant at St. Louis and at all four proposed sites. However, the decision has not yet been made as to which new plant or plants will be constructed.

Let us now show how 0-1 variables can be used in this **distribution system design problem** to develop a model for choosing the best plant locations and for determining how much to ship from each plant to each distribution center. We can use the following 0-1 variables to represent the plant construction decision.

FIGURE 7.7 THE NETWORK REPRESENTATION OF THE MARTIN-BECK COMPANY DISTRIBUTION SYSTEM PROBLEM

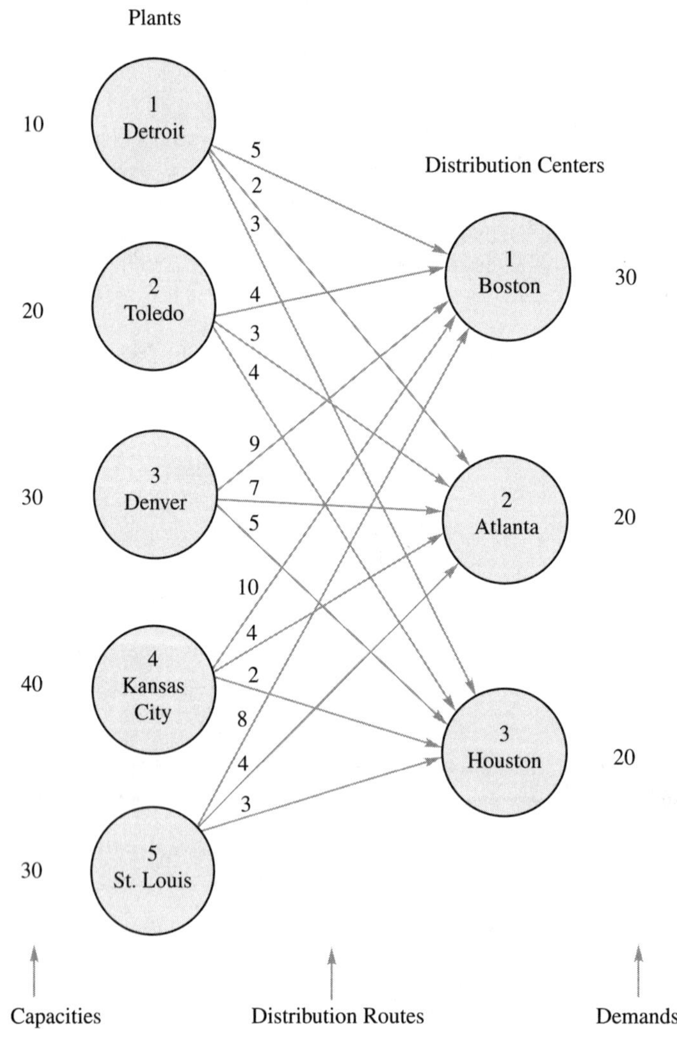

$$
\begin{aligned}
y_1 &= 1 \text{ if a plant is constructed in Detroit; 0 if not} \\
y_2 &= 1 \text{ if a plant is constructed in Toledo; 0 if not} \\
y_3 &= 1 \text{ if a plant is constructed in Denver; 0 if not} \\
y_4 &= 1 \text{ if a plant is constructed in Kansas City; 0 if not}
\end{aligned}
$$

The variables representing the amount shipped from each plant site to each distribution center are defined just as for a transportation problem.

$$
x_{ij} = \text{the units shipped in thousands from plant } i \text{ to distribution center } j
$$
$$
i = 1, 2, 3, 4, 5 \quad \text{and} \quad j = 1, 2, 3
$$

Using the shipping cost data in Table 7.2, the annual transportation cost in thousands of dollars is written

$$
\begin{aligned}
5x_{11} + 2x_{12} + 3x_{13} + 4x_{21} + 3x_{22} + 4x_{23} + 9x_{31} + 7x_{32} + 5x_{33} \\
+ 10x_{41} + 4x_{42} + 2x_{43} + 8x_{51} + 4x_{52} + 3x_{53}
\end{aligned}
$$

The annual fixed cost of operating the new plant or plants in thousands of dollars is written as

$$
175y_1 + 300y_2 + 375y_3 + 500y_4
$$

Note that the 0-1 variables are defined so that the annual fixed cost of operating the new plants is only calculated for the plant or plants that are actually constructed (i.e., $y_i = 1$). If a plant is not constructed, $y_i = 0$ and the corresponding annual fixed cost is \$0.

The Martin-Beck objective function is the sum of the annual transportation cost plus the annual fixed cost of operating the newly constructed plants.

Now let us consider the capacity constraints at the four proposed plants. Using Detroit as an example, we write the following constraint:

$$
x_{11} + x_{12} + x_{13} \leq 10y_1
$$

If the Detroit plant is constructed, $y_1 = 1$ and the total amount shipped from Detroit to the three distribution centers must be less than or equal to Detroit's 10,000-unit capacity. If the Detroit plant is not constructed, $y_1 = 0$ will result in a 0 capacity at Detroit. In this case, the variables corresponding to the shipments from Detroit must all equal zero: $x_{11} = 0$, $x_{12} = 0$, and $x_{13} = 0$. By placing all variables on the left-hand side of the constraints, we have the following Detroit capacity constraint:

$$
x_{11} + x_{12} + x_{13} - 10y_1 \leq 0 \quad \text{Detroit capacity}
$$

In a similar fashion, the capacity constraint for the proposed plant in Toledo can be written

$$
x_{21} + x_{22} + x_{23} - 20y_2 \leq 0 \quad \text{Toledo capacity}
$$

Similar constraints can be written for the proposed plants in Denver and Kansas City. Note that because a plant already exists in St. Louis, we do not define a 0-1 variable for this plant. Its capacity constraint can be written as follows:

$$
x_{51} + x_{52} + x_{53} \leq 30 \quad \text{St. Louis capacity}
$$

Three demand constraints will be needed, one for each of the three distribution centers. The demand constraint for the Boston distribution center with units in thousands is written as

$$x_{11} + x_{21} + x_{31} + x_{41} + x_{51} = 30 \quad \text{Boston demand}$$

Similar constraints appear for the Atlanta and Houston distribution centers.

The complete model for the Martin-Beck distribution system design problem is as follows:

$$\begin{aligned} \text{Min} \quad & 5x_{11} + 2x_{12} + 3x_{13} + 4x_{21} + 3x_{22} + 4x_{23} + 9x_{31} + 7x_{32} + 5x_{33} + 10x_{41} + 4x_{42} \\ & + 2x_{43} + 8x_{51} + 4x_{52} + 3x_{53} + 175y_1 + 300y_2 + 375y_3 + 500y_4 \end{aligned}$$

s.t.

$$\begin{array}{llll}
x_{11} + x_{12} + x_{13} & - 10y_1 & \leq 0 & \text{Detroit capacity} \\
x_{21} + x_{22} + x_{23} & - 20y_2 & \leq 0 & \text{Toledo capacity} \\
x_{31} + x_{32} + x_{33} & - 30y_3 & \leq 0 & \text{Denver capacity} \\
x_{41} + x_{42} + x_{43} & - 40y_4 & \leq 0 & \text{Kansas City capacity} \\
x_{51} + x_{52} + x_{53} & & \leq 30 & \text{St. Louis capacity} \\
x_{11} + x_{21} + x_{31} + x_{41} + x_{51} & & = 30 & \text{Boston demand} \\
x_{12} + x_{22} + x_{32} + x_{42} + x_{52} & & = 20 & \text{Atlanta demand} \\
x_{13} + x_{23} + x_{33} + x_{43} + x_{53} & & = 20 & \text{Houston demand}
\end{array}$$

$x_{ij} \geq 0$ for all i and j; $y_1, y_2, y_3, y_4 = 0, 1$

Using the integer linear programming module of The Management Scientist, we obtained the solution shown in Figure 7.8. The optimal solution calls for the construction of a plant in Kansas City ($y_4 = 1$); 20,000 units will be shipped from Kansas City to Atlanta ($x_{42} = 20$), 20,000 units will be shipped from Kansas City to Houston ($x_{43} = 20$), and 30,000 units will be shipped from St. Louis to Boston ($x_{51} = 30$). Note that the total cost of this solution including the fixed cost of $500,000 for the plant in Kansas City is $860,000.

This basic model can be expanded to accommodate distribution systems involving direct shipments from plants to warehouses, from plants to retail outlets, and multiple products.[2] Using the special properties of 0-1 variables, the model can also be expanded to accommodate a variety of configuration constraints on the plant locations. For example, suppose in another problem, site 1 was in Dallas and site 2 was in Fort Worth. A company might not want to locate plants in both Dallas and Fort Worth because the cities are so close together. To prevent this result from happening, the following constraint can be added to the model:

Problem 13, which is based on the Martin-Beck distribution system problem, provides additional practice involving 0-1 variables.

$$y_1 + y_2 \leq 1$$

This constraint allows either y_1 or y_2 to equal 1, but not both. If we had written the constraints as an equality, it would require that a plant be located in either Dallas or Fort Worth.

Bank Location

The long-range planning department for the Ohio Trust Company is considering expanding its operation into a 20-county region in northeastern Ohio (see Figure 7.9). Currently, Ohio Trust does not have a principal place of business in any of the 20 counties. According to the

[2] For computational reasons, it is usually preferable to replace the m plant capacity constraints with mn shipping route capacity constraints of the form $x_{ij} \leq \text{Min}\{s_i, d_j\}\, y_i$ for $i = 1, \ldots, m$, and $j = 1, \ldots, n$. The coefficient for y_i in each of these constraints is the smaller of the origin capacity (s_i) or the destination demand (d_j). These additional constraints often cause the solution of the LP Relaxation to be integer.

FIGURE 7.8 THE MANAGEMENT SCIENTIST SOLUTION FOR THE MARTIN-BECK COMPANY DISTRIBUTION SYSTEM PROBLEM

EXCEL file
Martin-Beck

```
OPTIMAL SOLUTION

Objective Function Value = 860.000

      Variable              Value
   --------------      ---------------
        X11                    0.000
        X12                    0.000
        X13                    0.000
        X21                    0.000
        X22                    0.000
        X23                    0.000
        X31                    0.000
        X32                    0.000
        X33                    0.000
        X41                    0.000
        X42                   20.000
        X43                   20.000
        X51                   30.000
        X52                    0.000
        X53                    0.000
        Y1                     0.000
        Y2                     0.000
        Y3                     0.000
        Y4                     1.000

     Constraint          Slack/Surplus
   --------------      ---------------
         1                     0.000
         2                     0.000
         3                     0.000
         4                     0.000
         5                     0.000
         6                     0.000
         7                     0.000
         8                     0.000
```

banking laws in Ohio, if a bank establishes a principal place of business (PPB) in any county, branch banks can be established in that county and in any adjacent county. However, to establish a new principal place of business, Ohio Trust must either obtain approval for a new bank from the state's superintendent of banks or purchase an existing bank.

Table 7.3 lists the 20 counties in the region and adjacent counties. For example, Ashtabula County is adjacent to Lake, Geauga, and Trumbull counties; Lake County is adjacent to Ashtabula, Cuyahoga, and Geauga counties; and so on.

As an initial step in its planning, Ohio Trust would like to determine the minimum number of PPBs necessary to do business throughout the 20-county region. A 0-1 integer

FIGURE 7.9 THE 20-COUNTY REGION IN NORTHEASTERN OHIO

programming model can be used to solve this **location problem** for Ohio Trust. We define the variables as

$$x_i = 1 \text{ if a PPB is established in county } i\text{; 0 otherwise}$$

To minimize the number of PPBs needed, we write the objective function as

$$\text{Min} \quad x_1 + x_2 + \cdots + x_{20}$$

The bank may locate branches in a county if the county contains a PPB or is adjacent to another county with a PPB. Thus, the linear program will need one constraint for each county. For example, the constraint for Ashtabula County is

$$x_1 + x_2 + x_{12} + x_{16} \geq 1 \quad \text{Ashtabula}$$

Note that satisfaction of this constraint ensures that a PPB will be placed in Ashtabula County *or* in one or more of the adjacent counties. This constraint thus guarantees that Ohio Trust will be able to place branch banks in Ashtabula County.

TABLE 7.3 COUNTIES IN THE OHIO TRUST EXPANSION REGION

Counties Under Consideration	Adjacent Counties (by Number)
1. Ashtabula	2, 12, 16
2. Lake	1, 3, 12
3. Cuyahoga	2, 4, 9, 10, 12, 13
4. Lorain	3, 5, 7, 9
5. Huron	4, 6, 7
6. Richland	5, 7, 17
7. Ashland	4, 5, 6, 8, 9, 17, 18
8. Wayne	7, 9, 10, 11, 18
9. Medina	3, 4, 7, 8, 10
10. Summit	3, 8, 9, 11, 12, 13
11. Stark	8, 10, 13, 14, 15, 18, 19, 20
12. Geauga	1, 2, 3, 10, 13, 16
13. Portage	3, 10, 11, 12, 15, 16
14. Columbiana	11, 15, 20
15. Mahoning	11, 13, 14, 16
16. Trumbull	1, 12, 13, 15
17. Knox	6, 7, 18
18. Holmes	7, 8, 11, 17, 19
19. Tuscarawas	11, 18, 20
20. Carroll	11, 14, 19

The complete statement of the bank location problem is

$$
\begin{aligned}
\text{Min} \quad & x_1 + x_2 + \quad \cdots \quad + x_{20} \\
\text{s.t.} \quad & \\
& x_1 + x_2 + x_{12} + x_{16} \geq 1 \quad \text{Ashtabula} \\
& x_1 + x_2 + x_3 + x_{12} \geq 1 \quad \text{Lake} \\
& \vdots \\
& x_{11} + x_{14} + x_{19} + x_{20} \geq 1 \quad \text{Carroll} \\
& x_i = 0, 1 \quad i = 1, 2, \ldots, 20
\end{aligned}
$$

We used The Management Scientist to solve this 20-variable, 20-constraint problem formulation. In Figure 7.10 we show a portion of the computer output. Note that the variable names correspond to the first four letters in the name of each county. Using the output, we see that the optimal solution calls for principal places of business in Ashland, Stark, and Geauga counties. With PPBs in these three counties, Ohio Trust can place branch banks in all 20 counties (see Figure 7.11). All other decision variables have an optimal value of zero, indicating that a PPB should not be placed in these counties. Clearly the integer programming model could be enlarged to allow for expansion into a larger area or throughout the entire state.

FIGURE 7.10 THE MANAGEMENT SCIENTIST SOLUTION FOR THE OHIO TRUST PPB LOCATION PROBLEM

EXCELfile
Ohio Trust

```
OPTIMAL SOLUTION

Objective Function Value = 3.000

        Variable              Value
     --------------      ---------------
          ASHT                    0.000
          LAKE                    0.000
          CUYA                    0.000
          LORA                    0.000
          HURO                    0.000
          RICH                    0.000
          ASHL                    1.000
          WAYN                    0.000
          MEDI                    0.000
          SUMM                    0.000
          STAR                    1.000
          GEAU                    1.000
          PORT                    0.000
          COLU                    0.000
          MAHO                    0.000
          TRUM                    0.000
          KNOX                    0.000
          HOLM                    0.000
          TUSC                    0.000
          CARR                    0.000
```

Product Design and Market Share Optimization

Conjoint analysis is a market research technique that can be used to learn how prospective buyers of a product value the product's attributes. In this section we will show how the results of conjoint analysis can be used in an integer programming model of a **product design and market share optimization problem.** We illustrate the approach by considering a problem facing Salem Foods, a major producer of frozen foods.

Salem Foods is planning to enter the frozen pizza market. Currently, two existing brands, Antonio's and King's, have the major share of the market. In trying to develop a sausage pizza that will capture a significant share of the market, Salem determined that the four most important attributes when consumers purchase a frozen sausage pizza are crust, cheese, sauce, and sausage flavor. The crust attribute has two levels (thin and thick); the cheese attribute has two levels (mozzarella and blend); the sauce attribute has two levels (smooth and chunky); and the sausage flavor attribute has three levels (mild, medium, and hot).

In a typical conjoint analysis, a sample of consumers is asked to express their preference for specially prepared pizzas with chosen levels for the attributes. Then regression analysis is used to determine the part-worth for each of the attribute levels. In essence, the part-worth is the utility value that a consumer attaches to each level of each attribute. A discussion of how to use regression analysis to compute the part-worths is beyond the scope

FIGURE 7.11 PRINCIPAL PLACE OF BUSINESS COUNTIES FOR OHIO TRUST

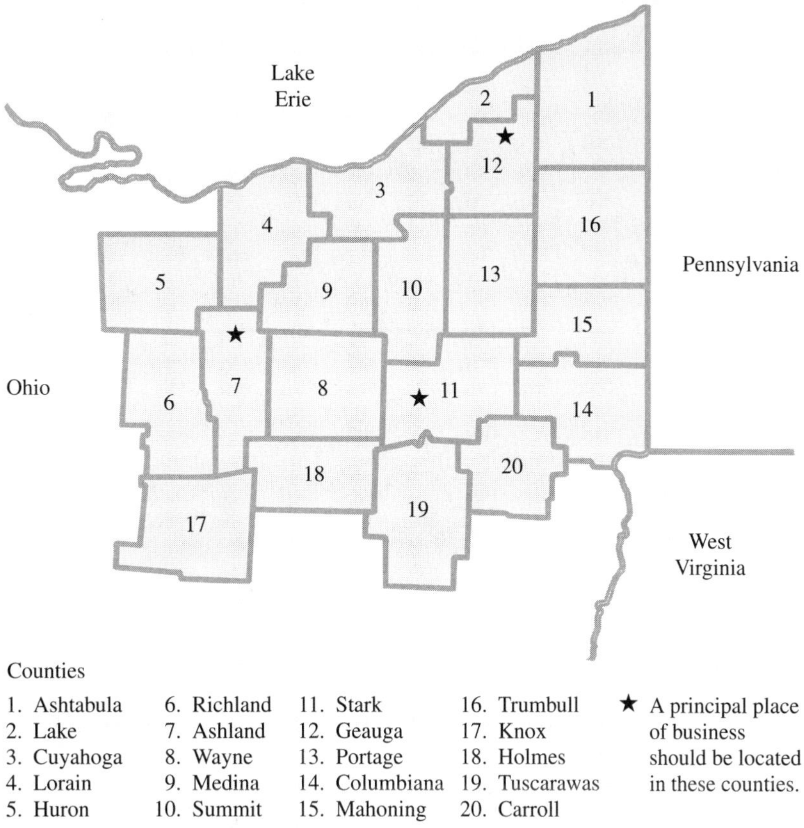

Lake Erie
Pennsylvania
Ohio
West Virginia
1
2
3
4
5
6
7
8
9
10
11
12
13
14
15
16
17
18
19
20
Counties
1. Ashtabula
2. Lake
3. Cuyahoga
4. Lorain
5. Huron
6. Richland
7. Ashland
8. Wayne
9. Medina
10. Summit
11. Stark
12. Geauga
13. Portage
14. Columbiana
15. Mahoning
16. Trumbull
17. Knox
18. Holmes
19. Tuscarawas
20. Carroll
★ A principal place of business should be located in these counties.

of this text, but we will show how the part-worths can be used to determine the overall value a consumer attaches to a particular pizza.

Table 7.4 shows the part-worths for each level of each attribute provided by a sample of eight potential Salem customers who are currently buying either King's or Antonio's pizza. For consumer 1 the part-worths for the crust attribute are 11 for thin crust and 2 for thick crust, indicating a preference for thin crust. For the cheese attribute, the part-worths are 6 for the mozzarella cheese and 7 for the cheese blend; thus, consumer 1 has a slight preference for the cheese blend. From the other part-worths, we see that consumer 1 shows a strong preference for the chunky sauce over the smooth sauce (17 to 3) and has a slight preference for the medium-flavored sausage. Note that consumer 2 shows a preference for the thin crust, the cheese blend, the chunky sauce, and mild-flavored sausage. The part-worths for the others consumers are interpreted in a similar manner.

The part-worths can be used to determine the overall value (utility) each consumer attaches to a particular type of pizza. For instance, consumer 1's current favorite pizza is the Antonio's brand, which has a thick crust, mozzarella cheese, chunky sauce, and medium-flavored sausage. We can determine consumer 1's utility for this particular type of pizza using the part-worths in Table 7.4. For consumer 1 the part-worths are 2 for thick crust, 6 for mozzarella cheese, 17 for chunky sauce, and 27 for medium-flavored sausage. Thus,

TABLE 7.4 PART-WORTHS FOR THE SALEM FOODS PROBLEM

	Crust		Cheese		Sauce		Sausage Flavor		
Consumer	**Thin**	**Thick**	**Mozzarella**	**Blend**	**Smooth**	**Chunky**	**Mild**	**Medium**	**Hot**
1	11	2	6	7	3	17	26	27	8
2	11	7	15	17	16	26	14	1	10
3	7	5	8	14	16	7	29	16	19
4	13	20	20	17	17	14	25	29	10
5	2	8	6	11	30	20	15	5	12
6	12	17	11	9	2	30	22	12	20
7	9	19	12	16	16	25	30	23	19
8	5	9	4	14	23	16	16	30	3

consumer 1's utility for the Antonio's brand pizza is 2 + 6 + 17 + 27 = 52. We can compute consumer 1's utility for a King's brand pizza in a similar manner. The King's brand pizza has a thin crust, a cheese blend, smooth sauce, and mild-flavored sausage. Because the part-worths for consumer 1 are 11 for thin crust, 7 for cheese blend, 3 for smooth sauce, and 26 for mild-flavored sausage, consumer 1's utility for the King's brand pizza is 11 + 7 + 3 + 26 = 47. In general, each consumer's utility for a particular type of pizza is just the sum of the appropriate part-worths.

In order to be successful with its brand, Salem Foods realizes that it must entice consumers in the marketplace to switch from their current favorite brand of pizza to the Salem product. That is, Salem must design a pizza (choose the type of crust, cheese, sauce, and sausage flavor) that will have the highest utility for enough people to ensure sufficient sales to justify making the product. Assuming the sample of eight consumers in the current study is representative of the marketplace for frozen sausage pizza, we can formulate and solve an integer programming model that can help Salem come up with such a design. In marketing literature, the problem being solved is called the *share of choices* problem.

The decision variables are defined as follows:

$$l_{ij} = 1 \text{ if Salem chooses level } i \text{ for attribute } j\text{; 0 otherwise}$$
$$y_k = 1 \text{ if consumer } k \text{ chooses the Salem brand; 0 otherwise}$$

The objective is to choose the levels of each attribute that will maximize the number of consumers preferring the Salem brand pizza. Because the number of customers preferring the Salem brand pizza is just the sum of the y_k variables, the objective function is

$$\text{Max} \quad y_1 + y_2 + \cdots + y_8$$

One constraint is needed for each consumer in the sample. To illustrate how the constraints are formulated, let us consider the constraint corresponding to consumer 1. For consumer 1, the utility of a particular type of pizza can be expressed as the sum of the part-worths:

$$\text{Utility for Consumer 1} = 11l_{11} + 2l_{21} + 6l_{12} + 7l_{22} + 3l_{13} + 17l_{23} + 26l_{14} + 27l_{24} + 8l_{34}$$

In order for consumer 1 to prefer the Salem pizza, the utility for the Salem pizza must be greater than the utility for consumer 1's current favorite. Recall that consumer 1's current favorite brand of pizza is Antonio's, with a utility of 52. Thus, consumer 1 will only purchase the Salem brand if the levels of the attributes for the Salem brand are chosen such that

$$11l_{11} + 2l_{21} + 6l_{12} + 7l_{22} + 3l_{13} + 17l_{23} + 26l_{14} + 27l_{24} + 8l_{34} > 52$$

Given the definitions of the y_k decision variables, we want $y_1 = 1$ when the consumer prefers the Salem brand and $y_1 = 0$ when the consumer does not prefer the Salem brand. Thus, we write the constraint for consumer 1 as follows:

$$11l_{11} + 2l_{21} + 6l_{12} + 7l_{22} + 3l_{13} + 17l_{23} + 26l_{14} + 27l_{24} + 8l_{34} \geq 1 + 52y_1$$

With this constraint, y_1 cannot equal 1 unless the utility for the Salem design (the left-hand side of the constraint) exceeds the utility for consumer 1's current favorite by at least 1. Because the objective function is to maximize the sum of the y_k variables, the optimization will seek a product design that will allow as many y_k as possible to equal 1.

Placing all the decision variables on the left-hand side of the constraint enables us to rewrite constraint 1 as follows:

$$11l_{11} + 2l_{21} + 6l_{12} + 7l_{22} + 3l_{13} + 17l_{23} + 26l_{14} + 27l_{24} + 8l_{34} - 52y_1 \geq 1$$

A similar constraint is written for each consumer in the sample. The coefficients for the l_{ij} variables in the utility functions are taken from Table 7.4 and the coefficients for the y_k variables are obtained by computing the overall utility of the consumer's current favorite brand of pizza. The following constraints correspond to the eight consumers in the study.

Antonio's brand is the current favorite pizza for consumers 1, 4, 6, 7, and 8. King's brand is the current favorite pizza for consumers 2, 3, and 5.

$$\begin{aligned}
11l_{11} + 2l_{21} + 6l_{12} + 7l_{22} + 3l_{13} + 17l_{23} + 26l_{14} + 27l_{24} + 8l_{34} - 52y_1 &\geq 1\\
11l_{11} + 7l_{21} + 15l_{12} + 17l_{22} + 16l_{13} + 26l_{23} + 14l_{14} + 1l_{24} + 10l_{34} - 58y_2 &\geq 1\\
7l_{11} + 5l_{21} + 8l_{12} + 14l_{22} + 16l_{13} + 7l_{23} + 29l_{14} + 16l_{24} + 19l_{34} - 66y_3 &\geq 1\\
13l_{11} + 20l_{21} + 20l_{12} + 17l_{22} + 17l_{13} + 14l_{23} + 25l_{14} + 29l_{24} + 10l_{34} - 83y_4 &\geq 1\\
2l_{11} + 8l_{21} + 6l_{12} + 11l_{22} + 30l_{13} + 20l_{23} + 15l_{14} + 5l_{24} + 12l_{34} - 58y_5 &\geq 1\\
12l_{11} + 17l_{21} + 11l_{12} + 9l_{22} + 2l_{13} + 30l_{23} + 22l_{14} + 12l_{24} + 20l_{34} - 70y_6 &\geq 1\\
9l_{11} + 19l_{21} + 12l_{12} + 16l_{22} + 16l_{13} + 25l_{23} + 30l_{14} + 23l_{24} + 19l_{34} - 79y_7 &\geq 1\\
5l_{11} + 9l_{21} + 4l_{12} + 14l_{22} + 23l_{13} + 16l_{23} + 16l_{14} + 30l_{24} + 3l_{34} - 59y_8 &\geq 1
\end{aligned}$$

Four more constraints must be added, one for each attribute. These constraints are necessary to ensure that one and only one level is selected for each attribute. For attribute 1 (crust), we must add the constraint

$$l_{11} + l_{21} = 1$$

Because l_{11} and l_{21} are both 0-1 variables, this constraint requires that one of the two variables equals 1 and the other equals 0. The following three constraints ensure that one and only one level is selected for each of the other three attributes.

$$\begin{aligned}
l_{12} + l_{22} &= 1\\
l_{13} + l_{23} &= 1\\
l_{14} + l_{24} + l_{34} &= 1
\end{aligned}$$

EXCELfile
Salem

The optimal solution (obtained using Excel Solver)[3] to this 17-variable, 12-constraint integer linear program is $l_{11} = l_{22} = l_{23} = l_{14} = 1$ and $y_1 = y_2 = y_6 = y_7 = 1$. The value of the optimal solution is 4, indicating that if Salem makes this type of pizza it will be preferable to the current favorite for four of the eight consumers. With $l_{11} = l_{22} = l_{23} = l_{14} = 1$, the pizza design that obtains the largest market share for Salem has a thin crust, a cheese blend, a chunky sauce, and mild-flavored sausage. Note also that with $y_1 = y_2 = y_6 = y_7 = 1$, consumers 1, 2, 6, and 7 will prefer the Salem pizza. With this information Salem may choose to market this type of pizza.

NOTES AND COMMENTS

1. Most practical applications of integer linear programming involve only 0-1 integer variables. Indeed, some mixed-integer computer codes are designed to handle only integer variables with binary values. However, if a clever mathematical trick is employed, these codes can still be used for problems involving general integer variables. The trick is called *binary expansion* and requires that an upper bound be established for each integer variable. More advanced texts on integer programming show how it can be done.
2. The Management Science in Action, Volunteer Scheduling for the Edmonton Folk Festival, describes how a series of three integer programming models was used to schedule volunteers. Two of the models employ 0-1 variables.
3. General-purpose mixed-integer linear programming codes and some spreadsheet packages can be used for linear programming problems, all-integer problems, and problems involving some continuous and some integer variables. General-purpose codes are seldom the fastest for solving problems with special structure (such as the transportation, assignment, and transshipment problems); however, unless the problems are very large, speed is usually not a critical issue. Thus, most practitioners prefer to use one general-purpose computer package that can be used on a variety of problems rather than to maintain a variety of computer programs designed for special problems.

MANAGEMENT SCIENCE IN ACTION

VOLUNTEER SCHEDULING FOR THE EDMONTON FOLK FESTIVAL*

The Edmonton Folk Festival is a four-day outdoor event that is run almost entirely by volunteers. In 2002, 1800 volunteers worked on 35 different crews and contributed more than 50,000 volunteer hours. With this many volunteers, coordination requires a major effort. For instance, in 2002, two volunteer coordinators used a trial-and-error procedure to develop schedules for the volunteers in the two gate crews. However, developing these schedules proved to be time consuming and frustrating; the coordinators spent as much time scheduling as they did supervising volunteers during the festival. To reduce the time spent on gate-crew scheduling, one of the coordinators asked the Centre for Excellence in Operations at the University of Alberta School of Business for help in automating the scheduling process. The Centre agreed to help.

The scheduling system developed consists of three integer programming models. Model 1 is used to determine daily shift schedules. This model determines the length of each shift (number of hours) and how many volunteers are needed for each shift to meet the peaks and valleys in demand. Model 2 is a binary integer program used to assign volunteers to shifts. The objective is to maximize volunteer preferences subject to several constraints, such

[3]We noted at the beginning of this chapter that some fairly small integer programs can be difficult to solve. The combinatorial structure of the share of choices problem in this section makes it too difficult for The Management Scientist. We have solved the Salem Foods problem using Premium Solver for Education. The Excel solution to this problem is contained on the CD that accompanies this text.

as number of hours worked, balance between morning and afternoon shifts, a mix of experienced and inexperienced volunteers on each shift, no conflicting shifts, and so on. Model 3 is used to allocate volunteers between the two gates.

The coordinators of the gate crews were pleased with the results provided by the models and learned to use them effectively. Vicki Fannon, the manager of volunteers for the festival, now has plans to expand the use of the integer programming models to the scheduling of other crews in the future.

*Based on L. Gordon and E. Erkut, "Improving Volunteer Scheduling for the Edmonton Folk Festival," *Interfaces* (September/October 2004): 367–376.

7.4 MODELING FLEXIBILITY PROVIDED BY 0-1 INTEGER VARIABLES

In Section 7.3 we presented four applications involving 0-1 integer variables. In this section we continue the discussion of the use of 0-1 integer variables in modeling. First, we show how 0-1 integer variables can be used to model multiple-choice and mutually exclusive constraints. Then, we show how 0-1 integer variables can be used to model situations in which k projects out of a set of n projects must be selected, as well as situations in which the acceptance of one project is conditional on the acceptance of another. We close the section with a cautionary note on the role of sensitivity analysis in integer linear programming.

Multiple-Choice and Mutually Exclusive Constraints

Recall the Ice-Cold Refrigerator capital budgeting problem introduced in Section 7.3. The decision variables were defined as

P = 1 if the plant expansion project is accepted; 0 if rejected
W = 1 if the warehouse expansion project is accepted; 0 if rejected
M = 1 if the new machinery project is accepted; 0 if rejected
R = 1 if the new product research project is accepted; 0 if rejected

Suppose that, instead of one warehouse expansion project, the Ice-Cold Refrigerator Company actually has three warehouse expansion projects under consideration. One of the warehouses *must* be expanded because of increasing product demand, but new demand isn't sufficient to make expansion of more than one warehouse necessary. The following variable definitions and **multiple-choice constraint** could be incorporated into the previous 0-1 integer linear programming model to reflect this situation. Let

W_1 = 1 if the original warehouse expansion project is accepted; 0 if rejected
W_2 = 1 if the second warehouse expansion project is accepted; 0 if rejected
W_3 = 1 if the third warehouse expansion project is accepted; 0 if rejected

The following multiple-choice constraint reflects the requirement that exactly one of these projects must be selected:

$$W_1 + W_2 + W_3 = 1$$

If W_1, W_2, and W_3 are allowed to assume only the values 0 or 1, then one and only one of these projects will be selected from among the three choices.

If the requirement that one warehouse must be expanded did not exist, the multiple-choice constraint could be modified as follows:

$$W_1 + W_2 + W_3 \leq 1$$

This modification allows for the case of no warehouse expansion ($W_1 = W_2 = W_3 = 0$) but does not permit more than one warehouse to be expanded. This type of constraint is often called a **mutually exclusive constraint.**

k Out of *n* Alternatives Constraint

An extension of the notion of a multiple-choice constraint can be used to model situations in which *k out of a set of n* projects must be selected—a ***k* out of *n* alternatives constraint.** Suppose that W_1, W_2, W_3, W_4, and W_5 represent five potential warehouse expansion projects and that two of the five projects must be accepted. The constraint that satisfies this new requirement is

$$W_1 + W_2 + W_3 + W_4 + W_5 = 2$$

If no more than two of the projects are to be selected, we would use the following less-than-or-equal-to constraint:

$$W_1 + W_2 + W_3 + W_4 + W_5 \leq 2$$

Again, each of these variables must be restricted to 0-1 values.

Conditional and Corequisite Constraints

Sometimes the acceptance of one project is conditional on the acceptance of another. For example, suppose for the Ice-Cold Refrigerator Company that the warehouse expansion project was conditional on the plant expansion project. That is, management will not consider expanding the warehouse unless the plant is expanded. With P representing plant expansion and W representing warehouse expansion, a **conditional constraint** could be introduced to enforce this requirement:

$$W \leq P$$

Both P and W must be 0 or 1; whenever P is 0, W will be forced to 0. When P is 1, W is also allowed to be 1; thus, both the plant and the warehouse can be expanded. However, we note that the preceding constraint does not force the warehouse expansion project (W) to be accepted if the plant expansion project (P) is accepted.

If the warehouse expansion project had to be accepted whenever the plant expansion project was, and vice versa, we would say that P and W represented **corequisite constraint** projects. To model such a situation, we simply write the preceding constraint as an equality:

$$W = P$$

Try Problem 7 for practice with the modeling flexibility provided by 0-1 variables.

The constraint forces P and W to take on the same value.

The Management Science in Action, Customer Order Allocation Model at Ketron, describes how the modeling flexibility provided by 0-1 variables helped Ketron build a customer order allocation model for a sporting goods company.

MANAGEMENT SCIENCE IN ACTION

CUSTOMER ORDER ALLOCATION MODEL AT KETRON*

Ketron Management Science provides consulting services for the design and implementation of mathematical programming applications. One such application involved the development of a mixed-integer programming model of the customer order allocation problem for a major sporting goods company. The sporting goods company markets approximately 300 products and has about 30 sources of supply (factory and warehouse locations). The problem is to determine how best to allocate customer orders to the various sources of supply such that the total manufacturing cost for the products ordered is minimized. Figure 7.12 provides a graphical representation of this problem. Note in the figure that each customer can receive shipments from only a few of the various sources of supply. For example, we see that customer 1 may be supplied by source A or B, customer 2 may be supplied only by source A, and so on.

The sporting equipment company classifies each customer order as either a "guaranteed" or "secondary" order. Guaranteed orders are single-source orders in that they must be filled by a single supplier to ensure that the complete order will be delivered to the customer at one time. This single-source requirement necessitates the use of 0-1 integer variables in the model. Approximately 80% of the company's orders are guaranteed orders. Secondary orders can be split among the various sources of supply. These orders are made by customers restocking inventory, and receiving partial shipments from different sources at different times is not a problem. The 0-1 variables are used to represent the assignment of a guaranteed order to a supplier and continuous variables are used to represent the secondary orders.

Constraints for the problem involve raw material capacities, manufacturing capacities, and individual product capacities. A fairly typical problem has about 800 constraints, 2000 0-1 assignment variables, and 500 continuous variables associated with the secondary orders. The customer order allocation problem is solved periodically as orders are received. In a typical period, between 20 and 40 customers are to be supplied. Because most customers require several products, usually between 600 and 800 orders must be assigned to the sources of supply.

*Based on information provided by J. A. Tomlin of Ketron Management Science.

FIGURE 7.12 GRAPHICAL REPRESENTATION OF THE CUSTOMER ORDER ALLOCATION PROBLEM

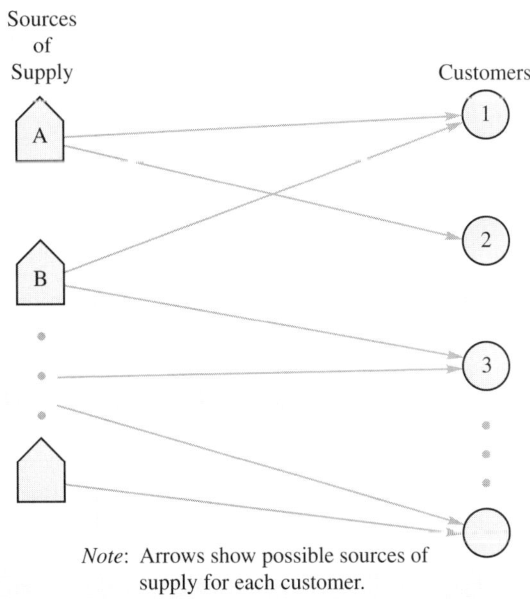

A Cautionary Note About Sensitivity Analysis

Sensitivity analysis often is more crucial for integer linear programming problems than for linear programming problems. A small change in one of the coefficients in the constraints can cause a relatively large change in the value of the optimal solution. To understand why, consider the following integer programming model of a simple capital budgeting problem involving four projects and a budgetary constraint for a single time period:

$$\begin{aligned} \text{Max} \quad & 40x_1 + 60x_2 + 70x_3 + 160x_4 \\ \text{s.t.} \quad & \\ & 16x_1 + 35x_2 + 45x_3 + 85x_4 \leq 100 \\ & x_1, x_2, x_3, x_4 = 0, 1 \end{aligned}$$

Dual prices cannot be used for integer programming sensitivity analysis because they are designed for linear programs. Multiple computer runs usually are necessary for sensitivity analysis of integer linear programs.

We can obtain the optimal solution to this problem by enumerating the alternatives. It is $x_1 = 1, x_2 = 1, x_3 = 1$, and $x_4 = 0$, with an objective function value of \$170. However, note that if the budget available is increased by \$1 (from \$100 to \$101), the optimal solution changes to $x_1 = 1$, $x_2 = 0$, $x_3 = 0$, and $x_4 = 1$, with an objective function value of \$200. That is, one additional dollar in the budget would lead to a \$30 increase in the return. Surely management, when faced with such a situation, would increase the budget by \$1. Because of the extreme sensitivity of the value of the optimal solution to the constraint coefficients, practitioners usually recommend re-solving the integer linear program several times with slight variations in the coefficients before attempting to choose the best solution for implementation.

SUMMARY

In this chapter, we introduced the important extension of linear programming referred to as *integer linear programming*. The only difference between the integer linear programming problems discussed in this chapter and the linear programming problems studied in previous chapters is that one or more of the variables must be integer. If all variables must be integer, we have an all-integer linear program. If some, but not necessarily all, variables must be integer, we have a mixed-integer linear program. Most integer programming applications involve 0-1, or binary, variables.

Studying integer linear programming is important for two major reasons. First, integer linear programming may be helpful when fractional values for the variables are not permitted. Rounding a linear programming solution may not provide an optimal integer solution; methods for finding optimal integer solutions are needed when the economic consequences of rounding are significant. A second reason for studying integer linear programming is the increased modeling flexibility provided through the use of 0-1 variables. We showed how 0-1 variables could be used to model important managerial considerations in capital budgeting, fixed cost, distribution system design, bank location, and product design/market share applications.

The number of applications of integer linear programming continues to grow rapidly. This growth is due in part to the availability of good integer linear programming software packages. As researchers develop solution procedures capable of solving larger integer linear programs and as computer speed increases, a continuation of the growth of integer programming applications is expected.

GLOSSARY

Integer linear program A linear program with the additional requirement that one or more of the variables must be integer.

All-integer linear program An integer linear program in which all variables are required to be integer.

LP Relaxation The linear program that results from dropping the integer requirements for the variables in an integer linear program.

Mixed-integer linear program An integer linear program in which some, but not necessarily all, variables are required to be integer.

0-1 integer linear program An all-integer or mixed-integer linear program in which the integer variables are only permitted to assume the values 0 or 1. Also called *binary integer program.*

Capital budgeting problem A 0-1 integer programming problem that involves choosing which projects or activities provide the best investment return.

Fixed cost problem A 0-1 mixed-integer programming problem in which the binary variables represent whether an activity, such as a production run, is undertaken (variable = 1) or not (variable = 0).

Distribution system design problem A mixed-integer linear program in which the binary integer variables usually represent sites selected for warehouses or plants and continuous variables represent the amount shipped over arcs in the distribution network.

Location problem A 0-1 integer programming problem in which the objective is to select the best locations to meet a stated objective. Variations of this problem (see the bank location problem in Section 7.3) are known as covering problems.

Product design and market share optimization problem Sometimes called the share of choices problem, it involves choosing a product design that maximizes the number of consumers preferring it.

Multiple-choice constraint A constraint requiring that the sum of two or more 0-1 variables equal 1. Thus, any feasible solution makes a choice of which variable to set equal to 1.

Mutually exclusive constraint A constraint requiring that the sum of two or more 0-1 variables be less than or equal to 1. Thus, if one of the variables equals 1, the others must equal 0. However, all variables could equal 0.

***k* out of *n* alternatives constraint** An extension of the multiple-choice constraint. This constraint requires that the sum of n 0-1 variables equal k.

Conditional constraint A constraint involving 0-1 variables that does not allow certain variables to equal 1 unless certain other variables are equal to 1.

Corequisite constraint A constraint requiring that two 0-1 variables be equal. Thus, they are both in or out of solution together.

PROBLEMS

1. Indicate which of the following is an all-integer linear program and which is a mixed-integer linear program. Write the LP Relaxation for the problem but do not attempt to solve.

   a. Max $30x_1 + 25x_2$

   s.t.

   $$\begin{aligned} 3x_1 + 1.5x_2 &\leq 400 \\ 1.5x_1 + 2x_2 &\leq 250 \\ 1x_1 + 1x_2 &\leq 150 \\ x_1, x_2 \geq 0 \text{ and } &x_2 \text{ integer} \end{aligned}$$

   b. Min $3x_1 + 4x_2$

   s.t.

   $$\begin{aligned} 2x_1 + 4x_2 &\geq 8 \\ 2x_1 + 6x_2 &\geq 12 \\ x_1, x_2 \geq 0 &\text{ and integer} \end{aligned}$$

2. Consider the following all-integer linear program.

   Max $5x_1 + 8x_2$

   s.t.

   $$\begin{aligned} 6x_1 + 5x_2 &\leq 30 \\ 9x_1 + 4x_2 &\leq 36 \\ 1x_1 + 2x_2 &\leq 10 \\ x_1, x_2 \geq 0 &\text{ and integer} \end{aligned}$$

   a. Graph the constraints for this problem. Use dots to indicate all feasible integer solutions.
   b. Find the optimal solution to the LP Relaxation. Round down to find a feasible integer solution.
   c. Find the optimal integer solution. Is it the same as the solution obtained in part (b) by rounding down?

3. Consider the following all-integer linear program.

   Max $1x_1 + 1x_2$

   s.t.

   $$\begin{aligned} 4x_1 + 6x_2 &\leq 22 \\ 1x_1 + 5x_2 &\leq 15 \\ 2x_1 + 1x_2 &\leq 9 \\ x_1, x_2 \geq 0 &\text{ and integer} \end{aligned}$$

   a. Graph the constraints for this problem. Use dots to indicate all feasible integer solutions.
   b. Solve the LP Relaxation of this problem.
   c. Find the optimal integer solution.

4. Consider the following all-integer linear program.

   Max $10x_1 + 3x_2$

   s.t.

   $$\begin{aligned} 6x_1 + 7x_2 &\leq 40 \\ 3x_1 + 1x_2 &\leq 11 \\ x_1, x_2 \geq 0 &\text{ and integer} \end{aligned}$$

a. Formulate and solve the LP Relaxation of the problem. Solve it graphically, and round down to find a feasible solution. Specify an upper bound on the value of the optimal solution.
b. Solve the integer linear program graphically. Compare the value of this solution with the solution obtained in part (a).
c. Suppose the objective function changes to Max $3x_1 + 6x_2$. Repeat parts (a) and (b).

5. Consider the following mixed-integer linear program.

$$\begin{aligned} \text{Max} \quad & 2x_1 + 3x_2 \\ \text{s.t.} \quad & \\ & 4x_1 + 9x_2 \leq 36 \\ & 7x_1 + 5x_2 \leq 35 \\ & x_1, x_2 \geq 0 \text{ and } x_1 \text{ integer} \end{aligned}$$

a. Graph the constraints for this problem. Indicate on your graph all feasible mixed-integer solutions.
b. Find the optimal solution to the LP Relaxation. Round the value of x_1 down to find a feasible mixed-integer solution. Is this solution optimal? Why or why not?
c. Find the optimal solution for the mixed-integer linear program.

6. Consider the following mixed-integer linear program.

$$\begin{aligned} \text{Max} \quad & 1x_1 + 1x_2 \\ \text{s.t.} \quad & \\ & 7x_1 + 9x_2 \leq 63 \\ & 9x_1 + 5x_2 \leq 45 \\ & 3x_1 + 1x_2 \leq 12 \\ & x_1, x_2 \geq 0 \text{ and } x_2 \text{ integer} \end{aligned}$$

a. Graph the constraints for this problem. Indicate on your graph all feasible mixed-integer solutions.
b. Find the optimal solution to the LP Relaxation. Round the value of x_2 down to find a feasible mixed-integer solution. Specify upper and lower bounds on the value of the optimal solution to the mixed-integer linear program.
c. Find the optimal solution to the mixed-integer linear program.

7. The following questions refer to a capital budgeting problem with six projects represented by 0-1 variables x_1, x_2, x_3, x_4, x_5, and x_6.
a. Write a constraint modeling a situation in which two of the projects 1, 3, 5, and 6 must be undertaken.
b. Write a constraint modeling a situation in which, if projects 3 and 5 must be undertaken, they must be undertaken simultaneously.
c. Write a constraint modeling a situation in which project 1 or 4 must be undertaken, but not both.
d. Write constraints modeling a situation where project 4 cannot be undertaken unless projects 1 and 3 also are undertaken.
e. Revise the requirement in part (d) to accommodate the case in which, when projects 1 and 3 are undertaken, project 4 also must be undertaken.

8. Spencer Enterprises must choose among a series of new investment alternatives. The potential investment alternatives, the net present value of the future stream of returns, the capital requirements, and the available capital funds over the next three years are summarized as follows:

	Net Present	Capital Requirements ($)		
Alternative	Value ($)	Year 1	Year 2	Year 3
Limited warehouse expansion	4,000	3,000	1,000	4,000
Extensive warehouse expansion	6,000	2,500	3,500	3,500
Test market new product	10,500	6,000	4,000	5,000
Advertising campaign	4,000	2,000	1,500	1,800
Basic research	8,000	5,000	1,000	4,000
Purchase new equipment	3,000	1,000	500	900
Capital funds available		10,500	7,000	8,750

a. Develop and solve an integer programming model for maximizing the net present value.
b. Assume that only one of the warehouse expansion projects can be implemented. Modify your model of part (a).
c. Suppose that, if test marketing of the new product is carried out, the advertising campaign also must be conducted. Modify your formulation of part (b) to reflect this new situation.

9. Hawkins Manufacturing Company produces connecting rods for 4- and 6-cylinder automobile engines using the same production line. The cost required to set up the production line to produce the 4-cylinder connecting rods is $2000, and the cost required to set up the production line for the 6-cylinder connecting rods is $3500. Manufacturing costs are $15 for each 4-cylinder connecting rod and $18 for each 6-cylinder connecting rod. Hawkins makes a decision at the end of each week as to which product will be manufactured the following week. If a production changeover is necessary from one week to the next, the weekend is used to reconfigure the production line. Once the line has been set up, the weekly production capacities are 6000 6-cylinder connecting rods and 8000 4-cylinder connecting rods. Let

x_4 = the number of 4-cylinder connecting rods produced next week
x_6 = the number of 6-cylinder connecting rods produced next week
s_4 = 1 if the production line is set up to produce the 4-cylinder connecting rods; 0 if otherwise
s_6 = 1 if the production line is set up to produce the 6-cylinder connecting rods; 0 if otherwise

a. Using the decision variables x_4 and s_4, write a constraint that limits next week's production of the 4-cylinder connecting rods to either 0 or 8000 units.
b. Using the decision variables x_6 and s_6, write a constraint that limits next week's production of the 6-cylinder connecting rods to either 0 or 6000 units.
c. Write three constraints that, taken together, limit the production of connecting rods for next week.
d. Write an objective function for minimizing the cost of production for next week.

10. Grave City is considering the relocation of several police substations to obtain better enforcement in high-crime areas. The locations under consideration together with the areas that can be covered from these locations are given in the following table.

Potential Locations for Substations	Areas Covered
A	1, 5, 7
B	1, 2, 5, 7
C	1, 3, 5
D	2, 4, 5
E	3, 4, 6
F	4, 5, 6
G	1, 5, 6, 7

a. Formulate an integer programming model that could be used to find the minimum number of locations necessary to provide coverage to all areas.
b. Solve the problem in part (a).

11. Hart Manufacturing makes three products. Each product requires manufacturing operations in three departments: A, B, and C. The labor-hour requirements, by department, are as follows:

Department	Product 1	Product 2	Product 3
A	1.50	3.00	2.00
B	2.00	1.00	2.50
C	0.25	0.25	0.25

During the next production period, the labor-hours available are 450 in department A, 350 in department B, and 50 in department C. The profit contributions per unit are $25 for product 1, $28 for product 2, and $30 for product 3.

a. Formulate a linear programming model for maximizing total profit contribution.
b. Solve the linear program formulated in part (a). How much of each product should be produced, and what is the projected total profit contribution?
c. After evaluating the solution obtained in part (b), one of the production supervisors noted that production setup costs had not been taken into account. She noted that setup costs are $400 for product 1, $550 for product 2, and $600 for product 3. If the solution developed in part (b) is to be used, what is the total profit contribution after taking into account the setup costs?
d. Management realized that the optimal product mix, taking setup costs into account, might be different from the one recommended in part (b). Formulate a mixed-integer linear program that takes setup costs into account. Management also stated that we should not consider making more than 175 units of product 1, 150 units of product 2, or 140 units of product 3.
e. Solve the mixed integer linear program formulated in part (d). How much of each product should be produced, and what is the projected total profit contribution? Compare this profit contribution to that obtained in part (c).

12. Yates Company supplies road salt to county highway departments. The company has three trucks, and the dispatcher is trying to schedule tomorrow's deliveries to Polk, Dallas, and Jasper counties. Two trucks have 15-ton capacities, and the third truck has a 30-ton capacity. Based on these truck capacities, two counties will receive 15 tons and the third will receive 30 tons of road salt. The dispatcher wants to determine how much to ship to each county. Let

$$P = \text{amount shipped to Polk County}$$
$$D = \text{amount shipped to Dallas County}$$
$$J = \text{amount shipped to Jasper County}$$

and

$$Y_i = \begin{cases} 1 \text{ if the 30-ton truck is assigned to county } i \\ 0 \text{ otherwise} \end{cases}$$

a. Use these variable definitions and write constraints that appropriately restrict the amount shipped to each county.
b. The cost of assigning the 30-ton truck to the three counties is $100 to Polk, $85 to Dallas, and $50 to Jasper. Formulate and solve a mixed-integer linear program to determine how much to ship to each county.

13. Recall the Martin-Beck Company distribution system problem in Section 7.3.
a. Modify the formulation shown in Section 7.3 to account for the policy restriction that one plant, but not two, must be located either in Detroit or in Toledo.
b. Modify the formulation shown in Section 7.3 to account for the policy restriction that no more than two plants can be located in Denver, Kansas City, and St. Louis.

14. An automobile manufacturer has five outdated plants: one each in Michigan, Ohio, and California and two in New York. Management is considering modernizing these plants to manufacture engine blocks and transmissions for a new model car. The cost to modernize each plant and the manufacturing capacity after modernization are as follows:

Plant	Cost ($ millions)	Engine Blocks (1000s)	Transmissions (1000s)
Michigan	25	500	300
New York	35	800	400
New York	35	400	800
Ohio	40	900	600
California	20	200	300

The projected needs are for total capacities of 900,000 engine blocks and 900,000 transmissions. Management wants to determine which plants to modernize to meet projected manufacturing needs and, at the same time, minimize the total cost of modernization.
a. Develop a table that lists every possible option available to management. As part of your table, indicate the total engine block capacity and transmission capacity for each possible option, whether the option is feasible based on the projected needs, and the total modernization cost for each option.
b. Based on your analysis in part (a), what recommendation would you provide management?

c. Formulate a 0-1 integer programming model that could be used to determine the optimal solution to the modernization question facing management.
d. Solve the model formulated in part (c) to provide a recommendation for management.

15. CHB, Inc., is a bank holding company that is evaluating the potential for expanding into a 13-county region in the southwestern part of the state. State law permits establishing branches in any county that is adjacent to a county in which a PPB (principal place of business) is located. The following map shows the 13-county region with the population of each county indicated.

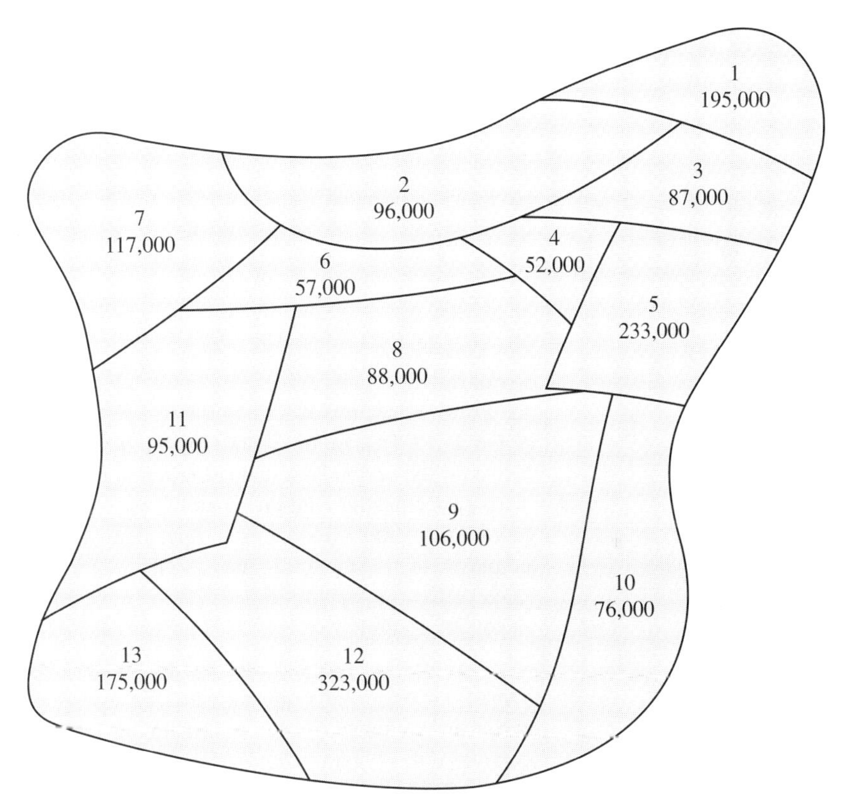

a. Assume that only one PPB can be established in the region. Where should it be located to maximize the population served? (*Hint:* Review the Ohio Trust formulation in Section 7.3. Consider minimizing the population not served, and introduce variable $y_i = 1$ if it is not possible to establish a branch in county i, and $y_i = 0$ otherwise.)
b. Suppose that two PPBs can be established in the region. Where should they be located to maximize the population served?
c. Management learned that a bank located in county 5 is considering selling. If CHB purchases this bank, the requisite PPB will be established in county 5, and a base for beginning expansion in the region will also be established. What advice would you give the management of CHB?

16. The Northshore Bank is working to develop an efficient work schedule for full-time and part-time tellers. The schedule must provide for efficient operation of the bank including adequate customer service, employee breaks, and so on. On Fridays the bank is open from 9:00 A.M. to 7:00 P.M. The number of tellers necessary to provide adequate customer service during each hour of operation is summarized here.

Time	Number of Tellers	Time	Number of Tellers
9:00 A.M.–10:00 A.M.	6	2:00 P.M.–3:00 P.M.	6
10:00 A.M.–11:00 A.M.	4	3:00 P.M.–4:00 P.M.	4
11:00 A.M.–Noon	8	4:00 P.M.–5:00 P.M.	7
Noon–1:00 P.M.	10	5:00 P.M.–6:00 P.M.	6
1:00 P.M.–2:00 P.M.	9	6:00 P.M.–7:00 P.M.	6

Each full-time employee starts on the hour and works a 4-hour shift, followed by 1 hour for lunch and then a 3-hour shift. Part-time employees work one 4-hour shift beginning on the hour. Considering salary and fringe benefits, full-time employees cost the bank $15 per hour ($105 a day), and part-time employees cost the bank $8 per hour ($32 per day).

a. Formulate an integer programming model that can be used to develop a schedule that will satisfy customer service needs at a minimum employee cost. (*Hint:* Let x_i = number of full-time employees coming on duty at the beginning of hour i and y_i = number of part-time employees coming on duty at the beginning of hour i.)
b. Solve the LP Relaxation of your model in part (a).
c. Solve for the optimal schedule of tellers. Comment on the solution.
d. After reviewing the solution to part (c), the bank manager realized that some additional requirements must be specified. Specifically, she wants to ensure that one full-time employee is on duty at all times and that there is a staff of at least five full-time employees. Revise your model to incorporate these additional requirements and solve for the optimal solution.

17. Refer to the Ohio Trust bank location problem introduced in Section 7.3. Table 7.3 shows the counties under consideration and the adjacent counties.

a. Write the complete integer programming model for expansion into the following counties only: Lorain, Huron, Richland, Ashland, Wayne, Medina, and Knox.
b. Use trial and error to solve the problem in part (a).
c. Use a computer program for integer programs to solve the problem.

18. Refer to the Salem Foods share of choices problem in Section 7.3 and address the following issues. It is rumored that King's is getting out of the frozen pizza business. If so, the major competitor for Salem Foods will be the Antonio's brand pizza.

a. Compute the overall utility for the Antonio's brand pizza for each of the consumers in Table 7.4.
b. Assume that Salem's only competitor is the Antonio's brand pizza. Formulate and solve the share of choices problem that will maximize market share. What is the best product design and what share of the market can be expected?

19. Burnside Marketing Research conducted a study for Barker Foods on some designs for a new dry cereal. Three attributes were found to be most influential in determining which cereal had the best taste: ratio of wheat to corn in the cereal flake, type of sweetener (sugar, honey, or artificial), and the presence or absence of flavor bits. Seven children participated in taste tests and provided the following part-worths for the attributes.

Child	Wheat/Corn Low	High	Sugar	Sweetener Honey	Artificial	Flavor Bits Present	Absent
1	15	35	30	40	25	15	9
2	30	20	40	35	35	8	11
3	40	25	20	40	10	7	14
4	35	30	25	20	30	15	18
5	25	40	40	20	35	18	14
6	20	25	20	35	30	9	16
7	30	15	25	40	40	20	11

a. Suppose the overall utility (sum of part-worths) of the current favorite cereal is 75 for each child. What is the product design that will maximize the share of choices for the seven children in the sample?
b. Assume the overall utility of the current favorite cereal for the first four children in the group is 70, and the overall utility of the current favorite cereal for the last three children in the group is 80. What is the product design that will maximize the share of choices for the seven children in the sample?

20. Refer to Problem 14. Suppose that management determined that its cost estimates to modernize the New York plants were too low. Specifically, suppose that the actual cost is $40 million to modernize each plant.
    a. What changes in your previous 0-1 integer linear programming model are needed to incorporate these changes in costs?
    b. For these cost changes, what recommendations would you now provide management regarding the modernization plan?
    c. Reconsider the solution obtained using the revised cost figures. Suppose that management decides that closing two plants in the same state is not acceptable. How could this policy restriction be added to your 0-1 integer programming model?
    d. Based on the cost revision and the policy restriction presented in part (c), what recommendations would you now provide management regarding the modernization plan?

21. The Bayside Art Gallery is considering installing a video camera security system to reduce its insurance premiums. A diagram of the eight display rooms that Bayside uses for exhibitions is shown in Figure 7.13; the openings between the rooms are numbered 1–13. A security firm proposed that two-way cameras be installed at some room openings. Each camera has the ability to monitor the two rooms between which the camera is located. For example, if a camera were located at opening number 4, rooms 1 and 4 would be covered; if a camera were located at opening 11, rooms 7 and 8 would be covered; and so on. Management decided not to locate a camera system at the entrance to the display rooms. The objective is to provide security coverage for all eight rooms using the minimum number of two-way cameras.
    a. Formulate a 0-1 integer linear programming model that will enable Bayside's management to determine the locations for the camera systems.
    b. Solve the model formulated in part (a) to determine how many two-way cameras to purchase and where they should be located.
    c. Suppose that management wants to provide additional security coverage for room 7. Specifically, management wants room 7 to be covered by two cameras. How would your model formulated in part (a) have to change to accommodate this policy restriction?
    d. With the policy restriction specified in part (c), determine how many two-way camera systems will need to be purchased and where they will be located.

FIGURE 7.13 DIAGRAM OF DISPLAY ROOMS FOR BAYSIDE ART GALLERY

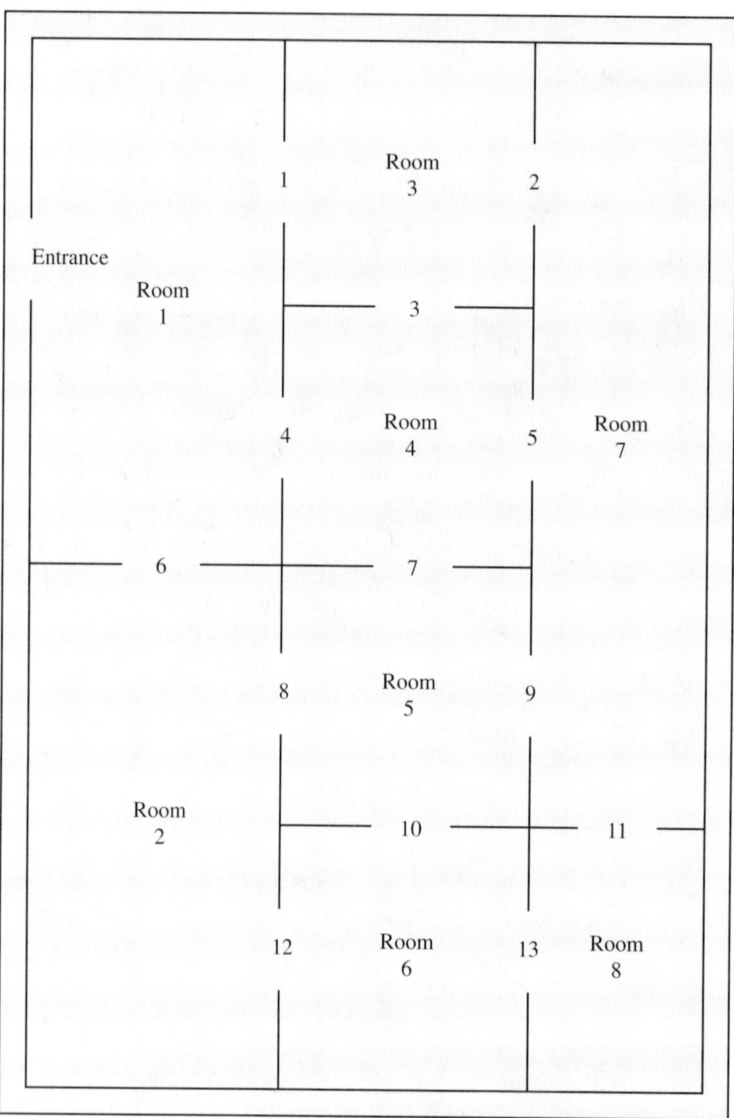

22. The Delta Group is a management consulting firm specializing in the health care industry. A team is being formed to study possible new markets, and a linear programming model has been developed for selecting team members. However, one constraint the president imposed is a team size of three, five, or seven members. The staff cannot figure out how to incorporate this requirement in the model. The current model requires that team members be selected from three departments and uses the following variable definitions.

x_1 = the number of employees selected from department 1
x_2 = the number of employees selected from department 2
x_3 = the number of employees selected from department 3

Show the staff how to write constraints that will ensure that the team will consist of three, five, or seven employees. The following integer variables should be helpful.

$$y_1 = \begin{cases} 1 & \text{if team size is 3} \\ 0 & \text{otherwise} \end{cases}$$

$$y_2 = \begin{cases} 1 & \text{if team size is 5} \\ 0 & \text{otherwise} \end{cases}$$

$$y_3 = \begin{cases} 1 & \text{if team size is 7} \\ 0 & \text{otherwise} \end{cases}$$

23. Roedel Electronics produces a variety of electrical components, including a remote controller for televisions and a remote controller for VCRs. Each controller consists of three subassemblies that are manufactured by Roedel: a base, a cartridge, and a keypad. Both controllers use the same base subassembly, but different cartridge and keypad subassemblies.

Roedel's sales forecast indicates that 7000 TV controllers and 5000 VCR controllers will be needed to satisfy demand during the upcoming Christmas season. Because only 500 hours of in-house manufacturing time are available, Roedel is considering purchasing some, or all, of the subassemblies from outside suppliers. If Roedel manufactures a subassembly in-house, it incurs a fixed setup cost as well as a variable manufacturing cost. The following table shows the setup cost, the manufacturing time per subassembly, the manufacturing cost per subassembly, and the cost to purchase each of the subassemblies from an outside supplier.

Subassembly	**Setup Cost ($)**	**Manufacturing Time per Unit (min.)**	**Manufacturing Cost per Unit ($)**	**Purchase Cost per Unit ($)**
Base	1000	0.9	0.40	0.65
TV cartridge	1200	2.2	2.90	3.45
VCR cartridge	1900	3.0	3.15	3.70
TV keypad	1500	0.8	0.30	0.50
VCR keypad	1500	1.0	0.55	0.70

a. Determine how many units of each subassembly Roedel should manufacture and how many units Roedel should purchase. What is the total manufacturing and purchase cost associated with your recommendation?

b. Suppose Roedel is considering purchasing new machinery to produce VCR cartridges. For the new machinery, the setup cost is $3000; the manufacturing time is 2.5 minutes per cartridge, and the manufacturing cost is $2.60 per cartridge. Assuming that the new machinery is purchased, determine how many units of each subassembly Roedel should manufacture and how many units of each subassembly Roedel should purchase. What is the total manufacturing and purchase cost associated with your recommendation? Do you think the new machinery should be purchased? Explain.

24. A mathematical programming system named SilverScreener uses a 0-1 integer programming model to help theater managers decide which movies to show on a weekly basis in a multiple-screen theater (*Interfaces,* May/June 2001). Suppose that management of Valley Cinemas would like to investigate the potential of using a similar scheduling system for their chain of multiple-screen theaters. Valley selected a small two-screen movie theater for the pilot testing and would like to develop an integer programming model to help schedule movies for the next four weeks. Six movies are available. The first week each

movie is available, the last week each movie can be shown, and the maximum number of weeks that each movie can run are shown here.

Movie	First Week Available	Last Week Available	Max. Run (weeks)
1	1	2	2
2	1	3	2
3	1	1	2
4	2	4	2
5	3	6	3
6	3	5	3

The overall viewing schedule for the theater is composed of the individual schedules for each of the six movies. For each movie a schedule must be developed that specifies the week the movie starts and the number of consecutive weeks it will run. For instance, one possible schedule for movie 2 is for it to start in week 1 and run for two weeks. Theater policy requires that once a movie is started it must be shown in consecutive weeks. It cannot be stopped and restarted again. To represent the schedule possibilities for each movie, the following decision variables were developed:

$$x_{ijw} = \begin{cases} 1 & \text{if movie } i \text{ is scheduled to start in week } j \text{ and run for } w \text{ weeks} \\ 0 & \text{otherwise} \end{cases}$$

For example, $x_{532} = 1$ means that the schedule selected for movie 5 is to begin in week 3 and run for two weeks. For each movie, a separate variable is given for each possible schedule.

a. Three schedules are associated with movie 1. List the variables that represent these schedules.
b. Write a constraint requiring that only one schedule be selected for movie 1.
c. Write a constraint requiring that only one schedule be selected for movie 5.
d. What restricts the number of movies that can be shown in week 1? Write a constraint that restricts the number of movies selected for viewing in week 1.
e. Write a constraint that restricts the number of movies selected for viewing in week 3.

25. East Coast Trucking provides service from Boston to Miami using regional offices located in Boston, New York, Philadelphia, Baltimore, Washington, Richmond, Raleigh, Florence, Savannah, Jacksonville, and Tampa. The number of miles between each of the regional offices is provided in the following table.

	New York	Philadelphia	Baltimore	Washington	Richmond	Raleigh	Florence	Savannah	Jacksonville	Tampa	Miami
Boston	211	320	424	459	565	713	884	1056	1196	1399	1669
New York		109	213	248	354	502	673	845	985	1188	1458
Philadelphia			104	139	245	393	564	736	876	1079	1349
Baltimore				35	141	289	460	632	772	975	1245
Washington					106	254	425	597	737	940	1210
Richmond						148	319	491	631	834	1104
Raleigh							171	343	483	686	956
Florence								172	312	515	785
Savannah									140	343	613
Jacksonville										203	473
Tampa											270

The company's expansion plans involve constructing service facilities in some of the cities where a regional office is located. Each regional office must be within 400 miles of a service facility. For instance, if a service facility is constructed in Richmond, it can provide service to regional offices located in New York, Philadelphia, Baltimore, Washington, Richmond, Raleigh, and Florence. Management would like to determine the minimum number of service facilities needed and where they should be located.

a. Formulate an integer linear program that can be used to determine the minimum number of service facilities needed and their location.
b. Solve the linear program formulated in part (a). How many service facilities are required, and where should they be located?
c. Suppose that each service facility can only provide service to regional offices within 300 miles. How many service facilities are required, and where should they be located?

Case Problem 1 TEXTBOOK PUBLISHING

ASW Publishing, Inc., a small publisher of college textbooks, must make a decision regarding which books to publish next year. The books under consideration are listed in the following table, along with the projected three-year sales expected from each book.

Book Subject	Type of Book	Projected Sales ($1000s)
Business calculus	New	20
Finite mathematics	Revision	30
General statistics	New	15
Mathematical statistics	New	10
Business statistics	Revision	25
Finance	New	18
Financial accounting	New	25
Managerial accounting	Revision	50
English literature	New	20
German	New	30

The books listed as revisions are texts that ASW already has under contract; these texts are being considered for publication as new editions. The books that are listed as new have been reviewed by the company, but contracts have not yet been signed.

Three individuals in the company can be assigned to these projects, all of whom have varying amounts of time available; John has 60 days available, and Susan and Monica both have 40 days available. The days required by each person to complete each project are shown in the following table. For instance, if the business calculus book is published, it will require 30 days of John's time and 40 days of Susan's time. An "X" indicates that the person will not be used on the project. Note that at least two staff members will be assigned to each project except the finance book.

Book Subject	John	Susan	Monica
Business calculus	30	40	X
Finite mathematics	16	24	X
General statistics	24	X	30

(continued)

Book Subject	John	Susan	Monica
Mathematical statistics	20	X	24
Business statistics	10	X	16
Finance	X	X	14
Financial accounting	X	24	26
Managerial accounting	X	28	30
English literature	40	34	30
German	X	50	36

ASW will not publish more than two statistics books or more than one accounting text in a single year. In addition, management decided that one of the mathematics books (business calculus or finite math) must be published, but not both.

Managerial Report

Prepare a report for the managing editor of ASW that describes your findings and recommendations regarding the best publication strategy for next year. In carrying out your analysis, assume that the fixed costs and the sales revenues per unit are approximately equal for all books; management is interested primarily in maximizing the total unit sales volume.

The managing editor also asked that you include recommendations regarding the following possible changes.

1. If it would be advantageous to do so, Susan can be moved off another project to allow her to work 12 more days.
2. If it would be advantageous to do so, Monica can also be made available for another 10 days.
3. If one or more of the revisions could be postponed for another year, should they be? Clearly the company will risk losing market share by postponing a revision.

Include details of your analysis in an appendix to your report.

Case Problem 2 YEAGER NATIONAL BANK

Using aggressive mail promotion with low introductory interest rates, Yeager National Bank (YNB) built a large base of credit card customers throughout the continental United States. Currently, all customers send their regular payments to the bank's corporate office located in Charlotte, North Carolina. Daily collections from customers making their regular payments are substantial, with an average of approximately $600,000. YNB estimates that it makes about 15 percent on its funds and would like to ensure that customer payments are credited to the bank's account as soon as possible. For instance, if it takes five days for a customer's payment to be sent through the mail, processed, and credited to the bank's account, YNB has potentially lost five days' worth of interest income. Although the time needed for this collection process cannot be completely eliminated, reducing it can be beneficial given the large amounts of money involved.

Instead of having all its credit card customers send their payments to Charlotte, YNB is considering having customers send their payments to one or more regional collection centers, referred to in the banking industry as lockboxes. Four lockbox locations have been proposed: Phoenix, Salt Lake City, Atlanta, and Boston. To determine which lockboxes to open and where lockbox customers should send their payments, YNB divided its customer base into five geographical regions: Northwest, Southwest, Central, Northeast, and Southeast. Every customer in the same region will be instructed to send his or her payment to the same lockbox. The following table shows the average number of days it takes before a customer's payment is credited to the bank's account when the payment is sent from each of the regions to each of the potential lockboxes.

Customer Zone	Location of Lockbox				Daily Collection ($1000s)
	Phoenix	**Salt Lake City**	**Atlanta**	**Boston**	
Northwest	4	2	4	4	80
Southwest	2	3	4	6	90
Central	5	3	3	4	150
Northeast	5	4	3	2	180
Southeast	4	6	2	3	100

Managerial Report

Dave Wolff, the vice president for cash management, asked you to prepare a report containing your recommendations for the number of lockboxes and the best lockbox locations. Mr. Wolff is primarily concerned with minimizing lost interest income, but he wants you to also consider the effect of an annual fee charged for maintaining a lockbox at any location. Although the amount of the fee is unknown at this time, we can assume that the fees will be in the range of $20,000 to $30,000 per location. Once good potential locations have been selected, Mr. Wolff will inquire as to the annual fees.

Case Problem 3 PRODUCTION SCHEDULING WITH CHANGEOVER COSTS

Buckeye Manufacturing produces heads for engines used in the manufacture of trucks. The production line is highly complex, and it measures 900 feet in length. Two types of engine heads are produced on this line: the P-Head and the H-Head. The P-Head is used in heavy-duty trucks and the H-Head is used in smaller trucks. Because only one type of head can be produced at a time, the line is set up to manufacture either the P-Head or the H-Head, but not both. Changeovers are made over a weekend; costs are $500 in going from a setup for the P-Head to a setup for the H-Head, and vice versa. When set up for the P-Head, the maximum production rate is 100 units per week and when set up for the H-Head, the maximum production rate is 80 units per week.

Buckeye just shut down for the week after using the line to produce the P-Head. The manager wants to plan production and changeovers for the next eight weeks. Currently, Buckeye's inventory consists of 125 P-Heads and 143 H-Heads. Inventory carrying costs are charged at an annual rate of 19.5 percent of the value of inventory. The production cost for the P-Head is $225, and the production cost for the H-Head is $310. The objective in developing a production schedule is to minimize the sum of production cost, plus inventory carrying cost, plus changeover cost.

Buckeye received the following requirements schedule from its customer (an engine assembly plant) for the next nine weeks.

	Product Demand	
Week	P-Head	H-Head
1	55	38
2	55	38
3	44	30
4	0	0
5	45	48
6	45	48
7	36	58
8	35	57
9	35	58

Safety stock requirements are such that week-ending inventory must provide for at least 80 percent of the next week's demand.

Managerial Report

Prepare a report for Buckeye's management with a production and changeover schedule for the next eight weeks. Be sure to note how much of the total cost is due to production, how much is due to inventory, and how much is due to changeover.

Appendix 7.1 EXCEL SOLUTION OF INTEGER LINEAR PROGRAMS

Worksheet formulation and solution for integer linear programs are similar to that for linear programming problems. Actually the worksheet formulation is exactly the same, but some additional information must be provided when setting up the **Solver Parameters** and **LP Simplex Solver Options** dialog boxes. First, constraints must be added in the **Solver Parameters** dialog box to identify the integer variables. In addition, the value for **Tolerance** under the **Integer** tab of the **LP Simplex Solver Options** dialog box may need to be adjusted to obtain a solution.

Let us demonstrate the Excel solution of an integer linear program by showing how Excel can be used to solve the Eastborne Realty problem. The worksheet with the optimal solution is shown in Figure 7.14. We will describe the key elements of the worksheet, describe how to obtain the solution, and then interpret the solution.

Formulation

The data and descriptive labels appear in cells A1:G7 of the worksheet in Figure 7.14. The screened cells in the lower portion of the worksheet contain the information required by the Excel Solver (decision variables, objective function, constraint left-hand sides, and constraint right-hand sides).

Decision Variables Cells B17:C17 are reserved for the decision variables. The optimal solution is to purchase four townhouses and two apartment buildings.

Objective Function The formula =SUMPRODUCT(B7:C7,B17:C17) has been placed into cell B13 to reflect the annual cash flow associated with the solution. The optimal solution provides an annual cash flow of $70,000.

Left-Hand Sides The left-hand sides for the three constraints are placed into cells F15:F17.

Cell F15 =SUMPRODUCT (B4:C4, $B$17:$C$17)
(Copy to sell F16)
Cell F17 =B17

FIGURE 7.14 EXCEL SOLUTION FOR THE EASTBORNE REALTY PROBLEM

EXCEL file
Eastborne

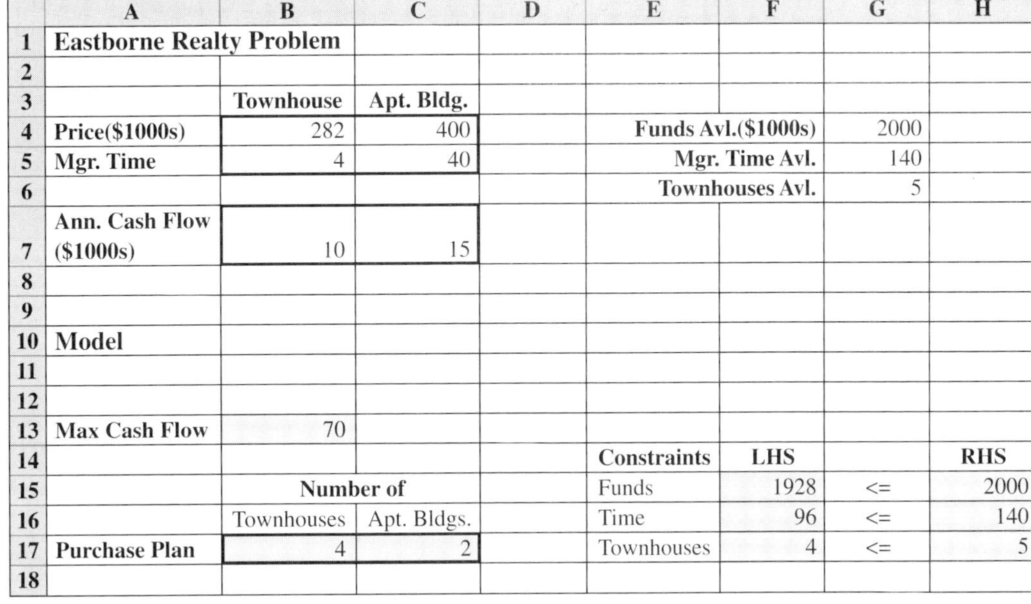

	A	B	C	D	E	F	G	H
1	**Eastborne Realty Problem**							
2								
3		**Townhouse**	**Apt. Bldg.**					
4	**Price($1000s)**	282	400			**Funds Avl.($1000s)**	2000	
5	**Mgr. Time**	4	40			**Mgr. Time Avl.**	140	
6						**Townhouses Avl.**	5	
7	**Ann. Cash Flow ($1000s)**	10	15					
8								
9								
10	**Model**							
11								
12								
13	**Max Cash Flow**	70						
14					**Constraints**	**LHS**		**RHS**
15		**Number of**			Funds	1928	<=	2000
16		Townhouses	Apt. Bldgs.		Time	96	<=	140
17	**Purchase Plan**	4	2		Townhouses	4	<=	5
18								

Right-Hand Sides The right-hand sides for the three constraints are placed into cells H15:H17.

Cell H15 =G4 (Copy to cells H16:H17)

Excel Solution

Excel 2007 Users: Select ***Add-ins,*** *then choose* ***Premium Solver.***

Begin the solution procedure by selecting **Premium Solver** from the **Tools** menu and entering the proper values into the **Solver Parameters** dialog box as shown in Figure 7.15.

FIGURE 7.15 SOLVER PARAMETERS DIALOG BOX FOR THE EASTBORNE REALTY PROBLEM

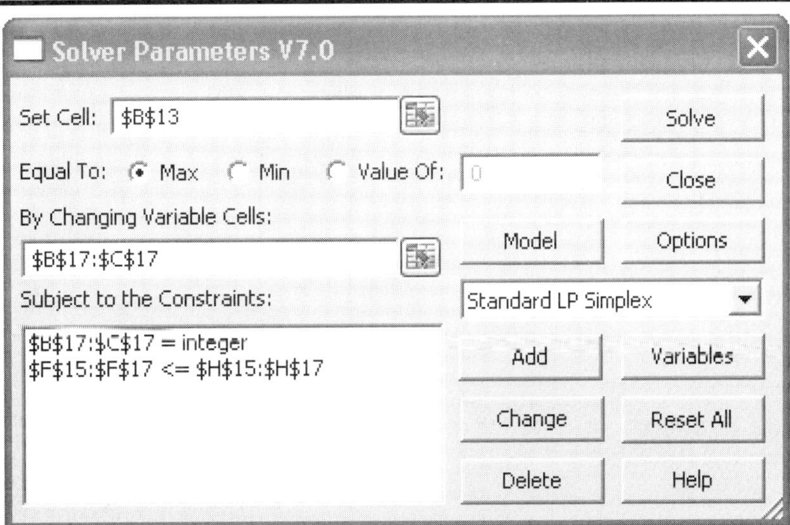

The first constraint shown is $B$17:$C$17 = integer. This constraint tells Solver that the decision variables in cell B17 and cell C17 must be integer. The integer requirement is created by using the **Add-Constraint** procedure. $B$17:$C17 is entered in the left-hand box of the **Cell Reference** area and **"int"** rather than <=, =, or => is selected as the form of the constraint. When **"int"** is selected, the term integer automatically appears as the right-hand side of the constraint. Figure 7.15 shows the additional information required to complete the **Solver Parameters** dialog box.

Next the **Options** button must be selected. The option **Assume Non-Negative** must be checked under the **General** tab of the **LP Simplex Solver Options** dialog box. Figure 7.16 shows the **LP Simplex Solver Options** dialog box for the Eastborne Realty problem after completing this step. Clicking **OK** in the **LP Simplex Solver Options** dialog box and selecting **Solve** in the **Solver Parameters** dialog box will instruct Solver to compute the optimal integer solution. The worksheet in Figure 7.14 shows that the optimal solution is to purchase four townhouses and two apartment buildings. The annual cash flow is $70,000.

FIGURE 7.16 SOLVER OPTIONS DIALOG BOX FOR THE EASTBORNE REALTY PROBLEM

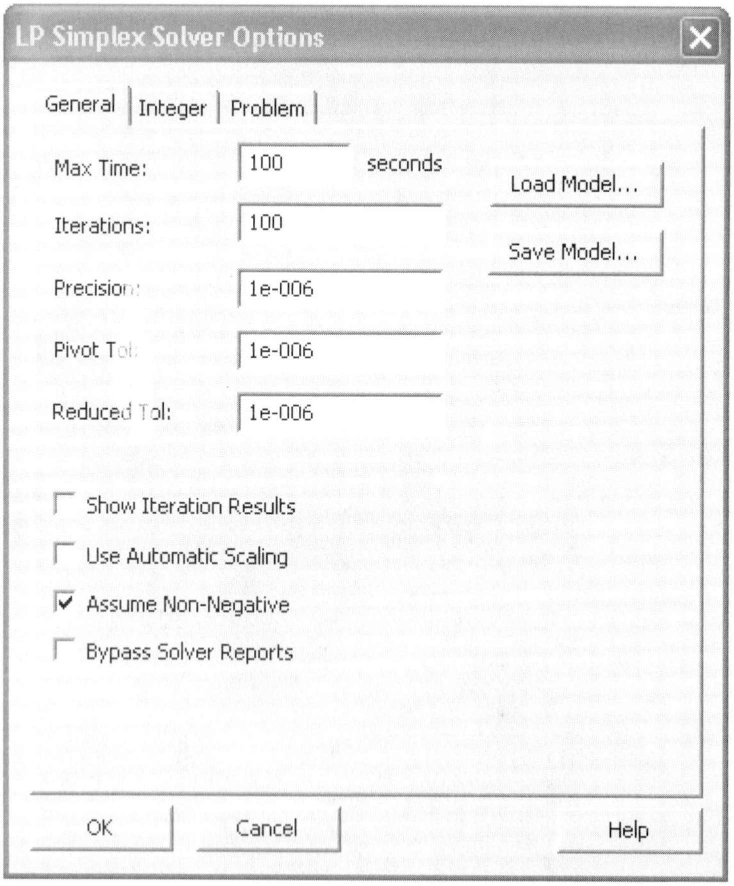

0-1 variables are identified with the "bin" designation in the Solver Parameters dialog box.

If binary variables are present in an integer linear programming problem, you must select the designation **"bin"** instead of **"int"** when setting up the constraints in the **Solver Parameters** dialog box.

The time required to obtain an optimal solution can be highly variable for integer linear programs. If an optimal solution cannot be found within a reasonable amount of time, the tolerance can be reset to 5 percent, or some higher value, so that the search procedure may stop when a near-optimal solution (within the tolerance of being optimal) has been found. To reset the tolerance, click the **Integer** tab in the **LP Simplex Solver Options** dialog box (see Figure 7.16). Then, when the new dialog box appears (see Figure 7.17), enter the desired value in the **Tolerance** box. Figure 7.17 shows a 0 in the **Tolerance** box for the Eastborne Realty problem. In a more difficult problem, .05 could be entered to allow the solution procedure to stop with a solution within 5 percent of optimal.

FIGURE 7.17 INTEGER OPTIONS DIALOG BOX FOR THE EASTBORNE REALTY PROBLEM

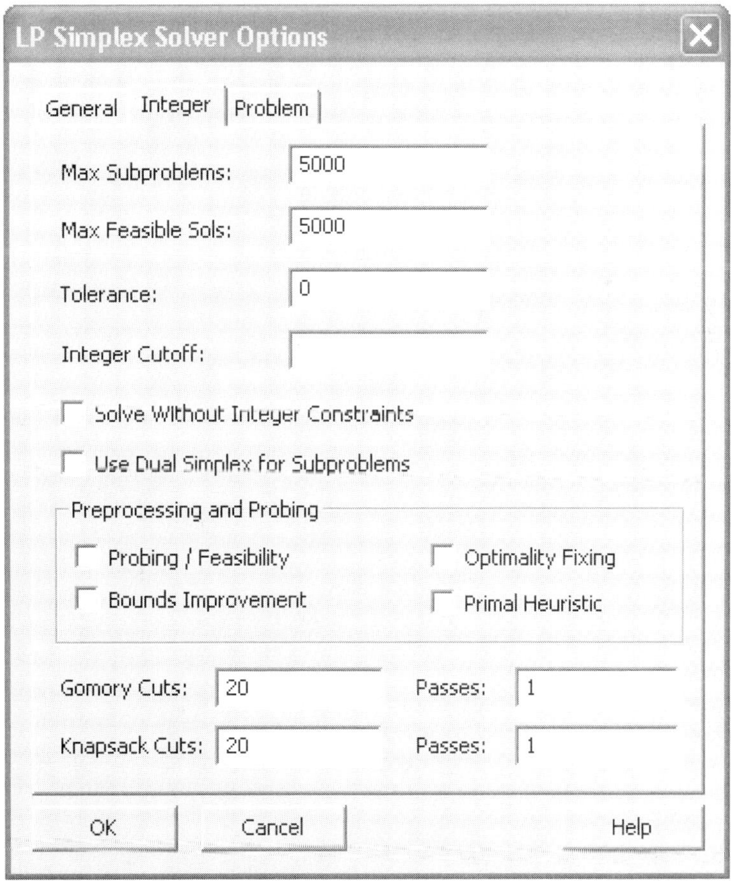

CHAPTER 13

Decision Analysis

CONTENTS

Decision analysis can be used to develop an optimal strategy when a decision maker is faced with several decision alternatives and an uncertain or risk-filled pattern of future events. For example, Ohio Edison used decision analysis to choose the best type of particulate control equipment for coal-fired generating units when it faced future uncertainties concerning sulfur content requirements, construction costs, and so on. The State of North Carolina used decision analysis in evaluating whether to implement a medical screening test to detect metabolic disorders in newborns. Thus, decision analysis repeatedly proves its value in decision making. The Management Science in Action, Decision Analysis at Eastman Kodak, describes how the use of decision analysis added approximately $1 billion in value.

Even when a careful decision analysis has been conducted, uncertain future events make the final consequence uncertain. In some cases, the selected decision alternative may provide good or excellent results. In other cases, a relatively unlikely future event may occur, causing the selected decision alternative to provide only fair or even poor results. The risk associated with any decision alternative is a direct result of the uncertainty associated with the final consequence. A good decision analysis includes risk analysis. Through risk analysis the decision maker is provided with probability information about the favorable as well as the unfavorable consequences that may occur.

MANAGEMENT SCIENCE IN ACTION

DECISION ANALYSIS AT EASTMAN KODAK*

Clemen and Kwit conducted a study to determine the value of decision analysis at the Eastman Kodak company. The study involved an analysis of 178 decision analysis projects over a 10-year period. The projects involved a variety of applications including strategy development, vendor selection, process analysis, new-product brainstorming, product-portfolio selection, and emission-reduction analysis. These projects required 14,372 hours of analyst time and the involvement of many other individuals at Kodak over the 10-year period. The shortest projects took less than 20 hours, and the longest projects took almost a year to complete.

Most decision analysis projects are one-time activities, which makes it difficult to measure the value added to the corporation. Clemen and Kwit used detailed records that were available and some innovative approaches to develop estimates of the incremental dollar value generated by the decision analysis projects. Their conservative estimate of the average value per project was $6.65 million and their optimistic estimate of the average value per project was $16.35 million. Their analysis led to the conclusion that all projects taken together added more than $1 billion in value to Eastman Kodak. Using these estimates, Clemen and Kwit concluded that decision analysis returned substantial value to the company. Indeed, they concluded that the value added by the projects was at least 185 times the cost of the analysts' time.

In addition to the monetary benefits, the authors point out that decision analysis adds value by facilitating discussion among stakeholders, promoting careful thinking about strategies, providing a common language for discussing the elements of a decision problem, and speeding implementation by helping to build consensus among decision makers. In commenting on the value of decision analysis at Eastman Kodak, Nancy L. S. Sousa said, "As General Manager, New Businesses, VP Health Imaging, Eastman Kodak, I encourage all of the business planners to use the decision and risk principles and processes as part of evaluating new business opportunities. The processes have clearly led to better decisions about entry and exit of businesses."

Although measuring the value of a particular decision analysis project can be difficult, it would be difficult to dispute the success that decision analysis had at Kodak.

*Based on Robert T. Clemen and Robert C. Kwit, "The Value of Decision Analysis at Eastman Kodak Company," *Interfaces* (September/October 2001): 74–92.

We begin the study of decision analysis by considering problems that involve reasonably few decision alternatives and reasonably few possible future events. Influence diagrams and payoff tables are introduced to provide a structure for the decision problem and to illustrate the fundamentals of decision analysis. We then introduce decision trees to show the sequential nature of decision problems. Decision trees are used to analyze more complex problems and to identify an optimal sequence of decisions, referred to as an optimal decision strategy. Sensitivity analysis shows how changes in various aspects of the problem affect the recommended decision alternative.

13.1 PROBLEM FORMULATION

The first step in the decision analysis process is problem formulation. We begin with a verbal statement of the problem. We then identify the **decision alternatives,** the uncertain future events, referred to as **chance events,** and the **consequences** associated with each decision alternative and each chance event outcome. Let us begin by considering a construction project of the Pittsburgh Development Corporation.

Pittsburgh Development Corporation (PDC) purchased land that will be the site of a new luxury condominium complex. The location provides a spectacular view of downtown Pittsburgh and the Golden Triangle where the Allegheny and Monongahela rivers meet to form the Ohio River. PDC plans to price the individual condominium units between $300,000 and $1,400,000.

PDC commissioned preliminary architectural drawings for three different projects: one with 30 condominiums, one with 60 condominiums, and one with 90 condominiums. The financial success of the project depends upon the size of the condominium complex and the chance event concerning the demand for the condominiums. The statement of the PDC decision problem is to select the size of the new luxury condominium project that will lead to the largest profit given the uncertainty concerning the demand for the condominiums.

Given the statement of the problem, it is clear that the decision is to select the best size for the condominium complex. PDC has the following three decision alternatives:

d_1 = a small complex with 30 condominiums
d_2 = a medium complex with 60 condominiums
d_3 = a large complex with 90 condominiums

A factor in selecting the best decision alternative is the uncertainty associated with the chance event concerning the demand for the condominiums. When asked about the possible demand for the condominiums, PDC's president acknowledged a wide range of possibilities, but decided that it would be adequate to consider two possible chance event outcomes: a strong demand and a weak demand.

In decision analysis, the possible outcomes for a chance event are referred to as the **states of nature.** The states of nature are defined so that one and only one of the possible states of nature will occur. For the PDC problem, the chance event concerning the demand for the condominiums has two states of nature:

s_1 = strong demand for the condominiums
s_2 = weak demand for the condominiums

Management must first select a decision alternative (complex size), then a state of nature follows (demand for the condominiums), and finally a consequence will occur. In this case, the consequence is PDC's profit.

Influence Diagrams

An **influence diagram** is a graphical device that shows the relationships among the decisions, the chance events, and the consequences for a decision problem. The **nodes** in an influence diagram represent the decisions, chance events, and consequences. Rectangles or squares depict **decision nodes,** circles or ovals depict **chance nodes,** and diamonds depict **consequence nodes.** The lines connecting the nodes, referred to as *arcs,* show the direction of influence that the nodes have on one another. Figure 13.1 shows the influence diagram for the PDC problem. The complex size is the decision node, demand is the chance node, and profit is the consequence node. The arcs connecting the nodes show that both the complex size and the demand influence PDC's profit.

Payoff Tables

Given the three decision alternatives and the two states of nature, which complex size should PDC choose? To answer this question, PDC will need to know the consequence associated with each decision alternative and each state of nature. In decision analysis, we refer to the consequence resulting from a specific combination of a decision alternative and a state of nature as a **payoff.** A table showing payoffs for all combinations of decision alternatives and states of nature is a **payoff table.**

Payoffs can be expressed in terms of profit, cost, time, distance, or any other measure appropriate for the decision problem being analyzed.

Because PDC wants to select the complex size that provides the largest profit, profit is used as the consequence. The payoff table with profits expressed in millions of dollars is shown in Table 13.1. Note, for example, that if a medium complex is built and demand turns out to be strong, a profit of $14 million will be realized. We will use the notation V_{ij} to denote the payoff associated with decision alternative *i* and state of nature *j*. Using Table 13.1, $V_{31} = 20$ indicates a payoff of $20 million occurs if the decision is to build a large complex (d_3) and the strong demand state of nature (s_1) occurs. Similarly, $V_{32} = -9$ indicates a loss of $9 million if the decision is to build a large complex (d_3) and the weak demand state of nature (s_2) occurs.

Decision Trees

A **decision tree** provides a graphical representation of the decision-making process. Figure 13.2 presents a decision tree for the PDC problem. Note that the decision tree shows the natural or logical progression that will occur over time. First, PDC must make a decision

FIGURE 13.1 INFLUENCE DIAGRAM FOR THE PDC PROJECT

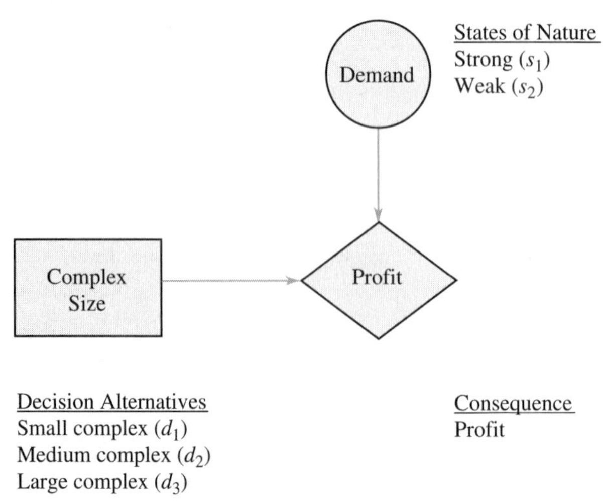

TABLE 13.1 PAYOFF TABLE FOR THE PDC CONDOMINIUM PROJECT (PAYOFFS IN $ MILLIONS)

	State of Nature	
Decision Alternative	Strong Demand s_1	Weak Demand s_2
Small complex, d_1	8	7
Medium complex, d_2	14	5
Large complex, d_3	20	−9

regarding the size of the condominium complex (d_1, d_2, or d_3). Then, after the decision is implemented, either state of nature s_1 or s_2 will occur. The number at each end point of the tree indicates the payoff associated with a particular sequence. For example, the topmost payoff of 8 indicates that an $8 million profit is anticipated if PDC constructs a small condominium complex (d_1) and demand turns out to be strong (s_1). The next payoff of 7 indicates an anticipated profit of $7 million if PDC constructs a small condominium complex (d_1) and demand turns out to be weak (s_2). Thus, the decision tree shows graphically the sequences of decision alternatives and states of nature that provide the six possible payoffs for PDC.

If you have a payoff table, you can develop a decision tree. Try Problem 1(a).

The decision tree in Figure 13.2 shows four nodes, numbered 1–4. Squares are used to depict decision nodes and circles are used to depict chance nodes. Thus, node 1 is a decision node, and nodes 2, 3, and 4 are chance nodes. The **branches,** which connect the nodes, leaving the decision node correspond to the decision alternatives. The branches leaving each chance node correspond to the states of nature. The payoffs are shown at the end of the states-of-nature branches. We now turn to the question: How can the decision maker use the information in the payoff table or the decision tree to select the best decision alternative? Several approaches may be used.

FIGURE 13.2 DECISION TREE FOR THE PDC CONDOMINIUM PROJECT (PAYOFFS IN $ MILLIONS)

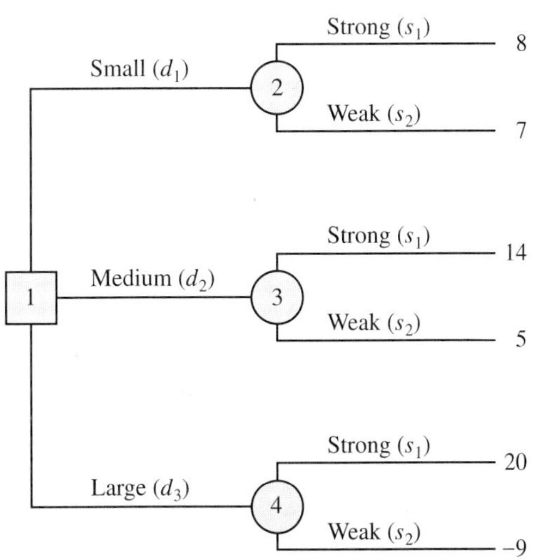

NOTES AND COMMENTS

1. Experts in problem solving agree that the first step in solving a complex problem is to decompose it into a series of smaller subproblems. Decision trees provide a useful way to show how a problem can be decomposed and the sequential nature of the decision process.
2. People often view the same problem from different perspectives. Thus, the discussion regarding the development of a decision tree may provide additional insight about the problem.

13.2 DECISION MAKING WITHOUT PROBABILITIES

Many people think of a good decision as one in which the consequence is good. However, in some instances, a good, well-thought-out decision may still lead to a bad or undesirable consequence.

In this section we consider approaches to decision making that do not require knowledge of the probabilities of the states of nature. These approaches are appropriate in situations in which the decision maker has little confidence in his or her ability to assess the probabilities, or in which a simple best-case and worst-case analysis is desirable. Because different approaches sometimes lead to different decision recommendations, the decision maker needs to understand the approaches available and then select the specific approach that, according to the decision maker's judgment, is the most appropriate.

Optimistic Approach

The **optimistic approach** evaluates each decision alternative in terms of the *best* payoff that can occur. The decision alternative that is recommended is the one that provides the best possible payoff. For a problem in which maximum profit is desired, as in the PDC problem, the optimistic approach would lead the decision maker to choose the alternative corresponding to the largest profit. For problems involving minimization, this approach leads to choosing the alternative with the smallest payoff.

For a maximization problem, the optimistic approach often is referred to as the maximax approach; for a minimization problem, the corresponding terminology is minimin.

To illustrate the optimistic approach, we use it to develop a recommendation for the PDC problem. First, we determine the maximum payoff for each decision alternative; then we select the decision alternative that provides the overall maximum payoff. These steps systematically identify the decision alternative that provides the largest possible profit. Table 13.2 illustrates these steps.

Because 20, corresponding to d_3, is the largest payoff, the decision to construct the large condominium complex is the recommended decision alternative using the optimistic approach.

Conservative Approach

The **conservative approach** evaluates each decision alternative in terms of the *worst* payoff that can occur. The decision alternative recommended is the one that provides the best of the worst possible payoffs. For a problem in which the output measure is profit, as in the PDC problem, the conservative approach would lead the decision maker to choose the alternative that

TABLE 13.2 MAXIMUM PAYOFF FOR EACH PDC DECISION ALTERNATIVE

Decision Alternative	Maximum Payoff	
Small complex, d_1	8	
Medium complex, d_2	14	
Large complex, d_3	20	← Maximum of the maximum payoff values

TABLE 13.3 MINIMUM PAYOFF FOR EACH PDC DECISION ALTERNATIVE

Decision Alternative	Minimum Payoff	
Small complex, d_1	7	← Maximum of the minimum payoff values
Medium complex, d_2	5	
Large complex, d_3	−9	

maximizes the minimum possible profit that could be obtained. For problems involving minimization, this approach identifies the alternative that will minimize the maximum payoff.

For a maximization problem, the conservative approach is often referred to as the maximin approach; for a minimization problem, the corresponding terminology is minimax.

To illustrate the conservative approach, we use it to develop a recommendation for the PDC problem. First, we identify the minimum payoff for each of the decision alternatives; then we select the decision alternative that maximizes the minimum payoff. Table 13.3 illustrates these steps for the PDC problem.

Because 7, corresponding to d_1, yields the maximum of the minimum payoffs, the decision alternative of a small condominium complex is recommended. This decision approach is considered conservative because it identifies the worst possible payoffs and then recommends the decision alternative that avoids the possibility of extremely "bad" payoffs. In the conservative approach, PDC is guaranteed a profit of at least $7 million. Although PDC may make more, it *cannot* make less than $7 million.

Minimax Regret Approach

The **minimax regret approach** to decision making is neither purely optimistic nor purely conservative. Let us illustrate the minimax regret approach by showing how it can be used to select a decision alternative for the PDC problem.

Suppose that PDC constructs a small condominium complex (d_1) and demand turns out to be strong (s_1). Table 13.1 showed that the resulting profit for PDC would be $8 million. However, given that the strong demand state of nature (s_1) has occurred, we realize that the decision to construct a large condominium complex (d_3), yielding a profit of $20 million, would have been the best decision. The difference between the payoff for the best decision alternative ($20 million) and the payoff for the decision to construct a small condominium complex ($8 million) is the **opportunity loss, or regret,** associated with decision alternative d_1 when state of nature s_1 occurs; thus, for this case, the opportunity loss or regret is $20 million − $8 million = $12 million. Similarly, if PDC makes the decision to construct a medium condominium complex (d_2) and the strong demand state of nature (s_1) occurs, the opportunity loss, or regret, associated with d_2 would be $20 million − $14 million = $6 million.

In general the following expression represents the opportunity loss, or regret.

$$R_{ij} = |V_j^* - V_{ij}| \tag{13.1}$$

where

R_{ij} = the regret associated with decision alternative d_i and state of nature s_j
V_j^* = the payoff value[1] corresponding to the best decision for the state of nature s_j
V_{ij} = the payoff corresponding to decision alternative d_i and state of nature s_j

[1]In maximization problems, V_j^* will be the largest entry in column j of the payoff table. In minimization problems, V_j^* will be the smallest entry in column j of the payoff table.

TABLE 13.4 OPPORTUNITY LOSS, OR REGRET, TABLE FOR THE PDC CONDOMINIUM PROJECT ($ MILLIONS)

	State of Nature	
Decision Alternative	**Strong Demand s_1**	**Weak Demand s_2**
Small complex, d_1	12	0
Medium complex, d_2	6	2
Large complex, d_3	0	16

Note the role of the absolute value in equation (13.1). For minimization problems, the best payoff, V_j^*, is the smallest entry in column j. Because this value always is less than or equal to V_{ij}, the absolute value of the difference between V_j^* and V_{ij} ensures that the regret is always the magnitude of the difference.

Using equation (4.1) and the payoffs in Table 13.1, we can compute the regret associated with each combination of decision alternative d_i and state of nature s_j. Because the PDC problem is a maximization problem, V_j^* will be the largest entry in column j of the payoff table. Thus, to compute the regret, we simply subtract each entry in a column from the largest entry in the column. Table 13.4 shows the opportunity loss, or regret, table for the PDC problem.

The next step in applying the minimax regret approach is to list the maximum regret for each decision alternative; Table 13.5 shows the results for the PDC problem. Selecting the decision alternative with the *minimum* of the *maximum* regret values—hence, the name *minimax regret*—yields the minimax regret decision. For the PDC problem, the alternative to construct the medium condominium complex, with a corresponding maximum regret of $6 million, is the recommended minimax regret decision.

For practice in developing a decision recommendation using the optimistic, conservative, and minimax regret approaches, try Problem 1 (part b).

Note that the three approaches discussed in this section provide different recommendations, which in itself isn't bad. It simply reflects the difference in decision-making philosophies that underlie the various approaches. Ultimately, the decision maker will have to choose the most appropriate approach and then make the final decision accordingly. The main criticism of the approaches discussed in this section is that they do not consider any information about the probabilities of the various states of nature. In the next section we discuss an approach that utilizes probability information in selecting a decision alternative.

13.3 DECISION MAKING WITH PROBABILITIES

In many decision-making situations, we can obtain probability assessments for the states of nature. When such probabilities are available, we can use the **expected value approach** to identify the best decision alternative. Let us first define the expected value of a decision alternative and then apply it to the PDC problem.

TABLE 13.5 MAXIMUM REGRET FOR EACH PDC DECISION ALTERNATIVE

Decision Alternative	**Maximum Regret**	
Small complex, d_1	12	
Medium complex, d_2	6	← Minimum of the maximum regret
Large complex, d_3	16	

Let

$$N = \text{the number of states of nature}$$
$$P(s_j) = \text{the probability of state of nature } s_j$$

Because one and only one of the N states of nature can occur, the probabilities must satisfy two conditions:

$$P(s_j) \geq 0 \qquad \text{for all states of nature} \tag{13.2}$$

$$\sum_{j=1}^{N} P(s_j) = P(s_1) + P(s_2) + \cdots + P(s_N) = 1 \tag{13.3}$$

The **expected value (EV)** of decision alternative d_i is defined as follows:

$$\text{EV}(d_i) = \sum_{j=1}^{N} P(s_j)V_{ij} \tag{13.4}$$

In words, the expected value of a decision alternative is the sum of weighted payoffs for the decision alternative. The weight for a payoff is the probability of the associated state of nature and therefore the probability that the payoff will occur. Let us return to the PDC problem to see how the expected value approach can be applied.

PDC is optimistic about the potential for the luxury high-rise condominium complex. Suppose that this optimism leads to an initial subjective probability assessment of 0.8 that demand will be strong (s_1) and a corresponding probability of 0.2 that demand will be weak (s_2). Thus, $P(s_1) = 0.8$ and $P(s_2) = 0.2$. Using the payoff values in Table 13.1 and equation (13.4), we compute the expected value for each of the three decision alternatives as follows:

$$\text{EV}(d_1) = 0.8(8) + 0.2(7) = 7.8$$
$$\text{EV}(d_2) = 0.8(14) + 0.2(5) = 12.2$$
$$\text{EV}(d_3) = 0.8(20) + 0.2(-9) = 14.2$$

Thus, using the expected value approach, we find that the large condominium complex, with an expected value of $14.2 million, is the recommended decision.

Can you now use the expected value approach to develop a decision recommendation? Try Problem 4.

The calculations required to identify the decision alternative with the best expected value can be conveniently carried out on a decision tree. Figure 13.3 shows the decision tree for the PDC problem with state-of-nature branch probabilities. Working backward through the decision tree, we first compute the expected value at each chance node. That is, at each chance node, we weight each possible payoff by its probability of occurrence. By doing so, we obtain the expected values for nodes 2, 3, and 4, as shown in Figure 13.4.

Because the decision maker controls the branch leaving decision node 1 and because we are trying to maximize the expected profit, the best decision alternative at node 1 is d_3. Thus, the decision tree analysis leads to a recommendation of d_3 with an expected value of $14.2 million. Note that this recommendation is also obtained with the expected value approach in conjunction with the payoff table.

Computer software packages are available to help in constructing more complex decision trees. See Appendix 13.1.

Other decision problems may be substantially more complex than the PDC problem, but if a reasonable number of decision alternatives and states of nature are present, you can use the decision tree approach outlined here. First, draw a decision tree consisting of

FIGURE 13.3 PDC DECISION TREE WITH STATE-OF-NATURE BRANCH PROBABILITIES

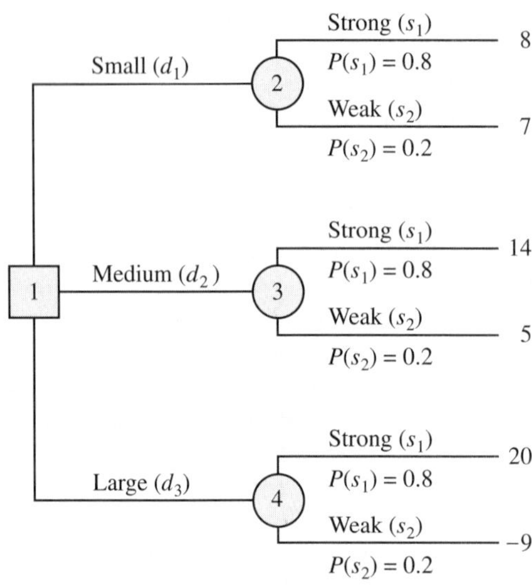

decision nodes, chance nodes, and branches that describe the sequential nature of the problem. If you use the expected value approach, the next step is to determine the probabilities for each of the states of nature and compute the expected value at each chance node. Then select the decision branch leading to the chance node with the best expected value. The decision alternative associated with this branch is the recommended decision.

The Management Science in Action, Early Detection of High-Risk Worker Disability Claims, describes how the Workers' Compensation Board of British Columbia used a decision tree and expected cost to help determine whether a short-term disability claim should be considered a high-risk or a low-risk claim.

FIGURE 13.4 APPLYING THE EXPECTED VALUE APPROACH USING A DECISION TREE

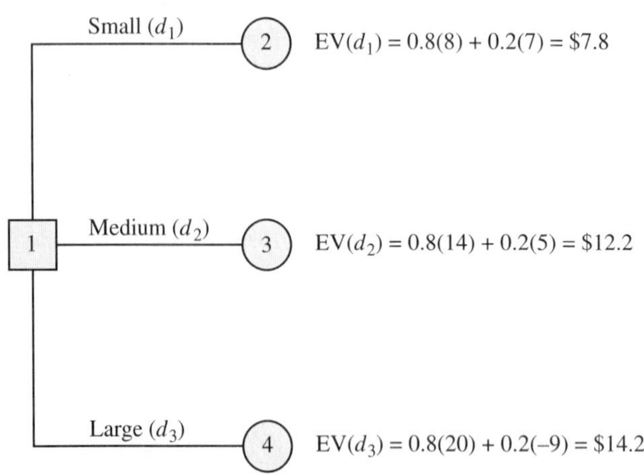

MANAGEMENT SCIENCE IN ACTION

EARLY DETECTION OF HIGH-RISK WORKER DISABILITY CLAIMS*

The Workers' Compensation Board of British Columbia (WCB) helps workers and employers maintain safe workplaces and helps injured workers obtain disability income and return to work safely. The funds used to make the disability compensation payments are obtained from assessments levied on employers. In return, employers receive protection from lawsuits arising from work-related injuries. In recent years, the WCB spent more than $1 billion on worker compensation and rehabilitation.

A short-term disability claim occurs when a worker suffers an injury or illness that results in temporary absence from work. Whenever a worker fails to recover completely from a short-term disability, the claim is reclassified as a long-term disability claim and more expensive long-term benefits are paid.

The WCB wanted a systematic way to identify short-term disability claims that posed a high financial risk of being converted to the more expensive long-term disability claims. If a short-term disability claim could be classified as high risk early in the process, a WCB management team could intervene and monitor the claim and the recovery process more closely. As a result, WCB could improve the management of the high-risk claims and reduce the cost of any subsequent long-term disability claims.

The WCB used a decision analysis approach to classify each new short-term disability claim as being either a high-risk claim or a low-risk claim. A decision tree consisting of two decision nodes and two states-of-nature nodes was developed. The two decision alternatives were: (1) Classify the new short-term claim as high-risk and intervene; (2) Classify the new short-term claim as low-risk and do not intervene. The two states of nature were: (1) The short-term claim converts to a long-term claim; (2) The short-term claim does not convert to a long-term claim. The characteristics of each new short-term claim were used to determine the probabilities for the states of nature. The payoffs were the disability claim costs associated with each decision alternative and each state-of-nature outcome. The objective of minimizing the expected cost determined whether a new short-term claim should be classified as high-risk.

Implementation of the decision analysis model improved the practice of claim management for the Workers' Compensation Board. Early intervention on the high-risk claims saved an estimated $4.7 million per year.

*Based on E. Urbanovich, E. Young, M. Puterman, and S. Fattedad, "Early Detection of High-Risk Claims at the Workers' Compensation Board of British Columbia," *Interfaces* (July/August 2003): 15–26.

Expected Value of Perfect Information

Suppose that PDC has the opportunity to conduct a market research study that would help evaluate buyer interest in the condominium project and provide information that management could use to improve the probability assessments for the states of nature. To determine the potential value of this information, we begin by supposing that the study could provide *perfect information* regarding the states of nature; that is, we assume for the moment that PDC could determine with certainty, prior to making a decision, which state of nature is going to occur. To make use of this perfect information, we will develop a decision strategy that PDC should follow once it knows which state of nature will occur. A decision strategy is simply a decision rule that specifies the decision alternative to be selected after new information becomes available.

To help determine the decision strategy for PDC, we reproduced PDC's payoff table as Table 13.6. Note that, if PDC knew for sure that state of nature s_1 would occur, the best decision alternative would be d_3, with a payoff of $20 million. Similarly, if PDC knew for sure that state of nature s_2 would occur, the best decision alternative would be d_1, with a payoff of $7 million. Thus, we can state PDC's optimal decision strategy when the perfect information becomes available as follows:

If s_1, select d_3 and receive a payoff of $20 million.
If s_2, select d_1 and receive a payoff of $7 million.

TABLE 13.6 PAYOFF TABLE FOR THE PDC CONDOMINIUM PROJECT ($ MILLIONS)

	State of Nature	
Decision Alternative	**Strong Demand s_1**	**Weak Demand s_2**
Small complex, d_1	8	7
Medium complex, d_2	14	5
Large complex, d_3	20	−9

What is the expected value for this decision strategy? To compute the expected value with perfect information, we return to the original probabilities for the states of nature: $P(s_1) = 0.8$, and $P(s_2) = 0.2$. Thus, there is a 0.8 probability that the perfect information will indicate state of nature s_1 and the resulting decision alternative d_3 will provide a $20 million profit. Similarly, with a 0.2 probability for state of nature s_2, the optimal decision alternative d_1 will provide a $7 million profit. Thus, from equation (13.4), the expected value of the decision strategy that uses perfect information is

$$0.8(20) + 0.2(7) = 17.4$$

We refer to the expected value of $17.4 million as the *expected value with perfect information* (EVwPI).

Earlier in this section we showed that the recommended decision using the expected value approach is decision alternative d_3, with an expected value of $14.2 million. Because this decision recommendation and expected value computation were made without the benefit of perfect information, $14.2 million is referred to as the *expected value without perfect information* (EVwoPI).

It would be worth $3.2 million for PDC to learn the level of market acceptance before selecting a decision alternative.

The expected value with perfect information is $17.4 million, and the expected value without perfect information is $14.2; therefore, the expected value of the perfect information (EVPI) is $17.4 − $14.2 = $3.2 million. In other words, $3.2 million represents the additional expected value that can be obtained if perfect information were available about the states of nature.

Generally speaking, a market research study will not provide "perfect" information; however, if the market research study is a good one, the information gathered might be worth a sizable portion of the $3.2 million. Given the EVPI of $3.2 million, PDC might seriously consider a market survey as a way to obtain more information about the states of nature.

In general, the **expected value of perfect information (EVPI)** is computed as follows:

$$\text{EVPI} = |\text{EVwPI} - \text{EVwoPI}| \tag{13.5}$$

where

EVPI = expected value of perfect information
EVwPI = expected value *with* perfect information about the states of nature
EVwoPI = expected value *without* perfect information about the states of nature

For practice in determining the expected value of perfect information, try Problem 14.

Note the role of the absolute value in equation (13.5). For minimization problems the expected value with perfect information is always less than or equal to the expected value without perfect information. In this case, EVPI is the magnitude of the difference between EVwPI and EVwoPI, or the absolute value of the difference as shown in equation (13.5).

NOTES AND COMMENTS

We restate the *opportunity loss,* or *regret,* table for the PDC problem (see Table 13.4) as follows.

	State of Nature	
	Strong Demand	**Weak Demand**
Decision Alternative	s_1	s_2
Small complex, d_1	12	0
Medium complex, d_2	6	2
Large complex, d_3	0	16

Using $P(s_1)$, $P(s_2)$, and the opportunity loss values, we can compute the *expected opportunity loss* (EOL) for each decision alternative. With $P(s_1) = 0.8$ and $P(s_2) = 0.2$, the expected opportunity loss for each of the three decision alternatives is

$$\text{EOL}(d_1) = 0.8(12) + 0.2(0) = 9.6$$
$$\text{EOL}(d_2) = 0.8(6) + 0.2(2) = 5.2$$
$$\text{EOL}(d_3) = 0.8(0) + 0.2(16) = 3.2$$

Regardless of whether the decision analysis involves maximization or minimization, the *minimum* expected opportunity loss always provides the best decision alternative. Thus, with $\text{EOL}(d_3) = 3.2$, d_3 is the recommended decision. In addition, the minimum expected opportunity loss always is *equal to the expected value of perfect information.* That is, EOL(best decision) = EVPI; for the PDC problem, this value is \$3.2 million.

13.4 RISK ANALYSIS AND SENSITIVITY ANALYSIS

Risk analysis helps the decision maker recognize the difference between the expected value of a decision alternative and the payoff that may actually occur. **Sensitivity analysis** also helps the decision maker by describing how changes in the state-of-nature probabilities and/or changes in the payoffs affect the recommended decision alternative.

Risk Analysis

A decision alternative and a state of nature combine to generate the payoff associated with a decision. The **risk profile** for a decision alternative shows the possible payoffs along with their associated probabilities.

Let us demonstrate risk analysis and the construction of a risk profile by returning to the PDC condominium construction project. Using the expected value approach, we identified the large condominium complex (d_3) as the best decision alternative. The expected value of \$14.2 million for d_3 is based on a 0.8 probability of obtaining a \$20 million profit and a 0.2 probability of obtaining a \$9 million loss. The 0.8 probability for the \$20 million payoff and the 0.2 probability for the −\$9 million payoff provide the risk profile for the large complex decision alternative. This risk profile is shown graphically in Figure 13.5.

Sometimes a review of the risk profile associated with an optimal decision alternative may cause the decision maker to choose another decision alternative even though the expected value of the other decision alternative is not as good. For example, the risk profile for the medium complex decision alternative (d_2) shows a 0.8 probability for a \$14 million payoff and 0.2 probability for a \$5 million payoff. Because no probability of a loss is associated with decision alternative d_2, the medium complex decision alternative would be judged less risky than the large complex decision alternative. As a result, a decision maker might prefer the less-risky medium complex decision alternative even though it has an expected value of \$2 million less than the large complex decision alternative.

Sensitivity Analysis

Sensitivity analysis can be used to determine how changes in the probabilities for the states of nature or changes in the payoffs affect the recommended decision alternative. In many cases, the probabilities for the states of nature and the payoffs are based on subjective

FIGURE 13.5 RISK PROFILE FOR THE LARGE COMPLEX DECISION ALTERNATIVE FOR THE PDC CONDOMINIUM PROJECT

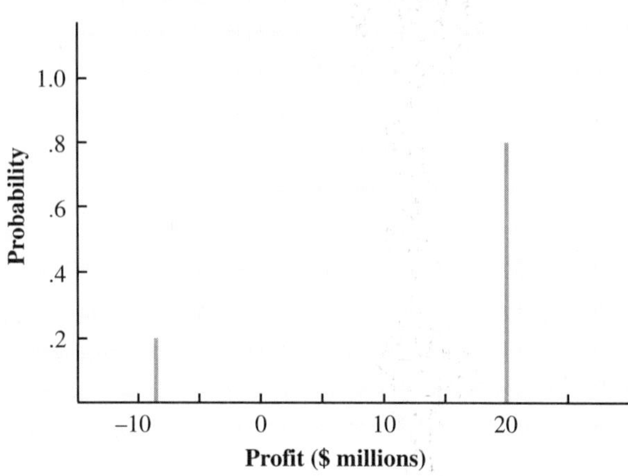

assessments. Sensitivity analysis helps the decision maker understand which of these inputs are critical to the choice of the best decision alternative. If a small change in the value of one of the inputs causes a change in the recommended decision alternative, the solution to the decision analysis problem is sensitive to that particular input. Extra effort and care should be taken to make sure the input value is as accurate as possible. On the other hand, if a modest to large change in the value of one of the inputs does not cause a change in the recommended decision alternative, the solution to the decision analysis problem is not sensitive to that particular input. No extra time or effort would be needed to refine the estimated input value.

One approach to sensitivity analysis is to select different values for the probabilities of the states of nature and the payoffs and then re-solve the decision analysis problem. If the recommended decision alternative changes, we know that the solution is sensitive to the changes made. For example, suppose that in the PDC problem the probability for a strong demand is revised to 0.2 and the probability for a weak demand is revised to 0.8. Would the recommended decision alternative change? Using $P(s_1) = 0.2$, $P(s_2) = 0.8$, and equation (13.4), the revised expected values for the three decision alternatives are

$$\begin{aligned} \text{EV}(d_1) &= 0.2(8) + 0.8(7) = 7.2 \\ \text{EV}(d_2) &= 0.2(14) + 0.8(5) = 6.8 \\ \text{EV}(d_3) &= 0.2(20) + 0.8(-9) = -3.2 \end{aligned}$$

With these probability assessments the recommended decision alternative is to construct a small condominium complex (d_1), with an expected value of $7.2 million. The probability of strong demand is only 0.2, so constructing the large condominium complex (d_3) is the least preferred alternative, with an expected value of −$3.2 million (a loss).

Computer software packages for decision analysis make it easy to calculate these revised scenarios.

Thus, when the probability of strong demand is large, PDC should build the large complex; when the probability of strong demand is small, PDC should build the small complex. Obviously, we could continue to modify the probabilities of the states of nature and learn even more about how changes in the probabilities affect the recommended decision alternative. The drawback to this approach is the numerous calculations required to evaluate the effect of several possible changes in the state-of-nature probabilities.

For the special case of two states of nature, a graphical procedure can be used to determine how changes for the probabilities of the states of nature affect the recommended decision alternative. To demonstrate this procedure, we let p denote the probability of state of nature s_1; that is, $P(s_1) = p$. With only two states of nature in the PDC problem, the probability of state of nature s_2 is

$$P(s_2) = 1 - P(s_1) = 1 - p$$

Using equation (13.4) and the payoff values in Table 13.1, we determine the expected value for decision alternative d_1 as follows:

$$\begin{aligned} \text{EV}(d_1) &= P(s_1)(8) + P(s_2)(7) \\ &= p(8) + (1 - p)(7) \\ &= 8p + 7 - 7p = p + 7 \end{aligned} \tag{13.6}$$

Repeating the expected value computations for decision alternatives d_2 and d_3, we obtain expressions for the expected value of each decision alternative as a function of p:

$$\text{EV}(d_2) = 9p + 5 \tag{13.7}$$

$$\text{EV}(d_3) = 29p - 9 \tag{13.8}$$

Thus, we have developed three equations that show the expected value of the three decision alternatives as a function of the probability of state of nature s_1.

We continue by developing a graph with values of p on the horizontal axis and the associated EVs on the vertical axis. Because equations (13.6), (13.7), and (13.8) are linear equations, the graph of each equation is a straight line. For each equation, we can obtain the line by identifying two points that satisfy the equation and drawing a line through the points. For instance, if we let $p = 0$ in equation (13.6), $\text{EV}(d_1) = 7$. Then, letting $p = 1$, $\text{EV}(d_1) = 8$. Connecting these two points, (0, 7) and (1, 8), provides the line labeled $\text{EV}(d_1)$ in Figure 13.6. Similarly, we obtain the lines labeled $\text{EV}(d_2)$ and $\text{EV}(d_3)$; these lines are the graphs of equations (13.7) and (13.8), respectively.

Figure 13.6 shows how the recommended decision changes as p, the probability of the strong demand state of nature (s_1), changes. Note that for small values of p, decision alternative d_1 (small complex) provides the largest expected value and is thus the recommended decision. When the value of p increases to a certain point, decision alternative d_2 (medium complex) provides the largest expected value and is the recommended decision. Finally, for large values of p, decision alternative d_3 (large complex) becomes the recommended decision.

The value of p for which the expected values of d_1 and d_2 are equal is the value of p corresponding to the intersection of the $\text{EV}(d_1)$ and the $\text{EV}(d_2)$ lines. To determine this value, we set $\text{EV}(d_1) = \text{EV}(d_2)$ and solve for the value of p:

$$\begin{aligned} p + 7 &= 9p + 5 \\ 8p &= 2 \\ p &= \frac{2}{8} = 0.25 \end{aligned}$$

FIGURE 13.6 EXPECTED VALUE FOR THE PDC DECISION ALTERNATIVES AS A FUNCTION OF p

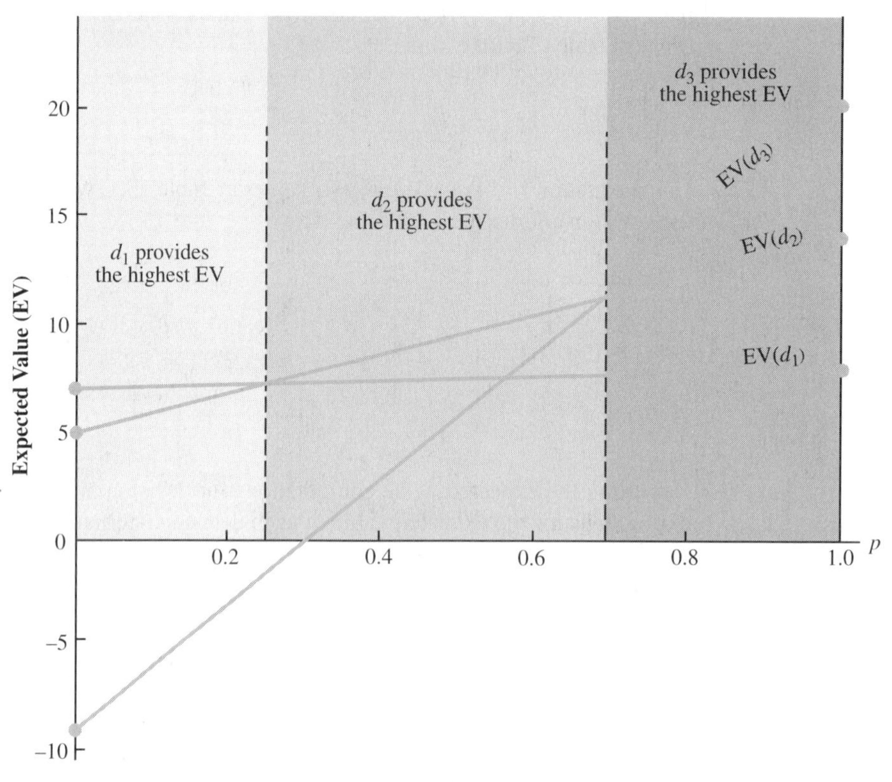

Graphical sensitivity analysis shows how changes in the probabilities for the states of nature affect the recommended decision alternative. Try Problem 8.

Hence, when $p = 0.25$, decision alternatives d_1 and d_2 provide the same expected value. Repeating this calculation for the value of p corresponding to the intersection of the EV(d_2) and EV(d_3) lines, we obtain $p = 0.70$.

Using Figure 13.6, we can conclude that decision alternative d_1 provides the largest expected value for $p \le 0.25$, decision alternative d_2 provides the largest expected value for $0.25 \le p \le 0.70$, and decision alternative d_3 provides the largest expected value for $p \ge 0.70$. Because p is the probability of state of nature s_1 and $(1 - p)$ is the probability of state of nature s_2, we now have the sensitivity analysis information that tells us how changes in the state-of-nature probabilities affect the recommended decision alternative.

Sensitivity analysis calculations can also be made for the values of the payoffs. In the original PDC problem, the expected values for the three decision alternatives were as follows: EV(d_1) = 7.8, EV(d_2) = 12.2, and EV(d_3) = 14.2. Decision alternative d_3 (large complex) was recommended. Note that decision alternative d_2 with EV(d_2) = 12.2 was the second best decision alternative. Decision alternative d_3 will remain the optimal decision alternative as long as EV(d_3) is greater than or equal to the expected value of the second best decision alternative. Thus, decision alternative d_3 will remain the optimal decision alternative as long as

$$\text{EV}(d_3) \ge 12.2 \tag{13.9}$$

Let

$$S = \text{the payoff of decision alternative } d_3 \text{ when demand is strong}$$
$$W = \text{the payoff of decision alternative } d_3 \text{ when demand is weak}$$

Using $P(s_1) = 0.8$ and $P(s_2) = 0.2$, the general expression for EV(d_3) is

$$\text{EV}(d_3) = 0.8S + 0.2W \tag{13.10}$$

Assuming that the payoff for d_3 stays at its original value of $-\$9$ million when demand is weak, the large complex decision alternative will remain optimal as long as

$$\text{EV}(d_3) = 0.8S + 0.2(-9) \geq 12.2 \tag{13.11}$$

Solving for S, we have

$$\begin{aligned} 0.8S - 1.8 &\geq 12.2 \\ 0.8S &\geq 14 \\ S &\geq 17.5 \end{aligned}$$

Recall that when demand is strong, decision alternative d_3 has an estimated payoff of \$20 million. The preceding calculation shows that decision alternative d_3 will remain optimal as long as the payoff for d_3 when demand is strong is at least \$17.5 million.

Assuming that the payoff for d_3 when demand is strong stays at its original value of \$20 million, we can make a similar calculation to learn how sensitive the optimal solution is with regard to the payoff for d_3 when demand is weak. Returning to the expected value calculation of equation (13.10), we know that the large complex decision alternative will remain optimal as long as

$$\text{EV}(d_3) = 0.8(20) + 0.2W \geq 12.2 \tag{13.12}$$

Solving for W, we have

$$\begin{aligned} 16 + 0.2W &\geq 12.2 \\ 0.2W &\geq -3.8 \\ W &\geq -19 \end{aligned}$$

Recall that when demand is weak, decision alternative d_3 has an estimated payoff of $-\$9$ million. The preceding calculation shows that decision alternative d_3 will remain optimal as long as the payoff for d_3 when demand is weak is at least $-\$19$ million.

Based on this sensitivity analysis, we conclude that the payoffs for the large complex decision alternative (d_3) could vary considerably and d_3 would remain the recommended decision alternative. Thus, we conclude that the optimal solution for the PDC decision problem is not particularly sensitive to the payoffs for the large complex decision alternative.

Sensitivity analysis can assist management in deciding whether more time and effort should be spent obtaining better estimates of payoffs and probabilities.

We note, however, that this sensitivity analysis has been conducted based on only one change at a time. That is, only one payoff was changed and the probabilities for the states of nature remained $P(s_1) = 0.8$ and $P(s_2) = 0.2$. Note that similar sensitivity analysis calculations can be made for the payoffs associated with the small complex decision alternative d_1 and the medium complex decision alternative d_2. However, in these cases, decision alternative d_3 remains optimal only if the changes in the payoffs for decision alternatives d_1 and d_2 meet the requirements that $\text{EV}(d_1) \le 14.2$ and $\text{EV}(d_2) \le 14.2$.

NOTES AND COMMENTS

1. Some decision analysis software automatically provide the risk profiles for the optimal decision alternative. These packages also allow the user to obtain the risk profiles for other decision alternatives. After comparing the risk profiles, a decision maker may decide to select a decision alternative with a good risk profile even though the expected value of the decision alternative is not as good as the optimal decision alternative.
2. A *tornado diagram,* a graphical display, is particularly helpful when several inputs combine to determine the value of the optimal solution. By varying each input over its range of values, we obtain information about how each input affects the value of the optimal solution. To display this information, a bar is constructed for the input with the width of the bar showing how the input affects the value of the optimal solution. The widest bar corresponds to the input that is most sensitive. The bars are arranged in a graph with the widest bar at the top, resulting in a graph that has the appearance of a tornado.

13.5 DECISION ANALYSIS WITH SAMPLE INFORMATION

In applying the expected value approach, we showed how probability information about the states of nature affects the expected value calculations and thus the decision recommendation. Frequently, decision makers have preliminary or **prior probability** assessments for the states of nature that are the best probability values available at that time. However, to make the best possible decision, the decision maker may want to seek additional information about the states of nature. This new information can be used to revise or update the prior probabilities so that the final decision is based on more accurate probabilities for the states of nature. Most often, additional information is obtained through experiments designed to provide **sample information** about the states of nature. Raw material sampling, product testing, and market research studies are examples of experiments (or studies) that may enable management to revise or update the state-of-nature probabilities. These revised probabilities are called **posterior probabilities.**

Let us return to the PDC problem and assume that management is considering a six-month market research study designed to learn more about potential market acceptance of the PDC condominium project. Management anticipates that the market research study will provide one of the following two results:

1. Favorable report: A significant number of the individuals contacted express interest in purchasing a PDC condominium.
2. Unfavorable report: Very few of the individuals contacted express interest in purchasing a PDC condominium.

Influence Diagram

By introducing the possibility of conducting a market research study, the PDC problem becomes more complex. The influence diagram for the expanded PDC problem is shown in Figure 13.7. Note that the two decision nodes correspond to the research study and the

FIGURE 13.7 INFLUENCE DIAGRAM FOR THE PDC PROBLEM WITH SAMPLE INFORMATION

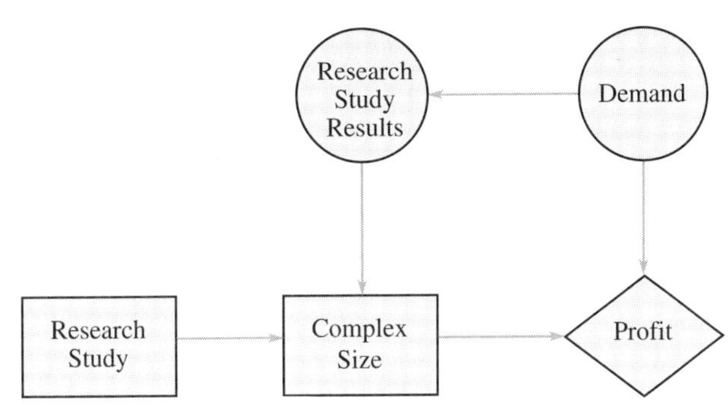

complex-size decisions. The two chance nodes correspond to the research study results and demand for the condominiums. Finally, the consequence node is the profit. From the arcs of the influence diagram, we see that demand influences both the research study results and profit. Although demand is currently unknown to PDC, some level of demand for the condominiums already exists in the Pittsburgh area. If existing demand is strong, the research study is likely to find a significant number of individuals who express an interest in purchasing a condominium. However, if the existing demand is weak, the research study is more likely to find a significant number of individuals who express little interest in purchasing a condominium. In this sense, existing demand for the condominiums will influence the research study results, and clearly, demand will have an influence upon PDC's profit.

The arc from the research study decision node to the complex-size decision node indicates that the research study decision precedes the complex-size decision. No arc spans from the research study decision node to the research study results node, because the decision to conduct the research study does not actually influence the research study results. The decision to conduct the research study makes the research study results available, but it does not influence the results of the research study. Finally, the complex-size node and the demand node both influence profit. Note that if a stated cost to conduct the research study were given, the decision to conduct the research study would also influence profit. In such a case, we would need to add an arc from the research study decision node to the profit node to show the influence that the research study cost would have on profit.

Decision Tree

The decision tree for the PDC problem with sample information shows the logical sequence for the decisions and the chance events in Figure 13.8.

First, PDC's management must decide whether the market research should be conducted. If it is conducted, PDC's management must be prepared to make a decision about the size of the condominium project if the market research report is favorable and, possibly, a different decision about the size of the condominium project if the market research report is unfavorable. In Figure 13.8, the squares are decision nodes and the circles are chance nodes. At each decision node, the branch of the tree that is taken is based on the decision made. At each chance node, the branch of the tree that is taken is based on probability or chance. For example, decision node 1 shows that PDC must first make the decision of whether to conduct the market research study. If the market research study is undertaken, chance node 2

FIGURE 13.8 THE PDC DECISION TREE INCLUDING THE MARKET RESEARCH STUDY

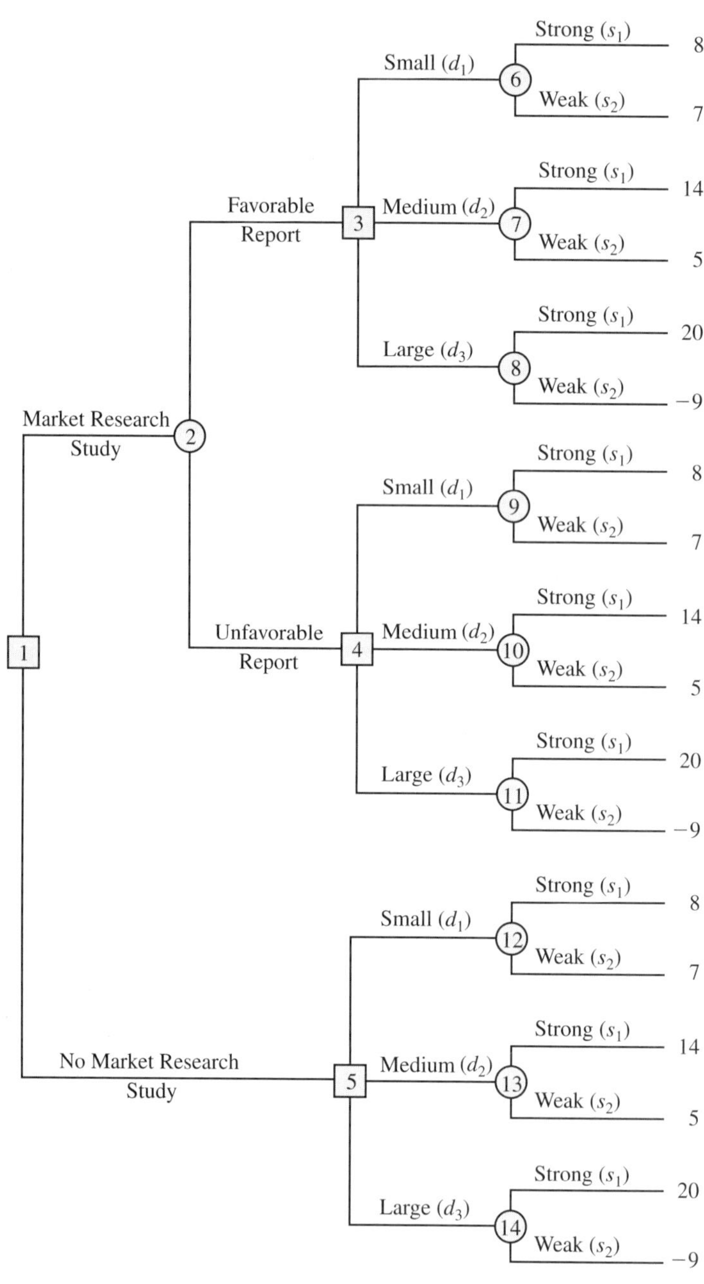

indicates that both the favorable report branch and the unfavorable report branch are not under PDC's control and will be determined by chance. Node 3 is a decision node, indicating that PDC must make the decision to construct the small, medium, or large complex if the market research report is favorable. Node 4 is a decision node showing that PDC must make the decision to construct the small, medium, or large complex if the market research report is unfavorable. Node 5 is a decision node indicating that PDC must make the decision to construct the small, medium, or large complex if the market research is not undertaken. Nodes 6 to 14 are chance nodes indicating that the strong demand or weak demand state-of-nature branches will be determined by chance.

We explain in Section 13.6 how these probabilities can be developed.

Analysis of the decision tree and the choice of an optimal strategy requires that we know the branch probabilities corresponding to all chance nodes. PDC has developed the following branch probabilities.

If the market research study is undertaken

$$P(\text{Favorable report}) = 0.77$$
$$P(\text{Unfavorable report}) = 0.23$$

If the market research report is favorable

$$P(\text{Strong demand given a favorable report}) = 0.94$$
$$P(\text{Weak demand given a favorable report}) = 0.06$$

If the market research report is unfavorable

$$P(\text{Strong demand given an unfavorable report}) = 0.35$$
$$P(\text{Weak demand given an unfavorable report}) = 0.65$$

If the market research report is not undertaken, the prior probabilities are applicable.

$$P(\text{Strong demand}) = 0.80$$
$$P(\text{Weak demand}) = 0.20$$

The branch probabilities are shown on the decision tree in Figure 13.9.

Decision Strategy

A **decision strategy** is a sequence of decisions and chance outcomes where the decisions chosen depend on the yet to be determined outcomes of chance events.

The approach used to determine the optimal decision strategy is based on a backward pass through the decision tree using the following steps:

1. At chance nodes, compute the expected value by multiplying the payoff at the end of each branch by the corresponding branch probabilities.
2. At decision nodes, select the decision branch that leads to the best expected value. This expected value becomes the expected value at the decision node.

Starting the backward pass calculations by computing the expected values at chance nodes 6 to 14 provides the following results.

$$\begin{aligned}
\text{EV(Node 6)} &= 0.94(8) + 0.06(7) = 7.94 \\
\text{EV(Node 7)} &= 0.94(14) + 0.06(5) = 13.46 \\
\text{EV(Node 8)} &= 0.94(20) + 0.06(-9) = 18.26 \\
\text{EV(Node 9)} &= 0.35(8) + 0.65(7) = 7.35 \\
\text{EV(Node 10)} &= 0.35(14) + 0.65(5) = 8.15 \\
\text{EV(Node 11)} &= 0.35(20) + 0.65(-9) = 1.15 \\
\text{EV(Node 12)} &= 0.80(8) + 0.20(7) = 7.80 \\
\text{EV(Node 13)} &= 0.80(14) + 0.20(5) = 12.20 \\
\text{EV(Node 14)} &= 0.80(20) + 0.20(-9) = 14.20
\end{aligned}$$

FIGURE 13.9 THE PDC DECISION TREE WITH BRANCH PROBABILITIES

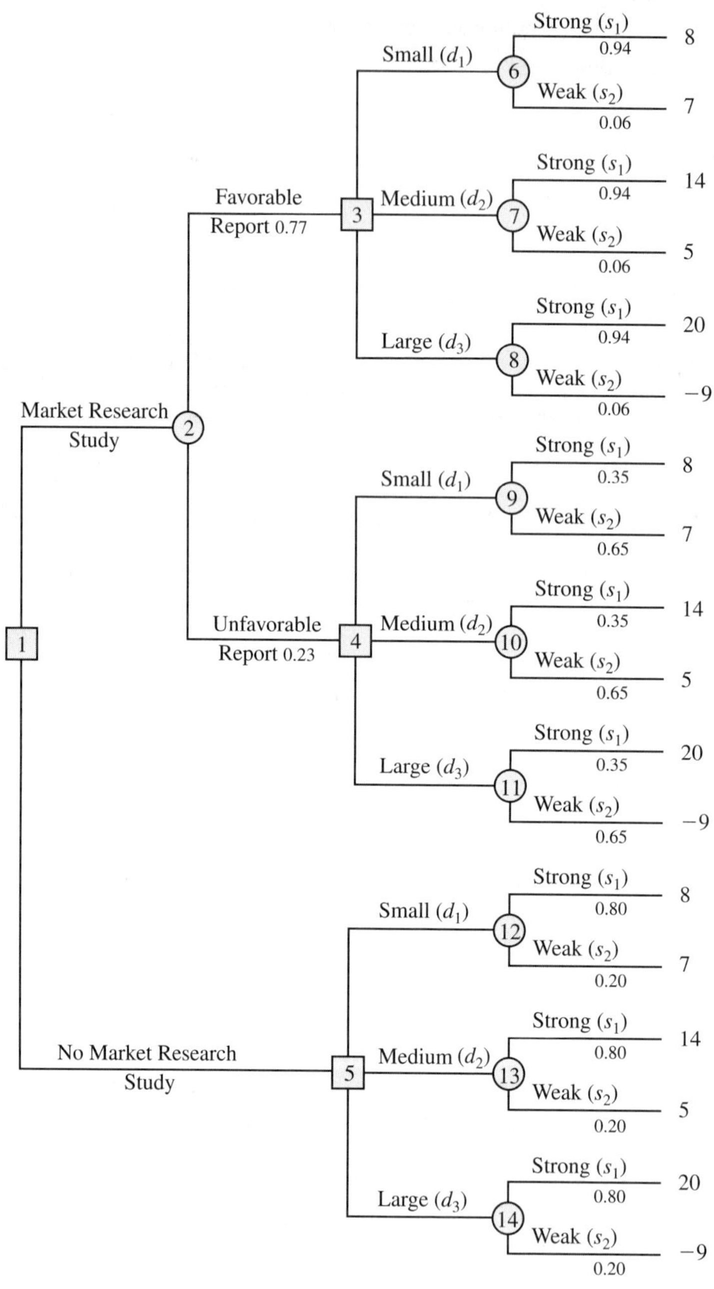

Figure 13.10 shows the reduced decision tree after computing expected values at these chance nodes.

Next, move to decision nodes 3, 4, and 5. For each of these nodes, we select the decision alternative branch that leads to the best expected value. For example, at node 3 we have the choice of the small complex branch with EV(Node 6) = 7.94, the medium complex branch with EV(Node 7) = 13.46, and the large complex branch with EV(Node 8) = 18.26.

FIGURE 13.10 PDC DECISION TREE AFTER COMPUTING EXPECTED VALUES AT CHANCE NODES 6 TO 14

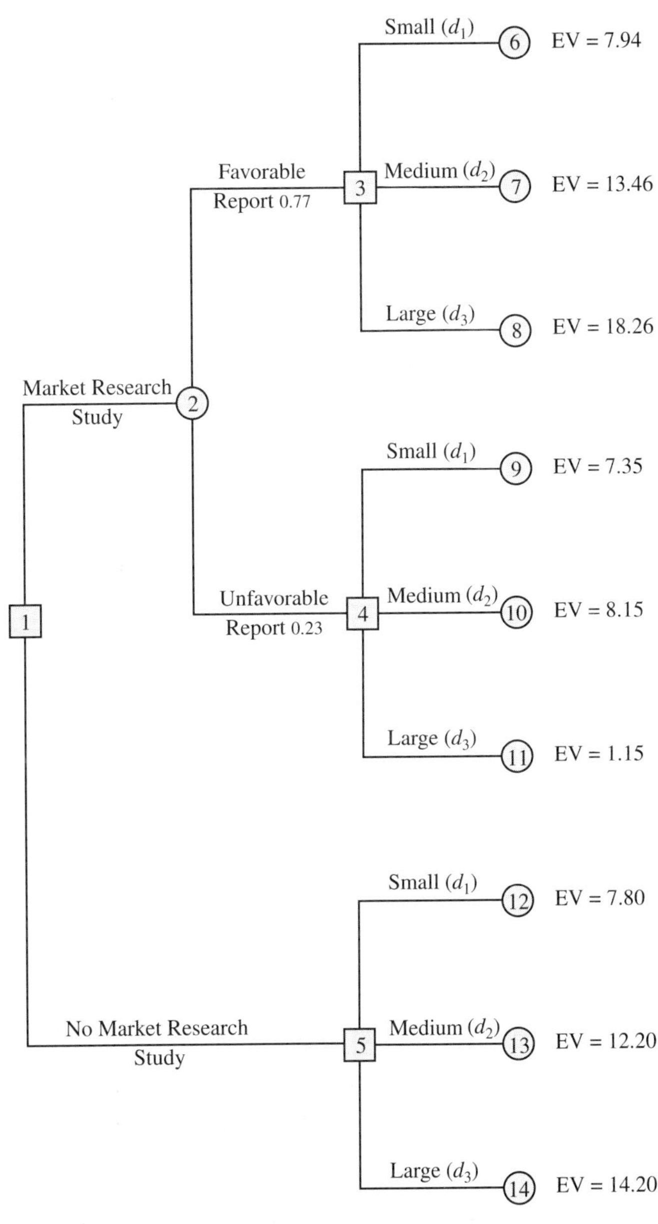

Thus, we select the large complex decision alternative branch and the expected value at node 3 becomes EV(Node 3) = 18.26.

For node 4, we select the best expected value from nodes 9, 10, and 11. The best decision alternative is the medium complex branch that provides EV(Node 4) = 8.15. For node 5, we select the best expected value from nodes 12, 13, and 14. The best decision alternative is the large complex branch that provides EV(Node 5) = 14.20. Figure 13.11 shows the reduced decision tree after choosing the best decisions at nodes 3, 4, and 5.

FIGURE 13.11 PDC DECISION TREE AFTER CHOOSING BEST DECISIONS AT NODES 3, 4, AND 5

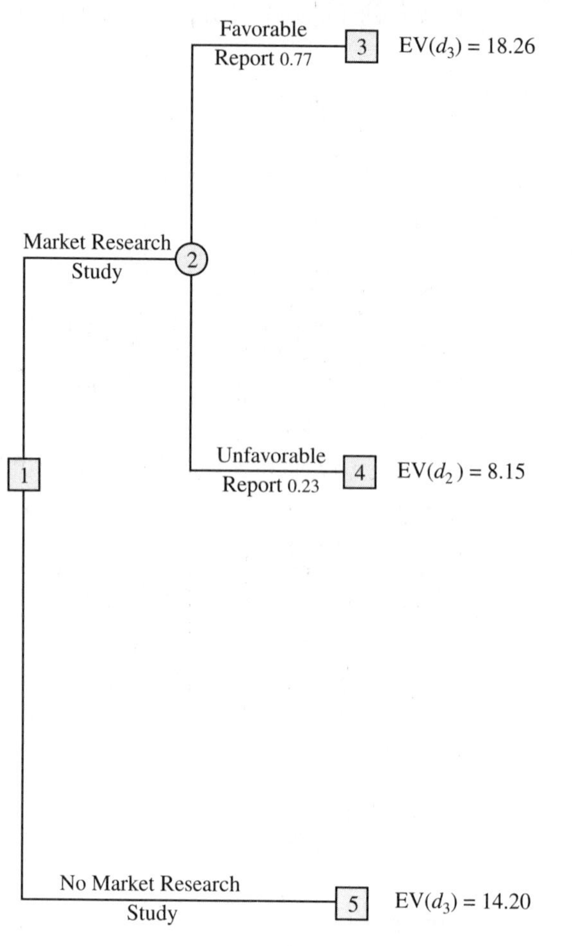

The expected value at chance node 2 can now be computed as follows:

$$\begin{aligned} \text{EV(Node 2)} &= 0.77\text{EV(Node 3)} + 0.23\text{EV(Node 4)} \\ &= 0.77(18.26) + 0.23(8.15) = 15.93 \end{aligned}$$

This calculation reduces the decision tree to one involving only the two decision branches from node 1 (see Figure 13.12).

Finally, the decision can be made at decision node 1 by selecting the best expected values from nodes 2 and 5. This action leads to the decision alternative to conduct the market research study, which provides an overall expected value of 15.93.

The optimal decision for PDC is to conduct the market research study and then carry out the following decision strategy:

If the market research is favorable, construct the large condominium complex.

If the market research is unfavorable, construct the medium condominium complex.

The analysis of the PDC decision tree describes the methods that can be used to analyze more complex sequential decision problems. First, draw a decision tree consisting of

FIGURE 13.12 PDC DECISION TREE REDUCED TO TWO DECISION BRANCHES

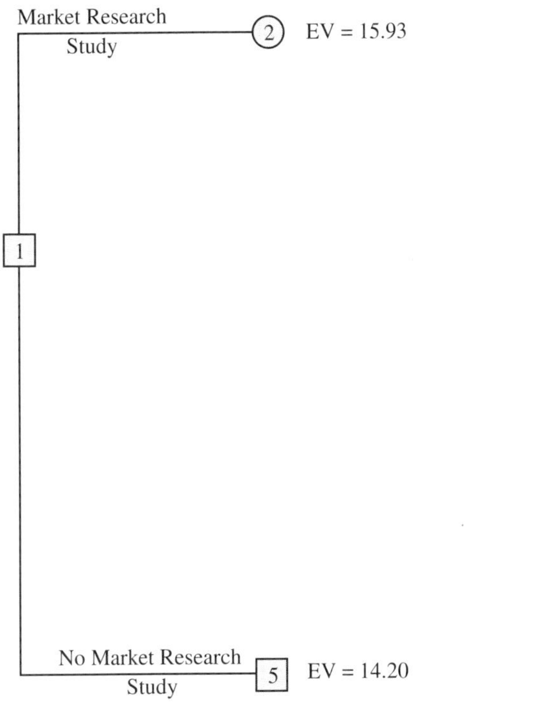

Problem 16 will test your ability to develop an optimal decision strategy.

decision and chance nodes and branches that describe the sequential nature of the problem. Determine the probabilities for all chance outcomes. Then, by working backward through the tree, compute expected values at all chance nodes and select the best decision branch at all decision nodes. The sequence of optimal decision branches determines the optimal decision strategy for the problem.

The Management Science in Action, New Drug Decision Analysis at Bayer Pharmaceuticals, describes how an extension of the decision analysis principles presented in this section enabled Bayer to make decisions about the development and marketing of a new drug.

Risk Profile

Figure 13.13 provides a reduced decision tree showing only the sequence of decision alternatives and chance events for the PDC optimal decision strategy. By implementing the optimal decision strategy, PDC will obtain one of the four payoffs shown at the terminal branches of the decision tree. Recall that a risk profile shows the possible payoffs with their associated probabilities. Thus, in order to construct a risk profile for the optimal decision strategy we will need to compute the probability for each of the four payoffs.

Note that each payoff results from a sequence of branches leading from node 1 to the payoff. For instance, the payoff of $20 million is obtained by following the upper branch from node 1, the upper branch from node 2, the lower branch from node 3, and the upper branch from node 8. The probability of following that sequence of branches can be found by multiplying the probabilities for the branches from the chance nodes in the sequence. Thus, the probability of the $20 million payoff is (0.77)(0.94) = 0.72. Similarly, the probabilities for each of the other payoffs are obtained by multiplying the probabilities for the

FIGURE 13.13 PDC DECISION TREE SHOWING ONLY BRANCHES ASSOCIATED WITH OPTIMAL DECISION STRATEGY

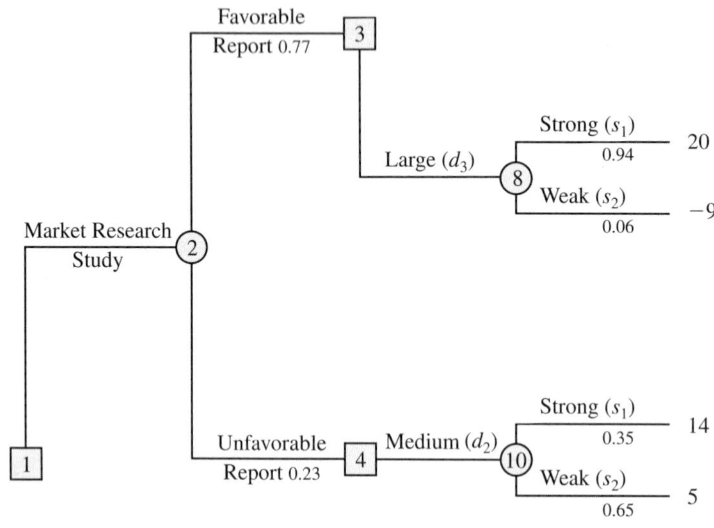

MANAGEMENT SCIENCE IN ACTION

NEW DRUG DECISION ANALYSIS AT BAYER PHARMACEUTICALS*

Drug development in the United States requires substantial investment and is very risky. It takes nearly 15 years to research and develop a new drug. The Bayer Biological Products (BP) group used decision analysis to evaluate the potential for a new blood-clot-busting drug. An influence diagram was used to describe the complex structure of the decision analysis process. Six key yes-or-no decision nodes were identified: (1) begin preclinical development, (2) begin testing in humans, (3) continue development into phase 3, (4) continue development into phase 4, (5) file a license application with the FDA, and (6) launch the new drug into the marketplace. More than 50 chance nodes appeared in the influence diagram. The chance nodes showed how uncertainties—related to factors such as direct labor costs, process development costs, market share, tax rate, and pricing—affected the outcome. Net present value provided the consequence and the decision-making criterion.

Probability assessments were made concerning both the technical risk and market risk at each stage of the process. The resulting sequential decision tree had 1955 possible paths that led to different net present value outcomes. Cost inputs, judgments of potential outcomes, and the assignment of probabilities helped evaluate the project's potential contribution. Sensitivity analysis was used to identify key variables that would require special attention by the project team and management during the drug development process. Application of decision analysis principles allowed Bayer to make good decisions about how to develop and market the new drug.

*Based on Jeffrey S. Stonebraker, "How Bayer Makes Decisions to Develop New Drugs," *Interfaces,* no. 6 (November/December 2002): 77–90.

branches from the chance nodes leading to the payoffs. Doing so, we find the probability of the −\$9 million payoff is (0.77)(0.06) = 0.05; the probability of the \$14 million payoff is (0.23)(0.35) = 0.08; and the probability of the \$5 million payoff is (0.23)(0.65) = 0.15. The following table showing the probability distribution for the payoffs for the PDC optimal decision strategy is the tabular representation of the risk profile for the optimal decision strategy.

FIGURE 13.14 RISK PROFILE FOR PDC CONDOMINIUM PROJECT WITH SAMPLE INFORMATION SHOWING PAYOFFS ASSOCIATED WITH OPTIMAL DECISION STRATEGY

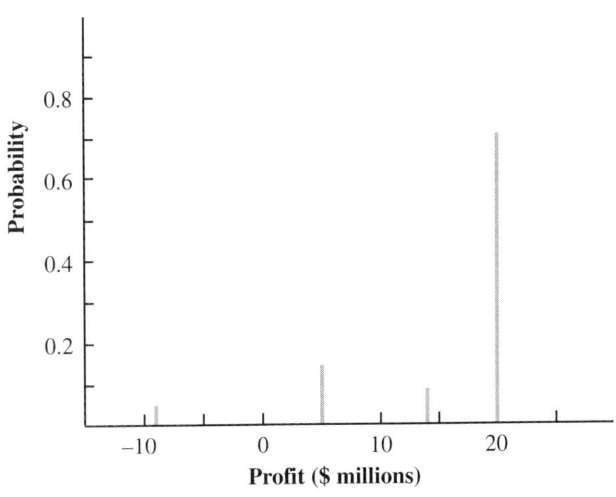

Payoff ($ millions)	Probability
−9	0.05
5	0.15
14	0.08
20	0.72
	1.00

Figure 13.14 provides a graphical representation of the risk profile. Comparing Figures 13.5 and 13.14, we see that the PDC risk profile is changed by the strategy to conduct the market research study. In fact, the use of the market research study lowered the probability of the $9 million loss from 0.20 to 0.05. PDC's management would most likely view that change as a significant reduction in the risk associated with the condominium project.

Expected Value of Sample Information

The EVSI = $1.73 million suggests PDC should be willing to pay up to $1.73 million to conduct the market research study.

In the PDC problem, the market research study is the sample information used to determine the optimal decision strategy. The expected value associated with the market research study is $15.93. In Section 13.3 we showed that the best expected value if the market research study is *not* undertaken is $14.20. Thus, we can conclude that the difference, $15.93 − $14.20 = $1.73, is the **expected value of sample information (EVSI).** In other words, conducting the market research study adds $1.73 million to the PDC expected value. In general, the expected value of sample information is as follows:

$$\text{EVSI} = |\text{EVwSI} - \text{EVwoSI}| \tag{13.13}$$

where

$$\text{EVSI} = \text{expected value of sample information}$$
$$\text{EVwSI} = \text{expected value } \textit{with} \text{ sample information about the states of nature}$$
$$\text{EVwoSI} = \text{expected value } \textit{without} \text{ sample information about the states of nature}$$

Note the role of the absolute value in equation (13.13). For minimization problems the expected value with sample information is always less than or equal to the expected value without sample information. In this case, EVSI is the magnitude of the difference between EVwSI and EVwoSI; thus, by taking the absolute value of the difference as shown in equation (13.13), we can handle both the maximization and minimization cases with one equation.

Efficiency of Sample Information

In Section 13.3 we showed that the expected value of perfect information (EVPI) for the PDC problem is \$3.2 million. We never anticipated that the market research report would obtain perfect information, but we can use an **efficiency** measure to express the value of the market research information. With perfect information having an efficiency rating of 100 percent, the efficiency rating E for sample information is computed as follows.

$$\text{E} = \frac{\text{EVSI}}{\text{EVPI}} \times 100 \tag{13.14}$$

For the PDC problem,

$$\text{E} = \frac{1.73}{3.2} \times 100 = 54.1\%$$

In other words, the information from the market research study is 54.1% as efficient as perfect information.

Low efficiency ratings for sample information might lead the decision maker to look for other types of information. However, high efficiency ratings indicate that the sample information is almost as good as perfect information and that additional sources of information would not yield significantly better results.

13.6 COMPUTING BRANCH PROBABILITIES

In Section 13.5 the branch probabilities for the PDC decision tree chance nodes were specified in the problem description. No computations were required to determine these probabilities. In this section we show how **Bayes' theorem** can be used to compute branch probabilities for decision trees.

The PDC decision tree is shown again in Figure 13.15. Let

$$F = \text{Favorable market research report}$$
$$U = \text{Unfavorable market research report}$$
$$s_1 = \text{Strong demand (state of nature 1)}$$
$$s_2 = \text{Weak demand (state of nature 2)}$$

FIGURE 13.15 THE PDC DECISION TREE

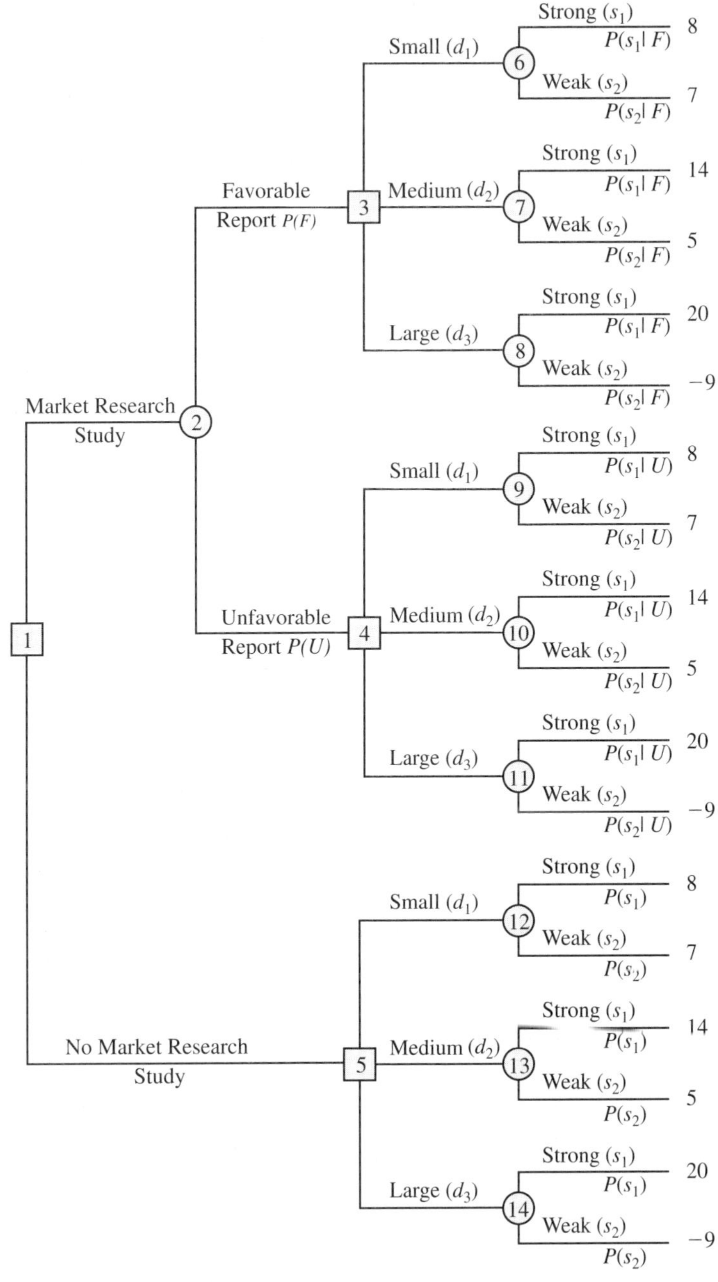

At chance node 2, we need to know the branch probabilities $P(F)$ and $P(U)$. At chance nodes 6, 7, and 8, we need to know the branch probabilities $P(s_1 \mid F)$, the probability of state of nature 1 given a favorable market research report, and $P(s_2 \mid F)$, the probability of state of nature 2 given a favorable market research report. $P(s_1 \mid F)$ and $P(s_2 \mid F)$ are referred to as *posterior probabilities* because they are conditional probabilities based on the outcome of the sample information. At chance nodes 9, 10, and 11, we need to know the branch probabilities $P(s_1 \mid U)$ and $P(s_2 \mid U)$; note that these are also posterior probabilities, denoting the probabilities of the two states of nature *given* that the market research report is unfavorable. Finally, at chance nodes 12, 13, and 14, we need the probabilities for the states of nature, $P(s_1)$ and $P(s_2)$, if the market research study is not undertaken.

In making the probability computations, we need to know PDC's assessment of the probabilities for the two states of nature, $P(s_1)$ and $P(s_2)$, which are the prior probabilities as discussed earlier. In addition, we must know the **conditional probability** of the market research outcomes (the sample information) *given* each state of nature. For example, we need to know the conditional probability of a favorable market research report given that the state of nature is strong demand for the PDC project; note that this conditional probability of F given state of nature s_1 is written $P(F \mid s_1)$. To carry out the probability calculations, we will need conditional probabilities for all sample outcomes given all states of nature, that is, $P(F \mid s_1)$, $P(F \mid s_2)$, $P(U \mid s_1)$, and $P(U \mid s_2)$. In the PDC problem, we assume that the following assessments are available for these conditional probabilities.

	Market Research	
State of Nature	**Favorable, F**	**Unfavorable, U**
Strong demand, s_1	$P(F \mid s_1) = 0.90$	$P(U \mid s_1) = 0.10$
Weak demand, s_2	$P(F \mid s_2) = 0.25$	$P(U \mid s_2) = 0.75$

Note that the preceding probability assessments provide a reasonable degree of confidence in the market research study. If the true state of nature is s_1, the probability of a favorable market research report is 0.90, and the probability of an unfavorable market research report is 0.10. If the true state of nature is s_2, the probability of a favorable market research report is 0.25, and the probability of an unfavorable market research report is 0.75. The reason for a 0.25 probability of a potentially misleading favorable market research report for state of nature s_2 is that when some potential buyers first hear about the new condominium project, their enthusiasm may lead them to overstate their real interest in it. A potential buyer's initial favorable response can change quickly to a "no thank you" when later faced with the reality of signing a purchase contract and making a down payment.

In the following discussion, we present a tabular approach as a convenient method for carrying out the probability computations. The computations for the PDC problem based on a favorable market research report (F) are summarized in Table 13.7. The steps used to develop this table are as follows.

Step 1. In column 1 enter the states of nature. In column 2 enter the *prior probabilities* for the states of nature. In column 3 enter the *conditional probabilities* of a favorable market research report (F) given each state of nature.

TABLE 13.7 BRANCH PROBABILITIES FOR THE PDC CONDOMINIUM PROJECT BASED ON A FAVORABLE MARKET RESEARCH REPORT

States of Nature s_j	Prior Probabilities $P(s_j)$	Conditional Probabilities $P(F \mid s_j)$	Joint Probabilities $P(F \cap s_j)$	Posterior Probabilities $P(s_j \mid F)$
s_1	0.8	0.90	0.72	0.94
s_2	0.2	0.25	0.05	0.06
	1.0		$P(F) = 0.77$	1.00

TABLE 13.8 BRANCH PROBABILITIES FOR THE PDC CONDOMINIUM PROJECT BASED ON AN UNFAVORABLE MARKET RESEARCH REPORT

States of Nature s_j	Prior Probabilities $P(s_j)$	Conditional Probabilities $P(U \mid s_j)$	Joint Probabilities $P(U \cap s_j)$	Posterior Probabilities $P(s_j \mid U)$
s_1	0.8	0.10	0.08	0.35
s_2	0.2	0.75	0.15	0.65
	1.0		$P(U) = 0.23$	1.00

Step 2. In column 4 compute the **joint probabilities** by multiplying the prior probability values in column 2 by the corresponding conditional probability values in column 3.

Step 3. Sum the joint probabilities in column 4 to obtain the probability of a favorable market research report, $P(F)$.

Step 4. Divide each joint probability in column 4 by $P(F) = 0.77$ to obtain the revised or *posterior probabilities*, $P(s_1 \mid F)$ and $P(s_2 \mid F)$.

Table 13.7 shows that the probability of obtaining a favorable market research report is $P(F) = 0.77$. In addition, $P(s_1 \mid F) = 0.94$ and $P(s_2 \mid F) = 0.06$. In particular, note that a favorable market research report will prompt a revised or posterior probability of 0.94 that the market demand of the condominium will be strong, s_1.

The tabular probability computation procedure must be repeated for each possible sample information outcome. Thus, Table 13.8 shows the computations of the branch probabilities of the PDC problem based on an unfavorable market research report. Note that the probability of obtaining an unfavorable market research report is $P(U) = 0.23$. If an unfavorable report is obtained, the posterior probability of a strong market demand, s_1, is 0.35 and of a weak market demand, s_2, is 0.65. The branch probabilities from Tables 13.7 and 13.8 were shown on the PDC decision tree in Figure 13.9.

Problem 23 asks you to compute the posterior probabilities.

The discussion in this section shows an underlying relationship between the probabilities on the various branches in a decision tree. To assume different prior probabilities, $P(s_1)$ and $P(s_2)$, without determining how these changes would alter $P(F)$ and $P(U)$, as well as the posterior probabilities $P(s_1 \mid F)$, $P(s_2 \mid F)$, $P(s_1 \mid U)$, and $P(s_2 \mid U)$, would be inappropriate.

The Management Science in Action, Medical Screening Test at Duke University Medical Center, shows how posterior probability information and decision analysis helped management understand the risks and costs associated with a new screening procedure.

MANAGEMENT SCIENCE IN ACTION

MEDICAL SCREENING TEST AT DUKE UNIVERSITY MEDICAL CENTER*

A medical screening test developed at the Duke University Medical Center involved using blood samples from newborns to screen for metabolic disorders. A positive test result indicated that a deficiency was present, while a negative test result indicated that a deficiency was not present. However, it was understood that the screening test was not a perfect predictor; that is, false-positive test results as well as false-negative test results were possible. A false-positive test result meant that the test detected a deficiency when in fact no deficiency was present. This case resulted in unnecessary further testing as well as unnecessary worry for the parents of the newborn. A false-negative test result meant that the test did not detect the presence of an existing deficiency. Using probability and decision analysis, a research team analyzed the role and value of the screening test.

(continued)

A decision tree with six nodes, 13 branches, and eight outcomes was used to model the screening test procedure. A decision node with the decision branches Test and No Test was placed at the start of the decision tree. Chance nodes and branches were used to describe the possible sequences of a positive test result, a negative test result, a deficiency present, and a deficiency not present.

The particular deficiency in question was rare, occurring at a rate of one case for every 250,000 newborns. Thus, the prior probability of a deficiency was 1/250,000 = 0.000004. Based on judgments about the probabilities of false-positive and false-negative test results, Bayes' theorem was used to calculate the posterior probability that a newborn with a positive test result actually had a deficiency. This posterior probability was 0.074. Thus, while a positive test result increased the probability the newborn had a deficiency from 0.000004 to 0.074, the probability that the newborn had a deficiency was still relatively low (0.074).

The probability information was helpful to doctors in reassuring worried parents that even though further testing was recommended, the chances were greater than 90% that a deficiency was not present. After the assignment of costs to the eight possible outcomes, decision analysis showed that the decision alternative to conduct the test provided the optimal decision strategy. The expected cost criterion established the expected cost to be approximately $6 per test. Decision analysis helped provide a realistic understanding of the risks and costs associated with the screening test.

*Based on James E. Smith and Robert L. Winkler, "Casey's Problem: Interpreting and Evaluating a New Test," *Interfaces* 29, no. 3 (May/June 1999): 63–76.

SUMMARY

Decision analysis can be used to determine a recommended decision alternative or an optimal decision strategy when a decision maker is faced with an uncertain and risk-filled pattern of future events. The goal of decision analysis is to identify the best decision alternative or the optimal decision strategy given information about the uncertain events and the possible consequences or payoffs. The uncertain future events are called chance events and the outcomes of the chance events are called states of nature.

We showed how influence diagrams, payoff tables, and decision trees could be used to structure a decision problem and describe the relationships among the decisions, the chance events, and the consequences. We presented three approaches to decision making without probabilities: the optimistic approach, the conservative approach, and the minimax regret approach. When probability assessments are provided for the states of nature, the expected value approach can be used to identify the recommended decision alternative or decision strategy.

In cases where sample information about the chance events is available, a sequence of decisions has to be made. First we must decide whether to obtain the sample information. If the answer to this decision is yes, an optimal decision strategy based on the specific sample information must be developed. In this situation, decision trees and the expected value approach can be used to determine the optimal decision strategy.

Even though the expected value approach can be used to obtain a recommended decision alternative or optimal decision strategy, the payoff that actually occurs will usually have a value different from the expected value. A risk profile provides a probability distribution for the possible payoffs and can assist the decision maker in assessing the risks associated with different decision alternatives. Finally, sensitivity analysis can be conducted to determine the effect changes in the probabilities for the states of nature and changes in the values of the payoffs have on the recommended decision alternative.

Decision analysis has been widely used in practice. The Management Science in Action, Investing in a Transmission System at Oglethorpe Power, describes the use of decision analysis to decide whether to invest in a major transmission system between Georgia and Florida.

MANAGEMENT SCIENCE IN ACTION

INVESTING IN A TRANSMISSION SYSTEM AT OGLETHORPE POWER*

Oglethorpe Power Corporation (OPC) provides wholesale electrical power to consumer-owned cooperatives in the state of Georgia. Florida Power Corporation proposed that OPC join in the building of a major transmission line from Georgia to Florida. Deciding whether to become involved in the building of the transmission line was a major decision for OPC because it would involve the commitment of substantial OPC resources. OPC worked with Applied Decision Analysis, Inc., to conduct a comprehensive decision analysis of the problem.

In the problem formulation step, three decisions were identified: (1) build a transmission line from Georgia to Florida; (2) upgrade existing transmission facilities; and (3) who would control the new facilities. Oglethorpe was faced with five chance events: (1) construction costs, (2) competition, (3) demand in Florida, (4) OPC's share of the operation, and (5) pricing. The consequence or payoff was measured in terms of dollars saved. The influence diagram for the problem had three decision nodes, five chance nodes, a consequence node, and several intermediate nodes that described intermediate calculations. The decision tree for the problem had more than 8000 paths from the starting node to the terminal branches.

An expected value analysis of the decision tree provided an optimal decision strategy for OPC. However, the risk profile for the optimal decision strategy showed that the recommended strategy was very risky and had a significant probability of increasing OPC's cost rather than providing a savings. The risk analysis led to the conclusion that more information about the competition was needed in order to reduce OPC's risk. Sensitivity analysis involving various probabilities and payoffs showed that the value of the optimal decision strategy was stable over a reasonable range of input values. The final recommendation from the decision analysis was that OPC should begin negotiations with Florida Power Corporation concerning the building of the new transmission line.

*Based on Adam Borison, "Oglethorpe Power Corporation Decides About Investing in a Major Transmission System," *Interfaces* (March/April 1995): 25–36.

GLOSSARY

Decision alternatives Options available to the decision maker.

Chance event An uncertain future event affecting the consequence, or payoff, associated with a decision.

Consequence The result obtained when a decision alternative is chosen and a chance event occurs. A measure of the consequence is often called a payoff.

States of nature The possible outcomes for chance events that affect the payoff associated with a decision alternative.

Influence diagram A graphical device that shows the relationship among decisions, chance events, and consequences for a decision problem.

Node An intersection or junction point of an influence diagram or a decision tree.

Decision nodes Nodes indicating points where a decision is made.

Chance nodes Nodes indicating points where an uncertain event will occur.

Consequence nodes Nodes of an influence diagram indicating points where a payoff will occur.

Payoff A measure of the consequence of a decision such as profit, cost, or time. Each combination of a decision alternative and a state of nature has an associated payoff (consequence).

Payoff table A tabular representation of the payoffs for a decision problem.

Decision tree A graphical representation of the decision problem that shows the sequential nature of the decision-making process.

Branch Lines showing the alternatives from decision nodes and the outcomes from chance nodes.

Optimistic approach An approach to choosing a decision alternative without using probabilities. For a maximization problem, it leads to choosing the decision alternative corresponding to the largest payoff; for a minimization problem, it leads to choosing the decision alternative corresponding to the smallest payoff.

Conservative approach An approach to choosing a decision alternative without using probabilities. For a maximization problem, it leads to choosing the decision alternative that maximizes the minimum payoff; for a minimization problem, it leads to choosing the decision alternative that minimizes the maximum payoff.

Minimax regret approach An approach to choosing a decision alternative without using probabilities. For each alternative, the maximum regret is computed, which leads to choosing the decision alternative that minimizes the maximum regret.

Opportunity loss, or regret The amount of loss (lower profit or higher cost) from not making the best decision for each state of nature.

Expected value approach An approach to choosing a decision alternative based on the expected value of each decision alternative. The recommended decision alternative is the one that provides the best expected value.

Expected value (EV) For a chance node, it is the weighted average of the payoffs. The weights are the state-of-nature probabilities.

Expected value of perfect information (EVPI) The expected value of information that would tell the decision maker exactly which state of nature is going to occur (i.e., perfect information).

Risk analysis The study of the possible payoffs and probabilities associated with a decision alternative or a decision strategy.

Sensitivity analysis The study of how changes in the probability assessments for the states of nature or changes in the payoffs affect the recommended decision alternative.

Risk profile The probability distribution of the possible payoffs associated with a decision alternative or decision strategy.

Prior probabilities The probabilities of the states of nature prior to obtaining sample information.

Sample information New information obtained through research or experimentation that enables an updating or revision of the state-of-nature probabilities.

Posterior (revised) probabilities The probabilities of the states of nature after revising the prior probabilities based on sample information.

Decision strategy A strategy involving a sequence of decisions and chance outcomes to provide the optimal solution to a decision problem.

Expected value of sample information (EVSI) The difference between the expected value of an optimal strategy based on sample information and the "best" expected value without any sample information.

Efficiency The ratio of EVSI to EVPI as a percentage; perfect information is 100% efficient.

Bayes' theorem A theorem that enables the use of sample information to revise prior probabilities.

Conditional probabilities The probability of one event given the known outcome of a (possibly) related event.

Joint probabilities The probabilities of both sample information and a particular state of nature occurring simultaneously.

PROBLEMS

1. The following payoff table shows profit for a decision analysis problem with two decision alternatives and three states of nature.

Decision Alternative	State of Nature s_1	s_2	s_3
d_1	250	100	25
d_2	100	100	75

   a. Construct a decision tree for this problem.
   b. If the decision maker knows nothing about the probabilities of the three states of nature, what is the recommended decision using the optimistic, conservative, and minimax regret approaches?

2. Suppose that a decision maker faced with four decision alternatives and four states of nature develops the following profit payoff table.

Decision Alternative	State of Nature s_1	s_2	s_3	s_4
d_1	14	9	10	5
d_2	11	10	8	7
d_3	9	10	10	11
d_4	8	10	11	13

   a. If the decision maker knows nothing about the probabilities of the four states of nature, what is the recommended decision using the optimistic, conservative, and minimax regret approaches?
   b. Which approach do you prefer? Explain. Is establishing the most appropriate approach before analyzing the problem important for the decision maker? Explain.
   c. Assume that the payoff table provides *cost* rather than profit payoffs. What is the recommended decision using the optimistic, conservative, and minimax regret approaches?

3. Southland Corporation's decision to produce a new line of recreational products resulted in the need to construct either a small plant or a large plant. The best selection of plant size depends on how the marketplace reacts to the new product line. To conduct an analysis, marketing management has decided to view the possible long-run demand as either low, medium, or high. The following payoff table shows the projected profit in millions of dollars:

Plant Size	Long-Run Demand Low	Medium	High
Small	150	200	200
Large	50	200	500

a. What is the decision to be made, and what is the chance event for Southland's problem?
b. Construct an influence diagram.
c. Construct a decision tree.
d. Recommend a decision based on the use of the optimistic, conservative, and minimax regret approaches.

4. The following profit payoff table was presented in Problem 1. Suppose that the decision maker obtained the probability assessments $P(s_1) = 0.65$, $P(s_2) = 0.15$, and $P(s_3) = 0.20$. Use the expected value approach to determine the optimal decision.

	State of Nature		
Decision Alternative	s_1	s_2	s_3
d_1	250	100	25
d_2	100	100	75

5. An investor wants to select one of seven mutual funds for the coming year. Data showing the percentage annual return for each fund during five typical one-year periods are shown here. The assumption is that one of these five-year periods will occur again during the coming year. Thus, years A, B, C, D, and E are the states of nature for the mutual fund decision.

	State of Nature				
Mutual Fund	Year A	Year B	Year C	Year D	Year E
Large-Cap Stock	35.3	20.0	28.3	10.4	−9.3
Mid-Cap Stock	32.3	23.2	−0.9	49.3	−22.8
Small-Cap Stock	20.8	22.5	6.0	33.3	6.1
Energy/Resources Sector	25.3	33.9	−20.5	20.9	−2.5
Health Sector	49.1	5.5	29.7	77.7	−24.9
Technology Sector	46.2	21.7	45.7	93.1	−20.1
Real Estate Sector	20.5	44.0	−21.1	2.6	5.1

a. Assume that the investor is conservative. What is the recommended mutual fund? Using this mutual fund, what are the minimum and maximum annual returns?
b. Suppose that an experienced financial analyst reviews the five states of nature and provides the following probabilities: 0.1, 0.3, 0.1, 0.1, and 0.4. Using the expected value, what is the recommended mutual fund? What is the expected annual return? Using this mutual fund, what are the minimum and maximum annual returns?
c. What is the expected annual return for the mutual fund recommended in part (a)? How much of an increase in the expected annual return can be obtained by following the recommendation in part (b)?
d. Which of the two mutual funds appears to have more risk? Why? Is the expected annual return greater for the mutual fund with more risk?
e. What mutual fund would you recommend to the investor? Explain.

6. Amy Lloyd is interested in leasing a new Saab and has contacted three automobile dealers for pricing information. Each dealer offered Amy a closed-end 36-month lease with no down payment due at the time of signing. Each lease includes a monthly charge and a mileage allowance. Additional miles receive a surcharge on a per-mile basis. The monthly lease cost, the mileage allowance, and the cost for additional miles follow:

Dealer	Monthly Cost	Mileage Allowance	Cost per Additional Mile
Forno Saab	$299	36,000	$0.15
Midtown Motors	$310	45,000	$0.20
Hopkins Automotive	$325	54,000	$0.15

Amy decided to choose the lease option that will minimize her total 36-month cost. The difficulty is that Amy is not sure how many miles she will drive over the next three years. For purposes of this decision she believes it is reasonable to assume that she will drive 12,000 miles per year, 15,000 miles per year, or 18,000 miles per year. With this assumption Amy estimated her total costs for the three lease options. For example, she figures that the Forno Saab lease will cost her $10,764 if she drives 12,000 miles per year, $12,114 if she drives 15,000 miles per year, or $13,464 if she drives 18,000 miles per year.

a. What is the decision, and what is the chance event?
b. Construct a payoff table for Amy's problem.
c. If Amy has no idea which of the three mileage assumptions is most appropriate, what is the recommended decision (leasing option) using the optimistic, conservative, and minimax regret approaches?
d. Suppose that the probabilities that Amy drives 12,000, 15,000, and 18,000 miles per year are 0.5, 0.4, and 0.1, respectively. What option should Amy choose using the expected value approach?
e. Develop a risk profile for the decision selected in part (d). What is the most likely cost, and what is its probability?
f. Suppose that after further consideration, Amy concludes that the probabilities that she will drive 12,000, 15,000, and 18,000 miles per year are 0.3, 0.4, and 0.3, respectively. What decision should Amy make using the expected value approach?

7. Hudson Corporation is considering three options for managing its data processing operation: continuing with its own staff, hiring an outside vendor to do the managing (referred to as *outsourcing*), or using a combination of its own staff and an outside vendor. The cost of the operation depends on future demand. The annual cost of each option (in thousands of dollars) depends on demand as follows.

	Demand		
Staffing Options	High	Medium	Low
Own staff	650	650	600
Outside vendor	900	600	300
Combination	800	650	500

a. If the demand probabilities are 0.2, 0.5, and 0.3, which decision alternative will minimize the expected cost of the data processing operation? What is the expected annual cost associated with that recommendation?
b. Construct a risk profile for the optimal decision in part (a). What is the probability of the cost exceeding $700,000?

8. The following payoff table shows the profit for a decision problem with two states of nature and two decision alternatives.

	State of Nature	
Decision Alternative	s_1	s_2
d_1	10	1
d_2	4	3

a. Use graphical sensitivity analysis to determine the range of probabilities of state of nature s_1 for which each of the decision alternatives has the largest expected value.
b. Suppose $P(s_1) = 0.2$ and $P(s_2) = 0.8$. What is the best decision using the expected value approach?
c. Perform sensitivity analysis on the payoffs for decision alternative d_1. Assume the probabilities are as given in part (b) and find the range of payoffs under states of nature s_1 and s_2 that will keep the solution found in part (b) optimal. Is the solution more sensitive to the payoff under state of nature s_1 or s_2?

9. Myrtle Air Express decided to offer direct service from Cleveland to Myrtle Beach. Management must decide between a full-price service using the company's new fleet of jet aircraft and a discount service using smaller capacity commuter planes. It is clear that the best choice depends on the market reaction to the service Myrtle Air offers. Management developed estimates of the contribution to profit for each type of service based upon two possible levels of demand for service to Myrtle Beach: strong and weak. The following table shows the estimated quarterly profits (in thousands of dollars).

	Demand for Service	
Service	**Strong**	**Weak**
Full price	\$960	−\$490
Discount	\$670	\$320

a. What is the decision to be made, what is the chance event, and what is the consequence for this problem? How many decision alternatives are there? How many outcomes are there for the chance event?
b. If nothing is known about the probabilities of the chance outcomes, what is the recommended decision using the optimistic, conservative, and minimax regret approaches?
c. Suppose that management of Myrtle Air Express believes that the probability of strong demand is 0.7 and the probability of weak demand is 0.3. Use the expected value approach to determine an optimal decision.
d. Suppose that the probability of strong demand is 0.8 and the probability of weak demand is 0.2. What is the optimal decision using the expected value approach?
e. Use graphical sensitivity analysis to determine the range of demand probabilities for which each of the decision alternatives has the largest expected value.

10. Video Tech is considering marketing one of two new video games for the coming holiday season: Battle Pacific or Space Pirates. Battle Pacific is a unique game and appears to have no competition. Estimated profits (in thousands of dollars) under high, medium, and low demand are as follows:

		Demand	
Battle Pacific	**High**	**Medium**	**Low**
Profit	\$1000	\$700	\$300
Probability	0.2	0.5	0.3

Video Tech is optimistic about its Space Pirates game. However, the concern is that profitability will be affected by a competitor's introduction of a video game viewed as similar to Space Pirates. Estimated profits (in thousands of dollars) with and without competition are as follows:

Space Pirates with Competition	Demand High	Demand Medium	Demand Low
Profit	$800	$400	$200
Probability	0.3	0.4	0.3

Space Pirates without Competition	Demand High	Demand Medium	Demand Low
Profit	$1600	$800	$400
Probability	0.5	0.3	0.2

a. Develop a decision tree for the Video Tech problem.
b. For planning purposes, Video Tech believes there is a 0.6 probability that its competitor will produce a new game similar to Space Pirates. Given this probability of competition, the director of planning recommends marketing the Battle Pacific video game. Using expected value, what is your recommended decision?
c. Show a risk profile for your recommended decision.
d. Use sensitivity analysis to determine what the probability of competition for Space Pirates would have to be for you to change your recommended decision alternative.

11. For the Pittsburgh Development Corporation problem in Section 13.3, the decision alternative to build the large condominium complex was found to be optimal using the expected value approach. In Section 13.4 we conducted a sensitivity analysis for the payoffs associated with this decision alternative. We found that the large complex remained optimal as long as the payoff for the strong demand was greater than or equal to $17.5 million and as long as the payoff for the weak demand was greater than or equal to −$19 million.
    a. Consider the medium complex decision. How much could the payoff under strong demand increase and still keep decision alternative d_3 the optimal solution?
    b. Consider the small complex decision. How much could the payoff under strong demand increase and still keep decision alternative d_3 the optimal solution?

12. The distance from Potsdam to larger markets and limited air service have hindered the town in attracting new industry. Air Express, a major overnight delivery service, is considering establishing a regional distribution center in Potsdam. However, Air Express will not establish the center unless the length of the runway at the local airport is increased. Another candidate for new development is Diagnostic Research, Inc. (DRI), a leading producer of medical testing equipment. DRI is considering building a new manufacturing plant. Increasing the length of the runway is not a requirement for DRI, but the planning commission feels that doing so will help convince DRI to locate their new plant in Potsdam. Assuming that the town lengthens the runway, the Potsdam planning commission believes that the probabilities shown in the following table are applicable.

	DRI Plant	**No DRI Plant**
Air Express Center	.30	.10
No Air Express Center	.40	.20

For instance, the probability that Air Express will establish a distribution center and DRI will build a plant is .30.

The estimated annual revenue to the town, after deducting the cost of lengthening the runway, is as follows:

	DRI Plant	No DRI Plant
Air Express Center	\$600,000	\$150,000
No Air Express Center	\$250,000	−\$200,000

If the runway expansion project is not conducted, the planning commission assesses the probability DRI will locate their new plant in Potsdam at 0.6; in this case, the estimated annual revenue to the town will be \$450,000. If the runway expansion project is not conducted and DRI does not locate in Potsdam, the annual revenue will be \$0 since no cost will have been incurred and no revenues will be forthcoming.

a. What is the decision to be made, what is the chance event, and what is the consequence?
b. Compute the expected annual revenue associated with the decision alternative to lengthen the runway.
c. Compute the expected annual revenue associated with the decision alternative to not lengthen the runway.
d. Should the town elect to lengthen the runway? Explain.
e. Suppose that the probabilities associated with lengthening the runway were as follows:

	DRI Plant	No DRI Plant
Air Express Center	.40	.10
No Air Express Center	.30	.20

What effect, if any, would this change in the probabilities have on the recommended decision?

13. Seneca Hill Winery recently purchased land for the purpose of establishing a new vineyard. Management is considering two varieties of white grapes for the new vineyard: Chardonnay and Riesling. The Chardonnay grapes would be used to produce a dry Chardonnay wine, and the Riesling grapes would be used to produce a semi-dry Riesling wine. It takes approximately four years from the time of planting before new grapes can be harvested. This length of time creates a great deal of uncertainty concerning future demand and makes the decision concerning the type of grapes to plant difficult. Three possibilities are being considered: Chardonnay grapes only; Riesling grapes only; and both Chardonnay and Riesling grapes. Seneca management decided that for planning purposes it would be adequate to consider only two demand possibilities for each type of wine: strong or weak. With two possibilities for each type of wine it was necessary to assess four probabilities. With the help of some forecasts in industry publications management made the following probability assessments.

	Riesling Demand	
Chardonnay Demand	**Weak**	**Strong**
Weak	0.05	0.50
Strong	0.25	0.20

Revenue projections show an annual contribution to profit of $20,000 if Seneca Hill only plants Chardonnay grapes and demand is weak for Chardonnay wine, and $70,000 if they only plant Chardonnay grapes and demand is strong for Chardonnay wine. If they only plant Riesling grapes, the annual profit projection is $25,000 if demand is weak for Riesling grapes and $45,000 if demand is strong for Riesling grapes. If Seneca plants both types of grapes, the annual profit projections are shown in the following table.

	Riesling Demand	
Chardonnay Demand	**Weak**	**Strong**
Weak	$22,000	$40,000
Strong	$26,000	$60,000

a. What is the decision to be made, what is the chance event, and what is the consequence? Identify the alternatives for the decisions and the possible outcomes for the chance events.
b. Develop a decision tree.
c. Use the expected value approach to recommend which alternative Seneca Hill Winery should follow in order to maximize expected annual profit.
d. Suppose management is concerned about the probability assessments when demand for Chardonnay wine is strong. Some believe it is likely for Riesling demand to also be strong in this case. Suppose the probability of strong demand for Chardonnay and weak demand for Riesling is 0.05 and that the probability of strong demand for Chardonnay and strong demand for Riesling is 0.40. How does this change the recommended decision? Assume that the probabilities when Chardonnay demand is weak are still 0.05 and 0.50.
e. Other members of the management team expect the Chardonnay market to become saturated at some point in the future, causing a fall in prices. Suppose that the annual profit projections fall to $50,000 when demand for Chardonnay is strong and Chardonnay grapes only are planted. Using the original probability assessments, determine how this change would affect the optimal decision.

14. The following profit payoff table was presented in Problems 1 and 4.

	State of Nature		
Decision Alternative	s_1	s_2	s_3
d_1	250	100	25
d_2	100	100	75

The probabilities for the states of nature are $P(s_1) = 0.65$, $P(s_2) = 0.15$, and $P(s_3) = 0.20$.

a. What is the optimal decision strategy if perfect information were available?
b. What is the expected value for the decision strategy developed in part (a)?
c. Using the expected value approach, what is the recommended decision without perfect information? What is its expected value?
d. What is the expected value of perfect information?

15. The Lake Placid Town Council decided to build a new community center to be used for conventions, concerts, and other public events, but considerable controversy surrounds the appropriate size. Many influential citizens want a large center that would be a showcase for the area. But the mayor feels that if demand does not support such a center, the community

will lose a large amount of money. To provide structure for the decision process, the council narrowed the building alternatives to three sizes: small, medium, and large. Everybody agreed that the critical factor in choosing the best size is the number of people who will want to use the new facility. A regional planning consultant provided demand estimates under three scenarios: worst case, base case, and best case. The worst-case scenario corresponds to a situation in which tourism drops significantly; the base-case scenario corresponds to a situation in which Lake Placid continues to attract visitors at current levels; and the best-case scenario corresponds to a significant increase in tourism. The consultant has provided probability assessments of 0.10, 0.60, and 0.30 for the worst-case, base-case, and best-case scenarios, respectively.

The town council suggested using net cash flow over a five-year planning horizon as the criterion for deciding on the best size. The following projections of net cash flow (in thousands of dollars) for a five-year planning horizon have been developed. All costs, including the consultant's fee, have been included.

	Demand Scenario		
Center Size	Worst Case	Base Case	Best Case
Small	400	500	660
Medium	−250	650	800
Large	−400	580	990

a. What decision should Lake Placid make using the expected value approach?
b. Construct risk profiles for the medium and large alternatives. Given the mayor's concern over the possibility of losing money and the result of part (a), which alternative would you recommend?
c. Compute the expected value of perfect information. Do you think it would be worth trying to obtain additional information concerning which scenario is likely to occur?
d. Suppose the probability of the worst-case scenario increases to 0.2, the probability of the base-case scenario decreases to 0.5, and the probability of the best-case scenario remains at 0.3. What effect, if any, would these changes have on the decision recommendation?
e. The consultant has suggested that an expenditure of $150,000 on a promotional campaign over the planning horizon will effectively reduce the probability of the worst-case scenario to zero. If the campaign can be expected to also increase the probability of the best-case scenario to 0.4, is it a good investment?

16. Consider a variation of the PDC decision tree shown in Figure 13.9. The company must first decide whether to undertake the market research study. If the market research study is conducted, the outcome will either be favorable (F) or unfavorable (U). Assume there are only two decision alternatives d_1 and d_2 and two states of nature s_1 and s_2. The payoff table showing profit is as follows:

	State of Nature	
Decision Alternative	s_1	s_2
d_1	100	300
d_2	400	200

a. Show the decision tree.
b. Using the following probabilities, what is the optimal decision strategy?

$P(F) = 0.56$	$P(s_1 \mid F) = 0.57$	$P(s_1 \mid U) = 0.18$	$P(s_1) = 0.40$
$P(U) = 0.44$	$P(s_2 \mid F) = 0.43$	$P(s_2 \mid U) = 0.82$	$P(s_2) = 0.60$

17. Hemmingway, Inc., is considering a \$5 million research and development (R&D) project. Profit projections appear promising, but Hemmingway's president is concerned because the probability that the R&D project will be successful is only 0.50. Secondly, the president knows that even if the project is successful, it will require that the company build a new production facility at a cost of \$20 million in order to manufacture the product. If the facility is built, uncertainty remains about the demand and thus uncertainty about the profit that will be realized. Another option is that if the R&D project is successful, the company could sell the rights to the product for an estimated \$25 million. Under this option, the company would not build the \$20 million production facility.

The decision tree is shown in Figure 13.16. The profit projection for each outcome is shown at the end of the branches. For example, the revenue projection for the high demand outcome is \$59 million. However, the cost of the R&D project (\$5 million) and the cost of the production facility (\$20 million) show the profit of this outcome to be \$59 − \$5 − \$20 = \$34 million. Branch probabilities are also shown for the chance events.

a. Analyze the decision tree to determine whether the company should undertake the R&D project. If it does, and if the R&D project is successful, what should the company do? What is the expected value of your strategy?
b. What must the selling price be for the company to consider selling the rights to the product?
c. Develop a risk profile for the optimal strategy.

FIGURE 13.16 DECISION TREE FOR HEMMINGWAY, INC.

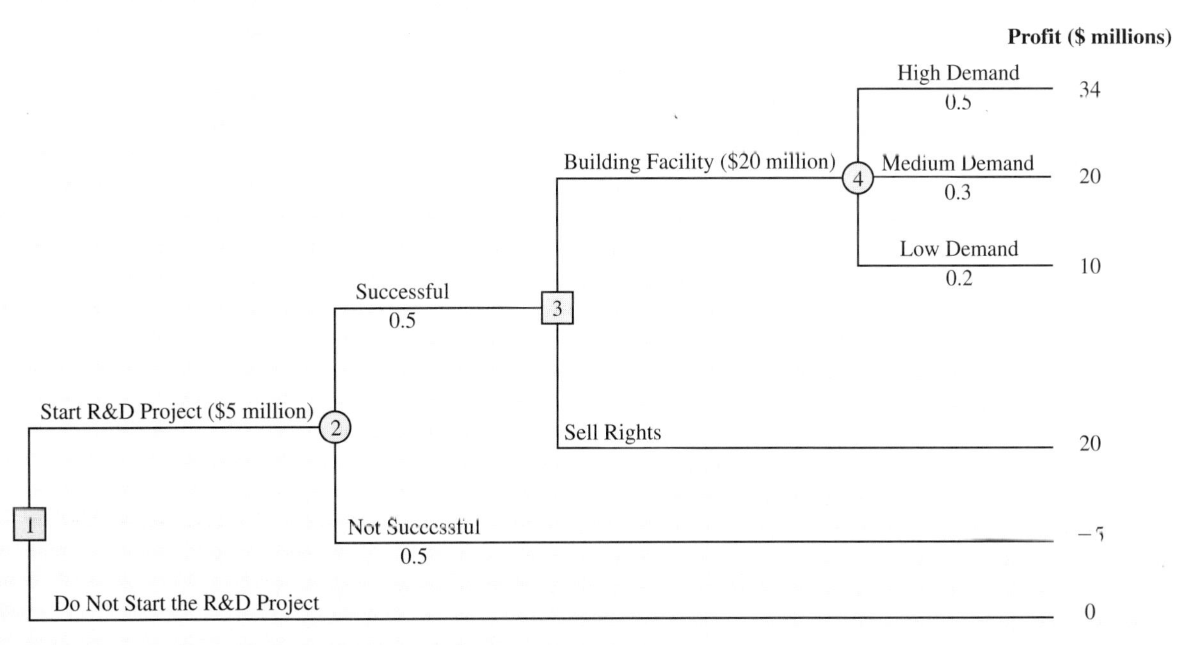

18. Dante Development Corporation is considering bidding on a contract for a new office building complex. Figure 13.17 shows the decision tree prepared by one of Dante's analysts. At node 1, the company must decide whether to bid on the contract. The cost of preparing the bid is $200,000. The upper branch from node 2 shows that the company has a 0.8 probability of winning the contract if it submits a bid. If the company wins the bid, it will have to pay $2,000,000 to become a partner in the project. Node 3 shows that the company will then consider doing a market research study to forecast demand for the office units prior to beginning construction. The cost of this study is $150,000. Node 4 is a chance node showing the possible outcomes of the market research study.

Nodes 5, 6, and 7 are similar in that they are the decision nodes for Dante to either build the office complex or sell the rights in the project to another developer. The decision to build the complex will result in an income of $5,000,000 if demand is high and $3,000,000 if demand is moderate. If Dante chooses to sell its rights in the project to another developer, income from the sale is estimated to be $3,500,000. The probabilities shown at nodes 4, 8, and 9 are based on the projected outcomes of the market research study.

a. Verify Dante's profit projections shown at the ending branches of the decision tree by calculating the payoffs of $2,650,000 and $650,000 for first two outcomes.
b. What is the optimal decision strategy for Dante, and what is the expected profit for this project?
c. What would the cost of the market research study have to be before Dante would change its decision about the market research study?
d. Develop a risk profile for Dante.

19. Hale's TV Productions is considering producing a pilot for a comedy series in the hope of selling it to a major television network. The network may decide to reject the series, but it may also decide to purchase the rights to the series for either one or two years. At this point

FIGURE 13.17 DECISION TREE FOR THE DANTE DEVELOPMENT CORPORATION

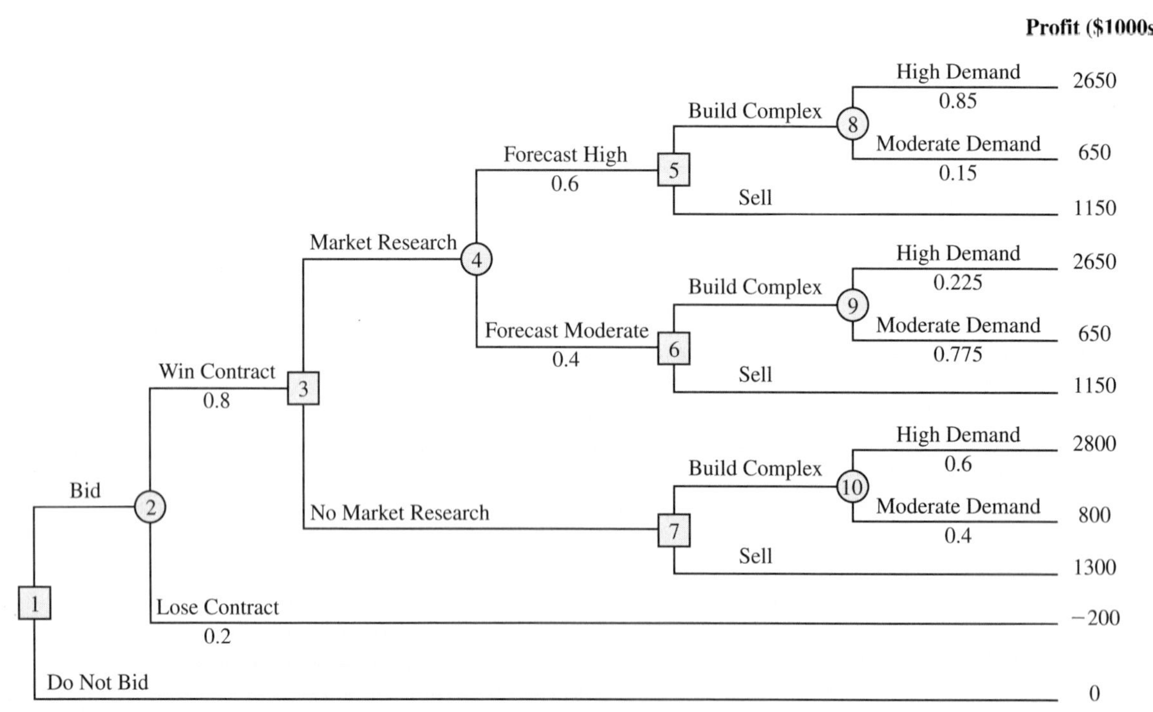

in time, Hale may either produce the pilot and wait for the network's decision or transfer the rights for the pilot and series to a competitor for $100,000. Hale's decision alternatives and profits (in thousands of dollars) are as follows:

	State of Nature		
Decision Alternative	**Reject, s_1**	**1 Year, s_2**	**2 Years, s_3**
Produce pilot, d_1	−100	50	150
Sell to competitor, d_2	100	100	100

The probabilities for the states of nature are $P(s_1) = 0.20$, $P(s_2) = 0.30$, and $P(s_3) = 0.50$. For a consulting fee of $5000, an agency will review the plans for the comedy series and indicate the overall chances of a favorable network reaction to the series. Assume that the agency review will result in a favorable (F) or an unfavorable (U) review and that the following probabilities are relevant.

$$P(F) = 0.69 \quad P(s_1 \mid F) = 0.09 \quad P(s_1 \mid U) = 0.45$$
$$P(U) = 0.31 \quad P(s_2 \mid F) = 0.26 \quad P(s_2 \mid U) = 0.39$$
$$P(s_3 \mid F) = 0.65 \quad P(s_3 \mid U) = 0.16$$

a. Construct a decision tree for this problem.
b. What is the recommended decision if the agency opinion is not used? What is the expected value?
c. What is the expected value of perfect information?
d. What is Hale's optimal decision strategy assuming the agency's information is used?
e. What is the expected value of the agency's information?
f. Is the agency's information worth the $5000 fee? What is the maximum that Hale should be willing to pay for the information?
g. What is the recommended decision?

20. Embassy Publishing Company received a six-chapter manuscript for a new college textbook. The editor of the college division is familiar with the manuscript and estimated a 0.65 probability that the textbook will be successful. If successful, a profit of $750,000 will be realized. If the company decides to publish the textbook and it is unsuccessful, a loss of $250,000 will occur.

Before making the decision to accept or reject the manuscript, the editor is considering sending the manuscript out for review. A review process provides either a favorable (F) or unfavorable (U) evaluation of the manuscript. Past experience with the review process suggests probabilities $P(F) = 0.7$ and $P(U) = 0.3$ apply. Let s_1 = the textbook is successful, and s_2 = the textbook is unsuccessful. The editor's initial probabilities of s_1 and s_2 will be revised based on whether the review is favorable or unfavorable. The revised probabilities are as follows.

$$P(s_1 \mid F) = 0.75 \quad P(s_1 \mid U) = 0.417$$
$$P(s_2 \mid F) = 0.25 \quad P(s_2 \mid U) = 0.583$$

a. Construct a decision tree assuming that the company will first make the decision of whether to send the manuscript out for review and then make the decision to accept or reject the manuscript.
b. Analyze the decision tree to determine the optimal decision strategy for the publishing company.
c. If the manuscript review costs $5000, what is your recommendation?
d. What is the expected value of perfect information? What does this EVPI suggest for the company?

21. A real estate investor has the opportunity to purchase land currently zoned residential. If the county board approves a request to rezone the property as commercial within the next year, the investor will be able to lease the land to a large discount firm that wants to open a new store on the property. However, if the zoning change is not approved, the investor will have to sell the property at a loss. Profits (in thousands of dollars) are shown in the following payoff table.

	State of Nature	
	Rezoning Approved	**Rezoning Not Approved**
Decision Alternative	s_1	s_2
Purchase, d_1	600	−200
Do not purchase, d_2	0	0

a. If the probability that the rezoning will be approved is 0.5, what decision is recommended? What is the expected profit?

b. The investor can purchase an option to buy the land. Under the option, the investor maintains the rights to purchase the land anytime during the next three months while learning more about possible resistance to the rezoning proposal from area residents. Probabilities are as follows.

Let H = High resistance to rezoning
L = Low resistance to rezoning

$$P(H) = 0.55 \qquad P(s_1 \mid H) = 0.18 \qquad P(s_2 \mid H) = 0.82$$
$$P(L) = 0.45 \qquad P(s_1 \mid L) = 0.89 \qquad P(s_2 \mid L) = 0.11$$

What is the optimal decision strategy if the investor uses the option period to learn more about the resistance from area residents before making the purchase decision?

c. If the option will cost the investor an additional $10,000, should the investor purchase the option? Why or why not? What is the maximum that the investor should be willing to pay for the option?

22. Lawson's Department Store faces a buying decision for a seasonal product for which demand can be high, medium, or low. The purchaser for Lawson's can order 1, 2, or 3 lots of the product before the season begins but cannot reorder later. Profit projections (in thousands of dollars) are shown.

	State of Nature		
	High Demand	**Medium Demand**	**Low Demand**
Decision Alternative	s_1	s_2	s_3
Order 1 lot, d_1	60	60	50
Order 2 lots, d_2	80	80	30
Order 3 lots, d_3	100	70	10

a. If the prior probabilities for the three states of nature are 0.3, 0.3, and 0.4, respectively, what is the recommended order quantity?

b. At each preseason sales meeting, the vice president of sales provides a personal opinion regarding potential demand for this product. Because of the vice president's enthusiasm and optimistic nature, the predictions of market conditions have always been either "excellent" (E) or "very good" (V). Probabilities are as follows.

$P(E) = 0.70$	$P(s_1 \mid E) = 0.34$	$P(s_1 \mid V) = 0.20$
$P(V) = 0.30$	$P(s_2 \mid E) = 0.32$	$P(s_2 \mid V) = 0.26$
	$P(s_3 \mid E) = 0.34$	$P(s_3 \mid V) = 0.54$

What is the optimal decision strategy?

c. Use the efficiency of sample information and discuss whether the firm should consider a consulting expert who could provide independent forecasts of market conditions for the product.

23. Suppose that you are given a decision situation with three possible states of nature: s_1, s_2, and s_3. The prior probabilities are $P(s_1) = 0.2$, $P(s_2) = 0.5$, and $P(s_3) = 0.3$. With sample information I, $P(I \mid s_1) = 0.1$, $P(I \mid s_2) = 0.05$, and $P(I \mid s_3) = 0.2$. Compute the revised or posterior probabilities: $P(s_1 \mid I)$, $P(s_2 \mid I)$, and $P(s_3 \mid I)$.

24. To save on expenses, Rona and Jerry agreed to form a carpool for traveling to and from work. Rona preferred to use the somewhat longer but more consistent Queen City Avenue. Although Jerry preferred the quicker expressway, he agreed with Rona that they should take Queen City Avenue if the expressway had a traffic jam. The following payoff table provides the one-way time estimate in minutes for traveling to or from work.

	State of Nature	
	Expressway Open	**Expressway Jammed**
Decision Alternative	s_1	s_2
Queen City Avenue, d_1	30	30
Expressway, d_2	25	45

Based on their experience with traffic problems, Rona and Jerry agreed on a 0.15 probability that the expressway would be jammed.

In addition, they agreed that weather seemed to affect the traffic conditions on the expressway. Let

C = clear
O = overcast
R = rain

The following conditional probabilities apply.

$P(C \mid s_1) = 0.8$	$P(O \mid s_1) = 0.2$	$P(R \mid s_1) = 0.0$
$P(C \mid s_2) = 0.1$	$P(O \mid s_2) = 0.3$	$P(R \mid s_2) = 0.6$

a. Use Bayes' theorem for probability revision to compute the probability of each weather condition and the conditional probability of the expressway open s_1 or jammed s_2 given each weather condition.

b. Show the decision tree for this problem.

c. What is the optimal decision strategy, and what is the expected travel time?

25. The Gorman Manufacturing Company must decide whether to manufacture a component part at its Milan, Michigan, plant or purchase the component part from a supplier. The resulting profit is dependent upon the demand for the product. The following payoff table shows the projected profit (in thousands of dollars).

	State of Nature		
	Low Demand	**Medium Demand**	**High Demand**
Decision Alternative	s_1	s_2	s_3
Manufacture, d_1	−20	40	100
Purchase, d_2	10	45	70

The state-of-nature probabilities are $P(s_1) = 0.35$, $P(s_2) = 0.35$, and $P(s_3) = 0.30$.

a. Use a decision tree to recommend a decision.

b. Use EVPI to determine whether Gorman should attempt to obtain a better estimate of demand.

c. A test market study of the potential demand for the product is expected to report either a favorable (F) or unfavorable (U) condition. The relevant conditional probabilities are as follows:

$$P(F \mid s_1) = 0.10 \qquad P(U \mid s_1) = 0.90$$
$$P(F \mid s_2) = 0.40 \qquad P(U \mid s_2) = 0.60$$
$$P(F \mid s_3) = 0.60 \qquad P(U \mid s_3) = 0.40$$

What is the probability that the market research report will be favorable?

d. What is Gorman's optimal decision strategy?

e. What is the expected value of the market research information?

f. What is the efficiency of the information?

Case Problem 1 PROPERTY PURCHASE STRATEGY

Glenn Foreman, president of Oceanview Development Corporation, is considering submitting a bid to purchase property that will be sold by sealed bid at a county tax foreclosure. Glenn's initial judgment is to submit a bid of $5 million. Based on his experience, Glenn estimates that a bid of $5 million will have a 0.2 probability of being the highest bid and securing the property for Oceanview. The current date is June 1. Sealed bids for the property must be submitted by August 15. The winning bid will be announced on September 1.

If Oceanview submits the highest bid and obtains the property, the firm plans to build and sell a complex of luxury condominiums. However, a complicating factor is that the property is currently zoned for single-family residences only. Glenn believes that a referendum could be placed on the voting ballot in time for the November election. Passage of the referendum would change the zoning of the property and permit construction of the condominiums.

The sealed-bid procedure requires the bid to be submitted with a certified check for 10% of the amount bid. If the bid is rejected, the deposit is refunded. If the bid is accepted, the deposit is the down payment for the property. However, if the bid is accepted and the bidder does not follow through with the purchase and meet the remainder of the financial obligation within six months, the deposit will be forfeited. In this case, the county will offer the property to the next highest bidder.

To determine whether Oceanview should submit the $5 million bid, Glenn conducted some preliminary analysis. This preliminary work provided an assessment of 0.3 for the probability that the referendum for a zoning change will be approved and resulted in the following estimates of the costs and revenues that will be incurred if the condominiums are built.

Cost and Revenue Estimates	
Revenue from condominium sales	\$15,000,000
Cost	
Property	\$5,000,000
Construction expenses	\$8,000,000

If Oceanview obtains the property and the zoning change is rejected in November, Glenn believes that the best option would be for the firm not to complete the purchase of the property. In this case, Oceanview would forfeit the 10 percent deposit that accompanied the bid.

Because the likelihood that the zoning referendum will be approved is such an important factor in the decision process, Glenn suggested that the firm hire a market research service to conduct a survey of voters. The survey would provide a better estimate of the likelihood that the referendum for a zoning change would be approved. The market research firm that Oceanview Development has worked with in the past has agreed to do the study for \$15,000. The results of the study will be available August 1, so that Oceanview will have this information before the August 15 bid deadline. The results of the survey will be either a prediction that the zoning change will be approved or a prediction that the zoning change will be rejected. After considering the record of the market research service in previous studies conducted for Oceanview, Glenn developed the following probability estimates concerning the accuracy of the market research information.

$$P(A \mid s_1) = 0.9 \qquad P(N \mid s_1) = 0.1$$
$$P(A \mid s_2) = 0.2 \qquad P(N \mid s_2) = 0.8$$

where

A = prediction of zoning change approval
N = prediction that zoning change will not be approved
s_1 = the zoning change is approved by the voters
s_2 = the zoning change is rejected by the voters

Managerial Report

Perform an analysis of the problem facing the Oceanview Development Corporation, and prepare a report that summarizes your findings and recommendations. Include the following items in your report:

1. A decision tree that shows the logical sequence of the decision problem
2. A recommendation regarding what Oceanview should do if the market research information is not available
3. A decision strategy that Oceanview should follow if the market research is conducted
4. A recommendation as to whether Oceanview should employ the market research firm, along with the value of the information provided by the market research firm

Include the details of your analysis as an appendix to your report.

Case Problem 2 LAWSUIT DEFENSE STRATEGY

John Campbell, an employee of Manhattan Construction Company, claims to have injured his back as a result of a fall while repairing the roof at one of the Eastview apartment buildings. He filed a lawsuit against Doug Reynolds, the owner of Eastview Apartments, asking for damages of $1,500,000. John claims that the roof had rotten sections and that his fall could have been prevented if Mr. Reynolds had told Manhattan Construction about the problem. Mr. Reynolds notified his insurance company, Allied Insurance, of the lawsuit. Allied must defend Mr. Reynolds and decide what action to take regarding the lawsuit.

Some depositions and a series of discussions took place between both sides. As a result, John Campbell offered to accept a settlement of $750,000. Thus, one option is for Allied to pay John $750,000 to settle the claim. Allied is also considering making John a counteroffer of $400,000 in the hope that he will accept a lesser amount to avoid the time and cost of going to trial. Allied's preliminary investigation shows that John's case is strong; Allied is concerned that John may reject their counteroffer and request a jury trial. Allied's lawyers spent some time exploring John's likely reaction if they make a counteroffer of $400,000.

The lawyers concluded that it is adequate to consider three possible outcomes to represent John's possible reaction to a counteroffer of $400,000: (1) John will accept the counteroffer and the case will be closed; (2) John will reject the counteroffer and elect to have a jury decide the settlement amount; or (3) John will make a counteroffer to Allied of $600,000. If John does make a counteroffer, Allied decided that they will not make additional counteroffers. They will either accept John's counteroffer of $600,000 or go to trial.

If the case goes to a jury trial, Allied considers three outcomes possible: (1) the jury may reject John's claim and Allied will not be required to pay any damages; (2) the jury will find in favor of John and award him $750,000 in damages; or (3) the jury will conclude that John has a strong case and award him the full amount of $1,500,000.

Key considerations as Allied develops its strategy for disposing of the case are the probabilities associated with John's response to an Allied counteroffer of $400,000 and the probabilities associated with the three possible trial outcomes. Allied's lawyers believe the probability that John will accept a counteroffer of $400,000 is 0.10, the probability that John will reject a counteroffer of $400,000 is 0.40, and the probability that John will, himself, make a counteroffer to Allied of $600,000 is 0.50. If the case goes to court, they believe that the probability the jury will award John damages of $1,500,000 is 0.30, the probability that the jury will award John damages of $750,000 is 0.50, and the probability that the jury will award John nothing is 0.20.

Managerial Report

Perform an analysis of the problem facing Allied Insurance and prepare a report that summarizes your findings and recommendations. Be sure to include the following items:

1. A decision tree
2. A recommendation regarding whether Allied should accept John's initial offer to settle the claim for $750,000
3. A decision strategy that Allied should follow if they decide to make John a counteroffer of $400,000
4. A risk profile for your recommended strategy

Appendix 13.1 DECISION ANALYSIS WITH TREEPLAN

Tutorial 9: Decision Analysis Using TreePlan

TreePlan* is an Excel add-in that can be used to develop decision trees for decision analysis problems. The software package is provided on the CD that accompanies this text. Instructions for installing TreePlan are included with the software. A manual containing

*TreePlan was developed by Professor Michael R. Middleton at the University of San Francisco and modified for use by Professor James E. Smith at Duke University. The TreePlan Web site is www.treeplan.com.

FIGURE 13.18 PDC DECISION TREE

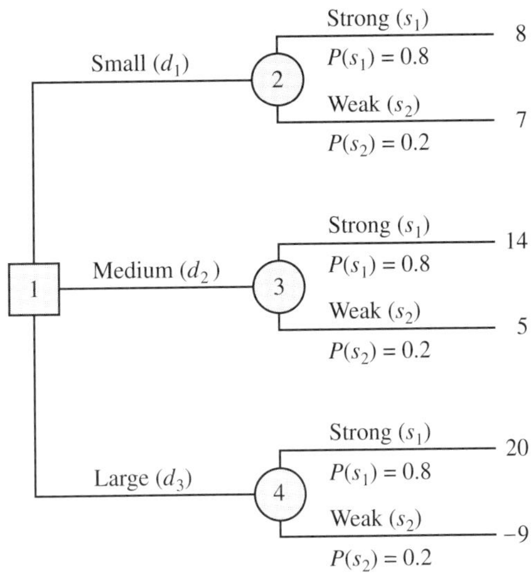

additional information on starting and using TreePlan is also included on the CD. In this appendix, we show how to use TreePlan to build a decision tree and solve the PDC problem presented in Section 13.3. The decision tree for the PDC problem is shown in Figure 13.18.

Getting Started: An Initial Decision Tree

We begin by assuming that TreePlan has been installed and an Excel worksheet is open. To build a TreePlan version of the PDC decision tree proceed as follows:

Step 1. Sclcct cell A1
Step 2. Select the **Tools** menu and choose **Decisloii Tree**
Step 3. When the **TreePlan New** dialog box appears:
Click **New Tree**

A decision tree with one decision node and two branches appears as follows:

	A	B	C	D	E	F	G
1							
2				Decision 1			
3							0
4				0	0		
5		1					
6	0						
7				Decision 2			
8							0
9				0	0		

Adding a Branch

The PDC problem has three decision alternatives (small, medium, and large condominium complexes), so we must add another decision branch to the tree.

Step 1. Select cell B5
Step 2. Select the **Tools** menu and choose **Decision Tree**
Step 3. When the **TreePlan Decision** dialog box appears:
Select **Add branch**
Click **OK**

A revised tree with three decision branches now appears in the Excel worksheet.

Naming the Decision Alternatives

The decision alternatives can be named by selecting the cells containing the labels Decision 1, Decision 2, and Decision 3, and then entering the corresponding PDC names Small, Medium, and Large. After naming the alternatives, the PDC tree with three decision branches appears as follows:

	A	B	C	D	E	F	G
1							
2				Small			
3							0
4				0	0		
5							
6							
7				Medium			
8		1					0
9	0			0	0		
10							
11							
12				Large			
13							0
14				0	0		

Adding Chance Nodes

The chance event for the PDC problem is the demand for the condominiums, which may be either strong or weak. Thus, a chance node with two branches must be added at the end of each decision alternative branch.

Step 1. Select cell F3
Step 2. Select the **Tools** menu and choose **Decision Tree**
Step 3. When the **TreePlan Terminal** dialog box appears:
Select **Change to event node**
Select **Two** in the **Branches** section
Click **OK**

The tree now appears as follows:

	A	B	C	D	E	F	G	H	I	J	K
1								0.5			
2								Event 4			
3											0
4				Small				0	0		
5											
6				0	0			0.5			
7								Event 5			
8											0
9								0	0		
10											
11		1									
12	0			Medium							
13											0
14				0	0						
15											
16											
17				Large							
18											0
19				0	0						

We next select the cells containing Event 4 and Event 5 and rename them Strong and Weak to provide the proper names for the PDC states of nature. After doing so we can copy the subtree for the chance node in cell F5 to the other two decision branches to complete the structure of the PDC decision tree.

Step 1. Select cell F5
Step 2. Select the **Tools** menu and choose **Decision Tree**
Step 3. When the **TreePlan Event** dialog box appears:
Select **Copy subtree**
Click **OK**
Step 4. Select cell F13
Step 5. Select the **Tools** menu and choose **Decision Tree**
Step 6. When the **TreePlan Terminal** dialog box appears:
Select **Paste subtree**
Click **OK**

This copy/paste procedure places a chance node at the end of the Medium decision branch. Repeating the same copy/paste procedure for the Large decision branch completes the structure of the PDC decision tree as shown in Figure 13.19.

Inserting Probabilities and Payoffs

TreePlan provides the capability of inserting probabilities and payoffs into the decision tree. In Figure 13.19, we see that TreePlan automatically assigned an equal probability 0.5 to each of the chance outcomes. For PDC, the probability of strong demand is 0.8 and the probability of weak demand is 0.2. We can select cells H1, H6, H11, H16, H21, and H26 and insert the appropriate probabilities. The payoffs for the chance outcomes are inserted in cells H4, H9, H14, H19, H24, and H29. After inserting the PDC probabilities and payoffs, the PDC decision tree appears as shown in Figure 13.20.

FIGURE 13.19 THE PDC DECISION TREE DEVELOPED BY TREEPLAN

	A	B	C	D	E	F	G	H	I	J	K
1								0.5			
2								Strong			
3											0
4				Small				0	0		
5											
6				0	0			0.5			
7								Weak			
8											0
9								0	0		
10											
11								0.5			
12								Strong			
13											0
14				Medium				0	0		
15		1									
16	0			0	0			0.5			
17								Weak			
18											0
19								0	0		
20											
21								0.5			
22								Strong			
23											0
24				Large				0	0		
25											
26				0	0			0.5			
27								Weak			
28											0
29								0	0		

Note that the payoffs also appear in the right-hand margin of the decision tree. The payoffs in the right margin are computed by a formula that adds the payoffs on all of the branches leading to the associated terminal node. For the PDC problem, no payoffs are associated with the decision alternatives branches so we leave the default values of zero in cells D6, D16, and D24. The PDC decision tree is now complete.

Interpreting the Result

When probabilities and payoffs are inserted, TreePlan automatically makes the backward pass computations necessary to determine the optimal solution. Optimal decisions are identified by the number in the corresponding decision node. In the PDC decision tree in Figure 13.20, cell B15 contains the decision node. Note that a 3 appears in this node, which tells us that decision alternative branch 3 provides the optimal decision. Thus, decision analysis recommends PDC construct the Large condominium complex. The expected value of this decision appears at the beginning of the tree in cell A16. Thus, we see the optimal expected value is \$14.2 million. The expected values of the other decision alternatives are displayed at the end of the corresponding decision branch. Thus, referring to cells E6 and E16, we see that the expected value of the Small complex is \$7.8 million and the expected value of the Medium complex is \$12.2 million.

FIGURE 13.20 THE PDC DECISION TREE WITH BRANCH PROBABILITIES AND PAYOFFS

EXCEL file
PDC Tree

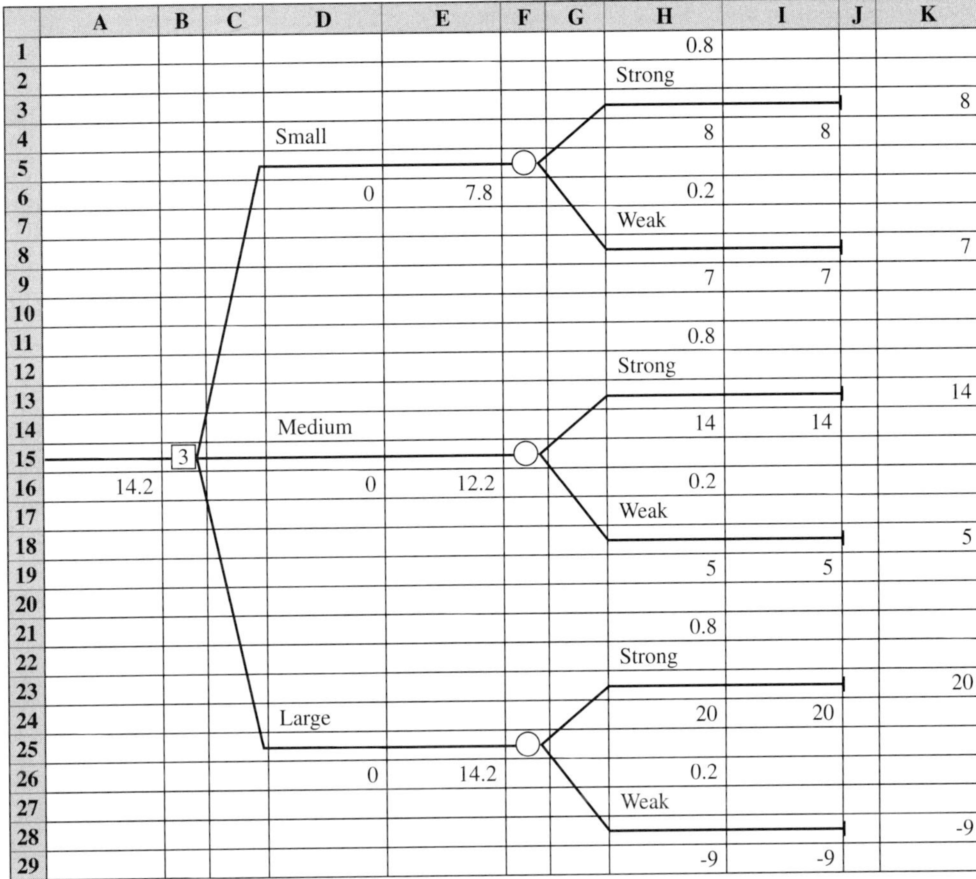

Other Options

TreePlan defaults to a maximization objective. If you would like a minimization objective, follow these steps:

Step 1. Select the **Tools** menu and choose **Decision Tree**
Step 2. Select **Options**
Step 3. Choose **Minimize (costs)**
Click **OK**

In using a TreePlan decision tree, we can modify probabilities and payoffs and quickly observe the impact of the changes on the optimal solution. Using this "what-if" type of sensitivity analysis, we can identify changes in probabilities and payoffs that would change the optimal decision. Also, because TreePlan is an Excel add-in, most of Excel's capabilities are available. For instance, we could use boldface to highlight the name of the optimal decision alternative on the final decision tree solution. A variety of other options TreePlan provides are contained in the TreePlan manual on the CD that accompanies this text. Computer software packages such as TreePlan make it easier to do a thorough analysis of a decision problem.

CHAPTER 15

Forecasting

CONTENTS

An essential aspect of managing any organization is planning for the future. Indeed, the long-run success of an organization depends on how well management is able to anticipate the future and develop appropriate strategies. Good judgment, intuition, and an awareness of the state of the economy may give a manager a rough idea or "feeling" of what is likely to happen in the future. However, converting this feeling into a number that can be used as next quarter's sales volume or next year's raw material cost per unit often is difficult. This chapter introduces several forecasting methods for that purpose.

Suppose that we have been asked to provide quarterly forecasts of the sales volume for a particular product during the coming year. Production schedules, raw material purchasing plans, inventory policies, and sales quotas will be affected by the quarterly forecasts that we provide. Consequently, poor forecasts may result in increased costs for the firm. How should we go about providing the quarterly sales volume forecasts?

Most companies can forecast total demand for all products, as a group, with errors of less than 5 percent. However, forecasting demand for individual products may result in significantly higher errors.

We will certainly want to review the actual sales data for the product in previous periods. Using these historical data, we can identify the general level of sales and any trend such as an increase or decrease in sales volume over time. A further review of the data might reveal a seasonal pattern such as peak sales occurring in the third quarter of each year and sales volume bottoming out during the first quarter. By reviewing historical data, we can often develop a better understanding of the pattern of past sales, leading to better predictions of future sales for the product.

The historical sales data form a time series. A **time series** is a set of observations of a variable measured at successive points in time or over successive periods of time. In this chapter we introduce several procedures for analyzing time series. The objective of such analyses is to provide good **forecasts** or predictions of future values of the time series.

A forecast is simply a prediction of what will happen in the future. Managers must learn to accept the fact that, regardless of the technique used, they will not be able to develop perfect forecasts.

Forecasting methods can be classified as quantitative or qualitative. Quantitative forecasting methods can be used when (1) past information about the variable being forecast is available, (2) the information can be quantified, and (3) a reasonable assumption is that the pattern of the past will continue into the future. In such cases, a forecast can be developed using a time series method or a causal method.

If the historical data are restricted to past values of the variable that we are trying to forecast, the forecasting procedure is called a **time series method.** The objective of time series methods is to discover a pattern in the historical data and then extrapolate this pattern into the future; the forecast is based solely on past values of the variable that we are trying to forecast and/or on past forecast errors. In this chapter we discuss three time series methods: smoothing (moving averages, weighted moving averages, and exponential smoothing), trend projection, and trend projection adjusted for seasonal influence.

Causal forecasting methods are based on the assumption that the variable we are trying to forecast exhibits a cause-effect relationship with one or more other variables. In this chapter we discuss the use of regression analysis as a causal forecasting method. For instance, the sales volume for many products is influenced by advertising expenditures, so regression analysis may be used to develop an equation showing how these two variables are related. Then, once the advertising budget has been set for the next period, we could substitute this value into the equation to develop a prediction or forecast of the sales volume for that period. Note that if a time series method had been used to develop the forecast, advertising expenditures would not even have been considered; that is, a time series method would have based the forecast solely on past sales.

Qualitative methods generally involve the use of expert judgment to develop forecasts. For instance, a panel of experts might develop a consensus forecast of the prime rate for a year from now. An advantage of qualitative procedures is that they can be applied when the information on the variable being forecast cannot be quantified and when historical data

FIGURE 15.1 AN OVERVIEW OF FORECASTING METHODS

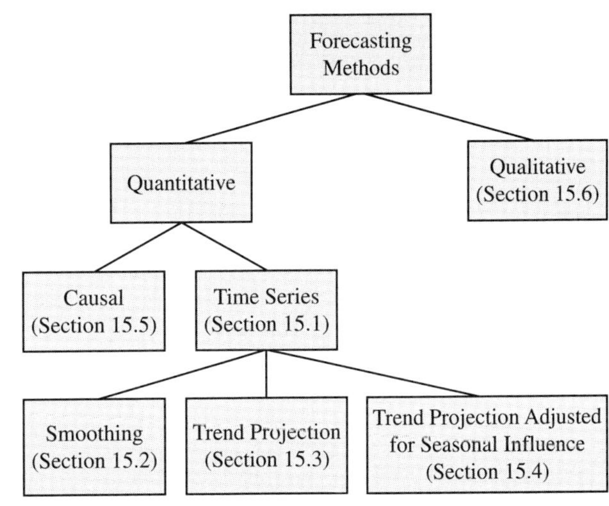

are either not applicable or not available. Figure 15.1 provides an overview of the types of forecasting methods.

Because all companies need to develop forecasts, forecasting is used in a wide variety of applications. For instance, the Management Science in Action, Forecasting Energy Needs in the Utility Industry, discusses the use of forecasting in the utility industry and a later Management Science in Action describes the forecasting of customer demand for one of the world's largest providers of badges that measure radioactive exposure.

MANAGEMENT SCIENCE IN ACTION

FORECASTING ENERGY NEEDS IN THE UTILITY INDUSTRY*

Duke Energy is a diversified energy company with a portfolio of natural gas and electric businesses and an affiliated real estate company. In 2006, Duke Energy merged with Cinergy of Cincinnati, Ohio, to create one of North America's largest energy companies with assets totaling more than $70 billion. As a result of this merger the Cincinnati Gas & Electric Company became part of Duke Energy. Today, Duke Energy services over 5.5 million retail electric and gas customers in North Carolina, South Carolina, Ohio, Kentucky, Indiana, and Ontario, Canada.

Forecasting in the utility industry offers some unique perspectives. Because electricity cannot take the form of finished goods or in-process inventories, this product must be generated to meet the instantaneous requirements of the customers. Electrical shortages are not just lost sales, but "brownouts" or "blackouts." This situation places an unusual burden on the utility forecaster. On the positive side, the demand for energy and the sale of energy are more predictable than for many other products. Also, unlike the situation in a multiproduct firm, a great amount of forecasting effort and expertise can be concentrated on the two products: gas and electricity.

The largest observed electric demand for any given period, such as an hour, a day, a month, or a year, is defined as the peak load. The forecast of the annual electric peak load guides the timing decision for constructing future generating units, and the financial impact of this decision is great. Obviously, a timing decision that leads to having the unit available no sooner than necessary is crucial.

The energy forecasts are important in other ways also. For example, purchases of coal as fuel for the generating units are based on the forecast

(continued)

levels of energy needed. The revenue from the electric operations of the company is determined from forecasted sales, which in turn enters into the planning of rate changes and external financing. These planning and decision-making processes are among the most important managerial activities in the company. It is imperative that the decision makers have the best forecast information available to assist them in arriving at these decisions.

*Based on information provided by Dr. Richard Evans of Cincinnati Gas & Electric Company, Cincinnati, Ohio.

15.1 COMPONENTS OF A TIME SERIES

The pattern or behavior of the data in a time series has several components. The usual assumption is that four separate components—trend, cyclical, seasonal, and irregular—combine to provide specific values for the time series.

Trend Component

In time series analysis, the measurements may be taken every hour, day, week, month, or year, or at any other regular interval. Although time series data generally exhibit random fluctuations, the time series may still show gradual shifts or movements to relatively higher or lower values over a longer period of time. The gradual shifting of the time series is referred to as the **trend** in the time series. This shifting or trend is usually the result of long-term factors such as changes in the population, demographic characteristics of the population, technology, and consumer preferences.

For example, a manufacturer of photographic equipment may observe substantial month-to-month variability in the number of cameras sold. However, in reviewing sales over the past 10 to 15 years, this manufacturer may note a gradual increase in the annual sales volume. Suppose that the sales volume was approximately 1700 cameras per month in 1997, 2300 cameras per month in 2002, and 2500 cameras per month in 2007. Although actual month-to-month sales volumes may vary substantially, this gradual growth in sales shows an upward trend for the time series. Figure 15.2 shows a straight line that may be a good approximation of the trend in camera sales. Although the trend for camera sales appears to be linear and increasing over time, sometimes the trend in a time series can be described better by some other pattern.

Figure 15.3 shows some other possible time series trend patterns. Part (a) shows a nonlinear trend; in this case, the time series shows little growth initially, then a period of rapid growth, and finally a leveling off. This trend pattern might be a good approximation of sales for a product from introduction through a growth period and into a period of market saturation. The linear decreasing trend in part (b) is useful for time series displaying a steady decline over time. The horizontal line in part (c) represents a time series that has no consistent increase or decrease over time and thus no trend.

Cyclical Component

Although a time series may exhibit a trend over long periods of time, all future values of the time series will not fall exactly on the trend line. In fact, time series often show alternating sequences of points below and above the trend line. Any recurring sequence of points above and below the trend line lasting more than one year can be attributed to the **cyclical component** of the time series. Figure 15.4 shows the graph of a time series with an obvious cyclical component. The observations are taken at intervals of one year.

Many time series exhibit cyclical behavior with regular runs of observations below and above the trend line. Generally, this component of the time series results from multiyear

FIGURE 15.2 LINEAR TREND OF CAMERA SALES

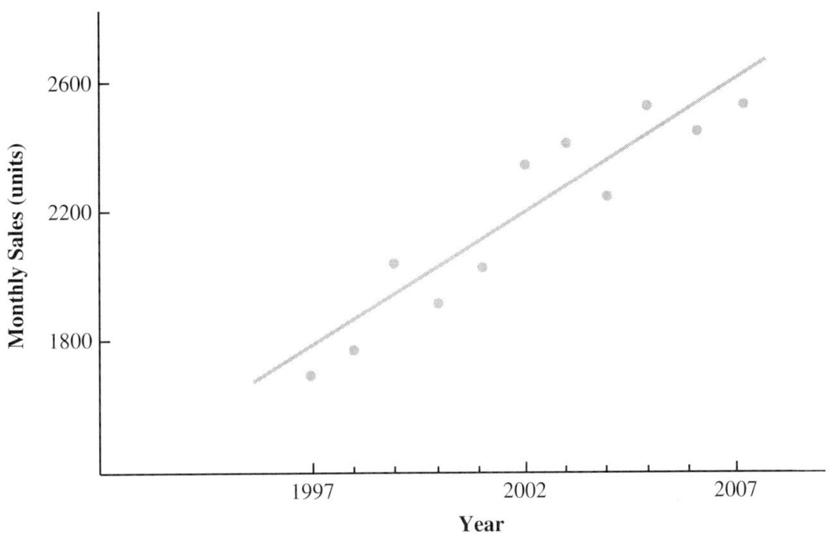

cyclical movements in the economy. For example, periods of modest inflation followed by periods of rapid inflation can lead to many time series that alternate below and above a generally increasing trend line (e.g., a time series for housing costs).

Seasonal Component

Whereas the trend and cyclical components of a time series are identified by analyzing multiyear movements in historical data, many time series show a regular pattern over one-year periods. For example, a manufacturer of swimming pools expects low sales activity in the fall and winter months, with peak sales occurring in the spring and summer months. Manufacturers of snow removal equipment and heavy clothing, however, expect just the opposite yearly pattern. Not surprisingly, the component of the time series that represents the variability in the data due to seasonal influences is called the **seasonal component.** Although we generally think of seasonal movement in a time series as occurring within one

FIGURE 15.3 EXAMPLES OF SOME POSSIBLE TIME SERIES TREND PATTERNS

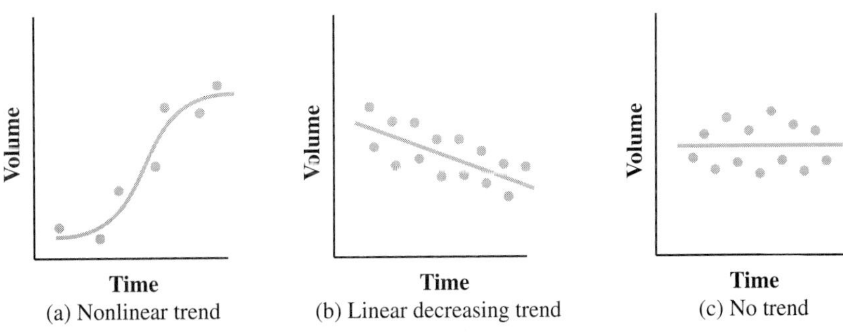

FIGURE 15.4 TREND AND CYCLICAL COMPONENTS OF A TIME SERIES (DATA POINTS ARE ONE YEAR APART)

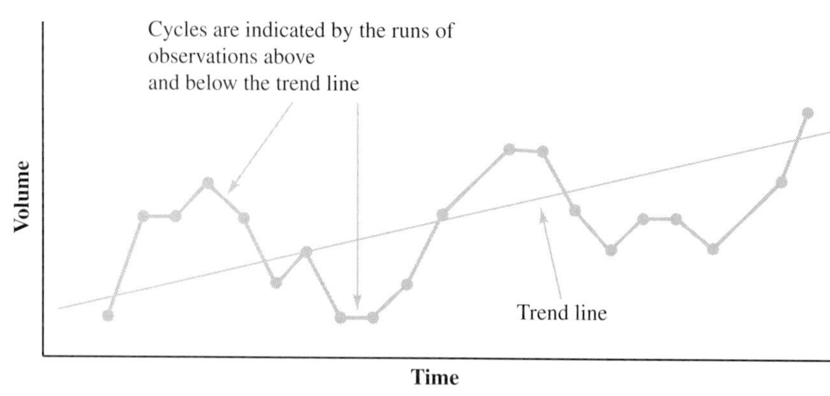

year, the seasonal component also may be used to represent any regularly repeating pattern that is less than one year in duration. For example, daily traffic volume data show within-the-day "seasonal" behavior, with peak levels during rush hours, moderate flow during the rest of the day, and light flow from midnight to early morning.

Irregular Component

The **irregular component** of the time series is the residual or "catchall" factor that includes deviations of actual time series values from those expected given the effects of the trend, cyclical, and seasonal components. It accounts for the random variability in the time series. The irregular component is caused by the short-term, unanticipated, and nonrecurring factors that affect the time series. Because this component accounts for the random variability in the time series, it is unpredictable. We cannot attempt to predict its impact on the time series.

15.2 SMOOTHING METHODS

Many manufacturing environments require forecasts for thousands of items weekly or monthly. Thus, in choosing a forecasting technique, simplicity and ease of use are important criteria. The data requirements for the techniques in this section are minimal, and the techniques are easy to use and understand.

In this section we discuss three forecasting methods: moving averages, weighted moving averages, and exponential smoothing. The objective of each of these methods is to "smooth out" the random fluctuations caused by the irregular component of the time series. Therefore, they are referred to as *smoothing methods*. Smoothing methods are appropriate for a stable time series—that is, one that exhibits no significant trend, cyclical, or seasonal effects—because they adapt well to changes in the level of the time series. However, without modification, they do not work as well when a significant trend and/or seasonal variation are present.

Smoothing methods are easy to use and generally provide a high level of accuracy for short-range forecasts such as a forecast for the next time period. One of the methods, exponential smoothing, has minimal data requirements and thus is a good method to use when forecasts are required for large numbers of items.

Moving Averages

The **moving averages** method uses the average of the *most recent n* data values in the time series as the forecast for the next period. Mathematically,

TABLE 15.1 GASOLINE SALES TIMES SERIES

Week	Sales (1000s of gallons)
1	17
2	21
3	19
4	23
5	18
6	16
7	20
8	18
9	22
10	20
11	15
12	22

$$\text{Moving average} = \frac{\sum(\text{most recent } n \text{ data values})}{n} \tag{15.1}$$

The term *moving* indicates that, as a new observation becomes available for the time series, it replaces the oldest observation in equation (15.1), and a new average is computed. As a result, the average will change, or move, as new observations become available.

To illustrate the moving averages method, consider the 12 weeks of data presented in Table 15.1 and Figure 15.5. These data show the number of gallons of gasoline sold by a

FIGURE 15.5 GRAPH OF GASOLINE SALES TIME SERIES

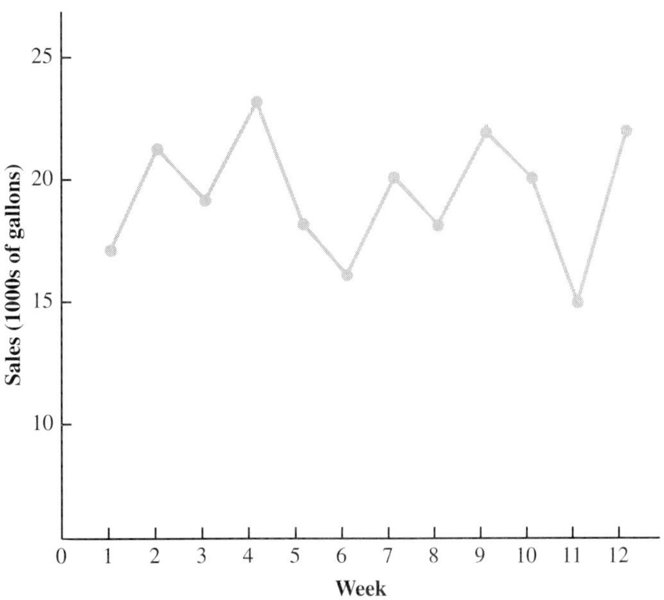

gasoline distributor in Bennington, Vermont, over the past 12 weeks. Figure 15.5 indicates that, although random variability is present, the time series appears to be stable over time. Thus, the smoothing methods of this section are applicable.

To use moving averages to forecast gasoline sales, we must first select the number of data values to be included in the moving average. For example, let us compute forecasts using a three-week moving average. The moving average calculation for the first three weeks of the gasoline sales time series is

$$\text{Moving average (weeks 1–3)} = \frac{17 + 21 + 19}{3} = 19$$

We then use this moving average value as the forecast for week 4. The actual value observed in week 4 is 23, so the forecast error in week 4 is $23 - 19 = 4$. In general, the error associated with a forecast is the difference between the observed value of the time series and the forecast.

The calculation for the second three-week moving average is

$$\text{Moving average (weeks 2–4)} = \frac{21 + 19 + 23}{3} = 21$$

Try Problem 1 for practice in using moving averages to compute a forecast.

Hence, the forecast for week 5 is 21, and the error associated with this forecast is $18 - 21 = -3$. Thus, the forecast error may be positive or negative, depending on whether the forecast is too low or too high. A complete summary of the three-week moving average calculations for the gasoline sales time series is shown in Table 15.2.

To forecast gasoline sales for week 13 using a three-week moving average, we need to compute the average of sales for weeks 10, 11, and 12. The calculation for this moving average is

$$\text{Moving average (weeks 10–12)} = \frac{20 + 15 + 22}{3} = 19$$

Hence, the forecast for week 13 is 19, or 19,000 gallons of gasoline. Figure 15.6 shows a graph of the original time series and the three-week moving average forecasts.

TABLE 15.2 SUMMARY OF THREE-WEEK MOVING AVERAGE CALCULATIONS

Week	Time Series Value	Moving Average Forecast	Forecast Error	Squared Forecast Error
1	17			
2	21			
3	19			
4	23	19	4	16
5	18	21	−3	9
6	16	20	−4	16
7	20	19	1	1
8	18	18	0	0
9	22	18	4	16
10	20	20	0	0
11	15	20	−5	25
12	22	19	3	9
		Totals	0	92

FIGURE 15.6 GRAPH OF GASOLINE SALES TIME SERIES AND THREE-WEEK MOVING AVERAGE FORECASTS

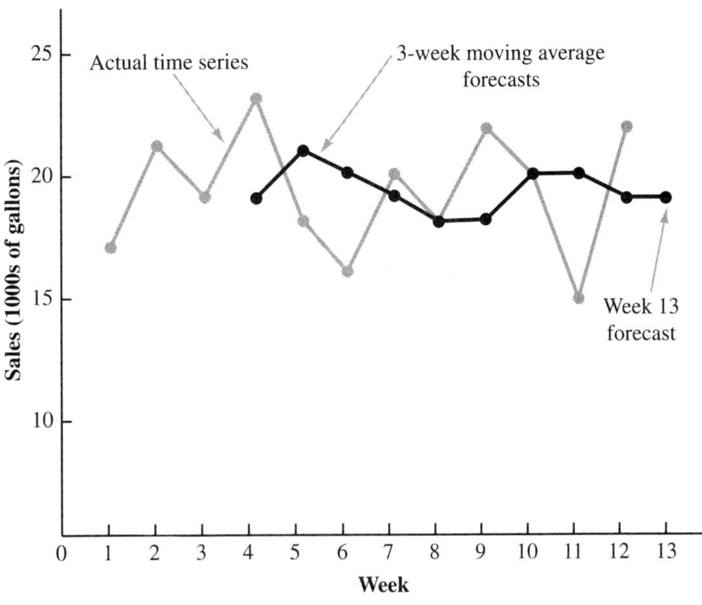

Forecast Accuracy An important consideration in selecting a forecasting method is the accuracy of the forecast. Clearly, we want forecast errors to be small. The last two columns of Table 15.2, which contain the forecast errors and the forecast errors squared, can be used to develop measures of forecast accuracy.

For the gasoline sales time series, we can use the last column of Table 15.2 to compute the average of the sum of the squared errors. Doing so, we obtain

$$\text{Average of the sum of squared errors} = \frac{92}{9} = 10.22$$

This average of the sum of squared errors is commonly referred to as the **mean squared error (MSE).** The MSE is an often-used measure of the accuracy of a forecasting method and is the one we use in this chapter.

Problem 2 will test your ability to use MSE as a measure of forecast accuracy.

As we indicated previously, to use the moving averages method, we must first select the number of data values to be included in the moving average. Not surprisingly, for a particular time series, different lengths of moving averages will affect the accuracy of the forecast. One possible approach to choosing the number of values to be included is to use trial and error to identify the length that minimizes the MSE. Then, if we assume that the length that is best for the past will also be best for the future, we would forecast the next value in the time series using the number of data values that minimized the MSE for the historical time series.

Weighted Moving Averages

In the moving averages method, each observation in the calculation receives the same weight. One variation, known as **weighted moving averages,** involves selecting different weights for each data value and then computing a weighted average of the most recent n data values as the forecast. In most cases, the most recent observation receives the most weight, and the weight decreases for older data values. For example, we can use the gasoline sales time series to illustrate the computation of a weighted three-week moving average, with the most recent observation receiving a weight three times as great as that given the oldest observation, and the next oldest observation receiving a weight twice as great as the oldest. For week 4 the computation is

$$\text{Weighted moving averages forecast for week 4} = \frac{3}{6}(19) + \frac{2}{6}(21) + \frac{1}{6}(17) = 19.33$$

Note that for the weighted moving average the sum of the weights is equal to 1. Actually, this condition was also true for the simple moving average: Each weight was ⅓. However, recall that the simple or unweighted moving average provided a forecast of 19.

Forecast Accuracy To use the weighted moving averages method, we must first select the number of data values to be included in the weighted moving average and then choose weights for each of the data values. In general, if we believe that the recent past is a better predictor of the future than the distant past, larger weights should be given to the more recent observations. However, when the time series is highly variable, selecting approximately equal weights for each data value may be best. Note that the only requirement in selecting the weights is that their sum must equal 1. To determine whether one particular combination of data values and weights provides a more accurate forecast than another combination, we will continue to use the MSE criterion as the measure of forecast accuracy. That is, if we assume that the combination that is best for the past will also be best for the future, we would use the combination of data values and weights that minimized MSE for the historical time series to forecast the next value in the time series.

Exponential Smoothing

Exponential smoothing is simple and has few data requirements. Thus, it is an inexpensive, useful approach for firms that make many forecasts each period.

Exponential smoothing uses a weighted average of past time series values as the forecast; it is a special case of the weighted moving averages method in which we select only one weight—the weight for the most recent observation. The weights for the other data values are automatically computed and get smaller and smaller as the observations move farther into the past. The basic exponential smoothing model is

$$F_{t+1} = \alpha Y_t + (1 - \alpha)F_t \qquad (15.2)$$

where

F_{t+1} = forecast of the time series for period $t + 1$
Y_t = actual value of the time series in period t
F_t = forecast of the time series for period t
α = smoothing constant ($0 \leq \alpha \leq 1$)

Equation (15.2) shows that the forecast for period $t + 1$ is a weighted average of the actual value in period t and the forecast for period t; note in particular that the weight given to the actual value in period t is α and that the weight given to the forecast in period t is $1 - \alpha$. We can demonstrate that the exponential smoothing forecast for any period also is a weighted average of *all the previous actual values* for the time series with a time series consisting of three periods of data: Y_1, Y_2, and Y_3. To start the calculations, we let F_1 equal the actual value of the time series in period 1; that is, $F_1 = Y_1$. Hence, the forecast for period 2

$$\begin{aligned} F_2 &= \alpha Y_1 + (1 - \alpha)F_1 \\ &= \alpha Y_1 + (1 - \alpha)Y_1 \\ &= Y_1 \end{aligned}$$

Thus, the exponential smoothing forecast for period 2 is equal to the actual value of the time series in period 1.

The forecast for period 3 is

$$F_3 = \alpha Y_2 + (1 - \alpha)F_2 = \alpha Y_2 + (1 - \alpha)Y_1$$

Finally, substituting this expression for F_3 in the expression for F_4, we obtain

$$\begin{aligned} F_4 &= \alpha Y_3 + (1 - \alpha)F_3 \\ &= \alpha Y_3 + (1 - \alpha)[\alpha Y_2 + (1 - \alpha)Y_1] \\ &= \alpha Y_3 + \alpha(1 - \alpha)Y_2 + (1 - \alpha)^2 Y_1 \end{aligned}$$

Hence, F_4 is a weighted average of the first three time series values. The sum of the coefficients, or weights, for Y_1, Y_2, and Y_3 equals 1. A similar argument can be made to show that, in general, any forecast F_{t+1} is a weighted average of all the previous time series values.

Despite the fact that exponential smoothing provides a forecast that is a weighted average of all past observations, all the past data do not need to be saved in order to compute the forecast for the next period. In fact, once the **smoothing constant** α has been selected, only two pieces of information are required to compute the forecast. Equation (15.2) shows that with a given α we can compute the forecast for period $t + 1$ simply by knowing the actual and forecast time series values for period t—that is, Y_t and F_t.

To illustrate the exponential smoothing approach to forecasting, consider the gasoline sales time series presented previously in Table 15.1 and Figure 15.5. As indicated, the exponential smoothing forecast for period 2 is equal to the actual value of the time series in period 1. Thus, with $Y_1 = 17$, we set $F_2 = 17$ to get the exponential smoothing computations started. From the time series data in Table 15.1, we find an actual time series value in period 2 of $Y_2 = 21$. Thus, period 2 has a forecast error of $21 - 17 = 4$.

Continuing with the exponential smoothing computations, using a smoothing constant of $\alpha = 0.2$, provides the forecast for period 3:

$$F_3 = 0.2Y_2 + 0.8F_2 = 0.2(21) + 0.8(17) = 17.8$$

Once the actual time series value in period 3, $Y_3 = 19$, is known, we can generate a forecast for period 4:

$$F_4 = 0.2Y_3 + 0.8F_3 = 0.2(19) + 0.8(17.8) = 18.04$$

By continuing the exponential smoothing calculations, we can determine the weekly forecast values and the corresponding weekly forecast errors, as shown in Table 15.3. Note that we have not shown an exponential smoothing forecast or the forecast error for period 1 because no forecast was made. For week 12, we have $Y_{12} = 22$ and $F_{12} = 18.48$. Can we use this information to generate a forecast for week 13 before the actual value of week 13 becomes known? Using the exponential smoothing model, we have

$$F_{13} = 0.2Y_{12} + 0.8F_{12} = 0.2(22) + 0.8(18.48) = 19.18$$

TABLE 15.3 SUMMARY OF THE EXPONENTIAL SMOOTHING FORECASTS AND FORECAST ERRORS FOR GASOLINE SALES WITH SMOOTHING CONSTANT $\alpha = 0.2$

Week (t)	Time Series Value (Y_t)	Exponential Smoothing Forecast (F_t)	Forecast Error ($Y_t - F_t$)
1	17		
2	21	17.00	4.00
3	19	17.80	1.20
4	23	18.04	4.96
5	18	19.03	−1.03
6	16	18.83	−2.83
7	20	18.26	1.74
8	18	18.61	−0.61
9	22	18.49	3.51
10	20	19.19	0.81
11	15	19.35	−4.35
12	22	18.48	3.52

Can you now use exponential smoothing to develop forecasts? Try Problem 4.

Thus, the exponential smoothing forecast of the amount sold in week 13 is 19.18, or 19,180 gallons of gasoline. With this forecast, the firm can make plans and decisions accordingly. The accuracy of the forecast will not be known until the end of week 13.

Figure 15.7 shows the plot of the actual and the forecast values from Table 15.3. Note in particular how the forecasts "smooth out" the irregular fluctuations in the time series.

FIGURE 15.7 GRAPH OF ACTUAL AND FORECAST GASOLINE SALES TIME SERIES WITH SMOOTHING CONSTANT $\alpha = 0.2$

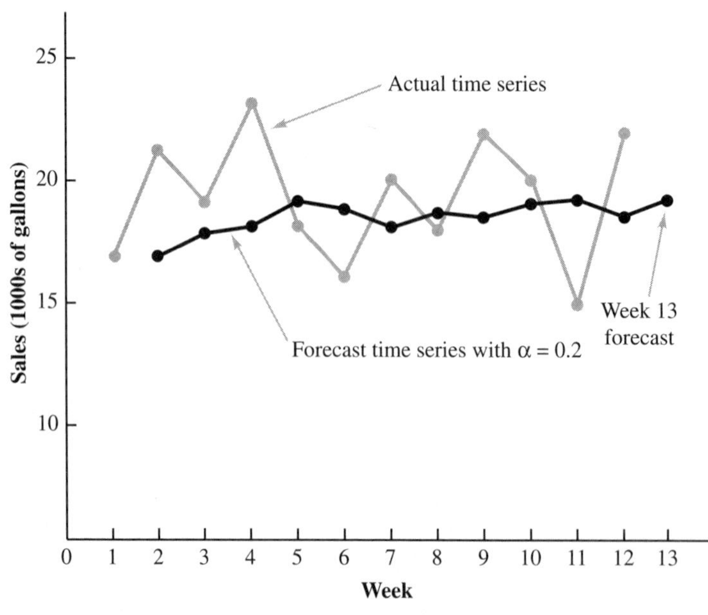

Forecast Accuracy In the preceding exponential smoothing calculations, we used a smoothing constant of $\alpha = 0.2$. Although any value of α between 0 and 1 is acceptable, some values will yield better forecasts than others. Insight into choosing a good value for α can be obtained by rewriting the basic exponential smoothing model as follows:

$$
\begin{aligned}
F_{t+1} &= \alpha Y_t + (1 - \alpha)F_t \\
&= \alpha Y_t + F_t - \alpha F_t \\
&= \underset{\text{Forecast in period } t}{F_t} + \alpha\underset{\text{Forecast error in period } t}{\underbrace{(Y_t - F_t)}}
\end{aligned}
\tag{15.3}
$$

Thus, the new forecast F_{t+1} is equal to the previous forecast F_t plus an adjustment, which is α times the most recent forecast error, $Y_t - F_t$. That is, the forecast in period $t + 1$ is obtained by adjusting the forecast in period t by a fraction of the forecast error. If the time series contains substantial random variability, a small value of the smoothing constant is preferred. The reason for this choice is that, because much of the forecast error is due to random variability, we do not want to overreact and adjust the forecasts too quickly. For a time series with relatively little random variability, larger values of the smoothing constant have the advantage of quickly adjusting the forecasts when forecasting errors occur and therefore allowing the forecast to react faster to changing conditions.

Problem 5 asks you to determine whether moving averages or exponential smoothing provides the best forecasts for a given set of data.

The criterion we use to determine a desirable value for the smoothing constant α is the same as the criterion we proposed earlier for determining the number of periods of data to include in the moving averages calculation. That is, we choose the value of α that minimizes the mean squared error. A summary of the MSE calculations for the exponential smoothing forecast of gasoline sales with $\alpha = 0.2$ is shown in Table 15.4. Note that there is one less squared error term than the number of periods of data because we had no past values with

TABLE 15.4 MEAN SQUARED ERROR COMPUTATIONS FOR FORECASTING GASOLINE SALES WITH $\alpha = 0.2$

Week (t)	Time Series Value (Y_t)	Forecast (F_t)	Forecast Error ($Y_t - F_t$)	Squared Forecast Error $(Y_t - F_t)^2$
1	17			
2	21	17.00	4.00	16.00
3	19	17.80	1.20	1.44
4	23	18.04	4.96	24.60
5	18	19.03	−1.03	1.06
6	16	18.83	−2.83	8.01
7	20	18.26	1.74	3.03
8	18	18.61	−0.61	0.37
9	22	18.49	3.51	12.32
10	20	19.19	0.81	0.66
11	15	19.35	−4.35	18.92
12	22	18.48	3.52	12.39
			Total	98.80

MSE = 98.80/11 = 8.98

TABLE 15.5 MEAN SQUARED ERROR COMPUTATIONS FOR FORECASTING GASOLINE SALES WITH $\alpha = 0.3$

Week (t)	Time Series Value (Y_t)	Forecast (F_t)	Forecast Error ($Y_t - F_t$)	Squared Forecast Error $(Y_t - F_t)^2$
1	17			
2	21	17.00	4.00	16.00
3	19	18.20	0.80	0.64
4	23	18.44	4.56	20.79
5	18	19.81	−1.81	3.28
6	16	19.27	−3.27	10.69
7	20	18.29	1.71	2.92
8	18	18.80	−0.80	0.64
9	22	18.56	3.44	11.83
10	20	19.59	0.41	0.17
11	15	19.71	−4.71	22.18
12	22	18.30	3.70	13.69
			Total	102.83

MSE = 102.83/11 = 9.35

which to make a forecast for period 1. Would a different value of α have provided better results in terms of a lower MSE value? Perhaps the most straightforward way to answer this question is simply to try another value for α. We then compare its mean squared error with the MSE value of 8.98, obtained using a smoothing constant of $\alpha = 0.2$.

The exponential smoothing results with $\alpha = 0.3$ are shown in Table 15.5. With MSE = 9.35, a smoothing constant of $\alpha = 0.3$ results in less forecast accuracy than a smoothing constant of $\alpha = 0.2$. Thus, we would be inclined to use the original smoothing constant of 0.2. Using a trial-and-error calculation with other values of α, we can find a "good" value for the smoothing constant. This value can be used in the exponential smoothing model to provide forecasts for the future. At a later date, after new time series observations have been obtained, we analyze the newly collected time series data to determine whether the smoothing constant should be revised to provide better forecasting results.

NOTES AND COMMENTS

1. Another commonly used measure of forecast accuracy is the **mean absolute deviation (MAD).** This measure is simply the average of the absolute values of all the forecast errors. Using the errors given in Table 15.2, we obtain

$$\text{MAD} = \frac{4 + 3 + 4 + 1 + 0 + 4 + 0 + 5 + 3}{9}$$
$$= 2.67$$

One major difference between the MSE and the MAD is that the MSE measure is influenced much more by large forecast errors than by small errors (for the MSE measure the errors are squared). The selection of the best measure of forecasting accuracy is not a simple matter. Indeed, forecasting experts often disagree as to which measure should be used. We use the MSE measure in this chapter.

2. Spreadsheet packages are an effective aid in choosing a good value of α for exponential smoothing and selecting weights for the weighted moving averages method. With the time series data and the forecasting formulas in the spreadsheets, you can experiment with different values of α (or moving average weights) and choose the value(s) providing the smallest MSE or MAD. In the chapter appendix, we show how this process can be done.

15.3 TREND PROJECTION

In this section we show how to forecast the values of a time series that exhibits a long-term linear trend. The type of time series for which the trend projection method is applicable shows a consistent increase or decrease over time. Because this type of time series is not stable, the smoothing methods described in the preceding section are not applicable.

Consider the time series for bicycle sales of a particular manufacturer over the past 10 years, as shown in Table 15.6 and Figure 15.8. Note that 21,600 bicycles were sold in year 1; 22,900 were sold in year 2; and so on. In year 10, the most recent year, 31,400 bicycles were sold. Although Figure 15.8 shows some up-and-down movement over the past 10 years, the time series for the number of bicycles sold seems to have an overall increasing or upward trend.

TABLE 15.6 BICYCLE SALES TIME SERIES

Year (t)	Sales (1000s) (Y_t)
1	21.6
2	22.9
3	25.5
4	21.9
5	23.9
6	27.5
7	31.5
8	29.7
9	28.6
10	31.4

FIGURE 15.8 GRAPH OF BICYCLE SALES TIME SERIES

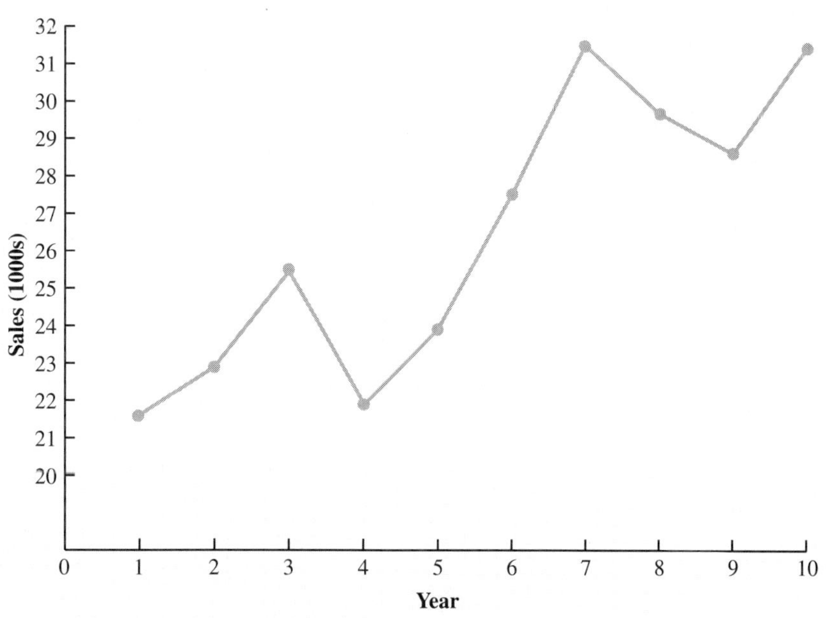

FIGURE 15.9 TREND REPRESENTED BY A LINEAR FUNCTION FOR BICYCLE SALES

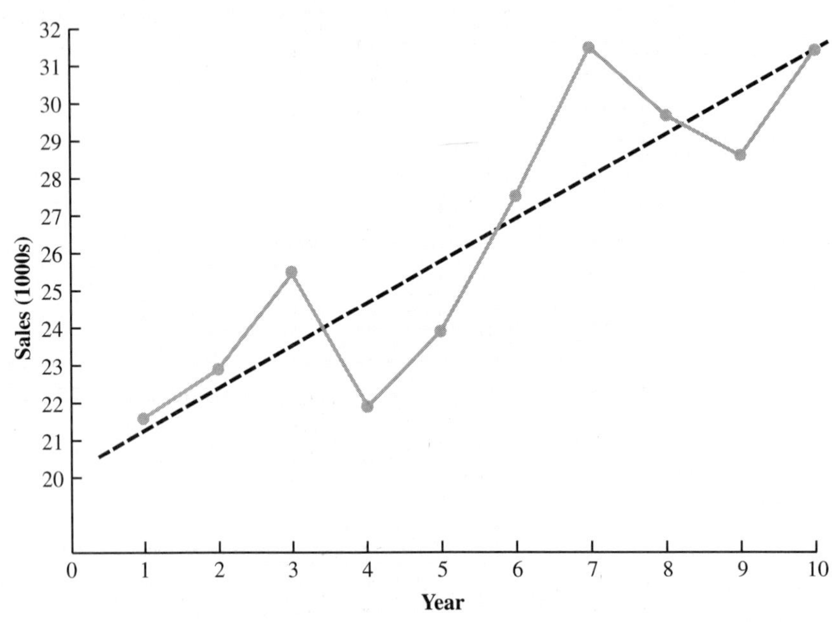

We do not want the trend component of a time series to follow each and every "up" and "down" movement. Rather, the trend component should reflect the gradual shifting—in this case, growth—of the time series values. After we view the time series data in Table 15.6 and the graph in Figure 15.8, we might agree that a linear trend as shown in Figure 15.9 provides a reasonable description of the long-run movement in the series.

We use the bicycle sales data to illustrate the calculations involved in applying regression analysis to identify a linear trend. For a linear trend, the estimated sales volume expressed as a function of time is

$$T_t = b_0 + b_1 t \tag{15.4}$$

where

T_t = trend value for bicycle sales in period t
b_0 = intercept of the trend line
b_1 = slope of the trend line

Note that, for the time series on bicycle sales, $t = 1$ corresponds to the oldest time series value and $t = 10$ corresponds to the most recent time series value. The equations for computing b_1 and b_0 are

$$b_1 = \frac{\Sigma t Y_t - (\Sigma t \Sigma Y_t)/n}{\Sigma t^2 - (\Sigma t)^2/n} \tag{15.5}$$

$$b_0 = \bar{Y} - b_1 \bar{t} \tag{15.6}$$

where

$$Y_t = \text{actual value of the time series in period } t$$
$$n = \text{number of periods}$$
$$\bar{Y} = \text{average value of the time series; that is, } \bar{Y} = \sum Y_t/n$$
$$\bar{t} = \text{average value of } t\text{; that is, } \bar{t} = \sum t/n$$

	t	Y_t	tY_t	t^2
	1	21.6	21.6	1
	2	22.9	45.8	4
	3	25.5	76.5	9
	4	21.9	87.6	16
	5	23.9	119.5	25
	6	27.5	165.0	36
	7	31.5	220.5	49
	8	29.7	237.6	64
	9	28.6	257.4	81
	10	31.4	314.0	100
Totals	55	264.5	1545.5	385

Using these relationships for b_0 and b_1 and the bicycle sales data of Table 15.6, we obtain the following calculations.

$$\bar{t} = \frac{55}{10} = 5.5$$

$$\bar{Y} = \frac{264.5}{10} = 26.45$$

$$b_1 = \frac{1545.5 - (55)(264.5)/10}{385 - (55)^2/10} = 1.10$$

$$b_0 = 26.45 - 1.10(5.5) = 20.4$$

Therefore,

$$T_t = 20.4 + 1.1t \tag{15.7}$$

is the equation for the linear trend component for the bicycle sales time series.

Try Problem 14 for practice in developing the equation for the linear trend component of a time series.

The slope of 1.1 in the trend equation indicates that over the past 10 years the firm has experienced an average growth in sales of about 1100 units per year. If we assume that the past 10-year trend in sales is a good indicator for the future, we can use equation (15.7) to project the trend component of the time series. For example, substituting $t = 11$ into equation (15.7) yields next year's trend projection, T_{11}:

$$T_{11} = 20.4 + 1.1(11) = 32.5$$

Thus, the trend component yields a sales forecast of 32,500 bicycles for next year.

FIGURE 15.10 SOME POSSIBLE FORMS OF NONLINEAR TREND PATTERNS

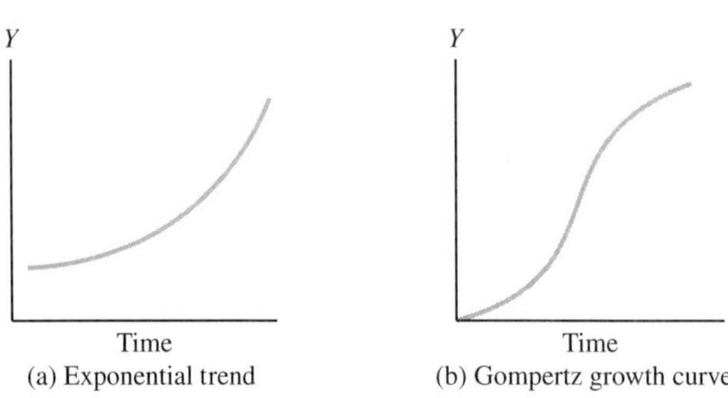

We can also use the trend line to forecast sales farther into the future. For instance, using equation (15.7), we develop forecasts for an additional 2 and 3 years into the future as follows:

$$T_{12} = 20.4 + 1.1(12) = 33.6$$
$$T_{13} = 20.4 + 1.1(13) = 34.7$$

The use of a linear function to model the trend is common. However, as we discussed earlier, sometimes time series exhibit a curvilinear (nonlinear) trend similar to those shown in Figure 15.10. More advanced texts discuss how to develop models for these more complex relationships.

15.4 TREND AND SEASONAL COMPONENTS

We have shown how to forecast the values of a time series that has a trend component. In this section we extend the discussion by showing how to forecast the values of a time series that has both trend and seasonal components.

Many situations in business and economics involve period-to-period comparisons. For instance, we might be interested to learn that unemployment is up 2% compared to last month, steel production is up 5% over last month, or that the production of electric power is down 3% from the previous month. Care must be exercised in using such information, however, because whenever a seasonal influence is present, such comparisons usually are not especially meaningful. For instance, the fact that electric power consumption is down by 3% from August to September might be only the seasonal effect associated with a decrease in the use of air conditioning and not because of a long-term decline in the use of electric power. Indeed, after adjusting for the seasonal effect, we might even find that the use of electric power has increased.

Removing the seasonal effect from a time series is known as *deseasonalizing the time series*. After we do so, period-to-period comparisons are more meaningful and can help identify whether a trend exists. The approach we take in this section is appropriate in situations when only seasonal effects are present or in situations when both seasonal and trend components are present. The first step is to compute seasonal indexes and use them to deseasonalize the data. Then, if a trend is apparent in the deseasonalized data, we use regression analysis on the deseasonalized data to estimate the trend.

Multiplicative Model

In addition to a trend component T and a seasonal component S, we assume that the time series also has an irregular component I. The irregular component accounts for the random effects in the time series that cannot be explained by the trend and seasonal components. Using T_t, S_t, and I_t to identify the trend, seasonal, and irregular components at time t, we assume that the actual time series value, denoted by Y_t, can be described by the **multiplicative time series model.**

$$Y_t = T_t \times S_t \times I_t \tag{15.8}$$

In this model, T_t is the trend measured in units of the item being forecast. However, the S_t and I_t components are measured in relative terms, with values above 1.00 indicating effects above the trend, and values below 1.00 indicating effects below the trend.

We illustrate the use of the multiplicative model with trend, seasonal, and irregular components by working with the quarterly data presented in Table 15.7 and Figure 15.11. These data show television set sales (in thousands of units) for a particular manufacturer over the past four years. We begin by showing how to identify the seasonal component of the time series.

Calculating the Seasonal Indexes

Figure 15.11 indicates that sales are lowest in the second quarter of each year, followed by higher sales levels in quarters 3 and 4. Thus, we conclude that a seasonal pattern exists for television set sales. We begin the computational procedure used to identify each quarter's seasonal influence by computing a moving average to isolate the combined seasonal and irregular components, S_t and I_t.

TABLE 15.7 QUARTERLY DATA FOR TELEVISION SET SALES

Year	Quarter	Sales (1000s)
1	1	4.8
	2	4.1
	3	6.0
	4	6.5
2	1	5.8
	2	5.2
	3	6.8
	4	7.4
3	1	6.0
	2	5.6
	3	7.5
	4	7.8
4	1	6.3
	2	5.9
	3	8.0
	4	8.4

FIGURE 15.11 GRAPH OF QUARTERLY TELEVISION SET SALES TIME SERIES

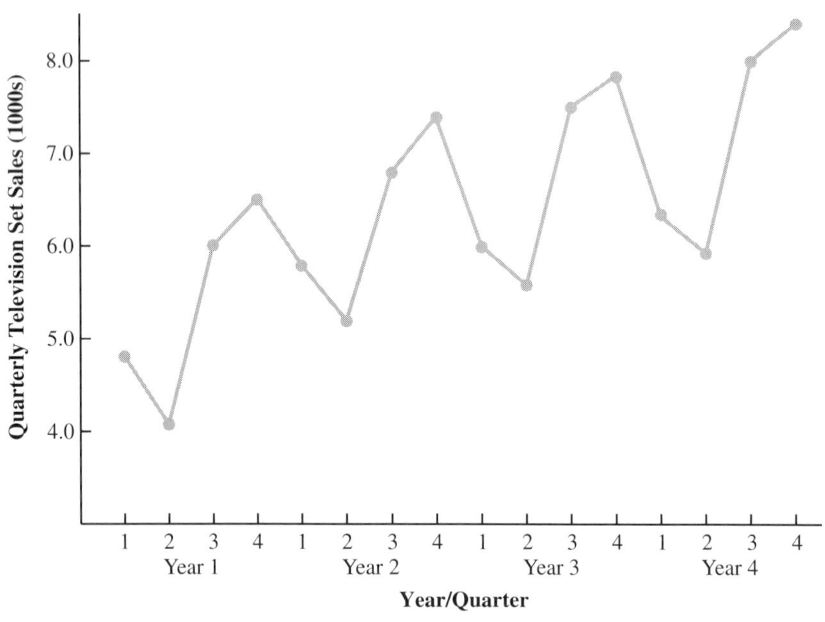

To do so, we use one year of data in each calculation. Because we are working with a quarterly series, we use four data values in each moving average. The moving average calculation for the first four quarters of the television set sales data is

$$\text{First moving average} = \frac{4.8 + 4.1 + 6.0 + 6.5}{4} = \frac{21.4}{4} = 5.35$$

Note that the moving average calculation for the first four quarters yields the average quarterly sales over year 1 of the time series. Continuing the moving average calculation, we next add the 5.8 value for the first quarter of year 2 and drop the 4.8 for the first quarter of year 1. Thus, the second moving average is

$$\text{Second moving average} = \frac{4.1 + 6.0 + 6.5 + 5.8}{4} = \frac{22.4}{4} = 5.6$$

Similarly, the third moving average calculation is $(16.0 + 6.5 + 5.8 + 5.2)/4 = 5.875$.

Before we proceed with the moving average calculations for the entire time series, we return to the first moving average calculation, which resulted in a value of 5.35. The 5.35 value represents an average quarterly sales volume (across all seasons) for year 1. As we look back at the calculation of the 5.35 value, associating 5.35 with the "middle" quarter of the moving average group makes sense. Note, however, that we encounter some difficulty in identifying the middle quarter; four quarters in the moving average allow for no middle quarter. The 5.35 value corresponds to the last half of quarter 2 and the first half of quarter 3. Similarly, if we go to the next moving average value of 5.60, the middle corresponds to the last half of quarter 3 and the first half of quarter 4.

Recall that the reason for computing moving averages is to isolate the combined seasonal and irregular components. However, the moving average values we computed do not correspond directly to the original quarters of the time series. We can resolve this difficulty by using the midpoints between successive moving average values. For example, because 5.35 corresponds to the first half of quarter 3 and 5.60 corresponds to the last half of quarter 3, we can use (5.35 + 5.60)/2 = 5.475 as the moving average value for quarter 3. Similarly, we associate a moving average value of (5.60 + 5.875)/2 = 5.738 with quarter 4. The result is a *centered moving average*. Table 15.8 shows a complete summary of the moving average and centered moving average calculations for the television set sales data.

If the number of data points in a moving average calculation is an odd number, the middle point will correspond to one of the periods in the time series. In such cases, we would not have to center the moving average values to correspond to a particular time period, as we did in the calculations in Table 15.8.

What do the centered moving averages in Table 15.8 tell us about this time series? Figure 15.12 shows plots of the actual time series values and the corresponding centered moving average. Note particularly how the centered moving average values tend to "smooth out" both the seasonal and irregular fluctuations in the time series. The moving average values computed for four quarters of data do not include the fluctuations due to seasonal influences because the seasonal effect has been averaged out. Each point in the centered moving average represents what the value of the time series would be without seasonal or irregular influences.

By dividing each time series observation by the corresponding centered moving average value, we can identify the seasonal-irregular effect in the time series. For example, the third quarter of year 1 shows 6.0/5.475 = 1.096 as the combined seasonal-irregular component. Table 15.9 summarizes the resulting seasonal-irregular values for the entire time series.

TABLE 15.8 CENTERED MOVING AVERAGE CALCULATIONS FOR THE TELEVISION SET SALES TIME SERIES

Year	Quarter	Sales (1000s)	Four-Quarter Moving Average	Centered Moving Average
1	1	4.8		
	2	4.1		
			5.350	
	3	6.0		5.475
			5.600	
	4	6.5		5.738
			5.875	
2	1	5.8		5.975
			6.075	
	2	5.2		6.188
			6.300	
	3	6.8		6.325
			6.350	
	4	7.4		6.400
			6.450	
3	1	6.0		6.538
			6.625	
	2	5.6		6.675
			6.725	
	3	7.5		6.763
			6.800	
	4	7.8		6.838
			6.875	
4	1	6.3		6.938
			7.000	
	2	5.9		7.075
			7.150	
	3	8.0		
	4	8.4		

FIGURE 15.12 GRAPH OF QUARTERLY TELEVISION SET SALES TIME SERIES AND CENTERED MOVING AVERAGE

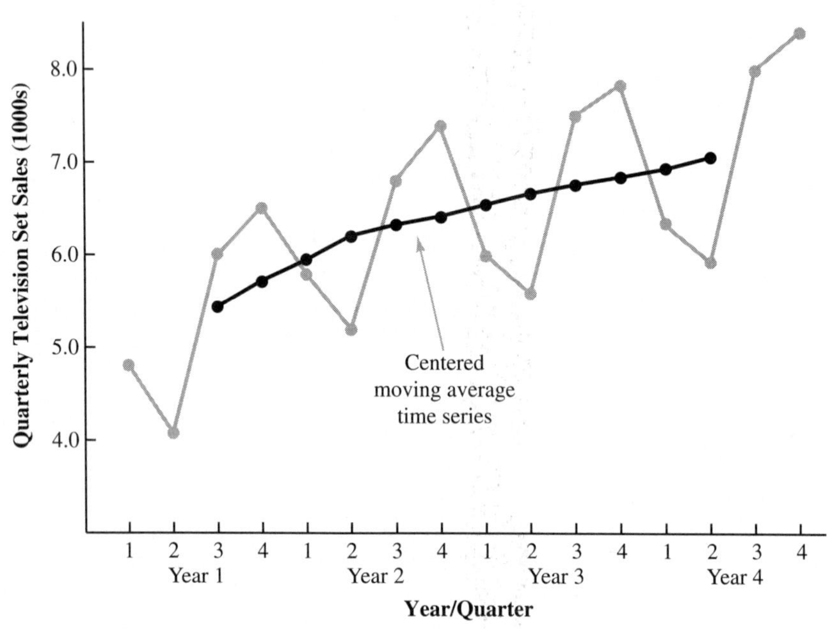

TABLE 15.9 SEASONAL-IRREGULAR VALUES FOR THE TELEVISION SET SALES TIME SERIES

Year	Quarter	Sales (1000s)	Centered Moving Average	Seasonal-Irregular Value
1	1	4.8		
	2	4.1		
	3	6.0	5.475	1.096
	4	6.5	5.738	1.133
2	1	5.8	5.975	0.971
	2	5.2	6.188	0.840
	3	6.8	6.325	1.075
	4	7.4	6.400	1.156
3	1	6.0	6.538	0.918
	2	5.6	6.675	0.839
	3	7.5	6.763	1.109
	4	7.8	6.838	1.141
4	1	6.3	6.938	0.908
	2	5.9	7.075	0.834
	3	8.0		
	4	8.4		

TABLE 15.10 SEASONAL INDEX CALCULATIONS FOR THE TELEVISION SET SALES TIME SERIES

Quarter	Seasonal-Irregular Component Values (S_tI_t)	Seasonal Index (S_t)
1	0.971, 0.918, 0.908	0.93
2	0.840, 0.839, 0.834	0.84
3	1.096, 1.075, 1.109	1.09
4	1.133, 1.156, 1.141	1.14

Consider the third quarter. The results from years 1, 2, and 3 show third-quarter values of 1.096, 1.075, and 1.109, respectively. Thus, in all cases the seasonal-irregular component appears to have an above average influence in the third quarter. The fluctuations over the three years can be attributed to the irregular component, so we can average the computed values to eliminate the irregular influence and obtain an estimate of the third-quarter seasonal influence:

$$\text{Seasonal effect of third quarter} = \frac{1.096 + 1.075 + 1.109}{3} = 1.09$$

We refer to 1.09 as the **seasonal index** for the third quarter. In Table 15.10 we summarize the calculations involved in computing the seasonal indexes for the television set sales time series. Thus, the seasonal indexes for all four quarters are: quarter 1, 0.93; quarter 2, 0.84; quarter 3, 1.09; and quarter 4, 1.14.

Interpretation of the values in Table 15.10 provides some observations about the "seasonal" component in television set sales. The best sales quarter is the fourth quarter, with sales averaging 14% above the average quarterly value. The worst, or slowest, sales quarter is the second quarter, with its seasonal index at 0.84, showing the sales average 16% below the average quarterly sales. The seasonal component corresponds to the intuitive expectation that television viewing interest and thus television purchase patterns tend to peak in the fourth quarter, with its coming winter season and fewer outdoor activities. The low second-quarter sales reflect the reduced television interest resulting from the spring and presummer activities of the potential customers.

Can you now compute and interpret seasonal indexes for a time series? Try Problem 25.

One final adjustment may be necessary in obtaining the seasonal indexes. The multiplicative model requires that the average seasonal index equal 1.00, so the sum of the four seasonal indexes in Table 15.10 must equal 4.00. In other words, the seasonal effects must even out over the year. The average of the seasonal indexes in our example is equal to 1.00, and hence, this type of adjustment is not necessary. In other cases, a slight adjustment may be necessary. To make the adjustment, multiply each seasonal index by the number of seasons divided by the sum of the unadjusted seasonal indexes. For instance, for quarterly data, multiply each seasonal index by 4/(sum of the unadjusted seasonal indexes). Some of the problems at the end of the chapter require this adjustment.

With deseasonalized data, comparing sales in successive periods makes sense. With data that have not been deseasonalized, relevant comparisons can often be made between sales in the current period and sales in the same period one year ago.

Deseasonalizing the Time Series

The purpose of finding seasonal indexes is to remove the seasonal effects from a time series. This process is referred to as *deseasonalizing* the time series. Economic time series adjusted for seasonal variations (**deseasonalized time series**) are reported in the *Survey of Current*

TABLE 15.11 DESEASONALIZED VALUES FOR THE TELEVISION SET SALES TIMES SERIES

Year	Quarter	Sales (1000s) (Y_t)	Seasonal Index (S_t)	Deseasonalized Sales ($Y_t/S_t = T_tI_t$)
1	1	4.8	0.93	5.16
	2	4.1	0.84	4.88
	3	6.0	1.09	5.50
	4	6.5	1.14	5.70
2	1	5.8	0.93	6.24
	2	5.2	0.84	6.19
	3	6.8	1.09	6.24
	4	7.4	1.14	6.49
3	1	6.0	0.93	6.45
	2	5.6	0.84	6.67
	3	7.5	1.09	6.88
	4	7.8	1.14	6.84
4	1	6.3	0.93	6.77
	2	5.9	0.84	7.02
	3	8.0	1.09	7.34
	4	8.4	1.14	7.37

Business, The Wall Street Journal, and *BusinessWeek.* Using the notation of the multiplicative model, we have

$$Y_t = T_t \times S_t \times I_t$$

By dividing each time series observation by the corresponding seasonal index, we remove the effect of season from the time series. The deseasonalized time series for television set sales is summarized in Table 15.11. A graph of the deseasonalized television set sales time series is shown in Figure 15.13.

Using Deseasonalized Time Series to Identify Trend

Although the graph in Figure 15.13 shows some up-and-down movement over the past 16 quarters, the time series seems to have an upward linear trend. To identify this trend, we use the same procedure as in the preceding section; in this case, the data used are quarterly deseasonalized sales values. Thus, for a linear trend, the estimated sales volume expressed as a function of time is

$$T_t = b_0 + b_1 t$$

where

T_t = trend value for television set sales in period t
b_0 = intercept of the trend line
b_1 = slope of the trend line

As before, $t = 1$ corresponds to the time of the first observation for the time series, $t = 2$ corresponds to the time of the second observation, and so on. Thus, for the deseasonalized television set sales time series, $t = 1$ corresponds to the first deseasonalized quarterly sales value and $t = 16$ corresponds to the most recent deseasonalized quarterly sales value. The equations for computing the values of b_0 and b_1 are

FIGURE 15.13 DESEASONALIZED TELEVISION SET SALES TIME SERIES

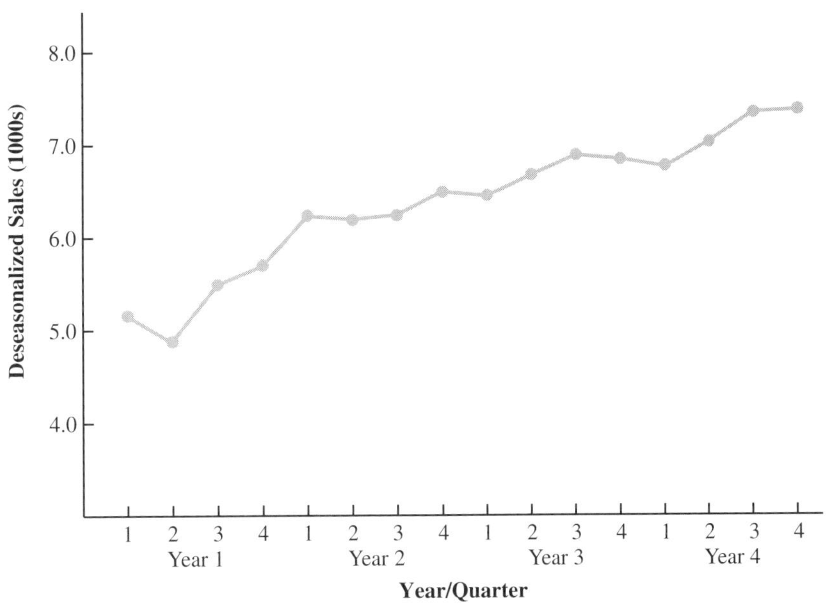

$$b_1 = \frac{\Sigma tY_t - (\Sigma t \Sigma Y_t)/n}{\Sigma t^2 - (\Sigma t)^2/n} \quad \text{and} \quad b_0 = \bar{Y} - b_1\bar{t}$$

Note, however, that Y_t now refers to the deseasonalized time series value at time t and not to the actual value of the time series. Using the given relationships for b_0 and b_1 and the deseasonalized sales data of Table 15.11, we make the following calculations.

	t	Y_t (deseasonalized)	tY_t	t^2
	1	5.16	5.16	1
	2	4.88	9.76	4
	3	5.50	16.50	9
	4	5.70	22.80	16
	5	6.24	31.20	25
	6	6.19	37.14	36
	7	6.24	43.68	49
	8	6.49	51.92	64
	9	6.45	58.05	81
	10	6.67	66.70	100
	11	6.88	75.68	121
	12	6.84	82.08	144
	13	6.77	88.01	169
	14	7.02	98.28	196
	15	7.34	110.10	225
	16	7.37	117.92	256
Totals	136	101.74	914.98	1496

$$\bar{t} = \frac{136}{16} = 8.5$$

$$\bar{Y} = \frac{101.74}{16} = 6.359$$

$$b_1 = \frac{914.98 - (136)(101.74)/16}{1496 - (136)^2/16} = 0.148$$

$$b_0 = 6.359 - 0.148(8.5) = 5.101$$

Therefore,

$$T_t = 5.101 + 0.148t$$

is the equation for the linear trend component of the time series.

The slope of 0.148 indicates that over the past 16 quarters the firm has experienced an average deseasonalized growth in sales of about 148 sets per quarter. If we assume that the past 16-quarter trend in sales data is a reasonably good indicator of the future, we can use this equation to project the trend component of the time series for future quarters. For example, substituting $t = 17$ into the equation yields next quarter's trend projection, T_{17}:

$$T_{17} = 5.101 + 0.148(17) = 7.617$$

Thus, the trend component yields a sales forecast of 7617 television sets for the next quarter. Similarly, the trend component produces sales forecasts of 7765, 7913, and 8061 television sets in quarters 18, 19, and 20, respectively.

Seasonal Adjustments

The final step in developing the forecast when both trend and seasonal components are present is to use the seasonal index to adjust the trend projection. Returning to the television set sales example, we have a trend projection for the next four quarters. Now we must adjust the forecast for the seasonal effect. The seasonal index for the first quarter of year 5 ($t = 17$) is 0.93, so we obtain the quarterly forecast by multiplying the forecast based on trend ($T_{17} = 7617$) times the seasonal index (0.93). Thus, the forecast for the next quarter is 7617(0.93) = 7084. Table 15.12 shows the quarterly forecast for quarters 17–20. The forecasts show the high-volume fourth quarter with a 9190-unit forecast and the low-volume second quarter with a 6523-unit forecast.

Applications that involve seasonal effects are commonplace. When dealing with data that have seasonal effects, firms must estimate the seasonal effects in order to obtain accurate forecasts. The Management Science in Action, Measuring and Reporting Radioactive Exposure, describes how one of the world's largest providers of dosimetry services was able to forecast demand for badges that measure radioactive exposure by using seasonal decomposition to capture the seasonality effect.

TABLE 15.12 QUARTERLY FORECASTS FOR THE TELEVISION SET SALES TIME SERIES

Year	Quarter	Trend Forecast	Seasonal Index (see Table 15.10)	Quarterly Forecast
5	1	7617	0.93	(7617)(0.93) = 7084
	2	7765	0.84	(7765)(0.84) = 6523
	3	7913	1.09	(7913)(1.09) = 8625
	4	8061	1.14	(8061)(1.14) = 9190

MANAGEMENT SCIENCE IN ACTION

MEASURING AND REPORTING RADIOACTIVE EXPOSURE*

U.S. federal law requires X-ray laboratories and nuclear plants to measure and report radioactive exposure for employees. Many organizations satisfy federal requirements by outsourcing the monitoring and reporting to firms that use thermoluminescent badges that record radioactive exposure for specified recording cycles of one month, three months, or six months.

The recording cycle for one of the world's largest providers of radiation dosimetry services begins with the shipment of customized badges to customers. When the customer receives the replenishment badges they collect the old badges and return them to the firm, which then measures the amount of radioactive exposure recorded on each badge. The variability in the time it takes customers to return badges, the fluctuating demand for badges from cycle to cycle, and the possible mishandling and wear of badges often affect the number of reusable badges for subsequent cycles. As a result it is difficult for the company to match the demand for customized badges with the supply of reusable badges. The company purchases new badges in order to supplement any shortfall of reusable badges.

One of the key factors in determining an effective new-badge purchasing system is the ability to forecast customer demand at the beginning of each recording cycle. Customers were classified into three groups based upon the length of their recording cycle: one, three, or six months. Historical data were used to create demand forecasts for each customer group using seasonal decomposition to capture the seasonality effect. The sum of the three customer group forecasts provided a forecast of total demand. Actual demand data for an 18-month period were used to estimate the seasonality effect. Tests with the forecasting model showed that it was able to capture the underlying seasonal factors and provide forecasts that were within 5% to 7% of the actual demand for the badges.

*Based on M. Bayiz and C. Tang, "An Integrated Planning System for Managing the Refurbishment of Thermoluminescent Badges," *Interfaces* (September/October 2004): 383–393.

Models Based on Monthly Data

In the preceding television set sales example we used quarterly data to illustrate the computation of seasonal indexes. However, many businesses use monthly rather than quarterly forecasts. In such cases, the procedures introduced in this section can be applied with minor modifications. First, a 12-month moving average replaces the four-quarter moving average; second, 12 monthly seasonal indexes, rather than the four quarterly indexes, must be computed. Other than these changes, the computational and forecasting procedures are identical.

Cyclical Component

Mathematically, the multiplicative model of equation (15.8) can be expanded to include a cyclical component as follows:

$$Y_t = T_t \times C_t \times S_t \times I_t \tag{15.9}$$

The cyclical component is attributable to multiyear cycles in the time series. It is analogous to the seasonal component but over a longer period of time. However, because of the length of time involved, obtaining enough relevant data to estimate the cyclical component often is difficult. Another difficulty is that the length of cycles usually varies. We leave further discussion of the cyclical component to texts on forecasting methods.

15.5 REGRESSION ANALYSIS

Regression analysis is a statistical technique that can be used to develop a mathematical equation showing how variables are related. In regression terminology, the variable that is being predicted is called the *dependent* or *response* variable. The variable or variables being used to predict the value of the dependent variable are called the *independent* or *predictor* variables. Regression analysis involving one independent variable and one dependent variable for which the relationship between the variables is approximated by a straight line is called *simple linear regression.* Regression analysis involving two or more independent variables is called *multiple regression analysis.* In Section 15.3 we utilized simple linear regression to fit a linear trend to the bicycle sales time series. Recall that we developed a linear equation relating bicycle sales to the time period. The number of bicycles sold isn't actually causally related to time; instead, time is a surrogate for variables to which the number of bicycles sold is actually related but which are either unknown or too difficult or costly to measure. Thus, the use of regression analysis for trend projection is not a causal forecasting method because only past values of sales, the variable being forecast, were used. When we use regression analysis to relate the variable that we want to forecast to other variables that are supposed to influence or explain that variable, it becomes a causal forecasting method.

Using Regression Analysis as a Causal Forecasting Method

To illustrate how regression analysis is used as a causal forecasting method, we consider the sales forecasting problem faced by Armand's Pizza Parlors, a chain of Italian restaurants doing business in a five-state area. The most successful locations have been near college campuses. The managers believe that quarterly sales for these restaurants (denoted by y) are related positively to the size of the student population (denoted by x); that is, restaurants near campuses with a large population tend to generate more sales than those located near campuses with a small population. Using regression analysis we can develop an equation showing how the dependent variable y is related to the independent variable x. This equation can then be used to forecast quarterly sales for restaurants located near college campuses given the size of the student population.

In situations where time series data are not available, regression analysis can still be used to develop a forecast. For instance, suppose that management wanted to forecast sales for a new restaurant they were considering opening near a college campus. Because no historical data are available on sales for a new restaurant, Armand's cannot use time series data to develop the forecast. But, as we will now illustrate, regression analysis can still be used to forecast quarterly sales.

To develop the equation relating quarterly sales and the size of the student population, Armand's collected data from a sample of 10 of its restaurants located near college campuses. These data are summarized in Table 15.13. For example, restaurant 1, with $y = 58$ and $x = 2$, had \$58,000 in quarterly sales and is located near a campus with 2000 students. Figure 15.14 shows graphically the data presented in Table 15.13. The size of the student population is shown on the horizontal axis, with quarterly sales shown on the vertical axis. This type of graph is called a *scatter diagram.* Usually the independent variable is plotted on the horizontal axis, and the dependent variable is plotted on the vertical axis. The advantage of a scatter diagram is that it provides an overview of the data and enables us to draw preliminary conclusions about a possible relationship between the variables.

What preliminary conclusions can we draw from Figure 15.14? Sales appear to be higher at campuses with larger student populations. Also, it appears that the relationship between the two variables can be approximated by a straight line; indeed, x and y appear to

TABLE 15.13 DATA ON QUARTERLY SALES AND STUDENT POPULATION FOR 10 RESTAURANTS

Restaurant	y = Quarterly Sales ($1000s)	x = Student Population (1000s)
1	58	2
2	105	6
3	88	8
4	118	8
5	117	12
6	137	16
7	157	20
8	169	20
9	149	22
10	202	26

be positively related. In Figure 15.15 we can draw a straight line through the data that appears to provide a good linear approximation of the relationship between the variables. Observe that the relationship isn't perfect. Indeed, few, if any, of the data fall exactly on the line. However, if we can develop the mathematical expression for this line, we may be able to use it to forecast the value of y corresponding to each possible value of x. The resulting equation of the line is called the *estimated regression equation.*

FIGURE 15.14 SCATTER DIAGRAM OF QUARTERLY SALES VERSUS STUDENT POPULATION

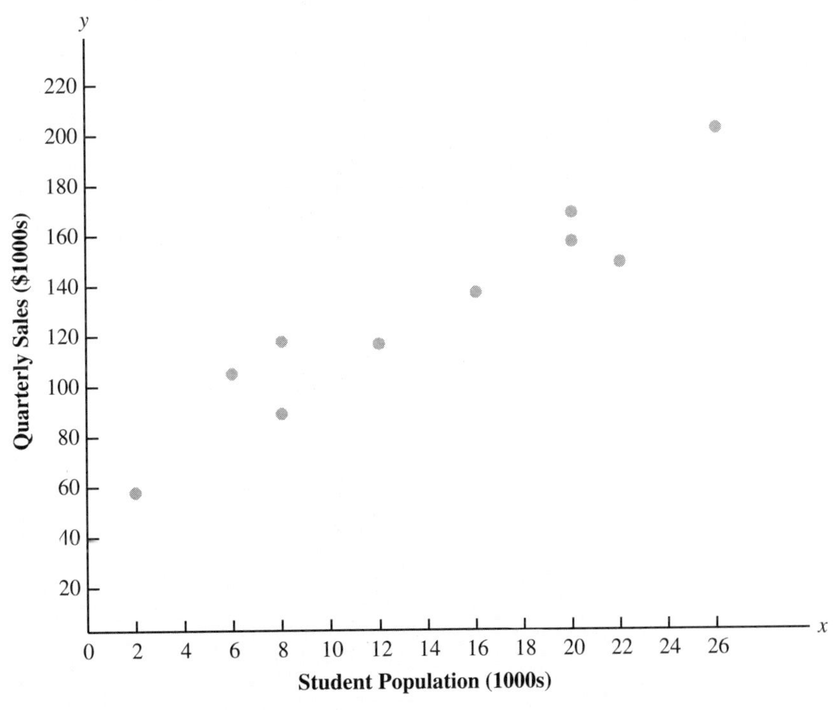

FIGURE 15.15 STRAIGHT-LINE APPROXIMATION FOR DATA ON QUARTERLY SALES AND STUDENT POPULATION

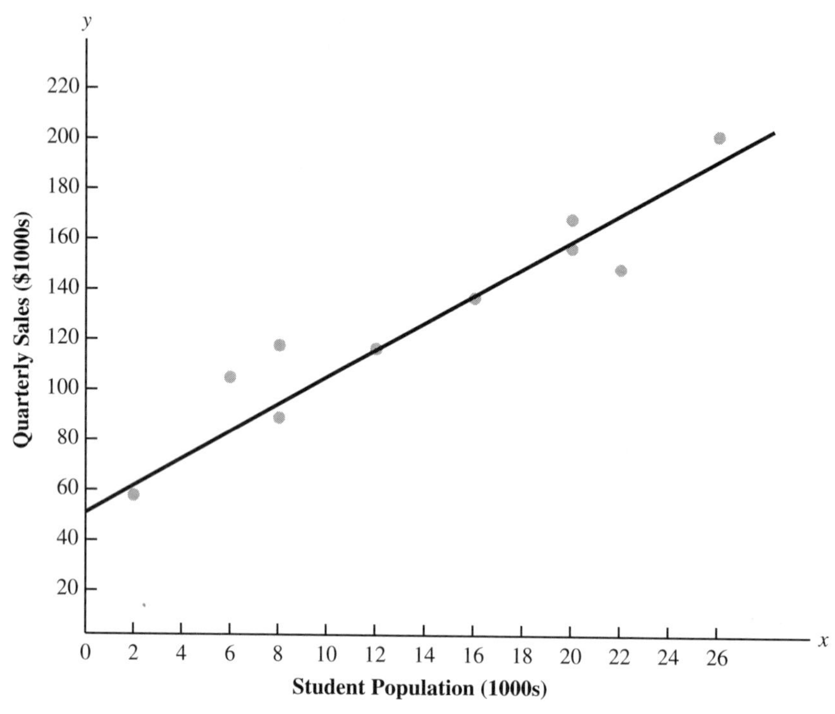

Using the least-squares method of estimation, the estimated regression equation is

$$\hat{y} = b_0 + b_1 x \tag{15.10}$$

where

$\hat{y}$ = estimated value of the dependent variable (quarterly sales)
b_0 = intercept of the estimated regression equation
b_1 = slope of the estimated regression equation
x = value of the independent variable (student population)

We use the sample data and the following equations to compute the intercept b_0 and slope b_1:

$$b_1 = \frac{\sum x_i y_i - (\sum x_i \sum y_i)/n}{\sum x_i^2 - (\sum x_i)^2/n} \tag{15.11}$$

$$b_0 = \bar{y} - b_1 \bar{x} \tag{15.12}$$

where

x_i = value of the independent variable for the ith observation
y_i = value of the dependent variable for the ith observation
$\bar{x}$ = mean value for the independent variable
$\bar{y}$ = mean value for the dependent variable
n = total number of observations

Some of the calculations necessary to develop the least-squares estimated regression equation for the data on student population and quarterly sales are shown in Table 15.14. Our example contains 10 restaurants or observations; hence, $n = 10$. Using equations (15.11) and (15.12), we can now compute the slope and intercept of the estimated regression equation. We calculate the slope b_1 as follows:

$$\begin{aligned} b_1 &= \frac{\Sigma x_i y_i - (\Sigma x_i \Sigma y_i)/n}{\Sigma x_i^2 - (\Sigma x_i)^2/n} \\ &= \frac{21{,}040 - (140)(1300)/10}{2528 - (140)^2/10} \\ &= \frac{2840}{568} \\ &= 5 \end{aligned}$$

We then calculate the intercept b_0 as follows:

$$\bar{x} = \frac{\Sigma x_i}{n} = \frac{140}{10} = 14$$

$$\bar{y} = \frac{\Sigma y_i}{n} = \frac{1300}{10} = 130$$

$$\begin{aligned} b_0 &= \bar{y} - b_1\bar{x} \\ &= 130 - 5(14) \\ &= 60 \end{aligned}$$

TABLE 15.14 CALCULATIONS FOR THE LEAST-SQUARES ESTIMATED REGRESSION EQUATION FOR ARMAND'S PIZZA PARLORS

Restaurant (i)		y_i	x_i	$x_i y_i$	x_i^2
1		58	2	116	4
2		105	6	630	36
3		88	8	704	64
4		118	8	944	64
5		117	12	1,404	144
6		137	16	2,192	256
7		157	20	3,140	400
8		169	20	3,380	400
9		149	22	3,278	484
10		202	26	5,252	676
	Totals	1300	140	21,040	2528

FIGURE 15.16 THE ESTIMATED REGRESSION EQUATION FOR ARMAND'S PIZZA PARLORS

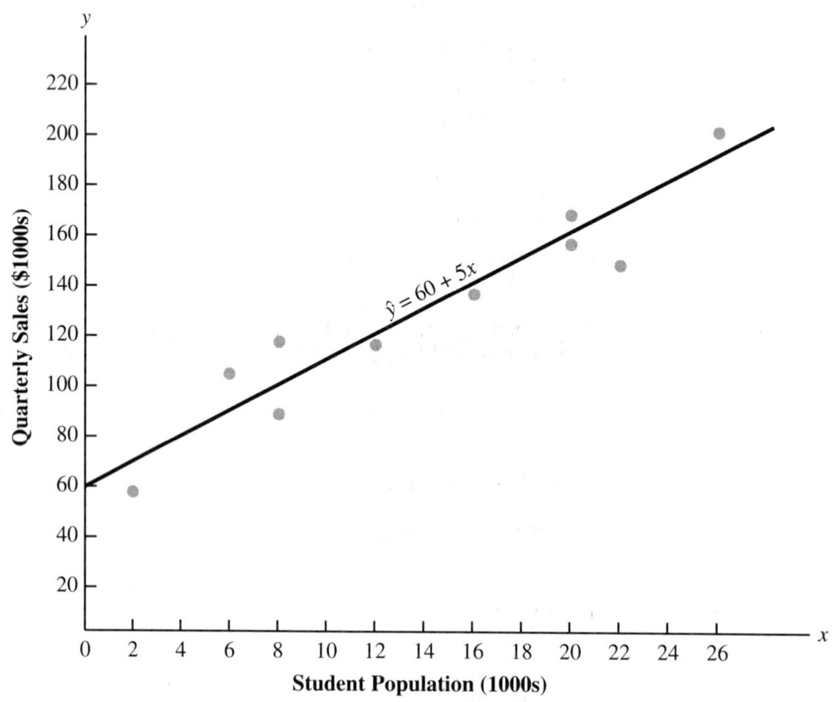

Thus, the estimated regression equation found by using the method of least squares is

$$\hat{y} = 60 + 5x$$

We show the graph of this equation in Figure 15.16.

The slope of the estimated regression equation ($b_1 = 5$) is positive, implying that, as student population increases, quarterly sales increase. In fact, we can conclude (because sales are measured in thousands of dollars and student population in thousands) that an increase in the student population of 1000 is associated with an increase of $5000 in expected quarterly sales; that is, quarterly sales are expected to increase by $5 per student.

If we believe that the least-squares estimated regression equation adequately describes the relationship between x and y, using the estimated regression equation to forecast the value of y for a given value of x seems reasonable. For example, if we wanted to forecast quarterly sales for a new restaurant to be located near a campus with 16,000 students, we would compute

Practice using regression analysis to develop a forecast by working Problem 33.

$$\hat{y} = 60 + 5(16) \\ = 140$$

Hence, we would forecast quarterly sales of $140,000.

The sales forecasting problem facing Armand's Pizza Parlors illustrates how simple linear regression analysis can be used to develop forecasts when time series data are not available. Multiple regression analysis also can be applied in these situations if additional data for other independent variables are available. For example, suppose that the management of Armand's Pizza Parlors also believes that the number of competitors near the college campus is related to quarterly sales. Intuitively, management believes that restaurants located near campuses with fewer competitors generate more sales revenue than those located near campuses with more competitors. With additional data, multiple regression analysis could be used to develop an equation relating quarterly sales to the size of the student population and the number of competitors.

Using Regression Analysis with Time Series Data

In Section 15.3 we fit a linear trend to the bicycle sales time series to show how simple linear regression analysis can be used to forecast future values of a time series when past values of the time series are available. Recall that for this problem the annual sales in year t was treated as the dependent variable and the year t was treated as the independent variable. The inherent complexity of most real-world problems necessitates the consideration of more than one independent variable to predict the dependent variable. We now consider how multiple regression analysis is used to develop forecasts when time series data are available.

To use multiple regression analysis, we need a sample of observations for the dependent variable and all the independent variables. In time series analysis, the n periods of time series data provide a sample of n observations for each variable. To describe the wide variety of regression-based models that can be developed, we use the following notation:

$$
\begin{aligned}
Y_t &= \text{actual value of the time series in period } t \\
x_{1t} &= \text{value of independent variable 1 in period } t \\
x_{2t} &= \text{value of independent variable 2 in period } t \\
&\ \ \vdots \\
x_{kt} &= \text{value of independent variable } k \text{ in period } t
\end{aligned}
$$

The n periods of data necessary to develop the estimated regression equation would appear as follows.

	Dependent Variable	Independent Variables				
Period	Y_t	x_{1t}	x_{2t}	x_{3t}	. . .	x_{kt}
1	Y_1	x_{11}	x_{21}	x_{31}	. . .	x_{k1}
2	Y_2	x_{12}	x_{22}	x_{32}	. . .	x_{k2}
.	.	.	.	.	. . .	.
.	.	.	.	.	. . .	.
.	.	.	.	.	. . .	.
n	Y_n	x_{1n}	x_{2n}	x_{3n}	. . .	x_{kn}

As you might imagine, a number of choices can be made when selecting the independent variables in a forecasting model. One possible choice is simply time. We made this choice in Section 15.3 when we estimated the trend of the time series using a linear function of the independent variable time. Letting

$$x_{1t} = t$$

we obtain an estimated regression equation of the form

$$\hat{Y}_t = b_0 + b_1 t$$

where $\hat{Y}_t$ is the estimate of the time series value Y_t and where b_0 and b_1 are the estimated regression coefficients. In a more complex model, additional terms could be added corresponding to time raised to other powers. For example, if

$$x_{2t} = t^2 \quad \text{and} \quad x_{3t} = t^3$$

the estimated regression equation would become

$$\begin{aligned}\hat{Y}_t &= b_0 + b_1 x_{1t} + b_2 x_{2t} + b_3 x_{3t} \\ &= b_0 + b_1 t + b_2 t^2 + b_3 t^3\end{aligned}$$

Note that this model provides a forecast of a time series with curvilinear characteristics over time.

Other regression-based forecasting models involve the use of a mixture of economic and demographic independent variables. For example, in forecasting the sale of refrigerators, we might select independent variables such as

x_{1t} = price in period t
x_{2t} = total industry sales in period $t - 1$
x_{3t} = number of building permits for new houses in period $t - 1$
x_{4t} = population forecast for period t
x_{5t} = advertising budget for period t

According to the usual multiple regression procedure, an estimated regression equation with five independent variables would be used to develop forecasts in this case.

Spyros Makridakis, a noted forecasting expert, conducted research showing that simple techniques usually outperform more complex procedures for short-term forecasting. Using a more sophisticated and expensive procedure will not guarantee better forecasts.

Whether a regression approach provides a good forecast depends largely on how well we are able to identify and obtain data for independent variables that are closely related to the time series. Generally, during the development of an estimated regression equation, we will want to consider many possible sets of independent variables. Thus, part of the regression analysis procedure should focus on the selection of the set of independent variables that provides the best forecasting model.

In the chapter introduction we stated that causal forecasting methods are based on the assumption that the variable we are trying to forecast exhibits a cause-effect relationship with one or more other variables. Regression analysis is the tool most often used in developing causal models. The related time series become the independent variables, and the time series being forecast is the dependent variable.

Another type of regression-based forecasting model occurs whenever all the independent variables are previous values of the same time series. For example, if the time series values are denoted $Y_1, Y_2, \ldots, Y_n$, we might try to find an estimated regression equation relating Y_t to the most recent time series values, Y_{t-1}, Y_{t-2}, and so on. For instance, if we use the actual values of the time series for the three most recent periods as independent variables, the estimated regression equation would be

$$\hat{Y}_t = b_0 + b_1 Y_{t-1} + b_2 Y_{t-2} + b_3 Y_{t-3}$$

Regression models such as this one in which the independent variables are previous values of the time series are referred to as **autoregressive models.**

Finally, another regression-based forecasting approach is one that incorporates a mixture of the independent variables previously discussed. For example, we might select a combination of time variables, some economic/demographic variables, and some previous values of the time series variable itself.

15.6 QUALITATIVE APPROACHES

If historical data are not available, managers may use a qualitative technique to develop forecasts. But the cost of using qualitative techniques can be high because of the time commitment required from the people involved.

In the preceding sections we discussed several types of quantitative forecasting methods. Most of these techniques require historical data on the variable of interest, so they cannot be applied when no historical data are available. Furthermore, even when such data are available, a significant change in environmental conditions affecting the time series may make the use of past data questionable in predicting future values of the time series. For example, a government-imposed gasoline rationing program would raise questions about the validity of a gasoline sales forecast based on historical data. Qualitative forecasting techniques offer an alternative in these and other cases.

Delphi Method

One of the most commonly used qualitative forecasting techniques is the **Delphi method.** This technique, originally developed by a research group at the Rand Corporation, attempts to develop forecasts through "group consensus." In its usual application, the members of a panel of experts—all of whom are physically separated from and unknown to each other—are asked to respond to a series of questionnaires. The responses from the first questionnaire are tabulated and used to prepare a second questionnaire that contains information and opinions of the entire group. Each respondent is then asked to reconsider and possibly revise his or her previous response in light of the group information provided. This process continues until the coordinator feels that some degree of consensus has been reached. The goal of the Delphi method is not to produce a single answer as output, but instead to produce a relatively narrow spread of opinions within which the majority of experts concurs.

Expert Judgment

Empirical evidence and theoretical arguments suggest that between 5 and 20 experts should be used in judgmental forecasting.

Qualitative forecasts often are based on the judgment of a single expert or represent the consensus of a group of experts. For example, each year a group of experts at Merrill Lynch gather to forecast the level of the Dow Jones Industrial Average and the prime rate for the next year. In doing so, the experts individually consider information that they believe will influence the stock market and interest rates; then they combine their conclusions into a forecast. No formal model is used, and no two experts are likely to consider the same information in the same way.

Expert judgment is a forecasting method that is often recommended when conditions in the past are not likely to hold in the future. Even though no formal quantitative model is used, expert judgment provides good forecasts in many situations.

Scenario Writing

The qualitative procedure referred to as **scenario writing** consists of developing a conceptual scenario of the future based on a well-defined set of assumptions. Different sets of assumptions lead to different scenarios. The job of the decision maker is to decide how likely each scenario is and then to make decisions accordingly.

Intuitive Approaches

Subjective, or *intuitive qualitative approaches*, are based on the ability of the human mind to process information that, in most cases, is difficult to quantify. These techniques are often used in group work, wherein a committee or panel seeks to develop new ideas or solve complex problems through a series of "brainstorming sessions." In such sessions, individuals are freed from the usual group restrictions of peer pressure and criticism because they can present any idea or opinion without regard to its relevancy and, even more importantly, without fear of criticism.

SUMMARY

In this chapter we discussed how forecasts can be developed to help managers develop appropriate strategies for the future. We began by defining a time series as a set of observations on a variable measured at successive points in time or over successive periods of time. A time series may involve four separate components: trend, seasonal, irregular, and cyclical. By isolating these components and measuring their apparent effects, future values of the time series can be forecast.

Quantitative forecasting methods include time series methods and causal methods. A time series method is appropriate when the historical data are restricted to past values of the variable being forecast. The three time series methods discussed in the chapter are smoothing (moving averages, weighted moving averages, and exponential smoothing), trend projection, and trend projection adjusted for seasonal influence.

Smoothing methods are appropriate for a stable time series; that is, one that exhibits no significant trend, cyclical, or seasonal effects. The moving averages approach consists of computing an average of past values and then using this average as the forecast for the next period. The weighted moving averages method allows for the possibility of unequal weights for the data; thus, the moving averages method is a special case of the weighted moving averages method in which all the weights are equal. Exponential smoothing also is a special case of the weighted moving averages method involving only one parameter: the weight for the most recent observation.

When a time series consists of random fluctuations around a long-term trend line, a linear equation may be used to estimate the trend. When seasonal effects are present, seasonal indexes can be computed and used to deseasonalize the data and to develop forecasts. When both seasonal and long-term trend effects are present, a trend line is fitted to the deseasonalized data; the seasonal indexes are then used to adjust the trend projections.

Causal forecasting methods are based on the assumption that the variable being forecast exhibits a cause-effect relationship with one or more other variables. A causal forecasting method is one that relates the variable being forecast to other variables that are thought to influence or explain it. Regression analysis is a causal forecasting method that can be used to develop forecasts when time series data are not available.

Qualitative forecasting methods may be used when little or no historical data are available. Qualitative forecasting methods also are considered most appropriate when the historical pattern of the time series is not expected to continue into the future.

GLOSSARY

Time series A set of observations of a variable measured at successive points in time or over successive periods of time.

Forecast A projection or prediction of future values of a time series.

Time series method Forecasting method that is based on the use of historical data that are restricted to past values of the variable we are trying to forecast.

Causal forecasting methods Forecasting methods that are based on the assumption that the variable we are trying to forecast exhibits a cause-effect relationship with one or more other variables.

Trend The gradual shift or movement of the time series to relatively higher or lower values over a longer period of time.

Cyclical component The component of the time series that accounts for the periodic above-trend and below-trend behavior of the time series lasting more than one year.

Seasonal component The component of the time series that represents the variability in the data due to seasonal influences.

Irregular component The component of the time series that accounts for the random variability in the time series.

Moving averages A smoothing method that uses the average of the most recent n data values in the time series as the forecast for the next period.

Mean squared error (MSE) An approach to measuring the accuracy of a forecasting model. This measure is the average of the sum of the squared differences between the actual time series values and the forecasted values.

Weighted moving averages A smoothing method that uses a weighted average of the most recent n data values as the forecast.

Exponential smoothing A smoothing method that uses a weighted average of past time series values as the forecast; it is a special case of the weighted moving averages method in which we select only one weight—the weight for the most recent observation.

Smoothing constant In the exponential smoothing model, the smoothing constant is the weight given to the actual value of the time series in period t.

Mean absolute deviation (MAD) A measure of forecast accuracy. The average of the absolute values of the forecast errors.

Multiplicative time series model A model that assumes that the separate components of the time series can be multiplied together to identify the actual time series value. When the four components of trend, cyclical, seasonal, and irregular are assumed present, we obtain $Y_t = T_t \times C_t \times S_t \times I_t$. When cyclical effects are not modeled, we obtain $Y_t = T_t \times S_t \times I_t$.

Seasonal index A measure of the seasonal effect on a time series. A seasonal index above 1 indicates a positive effect, a seasonal index of 1 indicates no seasonal effect, and a seasonal index less than 1 indicates a negative effect.

Deseasonalized time series A time series that has had the effect of season removed by dividing each original time series observation by the corresponding seasonal index.

Regression analysis A statistical technique used to develop a mathematical equation showing how variables are related.

Autoregressive model A regression model in which the independent variables are previous values of the time series.

Delphi method A qualitative forecasting method that obtains forecasts through group consensus.

Scenario writing A qualitative forecasting method that consists of developing a conceptual scenario of the future based on a well-defined set of assumptions.

PROBLEMS

1. Corporate Triple A Bond interest rates for 12 consecutive months are 9.5, 9.3, 9.4, 9.6, 9.8, 9.7, 9.8, 10.5, 9.9, 9.7, 9.6, and 9.6.
   a. Develop three- and four-month moving averages for this time series. Which moving average provides the better forecasts? Explain.
   b. What is the moving average forecast for the next month?

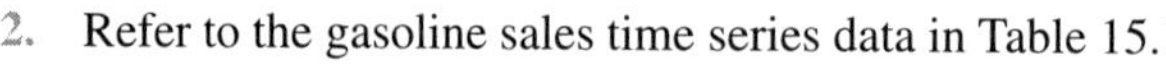

2. Refer to the gasoline sales time series data in Table 15.1.
   a. Compute four- and five-week moving averages for the time series.
   b. Compute the MSE for the four- and five-week moving average forecasts.
   c. What appears to be the best number of weeks of past data to use in the moving average computation? Remember that the MSE for the three-week moving average is 10.22.
3. Refer again to the gasoline sales time series data in Table 15.1.
   a. Use a weight of ½ for the most recent observation, ⅓ for the second most recent, and ⅙ for the third most recent to compute a three-week weighted moving average for the time series.
   b. Compute the MSE for the weighted moving average in part (a). Do you prefer this weighted moving average to the unweighted moving average? Remember that the MSE for the unweighted moving average is 10.22.
   c. Suppose that you are allowed to choose any weights as long as they sum to 1. Could you always find a set of weights that would make the MSE smaller for a weighted moving average than for an unweighted moving average? Why or why not?

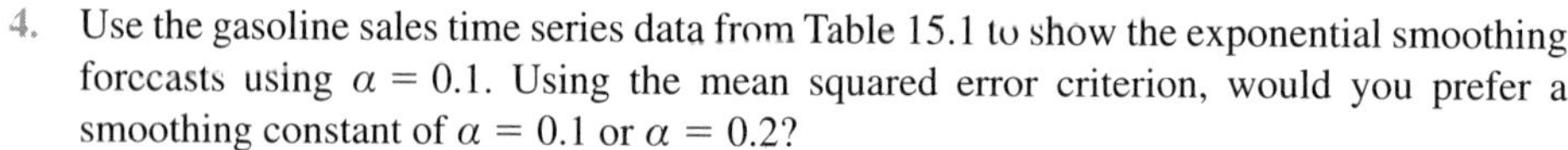

4. Use the gasoline sales time series data from Table 15.1 to show the exponential smoothing forecasts using $\alpha = 0.1$. Using the mean squared error criterion, would you prefer a smoothing constant of $\alpha = 0.1$ or $\alpha = 0.2$?

5. For the Hawkins Company, the monthly percentages of all shipments that were received on time over the past 12 months are 80, 82, 84, 83, 83, 84, 85, 84, 82, 83, 84, and 83.
   a. Compare a three-month moving average forecast with an exponential smoothing forecast for $\alpha = 0.2$. Which provides the better forecasts?
   b. What is the forecast for next month?
6. With a smoothing constant of $\alpha = 0.2$, equation (15.2) shows that the forecast for the 13th week of the gasoline sales data from Table 15.1 is given by $F_{13} = 0.2Y_{12} + 0.8F_{12}$. However, the forecast for week 12 is given by $F_{12} = 0.2Y_{11} + 0.8F_{11}$. Thus, we could combine these two results to write the forecast for the 13th week as

$$F_{13} = 0.2Y_{12} + 0.8(0.2Y_{11} + 0.8F_{11}) = 0.2Y_{12} + 0.16Y_{11} + 0.64F_{11}$$

   a. Make use of the fact that $F_{11} = 0.2Y_{10} + 0.8F_{10}$ (and similarly for F_{10} and F_9) and continue to expand the expression for F_{13} until you have written it in terms of the past data values Y_{12}, Y_{11}, Y_{10}, Y_9, and Y_8, and the forecast for period 8.
   b. Refer to the coefficients or weights for the past data values Y_{12}, Y_{11}, Y_{10}, Y_9, and Y_8; what observation can you make about how exponential smoothing weights past data values in arriving at new forecasts? Compare this weighting pattern with the weighting pattern of the moving averages method.

7. Alabama building contracts for a 12-month period (in millions of dollars) are 240, 350, 230, 260, 280, 320, 220, 310, 240, 310, 240, and 230.
   a. Compare a three-month moving average forecast with an exponential smoothing forecast using $\alpha = 0.2$. Which provides the better forecasts?
   b. What is the forecast for the next month?

8. Moving averages often are used to identify movements in stock prices. Daily closing prices (in dollars per share) for IBM for August 24, 2005, through September 16, 2005, follow (*Compustat,* February 26, 2006).

Day	Price ($)	Day	Price ($)
August 24	81.32	September 7	80.98
August 25	81.10	September 8	80.80
August 26	80.38	September 9	81.44
August 29	81.34	September 12	81.48
August 30	80.54	September 13	80.75
August 31	80.62	September 14	80.48
September 1	79.54	September 15	80.01
September 2	79.46	September 16	80.33
September 6	81.02		

   a. Use a three-month moving average to smooth the time series. Forecast the closing price for the next trading day.
   b. Use exponential smoothing with a smoothing constant of $\alpha = 0.6$ to smooth the time series. Forecast the closing price for the next trading day.
   c. Which of the two methods do you prefer? Why?

9. The following data represent 15 quarters of manufacturing capacity utilization (in percentages).

Quarter/Year	Utilization	Quarter/Year	Utilization
1/2004	82.5	1/2006	78.8
2/2004	81.3	2/2006	78.7
3/2004	81.3	3/2006	78.4
4/2004	79.0	4/2006	80.0
1/2005	76.6	1/2007	80.7
2/2005	78.0	2/2007	80.7
3/2005	78.4	3/2007	80.8
4/2005	78.0		

   a. Compute three- and four-quarter moving averages for this time series. Which moving average provides the better forecast for the fourth quarter of 2007?
   b. Use smoothing constants of $\alpha = 0.4$ and $\alpha = 0.5$ to develop forecasts for the fourth quarter of 2007. Which smoothing constant provides the better forecast?
   c. Based on the analyses in parts (a) and (b), which method—moving averages or exponential smoothing—provides the better forecast? Explain.

10. In 2005, Xerox Corporation's revenue from color products and services was $4.6 billion, or 30% of Xerox's total revenue. The following data show the quarterly percentage change in revenue for 12 quarters (*Democrat and Chronicle,* March 5, 2006).

Year	Quarter	% Growth
2003	1	15
	2	19
	3	15
	4	20
2004	1	26
	2	17
	3	18
	4	21
2005	1	15
	2	17
	3	22
	4	17

a. Use exponential smoothing to forecast this time series. Consider smoothing constants of $\alpha = 0.1$, $\alpha = 0.2$, and $\alpha = 0.3$. What value of the smoothing constant provides the best forecast?

b. What is the forecast of the percentage change for the first quarter of 2006?

11. The following table reports the percentage of stocks in a typical portfolio in nine quarters from 2005 to 2007.

Quarter	Stock %	Quarter	Stock %
1st—2005	29.8	2nd—2006	31.5
2nd—2005	31.0	3rd—2006	32.0
3rd—2005	29.9	4th—2006	31.9
4th—2005	30.1	1st—2007	30.0
1st—2006	32.2		

a. Use exponential smoothing to forecast this time series. Consider smoothing constants of $\alpha = 0.2$, 0.3, and 0.4. What value of the smoothing constant provides the best forecast?

b. What is the forecast of the percentage of assets committed to stocks for the second quarter of 2007?

12. United Dairies, Inc., supplies milk to several independent grocers throughout Dade County, Florida. Management wants to develop a forecast of the number of half-gallons of milk sold per week. Sales data (in units) for the past 12 weeks are as follows.

Week	Sales	Week	Sales
1	2750	7	3300
2	3100	8	3100
3	3250	9	2950
4	2800	10	3000
5	2900	11	3200
6	3050	12	3150

Use exponential smoothing, with $\alpha = 0.4$, to develop a forecast of demand for week 13.

13. Ten weeks of data on the Commodity Futures Index are 7.35, 7.40, 7.55, 7.56, 7.60, 7.52, 7.52, 7.70, 7.62, and 7.55.

a. Compute the exponential smoothing values for $\alpha = 0.2$.

b. Compute the exponential smoothing values for $\alpha = 0.3$.

c. Which exponential smoothing model provides the better forecasts? Forecast week 11.

14. The enrollment data (figures in thousands) for a state college for the past six years are shown.

Year	1	2	3	4	5	6
Enrollment	20.5	20.2	19.5	19.0	19.1	18.8

Develop the equation for the linear trend component for this time series. Comment on what is happening to enrollment at this institution.

15. Automobile sales at B. J. Scott Motors, Inc., provided the following 10-year time series.

Year	Sales	Year	Sales
1	400	6	260
2	390	7	300
3	320	8	320
4	340	9	340
5	270	10	370

Plot the time series, and comment on the appropriateness of a linear trend. What type of functional form would be best for the trend pattern of this time series?

16. The president of a small manufacturing firm has been concerned about the continual growth in manufacturing costs over the past several years. The following is a time series of the cost per unit (in dollars) for the firm's leading product over the past eight years.

Year	Cost per Unit ($)	Year	Cost per Unit ($)
1	20.00	5	26.60
2	24.50	6	30.00
3	28.20	7	31.00
4	27.50	8	36.00

a. Graph this time series. Does a linear trend appear?
b. Develop the equation for the linear trend component for the time series. What is the average cost increase per year?

17. The following data show the average monthly cellular telephone bill (*The New York Times Almanac*, 2006).

Year	Amount ($)
1998	39.43
1999	41.24
2000	45.27
2001	47.37
2002	48.40
2003	49.91

a. Graph this time series. Does a monthly trend appear to be present?
b. Develop a linear trend equation for this time series.
c. Use the trend equation to estimate the average monthly bill for 2004.
d. Would you feel comfortable using the linear trend equation to make forecasts for several years into the future? Explain.

18. FRED® (Federal Reserve Economic Data), a database of more than 3000 U.S. economic time series, can be used to access historical data on foreign exchange rates. The following data show the foreign exchange rate for the United States and Canada (http://research.stlouisfed.org/fred2/). The units for Rate are the number of Canadian dollars to one U.S. dollar.

Date	Rate
April 2005	1.2359
May 2005	1.2555
June 2005	1.2402
July 2005	1.2229
August 2005	1.2043
September 2005	1.1777
October 2005	1.1774
November 2005	1.1815
December 2005	1.1615
January 2006	1.1572

a. Graph this time series. Does a linear trend appear to be present?
b. Develop the equation for the linear trend component for the time series.
c. Use the trend equation to forecast the exchange rate for February 2006.
d. Would you feel comfortable in using the trend equation to forecast the exchange rate for July 2006?

19. The following data show the time series of the most recent quarterly capital expenditures (in billions of dollars) for the 1000 largest manufacturing firms: 24, 25, 23, 24, 22, 26, 28, 31, 29, 32, 37, and 42.
a. Develop a linear trend equation for the time series.
b. Graph the time series and the linear trend equation.
c. What appears to be happening to capital expenditures? What is the forecast one year, or four quarters, into the future?

20. The Costello Music Company has been in business for five years. During that time, the sales of pianos have grown from 12 units in the first year to 76 units in the most recent year. Fred Costello, the firm's owner, wants to develop a forecast of piano sales for the coming year based on the historical data shown.

Year	1	2	3	4	5
Sales	12	28	34	50	76

a. Graph this time series. Does a linear trend appear?
b. Develop the equation for the linear trend component for the time series. What is the average increase in sales per year for the firm?

21. Hudson Marine has been an authorized dealer for C&D marine radios for the past seven years. The number of radios sold each year is shown.

Year	1	2	3	4	5	6	7
Number Sold	35	50	75	90	105	110	130

a. Graph this time series. Does a linear trend appear?
b. Develop the equation for the linear trend component for the time series.
c. Use the linear trend developed in part (b) to prepare a forecast for sales in year 8.

22. The League of American Theatres and Producers, Inc., collects a variety of statistics for Broadway plays, such as gross revenue, playing time, and number of new productions. The following data show the season attendance (in millions) for Broadway shows from 1990 to 2001 (*The World Almanac 2002*).

Season	Attendance (in millions)	Season	Attendance (in millions)
1990–1991	7.3	1996–1997	10.6
1991–1992	7.4	1997–1998	11.5
1992–1993	7.9	1998–1999	11.7
1993–1994	8.1	1999–2000	11.4
1994–1995	9.0	2000–2001	11.9
1995–1996	9.5		

a. Plot the time series and comment on the appropriateness of a linear trend.
b. Develop the equation for the linear trend component for this time series.
c. What is the average increase in attendance per season?
d. Use the trend equation to forecast attendance for the 2001–2002 season.

23. The Garden Avenue Seven sells tapes of its musical performances. The following data show sales for the past 18 months. The group's manager wants an accurate method for forecasting future sales.

Month	Sales	Month	Sales	Month	Sales
1	293	7	381	13	549
2	283	8	431	14	544
3	322	9	424	15	601
4	355	10	433	16	587
5	346	11	470	17	644
6	379	12	481	18	660

a. Use exponential smoothing, with $\alpha = 0.3$, 0.4, and 0.5. Which value of α provides the best forecasts?
b. Use trend projection to provide a forecast. What is the value of MSE?
c. Which method of forecasting would you recommend to the manager? Why?

24. The Mayfair Department Store in Davenport, Iowa, is trying to determine the amount of sales lost while it was shut down because of summer floods. Sales data for January through June are shown.

Month	Sales ($1000s)
January	185.72
February	167.84
March	205.11
April	210.36
May	255.57
June	261.19

a. Use exponential smoothing, with $\alpha = 0.4$, to develop a forecast for July and August. (*Hint:* Use the forecast for July as the actual sales in July in developing the August forecast.) Comment on the use of exponential smoothing for forecasts more than one period into the future.
b. Use trend projection to forecast sales for July and August.
c. Mayfair's insurance company proposed a settlement based on lost sales of $240,000 in July and August. Is this amount fair? If not, what amount would you counter with?

25. The quarterly sales data (number of copies sold) for a college textbook over the past three years are as follows.

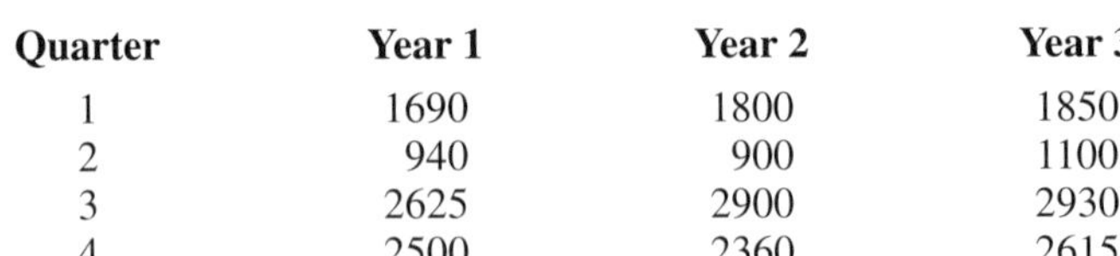

Quarter	Year 1	Year 2	Year 3
1	1690	1800	1850
2	940	900	1100
3	2625	2900	2930
4	2500	2360	2615

a. Show the four-quarter moving average values for this time series. Plot both the original time series and the moving averages on the same graph.
b. Compute seasonal indexes for the four quarters.
c. When does the textbook publisher experience the largest seasonal index? Does this result appear to be reasonable? Explain.

26. Identify the monthly seasonal indexes for the following three years of expenses for a six-unit apartment house in southern Florida. Use a 12-month moving average calculation.

Month	Year 1	Year 2	Year 3
January	170	180	195
February	180	205	210
March	205	215	230
April	230	245	280
May	240	265	290
June	315	330	390
July	360	400	420
August	290	335	330
September	240	260	290
October	240	270	295
November	230	255	280
December	195	220	250

27. Air pollution control specialists in southern California monitor the amount of ozone, carbon dioxide, and nitrogen dioxide in the air on an hourly basis. The hourly time series data exhibit seasonality, with the levels of pollutants showing similar patterns over the hours in the day. On July 15, 16, and 17, the observed levels of nitrogen dioxide in a city's downtown area for the 12 hours from 6:00 A.M. to 6:00 P.M. were as follows.

July 15	25	28	35	50	60	60	40	35	30	25	25	20
July 16	28	30	35	48	60	65	50	40	35	25	20	20
July 17	35	42	45	70	72	75	60	45	40	25	25	25

a. Identify the hourly seasonal indexes for the 12 hourly daily readings.
b. Based on the seasonal indexes in part (a), the trend equation developed for the deseasonalized data is $T_t = 32.983 + 0.3922t$. Using only the trend equation, develop forecasts for the 12 hours for July 18.
c. Use the seasonal indexes from part (a) to adjust the trend forecasts in part (b).

28. Refer to Problem 21. Suppose that the following are the quarterly sales data for the past seven years.

Year	Quarter 1	Quarter 2	Quarter 3	Quarter 4	Total Sales
1	6	15	10	4	35
2	10	18	15	7	50
3	14	26	23	12	75
4	19	28	25	18	90
5	22	34	28	21	105
6	24	36	30	20	110
7	28	40	35	27	130

a. Show the four-quarter moving average values for this time series. Plot both the original time series and the moving averages on the same graph.
b. Compute the seasonal indexes for the four quarters.
c. When does Hudson Marine experience the largest seasonal effect? Does this result seem reasonable? Explain.

29. Consider the Costello Music Company scenario presented in Problem 20 and the following quarterly sales data.

Year	Quarter 1	Quarter 2	Quarter 3	Quarter 4	Total Yearly Sales
1	4	2	1	5	12
2	6	4	4	14	28
3	10	3	5	16	34
4	12	9	7	22	50
5	18	10	13	35	76

a. Compute the seasonal indexes for the four quarters.
b. When does Costello Music experience the largest seasonal effect? Does this result appear to be reasonable? Explain.

30. Refer to the Hudson Marine data in Problem 28.
a. Deseasonalize the data, and use the deseasonalized time series to identify the trend.
b. Use the results of part (a) to develop a quarterly forecast for next year based on trend.
c. Use the seasonal indexes developed in Problem 28 to adjust the forecasts developed in part (b) to account for the effect of season.

31. Consider the Costello Music Company time series in Problem 29.
a. Deseasonalize the data, and use the deseasonalized time series to identify the trend.
b. Use the results of part (a) to develop a quarterly forecast for next year based on trend.
c. Use the seasonal indexes developed in Problem 29 to adjust the forecasts developed in part (b) to account for seasonal effects.

32. Electric power consumption is measured in kilowatt-hours (kWh). The local utility company has an interrupt program, whereby commercial customers who participate receive

favorable rates but must agree to cut back consumption if the utility requests them to do so. Timko Products cut back consumption at 12:00 noon Thursday. To assess the savings, the utility must estimate Timko's usage without the interrupt. The period of interrupted service was from noon to 8:00 P.M. Data on electric consumption for the past 72 hours is available.

Time Period	Monday	Tuesday	Wednesday	Thursday
12–4 A.M.	—	19,281	31,209	27,330
4–8 A.M.	—	33,195	37,014	32,715
8–12 noon	—	99,516	119,968	152,465
12–4 P.M.	124,299	123,666	156,033	
4–8 P.M.	113,545	111,717	128,889	
8–12 midnight	41,300	48,112	73,923	

a. Is there a seasonal effect over the 24-hour period? Compute seasonal indexes for the six 4-hour periods.
b. Use trend adjusted for seasonal factors to estimate Timko's normal usage over the period of interrupted service.

33. Eddie's Restaurants collected the following data on the relationship between advertising and sales at a sample of five restaurants.

Advertising Expenditures ($1000s)	1.0	4.0	6.0	10.0	14.0
Sales ($1000s)	19.0	44.0	40.0	52.0	53.0

a. Let x represent advertising expenditures and y represent sales. Use the method of least squares to develop a straight-line approximation of the relationship between the two variables.
b. Use the equation developed in part (a) to forecast sales for an advertising expenditure of $8000.

34. The management of a chain of fast-food restaurants wants to investigate the relationship between the daily sales volume (in dollars) of a company restaurant and the number of competitor restaurants within a 1-mile radius. The following data have been collected.

Number of Competitors Within 1 Mile	Sales ($)
1	3600
1	3300
2	3100
3	2900
3	2700
4	2500
5	2300
5	2000

a. Develop the least-squares estimated regression equation that relates daily sales volume to the number of competitor restaurants within a 1-mile radius.
b. Use the estimated regression equation developed in part (a) to forecast the daily sales volume for a particular company restaurant that has four competitors within a 1-mile radius.

35. The supervisor of a manufacturing process believed that assembly-line speed (in feet/minute) affected the number of defective parts found during on-line inspection. To test this theory,

management had the same batch of parts inspected visually at a variety of line speeds. The following data were collected.

Line Speed	Number of Defective Parts Found
20	21
20	19
40	15
30	16
60	14
40	17

a. Develop the estimated regression equation that relates line speed to the number of defective parts found.
b. Use the equation developed in part (a) to forecast the number of defective parts found for a line speed of 50 feet per minute.

Case Problem 1 FORECASTING SALES

The Vintage Restaurant is located on Captiva Island, a resort community near Fort Myers, Florida. The restaurant, which is owned and operated by Karen Payne, just completed its third year of operation. During this time, Karen sought to establish a reputation for the restaurant as a high-quality dining establishment that specializes in fresh seafood. The efforts made by Karen and her staff proved successful, and her restaurant is currently one of the best and fastest-growing restaurants on the island.

Karen concluded that, to plan better for the growth of the restaurant in the future, she needs to develop a system that will enable her to forecast food and beverage sales by month for up to one year in advance. Karen compiled the following data on total food and beverage sales for the three years of operation.

	Food and Beverage Sales for the Vintage Restaurant ($1000s)		
Month	First Year	Second Year	Third Year
January	242	263	282
February	235	238	255
March	232	247	265
April	178	193	205
May	184	193	210
June	140	149	160
July	145	157	166
August	152	161	174
September	110	122	126
October	130	130	148
November	152	167	173
December	206	230	235

Managerial Report

Perform an analysis of the sales data for the Vintage Restaurant. Prepare a report for Karen that summarizes your findings, forecasts, and recommendations. Include the following:

1. A graph of the time series.
2. An analysis of the seasonality of the data. Indicate the seasonal indexes for each month, and comment on the high seasonal and low seasonal sales months. Do the seasonal indexes make intuitive sense? Discuss.
3. Forecast sales for January through December of the fourth year.
4. Assume that January sales for the fourth year turned out to be $295,000. What was your forecast error? If this error is large, Karen may be puzzled about the difference between your forecast and the actual sales value. What can you do to resolve her uncertainty in the forecasting procedure?
5. Recommendations as to when the system that you developed should be updated to account for new sales data that will occur.
6. Include detailed calculations of your analysis in an appendix to your report.

Case Problem 2 FORECASTING LOST SALES

The Carlson Department Store suffered heavy damage when a hurricane struck on August 31, 2006. The store was closed for four months (September 2006 through December 2006), and Carlson is now involved in a dispute with its insurance company concerning the amount of lost sales during the time the store was closed. Two key issues must be resolved: (1) the amount of sales Carlson would have made if the hurricane had not struck; and (2) whether Carlson is entitled to any compensation for excess sales from increased business activity after the storm. More than $8 billion in federal disaster relief and insurance money came into the county, resulting in increased sales at department stores and numerous other businesses.

Table 15.15 shows the sales data for the 48 months preceding the storm. Table 15.16 reports total sales for the 48 months preceding the storm for all department stores in the

TABLE 15.15 SALES FOR CARLSON DEPARTMENT STORE, SEPTEMBER 2002 THROUGH AUGUST 2006

Month	2002	2003	2004	2005	2006
January		1.45	2.31	2.31	2.56
February		1.80	1.89	1.99	2.28
March		2.03	2.02	2.42	2.69
April		1.99	2.23	2.45	2.48
May		2.32	2.39	2.57	2.73
June		2.20	2.14	2.42	2.37
July		2.13	2.27	2.40	2.31
August		2.43	2.21	2.50	2.23
September	1.71	1.90	1.89	2.09	
October	1.90	2.13	2.29	2.54	
November	2.74	2.56	2.83	2.97	
December	4.20	4.16	4.04	4.35	

TABLE 15.16 DEPARTMENT STORE SALES FOR THE COUNTY, SEPTEMBER 2002 THROUGH DECEMBER 2006

Month	2002	2003	2004	2005	2006
January		46.8	46.8	43.8	48.0
February		48.0	48.6	45.6	51.6
March		60.0	59.4	57.6	57.6
April		57.6	58.2	53.4	58.2
May		61.8	60.6	56.4	60.0
June		58.2	55.2	52.8	57.0
July		56.4	51.0	54.0	57.6
August		63.0	58.8	60.6	61.8
September	55.8	57.6	49.8	47.4	69.0
October	56.4	53.4	54.6	54.6	75.0
November	71.4	71.4	65.4	67.8	85.2
December	117.6	114.0	102.0	100.2	121.8

county, as well as the total sales in the county for the four months the Carlson Department Store was closed. Management asks you to analyze these data and develop estimates of the lost sales at the Carlson Department Store for the months of September through December 2006. Management also wants to determine whether a case can be made for excess storm-related sales during the same period. If such a case can be made, Carlson is entitled to compensation for excess sales it would have earned in addition to ordinary sales.

Managerial Report

Prepare a report for the management of the Carlson Department Store that summarizes your findings, forecasts, and recommendations. Include the following:

1. An estimate of sales had there been no hurricane.
2. An estimate of countywide department store sales had there been no hurricane.
3. An estimate of lost sales for the Carlson Department Store for September through December 2006.

Appendix 15.1 USING EXCEL FOR FORECASTING

In this appendix we show how Excel can be used to develop forecasts using three forecasting methods: moving averages, exponential smoothing, and trend projection.

Moving Averages

To show how Excel can be used to develop forecasts using the moving averages method, we will develop a forecast for the gasoline sales time series in Table 15.1 and Figure 15.5. We assume that the user has entered the sales data for the 12 weeks into worksheet rows 1 through 12 of column A. The following steps can be used to produce a three-week moving average.

Step 1. Select the **Tools** menu
Step 2. Select the **Data Analysis** option

*Excel 2007 Users: To access the **Data Analysis** dialog box select the **Data** tab and click **Data Analysis** in the **Analysis** group.*

Step 3. When the **Data Analysis Tools** dialog box appears, choose **Moving Average**
Step 4. When the **Moving Average** dialog box appears:
Enter A1:A12 in the **Input Range** box
Enter 3 in the **Interval** box
Enter B1 in the **Output Range** box
Click **OK**

The three-week moving average forecasts will appear in column B of the worksheet. Note that forecasts for periods of other lengths can be computed easily by entering a different value in the **Interval** box.

Exponential Smoothing

To show how Excel can be used for exponential smoothing, we again develop a forecast for the gasoline sales time series in Table 15.1 and Figure 15.5. We assume that the user has entered the sales data for the 12 weeks into worksheet rows 1 through 12 of column A and that the smoothing constant is $\alpha = 0.2$. The following steps can be used to produce a forecast.

*Excel 2007 Users: To access the **Data Analysis** dialog box select the **Data** tab and click **Data Analysis** in the **Analysis** group.*

Step 1. Select the **Tools** menu
Step 2. Select the **Data Analysis** option
Step 3. When the **Data Analysis Tools** dialog box appears, choose **Exponential Smoothing**
Step 4. When the **Exponential Smoothing** dialog box appears:
Enter A1:A12 in the **Input Range** box
Enter 0.8 in the **Damping factor** box
Enter B1 in the **Output Range** box
Click **OK**

The exponential smoothing forecasts will appear in column B of the worksheet. Note that the value we entered in the **Damping factor** box is $1 - \alpha$; forecasts for other smoothing constants can be computed easily by entering a different value for $1 - \alpha$ in the **Damping factor** box.

Trend Projection

To show how Excel can be used for trend projection, we develop a forecast for the bicycle sales time series in Table 15.6 and Figure 15.8. We assume that the user has entered the year (1–10) for each observation into worksheet rows 1 through 10 of column A and the sales values into worksheet rows 1 through 10 of column B. The following steps can be used to produce a forecast for year 11 by trend projection.

*Excel 2007 Users: To access the **Insert Function** dialog box select the **Functions** tab and click **Insert Function** in the **Function Library** group.*

Step 1. Select an empty cell in the worksheet
Step 2. Select the **Insert** menu
Step 3. Choose the **Function** option
Step 4. When the **Insert Function** dialog box appears:
Choose **Statistical** in the **Select a category** box
Choose **Forecast** in the **Select a function** box
Click **OK**
Step 5. When the **Function Arguments** dialog box appears:
Enter 11 in the **x** box
Enter B1:B10 in the **Known y's** box
Enter A1:A10 in the **Known x's** box
Click **OK**

The forecast for year 11, in this case 32.5, will appear in the cell selected in step 1.

Appendix 15.2 USING CB PREDICTOR FOR FORECASTING

CB Predictor is an easy-to-use, graphically oriented forecasting add-in package. It is included as part of the Crystal Ball risk analysis package that accompanies the text. In this appendix, we show how CB Predictor can be used to develop forecasts using two forecasting methods: moving averages and exponential smoothing. We also briefly discuss some of the other forecasting techniques available using CB Predictor. Instructions for installing and starting CB Predictor are included with the Crystal Ball software.

Moving Averages

To show how CB Predictor can be used to develop forecasts using the moving averages method, we will develop a forecast for the gasoline sales time series in Table 15.1 and Figure 15.5. The labels Week and Sales are entered into cells A1:B1 of an Excel worksheet. To identify each of the 12 observations, we enter the numbers 1 through 12 into cells A2:A13. The corresponding sales data are entered in cells B2:B13. The following steps can be used to produce a three-week moving average.

Step 1. Select the **Run** menu
Step 2. Choose **CB Predictor**
Step 3. When the **Input Data** tab of the CB Predictor dialog box appears:
    Enter B1:B13 in the **Range** box
    Select **First row has headers**
    Select **Data in columns**
    Click **Next**
Step 4. When the **Data Attributes** tab of the CB Predictor dialog box appears:
    Select **weeks** from the **Data is in** list
    Select **with no seasonality (all seasonal methods skipped)**
    Click **Next**
Step 5. When the **Method Gallery** tab of the CB Predictor dialog box appears:
    Select **Single Moving Average**
    Double-click over the **Single Moving Average** method area
Step 6. When the **Single Moving Average** dialog box appears:
    Select **User defined**
    Enter 3 in the **Periods** box
    Click **OK**
Step 7. When the **Method Gallery** tab of the CB Predictor dialog box appears:
    Click **Next**
Step 8. When the **Results** tab of the CB Predictor dialog box appears:
    Enter 1 in the **Enter the number of periods to forecast** box
    Enter B14 in the **Paste forecasts at cell** box
    Click **Report**
    Click **Charts**
    Click **Results Table**
    Click **Methods Table**
    Click **Run**

The three-week moving average forecast of 19 for week 13 will appear in cell B14. Note that four new worksheets, labeled Report, Chart, Results Table, and Methods Table, appear as part of the CB Predictor output. Each of these worksheets provides details regarding the forecast results. For example, in the worksheet labeled Chart, CB Predictor provides a graph of the gasoline sales time series and the three-week moving average forecast similar to Figure 15.6 and a table of the time series data and the moving average forecast similar to Table 15.2. In the worksheet labeled Report, measures of forecast accuracy are also reported. One of these measures, RMSE = 3.1972, is just the square root of the MSE value that we used throughout the chapter.

Exponential Smoothing

To show how CB Predictor can be used for exponential smoothing, we again develop a forecast for the gasoline sales time series in Table 15.1 and Figure 15.5. The same worksheet that we used to develop a moving average forecast for gasoline sales applies: The labels Week and Sales are entered into cells A1:B1 of the worksheet, the numbers 1 through 12 are entered into cells A2:A13 to identify each of the 12 observations, and the sales data are entered in cells B2:B13. The following steps can be used to produce a forecast.

Step 1. Select the **Run** menu
Step 2. Choose **CB Predictor**
Step 3. When the **Input Data** tab of the CB Predictor dialog box appears:
Enter B1:B13 in the **Range** box
Select **First row has headers**
Select **Data in columns**
Click **Next**
Step 4. When the **Data Attributes** tab of the CB Predictor dialog box appears:
Select **weeks** from the **Data is in** list
Select **with no seasonality (all seasonal methods skipped)**
Click **Next**
Step 5. When the **Method Gallery** tab of the CB Predictor dialog box appears:
Select **Single Exp. Smoothing**
Double-click over the **Single Exp. Smoothing** method area
Step 6. When the **Single Exponential Smoothing** dialog box appears:
Select **User defined**
Enter .2 in the **Alpha** box
Click **OK**
Step 7. When the **Method Gallery** tab of the CB Predictor dialog box appears:
Click **Next**
Step 8. When the **Results** tab of the CB Predictor dialog box appears:
Enter 1 in the **Enter the number of periods to forecast** box
Enter B14 in the **Paste forecasts at cell** box
Click **Report**
Click **Charts**
Click **Results Table**
Click **Methods Table**
Click **Run**

The exponential smoothing forecast will appear in cell B14.

Other Forecasting Methods

In addition to moving averages and exponential smoothing, CB Predictor offers a variety of other forecasting methods that can be used for nonseasonal data with no trend, for nonseasonal data with trend, for seasonal data with no trend, and for seasonal data with trend. The "basic" models available in CB Predictor are the following:

	Nonseasonal		**Seasonal**	
No Trend	Single Moving Average	Single Exponential Smoothing	Seasonal Additive	Seasonal Multiplicative
Trend	Double Moving Average	Double Exponential Smoothing	Holt-Winters Additive	Holt-Winters Multiplicative

Thus, if the time series data contain both seasonal and trend components, the CB Predictor methods that are best designed to work for these situations are the Holt-Winters Additive method or the Holt-Winters Multiplicative method. Although a discussion of all the forecasting methods available using CB Predictor is beyond the scope of this text, more advanced books on forecasting discuss each of these techniques in detail.

Appendix D Self-Test Solutions and Answers to Even-Numbered Problems

Chapter 1

2. Define the problem; identify the alternatives; determine the criteria; evaluate the alternatives; choose an alternative

4. A quantitative approach should be considered because the problem is large, complex, important, new, and repetitive

6. Quicker to formulate, easier to solve, and/or more easily understood

8. a. Max $10x + 5y$
   s.t.
   $$5x + 2y \le 40$$
   $$x \ge 0,\ y \ge 0$$
   b. Controllable inputs: x and y
   Uncontrollable inputs: profit (10, 5), labor-hours (5, 2), and labor-hour availability (40)
   c. See Figure 1.8c
   d. $x = 0, y = 20$; Profit $= \$100$ (Solution by trial and error)
   e. Deterministic

10. a. Total units received $= x + y$
   b. Total cost $= 0.20x + 0.25y$
   c. $x + y = 5000$
   d. $x \le 4000$ Kansas City
   $y \le 3000$ Minneapolis
   e. Min $0.20x + 0.25y$
   s.t.
   $$\begin{aligned} x + y &= 5000 \\ x &\le 4000 \\ y &\le 3000 \\ x, y &\ge 0 \end{aligned}$$

FIGURE 1.8c SOLUTION

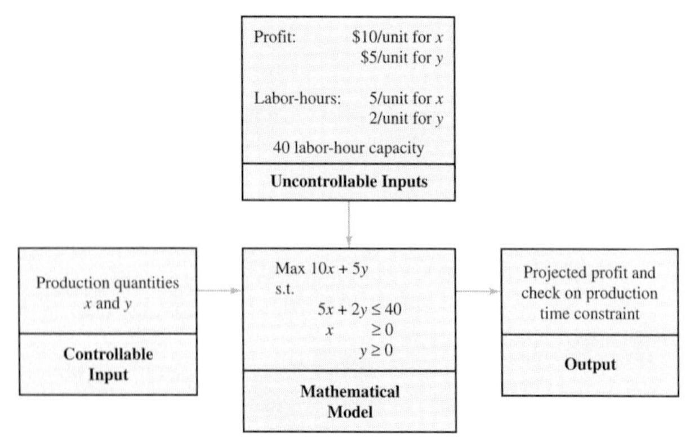

12. a. $TC = 1000 + 30x$
   b. $P = 40x - (1000 + 30x) = 10x - 1000$
   c. Break even when $P = 0$
   Thus, $10x - 1000 = 0$
   $$10x = 1000$$
   $$x = 100$$

14. a. 4706
   b. Loss of \$12,000
   c. \$23
   d. \$11,800 profit

16. a. Max $6x + 4y$
   b. $50x + 30y \le 80{,}000$
   $50x \le 50{,}000$
   $30y \le 45{,}000$

Chapter 2

1. Parts (a), (b), and (e) are acceptable linear programming relationships
   Part (c) is not acceptable because of $-2x_2^2$
   Part (d) is not acceptable because of $3\sqrt{x_1}$
   Part (f) is not acceptable because of $1x_1x_2$
   Parts (c), (d), and (f) could not be found in a linear programming model because they contain nonlinear terms

2. a.

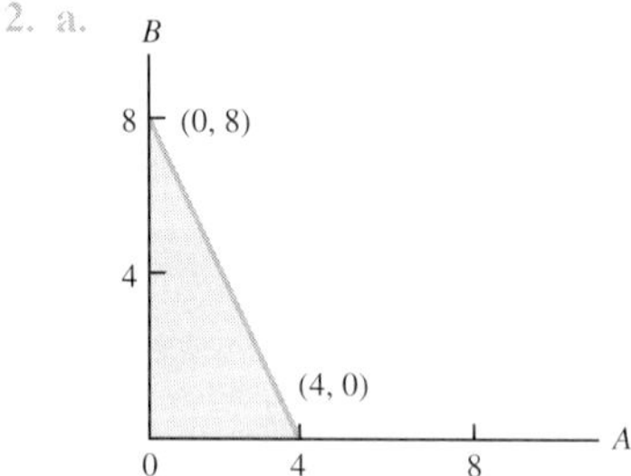

b.

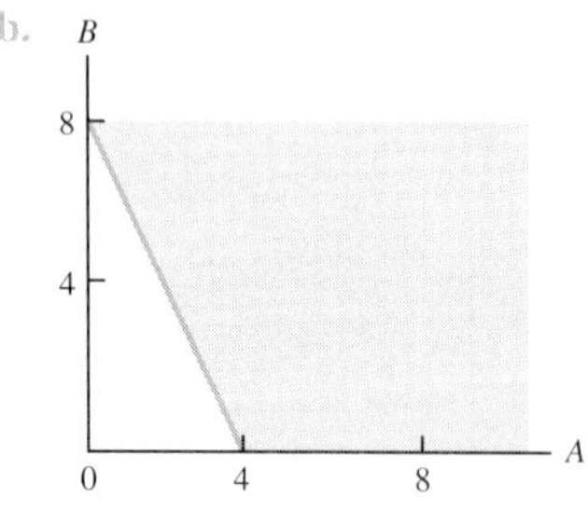

c.

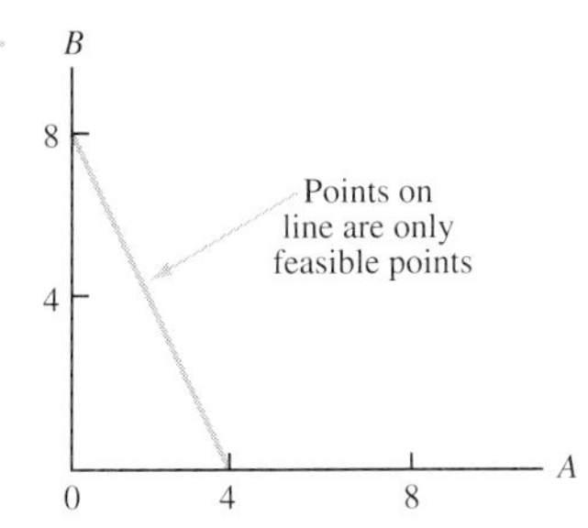

6. $7A + 10B = 420$
$6A + 4B = 420$
$-4A + 7B = 420$

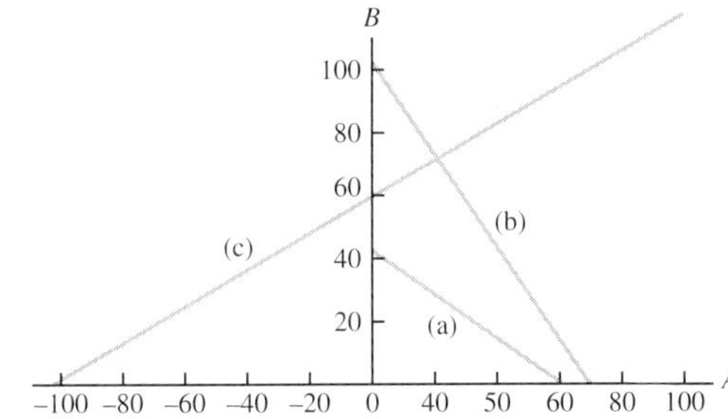

7.

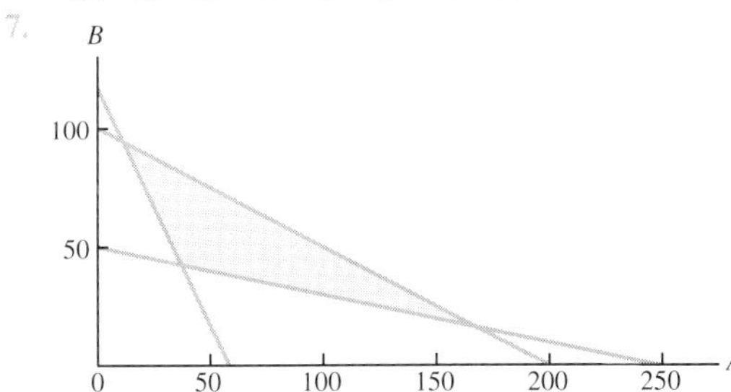

10.

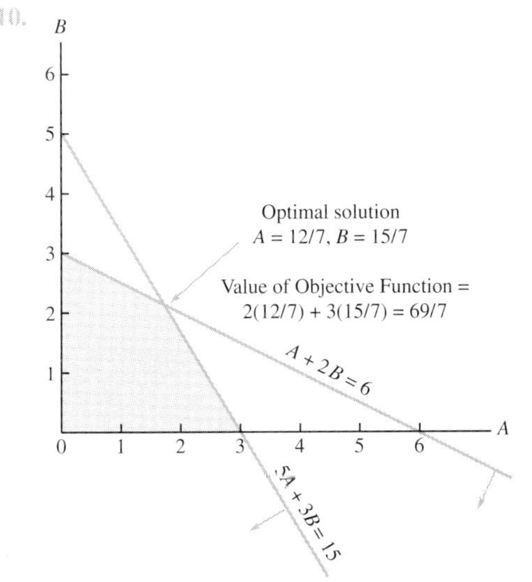

$$A + 2B = 6 \quad (1)$$
$$5A + 3B = 15 \quad (2)$$

Equation (1) times 5: $5A + 10B = 30 \quad (3)$

Equation (2) minus equation (3): $-7B = -15$

$B = 15/7$

From equation (1): $A = 6 - 2(15/7)$

$= 6 - 30/7 = 12/7$

12. a. $A = 3, B = 1.5$; value of optimal solution $= 13.5$
b. $A = 0, B = 3$; value of optimal solution $= 18$
c. Four: (0, 0), (4, 0), (3, 1.5), and (0.3)

13. a.

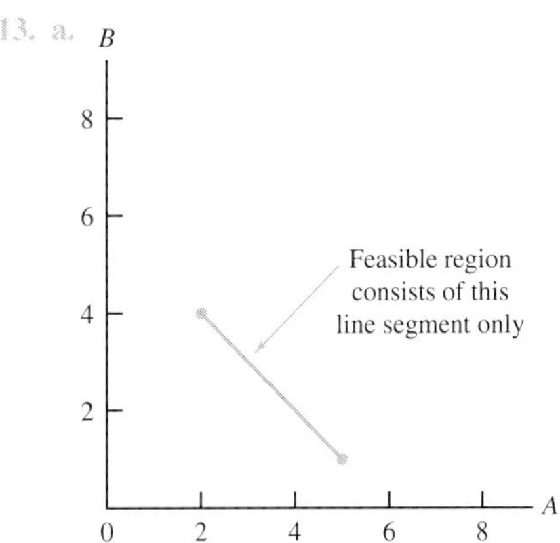

b. The extreme points are (5,1) and (2,4)

c.

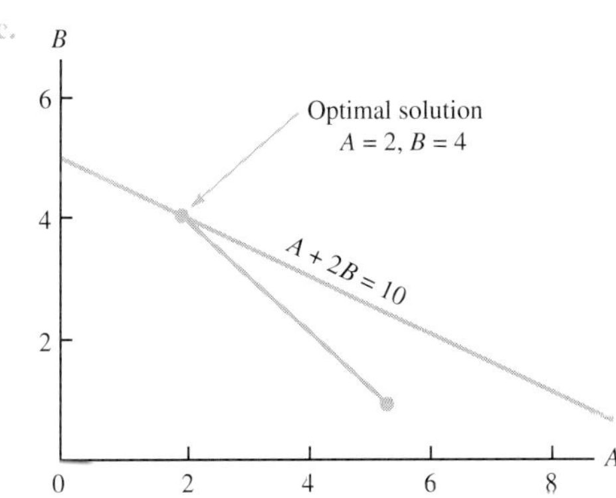

14. a. Let F = number of tons of fuel additive
S = number of tons of solvent base

Max $40F + 30S$

s.t.

$\frac{2}{5}F + \frac{1}{2}S \leq 200$ Material 1

$\frac{1}{5}S \leq 5$ Material 2

$\frac{3}{5}F + \frac{3}{10}S \leq 21$ Material 3

$F, S \geq 0$

b. $F = 25, S = 20$
c. Material 2:4 tons are used, 1 ton is unused
d. No redundant constraints

16. a. $3S + 9D$
b. (0, 540)
c. 90, 150, 348, 0

17. Max $5A + 2B + 0s_1 + 0s_2 + 0s_3$
s.t.

$$\begin{aligned} 1A - 2B + 1s_1 \quad &= 420 \\ 2A + 3B - \quad + 1s_2 \quad &= 610 \\ 6A - 1B + \quad + 1s_3 &= 125 \\ A, B, s_1, s_2, s_3 &\geq 0 \end{aligned}$$

18. b. $A = 18/7, B = 15/7$
c. 0, 0, 4/7

20. b. $A = 3.43, B = 3.43$
c. 2.86, 0, 1.43, 0

22. b.

Extreme Point	Coordinates	Profit ($)
1	(0, 0)	0
2	(1700, 0)	8500
3	(1400, 600)	9400
4	(800, 1200)	8800
5	(0, 1680)	6720

Extreme point 3 generates the highest profit
c. $A = 1400, C = 600$
d. Cutting and dyeing constraint and the packaging constraint
e. $A = 800, C = 1200$; profit = $9200

24. a. Let R = number of units of regular model
C = number of units of catcher's model

Max $5R + 8C$

$$\begin{aligned} 1R + \tfrac{3}{2}C &\leq 900 \quad \text{Cutting and sewing} \\ \tfrac{1}{2}R + \tfrac{1}{3}C &\leq 300 \quad \text{Finishing} \\ \tfrac{1}{8}R + \tfrac{1}{4}C &\leq 100 \quad \text{Packaging and shipping} \\ R, C &\geq 0 \end{aligned}$$

b.

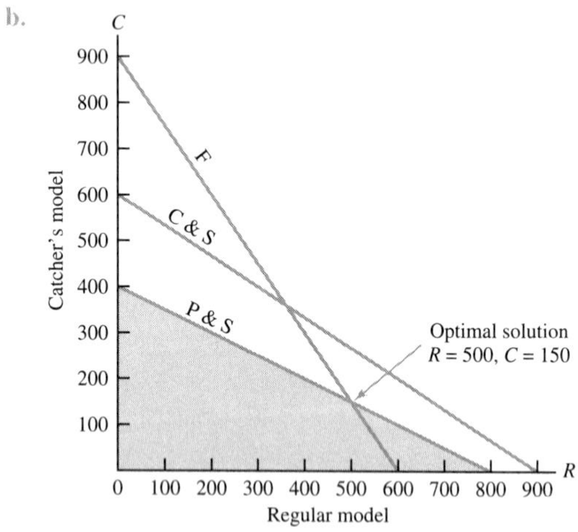

c. $5(500) + 8(150) = \$3,700$
d. C & S $1(500) + \tfrac{3}{2}(150) = 725$
F $\tfrac{1}{2}(500) + \tfrac{1}{3}(150) = 300$
P & S $\tfrac{1}{8}(500) + \tfrac{1}{4}(150) = 100$

e.

Department	Capacity	Usage	Slack
Cutting and sewing	900	725	175 hours
Finishing	300	300	0 hours
Packaging and shipping	100	100	0 hours

26. a. Max $50N + 80R$
s.t.

$$\begin{aligned} N + \quad R &= 1000 \\ N \quad &\geq 250 \\ R &\geq 250 \\ N - \quad 2R &\geq 0 \\ N, R &\geq 0 \end{aligned}$$

b. $N = 666.67, R = 333.33$; Audience exposure = 60,000

28. a. Max $1W + 1.25M$
s.t.

$$\begin{aligned} 5W + \quad 7M &\leq 4480 \\ 3W + \quad 1M &\leq 2080 \\ 2W + \quad 2M &\leq 1600 \\ W, M &\geq 0 \end{aligned}$$

b. $W = 560, M = 240$; Profit = 860

30. a. Max $15E + 18C$
s.t.

$$\begin{aligned} 40E + 25C &\leq 50,000 \\ 40E \quad &\geq 15,000 \\ 25C &\geq 10,000 \\ 25C &\leq 25,000 \\ E, C &\geq 0 \end{aligned}$$

c. (375, 400); (1000, 400); (625, 1000); (375, 1000)
d. $E = 625, C = 1000$
Total return = $27,375

31.

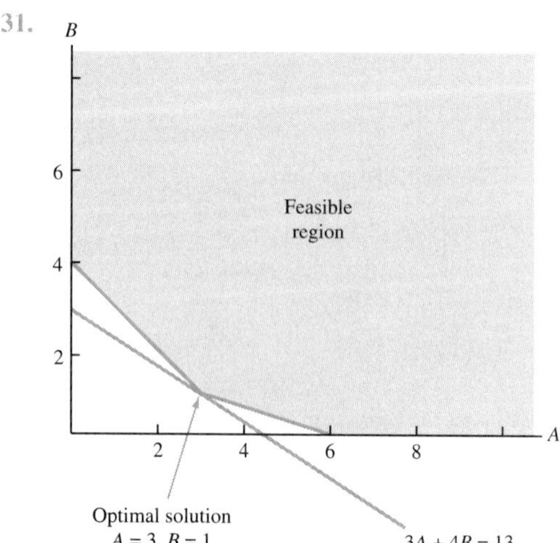

Objective function value = 13

32.

Extreme Points	Objective Function Value	Surplus Demand	Surplus Total Production	Slack Processing Time
(250, 100)	800	125	—	—
(125, 225)	925	—	—	125
(125, 350)	1300	—	125	—

34. a.

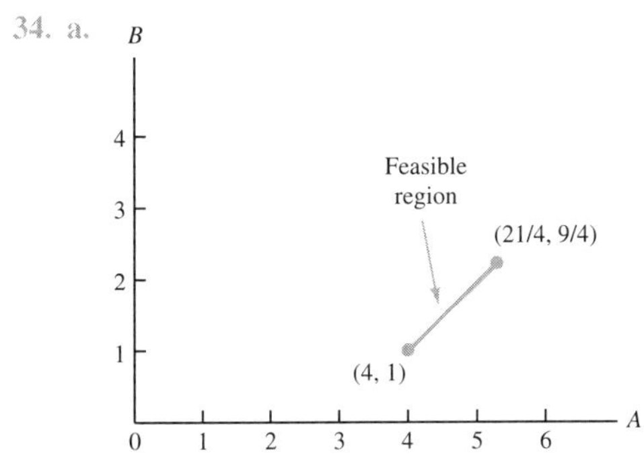

b. The two extreme points are

$(A = 4, B = 1)$ and $(A = 21/4, B = 9/4)$

c. The optimal solution (see part (a)) is $A = 4, B = 1$

35. a. Min $6A + 4B + 0s_1 + 0s_2 + 0s_3$

s.t.

$$\begin{aligned} 2A + 1B - s_1 \quad\quad\quad &= 12 \\ 1A + 1B \quad - s_2 \quad &= 10 \\ 1B \quad\quad + s_3 &= 4 \\ A, B, s_1, s_2, s_3 &\geq 0 \end{aligned}$$

b. The optimal solution is $A = 6, B = 4$

c. $s_1 = 4, s_2 = 0, s_3 = 0$

36. a. Min $10{,}000T + 8{,}000P$

s.t.

$$\begin{aligned} T \quad\quad &\geq 8 \\ P &\geq 10 \\ T + \quad P &\geq 25 \\ 3T + \quad 2P &\leq 84 \end{aligned}$$

c. (15, 10); (21.33, 10); (8, 30); (8, 17)

d. $T = 8, P = 17$

Total cost = $216,000

38. a. Min $7.50S + 9.00P$

s.t.

$$\begin{aligned} 0.10S + 0.30P &\geq 6 \\ 0.06S + 0.12P &\leq 3 \\ S + \quad P &= 30 \\ S, P &\geq 0 \end{aligned}$$

c. Optional solution is $S = 15, P = 15$

d. No

e. Yes

40. $P_1 = 30, P_2 = 25$; Cost = \$55

42.

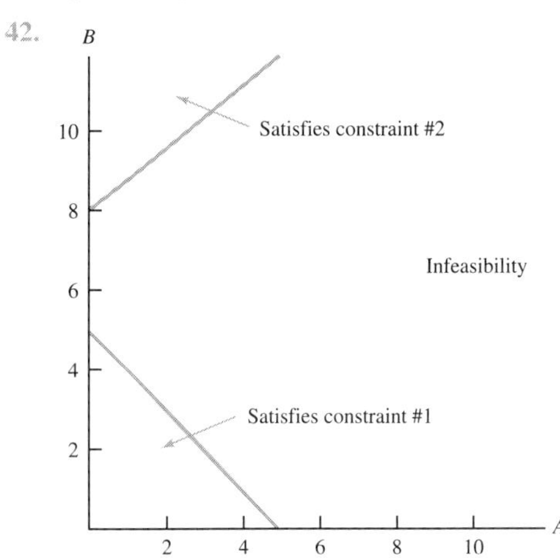

43.

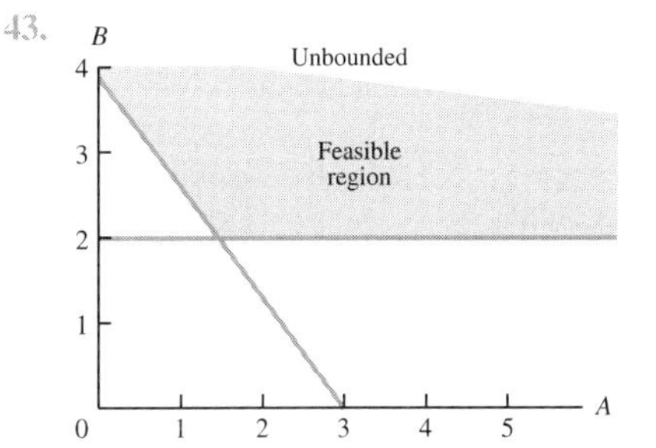

44. a. $A = 30/16, B = 30/16$; Value of optimal solution = $60/16$

b. $A = 0, B = 3$; Value of optimal solution = 6

46. a. 180, 20

b. Alternative optimal solutions

c. 120, 80

48. No feasible solution

50. $M = 65.45, R = 261.82$; Profit = \$45,818

52. $S = 384, O = 80$

54. a. Max $160M_1 + 345M_2$

s.t.

$$\begin{aligned} M_1 \quad\quad &\leq 15 \\ M_2 &\leq 10 \\ M_1 \quad\quad &\geq 5 \\ M_2 &\geq 5 \\ 40M_1 + 50M_2 &\leq 1000 \\ M_1, M_2 &\geq 0 \end{aligned}$$

b. $M_1 = 12.5, M_2 = 10$

Chapter 3

1. a.

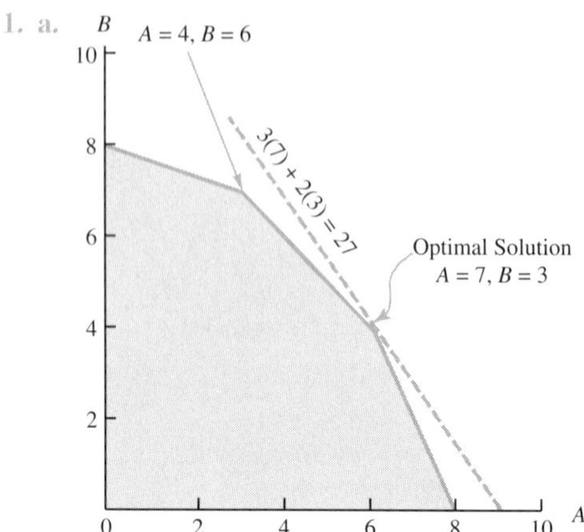

   b. The same extreme point, $A = 7$ and $B = 3$, remains optimal; value of the objective function becomes $5(7) + 2(3) = 41$
   c. A new extreme point, $A = 4$ and $B = 6$, becomes optimal; value of the objective function becomes $3(4) + 4(6) = 36$
   d. The objective coefficient range for variable A is 2 to 6; the optimal solution, $A = 7$ and $B = 3$, does not change The objective coefficient range for variable B is 1 to 3; re-solve the problem to find the new optimal solution

2. a. The feasible region becomes larger with the new optimal solution of $A = 6.5$ and $B = 4.5$
   b. Value of the optimal solution to the revised problem is $3(6.5) + 2(4.5) = 28.5$; the one-unit increase in the right-hand side of constraint 1 improves the value of the optimal solution by $28.5 - 27 = 1.5$; therefore, the dual price for constraint 1 is 1.5
   c. The right-hand-side range for constraint 1 is 8 to 11.2; as long as the right-hand side stays within this range, the dual price of 1.5 is applicable
   d. The improvement in the value of the optimal solution will be 0.5 for every unit increase in the right-hand side of constraint 2 as long as the right-hand side is between 18 and 30

4. a. $X = 2.5$, $Y = 2.5$
   b. -2
   c. 5 to 11
   d. -3 between 9 and 18

5. a. Regular glove = 500; Catcher's mitt = 150; Value = 3700
   b. The finishing, packaging, and shipping constraints are binding; there is no slack
   c. Cutting and sewing = 0
      Finishing = 3
      Packaging and shipping = 28
      Additional finishing time is worth \$3 per unit, and additional packaging and shipping time is worth \$28 per unit
   d. In the packaging and shipping department, each additional hour is worth \$28

6. a. 4 to 12
      3.33 to 10
   b. As long as the profit contribution for the regular glove is between \$4.00 and \$12.00, the current solution is optimal; as long as the profit contribution for the catcher's mitt stays between \$3.33 and \$10.00, the current solution is optimal; the optimal solution is not sensitive to small changes in the profit contributions for the gloves
   c. The dual prices for the resources are applicable over the following ranges:

Constraint	Right-Hand-Side Range
Cutting and sewing	725 to No upper limit
Finishing	133.33 to 400
Packaging and shipping	75 to 135

   d. Amount of increase = (28)(20) = \$560

8. a. More than \$7.00
   b. More than \$3.50
   c. None

10. a. $S = 4000$, $M = 10{,}000$; Total risk = 62,000
    b.

Variable	Objective Coefficient Range
S	3.75 to No upper limit
M	No lower limit to 6.4

    c. 5(4000) + 4(10,000) = \$60,000
    d. 60,000 / 1,200,000 = 0.05 or 5%
    e. 0.057 risk units
    f. 0.057(100) = 5.7%

12. a. $E = 80$, $S = 120$, $D = 0$
       Profit = \$16,440
    b. Fan motors and cooling coils
    c. Labor hours; 320 hours available
    d. Objective function coefficient range of optimality
       No lower limit to 159
       Because \$150 is in this range, the optimal solution would not change

13. a. Range of optimality
       E 47.5 to 75
       S 87 to 126
       D No lower limit to 159
    b.

Model	Profit	Change	Allowable Increase/Decrease	%
E	\$ 63	Increase \$6(100)	\$75 − \$63 = \$12	$\frac{6}{12}(100) = 50$
S	\$ 95	Decrease \$2	\$95 − \$87 = \$8	$\frac{2}{8}(100) = 25$
D	\$135	Increase \$4	\$159 − \$135 = \$24	$\frac{4}{24}(100) = 17$
				92

Because changes are 92% of allowable changes, the optimal solution of $E = 80$, $S = 120$, $D = 0$ will not change

The change in total profit will be

$$\begin{array}{lr} E \quad 80 \text{ units @ } +\$6 = & \$480 \\ S \quad 120 \text{ units @ } -\$2 = & -240 \\ \hline & \$240 \end{array}$$

$\therefore$ Profit = \$16,440 + \$240 = \$16,680

c. Range of feasibility

Constraint 1 160 to 280
Constraint 2 200 to 400
Constraint 3 2080 to No upper limit

d. Yes, Fan motors = 200 + 100 = 300 is outside the range of feasibility; the dual price will change

14\. a. Manufacture 100 cases of A and 60 cases of B, and purchase 90 cases of B; Total cost = \$2170
b. Demand for A, demand for B, assembly time
c. −12.25, −9.0, 0, .375
d. Assembly time constraint

16\. a. 100 suits, 150 sport coats
Profit = \$40,900
40 hours of cutting overtime
b. Optimal solution will not change
c. Consider ordering additional material
\$34.50 is the maximum price
d. Profit will improve by \$875

18\. a. The linear programming model is as follows:

$$\begin{aligned} \text{Min} \quad & 30AN + 50AO + 25BN + 40BO \\ \text{s.t.} \quad & \\ & AN + AO \geq 50{,}000 \\ & BN + BO \geq 70{,}000 \\ & AN + BN \leq 80{,}000 \\ & AO + BO \leq 60{,}000 \\ & AN, AO, BN, BO \geq 0 \end{aligned}$$

b. Optimal solution

	New Line	Old Line
Model A	50,000	0
Model B	30,000	40,000

Total cost: \$3,850,000

c. The first three constraints are binding
d. Because the dual price is positive, increasing the right-hand side of constraint 3 will *improve* the solution; thus, an increase in capacity for the new production line is desirable
e. Because constraint 4 is not a binding constraint, any increase in the production line capacity of the old production line will have no effect on the optimal solution; thus, increasing the capacity of the old production line results in no benefit
f. The reduced cost for model A made on the old production line is 5; thus, the cost would have to decrease by at least \$5 before any units of model A would be produced on the old production line
g. The right-hand-side range for constraint 2 shows a lower limit of 30,000; thus, if the minimum production requirement is reduced 10,000 units to 60,000, the dual price of −40 is applicable; thus, total cost would decrease by 10,000(40) = \$400,000

20\. a.

$$\begin{aligned} \text{Max} \quad & 0.07H + 0.12P + 0.09A \\ \text{s.t.} \quad & \\ & H + P + A = 1{,}000{,}000 \\ & 0.6H - 0.4P - 0.4A \geq 0 \\ & P - 0.6A \leq 0 \\ & H, P, A \geq 0 \end{aligned}$$

b. H = \$400,000, P = \$225,000, A = \$375,000
Total annual return = \$88,750
Annual percentage return = 8.875%
c. No change
d. Increase of \$890
e. Increase of \$312.50 or 0.031%

22\. a.

$$\begin{aligned} \text{Min} \quad & 30L + 25D + 18S \\ \text{s.t.} \quad & \\ & L + D + S = 100 \\ & 0.6L - 0.4D \geq 0 \\ & -0.15L - 0.15D + 0.85S \geq 0 \\ & -0.25L - 0.25D + S \leq 0 \\ & L \leq 50 \\ & L, D, S \geq 0 \end{aligned}$$

b. L = 48, D = 72, S = 30
Total cost = \$3780
c. No change
d. No change

24\. a. 333.3, 0, 833.3; Risk = 14,666.7; Return = 18,000 or 9%
b. 1000, 0, 0, 2500; Risk = 18,000; Return = 22,000 or 11%
c. \$4000

26\. a. Let M_1 = units of component 1 manufactured
M_2 = units of component 2 manufactured
M_3 = units of component 3 manufactured
P_1 = units of component 1 purchased
P_2 = units of component 2 purchased
P_3 = units of component 3 purchased

$$\begin{aligned} \text{Min} \quad & 4.50M_1 + 5.00M_2 + 2.75M_3 + 6.50P_1 + 8.80P_2 + 7.00P_3 \\ \text{s.t.} \quad & \\ & 2M_1 + 3M_2 + 4M_3 \leq 21{,}600 \quad \text{Production} \\ & 1M_1 + 1.5M_2 + 3M_3 \leq 15{,}000 \quad \text{Assembly} \\ & 1.5M_1 + 2M_2 + 5M_3 \leq 18{,}000 \quad \text{Testing/Packaging} \\ & 1M_1 + 1P_1 = 6{,}000 \quad \text{Component 1} \\ & 1M_2 + 1P_2 = 4{,}000 \quad \text{Component 2} \\ & 1M_3 + 1P_3 = 3{,}500 \quad \text{Component 3} \\ & M_1, M_2, M_3, P_1, P_2, P_3 \geq 0 \end{aligned}$$

b.

Source	Component 1	Component 2	Component 3
Manufacture	2000	4000	1400
Purchase	4000		2100

Total cost = \$73,550

c. Production: \$54.36 per hour
Testing & Packaging: \$ 7.50 per hour
d. Dual prices = −\$7.969; it would cost Benson \$7.969 to add a unit of component 2

28. b. $G = 120{,}000$; $S = 30{,}000$; $M = 150{,}000$
c. 0.15 to 0.60; No lower limit to 0.122; 0.02 to 0.20
d. 4668
e. $G = 48{,}000$; $S = 192{,}000$; $M = 60{,}000$
f. The client's risk index and the amount of funds available

30. a. $L = 3, N = 7, W = 5, S = 5$
b. Each additional minute of broadcast time increases cost by \$100
c. If local coverage is increased by 1 minute, total cost will increase by \$100
d. If the time devoted to local and national news is increased by 1 minute, total cost will increase by \$100
e. Increasing the sports by 1 minute will have no effect because the dual price is 0

32. a. Let P_1 = number of PT-100 battery packs produced at the Philippines plant
P_2 = number of PT-200 battery packs produced at the Philippines plant
P_3 = number of PT-300 battery packs produced at the Philippines plant
M_1 = number of PT-100 battery packs produced at the Mexico plant
M_2 = number of PT-200 battery packs produced at the Mexico plant
M_3 = number of PT-300 battery packs produced at the Mexico plant

$$
\begin{aligned}
\text{Min } & 1.13P_1 + 1.16P_2 + 1.52P_3 + 1.08M_1 + 1.16M_2 + 1.25M_3 \\
\text{s.t.} & \\
& P_1 + M_1 = 200{,}000 \\
& P_2 + M_2 = 100{,}000 \\
& P_3 + M_3 = 150{,}000 \\
& P_1 + P_2 \le 175{,}000 \\
& M_1 + M_2 \le 160{,}000 \\
& P_3 \le 75{,}000 \\
& M_3 \le 100{,}000 \\
& P_1, P_2, P_3, M_1, M_2, M_3 \ge 0
\end{aligned}
$$

b. The optimal solution is as follows:

	Philippines	Mexico
PT-100	40,000	160,000
PT-200	100,000	0
PT-300	50,000	100,000

Total production and transportation cost is \$535,000
c. The range of optimality for the objective function coefficient for P_1 shows a lower limit of \$1.08; thus, the production and/or shipping cost would have to decrease by at least 5 cents per unit
d. The range of optimality for the objective function coefficient for M_1 shows a lower limit of \$1.11; thus, the production and/or shipping cost would have to decrease by at least 5 cents per unit

Chapter 4

1. a. Let T = number of television advertisements
R = number of radio advertisements
N = number of newspaper advertisements

$$
\begin{aligned}
\text{Max } & 100{,}000T + 18{,}000R + 40{,}000N \\
\text{s.t.} & \\
& 2000T + 300R + 600N \le 18{,}200 \quad \text{Budget} \\
& T \le 10 \quad \text{Max TV} \\
& R \le 20 \quad \text{Max radio} \\
& N \le 10 \quad \text{Max news} \\
& -0.5T + 0.5R - 0.5N \le 0 \quad \text{Max 50\% radio} \\
& 0.9T - 0.1R - 0.1N \ge 0 \quad \text{Min 10\% TV} \\
& T, R, N \ge 0
\end{aligned}
$$

Solution:		Budget \$
	$T = 4$	\$ 8000
	$R = 14$	4200
	$N = 10$	6000
		\$18,200

Audience = 1,052,000
b. The dual price for the budget constraint is 51.30, meaning a \$100 increase in the budget should provide an increase in audience coverage of approximately 5130; the right-hand-side range for the budget constraint will show that this interpretation is correct

2. a. $x_1 = 77.89$, $x_2 = 63.16$, \$3284.21
b. Department A \$15.79; Department B \$47.37
c. $x_1 = 87.21$, $x_2 = 65.12$, \$3341.34
Department A 10 hours; Department B 3.2 hours

4. a. $x_1 = 500$, $x_2 = 300$, $x_3 = 200$, \$550
b. \$0.55
c. Aroma, 75; Taste 84.4
d. −\$0.60

6. 50 units of product 1; 0 units of product 2; 300 hours department A; 600 hours department B

8. Schedule 19 officers as follows:
3 begin at 8:00 A.M.; 3 begin at noon; 7 begin at 4:00 P.M.; 4 begin at midnight, 2 begin at 4:00 A.M.

9. a. Decision variables A, P, M, H, and G represent the fraction or proportion of the total investment in each alternative

$$
\begin{aligned}
\text{Max } & 0.073A + 0.103P + 0.064M + 0.075H + 0.045G \\
\text{s.t.} & \\
& A + P + M + H + G = 1 \\
& 0.5A + 0.5P - 0.5M - 0.5H \le 0 \\
& -0.5A - 0.5P + 0.5M + 0.5H \le 0 \\
& - 0.25M - 0.25H + G \ge 0 \\
& -0.6A + 0.4P \le 0 \\
& A, P, M, H, G \ge 0
\end{aligned}
$$

Objective function = 0.079; $A = 0.178$; $P = 0.267$; $M = 0.000$; $H = 0.444$; $G = 0.111$
b. Multiplying A, P, M, H, and G by the \$100,000 invested provides the following

Atlantic Oil	\$ 17,800
Pacific Oil	26,700
Huber Steel	44,400
Government bonds	11,100
	\$100,000

c. 0.079(\$100,000) = \$7900
d. The marginal rate of return is 0.079

10. a. 40.9%, 14.5%, 14.5%, 30.0%
Annual return = 5.4%
b. 0.0%, 36.0%, 36.0%, 28.0%
Annual return = 2.52%
c. 75.0%, 0.0%, 15.0%, 10.0%
Annual return = 8.2%
d. Yes

12.

Week	Buy	Sell	Store
1	80,000	0	100,000
2	0	0	100,000
3	0	100,000	0
4	25,000	0	25,000

14. b.

Quarter	Production	Ending Inventory
1	4000	2100
2	3000	1100
3	2000	100
4	1900	500

15. Let x_{11} = gallons of crude 1 used to produce regular
x_{12} = gallons of crude 1 used to produce high octane
x_{21} = gallons of crude 2 used to produce regular
x_{22} = gallons of crude 2 used to produce high octane

Min $0.10x_{11} + 0.10x_{12} + 0.15x_{21} + 0.15x_{22}$
s.t.

Each gallon of regular must have at least 40% A

$x_{11} + x_{21}$ = amount of regular produced
$0.4(x_{11} + x_{21})$ = amount of A required for regular
$0.2x_{11} + 0.50x_{21}$ = amount of A in $(x_{11} + x_{21})$ gallons of regular gas
$\therefore 0.2x_{11} + 0.50x_{21} \geq 0.4x_{11} + 0.40x_{21}$
$\therefore -0.2x_{11} + 0.10x_{21} \geq 0$

Each gallon of high octane can have at most 50% B

$x_{12} + x_{22}$ = amount high octane
$0.5(x_{12} + x_{22})$ = amount of B required for high octane
$0.60x_{12} + 0.30x_{22}$ = amount of B in $(x_{12} + x_{22})$ gallons of high octane
$\therefore 0.60x_{12} + 0.30x_{22} \leq 0.5x_{12} + 0.5x_{22}$
$\therefore 0.1x_{12} - 0.2x_{22} \leq 0$
$x_{11} + x_{21} \geq 800{,}000$
$x_{12} + x_{22} \geq 500{,}000$
$x_{11}, x_{12}, x_{21}, x_{22} \geq 0$

Optimal solution: $x_{11} = 266{,}667$, $x_{12} = 333{,}333$, $x_{21} = 533{,}333$, $x_{22} = 166{,}667$
Cost = \$165,000

16. x_i = number of 10-inch rolls processed by cutting alternative i
a. $x_1 = 0, x_2 = 125, x_3 = 500, x_4 = 1500, x_5 = 0, x_6 = 0, x_7 = 0$; 2125 rolls with waste of 750 inches
b. 2500 rolls with no waste; however, 1½-inch size is overproduced by 3000 units

18. a. 5 Super, 2 Regular, and 3 Econo-Tankers
Total cost \$583,000; monthly operating cost \$4650

19. a. Let x_{11} = amount of men's model in month 1
x_{21} = amount of women's model in month 1
x_{12} = amount of men's model in month 2
x_{22} = amount of women's model in month 2
s_{11} = inventory of men's model at end of month 1
s_{21} = inventory of women's model at end of month 1
s_{12} = inventory of men's model at end of month 2
s_{22} = inventory of women's model at end of month 2

Min $120x_{11} + 90x_{21} + 120x_{12} + 90x_{22} + 2.4s_{11} + 1.8s_{21} + 2.4s_{12} + 1.8s_{22}$
s.t.

$x_{11} - s_{11} = 130$
$x_{21} - s_{21} = 95$
$s_{11} + x_{12} - s_{12} = 200$
$s_{21} + x_{22} - s_{22} = 150$
} Satisfy demand

$s_{12} \geq 25$
$s_{22} \geq 25$
} Ending inventory requirement

Labor-hours: Men's 2.0 + 1.5 = 3.5
Women's 1.6 + 1.0 = 2.6

$3.5x_{11} + 2.6x_{21} \geq 900$
$3.5x_{11} + 2.6x_{21} \leq 1100$
$3.5x_{11} + 2.6x_{21} - 3.5x_{12} - 2.6x_{22} \leq 100$
$-3.5x_{11} - 2.6x_{21} + 3.5x_{12} + 2.6x_{22} \leq 100$
} Labor smoothing

$x_{11}, x_{12}, x_{21}, x_{22}, s_{11}, s_{12}, s_{21}, s_{22} \geq 0$

Solution: $x_{11} = 193$; $x_{21} = 95$; $x_{12} = 162$; $x_{22} = 175$
Total cost = \$67,156
Inventory levels: $s_{11} = 63$; $s_{12} = 25$; $s_{21} = 0$; $s_{22} = 25$
Labor levels: Previous 1000 hours
Month 1 922.25 hours
Month 2 1022.25 hours

b. To accommodate the new policy, the right-hand sides of the four labor-smoothing constraints must be changed to 950, 1050, 50, and 50, respectively; the new total cost is \$67,175

20. Produce 10,250 units in March, 10,250 units in April, and 12,000 units in May

22. b. 5, 515, 887 sq. in. of waste
Machine 3: 492 minutes

24. Investment strategy: 45.8% of A and 100% of B
Objective function = \$4340.40
Savings/Loan schedule

	Period 1	2	3	4
Savings	242.11	—	—	341.04
Funds from loan	—	200.00	127.58	—

Chapter 5

2. b. $E = 0.924$
   $wa = 0.074$
   $wc = 0.436$
   $we = 0.489$
   c. D is relatively inefficient
   Composite requires 92.4 of D's resources
   d. 34.37 patient days (65 or older)
   41.99 patient days (under 65)
   e. Hospitals A, C, and E

4. b. $E = 0.960$
   $wb = 0.074$
   $wc = 0.000$
   $wj = 0.436$
   $wn = 0.489$
   $ws = 0.000$
   c. Yes; $E = 0.960$
   d. More: \$220 profit per week
   Less: Hours of Operation 4.4 hours
   FTE Staff 2.6
   Supply Expense \$185.61
   d. Bardstown, Jeffersonville, and New Albany

6. a. 19, 18, 12, 18
   b. PCQ = 8 PMQ = 0 POQ = 27
   PCY = 4 PMY = 1 POY = 2
   NCQ = 6 NMQ = 23 NOQ = 2
   NCY = 4 NMY = 2 NOY = 1
   CMQ = 37 CMY = 2
   COQ = 11 COY = 3
   c. PCQ = 8 PMQ = 1 POQ = 3
   PCY = 4 PMY = 1 POY = 2
   NCQ = 6 NMQ = 3 NOQ = 2
   NCY = 4 NMY = 2 NOY = 1
   CMQ = 3 CMY = 2
   COQ = 7 COY = 3

8. b. 65.7% small-cap growth fund
   34.3% of the portfolio in a small-cap value
   Expected return = 18.5%
   c. 10% foreign stock
   50.8% small-cap growth fund
   39.2% of the portfolio in a small-cap value
   Expected return = 17.178%

10.

		Player B			
		b_1	b_2	b_3	Minimum
Player A	a_1	8	5	7	(5) ← Maximum
	a_2	2	4	10	4
	Maximum	8	(5) ↑ Minimum	7	

The game has a pure strategy: Player A strategy a_1; Player B strategy b_2; and value of game = 5

12. 2.5, 2.5, 1.5
    Strategy a_1 or a_2
    Expected payoff = 2.5

14. Pure strategies a_4 and b_3
    Value = 10

15. a. The maximum of the row minimums is not equal to the minimum of the column maximums, so a mixed strategy exists
    Linear program for Player A:

$$
\begin{array}{llr}
\text{Max} & GAINA & \\
\text{s.t.} & & \text{Player B strategy} \\
& 5PA2 + 2PA3 - GAINA \geq 0 & \text{(red chip)} \\
& -PA1 + 4PA2 + 3PA3 - GAINA \geq 0 & \text{(white chip)} \\
& 2PA1 - 3PA2 - 4PA3 - GAINA \geq 0 & \text{(blue chip)} \\
& PA1 + PA2 + PA3 = 1 & \\
& PA1, PA2, PA3 \geq 0 &
\end{array}
$$

    Player A: $P(\text{red}) = 0.7$, $P(\text{white}) = 0.3$, $P(\text{blue}) = 0.0$
    From dual prices:
    Player B: $P(\text{red}) = 0.0$, $P(\text{white}) = 0.5$, $P(\text{blue}) = 0.5$
    b. The value of the game is a 50-cent expected gain for Player A
    c. Player A

16. Company A: 0.0, 0.0, 0.8, 0.2
    Company B: 0.4, 0.6, 0.0, 0.0
    Expected gain for A = 2.8

Chapter 6

1.

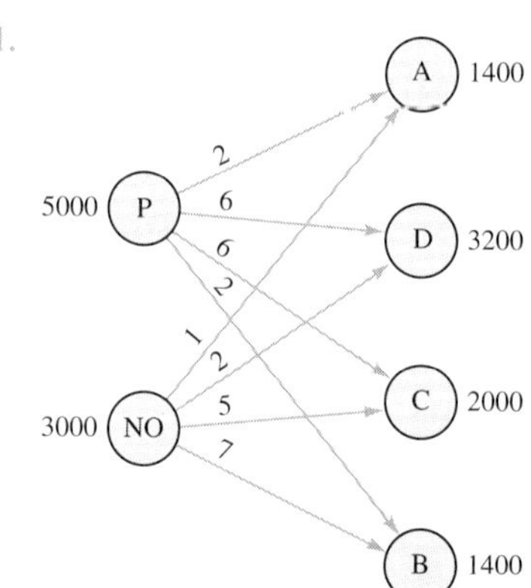

2. a. Let x_{11} = amount shipped from Jefferson City to Des Moines
   x_{12} = amount shipped from Jefferson City to Kansas City
   ⋮
   x_{23} = amount shipped from Omaha to St. Louis

$$
\begin{array}{ll}
\text{Min} & 14x_{11} + 9x_{12} + 7x_{13} + 8x_{21} + 10x_{22} + 5x_{23} \\
\text{s.t.} & \\
& x_{11} + x_{12} + x_{13} \leq 30 \\
& x_{21} + x_{22} + x_{23} \leq 20 \\
& x_{11} + x_{21} = 25 \\
& x_{12} + x_{22} = 15 \\
& x_{13} + x_{23} = 10 \\
& x_{11}, x_{12}, x_{13}, x_{21}, x_{22}, x_{23} \geq 0
\end{array}
$$

29. The capacitated transshipment problem to solve is given

Max x_{61}

s.t.

$$
\begin{aligned}
&x_{12} + x_{13} + x_{14} - x_{61} = 0 \\
&x_{24} + x_{25} - x_{12} - x_{42} = 0 \\
&x_{34} + x_{36} - x_{13} - x_{43} = 0 \\
&x_{42} + x_{43} + x_{45} + x_{46} - x_{14} - x_{24} - x_{34} - x_{54} = 0 \\
&x_{54} + x_{56} - x_{25} - x_{45} = 0 \\
&x_{61} - x_{36} + x_{46} - x_{56} = 0 \\
&x_{12} \le 2 \quad x_{13} \le 6 \quad x_{14} \le 3 \\
&x_{24} \le 1 \quad x_{25} \le 4 \\
&x_{34} \le 3 \quad x_{36} \le 2 \\
&x_{42} \le 1 \quad x_{43} \le 3 \quad x_{45} \le 1 \quad x_{46} \le 3 \\
&x_{54} \le 1 \quad x_{56} \le 6 \\
&x_{ij} \ge 0 \text{ for all } i, j
\end{aligned}
$$

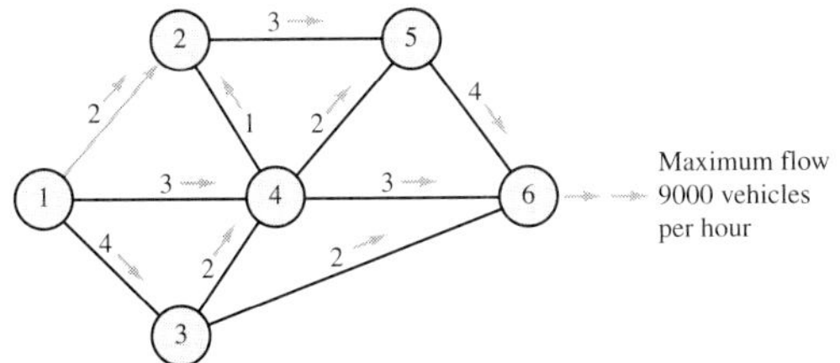

30. Maximal flow = 11,000 vehicles per hour

32. a. 10 hours; 10,000 gallons per hour
  b. 11.1 hours; flow reduced to 9000 gallons per hour

34. Maximal flow = 23 gallons/minute
  The total flow from 3 to 5 must be 5 gallons/minute

36. c. Regular-month 1: 275; overtime-month 1: 25; inventory at end of month 1: 150
  Regular-month 2: 200; overtime-month 2: 50; inventory at end of month 2: 150
  Regular-month 3: 100; overtime-month 3: 50; inventory at end of month 3: 0

Chapter 7

2. a.

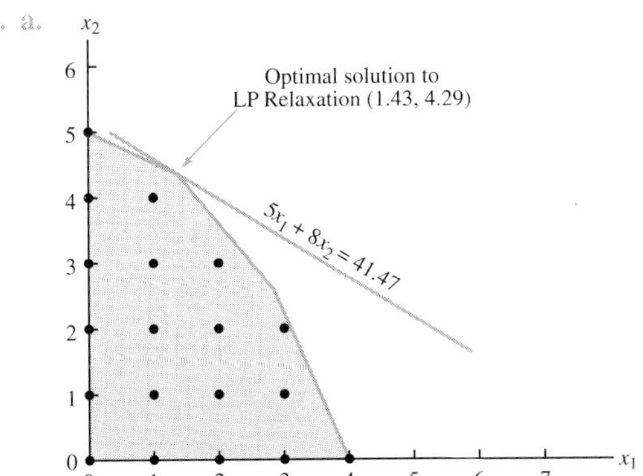

  b. The optimal solution to the LP Relaxation is given by $x_1 = 1.43$, $x_2 = 4.29$ with an objective function value of 41.47. Rounding down gives the feasible integer solution $x_1 = 1$, $x_2 = 4$; its value is 37

  c.

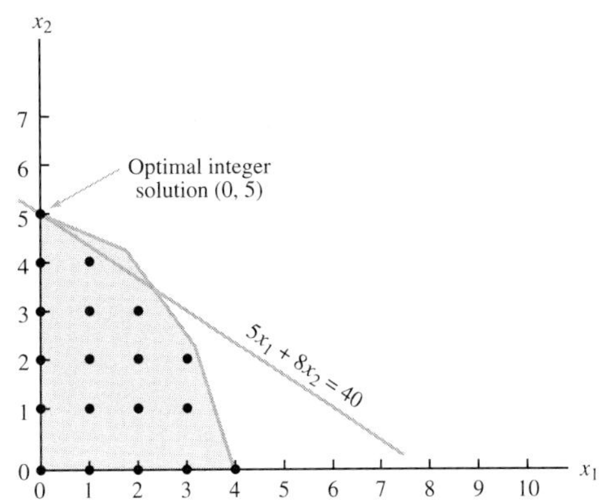

  The optimal solution is given by $x_1 = 0$, $x_2 = 5$; its value is 40. It is not the same solution as found by rounding down; it provides a 3-unit increase in the value of the objective function

4. a. $x_1 = 3.67$, $x_2 = 0$; Value = 36.7
  Rounded: $x_1 = 3$, $x_2 = 0$; Value = 30
  Lower bound = 30; Upper bound = 36.7
  b. $x_1 = 3$, $x_2 = 2$; Value = 36
  c. Alternative optimal solutions: $x_1 = 0$, $x_2 = 5$
  $x_1 = 2$, $x_2 = 4$

5. a. The feasible mixed-integer solutions are indicated by the boldface vertical lines in the graph

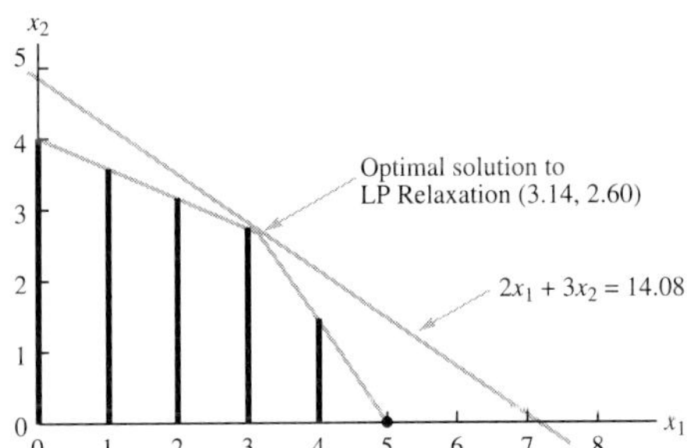

  b. The optimal solution to the LP Relaxation is given by $x_1 = 3.14$, $x_2 = 2.60$; its value is 14.08
  Rounding down the value of x_1 to find a feasible mixed-integer solution yields $x_1 = 3$, $x_2 = 2.60$ with a value of 13.8; this solution is clearly not optimal; with $x_1 = 3$, x_2 can be made larger without violating the constraints
  c. The optimal solution to the MILP is given by $x_1 = 3$, $x_2 = 2.67$; its value is 14, as shown in the following figure

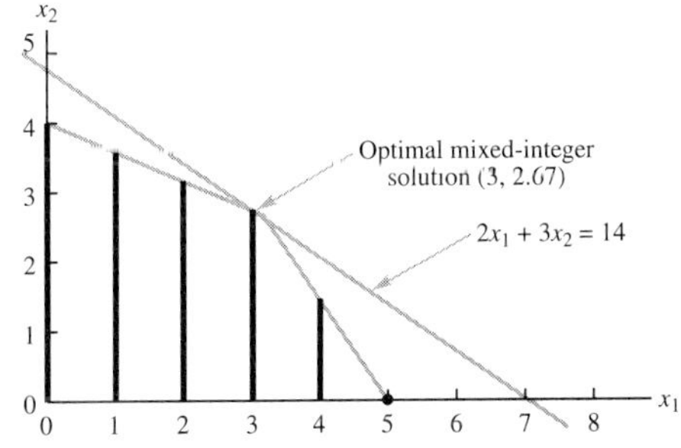

6. b. $x_1 = 1.96, x_2 = 5.48$; Value = 7.44
Rounded: $x_1 = 1.96, x_2 = 5$; Value = 6.96
Lower bound = 6.96; Upper bound = 7.44
c. $x_1 = 1.29, x_2 = 6$; Value = 7.29

7. a. $x_1 + x_3 + x_5 + x_6 = 2$
b. $x_3 - x_5 = 0$
c. $x_1 + x_4 = 1$
d. $x_4 \leq x_1$
$x_4 \leq x_3$
e. $x_4 \leq x_1$
$x_4 \leq x_3$
$x_4 \geq x_1 + x_3 - 1$

8. a. $x_3 = 1, x_4 = 1, x_6 = 1$; Value = 17,500
b. Add $x_1 + x_2 \leq 1$
c. Add $x_3 - x_4 = 0$

10. b. Choose locations B and E

12. a. $P \leq 15 + 15Y_P$
$D \leq 15 + 15Y_D$
$J \leq 15 + 15Y_J$
$Y_P + Y_D + Y_J \leq 1$
b. $P = 15, D = 15, J = 30$
$Y_P = 0, Y_D = 0, Y_J = 1$; Value = 50

13. a. Add the following multiple-choice constraint to the problem
$y_1 + y_2 = 1$
New optimal solution: $y_1 = 1$, $y_3 = 1$, $x_{12} = 10$, $x_{31} = 30$, $x_{52} = 10$, $x_{53} = 20$
Value = 940
b. Because one plant is already located in St. Louis, it is only necessary to add the following constraint to the model
$y_3 + y_4 \leq 1$
New optimal solution: $y_4 = 1$, $x_{42} = 20$, $x_{43} = 20$, $x_{51} = 30$
Value = 860

14. b. Modernize plants 1 and 3 or plants 4 and 5
d. Modernize plants 1 and 3

16. b. Use all part-time employees
Bring on as follows: 9:00 A.M.–6, 11:00 A.M.–2, 12:00 noon–6, 1:00 P.M.–1, 3:00 P.M.–6
Cost = $672
c. Same as in part (b)
d. New solution is to bring on 1 full-time employee at 9:00 A.M., 4 more at 11:00 A.M., and part-time employees as follows:
9:00 A.M.–5, 12:00 noon–5, and 3:00 P.M.–2

18. a. 52, 49, 36, 83, 39, 70, 79, 59
b. Thick crust, cheese blend, chunky sauce, medium sausage: Six of eight consumers will prefer this pizza (75%)

20. a. New objective function: Min $25x_1 + 40x_2 + 40x_3 + 40x_4 + 25x_5$
b. $x_4 = x_5 = 1$; modernize the Ohio and California plants
c. Add the constraint $x_2 + x_3 = 1$
d. $x_1 = x_3 = 1$

22. $x_1 + x_2 + x_3 = 3y_1 + 5y_2 + 7y_3$
$y_1 + y_2 + y_3 = 1$

24. a. $x_{111}, x_{112}, x_{121}$
b. $x_{111} + x_{112} + x_{121} \leq 1$
c. $x_{531} + x_{532} + x_{533} + x_{541} + x_{542} + x_{543} + x_{551} + x_{552} + x_{561} \leq 1$
d. Only two screens are available
e. $x_{213} + x_{222} + x_{231} + x_{422} + x_{431} + x_{531} + x_{532} + x_{533} + x_{631} + x_{632} + x_{633} \leq 2$

Chapter 8

2. a. $X = 4.32$ and $Y = 0.92$, for an optimal solution value of 4.84
b. The dual price on the constraint $X + 4Y \leq 8$ is 0.88, which is the decrease in the optimal objective function value if we increase the right-hand-side from 8 to 9
c. The new optimal objective function value is 4.0 so the actual decrease is only 0.84 rather than 0.88

4. a. $q_1 = 2150$
$q_2 = 100$
Gross profit = $1,235,000
b. $G = -1.5p_1^2 - .5p_2^2 + p_1p_2 + 2000p_1 + 3450p_2 - 11,465,000$
c. $p_1 = \$2725$ and $p_2 = \$6175$; $q_1 = 1185$ and $q_2 = 230$; $G = \$1,911,875$
d. Max $p_1q_1 + p_2q_2 - c_1 - c_2$
s.t.
$c_1 = 10000 + 1500q_1$
$c_2 = 30000 + 4000q_2$
$q_1 = 950 - 1.5p_1 + .7p_2$
$q_2 = 2500 + .3p_1 - .5p_2$

5. a. If $1000 is spent on radio and $1000 is spent on direct mail, simply substitute those values into the sales function:

$$S = -2R^2 - 10M^2 - 8RM + 18R + 34M$$
$$= -2(2^2) - 10(1^2) - 8(2)(1) + 18(2) + 34(1)$$
$$= 18$$

Sales = $18,000
b. Max $-2R^2 - 10M^2 - 8RM + 18R + 34M$
s.t.
$$R + M \leq 3$$
c. The optimal solution is Radio = $2500 and Direct mail = $500.
Total sales = $37,000

6. a. Without the global solver option turned on, LINGO returns $X = 4.978$ and $Y = 1.402$ for a value of 0.3088137E-08, which is a local minimum

FIGURE D12.18 WORKSHEET FOR THE CONTRACTOR BIDDING SIMULATION

	A	B	C	D	E	F	G	H	I
1	**Contractor Bidding**								
2									
3	**Contractor A (Uniform Distribution)**					**Contractor B (Normal Distribution)**			
4	Smallest Value		$600			Mean		$700	
5	Largest Value		$800			Standard Deviation		$50	
6									
7									
8	**Simulation**					**Results**			
9		Contractor	Contractor	Lowest		Contractor's	Number	Probability	
10	Trial	A's Bid	B's Bid	Bid		Bid	of Wins	of Winning	
11	1	$673	$720	$673		$650	628	0.628	
12	2	$757	$655	$655		$625	812	0.812	
13	3	$706	$791	$706		$615	875	0.875	
14	4	$638	$677	$638					
15									

a. The mean profit should be approximately $6000; simulation results will vary with most simulations having a mean profit between $5500 and $6500

b. 120 to 150 of the 500 simulation trials should show a loss; thus, the probability of a loss should be between 0.24 and 0.30

c. This project appears too risky

16. a. About 36% of simulation runs will show $130,000 as the winning bid

b. $150,000; $10,000

c. Recommended $140,000

18. Selected cell formulas for the worksheet shown in Figure D12.18 are as follows:

Cell	Formula
B11	=$C$4+RAND()*($C$5−$C$4)
C11	=NORMINV(RAND(),$H$4,$H$5)
D11	=MIN(B11:C11)
G11	=COUNTIF($D$11:$D$1010,">650")
H11	=G11/COUNT($D$11:$D$1010)

a. $650,000 should win roughly 600 to 650 of the 1000 times; the probability of winning the bid should be between 0.60 and 0.65

b. The probability of $625,000 winning should be roughly 0.82, and the probability of $615,000 winning should be roughly 0.88; a contractor's bid of $625,000 is recommended

20. a. Results vary with each simulation run

Approximate results: 50,000 provided $230,000
60,000 provided $190,000
70,000 less than $100,000

b. Recommend 50,000 units

c. Roughly 0.75

22. Very poor operation; some customers wait 30 minutes or more

24. b. Waiting time approximately 0.8 minutes

c. 30% to 35% of customers have to wait

Chapter 13

1. a.

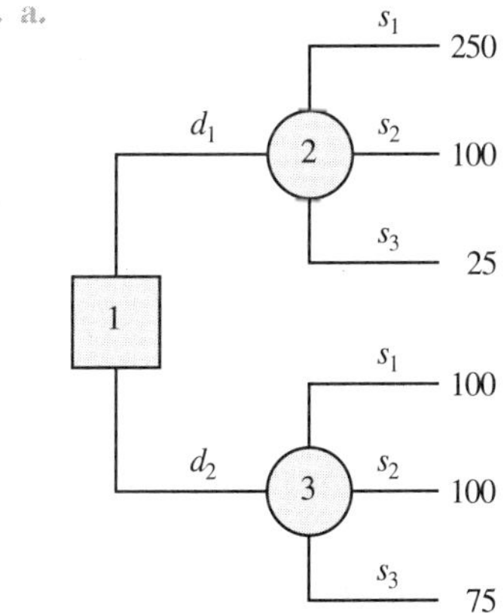

b.

Decision	Maximum Profit	Minimum Profit
d_1	250	25
d_2	100	75

Optimistic approach: Select d_1

Conservative approach: Select d_2

Regret or opportunity loss table:

Decision	s_1	s_2	s_3
d_1	0	0	50
d_2	150	0	0

Maximum regret: 50 for d_1 and 150 for d_2; select d_1

2. a. Optimistic: d_1
Conservative: d_3
Minimax regret: d_3
c. Optimistic: d_1
Conservative: d_2 or d_3
Minimax regret: d_2

3. a. Decision: choose the best plant size from the two alternatives: a small plant and a large plant
Chance event: market demand for the new product line with three possible outcomes (states of nature): low, medium, and high
b. Influence diagram:

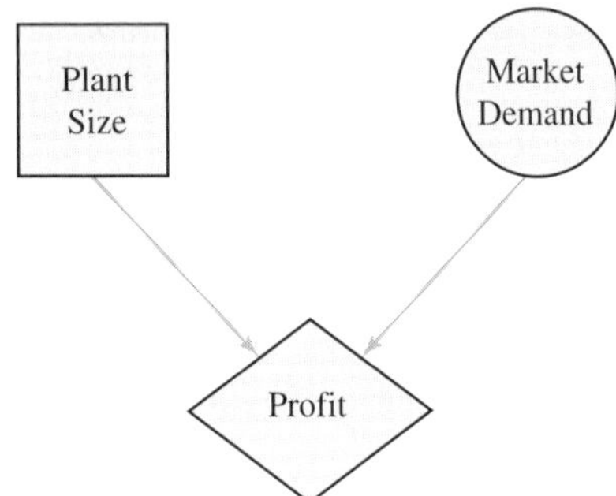

c.

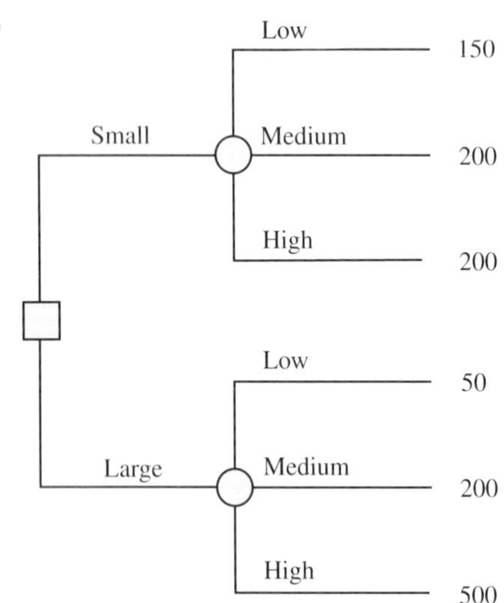

d.

Decision	Maximum Profit	Minimum Profit	Maximum Regret
Small	200	150	300
Large	500	50	100

Optimistic approach: Large plant
Conservative approach: Small plant
Minimax regret: Large plant

4. $EV(d_1) = 0.65(250) + 0.15(100) + 0.20(25) = 182.5$
$EV(d_2) = 0.65(100) + 0.15(100) + 0.20(75) = 95$
The optimal decision is d_1

6. a. Decision: Which lease option to choose
Chance event: Miles driven
b.

	Annual Miles Driven		
	12,000	15,000	18,000
Forno	10,764	12,114	13,464
Midtown	11,160	11,160	12,960
Hopkins	11,700	11,700	11,700

c. Optimistic: Forno Saab
Conservative: Hopkins Automotive
Minimax: Hopkins Automotive
d. Midtown Motors
e. Most likely: \$11,160; Probability = 0.9
f. Midtown Motors or Hopkins Automotive

7. a. EV(own staff) $= 0.2(650) + 0.5(650) + 0.3(600) = 635$
EV(outside vendor) $= 0.2(900) + 0.5(600) + 0.3(300) = 570$
EV(combination) $= 0.2(800) + 0.5(650) + 0.3(500) = 635$
Optimal decision: hire an outside vendor with an expected cost of \$570,000
b.

	Cost	Probability
Own staff	300	0.3
Outside vendor	600	0.5
Combination	900	0.2
		1.0

8. a. $EV(d_1) = p(10) + (1 - p)(1) = 9p + 1$
$EV(d_2) = p(4) + (1 - p)(3) = 1p + 3$

10
0 .25 1 p
Value of p for which EVs are equal

$9p + 1 = 1p + 3$ and hence $p = 0.25$
d_2 is optimal for $p \leq 0.25$, d_1 is optimal for $p \geq 0.25$

b. d_2
c. As long as the payoff for $s_1 \geq 2$, then d_2 is optimal

10. b. Space Pirates
EV = \$724,000
\$84,000 better than Battle Pacific
c.

\$200	0.18
\$400	0.32
\$800	0.30
\$1600	0.20

d. P(Competition) > 0.7273

12. a. Decision: Whether to lengthen the runway
Chance event: The location decisions of Air Express and DRI
Consequence: Annual revenue
b. \$255,000
c. \$270,000
d. No
e. Lengthen the runway

14. a. If s_1, then d_1; if s_2, then d_1 or d_2; if s_3, then d_2
b. EVwPI = 0.65(250) + 0.15(100) + 0.20(75) = 192.5
c. From the solution to Problem 4, we know that EV(d_1) = 182.5 and EV(d_2) = 95; thus, recommended decision is d_1; hence, EVwoPI = 182.5
d. EVPI = EVwPI − EVwoPI = 192.5 − 182.5 = 10

16. a.

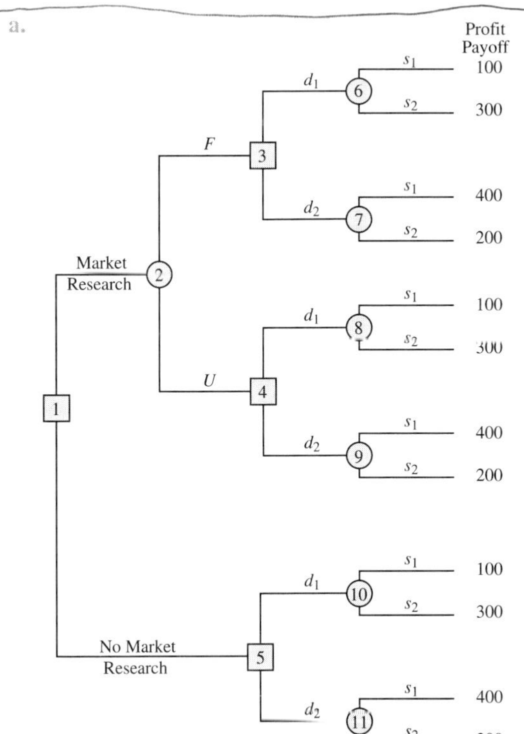

b. EV (node 6) = 0.57(100) + 0.43(300) = 186
EV (node 7) = 0.57(400) + 0.43(200) = 314
EV (node 8) = 0.18(100) + 0.82(300) = 264
EV (node 9) = 0.18(400) + 0.82(200) = 236
EV (node 10) = 0.40(100) + 0.60(300) = 220
EV (node 11) = 0.40(400) + 0.60(200) = 280

EV (node 3) = Max(186,314) = 314 d_2
EV (node 4) = Max(264,236) = 264 d_1
EV (node 5) = Max(220,280) = 280 d_2

EV (node 2) = 0.56(314) + 0.44(264) = 292
EV (node 1) = Max(292,280) = 292

∴ Market research
If favorable, decision d_2
If unfavorable, decision d_1

18. a. 5000 − 200 − 2000 − 150 = 2650
3000 − 200 − 2000 − 150 = 650
b. Expected values at nodes

8: 2350	5: 2350	9: 1100
6: 1150	10: 2000	7: 2000
4: 1870	3: 2000	2: 1560
1: 1560		

c. Cost would have to decrease by at least \$130,000
d.

Payoff (in millions)	Probability
−\$200	0.20
800	0.32
2800	0.48
	1.00

20. b. If Do Not Review, Accept
If Review and F, Accept
If Review and U, Accept
Always Accept
c. Do not review; EVSI = \$0
d. \$87,500; better method of predicting success

22. a. Order 2 lots; \$60,000
b. If E, order 2 lots
If V, order 1 lot
EV = \$60,500
c. EVPI = \$14,000
EVSI = \$500
Efficiency = 3.6%
Yes, use consultant

23.

State of Nature	$P(s_j)$	$P(I/s_j)$	$P(I \cap s_j)$	$P(s_j/I)$
s_1	0.2	0.10	0.020	0.1905
s_2	0.5	0.05	0.025	0.2381
s_3	0.3	0.20	0.060	0.5714
	1.0		$P(I)$ = 0.105	1.0000

24. a. 0.695, 0.215, 0.090
0.98, 0.02
0.79, 0.21
0.00, 1.00

c. If C, Expressway
If O, Expressway
If R, Queen City
26.6 minutes

Chapter 14

2. a. Let x_1 = number of shares of AGA Products purchased
x_2 = number of shares of Key Oil purchased
To obtain an annual return of exactly 9%:

$$0.06(50)x_1 + 0.10(100)x_2 = 0.09(50{,}000)$$
$$3x_1 + 10x_2 = 4500$$

To have exactly 60% of the total investment in Key Oil:

$$100x_2 = 0.60(50{,}000)$$
$$x_2 = 300$$

Therefore, we can write the goal programming model as follows:

Min $P_1(d_1^-) + P_2(d_2^+)$
s.t.

$50x_1 + 100x_2$	$\leq 50{,}000$	Funds available
$3x_1 + 10x_2 - d_1^+ + d_1^- =$	4,500	P_1 goal
$x_2 - d_2^+ + d_2^- =$	300	P_2 goal

$x_1, x_2, d_1^+, d_1^-, d_2^+, d_2^- \geq 0$

b. In the following graphical solution, $x_1 = 250$ and $x_2 = 375$

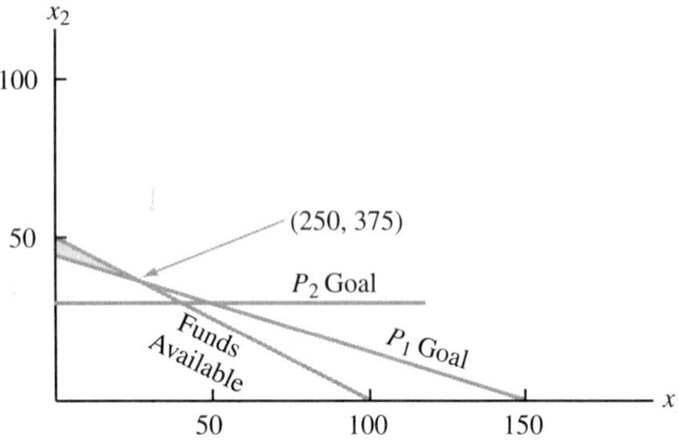

4. a. Min $P_1(d_1^-) + P_1(d_2^+) + P_2(d_3^-) + P_2(d_4^-) + P_3(d_5^-)$
s.t.

$$20x_1 + 30x_2 - d_1^+ + d_1^- = 4800$$
$$20x_1 + 30x_2 - d_2^+ + d_2^- = 6000$$
$$x_1 - d_3^+ + d_3^- = 100$$
$$x_2 - d_4^+ + d_4^- = 120$$
$$x_1 + x_2 - d_5^+ + d_5^- = 300$$
x_1, x_2, all deviation variables ≥ 0

b. $x_1 = 120, x_2 = 120$

6. a. Let x_1 = number of letters mailed to group 1 customers
x_2 = number of letters mailed to group 2 customers

Min $P_1(d_1^-) + P_1(d_2^-) + P_2(d_3^+)$
s.t.

$$x_1 - d_1^+ + d_1^- = 40{,}000$$
$$x_2 - d_2^+ + d_2^- = 50{,}000$$
$$x_1 + x_2 - d_3^+ + d_3^- = 70{,}000$$
x_1, x_2, all deviation variables ≥ 0

b. $x_1 = 40{,}000, x_2 = 50{,}000$
c. Optimal solution does not change

8. a. Min $d_1^- + d_1^+ + e_1^- + e_1^+ + d_2^- + d_2^+ + e_2^- + e_2^+ + d_3^- + d_3^+ + e_3^- + e_3^+$
s.t.

$$x_1 + d_1^- - d_1^+ = 1$$
$$x_2 + e_1^- - e_1^+ = 7$$
$$x_1 + d_2^- - d_2^+ = 5$$
$$x_2 + e_2^- - e_2^+ = 9$$
$$x_1 + d_3^- - d_3^+ = 6$$
$$x_2 + e_3^- - e_3^+ = 2$$
all variables ≥ 0

b. $x_1 = 5, x_2 = 7$

9. Scoring calculations

Criterion	Analyst Chicago	Accountant Denver	Auditor Houston
Career advancement	35	20	20
Location	10	12	8
Management	30	25	35
Salary	28	32	16
Prestige	32	20	24
Job security	8	10	16
Enjoyment of the work	28	20	20
Totals	171	139	139

The analyst position in Chicago is recommended

10. 178, 184, 151
Marysville

12. 170, 168, 190, 183
Handover College

14. a. 220 Bowrider (194)
b. 240 Sundancer (144)

16. Step 1: Column totals are $17/4$, $31/21$, and 12
Step 2:

Style	Accord	Saturn	Cavalier
Accord	$4/17$	$7/31$	$4/12$
Saturn	$12/17$	$21/31$	$7/12$
Cavalier	$1/17$	$3/31$	$1/12$

Step 3:

Style	Accord	Saturn	Cavalier	Row Average
Accord	0.235	0.226	0.333	0.265
Saturn	0.706	0.677	0.583	0.656
Cavalier	0.059	0.097	0.083	0.080

Consistency Ratio
Step 1:

$$0.265\begin{bmatrix}1\\3\\1/4\end{bmatrix} + 0.656\begin{bmatrix}1/3\\1\\1/7\end{bmatrix} + 0.080\begin{bmatrix}4\\7\\1\end{bmatrix}$$

$$\begin{bmatrix}0.265\\0.795\\0.066\end{bmatrix} + \begin{bmatrix}0.219\\0.656\\0.094\end{bmatrix} + \begin{bmatrix}0.320\\0.560\\0.080\end{bmatrix} = \begin{bmatrix}0.802\\2.007\\0.239\end{bmatrix}$$

Step 2: 0.802/0.265 = 3.028
2.007/0.656 = 3.062
0.239/0.080 = 3.007

Step 3: λ_{max} = (3.028 + 3.062 + 3.007)/3 = 3.032
Step 4: CI = (3.032 − 3)/2 = 0.016
Step 5: CR = 0.016/0.58 = 0.028
Because CR = 0.028 is less than 0.10, the degree of consistency exhibited in the pairwise comparison matrix for style is acceptable

18. a. 0.724, 0.193, 0.083
b. CR = 0.057, yes

20. a.

Flavor	A	B	C
A	1	3	2
B	1/3	1	5
C	1/2	1/5	1

b. Step 1: Column totals are 11/6, 21/5, and 8
Step 2:

Flavor	A	B	C
A	6/11	15/21	2/8
B	2/11	5/21	5/8
C	3/11	1/21	1/8

Step 3:

Flavor	A	B	C	Row Average
A	0.545	0.714	0.250	0.503
B	0.182	0.238	0.625	0.348
C	0.273	0.048	0.125	0.148

c. Step 1:

$$0.503\begin{bmatrix}1\\1/3\\1/2\end{bmatrix} + 0.348\begin{bmatrix}3\\1\\1/5\end{bmatrix} + 0.148\begin{bmatrix}2\\5\\1\end{bmatrix}$$

$$\begin{bmatrix}0.503\\0.168\\0.252\end{bmatrix} + \begin{bmatrix}1.044\\0.348\\0.070\end{bmatrix} + \begin{bmatrix}0.296\\0.740\\0.148\end{bmatrix} = \begin{bmatrix}1.845\\1.258\\0.470\end{bmatrix}$$

Step 2: 1.845/0.503 = 3.668
1.258/0.348 = 3.615
0.470/0.148 = 3.123

Step 3: λ_{max} = (3.668 + 3.615 + 3.123)/3 = 3.469
Step 4: CI = (3.469 − 3)/2 = 0.235
Step 5: CR = 0.235/0.58 = 0.415
Because CR = 0.415 is greater than 0.10, the individual's judgments are not consistent

22. a.

	D	S	N
D	1	1/4	1/7
S	4	1	1/3
N	7	3	1

b. 0.080, 0.265, 0.656
c. CR = 0.028, yes

24. Criteria: Yield and Risk
Step 1: Column totals are 1.5 and 3
Step 2:

	Yield	Risk	Priority
Yield	0.667	0.667	0.667
Risk	0.333	0.333	0.333

With only two criteria, CR = 0; no need to compute CR
Preceding calculations for Yield and Risk provide

Stocks	Yield Priority	Risk Priority
CCC	0.750	0.333
SRI	0.250	0.667

Overall Priorities:
CCC 0.667(0.750) + 0.333(0.333) = 0.611
SRI 0.667(0.250) + 0.333(0.667) = 0.389
CCC is preferred

26. a. Criterion: 0.608, 0.272, 0.120
Price: 0.557, 0.123, 0.320
Sound: 0.137, 0.239, 0.623
Reception: 0.579, 0.187, 0.046
b. 0.446, 0.162, 0.392
System A is preferred

Chapter 15

1. a.

Month	Time Series Value	3-Month Moving Average Forecast	$(\text{Error})^2$	4-Month Moving Average Forecast	$(\text{Error})^2$
1	9.5				
2	9.3				
3	9.4				
4	9.6	9.40	0.04		
5	9.8	9.43	0.14	9.45	0.12
6	9.7	9.60	0.01	9.53	0.03
7	9.8	9.70	0.01	9.63	0.03
8	10.5	9.77	0.53	9.73	0.59
9	9.9	10.00	0.01	9.95	0.00
10	9.7	10.07	0.14	9.98	0.08
11	9.6	10.03	0.18	9.97	0.14
12	9.6	9.73	0.02	9.92	0.10
		Totals	1.08		1.09

MSE(three-month) = 1.08/9 = 0.12
MSE(four-month) = 1.09/8 = 0.14
Use a three-month moving average

b. Forecast = (9.7 + 9.6 + 9.6)/3 = 9.63

2. a.

Week	Time Series Value	4-Week Moving Average Forecast	$(\text{Error})^2$	5-Week Moving Average Forecast	$(\text{Error})^2$
1	17				
2	21				
3	19				
4	23				
5	18	20.00	4.00		
6	16	20.25	18.06	19.60	12.96
7	20	19.00	1.00	19.40	0.36
8	18	19.25	1.56	19.20	1.44
9	22	18.00	16.00	19.00	9.00
10	20	19.00	1.00	18.80	1.44
11	15	20.00	25.00	19.20	17.64
12	22	18.75	10.56	19.00	9.00
		Totals	77.18		51.84

b. MSE(four-week) = 77.18/8 = 9.65
MSE(five-week) = 51.84/7 = 7.41

c. For the limited data provided, the five-week moving average provides the smallest MSE

4.

Week	Time Series Value	Forecast	Error	$(\text{Error})^2$
1	17			
2	21	17.00	4.00	16.00
3	19	17.40	1.60	2.56
4	23	17.56	5.44	29.59
5	18	18.10	−0.10	0.01
6	16	18.09	−2.09	4.37
7	20	17.88	2.12	4.49
8	18	18.10	−0.10	0.01
9	22	18.09	3.91	15.29
10	20	18.48	1.52	2.31
11	15	18.63	−3.63	13.18
12	22	18.27	3.73	13.91
			Total	101.72

MSE = 101.72/11 = 9.25
$\alpha = 0.2$ provided a lower MSE
Therefore, $\alpha = 0.2$ is better than $\alpha = 0.1$

5. a.

Month	Y_t	3-Month Moving Average Forecast	$(\text{Error})^2$	$\alpha = 2$ Forecast	$(\text{Error})^2$
1	80				
2	82			80.00	4.00
3	84			80.40	12.96
4	83	82.00	1.00	81.12	3.53
5	83	83.00	0.00	81.50	2.25
6	84	83.33	0.45	81.80	4.84
7	85	83.33	2.79	82.24	7.62
8	84	84.00	0.00	82.79	1.46
9	82	84.33	5.43	83.03	1.06
10	83	83.67	0.45	82.83	0.03
11	84	83.00	1.00	82.86	1.30
12	83	83.00	0.00	83.09	0.01
		Totals	11.12		39.06

MSE(three-month) = 11.12/9 = 1.24
MSE(α = 0.2) = 39.06/11 = 3.55
Use a three-month moving average

b. (83 + 84 + 83)/3 = 83.3

6. b. The more recent data receive the greater weight or importance in determining the forecast

8. a. 80.43
b. 80.31
c. exponential smoothing; smaller MSE

10. a. $\alpha = 0.3$
    b. 18.41

12. 3117.01

14. $\sum t = 21; \sum t^2 = 91; \sum Y_t = 117.1;$
    $\sum tY_t = 403.7; n = 6$

$$b_1 = \frac{\sum tY_t - (\sum t \sum Y_t)/n}{\sum t^2 - (\sum t)^2/n}$$

$$= \frac{403.7 - (21)(117.1)/6}{91 - (21)^2/6}$$

$$= -0.3514$$

$b_0 = \bar{Y} - b_1\bar{t} = 19.5167 - (-.3514)(3.5) = 20.7466$
$T_t = 20.7466 - 0.3514t$

Conclusion: Enrollment appears to be decreasing by an average of approximately 351 students per year

16. a. Linear trend appears to be reasonable
    b. $T_t = 19.993 + 1.774t$
    Average cost increase of $1.77 per unit per year

18. a. The graph shows a linear trend
    b. $T_t = 1.2622 - 0.0111t$
    c. 1.1401
    d. No

20. a. A linear trend appears to exist
    b. $T_t = -5 + 15t$
    Average increase in sales is 15 units per year

22. a. A linear trend appears to be appropriate
    b. $T_t = 6.4564 + 0.5345t$
    c. 0.5345 million
    d. 2001–2002 season: $T_{13} = 6.4564 + 0.5345(12) =$ 12.87 million

24. a. Forecast for July is 236.97; forecast for August is 236.97
    b. Forecast for July is 278.88; forecast for August is 297.33
    c. Not fair; it does not account for upward trend in sales

25. a. Four-quarter moving averages beginning with $(1690 + 940 + 2625 + 2500)/4 = 1938.75$
    Other moving averages are

1966.25	2002.50
1956.25	2052.50
2025.00	2060.00
1990.00	2123.75

b.

Quarter	Seasonal-Irregular Component Values		Seasonal Index	Adjusted Seasonal Index
1	0.904	0.900	0.9020	0.900
2	0.448	0.526	0.4970	0.486
3	1.344	1.453	1.3985	1.396
4	1.275	1.164	1.2195	1.217
		Total	4.0070	

Note: Adjustment for seasonal index = 4.000/4.007 = 0.9983

c. The largest seasonal effect is in the third quarter, which corresponds to the back-to-school demand during July, August, and September of each year

26. 0.707, 0.777, 0.827, 0.966, 1.016, 1.305, 1.494, 1.225, 0.976, 0.986, 0.936, 0.787

28. a. Selected centered moving averages for t = 5, 10, 15, and 20 are 11.125, 18.125, 22.875, and 27.000
    b. 0.899, 1.362, 1.118, 0.621
    c. Quarter 2, prior to summer boating season

30. a. $T_t = 6.329 + 1.055t$
    b. 36.92, 37.98, 39.03, 40.09
    c. 33.23, 51.65, 43.71, 24.86

32. a. Yes, there is a seasonal effect; seasonal indexes are 1.696, 1.458, 0.711, 0.326, 0.448, 1.362
    b. Forecast for 12–4 is 166,761.13; forecast for 4–8 is 146,052.99

33. a.

Restaurant (i)	x_i	y_i	$x_i y_i$	x_i^2
1	1	19	19	1
2	4	44	176	16
3	6	40	240	36
4	10	52	520	100
5	14	53	742	196
Totals	35	208	1697	349

$$\bar{x} = \frac{35}{5} = 7$$

$$\bar{y} = \frac{208}{5} = 41.6$$

$$b_1 = \frac{\Sigma x_i y_i - (\Sigma x_i \Sigma y_i)/n}{\Sigma x_i^2 - (\Sigma x_i)^2/n}$$
$$= \frac{1697 - (35)(208)/5}{349 - (35)^2/5}$$
$$= \frac{241}{104} = 2.317$$
$$b_0 = \bar{y} - b_1\bar{x} = 41.6 - 2.317(7) = 25.381$$
$$\hat{y} = 25.381 + 2.317x$$

b. $\hat{y} = 25.381 + 2.317(8) = 43.917$, or \$43,917

34. a. $\hat{y} = 37.666 - 3.222x$
b. \$3444

Chapter 16

2. a. 0.82
b. $\pi_1 = 0.5, \pi_2 = 0.5$
c. $\pi_1 = 0.6, \pi_2 = 0.4$

3. a. 0.10 as given by the transition probability
b. $\pi_1 = 0.90\pi_1 + 0.30\pi_2$ (1)
$\pi_2 = 0.10\pi_1 + 0.70\pi_2$ (2)
$\pi_1 + \pi_2 = 1$ (3)
Using (1) and (3),
$$0.10\pi_1 - 0.30\pi_2 = 0$$
$$0.10\pi_1 - 0.30(1 - \pi_1) = 0$$
$$0.10\pi_1 - 0.30 + 0.30\pi_1 = 0$$
$$0.40\pi_1 = 0.30$$
$$\pi_1 = 0.75$$
$$\pi_2 = (1 - \pi_1) = 0.25$$

4. a. $\pi_1 = 0.92, \pi_2 - 0.08$
b. \$85

6. a.

	City	Suburbs
City	0.98	0.02
Suburbs	0.01	0.99

b. $\pi_1 = 0.333, \pi_2 = 0.667$
c. City will decrease from 40% to 33%; suburbs will increase from 60% to 67%

7. a. $\pi_1 = 0.85\pi_1 + 0.20\pi_2 + 0.15\pi_3$ (1)
$\pi_2 = 0.10\pi_1 + 0.75\pi_2 + 0.10\pi_3$ (2)
$\pi_3 = 0.05\pi_1 + 0.05\pi_2 + 0.75\pi_3$ (3)
$\pi_1 + \pi_2 + \pi_3 = 1$ (4)
Using (1), (2), and (4) provides three equations with three unknowns; solving provides $\pi_1 = 0.548$, $\pi_2 = 0.286$, and $\pi_3 = 0.166$
b. 16.6% as given by π_3
c. Quick Stop should take
667 − 0.548(1000) = 119 Murphy's customers
and 333 − 0.286(1000) = 47 Ashley's customers
Total 166 Quick Stop customers

It will take customers from Murphy's and Ashley's

8. a. MDA
b. $\pi_1 = 1/3, \pi_2 = 2/3$

10. 3 − 1(0.59), 4 − 1(0.52)

11. $I = \begin{bmatrix} 1 & 0 \\ 0 & 1 \end{bmatrix} \quad Q = \begin{bmatrix} 0.25 & 0.25 \\ 0.05 & 0.25 \end{bmatrix}$

$$(I - Q) = \begin{bmatrix} 0.75 & -0.25 \\ -0.05 & 0.75 \end{bmatrix}$$
$$N = (I - Q)^{-1} = \begin{bmatrix} 1.3636 & 0.4545 \\ 0.0909 & 1.3636 \end{bmatrix}$$
$$NR = \begin{bmatrix} 1.3636 & 0.4545 \\ 0.0909 & 1.3636 \end{bmatrix}\begin{bmatrix} 0.5 & 0.0 \\ 0.5 & 0.2 \end{bmatrix} = \begin{bmatrix} 0.909 & 0.091 \\ 0.727 & 0.273 \end{bmatrix}$$
$$BNR = [4000 \quad 5000]\begin{bmatrix} 0.909 & 0.091 \\ 0.727 & 0.273 \end{bmatrix} = [7271 \quad 1729]$$

Estimate \$1729 in bad debts

12. 3580 will be sold eventually; 1420 will be lost

14. a. Graduate and drop out
b. P(Drop Out) = 0.15, P(Sophomore) = 0.10, P(Junior) = 0.75
c. 0.706, 0.294
d. Yes; P(Graduate) = 0.54
P(Drop Out) = 0.46
e. 1479 (74%) will graduate

Index

Note: Chapters 17–21 can be found on the CD-ROM included with this book. Index entries found in these chapters are denoted by chapter number, hyphen, and page number.

Page numbers followed by an **n** indicate a footnote.

D

M

N

O

T

ESSENTIALS OF STATISTICS FOR BUSINESS AND ECONOMICS 4e

David R. Anderson
University of Cincinnati

Dennis J. Sweeney
University of Cincinnati

Thomas A. Williams
Rochester Institute of Technology

Australia · Canada · Mexico · Singapore · Spain · United Kingdom · United States

Essentials of Statistics for Business and Economics, 4e

David R. Anderson, Dennis J. Sweeney, Thomas A. Williams

VP/Editorial Director:
Jack W. Calhoun

Sr. Acquisitions Editor:
Charles E. McCormick, Jr.

Developmental Editor:
Alisa Madden

Sr. Marketing Manager:
Larry Qualls

Sr. Production Editor:
Deanna Quinn

Technology Project Editor:
Chris Wittmer

Web Coordinator:
Kelly Reid

Manufacturing Coordinator:
Diane Lohman

Printer:
R. R. Donnelley
Willard, OH

Production House:
BookMasters, Inc.

Art Director:
Chris Miller

Cover Image:
© Digital Vision

Photography Manager:
John Hill

Printed in the United States of America
1 2 3 4 5 07 06 05 04

ISBN 0-324-22320-X (student edition package)
ISBN 0-324-22322-6 (book)
ISBN 0-324-22321-8 (CD)
ISBN 0-324-31734-4 (instructor edition package)

Library of Congress Control Number:
2004111060

For more information contact South-Western, 5191 Natorp Boulevard, Mason, Ohio 45040.
Or you can visit our Internet site at: http://www.swlearning.com

CHAPTER 10

Comparisons Involving Means

CONTENTS

STATISTICS *in* PRACTICE

FISONS CORPORATION
ROCHESTER, NEW YORK

Fisons Corporation, Rochester, New York, is a unit of Fisons Plc., UK. Fisons opened its U.S. operations in 1966.

Fisons Pharmaceutical Division uses extensive statistical procedures to test and develop new drugs. The testing process in the pharmaceutical industry usually consists of three stages: (1) preclinical testing, (2) testing for long-term usage and safety, and (3) clinical efficacy testing. At each successive stage, the chance that a drug will pass the rigorous tests decreases; however, the cost of further testing increases dramatically. Industry surveys indicate that on average the research and development for one new drug costs $250 million and takes 12 years. Hence, it is important to eliminate unsuccessful new drugs in the early stages of the testing process, as well as identify promising ones for further testing.

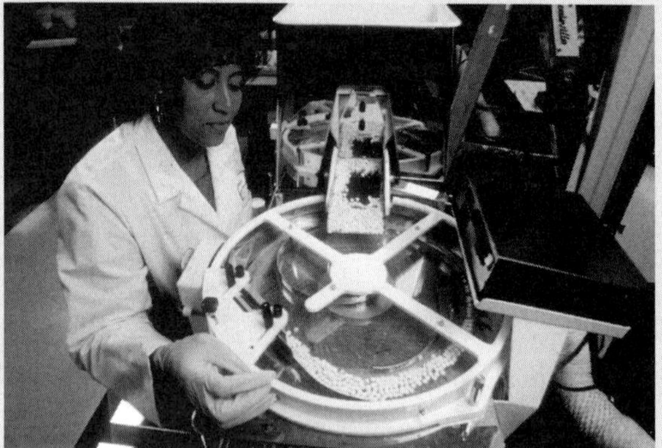

Statistical methods are used to test and develop new drugs. © Mark Richards/PhotoEdit.

Statistics plays a major role in pharmaceutical research, where government regulations are stringent and rigorously enforced. In preclinical testing, a two- or three-population statistical study typically is used to determine whether a new drug should continue to be studied in the long-term usage and safety program. The populations may consist of the new drug, a control, and a standard drug. The preclinical testing process begins when a new drug is sent to the pharmacology group for evaluation of efficacy—the capacity of the drug to produce the desired effects. As part of the process, a statistician is asked to design an experiment that can be used to test the new drug. The design must specify the sample size and the statistical methods of analysis. In a two-population study, one sample is used to obtain data on the efficacy of the new drug (population 1) and a second sample is used to obtain data on the efficacy of a standard drug (population 2). Depending on the intended use, the new and standard drugs are tested in such disciplines as neurology, cardiology, and immunology. In most studies, the statistical method involves hypothesis testing for the difference between the means of the new drug population and the standard drug population. If a new drug lacks efficacy or produces undesirable effects in comparison with the standard drug, the new drug is rejected and withdrawn from further testing. Only new drugs that show promising comparisons with the standard drugs are forwarded to the long-term usage and safety testing program.

Further data collection and multipopulation studies are conducted in the long-term usage and safety testing program and in the clinical testing programs. The Food and Drug Administration (FDA) requires that statistical methods be defined prior to such testing to avoid data-related biases. In addition, to avoid human biases, some of the clinical trials are double or triple blind. That is, neither the subject nor the investigator knows what drug is administered to whom. If the new drug meets all requirements in relation to the standard drug, a new drug application (NDA) is filed with the FDA. The application is rigorously scrutinized by statisticians and scientists at the agency.

In this chapter you will learn how to construct interval estimates and make hypothesis tests about means and proportions with two populations. Techniques will be presented for analyzing independent random samples as well as matched samples.

In Chapters 8 and 9 we showed how to develop interval estimates and conduct hypothesis tests for situations involving one population mean. In this chapter we extend our discussion of statistical inference to applications that compare the means of two or more populations. For example, we may want to develop an interval estimate of the difference between the mean starting salary for a population of men and the mean starting salary for a population of women or test the hypothesis that the mean number of hours between breakdowns is the same for four different machines. We begin by showing how to develop interval estimates and conduct hypothesis tests about the difference between two population means when the two population standard deviations are assumed known.

10.1 Inferences About the Difference Between Two Population Means: σ_1 and σ_2 Known

Letting μ_1 denote the mean of population 1 and μ_2 denote the mean of population 2, we will focus on inferences about the difference between the means: $\mu_1 - \mu_2$. To make an inference about this difference, we select a simple random sample of n_1 units from population 1 and a simple random sample of n_2 units from population 2. The two samples, taken separately and independently, are referred to as **independent simple random samples**. In this section, we assume information is available such that the two population standard deviations, σ_1 and σ_2, can be assumed known prior to collecting the samples. We refer to this situation as the σ_1 and σ_2 known case. In the following example we show how to compute a margin of error and develop an interval estimate of the difference between the two population means.

Interval Estimation of $\mu_1 - \mu_2$

Greystone Department Stores, Inc., operates two stores in Buffalo, New York: one is in the inner city and the other is in a suburban shopping center. The regional manager noticed that products that sell well in one store do not always sell well in the other. The manager believes this situation may be attributable to differences in customer demographics at the two locations. Customers may differ in age, education, income, and so on. Suppose the manager asks us to investigate the difference between the mean ages of the customers who shop at the two stores.

Let us define population 1 as all customers who shop at the inner-city store and population 2 as all customers who shop at the suburban store.

μ_1 = mean of population 1 (i.e., the mean age of all customers who shop at the inner-city store)

μ_2 = mean of population 2 (i.e., the mean age of all customers who shop at the suburban store)

The difference between the two population means is $\mu_1 - \mu_2$

To estimate $\mu_1 - \mu_2$, we select a simple random sample of n_1 customers from population 1 and a simple random sample of n_2 customers from population 2. We then compute the two sample means.

$\bar{x}_1$ = sample mean age for the simple random sample of n_1 inner-city customers

$\bar{x}_2$ = sample mean age for the simple random sample of n_2 suburban customers

The point estimator of the difference between the two population means is the difference between the two sample means.

POINT ESTIMATOR OF THE DIFFERENCE BETWEEN TWO POPULATION MEANS

$$\bar{x}_1 - \bar{x}_2 \tag{10.1}$$

Figure 10.1 provides an overview of the process used to estimate the difference between two population means based on two independent simple random samples.

FIGURE 10.1 ESTIMATING THE DIFFERENCE BETWEEN TWO POPULATION MEANS

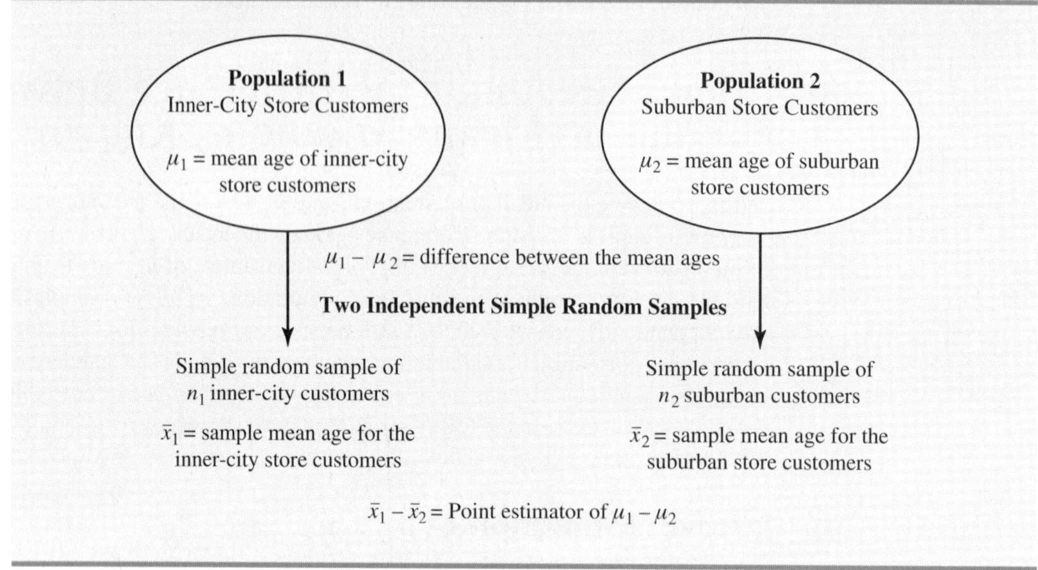

The standard error of $\bar{x}_1 - \bar{x}_2$ is the standard deviation of the sampling distribution of $\bar{x}_1 - \bar{x}_2$.

As with other point estimators, the point estimator $\bar{x}_1 - \bar{x}_2$ has a standard error that describes the variation in the sampling distribution of the estimator. With two independent simple random samples, the standard error of $\bar{x}_1 - \bar{x}_2$ is as follows:

$$\sigma_{\bar{x}_1 - \bar{x}_2} = \sqrt{\frac{\sigma_1^2}{n_1} + \frac{\sigma_2^2}{n_2}} \tag{10.2}$$

If both populations have a normal distribution, or if the sample sizes are large enough that the central limit theorem enables us to conclude that the sampling distributions of $\bar{x}_1$ and $\bar{x}_2$ can be approximated by a normal distribution, the sampling distribution of $\bar{x}_1 - \bar{x}_2$ will have a normal distribution with mean given by $\mu_1 - \mu_2$.

As we showed in Chapter 8, an interval estimate is given by a point estimate $\pm$ a margin of error. In the case of estimation of the difference between two population means, an interval estimate will take the following form:

$$\bar{x}_1 - \bar{x}_2 \pm \text{Margin of error}$$

With the sampling distribution of $\bar{x}_1 - \bar{x}_2$ having a normal distribution, we can write the margin of error as follows:

The margin of error is given by multiplying the standard error by $z_{\alpha/2}$.

$$\text{Margin of error} = z_{\alpha/2}\sigma_{\bar{x}_1 - \bar{x}_2} = z_{\alpha/2}\sqrt{\frac{\sigma_1^2}{n_1} + \frac{\sigma_2^2}{n_2}} \tag{10.3}$$

Thus the interval estimate of the difference between two population means is as follows:

INTERVAL ESTIMATE OF THE DIFFERENCE BETWEEN TWO POPULATION MEANS: σ_1 AND σ_2 KNOWN

$$\bar{x}_1 - \bar{x}_2 \pm z_{\alpha/2}\sqrt{\frac{\sigma_1^2}{n_1} + \frac{\sigma_2^2}{n_2}} \tag{10.4}$$

where $1 - \alpha$ is the confidence coefficient.

Let us return to the Greystone example. Based on data from previous customer demographic studies, the two population standard deviations are known with $\sigma_1 = 9$ years and $\sigma_2 = 10$ years. The data collected from the two independent simple random samples of Greystone customers provided the following results.

	Inner-City Store	Suburban Store
Sample Size	$n_1 = 36$	$n_2 = 49$
Sample Mean	$\bar{x}_1 = 40$ years	$\bar{x}_2 = 35$ years

Using expression (10.1), we find that the point estimate of the difference between the mean ages of the two populations is $\bar{x}_1 - \bar{x}_2 = 40 - 35 = 5$ years. Thus, we estimate that the customers at the inner-city store have a mean age five years greater than the mean age of the suburban store customers. We can now use expression (10.4) to compute the margin of error and provide the interval estimate of $\mu_1 - \mu_2$. Using 95% confidence and $z_{\alpha/2} = z_{.025} = 1.96$, we have

$$\bar{x}_1 - \bar{x}_2 \pm z_{\alpha/2}\sqrt{\frac{\sigma_1^2}{n_1} + \frac{\sigma_2^2}{n_2}}$$

$$40 - 35 \pm 1.96\sqrt{\frac{9^2}{36} + \frac{10^2}{49}}$$

$$5 \pm 4.06$$

Thus, the margin of error is 4.06 years and the 95% confidence interval estimate of the difference between the two population means is $5 - 4.06 = .94$ years to $5 + 4.06 = 9.06$ years.

Hypothesis Tests About $\mu_1 - \mu_2$

Let us consider hypothesis tests about the difference between two population means. Using D_0 to denote the hypothesized difference between μ_1 and μ_2, the three forms for a hypothesis test are as follows:

$$H_0: \mu_1 - \mu_2 \geq D_0 \qquad H_0: \mu_1 - \mu_2 \leq D_0 \qquad H_0: \mu_1 - \mu_2 = D_0$$
$$H_a: \mu_1 - \mu_2 < D_0 \qquad H_a: \mu_1 - \mu_2 > D_0 \qquad H_a: \mu_1 - \mu_2 \neq D_0$$

In many applications, $D_0 = 0$. Using the two-tailed test as an example, when $D_0 = 0$ the null hypothesis is $H_0: \mu_1 - \mu_2 = 0$. In this case, the null hypothesis is that μ_1 and μ_2 are equal. Rejection of H_0 leads to the conclusion that $H_a: \mu_1 - \mu_2 \neq 0$ is true; that is, μ_1 and μ_2 are not equal.

The steps for conducting hypothesis tests presented in Chapter 9 are applicable here. We must choose a level of significance, compute the value of the test statistic, and find the p-value to determine whether the null hypothesis should be rejected. With two independent simple random samples, we showed that the point estimator $\bar{x}_1 - \bar{x}_2$ has a standard error $\sigma_{\bar{x}_1 - \bar{x}_2}$ given by expression (10.2) and the distribution of $\bar{x}_1 - \bar{x}_2$ can be described by a normal distribution. In this case, the test statistic for the difference between two population means when σ_1 and σ_2 are known is as follows.

TEST STATISTIC FOR HYPOTHESIS TESTS ABOUT $\mu_1 - \mu_2$: σ_1 AND σ_2 KNOWN

$$z = \frac{(\bar{x}_1 - \bar{x}_2) - D_0}{\sqrt{\frac{\sigma_1^2}{n_1} + \frac{\sigma_2^2}{n_2}}} \qquad \textbf{(10.5)}$$

Let us demonstrate the use of this test statistic in the following hypothesis testing example.

As part of a study to evaluate differences in education quality between two training centers, a standardized examination is given to individuals who are trained at the centers. The difference between the mean examination scores is used to assess quality differences between the centers. The population means for the two centers are as follows.

μ_1 = the mean examination score for the population of individuals trained at center A

μ_2 = the mean examination score for the population of individuals trained at center B

We begin with the tentative assumption that no difference exists between the training quality provided at the two centers. Hence, in terms of the mean examination scores, the null hypothesis is that $\mu_1 - \mu_2 = 0$. If sample evidence leads to the rejection of this hypothesis, we will conclude that the mean examination scores differ for the two populations. This conclusion indicates a quality differential between the two centers and suggests that a follow-up study investigating the reason for the differential may be warranted. The null and alternative hypotheses for this two-tailed test are written as follows.

$$H_0: \mu_1 - \mu_2 = 0$$
$$H_a: \mu_1 - \mu_2 \neq 0$$

The standardized examination given previously in a variety of settings always resulted in an examination score standard deviation near 10 points. Thus, we will use this information to assume that the population standard deviations are known with $\sigma_1 = 10$ and $\sigma_2 = 10$. An $\alpha = .05$ level of significance is specified for the study.

ExamScores

Independent simple random samples of $n_1 = 30$ individuals from training center A and $n_2 = 40$ individuals from training center B are taken. The respective sample means are $\bar{x}_1 = 82$ and $\bar{x}_2 = 78$. Do these data suggest a significant difference between the population means at the two training centers? To help answer this question, we compute the test statistic using equation (10.5).

$$z = \frac{(\bar{x}_1 - \bar{x}_2) - D_0}{\sqrt{\dfrac{\sigma_1^2}{n_1} + \dfrac{\sigma_2^2}{n_2}}} = \frac{(82 - 78) - 0}{\sqrt{\dfrac{10^2}{30} + \dfrac{10^2}{40}}} = 1.66$$

Next let us compute the p-value for this two-tailed test. Because the test statistic z is in the upper tail, we first compute the area under the curve to the right of $z = 1.66$. Using the standard normal distribution table, the area between the mean and $z = 1.66$ is .4515. Thus, the area in the upper tail of the distribution is $.5000 - .4515 = .0485$. Because this test is a two-tailed test, we must double the tail area: p-value $= 2(.0485) = .0970$. Following the usual rule to reject H_0 if p-value $\leq \alpha$, we see that the p-value of .0970 does not allow us to reject H_0 at the .05 level of significance. The sample results do not provide sufficient evidence to conclude the training centers differ in quality.

In this chapter we will use the p-value approach to hypothesis testing as described in Chapter 9. However, if you prefer, the test statistic and the critical value rejection rule may be used. With $\alpha = .05$ and $z_{\alpha/2} = z_{.025} = 1.96$, the rejection rule employing the critical value approach would be to reject H_0 if $z \leq -1.96$ or if $z \geq 1.96$. With $z = 1.66$, we reach the same do-not-reject H_0 conclusion.

In the preceding example, we demonstrated a two-tailed hypothesis test about the difference between two population means. Lower tail and upper tail tests can also be considered. These tests use the same test statistic as given in equation (10.5). The procedure for computing the p-value and the rejection rules for these one-tailed tests are the same as those presented in Chapter 9.

Practical Advice

In most applications of the interval estimation and hypothesis testing procedures presented in this section, random samples with $n_1 \geq 30$ and $n_2 \geq 30$ are adequate. In cases where either or both sample sizes are less than 30, the distributions of the populations become important considerations. In general, with smaller sample sizes, it is more important for the analyst to be satisfied that it is reasonable to assume that the distributions of the two populations are at least approximately normal.

Exercises

Methods

1. Consider the following results for two independent random samples taken from two populations.

Sample 1	Sample 2
$n_1 = 50$	$n_2 = 35$
$\bar{x}_1 = 13.6$	$\bar{x}_2 = 11.6$
$\sigma_1 = 2.2$	$\sigma_2 = 3.0$

a. What is the point estimate of the difference between the two population means?
b. Provide a 90% confidence interval for the difference between the two population means.
c. Provide a 95% confidence interval for the difference between the two population means.

SELF test

2. Consider the following hypothesis test.

$$H_0: \mu_1 - \mu_2 \leq 0$$
$$H_a: \mu_1 - \mu_2 > 0$$

The following results are for two independent samples taken from the two populations.

Sample 1	Sample 2
$n_1 = 40$	$n_2 = 50$
$\bar{x}_1 = 25.2$	$\bar{x}_2 = 22.8$
$\sigma_1 = 5.2$	$\sigma_2 = 6.0$

a. What is the value of the test statistic?
b. What is the p-value?
c. With $\alpha = .05$, what is your hypothesis testing conclusion?

3. Consider the following hypothesis test.

$$H_0: \mu_1 - \mu_2 = 0$$
$$H_a: \mu_1 - \mu_2 \neq 0$$

The following results are for two independent samples taken from the two populations.

Sample 1	Sample 2
$n_1 = 80$	$n_2 = 70$
$\bar{x}_1 = 104$	$\bar{x}_2 = 106$
$\sigma_1 = 8.4$	$\sigma_2 = 7.6$

a. What is the value of the test statistic?
b. What is the p-value?
c. With $\alpha = .05$, what is your hypothesis testing conclusion?

Applications

4. Gasoline prices reached record high levels in 16 states during 2003 (*The Wall Street Journal,* March 7, 2003). Two of the affected states were California and Florida. The American Automobile Association reported a sample mean price of \$2.04 per gallon in California and a sample mean price of \$1.72 per gallon in Florida. Use a sample size of 40 for the California data and a sample size of 35 for the Florida data. Assume that prior studies indicating a population standard deviation of .10 in California and .08 in Florida are reasonable.
   a. What is a point estimate of the difference between the population mean prices per gallon in California and Florida?
   b. At 95% confidence, what is the margin of error?
   c. What is the 95% confidence interval estimate of the difference between the population mean prices per gallon in the two states?
5. A Cornell University study of wage differentials between men and women reported that one of the reasons wages for men are higher than wages for women is that men tend to have more years of work experience than women (*Business Week,* August 28, 2000). Assume the following sample summaries show the years of experience for each group.

Men	Women
$n_1 = 100$	$n_2 = 85$
$\bar{x}_1 = 14.9$ years	$\bar{x}_2 = 10.3$ years
$\sigma_1 = 5.2$ years	$\sigma_2 = 3.8$ years

   a. What is the point estimate of the difference between the two population means?
   b. At 95% confidence, what is the margin of error?
   c. What is the 95% confidence interval estimate of the difference between the two population means?
6. The nation's 40,000 mortgage brokerages are some of the most profitable small businesses in the United States. These low-profile companies find loans for customers in exchange for commissions. Mortgage Bankers Association of America provides data on the average size of loans handled by mortgage brokerages (*The Wall Street Journal,* February 24, 2003). Using sample data consistent with the Mortgage Bankers Association data, a sample of 270 loans made in 2002 provided a mean loan of \$175,000. Data for 2001 showed a sample of 250 loans made with a mean loan of \$165,000. Based on historical loan data, the population standard deviations for the loan amounts can be assumed known at \$55,000 in 2002 and \$50,000 in 2001. Do the sample data indicate an increase in the mean loan amount between 2001 and 2002? Use $\alpha = .05$.
7. During the 2003 season, Major League Baseball took steps to speed up the play of baseball games in order to maintain fan interest (*CNN Headline News,* September 30, 2003). The following results come from a sample of 60 games played during the summer of 2002 and a sample of 50 games played during the summer of 2003. The sample mean shows the mean duration of the games included in each sample.

2002 Season	2003 Season
$n_1 = 60$	$n_2 = 50$
$\bar{x}_1 = 2$ hours, 52 minutes	$\bar{x}_2 = 2$ hours, 46 minutes

a. A research hypothesis was that the steps taken during the 2003 season would reduce the population mean duration of baseball games. Formulate the null and alternative hypotheses.
b. What is the point estimate of the reduction in the mean duration of games during the 2003 season?
c. Historical data indicate a population standard deviation of 12 minutes is a reasonable assumption for both years. Conduct the hypothesis test and report the p-value. At a .05 level of significance, what is your conclusion?
d. Provide a 95% confidence interval estimate of the reduction in the mean duration of games during the 2003 season.
e. What was the percentage reduction in the mean time of baseball games during the 2003 season? Should management be pleased with the results of the statistical analysis? Discuss. Should the length of baseball games continue to be an issue in future years? Explain.

8. Arnold Palmer and Tiger Woods are two of the best golfers to ever play the game. To show how these two golfers would compare if both were playing at the top of their game, the following sample data provide the results of 18-hole scores during a PGA tournament competition. Palmer's scores are from his 1960 season, while Woods' scores are from his 1999 season (*Golf Magazine,* February 2000).

Arnold Palmer	Tiger Woods
$n_1 = 112$	$n_2 = 84$
$\bar{x}_1 = 69.95$	$\bar{x}_2 = 69.56$

Use the sample results to test the hypothesis of no difference between the population mean 18-hole scores for the two golfers.
a. Assume a population standard deviation of 2.5 for both golfers. What is the value of the test statistic?
b. What is the p-value?
c. At $\alpha = .01$, what is your conclusion?

Inferences About the Difference Between Two Population Means: σ_1 and σ_2 Unknown

In this section we extend the discussion of inferences about the difference between two population means to the case when the two population standard deviations, σ_1 and σ_2, are unknown. In this case, we will use the sample standard deviations, s_1 and s_2, to estimate the unknown population standard deviations. When we use the sample standard deviations, the interval estimation and hypothesis testing procedures will be based on the t distribution rather than the standard normal distribution.

Interval Estimation of $\mu_1 - \mu_2$

In the following example we show how to compute a margin of error and develop an interval estimate of the difference between two population means when σ_1 and σ_2 are unknown. Clearwater National Bank is conducting a study designed to identify differences between checking account practices by customers at two of its branch banks. A simple random sample of 28 checking accounts is selected from the Cherry Grove branch and an independent simple random sample of 22 checking accounts is selected from the Beechmont branch. The current checking account balance is recorded for each of the checking accounts. A summary of the account balances follows:

CheckAcct

	Cherry Grove	Beechmont
Sample Size	$n_1 = 28$	$n_2 = 22$
Sample Mean	$\bar{x}_1 = \$1025$	$\bar{x}_2 = \$910$
Sample Standard Deviation	$s_1 = \$150$	$s_2 = \$125$

Clearwater National Bank would like to estimate the difference between the mean checking account balance maintained by the population of Cherry Grove customers and the population of Beechmont customers. Let us develop the margin of error and an interval estimate of the difference between these two population means.

In Section 10.1, we provided the following interval estimate for the case when the population standard deviations, σ_1 and σ_2, are known.

$$\bar{x}_1 - \bar{x}_2 \pm z_{\alpha/2}\sqrt{\frac{\sigma_1^2}{n_1} + \frac{\sigma_2^2}{n_2}}$$

When σ_1 and σ_2 are estimated by s_1 and s_2, the t distribution is used to make inferences about the difference between two population means.

With σ_1 and σ_2 unknown, we will use the sample standard deviations s_1 and s_2 to estimate σ_1 and σ_2 and replace $z_{\alpha/2}$ with $t_{\alpha/2}$. As a result, the interval estimate of the difference between two population means is given by the following expression:

INTERVAL ESTIMATE OF THE DIFFERENCE BETWEEN TWO POPULATION MEANS: σ_1 AND σ_2 UNKNOWN

$$\bar{x}_1 - \bar{x}_2 \pm t_{\alpha/2}\sqrt{\frac{s_1^2}{n_1} + \frac{s_2^2}{n_2}} \tag{10.6}$$

where $1 - \alpha$ is the confidence coefficient.

In this expression, the use of the t distribution is an approximation, but it provides excellent results and is relatively easy to use. The only difficulty that we encounter in using expression (10.6) is determining the appropriate degrees of freedom for $t_{\alpha/2}$. Statistical software packages compute the appropriate degrees of freedom automatically. The formula used is as follows:

$$df = \frac{\left(\frac{s_1^2}{n_1} + \frac{s_2^2}{n_2}\right)^2}{\frac{1}{n_1 - 1}\left(\frac{s_1^2}{n_1}\right)^2 + \frac{1}{n_2 - 1}\left(\frac{s_2^2}{n_2}\right)^2} \tag{10.7}$$

Let us return to the Clearwater National Bank example and show how to use expression (10.6) to provide a 95% confidence interval estimate of the difference between the population mean checking account balances at the two branch banks. The sample data show $n_1 = 28$, $\bar{x}_1 = \$1025$, and $s_1 = \$150$ for the Cherry Grove branch, and $n_2 = 22$, $\bar{x}_2 = \$910$, and $s_2 = \$125$ for the Beechmont branch. The calculation for degrees of freedom for $t_{\alpha/2}$ is as follows:

$$df = \frac{\left(\frac{s_1^2}{n_1} + \frac{s_2^2}{n_2}\right)^2}{\frac{1}{n_1 - 1}\left(\frac{s_1^2}{n_1}\right)^2 + \frac{1}{n_2 - 1}\left(\frac{s_2^2}{n_2}\right)^2} = \frac{\left(\frac{150^2}{28} + \frac{125^2}{22}\right)^2}{\frac{1}{28 - 1}\left(\frac{150^2}{28}\right)^2 + \frac{1}{22 - 1}\left(\frac{125^2}{22}\right)^2} = 47.8$$

We round the noninteger degrees of freedom *down* to 47 to provide a slightly larger value of t and a more conservative interval estimate. Using the t distribution table with 47 degrees of freedom, we find $t_{.025} = 2.012$. Using expression (10.6), we develop the 95% confidence interval estimate of the difference between the two population means as follows.

$$\bar{x}_1 - \bar{x}_2 \pm t_{.025}\sqrt{\frac{s_1^2}{n_1} + \frac{s_2^2}{n_2}}$$

$$1025 - 910 \pm 2.012\sqrt{\frac{150^2}{28} + \frac{125^2}{22}}$$

$$115 \pm 78$$

The point estimate of the difference between the population mean checking account balances at the two branches is \$115. The margin of error is \$78, and the 95% confidence interval estimate of the difference between the two population means is 115 − 78 = \$37 to 115 + 78 = \$193.

This suggestion should help if you are using equation (10.7) to calculate the degrees of freedom by hand.

The computation of the degrees of freedom (equation (10.7)) is cumbersome if you are doing the calculation by hand, but it is easily implemented with a computer software package. However, note that the expressions s_1^2/n_1 and s_2^2/n_2 appear in both expression (10.6) and equation (10.7). These values only need to be computed once in order to evaluate both (10.6) and (10.7).

Hypothesis Tests About $\mu_1 - \mu_2$

Let us now consider hypothesis tests about the difference between the means of two populations when the population standard deviations σ_1 and σ_2 are unknown. Letting D_0 denote the hypothesized difference between μ_1 and μ_2, Section 10.1 showed that the test statistic used for the case where σ_1 and σ_2 are known is as follows.

$$z = \frac{(\bar{x}_1 - \bar{x}_2) - D_0}{\sqrt{\frac{\sigma_1^2}{n_1} + \frac{\sigma_2^2}{n_2}}}$$

The test statistic, z, follows the standard normal distribution.

When σ_1 and σ_2 are unknown, we use s_1 as an estimator of σ_1 and s_2 as an estimator of σ_2. Substituting these sample standard deviations for σ_1 and σ_2 provides the following test statistic when σ_1 and σ_2 are unknown.

TEST STATISTIC FOR HYPOTHESIS TESTS ABOUT $\mu_1 - \mu_2$: σ_1 AND σ_2 UNKNOWN

$$t = \frac{(\bar{x}_1 - \bar{x}_2) - D_0}{\sqrt{\frac{s_1^2}{n_1} + \frac{s_2^2}{n_2}}} \qquad \textbf{(10.8)}$$

The degrees of freedom for t are given by equation (10.7).

Let us demonstrate the use of this test statistic in the following hypothesis testing example.

Consider a new computer software package developed to help systems analysts reduce the time required to design, develop, and implement an information system. To evaluate the benefits of the new software package, a random sample of 24 systems analysts is selected. Each analyst is given specifications for a hypothetical information system. Then 12 of the analysts are instructed to produce the information system by using current technology. The other 12 analysts are trained in the use of the new software package and then instructed to use it to produce the information system.

This study involves two populations: a population of systems analysts using the current technology and a population of systems analysts using the new software package. In terms of the time required to complete the information system design project, the population means are as follows.

μ_1 = the mean project completion time for systems analysts using the current technology

μ_2 = the mean project completion time for systems analysts using the new software package

The researcher in charge of the new software evaluation project hopes to show that the new software package will provide a shorter mean project completion time. Thus, the researcher is looking for evidence to conclude that μ_2 is less than μ_1; in this case, the difference between the two population means, $\mu_1 - \mu_2$, will be greater than zero. The research hypothesis $\mu_1 - \mu_2 > 0$ is stated as the alternative hypothesis. Thus, the hypothesis test becomes

$$H_0\colon \mu_1 - \mu_2 \le 0$$
$$H_a\colon \mu_1 - \mu_2 > 0$$

We will use $\alpha = .05$ as the level of significance.

Suppose that the 24 analysts complete the study with the results shown in Table 10.1. Using the test statistic in equation (10.8), we have

$$t = \frac{(\bar{x}_1 - \bar{x}_2) - D_0}{\sqrt{\dfrac{s_1^2}{n_1} + \dfrac{s_2^2}{n_2}}} = \frac{(325 - 286) - 0}{\sqrt{\dfrac{40^2}{12} + \dfrac{44^2}{12}}} = 2.27$$

Computing the degrees of freedom using equation (10.7), we have

$$df = \frac{\left(\dfrac{s_1^2}{n_1} + \dfrac{s_2^2}{n_2}\right)^2}{\dfrac{1}{n_1 - 1}\left(\dfrac{s_1^2}{n_1}\right)^2 + \dfrac{1}{n_2 - 1}\left(\dfrac{s_2^2}{n_2}\right)^2} = \frac{\left(\dfrac{40^2}{12} + \dfrac{44^2}{12}\right)^2}{\dfrac{1}{12 - 1}\left(\dfrac{40^2}{12}\right)^2 + \dfrac{1}{12 - 1}\left(\dfrac{44^2}{12}\right)^2} = 21.8$$

Rounding down, we will use a t distribution with 21 degrees of freedom. This row of the t distribution table is as follows:

Area in Upper Tail	**.20**	**.10**	**.05**	**.025**	**.01**	**.005**
***t* Value (21 df)**	0.859	1.323	1.721	2.080	2.518	2.831

$t = 2.27$

Using the t distribution table, we can only determine a range for the p-value. Use of the computer is required to determine the exact p-value.

With an upper tail test, the p-value is the area in the upper tail to the right of $t = 2.27$. From the preceding results, we see that the p-value is between .025 and .01. Thus, the p-value is less than $\alpha = .05$ and H_0 is rejected. The sample results enable the researcher to conclude

TABLE 10.1 COMPLETION TIME DATA AND SUMMARY STATISTICS FOR THE SOFTWARE TESTING STUDY

CD file
SoftwareTest

	Current Technology	New Software
	300	274
	280	220
	344	308
	385	336
	372	198
	360	300
	288	315
	321	258
	376	318
	290	310
	301	332
	283	263
Summary Statistics		
Sample size	$n_1 = 12$	$n_2 = 12$
Sample mean	$\bar{x}_1 = 325$ hours	$\bar{x}_2 = 286$ hours
Sample standard deviation	$s_1 = 40$	$s_2 = 44$

that $\mu_1 - \mu_2 > 0$, or $\mu_1 > \mu_2$. Thus, the research study supports the conclusion that the new software package provides a smaller population mean completion time.

Minitab can be used to analyze data for testing hypotheses about the difference between two population means. The output comparing the current and new software technology is shown in Figure 10.2. The last line of the output shows $t = 2.27$ and p-value $= .017$. Note that Minitab used equation (10.7) to compute 21 degrees of freedom for this analysis.

Practical Advice

Whenever possible, equal sample sizes, $n_1 = n_2$, are recommended.

The interval estimation and hypothesis testing procedures presented in this section are robust and can be used with relatively small sample sizes. In most applications, equal or nearly equal sample sizes such that the total sample size $n_1 + n_2$ is at least 20 can be expected to provide very good results even if the populations are not normal. Larger sample sizes are recommended if the distributions of the populations are highly skewed or contain outliers. Smaller sample sizes should only be used if the analyst is satisfied that the distributions of the populations are at least approximately normal.

FIGURE 10.2 MINITAB OUTPUT FOR THE HYPOTHESIS TEST OF THE CURRENT AND NEW SOFTWARE TECHNOLOGY

```
Two-sample T for Current vs New

           N     Mean    StDev   SE Mean
Current   12    325.0     40.0        12
New       12    286.0     44.0        13

Difference = mu Current - mu New
Estimate for difference:  39.0000
95% lower bound for difference = 9.4643
T-Test of difference = 0 (vs >):  T-Value = 2.27  P-Value = 0.017  DF = 21
```

NOTES AND COMMENTS

Another approach used to make inferences about the difference between two population means when σ_1 and σ_2 are unknown is based on the assumption that the two population standard deviations are *equal* ($\sigma_1 = \sigma_2 = \sigma$). Under this assumption, the two sample standard deviations are combined to provide the following *pooled sample variance:*

$$s_p^2 = \frac{(n_1 - 1)s_1^2 + (n_2 - 1)s_2^2}{n_1 + n_2 - 2}$$

The t test statistic becomes

$$t = \frac{(\bar{x}_1 - \bar{x}_2) - D_0}{s_p\sqrt{\frac{1}{n_1} + \frac{1}{n_2}}}$$

and has $n_1 + n_2 - 2$ degrees of freedom. At this point, the computation of the p-value and the interpretation of the sample results are identical to the procedures discussed earlier in this section.

A difficulty with this procedure is that the assumption that the two population standard deviations are equal is usually difficult to verify. Unequal population standard deviations are frequently encountered. Using the pooled procedure may not provide satisfactory results especially if the sample sizes n_1 and n_2 are quite different.

The t procedure that we presented in this section does not require the assumption of equal population standard deviations and can be applied whether the population standard deviations are equal or not. It is a more general procedure and is recommended for most applications.

Exercises

Methods

9. Consider the following results for independent random samples taken from two populations.

Sample 1	Sample 2
$n_1 = 20$	$n_2 = 30$
$\bar{x}_1 = 22.5$	$\bar{x}_2 = 20.1$
$s_1 = 2.5$	$s_2 = 4.8$

a. What is the point estimate of the difference between the two population means?
b. What is the degrees of freedom for the t distribution?
c. At 95% confidence, what is the margin of error?
d. What is the 95% confidence interval for the difference between the two population means?

10. Consider the following hypothesis test.

$$H_0: \mu_1 - \mu_2 = 0$$
$$H_a: \mu_1 - \mu_2 \neq 0$$

The following results are from independent samples taken from two populations.

Sample 1	Sample 2
$n_1 = 35$	$n_2 = 40$
$\bar{x}_1 = 13.6$	$\bar{x}_2 = 10.1$
$s_1 = 5.2$	$s_2 = 8.5$

a. What is the value of the test statistic?
b. What is the degrees of freedom for the t distribution?
c. What is the p-value?
d. At $\alpha = .05$, what is your conclusion?

11. Consider the following data for two independent random samples taken from two normal populations.

Sample 1	10	7	13	7	9	8
Sample 2	8	7	8	4	6	9

a. Compute the two sample means.
b. Compute the two sample standard deviations.
c. What is the point estimate of the difference between the two population means?
d. What is the 90% confidence interval estimate of the difference between the two population means?

Applications

12. The U.S. Department of Transportation provides the number of miles that residents of the 75 largest metropolitan areas travel per day in a car. Suppose that for a simple random sample of 50 Buffalo residents the mean is 22.5 miles a day and the standard deviation is 8.4 miles a day, and for an independent simple random sample of 40 Boston residents the mean is 18.6 miles a day and the standard deviation is 7.4 miles a day.
    a. What is the point estimate of the difference between the mean number of miles that Buffalo residents travel per day and the mean number of miles that Boston residents travel per day?
    b. What is the 95% confidence interval for the difference between the two population means?

CD file
Cargo

13. FedEx and United Parcel Service (UPS) are the world's two leading cargo carriers by volume and revenue (*The Wall Street Journal,* January 27, 2004). According to the Airports Council International, the Memphis International Airport (FedEx) and the Louisville International Airport (UPS) are two of the ten largest cargo airports in the world. The following random samples show the tons of cargo per day handled by these airports. Data are in thousands of tons.

Memphis

9.1	15.1	8.8	10.0	7.5	10.5
8.3	9.1	6.0	5.8	12.1	9.3

Louisville

4.7	5.0	4.2	3.3	5.5
2.2	4.1	2.6	3.4	7.0

a. Compute the sample mean and sample standard deviation for each airport.
b. What is the point estimate of the difference between the two population means? Interpret this value in terms of the higher-volume airport and a comparison of the volume difference between the two airports.
c. Develop a 95% confidence interval of the difference between the daily population means for the two airports.

14. Coastal areas of the United States including Cape Cod, the Outer Banks, the Carolinas, and the Gulf Coast had relatively high population growth rates during the 1990s. Data were collected on residents living in the coastal communities as well as on residents living in noncoastal areas throughout the United States (*USA Today,* July 21, 2000). Assume that the following sample results were obtained on the ages of individuals in the two populations:

Coastal Areas	Noncoastal Areas
$n_1 = 150$	$n_2 = 175$
$\bar{x}_1 = 39.3$ years	$\bar{x}_2 = 35.4$ years
$s_1 = 16.8$ years	$s_2 = 15.2$ years

Test the hypothesis of no difference between the two population means. Use $\alpha = .05$.

a. Formulate the null and alternative hypotheses.
b. What is the value of the test statistic?
c. What is the p-value?
d. What is your conclusion?

15. Injuries to Major League Baseball players have been increasing in recent years. For the period 1992 to 2001, league expansion caused Major League Baseball rosters to increase 15%. However, the number of players being put on the disabled list due to injury increased 32% over the same period (*USA Today,* July 8, 2002). A research question addressed whether Major League Baseball players being put on the disabled list are on the list longer in 2001 than players put on the disabled list a decade earlier.

a. Using the population mean number of days a player is on the disabled list, formulate null and alternative hypotheses that can be used to test the research question.
b. Assume that the following data apply:

	2001 Season	1992 Season
Sample Players	$n_1 = 45$	$n_2 = 38$
Sample Mean Days	$\bar{x}_1 = 60$ days	$\bar{x}_2 = 51$ days
Sample Std Deviation	$s_1 = 18$ days	$s_2 = 15$ days

What is the point estimate of the difference between population mean days on the disabled list for 2001 compared to 1992? What is the percentage increase in the number of days on the disabled list?

c. Use $\alpha = .01$. What is your conclusion about number of days on the disabled list? What is the p-value?
d. Do these data suggest that Major League Baseball should be concerned about the situation?

SATVerbal

16. The College Board provided comparisons of Scholastic Aptitude Test (SAT) scores based on the highest level of education attained by the test taker's parents. A research hypothesis was that students whose parents had attained a higher level of education would on average score higher on the SAT. During 2003, the overall mean SAT verbal score was 507 (*The World Almanac 2004*). SAT verbal scores for independent samples of students follow. The first sample shows the SAT verbal test scores for students whose parents are college graduates with a bachelor's degree. The second sample shows the SAT verbal test scores for students whose parents are high school graduates but do not have a college degree.

Student's Parents			
College Grads		High School Grads	
485	487	442	492
534	533	580	478
650	526	479	425
554	410	486	485
550	515	528	390
572	578	524	535
497	448		
592	469		

a. Formulate the hypotheses that can be used to determine whether the sample data support the hypothesis that students show a higher population mean verbal score on the SAT if their parents attained a higher level of education.
b. What is the point estimate of the difference between the means for the two populations?
c. Compute the p-value for the hypothesis test.
d. At $\alpha = .05$, what is your conclusion?

17. Periodically, Merrill Lynch customers are asked to evaluate Merrill Lynch financial consultants and services (2000 Merrill Lynch Client Satisfaction Survey). Higher ratings on the client satisfaction survey indicate better service with 7 the maximum service rating. Independent samples of service ratings for two financial consultants are summarized here. Consultant A has 10 years of experience, whereas consultant B has 1 year of experience. Use $\alpha = .05$ and test to see whether the consultant with more experience has the higher population mean service rating.

Consultant A	Consultant B
$n_1 = 16$	$n_2 = 10$
$\bar{x}_1 = 6.82$	$\bar{x}_2 = 6.25$
$s_1 = .64$	$s_2 = .75$

a. State the null and alternative hypotheses.
b. Compute the value of the test statistic.
c. What is the p-value?
d. What is your conclusion?

18. Educational testing companies provide tutoring, classroom learning, and practice tests in an effort to help students perform better on tests such as the Scholastic Aptitude Test (SAT). The test preparation companies claim that their courses will improve SAT score performances by an average of 120 points (*The Wall Street Journal,* January 23, 2003). A researcher is uncertain of this claim and believes that 120 points may be an overstatement in an effort to encourage students to take the test preparation course. In an evaluation study of one test preparation service, the researcher collects SAT score data for 35 students who took the test preparation course and 48 students who did not take the course.

a. Formulate the hypotheses that can be used to test the researcher's belief that the improvement in SAT scores may be less than the stated average of 120 points.
b. Use $\alpha = .05$ and the following data. What is your conclusion?

	Course	No Course
Sample Mean	1058	983
Sample Standard Deviation	90	105

c. What is the point estimate of the improvement in the average SAT scores provided by the test preparation course? Provide a 95% confidence interval estimate of the improvement.
d. What advice would you have for the researcher after seeing the confidence interval?

10.3 Inferences About the Difference Between Two Population Means: Matched Samples

Suppose employees at a manufacturing company can use two different methods to perform a production task. To maximize production output, the company wants to identify the method with the smaller population mean completion time. Let μ_1 denote the population mean completion time for production method 1 and μ_2 denote the population mean completion time for production method 2. With no preliminary indication of the preferred production method, we begin by tentatively assuming that the two production methods have the same population mean completion time. Thus, the null hypothesis is $H_0: \mu_1 - \mu_2 = 0$. If this hypothesis is rejected, we can conclude that the population mean completion times differ. In this case, the method providing the smaller mean completion time would be recommended. The null and alternative hypotheses are written as follows.

$$H_0: \mu_1 - \mu_2 = 0$$
$$H_a: \mu_1 - \mu_2 \neq 0$$

In choosing the sampling procedure that will be used to collect production time data and test the hypotheses, we consider two alternative designs. One is based on independent samples and the other is based on **matched samples**.

1. *Independent sample design:* A simple random sample of workers is selected and each worker in the sample uses method 1. A second independent simple random sample of workers is selected and each worker in this sample uses method 2. The test of the difference between population means is based on the procedures in Section 10.2.
2. *Matched sample design:* One simple random sample of workers is selected. Each worker first uses one method and then uses the other method. The order of the two methods is assigned randomly to the workers, with some workers performing method 1 first and others performing method 2 first. Each worker provides a pair of data values, one value for method 1 and another value for method 2.

In the matched sample design the two production methods are tested under similar conditions (i.e., with the same workers); hence this design often leads to a smaller sampling error than the independent sample design. The primary reason is that in a matched sample design, variation between workers is eliminated because the same workers are used for both production methods.

Let us demonstrate the analysis of a matched sample design by assuming it is the method used to test the difference between population means for the two production methods. A random sample of six workers is used. The data on completion times for the six workers are given in Table 10.2. Note that each worker provides a pair of data values, one for each production method. Also note that the last column contains the difference in completion times d_i for each worker in the sample.

The key to the analysis of the matched sample design is to realize that we consider only the column of differences. Therefore, we have six data values (.6, −.2, .5, .3, .0, and .6) that will be used to analyze the difference between population means of the two production methods.

TABLE 10.2 TASK COMPLETION TIMES FOR A MATCHED SAMPLE DESIGN

Worker	Completion Time for Method 1 (minutes)	Completion Time for Method 2 (minutes)	Difference in Completion Times (d_i)
1	6.0	5.4	.6
2	5.0	5.2	−.2
3	7.0	6.5	.5
4	6.2	5.9	.3
5	6.0	6.0	.0
6	6.4	5.8	.6

Matched

Let μ_d = the mean of the *difference* values for the population of workers. With this notation, the null and alternative hypotheses are rewritten as follows.

$$H_0: \mu_d = 0$$
$$H_a: \mu_d \neq 0$$

Other than the use of the d notation, the formulas for the sample mean and sample standard deviation are the same ones used previously in the text.

If H_0 is rejected, we can conclude that the population mean completion times differ.

The d notation is a reminder that the matched sample provides *difference* data. The sample mean and sample standard deviation for the six difference values in Table 10.2 follow.

$$\bar{d} = \frac{\Sigma d_i}{n} = \frac{1.8}{6} = .30$$

$$s_d = \sqrt{\frac{\Sigma(d_i - \bar{d})^2}{n - 1}} = \sqrt{\frac{.56}{5}} = .335$$

It is not necessary to make the assumption that the population has a normal distribution if the sample size is large. Sample size guidelines for using the t distribution were presented in Chapters 8 and 9.

With the small sample of $n = 6$ workers, we need to make the assumption that the population of differences has a normal distribution. This assumption is necessary so that we may use the t distribution for hypothesis testing and interval estimation procedures. Based on this assumption, the following test statistic has a t distribution with $n - 1$ degrees of freedom.

$$t = \frac{\bar{d} - \mu_d}{s_d/\sqrt{n}} \tag{10.9}$$

Once the difference data are computed, the t distribution procedure for matched samples is the same as the one-population estimation and hypothesis testing procedures described in Chapters 8 and 9.

Let us use equation (10.9) to test the hypotheses $H_0: \mu_d = 0$ and $H_a: \mu_d \neq 0$, using $\alpha = .05$. Substituting the sample results $\bar{d} = .30$, $s_d = .335$, and $n = 6$ into equation (10.9), we compute the value of the test statistic.

$$t = \frac{\bar{d} - \mu_d}{s_d/\sqrt{n}} = \frac{.30 - 0}{.335/\sqrt{6}} = 2.20$$

Now let us compute the p-value for this two-tailed test. Because $t = 2.20 > 0$, the test statistic is in the upper tail of the t distribution. With $t = 2.20$, the area in the upper tail to the right of the test statistic can be found by using the t distribution table with degrees of freedom $= n - 1 = 6 - 1 = 5$. Information from the 5 degrees of freedom row of the t distribution table is as follows:

Area in Upper Tail	.20	.10	.05	.025	.01	.005
t Value (5 df)	0.920	1.476	2.015	2.571	3.365	4.032

$t = 2.20$

Thus, we see that the area in the upper tail is between .05 and .025. Because this test is a two-tailed test, we double these values to conclude that the p-value is between .10 and .05. This p-value is greater than $\alpha = .05$. Thus, the null hypothesis H_0: $\mu_d = 0$ is not rejected. Using Minitab and the data in Table 10.2, we find the p-value $= .080$.

In addition we can obtain an interval estimate of the difference between the two population means by using the single population methodology of Chapter 8. At 95% confidence, the calculation follows.

$$\bar{d} \pm t_{.025} \frac{s_d}{\sqrt{n}}$$

$$.3 \pm 2.571\left(\frac{.335}{\sqrt{6}}\right)$$

$$.3 \pm .35$$

Thus, the margin of error is .35 and the 95% confidence interval for the difference between the population means of the two production methods is $-.05$ minutes to .65 minutes.

NOTES AND COMMENTS

1. In the example presented in this section, workers performed the production task with first one method and then the other method. This example illustrates a matched sample design in which each sampled element (worker) provides a pair of data values. It is also possible to use different but "similar" elements to provide the pair of data values. For example, a worker at one location could be matched with a similar worker at another location (similarity based on age, education, gender, experience, etc.). The pairs of workers would provide the difference data that could be used in the matched sample analysis.
2. A matched sample procedure for inferences about two population means generally provides better precision than the independent sample approach, therefore it is the recommended design. However, in some applications the matching cannot be achieved, or perhaps the time and cost associated with matching are excessive. In such cases, the independent sample design should be used.

Exercises

Methods

19. Consider the following hypothesis test.

$$H_0: \mu_d \leq 0$$
$$H_a: \mu_d > 0$$

The following data are from matched samples taken from two populations.

	Population	
Element	1	2
1	21	20
2	28	26
3	18	18
4	20	20
5	26	24

a. Compute the difference value for each element.
b. Compute $\bar{d}$.
c. Compute the standard deviation s_d.
d. Conduct a hypothesis test using $\alpha = .05$. What is your conclusion?

20. The following data are from matched samples taken from two populations.

	Population	
Element	1	2
1	11	8
2	7	8
3	9	6
4	12	7
5	13	10
6	15	15
7	15	14

a. Compute the difference value for each element.
b. Compute $\bar{d}$.
c. Compute the standard deviation s_d.
d. What is the point estimate of the difference between the two population means?
e. Provide a 95% confidence interval for the difference between the two population means.

Applications

21. A market research firm used a sample of individuals to rate the purchase potential of a particular product before and after the individuals saw a new television commercial about the product. The purchase potential ratings were based on a 0 to 10 scale, with higher values indicating a higher purchase potential. The null hypothesis stated that the mean rating "after" would be less than or equal to the mean rating "before." Rejection of this hypothesis would show that the commercial improved the mean purchase potential rating. Use $\alpha = .05$ and the following data to test the hypothesis and comment on the value of the commercial.

	Purchase Rating			Purchase Rating	
Individual	After	Before	Individual	After	Before
1	6	5	5	3	5
2	6	4	6	9	8
3	7	7	7	7	5
4	4	3	8	6	6

22. A sample of 10 international telephone calls provided Sprint and WorldCom calling rates per minute for calls from the United States (*World Traveler,* July 2000).

Country	**Sprint**	**WorldCom**
Australia	.46	.26
Belgium	.69	.40
Brazil	.92	.53
Colombia	.55	.53
Denmark	.50	.26
France	.46	.26
Germany	.46	.26
Hong Kong	.92	.40
Japan	.69	.40
United Kingdom	.46	.26

Provide a 95% confidence interval estimate of the difference between the two population means.

23. Bank of America's Consumer Spending Survey collected data on annual credit card charges in seven different categories of expenditures: transportation, groceries, dining out, household expenses, home furnishings, apparel, and entertainment (*U.S. Airways Attaché,* December 2003). Using data from a sample of 42 credit card accounts, assume that each account was used to identify the annual credit card charges for groceries (population 1) and the annual credit card charges for dining out (population 2). Using the difference data, the sample mean difference was $\bar{d}$ = \$850, and the sample standard deviation was s_d = \$1123.
    a. Formulate the null and alternative hypotheses to test for no difference between the population mean credit card charges for groceries and the population mean credit card charges for dining out.
    b. Use a .05 level of significance. Can you conclude that the population means differ? What is the p-value?
    c. Which category, groceries or dining out, has a higher population mean annual credit card charge? What is the point estimate of the difference between the population means? What is the 95% confidence interval estimate of the difference between the population means?

24. Rental car gasoline prices per gallon were sampled at eight major airports. Data for Hertz and National car rental companies follow (*USA Today,* April 4, 2000).

Airport	**Hertz**	**National**
Boston Logan	1.55	1.56
Chicago O'Hare	1.62	1.59
Los Angeles	1.72	1.78
Miami	1.65	1.49
New York (JFK)	1.72	1.51
New York (LaGuardia)	1.67	1.50
Orange County, CA	1.68	1.77
Washington (Dulles)	1.52	1.41

Use α = .05 to test the hypothesis of no difference between the population mean prices per gallon for the two companies.

25. In recent years, a growing array of entertainment options competes for consumer time. By 2004, cable television and radio surpassed broadcast television, recorded music, and the daily newspaper to become the two entertainment media with the greatest usage (*The Wall Street Journal,* January 26, 2004). Researchers used a sample of 15 individuals and collected data on the hours per week spent watching cable television and hours per week spent listening to the radio.

TVRadio

Individual	Television	Radio	Individual	Television	Radio
1	22	25	9	21	21
2	8	10	10	23	23
3	25	29	11	14	15
4	22	19	12	14	18
5	12	13	13	14	17
6	26	28	14	16	15
7	22	23	15	24	23
8	19	21			

a. Use a .05 level of significance and test for a difference between the population mean usage for cable television and radio. What is the *p*-value?

b. What is the sample mean number of hours per week spent watching cable television? What is the sample mean number of hours per week spent listening to radio? Which medium has the greater usage?

26. StreetInsider.com reported 2002 earnings per share data for a sample of major companies (February 12, 2003). Prior to 2002, financial analysts predicted the 2002 earnings per share for these same companies (*Barron's,* September 10, 2001). Use the following data to comment on differences between actual and estimated earnings per share.

Earnings

Company	Actual	Predicted
AT&T	1.29	0.38
American Express	2.01	2.31
Citigroup	2.59	3.43
Coca-Cola	1.60	1.78
DuPont	1.84	2.18
Exxon-Mobil	2.72	2.19
General Electric	1.51	1.71
Johnson & Johnson	2.28	2.18
McDonald's	0.77	1.55
Wal-Mart	1.81	1.74

a. Use α = .05 and test for any difference between the population mean actual and population mean estimated earnings per share. What is the *p*-value? What is your conclusion?

b. What is the point estimate of the difference between the two means? Did the analysts tend to underestimate or overestimate the earnings?

c. At 95% confidence, what is the margin of error for the estimate in part (b)? What would you recommend based on this information?

10.4 Introduction to Analysis of Variance

Thus far we focused on statistical procedures used to compare two population means. In this section, we introduce **analysis of variance (ANOVA)** and show how it can be used to test the hypothesis that three or more population means are equal. We begin the discussion by considering a problem faced by National Computer Products, Inc.

National Computer Products, Inc. (NCP), manufactures printers and fax machines at plants located in Atlanta, Dallas, and Seattle. To measure how much employees at these plants know about total quality management, a random sample of six employees was selected from each plant and given a quality awareness examination. The examination scores obtained for these 18 employees are listed in Table 10.3. The sample means, sample variances, and sample standard deviations for each group are also provided. Managers want to use these data to test the hypothesis that the mean examination score is the same for all three plants.

We will define population 1 as all employees at the Atlanta plant, population 2 as all employees at the Dallas plant, and population 3 as all employees at the Seattle plant. Let

$$\mu_1 = \text{mean examination score for population 1}$$
$$\mu_2 = \text{mean examination score for population 2}$$
$$\mu_3 = \text{mean examination score for population 3}$$

Although we will never know the actual values of μ_1, μ_2, and μ_3, we want to use the sample results to test the following hypotheses.

If H_0 is rejected, we cannot conclude that all population means are different. Rejecting H_0 means that at least two population means have different values.

$$H_0\colon \mu_1 = \mu_2 = \mu_3$$
$$H_a\colon \text{Not all population means are equal}$$

As we will demonstrate shortly, analysis of variance is a statistical procedure that can be used to determine whether the observed differences in the three sample means are large enough to reject H_0.

In the introduction to this chapter we stated that analysis of variance can be used to analyze data obtained from both an observational study and an experimental study. In order to provide a common set of terminology for discussing the use of analysis of variance in both types of studies, we need to introduce the concepts of a response variable, a factor, and a treatment.

The two variables in the NCP example are plant location and score on the quality awareness examination. Because the objective is to determine whether the mean examination score is the same for plants located in Atlanta, Dallas, and Seattle, examination score is referred to as the dependent or *response variable* and plant location as the independent variable or *factor*. In general, the values of a factor selected for investigation are referred to as levels of the factor or *treatments*. Thus, in the NCP example the three treatments are Atlanta, Dallas, and Seattle. These three treatments define the populations of interest in the NCP example. For each treatment or population, the response variable is the examination score.

TABLE 10.3 EXAMINATION SCORES FOR 18 EMPLOYEES

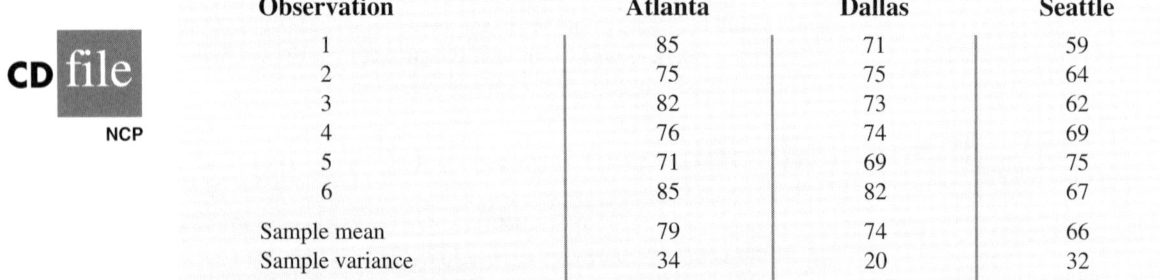

CD file NCP

Observation	Plant 1 Atlanta	Plant 2 Dallas	Plant 3 Seattle
1	85	71	59
2	75	75	64
3	82	73	62
4	76	74	69
5	71	69	75
6	85	82	67
Sample mean	79	74	66
Sample variance	34	20	32
Sample standard deviation	5.83	4.47	5.66

Assumptions for Analysis of Variance

Three assumptions are required to use analysis of variance.

If the sample sizes are equal, analysis of variance is not sensitive to departures from the assumption of normally distributed populations.

1. **For each population, the response variable is normally distributed.** Implication: In the NCP example, the examination scores (response variable) must be normally distributed at each plant.
2. **The variance of the response variable, denoted σ^2, is the same for all of the populations.** Implication: In the NCP example, the variance of examination scores must be the same for all three plants.
3. **The observations must be independent.** Implication: In the NCP example, the examination score for each employee must be independent of the examination score for any other employee.

A Conceptual Overview

If the means for the three populations are equal, we would expect the three sample means to be close together. In fact, the closer the three sample means are to one another, the more evidence we have for the conclusion that the population means are equal. Alternatively, the more the sample means differ, the more evidence we have for the conclusion that the population means are not equal. In other words, if the variability among the sample means is "small," it supports H_0; if the variability among the sample means is "large," it supports H_a.

If the null hypothesis, H_0: $\mu_1 = \mu_2 = \mu_3$, is true, we can use the variability among the sample means to develop an estimate of σ^2. First, note that if the assumptions for analysis of variance are satisfied, each sample will have come from the same normal distribution with mean μ and variance σ^2. Recall from Chapter 7 that the sampling distribution of the sample mean $\bar{x}$ for a simple random sample of size n from a normal population will be normally distributed with mean μ and variance σ^2/n. Figure 10.3 illustrates such a sampling distribution.

Thus, if the null hypothesis is true, we can think of each of the three sample means, $\bar{x}_1 = 79$, $\bar{x}_2 = 74$, and $\bar{x}_3 = 66$, from Table 10.3 as values drawn at random from the sampling distribution shown in Figure 10.3. In this case, the mean and variance of the three $\bar{x}$ values can be used to estimate the mean and variance of the sampling distribution. When the sample sizes are equal, as in the NCP example, the best estimate of the mean of the

FIGURE 10.3 SAMPLING DISTRIBUTION OF $\bar{x}$ GIVEN H_0 IS TRUE

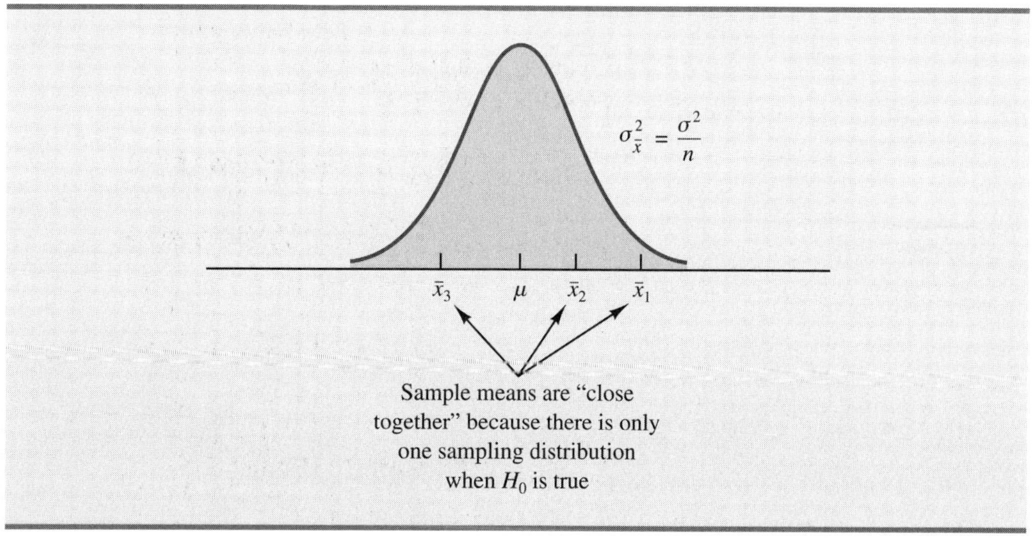

sampling distribution of $\bar{x}$ is the mean or average of the sample means. Thus, in the NCP example, an estimate of the mean of the sampling distribution of $\bar{x}$ is $(79 + 74 + 66)/3 = 73$. We refer to this estimate as the *overall sample mean.* An estimate of the variance of the sampling distribution of $\bar{x}$, $\sigma_{\bar{x}}^2$, is provided by the variance of the three sample means.

$$s_{\bar{x}}^2 = \frac{(79 - 73)^2 + (74 - 73)^2 + (66 - 73)^2}{3 - 1} = \frac{86}{2} = 43$$

Because $\sigma_{\bar{x}}^2 = \sigma^2/n$, solving for σ^2 gives

$$\sigma^2 = n\sigma_{\bar{x}}^2$$

Hence,

$$\text{Estimate of } \sigma^2 = n\,(\text{Estimate of } \sigma_{\bar{x}}^2) = ns_{\bar{x}}^2 = 6(43) = 258$$

The result, $ns_{\bar{x}}^2 = 258$, is referred to as the *between-treatments* estimate of σ^2.

The between-treatments estimate of σ^2 is based on the assumption that the null hypothesis is true. In this case, each sample comes from the same population, and there is only one sampling distribution of $\bar{x}$. To illustrate what happens when H_0 is false, suppose the population means all differ. Note that because the three samples are from normal populations with different means, they will result in three different sampling distributions. Figure 10.4 shows that in this case, the sample means are not as close together as they were when H_0 was true. Thus, $s_{\bar{x}}^2$ will be larger, causing the between-treatments estimate of σ^2 to be larger. In general, when the population means are not equal, the between-treatments estimate will overestimate the population variance σ^2.

The variation within each of the samples also has an effect on the conclusion we reach in analysis of variance. When a simple random sample is selected from each population, each of the sample variances provides an unbiased estimate of σ^2. Hence, we can combine or pool the individual estimates of σ^2 into one overall estimate. The estimate of σ^2 obtained in this way is called the *pooled* or *within-treatments* estimate of σ^2. Because each sample variance provides an estimate of σ^2 based only on the variation within each sample, the within-treatments estimate of σ^2 is not affected by whether the population means are equal.

FIGURE 10.4 SAMPLING DISTRIBUTIONS OF $\bar{x}$ GIVEN H_0 IS FALSE

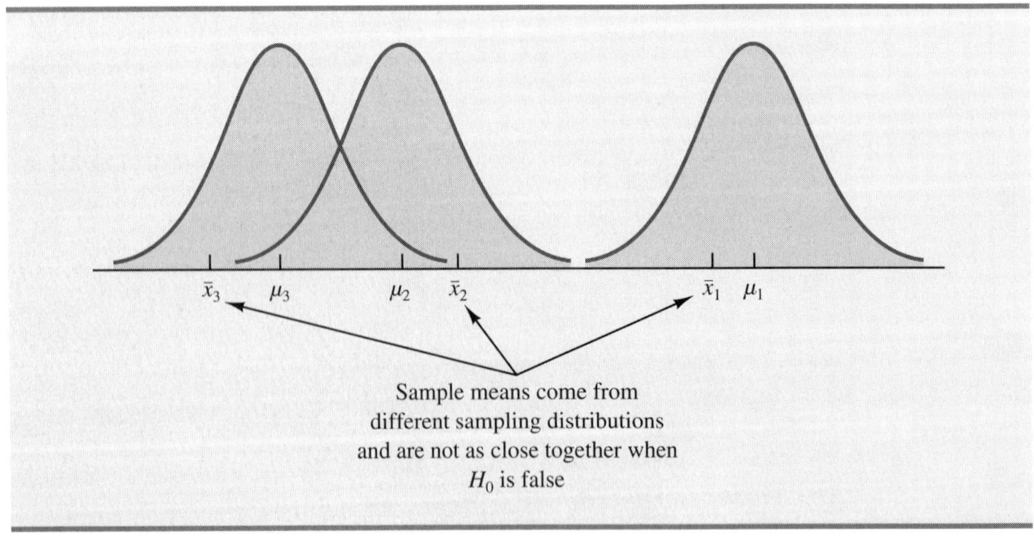

When the sample sizes are equal, the within-treatments estimate of σ^2 can be obtained by computing the average of the individual sample variances. For the NCP example we obtain

$$\text{Within-treatments estimate of } \sigma^2 = \frac{34 + 20 + 32}{3} = \frac{86}{3} = 28.67$$

In the NCP example, the between-treatments estimate of σ^2 (258) is much larger than the within-treatments estimate of σ^2 (28.67). In fact, the ratio of these two estimates is 258/28.67 = 9.00. Recall, however, that the between-treatments approach provides a good estimate of σ^2 only if the null hypothesis is true; if the null hypothesis is false, the between-treatments approach overestimates σ^2. The within-treatments approach provides a good estimate of σ^2 in either case. Thus, if the null hypothesis is true, the two estimates will be similar and their ratio will be close to 1. If the null hypothesis is false, the between-treatments estimate will be larger than the within-treatments estimate, and their ratio will be large. In the next section we will show how large this ratio must be to reject H_0.

In summary, the logic behind ANOVA is based on the development of two independent estimates of the common population variance σ^2. One estimate of σ^2 is based on the variability among the sample means themselves, and the other estimate of σ^2 is based on the variability of the data within each sample. By comparing these two estimates of σ^2, we will be able to determine whether the population means are equal.

NOTES AND COMMENTS

In Sections 10.1 and 10.2 we presented statistical methods for testing the hypothesis that two population means are equal. ANOVA can also be used to test the hypothesis that two population means are equal. In practice, however, analysis of variance is usually not used until dealing with three or more population means.

10.5 Analysis of Variance: Testing for the Equality of *k* Population Means

Analysis of variance can be used to test for the equality of k population means. The general form of the hypotheses tested is

$$H_0: \mu_1 = \mu_2 = \cdots = \mu_k$$
$$H_a: \text{Not all population means are equal}$$

where

$$\mu_j = \text{mean of the } j\text{th population}$$

We assume that a simple random sample of size n_j has been selected from each of the k populations or treatments. For the resulting sample data, let

$$x_{ij} = \text{value of observation } i \text{ for treatment } j$$
$$n_j = \text{number of observations for treatment } j$$
$$\bar{x}_j = \text{sample mean for treatment } j$$
$$s_j^2 = \text{sample variance for treatment } j$$
$$s_j = \text{sample standard deviation for treatment } j$$

The formulas for the sample mean and sample variance for treatment j are as follows.

$$\bar{x}_j = \frac{\sum_{i=1}^{n_j} x_{ij}}{n_j} \tag{10.10}$$

$$s_j^2 = \frac{\sum_{i=1}^{n_j} (x_{ij} - \bar{x}_j)^2}{n_j - 1} \tag{10.11}$$

The overall sample mean, denoted $\bar{\bar{x}}$, is the sum of all the observations divided by the total number of observations. That is,

$$\bar{\bar{x}} = \frac{\sum_{j=1}^{k}\sum_{i=1}^{n_j} x_{ij}}{n_T} \tag{10.12}$$

where

$$n_T = n_1 + n_2 + \cdots + n_k \tag{10.13}$$

If the size of each sample is n, $n_T = kn$; in this case equation (10.12) reduces to

$$\bar{\bar{x}} = \frac{\sum_{j=1}^{k}\sum_{i=1}^{n_j} x_{ij}}{kn} = \frac{\sum_{j=1}^{k}\sum_{i=1}^{n_j} x_{ij}/n}{k} = \frac{\sum_{j=1}^{k} \bar{x}_j}{k} \tag{10.14}$$

In other words, whenever the sample sizes are the same, the overall sample mean is just the average of the k sample means.

Because each sample in the NCP example consists of $n = 6$ observations, the overall sample mean can be computed by using equation (10.14). For the data in Table 10.3 we obtained the following result.

$$\bar{\bar{x}} = \frac{79 + 74 + 66}{3} = 73$$

If the null hypothesis is true ($\mu_1 = \mu_2 = \mu_3 = \mu$), the overall sample mean of 73 is the best estimate of the population mean μ.

Between-Treatments Estimate of Population Variance

In the preceding section, we introduced the concept of a between-treatments estimate of σ^2 and showed how to compute it when the sample sizes were equal. This estimate of σ^2 is called the *mean square due to treatments* and is denoted MSTR. The general formula for computing MSTR is

$$\text{MSTR} = \frac{\sum_{j=1}^{k} n_j(\bar{x}_j - \bar{\bar{x}})^2}{k - 1} \tag{10.15}$$

The numerator in equation (10.15) is called the *sum of squares due to treatments* and is denoted SSTR. The denominator, $k - 1$, represents the degrees of freedom associated with SSTR. Hence, the mean square due to treatments can be computed by the following formula.

MEAN SQUARE DUE TO TREATMENTS

$$\text{MSTR} = \frac{\text{SSTR}}{k - 1} \tag{10.16}$$

where

$$\text{SSTR} = \sum_{j=1}^{k} n_j(\bar{x}_j - \bar{\bar{x}})^2 \tag{10.17}$$

If H_0 is true, MSTR provides an unbiased estimate of σ^2. However, if the means of the k populations are not equal, MSTR is not an unbiased estimate of σ^2; in fact, in that case, MSTR should overestimate σ^2.

For the NCP data in Table 10.3, we obtain the following results.

$$\text{SSTR} = \sum_{j=1}^{k} n_j(\bar{x}_j - \bar{\bar{x}})^2 = 6(79 - 73)^2 + 6(74 - 73)^2 + 6(66 - 73)^2 = 516$$

$$\text{MSTR} = \frac{\text{SSTR}}{k - 1} = \frac{516}{2} = 258$$

Within-Treatments Estimate of Population Variance

Earlier, we introduced the concept of a within-treatments estimate of σ^2 and showed how to compute it when the sample sizes were equal. This estimate of σ^2 is called the *mean square due to error* and is denoted MSE. The general formula for computing MSE is

$$\text{MSE} = \frac{\sum_{j=1}^{k} (n_j - 1)s_j^2}{n_T - k} \tag{10.18}$$

The numerator in equation (10.18) is called the *sum of squares due to error* and is denoted SSE. The denominator of MSE, $n_T - k$, is the degrees of freedom associated with SSE. Hence, the formula for MSE can also be stated as follows.

MEAN SQUARE DUE TO ERROR

$$\text{MSE} = \frac{\text{SSE}}{n_T - k} \tag{10.19}$$

where

$$\text{SSE} = \sum_{j=1}^{k} (n_j - 1)s_j^2 \tag{10.20}$$

Note that MSE is based on the variation within each of the treatments; it is not influenced by whether the null hypothesis is true. Thus, MSE always provides an unbiased estimate of σ^2.

For the NCP data in Table 10.3 we obtain the following results

$$\text{SSE} = \sum_{j=1}^{k}(n_j - 1)s_j^2 = (6 - 1)34 + (6 - 1)20 + (6 - 1)32 = 430$$

$$\text{MSE} = \frac{\text{SSE}}{n_T - k} = \frac{430}{18 - 3} = \frac{430}{15} = 28.67$$

Comparing the Variance Estimates: The F Test

If the null hypothesis is true, MSTR and MSE provide two independent estimates of the population variance σ^2. When the null hypothesis is true and the ANOVA assumptions are valid, the sampling distribution of the ratio MSTR/MSE has an **F distribution** with $k - 1$ degrees of freedom in the numerator and $n_T - 1$ degrees of freedom in the denominator. The general shape of this F distribution is shown in Figure 10.5. If the null hypothesis is true, the value of MSTR/MSE should appear to be from this distribution. However, if the null hypothesis is false, the value of MSTR/MSE will be inflated because a large MSTR provides an overestimate of σ^2. The values of MSTR/MSE that lead to the rejection of the null hypothesis will be in the upper tail of the distribution shown in Figure 10.5.

With the decision to reject the null hypothesis H_0 based on the ratio MSTR/MSE, this ratio becomes the test statistic for the hypothesis test about the equality of k population means. The test statistic is as follows.

TEST STATISTIC FOR THE EQUALITY OF k POPULATION MEANS

$$F = \frac{\text{MSTR}}{\text{MSE}} \tag{10.21}$$

The F distribution has $k - 1$ degrees of freedom in the numerator and $n_T - k$ degrees of freedom in the denominator.

Let us return to the National Computer Products example and use a level of significance $\alpha = .05$ to conduct the hypothesis test. The null and alternative hypotheses are restated as follows:

$$H_0\text{: } \mu_1 = \mu_2 = \mu_3$$
$$H_a\text{: Not all population means are equal}$$

FIGURE 10.5 F DISTRIBUTION: THE SAMPLING DISTRIBUTION OF MSTR/MSE

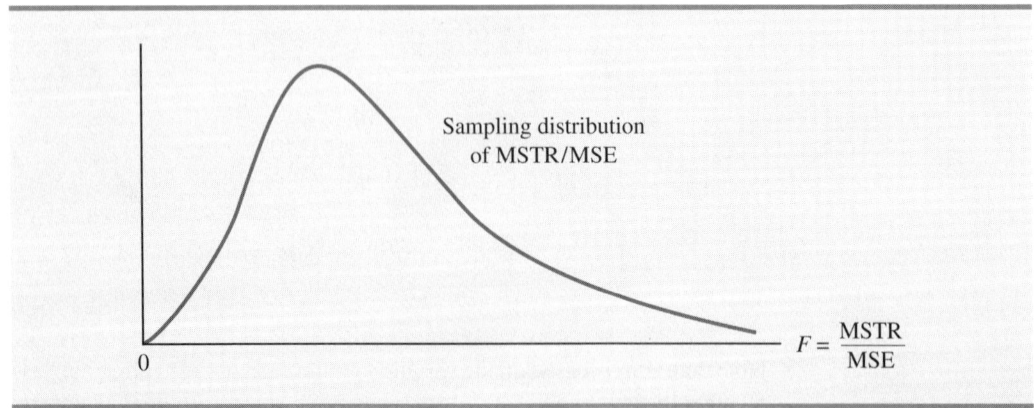

With the previously computed MSTR = 258 and MSE = 28.67, the value of the test statistic is

$$F = \frac{\text{MSTR}}{\text{MSE}} = \frac{258}{28.67} = 9$$

The numerator degrees of freedom is $k - 1 = 3 - 1 = 2$, and the denominator degrees of freedom is $n_T - k = 18 - 3 = 15$. Because we reject the null hypothesis for large values of the test statistic, we will compute the p-value as the upper tail area of the F distribution to the right of the test statistic $F = 9$. The usual hypothesis testing rule to reject H_0 if p-value $\leq \alpha$ applies.

Table 10.4 shows a portion of the F distribution table that will be helpful in this example. Using 2 numerator degrees of freedom and 15 denominator degrees of freedom, this table shows the following areas in the upper tail.

Area in Upper Tail	**.10**	**.05**	**.025**	**.01**
***F* Value ($df_1 = 2, df_2 = 15$)**	2.70	3.68	4.77	6.36

$F = 9$

Because $F = 9$ is greater than 6.36, the area in the upper tail at $F = 9$ is less than .01. Thus, the p-value is less than .01. With p-value $\leq \alpha = .05$, H_0 is rejected. The test provides sufficient evidence to conclude that the means of the three populations are not equal. In other words, analysis of variance supports the conclusion that the population mean examination scores at the three NCP plants are not equal.

Because the F table only provides values for upper tail areas of .10, .05, .025, and .01, we cannot determine the exact p-value directly from the table. Minitab or Excel provides the p-value as part of the standard ANOVA output. Appendixes 10.3 and 10.4 show the procedures that can be used. For the NCP example, the exact p-value corresponding to the test statistic $F = 9$ is .003.

As with other hypothesis testing procedures, the critical value approach may also be used. With $\alpha = .05$, the critical F value occurs with an area of .05 in the upper tail of an F distribution with 2 and 15 degrees of freedom. From the F distribution table, we find $F_{.05} = 3.68$. Hence, the appropriate upper tail rejection rule for the NCP example is

$$\text{Reject } H_0 \text{ if } F \geq 3.68$$

With $F = 9$, we reject H_0 and conclude that the means of the three populations are not equal. A summary of the overall procedure for testing for the equality of k population means follows.

TEST FOR THE EQUALITY OF k POPULATION MEANS

$$H_0\colon \mu_1 = \mu_2 = \cdots = \mu_k$$
$$H_a\colon \text{Not all population means are equal}$$

TEST STATISTIC

$$F = \frac{\text{MSTR}}{\text{MSE}}$$

REJECTION RULE

p-value approach: Reject H_0 if p value $\leq \alpha$
Critical value approach: Reject H_0 if $F \geq F_\alpha$

where the value of F_α is based on an F distribution with $k - 1$ numerator degrees of freedom and $n_T - k$ denominator degrees of freedom.

TABLE 10.4 SELECTED VALUES FROM THE *F* DISTRIBUTION TABLE

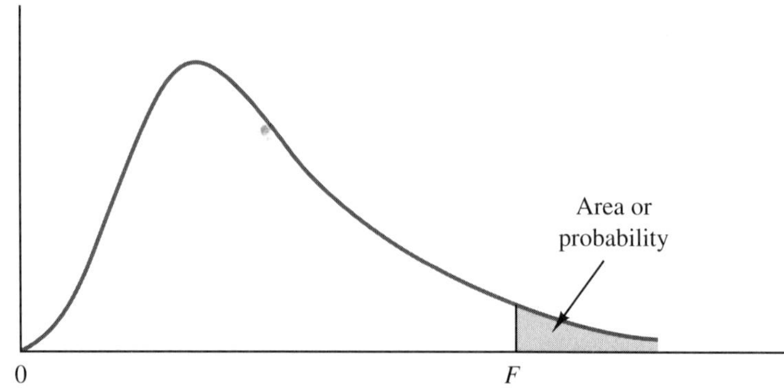

Denominator Degrees of Freedom	Area in Upper Tail	Numerator Degrees of Freedom				
		1	2	3	4	5
10	.10	3.29	2.92	2.73	2.61	2.52
	.05	4.96	4.10	3.71	3.48	3.33
	.025	6.94	5.46	4.83	4.47	4.24
	.01	10.04	7.56	6.55	5.99	5.64
15	.10	3.07	2.70	2.49	2.36	2.27
	.05	4.54	3.68	3.29	3.06	2.90
	.025	6.20	4.77	4.15	3.80	3.58
	.01	8.68	6.36	5.42	4.89	4.56
20	.10	2.97	2.59	2.38	2.25	2.16
	.05	4.35	3.49	3.10	2.87	2.71
	.025	5.87	4.46	3.86	3.51	3.29
	.01	8.10	5.85	4.94	4.43	4.10
25	.10	2.92	2.53	2.32	2.18	2.09
	.05	4.24	3.39	2.99	2.76	2.60
	.025	5.69	4.29	3.69	3.35	3.13
	.01	7.77	5.57	4.68	4.18	3.85
30	.10	2.88	2.49	2.28	2.14	2.05
	.05	4.17	3.32	2.92	2.69	2.53
	.025	5.57	4.18	3.59	3.25	3.03
	.01	7.56	5.39	4.51	4.02	3.70

Note: A more extensive table is provided as Table 4 of Appendix B.

ANOVA Table

The results of the preceding calculations can be displayed conveniently in a table referred to as the analysis of variance table, or **ANOVA table**. Table 10.5 is the analysis of variance table for the National Computer Products example. The sum of squares associated with the source of variation referred to as "Total" is called the *total sum of squares* (SST). Note that the results for the NCP example show SST = SSTR + SSE, and that the degrees of freedom associated with this total sum of squares is the sum of the degrees of freedom associated with the between-treatments estimate of σ^2 and the within-treatments estimate of σ^2.

TABLE 10.5 ANALYSIS OF VARIANCE TABLE FOR THE NCP EXAMPLE

Source of Variation	Sum of Squares	Degrees of Freedom	Mean Square	F
Treatments	516	2	258.00	9.00
Error	430	15	28.67	
Total	946	17		

We point out that SST divided by its degrees of freedom $n_T - 1$ is the overall sample variance that would be obtained if we treated the entire set of 18 observations as one data set. With the entire data set as one sample, the formula for computing the total sum of squares, SST, is

$$\text{SST} = \sum_{j=1}^{k}\sum_{i=1}^{n_j}(x_{ij} - \bar{\bar{x}})^2 \tag{10.22}$$

It can be shown that the results we observed for the analysis of variance table for the NCP example also apply to other problems. That is,

$$\text{SST} = \text{SSTR} + \text{SSE} \tag{10.23}$$

Analysis of variance can be thought of as a statistical procedure for partitioning the total sum of squares into separate components.

In other words, SST can be partitioned into two sums of squares: the sum of squares due to treatments and the sum of squares due to error. Note also that the degrees of freedom corresponding to SST, $n_T - 1$, can be partitioned into the degrees of freedom corresponding to SSTR, $k - 1$, and the degrees of freedom corresponding to SSE, $n_T - k$. The analysis of variance can be viewed as the process of **partitioning** the total sum of squares and the degrees of freedom into their corresponding sources: treatments and error. Dividing the sum of squares by the appropriate degrees of freedom provides the variance estimates and the F value used to test the hypothesis of equal population means.

Computer Results for Analysis of Variance

Because of the widespread availability of statistical computer packages, analysis of variance computations with large sample sizes or a large number of populations can be performed easily. In Figure 10.6 we show output for the NCP example obtained from the Minitab computer package. The first part of the computer output contains the familiar ANOVA table format. Comparing Figure 10.6 with Table 10.5, we see that the same information is available, although some of the headings are slightly different. The heading Source is used for the Source of Variation column, and Factor identifies the Treatments row. The Sum of Squares and Degrees of Freedom columns are interchanged, and a p-value is provided for the F test. Thus, at the $\alpha = .05$ level of significance, we reject H_0 because the p-value $= 0.003 \leq \alpha = .05$.

Note that following the ANOVA table the computer output contains the respective sample sizes, the sample means, and the standard deviations. In addition, Minitab provides a figure that shows individual 95% confidence interval estimates of each population mean. In developing these confidence interval estimates, Minitab uses MSE as the estimate of σ^2. Thus, the square root of MSE provides the best estimate of the population standard deviation σ. This estimate of σ on the computer output is Pooled StDev; it is equal to 5.354. To provide an illustration of how these interval estimates are developed, we will compute a 95% confidence interval estimate of the population mean for the Atlanta plant.

FIGURE 10.6 MINITAB OUTPUT FOR THE NCP ANALYSIS OF VARIANCE

```
Analysis of Variance
Source     DF        SS        MS         F        p
Factor      2     516.0     258.0      9.00    0.003
Error      15     430.0      28.7
Total      17     946.0
                                  Individual 95% Cis For Mean
                                  Based on Pooled StDev
 Level      N      Mean     StDev ---+---------+---------+---------+---
Atlanta     6    79.000     5.831                      (-----*-----)
Dallas      6    74.000     4.472             (-----*-----)
Seattle     6    66.000     5.657  (-----*-----)
                                  ---+---------+---------+---------+---
Pooled StDev =    5.354           63.0      70.0      77.0      84.0
```

From the study of interval estimation in Chapter 8, we know that the general form of an interval estimate of a population mean is

$$\bar{x} \pm t_{\alpha/2} \frac{s}{\sqrt{n}} \tag{10.24}$$

where s is the estimate of the population standard deviation σ. In the analysis of variance the best estimate of σ is provided by the square root of MSE or the Pooled StDev; therefore, we use a value of 5.354 for s in expression (10.24). The degrees of freedom for $t_{\alpha/2}$ is 15, the degrees of freedom associated with the within-treatments estimate of σ^2. Hence, at 95% confidence we have $t_{.025} = 2.131$ and

$$79 \pm 2.131 \frac{5.354}{\sqrt{6}} = 79 \pm 4.66$$

Thus, the individual 95% confidence interval for the Atlanta plant is from 79 − 4.66 = 74.34 to 79 + 4.66 = 83.66. Because the sample sizes are equal for the NCP example, the individual confidence intervals for the Dallas and Seattle plants are also constructed by adding and subtracting 4.66 from each sample mean. Thus, in the figure provided by Minitab we see that the widths of the confidence intervals are the same.

Exercises

Methods

27. Five observations were selected from each of three populations. The data obtained follow.

Observation	Sample 1	Sample 2	Sample 3
1	32	44	33
2	30	43	36
3	30	44	35

Observation	Sample 1	Sample 2	Sample 3
4	26	46	36
5	32	48	40
Sample mean	30	45	36
Sample variance	6.00	4.00	6.50

a. Compute the between-treatments estimate of σ^2.
b. Compute the within-treatments estimate of σ^2.
c. At the $\alpha = .05$ level of significance, can we reject the null hypothesis that the means of the three populations are equal?
d. Set up the ANOVA table for this problem.

28. Four observations were selected from each of three populations. The data obtained follow.

Observation	Sample 1	Sample 2	Sample 3
1	165	174	169
2	149	164	154
3	156	180	161
4	142	158	148
Sample mean	153	169	158
Sample variance	96.67	97.33	82.00

a. Compute the between-treatments estimate of σ^2.
b. Compute the within-treatments estimate of σ^2.
c. At the $\alpha = .05$ level of significance, can we reject the null hypothesis that the three population means are equal? Explain.
d. Set up the ANOVA table for this problem.

29. Samples were selected from three populations. The data obtained follow.

	Sample 1	Sample 2	Sample 3
	93	77	88
	98	87	75
	107	84	73
	102	95	84
		85	75
		82	
$\bar{x}_j$	100	85	79
s_j^2	35.33	35.60	43.50

a. Compute the between-treatments estimate of σ^2.
b. Compute the within-treatments estimate of σ^2.
c. At the $\alpha = .05$ level of significance, can we reject the null hypothesis that the three population means are equal? Explain.
d. Set up the ANOVA table for this problem.

30. A random sample of 16 observations was selected from each of four populations. A portion of the ANOVA table follows.

Source of Variation	Sum of Squares	Degrees of Freedom	Mean Square	F
Treatments			400	
Error				
Total	1500			

a. Provide the missing entries for the ANOVA table.
b. At the $\alpha = .05$ level of significance, can we reject the null hypothesis that the means of the four populations are equal?

31. Random samples of 25 observations were selected from each of three populations. For these data, SSTR = 120 and SSE = 216.
a. Set up the ANOVA table for this problem.
b. At the $\alpha = .05$ level of significance, can we reject the null hypothesis that the three population means are equal?

Applications

32. To test whether the mean time needed to mix a batch of material is the same for machines produced by three manufacturers, the Jacobs Chemical Company obtained the following data on the time (in minutes) needed to mix the material. Use these data to test whether the population mean times for mixing a batch of material differ for the three manufacturers. Use $\alpha = .05$.

	Manufacturer	
1	**2**	**3**
20	28	20
26	26	19
24	31	23
22	27	22

33. The Texas Transportation Institute at Texas A&M University conducted a survey to determine the number of hours per year drivers waste sitting in traffic. Of 75 urban areas studied, the most jammed urban area was Los Angeles where drivers wasted an average of 90 hours per year (*U.S. News & World Report,* October 13, 2003). Other jammed urban areas included Denver, Miami, and San Francisco. Assume sample data for six drivers in each of these cities show the following number of hours wasted per year sitting in traffic.

Denver	Miami	San Francisco
70	66	65
62	70	62
71	55	74
58	65	69
57	56	63
66	66	75

a. Compute the sample mean hours wasted per year for each of these urban areas.
b. Using $\alpha = .05$, test for significance differences among the population mean wasted time for these three urban areas. What is the p-value? What is your conclusion?

34. New York City, Boston, and the Silicon Valley of California are among the areas with the highest technology salaries in the United States (*USA Today,* February 28, 2002). The following sample data show individual annual salaries reported in thousands of dollars.

Technology

New York City	Boston	Silicon Valley
82	85	82
79	80	91
72	74	94
89	78	88
79	75	85
85	80	
	86	
	74	

Use $\alpha = .05$ and test for a significance difference among the population mean annual technology salaries for these three locations. What is the p-value? What is your conclusion? If a difference exists, which location appears to have the highest mean technology salary?

35. A study reported in the *Journal of Small Business Management* concluded that self-employed individuals experience higher job stress than individuals who are not self-employed. In this study job stress was assessed with a 15-item scale designed to measure various aspects of ambiguity and role conflict. Ratings for each of the 15 items were made using a scale of 1–5 indicating response options ranging from strong agreement to strong disagreement. The sum of the ratings for the 15 items for each individual surveyed is between 15 and 75, with higher values indicating a higher degree of job stress. Suppose that a similar approach, using a 20-item scale with 1–5 response options, was used to measure the job stress of individuals for 15 randomly selected real estate agents, 15 architects, and 15 stockbrokers. The results obtained follow.

Stress

Real Estate Agent	Architect	Stockbroker
81	43	65
48	63	48
68	60	57
69	52	91
54	54	70
62	77	67
76	68	83
56	57	75
61	61	53
65	80	71
64	50	54
69	37	72
83	73	65
85	84	58
75	58	58

Use $\alpha = .05$ to test for any significant difference in job stress among the three professions.

36. *Condé Nast Traveler* conducts an annual survey in which readers rate their favorite cruise ships. Ratings are provided for small ships (carrying up to 500 passengers), medium ships (carrying 500 to 1500 passengers), and large ships (carrying a minimum of 1500 passengers). The following data show the service ratings for eight randomly selected small ships, eight randomly selected medium ships, and eight randomly selected large ships. All ships are rated on a 100-point scale, with higher values indicating better service (*Condé Nast Traveler,* February 2003).

Ships

Small Ships		Medium Ships		Large Ships	
Name	**Rating**	**Name**	**Rating**	**Name**	**Rating**
Hanseactic	90.5	Amsterdam	91.1	Century	89.2
Mississippi Queen	78.2	Crystal Symphony	98.9	Disney Wonder	90.2
Philae	92.3	Maasdam	94.2	Enchantment of the Seas	85.9
Royal Clipper	95.7	Noordam	84.3	Grand Princess	84.2
Seabourn Pride	94.1	Royal Princess	84.8	Infinity	90.2
Seabourn Spirit	100	Ryndam	89.2	Legend of the Seas	80.6
Silver Cloud	91.8	Statendam	86.4	Paradise	75.8
Silver Wind	95	Veendam	88.3	Sun Princess	82.3

Use $\alpha = .05$ to test for any significant difference in the mean service ratings among the three sizes of cruise ships.

Summary

In this chapter we presented procedures for comparing two or more population means. First, we showed how to make inferences about the difference between two population means when independent simple random samples are selected. We considered the case where the population standard deviations, σ_1 and σ_2, could be assumed known. The standard normal distribution z was used to develop the interval estimate and served as the test statistic for hypothesis tests. We then considered the case where the population standard deviations were unknown and estimated by the sample standard deviations s_1 and s_2. In this case, the t distribution was used to develop the interval estimate and served as the test statistic for hypothesis tests.

Inferences about the difference between two population means were then discussed for the matched sample design. In the matched sample design each element provides a pair of data values, one from each population. The difference between the paired data values is then used in the statistical analysis. The matched sample design is generally preferred to the independent sample design because the matched-sample procedure often improves the precision of the estimate.

Finally, we showed how analysis of variance can be used to test for differences among three or more population means. The analysis of variance procedure uses two estimates of the population variance, σ^2. The ratio of these two estimates (the F statistic) can be used to provide the p-value and determine whether to reject the null hypothesis that the population means are equal.

Glossary

Independent simple random samples Samples selected from two populations in such a way that the elements making up one sample are chosen independently of the elements making up the other sample.

Matched samples Samples in which each data value of one sample is matched with a corresponding data value of the other sample.

Analysis of variance (ANOVA) A statistical technique that can be used to test the hypothesis that three or more population means are equal.

***F* distribution** A distribution based on the ratio of two independent estimates of the variance of a normal population. The distribution is used in hypothesis tests about the equality of k population means.

ANOVA table A table used to summarize the analysis of variance computations and results. It contains columns showing the source of variation, the sum of squares, the degrees of freedom, the mean square, and the F value.

Partitioning The process of allocating the total sum of squares and degrees of freedom to the various components.

Key Formulas

Point Estimator of the Difference Between Two Population Means

$$\bar{x}_1 - \bar{x}_2 \tag{10.1}$$

Standard Error of $\bar{x}_1 - \bar{x}_2$

$$\sigma_{\bar{x}_1 - \bar{x}_2} = \sqrt{\frac{\sigma_1^2}{n_1} + \frac{\sigma_2^2}{n_2}} \tag{10.2}$$

Interval Estimate of the Difference Between Two Population Means: σ_1 and σ_2 Known

$$\bar{x}_1 - \bar{x}_2 \pm z_{\alpha/2}\sqrt{\frac{\sigma_1^2}{n_1} + \frac{\sigma_2^2}{n_2}} \tag{10.4}$$

Test Statistic for Hypothesis Tests About $\mu_1 - \mu_2$: σ_1 and σ_2 Known

$$z = \frac{(\bar{x}_1 - \bar{x}_2) - D_0}{\sqrt{\frac{\sigma_1^2}{n_1} + \frac{\sigma_2^2}{n_2}}} \tag{10.5}$$

Interval Estimate of the Difference Between Two Population Means: σ_1 and σ_2 Unknown

$$\bar{x}_1 - \bar{x}_2 \pm t_{\alpha/2}\sqrt{\frac{s_1^2}{n_1} + \frac{s_2^2}{n_2}} \tag{10.6}$$

Degrees of Freedom for the t Distribution Using Two Independent Random Samples

$$df = \frac{\left(\frac{s_1^2}{n_1} + \frac{s_2^2}{n_2}\right)^2}{\frac{1}{n_1 - 1}\left(\frac{s_1^2}{n_1}\right)^2 + \frac{1}{n_2 - 1}\left(\frac{s_2^2}{n_2}\right)^2} \tag{10.7}$$

Test Statistic for Hypothesis Tests About $\mu_1 - \mu_2$: σ_1 and σ_2 Unknown

$$t = \frac{(\bar{x}_1 - \bar{x}_2) - D_0}{\sqrt{\frac{s_1^2}{n_1} + \frac{s_2^2}{n_2}}} \tag{10.8}$$

Test Statistic for Hypothesis Tests Involving Matched Samples

$$t = \frac{\bar{d} - \mu_d}{s_d/\sqrt{n}} \tag{10.9}$$

Sample Mean for Treatment j

$$\bar{x}_j = \frac{\sum_{i=1}^{n_j} x_{ij}}{n_j} \tag{10.10}$$

Sample Variance for Treatment j

$$s_j^2 = \frac{\sum_{i=1}^{n_j} (x_{ij} - \bar{x}_j)^2}{n_j - 1} \tag{10.11}$$

Overall Sample Mean

$$\bar{\bar{x}} = \frac{\sum_{j=1}^{k} \sum_{i=1}^{n_j} x_{ij}}{n_T} \tag{10.12}$$

$$n_T = n_1 + n_2 + \cdots + n_k \tag{10.13}$$

Mean Square Due to Treatments

$$\text{MSTR} = \frac{\text{SSTR}}{k - 1} \tag{10.16}$$

Sum of Squares Due to Treatments

$$\text{SSTR} = \sum_{j=1}^{k} n_j(\bar{x}_j - \bar{\bar{x}})^2 \tag{10.17}$$

Mean Square Due to Error

$$\text{MSE} = \frac{\text{SSE}}{n_T - k} \tag{10.19}$$

Sum of Squares Due to Error

$$\text{SSE} = \sum_{j=1}^{k} (n_j - 1)s_j^2 \tag{10.20}$$

Test Statistic for the Equality of k Population Means

$$F = \frac{\text{MSTR}}{\text{MSE}} \tag{10.21}$$

Total Sum of Squares

$$\text{SST} = \sum_{j=1}^{k} \sum_{i=1}^{n_j} (x_{ij} - \bar{\bar{x}})^2 \tag{10.22}$$

Partitioning of Sum of Squares

$$\text{SST} = \text{SSTR} + \text{SSE} \tag{10.23}$$

Supplementary Exercises

37. Safegate Foods, Inc., is redesigning the checkout lanes in its supermarkets throughout the country and is considering two designs. Tests on customer checkout times conducted at two stores where the two new systems have been installed result in the following summary of the data.

System A	System B
$n_1 = 120$	$n_2 = 100$
$\bar{x}_1 = 4.1$ minutes	$\bar{x}_2 = 3.4$ minutes
$\sigma_1 = 2.2$ minutes	$\sigma_2 = 1.5$ minutes

Test at the .05 level of significance to determine whether the population mean checkout times of the two systems differ. Which system is preferred?

38. Starting annual salaries for individuals with master's and bachelor's degrees in business were collected in two independent random samples. Use the following data to develop a 90% confidence interval estimate of the increase in starting salary that can be expected upon completion of a master's program.

Master's Degree	Bachelor's Degree
$n_1 = 60$	$n_2 = 80$
$\bar{x}_1 = \$45{,}000$	$\bar{x}_2 = \$35{,}000$
$\sigma_1 = \$4000$	$\sigma_2 = \$3500$

39. Three-megapixel digital cameras are typically the lightest, most compact, and easiest to use. However, if you plan to enlarge or crop images, you will probably want to spend more for a higher-resolution model. The following shows sample prices of five-megapixel and three-megapixel digital cameras (*Consumer Reports Buying Guide,* 2004).

Five-Megapixel		Three-Megapixel	
Model	**Price**	**Model**	**Price**
Nikon 5700	890	Kodak DX4330	280
Olympus C-5050	620	Canon A70	290
Sony DCS-F717	730	Sony DSC P8	370
Olympus C-5050	480	Minolta XI	400
Minolta 7Hi	1060	Sony DSC P72	310
HP 935	450	Nikon 3100	340
Pentax 550	540	Panasonic DMC-LC33	270
Canon S50	500	Pentax S	380
Kyocera TVS	890		
Minolta F300	440		

a. Provide a point estimate of the difference between population mean prices for the two types of digital cameras. What observation can you make about the price of the higher-quality five-megapixel model?

b. Develop a 95% confidence interval estimate of the difference between the two population mean prices.

40. Mutual funds are classified as *load* or *no-load* funds. Load funds require an investor to pay an initial fee based on a percentage of the amount invested in the fund. The no-load funds do not require this initial fee. Some financial advisors argue that the load mutual funds may be worth the extra fee because these funds provide a higher mean rate of return than the no-load mutual funds. A sample of 30 load mutual funds and a sample of 30 no-load mutual funds were selected. Data were collected on the annual return for the funds over a five-year period. The data are contained in the data set Mutual. The data for the first five load and first five no-load mutual funds are as follows.

Mutual

Mutual Funds—Load	Return	Mutual Funds—No Load	Return
American National Growth	15.51	Amana Income Fund	13.24
Arch Small Cap Equity	14.57	Berger One Hundred	12.13
Bartlett Cap Basic	17.73	Columbia International Stock	12.17
Calvert World International	10.31	Dodge & Cox Balanced	16.06
Colonial Fund A	16.23	Evergreen Fund	17.61

a. Formulate H_0 and H_a such that rejection of H_0 leads to the conclusion that the load mutual funds have a higher mean annual return over the five-year period.
b. Use the 60 mutual funds in the data set Mutual to conduct the hypothesis test. What is the p-value? At $\alpha = .05$, what is your conclusion?

41. The National Association of Home Builders provided data on the cost of the most popular home remodeling projects. Sample data on cost in thousands of dollars for two types of remodeling projects are as follows.

Kitchen	Master Bedroom	Kitchen	Master Bedroom
25.2	18.0	23.0	17.8
17.4	22.9	19.7	24.6
22.8	26.4	16.9	21.0
21.9	24.8	21.8	
19.7	26.9	23.6	

a. Develop a point estimate of the difference between the population mean remodeling costs for the two types of projects.
b. Develop a 90% confidence interval for the difference between the two population means.

42. Typical prices of single-family homes in the state of Florida are shown for a sample of 15 metropolitan areas (*Naples Daily News,* February 23, 2003). Data are in thousands of dollars.

Florida

Metropolitan Area	January 2003	January 2002
Daytona Beach	117	96
Fort Lauderdale	207	169
Fort Myers	143	129
Fort Walton Beach	139	134
Gainesville	131	119
Jacksonville	128	119
Lakeland	91	85
Miami	193	165
Naples	263	233
Ocala	86	90

Metropolitan Area	January 2003	January 2002
Orlando	134	121
Pensacola	111	105
Sarasota-Bradenton	168	141
Tallahassee	140	130
Tampa-St. Petersburg	139	129

a. Use a matched-sample analysis to develop a point estimate of the population mean one-year increase in the price of single-family homes in Florida.
b. Develop a 90% confidence interval estimate of the population mean one-year increase in the price of single-family homes in Florida.
c. What was the percentage increase over the one-year period?

43. *Money* magazine reports percentage returns and expense ratios for stock and bond funds. The following data are the expense ratios for 10 midcap stock funds, 10 small-cap stock funds, 10 hybrid stock funds, and 10 specialty stock funds (*Money,* March 2003).

Funds

Midcap	Small-Cap	Hybrid	Specialty
1.2	2.0	2.0	1.6
1.1	1.2	2.7	2.7
1.0	1.7	1.8	2.6
1.2	1.8	1.5	2.5
1.3	1.5	2.5	1.9
1.8	2.3	1.0	1.5
1.4	1.9	0.9	1.6
1.4	1.3	1.9	2.7
1.0	1.2	1.4	2.2
1.4	1.3	0.3	0.7

Use $\alpha = .05$ to test for any significant difference in the mean expense ratio among the four types of stock funds.

44. Buyers of sport utility vehicles (SUVs) and pickup trucks find a wide choice in today's marketplace. One of the factors important to many buyers is the resale value of the vehicle. The following table shows the resale value (%) after two years for 10 SUVs, 10 small pickup trucks, and 10 large pickup trucks (*Kiplinger's New Cars & Trucks 2000 Buyer's Guide*).

Trucks

Sport Utility	Resale Value	Small Pickup	Resale Value
Chevrolet Blazer LS	55	Chevrolet S-10 Extended Cab	46
Ford Explorer Sport	57	Dodge Dakota Club Cab Sport	53
GMC Yukon XL 1500	67	Ford Ranger XLT Regular Cab	48
Honda CR-V	65	Ford Ranger XLT Supercab	55
Isuzu VehiCross	62	GMC Sonoma Regular Cab	44
Jeep Cherokee Limited	57	Isuzu Hombre Spacecab	41
Mercury Mountaineer	59	Mazda B4000 SE Cab Plus	51
Nissan Pathfinder XE	54	Nissan Frontier XE Regular Cab	51
Toyota 4Runner	55	Toyota Tacoma Xtracab	49
Toyota RAV4	55	Toyota Tacoma Xtracab V6	50

(continued)

Full-Size Pickup	Resale Value
Chevrolet K2500	60
Chevrolet Silverado 2500 Ext	64
Dodge Ram 1500	54
Dodge Ram Quad Cab 2500	63
Dodge Ram Regular Cab 2500	59
Ford F150 XL	58
Ford F350 Super Duty Crew Cab XL	64
GMC New Sierra 1500 Ext Cab	68
Toyota Tundra Access Cab Limited	53
Toyota Tundra Regular Cab	58

At the $\alpha = .05$ level of significance, test for any significant difference in the mean resale value for the three types of vehicles.

45. Crown Plaza Hotels and Resorts offered special weekend rates at hotels at resorts nationwide. A sample of 30 properties from three regions of the country provided the following room rates (*USA Today*, April 14, 2000).

Resorts

West	Rate ($)	South	Rate ($)	Northeast	Rate ($)
Albuquerque	89	Atlanta	105	Albany	89
Irvine	79	Dallas	80	Boston	139
Las Vegas	119	Greenville	79	Hartford	85
Los Angeles	99	Houston	79	New York	159
Palo Alto	109	Jackson	69	Philadelphia	99
Phoenix	149	Macon	69	Pittsfield	99
Portland	79	Miami	89	Providence	149
San Francisco	139	Orlando	119	Washington	159
San Jose	99	Richmond	109	White Plains	109
Seattle	119	Tampa	119	Worchester	124

At the $\alpha = .05$ level of significance, test whether the mean rates are the same for the three regions.

46. The National Football League rates prospects by position on a scale that ranges from 5 to 9. The ratings are interpreted as follows: 8–9 should start the first year; 7.0–7.9 should start; 6.0–6.9 will make the team as backup; and 5.0–5.9 can make the club and contribute. The following table shows the ratings for three positions for 40 NFL prospects (*USA Today*, April 14, 2000). Does there appear to be any significant effect on the rating due to the player's position?

NFL

Wide Receiver		Guard		Offensive Tackle	
Name	Rating	Name	Rating	Name	Rating
Peter Warrick	9.0	Cosey Coleman	7.4	Chris Samuels	8.5
Plaxico Burress	8.8	Travis Claridge	7.0	Stockar McDougle	8.0
Sylvester Morris	8.3	Kaulana Noa	6.8	Chris McIngosh	7.8
Travis Taylor	8.1	Leander Jordan	6.7	Adrian Klemm	7.6
Laveranues Coles	8.0	Chad Clifton	6.3	Todd Wade	7.3
Dez White	7.9	Manula Savea	6.1	Marvel Smith	7.1
Jerry Porter	7.4	Ryan Johanningmeir	6.0	Michael Thompson	6.8
Ron Dugans	7.1	Mark Tauscher	6.0	Bobby Williams	6.8
Todd Pinkston	7.0	Blaine Saipaia	6.0	Darnell Alford	6.4

Wide Receiver		Guard		Offensive Tackle	
Name	**Rating**	**Name**	**Rating**	**Name**	**Rating**
Dennis Northcutt	7.0	Richard Mercier	5.8	Terrance Beadles	6.3
Anthony Lucas	6.9	Damion McIntosh	5.3	Tutan Reyes	6.1
Darrell Jackson	6.6	Jeno James	5.5	Greg Robinson-Ran	6.0
Danny Farmer	6.5	Al Jackson	5.5		
Sherrod Gideon	6.4				
Trevor Gaylor	6.2				

Case Problem 1 Par, Inc.

Par, Inc., is a major manufacturer of golf equipment. Management believes that Par's market share could be increased with the introduction of a cut-resistant, longer-lasting golf ball. Therefore, the research group at Par has been investigating a new golf ball coating designed to resist cuts and provide a more durable ball. The tests with the coating have been promising.

One of the researchers voiced concern about the effect of the new coating on driving distances. Par would like the new cut-resistant ball to offer driving distances comparable to those of the current-model golf ball. To compare the driving distances for the two balls, 40 balls of both the new and current models were subjected to distance tests. The testing was performed with a mechanical hitting machine so that any difference between the mean distances for the two models could be attributed to a difference in the two models. The results of the tests, with distances measured to the nearest yard, follow. These data are available on the CD that accompanies the text.

Golf

Model		Model		Model		Model	
Current	**New**	**Current**	**New**	**Current**	**New**	**Current**	**New**
264	277	270	272	263	274	281	283
261	269	287	259	264	266	274	250
267	263	289	264	284	262	273	253
272	266	280	280	263	271	263	260
258	262	272	274	260	260	275	270
283	251	275	281	283	281	267	263
258	262	265	276	255	250	279	261
266	289	260	269	272	263	274	255
259	286	278	268	266	278	276	263
270	264	275	262	268	264	262	279

Managerial Report

1. Formulate and present the rationale for a hypothesis test that Par could use to compare the driving distances of the current and new golf balls.
2. Analyze the data to provide the hypothesis testing conclusion. What is the p-value for your test? What is your recommendation for Par, Inc.?
3. Provide descriptive statistical summaries of the data for each model.
4. What is the 95% confidence interval for the population mean of each model, and what is the 95% confidence interval for the difference between the means of the two populations?
5. Do you see a need for larger sample sizes and more testing with the golf balls? Discuss.

Case Problem 2 Wentworth Medical Center

As part of a long-term study of individuals 65 years of age or older, sociologists and physicians at the Wentworth Medical Center in upstate New York investigated the relationship between geographic location and depression. A sample of 60 individuals, all in reasonably good health, was selected; 20 individuals were residents of Florida, 20 were residents of New York, and 20 were residents of North Carolina. Each of the individuals sampled was given a standardized test to measure depression. The data collected follow; higher test scores indicate higher levels of depression. These data are available on the data disk in the file Medical1.

A second part of the study considered the relationship between geographic location and depression for individuals 65 years of age or older who had a chronic health condition such as arthritis, hypertension, and/or heart ailment. A sample of 60 individuals with such conditions was identified. Again, 20 were residents of Florida, 20 were residents of New York, and 20 were residents of North Carolina. The levels of depression recorded for this study follow. These data are available on the CD accompanying the text in the file named Medical2.

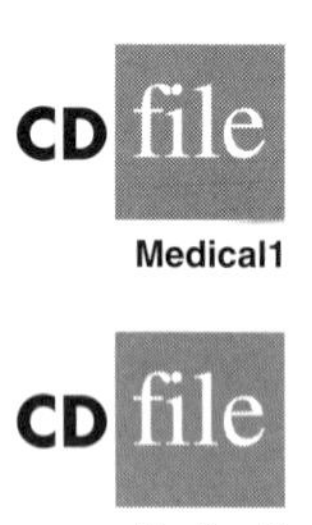

Data from Medical1			Data from Medical2		
Florida	New York	North Carolina	Florida	New York	North Carolina
3	8	10	13	14	10
7	11	7	12	9	12
7	9	3	17	15	15
3	7	5	17	12	18
8	8	11	20	16	12
8	7	8	21	24	14
8	8	4	16	18	17
5	4	3	14	14	8
5	13	7	13	15	14
2	10	8	17	17	16
6	6	8	12	20	18
2	8	7	9	11	17
6	12	3	12	23	19
6	8	9	15	19	15
9	6	8	16	17	13
7	8	12	15	14	14
5	5	6	13	9	11
4	7	3	10	14	12
7	7	8	11	13	13
3	8	11	17	11	11

Managerial Report

1. Use descriptive statistics to summarize the data from the two studies. What are your preliminary observations about the depression scores?
2. Use analysis of variance on both data sets. State the hypotheses being tested in each case. What are your conclusions?
3. Use inferences about individual treatment means where appropriate. What are your conclusions?
4. Discuss extensions of this study or other analyses that you feel might be helpful.

Case Problem 3 Compensation for ID Professionals

For the preceding 10 years *Industrial Distribution* tracked compensation of industrial distribution (ID) professionals. Results for the 358 respondents in the 1997 Annual Salary Survey showed that 27% of the respondents work for companies with sales over $40 million, with the typical ID professional working for a $12 million firm. Those who work for small to mid-sized companies (between $6 million and $20 million) report higher earnings than those in larger firms. The lowest paid employees work for firms with sales of less than $1 million. The typical outside salesperson made $50,000 in 1996, and the typical inside salesperson earned just $30,000 (*Industrial Distribution*, November 1997). Suppose that a local chapter of ID professionals in the greater San Francisco area conducted a survey of its membership to study the relationship, if any, between the years of experience and salary for individuals employed in outside and inside sales positions. On the survey, respondents were asked to specify one of three levels of years of experience: low (1–10 years), medium (11–20 years), and high (21 or more years). A portion of the data obtained follows. The complete data set, consisting of 120 observations, is available on the CD accompanying the text in the file named IDSalary.

IDSalary

Observation	Salary $	Position	Experience
1	28938	Inside	Medium
2	27694	Inside	Medium
3	45515	Outside	Low
4	27031	Inside	Medium
5	37283	Outside	Low
6	32718	Inside	Low
7	54081	Outside	High
8	23621	Inside	Low
9	47835	Outside	High
10	29768	Inside	Medium
.	.	.	.
.	.	.	.
.	.	.	.
115	33080	Inside	High
116	53702	Outside	Medium
117	58131	Outside	Medium
118	32788	Inside	High
119	28070	Inside	Medium
120	35259	Outside	Low

Managerial Report

1. Use descriptive statistics to summarize the data.
2. Develop a 95% confidence interval estimate of the mean annual salary for all salespersons, regardless of years of experience and type of position.
3. Develop a 95% confidence interval estimate of the mean salary for outside salespersons. Compare your results with the national value reported by *Industrial Distribution.*
4. Develop a 95% confidence interval estimate of the mean salary for inside salespersons. Compare your results with the national value reported by *Industrial Distribution.*
5. Ignoring the years of experience, develop a 95% confidence interval estimate of the mean difference between the annual salary for outside salespersons and the mean annual salary for inside salespersons. What is your conclusion?

6. Use analysis of variance to test for any significant differences due to position. Use a .05 level of significance, and for now, ignore the effect of years of experience.
7. Use analysis of variance to test for any significant differences due to years of experience. Use a .05 level of significance, and for now, ignore the effect of position.
8. At the .05 level of significance test for any significant differences due to position, years of experience, and interaction. Use inferences about individual treatment means where appropriate.

Appendix 10.1 Inferences About Two Populations Using Minitab

We describe the use of Minitab to develop interval estimates and conduct hypothesis tests about the difference between two population means and the difference between two population proportions. Minitab provides both interval estimation and hypothesis testing results within the same module. Thus, the Minitab procedure is the same for both types of inferences. In the examples that follow, we will demonstrate interval estimation and hypothesis testing for the same two samples. We note that Minitab does not provide a routine for inferences about the difference between two population means when the population standard deviations σ_1 and σ_2 are known.

Difference Between Two Population Means: σ_1 and σ_2 Unknown

CheckAcct

We will use the data for the checking account balances example presented in Section 10.2. The checking account balances at the Cherry Grove branch are in column C1, and the checking account balances at the Beechmont branch are in column C2. In this example, we will use the Minitab 2-Sample *t* procedure to provide a 95% confidence interval estimate of the difference between population means for the checking account balances at the two branch banks. The output of the procedure also provides the *p*-value for the hypothesis test: $H_0: \mu_1 - \mu_2 = 0$ versus $H_a: \mu_1 - \mu_2 \neq 0$. The following steps are necessary to execute the procedure:

Step 1. Select the **Stat** menu
Step 2. Choose **Basic Statistics**
Step 3. Choose **2-Sample t**
Step 4. When the 2-Sample t (Test and Confidence Interval) dialog box appears:
    Select **Samples in different columns**
    Enter C1 in the **First** box
    Enter C2 in the **Second** box
    Select **Options**
Step 5. When the 2-Sample t - Options dialog box appears:
    Enter 95 in the **Confidence level** box
    Enter 0 in the **Test difference** box
    Enter not equal in the **Alternative** box
    Click **OK**
Step 6. Click **OK**

The 95% confidence interval estimate is \$37 to \$193 as described in Section 10.2. The *p*-value = .005 shows the null hypothesis of equal population means can be rejected at the $\alpha = .01$ level of significance. In other applications, step 5 may be modified to provide different confidence levels, different hypothesized values, and different forms of the hypotheses.

Difference Between Two Population Means with Matched Samples

Matched

We use the data on production times in Table 10.2 to illustrate the matched sample procedure. The completion times for method 1 are entered into column C1 and the completion times for method 2 are entered into column C2. The Minitab steps for a matched sample are as follows:

Step 1. Select the **Stat** menu
Step 2. Choose **Basic Statistics**
Step 3. Choose **Paired t**
Step 4. When the Paired t (Test and Confidence Interval) dialog box appears:
Select **Samples in columns**
Enter C1 in the **First sample** box
Enter C2 in the **Second sample** box
Select **Options**
Step 5. When the Paired t - Options dialog box appears:
Enter 95 in the **Confidence level**
Enter 0 in the **Test mean** box
Enter not equal in the **Alternative** box
Click **OK**
Step 6. Click **OK**

Step 5 may be modified to provide different confidence levels, different hypothesized values, and different forms of the hypotheses.

Appendix 10.2 Inferences About Two Populations Using Excel

We describe the use of Excel to conduct hypothesis tests about the difference between two population means.* We begin with inferences about the difference between the means of two populations when the population standard deviations σ_1 and σ_2 are known.

Difference Between Two Population Means: σ_1 and σ_2 Known

ExamScores

We will use the examination scores for the two training centers discussed in Section 10.1. The label Center A is in cell A1 and the label Center B is in cell B1. The examination scores for center A are in cells A2:A31, and examination scores for center B are in cells B2:B41. The population standard deviations are assumed known with $\sigma_1 = 10$ and $\sigma_2 = 10$. The Excel routine will request the input of variances, which are $\sigma_1^2 = 100$ and $\sigma_2^2 = 100$. The following steps can be used to conduct a hypothesis test about the difference between the two population means.

Step 1. Select the **Tools** menu
Step 2. Choose **Data Analysis**
Step 3. When the Data Analysis dialog box appears:
Choose **z-Test: Two Sample for Means**
Click **OK**

*Excel's data analysis tools provide hypothesis testing procedures for the difference between two population means. However, there is no Excel routine for interval estimation of the difference between two population means.

Step 4. When the z-Test: Two Sample for Means dialog box appears:
Enter A1:A31 in the **Variable 1 Range** box
Enter B1:B41 in the **Variable 2 Range** box
Enter 0 in the **Hypothesized Mean Difference** box
Enter 100 in the **Variable 1 Variance** box
Enter 100 in the **Variable 2 Variance** box
Select **Labels**
Enter .05 in the **Alpha** box
Select **Output Range** and enter C1 in the box
Click **OK**

Difference Between Two Population Means: σ_1 and σ_2 Unknown

SoftwareTest

We use the data for the software testing study in Table 10.1. The data are already entered into an Excel worksheet with the label Current in cell A1 and the label New in cell B1. The completion times for the current technology are in cells A2:A13, and the completion times for the new software are in cells B2:B13. The following steps can be used to conduct a hypothesis test about the difference between two population means with σ_1 and σ_2 unknown.

Step 1. Select the **Tools** menu
Step 2. Choose **Data Analysis**
Step 3. When the Data Analysis dialog box appears:
Choose **t-Test: Two Sample Assuming Unequal Variances**
Click **OK**
Step 4. When the t-Test: Two Sample Assuming Unequal Variances dialog box appears:
Enter A1:A13 in the **Variable 1 Range** box
Enter B1:B13 in the **Variable 2 Range** box
Enter 0 in the **Hypothesized Mean Difference** box
Select **Labels**
Enter .05 in the **Alpha** box
Select **Output Range** and enter C1 in the box
Click **OK**

Difference Between Two Population Means with Matched Samples

Matched

We use the matched sample completion times in Table 10.2 to illustrate. The data are entered into a worksheet with the label Method 1 in cell A1 and the label Method 2 in cell B1. The completion times for method 1 are in cells A2:A7 and the completion times for method 2 are in cells B2:B7. The Excel procedure uses the steps previously described for the *t*-Test except the user chooses the **t-Test: Paired Two Sample for Means** data analysis tool in step 3. The variable 1 range is A1:A7 and the variable 2 range is B1:B7.

Appendix 10.3 Analysis of Variance with Minitab

NCP

To illustrate how Minitab can be used to test for the equality of *k* population means, we show how to test whether the mean examination score is the same at each plant in the National Computer Products example introduced in Section 10.4. The examination score data are entered into the first three columns of a Minitab worksheet; column 1 is labeled Atlanta, column 2 is labeled Dallas, and column 3 is labeled Seattle. The following steps produce the Minitab output in Figure 10.6.

Step 1. Select the **Stat** menu
Step 2. Choose **ANOVA**
Step 3. Choose **One-way (Unstacked)**
Step 4. When the One-way Analysis of Variance dialog box appears:
Enter C1-C3 in the **Responses (in separate columns)** box
Click **OK**

Appendix 10.4 Analysis of Variance with Excel

NCP

To illustrate how Excel can be used to test for the equality of k population means for both of these cases, we show how to test whether the mean examination score is the same at each plant in the National Computer Products example introduced in Section 10.4. The examination score data are entered into worksheet rows 2 to 7 of columns B, C, and D as shown in Figure 10.7; note that the cells in row 1 are labeled Atlanta, Dallas, and Seattle. The following steps are used to obtain the output shown in cells A9:G23; the ANOVA portion of this output corresponds to the ANOVA table shown in Table 10.5.

Step 1. Select the **Tools** menu
Step 2. Choose **Data Analysis**

FIGURE 10.7 EXCEL SOLUTION FOR THE NCP ANALYSIS OF VARIANCE EXAMPLE

	A	B	C	D	E	F	G	H
1	**Observation**	**Atlanta**	**Dallas**	**Seattle**				
2	1	85	71	59				
3	2	75	75	64				
4	3	82	73	62				
5	4	76	74	69				
6	5	71	69	75				
7	6	85	82	67				
8								
9	Anova: Single Factor							
10								
11	SUMMARY							
12	*Groups*	*Count*	*Sum*	*Average*	*Variance*			
13	Atlanta	6	474	79	34			
14	Dallas	6	444	74	20			
15	Seattle	6	396	66	32			
16								
17								
18	ANOVA							
19	*Source of Variation*	*SS*	*df*	*MS*	*F*	*P-value*	*F crit*	
20	Between Groups	516	2	258	9	0.0027	3.68	
21	Within Groups	430	15	28.6667				
22								
23	Total	946	17					
24								

Step 3. When the Data Analysis dialog box appears:
Choose **Anova: Single-Factor** from the list of Analysis Tools
Click **OK**

Step 4. When the Anova: Single-Factor dialog box appears:
Enter B1:D7 in the **Input Range** box
Select **Columns**
Select **Labels in First Row**
Select **Output Range** and enter A9 in the box
Click **OK**

CHAPTER 12

Simple Linear Regression

CONTENTS

STATISTICS *in* PRACTICE

ALLIANCE DATA SYSTEMS*
DALLAS, TEXAS

Alliance Data Systems (ADS) provides transaction processing, credit services, and marketing services for clients in the rapidly growing customer relationship management (CRM) industry. ADS clients are concentrated in four industries: retail, petroleum/convenience stores, utilities, and transportation. In 1983, Alliance began offering end-to-end credit processing services to the retail, petroleum, and casual dining industries; today they employ more than 6500 employees who provide services to clients around the world. Operating more than 140,000 point-of-sale terminals in the United States alone, ADS processes in excess of 2.5 billion transactions annually. The company ranks second in the United States in private label credit services by representing 49 private label programs with nearly 72 million cardholders. In 2001, ADS made an initial public offering and is now listed on the New York Stock Exchange.

As one of its marketing services, ADS designs direct mail campaigns and promotions. With its database containing information on the spending habits of more than 100 million consumers, ADS can target those consumers most likely to benefit from a direct mail promotion. The Analytical Development Group uses regression analysis to build models that measure and predict the responsiveness of consumers to direct market campaigns. Some regression models predict the probability of purchase for individuals receiving a promotion, and others predict the amount spent by those consumers making a purchase.

For one particular campaign, a retail store chain wanted to attract new customers. To predict the effect of the campaign, ADS analysts selected a sample from the consumer database, sent the sampled individuals promotional materials, and then collected transaction data on the consumers' response. Sample data were collected on the amount of purchase made by the consumers responding to the campaign, as well as a variety of consumer-specific variables thought to be useful in predicting sales. The consumer-specific variable that contributed most to predicting the amount purchased was the total amount of credit purchases at related stores over the past 39 months. ADS analysts developed an estimated regression equation relating the amount of purchase to the amount spent at related stores:

Alliance Data analysts discuss use of a regression model to predict sales for a direct marketing campaign. © Courtesy of Alliance Data Systems.

$$\hat{y} = 26.7 + 0.00205x$$

where

$$\hat{y} = \text{amount of purchase}$$
$$x = \text{amount spent at related stores}$$

Using this equation, we could predict that someone spending $10,000 over the past 39 months at related stores would spend $47.20 when responding to the direct mail promotion. In this chapter, you will learn how to develop this type of estimated regression equation.

The final model developed by ADS analysts also included several other variables that increased the predictive power of the preceding equation. Some of these variables included the absence/presence of a bank credit card, estimated income, and the average amount spent per trip at a selected store. In the following chapter, we will learn how such additional variables can be incorporated into a multiple regression model.

*The authors are indebted to Philip Clemance, director of analytical development at Alliance Data Systems, for providing this Statistics in Practice.

Managerial decisions often are based on the relationship between two or more variables. For example, after considering the relationship between advertising expenditures and sales, a marketing manager might attempt to predict sales for a given level of advertising expenditures. In another case, a public utility might use the relationship between the daily high temperature and the demand for electricity to predict electricity usage on the basis of next month's anticipated daily high temperatures. Sometimes a manager will rely on intuition to judge how two variables are related. However, if data can be obtained, a statistical procedure called *regression analysis* can be used to develop an equation showing how the variables are related.

The statistical methods used in studying the relationship between two variables were first employed by Sir Francis Galton (1822–1911). Galton was interested in studying the relationship between a father's height and the son's height. Galton's disciple, Karl Pearson (1857–1936), analyzed the relationship between the father's height and the son's height for 1078 pairs of subjects.

In regression terminology, the variable being predicted is called the **dependent variable**. The variable or variables being used to predict the value of the dependent variable are called the **independent variables**. For example, in analyzing the effect of advertising expenditures on sales, a marketing manager's desire to predict sales would suggest making sales the dependent variable. Advertising expenditure would be the independent variable used to help predict sales. In statistical notation, y denotes the dependent variable and x denotes the independent variable.

In this chapter we consider the simplest type of regression analysis involving one independent variable and one dependent variable in which the relationship between the variables is approximated by a straight line. It is called **simple linear regression**. Regression analysis involving two or more independent variables is called multiple regression analysis; multiple regression is covered in Chapter 13.

12.1 Simple Linear Regression Model

Armand's Pizza Parlors is a chain of Italian-food restaurants located in a five-state area. Armand's most successful locations are near college campuses. The managers believe that quarterly sales for these restaurants (denoted by y) are related positively to the size of the student population (denoted by x); that is, restaurants near campuses with a large student population tend to generate more sales than those located near campuses with a small student population. Using regression analysis, we can develop an equation showing how the dependent variable y is related to the independent variable x.

Regression Model and Regression Equation

In the Armand's Pizza Parlors example, the population consists of all the Armand's restaurants. For every restaurant in the population, a value of x (student population) corresponds to a value of y (quarterly sales). The equation that describes how y is related to x and an error term is called the **regression model**. The regression model used in simple linear regression follows.

SIMPLE LINEAR REGRESSION MODEL

$$y = \beta_0 + \beta_1 x + \epsilon \tag{12.1}$$

β_0 and β_1 are referred to as the parameters of the model, and ϵ (the Greek letter epsilon) is a random variable referred to as the error term. The error term accounts for the variability in y that cannot be explained by the linear relationship between x and y.

The population of all Armand's restaurants can also be viewed as a collection of subpopulations, one for each distinct value of x. For example, one subpopulation consists of all Armand's restaurants located near college campuses with 8000 students; another subpopulation consists of all Armand's restaurants located near college campuses with 9000 students; and so on. Each subpopulation has a corresponding distribution of y values. Thus, a distribution of y values is associated with restaurants located near campuses with 8000 students; a distribution of y values is associated with restaurants located near campuses with 9000 students; and so on. Each distribution of y values has its own mean or expected value. The equation that describes how the expected value of y, denoted $E(y)$, is related to x is called the **regression equation**. The regression equation for simple linear regression follows.

SIMPLE LINEAR REGRESSION EQUATION

$$E(y) = \beta_0 + \beta_1 x \quad \textbf{(12.2)}$$

The graph of the simple linear regression equation is a straight line; β_0 is the y-intercept of the regression line, β_1 is the slope, and $E(y)$ is the mean or expected value of y for a given value of x.

Examples of possible regression lines are shown in Figure 12.1. The regression line in Panel A shows that the mean value of y is related positively to x, with larger values of $E(y)$ associated with larger values of x. The regression line in Panel B shows the mean value of y is related negatively to x, with smaller values of $E(y)$ associated with larger values of x. The regression line in Panel C shows the case in which the mean value of y is not related to x; that is, the mean value of y is the same for every value of x.

Estimated Regression Equation

If the values of the population parameters β_0 and β_1 were known, we could use equation (12.2) to compute the mean value of y for a given value of x. In practice, the parameter values are not known, and must be estimated using sample data. Sample statistics (denoted b_0 and b_1) are computed as estimates of the population parameters β_0 and β_1. Substituting the values of the sample statistics b_0 and b_1 for β_0 and β_1 in the regression equation, we

FIGURE 12.1 POSSIBLE REGRESSION LINES IN SIMPLE LINEAR REGRESSION

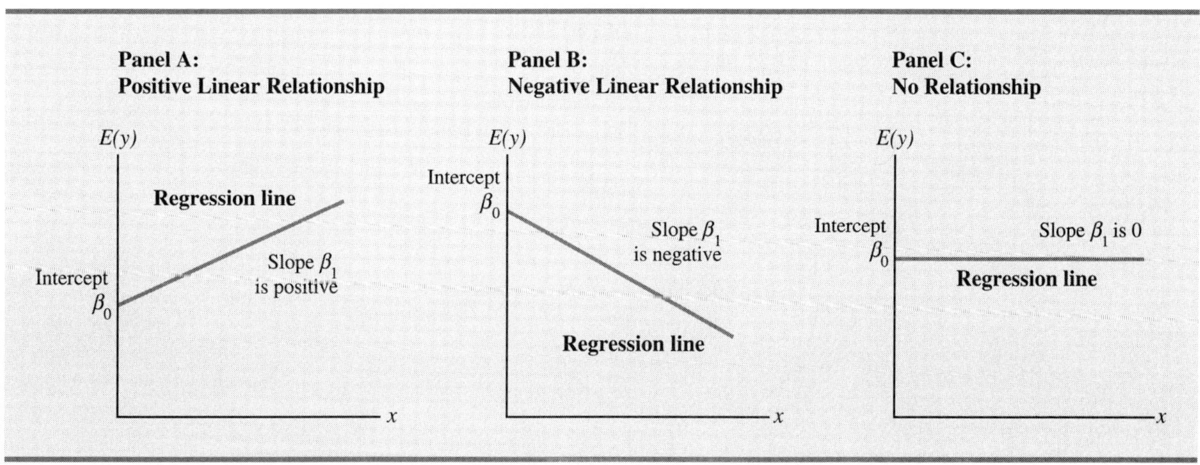

obtain the **estimated regression equation**. The estimated regression equation for simple linear regression follows.

ESTIMATED SIMPLE LINEAR REGRESSION EQUATION

$$\hat{y} = b_0 + b_1 x \tag{12.3}$$

The graph of the estimated simple linear regression equation is called the *estimated regression line*; b_0 is the y-intercept, and b_1 is the slope. In the next section, we show how the least squares method can be used to compute the values of b_0 and b_1 in the estimated regression equation.

In general, $\hat{y}$ is the point estimator of $E(y)$, the mean value of y for a given value of x. Thus, to estimate the mean or expected value of quarterly sales for all restaurants located near campuses with 10,000 students, Armand's would substitute the value of 10,000 for x in equation (12.3). In some cases, however, Armand's may be more interested in predicting sales for one particular restaurant. For example, suppose Armand's would like to predict quarterly sales for the restaurant located near Talbot College, a school with 10,000 students. As it turns out, the best estimate of y for a given value of x is also provided by $\hat{y}$. Thus, to predict quarterly sales for the restaurant located near Talbot College, Armand's would also substitute the value of 10,000 for x in equation (12.3).

Because the value of $\hat{y}$ provides both a point estimate of $E(y)$ for a given value of x and a point estimate of an individual value of y for a given value of x, we will refer to $\hat{y}$ simply as the *estimated value of y*. Figure 12.2 provides a summary of the estimation process for simple linear regression.

The estimation of β_0 and β_1 is a statistical process much like the estimation of μ discussed in Chapter 7. β_0 and β_1 are the unknown parameters of interest, and b_0 and b_1 are the sample statistics used to estimate the parameters.

FIGURE 12.2 THE ESTIMATION PROCESS IN SIMPLE LINEAR REGRESSION

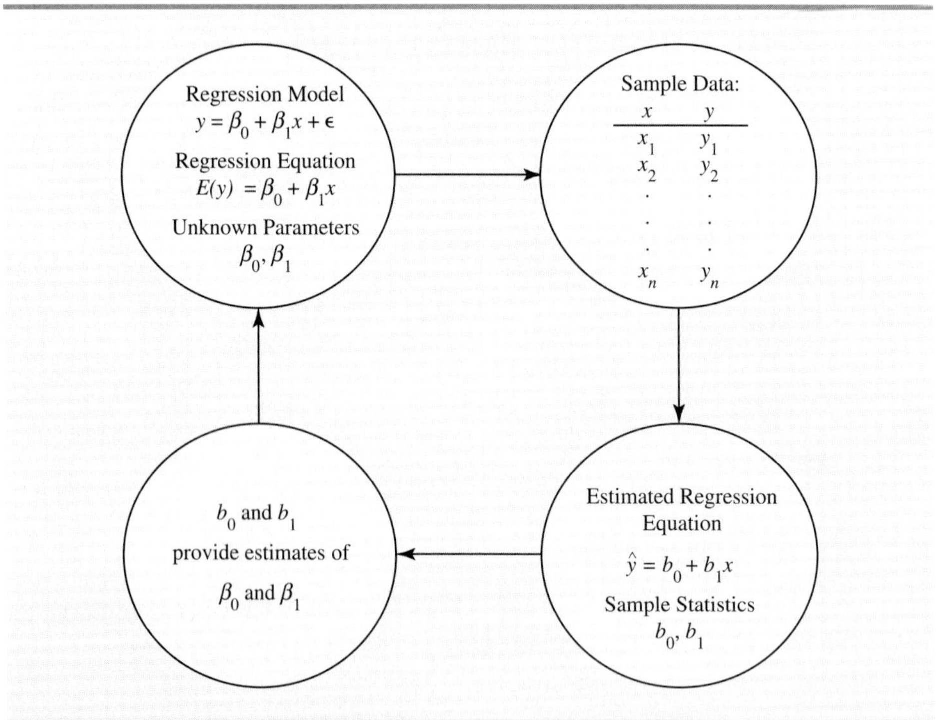

NOTES AND COMMENTS

1. Regression analysis cannot be interpreted as a procedure for establishing a cause-and-effect relationship between variables. It can only indicate how or to what extent variables are associated with each other. Any conclusions about cause and effect must be based upon the judgment of those individuals most knowledgeable about the application.
2. The regression equation in simple linear regression is $E(y) = \beta_0 + \beta_1 x$. More advanced texts in regression analysis often write the regression equation as $E(y|x) = \beta_0 + \beta_1 x$ to emphasize that the regression equation provides the mean value of y for a given value of x.

12.2 Least Squares Method

In simple linear regression, each observation consists of two values: one for the independent variable and one for the dependent variable.

The **least squares method** is a procedure for using sample data to find the estimated regression equation. To illustrate the least squares method, suppose data were collected from a sample of 10 Armand's Pizza Parlors restaurants located near college campuses. For the ith observation or restaurant in the sample, x_i is the size of the student population (in thousands) and y_i is the quarterly sales (in thousands of dollars). The values of x_i and y_i for the 10 restaurants in the sample are summarized in Table 12.1. We see that restaurant 1, with $x_1 = 2$ and $y_1 = 58$, is near a campus with 2000 students and has quarterly sales of \$58,000. Restaurant 2, with $x_2 = 6$ and $y_2 = 105$, is near a campus with 6000 students and has quarterly sales of \$105,000. The largest sales value is for restaurant 10, which is near a campus with 26,000 students and has quarterly sales of \$202,000.

Figure 12.3 is a scatter diagram of the data in Table 12.1. Student population is shown on the horizontal axis and quarterly sales is shown on the vertical axis. **Scatter diagrams** for regression analysis are constructed with the independent variable x on the horizontal axis and the dependent variable y on the vertical axis. The scatter diagram enables us to observe the data graphically and to draw preliminary conclusions about the possible relationship between the variables.

What preliminary conclusions can be drawn from Figure 12.3? Quarterly sales appear to be higher at campuses with larger student populations. In addition, for these data the relationship between the size of the student population and quarterly sales appears to be approximated by a straight line; indeed, a positive linear relationship is indicated between x

TABLE 12.1 STUDENT POPULATION AND QUARTERLY SALES DATA FOR 10 ARMAND'S PIZZA PARLORS

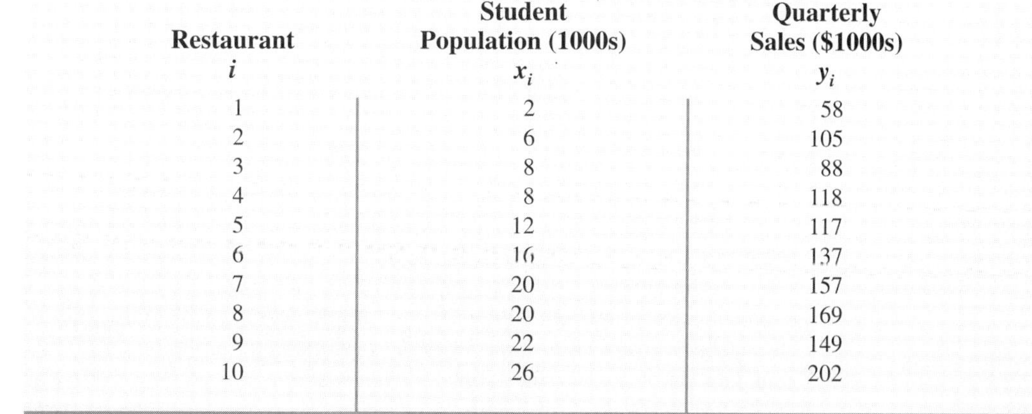

Restaurant i	Student Population (1000s) x_i	Quarterly Sales (\$1000s) y_i
1	2	58
2	6	105
3	8	88
4	8	118
5	12	117
6	16	137
7	20	157
8	20	169
9	22	149
10	26	202

Armand's

FIGURE 12.3 SCATTER DIAGRAM OF STUDENT POPULATION AND QUARTERLY SALES FOR ARMAND'S PIZZA PARLORS

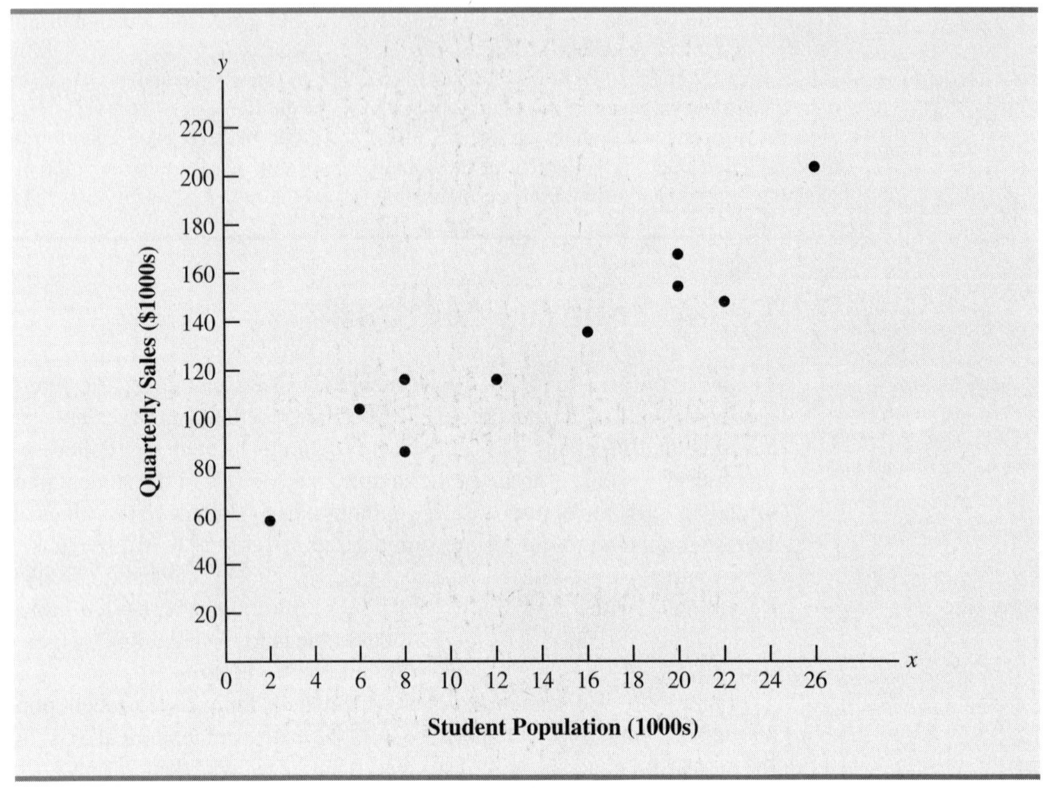

and y. We therefore choose the simple linear regression model to represent the relationship between quarterly sales and student population. Given that choice, our next task is to use the sample data in Table 12.1 to determine the values of b_0 and b_1 in the estimated simple linear regression equation. For the ith restaurant, the estimated regression equation provides

$$\hat{y}_i = b_0 + b_1 x_i \tag{12.4}$$

where

$\hat{y}_i$ = estimated value of quarterly sales ($1000s) for the ith restaurant
b_0 = the y-intercept of the estimated regression line
b_1 = the slope of the estimated regression line
x_i = size of the student population (1000s) for the ith restaurant

With y_i denoting the observed (actual) sales for restaurant i and $\hat{y}_i$ in equation (12.4) representing the estimated value of sales for restaurant i, every restaurant in the sample will have an observed value of sales y_i and an estimated value of sales $\hat{y}_i$. For the estimated regression line to provide a good fit to the data, we want the differences between the observed sales values and the estimated sales values to be small.

The least squares method uses the sample data to provide the values of b_0 and b_1 that minimize the *sum of the squares of the deviations* between the observed values of the dependent variable y_i and the estimated values of the dependent variable. The criterion for the least squares method is given by expression (12.5).

Carl Friedrich Gauss (1777–1855) proposed the least squares method.

LEAST SQUARES CRITERION

$$\min \Sigma(y_i - \hat{y}_i)^2 \tag{12.5}$$

where

y_i = observed value of the dependent variable for the ith observation
$\hat{y}_i$ = estimated value of the dependent variable for the ith observation

Differential calculus can be used to show that the values of b_0 and b_1 that minimize expression (12.5) can be found by using equations (12.6) and (12.7).

In computing b_1 with a calculator, carry as many significant digits as possible in the intermediate calculations. We recommend carrying at least four significant digits.

SLOPE AND y-INTERCEPT FOR THE ESTIMATED REGRESSION EQUATION*

$$b_1 = \frac{\Sigma(x_i - \bar{x})(y_i - \bar{y})}{\Sigma(x_i - \bar{x})^2} \tag{12.6}$$

$$b_0 = \bar{y} - b_1\bar{x} \tag{12.7}$$

where

x_i = value of the independent variable for the ith observation
y_i = value of the dependent variable for the ith observation
$\bar{x}$ = mean value for the independent variable
$\bar{y}$ = mean value for the dependent variable
n = total number of observations

Some of the calculations necessary to develop the least squares estimated regression equation for Armand's Pizza Parlors are shown in Table 12.2. With the sample of 10 restaurants, we have $n = 10$ observations. Because equations (12.6) and (12.7) require $\bar{x}$ and $\bar{y}$ we begin the calculations by computing $\bar{x}$ and $\bar{y}$.

$$\bar{x} = \frac{\Sigma x_i}{n} = \frac{140}{10} = 14$$

$$\bar{y} = \frac{\Sigma y_i}{n} = \frac{1300}{10} = 130$$

Using equations (12.6) and (12.7) and the information in Table 12.2, we can compute the slope and intercept of the estimated regression equation for Armand's Pizza Parlors. The calculation of the slope (b_1) proceeds as follows.

*An alternate formula for b_1 is

$$b_1 = \frac{\Sigma x_i y_i - (\Sigma x_i \Sigma y_i)/n}{\Sigma x_i^2 - (\Sigma x_i)^2/n}$$

This form of equation (12.6) is often recommended when using a calculator to compute b_1.

TABLE 12.2 CALCULATIONS FOR THE LEAST SQUARES ESTIMATED REGRESSION EQUATION FOR ARMAND'S PIZZA PARLORS

Restaurant i	x_i	y_i	$x_i - \bar{x}$	$y_i - \bar{y}$	$(x_i - \bar{x})(y_i - \bar{y})$	$(x_i - \bar{x})^2$
1	2	58	−12	−72	864	144
2	6	105	−8	−25	200	64
3	8	88	−6	−42	252	36
4	8	118	−6	−12	72	36
5	12	117	−2	−13	26	4
6	16	137	2	7	14	4
7	20	157	6	27	162	36
8	20	169	6	39	234	36
9	22	149	8	19	152	64
10	26	202	12	72	864	144
Totals	140	1300			2840	568
	Σx_i	Σy_i			$\Sigma(x_i - \bar{x})(y_i - \bar{y})$	$\Sigma(x_i - \bar{x})^2$

$$
\begin{aligned}
b_1 &= \frac{\Sigma(x_i - \bar{x})(y_i - \bar{y})}{\Sigma(x_i - \bar{x})^2} \\
&= \frac{2840}{568} \\
&= 5
\end{aligned}
$$

The calculation of the y-intercept (b_0) follows.

$$
\begin{aligned}
b_0 &= \bar{y} - b_1\bar{x} \\
&= 130 - 5(14) \\
&= 60
\end{aligned}
$$

Appendixes 12.1 and 12.2 show how Minitab and Excel can be used to obtain the estimated regression equation.

Thus, the estimated regression equation is

$$\hat{y} = 60 + 5x$$

Figure 12.4 shows the graph of this equation on the scatter diagram.

The slope of the estimated regression equation ($b_1 = 5$) is positive, implying that as student population increases, sales increase. In fact, we can conclude (based on sales measured in \$1000s and student population in 1000s) that an increase in the student population of 1000 is associated with an increase of \$5000 in expected sales; that is, quarterly sales are expected to increase by \$5 per student.

Using the estimated regression equation to make predictions outside the range of the values of the independent variable should be done with caution because outside that range we cannot be sure that the same relationship is valid.

If we believe the least squares estimated regression equation adequately describes the relationship between x and y, it would seem reasonable to use the estimated regression equation to predict the value of y for a given value of x. For example, if we wanted to predict quarterly sales for a restaurant to be located near a campus with 16,000 students, we would compute

$$\hat{y} = 60 + 5(16) = 140$$

Hence, we would predict quarterly sales of \$140,000 for this restaurant. In the following sections we will discuss methods for assessing the appropriateness of using the estimated regression equation for estimation and prediction.

FIGURE 12.4 GRAPH OF THE ESTIMATED REGRESSION EQUATION FOR ARMAND'S PIZZA PARLORS: $\hat{y} = 60 + 5x$

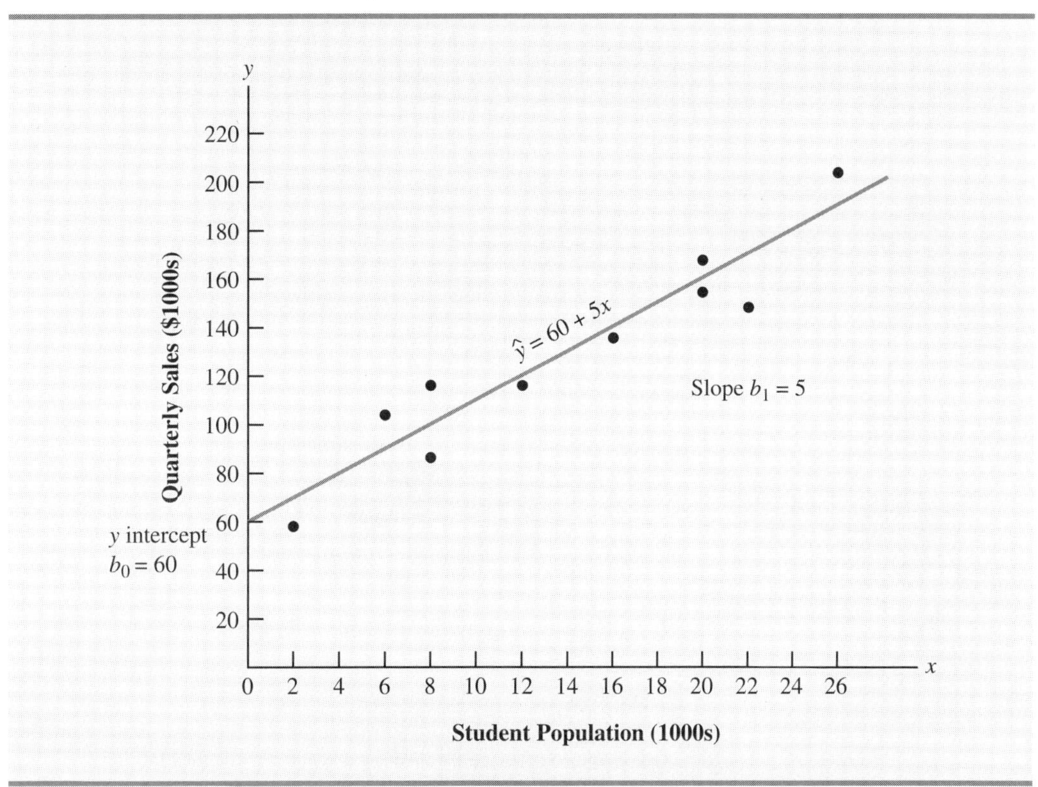

NOTES AND COMMENTS

The least squares method provides an estimated regression equation that minimizes the sum of squared deviations between the observed values of the dependent variable y_i and the estimated values of the dependent variable $\hat{y}_i$. This least squares criterion is used to choose the equation that provides the best fit. If some other criterion were used, such as minimizing the sum of the absolute deviations between y_i and $\hat{y}_i$, a different equation would be obtained. In practice, the least squares method is the most widely used.

Exercises

Methods

1. Given are five observations for two variables, x and y.

x_i	1	2	3	4	5
y_i	3	7	5	11	14

a. Develop a scatter diagram for these data.

b. What does the scatter diagram developed in part (a) indicate about the relationship between the two variables?

c. Try to approximate the relationship between x and y by drawing a straight line through the data.
d. Develop the estimated regression equation by computing the values of b_0 and b_1 using equations (12.6) and (12.7).
e. Use the estimated regression equation to predict the value of y when $x = 4$.

2. Given are five observations for two variables, x and y.

x_i	2	3	5	1	8
y_i	25	25	20	30	16

a. Develop a scatter diagram for these data.
b. What does the scatter diagram developed in part (a) indicate about the relationship between the two variables?
c. Try to approximate the relationship between x and y by drawing a straight line through the data.
d. Develop the estimated regression equation by computing the values of b_0 and b_1 using equations (12.6) and (12.7).
e. Use the estimated regression equation to predict the value of y when $x = 6$.

3. Given are five observations collected in a regression study on two variables.

x_i	2	4	5	7	8
y_i	2	3	2	6	4

a. Develop a scatter diagram for these data.
b. Develop the estimated regression equation for these data.
c. Use the estimated regression equation to predict the value of y when $x = 4$.

Applications

4. The following data were collected on the height (inches) and weight (pounds) of women swimmers.

Height	68	64	62	65	66
Weight	132	108	102	115	128

a. Develop a scatter diagram for these data with height as the independent variable.
b. What does the scatter diagram developed in part (a) indicate about the relationship between the two variables?
c. Try to approximate the relationship between height and weight by drawing a straight line through the data.
d. Develop the estimated regression equation by computing the values of b_0 and b_1.
e. If a swimmer's height is 63 inches, what would you estimate her weight to be?

5. Technological advances helped make inflatable paddlecraft suitable for backcountry use. These blow-up rubber boats, which can be rolled into a bundle not much bigger than a golf bag, are large enough to accommodate one or two paddlers and their camping gear. *Canoe & Kayak* magazine tested boats from nine manufacturers to determine how they would perform on a three-day wilderness paddling trip. One of the criteria in their evaluation was the baggage capacity of the boat, evaluated using a 4-point rating scale from 1 (lowest rating) to 4 (highest rating). The following data show the baggage capacity rating and the price of the boat (*Canoe & Kayak,* March 2003).

Boat	Baggage Capacity	Price ($)
S14	4	1595
Orinoco	4	1399
Outside Pro	4	1890
Explorer 380X	3	795
River XK2	2.5	600
Sea Tiger	4	1995
Maverik II	3	1205
Starlite 100	2	583
Fat Pack Cat	3	1048

a. Develop a scatter diagram for these data with baggage capacity rating as the independent variable.
b. What does the scatter diagram developed in part (a) indicate about the relationship between baggage capacity and price?
c. Draw a straight line through the data to approximate a linear relationship between baggage capacity and price.
d. Use the least squares method to develop the estimated regression equation.
e. Provide an interpretation for the slope of the estimated regression equation.
f. Predict the price for a boat with a baggage capacity rating of 3.

6. Wageweb conducts surveys of salary data and presents summaries on its Web site. Based on salary data as of October 1, 2002, Wageweb reported that the average annual salary for sales vice presidents was $142,111, with an average annual bonus of $15,432 (Wageweb.com, March 13, 2003). Assume the following data are a sample of the annual salary and bonus for 10 sales vice presidents. Data are in thousands of dollars.

Vice President	Salary	Bonus
1	135	12
2	115	14
3	146	16
4	167	19
5	165	22
6	176	24
7	98	7
8	136	17
9	163	18
10	119	11

a. Develop a scatter diagram for these data with salary as the independent variable.
b. What does the scatter diagram developed in part (a) indicate about the relationship between salary and bonus?
c. Use the least squares method to develop the estimated regression equation.
d. Provide an interpretation for the slope of the estimated regression equation.
e. Predict the bonus for a vice president with an annual salary of $120,000.

7. Would you expect more reliable cars to cost more? *Consumer Reports* rated 15 upscale sedans. Reliability was rated on a 5-point scale: poor (1), fair (2), good (3), very good (4), and excellent (5). The price and reliability rating for each of the 15 cars are shown (*Consumer Reports,* February 2004).

Cars

Make and Model	Reliability	Price ($)
Acura TL	4	33,150
BMW 330i	3	40,570
Lexus IS300	5	35,105
Lexus ES330	5	35,174
Mercedes-Benz C320	1	42,230
Lincoln LS Premium (V6)	3	38,225
Audi A4 3.0 Quattro	2	37,605
Cadillac CTS	1	37,695
Nissan Maxima 3.5 SE	4	34,390
Infiniti I35	5	33,845
Saab 9-3 Aero	3	36,910
Infiniti G35	4	34,695
Jaguar X-Type 3.0	1	37,995
Saab 9-5 Arc	3	36,955
Volvo S60 2.5T	3	33,890

a. Develop a scatter diagram for these data with the reliability rating as the independent variable.
b. Develop the least squares estimated regression equation.
c. Based upon your analysis, do you think more reliable cars cost more? Explain.
d. Estimate the price for an upscale sedan that has an average reliability rating.

8. Mountain bikes that cost less than $1000 now contain many of the high-quality components that until recently were only available on high-priced models. Today, even sub-$1000 models often offer supple suspensions, clipless pedals, and highly engineered frames. An interesting question is whether higher price still buys a higher level of handling, as measured by the bike's sidetrack capability. To measure sidetrack capability, *Outside Magazine* used a rating scale from 1 to 5, with 1 representing an average rating and 5 representing an excellent rating. The sidetrack capability and the price for 10 mountain bikes tested by *Outside Magazine* follow (*Outside Magazine Buyer's Guide,* 2001).

MtnBikes

Manufacturer and Model	Sidetrack Capability	Price ($)
Raleigh M80	1	600
Marin Bear Valley Feminina	1	649
GT Avalanche 2.0	2	799
Kona Jake the Snake	1	899
Schwinn Moab 2	3	950
Giant XTC NRS 3	4	1100
Fisher Paragon Genesisters	4	1149
Jamis Dakota XC	3	1300
Trek Fuel 90	5	1550
Specialized Stumpjumper M4	4	1625

a. Develop a scatter diagram for these data with sidetrack capability as the independent variable.
b. Does it appear that higher-priced models have a higher level of handling? Explain.
c. Develop the least squares estimated regression equation.
d. What is the estimated price for a mountain bike if it has a sidetrack capability rating of 4?

9. A sales manager collected the following data on annual sales and years of experience.

Salesperson	Years of Experience	Annual Sales ($1000s)
1	1	80
2	3	97
3	4	92
4	4	102
5	6	103
6	8	111
7	10	119
8	10	123
9	11	117
10	13	136

a. Develop a scatter diagram for these data with years of experience as the independent variable.
b. Develop an estimated regression equation that can be used to predict annual sales given the years of experience.
c. Use the estimated regression equation to predict annual sales for a salesperson with 9 years of experience.

10. *PC World* provided ratings for the top 15 notebook PCs (*PC World,* February 2000). The performance score is a measure of how fast a PC can run a mix of common business applications as compared to how fast a baseline machine can run them. For example, a PC with a performance score of 200 is twice as fast as the baseline machine. A 100-point scale was used to provide an overall rating for each notebook tested in the study. A score in the 90s is exceptional, while one in the 70s is above average. The performance scores and the overall ratings for the 15 notebooks follow.

PCs

Make and Model	Performance Score	Overall Rating
AMS Tech Roadster 15CTA380	115	67
Compaq Armada M700	191	78
Compaq Prosignia Notebook 150	153	79
Dell Inspiron 3700 C466GT	194	80
Dell Inspiron 7500 R500VT	236	84
Dell Latitude Cpi A366XT	184	76
Enpower ENP-313 Pro	184	77
Gateway Solo 9300LS	216	92
HP Pavilion Notebook PC	185	83
IBM ThinkPad I Series 1480	183	78
Micro Express NP7400	189	77
Micron TransPort NX PII-400	202	78
NEC Versa SX	192	78
Sceptre Soundx 5200	141	73
Sony VAIO PCG-F340	187	77

a. Develop a scatter diagram for these data with performance score as the independent variable.
b. Develop the least squares estimated regression equation.
c. Estimate the overall rating for a new PC that has a performance score of 225.

11. Although delays at major airports are now less frequent, it helps to know which airports are likely to throw off your schedule. In addition, if your plane is late arriving at a particular airport where you must make a connection, how likely is it that the departure will be

late and thus increase your chances of making the connection? The following data show the percentage of late arrivals and departures during August for 13 airports (*Business 2.0,* February 2002).

Airport

Airport	Late Arrivals (%)	Late Departures (%)
Atlanta	24	22
Charlotte	20	20
Chicago	30	29
Cincinnati	20	19
Dallas	20	22
Denver	23	23
Detroit	18	19
Houston	20	16
Minneapolis	18	18
Phoenix	21	22
Pittsburgh	25	22
Salt Lake City	18	17
St. Louis	16	16

a. Develop a scatter diagram for these data with the percentage of late arrivals as the independent variable.
b. What does the scatter diagram developed in part (a) indicate about the relationship between late arrivals and late departures?
c. Use the least squares method to develop the estimated regression equation.
d. Provide an interpretation for the slope of the estimated regression equation.
e. Suppose the percentage of late arrivals at the Philadelphia airport for August was 22%. What is an estimate of the percentage of late departures?

12. The following table gives the number of employees and the revenue (in millions of dollars) for 20 companies (*Fortune,* April 17, 2000).

EmpRev

Company	Employees	Revenue ($millions)
Sprint	77,600	19,930
Chase Manhattan	74,801	33,710
Computer Sciences	50,000	7,660
Wells Fargo	89,355	21,795
Sunbeam	12,200	2,398
CBS	29,000	7,510
Time Warner	69,722	27,333
Steelcase	16,200	2,743
Georgia-Pacific	57,000	17,796
Toro	1,275	4,673
American Financial	9,400	3,334
Fluor	53,561	12,417
Phillips Petroleum	15,900	13,852
Cardinal Health	36,000	25,034
Borders Group	23,500	2,999
MCI Worldcom	77,000	37,120
Consolidated Edison	14,269	7,491
IBP	45,000	14,075
Super Value	50,000	17,421
H&R Block	4,200	1,669

a. Develop a scatter diagram for these data with number of employees as the independent variable.
b. What does the scatter diagram developed in part (a) indicate about the relationship between number of employees and revenue?
c. Develop the estimated regression equation for these data.
d. Use the estimated regression equation to predict the revenue for a firm with 75,000 employees.

13. To the Internal Revenue Service, the reasonableness of total itemized deductions depends on the taxpayer's adjusted gross income. Large deductions, which include charity and medical deductions, are more reasonable for taxpayers with large adjusted gross incomes. If a taxpayer claims larger than average itemized deductions for a given level of income, the chances of an IRS audit are increased. Data (in thousands of dollars) on adjusted gross income and the average or reasonable amount of itemized deductions follow.

Adjusted Gross Income ($1000s)	Reasonable Amount of Itemized Deductions ($1000s)
22	9.6
27	9.6
32	10.1
48	11.1
65	13.5
85	17.7
120	25.5

a. Develop a scatter diagram for these data with adjusted gross income as the independent variable.
b. Use the least squares method to develop the estimated regression equation.
c. Estimate a reasonable level of total itemized deductions for a taxpayer with an adjusted gross income of $52,500. If this taxpayer claimed itemized deductions of $20,400, would the IRS agent's request for an audit appear justified? Explain.

14. Starting salaries for accountants and auditors in Rochester, New York, trail those of many U.S. cities. The following data show the starting salary (in thousands of dollars) and the cost of living index for Rochester and nine other metropolitan areas (*Democrat and Chronicle,* September 1, 2002). The cost of living index, based on a city's food, housing, taxes, and other costs, ranges from 0 (most expensive) to 100 (least expensive).

Salaries

Metropolitan Area	Index	Salary ($1000s)
Oklahoma City	82.44	23.9
Tampa/St. Petersburg/Clearwater	79.89	24.5
Indianapolis	55.53	27.4
Buffalo/Niagara Falls	41.36	27.7
Atlanta	39.38	27.1
Rochester	28.05	25.6
Sacramento	25.50	28.7
Raleigh/Durham/Chapel Hill	13.32	26.7
San Diego	3.12	27.8
Honolulu	0.57	28.3

a. Develop a scatter diagram for these data with the cost of living index as the independent variable.
b. Develop the estimated regression equation relating the cost of living index to the starting salary.
c. Estimate the starting salary for a metropolitan area with a cost of living index of 50.

12.3 Coefficient of Determination

For the Armand's Pizza Parlors example, we developed the estimated regression equation $\hat{y} = 60 + 5x$ to approximate the linear relationship between the size of the student population x and quarterly sales y. A question now is: How well does the estimated regression equation fit the data? In this section, we show that the **coefficient of determination** provides a measure of the goodness of fit for the estimated regression equation.

For the ith observation, the difference between the observed value of the dependent variable, y_i, and the estimated value of the dependent variable, $\hat{y}_i$, is called the ***i*th residual**. The ith residual represents the error in using $\hat{y}_i$ to estimate y_i. Thus, for the ith observation, the residual is $y_i - \hat{y}_i$. The sum of squares of these residuals or errors is the quantity that is minimized by the least squares method. This quantity, also known as the *sum of squares due to error*, is denoted by SSE.

SUM OF SQUARES DUE TO ERROR

$$\text{SSE} = \Sigma(y_i - \hat{y}_i)^2 \tag{12.8}$$

The value of SSE is a measure of the error in using the estimated regression equation to estimate the values of the dependent variable in the sample.

In Table 12.3 we show the calculations required to compute the sum of squares due to error for the Armand's Pizza Parlors example. For instance, for restaurant 1 the values of the independent and dependent variables are $x_1 = 2$ and $y_1 = 58$. Using the estimated regression equation, we find that the estimated value of quarterly sales for restaurant 1 is $\hat{y}_1 = 60 + 5(2) = 70$. Thus, the error in using $\hat{y}_1$ to estimate y_1 for restaurant 1 is $y_1 - \hat{y}_1 = 58 - 70 = -12$. The squared error, $(-12)^2 = 144$, is shown in the last column of Table 12.3. After computing and squaring the residuals for each restaurant in the sample, we sum them to obtain SSE = 1530. Thus, SSE = 1530 measures the error in using the estimated regression equation $\hat{y} = 60 + 5x$ to predict sales.

Now suppose we are asked to develop an estimate of quarterly sales without knowledge of the size of the student population. Without knowledge of any related variables, we would

TABLE 12.3 CALCULATION OF SSE FOR ARMAND'S PIZZA PARLORS

Restaurant i	x_i = Student Population (1000s)	y_i = Quarterly Sales ($1000s)	Predicted Sales $\hat{y}_i = 60 + 5x_i$	Error $y_i - \hat{y}_i$	Squared Error $(y_i - \hat{y}_i)^2$
1	2	58	70	−12	144
2	6	105	90	15	225
3	8	88	100	−12	144
4	8	118	100	18	324
5	12	117	120	−3	9
6	16	137	140	−3	9
7	20	157	160	−3	9
8	20	169	160	9	81
9	22	149	170	−21	441
10	26	202	190	12	144
					SSE = 1530

TABLE 12.4 COMPUTATION OF THE TOTAL SUM OF SQUARES FOR ARMAND'S PIZZA PARLORS

Restaurant i	x_i = Student Population (1000s)	y_i = Quarterly Sales ($1000s)	Deviation $y_i - \bar{y}$	Squared Deviation $(y_i - \bar{y})^2$
1	2	58	−72	5,184
2	6	105	−25	625
3	8	88	−42	1,764
4	8	118	−12	144
5	12	117	−13	169
6	16	137	7	49
7	20	157	27	729
8	20	169	39	1,521
9	22	149	19	361
10	26	202	72	5,184
				SST = 15,730

use the sample mean as an estimate of quarterly sales at any given restaurant. Table 12.2 shows that for the sales data, $\Sigma y_i = 1300$. Hence, the mean value of quarterly sales for the sample of 10 Armand's restaurants is $\bar{y} = \Sigma y_i/n = 1300/10 = 130$. In Table 12.4 we show the sum of squared deviations obtained by using the sample mean $\bar{y} = 130$ to estimate the value of quarterly sales for each restaurant in the sample. For the *i*th restaurant in the sample, the difference $y_i - \bar{y}$ provides a measure of the error involved in using $\bar{y}$ to estimate sales. The corresponding sum of squares, called the *total sum of squares,* is denoted SST.

TOTAL SUM OF SQUARES

$$\text{SST} = \Sigma(y_i - \bar{y})^2 \tag{12.9}$$

The sum at the bottom of the last column in Table 12.4 is the total sum of squares for Armand's Pizza Parlors; it is SST = 15,730.

In Figure 12.5 we show the estimated regression line $\hat{y} = 60 + 5x$ and the line corresponding to $\bar{y} = 130$. Note that the points cluster more closely around the estimated regression line than they do about the line $\bar{y} = 130$. For example, for the 10th restaurant in the sample we see that the error is much larger when $\bar{y} = 130$ is used as an estimate of y_{10} than when $\hat{y}_{10} = 60 + 5(26) = 190$ is used. We can think of SST as a measure of how well the observations cluster about the $\bar{y}$ line and SSE as a measure of how well the observations cluster about the $\hat{y}$ line.

To measure how much the $\hat{y}$ values on the estimated regression line deviate from $\bar{y}$, another sum of squares is computed. This sum of squares, called the *sum of squares due to regression,* is denoted SSR.

SUM OF SQUARES DUE TO REGRESSION

$$\text{SSR} = \Sigma(\hat{y}_i - \bar{y})^2 \tag{12.10}$$

FIGURE 12.5 DEVIATIONS ABOUT THE ESTIMATED REGRESSION LINE AND THE LINE $y = \bar{y}$ FOR ARMAND'S PIZZA PARLORS

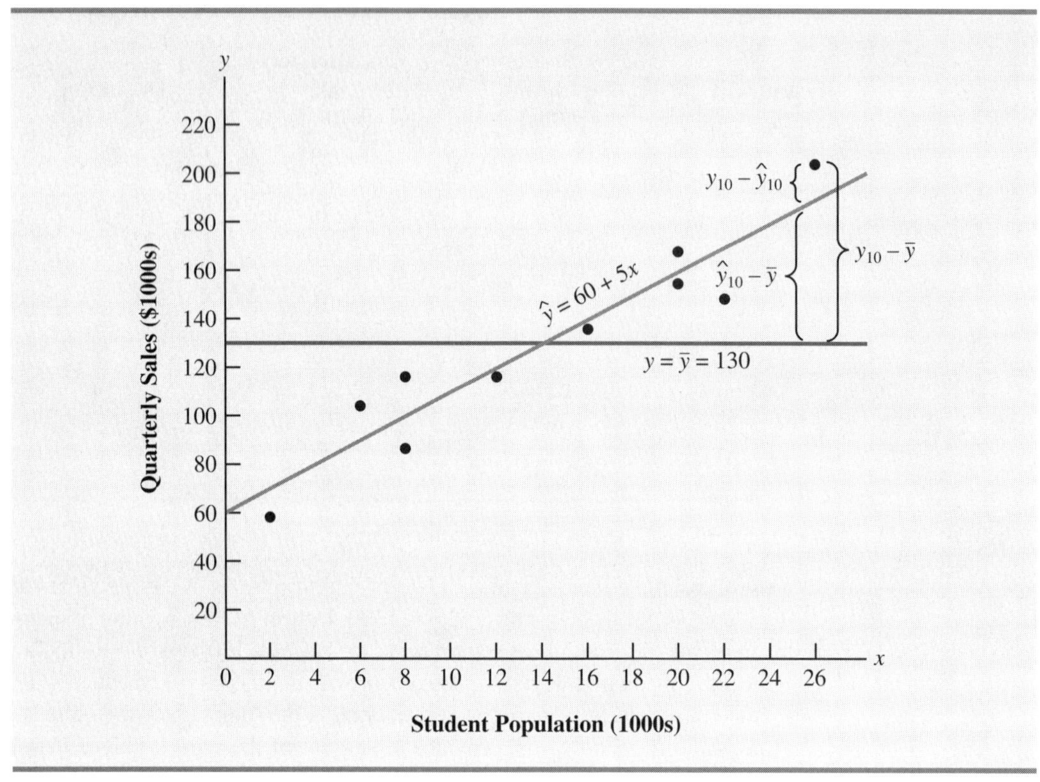

From the preceding discussion, we should expect that SST, SSR, and SSE are related. Indeed, the relationship among these three sums of squares provides one of the most important results in statistics.

SSR can be thought of as the explained portion of SST, and SSE can be thought of as the unexplained portion of SST.

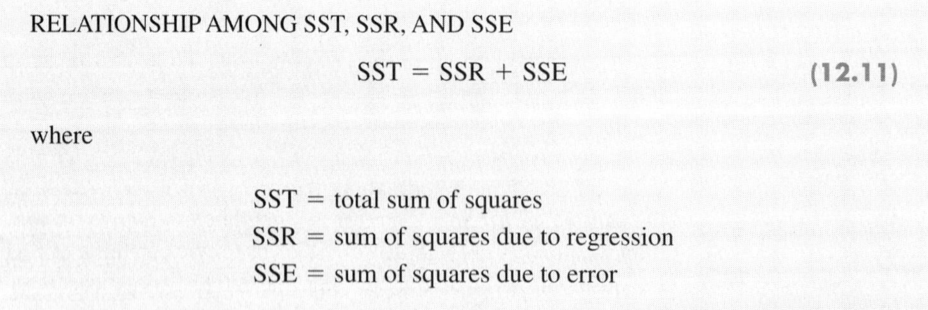

RELATIONSHIP AMONG SST, SSR, AND SSE

$$\text{SST} = \text{SSR} + \text{SSE} \tag{12.11}$$

where

SST = total sum of squares
SSR = sum of squares due to regression
SSE = sum of squares due to error

Equation (12.11) shows that the total sum of squares can be partitioned into two components, the regression sum of squares and the sum of squares due to error. Hence, if the values of any two of these sums of squares are known, the third sum of squares can be computed easily. For instance, in the Armand's Pizza Parlors example, we already know that SSE = 1530 and SST = 15,730; therefore, solving for SSR in equation (12.11), we find that the sum of squares due to regression is

$$\text{SSR} = \text{SST} - \text{SSE} = 15{,}730 - 1530 = 14{,}200$$

Now let us see how the three sums of squares, SST, SSR, and SSE, can be used to provide a measure of the goodness of fit for the estimated regression equation. The estimated regression equation would provide a perfect fit if every value of the dependent variable y_i happened to lie on the estimated regression line. In this case, $y_i - \hat{y}_i$ would be zero for each observation, resulting in SSE $= 0$. Because SST $=$ SSR $+$ SSE, we see that for a perfect fit SSR must equal SST, and the ratio (SSR/SST) must equal one. Poorer fits will result in larger values for SSE. Solving for SSE in equation (12.11), we see that SSE $=$ SST $-$ SSR. Hence, the largest value for SSE (and hence the poorest fit) occurs when SSR $= 0$ and SSE $=$ SST.

The ratio SSR/SST, which will take values between zero and one, is used to evaluate the goodness of fit for the estimated regression equation. This ratio is called the *coefficient of determination* and is denoted by r^2.

COEFFICIENT OF DETERMINATION

$$r^2 = \frac{\text{SSR}}{\text{SST}} \tag{12.12}$$

For the Armand's Pizza Parlors example, the value of the coefficient of determination is

$$r^2 = \frac{\text{SSR}}{\text{SST}} = \frac{14{,}200}{15{,}730} = .9027$$

When we express the coefficient of determination as a percentage, r^2 can be interpreted as the percentage of the total sum of squares that can be explained by using the estimated regression equation. For Armand's Pizza Parlors, we can conclude that 90.27% of the total sum of squares can be explained by using the estimated regression equation $\hat{y} = 60 + 5x$ to predict quarterly sales. In other words, 90.27% of the variability in sales can be explained by the linear relationship between the size of the student population and sales. We should be pleased to find such a good fit for the estimated regression equation.

Correlation Coefficient

In Chapter 3 we introduced the **correlation coefficient** as a descriptive measure of the strength of linear association between two variables, x and y. Values of the correlation coefficient are always between -1 and $+1$. A value of $+1$ indicates that the two variables x and y are perfectly related in a positive linear sense. That is, all data points are on a straight line that has a positive slope. A value of -1 indicates that x and y are perfectly related in a negative linear sense, with all data points on a straight line that has a negative slope. Values of the correlation coefficient close to zero indicate that x and y are not linearly related.

In Section 3.5 we presented the equation for computing the sample correlation coefficient. If a regression analysis has already been performed and the coefficient of determination r^2 computed, the sample correlation coefficient can be computed as follows.

SAMPLE CORRELATION COEFFICIENT

$$\begin{aligned} r_{xy} &= (\text{sign of } b_1)\sqrt{\text{Coefficient of determination}} \\ &= (\text{sign of } b_1)\sqrt{r^2} \end{aligned} \tag{12.13}$$

where

b_1 = the slope of the estimated regression equation $\hat{y} = b_0 + b_1x$

The sign for the sample correlation coefficient is positive if the estimated regression equation has a positive slope ($b_1 > 0$) and negative if the estimated regression equation has a negative slope ($b_1 < 0$).

For the Armand's Pizza Parlors example, the value of the coefficient of determination corresponding to the estimated regression equation $\hat{y} = 60 + 5x$ is .9027. Because the slope of the estimated regression equation is positive, equation (12.13) shows that the sample correlation coefficient is $+\sqrt{.9027} = +.9501$. With a sample correlation coefficient of $r_{xy} = +.9501$, we would conclude that a strong positive linear association exists between x and y.

In the case of a linear relationship between two variables, both the coefficient of determination and the sample correlation coefficient provide measures of the strength of the relationship. The coefficient of determination provides a measure between zero and one, whereas the sample correlation coefficient provides a measure between -1 and $+1$. Although the sample correlation coefficient is restricted to a linear relationship between two variables, the coefficient of determination can be used for nonlinear relationships and for relationships that have two or more independent variables. Thus, the coefficient of determination provides a wider range of applicability.

NOTES AND COMMENTS

1. In developing the least squares estimated regression equation and computing the coefficient of determination, we made no probabilistic assumptions about the error term ϵ, and no statistical tests for significance of the relationship between x and y were conducted. Larger values of r^2 imply that the least squares line provides a better fit to the data; that is, the observations are more closely grouped about the least squares line. But, using only r^2, we can draw no conclusion about whether the relationship between x and y is statistically significant. Such a conclusion must be based on considerations that involve the sample size and the properties of the appropriate sampling distributions of the least squares estimators.
2. As a practical matter, for typical data found in the social sciences, values of r^2 as low as .25 are often considered useful. For data in the physical and life sciences, r^2 values of .60 or greater are often found; in fact, in some cases, r^2 values greater than .90 can be found. In business applications, r^2 values vary greatly, depending on the unique characteristics of each application.

Exercises

Methods

15. The data from exercise 1 follow.

x_i	1	2	3	4	5
y_i	3	7	5	11	14

The estimated regression equation for these data is $\hat{y} = .20 + 2.60x$.

a. Compute SSE, SST, and SSR using equations (12.8), (12.9), and (12.10).
b. Compute the coefficient of determination r^2. Comment on the goodness of fit.
c. Compute the sample correlation coefficient.

16. The data from exercise 2 follow.

x_i	2	3	5	1	8
y_i	25	25	20	30	16

The estimated regression equation for these data is $\hat{y} = 30.33 - 1.88x$.

a. Compute SSE, SST, and SSR.
b. Compute the coefficient of determination r^2. Comment on the goodness of fit.
c. Compute the sample correlation coefficient.

17. The data from exercise 3 follow.

x_i	2	4	5	7	8
y_i	2	3	2	6	4

The estimated regression equation for these data is $\hat{y} = .75 + .51x$. What percentage of the total sum of squares can be accounted for by the estimated regression equation? What is the value of the sample correlation coefficient?

Applications

18. The following data are the monthly salaries y and the grade point averages x for students who obtained a bachelor's degree in business administration with a major in information systems. The estimated regression equation for these data is $\hat{y} = 1790.5 + 581.1x$.

GPA	Monthly Salary ($)	GPA	Monthly Salary ($)
2.6	3300	3.2	3500
3.4	3600	3.5	3900
3.6	4000	2.9	3600

a. Compute SST, SSR, and SSE.
b. Compute the coefficient of determination r^2. Comment on the goodness of fit.
c. What is the value of the sample correlation coefficient?

19. The data from exercise 7 follow:

Cars

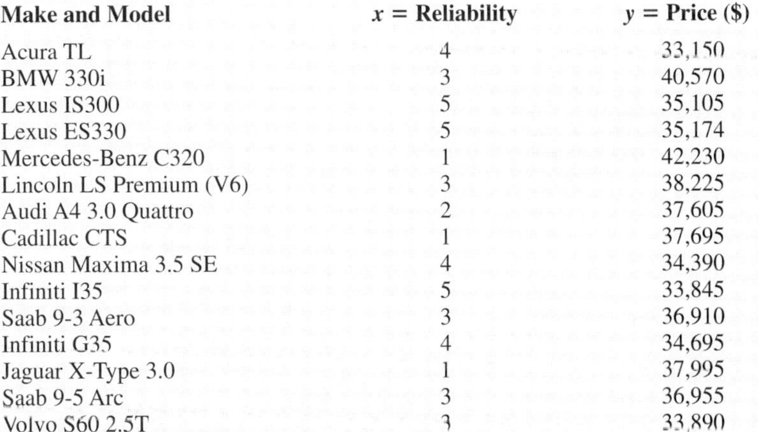

Make and Model	x = Reliability	y = Price ($)
Acura TL	4	33,150
BMW 330i	3	40,570
Lexus IS300	5	35,105
Lexus ES330	5	35,174
Mercedes-Benz C320	1	42,230
Lincoln LS Premium (V6)	3	38,225
Audi A4 3.0 Quattro	2	37,605
Cadillac CTS	1	37,695
Nissan Maxima 3.5 SE	4	34,390
Infiniti I35	5	33,845
Saab 9-3 Aero	3	36,910
Infiniti G35	4	34,695
Jaguar X-Type 3.0	1	37,995
Saab 9-5 Arc	3	36,955
Volvo S60 2.5T	3	33,890

The estimated regression equation for these data is $\hat{y} = 40{,}639 - 1301x$. What percentage of the total sum of squares can be accounted for by the estimated regression equation? Comment on the goodness of fit. What is the sample correlation coefficient?

20. The typical household income and typical home price for a sample of 18 cities follow (*Places Rated Almanac,* 2000). Data are in thousands of dollars.

Cities

City	Income	Home Price
Akron, OH	74.1	114.9
Atlanta, GA	82.4	126.9
Birmingham, AL	71.2	130.9
Bismarck, ND	62.8	92.8
Cleveland, OH	79.2	135.8
Columbia, SC	66.8	116.7
Denver, CO	82.6	161.9
Detroit, MI	85.3	145.0
Fort Lauderdale, FL	75.8	145.3
Hartford, CT	89.1	162.1
Lancaster, PA	75.2	125.9
Madison, WI	78.8	145.2
Naples, FL	100.0	173.6
Nashville, TN	77.3	125.9
Philadelphia, PA	87.0	151.5
Savannah, GA	67.8	108.1
Toledo, OH	71.2	101.1
Washington, DC	97.4	191.9

a. With these data, develop an estimated regression equation that could be used to estimate the typical home price for a city given the typical household income.
b. Compute r^2. Would you feel comfortable using this estimated regression equation to estimate the typical home price for a city?
c. Estimate the typical home price for a city with a typical household income of $95,000.

21. An important application of regression analysis in accounting is in the estimation of cost. By collecting data on volume and cost and using the least squares method to develop an estimated regression equation relating volume and cost, an accountant can estimate the cost associated with a particular manufacturing volume. Consider the following sample of production volumes and total cost data for a manufacturing operation.

Production Volume (units)	Total Cost ($)
400	4000
450	5000
550	5400
600	5900
700	6400
750	7000

a. With these data, develop an estimated regression equation that could be used to predict the total cost for a given production volume.
b. What is the variable cost per unit produced?
c. Compute the coefficient of determination. What percentage of the variation in total cost can be explained by production volume?
d. The company's production schedule shows 500 units must be produced next month. What is the estimated total cost for this operation?

22. *PC World* provided ratings for the top five small-office laser printers and five corporate laser printers (*PC World,* February 2003). The highest-rated small-office laser printer was the Minolta-QMS PagePro 1250W, with an overall rating of 91. The highest-rated corporate

laser printer, the Xerox Phaser 4400/N, had an overall rating of 83. The following data show the speed for plain text printing in pages per minute (ppm) and the price for each printer.

Printers

Name	Type	Speed (ppm)	Price ($)
Minolta-QMS PagePro 1250W	Small Office	12	199
Brother HL-1850	Small Office	10	499
Lexmark E320	Small Office	12.2	299
Minolta-QMS PagePro 1250E	Small Office	10.3	299
HP Laserjet 1200	Small Office	11.7	399
Xerox Phaser 4400/N	Corporate	17.8	1850
Brother HL-2460N	Corporate	16.1	1000
IBM Infoprint 1120n	Corporate	11.8	1387
Lexmark W812	Corporate	19.8	2089
Oki Data B8300n	Corporate	28.2	2200

a. Develop the estimated regression equation with speed as the independent variable.
b. Compute r^2. What percentage of the variation in cost can be explained by the printing speed?
c. What is the sample correlation coefficient between speed and price? Does it reflect a strong or weak relationship between printing speed and cost?

12.4 Model Assumptions

In conducting a regression analysis, we begin by making an assumption about the appropriate model for the relationship between the dependent and independent variable(s). For the case of simple linear regression, the assumed regression model is

$$y = \beta_0 + \beta_1 x + \epsilon$$

Then, the least squares method is used to develop values for b_0 and b_1, the estimates of the model parameters β_0 and β_1, respectively. The resulting estimated regression equation is

$$\hat{y} = b_0 + b_1 x$$

We saw that the value of the coefficient of determination (r^2) is a measure of the goodness of fit of the estimated regression equation. However, even with a large value of r^2, the estimated regression equation should not be used until further analysis of the appropriateness of the assumed model has been conducted. An important step in determining whether the assumed model is appropriate involves testing for the significance of the relationship. The tests of significance in regression analysis are based on the following assumptions about the error term ϵ.

ASSUMPTIONS ABOUT THE ERROR TERM ϵ IN THE REGRESSION MODEL

$$y = \beta_0 + \beta_1 x + \epsilon$$

1. The error term ϵ is a random variable with a mean or expected value of zero; that is, $E(\epsilon) = 0$.
   Implication: β_0 and β_1 are constants, therefore $E(\beta_0) = \beta_0$ and $E(\beta_1) = \beta_1$; thus, for a given value of x, the expected value of y is

$$E(y) = \beta_0 + \beta_1 x \tag{12.14}$$

As we indicated previously, equation (12.14) is referred to as the regression equation.

2. The variance of ϵ, denoted by σ^2, is the same for all values of x.
Implication: The variance of y about the regression line equals σ^2 and is the same for all values of x.
3. The values of ϵ are independent.
Implication: The value of ϵ for a particular value of x is not related to the value of ϵ for any other value of x; thus, the value of y for a particular value of x is not related to the value of y for any other value of x.
4. The error term ϵ is a normally distributed random variable.
Implication: Because y is a linear function of ϵ, y is also a normally distributed random variable.

Figure 12.6 illustrates the model assumptions and their implications; note that in this graphical interpretation, the value of $E(y)$ changes according to the specific value of x considered. However, regardless of the x value, the probability distribution of ϵ and hence the probability distributions of y are normally distributed, each with the same variance. The specific value of the error ϵ at any particular point depends on whether the actual value of y is greater than or less than $E(y)$.

At this point, we must keep in mind that we are also making an assumption or hypothesis about the form of the relationship between x and y. That is, we assume that a straight

FIGURE 12.6 ASSUMPTIONS FOR THE REGRESSION MODEL

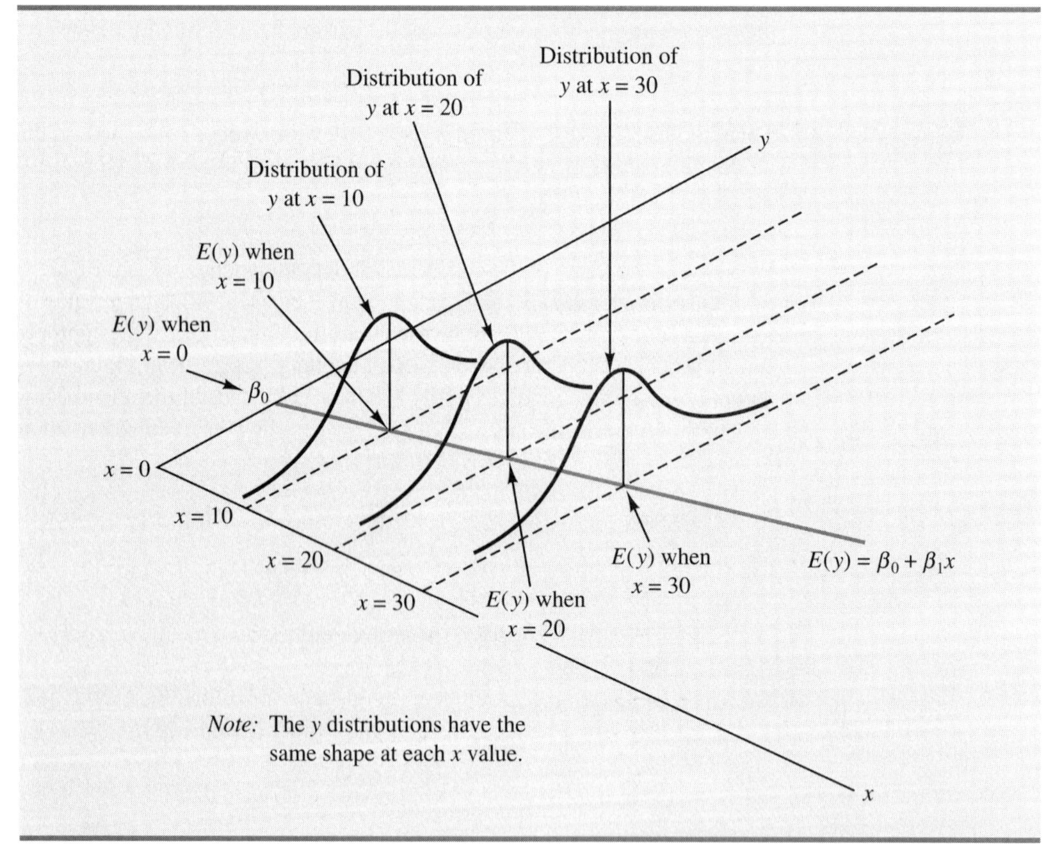

line represented by $\beta_0 + \beta_1 x$ is the basis for the relationship between the variables. We must not lose sight of the fact that some other model, for instance $y = \beta_0 + \beta_1 x^2 + \epsilon$, may turn out to be a better model for the underlying relationship.

12.5 Testing for Significance

In a simple linear regression equation, the mean or expected value of y is a linear function of x: $E(y) = \beta_0 + \beta_1 x$. If the value of β_1 is zero, $E(y) = \beta_0 + (0)x = \beta_0$. In this case, the mean value of y does not depend on the value of x and hence we would conclude that x and y are not linearly related. Alternatively, if the value of β_1 is not equal to zero, we would conclude that the two variables are related. Thus, to test for a significant regression relationship, we must conduct a hypothesis test to determine whether the value of β_1 is zero. Two tests are commonly used. Both require an estimate of σ^2, the variance of ϵ in the regression model.

Estimate of σ^2

From the regression model and its assumptions we can conclude that σ^2, the variance of ϵ, also represents the variance of the y values about the regression line. Recall that the deviations of the y values about the estimated regression line are called residuals. Thus, SSE, the sum of squared residuals, is a measure of the variability of the actual observations about the estimated regression line. The **mean square error** (MSE) provides the estimate of σ^2; it is SSE divided by its degrees of freedom.

With $\hat{y}_i = b_0 + b_1 x_i$, SSE can be written as

$$\text{SSE} = \Sigma(y_i - \hat{y}_i)^2 = \Sigma(y_i - b_0 - b_1 x_i)^2$$

Every sum of squares is associated with a number called its degrees of freedom. Statisticians have shown that SSE has $n - 2$ degrees of freedom because two parameters (β_0 and β_1) must be estimated to compute SSE. Thus, the mean square is computed by dividing SSE by $n - 2$. MSE provides an unbiased estimator of σ^2. Because the value of MSE provides an estimate of σ^2, the notation s^2 is also used.

MEAN SQUARE ERROR (ESTIMATE OF σ^2)

$$s^2 = \text{MSE} = \frac{\text{SSE}}{n - 2} \tag{12.15}$$

In Section 12.3 we showed that for the Armand's Pizza Parlors example, SSE = 1530; hence,

$$s^2 = \text{MSE} = \frac{1530}{8} = 191.25$$

provides an unbiased estimate of σ^2.

To estimate σ we take the square root of s^2. The resulting value, s, is referred to as the **standard error of the estimate**.

STANDARD ERROR OF THE ESTIMATE

$$s = \sqrt{\text{MSE}} = \sqrt{\frac{\text{SSE}}{n - 2}} \tag{12.16}$$

For the Armand's Pizza Parlors example, $s = \sqrt{\text{MSE}} = \sqrt{191.25} = 13.829$. In the following discussion, we use the standard error of the estimate in the tests for a significant relationship between x and y.

t Test

The simple linear regression model is $y = \beta_0 + \beta_1 x + \epsilon$. If x and y are linearly related, we must have $\beta_1 \neq 0$. The purpose of the t test is to see whether we can conclude that $\beta_1 \neq 0$. We will use the sample data to test the following hypotheses about the parameter β_1.

$$H_0: \beta_1 = 0$$
$$H_a: \beta_1 \neq 0$$

If H_0 is rejected, we will conclude that $\beta_1 \neq 0$ and that a statistically significant relationship exists between the two variables. However, if H_0 cannot be rejected, we will have insufficient evidence to conclude that a significant relationship exists. The properties of the sampling distribution of b_1, the least squares estimator of β_1, provide the basis for the hypothesis test.

First, let us consider what would happen if we used a different random sample for the same regression study. For example, suppose that Armand's Pizza Parlors used the sales records of a different sample of 10 restaurants. A regression analysis of this new sample might result in an estimated regression equation similar to our previous estimated regression equation $\hat{y} = 60 + 5x$. However, it is doubtful that we would obtain exactly the same equation (with an intercept of exactly 60 and a slope of exactly 5). Indeed, b_0 and b_1, the least squares estimators, are sample statistics with their own sampling distributions. The properties of the sampling distribution of b_1 follow.

SAMPLING DISTRIBUTION OF b_1

Expected Value

$$E(b_1) = \beta_1$$

Standard Deviation

$$\sigma_{b_1} = \frac{\sigma}{\sqrt{\Sigma(x_i - \bar{x})^2}} \tag{12.17}$$

Distribution Form

Normal

Note that the expected value of b_1 is equal to β_1, so b_1 is an unbiased estimator of β_1.

Because we do not know the value of σ, we develop an estimate of σ_{b_1}, denoted s_{b_1}, by estimating σ with s in equation (12.17). Thus, we obtain the following estimate of σ_{b_1}.

The standard deviation of b_1 is also referred to as the standard error of b_1. Thus, s_{b_1} provides an estimate of the standard error of b_1.

ESTIMATED STANDARD DEVIATION OF b_1

$$s_{b_1} = \frac{s}{\sqrt{\Sigma(x_i - \bar{x})^2}} \tag{12.18}$$

For Armand's Pizza Parlors, $s = 13.829$. Hence, using $\Sigma(x_i - \bar{x})^2 = 568$ as shown in Table 12.2, we have

$$s_{b_1} = \frac{13.829}{\sqrt{568}} = .5803$$

as the estimated standard deviation of b_1.

The t test for a significant relationship is based on the fact that the test statistic

$$\frac{b_1 - \beta_1}{s_{b_1}}$$

follows a t distribution with $n - 2$ degrees of freedom. If the null hypothesis is true, then $\beta_1 = 0$ and $t = b_1/s_{b_1}$.

Let us conduct this test of significance for Armand's Pizza Parlors at the $\alpha = .01$ level of significance. The test statistic is

$$t = \frac{b_1}{s_{b_1}} = \frac{5}{.5803} = 8.62$$

Appendixes 12.1 and 12.2 show how Minitab and Excel can be used to compute the p-value.

The t distribution table shows that with $n - 2 = 10 - 2 = 8$ degrees of freedom, $t = 3.355$ provides an area of .005 in the upper tail. Thus, the area in the upper tail of the t distribution corresponding to the test statistic $t = 8.62$ must be less than .005. Because this test is a two-tailed test, we double this value to conclude that the p-value associated with $t = 8.62$ must be less than $2(.005) = .01$. Minitab or Excel shows the p-value $= .000$. Because the p-value is less than $\alpha = .01$, we reject H_0 and conclude that β_1 is not equal to zero. This evidence is sufficient to conclude that a significant relationship exists between student population and quarterly sales. A summary of the t test for significance in simple linear regression follows.

t TEST FOR SIGNIFICANCE IN SIMPLE LINEAR REGRESSION

$$H_0: \beta_1 = 0$$
$$H_a: \beta_1 \neq 0$$

TEST STATISTIC

$$t = \frac{b_1}{s_{b_1}} \tag{12.19}$$

REJECTION RULE

p-value approach: Reject H_0 if p-value $\leq \alpha$

Critical value approach: Reject H_0 if $t \leq -t_{\alpha/2}$ or if $t \geq t_{\alpha/2}$

where $t_{\alpha/2}$ is based on a t distribution with $n - 2$ degrees of freedom.

Confidence Interval for β_1

The form of a confidence interval for β_1 is as follows:

$$b_1 \pm t_{\alpha/2} s_{b_1}$$

The point estimator is b_1 and the margin of error is $t_{\alpha/2}s_{b_1}$. The confidence coefficient associated with this interval is $1 - \alpha$, and $t_{\alpha/2}$ is the t value providing an area of $\alpha/2$ in the upper tail of a t distribution with $n - 2$ degrees of freedom. For example, suppose that we wanted to develop a 99% confidence interval estimate of β_1 for Armand's Pizza Parlors. From Table 2 of Appendix B we find that the t value corresponding to $\alpha = .01$ and $n - 2 = 10 - 2 = 8$ degrees of freedom is $t_{.005} = 3.355$. Thus, the 99% confidence interval estimate of β_1 is

$$b_1 \pm t_{\alpha/2}s_{b_1} = 5 \pm 3.355(.5803) = 5 \pm 1.95$$

or 3.05 to 6.95.

In using the t test for significance, the hypotheses tested were

$$H_0\colon \beta_1 = 0$$
$$H_a\colon \beta_1 \neq 0$$

At the $\alpha = .01$ level of significance, we can use the 99% confidence interval as an alternative for drawing the hypothesis testing conclusion for the Armand's data. Because 0, the hypothesized value of β_1, is not included in the confidence interval (3.05 to 6.95), we can reject H_0 and conclude that a significant statistical relationship exists between the size of the student population and quarterly sales. In general, a confidence interval can be used to test any two-sided hypothesis about β_1. If the hypothesized value of β_1 is contained in the confidence interval, do not reject H_0. Otherwise, reject H_0.

F Test

An F test, based on the F probability distribution, can also be used to test for significance in regression. With only one independent variable, the F test will provide the same conclusion as the t test; that is, if the t test indicates $\beta_1 \neq 0$ and hence a significant relationship, the F test will also indicate a significant relationship. But with more than one independent variable, only the F test can be used to test for an overall significant relationship.

The logic behind the use of the F test for determining whether the regression relationship is statistically significant is based on the development of two independent estimates of σ^2. We explained how MSE provides an estimate of σ^2. If the null hypothesis $H_0\colon \beta_1 = 0$ is true, the sum of squares due to regression, SSR, divided by its degrees of freedom provides another independent estimate of σ^2. This estimate is called the *mean square due to regression,* or simply the *mean square regression,* and is denoted MSR. In general,

$$\text{MSR} = \frac{\text{SSR}}{\text{Regression degrees of freedom}}$$

For the models we consider in this text, the regression degrees of freedom is always equal to the number of independent variables in the model:

$$\text{MSR} = \frac{\text{SSR}}{\text{Number of independent variables}} \tag{12.20}$$

Because we consider only regression models with one independent variable in this chapter, we have MSR = SSR/1 = SSR. Hence, for Armand's Pizza Parlors, MSR = SSR = 14,200.

If the null hypothesis ($H_0\colon \beta_1 = 0$) is true, MSR and MSE are two independent estimates of σ^2 and the sampling distribution of MSR/MSE follows an F distribution with numerator degrees of freedom equal to 1 and denominator degrees of freedom equal to $n - 2$. Therefore, when $\beta_1 = 0$, the value of MSR/MSE should be close to one. However, if the null hypothesis is false ($\beta_1 \neq 0$), MSR will overestimate σ^2 and the value of MSR/MSE will be inflated; thus, large values of MSR/MSE lead to the rejection of H_0 and the conclusion that the relationship between x and y is statistically significant.

Let us conduct the F test for the Armand's Pizza Parlors example. The test statistic is

In Section 10.4 we showed how to determine a p-value using the F distribution table.

$$F = \frac{\text{MSR}}{\text{MSE}} = \frac{14{,}200}{191.25} = 74.25$$

The F distribution table (Table 4 of Appendix B) shows that with one degree of freedom in the numerator and $n - 2 = 10 - 2 = 8$ degrees of freedom in the denominator, $F = 11.26$ provides an area of .01 in the upper tail. Thus, the area in the upper tail of the F distribution corresponding to the test statistic $F = 74.25$ must be less than .01. Thus, we conclude that the p-value must be less than .01. Minitab or Excel shows the p-value $= .000$. Because the p-value is less than $\alpha = .01$, we reject H_0 and conclude that a significant relationship exists between the size of the student population and quarterly sales. A summary of the F test for significance in simple linear regression follows.

The F test and the t test provide identical results for simple linear regression.

If H_0 is false, MSE *still provides an unbiased estimate of σ^2 and* MSR *overestimates σ^2. If H_0 is true, both* MSE *and* MSR *provide unbiased estimates of σ^2; in this case the value of* MSR/MSE *should be close to 1.*

F TEST FOR SIGNIFICANCE IN SIMPLE LINEAR REGRESSION

$$H_0\colon \beta_1 = 0$$
$$H_a\colon \beta_1 \neq 0$$

TEST STATISTIC

$$F = \frac{\text{MSR}}{\text{MSE}} \tag{12.21}$$

REJECTION RULE

p-value approach: Reject H_0 if p-value $\leq \alpha$
Critical value approach: Reject H_0 if $F \geq F_\alpha$

where F_α is based on an F distribution with 1 degree of freedom in the numerator and $n - 2$ degrees of freedom in the denominator.

In Chapter 10 we covered analysis of variance (ANOVA) and showed how an **ANOVA table** could be used to provide a convenient summary of the computational aspects of analysis of variance. A similar ANOVA table can be used to summarize the results of the F test for significance in regression. Table 12.5 is the general form of the ANOVA table for simple linear regression. Table 12.6 is the ANOVA table with the F test computations performed for Armand's Pizza Parlors. Regression, Error, and Total are the labels for the three sources of variation, with SSR, SSE, and SST appearing as the corresponding sum of squares in column 2. The degrees of freedom, 1 for SSR, $n - 2$ for SSE, and $n - 1$ for SST, are shown in column 3. Column 4 contains the values of MSR and MSE and column 5 contains the value of $F = \text{MSR}/\text{MSE}$. Almost all computer printouts of regression analysis include an ANOVA table summary of the F test for significance.

TABLE 12.5 GENERAL FORM OF THE ANOVA TABLE FOR SIMPLE LINEAR REGRESSION

In every analysis of variance table the total sum of squares is the sum of the regression sum of squares and the error sum of squares; in addition, the total degrees of freedom is the sum of the regression degrees of freedom and the error degrees of freedom.

Source of Variation	Sum of Squares	Degrees of Freedom	Mean Square	F
Regression	SSR	1	$\text{MSR} = \dfrac{\text{SSR}}{1}$	$F = \dfrac{\text{MSR}}{\text{MSE}}$
Error	SSE	$n - 2$	$\text{MSE} = \dfrac{\text{SSE}}{n - 2}$	
Total	SST	$n - 1$		

Some Cautions About the Interpretation of Significance Tests

Regression analysis, which can be used to identify how variables are associated with one another, cannot be used as evidence of a cause-and-effect relationship.

Rejecting the null hypothesis $H_0: \beta_1 = 0$ and concluding that the relationship between x and y is significant do not enable us to conclude that a cause-and-effect relationship is present between x and y. Concluding a cause-and-effect relationship is warranted only if the analyst can provide some type of theoretical justification that the relationship is in fact causal. In the Armand's Pizza Parlors example, we can conclude that there is a significant relationship between the size of the student population x and quarterly sales y; moreover, the estimated regression equation $\hat{y} = 60 + 5x$ provides the least squares estimate of the relationship. We cannot, however, conclude that changes in student population x *cause* changes in quarterly sales y just because we identified a statistically significant relationship. The appropriateness of such a cause-and-effect conclusion is left to supporting theoretical justification and to good judgment on the part of the analyst. Armand's managers felt that increases in the student population were a likely cause of increased quarterly sales. Thus, the result of the significance test enabled them to conclude that a cause-and-effect relationship was present.

In addition, just because we are able to reject $H_0: \beta_1 = 0$ and demonstrate statistical significance does not enable us to conclude that the relationship between x and y is linear. We can state only that x and y are related and that a linear relationship explains a significant portion of the variability in y over the range of values for x observed in the sample. Figure 12.7 illustrates this situation. The test for significance calls for the rejection of the null hypothesis $H_0: \beta_1 = 0$ and leads to the conclusion that x and y are significantly related, but the figure shows that the actual relationship between x and y is not linear. Although the

TABLE 12.6 ANOVA TABLE FOR THE ARMAND'S PIZZA PARLORS PROBLEM

Source of Variation	Sum of Squares	Degrees of Freedom	Mean Square	F
Regression	14,200	1	$\dfrac{14{,}200}{1} = 14{,}200$	$\dfrac{14{,}200}{191.25} = 74.25$
Error	1,530	8	$\dfrac{1530}{8} = 191.25$	
Total	15,730	9		

FIGURE 12.7 EXAMPLE OF A LINEAR APPROXIMATION OF A NONLINEAR RELATIONSHIP

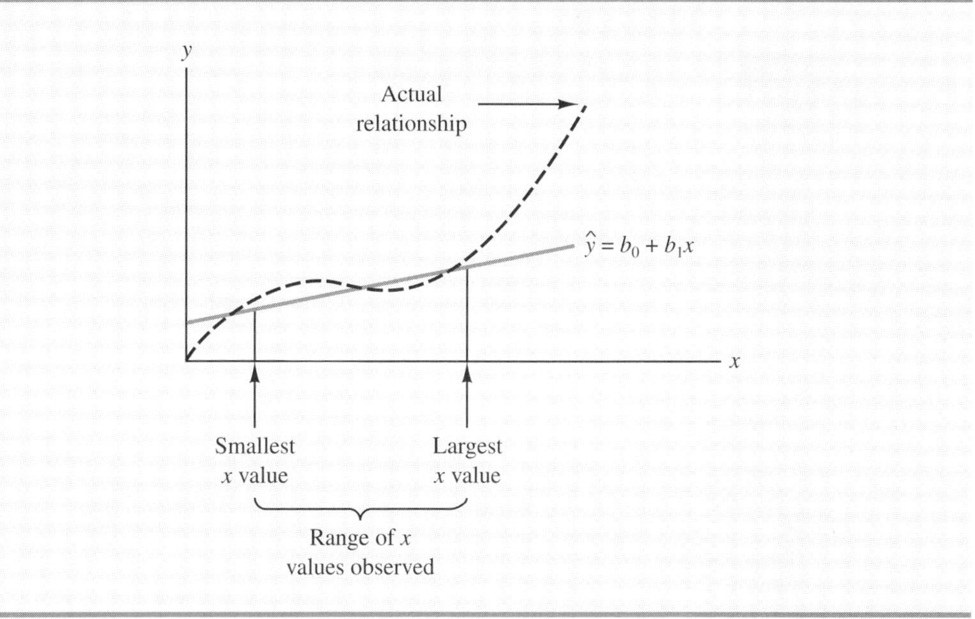

linear approximation provided by $\hat{y} = b_0 + b_1x$ is good over the range of x values observed in the sample, it becomes poor for x values outside that range.

Given a significant relationship, we should feel confident in using the estimated regression equation for predictions corresponding to x values within the range of the x values observed in the sample. For Armand's Pizza Parlors, this range corresponds to values of x between 2 and 26. Unless other reasons indicate that the model is valid beyond this range, predictions outside the range of the independent variable should be made with caution. For Armand's Pizza Parlors, because the regression relationship has been found significant at the .01 level, we should feel confident using it to predict sales for restaurants where the associated student population is between 2000 and 26,000.

NOTES AND COMMENTS

1. The assumptions made about the error term (Section 12.4) are what allow the tests of statistical significance in this section. The properties of the sampling distribution of b_1 and the subsequent t and F tests follow directly from these assumptions.
2. Do not confuse statistical significance with practical significance. With very large sample sizes, statistically significant results can be obtained for small values of b_1; in such cases, one must exercise care in concluding that the relationship has practical significance.
3. A test of significance for a linear relationship between x and y can also be performed by using the sample correlation coefficient r_{xy}. With ρ_{xy} denoting the population correlation coefficient, the hypotheses are as follows.

$$H_0: \rho_{xy} = 0$$
$$H_a: \rho_{xy} \neq 0$$

A significant relationship can be concluded if H_0 is rejected. The details of this test are provided in more advanced texts. However, the t and F tests presented previously in this section give the same result as the test for significance using the correlation coefficient. Conducting a test for significance using the correlation coefficient therefore is not necessary if a t or F test has already been conducted.

Exercises

Methods

23. The data from exercise 1 follow.

x_i	1	2	3	4	5
y_i	3	7	5	11	14

a. Compute the mean square error using equation (12.15).
b. Compute the standard error of the estimate using equation (12.16).
c. Compute the estimated standard deviation of b_1 using equation (12.18).
d. Use the t test to test the following hypotheses ($\alpha = .05$):

$$H_0: \beta_1 = 0$$
$$H_a: \beta_1 \neq 0$$

e. Use the F test to test the hypotheses in part (d) at a .05 level of significance. Present the results in the analysis of variance table format.

24. The data from exercise 2 follow.

x_i	2	3	5	1	8
y_i	25	25	20	30	16

a. Compute the mean square error using equation (12.15).
b. Compute the standard error of the estimate using equation (12.16).
c. Compute the estimated standard deviation of b_1 using equation (12.18).
d. Use the t test to test the following hypotheses ($\alpha = .05$):

$$H_0: \beta_1 = 0$$
$$H_a: \beta_1 \neq 0$$

e. Use the F test to test the hypotheses in part (d) at a .05 level of significance. Present the results in the analysis of variance table format.

25. The data from exercise 3 follow.

x_i	2	4	5	7	8
y_i	2	3	2	6	4

a. What is the value of the standard error of the estimate?
b. Test for a significant relationship by using the t test. Use $\alpha = .05$.
c. Use the F test to test for a significant relationship. Use $\alpha = .05$. What is your conclusion?

Applications

26. In exercise 18 the data on grade point average and monthly salary were as follows.

GPA	Monthly Salary ($)	GPA	Monthly Salary ($)
2.6	3300	3.2	3500
3.4	3600	3.5	3900
3.6	4000	2.9	3600

a. Does the t test indicate a significant relationship between grade point average and monthly salary? What is your conclusion? Use $\alpha = .05$.

b. Test for a significant relationship using the F test. What is your conclusion? Use $\alpha = .05$.

c. Show the ANOVA table.

27. *Outside Magazine* tested 10 different models of day hikers and backpacking boots. The following data show the upper support and price for each model tested. Upper support was measured using a rating from 1 to 5, with a rating of 1 denoting average upper support and a rating of 5 denoting excellent upper support (*Outside Magazine Buyer's Guide,* 2001).

CD file
Boots

Manufacturer and Model	Upper Support	Price ($)
Salomon Super Raid	2	120
Merrell Chameleon Prime	3	125
Teva Challenger	3	130
Vasque Fusion GTX	3	135
Boreal Maigmo	3	150
L.L. Bean GTX Super Guide	5	189
Lowa Kibo	5	190
Asolo AFX 520 GTX	4	195
Raichle Mt. Trail GTX	4	200
Scarpa Delta SL M3	5	220

a. Use these data to develop an estimated regression equation to estimate the price of a day hiker and backpacking boot given the upper support rating.

b. At the .05 level of significance, determine whether upper support and price are related.

c. Would you feel comfortable using the estimated regression equation developed in part (a) to estimate the price for a day hiker or backpacking boot given the upper support rating?

d. Estimate the price for a day hiker with an upper support rating of 4.

PCs

28. Refer to exercise 10, where an estimated regression equation relating the performance score and the overall rating for notebook PCs was developed. At the .05 level of significance, test whether performance score and overall rating are related. Show the ANOVA table. What is your conclusion?

29. Refer to exercise 21, where data on production volume and cost were used to develop an estimated regression equation relating production volume and cost for a particular manufacturing operation. Use $\alpha = .05$ to test whether the production volume is significantly related to the total cost. Show the ANOVA table. What is your conclusion?

30. Refer to exercise 22 where the following data were used to determine whether the price of a printer is related to the speed for plain text printing (*PC World,* February 2003).

Printers

Name	Type	Speed (ppm)	Price ($)
Minolta-QMS PagePro 1250W	Small Office	12	199
Brother HL-1850	Small Office	10	499
Lexmark E320	Small Office	12.2	299
Minolta-QMS PagePro 1250E	Small Office	10.3	299
HP Laserjet 1200	Small Office	11.7	399
Xerox Phaser 4400/N	Corporate	17.8	1850
Brother HL-2460N	Corporate	16.1	1000

(continued)

Name	Type	Speed (ppm)	Price ($)
IBM Infoprint 1120n	Corporate	11.8	1387
Lexmark W812	Corporate	19.8	2089
Oki Data B8300n	Corporate	28.2	2200

Does the evidence indicate a significant relationship between printing speed and price? Conduct the appropriate statistical test and state your conclusion. Use $\alpha = .05$.

31. Refer to exercise 20, where an estimated regression equation was developed relating typical household income and typical home price. Test whether the typical household income for a city and the typical home price are related at the .01 level of significance.

Using the Estimated Regression Equation for Estimation and Prediction

When using the simple linear regression model we are making an assumption about the relationship between x and y. We then use the least squares method to obtain the estimated simple linear regression equation. If a significant relationship exists between x and y, and the coefficient of determination shows that the fit is good, the estimated regression equation should be useful for estimation and prediction.

Point Estimation

In the Armand's Pizza Parlors example, the estimated regression equation $\hat{y} = 60 + 5x$ provides an estimate of the relationship between the size of the student population x and quarterly sales y. We can use the estimated regression equation to develop a point estimate of the mean value of y for a particular value of x or to predict an individual value of y corresponding to a given value of x. For instance, suppose Armand's managers want a point estimate of the mean quarterly sales for all restaurants located near college campuses with 10,000 students. Using the estimated regression equation $\hat{y} = 60 + 5x$, we see that for $x = 10$ (or 10,000 students), $\hat{y} = 60 + 5(10) = 110$. Thus, a point estimate of the mean quarterly sales for all restaurants located near campuses with 10,000 students is $110,000.

Now suppose Armand's managers want to predict sales for an individual restaurant located near Talbot College, a school with 10,000 students. In this case we are not interested in the mean value for all restaurants located near campuses with 10,000 students; we are just interested in predicting quarterly sales for one individual restaurant. As it turns out, the point estimate for an individual value of y is the same as the point estimate for the mean value of y. Hence, we would predict quarterly sales of $\hat{y} = 60 + 5(10) = 110$ or $110,000 for this one restaurant.

Interval Estimation

Confidence intervals and prediction intervals show the precision of the regression results. Narrower intervals provide a higher degree of precision.

Point estimates do not provide any information about the precision associated with an estimate. For that we must develop interval estimates much like those in Chapters 8, 10, and 11. The first type of interval estimate, a **confidence interval**, is an interval estimate of the *mean value of* y for a given value of x. The second type of interval estimate, a **prediction interval**, is used whenever we want an interval estimate of an *individual value of* y for a given value of x. The point estimate of the mean value of y is the same as the point estimate of an individual value of y. But, the interval estimates we obtain for the two cases are different. The margin of error is larger for a prediction interval.

Confidence Interval for the Mean Value of y

The estimated regression equation provides a point estimate of the mean value of y for a given value of x. In developing the confidence interval, we will use the following notation.

$$x_p = \text{the particular or given value of the independent variable } x$$
$$y_p = \text{the value of the dependent variable } y \text{ corresponding to the given } x_p$$
$$E(y_p) = \text{the mean or expected value of the dependent variable } y \text{ corresponding to the given } x_p$$
$$\hat{y}_p = b_0 + b_1 x_p = \text{the point estimate of } E(y_p) \text{ when } x = x_p$$

Using this notation to estimate the mean sales for all Armand's restaurants located near a campus with 10,000 students, we have $x_p = 10$, and $E(y_p)$ denotes the unknown mean value of sales for all restaurants where $x_p = 10$. The point estimate of $E(y_p)$ is provided by $\hat{y}_p = 60 + 5(10) = 110$.

In general, we cannot expect $\hat{y}_p$ to equal $E(y_p)$ exactly. If we want to make an inference about how close $\hat{y}_p$ is to the true mean value $E(y_p)$, we will have to estimate the variance of $\hat{y}_p$. The formula for estimating the variance of $\hat{y}_p$ given x_p, denoted by $s^2_{\hat{y}_p}$, is

$$s^2_{\hat{y}_p} = s^2\left[\frac{1}{n} + \frac{(x_p - \bar{x})^2}{\Sigma(x_i - \bar{x})^2}\right] \qquad \textbf{(12.22)}$$

The estimate of the standard deviation of $\hat{y}_p$ is given by the square root of equation (12.22).

$$s_{\hat{y}_p} = s\sqrt{\frac{1}{n} + \frac{(x_p - \bar{x})^2}{\Sigma(x_i - \bar{x})^2}} \qquad \textbf{(12.23)}$$

The computational results for Armand's Pizza Parlors in Section 12.5 provided $s = 13.829$. With $x_p = 10$, $\bar{x} = 14$, and $\Sigma(x_i - \bar{x})^2 = 568$, we can use equation (12.23) to obtain

$$s_{\hat{y}_p} = 13.829\sqrt{\frac{1}{10} + \frac{(10 - 14)^2}{568}}$$
$$= 13.829\sqrt{.1282} = 4.95$$

The general expression for a confidence interval follows.

The margin of error associated with this interval estimate is $t_{\alpha/2}s_{\hat{y}_p}$.

CONFIDENCE INTERVAL FOR $E(y_p)$

$$\hat{y}_p \pm t_{\alpha/2}s_{\hat{y}_p} \qquad \textbf{(12.24)}$$

where the confidence coefficient is $1 - \alpha$ and $t_{\alpha/2}$ is based on a t distribution with $n - 2$ degrees of freedom.

Using expression (12.24) to develop a 95% confidence interval of the mean quarterly sales for all Armand's restaurants located near campuses with 10,000 students, we need the value of t for $\alpha/2 = .025$ and $n - 2 = 10 - 2 = 8$ degrees of freedom. Using Table 2 of Appendix B, we have $t_{.025} = 2.306$. Thus, with $\hat{y}_p = 110$ and a margin of error of $t_{\alpha/2}s_{\hat{y}_p} = 2.306(4.95) = 11.415$, the 95% confidence interval estimate is

$$110 \pm 11.415$$

In dollars, the 95% confidence interval for the mean quarterly sales of all restaurants near campuses with 10,000 students is \$110,000 ± \$11,415. Therefore, the 95% confidence interval for the mean quarterly sales when the student population is 10,000 is \$98,585 to \$121,415.

Note that the estimated standard deviation of $\hat{y}_p$ given by equation (12.23) is smallest when $x_p = \bar{x}$ and the quantity $x_p - \bar{x} = 0$. In this case, the estimated standard deviation of $\hat{y}_p$ becomes

$$s_{\hat{y}_p} = s\sqrt{\frac{1}{n} + \frac{(\bar{x} - \bar{x})^2}{\Sigma(x_i - \bar{x})^2}} = s\sqrt{\frac{1}{n}}$$

This result implies that we can make the best or most precise estimate of the mean value of y whenever $x_p = \bar{x}$. In fact, the further x_p is from $\bar{x}$ the larger $x_p - \bar{x}$ becomes. As a result, confidence intervals for the mean value of y will become wider as x_p deviates more from $\bar{x}$. This pattern is shown graphically in Figure 12.8.

Prediction Interval for an Individual Value of *y*

Suppose that instead of estimating the mean value of sales for all Armand's restaurants located near campuses with 10,000 students, we want to estimate the sales for an individual restaurant located near Talbot College, a school with 10,000 students. As noted previously,

FIGURE 12.8 CONFIDENCE INTERVALS FOR THE MEAN SALES y AT GIVEN VALUES OF STUDENT POPULATION x

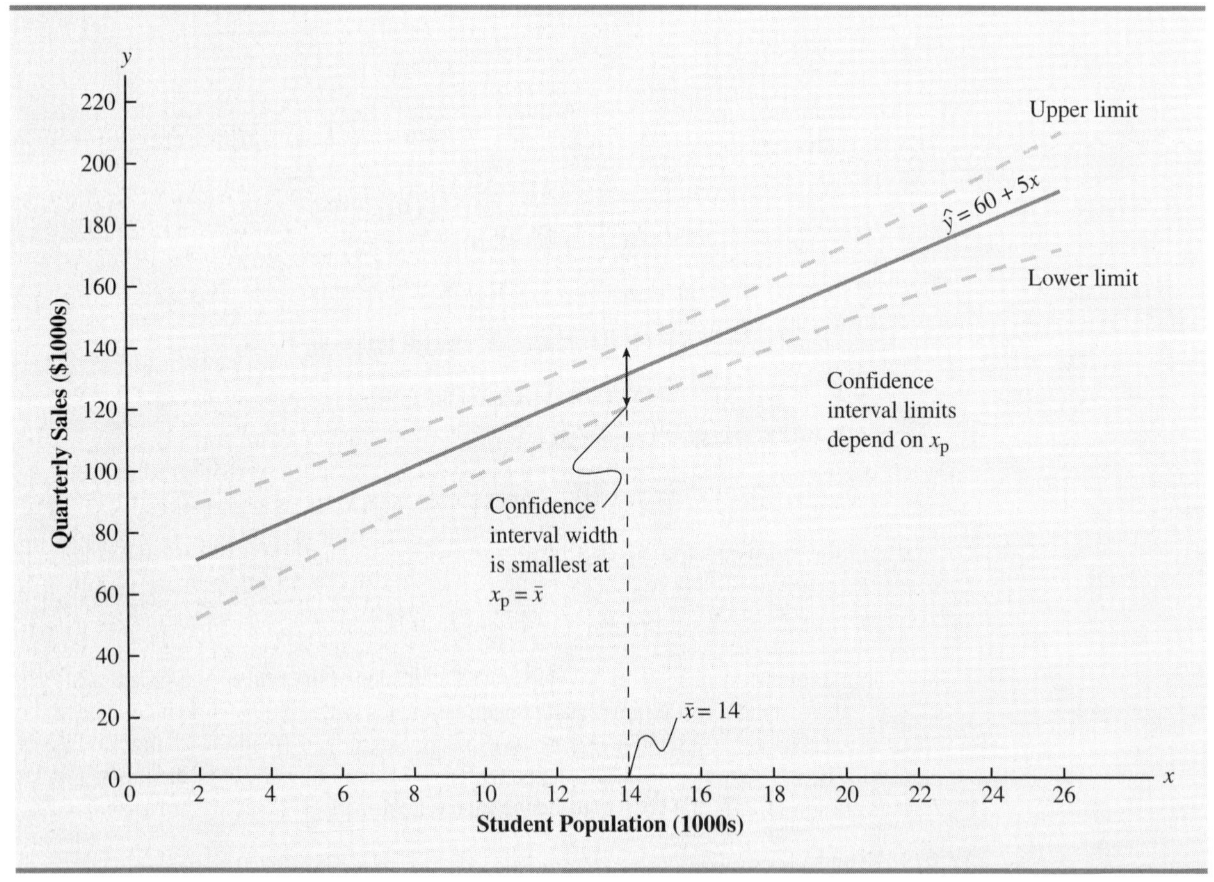

the point estimate of y_p, the value of y corresponding to the given x_p, is provided by the estimated regression equation $\hat{y}_p = b_0 + b_1x_p$. For the restaurant at Talbot College, we have $x_p = 10$ and a corresponding predicted quarterly sales of $\hat{y}_p = 60 + 5(10) = 110$, or \$110,000. Note that this value is the same as the point estimate of the mean sales for all restaurants located near campuses with 10,000 students.

To develop a prediction interval, we must first determine the variance associated with using $\hat{y}_p$ as an estimate of an individual value of y when $x = x_p$. This variance is made up of the sum of the following two components.

1. The variance of individual y values about the mean $E(y_p)$, an estimate of which is given by s^2
2. The variance associated with using $\hat{y}_p$ to estimate $E(y_p)$, an estimate of which is given by $s^2_{\hat{y}_p}$

The formula for estimating the variance of an individual value of y_p, denoted by s^2_{ind}, is

$$\begin{aligned} s^2_{\text{ind}} &= s^2 + s^2_{\hat{y}_p} \\ &= s^2 + s^2\left[\frac{1}{n} + \frac{(x_p - \bar{x})^2}{\Sigma(x_i - \bar{x})^2}\right] \\ &= s^2\left[1 + \frac{1}{n} + \frac{(x_p - \bar{x})^2}{\Sigma(x_i - \bar{x})^2}\right] \end{aligned} \tag{12.25}$$

Hence, an estimate of the standard deviation of an individual value of y_p is given by

$$s_{\text{ind}} = s\sqrt{1 + \frac{1}{n} + \frac{(x_p - \bar{x})^2}{\Sigma(x_i - \bar{x})^2}} \tag{12.26}$$

For Armand's Pizza Parlors, the estimated standard deviation corresponding to the prediction of sales for one specific restaurant located near a campus with 10,000 students is computed as follows.

$$\begin{aligned} s_{\text{ind}} &= 13.829\sqrt{1 + \frac{1}{10} + \frac{(10 - 14)^2}{568}} \\ &= 13.829\sqrt{1.1282} \\ &= 14.69 \end{aligned}$$

The general expression for a prediction interval follows.

The margin of error associated with this interval estimate is $t_{\alpha/2}s_{\text{ind}}$.

PREDICTION INTERVAL FOR y_p

$$\hat{y}_p \pm t_{\alpha/2}s_{\text{ind}} \tag{12.27}$$

where the confidence coefficient is $1 - \alpha$ and $t_{\alpha/2}$ is based on a t distribution with $n - 2$ degrees of freedom.

The 95% prediction interval for quarterly sales at Armand's Talbot College restaurant can be found by using $t_{.025} = 2.306$ and $s_{\text{ind}} = 14.69$. Thus, with $\hat{y}_p = 110$ and a margin of error of $t_{\alpha/2}s_{\text{ind}} = 2.306(14.69) = 33.875$, the 95% prediction interval is

$$110 \pm 33.875$$

FIGURE 12.9 CONFIDENCE AND PREDICTION INTERVALS FOR SALES y AT GIVEN VALUES OF STUDENT POPULATION x

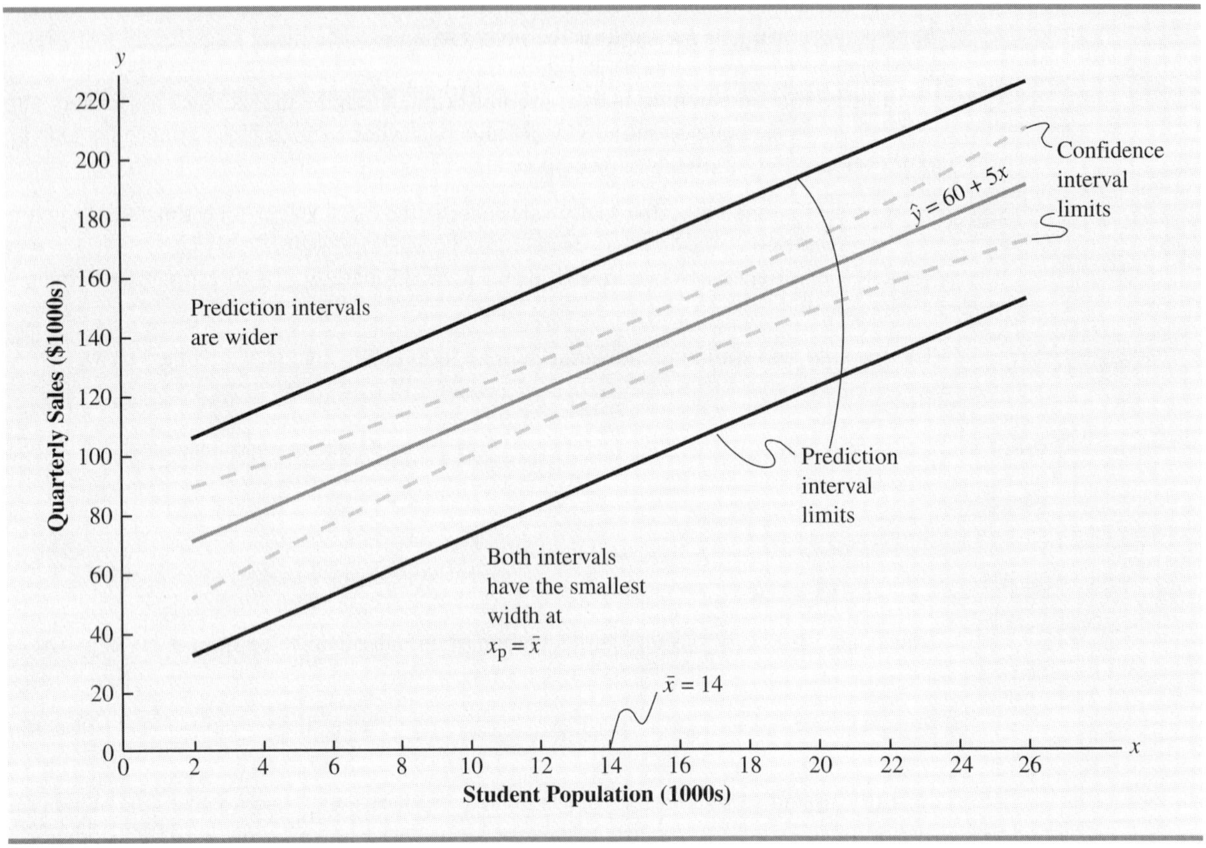

In dollars, this prediction interval is \$110,000 ± \$33,875 or \$76,125 to \$143,875. Note that the prediction interval for an individual restaurant located near a campus with 10,000 students is wider than the confidence interval for the mean sales of all restaurants located near campuses with 10,000 students. The difference reflects the fact that we are able to estimate the mean value of y more precisely than we can an individual value of y.

Both confidence interval estimates and prediction interval estimates are most precise when the value of the independent variable is $x_p = \bar{x}$. The general shapes of confidence intervals and the wider prediction intervals are shown together in Figure 12.9.

Exercises

Methods

32. The data from exercise 1 follow.

x_i	1	2	3	4	5
y_i	3	7	5	11	14

a. Use equation (12.23) to estimate the standard deviation of $\hat{y}_p$ when $x = 4$.
b. Use expression (12.24) to develop a 95% confidence interval for the expected value of y when $x = 4$.

c. Use equation (12.26) to estimate the standard deviation of an individual value of y when $x = 4$.
d. Use expression (12.27) to develop a 95% prediction interval for y when $x = 4$.

33. The data from exercise 2 follow.

x_i	2	3	5	1	8
y_i	25	25	20	30	16

a. Estimate the standard deviation of $\hat{y}_p$ when $x = 3$.
b. Develop a 95% confidence interval for the expected value of y when $x = 3$.
c. Estimate the standard deviation of an individual value of y when $x = 3$.
d. Develop a 95% prediction interval for y when $x = 3$.

34. The data from exercise 3 follow.

x_i	2	4	5	7	8
y_i	2	3	2	6	4

Develop the 95% confidence and prediction intervals when $x = 3$. Explain why these two intervals are different.

Applications

35. In exercise 18, the data on grade point average x and monthly salary y provided the estimated regression equation $\hat{y} = 1790.5 + 581.1x$.
a. Develop a 95% confidence interval for the mean starting salary for all students with a 3.0 GPA.
b. Develop a 95% prediction interval for the starting salary for Joe Heller, a student with a GPA of 3.0.

PCs

36. In exercise 10, data on the performance score (x) and the overall rating (y) for notebook PCs provided the estimated regression equation $\hat{y} = 51.819 + .1452x$ (*PC World,* February 2000).
a. Develop a point estimate of the overall rating for a PC with a performance score of 200.
b. Develop a 95% confidence interval for the mean overall score for all PCs with a performance score of 200.
c. Suppose that a new PC developed by Dell has a performance score of 200. Develop a 95% prediction interval for the overall score for this new PC.
d. Discuss the differences in your answers to parts (b) and (c).

37. In exercise 13, data were given on the adjusted gross income x and the amount of itemized deductions taken by taxpayers. Data were reported in thousands of dollars. With the estimated regression equation $\hat{y} = 4.68 + .16x$, the point estimate of a reasonable level of total itemized deductions for a taxpayer with an adjusted gross income of \$52,500 is \$13,080.
a. Develop a 95% confidence interval for the mean amount of total itemized deductions for all taxpayers with an adjusted gross income of \$52,500.
b. Develop a 95% prediction interval estimate for the amount of total itemized deductions for a particular taxpayer with an adjusted gross income of \$52,500.
c. If the particular taxpayer referred to in part (b) claimed total itemized deductions of \$20,400, would the IRS agent's request for an audit appear to be justified?
d. Use your answer to part (b) to give the IRS agent a guideline as to the amount of total itemized deductions a taxpayer with an adjusted gross income of \$52,500 should claim before an audit is recommended.

38. Refer to Exercise 21, where data on the production volume x and total cost y for a particular manufacturing operation were used to develop the estimated regression equation $\hat{y} = 1246.67 + 7.6x$.
a. The company's production schedule shows that 500 units must be produced next month. What is the point estimate of the total cost for next month?

b. Develop a 99% prediction interval for the total cost for next month.
c. If an accounting cost report at the end of next month shows that the actual production cost during the month was $6000, should managers be concerned about incurring such a high total cost for the month? Discuss.

39. Almost all U.S. light-rail systems use electric cars that run on tracks built at street level. The Federal Transit Administration claims light-rail is one of the safest modes of travel, with an accident rate of .99 accidents per million passenger miles as compared to 2.29 for buses. The following data show the miles of track and the weekday ridership in thousands of passengers for six light-rail systems (*USA Today,* January 7, 2003).

City	Miles of Track	Ridership (1000s)
Cleveland	15	15
Denver	17	35
Portland	38	81
Sacramento	21	31
San Diego	47	75
San Jose	31	30
St. Louis	34	42

a. Use these data to develop an estimated regression equation that could be used to predict the ridership given the miles of track.
b. Did the estimated regression equation provide a good fit? Explain.
c. Develop a 95% confidence interval for the mean weekday ridership for all light-rail systems with 30 miles of track.
d. Suppose that Charlotte is considering construction of a light-rail system with 30 miles of track. Develop a 95% prediction interval for the weekday ridership for the Charlotte system. Do you think that the prediction interval you developed would be of value to Charlotte planners in anticipating the number of weekday riders for their new light-rail system? Explain.

12.7 Computer Solution

Performing the regression analysis computations without the help of a computer can be quite time consuming. In this section we discuss how the computational burden can be minimized by using a computer software package such as Minitab.

We entered Armand's student population and sales data into a Minitab worksheet. The independent variable was named Pop and the dependent variable was named Sales to assist with interpretation of the computer output. Using Minitab, we obtained the printout for Armand's Pizza Parlors shown in Figure 12.10.* The interpretation of this printout follows.

1. Minitab prints the estimated regression equation as Sales = 60.0 + 5.00 Pop.
2. A table is printed that shows the values of the coefficients b_0 and b_1, the standard deviation of each coefficient, the t value obtained by dividing each coefficient value by its standard deviation, and the p-value associated with the t test. Because the p-value corresponding to $b_1 = 5.0000$ is zero (to three decimal places), the sample results indicate that the null hypothesis (H_0: $\beta_1 = 0$) should be rejected.

*The Minitab steps necessary to generate the output are given in Appendix 12.1.

FIGURE 12.10 MINITAB OUTPUT FOR THE ARMAND'S PIZZA PARLORS PROBLEM

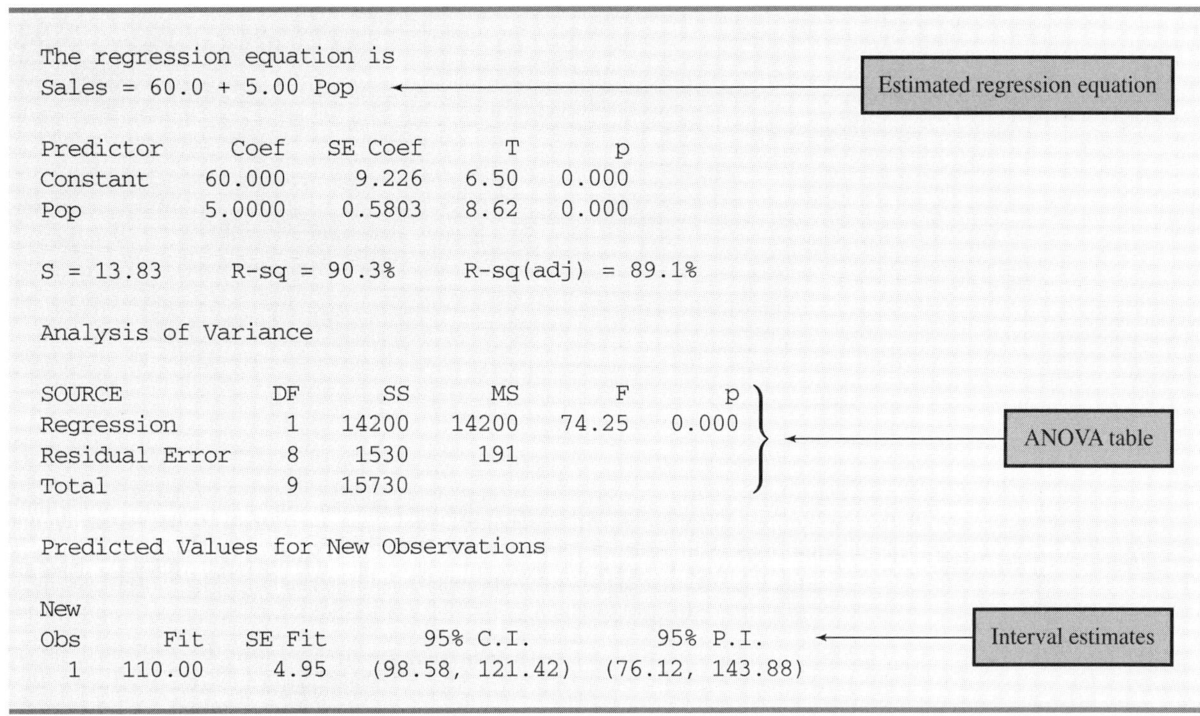

```
The regression equation is
Sales = 60.0 + 5.00 Pop

Predictor     Coef   SE Coef     T      p
Constant    60.000     9.226  6.50  0.000
Pop         5.0000    0.5803  8.62  0.000

S = 13.83    R-sq = 90.3%     R-sq(adj) = 89.1%

Analysis of Variance

SOURCE          DF     SS     MS      F      p
Regression       1  14200  14200  74.25  0.000
Residual Error   8   1530    191
Total            9  15730

Predicted Values for New Observations

New
Obs      Fit  SE Fit      95% C.I.          95% P.I.
  1   110.00    4.95  (98.58, 121.42)  (76.12, 143.88)
```


Alternatively, we could compare 8.62 (located in the t-ratio column) to the appropriate critical value. This procedure for the t test was described in Section 12.5.

3. Minitab prints the standard error of the estimate, $s = 13.83$, as well as information about the goodness of fit. Note that "R-sq = 90.3%" is the coefficient of determination expressed as a percentage.
4. The ANOVA table is printed below the heading Analysis of Variance. Minitab uses the label Residual Error for the error source of variation. Note that DF is an abbreviation for degrees of freedom and that MSR is given as 14,200 and MSE as 191. The ratio of these two values provides the F value of 74.25 and the corresponding p-value of 0.000. Because the p-value is zero (to three decimal places), the relationship between Sales and Pop is judged statistically significant.
5. The 95% confidence interval estimate of the expected sales and the 95% prediction interval estimate of sales for an individual restaurant located near a campus with 10,000 students are printed below the ANOVA table. The confidence interval is (98.58, 121.42) and the prediction interval is (76.12, 143.88) as we showed in Section 12.6.

Exercises

Applications

40. The commercial division of a real estate firm is conducting a regression analysis of the relationship between x, annual gross rents (in thousands of dollars), and y, selling price (in thousands of dollars), for apartment buildings. Data were collected on several properties recently sold and the following computer output was obtained.

```
The regression equation is
Y = 20.0 + 7.21 X

Predictor        Coef     SE Coef       T
Constant       20.000      3.2213    6.21
X               7.210      1.3626    5.29

Analysis of Variance

SOURCE             DF          SS
Regression          1     41587.3
Residual Error      7
Total               8     51984.1
```

a. How many apartment buildings were in the sample?
b. Write the estimated regression equation.
c. What is the value of s_{b_1}?
d. Use the F statistic to test the significance of the relationship at a .05 level of significance.
e. Estimate the selling price of an apartment building with gross annual rents of $50,000.

41. Following is a portion of the computer output for a regression analysis relating y = maintenance expense (dollars per month) to x = usage (hours per week) of a particular brand of computer terminal.

```
The regression equation is
Y = 6.1092 + .8951 X

Predictor        Coef     SE Coef
Constant       6.1092      0.9361
X              0.8951      0.1490

Analysis of Variance

SOURCE             DF          SS          MS
Regression          1     1575.76     1575.76
Residual Error      8      349.14       43.64
Total               9     1924.90
```

a. Write the estimated regression equation.
b. Use a t test to determine whether monthly maintenance expense is related to usage at the .05 level of significance.
c. Use the estimated regression equation to predict monthly maintenance expense for any terminal that is used 25 hours per week.

42. A regression model relating x, number of salespersons at a branch office, to y, annual sales at the office (in thousands of dollars), provided the following computer output from a regression analysis of the data.

```
The regression equation is
Y = 80.0 + 50.00 X

Predictor      Coef    SE Coef      T
Constant       80.0     11.333   7.06
X              50.0      5.482   9.12

Analysis of Variance

SOURCE          DF         SS        MS
Regression       1     6828.6    6828.6
Residual Error  28     2298.8      82.1
Total           29     9127.4
```

a. Write the estimated regression equation.
b. How many branch offices were involved in the study?
c. Compute the F statistic and test the significance of the relationship at a .05 level of significance.
d. Predict the annual sales at the Memphis branch office. This branch employs 12 salespersons.

43. Health experts recommend that runners drink 4 ounces of water every 15 minutes they run. Although handheld bottles work well for many types of runs, all-day cross-country runs require hip-mounted or over-the-shoulder hydration systems. In addition to carrying more water, hip-mounted or over-the-shoulder hydration systems offer more storage space for food and extra clothing. As the capacity increases, however, the weight and cost of these larger-capacity systems also increase. The following data show the weight (ounces) and the price for 26 hip-mounted or over-the-shoulder hydration systems (*Trail Runner Gear Guide,* 2003).

CD file
Hydration1

Model	Weight (oz.)	Price ($)
Fastdraw	3	10
Fastdraw Plus	4	12
Fitness	5	12
Access	7	20
Access Plus	8	25
Solo	9	25
Serenade	9	35
Solitaire	11	35
Gemini	21	45
Shadow	15	40
SipStream	18	60
Express	9	30
Lightning	12	40
Elite	14	60
Extender	16	65
Stinger	16	65
GelFlask Belt	3	20
GelDraw	1	7
GelFlask Clip-on Holster	2	10

(continued)

Model	Weight (oz.)	Price ($)
GelFlask Holster SS	1	10
Strider (W)	8	30
Walkabout (W)	14	40
Solitude I.C.E.	9	35
Getaway I.C.E.	19	55
Profile I.C.E.	14	50
Traverse I.C.E.	13	60

a. Use these data to develop an estimated regression equation that could be used to predict the price of a hydration system given its weight.
b. Test the significance of the relationship at the .05 level of significance.
c. Did the estimated regression equation provide a good fit? Explain.
d. Assume that the estimated regression equation developed in part (a) will also apply to hydration systems produced by other companies. Develop a 95% confidence interval estimate of the price for all hydration systems that weigh 10 ounces.
e. Assume that the estimated regression equation developed in part (a) will also apply to hydration systems produced by other companies. Develop a 95% prediction interval estimate of the price for the Back Draft system produced by Eastern Mountain Sports. The Back Draft system weighs 10 ounces.

44. Cushman & Wakefield, Inc., collects data showing the office building vacancy rates and rental rates for markets in the United States. The following data show the overall vacancy rates (%) and the average rental rates (per square foot) for the central business district for 18 selected markets.

OffRates

Market	Vacancy Rate (%)	Average Rate ($)
Atlanta	21.9	18.54
Boston	6.0	33.70
Hartford	22.8	19.67
Baltimore	18.1	21.01
Washington	12.7	35.09
Philadelphia	14.5	19.41
Miami	20.0	25.28
Tampa	19.2	17.02
Chicago	16.0	24.04
San Francisco	6.6	31.42
Phoenix	15.9	18.74
San Jose	9.2	26.76
West Palm Beach	19.7	27.72
Detroit	20.0	18.20
Brooklyn	8.3	25.00
Downtown, NY	17.1	29.78
Midtown, NY	10.8	37.03
Midtown South, NY	11.1	28.64

a. Develop a scatter diagram for these data; plot the vacancy rate on the horizontal axis.
b. Does there appear to be any relationship between vacancy rates and rental rates?
c. Develop the estimated regression equation that could be used to predict the average rental rate given the overall vacancy rate.
d. Test the significance of the relationship at the .05 level of significance.

e. Did the estimated regression equation provide a good fit? Explain.
f. Predict the expected rental rate for markets with a 25% vacancy rate in the central business district.
g. The overall vacancy rate in the central business district in Ft. Lauderdale is 11.3%. Predict the expected rental rate for Ft. Lauderdale.

12.8 Residual Analysis: Validating Model Assumptions

Residual analysis *is the primary tool for determining whether the assumed regression model is appropriate.*

As we noted previously, the *residual* for observation *i* is the difference between the observed value of the dependent variable (y_i) and the estimated value of the dependent variable ($\hat{y}_i$).

RESIDUAL FOR OBSERVATION *i*

$$y_i - \hat{y}_i \tag{12.28}$$

where

y_i = the observed value of the dependent variable
$\hat{y}_i$ = the estimated value of the dependent variable

In other words, the *i*th residual is the error resulting from using the estimated regression equation to predict the value of the dependent variable. The residuals for the Armand's Pizza Parlors example are computed in Table 12.7. The observed values of the dependent variable are in the second column and the estimated values of the dependent variable, obtained using the estimated regression equation $\hat{y} = 60 + 5x$, are in the third column. An analysis of the corresponding residuals in the fourth column will help determine whether the assumptions made about the regression model are appropriate.

Let us now review the regression assumptions for the Armand's Pizza Parlors example. A simple linear regression model was assumed.

$$y = \beta_0 + \beta_1 x + \epsilon \tag{12.29}$$

This model indicates that we assumed quarterly sales (y) to be a linear function of the size of the student population (x) plus an error term ϵ. In Section 12.4 we made the following assumptions about the error term ϵ.

1. $E(\epsilon) = 0$.
2. The variance of ϵ, denoted by σ^2, is the same for all values of x.
3. The values of ϵ are independent.
4. The error term ϵ has a normal distribution.

These assumptions provide the theoretical basis for the t test and the F test used to determine whether the relationship between x and y is significant, and for the confidence and prediction interval estimates presented in Section 12.6. If the assumptions about the error term ϵ appear questionable, the hypothesis tests about the significance of the regression relationship and the interval estimation results may not be valid.

The residuals provide the best information about ϵ; hence an analysis of the residuals is an important step in determining whether the assumptions for ϵ are appropriate. Much of

TABLE 12.7 RESIDUALS FOR ARMAND'S PIZZA PARLORS

Student Population x_i	Sales y_i	Estimated Sales $\hat{y}_i = 60 + 5x_i$	Residuals $y_i - \hat{y}_i$
2	58	70	−12
6	105	90	15
8	88	100	−12
8	118	100	18
12	117	120	−3
16	137	140	−3
20	157	160	−3
20	169	160	9
22	149	170	−21
26	202	190	12

residual analysis is based on an examination of graphical plots. In this section, we discuss the following residual plots.

1. A plot of the residuals against values of the independent variable x
2. A plot of residuals against the predicted values of the dependent variable $\hat{y}$

Residual Plot Against x

A **residual plot** against the independent variable x is a graph in which the values of the independent variable are represented by the horizontal axis and the corresponding residual values are represented by the vertical axis. A point is plotted for each residual. The first coordinate for each point is given by the value of x_i and the second coordinate is given by the corresponding value of the residual $y_i - \hat{y}_i$. For a residual plot against x with the Armand's Pizza Parlors data from Table 12.7, the coordinates of the first point are (2, −12), corresponding to $x_1 = 2$ and $y_1 - \hat{y}_1 = -12$; the coordinates of the second point are (6, 15), corresponding to $x_2 = 6$ and $y_2 - \hat{y}_2 = 15$, and so on. Figure 12.11 shows the resulting residual plot.

Before interpreting the results for this residual plot, let us consider some general patterns that might be observed in any residual plot. Three examples appear in Figure 12.12. If the assumption that the variance of ϵ is the same for all values of x and the assumed regression model is an adequate representation of the relationship between the variables, the residual plot should give an overall impression of a horizontal band of points such as the one in Panel A of Figure 12.12. However, if the variance of ϵ is not the same for all values of x—for example, if variability about the regression line is greater for larger values of x—a pattern such as the one in Panel B of Figure 12.12 could be observed. In this case, the assumption of a constant variance of ϵ is violated. Another possible residual plot is shown in Panel C. In this case, we would conclude that the assumed regression model is not an adequate representation of the relationship between the variables. A curvilinear regression model or multiple regression model should be considered.

Now let us return to the residual plot for Armand's Pizza Parlors shown in Figure 12.11. The residuals appear to approximate the horizontal pattern in Panel A of Figure 12.12. Hence, we conclude that the residual plot does not provide evidence that the assumptions

FIGURE 12.11 PLOT OF THE RESIDUALS AGAINST THE INDEPENDENT VARIABLE x FOR ARMAND'S PIZZA PARLORS

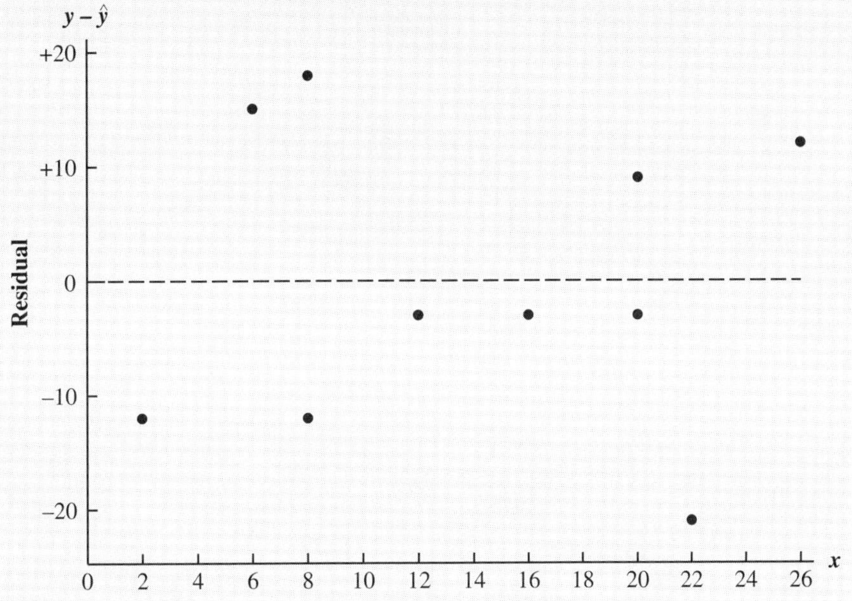

made for Armand's regression model should be challenged. At this point, we are confident in the conclusion that Armand's simple linear regression model is valid.

Experience and good judgment are always factors in the effective interpretation of residual plots. Seldom does a residual plot conform precisely to one of the patterns in Figure 12.12. Yet analysts who frequently conduct regression studies and frequently review residual plots become adept at understanding the differences between patterns that are reasonable and patterns that indicate the assumptions of the model should be questioned. A residual plot provides one technique to assess the validity of the assumptions for a regression model.

Residual Plot Against $\hat{y}$

Another residual plot represents the predicted value of the dependent variable $\hat{y}$ on the horizontal axis and the residual values on the vertical axis. A point is plotted for each residual. The first coordinate for each point is given by $\hat{y}_i$ and the second coordinate is given by the corresponding value of the ith residual $y_i - \hat{y}_i$. With the Armand's data from Table 12.7, the coordinates of the first point are (70, −12), corresponding to $\hat{y}_1 = 70$ and $y_1 - \hat{y}_1 = -12$; the coordinates of the second point are (90, 15), and so on. Figure 12.13 provides the residual plot. Note that the pattern of this residual plot is the same as the pattern of the residual plot against the independent variable x. It is not a pattern that would lead us to question the model assumptions. For simple linear regression, both the residual plot against x and the residual plot against $\hat{y}$ provide the same pattern. For multiple regression analysis, the residual plot against $\hat{y}$ is more widely used because of the presence of more than one independent variable.

FIGURE 12.12 RESIDUAL PLOTS FROM THREE REGRESSION STUDIES

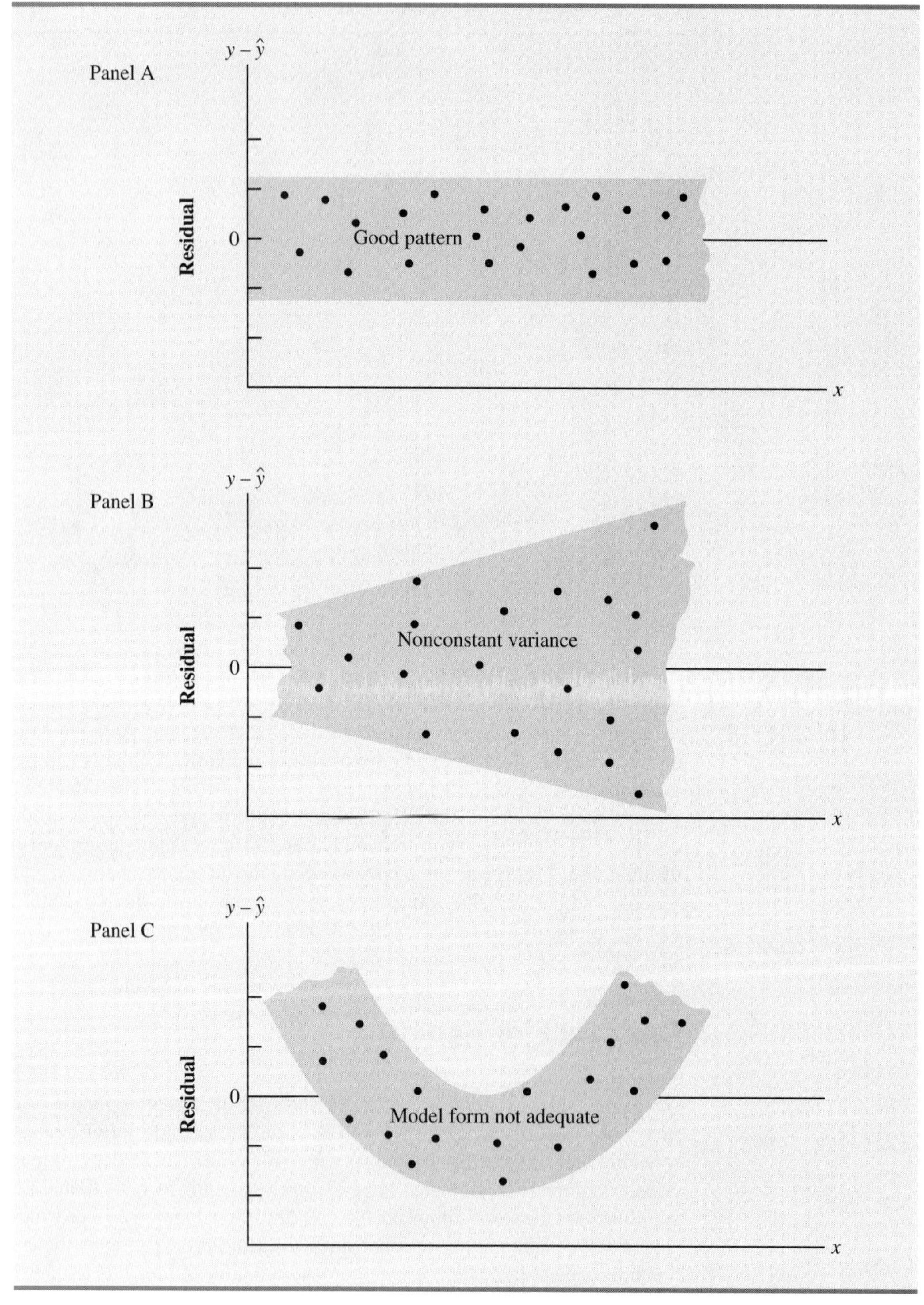

FIGURE 12.13 PLOT OF THE RESIDUALS AGAINST THE PREDICTED VALUES $\hat{y}$ FOR ARMAND'S PIZZA PARLORS

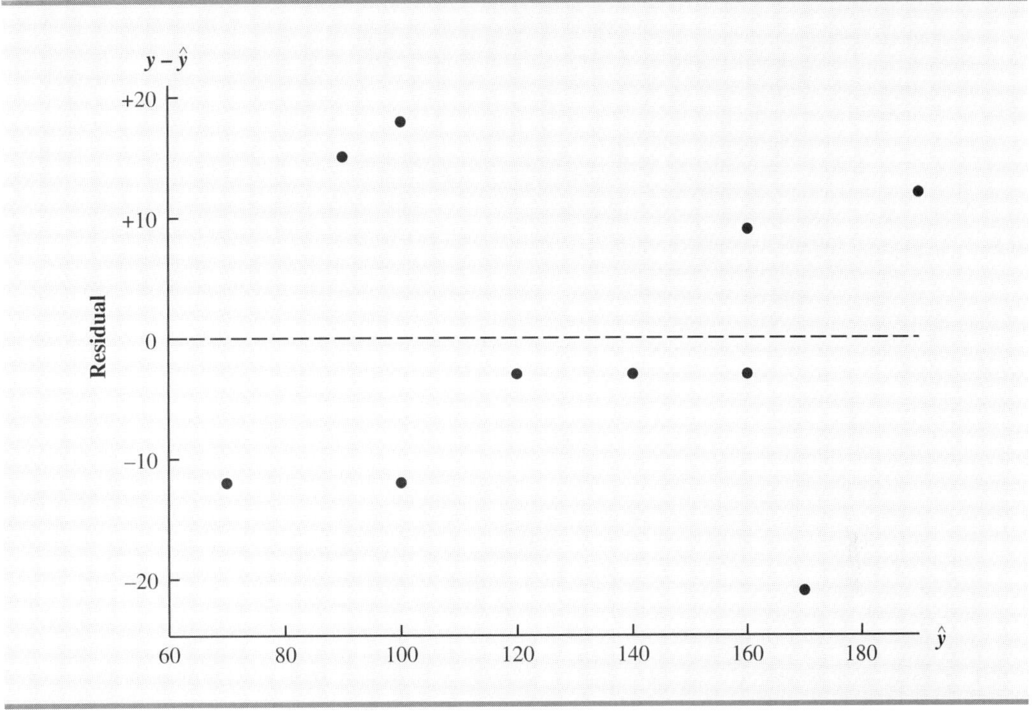

NOTES AND COMMENTS

1. We use residual plots to validate the assumptions of a regression model. If our review indicates that one or more assumptions are questionable, a different regression model or a transformation of the data should be considered. The appropriate corrective action when the assumptions are violated must be based on good judgment; recommendations from an experienced statistician can be valuable.
2. Analysis of residuals is the primary method statisticians use to verify that the assumptions associated with a regression model are valid. Even if no violations are found, it does not necessarily follow that the model will yield good predictions. However, if additional statistical tests support the conclusion of significance and the coefficient of determination is large, we should be able to develop good estimates and predictions using the estimated regression equation.

Exercises

Methods

SELF test

45. Given are data for two variables, x and y.

x_i	6	11	15	18	20
y_i	6	8	12	20	30

a. Develop an estimated regression equation for these data.
b. Compute the residuals.
c. Develop a plot of the residuals against the independent variable x. Do the assumptions about the error terms seem to be satisfied?

46. The following data were used in a regression study.

Observation	x_i	y_i	Observation	x_i	y_i
1	2	4	6	7	6
2	3	5	7	7	9
3	4	4	8	8	5
4	5	6	9	9	11
5	7	4			

a. Develop an estimated regression equation for these data.
b. Construct a plot of the residuals. Do the assumptions about the error term seem to be satisfied?

Applications

47. Data on advertising expenditures and revenue (in thousands of dollars) for the Four Seasons Restaurant follow.

Advertising Expenditures	Revenue
1	19
2	32
4	44
6	40
10	52
14	53
20	54

a. Let x equal advertising expenditures and y equal revenue. Use the method of least squares to develop a straight line approximation of the relationship between the two variables.
b. Test whether revenue and advertising expenditures are related at a .05 level of significance.
c. Construct a residual plot against the independent variable.
d. What conclusions can you draw from residual analysis? Should this model be used, or should we look for a better one?

48. Refer to exercise 9, where an estimated regression equation relating years of experience and annual sales was developed.
a. Compute the residuals and construct a residual plot for this problem.
b. Do the assumptions about the error terms seem reasonable in light of the residual plot?

49. American Depository Receipts (ADRs) are certificates traded on the NYSE representing shares of a foreign company held on deposit in a bank in its home country. The following table shows the price/earnings (P/E) ratio and the percentage return on investment (ROE) for 10 Indian companies that are likely new ADRs (*Bloomberg Personal Finance,* April 2000).

ADRs

Company	ROE	P/E
Bharti Televentures	6.43	36.88
Gujarat Ambuja Cements	13.49	27.03
Hindalco Industries	14.04	10.83

Company	ROE	P/E
ICICI	20.67	5.15
Mahanagar Telephone Nigam	22.74	13.35
NIIT	46.23	95.59
Pentamedia Graphics	28.90	54.85
Satyam Computer Services	54.01	189.21
Silverline Technologies	28.02	75.86
Videsh Sanchar Nigam	27.04	13.17

a. Use a computer package to develop an estimated regression equation relating y = P/E and x = ROE.
b. Construct a residual plot against the independent variable.
c. Do the assumptions about the error terms and model form seem reasonable in light of the residual plot?

Summary

In this chapter we showed how regression analysis can be used to determine how a dependent variable y is related to an independent variable x. In simple linear regression, the regression model is $y = \beta_0 + \beta_1 x + \epsilon$. The simple linear regression equation $E(y) = \beta_0 + \beta_1 x$ describes how the mean or expected value of y is related to x. We used sample data and the least squares method to develop the estimated regression equation $\hat{y} = b_0 + b_1 x$. In effect, b_0 and b_1 are the sample statistics used to estimate the unknown model parameters β_0 and β_1.

The coefficient of determination was presented as a measure of the goodness of fit for the estimated regression equation; it can be interpreted as the proportion of the variation in the dependent variable y that can be explained by the estimated regression equation. We reviewed correlation as a descriptive measure of the strength of a linear relationship between two variables.

The assumptions about the regression model and its associated error term ϵ were discussed, and t and F tests, based on those assumptions, were presented as a means for determining whether the relationship between two variables is statistically significant. We showed how to use the estimated regression equation to develop confidence interval estimates of the mean value of y and prediction interval estimates of individual values of y.

The chapter concluded with a section on the computer solution of regression problems and a section on the use of residual analysis to validate the model assumptions.

Glossary

Dependent variable The variable that is being predicted. It is denoted by y.

Independent variable The variable that is used to predict the value of the dependent variable. It is denoted by x.

Simple linear regression Regression analysis involving one independent variable and one dependent variable in which the relationship between the variables is approximated by a straight line.

Regression model The equation that describes how y is related to x and an error term; in simple linear regression, the regression model is $y = \beta_0 + \beta_1 x + \epsilon$.

Regression equation The equation that describes how the mean or expected value of the dependent variable is related to the independent variable; in simple linear regression, $E(y) = \beta_0 + \beta_1 x$.

Estimated regression equation The estimate of the regression equation developed from sample data by using the least squares method. For simple linear regression, the estimated regression equation is $\hat{y} = b_0 + b_1 x$.
Least squares method A procedure for using sample data to find the estimated regression equation. The objective is to minimize $\Sigma(y_i - \hat{y}_i)^2$.
Scatter diagram A graph of bivariate data in which the independent variable is on the horizontal axis and the dependent variable is on the vertical axis.
Coefficient of determination A measure of the goodness of fit of the estimated regression equation. It can be interpreted as the proportion of the variability in the dependent variable y that is explained by the estimated regression equation.
***i*th residual** The difference between the observed value of the dependent variable and the value predicted using the estimated regression equation; for the ith observation the ith residual is $y_i - \hat{y}_i$.
Correlation coefficient A measure of the strength of the linear relationship between two variables (previously discussed in Chapter 3).
Mean square error The unbiased estimate of the variance of the error term σ^2. It is denoted by MSE or s^2.
Standard error of the estimate The square root of the mean square error, denoted by s. It is the estimate of σ, the standard deviation of the error term ϵ.
ANOVA table The analysis of variance table used to summarize the computations associated with the F test for significance.
Confidence interval The interval estimate of the mean value of y for a given value of x.
Prediction interval The interval estimate of an individual value of y for a given value of x.
Residual analysis The primary tool for determining whether the assumed regression model is appropriate.
Residual plot Graphical representation of the residuals that can be used to determine whether the assumptions made about the regression model appear to be valid.

Key Formulas

Simple Linear Regression Model

$$y = \beta_0 + \beta_1 x + \epsilon \quad (12.1)$$

Simple Linear Regression Equation

$$E(y) = \beta_0 + \beta_1 x \quad (12.2)$$

Estimated Simple Linear Regression Equation

$$\hat{y} = b_0 + b_1 x \quad (12.3)$$

Least Squares Criterion

$$\min \Sigma(y_i - \hat{y}_i)^2 \quad (12.5)$$

Slope and *y*-Intercept for the Estimated Regression Equation

$$b_1 = \frac{\Sigma(x_i - \bar{x})(y_i - \bar{y})}{\Sigma(x_i - \bar{x})^2} \quad (12.6)$$

$$b_0 = \bar{y} - b_1 \bar{x} \quad (12.7)$$

Sum of Squares Due to Error

$$SSE = \Sigma(y_i - \hat{y}_i)^2 \tag{12.8}$$

Total Sum of Squares

$$SST = \Sigma(y_i - \bar{y})^2 \tag{12.9}$$

Sum of Squares Due to Regression

$$SSR = \Sigma(\hat{y}_i - \bar{y})^2 \tag{12.10}$$

Relationship Among SST, SSR, and SSE

$$SST = SSR + SSE \tag{12.11}$$

Coefficient of Determination

$$r^2 = \frac{SSR}{SST} \tag{12.12}$$

Sample Correlation Coefficient

$$\begin{aligned} r_{xy} &= (\text{sign of } b_1)\sqrt{\text{Coefficient of determination}} \\ &= (\text{sign of } b_1)\sqrt{r^2} \end{aligned} \tag{12.13}$$

Mean Square Error (Estimate of σ^2)

$$s^2 = MSE = \frac{SSE}{n - 2} \tag{12.15}$$

Standard Error of the Estimate

$$s = \sqrt{MSE} = \sqrt{\frac{SSE}{n - 2}} \tag{12.16}$$

Standard Deviation of b_1

$$\sigma_{b_1} = \frac{\sigma}{\sqrt{\Sigma(x_i - \bar{x})^2}} \tag{12.17}$$

Estimated Standard Deviation of b_1

$$s_{b_1} = \frac{s}{\sqrt{\Sigma(x_i - \bar{x})^2}} \tag{12.18}$$

***t* Test Statistic**

$$t = \frac{b_1}{s_{b_1}} \tag{12.19}$$

Mean Square Regression

$$MSR = \frac{SSR}{\text{Number of independent variables}} \tag{12.20}$$

***F* Test Statistic**

$$F = \frac{MSR}{MSE} \tag{12.21}$$

Estimated Standard Deviation of $\hat{y}_p$

$$s_{\hat{y}_p} = s\sqrt{\frac{1}{n} + \frac{(x_p - \bar{x})^2}{\Sigma(x_i - \bar{x})^2}} \tag{12.23}$$

Confidence Interval for $E(y_p)$

$$\hat{y}_p \pm t_{\alpha/2} s_{\hat{y}_p} \tag{12.24}$$

Estimated Standard Deviation of an Individual Value

$$s_{ind} = s\sqrt{1 + \frac{1}{n} + \frac{(x_p - \bar{x})^2}{\Sigma(x_i - \bar{x})^2}} \tag{12.26}$$

Prediction Interval for y_p

$$\hat{y}_p \pm t_{\alpha/2} s_{ind} \tag{12.27}$$

Residual for Observation i

$$y_i - \hat{y}_i \tag{12.28}$$

Supplementary Exercises

50. The data in the following table show the number of shares selling (millions) and the expected price (average of projected low price and projected high price) for 10 selected initial public stock offerings.

IPO

Company	Shares Selling	Expected Price ($)
American Physician	5.0	15
Apex Silver Mines	9.0	14
Dan River	6.7	15
Franchise Mortgage	8.75	17
Gene Logic	3.0	11
International Home Foods	13.6	19
PRT Group	4.6	13
Rayovac	6.7	14
RealNetworks	3.0	10
Software AG Systems	7.7	13

a. Develop an estimated regression equation with the number of shares selling as the independent variable and the expected price as the dependent variable.
b. At the .05 level of significance, is there a significant relationship between the two variables?
c. Did the estimated regression equation provide a good fit? Explain.
d. Use the estimated regression equation to estimate the expected price for a firm considering an initial public offering of 6 million shares.

51. Corporate share repurchase programs are often touted as a benefit for shareholders. But Robert Gabele, director of insider research for First Call/Thomson Financial, noted that many of these programs are undertaken solely to acquire stock for a company's incentive options for top managers. Across all companies, existing stock options in 1998 represented 6.2 percent of all common shares outstanding. The following data show the number of shares covered by option grants and the number of shares outstanding for 13 companies (*Bloomberg Personal Finance,* January/February 2000).

Options

Company	Shares of Option Grants Outstanding (millions)	Common Shares Outstanding (millions)
Adobe Systems	20.3	61.8
Apple Computer	52.7	160.9
Applied Materials	109.1	375.4
Autodesk	15.7	58.9
Best Buy	44.2	203.8
Fruit of the Loom	14.2	66.9
ITT Industries	18.0	87.9
Merrill Lynch	89.9	365.5
Novell	120.2	335.0
Parametric Technology	78.3	269.3
Reebok International	12.8	56.1
Silicon Graphics	52.6	188.8
Toys R Us	54.8	247.6

a. Develop the estimated regression equation that could be used to estimate the number of shares of option grants outstanding given the number of common shares outstanding.
b. Use the estimated regression equation to estimate the number of shares of option grants outstanding for a company that has 150 million shares of common stock outstanding.
c. Do you believe the estimated regression equation would provide a good prediction of the number of shares of option grants outstanding? Use r^2 to support your answer.

52. *Bloomberg Personal Finance* (July/August 2001) reported the market beta for Texas Instruments was 1.46. Market betas for individual stocks are determined by simple linear regression. For each stock, the dependent variable is its quarterly percentage return (capital appreciation plus dividends) minus the percentage return that could be obtained from a risk-free investment (the Treasury Bill rate is used as the risk-free rate). The independent variable is the quarterly percentage return (capital appreciation plus dividends) for the stock market (S&P 500) minus the percentage return from a risk-free investment. An estimated regression equation is developed with quarterly data; the market beta for the stock is the slope of the estimated regression equation (b_1). The value of the market beta is often interpreted as a measure of the risk associated with the stock. Market betas greater than 1 indicate that the stock is more volatile than the market average; market betas less than 1 indicate that the stock is less volatile than the market average. Suppose that the following figures are the differences between the percentage return and the risk-free return for 10 quarters for the S&P 500 and Horizon Technology.

S&P 500	Horizon
1.2	−0.7
−2.5	−2.0
−3.0	−5.5
2.0	4.7
5.0	1.8
1.2	4.1
3.0	2.6
−1.0	2.0
.5	−1.3
2.5	5.5

a. Develop an estimated regression equation that can be used to determine the market beta for Horizon Technology. What is Horizon Technology's market beta?
b. Test for a significant relationship at the .05 level of significance.
c. Did the estimated regression equation provide a good fit? Explain.
d. Use the market betas of Texas Instruments and Horizon Technology to compare the risk associated with the two stocks.

53. The Australian Public Service Commission's State of the Service Report 2002–2003 reported job satisfaction ratings for employees. One of the survey questions asked employees to choose the five most important workplace factors (from a list of factors) that most affected how satisfied they were with their job. Respondents were then asked to indicate their level of satisfaction with their top five factors. The following data show the percentage of employees who nominated the factor in their top five, and a corresponding satisfaction rating measured using the percentage of employees who nominated the factor in the top five and who were "very satisfied" or "satisfied" with the factor in their current workplace (http://www.apsc.gov.au/stateoftheservice).

JobSat

Workplace Factor	Top Five (%)	Satisfaction Rating (%)
Appropriate workload	30	49
Chance to be creative/innovative	38	64
Chance to make a useful contribution to society	40	67
Duties/expectations made clear	40	69
Flexible working arrangements	55	86
Good working relationships	60	85
Interesting work provided	48	74
Opportunities for career development	33	43
Opportunities to develop my skills	46	66
Opportunities to utilize my skills	50	70
Regular feedback/recognition for effort	42	53
Salary	47	62
Seeing tangible results from my work	42	69

a. Develop a scatter diagram with Top Five (%) on the horizontal axis and Satisfaction Rating (%) on the vertical axis.
b. What does the scatter diagram developed in part (a) indicate about the relationship between the two variables?
c. Develop the estimated regression equation that could be used to predict the Satisfaction Rating (%) given the Top Five (%).
d. Test for a significant relationship at the .05 level of significance.
e. Did the estimated regression equation provide a good fit? Explain.
f. What is the value of the sample correlation coefficient?

54. Jensen Tire & Auto is in the process of deciding whether to purchase a maintenance contract for its new computer wheel alignment and balancing machine. Managers feel that maintenance expense should be related to usage, and they collected the following information on weekly usage (hours) and annual maintenance expense (in hundreds of dollars).

Weekly Usage (hours)	Annual Maintenance Expense
13	17.0
10	22.0
20	30.0

Weekly Usage (hours)	Annual Maintenance Expense
28	37.0
32	47.0
17	30.5
24	32.5
31	39.0
40	51.5
38	40.0

a. Develop the estimated regression equation that relates annual maintenance expense to weekly usage.
b. Test the significance of the relationship in part (a) at a .05 level of significance.
c. Jensen expects to use the new machine 30 hours per week. Develop a 95% prediction interval for the company's annual maintenance expense.
d. If the maintenance contract costs $3000 per year, would you recommend purchasing it? Why or why not?

55. In a manufacturing process the assembly line speed (feet per minute) was thought to affect the number of defective parts found during the inspection process. To test this theory, managers devised a situation in which the same batch of parts was inspected visually at a variety of line speeds. They collected the following data.

Line Speed	Number of Defective Parts Found
20	21
20	19
40	15
30	16
60	14
40	17

a. Develop the estimated regression equation that relates line speed to the number of defective parts found.
b. At a .05 level of significance, determine whether line speed and number of defective parts found are related.
c. Did the estimated regression equation provide a good fit to the data?
d. Develop a 95% confidence interval to predict the mean number of defective parts for a line speed of 50 feet per minute.

56. A sociologist was hired by a large city hospital to investigate the relationship between the number of unauthorized days that employees are absent per year and the distance (miles) between home and work for the employees. A sample of 10 employees was chosen, and the following data were collected.

Distance to Work	Number of Days Absent
1	8
3	5
4	8
6	7
8	6

(continued)

Distance to Work	Number of Days Absent
10	3
12	5
14	2
14	4
18	2

a. Develop a scatter diagram for these data. Does a linear relationship appear reasonable? Explain.
b. Develop the least squares estimated regression equation.
c. Is there a significant relationship between the two variables? Use $\alpha = .05$.
d. Did the estimated regression equation provide a good fit? Explain.
e. Use the estimated regression equation developed in part (b) to develop a 95% confidence interval for the expected number of days absent for employees living 5 miles from the company.

57. The regional transit authority for a major metropolitan area wants to determine whether there is any relationship between the age of a bus and the annual maintenance cost. A sample of 10 buses resulted in the following data.

Age of Bus (years)	Maintenance Cost ($)
1	350
2	370
2	480
2	520
2	590
3	550
4	750
4	800
5	790
5	950

a. Develop the least squares estimated regression equation.
b. Test to see whether the two variables are significantly related with $\alpha = .05$.
c. Did the least squares line provide a good fit to the observed data? Explain.
d. Develop a 95% prediction interval for the maintenance cost for a specific bus that is 4 years old.

58. A marketing professor at Givens College is interested in the relationship between hours spent studying and total points earned in a course. Data collected on 10 students who took the course last quarter follow.

Hours Spent Studying	Total Points Earned
45	40
30	35
90	75
60	65
105	90
65	50
90	90
80	80
55	45
75	65

a. Develop an estimated regression equation showing how total points earned is related to hours spent studying.
b. Test the significance of the model with $\alpha = .05$.
c. Predict the total points earned by Mark Sweeney. He spent 95 hours studying.
d. Develop a 95% prediction interval for the total points earned by Mark Sweeney.

59. The Transactional Records Access Clearinghouse at Syracuse University reported data showing the odds of an Internal Revenue Service audit. The following table shows the average adjusted gross income reported and the percentage of the returns that were audited for 20 selected IRS districts.

CD file

IRSAudit

District	Adjusted Gross Income ($)	Percentage Audited
Los Angeles	36,664	1.3
Sacramento	38,845	1.1
Atlanta	34,886	1.1
Boise	32,512	1.1
Dallas	34,531	1.0
Providence	35,995	1.0
San Jose	37,799	0.9
Cheyenne	33,876	0.9
Fargo	30,513	0.9
New Orleans	30,174	0.9
Oklahoma City	30,060	0.8
Houston	37,153	0.8
Portland	34,918	0.7
Phoenix	33,291	0.7
Augusta	31,504	0.7
Albuquerque	29,199	0.6
Greensboro	33,072	0.6
Columbia	30,859	0.5
Nashville	32,566	0.5
Buffalo	34,296	0.5

a. Develop the estimated regression equation that could be used to predict the percentage audited given the average adjusted gross income reported.
b. At the .05 level of significance, determine whether the adjusted gross income and the percentage audited are related.
c. Did the estimated regression equation provide a good fit? Explain.
d. Use the estimated regression equation developed in part (a) to calculate a 95% confidence interval for the expected percentage audited for districts with an average adjusted gross income of $35,000.

Case Problem 1 Spending and Student Achievement

Is the educational achievement level of students related to how much the state in which they reside spends on education? In many communities taxpayers are asking this important question as school districts request tax revenue increases for education. In this case, you will be asked to analyze data on spending and achievement scores in order to determine whether there is any relationship between spending and student achievement in the public schools.

The federal government's National Assessment of Educational Progress (NAEP) program is frequently used to measure the educational achievement of students. Table 12.8 shows the total current spending per pupil per year, and the composite NAEP test score for 35 states that participated in the NAEP program. These data are available on the CD

TABLE 12.8 SPENDING PER PUPIL AND COMPOSITE TEST SCORES FOR STATES THAT PARTICIPATED IN THE NAEP PROGRAM

NAEP

State	Spending per Pupil ($)	Composite Test Score
Louisiana	4049	581
Mississippi	3423	582
California	4917	580
Hawaii	5532	580
South Carolina	4304	603
Alabama	3777	604
Georgia	4663	611
Florida	4934	611
New Mexico	4097	614
Arkansas	4060	615
Delaware	6208	615
Tennessee	3800	618
Arizona	4041	618
West Virginia	5247	625
Maryland	6100	625
Kentucky	5020	626
Texas	4520	627
New York	8162	628
North Carolina	4521	629
Rhode Island	6554	638
Washington	5338	639
Missouri	4483	641
Colorado	4772	644
Indiana	5128	649
Utah	3280	650
Wyoming	5515	657
Connecticut	7629	657
Massachusetts	6413	658
Nebraska	5410	660
Minnesota	5477	661
Iowa	5060	665
Montana	4985	667
Wisconsin	6055	667
North Dakota	4374	671
Maine	5561	675

accompanying the text in the file named NAEP. The composite test score is the sum of the math, science, and reading scores on the 1996 (1994 for reading) NAEP test. Pupils tested are in grade 8, except for reading, which is given to fourth-graders only. The maximum possible score is 1300. Table 12.9 shows the spending per pupil for 13 states that did not participate in relevant NAEP surveys. These data were reported in an article on spending and achievement level appearing in *Forbes* (November 3, 1997).

Managerial Report

1. Develop numerical and graphical summaries of the data.
2. Use regression analysis to investigate the relationship between the amount spent per pupil and the composite score on the NAEP test. Discuss your findings.

TABLE 12.9 SPENDING PER PUPIL FOR STATES THAT DID NOT PARTICIPATE IN THE NAEP PROGRAM

State	Spending per Pupil ($)
Idaho	3602
South Dakota	4067
Oklahoma	4265
Nevada	4658
Kansas	5164
Illinois	5297
New Hampshire	5387
Ohio	5438
Oregon	5588
Vermont	6269
Michigan	6391
Pennsylvania	6579
Alaska	7890

3. Do you think that the estimated regression equation developed for these data could be used to estimate the composite test scores for the states that did not participate in the NAEP program?
4. Suppose that you only considered states that spend at least $4000 per pupil but not more than $6000 per pupil. For these states, does the relationship between the two variables appear to be any different than for the complete data set? Discuss the results of your findings and whether you think deleting states with spending less than $4000 per year and more than $6000 per pupil is appropriate.
5. Develop estimates of the composite test scores for the states that did not participate in the NAEP program.
6. Based upon your analyses, do you think that the educational achievement level of students is related to how much the state spends on education?

Case Problem 2 U.S. Department of Transportation

As part of a study on transportation safety, the U.S. Department of Transportation collected data on the number of fatal accidents per 1000 licenses and the percentage of licensed drivers under the age of 21 in a sample of 42 cities. Data collected over a one-year period follow. These data are available on the CD accompanying the text in the file named Safety.

Safety

Percentage Under 21	Fatal Accidents per 1000 Licenses	Percentage Under 21	Fatal Accidents per 1000 Licenses
13	2.962	17	4.100
12	0.708	8	2.190
8	0.885	16	3.623
12	1.652	15	2.623
11	2.091	9	0.835
17	2.627	8	0.820
18	3.830	14	2.890
8	0.368	8	1.267

(continued)

Percentage Under 21	Fatal Accidents per 1000 Licenses	Percentage Under 21	Fatal Accidents per 1000 Licenses
13	1.142	15	3.224
8	0.645	10	1.014
9	1.028	10	0.493
16	2.801	14	1.443
12	1.405	18	3.614
9	1.433	10	1.926
10	0.039	14	1.643
9	0.338	16	2.943
11	1.849	12	1.913
12	2.246	15	2.814
14	2.855	13	2.634
14	2.352	9	0.926
11	1.294	17	3.256

Managerial Report

1. Develop numerical and graphical summaries of the data.
2. Use regression analysis to investigate the relationship between the number of fatal accidents and the percentage of drivers under the age of 21. Discuss your findings.
3. What conclusion and recommendations can you derive from your analysis?

Case Problem 3 Alumni Giving

Alumni donations are an important source of revenue for colleges and universities. If administrators could determine the factors that influence increases in the percentage of alumni who make a donation, they might be able to implement policies that could lead to increased revenues. Research shows that students who are more satisfied with their contact with teachers are more likely to graduate. As a result, one might suspect that smaller class sizes and lower student-faculty ratios might lead to a higher percentage of satisfied graduates, which in turn might lead to increases in the percentage of alumni who make a donation. Table 12.10 shows data for 48 national universities (*America's Best Colleges,* Year 2000 Edition). The column labeled % of Classes Under 20 shows the percentage of classes offered with fewer than 20 students. The column labeled Student/Faculty Ratio is the number of students enrolled divided by the total number of faculty. Finally, the column labeled Alumni Giving Rate is the percentage of alumni that made a donation to the university.

Managerial Report

1. Develop numerical and graphical summaries of the data.
2. Use regression analysis to develop an estimated regression equation that could be used to predict the alumni giving rate given the percentage of classes with fewer than 20 students.
3. Use regression analysis to develop an estimated regression equation that could be used to predict the alumni giving rate given the student-faculty ratio.
4. Which of the two estimated regression equations provides the best fit? For this estimated regression equation, perform an analysis of the residuals and discuss your findings and conclusions.
5. What conclusions and recommendations can you derive from your analysis?

Alumni

TABLE 12.10 DATA FOR 48 NATIONAL UNIVERSITIES

	% of Classes Under 20	Student/Faculty Ratio	Alumni Giving Rate
Boston College	39	13	25
Brandeis University	68	8	33
Brown University	60	8	40
California Institute of Technology	65	3	46
Carnegie Mellon University	67	10	28
Case Western Reserve Univ.	52	8	31
College of William and Mary	45	12	27
Columbia University	69	7	31
Cornell University	72	13	35
Dartmouth College	61	10	53
Duke University	68	8	45
Emory University	65	7	37
Georgetown University	54	10	29
Harvard University	73	8	46
Johns Hopkins University	64	9	27
Lehigh University	55	11	40
Massachusetts Inst. of Technology	65	6	44
New York University	63	13	13
Northwestern University	66	8	30
Pennsylvania State Univ.	32	19	21
Princeton University	68	5	67
Rice University	62	8	40
Stanford University	69	7	34
Tufts University	67	9	29
Tulane University	56	12	17
U. of California–Berkeley	58	17	18
U. of California–Davis	32	19	7
U. of California–Irvine	42	20	9
U. of California–Los Angeles	41	18	13
U. of California–San Diego	48	19	8
U. of California–Santa Barbara	45	20	12
U. of Chicago	65	4	36
U. of Florida	31	23	19
U. of Illinois–Urbana Champaign	29	15	23
U. of Michigan–Ann Arbor	51	15	13
U. of North Carolina–Chapel Hill	40	16	26
U. of Notre Dame	53	13	49
U. of Pennsylvania	65	7	41
U. of Rochester	63	10	23
U. of Southern California	53	13	22
U. of Texas–Austin	39	21	13
U. of Virginia	44	13	28
U. of Washington	37	12	12
U. of Wisconsin–Madison	37	13	13
Vanderbilt University	68	9	31
Wake Forest University	59	11	38
Washington University–St. Louis	73	7	33
Yale University	77	7	50

Case Problem 4 Major League Baseball Team Values

A group led by John Henry paid $700 million to purchase the Boston Red Sox, even though the Red Sox have not won the World Series since 1918 and posted an operating loss of $11.4 million for 2001. Moreover, *Forbes* magazine estimates that the current value of the team is actually $426 million. *Forbes* attributes the difference between the current value for a team and the price investors are willing to pay to the fact that the purchase of a team often includes the acquisition of a grossly undervalued cable network. For instance, in purchasing the Boston Red Sox, the new owners also got an 80% interest in the New England Sports Network. Table 12.11 shows data for the 30 major league teams (*Forbes,* April 15, 2002). The column labeled Value contains the values of the teams based on current stadium deals, without deduction for debt. The column labeled Income indicates the earnings before interest, taxes, and depreciation.

Managerial Report

1. Develop numerical and graphical summaries of the data.
2. Use regression analysis to investigate the relationship between value and income. Discuss your findings.

MLB

TABLE 12.11 DATA FOR MAJOR LEAGUE BASEBALL TEAMS

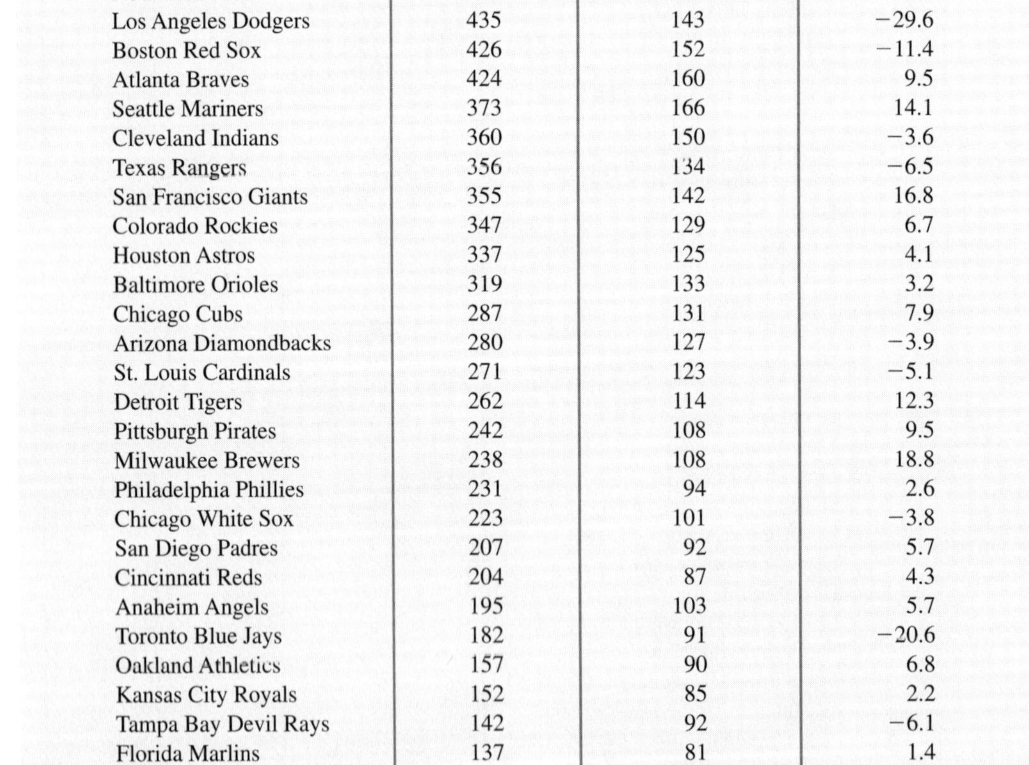

Team	Value	Revenue	Income
New York Yankees	730	215	18.7
New York Mets	482	169	14.3
Los Angeles Dodgers	435	143	−29.6
Boston Red Sox	426	152	−11.4
Atlanta Braves	424	160	9.5
Seattle Mariners	373	166	14.1
Cleveland Indians	360	150	−3.6
Texas Rangers	356	134	−6.5
San Francisco Giants	355	142	16.8
Colorado Rockies	347	129	6.7
Houston Astros	337	125	4.1
Baltimore Orioles	319	133	3.2
Chicago Cubs	287	131	7.9
Arizona Diamondbacks	280	127	−3.9
St. Louis Cardinals	271	123	−5.1
Detroit Tigers	262	114	12.3
Pittsburgh Pirates	242	108	9.5
Milwaukee Brewers	238	108	18.8
Philadelphia Phillies	231	94	2.6
Chicago White Sox	223	101	−3.8
San Diego Padres	207	92	5.7
Cincinnati Reds	204	87	4.3
Anaheim Angels	195	103	5.7
Toronto Blue Jays	182	91	−20.6
Oakland Athletics	157	90	6.8
Kansas City Royals	152	85	2.2
Tampa Bay Devil Rays	142	92	−6.1
Florida Marlins	137	81	1.4
Minnesota Twins	127	75	3.6
Montreal Expos	108	63	−3.4

3. Use regression analysis to investigate the relationship between value and revenue. Discuss your findings.
4. What conclusions and recommendations can you derive from your analysis?

Appendix 12.1 Regression Analysis with Minitab

Armand's

In Section 12.7 we discussed the computer solution of regression problems by showing Minitab's output for the Armand's Pizza Parlors problem. In this appendix, we describe the steps required to generate the Minitab computer solution. First, the data must be entered in a Minitab worksheet. Student population data are entered in column C1 and quarterly sales data are entered in column C2. The variable names Pop and Sales are entered as the column headings on the worksheet. In subsequent steps, we refer to the data by using the variable names Pop and Sales or the column indicators C1 and C2. The following steps describe how to use Minitab to produce the regression results shown in Figure 12.10.

Step 1. Select the **Stat** menu
Step 2. Select the **Regression** menu
Step 3. Choose **Regression**
Step 4. When the Regression dialog box appears:
Enter Sales in the **Response** box
Enter Pop in the **Predictors** box
Click the **Options** button
When the Regression-Options dialog box appears:
Enter 10 in the **Prediction intervals for new observations** box
Click **OK**
When the Regression dialog box reappears:
Click **OK**

The Minitab regression dialog box provides additional capabilities that can be obtained by selecting the desired options. For instance, to obtain a residual plot that shows the predicted value of the dependent variable $\hat{y}$ on the horizontal axis and the residual values on the vertical axis, step 4 would be as follows:

Step 4. When the Regression dialog box appears:
Enter Sales in the **Response** box
Enter Pop in the **Predictors** box
Click the **Graphs** button
When the Regression-Graphs dialog box appears:
Select **Regular** under Residuals for Plots
Select **Residuals versus fits** under Residual Plots
Click **OK**
When the Regression dialog box reappears:
Click **OK**

Appendix 12.2 Regression Analysis with Excel

Armand's

In this appendix we will illustrate how Excel's Regression tool can be used to perform the regression analysis computations for the Armand's Pizza Parlors problem. Refer to Figure 12.14 as we describe the steps involved. The labels Restaurant, Population, and Sales are entered into cells A1:C1 of the worksheet. To identify each of the 10 observations, we entered the

FIGURE 12.14 EXCEL SOLUTION TO THE ARMAND'S PIZZA PARLORS PROBLEM

	A	B	C	D	E	F	G	H	I	J
1	**Restaurant**	**Population**	**Sales**							
2	1	2	58							
3	2	6	105							
4	3	8	88							
5	4	8	118							
6	5	12	117							
7	6	16	137							
8	7	20	157							
9	8	20	169							
10	9	22	149							
11	10	26	202							
12										
13	SUMMARY OUTPUT									
14										
15	*Regression Statistics*									
16	Multiple R	0.9501								
17	R Square	0.9027								
18	Adjusted R Square	0.8906								
19	Standard Error	13.8293								
20	Observations	10								
21										
22	ANOVA									
23		*df*	*SS*	*MS*	*F*	*Significance F*				
24	Regression	1	14200	14200	74.2484	2.55E-05				
25	Residual	8	1530	191.25						
26	Total	9	15730							
27										
28		*Coefficients*	*Standard Error*	*t Stat*	*P-value*	*Lower 95%*	*Upper 95%*	*Lower 99.0%*	*Upper 99.0%*	
29	Intercept	60	9.2260	6.5033	0.0002	38.7247	81.2753	29.0431	90.9569	
30	Population	5	0.5803	8.6167	2.55E-05	3.6619	6.3381	3.0530	6.9470	
31										

numbers 1 through 10 into cells A2:A11. The sample data are entered into cells B2:C11. The following steps describe how to use Excel to produce the regression results.

Step 1. Select the **Tools** menu
Step 2. Choose **Data Analysis**
Step 3. Choose **Regression** from the list of Analysis Tools
Step 4. Click **OK**
Step 5. When the Regression dialog box appears:
Enter C1:C11 in the **Input Y Range** box
Enter B1:B11 in the **Input X Range** box
Select **Labels**
Select **Confidence Level**
Enter 99 in the **Confidence Level** box
Select **Output Range**

Enter A13 in the **Output Range** box
(Any upper-left-hand corner cell indicating where the output is to begin may be entered here.)
Click **OK**

The first section of the output, titled *Regression Statistics,* contains summary statistics such as the coefficient of determination (R Square). The second section of the output, titled ANOVA, contains the analysis of variance table. The last section of the output, which is not titled, contains the estimated regression coefficients and related information. We will begin our discussion of the interpretation of the regression output with the information contained in cells A28:I30.

Interpretation of Estimated Regression Equation Output

The y-intercept of the estimated regression line, $b_0 = 60$, is shown in cell B29, and the slope of the estimated regression line, $b_1 = 5$, is shown in cell B30. The label Intercept in cell A29 and the label Population in cell A30 are used to identify these two values.

In Section 12.5 we showed that the estimated standard deviation of b_1 is $s_{b_1} = .5803$. Note that the value in cell C30 is .5803. The label Standard Error in cell C28 is Excel's way of indicating that the value in cell C30 is the standard error, or standard deviation, of b_1. Recall that the t test for a significant relationship required the computation of the t statistic, $t = b_1/s_{b_1}$. For the Armand's data, the value of t that we computed was $t = 5/.5803 = 8.62$. The label in cell D28, *t Stat,* reminds us that cell D30 contains the value of the t test statistic.

The value in cell E30 is the p-value associated with the t test for significance. Excel has displayed the p-value in cell E30 using scientific notation. To obtain the decimal value, we move the decimal point 5 places to the left, obtaining a value of .0000255. Because the p-value $= .0000255 < \alpha = .01$, we can reject H_0 and conclude that we have a significant relationship between student population and quarterly sales.

The information in cells F28:I30 can be used to develop confidence interval estimates of the y-intercept and slope of the estimated regression equation. Excel always provides the lower and upper limits for a 95% confidence interval. Recall that in step 4 we selected Confidence Level and entered 99 in the Confidence Level box. As a result, Excel's Regression tool also provides the lower and upper limits for a 99% confidence interval. The value in cell H30 is the lower limit for the 99% confidence interval estimate of β_1 and the value in cell I30 is the upper limit. Thus, after rounding, the 99% confidence interval estimate of β_1 is 3.05 to 6.95. The values in cells F30 and G30 provide the lower and upper limits for the 95% confidence interval. Thus, the 95% confidence interval is 3.66 to 6.34.

Interpretation of ANOVA Output

The information in cells A22:F26 is a summary of the analysis of variance computations. The three sources of variation are labeled Regression, Residual, and Total. The label *df* in cell B23 stands for degrees of freedom, the label *SS* in cell C23 stands for sum of squares, and the label *MS* in cell D23 stands for mean square.

In Section 12.5 we stated that the mean square error, obtained by dividing the error or residual sum of squares by its degrees of freedom, provides an estimate of σ^2. The value in cell D25, 191.25, is the mean square error for the Armand's regression output. In Section 12.5 we showed that an F test could also be used to test for significance in regression. The value in cell F24, .0000255, is the p-value associated with the F test for significance. Because the p-value $= .0000255 < \alpha = .01$, we can reject H_0 and conclude that we have a

The label Significance F may be more meaningful if you think of the value in cell F24 as the observed level of significance for the F test.

significant relationship between student population and quarterly sales. The label Excel uses to identify the p-value for the F test for significance, shown in cell F23, is *Significance F.*

Interpretation of Regression Statistics Output

The coefficient of determination, .9027, appears in cell B17; the corresponding label, R Square, is shown in cell A17. The square root of the coefficient of determination provides the sample correlation coefficient of .9501 shown in cell B16. Note that Excel uses the label Multiple R (cell A16) to identify this value. In cell A19, the label Standard Error is used to identify the value of the standard error of the estimate shown in cell B19. Thus, the standard error of the estimate is 13.8293. We caution the reader to keep in mind that in the Excel output, the label Standard Error appears in two different places. In the Regression Statistics section of the output, the label Standard Error refers to the estimate of σ. In the Estimated Regression Equation section of the output the label *Standard Error* refers to s_{b_1}, the standard deviation of the sampling distribution of b_1.

CHAPTER 13

Multiple Regression

CONTENTS

STATISTICS *in* PRACTICE

INTERNATIONAL PAPER*
PURCHASE, NEW YORK

International Paper is the world's largest paper and forest products company. The company employs more than 117,000 people in its operations in nearly 50 countries, and exports its products to more than 130 nations. International Paper produces building materials such as lumber and plywood; consumer packaging materials such as disposable cups and containers; industrial packaging materials such as corrugated boxes and shipping containers; and a variety of papers for use in photocopiers, printers, books, and advertising materials.

To make paper products, pulp mills process wood chips and chemicals to produce wood pulp. The wood pulp is then used at a paper mill to produce paper products. In the production of white paper products, the pulp must be bleached to remove any discoloration. A key bleaching agent used in the process is chlorine dioxide, which, because of its combustible nature, is usually produced at a pulp mill facility and then piped in solution form into the bleaching tower of the pulp mill. To improve one of the processes used to produce chlorine dioxide, researchers studied the process's control and efficiency. One aspect of the study looked at the chemical-feed rate for chlorine dioxide production.

To produce the chlorine dioxide, four chemicals flow at metered rates into the chlorine dioxide generator. The chlorine dioxide produced in the generator flows to an absorber where chilled water absorbs the chlorine dioxide gas to form a chlorine dioxide solution. The solution is then piped into the paper mill. A key part of controlling the process involves the chemical-feed rates. Historically, experienced operators set the chemical-feed rates, but this approach led to overcontrol by the operators. Consequently, chemical engineers at the mill requested that a set of control equations, one for each chemical feed, be developed to aid the operators in setting the rates.

*The authors are indebted to Marian Williams and Bill Griggs for providing this Statistics in Practice. This application was originally developed at Champion International Corporation, which became part of International Paper in 2000.

Multiple regression analysis assisted in the development of a better bleaching process for making white paper products. © Lester Lefkowitz/Corbis.

Using multiple regression analysis, statistical analysts developed an estimated multiple regression equation for each of the four chemicals used in the process. Each equation related the production of chlorine dioxide to the amount of chemical used and the concentration level of the chlorine dioxide solution. The resulting set of four equations was programmed into a microcomputer at each mill. In the new system, operators enter the concentration of the chlorine dioxide solution and the desired production rate; the computer software then calculates the chemical feed needed to achieve the desired production rate. After the operators began using the control equations, the chlorine dioxide generator efficiency increased, and the number of times the concentrations fell within acceptable ranges increased significantly.

This example shows how multiple regression analysis can be used to develop a better bleaching process for producing white paper products. In this chapter we will discuss how computer software packages are used for such purposes. Most of the concepts introduced in Chapter 12 for simple linear regression can be directly extended to the multiple regression case.

In Chapter 12 we presented simple linear regression and demonstrated its use in developing an estimated regression equation that describes the relationship between two variables. Recall that the variable being predicted or explained is called the dependent variable and the variable being used to predict or explain the dependent variable is called the independent variable. In this chapter we continue our study of regression analysis by considering situations involving two or more independent variables. This subject area, called **multiple regression analysis**, enables us to consider more factors and thus obtain better estimates than are possible with simple linear regression.

13.1 Multiple Regression Model

Multiple regression analysis is the study of how a dependent variable y is related to two or more independent variables. In the general case, we will use p to denote the number of independent variables.

Regression Model and Regression Equation

The concepts of a regression model and a regression equation introduced in the preceding chapter are applicable in the multiple regression case. The equation that describes how the dependent variable y is related to the independent variables $x_1, x_2, \ldots x_p$ and an error term is called the **multiple regression model**. We begin with the assumption that the multiple regression model takes the following form.

MULTIPLE REGRESSION MODEL

$$y = \beta_0 + \beta_1 x_1 + \beta_2 x_2 + \cdots + \beta_p x_p + \epsilon \quad \textbf{(13.1)}$$

In the multiple regression model, $\beta_0, \beta_1, \beta_2, \ldots, \beta_p$ are the parameters and ϵ (the Greek letter epsilon) is a random variable. A close examination of this model reveals that y is a linear function of $x_1, x_2, \ldots, x_p$ (the $\beta_0 + \beta_1 x_1 + \beta_2 x_2 + \cdots + \beta_p x_p$ part) plus an error term ϵ. The error term accounts for the variability in y that cannot be explained by the linear effect of the p independent variables.

In Section 13.4 we will discuss the assumptions for the multiple regression model and ϵ. One of the assumptions is that the mean or expected value of ϵ is zero. A consequence of this assumption is that the mean or expected value of y, denoted $E(y)$, is equal to $\beta_0 + \beta_1 x_1 + \beta_2 x_2 + \cdots + \beta_p x_p$. The equation that describes how the mean value of y is related to $x_1, x_2, \ldots, x_p$ is called the **multiple regression equation**.

MULTIPLE REGRESSION EQUATION

$$E(y) = \beta_0 + \beta_1 x_1 + \beta_2 x_2 + \cdots + \beta_p x_p \quad \textbf{(13.2)}$$

Estimated Multiple Regression Equation

If the values of $\beta_0, \beta_1, \beta_2, \ldots, \beta_p$ were known, equation (13.2) could be used to compute the mean value of y at given values of $x_1, x_2, \ldots, x_p$. Unfortunately, these parameter values will not, in general, be known and must be estimated from sample data. A simple random sample is used to compute sample statistics $b_0, b_1, b_2, \ldots, b_p$ that are used as the point estimators of the parameters $\beta_0, \beta_1, \beta_2, \ldots, \beta_p$. These sample statistics provide the following **estimated multiple regression equation**.

ESTIMATED MULTIPLE REGRESSION EQUATION

$$\hat{y} = b_0 + b_1x_1 + b_2x_2 + \cdots + b_px_p \tag{13.3}$$

where

$b_0, b_1, b_2, \ldots, b_p$ are the estimates of $\beta_0, \beta_1, \beta_2, \ldots, \beta_p$
$\hat{y}$ = estimated value of the dependent variable

The estimation process for multiple regression is shown in Figure 13.1.

13.2 Least Squares Method

In Chapter 12, we used the **least squares method** to develop the estimated regression equation that best approximated the straight-line relationship between the dependent and independent variables. This same approach is used to develop the estimated multiple regression equation. The least squares criterion is restated as follows.

LEAST SQUARES CRITERION

$$\min \Sigma(y_i - \hat{y}_i)^2 \tag{13.4}$$

FIGURE 13.1 THE ESTIMATION PROCESS FOR MULTIPLE REGRESSION

In simple linear regression, b_0 and b_1 were the sample statistics used to estimate the parameters β_0 and β_1. Multiple regression analysis parallels this statistical inference process, with $b_0, b_1, b_2, \ldots b_p$ denoting the sample statistics used to estimate the parameters $\beta_0, \beta_1, \beta_2, \ldots, \beta_p$.

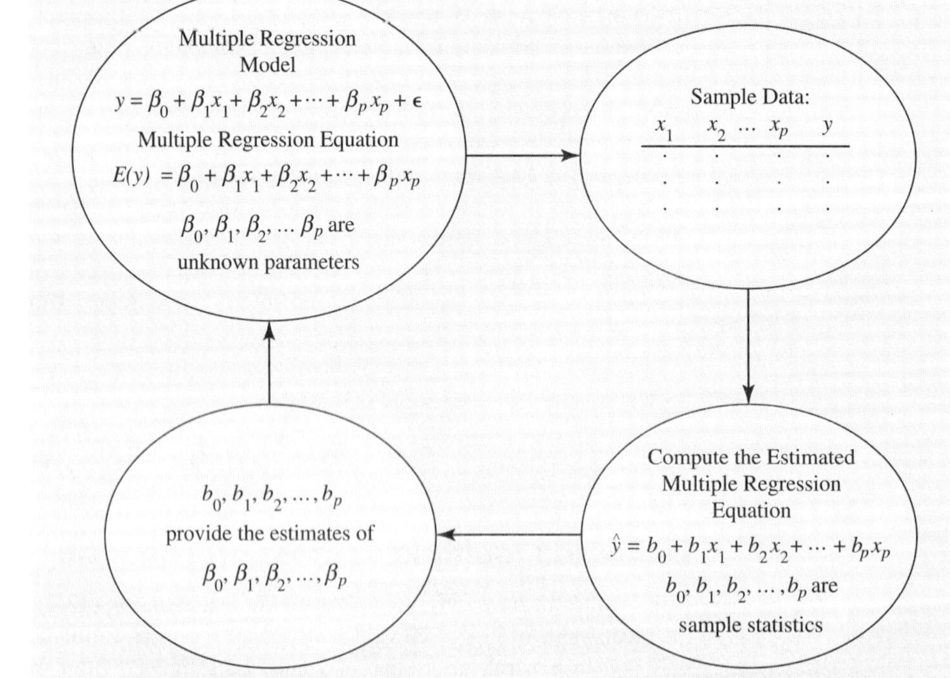

where

y_i = observed value of the dependent variable for the ith observation
$\hat{y}_i$ = estimated value of the dependent variable for the ith observation

The estimated values of the dependent variable are computed by using the estimated multiple regression equation,

$$\hat{y} = b_0 + b_1x_1 + b_2x_2 + \cdots + b_px_p$$

As expression (13.4) shows, the least squares method uses sample data to provide the values of $b_0, b_1, b_2, \ldots, b_p$ that make the sum of squared residuals [the deviations between the observed values of the dependent variable (y_i) and the estimated values of the dependent variable ($\hat{y}_i$)] a minimum.

In Chapter 12 we presented formulas for computing the least squares estimators b_0 and b_1 for the estimated simple linear regression equation $\hat{y} = b_0 + b_1x$. With relatively small data sets, we were able to use those formulas to compute b_0 and b_1 by manual calculations. In multiple regression, however, the presentation of the formulas for the regression coefficients $b_0, b_1, b_2, \ldots, b_p$ involves the use of matrix algebra and is beyond the scope of this text. Therefore, in presenting multiple regression, we focus on how computer software packages can be used to obtain the estimated regression equation and other information. The emphasis will be on how to interpret the computer output rather than on how to make the multiple regression computations.

An Example: Butler Trucking Company

As an illustration of multiple regression analysis, we will consider a problem faced by the Butler Trucking Company, an independent trucking company in southern California. A major portion of Butler's business involves deliveries throughout its local area. To develop better work schedules, the managers want to estimate the total daily travel time for their drivers.

Initially the managers believed that the total daily travel time would be closely related to the number of miles traveled in making the daily deliveries. A simple random sample of 10 driving assignments provided the data shown in Table 13.1 and the scatter diagram shown in Figure 13.2. After reviewing this scatter diagram, the managers hypothesized that the simple linear regression model $y = \beta_0 + \beta_1x_1 + \epsilon$ could be used to describe the relationship between the total travel time (y) and the number of miles traveled (x_1). To estimate

TABLE 13.1 PRELIMINARY DATA FOR BUTLER TRUCKING

Butler

Driving Assignment	x_1 = Miles Traveled	y = Travel Time (hours)
1	100	9.3
2	50	4.8
3	100	8.9
4	100	6.5
5	50	4.2
6	80	6.2
7	75	7.4
8	65	6.0
9	90	7.6
10	90	6.1

FIGURE 13.2 SCATTER DIAGRAM OF PRELIMINARY DATA FOR BUTLER TRUCKING

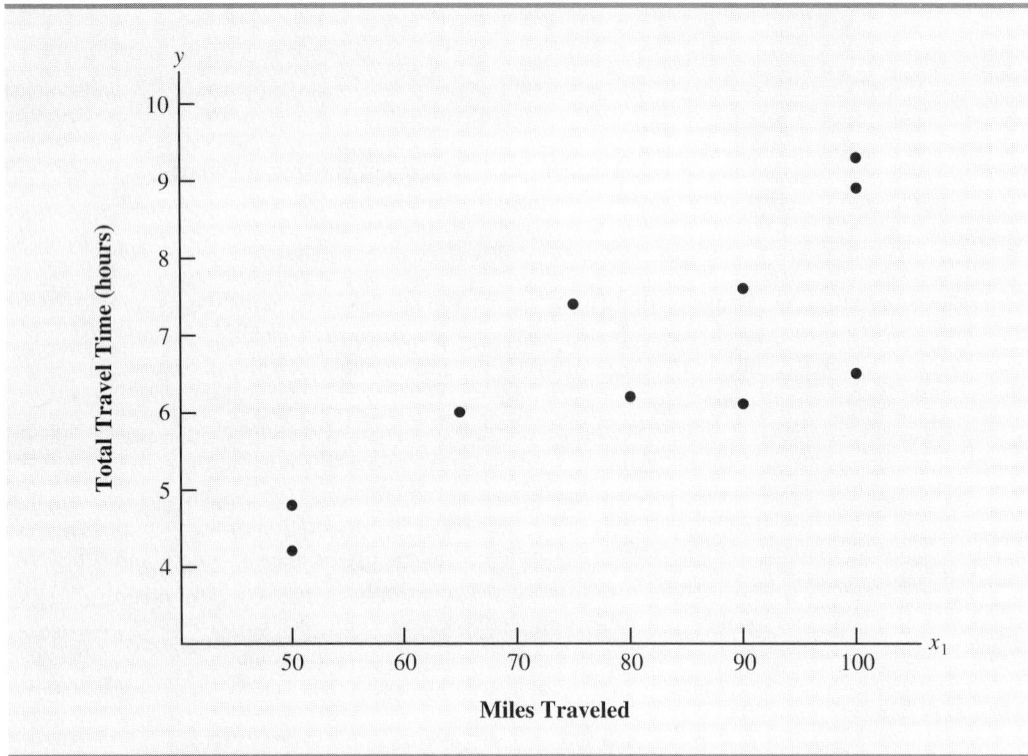

the parameters β_0 and β_1, the least squares method was used to develop the estimated regression equation.

$$\hat{y} = b_0 + b_1 x_1 \tag{13.5}$$

In Figure 13.3, we show the Minitab computer output from applying simple linear regression to the data in Table 13.1. The estimated regression equation is

$$\hat{y} = 1.27 + .0678x_1$$

At the .05 level of significance, the F value of 15.81 and its corresponding p-value of .004 indicate that the relationship is significant; that is, we can reject H_0: $\beta_1 = 0$ because the p-value is less than $\alpha = .05$. Note that the same conclusion is obtained from the t value of 3.98 and its associated p-value of .004. Thus, we can conclude that the relationship between the total travel time and the number of miles traveled is significant; longer travel times are associated with more miles traveled. With a coefficient of determination (expressed as a percentage) of R-sq = 66.4%, we see that 66.4% of the variability in travel time can be explained by the linear effect of the number of miles traveled. This finding is fairly good, but the managers might want to consider adding a second independent variable to explain some of the remaining variability in the dependent variable.

In attempting to identify another independent variable, the managers felt that the number of deliveries could also contribute to the total travel time. The Butler Trucking data, with the number of deliveries added, are shown in Table 13.2. The Minitab computer solution with both miles traveled (x_1) and number of deliveries (x_2) as independent variables is shown in Figure 13.4. The estimated regression equation is

$$\hat{y} = -.869 + .0611x_1 + .923x_2 \tag{13.6}$$

FIGURE 13.3 MINITAB OUTPUT FOR BUTLER TRUCKING WITH ONE INDEPENDENT VARIABLE

In the Minitab output the variable names Miles *and* Time *were entered as the column headings on the worksheet; thus,* x_1 = Miles *and* y = Time.

```
The regression equation is
Time = 1.27 + 0.0678 Miles

Predictor       Coef   SE Coef     T      p
Constant       1.274     1.401  0.91  0.390
Miles        0.06783   0.01706  3.98  0.004

S = 1.002    R-sq = 66.4%    R-sq(adj) = 62.2%

Analysis of Variance

SOURCE           DF      SS      MS      F      p
Regression        1  15.871  15.871  15.81  0.004
Residual Error    8   8.029   1.004
Total             9  23.900
```

In the next section we will discuss the use of the coefficient of multiple determination in measuring how good a fit is provided by this estimated regression equation. Before doing so, let us examine more carefully the values of $b_1 = .0611$ and $b_2 = .923$ in equation (13.6).

Note on Interpretation of Coefficients

One observation can be made at this point about the relationship between the estimated regression equation with only the miles traveled as an independent variable and the equation that includes the number of deliveries as a second independent variable. The value of b_1 is not the same in both cases. In simple linear regression, we interpret b_1 as an estimate of the change in y for a one-unit change in the independent variable. In multiple regression analysis, this interpretation must be modified somewhat. That is, in multiple regression analysis, we interpret each regression coefficient as follows: b_i represents an estimate of the change in y corresponding to a one-unit change in x_i when all other independent variables are held constant. In the Butler Trucking example involving two independent variables, $b_1 = .0611$. Thus,

TABLE 13.2 DATA FOR BUTLER TRUCKING WITH MILES TRAVELED (x_1) AND NUMBER OF DELIVERIES (x_2) AS THE INDEPENDENT VARIABLES

Butler

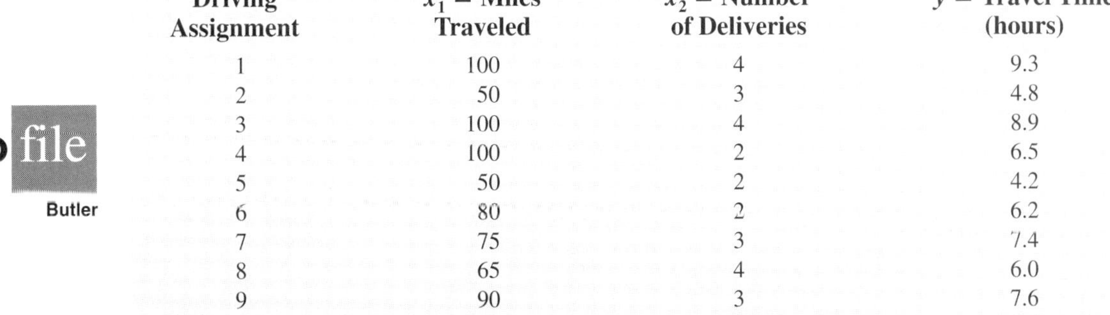

Driving Assignment	x_1 = Miles Traveled	x_2 = Number of Deliveries	y = Travel Time (hours)
1	100	4	9.3
2	50	3	4.8
3	100	4	8.9
4	100	2	6.5
5	50	2	4.2
6	80	2	6.2
7	75	3	7.4
8	65	4	6.0
9	90	3	7.6
10	90	2	6.1

FIGURE 13.4 MINITAB OUTPUT FOR BUTLER TRUCKING WITH TWO INDEPENDENT VARIABLES

```
The regression equation is
Time = - 0.869 + 0.0611 Miles + 0.923 Deliveries

Predictor        Coef     SE Coef      T      p
Constant      -0.8687      0.9515  -0.91  0.392
Miles        0.061135    0.009888   6.18  0.000
Deliveries     0.9234      0.2211   4.18  0.004

S = 0.5731   R-sq = 90.4%   R-sq(adj) = 87.6%

Analysis of Variance

SOURCE          DF      SS      MS      F      p
Regression       2  21.601  10.800  32.88  0.000
Residual Error   7   2.299   0.328
Total            9  23.900
```

In the Minitab output the variable names Miles, Deliv, and Time were entered as the column headings on the worksheet; thus, x_1 = Miles, x_2 = Deliv, *and* y = Time.

.0611 hours is an estimate of the expected increase in travel time corresponding to an increase of 1 mile in the distance traveled when the number of deliveries is held constant. Similarly, because $b_2 = .923$, an estimate of the expected increase in travel time corresponding to an increase of one delivery when the number of miles traveled is held constant is .923 hours.

Exercises

Note to student: The exercises involving data in this and subsequent sections were designed to be solved using a computer software package.

Methods

1. The estimated regression equation for a model involving two independent variables and 10 observations follows.

$$\hat{y} = 29.1270 + .5906x_1 + .4980x_2$$

   a. Interpret b_1 and b_2 in this estimated regression equation.
   b. Estimate y when $x_1 = 180$ and $x_2 = 310$.

Exer2

2. Consider the following data for a dependent variable y and two independent variables, x_1 and x_2.

x_1	x_2	y
30	12	94
47	10	108
25	17	112
51	16	178
40	5	94
51	19	175
74	7	170
36	12	117
59	13	142
76	16	211

a. Develop an estimated regression equation relating y to x_1. Estimate y if $x_1 = 45$.
b. Develop an estimated regression equation relating y to x_2. Estimate y if $x_2 = 15$.
c. Develop an estimated regression equation relating y to x_1 and x_2. Estimate y if $x_1 = 45$ and $x_2 = 15$.

3. In a regression analysis involving 30 observations, the following estimated regression equation was obtained.

$$\hat{y} = 17.6 + 3.8x_1 - 2.3x_2 + 7.6x_3 + 2.7x_4$$

a. Interpret b_1, b_2, b_3, and b_4 in this estimated regression equation.
b. Estimate y when $x_1 = 10$, $x_2 = 5$, $x_3 = 1$, and $x_4 = 2$.

Applications

4. A shoe store developed the following estimated regression equation relating sales to inventory investment and advertising expenditures.

$$\hat{y} = 25 + 10x_1 + 8x_2$$

where

x_1 = inventory investment ($1000s)
x_2 = advertising expenditures ($1000s)
y = sales ($1000s)

a. Estimate sales resulting from a $15,000 investment in inventory and an advertising budget of $10,000.
b. Interpret b_1 and b_2 in this estimated regression equation.

5. The owner of Showtime Movie Theaters, Inc., would like to estimate weekly gross revenue as a function of advertising expenditures. Historical data for a sample of eight weeks follow.

Showtime

Weekly Gross Revenue ($1000s)	Television Advertising ($1000s)	Newspaper Advertising ($1000s)
96	5.0	1.5
90	2.0	2.0
95	4.0	1.5
92	2.5	2.5
95	3.0	3.3
94	3.5	2.3
94	2.5	4.2
94	3.0	2.5

a. Develop an estimated regression equation with the amount of television advertising as the independent variable.
b. Develop an estimated regression equation with both television advertising and newspaper advertising as the independent variables.
c. Is the estimated regression equation coefficient for television advertising expenditures the same in part (a) and in part (b)? Interpret the coefficient in each case.
d. What is the estimate of the weekly gross revenue for a week when $3500 is spent on television advertising and $1800 is spent on newspaper advertising?

6. In baseball, a team's success is often thought to be a function of the team's hitting performance and pitching performance. One measure of hitting performance is the number of home runs the team has, and one measure of pitching performance is the earned run average for the team's pitching staff. It is generally believed that teams that hit more home runs and have a lower earned run average will win a higher percentage of the games played. The following data show the percentage of games won (PCT), the number of team home runs (HR), and the earned run average (ERA) for the 16 teams in the National League for the 2003 Major League Baseball season (http://www.usatoday, January 7, 2004).

MLB

Team	PCT	HR	ERA	Team	PCT	HR	ERA
Arizona	0.519	152	3.857	Milwaukee	0.420	196	5.058
Atlanta	0.623	235	4.106	Montreal	0.512	144	4.027
Chicago	0.543	172	3.842	New York	0.410	124	4.517
Cincinnati	0.426	182	5.127	Philadelphia	0.531	166	4.072
Colorado	0.457	198	5.269	Pittsburgh	0.463	163	4.664
Florida	0.562	157	4.059	San Diego	0.395	128	4.904
Houston	0.537	191	3.880	San Francisco	0.621	180	3.734
Los Angeles	0.525	124	3.162	St. Louis	0.525	196	4.642

a. Determine the estimated regression equation that could be used to predict the percentage of games won given the number of team home runs.
b. Determine the estimated regression equation that could be used to predict the percentage of games won given the earned run average for the team's pitching staff.
c. Determine the estimated regression equation that could be used to predict the percentage of games won given the number of team home runs and the earned run average for the team's pitching staff.
d. For the 2003 season San Diego won only 39.5% of the games they played, the lowest in the National League. To improve next year's record, the team is trying to acquire new players who will increase the number of team home runs to 180 and decrease the earned run average for the team's pitching staff to 4.0. Use the estimated regression equation developed in part (c) to estimate the percentage of games San Diego will win if they have 180 team home runs and have an earned run average of 4.0.

7. Designers of backpacks use exotic material such as supernylon Delrin, high-density polyethylene, aircraft aluminum, and thermomolded foam to make packs that fit comfortably and distribute weight to eliminate pressure points. The following data show the capacity (cubic inches), comfort rating, and price for 10 backpacks tested by *Outside Magazine*. Comfort was measured using a rating from 1 to 5, with a rating of 1 denoting average comfort and a rating of 5 denoting excellent comfort (*Outside Buyer's Guide,* 2001).

Backpack

Manufacturer and Model	Capacity	Comfort	Price ($)
Camp Trails Paragon II	4330	2	190
EMS 5500	5500	3	219
Lowe Alpomayo 90+20	5500	4	249
Marmot Muir	4700	3	249
Kelly Bigfoot 5200	5200	4	250
Gregory Whitney	5500	4	340
Osprey 75	4700	4	389
Arc'Teryx Bora 95	5500	5	395
Dana Design Terraplane LTW	5800	5	439
The Works @ Mystery Ranch Jazz	5000	5	525

a. Determine the estimated regression equation that can be used to predict the price of a backpack given the capacity and the comfort rating.
b. Interpret b_1 and b_2.
c. Predict the price for a backpack with a capacity of 4500 cubic inches and a comfort rating of 4.

8. The following table gives the annual return, the safety rating (0 = riskiest, 10 = safest), and the annual expense ratio for 20 foreign funds (*Mutual Funds,* March 2000).

CD file ForFunds

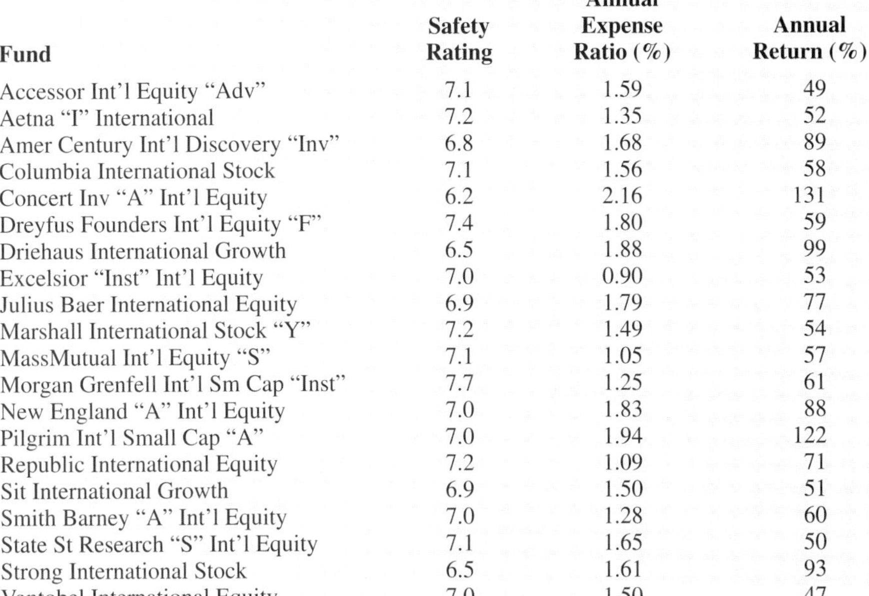

Fund	Safety Rating	Annual Expense Ratio (%)	Annual Return (%)
Accessor Int'l Equity "Adv"	7.1	1.59	49
Aetna "I" International	7.2	1.35	52
Amer Century Int'l Discovery "Inv"	6.8	1.68	89
Columbia International Stock	7.1	1.56	58
Concert Inv "A" Int'l Equity	6.2	2.16	131
Dreyfus Founders Int'l Equity "F"	7.4	1.80	59
Driehaus International Growth	6.5	1.88	99
Excelsior "Inst" Int'l Equity	7.0	0.90	53
Julius Baer International Equity	6.9	1.79	77
Marshall International Stock "Y"	7.2	1.49	54
MassMutual Int'l Equity "S"	7.1	1.05	57
Morgan Grenfell Int'l Sm Cap "Inst"	7.7	1.25	61
New England "A" Int'l Equity	7.0	1.83	88
Pilgrim Int'l Small Cap "A"	7.0	1.94	122
Republic International Equity	7.2	1.09	71
Sit International Growth	6.9	1.50	51
Smith Barney "A" Int'l Equity	7.0	1.28	60
State St Research "S" Int'l Equity	7.1	1.65	50
Strong International Stock	6.5	1.61	93
Vontobel International Equity	7.0	1.50	47

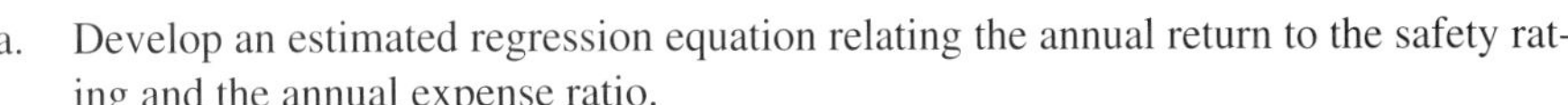

a. Develop an estimated regression equation relating the annual return to the safety rating and the annual expense ratio.
b. Estimate the annual return for a firm that has a safety rating of 7.5 and annual expense ratio of 2.

9. Two experts provided subjective lists of school districts that they think are among the best in the country. For each school district the average class size, the combined SAT score, and the percentage of students who attended a four-year college were provided.

District	Average Class Size	Combined SAT Score	% Attend Four-Year College
Blue Springs, MO	25	1083	74
Garden City, NY	18	997	77
Indianapolis, IN	30	716	40
Newport Beach, CA	26	977	51
Novi, MI	20	980	53
Piedmont, CA	28	1042	75
Pittsburg, PA	21	983	66
Scarsdale, NY	20	1110	87
Wayne, PA	22	1040	85
Weston, MA	21	1031	89
Farmingdale, NY	22	947	81

(continued)

District	Average Class Size	Combined SAT Score	% Attend Four-Year College
Mamaroneck, NY	20	1000	69
Mayfield, OH	24	1003	48
Morristown, NJ	22	972	64
New Rochelle, NY	23	1039	55
Newtown Square, PA	17	963	79
Omaha, NE	23	1059	81
Shaker Heights, OH	23	940	82

a. Using these data, develop an estimated regression equation relating the percentage of students who attend a four-year college to the average class size and the combined SAT score.
b. Estimate the percentage of students who attend a four-year college if the average class size is 20 and the combined SAT score is 1000.

10. The National Basketball Association (NBA) records a variety of statistics for each team. Four of these statistics are the percentage of games won (PCT), the percentage of field goals made by the team (FG%), the percentage of three-point shots made by the team's opponent (Opp 3 Pct%), and the number of turnovers committed by the team's opponent (Opp TO). The following data show the values of these statistics for the 29 teams in the NBA for a portion of the 2004 season (http://www.nba.com, January 3, 2004).

NBA

Team	PCT	FG%	Opp 3 Pt%	Opp TO	Team	PCT	FG%	Opp 3 Pt%	Opp TO
Atlanta	0.265	0.435	0.346	13.206	Minnesota	0.677	0.473	0.348	13.839
Boston	0.471	0.449	0.369	16.176	New Jersey	0.563	0.435	0.338	17.063
Chicago	0.313	0.417	0.372	15.031	New Orleans	0.636	0.421	0.330	16.909
Cleveland	0.303	0.438	0.345	12.515	New York	0.412	0.442	0.330	13.588
Dallas	0.581	0.439	0.332	15.000	Orlando	0.242	0.417	0.360	14.242
Denver	0.606	0.431	0.366	17.818	Philadelphia	0.438	0.428	0.364	16.938
Detroit	0.606	0.423	0.262	15.788	Phoenix	0.364	0.438	0.326	16.515
Golden State	0.452	0.445	0.384	14.290	Portland	0.484	0.447	0.367	12.548
Houston	0.548	0.426	0.324	13.161	Sacramento	0.724	0.466	0.327	15.207
Indiana	0.706	0.428	0.317	15.647	San Antonio	0.688	0.429	0.293	15.344
L.A. Clippers	0.464	0.424	0.326	14.357	Seattle	0.533	0.436	0.350	16.767
L.A. Lakers	0.724	0.465	0.323	16.000	Toronto	0.516	0.424	0.314	14.129
Memphis	0.485	0.432	0.358	17.848	Utah	0.531	0.456	0.368	15.469
Miami	0.424	0.410	0.369	14.970	Washington	0.300	0.411	0.341	16.133
Milwaukee	0.500	0.438	0.349	14.750					

a. Determine the estimated regression equation that can be used to predict the percentage of games won given the percentage of field goals made by the team.
b. Provide an interpretation for the slope of the estimated regression equation developed in part (a).
c. Determine the estimated regression equation that can be used to predict the percentage of games won given the percentage of field goals made by the team, the percentage of three-point shots made by the team's opponent, and the number of turnovers committed by the team's opponent.
d. Discuss the practical implications of the estimated regression equation developed in part (c).
e. Estimate the percentage of games won for a team with the following values for the three independent variables: FG% = .45, Opp 3 Pt% = .34, and Opp TO = 17.

13.3 Multiple Coefficient of Determination

In simple linear regression we showed that the total sum of squares can be partitioned into two components: the sum of squares due to regression and the sum of squares due to error. The same procedure applies to the sum of squares in multiple regression.

RELATIONSHIP AMONG SST, SSR, AND SSE

$$\text{SST} = \text{SSR} + \text{SSE} \tag{13.7}$$

where

$$\begin{aligned} \text{SST} &= \text{total sum of squares} = \Sigma(y_i - \bar{y})^2 \\ \text{SSR} &= \text{sum of squares due to regression} = \Sigma(\hat{y}_i - \bar{y})^2 \\ \text{SSE} &= \text{sum of squares due to error} = \Sigma(y_i - \hat{y}_i)^2 \end{aligned}$$

Because of the computational difficulty in computing the three sums of squares, we rely on computer packages to determine those values. The analysis of variance part of the Minitab output in Figure 13.4 shows the three values for the Butler Trucking problem with two independent variables: SST = 23.900, SSR = 21.601, and SSE = 2.299. With only one independent variable (number of miles traveled), the Minitab output in Figure 13.3 shows that SST = 23.900, SSR = 15.871, and SSE = 8.029. The value of SST is the same in both cases because it does not depend on $\hat{y}$, but SSR increases and SSE decreases when a second independent variable (number of deliveries) is added. The implication is that the estimated multiple regression equation provides a better fit for the observed data.

In Chapter 14, we used the coefficient of determination, $r^2 = \text{SSR/SST}$, to measure the goodness of fit for the estimated regression equation. The same concept applies to multiple regression. The term **multiple coefficient of determination** indicates that we are measuring the goodness of fit for the estimated multiple regression equation. The multiple coefficient of determination, denoted R^2, is computed as follows.

MULTIPLE COEFFICIENT OF DETERMINATION

$$R^2 = \frac{\text{SSR}}{\text{SST}} \tag{13.8}$$

The multiple coefficient of determination can be interpreted as the proportion of the variability in the dependent variable that can be explained by the estimated multiple regression equation. Hence, when multiplied by 100, it can be interpreted as the percentage of the variability in y that can be explained by the estimated regression equation.

In the two-independent-variable Butler Trucking example, with SSR = 21.601 and SST = 23.900, we have

$$R^2 = \frac{21.601}{23.900} = .904$$

Therefore, 90.4% of the variability in travel time y is explained by the estimated multiple regression equation with miles traveled and number of deliveries as the independent variables. In Figure 13.4, we see that the multiple coefficient of determination is also provided by the Minitab output; it is denoted by R-sq = 90.4%.

Adding independent variables causes the prediction errors to become smaller, thus reducing the sum of squares due to error, SSE. Because SSR = SST − SSE, when SSE becomes smaller, SSR becomes larger, causing R^2 = SSR/SST to increase.

Figure 13.3 shows that the R-sq value for the estimated regression equation with only one independent variable, number of miles traveled (x_1), is 66.4%. Thus, the percentage of the variability in travel times that is explained by the estimated regression equation increases from 66.4% to 90.4% when number of deliveries is added as a second independent variable. In general, R^2 always increases as independent variables are added to the model.

Many analysts prefer adjusting R^2 for the number of independent variables to avoid overestimating the impact of adding an independent variable on the amount of variability explained by the estimated regression equation. With n denoting the number of observations and p denoting the number of independent variables, the **adjusted multiple coefficient of determination** is computed as follows.

If a variable is added to the model, R^2 becomes larger even if the variable added is not statistically significant. The adjusted multiple coefficient of determination compensates for the number of independent variables in the model.

ADJUSTED MULTIPLE COEFFICIENT OF DETERMINATION

$$R_a^2 = 1 - (1 - R^2)\frac{n - 1}{n - p - 1} \tag{13.9}$$

For the Butler Trucking example with $n = 10$ and $p = 2$, we have

$$R_a^2 = 1 - (1 - .904)\frac{10 - 1}{10 - 2 - 1} = .88$$

Thus, after adjusting for the two independent variables, we have an adjusted multiple coefficient of determination of .88. This value is provided by the Minitab output in Figure 13.4 as R-sq(adj) = 87.6%; the value we calculated differs because we used a rounded value of R^2 in the calculation.

NOTES AND COMMENTS

If the value of R^2 is small and the model contains a large number of independent variables, the adjusted coefficient of determination can take a negative value; in such cases, Minitab sets the adjusted coefficient of determination to zero.

Exercises

Methods

11. In exercise 1, the following estimated regression equation based on 10 observations was presented.

$$\hat{y} = 29.1270 + .5906x_1 + .4980x_2$$

The values of SST and SSR are 6724.125 and 6216.375, respectively.

a. Find SSE.
b. Compute R^2.
c. Compute R_a^2.
d. Comment on the goodness of fit.

12. In exercise 2, 10 observations were provided for a dependent variable y and two independent variables x_1 and x_2; for these data SST = 15,182.9, and SSR = 14,052.2.
    a. Compute R^2.
    b. Compute R_a^2.
    c. Does the estimated regression equation explain a large amount of the variability in the data? Explain.
13. In exercise 3, the following estimated regression equation based on 30 observations was presented.

$$\hat{y} = 17.6 + 3.8x_1 - 2.3x_2 + 7.6x_3 + 2.7x_4$$

    The values of SST and SSR are 1805 and 1760, respectively.
    a. Compute R^2.
    b. Compute R_a^2.
    c. Comment on the goodness of fit.

Applications

14. In exercise 4, the following estimated regression equation relating sales to inventory investment and advertising expenditures was given.

$$\hat{y} = 25 + 10x_1 + 8x_2$$

    The data used to develop the model came from a survey of 10 stores; for those data, SST = 16,000 and SSR = 12,000.
    a. For the estimated regression equation given, compute R^2.
    b. Compute R_a^2.
    c. Does the model appear to explain a large amount of variability in the data? Explain.

SELF test

15. In exercise 5, the owner of Showtime Movie Theaters, Inc., used multiple regression analysis to predict gross revenue (y) as a function of television advertising (x_1) and newspaper advertising (x_2). The estimated regression equation was

$$\hat{y} = 83.2 + 2.29x_1 + 1.30x_2$$

CD file

Showtime

    The computer solution provided SST = 25.5 and SSR = 23.435.
    a. Compute and interpret R^2 and R_a^2.
    b. When television advertising was the only independent variable, $R^2 = .653$ and $R_a^2 = .595$. Do you prefer the multiple regression results? Explain.

MLB

16. In exercise 6, data were given on the percentage of games won, the number of team home runs, and the earned run average for the team's pitching staff for the 16 teams in the National League for the 2003 Major League Baseball season (http://www.usatoday, January 7, 2004).
    a. Did the estimated regression equation that uses only the number of home runs as the independent variable to predict the percentage of games won provide a good fit? Explain.
    b. Discuss the benefits of using both the number of home runs and the earned run average to predict the percentage of games won.

Schools

17. In exercise 9, an estimated regression equation was developed relating the percentage of students who attend a four-year college to the average class size and the combined SAT score.
    a. Compute and interpret R^2 and R_a^2.
    b. Does the estimated regression equation provide a good fit to the data? Explain.

NBA

18. Refer to exercise 10, where data were reported on a variety of statistics for the 29 teams in the National Basketball Association for a portion of the 2004 season (http://www.nba.com, January 3, 2004).
    a. In part (c) of exercise 10, an estimated regression equation was developed relating the percentage of games won given the percentage of field goals made by the team, the percentage of three-point shots made by the team's opponent, and the number of turnovers committed by the team's opponent. What are the values of R^2 and R_a^2?
    b. Does the estimated regression equation provide a good fit to the data? Explain.

Model Assumptions

In Section 13.1 we introduced the following multiple regression model.

MULTIPLE REGRESSION MODEL

$$y = \beta_0 + \beta_1 x_1 + \beta_2 x_2 + \cdots + \beta_p x_p + \epsilon \quad \textbf{(13.10)}$$

The assumptions about the error term ϵ in the multiple regression model parallel those for the simple linear regression model.

ASSUMPTIONS ABOUT THE ERROR TERM ϵ IN THE MULTIPLE REGRESSION MODEL $y = \beta_0 + \beta_1 x_1 + \cdots + \beta_p x_p + \epsilon$

1. The error ϵ is a random variable with mean or expected value of zero; that is, $E(\epsilon) = 0$.
   Implication: For given values of $x_1, x_2, \ldots, x_p$, the expected, or average, value of y is given by

$$E(y) = \beta_0 + \beta_1 x_1 + \beta_2 x_2 + \cdots + \beta_p x_p \quad \textbf{(13.11)}$$

   Equation (13.11) is the multiple regression equation we introduced in Section 13.1. In this equation, $E(y)$ represents the average of all possible values of y that might occur for the given values of $x_1, x_2, \ldots, x_p$.
2. The variance of ϵ is denoted by σ^2 and is the same for all values of the independent variables $x_1, x_2, \ldots, x_p$.
   Implication: The variance of y about the regression line equals σ^2 and is the same for all values of $x_1, x_2, \ldots, x_p$.
3. The values of ϵ are independent.
   Implication: The size of the error for a particular set of values for the independent variables is not related to the size of the error for any other set of values.
4. The error ϵ is a normally distributed random variable reflecting the deviation between the y value and the expected value of y given by $\beta_0 + \beta_1 x_1 + \beta_2 x_2 + \cdots + \beta_p x_p$.
   Implication: Because $\beta_0, \beta_1, \ldots, \beta_p$ are constants for the given values of $x_1, x_2, \ldots, x_p$, the dependent variable y is also a normally distributed random variable.

To obtain more insight about the form of the relationship given by equation (13.11), consider the following two-independent-variable multiple regression equation.

$$E(y) = \beta_0 + \beta_1 x_1 + \beta_2 x_2$$

The graph of this equation is a plane in three-dimensional space. Figure 13.5 provides an example of such a graph. Note that the value of ϵ shown is the difference between the actual y value and the expected value of y, $E(y)$, when $x_1 = x_1^*$ and $x_2 = x_2^*$.

In regression analysis, the term *response variable* is often used in place of the term *dependent variable.* Furthermore, since the multiple regression equation generates a plane or surface, its graph is called a *response surface.*

FIGURE 13.5 GRAPH OF THE REGRESSION EQUATION FOR MULTIPLE REGRESSION ANALYSIS WITH TWO INDEPENDENT VARIABLES

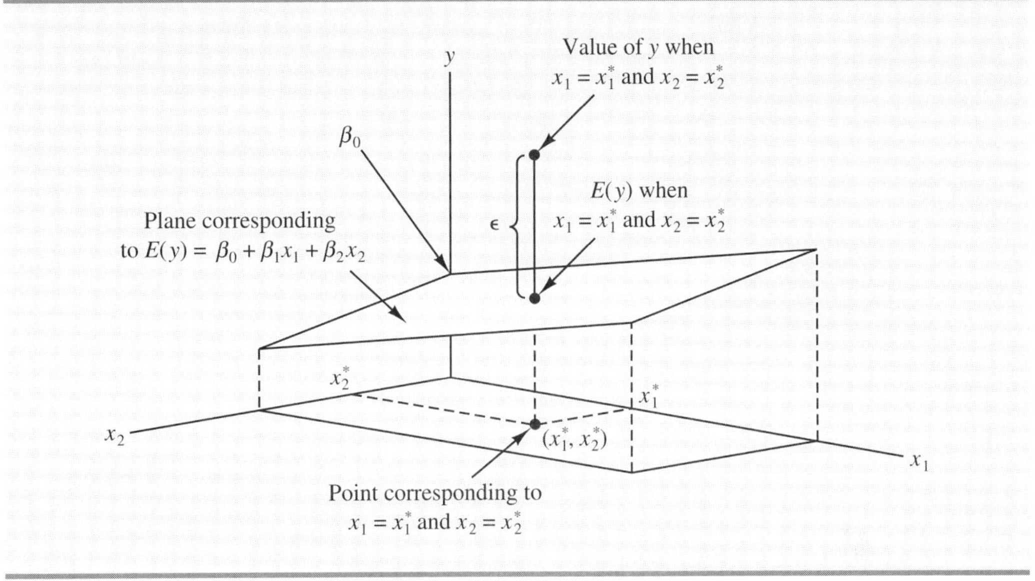

13.5 Testing for Significance

In this section we show how to conduct significance tests for a multiple regression relationship. The significance tests we used in simple linear regression were a *t* test and an *F* test. In simple linear regression, both tests provide the same conclusion; that is, if the null hypothesis is rejected, we conclude that $\beta_1 \neq 0$. In multiple regression, the *t* test and the *F* test have different purposes.

1. The *F* test is used to determine whether a significant relationship exists between the dependent variable and the set of all the independent variables; we will refer to the *F* test as the test for *overall significance.*
2. If the *F* test shows an overall significance, the *t* test is used to determine whether each of the individual independent variables is significant. A separate *t* test is conducted for each of the independent variables in the model; we refer to each of these *t* tests as a test for *individual significance.*

In the material that follows, we will explain the *F* test and the *t* test and apply each to the Butler Trucking Company example.

F Test

The multiple regression model as defined in Section 13.4 is

$$y = \beta_0 + \beta_1 x_1 + \beta_2 x_2 + \cdots + \beta_p x_p + \epsilon$$

The hypotheses for the *F* test involve the parameters of the multiple regression model.

$$H_0\colon \beta_1 = \beta_2 = \cdots = \beta_p = 0$$
$$H_a\colon \text{One or more of the parameters is not equal to zero}$$

If H_0 is rejected, the test gives us sufficient statistical evidence to conclude that one or more of the parameters is not equal to zero and that the overall relationship between y and the set of independent variables $x_1, x_2, \ldots, x_p$ is significant. However, if H_0 cannot be rejected, we do not have sufficient evidence to conclude that a significant relationship is present.

Before describing the steps of the F test, we need to review the concept of *mean square.* A mean square is a sum of squares divided by its corresponding degrees of freedom. In the multiple regression case, the total sum of squares has $n - 1$ degrees of freedom, the sum of squares due to regression (SSR) has p degrees of freedom, and the sum of squares due to error has $n - p - 1$ degrees of freedom. Hence, the mean square due to regression (MSR) is SSR/p and the mean square due to error (MSE) is SSE/$(n - p - 1)$.

$$\text{MSR} = \frac{\text{SSR}}{p} \tag{13.12}$$

and

$$\text{MSE} = \frac{\text{SSE}}{n - p - 1} \tag{13.13}$$

As discussed in Chapter 12, MSE provides an unbiased estimate of σ^2, the variance of the error term ϵ. If H_0: $\beta_1 = \beta_2 = \cdots = \beta_p = 0$ is true, MSR also provides an unbiased estimate of σ^2, and the value of MSR/MSE should be close to 1. However, if H_0 is false, MSR overestimates σ^2 and the value of MSR/MSE becomes larger. To determine how large the value of MSR/MSE must be to reject H_0, we make use of the fact that if H_0 is true and the assumptions about the multiple regression model are valid, the sampling distribution of MSR/MSE is an F distribution with p degrees of freedom in the numerator and $n - p - 1$ in the denominator. A summary of the F test for significance in multiple regression follows.

F TEST FOR OVERALL SIGNIFICANCE

H_0: $\beta_1 = \beta_2 = \cdots = \beta_p = 0$

H_a: One or more of the parameters is not equal to zero

TEST STATISTIC

$$F = \frac{\text{MSR}}{\text{MSE}} \tag{13.14}$$

REJECTION RULE

p-value approach:	Reject H_0 if p-value $\leq \alpha$
Critical value approach:	Reject H_0 if $F \geq F_\alpha$

where F_α is based on an F distribution with p degrees of freedom in the numerator and $n - p - 1$ degrees of freedom in the denominator.

Let us apply the F test to the Butler Trucking Company multiple regression problem. With two independent variables, the hypotheses are written as follows.

H_0: $\beta_1 = \beta_2 = 0$

H_a: β_1 and/or β_2 is not equal to zero

Figure 13.6 is the Minitab output for the multiple regression model with miles traveled (x_1) and number of deliveries (x_2) as the two independent variables. In the analysis of variance part of the output, we see that MSR = 10.8 and MSE = .328. Using equation (13.14), we obtain the test statistic.

$$F = \frac{10.8}{.328} = 32.9$$

FIGURE 13.6 MINITAB OUTPUT FOR BUTLER TRUCKING WITH TWO INDEPENDENT VARIABLES, MILES TRAVELED (x_1) AND NUMBER OF DELIVERIES (x_2)

```
The regression equation is
Time = - 0.869 + 0.0611 Miles + 0.923 Deliveries

Predictor         Coef   SE Coef      T      p
Constant       -0.8687    0.9515  -0.91  0.392
Miles         0.061135  0.009888   6.18  0.000
Deliveries      0.9234    0.2211   4.18  0.004

S = 0.5731   R-sq = 90.4%   R-sq(adj) = 87.6%

Analysis of Variance

SOURCE            DF      SS      MS      F      p
Regression         2  21.601  10.800  32.88  0.000
Residual Error     7   2.299   0.328
Total              9  23.900
```

Note that the F value on the Minitab output is $F = 32.88$; the value we calculated differs because we used rounded values for MSR and MSE in the calculation. Using $\alpha = .01$, the p-value $= 0.000$ in the last column of the analysis of variance table (Figure 13.6) indicates that we can reject H_0: $\beta_1 = \beta_2 = 0$ because the p-value is less than $\alpha = .01$. Alternatively, Table 4 of Appendix B shows that with two degrees of freedom in the numerator and seven degrees of freedom in the denominator, $F_{.01} = 9.55$. With $32.9 > 9.55$, we reject H_0: $\beta_1 = \beta_2 = 0$ and conclude that a significant relationship is present between travel time y and the two independent variables, miles traveled and number of deliveries.

As noted previously, the mean square error provides an unbiased estimate of σ^2, the variance of the error term ϵ. Referring to Figure 13.6, we see that the estimate of σ^2 is MSE $= .328$. The square root of MSE is the estimate of the standard deviation of the error term. As defined in Section 12.5, this standard deviation is called the standard error of the estimate and is denoted s. Hence, we have $s = \sqrt{\text{MSE}} = \sqrt{.328} = .573$. Note that the value of the standard error of the estimate appears in the Minitab output in Figure 13.6.

Table 13.3 is the general analysis of variance (ANOVA) table that provides the F test results for a multiple regression model. The value of the F test statistic appears in the last column and can be compared to F_α with p degrees of freedom in the numerator and $n - p - 1$ degrees of freedom in the denominator to make the hypothesis test conclusion. By reviewing the Minitab output for Butler Trucking Company in Figure 13.6, we see that

TABLE 13.3 ANOVA TABLE FOR A MULTIPLE REGRESSION MODEL WITH p INDEPENDENT VARIABLES

Source	Sum of Squares	Degrees of Freedom	Mean Square	F
Regression	SSR	p	$\text{MSR} = \dfrac{\text{SSR}}{p}$	$F = \dfrac{\text{MSR}}{\text{MSE}}$
Error	SSE	$n - p - 1$	$\text{MSE} = \dfrac{\text{SSE}}{n - p - 1}$	
Total	SST	$n - 1$		

Minitab's analysis of variance table contains this information. Moreover, Minitab also provides the p-value corresponding to the F test statistic.

t Test

If the F test shows that the multiple regression relationship is significant, a t test can be conducted to determine the significance of each of the individual parameters. The t test for individual significance follows.

t TEST FOR INDIVIDUAL SIGNIFICANCE

For any parameter β_i

$$H_0: \beta_i = 0$$
$$H_a: \beta_i \neq 0$$

TEST STATISTIC

$$t = \frac{b_i}{s_{b_i}} \tag{13.15}$$

REJECTION RULE

p-value approach:	Reject H_0 if p-value $\leq \alpha$
Critical value approach:	Reject H_0 if $t \leq -t_{\alpha/2}$ or if $t \geq t_{\alpha/2}$

where $t_{\alpha/2}$ is based on a t distribution with $n - p - 1$ degrees of freedom.

In the test statistic, s_{b_i} is the estimate of the standard deviation of b_i. The value of s_{b_i} will be provided by the computer software package.

Let us conduct the t test for the Butler Trucking regression problem. Refer to the section of Figure 13.6 that shows the Minitab output for the t-ratio calculations. Values of b_1, b_2, s_{b_1}, and s_{b_2} are as follows.

$$b_1 = .061135 \quad s_{b_1} = .009888$$
$$b_2 = .9234 \quad s_{b_2} = .2211$$

Using equation (13.15), we obtain the test statistic for the hypotheses involving parameters β_1 and β_2.

$$t = .061135/.009888 = 6.18$$
$$t = .9234/.2211 = 4.18$$

Note that both of these t-ratio values and the corresponding p-values are provided by the Minitab output in Figure 13.6. Using $\alpha = .01$, the p-values of .000 and .004 on the Minitab output indicate that we can reject H_0: $\beta_1 = 0$ and H_0: $\beta_2 = 0$. Hence, both parameters are statistically significant. Alternatively, Table 2 of Appendix B shows that with $n - p - 1 = 10 - 2 - 1 = 7$ degrees of freedom, $t_{.005} = 3.499$. With $6.18 > 3.499$, we reject H_0: $\beta_1 = 0$. Similarly, with $4.18 > 3.499$, we reject H_0: $\beta_2 = 0$.

Multicollinearity

We used the term *independent variable* in regression analysis to refer to any variable being used to predict or explain the value of the dependent variable. The term does not mean, however, that the independent variables themselves are independent in any statistical sense. On the contrary, most independent variables in a multiple regression problem are correlated to some degree with one another. For example, in the Butler Trucking example involving the two independent variables x_1 (miles traveled) and x_2 (number of deliveries), we could treat the miles traveled as the dependent variable and the number of deliveries as the independent variable to determine whether those two variables are themselves related. We could then compute the sample correlation coefficient $r_{x_1x_2}$ to determine the extent to which the variables are related. Doing so yields $r_{x_1x_2} = .16$. Thus, we find some degree of linear association between the two independent variables. In multiple regression analysis, **multicollinearity** refers to the correlation among the independent variables.

To provide a better perspective of the potential problems of multicollinearity, let us consider a modification of the Butler Trucking example. Instead of x_2 being the number of deliveries, let x_2 denote the number of gallons of gasoline consumed. Clearly, x_1 (the miles traveled) and x_2 are related; that is, we know that the number of gallons of gasoline used depends on the number of miles traveled. Hence, we would conclude logically that x_1 and x_2 are highly correlated independent variables.

When the independent variables are highly correlated, it is not possible to determine the separate effect of any particular independent variable on the dependent variable.

Assume that we obtain the equation $\hat{y} = b_0 + b_1x_1 + b_2x_2$ and find that the F test shows the relationship to be significant. Then suppose we conduct a t test on β_1 to determine whether $\beta_1 \neq 0$, and we cannot reject H_0: $\beta_1 = 0$. Does this result mean that travel time is not related to miles traveled? Not necessarily. What it probably means is that with x_2 already in the model, x_1 does not make a significant contribution to determining the value of y. This interpretation makes sense in our example; if we know the amount of gasoline consumed, we do not gain much additional information useful in predicting y by knowing the miles traveled. Similarly, a t test might lead us to conclude $\beta_2 = 0$ on the grounds that, with x_1 in the model, knowledge of the amount of gasoline consumed does not add much.

To summarize, in t tests for the significance of individual parameters, the difficulty caused by multicollinearity is that it is possible to conclude that none of the individual parameters are significantly different from zero when an F test on the overall multiple regression equation indicates a significant relationship. This problem is avoided when there is little correlation among the independent variables.

A sample correlation coefficient greater than +0.70 or less than −0.70 for two independent variables is a rule of thumb warning of potential problems with multicollinearity.

Statisticians have developed several tests for determining whether multicollinearity is high enough to cause problems. According to the rule of thumb test, multicollinearity is a potential problem if the absolute value of the sample correlation coefficient exceeds .7 for any two of the independent variables. The other types of tests are more advanced and beyond the scope of this text.

If possible, every attempt should be made to avoid including independent variables that are highly correlated. In practice, however, strict adherence to this policy is rarely possible. When decision makers have reason to believe substantial multicollinearity is present, they must realize that separating the effects of the individual independent variables on the dependent variable is difficult.

NOTES AND COMMENTS

Ordinarily, multicollinearity does not affect the way in which we perform our regression analysis or interpret the output from a study. However, when multicollinearity is severe—that is, when two or more of the independent variables are highly correlated with one another—we can have difficulty interpreting the results of t tests on the individual parameters. In addition to the type of problem illustrated in this section, severe cases of multicollinearity have been shown to result in least squares estimates that have the wrong sign. That is, in simulated studies where researchers created the underlying regression model and then applied the least squares technique to develop estimates of β_0, β_1, β_2, and so on, it has been shown that under conditions of high multicollinearity the least squares estimates can have a sign opposite that of the parameter being estimated. For example, β_2 might actually be +10 and b_2, its estimate, might turn out to be −2. Thus, little faith can be placed in the individual coefficients if multicollinearity is present to a high degree.

Exercises

Methods

19. In exercise 1, the following estimated regression equation based on 10 observations was presented.

$$\hat{y} = 29.1270 + .5906x_1 + .4980x_2$$

Here SST = 6724.125, SSR = 6216.375, $s_{b_1} = .0813$, and $s_{b_2} = .0567$.

a. Compute MSR and MSE.
b. Compute F and perform the appropriate F test. Use $\alpha = .05$.
c. Perform a t test for the significance of β_1. Use $\alpha = .05$.
d. Perform a t test for the significance of β_2. Use $\alpha = .05$.

20. Refer to the data presented in exercise 2. The estimated regression equation for these data is

$$\hat{y} = -18.4 + 2.01x_1 + 4.74x_2$$

Here SST = 15,182.9, SSR = 14,052.2, $s_{b_1} = .2471$, and $s_{b_2} = .9484$.

a. Test for a significant relationship among x_1, x_2, and y. Use $\alpha = .05$.
b. Is β_1 significant? Use $\alpha = .05$.
c. Is β_2 significant? Use $\alpha = .05$.

21. The following estimated regression equation was developed for a model involving two independent variables.

$$\hat{y} = 40.7 + 8.63x_1 + 2.71x_2$$

After x_2 was dropped from the model, the least squares method was used to obtain an estimated regression equation involving only x_1 as an independent variable.

$$\hat{y} = 42.0 + 9.01x_1$$

a. Give an interpretation of the coefficient of x_1 in both models.
b. Could multicollinearity explain why the coefficient of x_1 differs in the two models? If so, how?

Applications

22. In exercise 4 the following estimated regression equation relating sales to inventory investment and advertising expenditures was given.

$$\hat{y} = 25 + 10x_1 + 8x_2$$

The data used to develop the model came from a survey of 10 stores; for these data SST = 16,000 and SSR = 12,000.

a. Compute SSE, MSE, and MSR.
b. Use an F test and a .05 level of significance to determine whether there is a relationship among the variables.

23. Refer to exercise 5.

a. Use $\alpha = .01$ to test the hypotheses

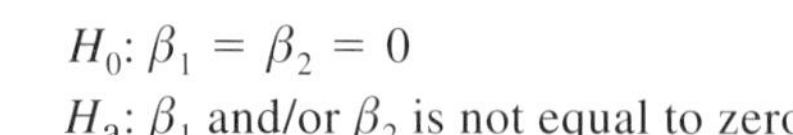

$$H_0: \beta_1 = \beta_2 = 0$$
$$H_a: \beta_1 \text{ and/or } \beta_2 \text{ is not equal to zero}$$

Showtime

for the model $y = \beta_0 + \beta_1 x_1 + \beta_2 x_2 + \epsilon$, where

$$x_1 = \text{television advertising (\$1000s)}$$
$$x_2 = \text{newspaper advertising (\$1000s)}$$

b. Use $\alpha = .05$ to test the significance of β_1. Should x_1 be dropped from the model?
c. Use $\alpha = .05$ to test the significance of β_2. Should x_2 be dropped from the model?

CD file

MLB

24. Refer to the data in exercise 6. Use the number of team home runs and the earned run average for the team's pitching staff to predict the percentage of games won.
    a. Use the F test to determine the overall significance of the relationship. What is your conclusion at the .05 level of significance?
    b. Use the t test to determine the significance of each independent variable. What is your conclusion at the .05 level of significance?

25. *Barron's* conducts an annual review of online brokers, including both brokers that can be accessed via a Web browser, as well as direct-access brokers that connect customers directly with the broker's network server. Each broker's offerings and performance are evaluated in six areas, using a point value of 0–5 in each category. The results are weighted to obtain an overall score, and a final star rating, ranging from zero to five stars, is assigned to each broker. Trade execution, ease of use, and range of offerings are three of the areas evaluated. A point value of 5 in the trade execution area means the order entry and execution process flowed easily from one step to the next. A value of 5 in the ease of use area means that the site was easy to use and can be tailored to show what the user wants to see. A value of 5 in the range offerings area means that all of the investment transactions can be executed online. The following data show the point values for trade execution, ease of use, range of offerings, and the star rating for a sample of 10 of the online brokers that *Barron's* evaluated (*Barron's,* March 10, 2003).

Brokers

Broker	Trade Execution	Use	Range	Rating
Wall St. Access	3.7	4.5	4.8	4.0
E*TRADE (Power)	3.4	3.0	4.2	3.5
E*TRADE (Standard)	2.5	4.0	4.0	3.5
Preferred Trade	4.8	3.7	3.4	3.5
my Track	4.0	3.5	3.2	3.5
TD Waterhouse	3.0	3.0	4.6	3.5
Brown & Co.	2.7	2.5	3.3	3.0
Brokerage America	1.7	3.5	3.1	3.0
Merrill Lynch Direct	2.2	2.7	3.0	2.5
Strong Funds	1.4	3.6	2.5	2.0

a. Determine the estimated regression equation that can be used to predict the star rating given the point values for execution, ease of use, and range of offerings.
b. Use the F test to determine the overall significance of the relationship. What is the conclusion at the .05 level of significance?
c. Use the t test to determine the significance of each independent variable. What is your conclusion at the .05 level of significance?
d. Remove any independent variable that is not significant from the estimated regression equation. What is your recommended estimated regression equation? Compare the R^2 with the value of R^2 from part (a). Discuss the differences.

NBA

26. In exercise 10 an estimated regression equation was developed relating the percentage of games won given the percentage of field goals made by the team, the percentage of three-point shots made by the team's opponent, and the number of turnovers committed by the team's opponent.
    a. Use the F test to determine the overall significance of the relationship. What is your conclusion at the .05 level of significance?
    b. Use the t test to determine the significance of each independent variable. What is your conclusion at the .05 level of significance?

13.6 Using the Estimated Regression Equation for Estimation and Prediction

The procedures for estimating the mean value of y and predicting an individual value of y in multiple regression are similar to those in regression analysis involving one independent variable. First, recall that in Chapter 12 we showed that the point estimate of the expected value of y for a given value of x was the same as the point estimate of an individual value of y. In both cases, we used $\hat{y} = b_0 + b_1x$ as the point estimate.

In multiple regression we use the same procedure. That is, we substitute the given values of $x_1, x_2, \ldots, x_p$ into the estimated regression equation and use the corresponding value of $\hat{y}$ as the point estimate. Suppose that for the Butler Trucking example we want to use the estimated regression equation involving x_1 (miles traveled) and x_2 (number of deliveries) to develop two interval estimates:

1. A *confidence interval* of the mean travel time for all trucks that travel 100 miles and make two deliveries
2. A *prediction interval* of the travel time for *one specific* truck that travels 100 miles and makes two deliveries

Using the estimated regression equation $\hat{y} = -.869 + .0611x_1 + .923x_2$ with $x_1 = 100$ and $x_2 = 2$, we obtain the following value of $\hat{y}$.

$$\hat{y} = -.869 + .0611(100) + .923(2) = 7.09$$

Hence, the point estimate of travel time in both cases is approximately seven hours.

To develop interval estimates for the mean value of y and for an individual value of y, we use a procedure similar to that for regression analysis involving one independent variable. The formulas required are beyond the scope of the text, but computer packages for multiple regression analysis will often provide confidence intervals once the values of $x_1, x_2, \ldots, x_p$ are specified by the user. In Table 13.4 we show the 95% confidence and prediction intervals for the Butler Trucking example for selected values of x_1 and x_2; these values were obtained using Minitab. Note that the interval estimate for an individual value of y is wider than the interval estimate for the expected value of y. This difference simply reflects the fact that for given values of x_1 and x_2 we can estimate the mean travel time for all trucks with more precision than we can predict the travel time for one specific truck.

TABLE 13.4 THE 95% CONFIDENCE AND PREDICTION INTERVALS FOR BUTLER TRUCKING

Value of	Value of	Confidence Interval		Prediction Interval	
x_1	x_2	**Lower Limit**	**Upper Limit**	**Lower Limit**	**Upper Limit**
50	2	3.146	4.924	2.414	5.656
50	3	4.127	5.789	3.368	6.548
50	4	4.815	6.948	4.157	7.607
100	2	6.258	7.926	5.500	8.683
100	3	7.385	8.645	6.520	9.510
100	4	8.135	9.742	7.362	10.515

Exercises

Methods

27. In exercise 1, the following estimated regression equation based on 10 observations was presented.

$$\hat{y} = 29.1270 + .5906x_1 + .4980x_2$$

a. Develop a point estimate of the mean value of y when $x_1 = 180$ and $x_2 = 310$.
b. Develop a point estimate for an individual value of y when $x_1 = 180$ and $x_2 = 310$.

SELF test

28. Refer to the data in exercise 2. The estimated regression equation for those data is

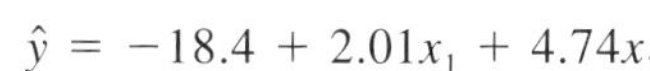

$$\hat{y} = -18.4 + 2.01x_1 + 4.74x_2$$

a. Develop a 95% confidence interval for the mean value of y when $x_1 = 45$ and $x_2 = 15$.
b. Develop a 95% prediction interval for y when $x_1 = 45$ and $x_2 = 15$.

Applications

SELF test

29. In exercise 5, the owner of Showtime Movie Theaters, Inc., used multiple regression analysis to predict gross revenue (y) as a function of television advertising (x_1) and newspaper advertising (x_2). The estimated regression equation was

$$\hat{y} = 83.2 + 2.29x_1 + 1.30x_2$$

CD file
Showtime

a. What is the gross revenue expected for a week when \$3500 is spent on television advertising ($x_1 = 3.5$) and \$1800 is spent on newspaper advertising ($x_2 = 1.8$)?
b. Provide a 95% confidence interval for the mean revenue of all weeks with the expenditures listed in part (a).
c. Provide a 95% prediction interval for next week's revenue, assuming that the advertising expenditures will be allocated as in part (a).

Schools

30. In exercise 9, an estimated regression equation was developed relating the percentage of students who attend a four-year college to the average class size and the combined SAT score.
a. Develop a 95% confidence interval for the mean percentage of students who attend a four-year college for a school district that has an average class size of 25 and whose students have a combined SAT score of 1000.
b. Suppose that a school district in Conway, South Carolina, has an average class size of 25 and a combined SAT score of 950. Develop a 95% prediction interval for the percentage of students who attend a four-year college.

31. The Buyer's Guide section of the Web site for *Car and Driver* magazine provides reviews and road tests for cars, trucks, SUVs, and vans. The average ratings of overall quality, vehicle styling, braking, handling, fuel economy, interior comfort, acceleration, dependability, fit and finish, transmission, and ride are summarized for each vehicle using a scale ranging from 1 (worst) to 10 (best). A portion of the data for 14 Sports/GT cars is shown here (http://www.caranddriver, January 7, 2004).

SportsCar

Sports/GT	Overall	Handling	Dependability	Fit and Finish
Acura 3.2CL	7.80	7.83	8.17	7.67
Acura RSX	9.02	9.46	9.35	8.97
Audi TT	9.00	9.58	8.74	9.38
BMW 3-Series/M3	8.39	9.52	8.39	8.55
Chevrolet Corvette	8.82	9.64	8.54	7.87

(continued)

Sports/GT	Overall	Handling	Dependability	Fit and Finish
Ford Mustang	8.34	8.85	8.70	7.34
Honda Civic Si	8.92	9.31	9.50	7.93
Infinity G35	8.70	9.34	8.96	8.07
Mazda RX-8	8.58	9.79	8.96	8.12
Mini Cooper	8.76	10.00	8.69	8.33
Mitsubishi Eclipse	8.17	8.95	8.25	7.36
Nissan 350Z	8.07	9.35	7.56	8.21
Porsche 911	9.55	9.91	8.86	9.55
Toyota Celica	8.77	9.29	9.04	7.97

a. Develop an estimated regression equation using handling, dependability, and fit and finish to predict overall quality.
b. Another Sports/GT car rated by *Car and Driver* is the Honda Accord. The ratings for handling, dependability, and fit and finish for the Honda Accord were 8.28, 9.06, and 8.07, respectively. Estimate the overall rating for this car.
c. Provide a 95% confidence interval for overall quality for all sports and GT cars with the characteristics listed in part (b).
d. Provide a 95% prediction interval for overall quality for the Honda Accord described in part (b).
e. The overall rating reported by *Car and Driver* for the Honda Accord was 8.65. How does this rating compare to the estimates you developed in parts (b) and (d)?

13.7 Qualitative Independent Variables

The independent variables may be qualitative or quantitative.

Thus far, the examples we considered involved quantitative independent variables such as student population, distance traveled, and number of deliveries. In many situations, however, we must work with **qualitative independent variables** such as gender (male, female), method of payment (cash, credit card, check), and so on. The purpose of this section is to show how qualitative variables are handled in regression analysis. To illustrate the use and interpretation of a qualitative independent variable, we will consider a problem facing the managers of Johnson Filtration, Inc.

An Example: Johnson Filtration, Inc.

Johnson Filtration, Inc., provides maintenance service for water-filtration systems throughout southern Florida. Customers contact Johnson with requests for maintenance service on their water-filtration systems. To estimate the service time and the service cost, Johnson's managers want to predict the repair time necessary for each maintenance request. Hence, repair time in hours is the dependent variable. Repair time is believed to be related to two factors, the number of months since the last maintenance service and the type of repair problem (mechanical or electrical). Data for a sample of 10 service calls are reported in Table 13.5.

Let y denote the repair time in hours and x_1 denote the number of months since the last maintenance service. The regression model that uses only x_1 to predict y is

$$y = \beta_0 + \beta_1 x_1 + \epsilon$$

Using Minitab to develop the estimated regression equation, we obtained the output shown in Figure 13.7. The estimated regression equation is

$$\hat{y} = 2.15 + .304x_1 \qquad (13.16)$$

TABLE 13.5 DATA FOR THE JOHNSON FILTRATION EXAMPLE

Service Call	Months Since Last Service	Type of Repair	Repair Time in Hours
1	2	Electrical	2.9
2	6	Mechanical	3.0
3	8	Electrical	4.8
4	3	Mechanical	1.8
5	2	Electrical	2.9
6	7	Electrical	4.9
7	9	Mechanical	4.2
8	8	Mechanical	4.8
9	4	Electrical	4.4
10	6	Electrical	4.5

At the .05 level of significance, the *p*-value of .016 for the *t* (or *F*) test indicates that the number of months since the last service is significantly related to repair time. R-sq = 53.4% indicates that x_1 alone explains 53.4% of the variability in repair time.

To incorporate the type of repair into the regression model, we define the following variable.

$$x_2 = \begin{cases} 0 \text{ if the type of repair is mechanical} \\ 1 \text{ if the type of repair is electrical} \end{cases}$$

In regression analysis x_2 is called a **dummy** or ***indicator* variable**. Using this dummy variable, we can write the multiple regression model as

$$y = \beta_0 + \beta_1 x_1 + \beta_2 x_2 + \epsilon$$

Table 13.6 is the revised data set that includes the values of the dummy variable. Using Minitab and the data in Table 13.6, we can develop estimates of the model parameters. The Minitab output in Figure 13.8 shows that the estimated multiple regression equation is

$$\hat{y} = .93 + .388x_1 + 1.26x_2 \qquad \textbf{(13.17)}$$

FIGURE 13.7 MINITAB OUTPUT FOR JOHNSON FILTRATION WITH MONTHS SINCE LAST SERVICE (x_1) AS THE INDEPENDENT VARIABLE

In the Minitab output the variable names Months *and* Time *were entered as the column headings on the worksheet; thus,* x_1 = Months *and* y = Time.

```
The regression equation is
Time = 2.15 + 0.304 Months

Predictor    Coef   SE Coef     T      p
Constant   2.1473    0.6050  3.55  0.008
Months     0.3041    0.1004  3.03  0.016

S = 0.7810   R-sq = 53.4%   R-sq(adj) = 47.6%

Analysis of Variance

SOURCE          DF       SS      MS     F      p
Regression       1   5.5960  5.5960  9.17  0.016
Residual Error   8   4.8800  0.6100
Total            9  10.4760
```

TABLE 13.6 DATA FOR THE JOHNSON FILTRATION EXAMPLE WITH TYPE OF REPAIR INDICATED BY A DUMMY VARIABLE ($x_2 = 0$ FOR MECHANICAL; $x_2 = 1$ FOR ELECTRICAL)

Johnson

Customer	Months Since Last Service (x_1)	Type of Repair (x_2)	Repair Time in Hours (y)
1	2	1	2.9
2	6	0	3.0
3	8	1	4.8
4	3	0	1.8
5	2	1	2.9
6	7	1	4.9
7	9	0	4.2
8	8	0	4.8
9	4	1	4.4
10	6	1	4.5

At the .05 level of significance, the p-value of .001 associated with the F test ($F = 21.36$) indicates that the regression relationship is significant. The t test part of the printout in Figure 13.8 shows that both months since last service (p-value = .000) and type of repair (p-value = .005) are statistically significant. In addition, R-sq = 85.9% and R-sq(adj) = 81.9% indicate that the estimated regression equation does a good job of explaining the variability in repair times. Thus, equation (13.17) should prove helpful in estimating the repair time necessary for the various service calls.

Interpreting the Parameters

The multiple regression equation for the Johnson Filtration example is

$$E(y) = \beta_0 + \beta_1 x_1 + \beta_2 x_2 \qquad (13.18)$$

FIGURE 13.8 MINITAB OUTPUT FOR JOHNSON FILTRATION WITH MONTHS SINCE LAST SERVICE (x_1) AND TYPE OF REPAIR (x_2) AS THE INDEPENDENT VARIABLES

In the Minitab output the variable names Months, Type, *and* Time *were entered as the column headings on the worksheet; thus,* x_1 = Months, x_2 = Type, *and* y = Time.

```
The regression equation is
Time = 0.930 + 0.388 Months + 1.26 Type

Predictor       Coef   SE Coef      T      p
Constant      0.9305    0.4670   1.99  0.087
Months       0.38762   0.06257   6.20  0.000
Type          1.2627    0.3141   4.02  0.005

S = 0.4590   R-sq = 85.9%   R-sq(adj) = 81.9%

Analysis of Variance

SOURCE          DF       SS      MS      F      p
Regression       2   9.0009  4.5005  21.36  0.001
Residual Error   7   1.4751  0.2107
Total            9  10.4760
```

To understand how to interpret the parameters β_0, β_1, and β_2 when a qualitative variable is present, consider the case when $x_2 = 0$ (mechanical repair). Using $E(y \mid \text{mechanical})$ to denote the mean or expected value of repair time *given* a mechanical repair, we have

$$E(y \mid \text{mechanical}) = \beta_0 + \beta_1 x_1 + \beta_2(0) = \beta_0 + \beta_1 x_1 \tag{13.19}$$

Similarly, for an electrical repair ($x_2 = 1$), we have

$$\begin{aligned} E(y \mid \text{electrical}) &= \beta_0 + \beta_1 x_1 + \beta_2(1) = \beta_0 + \beta_1 x_1 + \beta_2 \\ &= (\beta_0 + \beta_2) + \beta_1 x_1 \end{aligned} \tag{13.20}$$

Comparing equations (13.19) and (13.20), we see that the mean repair time is a linear function of x_1 for both mechanical and electrical repairs. The slope of both equations is β_1, but the y-intercept differs. The y-intercept is β_0 in equation (13.19) for mechanical repairs and $(\beta_0 + \beta_2)$ in equation (13.20) for electrical repairs. The interpretation of β_2 is that it indicates the difference between the mean repair time for an electrical repair and the mean repair time for a mechanical repair.

If β_2 is positive, the mean repair time for an electrical repair will be greater than that for a mechanical repair; if β_2 is negative, the mean repair time for an electrical repair will be less than that for a mechanical repair. Finally, if $\beta_2 = 0$, there is no difference in the mean repair time between electrical and mechanical repairs and the type of repair is not related to the repair time.

Using the estimated multiple regression equation $\hat{y} = .93 + .388x_1 + 1.26x_2$, we see that .93 is the estimate of β_0 and 1.26 is the estimate of β_2. Thus, when $x_2 = 0$ (mechanical repair)

$$\hat{y} = .93 + .388x_1 \tag{13.21}$$

and when $x_2 = 1$ (electrical repair)

$$\begin{aligned} \hat{y} &= .93 + .388x_1 + 1.26(1) \\ &= 2.19 + .388x_1 \end{aligned} \tag{13.22}$$

In effect, the use of a dummy variable for type of repair provides two equations that can be used to predict the repair time, one corresponding to mechanical repairs and one corresponding to electrical repairs. In addition, with $b_2 = 1.26$, we learn that, on average, electrical repairs require 1.26 hours longer than mechanical repairs.

Figure 13.9 is the plot of the Johnson data from Table 13.6. Repair time in hours (y) is represented by the vertical axis and months since last service (x_1) is represented by the horizontal axis. A data point for a mechanical repair is indicated by an M and a data point for an electrical repair is indicated by an E. Equations (13.21) and (13.22) are plotted on the graph to show graphically the two equations that can be used to predict the repair time, one corresponding to mechanical repairs and one corresponding to electrical repairs.

More Complex Qualitative Variables

A qualitative variable with k levels must be modeled using k − 1 dummy variables. Care must be taken in defining and interpreting the dummy variables.

Because the qualitative variable for the Johnson Filtration example had two levels (mechanical and electrical), defining a dummy variable with zero indicating a mechanical repair and one indicating an electrical repair was easy. However, when a qualitative variable has more than two levels, care must be taken in both defining and interpreting the dummy variables. As we will show, if a qualitative variable has k levels, $k - 1$ dummy variables are required, with each dummy variable being coded as 0 or 1.

For example, suppose a manufacturer of copy machines organized the sales territories for a particular state into three regions: A, B, and C. The managers want to use regression analysis to help predict the number of copiers sold per week. With the number of units sold as the dependent variable, they are considering several independent variables (the number of sales personnel, advertising expenditures, and so on). Suppose the managers believe sales region is also an important factor in predicting the number of copiers sold. Because sales

FIGURE 13.9 SCATTER DIAGRAM FOR THE JOHNSON FILTRATION REPAIR DATA FROM TABLE 13.6

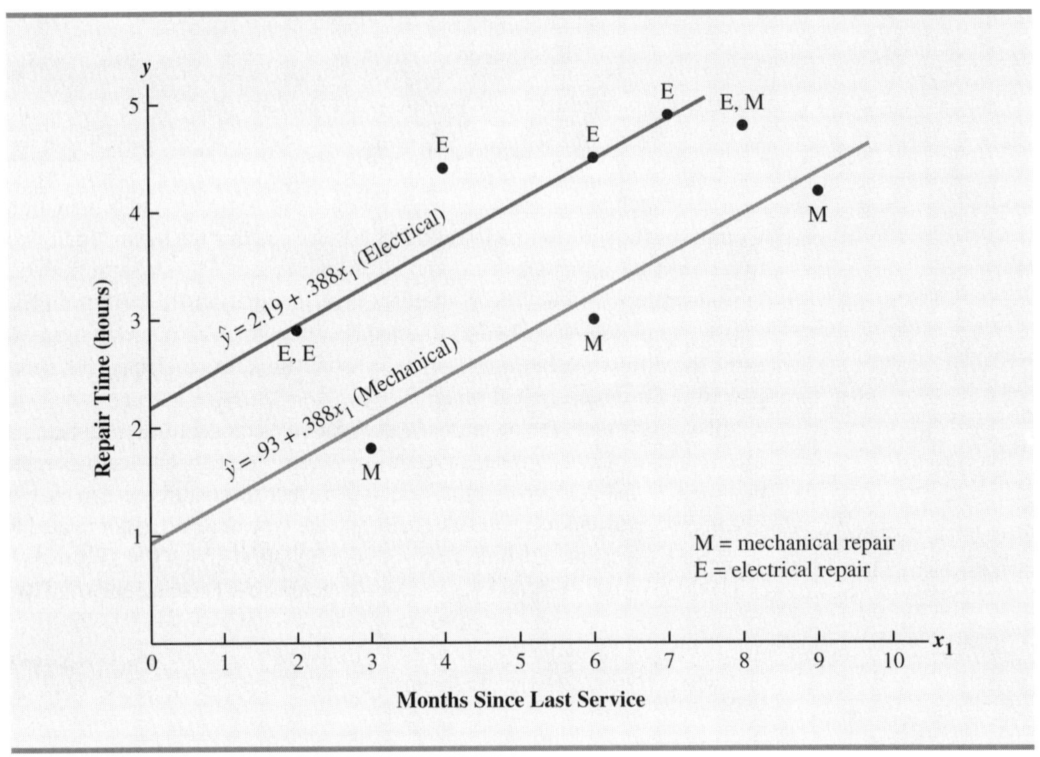

region is a qualitative variable with three levels, A, B, and C, we will need 3 − 1 = 2 dummy variables to represent the sales region. Each variable can be coded 0 or 1 as follows.

$$x_1 = \begin{cases} 1 \text{ if sales region B} \\ 0 \text{ otherwise} \end{cases}$$

$$x_2 = \begin{cases} 1 \text{ if sales region C} \\ 0 \text{ otherwise} \end{cases}$$

With this definition, we have the following values of x_1 and x_2.

Region	x_1	x_2
A	0	0
B	1	0
C	0	1

Observations corresponding to region A would be coded $x_1 = 0, x_2 = 0$; observations corresponding to region B would be coded $x_1 = 1, x_2 = 0$; and observations corresponding to region C would be coded $x_1 = 0, x_2 = 1$.

The regression equation relating the expected value of the number of units sold, $E(y)$, to the dummy variables would be written as

$$E(y) = \beta_0 + \beta_1 x_1 + \beta_2 x_2$$

To help us interpret the parameters β_0, β_1, and β_2, consider the following three variations of the regression equation.

$$E(y \mid \text{region A}) = \beta_0 + \beta_1(0) + \beta_2(0) = \beta_0$$
$$E(y \mid \text{region B}) = \beta_0 + \beta_1(1) + \beta_2(0) = \beta_0 + \beta_1$$
$$E(y \mid \text{region C}) = \beta_0 + \beta_1(0) + \beta_2(1) = \beta_0 + \beta_2$$

Thus, β_0 is the mean or expected value of sales for region A; β_1 is the difference between the mean number of units sold in region B and the mean number of units sold in region A; and β_2 is the difference between the mean number of units sold in region C and the mean number of units sold in region A.

Two dummy variables were required because sales region is a qualitative variable with three levels. But the assignment of $x_1 = 0, x_2 = 0$ to indicate region A, $x_1 = 1, x_2 = 0$ to indicate region B, and $x_1 = 0, x_2 = 1$ to indicate region C was arbitrary. For example, we could have chosen $x_1 = 1, x_2 = 0$ to indicate region A, $x_1 = 0, x_2 = 0$ to indicate region B, and $x_1 = 0, x_2 = 1$ to indicate region C. In that case, β_1 would have been interpreted as the mean difference between regions A and B and β_2 as the mean difference between regions C and B.

The important point to remember is that when a qualitative variable has k levels, $k - 1$ dummy variables are required in the multiple regression analysis. Thus, if the sales region example had a fourth region, labeled D, three dummy variables would be necessary. For example, the three dummy variables can be coded as follows.

$$x_1 = \begin{cases} 1 \text{ if sales region B} \\ 0 \text{ otherwise} \end{cases} \quad x_2 = \begin{cases} 1 \text{ if sales region C} \\ 0 \text{ otherwise} \end{cases} \quad x_3 = \begin{cases} 1 \text{ if sales region D} \\ 0 \text{ otherwise} \end{cases}$$

Exercises

Methods

32. Consider a regression study involving a dependent variable y, a quantitative independent variable x_1, and a qualitative variable with two levels (level 1 and level 2).
    a. Write a multiple regression equation relating x_1 and the qualitative variable to y.
    b. What is the expected value of y corresponding to level 1 of the qualitative variable?
    c. What is the expected value of y corresponding to level 2 of the qualitative variable?
    d. Interpret the parameters in your regression equation.
33. Consider a regression study involving a dependent variable y, a quantitative independent variable x_1, and a qualitative independent variable with three possible levels (level 1, level 2, and level 3).
    a. How many dummy variables are required to represent the qualitative variable?
    b. Write a multiple regression equation relating x_1 and the qualitative variable to y.
    c. Interpret the parameters in your regression equation.

Applications

34. Management proposed the following regression model to predict sales at a fast-food outlet.

$$y = \beta_0 + \beta_1 x_1 + \beta_2 x_2 + \beta_3 x_3 + \epsilon$$

where

$$x_1 = \text{number of competitors within one mile}$$
$$x_2 = \text{population within 1 mile (1000s)}$$
$$x_3 = \begin{cases} 1 \text{ if drive-up window present} \\ 0 \text{ otherwise} \end{cases}$$
$$y = \text{sales (\$1000s)}$$

The following estimated regression equation was developed after 20 outlets were surveyed.

$$\hat{y} = 10.1 - 4.2x_1 + 6.8x_2 + 15.3x_3$$

a. What is the expected amount of sales attributable to the drive-up window?
b. Predict sales for a store with two competitors, a population of 8000 within 1 mile, and no drive-up window.
c. Predict sales for a store with one competitor, a population of 3000 within 1 mile, and a drive-up window.

35. Refer to the Johnson Filtration problem introduced in this section. Suppose that in addition to information on the number of months since the machine was serviced and whether a mechanical or an electrical failure had occurred, the managers obtained a list showing which repairperson performed the service. The revised data follow.

CD file

Repair

Repair Time in Hours	Months Since Last Service	Type of Repair	Repairperson
2.9	2	Electrical	Dave Newton
3.0	6	Mechanical	Dave Newton
4.8	8	Electrical	Bob Jones
1.8	3	Mechanical	Dave Newton
2.9	2	Electrical	Dave Newton
4.9	7	Electrical	Bob Jones
4.2	9	Mechanical	Bob Jones
4.8	8	Mechanical	Bob Jones
4.4	4	Electrical	Bob Jones
4.5	6	Electrical	Dave Newton

a. Ignore for now the months since the last maintenance service (x_1) and the repairperson who performed the service. Develop the estimated simple linear regression equation to predict the repair time (y) given the type of repair (x_2). Recall that $x_2 = 0$ if the type of repair is mechanical and 1 if the type of repair is electrical.
b. Does the equation that you developed in part (a) provide a good fit for the observed data? Explain.
c. Ignore for now the months since the last maintenance service and the type of repair associated with the machine. Develop the estimated simple linear regression equation to predict the repair time given the repairperson who performed the service. Let $x_3 = 0$ if Bob Jones performed the service and $x_3 = 1$ if Dave Newton performed the service.
d. Does the equation that you developed in part (c) provide a good fit for the observed data? Explain.

36. This problem is an extension of the situation described in exercise 35.

CD file

Repair

a. Develop the estimated regression equation to predict the repair time given the number of months since the last maintenance service, the type of repair, and the repairperson who performed the service.
b. At the .05 level of significance, test whether the estimated regression equation developed in part (a) represents a significant relationship between the independent variables and the dependent variable.
c. Is the addition of the independent variable x_3, the repairperson who performed the service, statistically significant? Use $\alpha = .05$. What explanation can you give for the results observed?

37. The National Football League rates prospects by position on a scale that ranges from 5 to 9. The ratings are interpreted as follows: 8–9 should start the first year; 7.0–7.9 should start; 6.0–6.9 will make the team as backup; and 5.0–5.9 can make the club and contribute. The following table shows the position, weight, speed (for 40 yards), and ratings for 25 NFL prospects (*USA Today*, April 14, 2000).

Football

Name	Position	Weight (pounds)	Speed (seconds)	Rating
Cosey Coleman	Guard	322	5.38	7.4
Travis Claridge	Guard	303	5.18	7.0
Kaulana Noa	Guard	317	5.34	6.8
Leander Jordan	Guard	330	5.46	6.7
Chad Clifton	Guard	334	5.18	6.3
Manula Savea	Guard	308	5.32	6.1
Ryan Johanningmeir	Guard	310	5.28	6.0
Mark Tauscher	Guard	318	5.37	6.0
Blaine Saipaia	Guard	321	5.25	6.0
Richard Mercier	Guard	295	5.34	5.8
Damion McIntosh	Guard	328	5.31	5.3
Jeno James	Guard	320	5.64	5.0
Al Jackson	Guard	304	5.20	5.0
Chris Samuels	Offensive tackle	325	4.95	8.5
Stockar McDougle	Offensive tackle	361	5.50	8.0
Chris McIngosh	Offensive tackle	315	5.39	7.8
Adrian Klemm	Offensive tackle	307	4.98	7.6
Todd Wade	Offensive tackle	326	5.20	7.3
Marvel Smith	Offensive tackle	320	5.36	7.1
Michael Thompson	Offensive tackle	287	5.05	6.8
Bobby Williams	Offensive tackle	332	5.26	6.8
Darnell Alford	Offensive tackle	334	5.55	6.4
Terrance Beadles	Offensive tackle	312	5.15	6.3
Tutan Reyes	Offensive tackle	299	5.35	6.1
Greg Robinson-Ran	Offensive tackle	333	5.59	6.0

a. Develop a dummy variable that will account for the player's position.
b. Develop an estimated regression equation to show how rating is related to position, weight, and speed.
c. At the .05 level of significance, test whether the estimated regression equation developed in part (b) indicates a significant relationship between the independent variables and the dependent variable.
d. Does the estimated regression equation provide a good fit for the observed data? Explain.
e. Is position a significant factor in the player's rating? Use $\alpha = .05$. Explain.
f. Suppose a new offensive tackle prospect who weighs 300 pounds ran the 40 yards in 5.1 seconds. Use the estimated regression equation developed in part (b) to estimate the rating for this player.

38. A 10-year study conducted by the American Heart Association provided data on how age, blood pressure, and smoking relate to the risk of strokes. Assume that the following data are from a portion of this study. Risk is interpreted as the probability (times 100) that the patient will have a stroke over the next 10-year period. For the smoking variable, define a dummy variable with 1 indicating a smoker and 0 indicating a nonsmoker.

Stroke

Risk	Age	Pressure	Smoker
12	57	152	No
24	67	163	No
13	58	155	No
56	86	177	Yes
28	59	196	No
51	76	189	Yes

(continued)

Risk	Age	Pressure	Smoker
18	56	155	Yes
31	78	120	No
37	80	135	Yes
15	78	98	No
22	71	152	No
36	70	173	Yes
15	67	135	Yes
48	77	209	Yes
15	60	199	No
36	82	119	Yes
8	66	166	No
34	80	125	Yes
3	62	117	No
37	59	207	Yes

a. Develop an estimated regression equation that relates risk of a stroke to the person's age, blood pressure, and whether the person is a smoker.
b. Is smoking a significant factor in the risk of a stroke? Explain. Use $\alpha = .05$.
c. What is the probability of a stroke over the next 10 years for Art Speen, a 68-year-old smoker who has blood pressure of 175? What action might the physician recommend for this patient?

Summary

In this chapter, we introduced multiple regression analysis as an extension of simple linear regression analysis presented in Chapter 12. Multiple regression analysis enables us to understand how a dependent variable is related to two or more independent variables. The multiple regression equation $E(y) = \beta_0 + \beta_1 x_1 + \beta_2 x_2 + \cdots + \beta_p x_p$ shows that the expected value or mean value of the dependent variable y is related to the values of the independent variables $x_1, x_2, \ldots, x_p$. Sample data and the least squares method are used to develop the estimated multiple regression equation $\hat{y} = b_0 + b_1 x_1 + b_2 x_2 + \ldots + b_p x_p$. In effect $b_0, b_1, b_2, \ldots, b_p$ are sample statistics used to estimate the unknown model parameters $\beta_0, \beta_1, \beta_2, \ldots, \beta_p$. Computer printouts were used throughout the chapter to emphasize the fact that statistical software packages are the only realistic means of performing the numerous computations required in multiple regression analysis.

The multiple coefficient of determination was presented as a measure of the goodness of fit of the estimated regression equation. It determines the proportion of the variation of y that can be explained by the estimated regression equation. The adjusted multiple coefficient of determination is a similar measure of goodness of fit that adjusts for the number of independent variables and thus avoids overestimating the impact of adding more independent variables.

An F test and a t test were presented as ways to determine statistically whether the relationship among the variables is significant. The F test is used to determine whether there is a significant overall relationship between the dependent variable and the set of all independent variables. The t test is used to determine whether there is a significant relationship between the dependent variable and an individual independent variable given the other independent variables in the regression model. Correlation among the independent variables, known as multicollinearity, was discussed.

The chapter concluded with a section on how dummy variables can be used to incorporate qualitative independent variables into multiple regression analysis.

Glossary

Multiple regression analysis Regression analysis involving two or more independent variables.
Multiple regression model The mathematical equation that describes how the dependent variable y is related to the independent variables $x_1, x_2, \ldots, x_p$ and an error term ϵ.
Multiple regression equation The mathematical equation that describes how the mean or expected value of the dependent variable y is related to the values of the independent variables; that is, $E(y) = \beta_0 + \beta_1 x_1 + \beta_2 x_2 + \ldots + \beta_p x_p$.
Estimated multiple regression equation The estimate of the multiple regression equation based on sample data and the least squares method; it is $\hat{y} = b_0 + b_1 x_1 + b_2 x_2 + \ldots + b_p x_p$.
Least squares method The method used to develop the estimated regression equation. It minimizes the sum of squared residuals (the deviations between the observed values of the dependent variable, y_i, and the estimated values of the dependent variable, $\hat{y}_i$).
Multiple coefficient of determination A measure of the goodness of fit of the estimated multiple regression equation. It can be interpreted as the proportion of the variability in the dependent variable that is explained by the estimated regression equation.
Adjusted multiple coefficient of determination A measure of the goodness of fit of the estimated multiple regression equation that adjusts for the number of independent variables in the model and thus avoids overestimating the impact of adding more independent variables.
Multicollinearity The term used to describe the correlation among the independent variables.
Qualitative independent variable An independent variable with qualitative data.
Dummy variable A variable used to model the effect of qualitative independent variables. A dummy variable may take only the value zero or one.

Key Formulas

Multiple Regression Model

$$y = \beta_0 + \beta_1 x_1 + \beta_2 x_2 + \cdots + \beta_p x_p + \epsilon \qquad \textbf{(13.1)}$$

Multiple Regression Equation

$$E(y) = \beta_0 + \beta_1 x_1 + \beta_2 x_2 + \cdots + \beta_p x_p \qquad \textbf{(13.2)}$$

Estimated Multiple Regression Equation

$$\hat{y} = b_0 + b_1 x_1 + b_2 x_2 + \cdots + b_p x_p \qquad \textbf{(13.3)}$$

Least Squares Criterion

$$\min \Sigma(y_i - \hat{y}_i)^2 \qquad \textbf{(13.4)}$$

Relationship Among SST, SSR, and SSE

$$\text{SST} = \text{SSR} + \text{SSE} \qquad \textbf{(13.7)}$$

Multiple Coefficient of Determination

$$R^2 = \frac{\text{SSR}}{\text{SST}} \qquad \textbf{(13.8)}$$

Adjusted Multiple Coefficient of Determination

$$R_a^2 = 1 - (1 - R^2)\frac{n - 1}{n - p - 1} \qquad \textbf{(13.9)}$$

Mean Square Regression

$$\text{MSR} = \frac{\text{SSR}}{p} \tag{13.12}$$

Mean Square Error

$$\text{MSE} = \frac{\text{SSE}}{n - p - 1} \tag{13.13}$$

***F* Test Statistic**

$$F = \frac{\text{MSR}}{\text{MSE}} \tag{13.14}$$

***t* Test Statistic**

$$t = \frac{b_i}{s_{b_i}} \tag{13.15}$$

Supplementary Exercises

39. The admissions officer for Clearwater College developed the following estimated regression equation relating the final college GPA to the student's SAT mathematics score and high-school GPA.

$$\hat{y} = -1.41 + .0235x_1 + .00486x_2$$

where

$$x_1 = \text{high-school grade point average}$$
$$x_2 = \text{SAT mathematics score}$$
$$y = \text{final college grade point average}$$

a. Interpret the coefficients in this estimated regression equation.
b. Estimate the final college GPA for a student who has a high-school average of 84 and a score of 540 on the SAT mathematics test.

40. The personnel director for Electronics Associates developed the following estimated regression equation relating an employee's score on a job satisfaction test to his or her length of service and wage rate.

$$\hat{y} = 14.4 - 8.69x_1 + 13.5x_2$$

where

$$x_1 = \text{length of service (years)}$$
$$x_2 = \text{wage rate (dollars)}$$
$$y = \text{job satisfaction test score (higher scores indicate greater job satisfaction)}$$

a. Interpret the coefficients in this estimated regression equation.
b. Develop an estimate of the job satisfaction test score for an employee who has four years of service and makes \$6.50 per hour.

41. A partial computer output from a regression analysis follows.

```
The regression equation is
Y = 8.103 + 7.602 X1 + 3.111 X2

Predictor        Coef       SE Coef       T
Constant       _______       2.667      _____
X1             _______       2.105      _____
X2             _______       0.613      _____

S = 3.335      R-sq = 92.3%      R-sq(adj) = ____%

Analysis of Variance

SOURCE            DF        SS        MS        F
Regression       _____     1612     _____     _____
Residual Error    12      _____     _____
Total            _____    _____
```

a. Compute the appropriate t-ratios.
b. Test for the significance of β_1 and β_2 at $\alpha = .05$.
c. Compute the entries in the DF, SS, and MS columns.
d. Compute R_a^2.

42. Recall that in exercise 39, the admissions officer for Clearwater College developed the following estimated regression equation relating final college GPA to the student's SAT mathematics score and high-school GPA.

$$\hat{y} = -1.41 + .0235x_1 + .00486x_2$$

where

x_1 = high-school grade point average
x_2 = SAT mathematics score
y = final college grade point average

A portion of the Minitab computer output follows.

```
The regression equation is
Y = -1.41 + .0235 X1 + .00486 X2

Predictor        Coef        SE Coef       T
Constant       -1.4053       0.4848      _____
X1             0.023467      0.008666    _____
X2             _______       0.001077    _____

S = 0.1298      R-sq = _____      R-sq(adj) = _____

Analysis of Variance

SOURCE            DF        SS         MS        F
Regression       _____    1.76209    _____     _____
Residual Error   _____    _______    _____
Total              9      1.88000
```

a. Complete the missing entries in this output.
b. Compute F and test at a .05 level of significance to see whether a significant relationship is present.
c. Did the estimated regression equation provide a good fit to the data? Explain.
d. Use the t test and $\alpha = .05$ to test H_0: $\beta_1 = 0$ and H_0: $\beta_2 = 0$.

43. Recall that in exercise 40 the personnel director for Electronics Associates developed the following estimated regression equation relating an employee's score on a job satisfaction test to length of service and wage rate.

$$\hat{y} = 14.4 - 8.69x_1 + 13.5x_2$$

where

x_1 = length of service (years)
x_2 = wage rate (dollars)
y = job satisfaction test score (higher scores indicate greater job satisfaction)

A portion of the Minitab computer output follows.

```
The regression equation is
Y = 14.4 - 8.69 X1 + 13.52 X2

Predictor          Coef        SE Coef         T
Constant         14.448          8.191      1.76
X1               ______          1.555     _____
X2               13.517          2.085     _____

S = 3.773      R-sq - ______%  R-sq(adj) = ______%

Analysis of Variance

SOURCE              DF          SS          MS          F
Regression           2       _____       _____      _____
Residual Error   _____       71.17       _____
Total                7       720.0
```

a. Complete the missing entries in this output.
b. Compute F and test using $\alpha = .05$ to see whether a significant relationship is present.
c. Did the estimated regression equation provide a good fit to the data? Explain.
d. Use the t test and $\alpha = .05$ to test H_0: $\beta_1 = 0$ and H_0: $\beta_2 = 0$.

44. *SmartMoney* magazine evaluated 65 metropolitan areas to determine where home values are headed. An ideal city would get a score of 100 if all factors measured were as favorable as possible. Areas with a score of 60 or greater are considered to be primed for price appreciation, and areas with a score of below 50 may see housing values erode. Two of the factors evaluated were the recession resistance of the area and its affordability. Both of these factors were rated using a scale ranging from 0 (low score) to 10 (high score). The data obtained for a sample of 20 cities evaluated by *SmartMoney* follow (*SmartMoney*, February 2002).

HomeValue

Metro Area	Recession Resistance	Affordability	Score
Tucson	10	7	70.7
Fort Worth	10	7	68.5
San Antonio	6	8	65.5
Richmond	8	6	63.6
Indianapolis	4	8	62.5
Philadelphia	0	10	61.9
Atlanta	2	6	60.7
Phoenix	4	5	60.3
Cincinnati	2	7	57.0
Miami	6	5	56.5
Hartford	0	7	56.2
Birmingham	0	8	55.7
San Diego	8	2	54.6
Raleigh	2	7	50.9
Oklahoma City	1	6	49.6
Orange County	4	2	49.1
Denver	4	4	48.6
Los Angeles	0	7	45.7
Detroit	0	5	44.3
New Orleans	0	5	41.2

a. Develop an estimated regression equation that can be used to predict the score given the recession resistance rating. At the .05 level of significance, test for a significant relationship.
b. Did the estimated regression equation developed in part (a) provide a good fit to the data? Explain.
c. Develop an estimated regression equation that can be used to predict the score given the recession resistance rating and the affordability rating. At the .05 level of significance, test for overall significance.

45. Today's marketplace offers a wide choice to buyers of sport utility vehicles (SUVs) and pickup trucks. An important factor to many buyers is the resale value of the vehicle. The following table shows the resale value (%) after two years and the suggested retail price for 10 SUVs, 10 small pickup trucks, and 10 large pickup trucks (*Kiplinger's New Cars & Trucks 2000 Buyer's Guide*).

Trucks

Make and Model	Type of Vehicle	Suggested Retail Price ($)	Resale Value (%)
Chevrolet Blazer LS	Sport utility	19,495	55
Ford Explorer Sport	Sport utility	20,495	57
GMC Yukon XL 1500	Sport utility	26,789	67
Honda CR-V	Sport utility	18,965	65
Isuzu VehiCross	Sport utility	30,186	62
Jeep Cherokee Limited	Sport utility	25,745	57
Mercury Mountaineer Monterrey	Sport utility	29,895	59
Nissan Pathfinder XE	Sport utility	26,919	54
Toyota 4Runner	Sport utility	22,418	55
Toyota RAV4	Sport utility	17,148	55
Chevrolet S-10 Extended Cab	Small pickup	18,847	46
Dodge Dakota Club Cab Sport	Small pickup	16,870	53
Ford Ranger XLT Regular Cab	Small pickup	18,510	48

(continued)

Make and Model	Type of Vehicle	Suggested Retail Price ($)	Resale Value (%)
Ford Ranger XLT Supercab	Small pickup	20,225	55
GMC Sonoma Regular Cab	Small pickup	16,938	44
Isuzu Hombre Spacecab	Small pickup	18,820	41
Mazda B4000 SE Cab Plus	Small pickup	23,050	51
Nissan Frontier XE Regular Cab	Small pickup	12,110	51
Toyota Tacoma Xtracab	Small pickup	18,228	49
Toyota Tacoma Xtracab V6	Small pickup	19,318	50
Chevrolet K2500	Full-size pickup	24,417	60
Chevrolet Silverado 2500 Ext	Full-size pickup	24,140	64
Dodge Ram 1500	Full-size pickup	17,460	54
Dodge Ram Quad Cab 2500	Full-size pickup	32,770	63
Dodge Ram Regular Cab 2500	Full-size pickup	23,140	59
Ford F150 XL	Full-size pickup	22,875	58
Ford F350 Super Duty Crew Cab XL	Full-size pickup	34,295	64
GMC New Sierra 1500 Ext Cab	Full-size pickup	27,089	68
Toyota Tundra Access Cab Limited	Full-size pickup	25,605	53
Toyota Tundra Regular Cab	Full-size pickup	15,835	58

a. Develop an estimated regression equation that can be used to predict the resale value given the suggested retail price. At the .05 level of significance, test for a significant relationship.
b. Did the estimated regression equation developed in part (a) provide a good fit to the data? Explain.
c. Develop an estimated regression equation that can be used to predict the resale value given the suggested retail price and the type of vehicle.
d. Use the F test to determine the significance of the regression results. At a .05 level of significance, what is your conclusion?

46. The U.S. Department of Energy's *Fuel Economy Guide* provides fuel efficiency data for cars and trucks. A portion of the data for 35 standard pickup trucks produced by Chevrolet and General Motors follows (http://www.fueleconomy.gov, March 21, 2003). The column labeled Drive identifies whether the vehicle has two-wheel drive (2WD) or four-wheel drive (4WD). The column labeled Displacement shows the engine's displacement in liters, the column labeled Cylinders specifies the number of cylinders the engine has, and the column labeled Transmission shows whether the truck has an automatic transmission or a manual transmission. The column labeled City MPG shows the fuel efficiency rating for the truck for city driving in terms of miles per gallon (mpg).

FuelEcon

Truck	Name	Drive	Displacement	Cylinders	Transmission	City MPG
1	C1500 Silverado	2WD	4.3	6	Auto	15
2	C1500 Silverado	2WD	4.3	6	Manual	15
3	C1500 Silverado	2WD	4.8	8	Auto	15
4	C1500 Silverado	2WD	4.8	8	Manual	16
5	C1500 Silverado	2WD	5.3	8	Auto	11
.	.	.	.	.	.	.
.	.	.	.	.	.	.
32	K1500 Sierra	4WD	5.3	8	Auto	15
33	K1500 Sierra	4WD	5.3	8	Auto	15
34	Sonoma	4WD	4.3	6	Auto	17
35	Sonoma	4WD	4.3	6	Manual	15

a. Develop an estimated regression equation that can be used to predict the fuel efficiency for city driving given the engine's displacement. Test for significance using $\alpha = .05$.
b. Consider the addition of the dummy variable Drive4, where the value of Drive4 is 0 if the truck has two-wheel drive and 1 if the truck has four-wheel drive. Develop the estimated regression equation that can be used to predict the fuel efficiency for city driving given the engine's displacement and the dummy variable Drive4.
c. Use $\alpha = .05$ to determine whether the dummy variable added in part (b) is significant.
d. Consider the addition of the dummy variable EightCyl, where the value of EightCyl is 0 if the truck's engine has six cylinders and 1 if the truck's engine has eight cylinders. Develop the estimated regression equation that can be used to predict the fuel efficiency for city driving given the engine's displacement and the dummy variables Drive4 and EightCyl.
e. For the estimated regression equation developed in part (d), test for overall significance and individual significance using $\alpha = .05$.

Case Problem 1 Consumer Research, Inc.

Consumer Research, Inc., is an independent agency that conducts research on consumer attitudes and behaviors for a variety of firms. In one study, a client asked for an investigation of consumer characteristics that can be used to predict the amount charged by credit card users. Data were collected on annual income, household size, and annual credit card charges for a sample of 50 consumers. The following data are on the CD accompanying the text in the data set named Consumer.

Consumer

Income ($1000s)	Household Size	Amount Charged ($)	Income ($1000s)	Household Size	Amount Charged ($)
54	3	4016	54	6	5573
30	2	3159	30	1	2583
32	4	5100	48	2	3866
50	5	4742	34	5	3586
31	2	1864	67	4	5037
55	2	4070	50	2	3605
37	1	2731	67	5	5345
40	2	3348	55	6	5370
66	4	4764	52	2	3890
51	3	4110	62	3	4705
25	3	4208	64	2	4157
48	4	4219	22	3	3579
27	1	2477	29	4	3890
33	2	2514	39	2	2972
65	3	4214	35	1	3121
63	4	4965	39	4	4183
42	6	4412	54	3	3730
21	2	2448	23	6	4127
44	1	2995	27	2	2921
37	5	4171	26	7	4603
62	6	5678	61	2	4273
21	3	3623	30	2	3067
55	7	5301	22	4	3074
42	2	3020	46	5	4820
41	7	4828	66	4	5149

Managerial Report

1. Use methods of descriptive statistics to summarize the data. Comment on the findings.
2. Develop estimated regression equations, first using annual income as the independent variable and then using household size as the independent variable. Which variable is the better predictor of annual credit card charges? Discuss your findings.
3. Develop an estimated regression equation with annual income and household size as the independent variables. Discuss your findings.
4. What is the predicted annual credit card charge for a three-person household with an annual income of $40,000?
5. Discuss the need for other independent variables that could be added to the model. What additional variables might be helpful?

Case Problem 2 Predicting Student Proficiency Test Scores

In order to predict how a school district would have scored when accounting for poverty and other income measures, *The Cincinnati Enquirer* gathered data from the Ohio Department of Education's Education Management Services and the Ohio Department of Taxation (*The Cincinnati Enquirer*, November 30, 1997). First, the newspaper obtained passage-rate data on the math, reading, science, writing, and citizenship proficiency exams given to fourth-, sixth-, ninth-, and 12th-graders in early 1996. By combining these data, they computed an overall percentage of students that passed the tests for each district.

The percentage of a school district's students on Aid for Dependent Children (ADC), the percentage who qualify for free or reduced-price lunches, and the district's median family income were also recorded. A portion of the data collected for the 608 school districts follows. The complete data set is available on the CD accompanying the text in the data set named Enquirer.

CD file

Enquirer

Rank	School District	County	% Passed	% on ADC	% Free Lunch	Median Income ($)
1	Ottawa Hills Local	Lucas	93.85	0.11	0.00	48231
2	Wyoming City	Hamilton	93.08	2.95	4.59	42672
3	Oakwood City	Montgomery	92.92	0.20	0.38	42403
4	Madeira City	Hamilton	92.37	1.50	4.83	32889
5	Indian Hill Ex Vill	Hamilton	91.77	1.23	2.70	44135
6	Solon City	Cuyahoga	90.77	0.68	2.24	34993
7	Chagrin Falls Ex Vill	Cuyahoga	89.89	0.47	0.44	38921
8	Mariemont City	Hamilton	89.80	3.00	2.97	31823
9	Upper Arlington City	Franklin	89.77	0.24	0.92	38358
10	Granville Ex Vill	Licking	89.22	1.14	0.00	36235
⋮	⋮	⋮	⋮	⋮	⋮	⋮

The data have been ranked based on the values in the column labeled % Passed; these data are the overall percentage of students passing the tests. Data in the column labeled % on ADC are the percentage of each school district's students on ADC, and the data in the column labeled % Free Lunch are the percentage of students who qualify for free or reduced-price lunches. The column labeled Median Income shows each district's median family income. Also shown for each school district is the county in which the school district is located. Note that in some cases the value in the % Free Lunch column is 0, indicating that the district did not participate in the free lunch program.

Managerial Report

Use the methods presented in this and previous chapters to analyze this data set. Present a summary of your analysis, including key statistical results, conclusions, and recommendations, in a managerial report. Include any technical material you feel is appropriate in an appendix.

Case Problem 3 Alumni Giving

Alumni donations are an important source of revenue for colleges and universities. If administrators could determine the factors that could lead to increases in the percentage of alumni who make a donation, they might be able to implement policies that could lead to increased revenues. Research shows that students who are more satisfied with their contact with teachers are more likely to graduate. As a result, one might suspect that smaller class sizes and lower student-faculty ratios might lead to a higher percentage of satisfied graduates, which in turn might lead to increases in the percentage of alumni who make a donation. Table 13.7 shows data for 48 national universities (*America's Best Colleges,* Year 2000 Edition). The column labeled Graduation Rate is the percentage of students who initially enrolled at the university and graduated. The column labeled % of Classes Under 20 shows the percentage of classes offered with fewer than 20 students. The column labeled Student-Faculty Ratio is the number of students enrolled divided by the total number of faculty. Finally, the column labeled Alumni Giving Rate is the percentage of alumni who made a donation to the university.

Managerial Report

1. Use methods of descriptive statistics to summarize the data.
2. Develop an estimated regression equation that can be used to predict the alumni giving rate given the number of students who graduate. Discuss your findings.
3. Develop an estimated regression equation that could be used to predict the alumni giving rate using the data provided.
4. What conclusions and recommendations can you derive from your analysis?

Appendix 13.1 Multiple Regression with Minitab

Butler

In Section 13.2 we discussed the computer solution of multiple regression problems by showing Minitab's output for the Butler Trucking Company problem. In this appendix we describe the steps required to generate the Minitab computer solution. First, the data must be entered in a Minitab worksheet. The miles traveled are entered in column C1, the number of deliveries are entered in column C2, and the travel times (hours) are entered in column C3. The variable names Miles, Deliv, and Time were entered as the column headings on the worksheet. In subsequent steps, we refer to the data by using the variable names Miles, Deliv, and Time or the column indicators C1, C2, and C3. The following steps describe how to use Minitab to produce the regression results shown in Figure 13.4.

Step 1. Select the **Stat** menu
Step 2. Select the **Regression** menu
Step 3. Choose **Regression**
Step 4. When the **Regression** dialog box appears
Enter Time in the **Response** box
Enter Miles and Deliv in the **Predictors** box
Click **OK**

TABLE 13.7 DATA FOR 48 NATIONAL UNIVERSITIES

Alumni

University	State	Graduation Rate	% of Classes Under 20	Student-Faculty Ratio	Alumni Giving Rate
Boston College	MA	85	39	13	25
Brandeis University	MA	79	68	8	33
Brown University	RI	93	60	8	40
California Institute of Technology	CA	85	65	3	46
Carnegie Mellon University	PA	75	67	10	28
Case Western Reserve Univ.	OH	72	52	8	31
College of William and Mary	VA	89	45	12	27
Columbia University	NY	90	69	7	31
Cornell University	NY	91	72	13	35
Dartmouth College	NH	94	61	10	53
Duke University	NC	92	68	8	45
Emory University	GA	84	65	7	37
Georgetown University	PA	91	54	10	29
Harvard University	MA	97	73	8	46
Johns Hopkins University	MD	89	64	9	27
Lehigh University	PA	81	55	11	40
Massachusetts Inst. of Technology	MA	92	65	6	44
New York University	NY	72	63	13	13
Northwestern University	IL	90	66	8	30
Pennsylvania State Univ.	PA	80	32	19	21
Princeton University	NJ	95	68	5	67
Rice University	TX	92	62	8	40
Stanford University	CA	92	69	7	34
Tufts University	MA	87	67	9	29
Tulane University	LA	72	56	12	17
U. of California–Berkeley	CA	83	58	17	18
U. of California–Davis	CA	74	32	19	7
U. of California–Irvine	CA	74	42	20	9
U. of California–Los Angeles	CA	78	41	18	13
U. of California–San Diego	CA	80	48	19	8
U. of California–Santa Barbara	CA	70	45	20	12
U. of Chicago	IL	84	65	4	36
U. of Florida	FL	67	31	23	19
U. of Illinois–Urbana Champaign	IL	77	29	15	23
U. of Michigan–Ann Arbor	MI	83	51	15	13
U. of North Carolina–Chapel Hill	NC	82	40	16	26
U. of Notre Dame	IN	94	53	13	49
U. of Pennsylvania	PA	90	65	7	41
U. of Rochester	NY	76	63	10	23
U. of Southern California	CA	70	53	13	22
U. of Texas–Austin	TX	66	39	21	13
U. of Virginia	VA	92	44	13	28
U. of Washington	WA	70	37	12	12
U. of Wisconsin–Madison	WI	73	37	13	13
Vanderbilt University	TN	82	68	9	31
Wake Forest University	NC	82	59	11	38
Washington University–St. Louis	MO	86	73	7	33
Yale University	CT	94	77	7	50

Appendix 13.2 Multiple Regression with Excel

Butler

In Section 13.2 we discussed the computer solution of multiple regression problems by showing Minitab's output for the Butler Trucking Company problem. In this appendix we describe how to use Excel's Regression tool to develop the estimated multiple regression equation for the Butler Trucking problem. Refer to Figure 13.10 as we describe the tasks involved. First, the labels Assignment, Miles, Deliveries, and Time are entered into cells A1:D1 of the worksheet, and the sample data into cells B2:D11. The numbers 1–10 in cells A2:A11 identify each observation.

The following steps describe how to use the Regression tool for the multiple regression analysis.

Step 1. Select the **Tools** menu
Step 2. Choose **Data Analysis**
Step 3. Choose **Regression** from the list of Analysis Tools

FIGURE 13.10 EXCEL OUTPUT FOR BUTLER TRUCKING WITH TWO INDEPENDENT VARIABLES

	A	B	C	D	E	F	G	H	I
1	Assignment	Miles	Deliveries	Time					
2	1	100	4	9.3					
3	2	50	3	4.8					
4	3	100	4	8.9					
5	4	100	2	6.5					
6	5	50	2	4.2					
7	6	80	2	6.2					
8	7	75	3	7.4					
9	8	65	4	6					
10	9	90	3	7.6					
11	10	90	2	6.1					
12									
13	SUMMARY OUTPUT								
14									
15	*Regression Statistics*								
16	Multiple R	0.9507							
17	R Square	0.9038							
18	Adjusted R Square	0.8763							
19	Standard Error	0.5731							
20	Observations	10							
21									
22	ANOVA								
23		*df*	*SS*	*MS*	*F*	*Significance F*			
24	Regression	2	21.6006	10.8003	32.8784	0.0003			
25	Residual	7	2.2994	0.3285					
26	Total	9	23.9						
27									
28		*Coefficients*	*Standard Error*	*t Stat*	*P-value*	*Lower 95%*	*Upper 95%*	*Lower 99.0%*	*Upper 99.0%*
29	Intercept	-0.8687	0.9515	-0.9129	0.3916	-3.1188	1.3813	-4.1986	2.4612
30	Miles	0.0611	0.0099	6.1824	0.0005	0.0378	0.0845	0.0265	0.0957
31	Deliveries	0.9234	0.2211	4.1763	0.0042	0.4006	1.4463	0.1496	1.6972

Step 4. When the Regression dialog box appears
Enter D1:D11 in the **Input Y Range** box
Enter B1:C11 in the **Input X Range** box
Select **Labels**
Select **Confidence Level**
Enter 99 in the **Confidence Level** box
Select **Output Range**
Enter A13 in the **Output Range** box (to identify the upper left corner of the section of the worksheet where the output will appear)
Click **OK**

In the Excel output shown in Figure 13.10 the label for the independent variable x_1 is Miles (see cell A30), and the label for the independent variable x_2 is Deliveries (see cell A31). The estimated regression equation is

$$\hat{y} = -.8687 + .0611x_1 + .9234x_2$$

Note that using Excel's Regression tool for multiple regression is almost the same as using it for simple linear regression. The major difference is that in the multiple regression case a larger range of cells is required in order to identify the independent variables.

Appendix B: Tables

TABLE 1 STANDARD NORMAL DISTRIBUTION

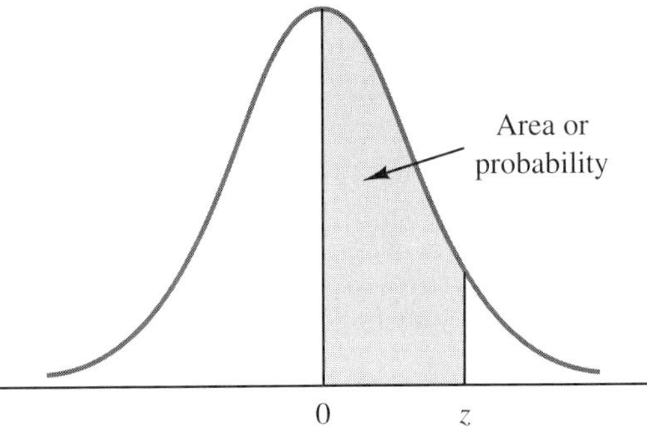

Entries in the table give the area under the curve between the mean and z standard deviations above the mean. For example, for $z = 1.25$ the area under the curve between the mean and z is .3944.

z	.00	.01	.02	.03	.04	.05	.06	.07	.08	.09
.0	.0000	.0040	.0080	.0120	.0160	.0199	.0239	.0279	.0319	.0359
.1	.0398	.0438	.0478	.0517	.0557	.0596	.0636	.0675	.0714	.0753
.2	.0793	.0832	.0871	.0910	.0948	.0987	.1026	.1064	.1103	.1141
.3	.1179	.1217	.1255	.1293	.1331	.1368	.1406	.1443	.1480	.1517
.4	.1554	.1591	.1628	.1664	.1700	.1736	.1772	.1808	.1844	.1879
.5	.1915	.1950	.1985	.2019	.2054	.2088	.2123	.2157	.2190	.2224
.6	.2257	.2291	.2324	.2357	.2389	.2422	.2454	.2486	.2517	.2549
.7	.2580	.2611	.2642	.2673	.2704	.2734	.2764	.2794	.2823	.2852
.8	.2881	.2910	.2939	.2967	.2995	.3023	.3051	.3078	.3106	.3133
.9	.3159	.3186	.3212	.3238	.3264	.3289	.3315	.3340	.3365	.3389
1.0	.3413	.3438	.3461	.3485	.3508	.3531	.3554	.3577	.3599	.3621
1.1	.3643	.3665	.3686	.3708	.3729	.3749	.3770	.3790	.3810	.3830
1.2	.3849	.3869	.3888	.3907	.3925	.3944	.3962	.3980	.3997	.4015
1.3	.4032	.4049	.4066	.4082	.4099	.4115	.4131	.4147	.4162	.4177
1.4	.4192	.4207	.4222	.4236	.4251	.4265	.4279	.4292	.4306	.4319
1.5	.4332	.4345	.4357	.4370	.4382	.4394	.4406	.4418	.4429	.4441
1.6	.4452	.4463	.4474	.4484	.4495	.4505	.4515	.4525	.4535	.4545
1.7	.4554	.4564	.4573	.4582	.4591	.4599	.4608	.4616	.4625	.4633
1.8	.4641	.4649	.4656	.4664	.4671	.4678	.4686	.4693	.4699	.4706
1.9	.4713	.4719	.4726	.4732	.4738	.4744	.4750	.4756	.4761	.4767
2.0	.4772	.4778	.4783	.4788	.4793	.4798	.4803	.4808	.4812	.4817
2.1	.4821	.4826	.4830	.4834	.4838	.4842	.4846	.4850	.4854	.4857
2.2	.4861	.4864	.4868	.4871	.4875	.4878	.4881	.4884	.4887	.4890
2.3	.4893	.4896	.4898	.4901	.4904	.4906	.4909	.4911	.4913	.4916
2.4	.4918	.4920	.4922	.4925	.4927	.4929	.4931	.4932	.4934	.4936
2.5	.4938	.4940	.4941	.4943	.4945	.4946	.4948	.4949	.4951	.4952
2.6	.4953	.4955	.4956	.4957	.4959	.4960	.4961	.4962	.4963	.4964
2.7	.4965	.4966	.4967	.4968	.4969	.4970	.4971	.4972	.4973	.4974
2.8	.4974	.4975	.4976	.4977	.4977	.4978	.4979	.4979	.4980	.4981
2.9	.4981	.4982	.4982	.4983	.4984	.4984	.4985	.4985	.4986	.4986
3.0	.4987	.4987	.4987	.4988	.4988	.4989	.4989	.4989	.4990	.4990

TABLE 2 t DISTRIBUTION

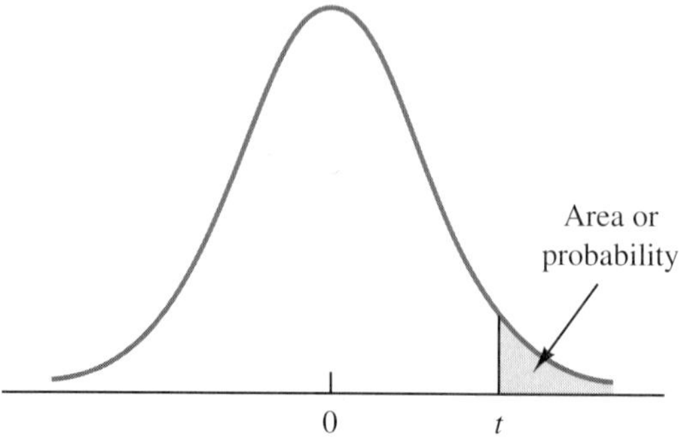

Entries in the table give t values for an area or probability in the upper tail of the t distribution. For example, with 10 degrees of freedom and a .05 area in the upper tail, $t_{.05} = 1.812$.

Degrees of Freedom	Area in Upper Tail					
	.20	.10	.05	.025	.01	.005
1	1.376	3.078	6.314	12.706	31.821	63.656
2	1.061	1.886	2.920	4.303	6.965	9.925
3	.978	1.638	2.353	3.182	4.541	5.841
4	.941	1.533	2.132	2.776	3.747	4.604
5	.920	1.476	2.015	2.571	3.365	4.032
6	.906	1.440	1.943	2.447	3.143	3.707
7	.896	1.415	1.895	2.365	2.998	3.499
8	.889	1.397	1.860	2.306	2.896	3.355
9	.883	1.383	1.833	2.262	2.821	3.250
10	.879	1.372	1.812	2.228	2.764	3.169
11	.876	1.363	1.796	2.201	2.718	3.106
12	.873	1.356	1.782	2.179	2.681	3.055
13	.870	1.350	1.771	2.160	2.650	3.012
14	.868	1.345	1.761	2.145	2.624	2.977
15	.866	1.341	1.753	2.131	2.602	2.947
16	.865	1.337	1.746	2.120	2.583	2.921
17	.863	1.333	1.740	2.110	2.567	2.898
18	.862	1.330	1.734	2.101	2.552	2.878
19	.861	1.328	1.729	2.093	2.539	2.861
20	.860	1.325	1.725	2.086	2.528	2.845
21	.859	1.323	1.721	2.080	2.518	2.831
22	.858	1.321	1.717	2.074	2.508	2.819
23	.858	1.319	1.714	2.069	2.500	2.807
24	.857	1.318	1.711	2.064	2.492	2.797
25	.856	1.316	1.708	2.060	2.485	2.787
26	.856	1.315	1.706	2.056	2.479	2.779
27	.855	1.314	1.703	2.052	2.473	2.771
28	.855	1.313	1.701	2.048	2.467	2.763
29	.854	1.311	1.699	2.045	2.462	2.756
30	.854	1.310	1.697	2.042	2.457	2.750
31	.853	1.309	1.696	2.040	2.453	2.744
32	.853	1.309	1.694	2.037	2.449	2.738
33	.853	1.308	1.692	2.035	2.445	2.733
34	.852	1.307	1.691	2.032	2.441	2.728

TABLE 2 *t* DISTRIBUTION (*Continued*)

Degrees of Freedom	Area in Upper Tail .20	.10	.05	.025	.01	.005
35	.852	1.306	1.690	2.030	2.438	2.724
36	.852	1.306	1.688	2.028	2.434	2.719
37	.851	1.305	1.687	2.026	2.431	2.715
38	.851	1.304	1.686	2.024	2.429	2.712
39	.851	1.304	1.685	2.023	2.426	2.708
40	.851	1.303	1.684	2.021	2.423	2.704
41	.850	1.303	1.683	2.020	2.421	2.701
42	.850	1.302	1.682	2.018	2.418	2.698
43	.850	1.302	1.681	2.017	2.416	2.695
44	.850	1.301	1.680	2.015	2.414	2.692
45	.850	1.301	1.679	2.014	2.412	2.690
46	.850	1.300	1.679	2.013	2.410	2.687
47	.849	1.300	1.678	2.012	2.408	2.685
48	.849	1.299	1.677	2.011	2.407	2.682
49	.849	1.299	1.677	2.010	2.405	2.680
50	.849	1.299	1.676	2.009	2.403	2.678
51	.849	1.298	1.675	2.008	2.402	2.676
52	.849	1.298	1.675	2.007	2.400	2.674
53	.848	1.298	1.674	2.006	2.399	2.672
54	.848	1.297	1.674	2.005	2.397	2.670
55	.848	1.297	1.673	2.004	2.396	2.668
56	.848	1.297	1.673	2.003	2.395	2.667
57	.848	1.297	1.672	2.002	2.394	2.665
58	.848	1.296	1.672	2.002	2.392	2.663
59	.848	1.296	1.671	2.001	2.391	2.662
60	.848	1.296	1.671	2.000	2.390	2.660
61	.848	1.296	1.670	2.000	2.389	2.659
62	.847	1.295	1.670	1.999	2.388	2.657
63	.847	1.295	1.669	1.998	2.387	2.656
64	.847	1.295	1.669	1.998	2.386	2.655
65	.847	1.295	1.669	1.997	2.385	2.654
66	.847	1.295	1.668	1.997	2.384	2.652
67	.847	1.294	1.668	1.996	2.383	2.651
68	.847	1.294	1.668	1.995	2.382	2.650
69	.847	1.294	1.667	1.995	2.382	2.649
70	.847	1.294	1.667	1.994	2.381	2.648
71	.847	1.294	1.667	1.994	2.380	2.647
72	.847	1.293	1.666	1.993	2.379	2.646
73	.847	1.293	1.666	1.993	2.379	2.645
74	.847	1.293	1.666	1.993	2.378	2.644
75	.846	1.293	1.665	1.992	2.377	2.643
76	.846	1.293	1.665	1.992	2.376	2.642
77	.846	1.293	1.665	1.991	2.376	2.641
78	.846	1.292	1.665	1.991	2.375	2.640
79	.846	1.292	1.664	1.990	2.374	2.639

TABLE 2 t DISTRIBUTION (*Continued*)

Degrees of Freedom	Area in Upper Tail					
	.20	**.10**	**.05**	**.025**	**.01**	**.005**
80	.846	1.292	1.664	1.990	2.374	2.639
81	.846	1.292	1.664	1.990	2.373	2.638
82	.846	1.292	1.664	1.989	2.373	2.637
83	.846	1.292	1.663	1.989	2.372	2.636
84	.846	1.292	1.663	1.989	2.372	2.636
85	.846	1.292	1.663	1.988	2.371	2.635
86	.846	1.291	1.663	1.988	2.370	2.634
87	.846	1.291	1.663	1.988	2.370	2.634
88	.846	1.291	1.662	1.987	2.369	2.633
89	.846	1.291	1.662	1.987	2.369	2.632
90	.846	1.291	1.662	1.987	2.368	2.632
91	.846	1.291	1.662	1.986	2.368	2.631
92	.846	1.291	1.662	1.986	2.368	2.630
93	.846	1.291	1.661	1.986	2.367	2.630
94	.845	1.291	1.661	1.986	2.367	2.629
95	.845	1.291	1.661	1.985	2.366	2.629
96	.845	1.290	1.661	1.985	2.366	2.628
97	.845	1.290	1.661	1.985	2.365	2.627
98	.845	1.290	1.661	1.984	2.365	2.627
99	.845	1.290	1.660	1.984	2.364	2.626
100	.845	1.290	1.660	1.984	2.364	2.626
∞	.842	1.282	1.645	1.960	2.326	2.576

TABLE 3 CHI-SQUARE DISTRIBUTION

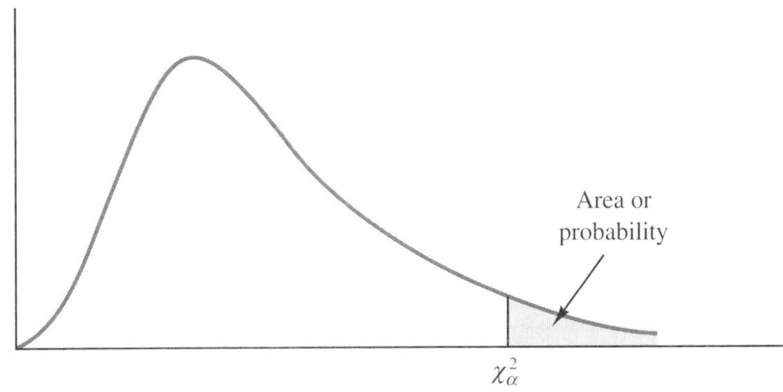

Entries in the table give χ^2_α values, where α is the area or probability in the upper tail of the chi-square distribution. For example, with 10 degrees of freedom and a .01 area in the upper tail, $\chi^2_{.01} = 23.209$.

Degrees of Freedom	Area in Upper Tail									
	.995	.99	.975	.95	.90	.10	.05	.025	.01	.005
1	.000	.000	.001	.004	.016	2.706	3.841	5.024	6.635	7.879
2	.010	.020	.051	.103	.211	4.605	5.991	7.378	9.210	10.597
3	.072	.115	.216	.352	.584	6.251	7.815	9.348	11.345	12.838
4	.207	.297	.484	.711	1.064	7.779	9.488	11.143	13.277	14.860
5	.412	.554	.831	1.145	1.610	9.236	11.070	12.832	15.086	16.750
6	.676	.872	1.237	1.635	2.204	10.645	12.592	14.449	16.812	18.548
7	.989	1.239	1.690	2.167	2.833	12.017	14.067	16.013	18.475	20.278
8	1.344	1.647	2.180	2.733	3.490	13.362	15.507	17.535	20.090	21.955
9	1.735	2.088	2.700	3.325	4.168	14.684	16.919	19.023	21.666	23.589
10	2.156	2.558	3.247	3.940	4.865	15.987	18.307	20.483	23.209	25.188
11	2.603	3.053	3.816	4.575	5.578	17.275	19.675	21.920	24.725	26.757
12	3.074	3.571	4.404	5.226	6.304	18.549	21.026	23.337	26.217	28.300
13	3.565	4.107	5.009	5.892	7.041	19.812	22.362	24.736	27.688	29.819
14	4.075	4.660	5.629	6.571	7.790	21.064	23.685	26.119	29.141	31.319
15	4.601	5.229	6.262	7.261	8.547	22.307	24.996	27.488	30.578	32.801
16	5.142	5.812	6.908	7.962	9.312	23.542	26.296	28.845	32.000	34.267
17	5.697	6.408	7.564	8.672	10.085	24.769	27.587	30.191	33.409	35.718
18	6.265	7.015	8.231	9.390	10.865	25.989	28.869	31.526	34.805	37.156
19	6.844	7.633	8.907	10.117	11.651	27.204	30.144	32.852	36.191	38.582
20	7.434	8.260	9.591	10.851	12.443	28.412	31.410	34.170	37.566	39.997
21	8.034	8.897	10.283	11.591	13.240	29.615	32.671	35.479	38.932	41.401
22	8.643	9.542	10.982	12.338	14.041	30.813	33.924	36.781	40.289	42.796
23	9.260	10.196	11.689	13.091	14.848	32.007	35.172	38.076	41.638	44.181
24	9.886	10.856	12.401	13.848	15.659	33.196	36.415	39.364	42.980	45.558
25	10.520	11.524	13.120	14.611	16.473	34.382	37.652	40.646	44.314	46.928
26	11.160	12.198	13.844	15.379	17.292	35.563	38.885	41.923	45.642	48.290
27	11.808	12.878	14.573	16.151	18.114	36.741	40.113	43.195	46.963	49.645
28	12.461	13.565	15.308	16.928	18.939	37.916	41.337	44.461	48.278	50.994
29	13.121	14.256	16.047	17.708	19.768	39.087	42.557	45.722	49.588	52.335

TABLE 3 CHI-SQUARE DISTRIBUTION (*Continued*)

Degrees of Freedom	Area in Upper Tail									
	.995	**.99**	**.975**	**.95**	**.90**	**.10**	**.05**	**.025**	**.01**	**.005**
30	13.787	14.953	16.791	18.493	20.599	40.256	43.773	46.979	50.892	53.672
35	17.192	18.509	20.569	22.465	24.797	46.059	49.802	53.203	57.342	60.275
40	20.707	22.164	24.433	26.509	29.051	51.805	55.758	59.342	63.691	66.766
45	24.311	25.901	28.366	30.612	33.350	57.505	61.656	65.410	69.957	73.166
50	27.991	29.707	32.357	34.764	37.689	63.167	67.505	71.420	76.154	79.490
55	31.735	33.571	36.398	38.958	42.060	68.796	73.311	77.380	82.292	85.749
60	35.534	37.485	40.482	43.188	46.459	74.397	79.082	83.298	88.379	91.952
65	39.383	41.444	44.603	47.450	50.883	79.973	84.821	89.177	94.422	98.105
70	43.275	45.442	48.758	51.739	55.329	85.527	90.531	95.023	100.425	104.215
75	47.206	49.475	52.942	56.054	59.795	91.061	96.217	100.839	106.393	110.285
80	51.172	53.540	57.153	60.391	64.278	96.578	101.879	106.629	112.329	116.321
85	55.170	57.634	61.389	64.749	68.777	102.079	107.522	112.393	118.236	122.324
90	59.196	61.754	65.647	69.126	73.291	107.565	113.145	118.136	124.116	128.299
95	63.250	65.898	69.925	73.520	77.818	113.038	118.752	123.858	129.973	134.247
100	67.328	70.065	74.222	77.929	82.358	118.498	124.342	129.561	135.807	140.170

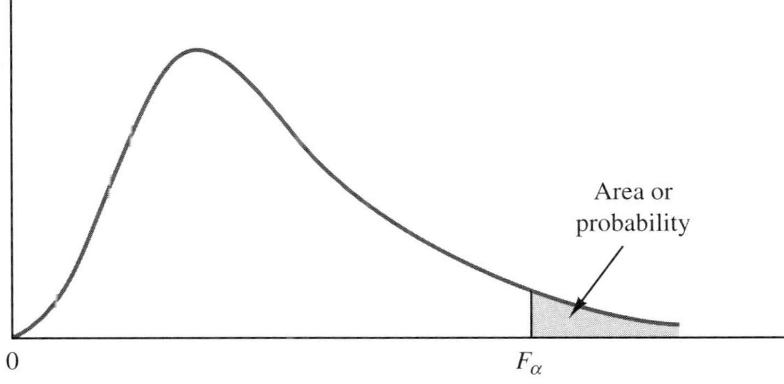

Entries in the table give F_α values, where α is the area or probability in the upper tail of the F distribution. For example, with 4 numerator degrees of freedom, 8 denominator degrees of freedom, and a .05 area in the upper tail, $F_{.05} = 3.84$.

Denominator Degrees of Freedom	Area in Upper Tail	Numerator Degrees of Freedom																	
		1	2	3	4	5	6	7	8	9	10	15	20	25	30	40	60	100	1000
1	.10	39.86	49.50	53.59	55.83	57.24	58.20	58.91	59.44	59.86	60.19	61.22	61.74	62.05	62.26	62.53	62.79	63.01	63.30
	.05	161.45	199.50	215.71	224.58	230.16	233.99	236.77	238.88	240.54	241.88	245.95	248.02	249.26	250.10	251.14	252.20	253.04	254.19
	.025	647.79	799.48	864.15	899.60	921.83	937.11	948.20	956.64	963.28	968.63	984.87	993.08	998.09	1001.40	1005.60	1009.79	1013.16	1017.76
	.01	4052.18	4999.34	5403.53	5624.26	5763.96	5858.95	5928.33	5980.95	6022.40	6055.93	6156.97	6208.66	6239.86	6260.35	6286.43	6312.97	6333.92	6362.80
2	.10	8.53	9.00	9.16	9.24	9.29	9.33	9.35	9.37	9.38	9.39	9.42	9.44	9.45	9.46	9.47	9.47	9.48	9.49
	.05	18.51	19.00	19.16	19.25	19.30	19.33	19.35	19.37	19.38	19.40	19.43	19.45	19.46	19.46	19.47	19.48	19.49	19.49
	.025	38.51	39.00	39.17	39.25	39.30	39.33	39.36	39.37	39.39	39.40	39.43	39.45	39.46	39.46	39.47	39.48	39.49	39.50
	.01	98.50	99.00	99.16	99.25	99.30	99.33	99.36	99.38	99.39	99.40	99.43	99.45	99.46	99.47	99.48	99.48	99.49	99.50
3	.10	5.54	5.46	5.39	5.34	5.31	5.28	5.27	5.25	5.24	5.23	5.20	5.18	5.17	5.17	5.16	5.15	5.14	5.13
	.05	10.13	9.55	9.28	9.12	9.01	8.94	8.89	8.85	8.81	8.79	8.70	8.66	8.63	8.62	8.59	8.57	8.55	8.53
	.025	17.44	16.04	15.44	15.10	14.88	14.73	14.62	14.54	14.47	14.42	14.25	14.17	14.12	14.08	14.04	13.99	13.96	13.91
	.01	34.12	30.82	29.46	28.71	28.24	27.91	27.67	27.49	27.34	27.23	26.87	26.69	26.58	26.50	26.41	26.32	26.24	26.14
4	.10	4.54	4.32	4.19	4.11	4.05	4.01	3.98	3.95	3.94	3.92	3.87	3.84	3.83	3.82	3.80	3.79	3.78	3.76
	.05	7.71	6.94	6.59	6.39	6.26	6.16	6.09	6.04	6.00	5.96	5.86	5.80	5.77	5.75	5.72	5.69	5.66	5.63
	.025	12.22	10.65	9.98	9.60	9.36	9.20	9.07	8.98	8.90	8.84	8.66	8.56	8.50	8.46	8.41	8.36	8.32	8.26
	.01	21.20	18.00	16.69	15.98	15.52	15.21	14.98	14.80	14.66	14.55	14.20	14.02	13.91	13.84	13.75	13.65	13.58	13.47
5	.10	4.06	3.78	3.62	3.52	3.45	3.40	3.37	3.34	3.32	3.30	3.324	3.21	3.19	3.17	3.16	3.14	3.13	3.11
	.05	6.61.	5.79	5.41	5.19	5.05	4.95	4.88	4.82	4.77	4.74	4.62	4.56	4.52	4.50	4.46	4.43	4.41	4.37
	.025	10.01	8.43	7.76	7.39	7.15	6.98	6.85	6.76	6.68	6.62	6.43	6.33	6.27	6.23	6.18	6.12	6.08	6.02
	.01	16.26	13.27	12.06	11.39	10.97	10.67	10.46	10.29	10.16	10.05	9.72	9.55	9.45	9.38	9.29	9.20	9.13	9.03

TABLE 4 *F* DISTRIBUTION (*Continued*)

Denominator Degrees of Freedom	Area in Upper Tail	Numerator Degrees of Freedom																	
		1	2	3	4	5	6	7	8	9	10	15	20	25	30	40	60	100	1000
6	.10	3.78	3.46	3.29	3.18	3.11	3.05	3.01	2.98	2.96	2.94	2.87	2.84	2.81	2.80	2.78	2.76	2.75	2.72
	.05	5.99	5.14	4.76	4.53	4.39	4.28	4.21	4.15	4.10	4.06	3.94	3.87	3.83	3.81	3.77	3.74	3.71	3.67
	.025	8.81	7.26	6.60	6.23	5.99	5.82	5.70	5.60	5.52	5.46	5.27	5.17	5.11	5.07	5.01	4.96	4.92	4.86
	.01	13.75	10.92	9.78	9.15	8.75	8.47	8.26	8.10	7.98	7.87	7.56	7.40	7.30	7.23	7.14	7.06	6.99	6.89
7	.10	3.59	3.26	3.07	2.96	2.88	2.83	2.78	2.75	2.72	2.70	2.63	2.59	2.57	2.56	2.54	2.51	2.50	2.47
	.05	5.59	4.74	4.35	4.12	3.97	3.87	3.79	3.73	3.68	3.64	3.51	3.44	3.40	3.38	3.34	3.30	3.27	3.23
	.025	8.07	6.54	5.89	5.52	5.29	5.12	4.99	4.90	4.82	4.76	4.57	4.47	4.40	4.36	4.31	4.25	4.21	4.15
	.01	12.25	9.55	8.45	7.85	7.46	7.19	6.99	6.84	6.72	6.62	6.31	6.16	6.06	5.99	5.91	5.82	5.75	5.66
8	.10	3.46	3.11	2.92	2.81	2.73	2.67	2.62	2.59	2.56	2.54	2.46	2.42	2.40	2.38	2.36	2.34	2.32	2.30
	.05	5.32	4.46	4.07	3.84	3.69	3.58	3.50	3.44	3.39	3.35	3.22	3.15	3.11	3.08	3.04	3.01	2.97	2.93
	.025	7.57	6.06	5.42	5.05	4.82	4.65	4.53	4.43	4.36	4.30	4.10	4.00	3.94	3.89	3.84	3.78	3.74	3.68
	.01	11.26	8.65	7.59	7.01	6.63	6.37	6.18	6.03	5.91	5.81	5.52	5.36	5.26	5.20	5.12	5.03	4.96	4.87
9	.10	3.36	3.01	2.81	2.69	2.61	2.55	2.51	2.47	2.44	2.42	2.34	2.30	2.27	2.25	2.23	2.21	2.19	2.16
	.05	5.12	4.26	3.86	3.63	3.48	3.37	3.29	3.23	3.18	3.14	3.01	2.94	2.89	2.86	2.83	2.79	2.76	2.71
	.025	7.21	5.71	5.08	4.72	4.48	4.32	4.20	4.10	4.03	3.96	3.77	3.67	3.60	3.56	3.51	3.45	3.40	3.34
	.01	10.56	8.02	6.99	6.42	6.06	5.80	5.61	5.47	5.35	5.26	4.96	4.81	4.71	4.65	4.57	4.48	4.41	4.32
10	.10	3.29	2.92	2.73	2.61	2.52	2.46	2.41	2.38	2.35	2.32	2.24	2.20	2.17	2.16	2.13	2.11	2.09	2.06
	.05	4.96	4.10	3.71	3.48	3.33	3.22	3.14	3.07	3.02	2.98	2.85	2.77	2.73	2.70	2.66	2.62	2.59	2.54
	.025	6.94	5.46	4.83	4.47	4.24	4.07	3.95	3.85	3.78	3.72	3.52	3.42	3.35	3.31	3.26	3.20	3.15	3.09
	.01	10.04	7.56	6.55	5.99	5.64	5.39	5.20	5.06	4.94	4.85	4.56	4.41	4.31	4.25	4.17	4.08	4.01	3.92
11	.10	3.23	2.86	2.66	2.54	2.45	2.39	2.34	2.30	2.27	2.25	2.17	2.12	2.10	2.08	2.05	2.03	2.01	1.98
	.05	4.84	3.98	3.59	3.36	3.20	3.09	3.01	2.95	2.90	2.85	2.72	2.65	2.60	2.57	2.53	2.49	2.46	2.41
	.025	6.72	5.26	4.63	4.28	4.04	3.88	3.76	3.66	3.59	3.53	3.33	3.23	3.16	3.12	3.06	3.00	2.96	2.89
	.01	9.65	7.21	6.22	5.67	5.32	5.07	4.89	4.74	4.63	4.54	4.25	4.10	4.01	3.94	3.86	3.78	3.71	3.61
12	.10	3.18	2.81	2.61	2.48	2.39	2.33	2.28	2.24	2.21	2.19	2.10	2.06	2.03	2.01	1.99	1.96	1.94	1.91
	.05	4.75	3.89	3.49	3.26	3.11	3.00	2.91	2.85	2.80	2.75	2.62	2.54	2.50	2.47	2.43	2.38	2.35	2.30
	.025	6.55	5.10	4.47	4.12	3.89	3.73	3.61	3.51	3.44	3.37	3.18	3.07	3.01	2.96	2.91	2.85	2.80	2.73
	.01	9.33	6.93	5.95	5.41	5.06	4.82	4.64	4.50	4.39	4.30	4.01	3.86	3.76	3.70	3.62	3.54	3.47	3.37
13	.10	3.14	2.76	2.56	2.43	2.35	2.28	2.23	2.20	2.16	2.14	2.05	2.01	1.98	1.96	1.93	1.90	1.88	1.85
	.05	4.67	3.81	3.41	3.18	3.03	2.92	2.83	2.77	2.71	2.67	2.53	2.46	2.41	2.38	2.34	2.30	2.26	2.21
	.025	6.41	4.97	4.35	4.00	3.77	3.60	3.48	3.39	3.31	3.25	3.05	2.95	2.88	2.84	2.78	2.72	2.67	2.60
	.01	9.07	6.70	5.74	5.21	4.86	4.62	4.44	4.30	4.19	4.10	3.82	3.66	3.57	3.51	3.43	3.34	3.27	3.18
14	.10	3.10	2.73	2.52	2.39	2.31	2.24	2.19	2.15	2.12	2.10	2.01	1.96	1.93	1.99	1.89	1.86	1.83	1.80
	.05	4.60	3.74	3.34	3.11	2.96	2.85	2.76	2.70	2.65	2.60	2.46	2.39	2.34	2.31	2.27	2.22	2.19	2.14
	.025	6.30	4.86	4.24	3.89	3.66	3.50	3.38	3.29	3.21	3.15	2.95	2.84	2.78	2.73	2.67	2.61	2.56	2.50
	.01	8.86	6.51	5.56	5.04	4.69	4.46	4.28	4.14	4.03	3.94	3.66	3.51	3.41	3.35	3.27	3.18	3.11	3.02
15	.10	3.07	2.70	2.49	2.36	2.27	2.21	2.16	2.12	2.09	2.06	1.97	1.92	1.89	1.87	1.85	1.82	1.79	1.76
	.05	4.54	3.68	3.29	3.06	2.90	2.79	2.71	2.64	2.59	2.54	2.40	2.33	2.28	2.25	2.20	2.16	2.12	2.07
	.025	6.20	4.77	4.15	3.80	3.58	3.41	3.29	3.20	3.12	3.06	2.86	2.76	2.69	2.64	2.59	2.52	2.47	2.40
	.01	8.68	6.36	5.42	4.89	4.56	4.32	4.14	4.00	3.89	3.80	3.52	3.37	3.28	3.21	3.13	3.05	2.98	2.88

Denominator Degrees of Freedom	Area in Upper Tail	Numerator Degrees of Freedom																	
		1	2	3	4	5	6	7	8	9	10	15	20	25	30	40	60	100	1000
16	.10	3.05	2.67	2.46	2.33	2.24	2.18	2.13	2.09	2.06	2.03	1.94	1.89	1.86	1.84	1.81	1.78	1.76	1.72
	.05	4.49	3.63	3.24	3.01	2.85	2.74	2.66	2.59	2.54	2.49	2.35	2.28	2.23	2.19	2.15	2.11	2.07	2.02
	.025	6.12	4.69	4.08	3.73	3.50	3.34	3.22	3.12	3.05	2.99	2.79	2.68	2.61	2.57	2.51	2.45	2.40	2.32
	.01	8.53	6.23	5.29	4.77	4.44	4.20	4.03	3.89	3.78	3.69	3.41	3.26	3.16	3.10	3.02	2.93	2.86	2.76
17	.10	3.03	2.64	2.44	2.31	2.22	2.15	2.10	2.06	2.03	2.00	1.91	1.86	1.83	1.81	1.78	1.75	1.73	1.69
	.05	4.45	3.59	3.20	2.96	2.81	2.70	2.61	2.55	2.49	2.45	2.31	2.23	2.18	2.15	2.10	2.06	2.02	1.97
	.025	6.04	4.62	4.01	3.66	3.44	3.28	3.16	3.06	2.98	2.92	2.72	2.62	2.55	2.50	2.44	2.38	2.33	2.26
	.01	8.40	6.11	5.19	4.67	4.34	4.10	3.93	3.79	3.68	3.59	3.31	3.16	3.07	3.00	2.92	2.83	2.76	2.66
18	.10	3.01	2.62	2.42	2.29	2.20	2.13	2.08	2.04	2.00	1.98	1.89	1.84	1.80	1.78	1.75	1.72	1.70	1.66
	.05	4.41	3.55	3.16	2.93	2.77	2.66	2.58	2.51	2.46	2.41	2.27	2.19	2.14	2.11	2.06	2.02	1.98	1.92
	.025	5.98	4.56	3.95	3.61	3.38	3.22	3.10	3.01	2.93	2.87	2.67	2.56	2.49	2.44	2.38	2.32	2.27	2.20
	.01	8.29	6.01	5.09	4.58	4.25	4.01	3.84	3.71	3.60	3.51	3.23	3.08	2.98	2.92	2.84	2.75	2.68	2.58
19	.10	2.99	2.61	2.40	2.27	2.18	2.11	2.06	2.02	1.98	1.96	1.86	1.81	1.78	1.76	1.73	1.70	1.67	1.64
	.05	4.38	3.52	3.13	2.90	2.74	2.63	2.54	2.48	2.42	2.38	2.23	2.16	2.11	2.07	2.03	1.98	1.94	1.88
	.025	5.92	4.51	3.90	3.56	3.33	3.17	3.05	2.96	2.88	2.82	2.62	2.51	2.44	2.39	2.33	2.27	2.22	2.14
	.01	8.18	5.93	5.01	4.50	4.17	3.94	3.77	3.63	3.52	3.43	3.15	3.00	2.91	2.84	2.76	2.67	2.60	2.50
20	.10	2.97	2.59	2.38	2.25	2.16	2.09	2.04	2.00	1.96	1.94	1.84	1.79	1.76	1.74	1.71	1.68	1.65	1.61
	.05	4.35	3.49	3.10	2.87	2.71	2.60	2.51	2.45	2.39	2.35	2.20	2.12	2.07	2.04	1.99	1.95	1.91	1.85
	.025	5.87	4.46	3.86	3.51	3.29	3.13	3.01	2.91	2.84	2.77	2.57	2.46	2.40	2.35	2.29	2.22	2.17	2.09
	.01	8.10	5.85	4.94	4.43	4.10	3.87	3.70	3.56	3.46	3.37	3.09	2.94	2.84	2.78	2.69	2.61	2.54	2.43
21	.10	2.96	2.57	2.36	2.23	2.14	2.08	2.02	1.98	1.95	1.92	1.83	1.78	1.74	1.72	1.69	1.66	1.63	1.59
	.05	4.32	3.47	3.07	2.84	2.68	2.57	2.49	2.42	2.37	2.32	2.18	2.10	2.05	2.01	1.96	1.92	1.88	1.82
	.025	5.83	4.42	3.82	3.48	3.25	3.09	2.97	2.87	2.80	2.73	2.53	2.42	2.36	2.31	2.25	2.18	2.13	2.05
	.01	8.02	5.78	4.87	4.37	4.04	3.81	3.64	3.51	3.40	3.31	3.03	2.88	2.79	2.72	2.64	2.55	2.48	2.37
22	.10	2.95	2.56	2.35	2.22	2.13	2.06	2.01	1.97	1.93	1.90	1.81	1.76	1.73	1.70	1.67	1.64	1.61	1.57
	.05	4.30	3.44	3.05	2.82	2.66	2.55	2.46	2.40	2.34	2.30	2.15	2.07	2.02	1.98	1.94	1.89	1.85	1.79
	.025	5.79	4.38	3.78	3.44	3.22	3.05	2.93	2.84	2.76	2.70	2.50	2.39	2.32	2.27	2.21	2.14	2.09	2.01
	.01	7.95	5.72	4.82	4.31	3.99	3.76	3.59	3.45	3.35	3.26	2.98	2.83	2.73	2.67	2.58	2.50	2.42	2.32
23	.10	2.94	2.55	2.34	2.21	2.11	2.05	1.99	1.95	1.92	1.89	1.80	1.74	1.71	1.69	1.66	1.62	1.59	1.55
	.05	4.28	3.42	3.03	2.80	2.64	2.53	2.44	2.37	2.32	2.27	2.13	2.05	2.00	1.96	1.91	1.86	1.82	1.76
	.025	5.75	4.35	3.75	3.41	3.18	3.02	2.90	2.81	2.73	2.67	2.47	2.36	2.29	2.24	2.18	2.11	2.06	1.98
	.01	7.88	5.66	4.76	4.26	3.94	3.71	3.54	3.41	3.30	3.21	2.93	2.78	2.69	2.62	2.54	2.45	2.37	2.27
24	.10	2.93	2.54	2.33	2.19	2.10	2.04	1.98	1.94	1.91	1.88	1.78	1.73	1.70	1.67	1.64	1.61	1.58	1.54
	.05	4.26	3.40	3.01	2.78	2.62	2.51	2.42	2.36	2.30	2.25	2.11	2.03	1.97	1.94	1.89	1.84	1.80	1.74
	.025	5.72	4.32	3.72	3.38	3.15	2.99	2.87	2.78	2.70	2.64	2.44	2.33	2.26	2.21	2.15	2.08	2.02	1.94
	.01	7.82	5.61	4.72	4.22	3.90	3.67	3.50	3.36	3.26	3.17	2.89	2.74	2.64	2.58	2.49	2.40	2.33	2.22

TABLE 4 *F* DISTRIBUTION (*Continued*)

Denominator Degrees of Freedom	Area in Upper Tail	Numerator Degrees of Freedom																	
		1	2	3	4	5	6	7	8	9	10	15	20	25	30	40	60	100	1000
25	.10	2.92	2.53	2.32	2.18	2.09	2.02	1.97	1.93	1.89	1.87	1.77	1.72	1.68	1.66	1.63	1.59	1.56	1.52
	.05	4.24	3.39	2.99	2.76	2.60	2.49	2.40	2.34	2.28	2.24	2.09	2.01	1.96	1.92	1.87	1.82	1.78	1.72
	.025	5.69	4.29	3.69	3.35	3.13	2.97	2.85	2.75	2.68	2.61	2.41	2.30	2.23	2.18	2.12	2.05	2.00	1.91
	.01	7.77	5.57	4.68	4.18	3.85	3.63	3.46	3.32	3.22	3.13	2.85	2.70	2.60	2.54	2.45	2.36	2.29	2.18
26	.10	2.91	2.52	2.31	2.17	2.08	2.01	1.96	1.92	1.88	1.86	1.76	1.71	1.67	1.65	1.61	1.58	1.55	1.51
	.05	4.23	3.37	2.98	2.74	2.59	2.47	2.39	2.32	2.27	2.22	2.07	1.99	1.94	1.90	1.85	1.80	1.76	1.70
	.025	5.66	4.27	3.67	3.33	3.10	2.94	2.82	2.73	2.65	2.59	2.39	2.28	2.21	2.16	2.09	2.03	1.97	1.89
	.01	7.72	5.53	4.64	4.14	3.82	3.59	3.42	3.29	3.18	3.09	2.81	2.66	2.57	2.50	2.42	2.33	2.25	2.14
27	.10	2.90	2.51	2.30	2.17	2.07	2.00	1.95	1.91	1.87	1.85	1.75	1.70	1.66	1.64	1.60	1.57	1.54	1.50
	.05	4.21	3.35	2.96	2.73	2.57	2.46	2.37	2.31	2.25	2.20	2.06	1.97	1.92	1.88	1.84	1.79	1.74	1.68
	.025	5.63	4.24	3.65	3.31	3.08	2.92	2.80	2.71	2.63	2.57	2.36	2.25	2.18	2.13	2.07	2.00	1.94	1.86
	.01	7.68	5.49	4.60	4.11	3.78	3.56	3.39	3.26	3.15	3.06	2.78	2.63	2.54	2.47	2.38	2.29	2.22	2.11
28	.10	2.89	2.50	2.29	2.16	[illegible]	[illegible]	1.94	1.90	1.87	1.84	1.74	1.69	1.65	1.63	1.59	1.56	1.53	1.48
	.05	4.20	3.34	2.95	2.71	2.56	2.45	2.36	2.29	2.24	2.19	2.04	1.96	1.91	1.87	1.82	1.77	1.73	1.66
	.025	5.61	4.22	3.63	3.29	3.06	2.90	2.78	2.69	2.61	2.55	2.34	2.23	2.16	2.11	2.05	1.98	1.92	1.84
	.01	7.64	5.45	4.57	4.07	3.75	3.53	3.36	3.23	3.12	3.03	2.75	2.60	2.51	2.44	2.35	2.26	2.19	2.08
29	.10	2.89	2.50	2.28	2.15	2.06	1.99	1.93	1.89	1.86	1.83	1.73	1.68	1.64	1.62	1.58	1.55	1.52	1.47
	.05	4.18	3.33	2.93	2.70	2.55	2.43	2.35	2.28	2.22	2.18	2.03	1.94	1.89	1.85	1.81	1.75	1.71	1.65
	.025	5.59	4.20	3.61	3.27	3.04	2.88	2.76	2.67	2.59	2.53	2.32	2.21	2.14	2.09	2.03	1.96	1.90	1.82
	.01	7.60	5.42	4.54	4.04	3.73	3.50	3.33	3.20	3.09	3.00	2.73	2.57	2.48	2.41	2.33	2.23	2.16	2.05
30	.10	2.88	2.49	2.28	2.14	2.05	1.98	1.93	1.88	1.85	1.82	1.72	1.67	1.63	1.61	1.57	1.54	1.51	1.46
	.05	4.17	3.32	2.92	2.69	2.53	2.42	2.33	2.27	2.21	2.16	2.01	1.93	1.88	1.84	1.79	1.74	1.70	1.63
	.025	5.57	4.18	3.59	3.25	3.03	2.87	2.75	2.65	2.57	2.51	2.31	2.20	2.12	2.07	2.01	1.94	1.88	1.80
	.01	7.56	5.39	4.51	4.02	3.70	3.47	3.30	3.17	3.07	2.98	2.70	2.55	2.45	2.39	2.30	2.21	2.13	2.02
40	.10	2.84	2.44	2.23	2.09	2.00	1.93	1.87	1.83	1.79	1.76	1.66	1.61	1.57	1.54	1.51	1.47	1.43	1.38
	.05	4.08	3.23	2.84	2.61	2.45	2.34	2.25	2.18	2.12	2.08	1.92	1.84	1.78	1.74	1.69	1.64	1.59	1.52
	.025	5.42	4.05	3.46	3.13	2.90	2.74	2.62	2.53	2.45	2.39	2.18	2.07	1.99	1.94	1.88	1.80	1.74	1.65
	.01	7.31	5.18	4.31	3.83	3.51	3.29	3.12	2.99	2.89	2.80	2.52	2.37	2.27	2.20	2.11	2.02	1.94	1.82
60	.10	2.79	2.39	2.18	2.04	1.95	1.87	1.82	1.77	1.74	1.71	1.60	1.54	1.50	1.48	1.44	1.40	1.36	1.30
	.05	4.00	3.15	2.76	2.53	2.37	2.25	2.17	2.10	2.04	1.99	1.84	1.75	1.69	1.65	1.59	1.53	1.48	1.40
	.025	5.29	3.93	3.34	3.01	2.79	2.63	2.51	2.41	2.33	2.27	2.06	1.94	1.87	1.82	1.74	1.67	1.60	1.49
	.01	7.08	4.98	4.13	3.65	3.34	3.12	2.95	2.82	2.72	2.63	2.35	2.20	2.10	2.03	1.94	1.84	1.75	1.62
100	.10	2.76	2.36	2.14	2.00	1.91	1.83	1.78	1.73	1.69	1.66	1.56	1.49	1.45	1.42	1.38	1.34	1.29	1.22
	.05	3.94	3.09	2.70	2.46	2.31	2.19	2.10	2.03	1.97	1.93	1.77	1.68	1.62	1.57	1.52	1.45	1.39	1.30
	.025	5.18	3.83	3.25	2.92	2.70	2.54	2.42	2.32	2.24	2.18	1.97	1.85	1.77	1.71	1.64	1.56	1.48	1.36
	.01	6.90	4.82	3.98	3.51	3.21	2.99	2.82	2.69	2.59	2.50	2.22	2.07	1.97	1.89	1.80	1.69	1.60	1.45
1000	.10	2.71	2.31	2.09	1.95	1.85	1.78	1.72	1.68	1.64	1.61	1.49	1.43	1.38	1.35	1.30	1.25	1.20	1.08
	.05	3.85	3.00	2.61	2.38	2.22	2.11	2.02	1.95	1.89	1.84	1.68	1.58	1.52	1.47	1.41	1.33	1.26	1.11
	.025	5.04	3.70	3.13	2.80	2.58	2.42	2.30	2.20	2.13	2.06	1.85	1.72	1.64	1.58	1.50	1.41	1.32	1.13
	.01	6.66	4.63	3.80	3.34	3.04	2.82	2.66	2.53	2.43	2.34	2.06	1.90	1.79	1.72	1.61	1.50	1.38	1.16

Appendix D: Self-Test Solutions and Answers to Even-Numbered Exercises

Chapter 1

2. a. 9
b. 4
c. Qualitative: country and room rate
Quantitative: number of rooms and overall score
d. Country is nominal; room rate is ordinal; number of rooms is ratio; overall score is interval

3. a. Average number of rooms = 808/9 = 89.78, or approximately 90 rooms
b. Average overall score = 732.1/9 = 81.3
c. 2 of 9 are located in England; approximately 22%
d. 4 of 9 have a room rate of $$; approximately 44%

4. a. 10
b. All brands of minisystems manufactured
c. $314
d. $314

6. Questions a, c, and d provide quantitative data
Questions b and e provide qualitative data

8. a. 1005
b. Qualitative
c. Percentages
d. Approximately 291

10. a. Quantitative; ratio
b. Qualitative; nominal
c. Qualitative; ordinal
d. Quantitative; ratio
e. Qualitative; nominal

12. a. All visitors to Hawaii
b. Yes
c. First and fourth questions provide quantitative data
Second and third questions provide qualitative data

13. a. Quantitative
b. Time series with 6 observations
c. Earnings for Volkswagen
d. An increase would be expected in 2003, but it appears that the rate of increase is slowing

14. a. Qualitative

16. a. Product taste tests and test marketing
b. Specially designed statistical studies

18. a. 36%
b. 189
c. Qualitative

20. a. 43% of managers were bullish or very bullish, and 21% of managers expected health care to be the leading industry over the next 12 months.
b. The average 12-month return estimate is 11.2% for the population of investment managers.
c. The sample average of 2.5 years is an estimate of how long the population of investment managers think it will take to resume sustainable growth.

22. a. All registered voters in California
b. Registered voters contacted by the Policy Institute
c. Too time consuming and costly to reach the entire population

24. a. Correct
b. Incorrect
c. Correct
d. Incorrect
e. Incorrect

Chapter 2

2. a. .20
b. 40
c/d.

Class	Frequency	Percent Frequency
A	44	22
B	36	18
C	80	40
D	40	20
Total	200	100

3. a. $360° \times 58/120 = 174°$
b. $360° \times 42/120 = 126°$
c.

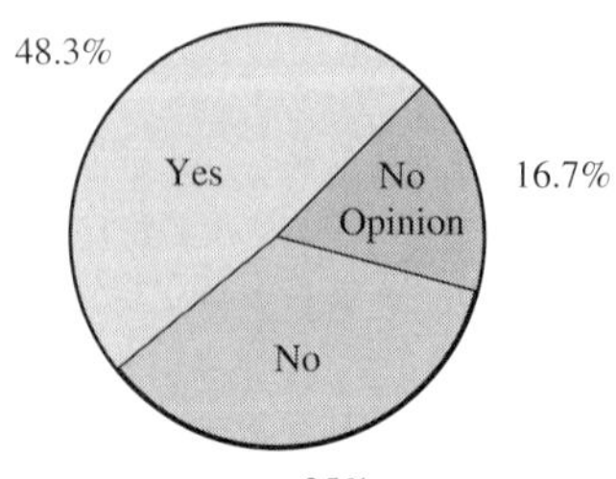

d.

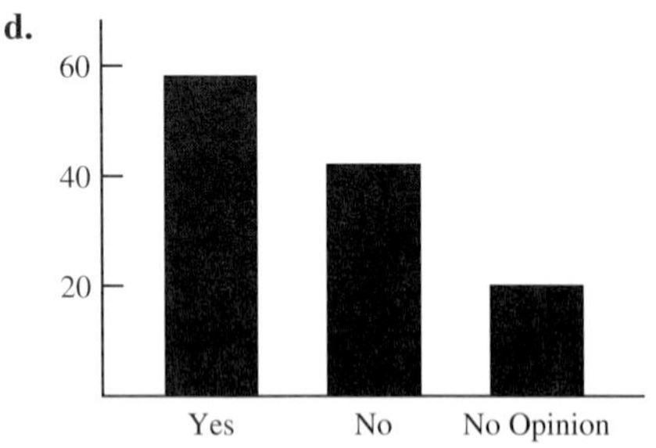

4. a. Qualitative

b.

TV Show	Frequency	Percent Frequency
CSI	18	36
ER	11	22
Friends	15	30
Raymond	6	12
Total	50	100

d. CSI had the largest; Friends was second

6. a.

Book	Frequency	Percent Frequency
7 Habits	10	16.66
Millionaire	16	26.67
Motley	9	15.00
Dad	13	21.67
WSJ Guide	6	10.00
Other	6	10.00
Total	60	100.00

b. First 5: *Millionaire, Dad, 7 Habits, Motley, WSJ Guide*

c. 48.33%

7.

Rating	Frequency	Relative Frequency
Outstanding	19	.38
Very good	13	.26
Good	10	.20
Average	6	.12
Poor	2	.04

Management should be pleased with these results: 64% of the ratings are very good to outstanding, and 84% of the ratings are good or better; comparing these ratings to previous results will show whether the restaurant is making improvements in its customers' ratings of food quality

8. a.

Position	Frequency	Relative Frequency
P	17	.309
H	4	.073
1	5	.091
2	4	.073
3	2	.036
S	5	.091
L	6	.109
C	5	.091
R	7	.127
Totals	55	1.000

b. Pitcher

c. 3rd base

d. Right field

e. Infielders 16 to outfielders 18

10. a. The data are ordinal; they simply provide quality classifications.

b.

Response	Frequency	Relative Frequency
3	2	.03
4	4	.07
5	12	.20
6	24	.40
7	18	.30
Totals	60	1.00

12.

Class	Cumulative Frequency	Cumulative Relative Frequency
≤19	10	.20
≤29	24	.48
≤39	41	.82
≤49	48	.96
≤59	50	1.00

14. b/c.

Class	Frequency	Percent Frequency
6.0–7.9	4	20
8.0–9.9	2	10
10.0–11.9	8	40
12.0–13.9	3	15
14.0–15.9	3	15
Totals	20	100

15. a/b.

Waiting Time	Frequency	Relative Frequency
0–4	4	.20
5–9	8	.40
10–14	5	.25
15–19	2	.10
20–24	1	.05
Totals	20	1.00

c/d.

Waiting Time	Cumulative Frequency	Cumulative Relative Frequency
≤4	4	.20
≤9	12	.60
≤14	17	.85
≤19	19	.95
≤24	20	1.00

e. 12/20 = .60

16. a. Adjusted Gross Income

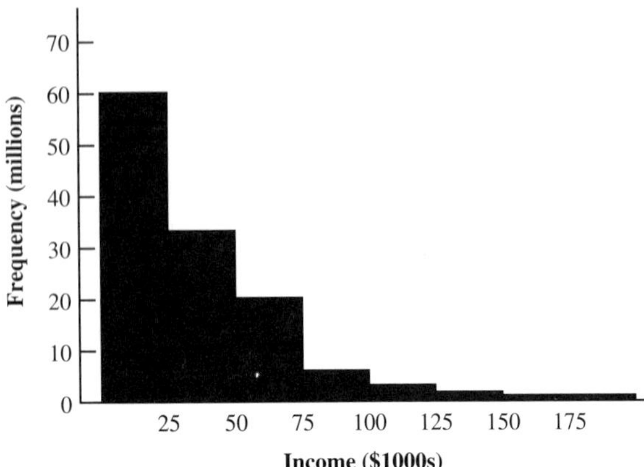

Histogram is skewed to the right

b. Exam Scores

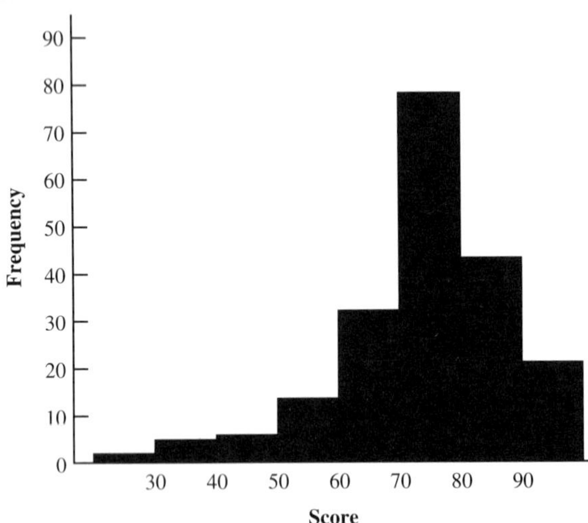

Histogram is skewed to the left

c.

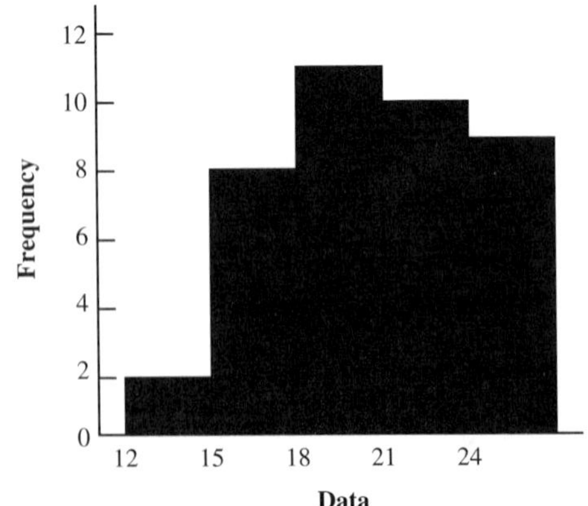

Histogram skewed slightly to the left, but roughly symmetric

18. a. Lowest salary: $93,000
Highest salary: $178,000

b.

Salary ($1000s)	Frequency	Relative Frequency	Percent Frequency
91–105	4	0.08	8
106–120	5	0.10	10
121–135	11	0.22	22
136–150	18	0.36	36
151–165	9	0.18	18
166–180	3	0.06	6
Total	50	1.00	100

c. 20/50
d. 24%

20. a.

Price	Frequency	Percent Frequency
30–39.99	7	35
40–49.99	5	25
50–59.99	2	10
60–69.99	3	15
70–79.99	3	15
Total	20	100

c. Fleetwood Mac, Harper/Johnson

22.

5	7 8
6	4 5 8
7	0 2 2 5 5 6 8
8	0 2 3 5

23. Leaf unit = .1

6	3
7	5 5 7
8	1 3 4 8
9	3 6
10	0 4 5
11	3

24. Leaf unit = 10

11	6
12	0 2
13	0 6 7
14	2 2 7
15	5
16	0 2 8
17	0 2 3

25.

9	8 9
10	2 4 6 6
11	4 5 7 8 8 9
12	2 4 5 7
13	1 2
14	4
15	1

26. a.

1	0 3 7 7
2	4 5 5
3	0 0 5 5 9
4	0 0 0 5 5 8
5	0 0 0 4 5 5

b.

0	5 7
1	0 1 1 3 4
1	5 5 5 8
2	0 0 0 0 0 0
2	5 5
3	0 0 0
3	6
4	
4	
5	
5	
6	3

28. a.

2	14
2	67
3	011123
3	5677
4	003333344
4	6679
5	00022
5	5679
6	14
6	6
7	2

b. 40–44 with 9

c. 43 with 5

d. 10%; relative small participation in the race

29. a.

x \ y	1	2	Total
A	5	0	5
B	11	2	13
C	2	10	12
Total	18	12	30

b.

x \ y	1	2	Total
A	100.0	0.0	100.0
B	84.6	15.4	100.0
C	16.7	83.3	100.0

c.

x \ y	1	2
A	27.8	0.0
B	61.1	16.7
C	11.1	83.3
Total	100.0	100.0

d. *A* values are always in $y = 1$
B values are most often in $y = 1$
C values are most often in $y = 2$

30. a.

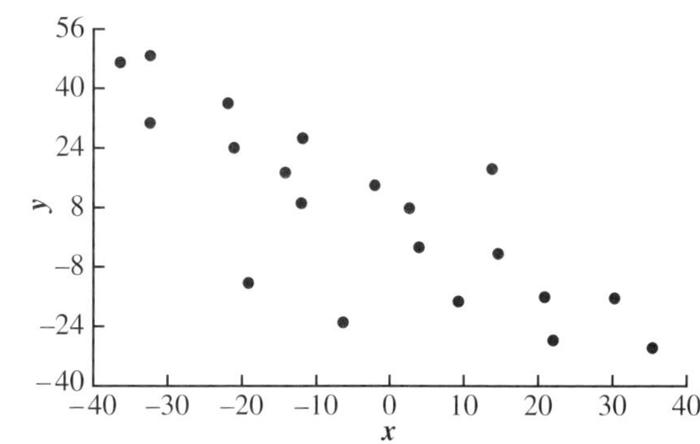

b. A negative relationship between *x* and *y*; *y* decreases as *x* increases

32. a.

	Household Income ($1000s)					
Education Level	Under 25	25.0–49.9	50.0–74.9	75.0–99.9	100 or more	Total
Not H.S. Graduate	32.70	14.82	8.27	5.02	2.53	15.86
H.S. Graduate	35.74	35.56	31.48	25.39	14.47	30.78
Some College	21.17	29.77	30.25	29.82	22.26	26.37
Bachelor's Degree	7.53	14.43	20.56	25.03	33.88	17.52
Beyond Bach. Deg.	2.86	5.42	9.44	14.74	26.86	9.48
Total	100.00	100.00	100.00	100.00	100.00	100.00

15.86% of the heads of households did not graduate from high school

b. 26.86%, 39.72%

34. a.

	EPS Rating					
Sales/Margins/ROE	0–19	20–39	40–59	60–79	80–100	Total
A				1	8	9
B		1	4	5	2	12
C	1		1	2	3	7
D	3	1		1		5
E		2	1			3
Total	4	4	6	9	13	36

b.

Sales/ Margins/ ROE	EPS Rating 0–19	20–39	40–59	60–79	80–100	Total
A				11.11	88.89	100
B		8.33	33.33	41.67	16.67	100
C	14.29		14.29	28.57	42.86	100
D	60.00	20.00		20.00		100
E		66.67	33.33			100

Higher EPS ratings seem to be associated with higher ratings on Sales/Margins/ROE

36. b. No apparent relationship

38. a.

Vehicle	Frequency	Percent Frequency
Accord	6	12
Camry	7	14
F-Series	14	28
Ram	10	20
Silverado	13	26

b. Ford F-Series and the Toyota Camry

40. a.

Response	Frequency	Percent Frequency
Accuracy	16	16
Approach shots	3	3
Mental approach	17	17
Power	8	8
Practice	15	15
Putting	10	10
Short game	24	24
Strategic decisions	7	7
Total	100	100

b. Poor short game, poor mental approach, lack of accuracy, and limited practice

42. a/b.

Closing Price	Freq.	Rel. Freq.	Cum. Freq.	Cum. Rel. Freq.
0–9.99	9	.225	9	.225
10–19.99	10	.250	19	.475
20–29.99	5	.125	24	.600
30–39.99	11	.275	35	.875
40–49.99	2	.050	37	.925
50–59.99	2	.050	39	.975
60–69.99	0	.000	39	.975
70–79.99	1	.025	40	1.000
Total	40	1.000		

44.

Income ($)	Frequency	Relative Frequency
18,000–21,999	13	0.255
22,000–25,999	20	0.392
26,000–29,999	12	0.235
30,000–33,999	4	0.078
34,000–37,999	2	0.039
Total	51	1.000

46. a. High Temperature

3 |
4 |
5 | 7
6 | 1 4 4 4 4 6 8
7 | 3 5 7 9
8 | 0 1 1 4 6
9 | 0 2 3

b. Low Temperature

3 | 9
4 | 3 6 8
5 | 0 0 0 2 4 4 5 5 7 9
6 | 1 8
7 | 2 4 5 5
8 |
9 |

c. The range of low temperatures is below the range of high temperatures

d. 8 cities

e.

Temperature	Frequency High Temp.	Low Temp.
30–39	0	1
40–49	0	3
50–59	1	10
60–69	7	2
70–79	4	4
80–89	5	0
90–99	3	0
Total	20	20

48. a.

Occupation	Satisfaction Score 30–39	40–49	50–59	60–69	70–79	80–89	Total
Cabinetmaker			2	4	3	1	10
Lawyer	1	5	2	1	1		10
Physical Therapist			5	2	1	2	10
Systems Analyst		2	1	4	3		10
Total	1	7	10	11	8	3	40

b.

Occupation	Satisfaction Score 30–39	40–49	50–59	60–69	70–79	80–89	Total
Cabinetmaker			20	40	30	10	100
Lawyer	10	50	20	10	10		100
Physical Therapist			50	20	10	20	100
Systems Analyst		20	10	40	30		100

c. Cabinetmakers seem to have the highest job satisfaction scores; lawyers seem to have the lowest

50. a. Row totals: 247; 54; 82; 121
Column totals: 149; 317; 17; 7; 14

b.

Year	Freq.	Fuel	Freq.
1973 or before	247	Elect.	149
1974–79	54	Nat. Gas	317
1980–86	82	Oil	17
1987–91	121	Propane	7
Total	504	Other	14
		Total	504

c. Crosstabulation of column percentages

Year Constructed	Fuel Type Elect.	Nat. Gas	Oil	Propane	Other
1973 or before	26.9	57.7	70.5	71.4	50.0
1974–1979	16.1	8.2	11.8	28.6	0.0
1980–1986	24.8	12.0	5.9	0.0	42.9
1987–1991	32.2	22.1	11.8	0.0	7.1
Total	100.0	100.0	100.0	100.0	100.0

d. Crosstabulation of row percentages.

Year Constructed	Fuel Type Elect.	Nat. Gas	Oil	Propane	Other	Total
1973 or before	16.2	74.1	4.9	2.0	2.8	100.0
1974–1979	44.5	48.1	3.7	3.7	0.0	100.0
1980–1986	45.1	46.4	1.2	0.0	7.3	100.0
1987–1991	39.7	57.8	1.7	0.0	0.8	100.0

52. a. Crosstabulation of market value and profit

Market Value ($1000s)	Profit ($1000s) 0–300	300–600	600–900	900–1200	Total
0–8000	23	4			27
8000–16,000	4	4	2	2	12
16,000–24,000		2	1	1	4
24,000–32,000		1	2	1	4
32,000–40,000		2	1		3
Total	27	13	6	4	50

b. Crosstabulation of row percentages

Market Value ($1000s)	Profit ($1000s) 0–300	300–600	600–900	900–1200	Total
0–8000	85.19	14.81	0.00	0.00	100
8000–16,000	33.33	33.33	16.67	16.67	100
16,000–24,000	0.00	50.00	25.00	25.00	100
24,000–32,000	0.00	25.00	50.00	25.00	100
32,000–40,000	0.00	66.67	33.33	0.00	100

c. A positive relationship is indicated between profit and market value; as profit goes up, market value goes up

54. b. A positive relationship is demonstrated between market value and stockholders' equity

Chapter 3

2. 16, 16.5

3. Arrange data in order: 15, 20, 25, 25, 27, 28, 30, 34

$i = \frac{20}{100}(8) = 1.6$; round up to position 2

20th percentile = 20

$i = \frac{25}{100}(8) = 2$; use positions 2 and 3

$$\text{25th percentile} = \frac{20 + 25}{2} = 22.5$$

$i = \frac{65}{100}(8) = 5.2$; round up to position 6

65th percentile = 28

$i = \frac{75}{100}(8) = 6$; use positions 6 and 7

$$\text{75th percentile} = \frac{28 + 30}{2} = 29$$

4. 59.727, 57, 53

6. a. 422
b. 380
c. 690
d. Not using capacity

8. a. $\bar{x} = \frac{\Sigma x_i}{n} = \frac{695}{20} = 34.75$

Mode = 25 (appears three times)

b. Data in order: 18, 20, 25, 25, 25, 26, 27, 27, 28, 33, 36, 37, 40, 40, 42, 45, 46, 48, 53, 54

Median (10th and 11th positions)

$$\frac{33 + 36}{2} = 34.5$$

At-home workers are slightly younger

c. $i = \frac{25}{100}(20) = 5$; use positions 5 and 6

$$Q_1 = \frac{25 + 26}{2} = 25.5$$

$i = \frac{75}{100}(20) = 15$; use positions 15 and 16

$Q_3 = \frac{42 + 45}{2} = 43.5$

d. $i = \frac{32}{100}(20) = 6.4$; round up to position 7

32nd percentile = 27

At least 32% of the people are 27 or younger

10. a. 76, 76

b. 39, 37.5

c. Yes; emergency wait too long

12. a. $639

b. 98.8 pictures

c. 110.2 minutes

14. 16, 4

15. Range = 34 − 15 = 19

Arrange data in order: 15, 20, 25, 25, 27, 28, 30, 34

$i = \frac{25}{100}(8) = 2;\ Q_1 = \frac{20 + 25}{2} = 22.5$

$i = \frac{75}{100}(8) = 6;\ Q_3 = \frac{28 + 30}{2} = 29$

$IQR = Q_3 - Q_1 = 29 - 22.5 = 6.5$

$\bar{x} = \frac{\Sigma x_i}{n} = \frac{204}{8} = 25.5$

x_i	$(x_i - \bar{x})$	$(x_i - \bar{x})^2$
27	1.5	2.25
25	−.5	.25
20	−5.5	30.25
15	−10.5	110.25
30	4.5	20.25
34	8.5	72.25
28	2.5	6.25
25	−.5	.25
		242.00

$$s^2 = \frac{\Sigma(x_i - \bar{x})^2}{n - 1} = \frac{242}{8 - 1} = 34.57$$

$$s = \sqrt{34.57} = 5.88$$

16. a. Range = 190 − 168 = 22

b. $\bar{x} = \frac{\Sigma x_i}{n} = \frac{1068}{6} = 178$

$$s^2 = \frac{\Sigma(x_i - \bar{x})^2}{n - 1}$$

$$= \frac{4^2 + (-10)^2 + 6^2 + 12^2 + (-8)^2 + (-4)^2}{6 - 1}$$

$$= \frac{376}{5} = 75.2$$

c. $s = \sqrt{75.2} = 8.67$

d. $\frac{s}{\bar{x}}(100) = \frac{8.67}{178}(100\%) = 4.87\%$

18. a. 38, 97, 9.85

b. Eastern shows more variation

20. *Dawson:* range = 2, $s = .67$

Clark: range = 8, $s = 2.58$

22. a. 45.05, 23.98; 57.50, 11.475

b. 190.67, 13.81; 140.63, 11.86

c. 38.02%; 57.97%

d. Greater for broker-assisted trades

24. *Quarter-milers:* $s = .0564$, Coef. of Var. = 5.8%

Milers: $s = .1295$, Coef. of Var. = 2.9%

26. .20, 1.50, 0, −.50, −2.20

27. Chebyshev's theorem: *at least* $(1 - 1/z^2)$

a. $z = \frac{40 - 30}{5} = 2;\ 1 - \frac{1}{(2)^2} = .75$

b. $z = \frac{45 - 30}{5} = 3;\ 1 - \frac{1}{(3)^2} = .89$

c. $z = \frac{38 - 30}{5} = 1.6;\ 1 - \frac{1}{(1.6)^2} = .61$

d. $z = \frac{42 - 30}{5} = 2.4;\ 1 - \frac{1}{(2.4)^2} = .83$

e. $z = \frac{48 - 30}{5} = 3.6;\ 1 - \frac{1}{(3.6)^2} = .92$

28. a. 95%

b. Almost all

c. 68%

29. a. $z = 2$ standard deviations

$1 - \frac{1}{z^2} = 1 - \frac{1}{2^2} = \frac{3}{4}$; at least 75%

b. $z = 2.5$ standard deviations

$1 - \frac{1}{z^2} = 1 - \frac{1}{2.5^2} = .84$; at least 84%

c. $z = 2$ standard deviations

Empirical rule: 95%

30. a. 68%

b. 81.5%

c. 2.5%

32. a. −.67

b. 1.50

c. Neither an outlier

d. Yes; $z = 8.25$

34. a. 76.5, 7

b. 16%, 2.5%

c. 12.2, 7.89; no

36. 15, 22.5, 26, 29, 34

38. Arrange data in order: 5, 6, 8, 10, 10, 12, 15, 16, 18

$i = \frac{25}{100}(9) = 2.25$; round up to position 3

$Q_1 = 8$

Median (5th position) = 10

$i = \frac{75}{100}(9) = 6.75$; round up to position 7

$Q_3 = 15$

5-number summary: 5, 8, 10, 15, 18

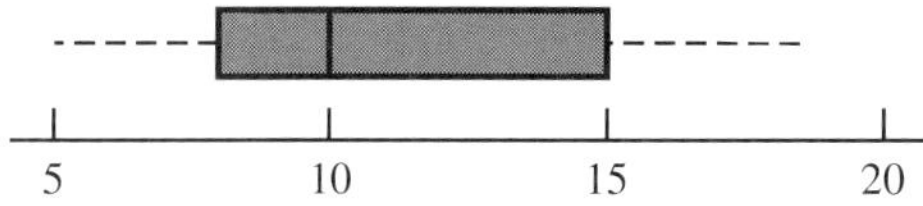

40. a. 619, 725, 1016, 1699, 4450

b. Limits: 0, 3160

c. Yes

d. No

41. a. Arrange data in order low to high

$i = \frac{25}{100}(21) = 5.25$; round up to 6th position

$Q_1 = 1872$

Median (11th position) = 4019

$i = \frac{75}{100}(21) = 15.75$; round up to 16th position

$Q_3 = 8305$

5-number summary: 608, 1872, 4019, 8305, 14138

b. $\text{IQR} = Q_3 - Q_1 = 8305 - 1872 = 6433$

Lower limit: $1872 - 1.5(6433) = -7777$

Upper limit: $8305 + 1.5(6433) = 17{,}955$

c. No; data are within limits

d. $41{,}138 > 27{,}604$; 41,138 would be an outlier; data value would be reviewed and corrected

e.

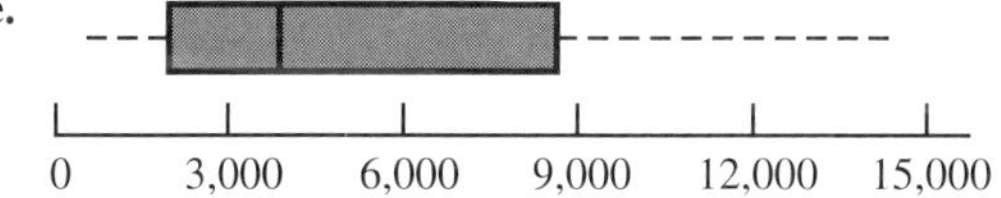

42. a. 61

b. 34, 45, 61, 90, 126

c. No; upper limit = 157.5

44. a. 18.2, 15.35

b. 11.7, 23.5

c. 3.4, 11.7, 15.35, 23.5, 41.3

d. Yes; Alger Small Cap 41.3

45. b. There appears to be a negative linear relationship between x and y

c.

x_i	y_i	$x_i - \bar{x}$	$y_i - \bar{y}$	$(x_i - \bar{x})(y_i - \bar{y})$
4	50	−4	4	−16
6	50	−2	4	−8
11	40	3	−6	−18
3	60	−5	14	−70
16	30	8	−16	−128
40	230	0	0	−240

$\bar{x} = 8$; $\bar{y} = 46$

$$s_{xy} = \frac{\Sigma(x_i - \bar{x})(y_i - \bar{y})}{n - 1} = \frac{-240}{4} = -60$$

The sample covariance indicates a negative linear association between x and y

d. $r_{xy} = \frac{s_{xy}}{s_x s_y} = \frac{-60}{(5.43)(11.40)} = -.969$

The sample correlation coefficient of −.969 is indicative of a strong negative linear relationship

46. b. There appears to be a positive linear relationship between x and y

c. $s_{xy} = 26.5$

d. $r_{xy} = .693$

48. −.91; negative relationship

50. a. .92

b. Strong positive linear relationship

52. a. 3.69

b. 3.175

53. a.

f_i	M_i	$f_i M_i$
4	5	20
7	10	70
9	15	135
5	20	100
25		325

$$\bar{x} = \frac{\Sigma f_i M_i}{n} = \frac{325}{25} = 13$$

b.

f_i	M_i	$(M_i - \bar{x})$	$(M_i - \bar{x})^2$	$f_i(M_i - \bar{x})^2$
4	5	−8	64	256
7	10	−3	9	63
9	15	2	4	36
5	20	7	49	245
25				600

$$s^2 = \frac{\Sigma f_i(M_i - \bar{x})^2}{n - 1} = \frac{600}{25 - 1} = 25$$

$$s = \sqrt{25} = 5$$

54. a.

Grade x_i	Weight w_i
4 (A)	9
3 (B)	15
2 (C)	33
1 (D)	3
0 (F)	0
	60 credit hours

$$\bar{x} = \frac{\Sigma w_i x_i}{\Sigma w_i} = \frac{9(4) + 15(3) + 33(2) + 3(1)}{9 + 15 + 33 + 3} = \frac{150}{60} = 2.5$$

b. Yes

56. 10.74, 25.63, 5.06; Estimate = 1288.8

58. a. 1800, 1351
b. 387, 1710
c. 7280, 1323
d. 3,675,303, 1917
e. 9271.01, 96.29
f. High positive
g. Using a box plot: 4135 and 7450

60. a. 2.3, 1.85
b. 1.90, 1.38
c. Altria Group 5%
d. −.51, below mean
e. 1.02, above mean
f. No

62. a. $\bar{x} = 83.135$, $s = 16.173$
b. \$50,789 to \$115,481
c. Same range as in part (b); higher probability
d. Danbury, CT, is an outlier

64. a. 502.67; positive linear relationship
b. .933

66. b. .9856, strong positive relationship

68. a. 817
b. 833

70. a. 60.68
b. $s^2 = 31.23$; $s = 5.59$

Chapter 4

2. $\binom{6}{3} = \frac{6!}{3!3!} = \frac{6 \cdot 5 \cdot 4 \cdot 3 \cdot 2 \cdot 1}{(3 \cdot 2 \cdot 1)(3 \cdot 2 \cdot 1)} = 20$

ABC	ACE	BCD	BEF
ABD	ACF	BCE	CDE
ABE	ADE	BCF	CDF
ABF	ADF	BDE	CEF
ACD	AEF	BDF	DEF

4. b. (H,H,H), (H,H,T), (H,T,H), (H,T,T), (T,H,H), (T,H,T), (T,T,H), (T,T,T)
c. ⅛

6. $P(E_1) = .40$, $P(E_2) = .26$, $P(E_3) = .34$
The relative frequency method was used

8. a. 4: Commission Positive—Council Approves
Commission Positive—Council Disapproves
Commission Negative—Council Approves
Commission Negative—Council Disapproves

9. $\binom{50}{4} = \frac{50!}{4!46!} = \frac{50 \cdot 49 \cdot 48 \cdot 47}{4 \cdot 3 \cdot 2 \cdot 1} = 230{,}300$

10. a. Use the relative frequency approach
$P(\text{California}) = 1{,}434/2{,}374 = .60$
b. Number not from four states
$= 2{,}374 - 1{,}434 - 390 - 217 - 112$
$= 221$
$P(\text{Not from 4 states}) = 221/2{,}374 = .09$
c. $P(\text{Not in early stages}) = 1 - .22 = .78$
d. Estimate of number of Massachusetts' companies in early stage of development = (.22)390 ≈ 86
e. If we assume the size of the awards did not differ by state, we can multiply the probability an award went to Colorado by the total venture funds disbursed to get an estimate

Estimate of Colorado funds = (112/2374)(\$32.4)
= \$1.53 billion

Authors' Note: The actual amount going to Colorado was \$1.74 billion

12. a. 2,869,685
b. 1/2,869,685
c. 1/120,526,770

14. a. ¼
b. ½
c. ¾

15. a. S = (ace of clubs, ace of diamonds, ace of hearts, ace of spades)
b. S = (2 of clubs, 3 of clubs, . . . , 10 of clubs, J of clubs, Q of clubs, K of clubs, A of clubs)
c. There are 12; jack, queen, or king in each of the four suits
d. For (a): 4/52 = 1/13 = .08
For (b): 13/52 = 1/4 = .25
For (c): 12/52 = .23

16. a. 36
c. ⅙
d. $\frac{5}{18}$
e. No; $P(\text{odd}) = P(\text{even}) = \frac{1}{2}$
f. Classical

17. a. (4, 6), (4, 7), (4, 8)
b. .05 + .10 + .15 = .30
c. (2, 8), (3, 8), (4, 8)
d. .05 + .05 + .15 = .25
e. .15

18. a. $P(0) = .05$
b. $P(4 \text{ or } 5) = .20$
c. $P(0, 1, \text{ or } 2) = .55$

20. a. .112
b. .086
c. .49

22. a. .40, .40, .60
b. .80, yes
c. $A^c = (E_3, E_4, E_5)$; $C^c = (E_1, E_4)$;
$P(A^c) = .60$; $P(C^c) = .40$
d. (E_1, E_2, E_5); .60
e. .80

23. a. $P(A) = P(E_1) + P(E_4) + P(E_6)$
$= .05 + .25 + .10 = .40$
$P(B) = P(E_2) + P(E_4) + P(E_7)$
$= .20 + .25 + .05 = .50$
$P(C) = P(E_2) + P(E_3) + P(E_5) + P(E_7)$
$= .20 + .20 + .15 + .05 = .60$

b. $A \cup B = \{E_1, E_2, E_4, E_6, E_7\}$;
$P(A \cup B) = P(E_1) + P(E_2) + P(E_4) + P(E_6) + P(E_7)$
$= .05 + .20 + .25 + .10 + .05$
$= .65$

c. $A \cap B = \{E_4\}$; $P(A \cap B) = P(E_4) = .25$

d. Yes, they are mutually exclusive

e. $B^c = \{E_1, E_3, E_5, E_6\}$;
$P(B^c) = P(E_1) + P(E_3) + P(E_5) + P(E_6)$
$= .05 + .20 + .15 + .10$
$= .50$

24. a. .05
b. .70

26. a. .30, .23
b. .17
c. .64

28. Let B = rented a car for business reasons
P = rented a car for personal reasons

a. $P(B \cup P) = P(B) + P(P) - P(B \cap P)$
$= .540 + .458 - .300$
$= .698$

b. $P(\text{Neither}) = 1 - .698 = .302$

30. a. $P(A \mid B) = \dfrac{P(A \cap B)}{P(B)} = \dfrac{.40}{.60} = .6667$

b. $P(B \mid A) = \dfrac{P(A \cap B)}{P(A)} = \dfrac{.40}{.50} = .80$

c. No, because $P(A \mid B) \neq P(A)$

32. a.

	Yes	No	Total
18 to 34	.375	.085	.46
35 and over	.475	.065	.54
Total	.850	.150	1.00

b. 46% 18 to 34; 54% 35 and over
c. .15
d. .1848
e. .1204
f. .5677
g. Higher probability of No for 18 to 34

33. a.

	Reason for Applying			
	Quality	**Cost/ Convenience**	**Other**	**Total**
Full-time	.218	.204	.039	.461
Part-time	.208	.307	.024	.539
Total	.426	.511	.063	1.000

b. A student is most likely to cite cost or convenience as the first reason (probability = .511); school quality is the reason cited by the second largest number of students (probability = .426)

c. $P(\text{quality} \mid \text{full-time}) = .218/.461 = .473$

d. $P(\text{quality} \mid \text{part-time}) = .208/.539 = .386$

e. For independence, we must have $P(A)P(B) = P(A \cap B)$; from the table

$P(A \cap B) = .218$, $P(A) = .461$, $P(B) = .426$
$P(A)P(B) = (.461)(.426) = .196$

Because $P(A)P(B) \neq P(A \cap B)$, the events are not independent

34. a. .44
b. .15
c. .136
d. .106
e. .0225
f. .0025

36. a. .7921
b. .9879
c. .0121
d. .3364, .8236, .1764
Don't foul Reggie Miller

38. a. .0209
b. .0141, .027
c. No
d. .0202, .0458
e. Yes

39. a. Yes, because $P(A_1 \cap A_2) = 0$

b. $P(A_1 \cap B) = P(A_1)P(B \mid A_1) = .40(.20) = .08$
$P(A_2 \cap B) = P(A_2)P(B \mid A_2) = .60(.05) = .03$

c. $P(B) = P(A_1 \cap B) + P(A_2 \cap B) = .08 + .03 = .11$

d. $P(A_1 \mid B) = \dfrac{.08}{.11} = .7273$

$P(A_2 \mid B) = \dfrac{.03}{.11} = .2727$

40. a. .10, .20, .09
b. .51
c. .26, .51, .23

42. M = missed payment
D_1 = customer defaults
D_2 = customer does not default
$P(D_1) = .05$, $P(D_2) = .95$, $P(M \mid D_2) = .2$, $P(M \mid D_1) = 1$

a. $P(D_1 \mid M) = \dfrac{P(D_1)P(M \mid D_1)}{P(D_1)P(M \mid D_1) + P(D_2)P(M \mid D_2)}$

$= \dfrac{(.05)(1)}{(.05)(1) + (.95)(.2)}$

$= \dfrac{.05}{.24} = .21$

b. Yes, the probability of default is greater than .20

44. a. .47, .53, .50, .45
b. .4963
c. .4463
d. 47%, 53%

46. a. .68
b. 52
c. 10

48. a. 315
b. .29
c. No
d. Republicans

50. a. .76
b. .24

52. b. .2022
c. .4618
d. .4005

54. a. .49
b. .44
c. .54
d. No
e. Yes

56. a. .25
b. .125
c. .0125
d. .10
e. No

58. 3.44%

60. a. .40
b. .67

Chapter 5

1. a. Head, Head (H, H)
Head, Tail (H, T)
Tail, Head (T, H)
Tail, Tail (T, T)
b. x = number of heads on two coin tosses
c.

Outcome	Values of x
(H, H)	2
(H, T)	1
(T, H)	1
(T, T)	0

d. Discrete; it may assume 3 values: 0, 1, and 2

2. a. x = time in minutes to assemble product
b. Any positive value: $x > 0$
c. Continuous

3. Let Y = position is offered
N = position is not offered
a. $S = \{(Y, Y, Y), (Y, Y, N), (Y, N, Y), (Y, N, N), (N, Y, Y), (N, Y, N), (N, N, Y), (N, N, N)\}$
b. Let N = number of offers made; N is a discrete random variable
c.

Experimental Outcome	(Y, Y, Y)	(Y, Y, N)	(Y, N, Y)	(Y, N, N)	(N, Y, Y)	(N, Y, N)	(N, N, Y)	(N, N, N)
Value of N	3	2	2	1	2	1	1	0

4. $x = 0, 1, 2, \ldots, 12$

6. a. $0, 1, 2, \ldots, 20$; discrete
b. $0, 1, 2, \ldots$; discrete
c. $0, 1, 2, \ldots, 50$; discrete
d. $0 \leq x \leq 8$; continuous
e. $x > 0$; continuous

7. a. $f(x) \geq 0$ for all values of x
$\Sigma f(x) = 1$; therefore, it is a valid probability distribution
b. Probability $x = 30$ is $f(30) = .25$
c. Probability $x \leq 25$ is $f(20) + f(25) = .20 + .15 = .35$
d. Probability $x > 30$ is $f(35) = .40$

8. a.

x	$f(x)$
1	3/20 = .15
2	5/20 = .25
3	8/20 = .40
4	4/20 = .20
	Total 1.00

b.

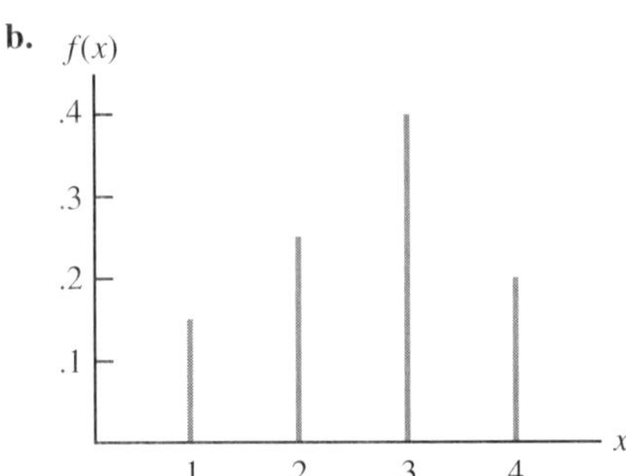

c. $f(x) \geq 0$ for $x = 1, 2, 3, 4$
$\Sigma f(x) = 1$

10. a.

x	1	2	3	4	5
$f(x)$	.05	.09	.03	.42	.41

b.

x	1	2	3	4	5
$f(x)$	.04	.10	.12	.46	.28

c. .83
d. .28
e. Senior executives more satisfied

12. a. Yes
b. .65

14. a. .05
b. .70
c. .40

16. a.

y	$f(y)$	$yf(y)$
2	.20	.40
4	.30	1.20
7	.40	2.80
8	.10	.80
Totals	1.00	5.20

$$E(y) = \mu = 5.20$$

b.

y	$y - \mu$	$(y - \mu)^2$	$f(y)$	$(y - \mu)^2 f(y)$
2	−3.20	10.24	.20	2.048
4	−1.20	1.44	.30	.432
7	1.80	3.24	.40	1.296
8	2.80	7.84	.10	.784
			Total	4.560

$$\text{Var}(y) = 4.56$$
$$\sigma = \sqrt{4.56} = 2.14$$

18. a/b.

x	$f(x)$	$xf(x)$	$x - \mu$	$(x - \mu)^2$	$(x - \mu)^2 f(x)$
0	0.04	0.00	−1.84	3.39	0.12
1	0.34	0.34	−0.84	0.71	0.24
2	0.41	0.82	0.16	0.02	0.01
3	0.18	0.53	1.16	1.34	0.24
4	0.04	0.15	2.16	4.66	0.17
Total	1.00	1.84 ↑ $E(x)$			0.79 ↑ Var(x)

c/d.

y	$f(y)$	$yf(y)$	$y - \mu$	$(y - \mu)^2$	$y - \mu^2 f(y)$
0	0.00	0.00	−2.93	8.58	0.01
1	0.03	0.03	−1.93	3.72	0.12
2	0.23	0.45	−0.93	0.86	0.20
3	0.52	1.55	0.07	0.01	0.00
4	0.22	0.90	1.07	1.15	0.26
Total	1.00	2.93 ↑ $E(y)$			0.59 ↑ Var(y)

e. The number of bedrooms in owner-occupied houses is greater than in renter-occupied houses; the expected number of bedrooms is 1.09 = 2.93 − 1.84 greater and the variability in the number of bedrooms is less for the owner-occupied houses

20. a. 166
b. −94; concern is to protect against the expense of a big accident

22. a. 445
b. \$1250 loss

24. a. Medium: 145; large: 140
b. Medium: 2725; large: 12,400

25. a.

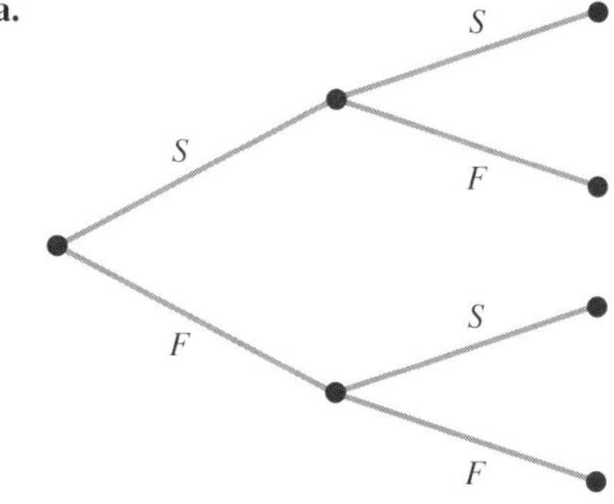

b. $f(1) = \binom{2}{1}(.4)^1(.6)^1 = \frac{2!}{1!1!}(.4)(.6) = .48$

c. $f(0) = \binom{2}{0}(.4)^0(.6)^2 = \frac{2!}{0!2!}(1)(.36) = .36$

d. $f(2) = \binom{2}{2}(.4)^2(.6)^0 = \frac{2!}{2!0!}(.16)(.1) = .16$

e. $P(x \geq 1) = f(1) + f(2) = .48 + .16 = .64$

f. $E(x) = np = 2(.4) = .8$
$\text{Var}(x) = np(1 - p) = 2(.4)(.6) = .48$
$\sigma = \sqrt{.48} = .6928$

26. a. $f(0) = .3487$
b. $f(2) = .1937$
c. .9298
d. .6513
e. 1
f. $\sigma^2 = .9000, \sigma = .9487$

28. a. .2789
b. .4181
c. .0733

30. a. Probability of a defective part being produced must be .03 for each part selected; parts must be selected independently
b. Let D = defective
G = not defective

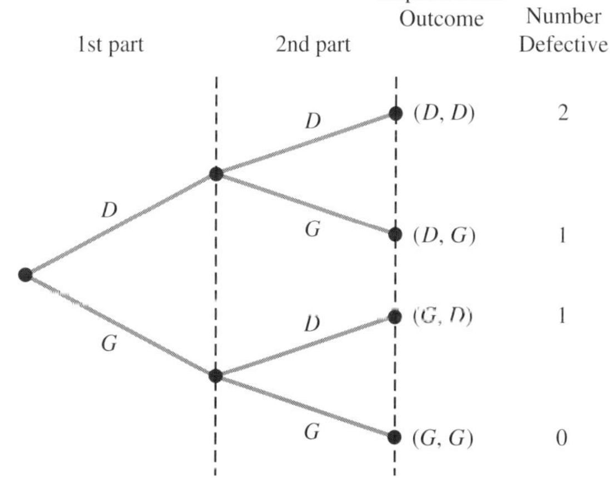

c. Two outcomes result in exactly one defect

d. $P(\text{no defects}) = (.97)(.97) = .9409$

$P(1 \text{ defect}) = 2(.03)(.97) = .0582$

$P(2 \text{ defects}) = (.03)(.03) = .0009$

32. a. .90
b. .99
c. .999
d. Yes

34. a. .0634
b. .0634
c. .9729

38. a. $f(x) = \dfrac{3^x e^{-3}}{x!}$

b. .2241
c. .1494
d. .8008

39. a. $f(x) = \dfrac{2^x e^{-2}}{x!}$

b. $\mu = 6$ for 3 time periods

c. $f(x) = \dfrac{6^x e^{-6}}{x!}$

d. $f(2) = \dfrac{2^2 e^{-2}}{2!} = \dfrac{4(.1353)}{2} = .2706$

e. $f(6) = \dfrac{6^6 e^{-6}}{6!} = .1606$

f. $f(5) = \dfrac{4^5 e^{-4}}{5!} = .1563$

40. a. $\mu = 48(5/60) = 4$

$f(3) = \dfrac{4^3 e^{-4}}{3!} = \dfrac{(64)(.0183)}{6} = .1952$

b. $\mu = 48(15/60) = 12$

$f(10) = \dfrac{12^{10} e^{-12}}{10!} = .1048$

c. $\mu = 48(5/60) = 4$; one can expect four callers to be waiting after 5 minutes

$f(0) = \dfrac{4^0 e^{-4}}{0!} = .0183$; the probability none will be waiting after 5 minutes is .0183

d. $\mu = 48(3/60) = 2.4$

$f(0) = \dfrac{2.4^0 e^{-2.4}}{0!} = .0907$; the probability of no interruptions in 3 minutes is .0907

42. a. $f(0) = \dfrac{7^0 e^{-7}}{0!} = e^{-7} = .0009$

b. probability $= 1 - [f(0) + f(1)]$

$f(1) = \dfrac{7^1 e^{-7}}{1!} = 7e^{-7} = .0064$

probability $= 1 - [.0009 + .0064] = .9927$

c. $\mu = 3.5$

$f(0) = \dfrac{3.5^0 e^{-3.5}}{0!} = e^{-3.5} = .0302$

probability $= 1 - f(0) = 1 - .0302 = .9698$

d.

$$\begin{aligned}\text{probability} &= 1 - [f(0) + f(1) + f(2) + f(3) + f(4)]\\ &= 1 - [.0009 + .0064 + .0223 + .0521 + .0912]\\ &= .8271\end{aligned}$$

44. a. $\mu = 1.25$
b. .2865
c. .3581
d. .3554

46. a. $f(1) = \dfrac{\binom{3}{1}\binom{10-3}{4-1}}{\binom{10}{4}} = \dfrac{\left(\frac{3!}{1!2!}\right)\left(\frac{7!}{3!4!}\right)}{\frac{10!}{4!6!}}$

$= \dfrac{(3)(35)}{210} = .50$

b. $f(2) = \dfrac{\binom{3}{2}\binom{10-3}{2-2}}{\binom{10}{2}} = \dfrac{(3)(1)}{45} = .067$

c. $f(0) = \dfrac{\binom{3}{0}\binom{10-3}{2-0}}{\binom{10}{2}} = \dfrac{(1)(21)}{45} = .4667$

d. $f(2) = \dfrac{\binom{3}{2}\binom{10-3}{4-2}}{\binom{10}{4}} = \dfrac{(3)(21)}{210} = .30$

48. a. .5250
b. .1833

50. $N = 60, n = 10$

a. $r = 20, x - 0$

$$\begin{aligned}f(0) &= \frac{\binom{20}{0}\binom{40}{10}}{\binom{60}{10}} = \frac{(1)\left(\frac{40!}{10!30!}\right)}{\frac{60!}{10!50!}}\\ &= \left(\frac{40!}{10!30!}\right)\left(\frac{10!50!}{60!}\right)\\ &= \frac{40\cdot39\cdot38\cdot37\cdot36\cdot35\cdot34\cdot33\cdot32\cdot31}{60\cdot59\cdot58\cdot57\cdot56\cdot55\cdot54\cdot53\cdot52\cdot51}\\ &\approx .01\end{aligned}$$

b. $r = 20, x = 1$

$$\begin{aligned}f(1) &= \frac{\binom{20}{1}\binom{40}{9}}{\binom{60}{10}} = 20\left(\frac{40!}{9!31!}\right)\left(\frac{10!50!}{60!}\right)\\ &\approx .07\end{aligned}$$

c. $1 - f(0) - f(1) = 1 - .08 = .92$

d. Same as the probability one will be from Hawaii; in part (b) it was equal to approximately .07

52. a. .5333
b. .6667
c. .7778
d. $n = 7$

54. a.

x	1	2	3	4	5
$f(x)$	.24	.21	.10	.21	.24

b. 3.00, 2.34
c. Bonds: $E(x) = 1.36$, $\text{Var}(x) = .23$
Stocks: $E(x) = 4$, $\text{Var}(x) = 1$

56. a. .0596
b. .3585
c. 100
d. 9.7468

58. a. .9510
b. .0480
c. .0490

60. a. 240
b. 12.9615
c. 12.9615

62. .1912

64. a. .2240
b. .5767

66. a. .4667
b. .4667
c. .0667

Chapter 6

1. a.

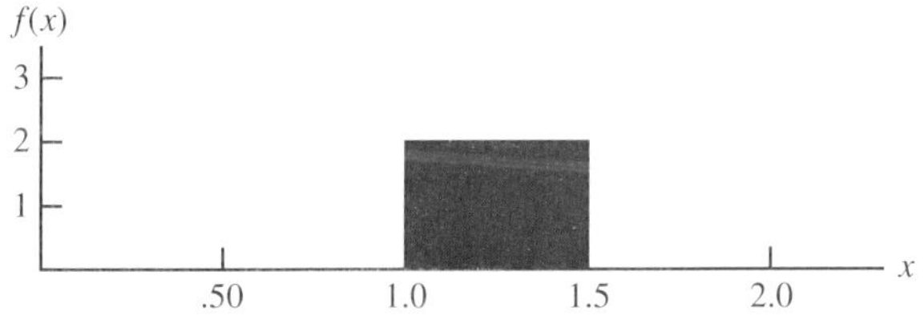

f(x)
3
2
1
.50 1.0 1.5 2.0 x

b. $P(x = 1.25) = 0$; the probability of any single point is zero because the area under the curve above any single point is zero
c. $P(1.0 \leq x \leq 1.25) = 2(.25) = .50$
d. $P(1.20 < x < 1.5) = 2(.30) = .60$

2. b. .50
c. .60
d. 15
e. 8.33

4. a.

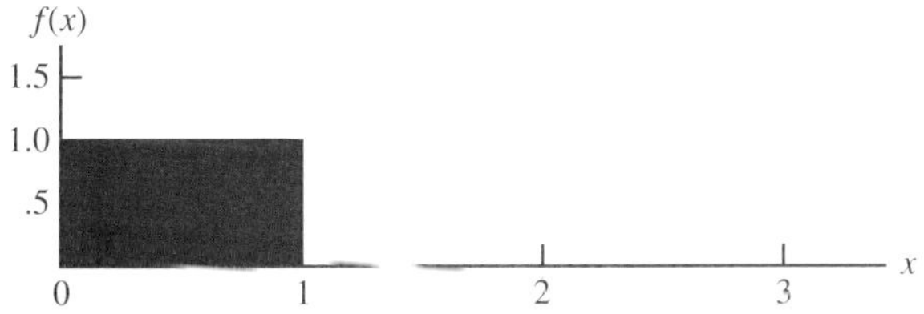

f(x)
1.5
1.0
.5
0 1 2 3 x

b. $P(.25 < x < .75) = 1(.50) = .50$
c. $P(x \leq .30) = 1(.30) = .30$
d. $P(x > .60) = 1(.40) = .40$

6. a. .40
b. .64
c. .68

10. a. .3413
b. .4332
c. .4772
d. .4938

12. a. .2967
b. .4418
c. .3300
d. .5910
e. .8849
f. .2389

13. a. $.6879 - .0239 = .6640$
b. $.8888 - .6985 = .1903$
c. $.9599 - .8508 = .1091$

14. a. $z = 1.96$
b. $z = .61$
c. $z = 1.12$
d. $z = .44$

15. a. Look in the table for an area of $.5000 - .2119 = .2881$; $z = .80$ cuts off an area of .2119 in the upper tail; thus, for an area of .2119 in the lower tail, $z = -.80$
b. Look in the table for an area of $.9030/2 = .4515$; $z = 1.66$
c. Look in the table for an area of $.2052/2 = .1026$; $z = .26$
d. Look in the table for an area of .4948; $z = 2.56$
e. Look in the table for an area of .1915; because the value we are seeking is below the mean, the z value must be negative; thus, $z = -.50$

16. a. $z = 2.33$
b. $z = 1.96$
c. $z = 1.645$
d. $z = 1.28$

18. $\mu = 30$ and $\sigma = 8.2$

a. At $x = 40$, $z = \dfrac{40 - 30}{8.2} = 1.22$

$P(z \leq 1.22) = .5000 + .3888 = .8888$
$P(x \geq 40) = 1.000 - .8888 = .1112$

b. At $x = 20$, $z = \dfrac{20 - 30}{8.2} = -1.22$

$P(z > -1.22) = .5000 + .3888 = .8888$
$P(x \leq 20) = 1.0000 - .8888 = .1112$

c. A z-value of 1.28 cuts off an area of approximately 10% in the upper tail
$x = 30 + 8.2(1.28)$
$= 40.50$
A stock price of \$40.50 or higher will put a company in the top 10%

20. a. .0885
b. 12.51%
c. 93.8 hours or more

22. a. .4194
b. \$517.44 or more
c. .0166

24. a. 902.75, 114.185
b. .1841
c. .1977
d. 1,091 million

26. a. $\mu = np = 100(.20) = 20$
$\sigma^2 = np(1 - p) = 100(.20)(.80) = 16$
$\sigma = \sqrt{16} = 4$
b. Yes, because $np = 20$ and $n(1 - p) = 80$
c. $P(23.5 \leq x \leq 24.5)$
$z = \dfrac{24.5 - 20}{4} = +1.13$ Area = .3708
$z = \dfrac{23.5 - 20}{4} = +.88$ Area = .3106
$P(23.5 \leq x \leq 24.5) = .3708 - .3106 = .0602$
d. $P(17.5 \leq x \leq 22.5)$
$z = \dfrac{17.5 - 20}{4} = -.63$ Area = .2357
$z = \dfrac{22.5 - 20}{4} = +.63$ Area = .2357
$P(17.5 \leq x \leq 22.5) = .2357 + .2357 = .4714$
e. $P(x \leq 15.5)$
$z = \dfrac{15.5 - 20}{4} = -1.13$ Area = .3708
$P(x \leq 15.5) = .5000 - .3708 = .1292$

28. a. .1867
b. 125
c. It's a toss-up

30. a. 220
b. .0392
c. .8962

32. a. .5276
b. .3935
c. .4724
d. .1341

33. a. $P(x \leq x_0) = 1 - e^{-x_0/3}$
b. $P(x \leq 2) = 1 - e^{-2/3} = 1 - .5134 = .4866$
c. $P(x \geq 3) = 1 - P(x \leq 3) = 1 - (1 - e^{-3/3})$
$= e^{-1} = .3679$
d. $P(x \leq 5) = 1 - e^{-5/3} = 1 - .1889 = .8111$
e. $P(2 \leq x \leq 5) = P(x \leq 5) - P(x \leq 2)$
$= .8111 - .4866 = .3245$

34. a. .3935
b. .2231
c. .3834

35. a.

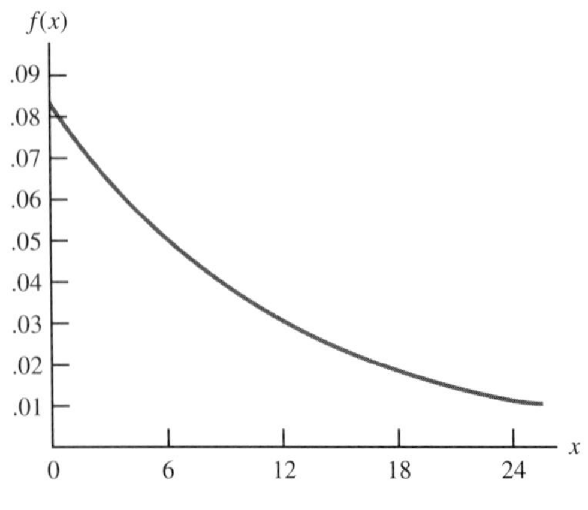

b. $P(x \leq 12) = 1 - e^{-12/12} = 1 - .3679 = .6321$
c. $P(x \leq 6) = 1 - e^{-6/12} = 1 - .6065 = .3935$
d. $P(x \geq 30) = 1 - P(x < 30)$
$= 1 - (1 - e^{-30/12})$
$= .0821$

36. a. 50 hours
b. .3935
c. .1353

38. a. $f(x) = 30e^{-30x}$
b. .0821
c. .7135

40. a. \$3780 or less
b. 19.22%
c. \$8167.50

42. a. 3229
b. .2244
c. \$12,382 or more

44. a. .0228
b. \$50

46. a. 38.3%
b. 3.59% better, 96.41% worse
c. 38.21%

48. $\mu = 19.23$ ounces

50. a. Lose \$240
b. .1788
c. .3557
d. .0594

52. a. $\frac{1}{7}$ minute
b. $7e^{-7x}$
c. .0009
d. .2466

54. a. 2 minutes
b. .2212
c. .3935
d. .0821

Chapter 7

1. a. AB, AC, AD, AE, BC, BD, BE, CD, CE, DE
b. With 10 samples, each has a $\frac{1}{10}$ probability
c. E and C because 8 and 0 do not apply; 5 identifies E; 7 does not apply; 5 is skipped because E is already in the sample; 3 identifies C; 2 is not needed because the sample of size 2 is complete

2. 22, 147, 229, 289

3. 459, 147, 385, 113, 340, 401, 215, 2, 33, 348

4. a. Nasdaq 100, Oracle, Microsoft, Lucent, Applied Materials
b. 252

6. 2782, 493, 825, 1807, 289

8. Maryland, Iowa, Florida State, Virginia, Pittsburgh, Oklahoma

10. a. finite; **b.** infinite; **c.** infinite; **d.** infinite; **e.** finite

11. a. $\bar{x} = \frac{\Sigma x_i}{n} = \frac{54}{6} = 9$

b. $s = \sqrt{\frac{\Sigma(x_i - \bar{x})^2}{n - 1}}$

$\Sigma(x_i - \bar{x})^2 = (-4)^2 + (-1)^2 + 1^2 + (-2)^2 + 1^2 + 5^2$
$= 48$

$s = \sqrt{\frac{48}{6 - 1}} = 3.1$

12. a. .50
b. .3667

13. a. $\bar{x} = \frac{\Sigma x_i}{n} = \frac{465}{5} = 93$

b.

	x_i	$(x_i - \bar{x})$	$(x_i - \bar{x})^2$
	94	+1	1
	100	+7	49
	85	−8	64
	94	+1	1
	92	−1	1
Totals	465	0	116

$s = \sqrt{\frac{\Sigma(x_i - \bar{x})^2}{n - 1}} = \sqrt{\frac{116}{4}} = 5.39$

14. a. .45
b. .15
c. .45

16. a. .10
b. 20
c. .72

18. a. 200
b. 5
c. Normal with $E(\bar{x}) = 200$ and $\sigma_{\bar{x}} = 5$
d. The probability distribution of $\bar{x}$

19. a. The sampling distribution is normal with:

$E(\bar{x}) = \mu = 200$

$\sigma_{\bar{x}} = \frac{\sigma}{\sqrt{n}} = \frac{50}{\sqrt{100}} = 5$

For +5, $(\bar{x} - \mu) = 5$,

$z = \frac{\bar{x} - \mu}{\sigma_{\bar{x}}} = \frac{5}{5} = 1$

Area = 2(.3413) = .6826

b. For ±10, $(\bar{x} - \mu) = 10$,

$z = \frac{\bar{x} - \mu}{\sigma_{\bar{x}}} = \frac{10}{5} = 2$

Area = 2(.4772) = .9544

20. 3.54, 2.50, 2.04, 1.77
$\sigma_{\bar{x}}$ decreases as n increases

22. a. Normal with $E(\bar{x}) = 51{,}800$ and $\sigma_{\bar{x}} = 516.40$
b. $\sigma_{\bar{x}}$ decreases to 365.15
c. $\sigma_{\bar{x}}$ decreases as n increases

23. a.

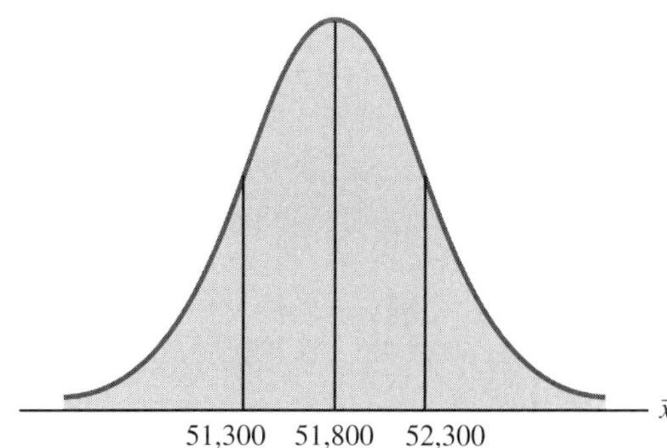

$\sigma_{\bar{x}} = \frac{\sigma}{\sqrt{n}} = \frac{4000}{\sqrt{60}} = 516.40$

$z = \frac{52{,}300 - 51{,}800}{516.40} = +.97$

Area = 2(.3340) = .6680

b. $\sigma_{\bar{x}} = \frac{\sigma}{\sqrt{n}} = \frac{4000}{\sqrt{120}} = 365.15$

$z = \frac{52{,}300 - 51{,}800}{365.15} = +1.37$

Area = 2(.4147) = .8294

24. a. Normal with $E(\bar{x}) = 4260$ and $\sigma_{\bar{x}} = 127.28$
b. .95
c. .5704

26. a. .5034, .6212, .7888, .9232, .9876
b. Higher probability within ±250

28. a. Normal with $E(\bar{x}) = 687$ and $\sigma_{\bar{x}} = 34.29$
b. .9964
c. .5346
d. Increase the sample size

30. a. $n/N = .01$; no
b. 1.29, 1.30; little difference
c. .8764

32. a. $E(\bar{p}) = .40$

$\sigma_{\bar{p}} = \sqrt{\frac{p(1 - p)}{n}} = \sqrt{\frac{(.40)(.60)}{200}} = .0346$

$z = \frac{\bar{p} - p}{\sigma_{\bar{p}}} = \frac{.03}{.0346} = .87$

Area = 2(.3078) = .6156

b. $z = \frac{\bar{p} - p}{\sigma_{\bar{p}}} = \frac{.05}{.0346} = 1.44$

Area = 2(.4251) = .8502

34. a. .6156
b. .7814
c. .9488
d. .9942
e. Higher probability with larger n

35. a.

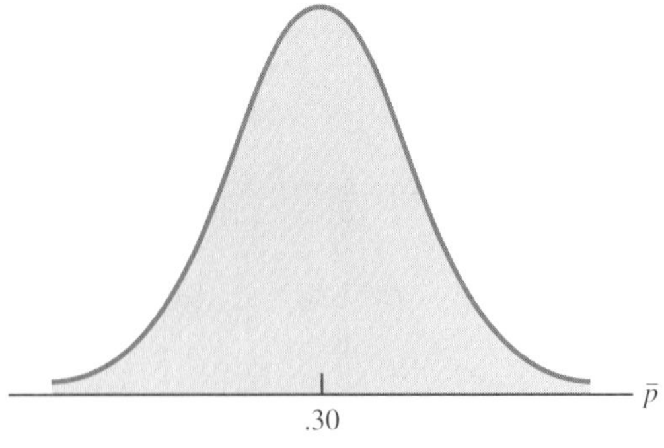

$$\sigma_{\bar{p}} = \sqrt{\frac{p(1-p)}{n}} = \sqrt{\frac{.30(.70)}{100}} = .0458$$

The normal distribution is appropriate because $np = 100(.30) = 30$ and $n(1-p) = 100(.70) = 70$ are both greater than 5

b. $P(.20 \le \bar{p} \le .40) = ?$

$$z = \frac{.40 - .30}{.0458} = 2.18$$

$$\text{Area} = 2(.4854) = .9708$$

c. $P(.25 \le \bar{p} \le .35) = ?$

$$z = \frac{.35 - .30}{.0458} = 1.09$$

$$\text{Area} = 2(.3621) = .7242$$

36. a. Normal with $E(\bar{p}) = .56$ and $\sigma_{\bar{p}} = .0287$
b. .7062
c. .8612, .9438

38. a. Normal with $E(\bar{p}) = .56$ and $\sigma_{\bar{p}} = .0248$
b. .5820
c. .8926

40. a. Normal with $E(\bar{p}) - .76$ and $\sigma_{\bar{p}} = .0214$
b. .8384
c. .9452

42. 112, 145, 73, 324, 293, 875, 318, 618

44. a. Normal with $E(\bar{x}) = 115.50$ and $\sigma_{\bar{x}} = 5.53$
b. .9298
c. .0026

46. a. 707
b. .50
c. .8414
d. .9544

48. a. 625
b. .7888

50. a. Normal with $E(\bar{p}) = .305$ and $\sigma_{\bar{p}} = .0326$
b. .7814
c. .4582

52. a. .9606
b. .0495

54. a. 48
b. Normal, $E(\bar{p}) = .25$, $\sigma_{\bar{p}} = .0625$
c. .2119

Chapter 8

2. Use $\bar{x} \pm z_{\alpha/2}(\sigma/\sqrt{n})$
a. $32 \pm 1.645\ (6/\sqrt{50})$
32 ± 1.4; 30.6 to 33.4
b. $32 \pm 1.96(6/\sqrt{50})$
32 ± 1.66; 30.34 to 33.66
c. $32 \pm 2.576(6/\sqrt{50})$
32 ± 2.19; 29.81 to 34.19

4. 54

5. a. $1.96\sigma/\sqrt{n} = 1.96(5/\sqrt{49}) = 1.40$
b. 24.80 ± 1.40; 23.40 to 26.20

6. 8.1 to 8.9

8. a. Population is at least approximately normal
b. 3.1
c. 4.1

10. a. \$113,638 to \$124,672
b. \$112,581 to \$125,729
c. \$110,515 to \$127,795
d. Width increases as confidence level increases

12. a. 2.179
b. −1.676
c. 2.457
d. −1.708 and 1.708
e. −2.014 and 2.014

13. a. $\bar{x} = \dfrac{\Sigma x_i}{n} = \dfrac{80}{8} = 10$

b. $s = \sqrt{\dfrac{\Sigma(x_i - \bar{x})^2}{n-1}} = \sqrt{\dfrac{84}{7}} = 3.46$

c. $t_{.025}\left(\dfrac{s}{\sqrt{n}}\right) - 2.365\left(\dfrac{3.46}{\sqrt{8}}\right) = 2.9$

d. $\bar{x} \pm t_{.025}\left(\dfrac{s}{\sqrt{n}}\right)$

10 ± 2.9 (7.1 to 12.9)

14. a. 21.5 to 23.5
b. 21.3 to 23.7
c. 20.9 to 24.1
d. A larger margin of error and a wider interval

15. $\bar{x} \pm t_{\alpha/2}(s/\sqrt{n})$
90% confidence: $df = 64$ and $t_{.05} = 1.669$

$$19.5 \pm 1.669\left(\frac{5.2}{\sqrt{65}}\right)$$

19.5 ± 1.08 (18.42 to 20.58)
95% confidence: $df = 64$ and $t_{.025} = 1.998$

$$19.5 \pm 1.998\left(\frac{5.2}{\sqrt{65}}\right)$$

19.5 ± 1.29 (18.21 to 20.79)

16. a. 1.69
b. 47.31 to 50.69
c. Fewer hours and higher cost for United

18. a. 3.8
b. .84

c. 2.96 to 4.64
d. Larger n next time

20. 6.28 to 6.78

22. a. 3.35
b. 2.40 to 4.30

24. a. Planning value of $\sigma = \frac{\text{Range}}{4} = \frac{36}{4} = 9$

b. $n = \frac{z_{.025}^2\sigma^2}{E^2} = \frac{(1.96)^2(9)^2}{(3)^2} = 34.57$; use $n = 35$

c. $n = \frac{(1.96)^2(9)^2}{(2)^2} = 77.79$; use $n = 78$

25. a. Use $n = \frac{z_{\alpha/2}^2\sigma^2}{E^2}$

$n = \frac{(1.96)^2(6.82)^2}{(1.5)^2} = 79.41$; use $n = 80$

b. $n = \frac{(1.645)^2(6.82)^2}{(2)^2} = 31.47$; use $n = 32$

26. a. 340
b. 1358
c. 8487

28. a. 343
b. 487
c. 840
d. n gets larger; no to 99% confidence

30. 81

31. a. $\bar{p} = \frac{100}{400} = .25$

b. $\sqrt{\frac{\bar{p}(1-\bar{p})}{n}} = \sqrt{\frac{.25(.75)}{400}} = .0217$

c. $\bar{p} \pm z_{.025}\sqrt{\frac{\bar{p}(1-\bar{p})}{n}}$

$.25 \pm 1.96(.0217)$

$.25 \pm .0424$; .2076 to .2924

32. a. .6733 to .7267
b. .6682 to .7318

34. 1068

35. a. $\bar{p} = \frac{281}{611} = .4599$ (46%)

b. $z_{.05}\sqrt{\frac{\bar{p}(1-\bar{p})}{n}} = 1.645\sqrt{\frac{.4599(1-.4599)}{611}} = .0332$

c. $\bar{p} \pm .0332$
$.4599 \pm .0332$ (.4267 to .4931)

36. a. .4393
b. .3870 to .4916

38. a. .0430
b. .2170 to .3030
c. 822

39. a. $n = \frac{1.96^2 p^*(1-p^*)}{E^2}$

$n = \frac{1.96^2(.33)(.67)}{(.03)^2} = 943.75$; use $n = 944$

b. $n = \frac{2.576^2(.33)(.67)}{(.03)^2} = 1630.19$; use $n = 1631$

40. .0267, (.8333 to .8867)

42. a. .0442
b. 601, 1068, 2401, 9604

44. a. 2009
b. 47,991 to 52,009

46. a. 998
b. \$24,479 to \$26,455
c. \$93.5 million
d. Yes; \$21.4 (30%) over *Lost World*

48. a. 14 minutes
b. 13.38 to 14.62
c. 32 per day
d. Staff reduction

50. 37

52. 176

54. a. .5420
b. .0508
c. .4912 to .5928

56. a. .68
b. .6391 to .7209

58. a. 1267
b. 1509

60. a. .3101
b. .2898 to .3304
c. 8219; no, this sample size is unnecessarily large

Chapter 9

2. a. $H_0: \mu \leq 14$
$H_a: \mu > 14$
b. No evidence that the new plan increases sales
c. The research hypothesis $\mu > 14$ is supported; the new plan increases sales

4. a. $H_0: \mu \geq 220$
$H_a: \mu < 220$

5. a. Rejecting $H_0: \mu \leq 56.2$ when it is true
b. Accepting $H_0: \mu \leq 56.2$ when it is false

6. a. $H_0: \mu \leq 1$
$H_a: \mu > 1$
b. Claiming $\mu > 1$ when it is not true
c. Claiming $\mu \leq 1$ when it is not true

8. a. $H_0: \mu \geq 220$
$H_a: \mu < 220$
b. Claiming $\mu < 220$ when it is not true
c. Claiming $\mu \geq 220$ when it is not true

10. a. $z = \dfrac{\bar{x} - \mu_0}{\sigma/\sqrt{n}} = \dfrac{26.4 - 25}{6/\sqrt{40}} = 1.48$

b. Area = .4306
p-value = .5000 − .4306 = .0694

c. p-value > .01, do not reject H_0

d. Reject H_0 if $z \geq 2.33$
1.48 < 2.33, do not reject H_0

11. a. $z = \dfrac{\bar{x} - \mu_0}{\sigma/\sqrt{n}} = \dfrac{14.15 - 15}{3/\sqrt{50}} = -2.00$

b. Area = .4772
p-value = 2(.5000 − .4772) = .0456

c. p-value ≤ .05, reject H_0

d. Reject H_0 if $z \leq -1.96$ or $z \geq 1.96$
−2.00 ≤ −1.96, reject H_0

12. a. .1056; do not reject H_0
b. .0062; reject H_0
c. ≈ 0; reject H_0
d. .7967; do not reject H_0

14. a. .3844; do not reject H_0
b. .0074; reject H_0
c. .0836; do not reject H_0

15. a. $H_0: \mu \geq 1056$
$H_a: \mu < 1056$

b. $z = \dfrac{\bar{x} - \mu_0}{\sigma/\sqrt{n}} = \dfrac{910 - 1056}{1600/\sqrt{400}} = -1.83$
p-value = .5000 − .4664 = .0336

c. p-value ≤ .05, reject H_0. The mean refund of "last-minute" filers is less than $1056

d. Reject H_0 if $z \leq -1.645$
−1.83 ≤ −1.645, reject H_0

16. a. $H_0: \mu \leq 895$
$H_a: \mu > 895$
b. .1170
c. Do not reject H_0
d. Withhold judgment; collect more data

18. a. $H_0: \mu = 4.1$
$H_a: \mu \neq 4.1$
b. −2.21, .0272
c. Reject H_0

20. a. $H_0: \mu \geq 181{,}900$
$H_a: \mu < 181{,}900$
b. −2.93
c. .0017
d. Reject H_0

22. a. $H_0: \mu = 8$
$H_a: \mu \neq 8$
b. .1706
c. Do not reject H_0
d. 7.83 to 8.97; Yes

24. a. $t = \dfrac{\bar{x} - \mu_0}{s/\sqrt{n}} = \dfrac{17 - 18}{4.5/\sqrt{48}} = -1.54$

b. Degrees of freedom = $n - 1 = 47$
Area in lower tail is between .05 and .10
p-value (two-tail) is between .10 and .20

c. p-value > .05; do not reject H_0

d. With $df = 47$, $t_{.025} = 2.012$
Reject H_0 if $t \leq -2.012$ or $t \geq 2.012$
$t = -1.54$; do not reject H_0

26. a. Between .02 and .05; reject H_0
b. Between .01 and .02; reject H_0
c. Between .10 and .20; do not reject H_0

27. a. $H_0: \mu \geq 238$
$H_a: \mu < 238$

b. $t = \dfrac{\bar{x} - \mu_0}{s/\sqrt{n}} = \dfrac{231 - 238}{80/\sqrt{100}} = -.88$
Degrees of freedom = $n - 1 = 99$
p-value is between .10 and .20

c. p-value > .05; do not reject H_0
Cannot conclude mean weekly benefit in Virginia is less than the national mean

d. $df = 99$ $t_{.05} = -1.66$
Reject H_0 if $t \leq -1.66$
−.88 > −1.66; do not reject H_0

28. a. $H_0: \mu \leq 3530$
$H_a: \mu > 3530$
b. Between .005 and .01
c. Reject H_0

30. a. $H_0: \mu = 600$
$H_a: \mu \neq 600$
b. Between .20 and .40
c. Do not reject H_0
d. A larger sample size

32. a. $H_0: \mu = 10{,}192$
$H_a: \mu \neq 10{,}192$
b. Between .02 and .05
c. Reject H_0

34. a. $H_0: \mu = 2$
$H_a: \mu \neq 2$
b. 2.2
c. .52
d. Between .20 and .40
e. Do not reject H_0

36. a. $z = \dfrac{\bar{p} - p_0}{\sqrt{\dfrac{p_0(1 - p_0)}{n}}} = \dfrac{.68 - .75}{\sqrt{\dfrac{.75(1 - .75)}{300}}} = -2.80$

p-value = .5000 − .4974 = .0026
p-value ≤ .05; reject H_0

b. $z = \dfrac{.72 - .75}{\sqrt{\dfrac{.75(1 - .75)}{300}}} = -1.20$

p-value = .5000 − .3849 = .1151
p-value > .05; do not reject H_0

c. $z = \dfrac{.70 - .75}{\sqrt{\dfrac{.75(1 - .75)}{300}}} = -2.00$

p-value $= .5000 - .4772 = .0228$

p-value $\leq .05$; reject H_0

d. $z = \dfrac{.77 - .75}{\sqrt{\dfrac{.75(1 - .75)}{300}}} = .80$

p-value $= .5000 + .2881 = .7881$

p-value $> .05$; do not reject H_0

38. a. H_0: $p = .64$
H_a: $p \neq .64$

b. $\bar{p} = 52/100 = .52$

$$z = \frac{\bar{p} - p_0}{\sqrt{\dfrac{p_0(1 - p_0)}{n}}} = \frac{.52 - .64}{\sqrt{\dfrac{.64(1 - .64)}{100}}} = -2.50$$

Area $= .4938$

p-value $= 2(.5000 - .4938) = .0124$

c. p-value $\leq .05$; reject H_0
Proportion differs from the reported .64

d. Yes, because $\bar{p} = .52$ indicates that fewer believe the supermarket brand is as good as the name brand

40. a. .2702

b. H_0: $p \leq .22$
H_a: $p > .22$
p-value ≈ 0; reject H_0

c. Helps evaluate the effectiveness of commercials

42. H_0: $p \leq .24$
H_a: $p > .24$
p-value $= .0023$; reject H_0

44. a. H_0: $p \leq .51$
H_a: $p > .51$

b. $\bar{p} = .58$, p-value $= .0026$

c. Reject H_0

46. a. H_0: $\mu = 16$
H_a: $\mu \neq 16$

b. .0286; reject H_0
Readjust line

c. .2186; do not reject H_0
Continue operation

d. $z = 2.19$; reject H_0
$z = -1.23$; do not reject H_0
Yes, same conclusion

48. a. H_0: $\mu \leq 45{,}250$
H_a: $\mu > 45{,}250$

b. .0034

c. Reject H_0

50. $t = -.93$
p-value between .20 and .40
Do not reject H_0

52. $t = 2.26$
p-value between .01 and .025
Reject H_0

54. a. H_0: $p \leq .50$
H_a: $p > .50$

b. .64

c. .0026; reject H_0

56. a. H_0: $p \leq .50$
H_a: $p > .50$

b. .6381

c. .0023; reject H_0

58. H_0: $p \geq .90$
H_a: $p < .90$
p-value $= .0808$
Do not reject H_0

Chapter 10

1. a. $\bar{x}_1 - \bar{x}_2 = 13.6 - 11.6 = 2$

b. $z_{\alpha/2} = z_{.05} = 1.645$

$$\bar{x}_1 - \bar{x}_2 \pm 1.645\sqrt{\frac{\sigma_1^2}{n_1} + \frac{\sigma_2^2}{n_2}}$$

$$2 \pm 1.645\sqrt{\frac{(2.2)^2}{50} + \frac{(3)^2}{35}}$$

$2 \pm .98$ (1.02 to 2.98)

c. $z_{\alpha/2} = z_{.05} = 1.96$

$$2 \pm 1.96\sqrt{\frac{(2.2)^2}{50} + \frac{(3)^2}{35}}$$

2 ± 1.17 (.83 to 3.17)

2. a. $z = \dfrac{(\bar{x}_1 - \bar{x}_2) - D_0}{\sqrt{\dfrac{\sigma_1^2}{n_1} + \dfrac{\sigma_2^2}{n_2}}} = \dfrac{(25.2 - 22.8) - 0}{\sqrt{\dfrac{(5.2)^2}{40} + \dfrac{(6)^2}{50}}} = 2.03$

b. p-value $= .5000 - .4788 = .0212$

c. p-value $\leq .05$; reject H_0

4. a. $\bar{x}_1 - \bar{x}_2 = 2.04 - 1.72 = .32$

b. $z_{.025}\sqrt{\dfrac{\sigma_1^2}{n_1} + \dfrac{\sigma_2^2}{n_2}} = 1.96\sqrt{\dfrac{(.10)^2}{40} + \dfrac{(.08)^2}{35}} = .04$

c. $.32 \pm .04$ (.28 to .36)

6. p-value $= .015$
Reject H_0; an increase

8. a. 1.08

b. .2802

c. Do not reject H_0; cannot conclude a difference exists

9. a. $\bar{x}_1 - \bar{x}_2 = 22.5 - 20.1 = 2.4$

b. $$df = \frac{\left(\dfrac{s_1^2}{n_1} + \dfrac{s_2^2}{n_2}\right)^2}{\dfrac{1}{n_1 - 1}\left(\dfrac{s_1^2}{n_1}\right)^2 + \dfrac{1}{n_2 - 1}\left(\dfrac{s_2^2}{n_2}\right)^2}$$

$$= \frac{\left(\dfrac{2.5^2}{20} + \dfrac{4.8^2}{30}\right)^2}{\dfrac{1}{19}\left(\dfrac{2.5^2}{20}\right)^2 + \dfrac{1}{29}\left(\dfrac{4.8^2}{30}\right)^2} = 45.8$$

c. $df = 45$, $t_{.025} = 2.014$

$$t_{.025}\sqrt{\frac{s_1^2}{n_1}+\frac{s_2^2}{n_2}} = 2.014\sqrt{\frac{2.5^2}{20}+\frac{4.8^2}{30}} = 2.1$$

d. 2.4 ± 2.1 (.3 to 4.5)

10. a. $$t = \frac{(\bar{x}_1 - \bar{x}_2) - 0}{\sqrt{\frac{s_1^2}{n_1}+\frac{s_2^2}{n_2}}} = \frac{(13.6 - 10.1) - 0}{\sqrt{\frac{5.2^2}{35}+\frac{8.5^2}{40}}} = 2.18$$

b. $$df = \frac{\left(\frac{s_1^2}{n_1}+\frac{s_2^2}{n_2}\right)^2}{\frac{1}{n_1-1}\left(\frac{s_1^2}{n_1}\right)^2+\frac{1}{n_2-1}\left(\frac{s_2^2}{n_2}\right)^2}$$

$$= \frac{\left(\frac{5.2^2}{35}+\frac{8.5^2}{40}\right)^2}{\frac{1}{34}\left(\frac{5.2^2}{35}\right)^2+\frac{1}{39}\left(\frac{8.5^2}{40}\right)^2} = 65.7$$

Use $df = 65$

c. $df = 65$, area in tail is between .01 and .025
two-tail p-value is between .02 and .05.

d. p-value $\leq .05$; reject H_0

12. a. $\bar{x}_1 - \bar{x}_2 = 22.5 - 18.6 = 3.9$ miles

b. $$df = \frac{\left(\frac{s_1^2}{n_1}+\frac{s_2^2}{n_2}\right)^2}{\frac{1}{n_1-1}\left(\frac{s_1^2}{n_1}\right)^2+\frac{1}{n_2-1}\left(\frac{s_2^2}{n_2}\right)^2}$$

$$= \frac{\left(\frac{8.4^2}{50}+\frac{7.4^2}{40}\right)^2}{\frac{1}{49}\left(\frac{8.4^2}{50}\right)^2+\frac{1}{39}\left(\frac{7.4^2}{40}\right)^2} = 87.1$$

Use $df = 87$, $t_{.025} = 1.988$

$$3.9 \pm 1.988\sqrt{\frac{8.4^2}{50}+\frac{7.4^2}{40}}$$

3.9 ± 3.3 (.6 to 7.2)

14. a. $H_0: \mu_1 - \mu_2 = 0$
$H_a: \mu_1 - \mu_2 \neq 0$

b. 2.18

c. Between .02 and .05

d. Reject H_0; mean ages differ

16. a. $H_0: \mu_1 - \mu_2 \leq 0$
$H_a: \mu_1 - \mu_2 > 0$

b. 38

c. $t = 1.80$, $df = 25$
p-value between .025 and .05

d. Reject H_0; conclude higher mean score if college grad

18. a. $H_0: \mu_1 - \mu_2 \geq 120$
$H_a: \mu_1 - \mu_2 < 120$

b. -2.10
Between .01 and .025

c. 32 to 118

d. Larger sample size

19. a. 1, 2, 0, 0, 2

b. $\bar{d} = \Sigma d_i/n = 5/5 = 1$

c. $$s_d = \sqrt{\frac{\Sigma(d_i - \bar{d})^2}{n-1}} = \sqrt{\frac{4}{5-1}} = 1$$

d. $$t = \frac{\bar{d} - \mu}{s_d/\sqrt{n}} = \frac{1-0}{1/\sqrt{5}} = 2.24$$

$df = n - 1 = 4$
p-value is between .025 and .05
p-value $\leq .05$; reject H_0

20. a. 3, −1, 3, 5, 3, 0, 1

b. 2

c. 2.08

d. 2

e. .07 to 3.93

21. $H_0: \mu_d \leq 0$
$H_a: \mu_d > 0$
$\bar{d} = .625$
$s_d = 1.30$

$$t = \frac{\bar{d} - \mu_d}{s_d/\sqrt{n}} = \frac{.625 - 0}{1.30/\sqrt{8}} = 1.36$$

$df = n - 1 = 7$
p-value is between .10 and .20
p-value $> .05$; do not reject H_0

22. .16 to .35

24. $t = 1.63$
p-value between .10 and .20
Do not reject H_0

26. a. $t = -.60$
p-value greater than .40
Do not reject H_0

b. .103

c. .39; larger sample size

27. a. $\bar{\bar{x}} = (30 + 45 + 36)/3 = 37$

$$\text{SSTR} = \sum_{j=1}^{k} n_j(\bar{x}_j - \bar{\bar{x}})^2$$
$$= 5(30 - 37)^2 + 5(45 - 37)^2 + 5(36 - 37)^2$$
$$= 570$$

$$\text{MSTR} = \frac{\text{SSTR}}{k-1} = \frac{570}{2} = 285$$

b. $$\text{SSE} = \sum_{j=1}^{k}(n_j - 1)s_j^2$$
$$= 4(6) + 4(4) + 4(6.5) = 66$$

$$\text{MSE} = \frac{\text{SSE}}{n_T - k} = \frac{66}{15-3} = 5.5$$

c. $$F = \frac{\text{MSTR}}{\text{MSE}} = \frac{285}{5.5} = 51.82$$

From the F table (2 degrees of freedom numerator and 12 denominator), p-value is less than .01

Because p-value $\leq \alpha = 0.5$, we reject the null hypothesis that the means of the three populations are equal

d.

Source of Variation	Sum of Squares	Degrees of Freedom	Mean Square	F
Treatments	570	2	285	51.82
Error	66	12	5.5	
Total	636	14		

28. a. MSTR = 268
b. MSE = 92
c. Cannot reject H_0 because p-value is greater than .10
d.

Source of Variation	Sum of Squares	Degrees of Freedom	Mean Square	F
Treatments	536	2	268	2.91
Error	828	9	92	
Total	1364	11		

30. a. 1200, 3
300, 12
$F = 16$
b. Reject H_0 because p-value is less than .01

32.

	Mfg 1	Mfg 2	Mfg 3
Sample mean	23	28	21
Sample variance	6.67	4.67	3.33

$$\bar{\bar{x}} = (23 + 28 + 21)/3 = 24$$

$$\text{SSTR} = \sum_{j=1}^{k} n_j(\bar{x}_j - \bar{\bar{x}})^2 = 4(23 - 24)^2 + 4(28 - 24)^2 + 4(21 - 24)^2 = 104$$

$$\text{MSTR} = \frac{\text{SSTR}}{k - 1} = \frac{104}{2} = 52$$

$$\text{SSE} = \sum_{j=1}^{k} (n_j - 1)s_j^2 = 3(6.67) + 3(4.67) + 3(3.33) = 44.01$$

$$\text{MSE} = \frac{\text{SSE}}{n_T - k} = \frac{44.01}{12 - 3} = 4.89$$

$$F = \frac{\text{MSTR}}{\text{MSE}} = \frac{52}{4.89} = 10.63$$

From the F table (2 degrees of freedom numerator and 9 denominator), p-value is less than .01

Because p value $\le \alpha = .05$, we reject the null hypothesis that the mean time needed to mix a batch of material is the same for each manufacturer

34. Sample means: 81, 79, 88; $F = 4.99$
p-value is between .025 and .05
Significant difference; Silicon Valley

36. Significant; $F = 3.70$
p-value is between .025 and .05

38. 8934 to 11,066

40. a. $H_0\colon \mu_1 - \mu_2 \le 0$
$H_a\colon \mu_1 - \mu_2 > 0$
b. $t = .60$, $df = 57$
p-value greater than .20
Do not reject H_0

42. a. 15 (or $15,000)
b. 9.81 to 20.19
c. 11.5%

44. Sample means: 58.6, 48.8, 60.1; $F = 18.59$
p-value ≈ 0; significant difference

46. Sample means: 7.41, 6.11, 7.06; $F = 9.33$
p-value < .01; significant difference

Chapter 11

2. a. $\bar{p} = \dfrac{n_1\bar{p}_1 + n_2\bar{p}_2}{n_1 + n_2} = \dfrac{200(.22) + 300(.16)}{200 + 300} = .1840$

$$z = \frac{\bar{p}_1 - \bar{p}_2}{\sqrt{\bar{p}(1 - \bar{p})\left(\frac{1}{n_1} + \frac{1}{n_2}\right)}} = \frac{.22 - .16}{\sqrt{.1840(1 - .1840)\left(\frac{1}{200} + \frac{1}{300}\right)}} = 1.70$$

p-value = .5000 − .4554 = .0446
b. p-value ≤ .05; reject H_0

3. $\bar{p}_1 = 220/400 = .55$ $\quad \bar{p}_2 = 192/400 = .48$

$$\bar{p}_1 - \bar{p}_2 \pm z_{.025}\sqrt{\frac{\bar{p}_1(1 - \bar{p}_1)}{n_1} + \frac{\bar{p}_2(1 - \bar{p}_2)}{n_2}}$$

$$.55 - .48 \pm 1.96\sqrt{\frac{.55(1 - .55)}{400} + \frac{.48(1 - .48)}{400}}$$

.07 ± .0691 (.0009 to .1391)
7% more executives are predicting an increase in full-time jobs; the confidence interval shows the difference may be from 0% to 14%

4. a. .46, .28
b. .18
c. .0777
d. .1023 to .2577, higher for Republicans

6. a. .803
b. .849
c. $H_0\colon p_1 - p_2 \ge 0$
$H_a\colon p_1 - p_2 < 0$
d. p-value = .0104
Reject H_0

8. a. $H_0\colon p_1 - p_2 = 0$
$H_a\colon p_1 - p_2 \ne 0$
b. .13

c. .0404; conclude difference exists
d. Yes; attracting younger age group

10. p-value = .0322
Reject H_0

11. a. Expected frequencies: $e_1 = 200(.40) = 80$
$e_2 = 200(.40) = 80$
$e_3 = 200(.20) = 40$
Actual frequencies: $f_1 = 60, f_2 = 120, f_3 = 20$

$$\chi^2 = \frac{(60-80)^2}{80} + \frac{(120-80)^2}{80} + \frac{(20-40)^2}{40}$$
$$= \frac{400}{80} + \frac{1600}{80} + \frac{400}{40}$$
$$= 5 + 20 + 10 = 35$$

Degrees of freedom: $k - 1 = 2$
$\chi^2 = 35$ shows p-value ≈ 0
p-value $\leq .01$; reject H_0

b. Reject H_0 if $\chi^2 \geq 9.210$
$\chi^2 = 35$; reject H_0

12. $\chi^2 = 15.33$, $df = 3$
p-value less than .005
Reject H_0

13. H_0: $p_{\text{ABC}} = .29, p_{\text{CBS}} = .28, p_{\text{NBC}} = .25, p_{\text{IND}} = .18$
H_a: The proportions are not
$p_{\text{ABC}} = .29, p_{\text{CBS}} = .28, p_{\text{NBC}} = .25, p_{\text{IND}} = .18$
Expected frequencies: $300(.29) = 87$, $300(.28) = 84$
$300(.25) = 75$, $300(.18) = 54$
$e_1 = 87, e_2 = 84, e_3 = 75, e_4 = 54$
Actual frequencies: $f_1 = 95, f_2 = 70, f_3 = 89, f_4 = 46$

$$\chi^2 = \frac{(95-87)^2}{87} + \frac{(70-84)^2}{84} + \frac{(89-75)^2}{75} + \frac{(46-54)^2}{54} = 6.87$$

Degrees of freedom: $k - 1 = 3$
$\chi^2 = 6.87$, p-value between .05 and .10
Do not reject H_0

14. $\chi^2 = 29.51$, $df = 5$
p-value ≈ 0
Reject H_0

16. a. $\chi^2 = 12.21$, $df = 3$
p-value is between .005 and .01
Conclude difference for 2003
b. 21%, 30%, 15%, 34%
Increased use of debit card
c. 51%

18. $\chi^2 = 16.31$, $df = 3$
p-value less than .005
Reject H_0

19. H_0: The column variable is independent of the row variable
H_a: The column variable is not independent of the row variable

Expected frequencies:

	A	B	C
P	28.5	39.9	45.6
Q	21.5	30.1	34.4

$$\chi^2 = \frac{(20-28.5)^2}{28.5} + \frac{(44-39.9)^2}{39.9} + \frac{(50-46.5)^2}{45.6} + \frac{(30-21.5)^2}{21.5} + \frac{(26-30.1)^2}{30.1} + \frac{(30-34.4)^2}{34.4}$$
$$= 7.86$$

Degrees of freedom: $(2 - 1)(3 - 1) = 2$
$\chi^2 = 7.86$, p-value between .01 and .025
Reject H_0

20. $\chi^2 = 19.77$, $df = 4$
p-value less than .005
Reject H_0

21. H_0: Type of ticket purchased is independent of the type of flight
H_a: Type of ticket purchased is not independent of the type of flight

Expected frequencies:
$e_{11} = 35.59$ $e_{12} = 15.41$
$e_{21} = 150.73$ $e_{22} = 65.27$
$e_{31} = 455.68$ $e_{32} = 197.32$

Ticket	Flight	Observed Frequency (f_i)	Expected Frequency (e_i)	$(f_i - e_i)^2/e_i$
First	Domestic	29	35.59	1.22
First	International	22	15.41	2.82
Business	Domestic	95	150.73	20.61
Business	International	121	65.27	47.59
Full-fare	Domestic	518	455.68	8.52
Full-fare	International	135	197.32	19.68
Totals		920		$\chi^2 = 100.43$

Degrees of freedom: $(3 - 1)(2 - 1) = 2$
$\chi^2 = 100.43$, p-value ≈ 0
Reject H_0

22. a. $\chi^2 = 7.36$, $df = 2$
p-value between .025 and .05
Reject H_0
b. Domestic 47.2%

24. a. $\chi^2 = 10.60$, $df = 4$
p-value between .025 and .05
Reject H_0; not independent
b. Higher negative effect on grades as hours increase

26. a. $\chi^2 = 7.85$, $df = 3$
p-value between .025 and .05
Reject H_0
b. Pharmaceutical, 98.6%

28. a. $H_0: p_1 - p_2 = 0$
$H_a: p_1 - p_2 \neq 0$
b. .31, .26
c. $z = 2.04$; p-value = .0414
Reject H_0; conclude difference
d. .0475, .0025 to .0975

30. $z = 2.37$; p-value = .0178
Reject H_0

32. a. .16
b. $H_0: p_1 - p_2 \leq 0$
$H_a: p_1 - p_2 > 0$
c. $z = 3.49$; p-value ≈ 0
Reject H_0

34. $\chi^2 = 4.64$, $df = 2$
p-value between .05 and .10
Do not reject H_0

36. $\chi^2 = 42.53$, $df = 4$
p-value ≈ 0; reject H_0

38. $\chi^2 = 23.37$, $df = 3$
p-value ≈ 0; reject H_0

40. a. $\chi^2 = 12.86$, $df = 2$
p-value less than .005
Reject H_0
b. 66.9, 30.3, 2.9
54.0, 42.0, 4.0

42. a. 24.01, 41.16, 20.46, 8.37
Last entry combines 3 and 4
b. $\chi^2 = 6.17$, $df = 3$
p-value greater than .10
Do not reject H_0; binomial

Chapter 12

1. a.

b. There appears to be a linear relationship between x and y
c. Many different straight lines can be drawn to provide a linear approximation of the relationship between x and y; in part (d) we will determine the equation of a straight line that "best" represents the relationship according to the least squares criterion
d. Summations needed to compute the slope and y-intercept:
$\Sigma x_i = 15$, $\Sigma y_i = 40$, $\Sigma(x_i - \bar{x})(y_i - \bar{y}) = 26$, $\Sigma(x_i - \bar{x})^2 = 10$

$$b_1 = \frac{\Sigma(x_i - \bar{x})(y_i - \bar{y})}{\Sigma(x_i - \bar{x})^2} = \frac{26}{10} = 2.6$$

$b_0 = \bar{y} - b_1\bar{x} = 8 - (2.6)(3) = 0.2$
$\hat{y} = 0.2 - 2.6x$
e. $\hat{y} = .2 + 2.6x = .2 + 2.6(4) = 10.6$

2. b. There appears to be a linear relationship between x and y
d. $\hat{y} = 30.33 - 1.88x$
e. 19.05

4. a.

b. It indicates there may be a linear relationship between height and weight
c. Many different straight lines can be drawn to provide a linear approximation of the relationship between height and weight; in part (d) we will determine the equation of a straight line that "best" represents the relationship according to the least squares criterion
d. Summations needed to compute the slope and y-intercept:
$\Sigma x_i = 325$, $\Sigma y_i = 585$, $\Sigma(x_i - \bar{x})(y_i - \bar{y}) = 110$, $\Sigma(x_i - \bar{x})^2 = 20$

$$b_1 = \frac{\Sigma(x_i - \bar{x})(y_i - \bar{y})}{\Sigma(x_i - \bar{x})^2} = \frac{110}{20} = 5.5$$

$b_0 = \bar{y} - b_1\bar{x} = 117 - (5.5)(65) = -240.5$
$\hat{y} = -240.5 + 5.5x$
e. $\hat{y} = -240.5 + 5.5(63) = 106$
The estimate of weight is 106 pounds

6. c. $\hat{y} = -10.16 + .18x$
e. 11.95 or approximately $12,000

8. c. $\hat{y} = 490.21 + 204.24x$
d. $1307

10. b. $\hat{y} = 51.82 + .145x$
c. 84.4

12. c. $\hat{y} = 1293 + .3165x$
d. 25,031

14. b. $\hat{y} = 28.30 - .0415x$
c. 26.2

15. a. $\hat{y}_i = .2 + 2.6x_i$ and $\bar{y} = 8$

x_i	y_i	$\hat{y}_i$	$y_i - \hat{y}_i$	$(y_i - \hat{y}_i)^2$	$y_i - \bar{y}$	$(y_i - \bar{y})^2$
1	3	2.8	.2	.04	−5	25
2	7	5.4	1.6	2.56	−1	1
3	5	8.0	−3.0	9.00	−3	9
4	11	10.6	.4	.16	3	9
5	14	13.2	.8	.64	6	36
				SSE = 12.40		SST = 80

SSR = SST − SSE = 80 − 12.4 = 67.6

b. $r^2 = \dfrac{\text{SSR}}{\text{SST}} = \dfrac{67.6}{80} = .845$

The least squares line provided a good fit; 84.5% of the variability in y has been explained by the least squares line

c. $r = \sqrt{.845} = +.9192$

d. $t = \dfrac{b_1 - \beta_1}{s_{b_1}} = \dfrac{2.6 - 0}{.643} = 4.04$

From the t table (3 degrees of freedom), area in tail is between .01 and .025

p-value is between .02 and .05

Actual p-value = .0272

Because p-value $\leq \alpha$, we reject H_0: $\beta_1 = 0$

e. $\text{MSR} = \dfrac{\text{SSR}}{1} = 67.6$

$$F = \frac{\text{MSR}}{\text{MSE}} = \frac{67.6}{4.133} = 16.36$$

From the F table (1 degree of freedom numerator and 3 denominator), p-value is between .025 and .05

Actual p-value = .0272

Because p-value $\leq \alpha$, we reject H_0: $\beta_1 = 0$

Source of Variation	Sum of Squares	Degrees of Freedom	Mean Square	F
Regression	67.6	1	67.6	16.36
Error	12.4	3	4.133	
Total	80	4		

16. a. SSE = 6.3325, SST = 114.80, SSR = 108.47

b. $r^2 = .945$

c. $r = -.9721$

18. a. The estimated regression equation and the mean for the dependent variable:

$\hat{y} = 1790.5 + 581.1x, \quad \bar{y} = 3650$

The sum of squares due to error and the total sum of squares:

$\text{SSE} = \Sigma(y_i - \hat{y}_i)^2 = 85{,}135.14$

$\text{SST} = \Sigma(y_i - \bar{y})^2 = 335{,}000$

Thus, SSR = SST − SSE

= 335,000   85,135.14 = 249,864.86

b. $r^2 = \dfrac{\text{SSR}}{\text{SST}} = \dfrac{249{,}864.86}{335{,}000} = .746$

The least squares line accounted for 74.6% of the total sum of squares

c. $r = \sqrt{.746} = +.8637$

20. a. $\hat{y} = -48.11 + 2.3325x$

b. $r^2 = .82$

c. $173,500

22. a. $\hat{y} = -745.80 + 117.917x$

b. $r^2 = .7071$

c. $r = +.84$

23. a. $s^2 = \text{MSE} = \dfrac{\text{SSE}}{n-2} = \dfrac{12.4}{3} = 4.133$

b. $s = \sqrt{\text{MSE}} = \sqrt{4.133} = 2.033$

c. $\Sigma(x_i - \bar{x})^2 = 10$

$$s_{b_1} = \frac{s}{\sqrt{\Sigma(x_i - \bar{x})^2}} = \frac{2.033}{\sqrt{10}} = .643$$

24. a. 2.11

b. 1.453

c. .262

d. Significant; p-value is less than .01

e. Significant; p-value is less than .01

26. a. $s^2 = \text{MSE} = \dfrac{\text{SSE}}{n-2} = \dfrac{85{,}135.14}{4} = 21{,}283.79$

$s = \sqrt{\text{MSE}} = \sqrt{21{,}283.79} = 145.89$

$\Sigma(x_i - \bar{x})^2 = .74$

$$s_{b_1} = \frac{s}{\sqrt{\Sigma(x_i - \bar{x})^2}} = \frac{145.89}{\sqrt{.74}} = 169.59$$

$$t = \frac{b_1 - \beta_1}{s_{b_1}} = \frac{581.08 - 0}{169.59} = 3.43$$

From the t table (4 degrees of freedom), area in tail is between .01 and .025

p-value is between .02 and .05

Actual p-value = .0266

Because p-value $\leq \alpha$, we reject H_0: $\beta_1 = 0$

b. $\text{MSR} = \dfrac{\text{SSR}}{1} = \dfrac{249{,}864.86}{1} = 249{,}864.86$

$$F = \frac{\text{MSR}}{\text{MSE}} = \frac{249{,}864.86}{21{,}283.79} = 11.74$$

From the F table (1 degree of freedom numerator and 4 denominator), p-value is between .025 and .05

Actual p-value = .0266

Because p-value $\leq \alpha$, we reject H_0: $\beta_1 = 0$

c.

Source of Variation	Sum of Squares	Degrees of Freedom	Mean Square	F
Regression	29,864.86	1	29,864.86	11.74
Error	85,135.14	4	21,283.79	
Total	335,000	5		

28. They are related; p-value is less than .01

30. Significant; p-value is less than .01

32. a. $s = 2.033$

$\bar{x} = 3, \Sigma(x_i - \bar{x})^2 = 10$

$$s_{\hat{y}_p} = s\sqrt{\frac{1}{n} + \frac{(x_p - \bar{x})^2}{\Sigma(x_i - \bar{x})^2}}$$

$$= 2.033\sqrt{\frac{1}{5} + \frac{(4-3)^2}{10}} = 1.11$$

b. $\hat{y} = .2 + 2.6x = .2 + 2.6(4) = 10.6$

$\hat{y}_p \pm t_{\alpha/2} s_{\hat{y}_p}$

$10.6 \pm 3.182(1.11)$

10.6 ± 3.53, or 7.07 to 14.13

c. $$s_{\text{ind}} = s\sqrt{1 + \frac{1}{n} + \frac{(x_p - \bar{x})^2}{\Sigma(x_i - \bar{x})^2}}$$

$$= 2.033\sqrt{1 + \frac{1}{5} + \frac{(4-3)^2}{10}} = 2.32$$

d. $\hat{y}_p \pm t_{\alpha/2} s_{\text{ind}}$

$10.6 \pm 3.182(2.32)$

10.6 ± 7.38, or 3.22 to 17.98

34. Confidence interval: −.4 to 4.98

Prediction interval: −2.27 to 7.31

35. a. $s = 145.89, \bar{x} = 3.2, \Sigma(x_i - \bar{x})^2 = .74$

$\hat{y} = 1790.5 + 581.1x = 1790.5 + 581.1(3)$

$= 3533.8$

$$s_{\hat{y}_p} = s\sqrt{\frac{1}{n} + \frac{(x_p - \bar{x})^2}{\Sigma(x_i - \bar{x})^2}}$$

$$= 145.89\sqrt{\frac{1}{6} + \frac{(3-3.2)^2}{.74}} = 68.54$$

$\hat{y}_p \pm t_{\alpha/2} s_{\hat{y}_p}$

$3533.8 \pm 2.776(68.54)$

3533.8 ± 190.27, or \$3343.53 to \$3724.07

b. $$s_{\text{ind}} = s\sqrt{1 + \frac{1}{n} + \frac{(x_p - \bar{x})^2}{\Sigma(x_i - \bar{x})^2}}$$

$$= 145.89\sqrt{1 + \frac{1}{6} + \frac{(3-3.2)^2}{.74}} = 161.19$$

$\hat{y}_p \pm t_{\alpha/2} s_{\text{ind}}$

$3533.8 \pm 2.776(161.19)$

3533.8 ± 447.46, or \$3086.34 to \$3981.26

36. a. 80.86

b. 78.58 to 83.14

c. 72.92 to 88.80

38. a. \$5046.67

b. \$3815.10 to \$6278.24

c. Not out of line

40. a. 9

b. $\hat{y} = 20.0 + 7.21x$

c. 1.3626

d. SSE = SST − SSR = 51,984.1 − 41,587.3 = 10,396.8

MSE = 10,396.8/7 = 1485.3

$$F = \frac{\text{MSR}}{\text{MSE}} = \frac{41,587.3}{1485.3} = 28.0$$

From the F table (1 degree of freedom numerator and 7 denominator), p-value is less than .01

Actual p-value = .0011

Because p-value $\le \alpha = .05$, we reject H_0: $\beta_1 = 0$

e. $\hat{y} = 20.0 + 7.21(50) = 380.5$, or \$380,500

42. a. $\hat{y} = 80.0 + 50.0x$

b. 30

c. Significant; p-value is less than .01

d. \$680,000

44. b. Yes

c. $\hat{y} = 37.1 - .779x$

d. Significant; p-value = 0.003

e. $r^2 = .434$; not a good fit

f. \$12.27 to \$22.90

g. \$17.47 to \$39.05

45. a. $\Sigma x_i = 70, \quad \Sigma y_i = 76, \quad \Sigma(x_i - \bar{x})(y_i - \bar{y}) = 200,$
$\Sigma(x_i - \bar{x})^2 = 126$

$$b_1 = \frac{\Sigma(x_i - \bar{x})(y_i - \bar{y})}{\Sigma(x_i - \bar{x})^2} = \frac{200}{126} = 1.5873$$

$b_0 = \bar{y} - b_1\bar{x} = 15.2 - (1.5873)(14) = -7.0222$

$\hat{y} = -7.02 + 1.59x$

b.

x_i	y_i	$\hat{y}_i$	$y_i - \hat{y}_i$
6	6	2.52	3.48
11	8	10.47	−2.47
15	12	16.83	−4.83
18	20	21.60	−1.60
20	30	24.78	5.22

c.

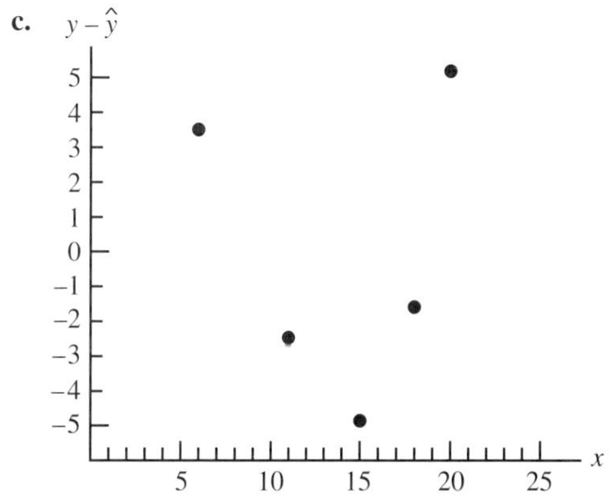

With only five observations, it is difficult to determine whether the assumptions are satisfied; however, the plot does suggest curvature in the residuals, which would indicate that the error term assumptions are not satisfied; the scatter diagram for these data also indicates that the underlying relationship between x and y may be curvilinear

46. a. $\hat{y} = 2.32 + .64x$

b. No; the variance does not appear to be the same for all values of x

47. a. Let x = advertising expenditures and y = revenue

$\hat{y} = 29.4 + 1.55x$

b. SST = 1002, SSE = 310.28, SSR = 691.72

$$\text{MSR} = \frac{\text{SSR}}{1} = 691.72$$

$$\text{MSE} = \frac{\text{SSE}}{n - 2} = \frac{310.28}{5} = 62.0554$$

$$F = \frac{\text{MSR}}{\text{MSE}} = \frac{691.72}{62.0554} = 11.15$$

From the F table (1 degree of freedom numerator and 5 denominator), p-value is between .01 and .025

Actual p-value = .0206

Because p-value $\leq \alpha = .05$, we conclude that the two variables are related

c.

x_i	y_i	$\hat{y}_i = 29.40 + 1.55x_i$	$y_i - \hat{y}_i$
1	19	30.95	−11.95
2	32	32.50	−.50
4	44	35.60	8.40
6	40	38.70	1.30
10	52	44.90	7.10
14	53	51.10	1.90
20	54	60.40	−6.40

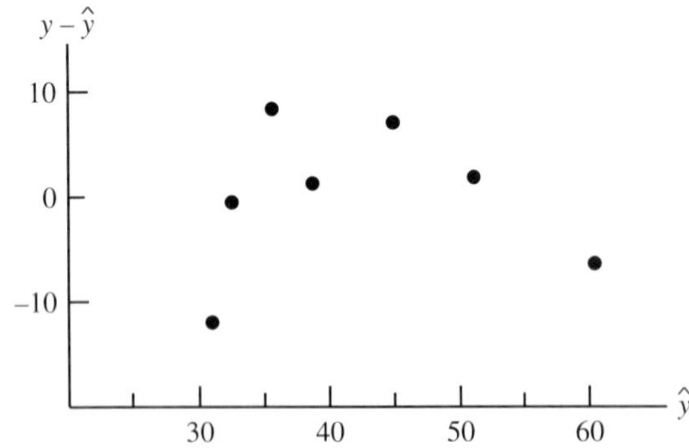

d. The residual plot leads us to question the assumption of a linear relationship between x and y; even though the relationship is significant at the $\alpha = .05$ level, it would be extremely dangerous to extrapolate beyond the range of the data

48. b. Yes

50. a. $\hat{y} = 9.26 + .711x$

b. Significant; p-value = .001

c. $r^2 = .744$; good fit

d. \$13.53

52. a. Market beta = .95

b. Significant; p-value = .029

c. $r^2 = .470$; not a good fit

d. Texas Instruments has a higher risk

54. a. $\hat{y} = 10.5 + .953x$

b. Significant relationship; p-value = .000

c. \$2874 to \$4952

d. Yes

56. a. Negative linear relationship

b. $\hat{y} = 8.10 - .344x$

c. Significant; p-value = .002

d. $r^2 = .711$; reasonably good fit

e. 5.2 to 7.6 days

58. a. $\hat{y} = 5.85 + .830x$

b. Significant; p-value = .000

c. 84.65 points

d. 65.35 to 103.96

Chapter 13

2. a. The estimated regression equation is
$\hat{y} = 45.06 + 1.94x_1$
An estimate of y when $x_1 = 45$ is
$\hat{y} = 45.06 + 1.94(45) = 132.36$

b. The estimated regression equation is
$\hat{y} = 85.22 + 4.32x_2$
An estimate of y when $x_2 = 15$ is
$\hat{y} = 85.22 + 4.32(15) = 150.02$

c. The estimated regression equation is
$\hat{y} = -18.37 + 2.01x_1 + 4.74x_2$
An estimate of y when $x_1 = 45$ and $x_2 = 15$ is
$\hat{y} = -18.37 + 2.01(45) + 4.74(15) = 143.18$

4. a. \$255,000

5. a. The Minitab output is shown in Figure D13.5a

b. The Minitab output is shown in Figure D13.5b

c. It is 1.60 in part (a) and 2.29 in part (b); in part (a) the coefficient is an estimate of the change in revenue due to a one-unit change in television advertising expenditures; in part (b) it represents an estimate of the change in revenue due to a one-unit change in television advertising expenditures when the amount of newspaper advertising is held constant

d. Revenue = 83.2 + 2.29(3.5) + 1.30(1.8) = 93.56 or \$93,560

6. a. PCT = .354 + .000888 HR

b. PCT = .865 − .0837 ERA

c. PCT = .709 + .00140 HR − .103 ERA

d. 54.9%

8. a. Return = 247 − 32.8 Safety + 34.6 ExpRatio

b. 70.2

FIGURE D13.5a

```
The regression equation is
Revenue = 88.6 + 1.60 TVAdv

Predictor       Coef    SE Coef       T       p
Constant      88.638      1.582   56.02   0.000
TVAdv         1.6039     0.4778    3.36   0.015

S = 1.215      R-sq = 65.3%     R-sq(adj) = 59.5%

Analysis of Variance

SOURCE            DF        SS        MS       F       p
Regression         1    16.640    16.640   11.27   0.015
Residual Error     6     8.860     1.477
Total              7    25.500
```

FIGURE D13.5b

```
The regression equation is
Revenue = 83.2 + 2.29 TVAdv + 1.30 NewsAdv

Predictor       Coef    SE Coef       T       p
Constant      83.230      1.574   52.88   0.000
TVAdv         2.2902     0.3041    7.53   0.001
NewsAdv       1.3010     0.3207    4.06   0.010

S = 0.6426      R-sq = 91.9%     R-sq(adj) = 88.7%

Analysis of Variance

SOURCE            DF        SS        MS       F       p
Regression         2    23.435    11.718   28.38   0.002
Residual Error     5     2.065     0.413
Total              7    25.500
```

10. a. PCT = −1.22 + 3.96 FG%

b. An increase of .01 in FG% will increase PCT by approximately .04

c. PCT = −1.23 + 4.82 FG% − 2.59 Opp 3 Pt% + .0344 Opp TO

e. .6432

12. a. $R^2 = \dfrac{\text{SSR}}{\text{SST}} = \dfrac{14{,}052.2}{15{,}182.9} = .926$

b. $R_a^2 = 1 - (1 - R^2)\dfrac{n-1}{n-p-1}$

$= 1 - (1 - .926)\dfrac{10-1}{10-2-1} = .905$

c. Yes; after adjusting for the number of independent variables in the model, we see that 90.5% of the variability in y has been accounted for

14. a. .75

b. .68

15. a. $R^2 = \dfrac{\text{SSR}}{\text{SST}} = \dfrac{23.435}{25.5} = .919$

$R_a^2 = 1 - (1 - R^2)\dfrac{n-1}{n-p-1}$

$= 1 - (1 - .919)\dfrac{8-1}{8-2-1} = .887$

b. Multiple regression analysis is preferred because both R^2 and R_a^2 show an increased percentage of the variability of y explained when both independent variables are used

16. a. No, $R^2 = .153$

b. Better fit with multiple regression

18. a. $R^2 = .564$, $R_a^2 = .511$
b. The fit is not very good

19. a. $\text{MSR} = \frac{\text{SSR}}{p} = \frac{6216.375}{2} = 3108.188$

$\text{MSE} = \frac{\text{SSE}}{n - p - 1} = \frac{507.75}{10 - 2 - 1} = 72.536$

b. $F = \frac{\text{MSR}}{\text{MSE}} = \frac{3108.188}{72.536} = 42.85$

From the F table (2 degrees of freedom numerator and 7 denominator), p-value is less than .01

Because p-value $\leq \alpha$, the overall model is significant

c. $t = \frac{b_1}{s_{b_1}} = \frac{.5906}{.0813} = 7.26$

p-value is less than .01

Because p-value $\leq \alpha$, β_1 is significant

d. $t = \frac{b_2}{s_{b_2}} = \frac{.4980}{.0567} = 8.78$

p-value is less than .01

Because p-value $\leq \alpha$, β_2 is significant

20. a. Significant; p-value = .000
b. Significant; p-value = .000
c. Significant; p-value = .002

22. a. SSE = 4000, $s^2 = 571.43$,
MSR = 6000
b. Significant; p-value is less than .01

23. a. $F = 28.38$
p-value = .002
Because p-value $\leq \alpha$, there is a significant relationship

b. $t = 7.53$
p-value = .001
Because p-value $\leq \alpha$, β_1 is significant and x_1 should not be dropped from the model

c. $t = 4.06$
p-value = .010
Because p-value $\leq \alpha$, β_2 is significant and x_2 should not be dropped from the model

24. a. Reject H_0: $\beta_1 = \beta_2 = 0$; p-value = .000
b. HR: Reject H_0: $\beta_1 = 0$; p-value = .000
ERA: Reject H_0: $\beta_2 = 0$; p-value = .000

26. a. Significant; p-value = .000
b. All of the independent variables are significant

28. a. Using Minitab, the 95% confidence interval is 132.16 to 154.15
b. Using Minitab, the 95% prediction interval is 111.15 at 175.17

29. a. See Minitab output in Figure D13.5b.
$\hat{y} = 83.230 + 2.2902(3.5) + 1.3010(1.8) = 93.588$ or $93,588
b. Minitab results: 92.840 to 94.335, or $92,840 to $94,335
c. Minitab results: 91.774 to 95.401, or $91,774 to $95,401

30. a. 58.37% to 75.03%
b. 35.24% to 90.59%

32. a. $E(y) = \beta_0 + \beta_1 x_1 + \beta_2 x_2$

where $x_2 = \begin{cases} 0 \text{ if level 1} \\ 1 \text{ if level 2} \end{cases}$

b. $E(y) = \beta_0 + \beta_1 x_1 + \beta_2(0) = \beta_0 + \beta_1 x_1$
c. $E(y) = \beta_0 + \beta_1 x_1 + \beta_2(1) = \beta_0 + \beta_1 x_1 + \beta_2$
d. $\beta_2 = E(y \mid \text{level 2}) - E(y \mid \text{level 1})$
β_1 is the change in $E(y)$ for a 1-unit change in x_1 holding x_2 constant

34. a. $15,300, because $b_3 = 15.3$
b. $\hat{y} = 10.1 - 4.2(2) + 6.8(8) + 15.3(0) = 56.1$
Sales prediction: $56,100
c. $\hat{y} = 10.1 - 4.2(1) + 6.8(3) + 15.3(1) = 41.6$
Sales prediction: $41,600

36. a. $\hat{y} = 1.86 + 0.291$ Months $+ 1.10$ Type $- 0.609$ Person
b. Significant; p-value = .002
c. Person is not significant; p-value = .167

38. a. $\hat{y} = -91.8 + 1.08$ Age $+ .252$ Pressure $+ 8.74$ Smoker
b. Significant; p-value = .01
c. 95% prediction interval is 21.35 to 47.18 or a probability of .2135 to .4718; quit smoking and begin some type of treatment to reduce his blood pressure

40. b. 67.39

42. a. $\hat{y} = -1.41 + .0235x_1 + .00486x_2$
b. Significant
c. $R^2 = .937$; $R_a^2 = 9.19$; good fit
d. Both significant

44. a. Score = 50.6 + 1.56 RecRes
b. $r^2 = .431$; not a good fit
c. Score = 33.5 + 1.90 RecRes + 2.61 Afford
Significant
$R_2^2 = .784$; much better fit

46. a. CityMPG = 24.1 − 2.10 Displace
Significant; p-value = .000
b. CityMPG = 26.4 − 2.44 Displace − 1.20 Drive4
c. Significant; p-value = .016
d. CityMPG = 33.3 − 4.15 Displace − 1.24 Drive4 + 2.16 EightCyl
e. Significant overall and individually

Index

A

B

C

D

E

F

L

M

N

Q

R

S

T

U

V

W

Z